THE LAW OF BUSINESS ORGANIZATIONS

CASES, MATERIALS, AND PROBLEMS

Twelfth Edition

■ ■ ■

by

Robert W. Hamilton

Minerva House Drysdale Regents
Chair in Law Emeritus
The University of Texas at Austin

Jonathan R. Macey

Sam Harris Professor of Corporate Law,
Corporate Finance and Securities Law
Yale Law School

Douglas K. Moll

Beirne, Maynard & Parsons, L.L.P. Professor of Law
University of Houston Law Center

AMERICAN CASEBOOK SERIES®

WEST
ACADEMIC
PUBLISHING

American Casebook Series is a trademark registered in the U.S. Patent and Trademark Office.

COPYRIGHT © 1976, 1981, 1986, 1990, 1994 WEST PUBLISHING CO.
© West, a Thomson business, 1998, 2001, 2003, 2005, 2007
© 2010 Thomson Reuters
© 2014 LEG, Inc. d/b/a West Academic
    444 Cedar Street, Suite 700
    St. Paul, MN 55101
    1-877-888-1330

West, West Academic Publishing, and West Academic are trademarks of West Publishing Corporation, used under license.

Printed in the United States of America

ISBN: 978-0-314-28563-8

PREFACE

This book is designed for introductory courses in the law of business associations. It may also be used for more focused courses on corporations or unincorporated business associations. With a minimum of adjustment, it may be used in courses covering from two to six credit hours.

We are strongly of the view that the modern law of business associations can be most effectively taught only in the context of a specific set of statutes. The accompanying statutory supplement contains all of the statutes that students will need when using this book as well as portions of the official commentary.

In the preparation of this book, a number of stylistic conventions have been used. Ellipses ("* * *") indicate textual omissions in cases and materials. Citations and footnotes, however, are usually omitted without indication. Any footnotes that remain retain their original numbers. Text added by the undersigned authors to cases and materials is typically contained within square brackets, while footnotes added by the undersigned authors are designated by letters (a–z in each Chapter, followed if needed by aa–zz, then aaa–zzz).

Finally, we would like to thank Judy Dodson, Professor Hamilton's patient secretary, who prepared the original text of this book. We also want to acknowledge the assistance of Allison Harlow, Cornell Law School class of 2001; Jeff Hanson and Rudy Koch, Cornell Law School class of 2003; Christine Harlow, Cornell Law School class of 2004; Eric Rosenstock, Yale Law School class of 2005; Mark Cho, Sabrina Glaser, and Robin Preussell, Yale Law School class of 2006; Stephanie Biederman and Johanna Spellman, Yale Law School class of 2007; Zoë Klugman, University of Pennsylvania Law School class of 2009; Andrew Geiring, Yale Law School class of 2011; Robin Lowe Clarkson, University of Houston Law Center class of 2010; Andrea Marks and Robert Slater, University of Houston Law Center class of 2011; and Jillian Rae, University of Houston Law Center class of 2013. These students performed able research, recorded innumerable changes, ensured consistency of form throughout, and checked galleys and page proofs.

Acknowledgements

Permission to use copyrighted materials is gratefully acknowledged from Albany Law Review, American Business Law Journal, American Enterprise Institute, American Law Institute, Annual Survey of American Law, Arizona Law Review, Brooklyn Law Review, Bureau of National Affairs, Inc., Cardozo Law Review, Case Western Reserve Law Review, Catholic University Law Review, CBIZ Valuation Group, Inc.,

University of Chicago Law Review, University of Chicago Press, Cincinnati Law Review, Cleveland State Law Review, Columbia Law Review, Cornell Law Review, Delaware Journal of Corporate Law, Directors of the Columbia Law Review, Duke Law Journal, Fordham Law Review, George Mason Law Review, Georgetown Law Journal, Georgia Law Review, The Hartford Courant, Harvard Business School Publishing Corporation, Harvard Law Review, Harvard University Press, University of Illinois Law Review, Journal of Corporate Finance, Journal of Corporation Law, Journal of Small and Emerging Business Law, University of Miami Law Review, University of Michigan Journal of Law Reform, Michigan Law Review, Minnesota Law Review, National Association for Law Placement, National Law Journal, NCCUSL, New York Stock Exchange, New York Times, North Carolina Law Review, Oklahoma City University Law Review, Penguin, USA, University of Pennsylvania Law Review, Practical Accountant, Prentice Hall Law and Business, Stanford Law Review, Texas Law Review, Vanderbilt Law Review, Wake Forest Law Review, Wall Street Journal, West Publishing, Wisconsin Law Review, Yale Law Journal, Barbara Aldave, Chancellor William T. Allen, Norwood P. Beveridge, Bernard S. Black, Margaret M. Blair, Dennis J. Block, Richard A. Booth, Douglas M. Branson, James R. Burkhard, William J. Carney, Pat K. Chew, John C. Coffee, Jr., Frank H. Easterbrook, Melvin A. Eisenberg, Richard A. Epstein, Edward A. Fallone, Allen Ferrell, Daniel R. Fischel, Geoffrey D. Genz, David D. Haddock, Susan Pace Hamill, James J. Hanks, Jr., Charles Hansen, Henry Hansmann, Harry J. Haynsworth, Allan Ickowitz, Dennis S. Karjala, Edmund W. Kitch, Richard H. Koppes, Reinier Kraakman, Jake Krocheski, James G. Leyden, Jr., Bayless Manning, Lawrence E. Mitchell, Joseph P. Monteleone, Stephen Norman, Adam C. Pritchard, Larry E. Ribstein, Roberta Romano, G. Santangelo, A. A. Sommer, Jr., Lynn A. Stout, and E. Norman Veasey.

ROBERT W. HAMILTON

JONATHAN R. MACEY

DOUGLAS K. MOLL

May 2014

SUMMARY OF CONTENTS

TABLE OF CONTENTS

TABLE OF CASES

The principal cases are in bold type.

———

THE LAW OF BUSINESS ORGANIZATIONS

CASES, MATERIALS, AND PROBLEMS

Twelfth Edition

CHAPTER 1

INTRODUCTION: BUSINESS FORMS AND BUSINESS TAXATION

■ ■ ■

A. THE SUBJECT IN GENERAL

The subject of this book is the legal environment in which business in the United States is conducted either by a single individual or cooperatively by a few or many individuals. "Business" is a broad term describing an extremely wide range of activities. At one extreme is the summer lemonade stand opened for one afternoon by an enterprising eleven-year-old. At the other is the Wal-Mart Corporation, which in 2013 had net sales of $466.1 billion and operating income of $27.8 billion, with more than 10,700 stores in 27 countries and 2.2 million employees.

Business associations can be classified and analyzed in myriad ways, including by the legal form of the business. The lemonade stand is an example of a *sole proprietorship*. Wal-Mart, by contrast, is organized as a *corporation*. Other traditional forms of business are the *general partnership* and the *limited partnership*. In the 1990s, new forms of business were created with names confusingly similar to the limited partnership: the *limited liability company,* the *limited liability partnership,* and in some states, the *limited liability limited partnership.* As you will learn, the differences between these various legal forms are significant.

Classification by legal form naturally breaks into two categories: (1) *corporations* and (2) *unincorporated associations*, e.g., proprietorships, partnerships, limited liability companies, etc. A further method of classification, and the one basically followed in this book, is to divide business organizations on the basis of whether they are *closely held* or *publicly held.* In general, a closely held firm is a business with relatively few owners whose ownership interests are not publicly traded on an established market (e.g., a law partnership or a local air conditioning corporation). In contrast, a publicly held firm is a business that typically has a large number of owners with ownership interests that are routinely bought and sold on a public market (e.g., Wal-Mart).

Closely held firms may be organized as corporations or unincorporated associations. Virtually all publicly held firms, however, are organized as corporations, and such firms confront certain management, control, and regulatory issues that are largely inapplicable to closely held firms. Closely held firms that are organized as corporations, however, are similar in formal respects to publicly held corporations.

The closely held/publicly held classification does have disadvantages: it ignores the fact that in the real world there is a continuum of business size, complexity, and ownership, and it treats the world of business as polar rather than continuous. This classification also tends to hide the fact that closely and publicly held firms draw from a common reservoir of principles and tradition, particularly with respect to the use of the corporate form, and each therefore to some extent influences the other.

Developments during the last three decades have greatly increased the attractiveness of unincorporated forms for closely held firms. The most important developments are (1) the creation of new unincorporated business forms that grant the advantage of limited liability for all owners of the business, and (2) changes in the regulations promulgated under the Internal Revenue Code that give unincorporated firms and their owners considerable freedom in electing how their income is to be taxed. The net result undoubtedly is to encourage firms with few owners to use unincorporated business forms.

B. AN INTRODUCTION TO BUSINESS FORMS

Chapter Two of this book examines the law of agency—the law governing the relationships between principals, agents, and third parties. Although agency law applies to all forms of business, it is frequently invoked when dealing with the most basic (and most common) form—the *sole proprietorship*. A sole proprietorship is a business owned by a single individual that is not operated as a corporation or other special legal form. The major advantage of a sole proprietorship is that it is easy to establish—the proprietor simply begins to conduct business. In some jurisdictions, a proprietor using an assumed name for the business must also file an "assumed name" or "fictitious name" certificate with the county clerk specifying the name of the owner and the name of the business. The major disadvantage of a sole proprietorship is that the owner has unlimited personal liability for the obligations of the business. Debts of the business, in other words, are viewed by the law as debts of the owner, and the owner's personal assets are at risk in lawsuits arising out of business activities. When a sole proprietor engages others to help conduct the business, such as employees, the relationships between (1) the employee (the agent) and the employer/proprietor (the principal), (2) the employee and third parties the employee has dealt with on behalf of the employer, and (3) the employer and third parties the employee has dealt with on behalf of the employer, are, in many respects, governed by agency law. Agency law is also important because it serves as the foundation for many of the legal principles associated with the other business forms discussed in this book.

Chapter Three explores the *general partnership*—an association of two or more persons to carry on, as co-owners, a business for profit. Among the modern forms of business organization that involve two or more owners, the general partnership is unique in that it can be informally created. Put differently, establishing a general partnership does not require the filing of an organizational document with the state. So long as two or more persons are carrying on, as co-owners, a business for profit, a general partnership is created—regardless of whether the co-owners intended that result.

Some statutes view a general partnership as a separate legal entity whose identity is distinct from that of its owners (known as "partners"). Other statutes view a general partnership as an aggregate of the individual partners with no legal differentiation between the business and the partners themselves. Under either view, all of the partners in a general partnership have the right to participate in the management of the business. Moreover, the general partnership form provides partners with a relatively easy exit from the venture, as a partner's withdrawal typically causes a buyout of the partner's interest or the dissolution of the partnership itself. The general partnership is also characterized by structural flexibility (the partners can contractually arrange to run the business largely as they see fit), restricted transferability of ownership interests (a transferee of a partnership interest can only become a partner with the unanimous consent of the other partners), and pass-through taxation (partnership income is only taxed at the partner level, rather than "doubly taxed" at both the partnership and the partner levels). Like a sole proprietorship, however, the primary downside of a general partnership is that the law imposes unlimited personal liability on partners for the obligations of the partnership. Further, the easy exit from the general partnership makes it a rather unstable business form in certain circumstances—a situation which may be unsuitable for particular types of ventures.

Chapters 4–17 examine the *corporation* form of business. In economic terms, the corporation dwarfs in importance all other business forms combined. Under all corporation statutes, a corporation is viewed as a separate legal entity whose identity is distinct from that of its owners (known as "shareholders"). This notion that a corporation is an entity independent of its shareholders is deeply ingrained. The corporation itself enters into contracts, borrows money, owns property, sues and defends, and otherwise conducts its business as if it were a real person.

Many of the basic attributes of the corporation form are diametrically opposed to the basic attributes of the general partnership form. Examples include the following:

(a) A corporation is consciously formed by filing an organizational document with the state.

(b) Shareholders have no right to participate in the management of the business (except in certain extraordinary situations, such as mergers).

(c) A shareholder in a corporation typically has no ability to compel a buyout of his ownership interest or the dissolution of the firm.

(d) Ownership interests in a corporation may be freely and fully transferred without the consent of the other shareholders (although finding a buyer may be difficult in a closely held corporation where, by definition, there is no public market for the company's ownership interests).

(e) The income of a corporation is taxed twice—once at the corporation level, and a second time at the shareholder level. Stated differently, the corporation pays taxes on its income, and the shareholders pay taxes on that income again when (and if) the income is distributed to them. Whether this tax treatment is advantageous or disadvantageous depends heavily on the individual and corporate tax rates that exist at the time, as well as on the financial circumstances of the shareholders. In today's tax climate, however, this "double taxation" is usually undesirable. Aside from income taxes, corporations (but not partnerships) are also subject to state franchise taxes—taxes imposed for the privilege of organizing a business in a state.

(f) A corporation provides its shareholders with limited liability for the obligations of the business. In a lawsuit against a corporation, a shareholder's personal assets are not at risk; instead, the most that a shareholder can lose is the amount of his investment. This limited liability is one of the most important benefits of operating a business as a corporation.

Chapter 18 begins the exploration of the "hybrid" business organizations—i.e., business structures that combine attributes of the general partnership and corporation forms. In particular, Chapter 18 addresses the *limited partnership*—a partnership comprised of two classes of partners, general and limited, that is formed by filing an organizational document with the state. Like a general partnership, general partners in a limited partnership have unlimited personal liability for the venture's obligations (although individual liability concerns are significantly lessened by the common use of limited liability entities as general partners). Like a corporation, limited partners in a limited partnership have limited liability for the venture's obligations (although, under many statutes, that limited liability can be forfeited in certain circumstances if a limited partner participates in the control of the business). In a limited partnership, the limited partners are largely passive investors while the general partners manage the business. As with a general partnership, a limited partnership is characterized by structural flexibility, restricted transferability of ownership interests, and pass-through taxation. Exit rights, however, tend to be more restricted in the limited partnership form.

Chapter 19 addresses the *limited liability partnership* ("LLP"). The LLP is a general partnership that, depending on the relevant statute, provides the partners with limited liability for the partnership's tort obligations or for both its tort and contract obligations. Chapter 19 also addresses the *limited liability limited partnership* ("LLLP")—a limited partnership that provides LLP-like limited liability protection to some or all of the partners. The filing of an organizational document with the state is required to establish both of these business forms.

Chapter 20 examines the *limited liability company* ("LLC"). An LLC is a business organization, formed by a required state filing, that adopts many of the best features of the corporation and partnership forms. Like a corporation, an LLC is a legal entity that is separate and distinct from its owners (known as "members"). An LLC can be structured to provide management rights to members or to a designated group of managers, and it offers limited liability to the members for all of the venture's obligations (regardless of whether the members participate in the control of the business). Exit rights in an LLC tend to be restricted in a corporate-like manner, as many statutes prevent a minority member from demanding a buyout of his interest or from compelling dissolution of the enterprise. Like a partnership, an LLC is characterized by structural flexibility, restricted transferability of ownership interests, and pass-through taxation. Along with avoiding double taxation with respect to income taxes, LLCs in most states avoid franchise taxes as well. Because of this favorable combination of attributes, the LLC has emerged as the preferred business form for many closely held ventures.

C. THE STATUTES

Unlike subjects such as property and torts, the subject of business associations is largely governed by statute. This is true not only in the large commercial states such as California, New York, and Texas, but in the smaller states as well. Answers to many questions must be found in the statutes and cannot be answered solely on the basis of common sense or prior judicial decision. In this respect, the law of business associations is similar to many other areas of law in the modern commercial and government-oriented society.

An experienced attorney does not attempt to memorize the detailed provisions of the numerous complex statutes and regulations with which he or she must be familiar. Rather, the attorney becomes generally familiar with the provisions and keeps copies of them available for easy reference. Each student should follow approximately the same process.

Thus, statutory references should be looked up in the Supplement, as the materials cannot be fully understood without doing so.

The statutes in most jurisdictions today are modern and draw from a common core of model and uniform statutes. One should not assume, however, that statutes always clarify and simplify. In specific circumstances, statutory language may appear to require an unjust or unreasonable result. This is more likely to be true in jurisdictions that have not drawn from the common core of model and uniform statutes, but it is true in some circumstances under the model and uniform statutes as well.

D. FEDERAL INCOME TAXATION: BASIC PRINCIPLES

Trends in the law of business associations can be understood only if one has a passing familiarity with the modern federal income tax structure. Moreover, when considering taxes in the business context, one must take into account not only the taxation of the business itself, but also the relationship with the taxation of the individual owners. This Section provides a basic introduction to these topics. As you proceed through the various business associations discussed in this book, you may find it useful to return to this discussion.

Initially, all businesses compute income for tax purposes in the same manner, deducting business expenses from receipts in order to compute taxable income. After determination of the business's taxable income, however, the tax treatment to some extent depends on the business form.

In broad terms, the Internal Revenue Code recognizes two distinct methods of taxing business income, which are generally described as "corporate" and "partnership" taxation. Corporate income taxation is described in Subchapters C and S of the Internal Revenue Code, while partnership income taxation is described in Subchapter K. The differences between these two basic methods of taxing business income drive the selection of business form for specific enterprises.

1. CORPORATE TAX RATES

Corporations historically have been treated as separate taxable entities under the Internal Revenue Code with their own sets of rules and tax schedules. The rates applicable to traditional corporations are set forth in Subchapter C. In 2014, corporations were subject to tax on income at the following rates:[a]

---

[a] This table is a composite table building in special surtaxes at the $100,000 and $15,000,000 levels.

Table 1

2014 Corporate Tax Rates

If Taxable Income Is Over	But Not Over	The Tax Is	Of the Amount Over
–0–	$50,000	15%	–0–
$50,000	$75,000	$7,500 + 25%	$50,000
$75,000	$100,000	$13,750 + 34%	$75,000
$100,000	$335,000	$22,250 + 39%	$100,000
$335,000	$10,000,000	$113,900 + 34%	$335,000
$10,000,000	$15,000,000	$3,400,000 + 35%	$10,000,000
$15,000,000	$18,333,333	$5,150,000 + 38%	$15,000,000
$18,333,333	_____	$6,416,667 + 35%	$18,333,333

NOTES

(1) It is important to distinguish between *marginal* tax rates and *average* tax rates. The *marginal* tax rate applicable to a corporation with exactly $75,000 of income is 34 percent because that is the rate applicable to each additional dollar of taxable income that the corporation earns above $75,000 (up to $100,000). The *average* tax rate on such income, however, is 18.33 percent because a corporation's tax bill on exactly $75,000 of taxable income is $13,750 (15 percent of $50,000 plus 25 percent of $25,000). A corporation with precisely $100,000 of taxable income owes $22,250; that is an average rate of 22.25 percent, but the marginal tax rate on each additional dollar of income is 39 percent up to $335,000.

(2) Where do the mysterious numbers $7,500 and $13,750 in Table 1 come from? Hint: calculate the precise tax due on $50,000 of income taxed at 15 percent; then calculate the precise tax due on an additional $25,000 of income taxed at 25 percent.

(3) The tax structure for corporations in general is mildly "progressive" because additional income is taxed at increasingly higher rates. A tax structure is "regressive" if lower amounts of income are taxed at higher rates than higher amounts of income. When a corporation's income is in the $100,000–$335,000 range, it is subject to a marginal rate of 39 percent; above $335,000 the rate reverts to 34 percent. (There is a similar pattern at the $15,000,000–$18,333,333 range. The marginal tax rate rises to 38 percent and then drops back to 35 percent.) These declines in marginal rates may be viewed as regressive even though the average rate of taxation on corporate income can never exceed 34 percent at any level of income up to $10,000,000, or 35 percent at any level of income. These special surtaxes on corporations are designed to gradually eliminate the benefit of the lower brackets for corporations that have incomes over $100,000 and $15,000,000 respectively.

(4) Corporations subject to the tax rates set forth in Table 1 are called C corporations, named after Subchapter C of the Internal Revenue Code. The taxation of S corporations is discussed below.

2.   INDIVIDUAL TAX RATES

There are four different individual income tax rate schedules based primarily on marital status, plus elaborate sets of tax tables based on the rate schedules that are used mostly by persons with relatively small incomes. In addition, there is a special tax schedule for the income of trusts and estates. For purposes of considering the interaction of personal and corporate tax rates upon business income, however, a detailed consideration of this complex structure is unnecessary. Instead, by way of illustration, consider the tax schedule for married taxpayers filing a joint return:

Table 2

2014 Income Tax Rates
(Married Taxpayers Filing Joint Return)

If taxable income is:	The tax is:
Not over $18,150	10% of taxable income
Over $18,150 but not over $73,800	$1,815 + 15% of excess over $18,150
Over $73,800 but not over $148,850	$10,162.50 + 25% of excess over $73,800
Over $148,850 but not over $226,850	$28,925 + 28% of excess over $148,850
Over $226,850 but not over $405,100	$50,765 + 33% of excess over $226,850
Over $405,100 but not over $457,600	$109,587.50 + 35% of excess over $405,100
Over $457,600	$127,962.50 + 39.6% of excess over $457,600

NOTE

In the years during and after World War II, marginal rates on individual taxpayers were extremely high by modern standards—the top bracket rising above 90 percent. As late as 1980, the highest marginal rate for joint returns was 70 percent for taxable income in excess of $215,400. A major policy implemented by the Reagan administration in the 1980s was to reduce high marginal rates. This policy resulted in a maximum marginal rate of 28 percent in the significant 1986 Tax Reform Act. Between 1986 and the present, however, the general trend has been toward higher marginal rates.

3.   THE TAXATION OF CAPITAL GAINS AND LOSSES

Before 1986, at the same time that the maximum tax rates of 70 percent or more were in effect, the maximum tax rate on a different form of income—long-term capital gains arising from the sale or exchange of capital assets held for more than 6 months—was only 25 percent. Capital assets are assets held for profit-making or investment purposes. In general, most assets other than inventory and property used in the active conduct of a trade or business are capital assets. This dramatic difference in rates created strong incentives to structure transactions or establish strategies that transmuted ordinary income into long-term capital gains in order to make the 25 percent rate (rather than the 70 percent rate) applicable. To a somewhat lesser extent, this same incentive exists today.

The technical rules with respect to the treatment of capital gains were relatively complex before 1986 and are even more complex today. Long-term capital gains or losses are presently defined as gains or losses from the sale or exchange of capital assets held for more than one year. In 2014, the maximum tax rate on long-term capital gains with respect to most assets was 20 percent. Short-term capital gains are taxed at ordinary income tax rates. Capital losses are available to offset capital gains plus up to $3,000 of ordinary income in any year; excess capital losses may be carried over to offset capital gains in future years. In making these various calculations and determining the net amount of gain or loss (as well as the short-term or long-term character of the gain or loss), short-term gains and losses are separately netted to determine the net short-term capital gain or loss. Long-term capital gains and losses are netted in the same manner to establish the net long-term gain or loss. The two are then combined to determine the net capital gain or loss for the year.

4.   THE TAXATION OF PROPRIETORSHIPS, PARTNERSHIPS, AND CORPORATIONS

(1) **Proprietorships**. Consider first the tax treatment of a proprietorship—a business wholly owned by a single individual.

ROBERT W. HAMILTON, BUSINESS ORGANIZATIONS: UNINCORPORATED BUSINESSES AND CLOSELY HELD CORPORATIONS
Pages 46–47 (1996).

A proprietorship is not a separate taxable entity. Its income or loss is reported on the proprietor's personal income tax return. For example, if a proprietor files a joint return with his or her spouse, the business income or loss of each proprietorship owned by either or both of them must be included in that joint return.

The manner of reporting the income and expenses of a proprietorship is interesting because it reflects a pragmatic compromise between the legal view that a proprietorship is not a separate entity from its owner and the economic view that the proprietorship's financial affairs should not be intermixed with the proprietor's personal affairs. The Internal Revenue Code requires an individual taxpayer who is also an entrepreneur to file the long-form personal income tax return—the form 1040. The Internal Revenue Code also requires a separate tax form, Schedule C, to be prepared to record the gain or loss from each business owned by the taxpayer. Schedule C must be attached to the taxpayer's form 1040 and the income or loss of the proprietorship is added to or subtracted from the proprietor's other income in order to determine her final liability to Uncle Sam. A separate Schedule C must be filed for each business. State income taxation works much the same way (though many states base their tax on the taxpayer's federal tax return and do not require a completely separate accounting of income or loss). * * *

Every entrepreneur operating a sole proprietorship must also take into account the requirements of the Self Employment Contributions Act of 1954 ["SECA"], imposing a tax on Schedule C income equal (in [2014]) to 12.4 percent of proprietorship income up to [$117,000] for [social security] and an additional uncapped [2.9 percent] for Medicare. If the entrepreneur is also an employee of another firm, the [social security] tax is applied first against the salary of the employee and the proprietorship income is taxed only to the extent the salary is less than [$117,000].

————

(2) **Unincorporated Business Forms.** Under regulations adopted by the Treasury Department in 1997, an unincorporated business entity (including a business entity formed under state law as a general partnership, limited partnership, limited liability partnership, or limited liability company) that has at least two owners generally will be classified for federal income tax purposes as a partnership, and therefore will be subject to taxation under Subchapter K of the Internal Revenue Code. Alternatively, the entity may elect to be classified for federal income tax purposes as a corporation. An unincorporated business entity that has a single owner generally will be disregarded as an entity separate from its owner for federal income tax purposes (i.e., its activities will be treated in the same manner as a sole proprietorship or branch or division of the owner), unless the entity elects to be classified for federal income tax purposes as a corporation. Because it is largely elective, this tax classification regime is commonly referred to as "check the box." There is a statutory exception to this elective regime in the case of publicly traded partnerships, which generally will be classified for federal income tax purposes as corporations.

Under the partnership tax regime of Subchapter K, the partnership itself does not pay any tax. It does, however, compute its taxable income and file an informational return (Form 1065) with the IRS. For federal income tax purposes, the income or loss reported by the partnership is "passed through" to the partners in accordance with the partnership agreement. The partnership must provide each partner with a statement (Form K–1) informing the partner of her respective share of the partnership's income and deductions. Each partner must then include these amounts directly on her income tax return. Taxation is therefore imposed solely at the level of owners and not at the entity level.

It is important to appreciate that while both proprietorships and unincorporated business forms are taxed as extensions of the individual taxpayers who are the owners of the enterprise, the amounts allocated are based on the income calculations of the proprietorship or unincorporated business form and not on the amounts actually distributed in cash or property to the proprietor, partner, or member. There will be tax to pay on business income, in other words, even though the business has not actually distributed any of that income to its owners.

The apparent simplicity of the pass-through tax treatment provided by Subchapter K is quite deceptive. The allocation of losses among general partners, in particular, opened the door to tax avoidance on a major scale. With the development of limited liability for owners in limited liability companies and limited liability partnerships, partnership taxation easily became the most complex area of tax law. *See, e.g.,* Christine R. Strong and Susan P. Hamill, *Allocations Attributable to Partner Nonrecourse Liabilities: Issues Revealed by LLCs and LLPs,* 51 ALA. L. REV. 603 (2000).

In general terms, the SECA tax is imposed on general partners, I.R.C. § 1402(a), but not on limited partners unless the payments constitute "guaranteed payments." I.R.C. § 1402(a)(13). The SECA tax is applicable to earnings of individual members of limited liability companies to the extent attributable to a trade or business.

(3) **C Corporations.** As mentioned above, C corporations have their own special tax schedule. When comparing the tax consequences of conducting a business in a corporate or unincorporated form, however, it is essential to recognize that the corporate rate is not in lieu of, but is in addition to, the tax on the ultimate shareholders. There is, in short, double taxation of business earnings if a C corporation makes distributions to shareholders.

An example should make this clear. If a C corporation has taxable income of precisely $1,000,000, the corporation must pay a corporate income tax of $340,000, which leaves $660,000 available for distribution to the shareholders. If the corporation then distributes the $660,000 to its shareholders, all of whom are in the 39.6 percent bracket, the shareholders in the aggregate will owe another $261,360, for a total tax bill at both levels (entity and owner) of $601,360. In contrast, if the business were conducted in an unincorporated form, there is no tax at all at the entity level, and the maximum owner-level tax (calculated at the rate of 39.6 percent) would be $396,000. In other words, on the assumption that all income is to be distributed to shareholders, the failure to obtain pass-through tax treatment results in $205,360 of additional federal income tax in a single year. Indeed, assuming corporate and individual taxpayers at the highest levels of income, the combined tax rate on a distribution by a C corporation that is subject to the 35 percent rate to its shareholders who are all in the 39.6 percent bracket is about 61 percent. Thus, there is approximately a 21 percent differential or bias against C corporation tax status at the highest levels of income.[b]

(4) **S Corporations.** The double tax treatment of C corporations was widely viewed by shareholders in closely held corporations as unfair and discriminatory. In the 1950s, Subchapter S was added to the Internal Revenue Code to give some relief from the double tax treatment. Subchapter S requires an affirmative election by the corporation and is not available to all closely held corporations. A corporation that makes this election is called an "S corporation" or a "sub S corporation."

The S corporation election is a tax election and not a corporate law election: an S corporation possesses all of the normal attributes of a corporation under state law, but is taxed in a different way than C corporations. To be eligible for S corporation treatment, corporations must not have more than 100 shareholders. (The maximum number of shareholders in an S corporation was originally set at ten and has gradually increased over the years.) An S corporation, in addition to meeting the maximum 100-shareholder requirement, is prohibited from having shareholders who are nonresident aliens or who are non-individuals (with certain exceptions), and it may not have issued more than one class of stock (except for classes of common stock that differ only in voting rights). There is no maximum size limitation for S corporations in terms of assets or revenues, though doubtless most of them are comparatively small on these measures.

S corporations are taxed on a modified pass-through basis that is similar in many respects to unincorporated business taxation. The corporation files a return showing the earnings allocable to each shareholder, and the shareholder must include that amount in her personal income tax return. That amount is includible whether or not any distributions are made by the corporation. The tax treatment of S

---

[b]   Many corporate dividends are "qualified dividends" which are taxed at the lower capital gains rate. Thus, although there is still a double taxation of business earnings, the shareholder-level tax may be lower than this example suggests. In fact, when small amounts of corporate income are combined with qualified dividends, the double taxation associated with C corporation status may produce a lower total tax bill than pass-through treatment.

corporations is not identical to that of unincorporated business forms, however, and in several respects it is less advantageous to the taxpayer than what Subchapter K would provide. Nevertheless, an S corporation does have the basic feature of pass-through taxation that is typical of unincorporated business forms. As a result, it is a plausible alternative to a partnership from a tax standpoint.

NOTES

(1) The tax treatment of C corporations has been the subject of considerable theoretical discussion, both historically and at present. At the beginning of President Reagan's second term, there was a brief flirtation with the idea that the corporate income tax should be abolished. As the compromises that eventually became the Tax Reform Act of 1986 were hammered out, however, this idea was abandoned. Instead, there was increased reliance on the corporate income tax as a source of revenue.

(2) There have been numerous proposals over the years to "integrate" the corporate and individual income tax structures in order to eliminate the double tax on corporate income. Other industrialized countries generally do not have a double tax structure. President Reagan's proposal to repeal the corporate income tax is one example of such a proposal. Alternatively, one could eliminate dividends from the taxable income of shareholders. Yet another approach would treat the payment of tax by a corporation as a kind of withholding tax with respect to income ultimately distributed to shareholders. Finally, another approach would in effect extend S corporation tax treatment to all corporations. These proposals have formidable problems because of the different types of taxpayers, tax-exempt entities, foreign shareholders, and the like. For interesting analyses of the double tax structure and the problems of integration proposals, see AMERICAN LAW INSTITUTE, FEDERAL INCOME TAX PROJECT: REPORTER'S STUDY OF CORPORATE TAX INTEGRATION (1993); U.S. DEP'T OF THE TREASURY, INTEGRATION OF THE INDIVIDUAL AND CORPORATE TAX SYSTEMS: TAXING BUSINESS INCOME ONCE (1992).

5.   TAX PLANNING FOR BUSINESSES

Tax planning for businesses involves several considerations. First, everyone has to pay taxes on their income, or at least account to the federal government by filing a tax return. In this respect, taxation is more immediate and certain than the risk of unlimited liability for owners. The danger that a business may incur a liability in excess of business assets may or may not materialize depending upon what happens in the future. Liability for taxes, however, is a certainty. Tax planning, therefore, is a routine and often dominant aspect of every significant business venture.

Second, taxpayers quite legitimately expect to minimize their tax liability to the extent they may legally do so. There is a basic distinction between legitimate tax avoidance (usually called "tax planning") on the one hand, and tax evasion that may lead to fraud penalties (or worse) on the other.[c] The selection of a business form in order to take advantage of a difference in taxation is clearly permissible tax planning.

Third, in tax planning, one must usually concentrate on the marginal rate of taxation and not the average rate. For example, an individual considering an investment in a business venture may already have income from other sources that exceeds $73,800. Every dollar of income obtained from the business venture, therefore, will be taxed at 25 percent or more. Where there are several different investors or owners, they are likely to be in different individual tax brackets. Generally, the strategy that minimizes the tax obligations of the investor or owner who is in the highest tax bracket will be followed, although that is not always true.[d]

Fourth, in selecting the form of business, the total tax liability of both business and owners must be taken into account.[e] As illustrated by the above double tax versus pass-through example, under current tax rates, it is usually advantageous to conduct a small business in a form that permits pass-through tax treatment.[f]

---

[c] The claiming of personal exemptions for household pets is an example of criminal tax evasion, while electing S corporation status is an example of acceptable tax avoidance. While this may seem obvious, the line between legitimate avoidance and improper evasion is often shadowy.

[d] A revised version of the "Golden Rule" for business is "He who has the gold, rules." Typically, the person in the highest tax bracket will be contributing capital that is essential for the success of the enterprise, and hence his tax minimization becomes the goal of tax planning.

[e] With respect to a newly formed corporation, the entity will be taxed at the 15 percent rate for income up to $50,000, although the 5 percent surtax will wipe out the benefit of that lower tax rate after the corporation's taxable income grows. Because new businesses may be placed in several different corporations, however, multiple uses of the 15 percent bracket may be available in certain situations.

[f] When (a) a business produces relatively small amounts of income, (b) an individual owner is in a high marginal tax bracket, and (c) there is no short-term need for the business to distribute its income, a C corporation may produce a lower combined tax bill than a pass-through entity. For example, assume that a C corporation earns only enough income to be taxed at the low 15 percent and 25 percent brackets. Assume further that the corporation retains its income over the years and makes no distributions to the shareholders. Ultimately, the stock of the corporation is sold with the gain taxed at the long-term capital gains rate of 20 percent. (Alternatively, the stock may be held until the death of the shareholder, where the step-up in basis permits the capital gains tax to be avoided entirely.) Paying the entity-level tax at the low rates plus the 20 percent capital gains rate may produce a smaller overall tax bill than if the business were conducted in a pass-through form (with the shareholder paying taxes on the business income at, say, a 39.6 percent marginal rate). This tax planning strategy is commonly known as the "accumulation/bail-out" strategy.

CHAPTER 2

AGENCY

■ ■ ■

A. INTRODUCTION[a]

The law of agency is the law of delegation—i.e., the legal principles that govern the ability of one person (the principal) to have another person (the agent) act on his behalf. Basic agency relationships underlie virtually all commercial dealings in the modern world. For example, the relationship between a sole proprietor and his employees is governed by the law of agency, as is the relationship between a corporation and its officers. The agency relationship is not a form of business organization in and of itself; instead, agency is the mechanism by which business organizations function. To take an obvious example, a corporation—an artificial legal construct that has no physical being of its own—can act only through agents for everything it does. Whether the corporation is writing a check, selling a product, or entering into a multi-billion dollar merger, the law of agency is involved.

Agency concepts explicitly appear in the statutory schemes of many business organizations. In the general partnership, for example, partners are agents with apparent authority to bind the partnership for acts in the ordinary course of the partnership business.[b] While this principle presents itself as a partnership doctrine (it is in the partnership statute after all), and while it could be studied purely as a matter of partnership law, it is far easier to understand it if one is familiar with the agency concepts from which the principle derived. Even when the relevant business organization statute does not explicitly incorporate an agency concept, the common law of agency will apply unless it is clearly displaced by the statutory scheme at issue. Section 104(a) of the Revised Uniform Partnership Act, for example, indicates that "[u]nless displaced by particular provisions of this [Act], the principles of law and equity supplement this [Act]," and the comment states that the law of agency is encompassed within these supplementary principles. As a further example, § 301 of the Revised Uniform Limited Liability Company Act explicitly defers to the law of agency. In short, the

---

[a] A good portion of the material in this Chapter is taken from ROBERT W. HAMILTON, BUSINESS ORGANIZATIONS: UNINCORPORATED BUSINESSES AND CLOSELY HELD CORPORATIONS (1996). The material is reprinted with permission of Aspen Law and Business. Modifications and additions have been made for editorial purposes and to include material on the Third Restatement of Agency.

[b] *See, e.g.*, RUPA § 301.

study of agency law is directly related to the study of modern business organizations.

The principal sources of agency law today are the Second and Third Restatements of Agency. The American Law Institute—an association of lawyers, academics, and judges—authored the Restatements of Agency and, like all Restatements, their text and comments represent an effort to capture the law as developed by the courts. The Second Restatement of Agency was published in 1958, and the Third Restatement of Agency was published in 2006. Although the Restatements are not binding authorities, they are very influential and persuasive to many courts.

Because of the relatively recent publication of the Third Restatement, most of the existing case law deals with the Second Restatement. Nevertheless, the basic principles of the Second and Third Restatements are largely the same. The materials in this Chapter will discuss and cite both versions.

B. THE CREATION OF THE AGENCY RELATIONSHIP

The Second Restatement defines *agency* as the "fiduciary relation which results from the manifestation of consent by one person to another that the other shall act on his behalf and subject to his control, and consent by the other so to act."[c] The person who is acting for another is the *agent*; the person for whom the agent is acting is the *principal*. Parsing the definition of agency reveals three elements of an agency relationship: (1) consent by the principal and the agent; (2) action by the agent on behalf of the principal; and (3) control by the principal. These elements reveal the general policy thrust of agency law—if there is mutual consent to an arrangement involving an agent acting to further the principal's interest and subject to the principal's control, then it is appropriate to make the principal liable for the agent's actions.

Consent: Consent of both the principal and the agent is necessary to form an agency relationship. More specifically, both the principal and the agent must consent to the agent acting on the principal's behalf and subject to the principal's control. Thus, agency is a consensual relationship in which one person agrees to act for the benefit of, and subject to the control of, another person.

The principal must manifest (or convey) his consent to the agent. This required manifestation of consent may be written, oral, or implied from the parties' conduct. The agent's consent may also be established by written or oral statements, or by implication from the parties' conduct.[d] Thus, if *P*

---

c   RESTATEMENT (SECOND) OF AGENCY § 1 (1958); *see* RESTATEMENT (THIRD) OF AGENCY § 1.01 (2006).

d   *See, e.g.*, RESTATEMENT (THIRD) OF AGENCY § 1.03 (2006).

asks *A* to complete a task pursuant to *P*'s instructions, and *A* does so, an agency relationship has been created even if *A* did not expressly communicate to *P* his agreement to perform the task.

On behalf of: The agent must be acting on the principal's behalf. This requirement is generally understood to mean that the agent must be acting *primarily* for the benefit of the principal rather than for the benefit of the agent or some other party.[e] This element is critical to the agency definition, as it allows courts to distinguish the agency relationship from more garden-variety exchanges of compensation for services where we would not expect an agency relationship to arise. Simply acting in a way that benefits another, in other words, even when there is control, is insufficient to establish an agency relationship; instead, a court must believe that the agent was acting primarily for the benefit of the other person (the principal).

For example, suppose that a homeowner calls an electrician to install a new chandelier. One might plausibly argue that the electrician has agreed to act subject to the homeowner's control in several respects—e.g., the homeowner has specified the particular task, the homeowner may have required a particular time and date for the service, and the homeowner may want the chandelier hung in a particular manner. Nevertheless, absent extraordinary facts, the electrician's services would be considered primarily for his own benefit, largely because the electrician sets the price for his services and retains the profits from his labor. From a policy standpoint, this conclusion is sensible, as we would not expect an electrician to have a fiduciary duty of loyalty to his customer, or for the customer to be liable for the electrician's negligence, or for any of the other onerous obligations of the agency relationship to apply.[f]

Control: The agent must act subject to the principal's control, but the degree of control exercised by the principal does not have to be significant. As one court observed:

> The control a principal must exercise over an agent in order to evidence an agency relationship is not so comprehensive. A principal need not exercise physical control over the actions of its agent in order for an agency relationship to exist; rather, the

---

[e]   *See* J. DENNIS HYNES & MARK J. LOEWENSTEIN, AGENCY, PARTNERSHIP, AND THE LLC: THE LAW OF UNINCORPORATED BUSINESS ENTERPRISES: CASES, MATERIALS, PROBLEMS 17 (7th ed. 2007) ("'On the principal's behalf' and acting 'primarily' for the principal's benefit are different ways of expressing the same requirement. Merely benefitting another by one's conduct does not qualify. It is too far removed in degree."); *cf.* RESTATEMENT (SECOND) OF AGENCY § 13 cmt. a (1958) ("The agreement to act on behalf of the principal causes the agent to be a fiduciary, that is, a person having a duty, created by his undertaking, to act primarily for the benefit of another in matters connected with his undertaking.").

[f]   Does the fact that an agent is compensated indicate that the agent is acting primarily for his own benefit rather than that of the principal? A paid agent is in some sense acting on his own behalf in order to earn the promised compensation; nevertheless, "compensation is earned by acting in a manner that advances the interest of the principal, and thus the paid agent is considered to be *primarily* acting for the benefit of another." HYNES & LOEWENSTEIN, *supra* note e, at 17.

agent must be subject to the principal's control over the result or ultimate objectives of the agency relationship.

* * *

In sum, the control a principal exercises over its agent is not defined rigidly to mean control over the minutia of the agent's actions, such as the agent's physical conduct * * *. The level of control may be very attenuated with respect to the details. However, the principal must have ultimate responsibility to control the end result of his or her agent's actions; such control may be exercised by prescribing the agents' obligations or duties before or after the agent acts, or both.[g]

Thus, the requisite level of control may be found simply by the fact that the principal has specified the task that the agent should perform, even if the principal has not prescribed the details of how the task should be accomplished.

In addition to these three elements, it is important to note that the agency definition uses the term "person" to refer to both agents and principals. Both the Second and Third Restatements define "person" to include individuals as well as organizations.[h] Thus, agency relationships are not limited to natural persons; indeed, artificial entities such as corporations, trusts, partnerships, or limited liability companies may act as principals or as agents.

Keep in mind that, if the legal definition of agency has been met through satisfaction of the above elements, an agency relationship is present regardless of whether the parties intended to create such a relationship (and regardless of what they call it):

Agency is a legal concept which depends upon the existence of required factual elements: the manifestation by the principal that the agent shall act for him, the agent's acceptance of the undertaking and the understanding of the parties that the principal is to be in control of the undertaking. The relation which the law calls agency does not depend upon the intent of the parties to create it, nor their belief that they have done so. To constitute the relation, there must be an agreement, but not necessarily a contract, between the parties; if the agreement results in the factual relation between them to which are attached the legal consequences of agency, an agency exists although the parties did not call it agency and did not intend the

---

[g] Green v. H&R Block, Inc., 735 A.2d 1039, 1050–51 (Md. 1999); *see also* RESTATEMENT (SECOND) OF AGENCY § 14 cmt. a (1958) ("The control of the principal does not, however, include control at every moment; its exercise may be very attenuated and, as where the principal is physically absent, may be ineffective.").

[h] *See* RESTATEMENT (SECOND) OF AGENCY § 1 cmt. a (1958); RESTATEMENT (THIRD) OF AGENCY § 1.04(5) (2006).

legal consequences of the relation to follow. Thus, when one who asks a friend to do a slight service for him, such as to return for credit goods recently purchased from a store, neither one may have any realization that they are creating an agency relation or be aware of the legal obligations which would result from performance of the service.[i]

C. LIABILITY FROM THE AGENCY RELATIONSHIP

What liability is created when an agent interacts with a third party? This is the most common question that arises out of a principal-agent relationship. Both tort and contract liability will be discussed below.

1. TORT LIABILITY FROM THE AGENCY RELATIONSHIP

A general tenet of agency law is that a principal has the right to control the conduct of an agent with respect to matters entrusted to the agent.[j] The principal can determine what the ultimate goal is, and the agent must strive to meet that goal. The degree of control that the principal has over the acts of the agent may vary widely within the agency relationship. In this respect, the Second Restatement distinguishes between a master/servant relationship and an independent contractor relationship.[k]

A *master* is a principal who "employs an agent to perform service in his affairs and who controls or has the right to control the physical conduct of the other in the performance of the service." A *servant* is an agent so employed by a master.[l] In some sense, the use of the words master and servant for this relationship is unfortunate because those words may imply servility, household service, or manual labor. The relationship is not so limited; indeed, under these definitions, most employment relationships are technically master/servant relationships.[m] An *independent contractor* is a "person who contracts with another to do something for him but who is not controlled by the other nor subject to the other's right to control with

---

[i]   RESTATEMENT (SECOND) OF AGENCY § 1 cmt. b (1958); *see* RESTATEMENT (THIRD) OF AGENCY § 1.02 (2006).

[j]   *See* RESTATEMENT (SECOND) OF AGENCY § 14 (1958); RESTATEMENT (THIRD) OF AGENCY § 1.01 (2006).

[k]   *See* RESTATEMENT (SECOND) OF AGENCY § 2 (1958).

[l]   *See id.* §§ 2, 220(1). Thus, a master is a subcategory of principal, and a servant is a subcategory of agent. *See id.* § 2 cmt. a.

[m]   *See, e.g., id.* § 220 cmt. a ("The word [servant] indicates the closeness of the relation between the one giving and the one receiving the service rather than the nature of the service or the importance of the one giving it. Thus, ship captains and managers of great corporations are normally superior servants, differing only in the dignity and importance of their positions from those working under them. The rules for determining the liability of the employer for the conduct of both superior servants and the humblest employees are the same * * *.").

respect to his physical conduct in the performance of the undertaking."[n] In general, if a person is subject to the control of another as to the means used to achieve a particular result, he is a servant. By contrast, if a person is subject to the control of another as to his results only (but not over how to achieve those results), he is an independent contractor.[o]

Example: General Motors Corporation employs an individual to serve as head designer of a new automobile. His salary is $300,000 per year. The designer is a "servant" in the Second Restatement terminology and General Motors is his "master." As evidence, consider this possible scenario: the chief executive officer of General Motors comes to the designer and says, "John, the board of directors liked your sketches for the new convertible. They feel, however, that it looks a little boxy and they think the headlights are too conspicuous. Please streamline it a little more and move the headlights into the front fenders." What should the head designer do? He makes the changes that are requested, thereby indicating that he is a servant.

Example: A builder enters into a contract with the owner of a lot to build a house on the lot in accordance with certain plans and specifications prepared by an architect. The builder is an independent contractor. He is employed merely to accomplish a specific result and is not otherwise subject to the owner's control.

Example: A broker enters into a contract to sell goods for a manufacturer. His arrangement involves the receipt of a salary plus a commission on each sale, but the broker has discretion as to how to conduct his business. He determines which cities to visit and who to contact. He uses his own automobile to visit prospects. The broker is an independent contractor because the manufacturer does not control the details of how the broker conducts his day-to-day business.[p]

The classification of an agent as a servant or an independent contractor is important primarily because different rules apply with respect to the principal's liability for harm caused by the agent's tortious conduct.

---

[n]   *Id.* § 2(3).

[o]   Uncertainty may sometimes exist as to whether a person is a servant or an independent contractor. The Second Restatement of Agency contains a somewhat dated provision that provides guidance for this determination. *See* RESTATEMENT (SECOND) OF AGENCY § 220(2) (1958). A more modern list might include factors such as whether the employer files a W-4 form for the employee, whether the employee is listed as such on insurance forms, and the like.

[p]   While all servants are agents, an independent contractor may or may not be an agent. *See id.* § 2. In general, a non-agent independent contractor exists when one or more of the basic elements of the agency relationship are absent—e.g., when there is insufficient control over the contractor, or when the contractor is acting primarily in his own interests. *See, e.g.*, Kemether v. Pa. Interscholastic Athletic Ass'n, Inc., 15 F. Supp. 2d 740, 748 (E.D. Pa. 1998) ("Where prerequisites of agency, such as control, are not satisfied, a non-agent independent contractor relationship may exist: A person who contracts to accomplish something for another or to deliver something to another, but who is not acting as a fiduciary for the other is a non-agent contractor. He may be anyone who has made a contract and who is not an agent." (internal quotation omitted)). In this Chapter, we are concerned only with independent contractors who would also be legally characterized as agents.

While a master is liable for torts committed by a servant within the scope of his employment, a principal is generally not liable for torts committed by an independent contractor in connection with his work.[q] Thus, the determination of whether a person is a servant or an independent contractor can be outcome-determinative in a particular dispute.

Example: *P*, the owner of a successful retail operation with two stores, hires *D* to drive her delivery truck and to deliver goods to her two stores. Before doing so, *P* checks *D*'s driving record and arranges for him to go to a driving school for truck drivers. *D*'s record shows that he has had no accidents for 20 years, and he completes the driving school program without difficulty. Three weeks later, while driving *P*'s delivery truck, *D* is negligent and has a serious accident, injuring *T*. *P* is liable to *T* for his injuries.

In this example, *D* is a servant, and *P*'s liability is independent of whether *P* exercised due care in hiring *D*, or even whether she knew that *D* was her employee at all. *P*'s liability, however, only applies to actions within the scope of *D*'s employment. *P*'s liability in this situation may be described as "vicarious liability" and the consequence of "respondeat superior." *Vicarious liability* refers to the imposition of liability on one person for the actionable conduct of another. *Respondeat superior* is a Latin phrase that means "let the master respond."

Example: The manufacturer's broker, who is selling goods in one of the above examples, has an automobile accident while driving his own car to visit a prospect. The manufacturer is not liable for injuries to third persons arising from the accident. The same would be true of a person injured by the builder in the above example while working on the owner's house. Because the broker and the builder are both independent contractors, the general rule of non-liability for the principal applies.

Of course, the broker and the builder themselves would both be personally liable for the injuries that they caused in these examples, as a person is always responsible for his own torts. *D*, the servant in the above delivery truck example, would also be personally liable for *T*'s injuries, since he too is a tortfeasor. This illustrates the difference between direct liability (a person is always responsible for his own torts) and vicarious liability (a person is sometimes, but not always, responsible for the torts of another).[r]

---

[q] *See* RESTATEMENT (SECOND) OF AGENCY §§ 219, 250 (1958); *cf.* RESTATEMENT (THIRD) OF AGENCY § 7.07 (2006) (imposing similar liability rules but not using the terms "master," "servant," or "independent contractor").

[r] *See* RESTATEMENT (SECOND) OF AGENCY § 343 (1958); RESTATEMENT (THIRD) OF AGENCY § 7.01 (2006). Similarly, while agency concepts may make a principal vicariously liable for the acts of an agent, the principal may also be directly liable for the principal's own tortious behavior (e.g., negligent hiring or negligent supervision). *See, e.g.,* RESTATEMENT (SECOND) OF AGENCY § 213 (1958); RESTATEMENT (THIRD) OF AGENCY §§ 7.03(1), 7.05 (2006).

The Third Restatement does not use the terms "master," "servant," or "independent contractor." Instead, the Third Restatement simply defines an "employee" as "an agent whose principal controls or has the right to control the manner and means of the agent's performance of work," and it provides that "[a]n employer is subject to vicarious liability for a tort committed by its employee acting within the scope of employment."[s] Under the Third Restatement, therefore, there are "employee agents" and "nonemployee agents," with the latter term analogous to the "independent contractor" language of the Second Restatement.

NOTES

(1) As further justification for the doctrine of respondeat superior, consider the following:

> What has emerged as the modern justification for vicarious liability is a rule of policy, a deliberate allocation of a risk. The losses caused by the torts of employees, which as a practical matter are sure to occur in the conduct of the employer's enterprise, are placed upon that enterprise itself, as a required cost of doing business. They are placed upon the employer because, having engaged in an enterprise, which will on the basis of all past experience involve harm to others through the torts of employees, and sought to profit by it, it is just that he, rather than the innocent injured plaintiff, should bear them; and because he is better able to absorb them, and to distribute them, through prices, rates or liability insurance, to the public, and so to shift them to society, to the community at large. Added to this is the makeweight argument that an employer who is held strictly liable is under the greatest incentive to be careful in the selection, instruction and supervision of his servants, and to take every precaution to see that the enterprise is conducted safely.

W. PAGE KEETON ET AL., PROSSER AND KEETON ON THE LAW OF TORTS § 69, at 500–01 (5th ed. 1984).

(2) For guidance on whether a servant/employee's actions are within the scope of his employment, see RESTATEMENT (SECOND) OF AGENCY §§ 228–237 (1958); RESTATEMENT (THIRD) OF AGENCY § 7.07(2) (2006).

(3) As mentioned, the general rule is that a principal is not liable for torts committed by an independent contractor. In *Anderson v. Marathon Petroleum Co.*, 801 F.2d 936 (7th Cir. 1986), the Seventh Circuit explained the rationale for this rule:

> Generally a principal is not liable for an independent contractor's torts even if they are committed in the performance of the contract and even though a principal is liable under the doctrine of respondeat superior for the torts of his employees if committed in

---

[s]   RESTATEMENT (THIRD) OF AGENCY § 7.07 (2006).

the furtherance of their employment. The reason for distinguishing the independent contractor from the employee is that, by definition of the relationship between a principal and an independent contractor, the principal does not supervise the details of the independent contractor's work and therefore is not in a good position to prevent negligent performance, whereas the essence of the contractual relationship known as employment is that the employee surrenders to the employer the right to direct the details of his work, in exchange for receiving a wage. The independent contractor commits himself to providing a specified output, and the principal monitors the contractor's performance not by monitoring inputs—i.e., supervising the contractor—but by inspecting the contractually specified output to make sure it conforms to the specifications. This method of monitoring works fine if it is feasible for the principal to specify and monitor output, but sometimes it is not feasible, particularly if the output consists of the joint product of many separate producers whose specific contributions are difficult (sometimes impossible) to disentangle. In such a case it may be more efficient for the principal to monitor inputs rather than output—the producers rather than the product. By becoming an employee a producer in effect submits himself to that kind of monitoring, receiving payment for the work he puts in rather than for the output he produces.

Since an essential element of the employment relationship is thus the employer's monitoring of the employee's work, a principal who is not knowledgeable about the details of some task is likely to delegate it to an independent contractor. Hence in general, though of course not in every case, the principal who uses an independent contractor will not be as well placed as an employer would be to monitor the work and make sure it is done safely. This is the reason as we have said for not making the principal vicariously liable for the torts of his independent contractors.

Id. at 938–39.

Despite this general rule, there are circumstances where liability is imposed on a principal for the torts of an independent contractor. *See, e.g.,* RESTATEMENT (SECOND) OF AGENCY §§ 212, 214–216, 250–267 (1958); RESTATEMENT (THIRD) OF AGENCY §§ 7.03–7.06, 7.08 (2006). Examples of such circumstances include nondelegable duties (such as duties associated with abnormally dangerous activities), torts that are authorized by the principal, and fraud or misrepresentation (in some situations) by the agent.

2. CONTRACT LIABILITY FROM THE AGENCY RELATIONSHIP

A contractual transaction between an agent and a third party may impose liability upon the principal, the third party, and/or the agent. This liability inquiry is often affected by the type of principal that is present in the transaction: (1) a "disclosed" principal; (2) a "partially disclosed" principal; or (3) an "undisclosed" principal.

A principal is *disclosed* if, at the time of the agent's transaction, the third party has notice that the agent is acting for a principal and has notice of the principal's identity.[t] It may be, of course, that in a specific situation, a third person does not actually know who the principal is, but should be able to reasonably infer the identity of the principal from the information at hand. This is still a disclosed principal situation.[u]

A principal is *partially disclosed* if, at the time of the agent's transaction, the third party has notice that the agent is or may be acting for a principal, but has no notice of the principal's identity.[v]

Example: *A* offers to sell goods to *TP*, truthfully advising him that *A* is the representative of a well-known manufacturer. The identity of the manufacturer is not disclosed. The manufacturer is a partially disclosed principal.

A principal is *undisclosed* if, at the time of the agent's transaction, the third party has no notice that the agent is acting for a principal.[w] In effect, the third party is dealing with the agent as though the agent is the real party in interest.

a. Liability of the Principal to the Third Party

A principal will be liable on a contract between the agent and a third party when the agent acts with actual authority, apparent authority, or inherent authority. Even when the agent lacks one of these three types of authority, the principal may be liable under the doctrines of estoppel or ratification.

(1) Actual Authority

Actual authority (often described as *express authority* or simply by the words "authority" or "authorized") arises from the manifestation of a *principal to an agent* that the agent has power to deal with others as a representative of the principal.[x] An agent who agrees to act in accordance with that manifestation has actual authority to so act, and his actions

---

[t]   *See* RESTATEMENT (SECOND) OF AGENCY § 4(1) (1958); RESTATEMENT (THIRD) OF AGENCY § 1.04(2)(a) (2006).

[u]   *See* RESTATEMENT (SECOND) OF AGENCY § 9(1) (1958); RESTATEMENT (THIRD) OF AGENCY § 1.04(4) (2006).

[v]   *See* RESTATEMENT (SECOND) OF AGENCY § 4(2) (1958). Instead of the term "partially disclosed" principal, the Third Restatement uses the term "unidentified" principal. *See* RESTATEMENT (THIRD) OF AGENCY § 1.04(2)(c) (2006).

[w]   *See* RESTATEMENT (SECOND) OF AGENCY § 4(3) (1958); RESTATEMENT (THIRD) OF AGENCY § 1.04(2)(b) (2006).

[x]   *See* RESTATEMENT (SECOND) OF AGENCY §§ 7, 26, 32–34 (1958); RESTATEMENT (THIRD) OF AGENCY §§ 2.01–2.02, 3.01 (2006).

without more bind the principal.[y] Put differently, if the principal's words or conduct would lead a reasonable person in the agent's position to believe that the agent has authority to act on the principal's behalf, the agent has actual authority to bind the principal.[z]

Example: *P*, the owner of two retail stores, employs *C* to serve as credit manager. *P* has orally given *C* the authority to review and approve requests from customers for the extension of credit. *C* reviews the application of *Y* and approves him for the extension of credit. *C* has actual authority to approve *Y*, and *P* is bound by *C*'s decision.

Example: *P* goes to an office where, as he knows, several brokers have desks, and leaves upon the desk of *A*, thinking it to be the desk of *X*, a note signed by *P*, which states: "I authorize you to contract in my name for the purchase of 100 shares of Western Union stock at today's market." Unaware of the mistake, *A* comes to work, finds the note, and makes a contract with *T* in *P*'s name for the purchase of the shares. *A* has actual authority to make the contract, and *P* is bound by *A*'s action.

Actual authority may be *express* (e.g., oral or written statements, including provisions in the company's organizational documents) or *implied* (e.g., inferred from the principal's prior acts).[aa]

Example: *P* is an elderly person living alone. He is befriended by *A*, a neighbor. *A* does errands for *P*, going to the store, helping *P* go to the doctor, and so forth. *P* has long had a charge account at the local grocery store that *A* has used frequently to charge groceries for *P*. The approval by *P* of *A*'s prior transactions would lead a reasonable person in *A*'s position to believe that he had authority to buy groceries for *P* in the future. This is implied actual authority based on *P*'s acceptance of the groceries in the past.[bb]

A common type of implied actual authority is incidental authority. *Incidental authority* is simply authority to do incidental acts that are

---

[y] *See* RESTATEMENT (SECOND) OF AGENCY §§ 144, 186 (1958); RESTATEMENT (THIRD) OF AGENCY §§ 6.01–6.03 (2006).

[z] *See* RESTATEMENT (SECOND) OF AGENCY §§ 7, 26 (1958); RESTATEMENT (THIRD) OF AGENCY §§ 2.01–2.02, 3.01 (2006).

[aa] *See* RESTATEMENT (SECOND) OF AGENCY § 7 cmt. c (1958) ("It is possible for a principal to specify minutely what the agent is to do. To the extent that he does this, the agent may be said to have express authority. But most authority is created by implication. * * * [Such authority may be] implied or inferred from the words used, from customs and from the relations of the parties. [It is] described as 'implied authority.' "); RESTATEMENT (THIRD) OF AGENCY § 2.02 (2006) (noting that an agent has actual authority "to take action designated or implied" in the principal's manifestations to the agent).

[bb] *Cf.* RESTATEMENT (SECOND) OF AGENCY § 43(2) (1958) ("Acquiescence by the principal in a series of acts by the agent indicates authorization to perform similar acts in the future."); RESTATEMENT (THIRD) OF AGENCY § 2.02 cmt. f (2006) ("On prior occasions the principal may have affirmatively approved of the agent's unauthorized act or silently acquiesced in it by failing to voice affirmative disapproval. This history is likely to influence the agent's subsequent interpretation of instructions. If the principal's subsequent instructions do not address the history, the agent may well infer from the principal's silence that the principal will not demand compliance with the instructions to any degree greater than the principal has done in the past.").

related to a transaction that is authorized. As the Third Restatement explains:

> If a principal's manifestation to an agent expresses the principal's wish that something be done, it is natural to assume that the principal wishes, as an incidental matter, that the agent take the steps necessary and that the agent proceed in the usual and ordinary way, if such has been established, unless the principal directs otherwise. The underlying assumptions are that the principal does not wish to authorize what cannot be achieved if necessary steps are not taken by the agent, and that the principal's manifestation often will not specify all steps necessary to translate it into action.[cc]

***Example*:** *P* authorizes *A* to purchase and obtain goods for him but does not give him money to pay for them. There being no arrangement that *A* is to supply the money or buy upon his own credit, *A* has authority to buy upon *P's* credit.

***Example*:** *P* directs *A* to sell goods by auction at a designated time and place. *P* and *A* both know that a statute forbids anyone but a licensed auctioneer to conduct sales by auction. Nothing to the contrary appearing, *A*'s authority includes authority to employ a licensed auctioneer.

(2) Apparent Authority & Estoppel

Apparent authority arises from the manifestation of a *principal to a third party* that another person is authorized to act as an agent for the principal.[dd] That other person has apparent authority and an act by him within the scope of that apparent authority binds the principal.[ee] Put differently, if the principal's words or conduct would lead a reasonable person in the third party's position to believe that the agent (or other person) has authority to act on the principal's behalf, the agent (or other person) has apparent authority to bind the principal.[ff]

Apparent authority commonly arises when a principal creates the impression that broad authority exists in an agent when in fact it does not. The theory is that if a third party relies on the appearance of authority, the third party may hold the principal liable for the action of

---

[cc] RESTATEMENT (THIRD) OF AGENCY § 2.02 cmt. d (2006); *see also id.* § 2.02(1) (stating that "[a]n agent has actual authority to take * * * acts necessary or incidental to achieving the principal's objectives"); RESTATEMENT (SECOND) OF AGENCY § 35 (1958) ("Unless otherwise agreed, authority to conduct a transaction includes authority to do acts which are incidental to it, usually accompany it, or are reasonably necessary to accomplish it.").

[dd] *See* RESTATEMENT (SECOND) OF AGENCY §§ 8, 27, 49 (1958); RESTATEMENT (THIRD) OF AGENCY §§ 2.03, 3.03 (2006).

[ee] *See* RESTATEMENT (SECOND) OF AGENCY § 159 (1958); RESTATEMENT (THIRD) OF AGENCY §§ 6.01–6.02 (2006).

[ff] *See* RESTATEMENT (SECOND) OF AGENCY §§ 8, 27, 49 (1958); RESTATEMENT (THIRD) OF AGENCY §§ 2.03, 3.03 (2006).

the agent. As mentioned, the principal is bound by the agent's conduct within the scope of the agent's apparent authority, even though the conduct was not actually authorized by the principal.

Example: *P* gives *A*, an agent who is authorized to sell a piece of property on behalf of *P*, specific instructions as to various terms of the sale, including the minimum price ($300,000) *P* is willing to accept. *P* informs possible buyers that *A* is his selling agent but obviously does not communicate *A*'s specific instructions to anyone but *A* (because to do so would be a virtual blueprint to possible buyers as to how to buy the property as cheaply as possible). *A* has actual authority to enter into a contract to sell the property only at a price equal to or higher than $300,000. *A* has apparent authority, however, to sell the property at any price given that *P* has represented to possible buyers that *A* is his agent.

Example: *A* signs a contract on behalf of *P* to sell *P*'s property to *TP* for $275,000. *P* is bound on that contract because the action was within *A*'s apparent authority. Nevertheless, *A* has violated his instructions and is liable to *P* for the loss incurred.[gg]

The major difference between apparent authority and actual authority is that actual authority flows from the principal to the agent, while apparent authority flows from the principal to the third party. As previously mentioned, if the principal's words or conduct would lead a reasonable person in the *agent's* position to believe that the agent has authority to act on the principal's behalf, the agent has actual authority, but if the principal's words or conduct would lead a reasonable person in the *third party's* position to believe that the agent (or other person) has authority to act on the principal's behalf, the agent (or other person) has apparent authority.

In some circumstances, the scope of an agent's apparent authority will be equivalent to the scope of the agent's actual authority. For example, when a principal sends identical letters describing the agent's authority and its limits to both the agent and the third party, actual and apparent authority are co-extensive (assuming no other facts). As the above examples indicate, however, the scope of actual and apparent authority will not always be the same. It is, therefore, important to distinguish between the concepts and to recognize that liability for the principal may arise from statements or other manifestations made by the principal to an agent (actual authority), and/or from statements or other manifestations made by the principal to a third party (apparent authority).

[gg] *See* Chapter 2, Section D(1).

NOTES

(1) Apparent authority can exist even in the absence of a principal-agent relationship. For example, apparent authority can arise when a person falsely represents to a third party that someone else is his agent. *See, e.g.*, RESTATEMENT (THIRD) OF AGENCY § 2.03 (2006) ("Apparent authority is the power held by an agent *or other actor* to affect a principal's legal relations with third parties when a third party reasonably believes *the actor* has authority to act on behalf of the principal and that belief is traceable to the principal's manifestations."); *id.* § 2.03 cmt. a ("The [apparent authority] definition in this section does not presuppose the present or prior existence of an agency relationship * * *. The definition thus applies to actors who appear to be agents but are not, as well as to agents who act beyond the scope of their actual authority."); *see also* RESTATEMENT (SECOND) OF AGENCY § 27 (1958) (describing apparent authority and noting that it is created by the principal's conduct "which, reasonably interpreted, causes the third person to believe that the principal consents to have the act done on his behalf by *the person* purporting to act for him").

(2) Apparent authority is based on the principal's manifestations to a third party. Thus, apparent authority cannot be created by the mere representations of an agent or other actor. Not even the most convincing and persuasive person can create an agency or apparent agency relationship entirely on his own.

Example: John is a smooth-talking con man. He becomes friends with X and represents to X that he is an agent for General Motors seeking possible owners of new car franchises. John is very convincing, showing forged letters on GM letterhead, a forged identification card, and so forth. He persuades X that he will obtain a franchise for X if X will pay $250,000. X does so. John disappears with X's money. General Motors is not obligated to grant a franchise to X and is not otherwise liable for X's loss.

(3) Apparent authority may be established through the agent's title or position. Indeed, it is somewhat common for a third party to argue that the agent's title or position, which was given to him by the principal, created a reasonable belief in the third party that the agent was authorized to act for the principal in ways that are typical of someone who holds that title or position. This notion that title or position conveys authority can also be used to establish actual authority to the extent that the agent reasonably believes that he has authority to act based on the title or position given to him by the principal.

For example, if P appoints A as "Treasurer," and nothing more is stated, A will reasonably believe that he has the authority that Treasurers typically have, and third parties who deal with A (and are aware of his position) will reasonably believe the same. If P tells A that he will not have authority to write checks on the company's account, A will not have actual authority to do so. Assuming that a Treasurer typically has the power to write company checks, however, A will have apparent authority to write checks with respect to third parties who are aware of his position but are unaware of the limitation on his authority. *See, e.g.*, RESTATEMENT (SECOND) OF AGENCY § 27 cmt. a ("[A]s in the case of authority, apparent authority can be created by appointing a person to a position, such as that of manager or treasurer, which carries with it generally recognized duties; to those who know of the appointment there is apparent authority to do the things ordinarily entrusted to one occupying such a position, regardless of unknown limitations which are imposed upon the particular agent."); *id.* § 49 cmt. c ("Acts are interpreted in the light of ordinary human experience. If a principal puts an agent into, or knowingly permits him to occupy, a position in which according to the ordinary habits of persons in the locality, trade or profession, it is usual for such an agent to have a particular kind of authority, anyone dealing with him is justified in inferring that he has such authority, in the absence of reason to know otherwise. The content of such apparent authority is a matter to be determined from the facts.").

(4) The doctrine of estoppel is closely related to the concept of apparent authority. Both doctrines focus on holding the principal responsible for a third party's belief that a person is authorized to act on the principal's behalf. *Compare* RESTATEMENT (SECOND) OF AGENCY §§ 27, 49 (1958) (discussing apparent authority), *and* RESTATEMENT (THIRD) OF AGENCY §§ 2.03, 3.03 (2006) (same), *with* RESTATEMENT (SECOND) OF AGENCY § 8B (1958) (discussing estoppel), *and* RESTATEMENT (THIRD) OF AGENCY § 2.05 (2006) (same). The doctrines, however, are distinct. The doctrine of apparent authority holds the principal responsible for the third party's belief because of the principal's manifestations of authority to the third party. By contrast, the doctrine of estoppel applies when the principal has not made any manifestations of authority to the third party at all. Instead, the principal is held responsible under the estoppel doctrine because the principal contributed to the third party's belief or failed to dispel it:

> * * * The [estoppel] doctrine is applicable when the person against whom estoppel is asserted has made no manifestation that an actor has authority as an agent but is responsible for the third party's belief that an actor is an agent and the third party has justifiably been induced by that belief to undergo a detrimental change in position. Most often the person estopped will be responsible for the third party's erroneous belief as the consequence of a failure to use reasonable care, either to prevent circumstances that foreseeably led to the belief, or to correct the belief once on notice of it. * * *

RESTATEMENT (THIRD) OF AGENCY § 2.05 cmt. c (2006). Thus, the estoppel doctrine may apply when apparent authority is unavailable. Consider the following example:

> P has two coagents, A and B. P has notice that B, acting without actual or apparent authority, has represented to T that A has authority to enter into a transaction that is contrary to P's instructions. T does not know that P's instructions forbid A from

engaging in the transaction. T cannot establish conduct by P on the basis of which T could reasonably believe that A has the requisite authority. T can, however, establish that P had notice of B's representation and that it would have been easy for P to inform T of the limits on A's authority. T detrimentally changes position in reliance on B's representation by making a substantial down payment. If it is found that T's action was justifiable, P is estopped to deny B's authority to make the representation.

Id. § 2.05 illus. 1; *see also id.* § 2.05 cmt. d ("The doctrine stated in this section may estop a person from denying the existence of an agency relationship with an actor when the third party would be unable to establish either the existence of a relationship of agency between the actor and the person estopped * * * or a manifestation of authority sufficient to create apparent authority * * *.").

(5) Apparent authority and estoppel also differ to the extent that apparent authority may be created without the need to establish a detrimental change in position. *See, e.g.*, RESTATEMENT (SECOND) OF AGENCY § 8B cmt. b (1958) ("If the claim of a party to a transaction is based solely upon estoppel, he must prove a change of position which is not required in the case of apparent authority."); RESTATEMENT (THIRD) OF AGENCY § 2.03 cmt. e (2006) ("To establish that an agent acted with apparent authority, it is not necessary for the plaintiff to establish that the principal's manifestation induced the plaintiff to make a detrimental change in position, in contrast to the showing required by the estoppel doctrine[ ].").

(3) Inherent Authority

According to the Second Restatement, the term "inherent agency power" (typically referred to as *inherent authority*) is used to describe "the power of an agent which is derived not from authority, apparent authority or estoppel, but solely from the agency relation and exists for the protection of persons harmed by or dealing with a servant or other agent."[hh] That definition indicates that inherent authority is a distinct type of authority, but it says very little about when it arises.

Later sections, however, provide further guidance. A general agent[ii] for a disclosed or partially disclosed principal has inherent authority to bind the principal "for acts done on his [the principal's] account which usually accompany or are incidental to transactions which the agent is authorized to conduct if, although they are forbidden by the principal, the other party reasonably believes that the agent is authorized to do them and has no notice that he is not so authorized."[jj]

[hh] RESTATEMENT (SECOND) OF AGENCY § 8A (1958).

[ii] A "general agent" is "an agent authorized to conduct a series of transactions involving a continuity of service." *Id.* § 3(1).

[jj] *Id.* § 161.

Example: *P* hires *A* to manage a branch store of *P*'s retail operations. *A* has authority to manage the store on a day-to-day basis but is told expressly that he has no authority to mark down the prices of goods without the prior approval of *P*. *A* nevertheless marks down slow-moving goods which are sold to third persons. There is no actual authority, but *P* is bound by inherent authority if the act of marking down prices usually accompanies managerial duties, and if a third party reasonably believed that *A* was authorized to do such an act.

In the above example, can an argument be made that there was apparent authority? After all, the principal gave *A* the position of "manager," and it may be reasonable for third parties who know that *A* is a manager to believe that he has authority to mark down prices.[kk] In situations involving a disclosed or partially disclosed principal, therefore, the concepts of apparent authority and inherent authority may overlap.

In an undisclosed principal situation, however, inherent authority has independent significance. After all, apparent authority involves a third party who reasonably believes, based on the principal's manifestations, that a person was authorized to act on the principal's behalf.[ll] In an undisclosed principal situation, therefore, there can be no apparent authority, as the third party has no idea that a principal is involved in the transaction.[mm] Even in the absence of actual and apparent authority, however, an undisclosed principal can still be bound via inherent authority. Indeed, "[a] general agent for an undisclosed principal authorized to conduct transactions subjects his principal to liability for acts done on his account, if usual or necessary in such transactions, although forbidden by the principal to do them."[nn]

Example: *P* employs *A* to manage his cigar bar, directing *A* to represent that he (*A*) is the owner, and to purchase no goods for the business except alcohol and bottled water, with all other goods to be supplied by *P*. *A* purchases cigars from *T* for the business. *P* is subject to liability to *T* for the price of the cigars.

[kk] *See* Chapter 2, Section C(2)(a)(2).

[ll] *See* Chapter 2, Section C(2)(a)(2).

[mm] *See* RESTATEMENT (SECOND) OF AGENCY § 194 cmt. a (1958) ("Since apparent authority is the power which results from acts which appear to the third person to be authorized by the principal, if such person does not know of the existence of a principal there can be no apparent authority."); RESTATEMENT (THIRD) OF AGENCY § 2.03 cmt. f (2006) ("In contrast, apparent authority is not present when a third party believes that an interaction is with an actor who is a principal. If a third party believes that an actor represents no one else's interests, the third party does not have a reasonable belief in the actor's power to affect anyone else's legal position.").

[nn] RESTATEMENT (SECOND) OF AGENCY § 194 (1958); *see also id.* § 195 (discussing the inherent authority of manager-agents in an undisclosed principal situation); *cf.* RESTATEMENT (THIRD) OF AGENCY § 2.06(2) (2006) (preserving what is effectively inherent authority (although not designated as such) in undisclosed principal situations).

NOTES

(1) What is the rationale for inherent authority? Consider the following:

> The principles of agency have made it possible for persons to utilize the services of others in accomplishing far more than could be done by their unaided efforts. * * * Partnerships and corporations, through which most of the work of the world is done today, depend for their existence upon agency principles. The rules designed to promote the interests of these enterprises are necessarily accompanied by rules to police them. It is inevitable that in doing their work, either through negligence or excess of zeal, agents will harm third persons or will deal with them in unauthorized ways. It would be unfair for an enterprise to have the benefit of the work of its agents without making it responsible to some extent for their excesses and failures to act carefully. The answer of the common law has been the creation of special agency powers or, to phrase it otherwise, the imposition of liability upon the principal because of unauthorized or negligent acts of his servants and other agents. These powers or liabilities are created by the courts primarily for the protection of third persons, either those who are harmed by the agent or those who deal with the agent. In the long run, however, they [i]nure to the benefit of the business world and hence to the advantage of employers as a class, the members of which are plaintiffs as well as defendants in actions brought upon unauthorized transactions conducted by agents.

RESTATEMENT (SECOND) OF AGENCY § 8A cmt. a (1958); *see also id.* § 161 cmt. a ("The basis of the [inherent authority] liability stated in this Section is comparable to the liability of a master for the torts of his servant. * * * In the case of the master, it is thought fair that one who benefits from the enterprise and has a right to control the physical activities of those who make the enterprise profitable, should pay for the physical harm resulting from the errors and derelictions of the servants while doing the kind of thing which makes the enterprise successful. * * * Commercial convenience requires that the principal should not escape liability where there have been deviations from the usually granted authority by persons who are such essential parts of his business enterprise. In the long run it is of advantage to business, and hence to employers as a class, that third persons should not be required to scrutinize too carefully the mandates of permanent or semi-permanent agents who do no more than what is usually done by agents in similar positions.").

(2) The Third Restatement does not recognize "inherent authority" as an independent concept:

> The term "inherent agency power," used in Restatement Second, Agency, and defined therein by § 8A, is not used in this Restatement. Inherent agency power is defined as "a term used * * * to indicate the power of an agent which is derived not from

authority, apparent authority or estoppel, but solely from the agency relation and exists for the protection of persons harmed by or dealing with a servant or other agent." Other doctrines stated in this Restatement encompass the justifications underpinning § 8A, including the importance of interpretation by the agent in the agent's relationship with the principal, as well as the doctrines of apparent authority, estoppel, and restitution.

RESTATEMENT (THIRD) OF AGENCY § 2.01 cmt. b (2006). *But see id.* § 2.06(2) (preserving what is effectively inherent authority (although not designated as such) in undisclosed principal situations).

(4) Ratification

Even if an agent acts without authority, the principal will be liable to a third party if (1) the agent purports to act (or, under the Third Restatement, acts) on the principal's behalf, and (2a) the principal affirmatively treats the agent's act as authorized (*express ratification*), or (2b) the principal engages in conduct that is justifiable only if the principal is treating the agent's act as authorized (*implied ratification*).[oo] Significantly, ratification does not occur unless the principal, at the time of the ratification, is fully aware of all of the material facts involved in the original transaction.[pp]

Express ratification most commonly occurs through oral or written statements (e.g., a company resolution).[qq] Implied ratification most commonly occurs when the principal has knowledge of an unauthorized transaction entered into purportedly on his behalf, but the principal nevertheless accepts the benefits of the transaction.[rr]

Example: *P* owns an advertising agency and employs *A* to service existing accounts by purchasing space in advertising media. *A* does not have authority to set terms with clients. *A* executes an agreement with *T* that commits *P* to develop a new advertising campaign for *T*. *P* learns of the agreement and then accepts and retains advance payment made by *T* for the new advertising campaign. By accepting and retaining the payment, *P* has ratified the unauthorized agreement made by *A*.

[oo] *See* RESTATEMENT (SECOND) OF AGENCY §§ 82–83, 85, 100, 143 (1958); RESTATEMENT (THIRD) OF AGENCY §§ 4.01–4.03 (2006). Under the Second Restatement, ratification can occur only if the agent purports to act on the principal's behalf, but under the Third Restatement, ratification can occur if the agent acts or purports to act on the principal's behalf. *Compare* RESTATEMENT (SECOND) OF AGENCY § 85(1) (1958) *with* RESTATEMENT (THIRD) OF AGENCY § 4.03 (2006). For the significance of this point, please see the "Notes" following this Section.

[pp] *See* RESTATEMENT (SECOND) OF AGENCY § 91 (1958); RESTATEMENT (THIRD) OF AGENCY § 4.06 (2006).

[qq] *Cf.* RESTATEMENT (SECOND) OF AGENCY § 93 (1958); RESTATEMENT (THIRD) OF AGENCY § 4.01(2) (2006).

[rr] *Cf.* RESTATEMENT (SECOND) OF AGENCY §§ 98–99 (1958); RESTATEMENT (THIRD) OF AGENCY § 4.01 cmt. g (2006) ("A person may ratify an act * * * by receiving or retaining benefits it generates if the person has knowledge of material facts * * * and no independent claim to the benefit.").

Example: Without authority to bind *P*, *A* purports to rent machinery from *T* for *P*. *A* delivers the machinery to *P*, representing that *T* has loaned the machinery to *P* without requiring compensation. *P* uses the machinery. There is no ratification by *P* because he was unaware of the material facts related to the rental transaction.

Ratification occurs as soon as the principal objectively manifests his acceptance of the transaction, even if the fact of ratification is not communicated to the third party, the agent, or any other person.[ss] When ratification occurs, the effect is to validate the contract as if it were originally authorized by the principal. Thus, ratification imposes liability upon a principal in the same manner as if the principal had actually authorized the contract in the first place.[tt] Nevertheless, ratification is not effective unless it occurs before the third party has withdrawn from the transaction. Similarly, ratification is ineffective if it would be unfair to the third party as a result of changed circumstances.[uu]

NOTES

(1) What function does ratification serve? Consider the following:

> Ratification often serves the function of clarifying situations of ambiguous or uncertain authority. A principal's ratification confirms or validates an agent's right to have acted as the agent did. That is, an agent's action may have been effective to bind the principal to the third party, and the third party to the principal, because the agent acted with apparent authority. If the principal ratifies the agent's act, it is thereafter not necessary to establish that the agent acted with apparent authority. Moreover, by replicating the effects of actual authority, the principal's ratification eliminates claims the principal would otherwise have against the agent for acting without actual authority. The principal's ratification may also eliminate claims that third parties could assert against the agent when the agent has purported to be authorized to bind the principal but the principal is not bound. * * *

RESTATEMENT (THIRD) OF AGENCY § 4.01 cmt. b (2006).

(2) Ratification cannot operate to prejudice the rights of persons who are not parties to the transaction, but who acquired rights or other interests in the subject matter of the transaction before the ratification occurred. *See*

[ss] *See* RESTATEMENT (SECOND) OF AGENCY § 95 (1958); RESTATEMENT (THIRD) OF AGENCY § 4.01 cmt. d (2006) ("Ratification requires an objectively or externally observable indication that a person consents that another's prior act shall affect the person's legal relations. To constitute ratification, the consent need not be communicated to the third party or the agent. This is so because the focal point of ratification is an observable indication that the principal has exercised choice and has consented.").

[tt] *See* RESTATEMENT (SECOND) OF AGENCY §§ 82, 100, 143 (1958); RESTATEMENT (THIRD) OF AGENCY §§ 4.01(1), 4.02(1) (2006).

[uu] *See* RESTATEMENT (SECOND) OF AGENCY §§ 88–89 (1958); RESTATEMENT (THIRD) OF AGENCY § 4.05 (2006).

RESTATEMENT (SECOND) OF AGENCY § 101(c) (1958); RESTATEMENT (THIRD) OF AGENCY § 4.02(2)(c) (2006).

Example: Purporting to act for *P* but without power to bind him, *A* makes a contract for the sale of *P*'s land to *T*. *B*, not knowing this, offers *P* a smaller price than that called for by *T*'s contract. *P* accepts *B*'s offer; then learning of the contract with *T*, ratifies that. *B* is entitled to the land. *P* is subject to liability to *T* on the contract.

(3) As mentioned, ratification requires an agent to purport to act on the principal's behalf. *See* RESTATEMENT (SECOND) OF AGENCY § 85(1) (1958). Under the Second Restatement, therefore, there can be no ratification by an undisclosed principal. By definition, in an undisclosed principal situation, a third party has no notice that the agent is acting for a principal; thus, the agent is not purporting to act on the principal's behalf.

The Third Restatement changes this rule and allows ratification by an undisclosed principal by stating that "[a] person may ratify an act if the actor *acted or purported to act* as an agent on the person's behalf." RESTATEMENT (THIRD) OF AGENCY § 4.03 (2006) (emphasis added). Because an agent for an undisclosed principal acts on the principal's behalf (even though he does not purport to do so), ratification by an undisclosed principal is permissible. *See id.* § 4.03 cmt. b ("The formulation in this section does not distinguish among disclosed principals, unidentified principals, and undisclosed principals. It is contrary to the rule in Restatement Second, Agency § 85(1), which states that an act may be ratified only if the actor purported to act as an agent. That rule limited ratification to situations in which the principal was disclosed or unidentified. * * * In contrast, under the formulation in this section, an undisclosed principal may ratify an agent's unauthorized act.").

b. Liability of the Third Party to the Principal

When an agent makes a contract for a disclosed or partially disclosed principal, the third party is liable to the principal if the agent acted with authority (actual, apparent, or, under the Second Restatement, inherent), so long as the principal is not excluded as a party by the form or terms of the contract.^{vv} When an agent makes a contract for an undisclosed principal, the third party is liable to the principal if the agent had authority (actual or, under the Second Restatement, inherent), so long as the principal is not excluded by the form or terms of the contract, the existence of the principal is not fraudulently concealed, and there is no set-off or similar defense against the agent.^{ww}

[vv] *See* RESTATEMENT (SECOND) OF AGENCY §§ 292–293 (1958); RESTATEMENT (THIRD) OF AGENCY §§ 6.01(1), 6.02(1) (2006). Because ratification functions as a substitute for actual authority, ratification by the principal would also seem to bind the third party if such ratification would not be unfair to the third party as a result of changed circumstances. *See* Chapter 2, Section C(2)(a)(4).

[ww] *See* RESTATEMENT (SECOND) OF AGENCY §§ 302–304, 306, 308 (1958); RESTATEMENT (THIRD) OF AGENCY §§ 6.03, 6.06, 6.11(4) (2006). As mentioned, apparent authority is inapplicable in the undisclosed principal situation. *See* Chapter 2, Section C(2)(a)(3). Once again,

The fraudulent concealment exception merits some additional discussion. When an agent contracting on behalf of an undisclosed principal falsely represents that the agent is not acting for a principal (i.e., the agent falsely represents that he is acting solely for himself), the Second and Third Restatements both provide that the third party can avoid the contract if the principal or the agent had notice that the third party would not have dealt with the principal.[xx]

Example: With authorization from P, his undisclosed principal, A contracts with T to sell and deliver to T 1000 shares in a corporation. Having no reason to suppose that T is unwilling to deal with P, A denies the existence of P and affirmatively represents that he is acting solely for himself. P can enforce this contract.

Example: Same facts as above, except that A knows that T would not enter into any transaction with him if T knew that P was the principal. A denies the existence of P and makes his affirmative representation for this reason. P cannot enforce this contract if T elects to rescind.

Example: Same facts as the first example, except that A has no reason to believe that T would be unwilling to contract with P but this fact is known to P, who employed A for the purpose of concealing P's interest in the transaction from T. P cannot enforce this contract if T elects to rescind.

Despite the general rules stated above, an undisclosed principal cannot bind a third party to a contract if the principal's role in the contract substantially changes the third party's rights or obligations:

> The nature of the performance that a contract requires determines whether performance by an undisclosed principal will be effective as performance under the contract and whether an undisclosed principal can require that the third party render performance to the principal. Performance by an undisclosed principal is not effective as performance under a contract if the third party has a substantial interest in receiving performance from the agent who made the contract. This limit corresponds to the limit on delegability of performance of a duty as stated in [the Second Restatement of Contracts]. * * * The nature of the performance that a contract requires from a third party determines whether an undisclosed principal is entitled to receive that performance. An undisclosed principal may not

---

because ratification functions as a substitute for actual authority, ratification by the principal would also seem to bind the third party if such ratification would not be unfair to the third party as a result of changed circumstances. *See* Chapter 2, Section C(2)(a)(4). Only the Third Restatement, however, recognizes ratification in an undisclosed principal situation. *See* Chapter 2, Section C(2)(a)(4).

[xx] *See* RESTATEMENT (SECOND) OF AGENCY § 304 (1958); RESTATEMENT (THIRD) OF AGENCY § 6.11(4) (2006).

require that a third party render performance to the principal if rendering performance to the principal would materially change the nature of the third party's duty, materially increase the burden or risk imposed on the third party, or materially impair the third party's chance of receiving return performance. These limits correspond to the limits imposed on assignment of a contractual right.[yy]

c.   Liability of the Agent to the Third Party

If an agent contracts with a third party on behalf of a disclosed principal, the general rule is that the agent is not a party to the contract and is not liable to the third party.[zz] This result is consistent with the third party's expectations—i.e., the third party expected that he was entering into a contract with the principal and not with the agent.

Example: P instructs A to purchase a computer on P's behalf. A goes to T's computer store and represents to T that he is buying for the account of P. A contract is entered into. P is liable on the contract, but A is not.

If an agent contracts with a third party on behalf of a partially disclosed or undisclosed principal, the general rule is that the agent is a party to the contract and is liable to the third party (regardless of whether the principal is also liable to the third party).[aaa] The third party's right to hold the agent responsible on contracts with partially disclosed principals is based on the common sense notion that a third party normally would not agree to look solely to a person whose identity is unknown for performance of the contract. If the third party does not know the identity of the principal, the third party cannot investigate the solvency and reliability of the principal; thus, the third party probably expected the agent to be liable. Similarly, the third party's right to hold the agent responsible on contracts with undisclosed principals is also consistent with the third party's expectations—i.e., the third party expected the agent to be a party to the contract because the agent presented the deal as if he were acting for himself. Moreover, if the third party is unaware of the principal's existence, the third party must be relying on the agent's solvency and reliability when entering into the contract.

Example: P, a well-known manufacturer, instructs A to offer to sell goods on P's behalf to T without revealing P's identity. A makes the offer and truthfully advises T that A is making the offer on behalf of a well-

---

[yy] RESTATEMENT (THIRD) OF AGENCY § 6.03 cmt. d (2006); *see* RESTATEMENT (SECOND) OF AGENCY §§ 309–310 (1958).

[zz] *See* RESTATEMENT (SECOND) OF AGENCY § 320 (1958); RESTATEMENT (THIRD) OF AGENCY § 6.01(2) (2006).

[aaa] *See* RESTATEMENT (SECOND) OF AGENCY § 321–322 (1958); RESTATEMENT (THIRD) OF AGENCY § 6.02(2), 6.03(2), 6.09 (2006).

known manufacturer. *A* does not disclose *P*'s identity. *T* accepts the offer. Both *P* and *A* are liable on the contract.

    Example: Same facts as above, but *A* offers to sell the goods to *T* without disclosing that they are *P*'s goods and that he is selling the goods on *P*'s behalf. *T* accepts the offer. Both *P* and *A* are liable on the contract.

    An agent who purports to act on behalf of a principal makes an implied warranty of authority to a third party. If the agent lacks the power to bind the principal, the agent is liable to the third party for breach of the implied warranty (unless the agent conveyed that he was not making such a warranty or the third party knew that the agent had no authority).**bbb** The agent may also be liable to the third party under a theory that he has tortiously misrepresented his authority.**ccc**

    Example: *A*, a mortgage broker claiming to act as agent for *P* Corporation, makes an oral contract to sell mortgage-backed securities owned by *P* Corporation to *T* Bank. *A* acted without actual, apparent, or inherent authority. *A* is subject to liability to *T* Bank for loss to *T* Bank resulting from *T* Bank's reliance on *A*'s implied representation that *A* had power to bind *P* Corporation.

NOTE

    If an agent becomes a party to a contract under the general rules stated above, and if the third party breaches the contract in some manner, the third party may be liable to the agent. *See, e.g.*, RESTATEMENT (THIRD) OF AGENCY § 6.03 cmt. e (2006) ("As a party to a contract made on behalf of an undisclosed principal, an agent may sue the third party in the agent's own name.").

D. DUTIES OF THE AGENT AND THE PRINCIPAL TO EACH OTHER

1. THE AGENT'S DUTIES TO THE PRINCIPAL

    An agency relationship has the important characteristic of being a *fiduciary* relationship. An agent is a fiduciary with respect to matters within the scope of his agency.**ddd** Basically, this means that an agent is held to a very high standard of conduct in carrying out his tasks for the principal. In general, an agent's duties require the agent to act *loyally* and *carefully* when acting within the scope of the agency. Some examples

---

    bbb *See* RESTATEMENT (SECOND) OF AGENCY § 329 (1958); RESTATEMENT (THIRD) OF AGENCY § 6.10 (2006).

    ccc *See* RESTATEMENT (SECOND) OF AGENCY § 330 (1958); RESTATEMENT (THIRD) OF AGENCY § 6.10 cmt. a (2006) ("An agent who falsely warrants authority may be subject to liability for fraud or negligent misrepresentation.").

    ddd *See* RESTATEMENT (SECOND) OF AGENCY § 13 (1958); RESTATEMENT (THIRD) OF AGENCY §§ 1.01, 8.01 (2006).

of this loyalty obligation include the following: (1) an agent is accountable to the principal for any profits arising out of the transactions he is to conduct on the principal's behalf;[eee] (2) an agent must act solely for the benefit of the principal and not to benefit himself or someone else other than the principal;[fff] (3) an agent must refrain from dealing with his principal as an adverse party or from acting on behalf of an adverse party;[ggg] (4) an agent may not compete with his principal concerning the subject matter of the agency;[hhh] and (5) an agent may not use the principal's property (including confidential information) for the agent's own purposes or a third party's purposes.[iii]

As mentioned, the agency relationship requires an agent to act carefully as well. An agent "has a duty to the principal to act with the care, competence, and diligence normally exercised by agents in similar circumstances."[jjj] Moreover, "[i]f an agent claims to possess special skills or knowledge, the agent has a duty to the principal to act with the care, competence, and diligence normally exercised by agents with such skills or knowledge."[kkk]

In many circumstances, an agent also has a duty to disclose information to the principal. The agent must "use reasonable efforts to give his principal information which is relevant to affairs entrusted to him and which, as the agent has notice, the principal would desire to have and which can be communicated without violating a superior duty to a third person."[lll] This disclosure obligation between parties in a fiduciary relationship differs dramatically from the lack of any duty to volunteer information in an arm's length transaction.

Example: *M* is looking for a site for his plant. He learns that *O* has a site for sale. The asking price is $250,000. *M* and *O* negotiate and agree upon a price of $247,500. In this negotiation, *O* does not disclose that he purchased the site for $150,000 a few days before—information that would have been relevant to *M*'s decision to agree to the $247,500 price.

[eee] *See* RESTATEMENT (SECOND) OF AGENCY § 388 (1958); RESTATEMENT (THIRD) OF AGENCY §§ 8.02, 8.06.

[fff] *See* RESTATEMENT (SECOND) OF AGENCY § 387 (1958); RESTATEMENT (THIRD) OF AGENCY §§ 8.01, 8.06 (2006).

[ggg] *See* RESTATEMENT (SECOND) OF AGENCY §§ 389, 391 (1958); RESTATEMENT (THIRD) OF AGENCY §§ 8.03, 8.06 (2006).

[hhh] *See* RESTATEMENT (SECOND) OF AGENCY § 393 (1958); RESTATEMENT (THIRD) OF AGENCY §§ 8.04, 8.06 (2006).

[iii] *See* RESTATEMENT (SECOND) OF AGENCY §§ 395–396, 398, 402, 404, 422–423 (1958); RESTATEMENT (THIRD) OF AGENCY §§ 8.05, 8.06, 8.12 (2006).

[jjj] RESTATEMENT (THIRD) OF AGENCY § 8.08 (2006); *see* RESTATEMENT (SECOND) OF AGENCY § 379 (1958).

[kkk] RESTATEMENT (THIRD) OF AGENCY § 8.08 (2006); *see* RESTATEMENT (SECOND) OF AGENCY § 379 (1958).

[lll] RESTATEMENT (SECOND) OF AGENCY § 381 (1958); *see id.* § 390 (imposing a duty to disclose on an agent who acts as an adverse party with the principal's consent); RESTATEMENT (THIRD) OF AGENCY §§ 8.06, 8.11 (2006).

O's failure to disclose this information is not a breach of any duty and *M* may not rescind the transaction.

Example: *P* retains *A* to purchase a suitable manufacturing site for him. *A* owns a suitable site which he offers to *P* for $250,000, a fair price. *A* tells *P* all of the relevant facts, but *A* fails to mention that *A* purchased the site for $150,000 only a short time ago. *A* has breached his duty and the transaction may be rescinded by *P*.

An agent also has a duty to act only as authorized by the principal.[mmm] It should come as no surprise, therefore, that an agent acting without actual authority is liable to his principal for any loss suffered by the principal (e.g., if an agent lacking actual authority binds the principal via apparent authority).[nnn]

Example: *A* acts as *P* Insurance Company's agent for purposes of issuing policies of workers' compensation insurance. *A* issues a binder policy to *T*. *A* acts with apparent authority in issuing the policy but *A* issues it in a manner clearly prohibited by *A*'s agency agreement with *P*. *E*, an employee of *T*, suffers a job-related injury. *P* must pay the claim even though *A* exceeded *A*'s actual authority in issuing the insurance policy to *T*. *A* is subject to liability to *P* for the amount of *T*'s claim against *P*. *A* is also subject to liability for any costs *P* incurs in opposing *T*'s claim.

2. THE PRINCIPAL'S DUTIES TO THE AGENT

A principal's duties to an agent are not fiduciary in nature, as fiduciary responsibilities run only from the agent to the principal.[ooo] Nevertheless, a principal has several obligations to an agent. For example, a principal must perform his contractual commitments to the agent, must not unreasonably interfere with the agent's work, and must generally act fairly and in good faith towards the agent.[ppp] Perhaps most importantly, if the agent incurs expenses or suffers other losses in

---

[mmm] *See* RESTATEMENT (SECOND) OF AGENCY §§ 383, 385 (1958); RESTATEMENT (THIRD) OF AGENCY § 8.09 (2006).

[nnn] *See* RESTATEMENT (SECOND) OF AGENCY §§ 399, 401 (1958); RESTATEMENT (THIRD) OF AGENCY § 8.09 (2006); *id.* § 8.09 cmt. b ("If an agent takes action beyond the scope of the agent's actual authority, the agent is subject to liability to the principal for loss caused the principal. The principal's loss may stem from actions taken by the agent with apparent authority, on the basis of which the principal became subject to liability to third parties. The principal's loss may include costs the principal incurs in defending against lawsuits brought against the principal by third parties."); *see also id.* ("If an agent's action beyond the scope of the agent's actual authority causes loss to the principal, the agent is subject to liability to the principal for that loss even though the loss would have been greater had the agent acted consistently with the agent's actual authority. Were the rule otherwise, an agent might be tempted to act or to continue to act without actual authority in the hope that matters will turn out sufficiently well that the principal will not suffer loss. Moreover, the underlying premise of a relationship of agency is action by the agent that is consistent with the principal's manifestation of assent, not whether an agent's action is in fact beneficial to the principal.").

[ooo] *See* Chapter 2, Section D(1).

[ppp] *See* RESTATEMENT (SECOND) OF AGENCY §§ 432–437, 441 (1958); RESTATEMENT (THIRD) OF AGENCY §§ 8.13, 8.15 (2006).

carrying out the principal's instructions, the principal has a duty to indemnify the agent.qqq

E. TERMINATION OF THE AGENT'S POWER

As previously discussed, the relationship between an agent and a principal is a consensual one.rrr Actual authority from that relationship terminates when the objective of the relationship has been achieved, when the principal or the agent dies, and in a variety of other circumstances.sss Actual authority also terminates when the principal revokes it or the agent renounces it.ttt If the agency relationship is based on contract, however, the decision to terminate actual authority may be a breach of that contract. Nevertheless, actual authority has ended, even though contractual liability may exist for its termination.uuu Stated differently, a principal or an agent always has the power to terminate actual authority, but he may not have the right.

Example: *P*, who owns a hotel, retains *A* Corp. to manage it. *P* and *A* Corp. enter into an agreement providing that, in exchange for *A* Corp.'s management services, *A* Corp. will receive a commission equal to five percent of the hotel's gross revenues. The agreement further provides that *A* Corp.'s authority shall be irrevocable by *P* for a period of 10 years. Two years later, *P* revokes. *A* Corp.'s actual authority is terminated, although *A* Corp. may have claims against *P* for breach of contract.

Because an inference of apparent authority may be based on the existence of prior actual authority, the termination of actual authority does not itself eliminate the apparent authority of an agent. It may be necessary to give notice of termination to third parties who dealt with the agent or who otherwise continue to believe that the principal has authorized the agent to act.vvv

---

qqq *See* RESTATEMENT (SECOND) OF AGENCY §§ 438–440 (1958); RESTATEMENT (THIRD) OF AGENCY § 8.14 (2006).

rrr *See* Chapter 2, Section B.

sss *See* RESTATEMENT (SECOND) OF AGENCY §§ 105–124 (1958); RESTATEMENT (THIRD) OF AGENCY §§ 3.06–3.10 (2006).

ttt *See* RESTATEMENT (SECOND) OF AGENCY § 117–119 (1958); RESTATEMENT (THIRD) OF AGENCY §§ 3.09–3.10 (2006).

uuu *See* RESTATEMENT (SECOND) OF AGENCY § 118 (1958); *id.* § 118 cmt. b ("The principal has power to revoke [authority] and the agent has power to renounce [authority], although doing so is in violation of a contract between the parties and although the authority is expressed to be irrevocable. A statement in a contract that the authority cannot be terminated by either party is effective only to create liability for its wrongful termination."); RESTATEMENT (THIRD) OF AGENCY § 3.10(1) (2006); *id.* § 3.10 cmt. b ("A principal has power to revoke an agent's actual authority and the agent has power to renounce it. The power is not extinguished because an agreement between principal and agent states that the agent's actual authority shall be irrevocable or shall not be revoked except under specified circumstances. * * * Exercising the power to revoke or renounce may constitute a breach of contract.").

vvv *See* RESTATEMENT (SECOND) OF AGENCY §§ 124A, 125 (1958); RESTATEMENT (THIRD) OF AGENCY § 3.11 (2006).

CHAPTER 3

THE GENERAL PARTNERSHIP

■ ■ ■

A. INTRODUCTION

There are many business organizations that have the partnership structure. This Chapter focuses on the general partnership, which can be thought of as the basic partnership form. Other partnership structures, such as the limited partnership and the limited liability partnership, are discussed in later Chapters.

The law governing general partnerships is largely derived from statute. The National Conference of Commissioners on Uniform State Laws ("NCCUSL") promulgated the Uniform Partnership Act ("UPA") in 1914. With the exception of Louisiana, UPA was adopted in every state. In 1992, NCCUSL promulgated a revision of UPA. This revised act was itself amended in 1993, 1994, 1996, and 1997, and the final 1997 act has become known as the Revised Uniform Partnership Act ("RUPA"). As of this writing, some version of RUPA has been adopted by thirty-seven states as well as the District of Columbia and the Virgin Islands.

Despite the prevalence of RUPA in this country, the materials in this Chapter will discuss both UPA and RUPA. There are several reasons for this dual treatment. First, UPA is still the law in some commercially important states, such as New York. Second, UPA and RUPA share many common principles. Because there is far more UPA case law than RUPA case law, however, many of the primary materials that are useful for teaching the basic principles of partnership law are UPA-based. Third, it is easier to understand many of the significant changes in RUPA, particularly the dissociation and dissolution provisions, if one has a working knowledge of how those issues are dealt with under UPA.

B. FORMATION

1. THE DEFINITION OF PARTNERSHIP

The general partnership is unique among business organizations with two or more owners because its formation does not require a public filing with the state. Instead, under UPA, a general partnership is formed whenever there is an "association of two or more persons to carry on as co-owners a business for profit." UPA § 6; *see* RUPA § 202(a) (defining a partnership as an "association of two or more persons to carry on as co-owners a business for profit * * * whether or not the persons intend to form a partnership"). Both UPA and RUPA contain rules for assisting in the determination of whether a partnership has been formed. *See* UPA § 7; RUPA § 202(c). The most important of these rules indicates that a person who receives a share of the profits of a business is presumed to be a partner in the business, unless the profits were received in payment of a debt, as wages, or for other listed exceptions. *See* UPA § 7(4); RUPA § 202(c)(3).

Because the formation of a general partnership simply requires a business relationship to fall within the statutory definition, a general partnership can be created even if the partners do not realize that they are forming such an enterprise. *See, e.g.*, Byker v. Mannes, 641 N.W.2d 210, 215–16 (Mich. 2002) ("The statutory language is devoid of any requirement that the individuals have the subjective intent to create a partnership. Stated more plainly, the statute does not require partners to be aware of their status as 'partners' in order to have a legal partnership. * * * Thus, one analyzes whether the parties acted as partners, not whether they subjectively intended to create, or not to create, a partnership."); *see also* Hilco Prop. Servs., Inc. v. United States, 929 F. Supp. 526, 536–37 (D.N.H. 1996) ("The conduct of the parties and the circumstances surrounding their relationship and transactions control the factual question of whether a partnership existed * * *. And although the question of intent is a crucial part of the calculus, 'the only necessary intent * * * is an intent to do those things which constitute a partnership.' "). The implications of this proposition are discussed in the materials below.

> ## MARTIN V. PEYTON
> Court of Appeals of New York, 1927.
> 158 N.E. 77.

Action by Charles S. Martin against William C. Peyton and others. A judgment of the Special Term, entered on the report of a referee in favor of the defendants was affirmed by the Appellate Division and plaintiff appeals. Affirmed.

ANDREWS, J.

* * * Today only those who are partners between themselves may be charged for partnership debts by others. [UPA § 7]. There is one exception. Now and then a recovery is allowed where in truth such relationship is absent. This is because the debtor may not deny the claim. [UPA § 16].

Partnership results from contract, express or implied. If denied, it may be proved by the production of some written instrument, by testimony as to some conversation, by circumstantial evidence. If nothing else appears, the receipt by the defendant of a share of the profits of the business is enough. [UPA § 7].

Assuming some written contract between the parties, the question may arise whether it creates a partnership. If it be complete, if it expresses in good faith the full understanding and obligation of the parties, then it is for the court to say whether a partnership exists. It may, however, be a mere sham intended to hide the real relationship. Then other results follow. In passing upon it, effect is to be given to each provision. Mere words will not blind us to realities. Statements that no partnership is intended are not conclusive. If as a whole a contract contemplates an association of two or more persons to carry on as co-owners a business for profit, a partnership there is. [UPA § 6]. On the other hand, if it be less than this, no partnership exists. Passing on the contract as a whole, an arrangement for sharing profits is to be considered. It is to be given its due weight. But it is to be weighed in connection with all the rest. It is not decisive. It may be merely the method adopted to pay a debt or wages, as interest on a loan or for other reasons.

An existing contract may be modified later by subsequent agreement, oral or written. A partnership may be so created where there was none before. And again, that the original agreement has been so modified may be proved by circumstantial evidence—by showing the conduct of the parties.

In the case before us, the claim that the defendants became partners in the firm of Knauth, Nachod & Kuhne ["K. N. & K."], doing business as bankers and brokers, depends upon the interpretation of certain instruments. There is nothing in their subsequent acts determinative of or indeed material upon this question. And we are relieved of questions that sometimes arise. "The plaintiff's position is not," we are told, "that the agreements of June 4, 1921, were a false expression or incomplete expression of the intention of the parties. We say that they express defendants' intention and that that intention was to create a relationship which as a matter of law constitutes a partnership." Nor may the claim of the plaintiff be rested on any question of estoppel. "The plaintiff's claim," he stipulates, "is a claim of actual partnership, not of partnership by estoppel, and liability is not sought to be predicated upon [§ 16] of the [1914 Uniform] Partnership [Act]."

Remitted then, as we are, to the documents themselves, we refer to circumstances surrounding their execution only so far as is necessary to make them intelligible. And we are to remember that although the intention of the parties to avoid liability as partners is clear, although in language precise and definite they deny any design to then join the firm of K. N. & K.; although they say their interests in profits should be construed merely as a measure of compensation for loans, not an interest in profits as such; although they provide that they shall not be liable for any losses or treated as partners, the question still remains whether in fact they agree to so associate themselves with the firm as to "carry on as co-owners a business for profit."

In the spring of 1921 the firm of K. N. & K. found itself in financial difficulties. John R. Hall was one of the partners. He was a friend of Mr. Peyton. From him he obtained the loan of almost $500,000 of Liberty bonds, which K. N. & K. might use as collateral to secure bank advances. This, however, was not sufficient. The firm and its members had engaged in unwise speculations, and it was deeply involved. Mr. Hall was also intimately acquainted with George W. Perkins, Jr., and with Edward W. Freeman. He also knew Mrs. Peyton and Mrs. Perkins and Mrs. Freeman. All were anxious to help him. He therefore, representing K. N. & K., entered into negotiations with them. While they were pending a proposition was made that Mr. Peyton, Mr. Perkins, and Mr. Freeman, or some of them, should become partners. It met a decided refusal. Finally an agreement was reached. It is expressed in three documents, executed on the same day, all a part of the one transaction. They were drawn with care and are unambiguous. We shall refer to them as "the agreement," "the indenture," and "the option."

We have no doubt as to their general purpose. The respondents were to loan K. N. & K. $2,500,000 worth of liquid securities, which were to be returned to them on or before April 15, 1923. The firm might hypothecate them to secure loans totaling $2,000,000, using the proceeds as its business necessities required. To insure respondents against loss K. N. & K. were to turn over to them a large number of their own securities which may have been valuable, but which were of so speculative a nature that they could not be used as collateral for bank loans. In compensation for the loan, the respondents were to receive 40 [percent] of the profits of the firm until the return was made, not exceeding, however, $500,000, and not less than $100,000. Merely because the transaction involved the transfer of securities and not of cash does not prevent its being a loan * * *. The respondents also were given an option to join the firm if they, or any of them, expressed a desire to do so before June 4, 1923.

Many other detailed agreements are contained in the papers. Are they such as may be properly inserted to protect the lenders? Or do they go further? Whatever their purpose, did they in truth associate the respondents with the firm so that they and it together thereafter carried on as co-owners a business for profit? The answer depends upon an analysis of these various provisions.

As representing the lenders, Mr. Peyton and Mr. Freeman are called "trustees." The loaned securities when used as collateral are not to be mingled with other securities of K. N. & K., and the trustees at all times are to be kept informed of all transactions affecting them. To them shall be paid all dividends and income accruing therefrom. They may also substitute for any of the securities loaned securities of equal value. With their consent the firm may sell any of its securities held by the respondents, the proceeds to go, however, to the trustees. In other similar ways the trustees may deal with these same securities, but the securities loaned shall always be sufficient in value to permit of their hypothecation for $2,000,000. If they rise in price, the excess may be withdrawn by the defendants. If they fall, they shall make good the deficiency.

So far, there is no hint that the transaction is not a loan of securities with a provision for compensation. Later a somewhat closer connection with the firm appears. Until the securities are returned, the directing management of the firm is to be in the hands of John R. Hall, and his life is to be insured for $1,000,000, and the policies are to be assigned as further collateral security to the trustees. These requirements are not unnatural. Hall was the one known and trusted by the defendants. Their acquaintance with the other members of the firm was of the slightest. These others had brought an old and established business to the verge of bankruptcy. As the respondents knew, they also had engaged in unsafe speculation. The respondents were about to loan $2,500,000 of good securities. As collateral they were to receive others of problematical value. What they required seems but ordinary caution. Nor does it imply an association in the business.

The trustees are to be kept advised as to the conduct of the business and consulted as to important matters. They may inspect the firm books and are entitled to any information they think important. Finally, they may veto any business they think highly speculative or injurious. Again we hold this but a proper precaution to safeguard the loan. The trustees may not initiate any transaction as a partner may do. They may not bind the firm by any action of their own. Under the circumstances the safety of the loan depended upon the business success of K. N. & K. This success was likely to be compromised by the inclination of its members to engage in speculation. No longer, if the respondents were to be protected, should it be allowed. The trustees therefore might prohibit it, and that their prohibition might be effective, information was to be furnished them. Not dissimilar agreements have been held proper to guard the interests of the lender.

As further security each member of K. N. & K. is to assign to the trustees their interest in the firm. No loan by the firm to any member is permitted and the amount each may draw is fixed. No other distribution of profits is to be made. So that realized profits may be calculated the existing capital is stated to be $700,000, and profits are to be realized as promptly as good business practice will permit. In case the trustees think this is not done, the question is left to them and to Mr. Hall, and if they differ then to an arbitrator. There is no obligation that the firm shall continue the business. It may dissolve at any time. Again we conclude there is nothing here not properly adapted to secure the interest of the respondents as lenders. If their compensation is dependent on a percentage of the profits, still provision must be made to define what these profits shall be.

The "indenture" is substantially a mortgage of the collateral delivered by K. N. & K. to the trustees to secure the performance of the "agreement." It certainly does not strengthen the claim that the respondents were partners.

Finally we have the "option." It permits the respondents, or any of them, or their assignees or nominees to enter the firm at a later date if they desire to do so by buying 50 [percent] or less of the interests therein of all or any of the members at a stated price. Or a corporation may, if the respondents and the members agree, be formed in place of the firm. Meanwhile, apparently with the design of protecting the firm business against improper or ill-judged action which might render the option valueless, each member of the firm is to place his resignation in the hands of Mr. Hall. If at any time he and the trustees agree that such resignation should be accepted, that member shall then retire, receiving the value of his interest calculated as of the date of such retirement.

This last provision is somewhat unusual, yet it is not enough in itself to show that on June 4, 1921, a present partnership was created, nor taking these various papers as a whole do we reach such a result. It is quite true that even if one or two or three like provisions contained in such a contract do not require this conclusion, yet it is also true that when taken together a point may come where stipulations immaterial separately cover so wide a field that we should hold a partnership exists. As in other branches of the law, a question of degree is often the determining factor. Here that point has not been reached.

The judgment appealed from should be affirmed, with costs.

CARDOZO, C.J., and POUND, LEHMAN, KELLOGG, and O'BRIEN, JJ., concur.

NOTES

(1) Why is the plaintiff arguing that Peyton, Perkins, and Freeman are partners of the firm? Put differently, if the argument is credited, how will it help the plaintiff? *See* UPA §§ 13–15; RUPA §§ 305–306.

(2) What facts suggest that Peyton, Perkins, and Freeman are partners of the firm? Why did the court find those facts to be insufficient?

(3) In *Lupien v. Malsbenden*, 477 A.2d 746 (Me. 1984), the plaintiff entered into a written agreement with Steven Cragin, doing business as York

Motor Mart, for the construction of a Bradley automobile.[a] The plaintiff paid a total of $4,450 of the $8,020 purchase price, but the Bradley was never received. *See id.* at 747. After Cragin disappeared, a suit was filed against Frederick Malsbenden on the theory that he was a partner of Cragin in the business. *See id.* at 747 & n.1. The court upheld a jury verdict in the plaintiff's favor:

> Here the trial justice concluded that, notwithstanding Malsbenden's assertion that he was only a "banker," his "total involvement" in the Bradley operation was that of a partner. The testimony at trial, both respecting Malsbenden's financial interest in the enterprise and his involvement in day-to-day business operations, amply supported the Superior Court's conclusion. Malsbenden had a financial interest of $85,000 in the Bradley portion of York Motor Mart's operations. Although Malsbenden termed the investment a loan, significantly he conceded that the "loan" carried no interest. His "loan" was not made in the form of a fixed payment or payments, but was made to the business, at least in substantial part, in the form of day-to-day purchases of Bradley kits, other parts and equipment, and in the payment of wages. Furthermore, the "loan" was not to be repaid in fixed amounts or at fixed times, but rather only upon the sale of Bradley automobiles.

> The evidence also showed that, unlike a banker, Malsbenden had the right to participate in control of the business and in fact did so on a day-to-day basis. According to Urbin Savaria, who worked at York Motor Mart from late April through June 1980, Malsbenden during that time opened the business establishment each morning, remained present through part of every day, had final say on the ordering of parts, paid for parts and equipment, and paid Savaria's salary. On plaintiff's frequent visits to York Motor Mart, he generally dealt with Malsbenden because Cragin was not present. It was Malsbenden who insisted that plaintiff trade in his truck prior to the completion of the Bradley because the proceeds from the sale of the truck were needed to complete the Bradley. When it was discovered that the "demo" Bradley [had] given to plaintiff while he awaited completion of his car actually belonged to a third party, it was Malsbenden who bought the car for plaintiff's use. As of three years after the making of the contract now in litigation, Malsbenden was still doing business at York Motor Mart, "just disposing of property."

> Malsbenden and Cragin may well have viewed their relationship to be that of creditor-borrower, rather than a partnership. At trial Malsbenden so asserts, and Cragin's departure from the scene in the spring of 1980 deprives us of the benefit of his view of his business arrangement with Malsbenden. In any event,

---

[a]   According to the court, "[a] Bradley automobile is a 'kit car' constructed on a Volkswagen chassis." *Id.* at 747 n.2.

whatever the intent of these two men as to their respective involvements in the business of making and selling Bradley cars, there is no clear error in the Superior Court's finding that the Bradley car operation represented a pooling of Malsbenden's capital and Cragin's automotive skills, with joint control over the business and intent to share the fruits of the enterprise. As a matter of law, that arrangement amounted to a partnership * * *.

Id. at 748–49. Is *Lupien* consistent with *Martin*?

(4) UPA recognizes that partners need not be individuals; they may be corporations, partnerships, or other types of associations. *See* UPA §§ 2, 6. RUPA also provides for non-individual partners. *See* RUPA § 101(6), (10).

2.   THE PARTNERSHIP AGREEMENT

As a general matter, once a partnership has been formed, the partnership's operation is governed by the provisions of the applicable statute. For example, UPA indicates that partners share equally in the profits and losses of the partnership, and it directs that every partner has the right to participate in the management of the partnership. *See* UPA § 18(a), (e); RUPA § 401(b), (f). It is important to note, however, that almost all of the statutory provisions function merely as default rules that can be altered by the agreement of the partners. *See* RUPA § 103.[b] Thus, partners in a general partnership can largely structure their business as they see fit.

RUPA makes clear that a partnership agreement may be written, oral, or implied among the partners. *See* RUPA § 101(7). (UPA has no analogous provision). Although it is not necessary for a partnership agreement to be in writing, it is usually desirable. For example, one major advantage of having a written agreement is that it may avoid future disputes over what the business arrangement actually was. As another example, a partner may wish to lend rather than to contribute specific property to a partnership. A written agreement clearly identifying which property is contributed and which is loaned is critical to protect the partner's interest in the loaned property.

When real estate is to be contributed as partnership property or the agreement includes a term of more than one year, a written agreement may be necessary to comply with the statute of frauds. In *Gano v. Jamail*, 678 S.W.2d 152 (Tex. App. 1984), for example, Gano claimed that he was made a partner by oral agreement in Jamail's one-person law practice in 1969 on a fifty percent participation basis, after which the firm was known as "Jamail and Gano." In 1978, Jamail terminated the arrangement, and Gano brought suit on the alleged partnership

---

[b]   UPA has no analogous provision to RUPA § 103. Nevertheless, some UPA provisions explicitly indicate that they can be altered by an agreement between the partners. *See, e.g.,* UPA §§ 18–19.

agreement. Gano lost because of the one-year provision of the statute of frauds. The court accepted the argument that the firm "was involved almost exclusively in a personal injury practice in which cases were based on contingent fee contracts, and almost always took more than a year to conclude," and the agreement contemplated that the partnership was to last until all of the cases signed up during the partnership were resolved. *Id.* at 154.

A written partnership agreement is also advantageous to the attorney: not only may it justify a somewhat higher fee, but it also places suggestions and advice in concrete form so as to safeguard against misunderstandings. More generally, and as mentioned, in the absence of a written or other agreement, the relationship between the partners will be governed by the provisions of the applicable state partnership statute. It is unlikely that the provisions of the statute will reflect all of the expectations and understandings among the partners. In short, the advantages of a written agreement are so substantial that lawyers who do not advise their clients to at least *consider* a written agreement before entering into a partnership risk a malpractice suit.

3. ENTITY v. AGGREGATE VIEWS

Is a general partnership a legal entity that is separate and distinct from the partners themselves, or is a partnership simply an aggregate of its partners with no separate legal status? A number of issues turn on the answer to this question. For example, can a partnership sue or be sued in its own name? Can it hold property of its own? Only if the partnership is viewed as a distinct legal entity would the answer to these questions appear to be yes.

In general, UPA adopts an aggregate view of the partnership and rejects the notion that a partnership is a legal entity. For example, UPA § 29 indicates that a partnership is dissolved whenever any partner ceases to be associated in the carrying on of the business. If a partnership were a separate legal entity, the departure of a partner would not have to affect the existence of the partnership itself. If a partnership were simply an aggregate of its partners, however, then the departure of one of the partners would necessarily change the aggregate. It would make sense to conclude, as UPA § 29 does, that the former aggregate partnership no longer exists.

This aggregate view of the partnership has produced some controversial judicial decisions. In *Fairway Development Co. v. Title Insurance Co. of Minnesota*, 621 F. Supp. 120 (N.D. Ohio 1985), a general partnership consisting of Thomas Bernabei, James Serra, and Howard Wenger purchased a title guaranty policy. The defendant, Title Insurance Company, attempted to avoid payment under the policy on the theory that the insured partnership no longer existed:

Defendant seeks summary judgment on plaintiff's complaint * * *. [D]efendant asserts that it is liable under the title guaranty policy in question only to the named party guaranteed. Defendant asserts that it originally guaranteed a general partnership, which it refers to as Fairway Development I, consisting of three partners: Thomas M. Bernabei, James V. Serra, Jr., and Howard J. Wenger. Defendant states that each of these three men contributed to the partnership's capital and shared in the partnership's profits and losses equally. Defendant argues that Fairway Development I commenced on October 15, 1979 and terminated on May 20, 1981, when two partners in Fairway Development I, Bernabei and Serra, sold and transferred their respective undivided one-third interests in the partnership to the remaining partner, Wenger, and a third-party purchaser, James E. Valentine. Defendant argues that a new partnership resulted from this sale, called Fairway Development II. Defendant concludes that it cannot be held liable to the plaintiff since it is not in privity with the plaintiff as the named party guaranteed. Defendant argues that the named party guaranteed was Fairway Development I, a partnership which dissolved in 1981 upon formation of Fairway Development II, and that its liability does not extend to Fairway Development II.

Id. at 121. The plaintiff contended that "the facts are clear that there was an intent between the partners of what defendant calls Fairway Development I and II to continue the operation of the Fairway Development Company following the sale by Bernabei and Serra of their interests to Wenger and Valentine without dissolving the partnership." *Id.* at 122. Similarly, the plaintiff argued that "Fairway Development II has continued to carry on the stated purpose of Fairway Development I, which is really just an expansion of the purpose set forth in the partnership agreement for Fairway Development I, the acquisition and development of real estate." *Id.*

After reviewing various sections of the UPA-based Ohio partnership statute, the court sided with the defendant insurance company:

* * * The Court's review of the applicable statutory law supports a finding that the common law rule that "a dissolution occurs and a new partnership is formed whenever a partner retires or a new partner is admitted," *see Shunk v. Shunk Manufacturing Co.,* 86 Ohio App. 467, 476, 93 N.E.2d 321 (3rd Dist. 1949), citing *Snyder Manufacturing Co. v. Snyder,* 54 Ohio St. 86, 43 N.E. 325 (1896), survives the enactment of the Ohio Uniform Partnership Law.

* * *

*** The Court's conclusion accords with the aggregate theory of partnership, which, applied to this case, recognizes Fairway Development I not as an entity in itself, but as a partnership made up of three members, Bernabei, Serra, and Wenger. That partnership ceased when the membership of the partnership changed.

* * *

The Court finds that the law as applicable to the facts of this case supports a finding that the named party guaranteed in the contract in question is not the plaintiff, and that the plaintiff is a new partnership which followed the termination of Fairway Development I. * * *

* * *

* * * [T]he Court holds that the terms of the title guaranty extended only to the named party guaranteed, that party being Fairway Development I, and that Fairway Development II therefore has no standing to sue the defendant for breach of the contract in question. Defendant's motion for summary judgment is therefore granted.

Id. at 123–25.

NOTES

(1) Along with UPA § 29, § 41(1) also suggests an aggregate view of the partnership. Can you explain why?

(2) Given the result in *Fairway*, aren't all contracts entered into by UPA partnerships in jeopardy? How can UPA partnerships protect their contracts from *Fairway*-like consequences?

(3) UPA is silent on whether a partnership may sue or be sued in its own name, presumably because UPA largely adopts an aggregate view of the partnership. Nevertheless, many UPA jurisdictions have enacted provisions—usually in the state's partnership statute or rules of civil procedure—that explicitly permit the partnership to sue or be sued in its own name. Absent such provisions, all of the partners must be joined as plaintiffs in lawsuits seeking to assert the partnership's rights. Similarly, absent such provisions, some or all of the individual partners (depending upon whether the partners have joint liability or joint and several liability) must be sued to enforce an obligation owed by the partnership. *See* Chapter 3, Section D(3)(b).

(4) RUPA explicitly adopts an entity view of the partnership. RUPA § 201 states that "[a] partnership is an entity distinct from its partners," and the comment mentions that "RUPA embraces the entity theory of the partnership." This entity view simplifies many of the practical problems caused by the aggregate perspective. *See, e.g.,* RUPA § 307(a) (stating that

"[a] partnership may sue and be sued in the name of the partnership"); *see also id.* § 203 ("Property acquired by a partnership is property of the partnership and not of the partners individually.").

4. PARTNERSHIP BY ESTOPPEL

SMITH V. KELLEY

Court of Appeals of Kentucky, 1971.
465 S.W.2d 39.

CLAY, COMMISSIONER.

Appellant [Smith] brought this suit for a partnership accounting. The Chancellor adjudged no partnership existed and dismissed appellant's claim. Appellant contends on appeal that the judgment is "erroneous."

With one exception, there is little dispute about the facts. In 1964 appellees Kelley and Galloway were partners in an accounting business. Appellant left another firm and came to work for them. For three and one-half years appellant drew $1,000 a month, plus $100 a month for travel expenses. At the end of each year he was paid a relatively small additional sum as a bonus out of the profits of the business. Not until appellant left the Kelley-Galloway firm in 1968 did he make any claim that he was entitled to a fixed percentage of the profits. In this lawsuit he asserts he had a twenty-percent interest therein.

There was no writing evidencing a partnership agreement. However, during the years appellant worked for the firm he was held out to the public as a partner. In a contract entered into between Kelley, Galloway, appellant and a third party, appellant was designated a partner. Partnership tax returns listed him as such; so did a statement filed with the Kentucky Board of Accountancy. In a suit filed in the circuit court against a third party he was designated a partner.

On the other hand, Kelley, Galloway and another employee of the firm testified there was no agreement that Smith would be a partner or have a right to share in the profits; he made no contribution to the assets of the partnership; he took no part in the management; he had no authority to hire or fire employees or to make purchases for the firm; he did not sign any notes when the firm was borrowing money; and he was not obligated to stand [for] any losses of the firm.

A partnership is a contractual relationship and the intention to create it is necessary. As to third parties, a partnership may arise by estoppel, but our question is whether the parties intended to and did create such a relationship as would entitle appellant to share in the profits.

The Chancellor found that the original partners had at no time agreed that appellant would be entitled to share in a percentage of the profits. This was a matter of credibility and the Chancellor, who heard the evidence, chose to believe appellees. His finding on this point was not clearly erroneous and would seem to be dispositive of the case. In addition however, the conduct of the parties over a three-and-one-half-year period confirms the conclusion that, though appellant was held out to the public as a partner, between themselves a partnership relationship was not intended to be and was not created. We find no error in the court's findings of fact or conclusions of law.

* * *

We have examined the [1914] Uniform Partnership Act, and particularly [§§ 6, 7(1), 7(4), 18(a), 18(e), 18(g)], and find the trial court's decision took cognizance of the essential elements of a partnership therein prescribed.

The judgment is affirmed.

NOTES

(1) Do you agree with the court's conclusion that Smith was not a partner in the Kelley-Galloway partnership? *See* UPA §§ 6–7; RUPA § 202. What was Smith hoping to gain with the assertion that he was a partner? *See* UPA § 18(a); RUPA § 401(b).

(2) Assume that a client of the Kelley-Galloway accounting firm sues the partnership for malpractice and adds Smith as a defendant. Is Smith potentially liable? *See* UPA § 16; RUPA § 308.

(3) RUPA clearly indicates that, except as provided in § 308, "persons who are not partners as to each other [under § 202] are not liable as partners to other persons." RUPA § 308(e); *see also id.* § 308 cmt. (noting that § 308(a) "is the exclusive basis for imposing liability as a partner on persons who are not partners in fact").

C. MANAGEMENT AND OPERATION

SUMMERS V. DOOLEY
Supreme Court of Idaho, 1971.
481 P.2d 318.

DONALDSON, JUSTICE.

This lawsuit, tried in the district court, involves a claim by one partner against the other for $6,000. The complaining partner asserts that he has been required to pay out more than $11,000 in expenses without any reimbursement from either the partnership funds or his partner. The expenditure in question was incurred by the complaining partner (John Summers, plaintiff-appellant) for the purpose of hiring an additional employee. * * *

The pertinent facts leading to this lawsuit are as follows. Summers entered [into] a partnership agreement with Dooley (defendant-respondent) in 1958 for the purpose of operating a trash collection business. The business was operated by the two men and when either was unable to work, the nonworking partner provided a replacement at his own expense. In 1962, Dooley became unable to work and, at his own expense, hired an employee to take his place. In July, 1966, Summers approached his partner Dooley regarding the hiring of an additional employee but Dooley refused. Nevertheless, on his own initiative, Summers hired the man and paid him out of his own pocket. Dooley, upon discovering that Summers had hired an additional man, objected, stating that he did not feel additional labor was necessary and refused to pay for the new employee out of the partnership funds. Summers continued to operate the business using the third man and in October of 1967 instituted suit in the district court for $6,000 against his partner, the gravamen of the complaint being that Summers has been required to pay out more than $11,000 in expenses, incurred in the hiring of the additional man, without any reimbursement from either the partnership funds or his partner. After trial before the court, sitting without a jury, Summers * * * has appealed. He urges in essence that the trial court erred by failing to conclude that he should be reimbursed for expenses and costs connected in the employment of extra help in the partnership business.

The principal thrust of appellant's contention is that in spite of the fact that one of the two partners refused to consent to the hiring of additional help, nonetheless, the non-consenting partner retained profits earned by the labors of the third man and therefore the non-consenting partner should be estopped from denying the need and value of the employee, and has by his behavior ratified the act of the other partner who hired the additional man.

The issue presented for decision by this appeal is whether an equal partner in a two man partnership has the authority to hire a new employee in disregard of the objection of the other partner and then attempt to charge the dissenting partner with the costs incurred as a result of his unilateral decision.

The State of Idaho has enacted specific statutes with respect to the legal concept known as 'partnership.' Therefore any solution of partnership problems should logically begin with an application of the relevant code provision.

In the instant case the record indicates that although Summers requested his partner Dooley to agree to the hiring of a third man, such requests were not honored. In fact Dooley made it clear that he was "voting no" with regard to the hiring of an additional employee.

An application of the relevant statutory provisions and pertinent case law to the factual situation presented by the instant case indicates that the trial court was correct in its disposal of the issue since a majority of the partners did not consent to the hiring of the third man. [UPA § 18(h)] provides:

> "Any difference arising as to ordinary matters connected with the partnership business may be decided by a *majority of the partners* * * *." (emphasis supplied)

It is the opinion of this Court that the preceding statute is of a mandatory rather than permissive nature. This conclusion is based upon the following reasoning. Whether a statute is mandatory or directory does not depend upon its form, but upon the intention of the legislature, to be ascertained from a consideration of the entire act, its nature, its object, and the consequences that would result from construing it one way or the other.

* * * A careful reading of the statutory provision [UPA § 18] indicates that subsection [(e)] bestows *equal rights in the management and conduct of the partnership business* upon all of the partners. The concept of equality between partners with respect to management of business affairs is a central theme and recurs throughout the Uniform Partnership law, which has been enacted in this jurisdiction. Thus the only reasonable interpretation of [UPA § 18(h)] is that business differences must be decided by a majority of the partners provided no other agreement between the partners speaks to the issues.

A noted scholar has dealt precisely with the issue to be decided.

> "* * * if the partners are equally divided, those who forbid a change must have their way." Walter B. Lindley, A Treatise on the Law of Partnership, Ch. II, § III, ¶ 24–8, p. 403 (1924).

> * * *

In the case at bar one of the partners continually voiced objection to the hiring of the third man. He did not sit idly by and acquiesce in the actions of his partner. Under these circumstances it is manifestly unjust to permit recovery of an expense which was incurred individually and not for the benefit of the partnership but rather for the benefit of one partner.

Judgment affirmed. * * *

NOTES

(1) What vote is required to authorize an ordinary business matter in a general partnership? *See* UPA § 18(h); RUPA § 401(j). Is this a default rule that the partners can alter by agreement? If so, is it an appropriate default rule?

(2) What vote is required to authorize an extraordinary business matter in a general partnership? *See* UPA § 18(h); RUPA § 401(j) & cmt. 11.

(3) UPA § 18(e) provides that "[a]ll partners have equal rights in the management and conduct of the partnership business." This provision "has been interpreted broadly to mean that, absent contrary agreement, each partner has a continuing right to participate in the management of the partnership and to be informed about the partnership business, even if his assent to partnership business decisions is not required." RUPA § 401 cmt. 7. RUPA § 401(f) is based on UPA § 18(e).

(4) Summers and Dooley clearly disagreed on hiring the additional employee. Was there any basis for Summers to argue that he had actual authority to hire the employee? Consider *Parks v. Riverside Insurance Co. of America*, 308 F.2d 175 (10th Cir. 1962):

> It is, of course, well settled that in the absence of an agreement, express or implied, to the contrary, each partner is entitled to participate in the management of the partnership business and has an equal vote therein, but it is likewise well settled, as we think the Oklahoma Uniform Partnership Act recognizes, that partners may agree that, as among themselves, one or more of them shall have exclusive control over the management of the partnership business, and that an agreement for exclusive control of the management of the business by one partner may be implied from the course of conduct of the parties.

Id. at 180.

(5) If Summers is correct that Dooley "retained profits earned by the labors" of the additional employee, why did the court seemingly reject Summers' argument that Dooley "has by his behavior ratified the act of the other partner [Summers] who hired the additional man?"

NATIONAL BISCUIT CO. V. STROUD

Supreme Court of North Carolina, 1959.
106 S.E.2d 692.

PARKER, JUSTICE.

C.N. Stroud and Earl Freeman entered into a general partnership to sell groceries under the firm name of Stroud's Food Center. There is nothing in the agreed statement of facts to indicate or suggest that Freeman's power and authority as a general partner were in any way restricted or limited by the articles of partnership in respect to the ordinary and legitimate business of the partnership. Certainly, the purchase and sale of bread were ordinary and legitimate business of Stroud's Food Center during its continuance as a going concern.

Several months prior to February 1956 Stroud advised plaintiff that he personally would not be responsible for any additional bread sold by plaintiff to Stroud's Food Center. After such notice to plaintiff, it from 6 February 1956 to 25 February 1956, at the request of Freeman, sold and delivered bread in the amount of $171.04 to Stroud's Food Center.

In Johnson v. Bernheim, 76 N.C. 139, this Court said: "A and B are general partners to do some given business; the partnership is, by operation of law, a power to each to bind the partnership in any manner legitimate to the business. If one partner go[es] to a third person to buy an article on time for the partnership, the other partner cannot prevent it by writing to the third person not to sell to him on time; or, if one party attempt[s] to buy for cash, the other has no right to require that it shall be on time. And what is true in regard to buying is true in regard to selling. What either partner does with a third person is binding on the partnership. It is otherwise where the partnership is not general, but is upon special terms, as that purchases and sales must be with and for cash. There the power to each is special, in regard to all dealings with third persons at least who have notice of the terms." There is contrary authority. 68 C.J.S. Partnership § 143, pp. 578–579. However, this text of C.J.S. does not mention the effect of the provisions of the Uniform Partnership Act.

The General Assembly of North Carolina in 1941 enacted a Uniform Partnership Act, which became effective 15 March 1941. G.S. Ch. 59, Partnership, Art. 2. * * *

[The Court quotes UPA §§ 9(1), 9(4), 18(e), 18(h) and the North Carolina version of UPA § 15, which reads, "All partners are jointly and severally liable for the acts and obligations of the partnership."]

Freeman as a general partner with Stroud, with no restrictions on his authority to act within the scope of the partnership business, so far as the agreed statement of facts shows, had under the Uniform Partnership Act "equal rights in the management and conduct of the partnership business." Under [UPA § 18(h)] Stroud, his co-partner, could not restrict the power and authority of Freeman to buy bread for the partnership as a going concern, for such a purchase was an "ordinary matter connected with the partnership business," for the purpose of its business and within its scope, because in the very nature of things Stroud was not, and could not be, a majority of the partners. Therefore, Freeman's purchases of bread from plaintiff for Stroud's Food Center as a going concern bound the partnership and his co-partner Stroud. * * *

In Crane on Partnership, 2d Ed., p. 277, it is said: "In cases of an even division of the partners as to whether or not an act within the scope of the business should be done, of which disagreement a third person has knowledge, it seems that logically no restriction can be placed upon the power to act. The partnership being a going concern, activities within the scope of the business should not be limited, save by the expressed will of the majority deciding a disputed question; half of the members are not a majority." * * *

At the close of business on 25 February 1956, Stroud and Freeman by agreement dissolved the partnership. By their dissolution agreement all of the partnership assets, including cash on hand, bank deposits and all accounts receivable, with a few exceptions, were assigned to Stroud, who bound himself by such written dissolution agreement to liquidate the firm's assets and discharge its liabilities. It would seem a fair inference from the agreed statement of facts that the partnership got the benefit of the bread sold and delivered by plaintiff to Stroud's Food Center, at Freeman's request, from 6 February 1956 to 25 February 1956. But whether it did or not, Freeman's acts, as stated above, bound the partnership and Stroud.

The judgment of the court below is affirmed.

NOTES

(1) Is *Stroud* consistent with *Summers v. Dooley*?

(2) Can the result in *Stroud* be justified on actual authority grounds? On apparent authority grounds? *See* UPA § 9; RUPA § 301.

(3) As the prior note suggests, both actual and apparent authority are frequently implicated in the partnership setting. For example, if Freeman had been an employee or agent of Stroud rather than a partner, it is clear that Stroud could have revoked any actual authority that Freeman might have possessed to bind Stroud to a purchase of bread simply by notifying Freeman. Despite such notice, however, Freeman might still have apparent authority to bind Stroud to a purchase of bread unless National Biscuit was advised of the revocation of authority.

(4) What should a person in Stroud's position do if he no longer trusts his co-partner and wishes to avoid liability for future bread purchases by the partnership? *See* UPA §§ 31(1)(b), 35(1)(b); RUPA §§ 601(1), 703, 704.

(5) Under UPA § 9, a partner has authority to bind the partnership for any act that is "apparently carrying on in the usual way the business of the partnership." While this language would presumably encompass an act within the apparent course of business of the partner's firm, it is unclear whether it would also encompass an act that is not within the apparent course of business of the partner's firm, but that is within the apparent course of business of other firms engaged in a similar line of business. There is authority under UPA for this broader construction. *See, e.g.,* Burns v. Gonzalez, 439 S.W.2d 128, 131 (Tex. Civ. App. 1969) ("As we interpret [UPA] Sec. 9(1), the act of a partner binds the firm, absent an express limitation of authority known to the party dealing with such partner, if such act is for the purpose of 'apparently carrying on' the business of the partnership in the way in which other firms engaged in the same business in the locality usually transact business, or in the way in which the particular partnership usually

[handwritten margin note:] Third party is asking for relief in this case. In Summers the partner was requesting relief—

transacts its business."). RUPA § 301(1) makes clear that a partner has authority to bind the partnership for any act that is "apparently carrying on in the ordinary course the partnership business or business of the kind carried on by the partnership."

(6) As discussed in Section B(2), the substantive rules governing the internal affairs of a partnership may generally be altered by agreement of the partners. *See* RUPA § 103. Can the partners agree to eliminate the apparent authority granted to partners in UPA § 9 and RUPA § 301? *See* RUPA § 103(b)(10).

(7) RUPA permits a partnership to publicly file a "statement of partnership authority." *See* RUPA § 303. According to the comment, § 303 "provides for an optional statement of partnership authority specifying the names of the partners authorized to execute instruments transferring real property held in the name of the partnership," and it "may also grant supplementary authority to partners, or limit their authority, to enter into other transactions on behalf of the partnership." UPA has no similar provision.

Does RUPA § 303 mean that National Biscuit would have to check the public filings before it can safely sell bread on credit to a business such as Stroud's Food Center? With respect to real estate transfers by partnerships, does § 303 create one more piece of paper that a title examiner must review?

D. FINANCIAL RIGHTS AND OBLIGATIONS

1. PARTNERSHIP ACCOUNTING

From an accounting standpoint, the business of the partnership is distinct from the financial affairs of the individual partners. The interests of the partners are usually reflected in capital accounts which are adjusted periodically for income, draws, and contributions or withdrawals of capital. A capital account essentially sets forth the partner's ownership interest in the partnership. RUPA § 401 describes how each partner's capital account is constructed and maintained: that account equals the capital contributed by the partner less the amount of any distributions to the partner plus the partner's share of the profits less the partner's share of the losses. A partner's capital account may be negative from time to time; upon the final settlement of accounts when the partnership is terminated, a partner with a negative capital account must pay the partnership that amount. *See id.* § 807(b). It is not essential that the partnership actually maintain a formal capital account for each partner, but all except the most informal partnerships do so.

In most respects, financial accounting for partnerships closely resembles corporate accounting for profits, losses, assets, and liabilities. A simple illustration based on the first year's successful operation of a business called the AB Software Store is helpful.

(1) Income Statement

AB SOFTWARE STORE
Statement of Profit and Loss for Year Ending December 31, 2014

Sales	$417,000	
Cost of Sales	270,000	
GROSS PROFIT		$147,000
Other Expenses:		
Advertising	8,000	
Rentals	24,000	
Depreciation	5,000	
Salaries	32,000	
Miscellaneous	18,000	87,000
NET PROFIT		$60,000

(2) Balance Sheet

AB SOFTWARE STORE
Balance Sheet, December 31, 2014

Assets		Liabilities	
Cash	$19,000	Accounts Payable	$73,000
Accounts Receivable	93,000	Note Payable to A	25,000
Inventory	95,000		
Fixtures (Net of depreciation)	42,000		
Truck (Net of depreciation)	9,000	**Equity**	
		Partner's Capital	160,000
	$258,000		$258,000

(3) Capital Accounts for 2014

	Opening	Income for Year	Draws for Year	Closing
A	$100,000	$30,000	–0–	$130,000
B	–0–	30,000	–0–	30,000
				$160,000

ROBERT W. HAMILTON AND RICHARD A. BOOTH, BUSINESS BASICS FOR LAW STUDENTS: ESSENTIAL CONCEPTS AND APPLICATIONS

Pages 118–23 (4th ed. 2006).[c]

The starting point of the whole subject of accountancy is a very simple equation:

$$\text{equity} = \text{assets} - \text{liabilities}$$

Equity in this equation has nothing to do with the historical courts of equity or with notions of fairness or simple justice: It means ownership or net worth. This equation simply states that the net worth of a business is equal to its assets minus its liabilities.

A balance sheet is in many ways the most fundamental financial statement: It is simply a restatement of this fundamental equation in the form:

$$\text{assets} = \text{liabilities} + \text{equity}$$

A balance sheet simply is a presentation of this equation in a chart form.

Assets	Liabilities Equity
Total	Total

Every balance sheet, whether it is for General Motors or the smallest retail grocery store, is based on this format.

The asset side of a balance sheet is sometimes referred to as the left-hand side * * * [and] the liability/equity side is sometimes called the right-hand side * * *.

There are four fundamental premises underlying financial accounting that can readily be grasped from this simple introduction. First, financial accounting assumes that the business that is the subject of the financial statements is an entity. A person may own several different businesses; if each business maintains its own records, it will be on the assumption that each is independent from the person's other businesses. The equity referred to in that business's balance sheet will be limited to the person's investment in that single business. If a person owns two businesses that keep separate financial records, a debt that one business owes to the other will be reflected as an asset on one balance sheet and a liability on the other.

---

    [c] Reprinted with the permission of Aspen Law & Business/Panel Publishers, a division of Aspen Publishers, Inc.

Second, all entries must be in terms of dollars (at least in the United States). All property, tangible or intangible, and obligations shown on a balance sheet must be expressed in dollars, either historical cost or fair market value or some other method of valuation. Many "assets" or "liabilities" of a business, however, are not reflected at all. A person's friendly smile may be an asset in a sense, but will not appear on a balance sheet because a dollar value is not normally given to a smile. Assets, such as a debt owed to the company or rights to a patent, on the other hand, do appear in balance sheets. Similarly, a company may have a reputation for sharp practices or questionable dealing. Although that reputation is doubtless a liability in a sense, it is not the type of liability that appears on a balance sheet. A liability in the balance sheet sense is a recognized debt or obligation to someone else, payable either in money or in something reducible to money. Not all liabilities that in the legal or lay sense meet this test are recognized as liabilities in the accounting sense.

Third, a balance sheet must balance. The fundamental accounting equation itself states an equality: The two sides of the balance sheet restate that equality in somewhat reorganized form. A balance sheet therefore is itself an equality, and the sum of the left-hand side of the balance sheet must precisely equal the sum of the right-hand side. Indeed, when accountants are involved in auditing a complex business, they take advantage of this characteristic by running trial balances on their work to make sure that they have not inadvertently transposed or omitted figures: The mathematical equality of the two sides of the balance sheet provides a check on the accuracy of the accountant's labors. In short, if a balance sheet doesn't balance, there is a mistake somewhere.

Fourth, every transaction that a business enters into must be recorded in at least two ways if the balance sheet is to continue to balance. This last point underlies the concept of that mysterious (and somewhat illicit sounding) subject, double entry bookkeeping, and is the cornerstone on which modern accounting is built.

Assume that we have a new business that is just starting out, in which the owner has invested $10,000 in cash (for this purpose it makes no difference whether the business is going to be conducted in the form of a proprietorship, partnership, or corporation; all that is important is that it will be accounted for as an entity separate from the owner). The opening balance sheet will look like this:

Assets		Liabilities	–0–
Cash	10,000	Equity	10,000
Total	10,000	Total	10,000

Now let us assume that the owner buys a used truck for $3,000 cash. The effect of this transaction is to reduce cash by $3,000 and create a new asset on the balance sheet:

Assets		Liabilities	–0–
Cash	7,000		
Used Truck	3,000	Equity	10,000
Total	10,000	Total	10,000

Voila! The balance sheet still balances. Next, let us assume that the owner goes down to the bank and borrows an additional $1,000. This also has a dual effect: It increases cash by $1,000 (because the business is receiving the proceeds of the loan) and increases liabilities by $1,000 (because the business thereafter must repay the loan). Yet another balance sheet can be created showing the additional effect of this second transaction:

Assets		Liabilities	
Cash	8,000	Debt to Bank	1,000
Used Truck	3,000	Equity	10,000
Total	11,000	Total	11,000

Further insights should be evident from these two examples: First, a balance sheet records a situation at one instant in time. It is a static concept, an equilibrium that exists at one point in time rather than a record of change from an earlier period. Put another way, every transaction potentially creates a different or new balance sheet when the transaction is recorded. Second, the bottom line of a balance sheet— $11,000 in this example—is not itself a meaningful figure, because transactions such as the bank loan that do not affect the real worth of the business to the owners may increase or decrease the bottom line.

* * *

The two transactions described above—the purchase of a used truck and a short-term bank loan—involve a reshuffling of assets and liabilities. From an accounting standpoint, the owner of the business is neither richer nor poorer as a result of them. However, most transactions that a business enters into are of a different type: They involve ordinary business operations leading to a profit or loss in the current accounting period. Consider a simple example. Suppose the business described above involves hauling things in the truck for customers. Thus, the company hires a truck driver at a cost of $200 per day to drive the truck and pick up and deliver for it. During that first day the truck driver works very hard and for long hours making deliveries for which the business is paid $500. It is simple to create a profit and loss statement or income statement for the business for the one day of operation. "Profit and loss" and "income" are synonyms for this purpose. The basic formula is:

$$\text{income} = \text{revenues} - \text{expenses}$$

Obviously, the business had income of $300 ($500 of revenue minus $200 of expense for the truck driver) for its first day of operation. There may have been other expenses as well that arguably should be charged to that first day of operation, but for simplicity we are ignoring that possibility.

At first glance the income statement appears to have nothing to do with the balance sheet described in the previous section. It is possible, however, to create a new balance sheet to reflect each of these transactions.

First, the payment of the $200 to the truck driver involves a cash payment of $200 by the business; it is easy to record that. But where should the offsetting entry be? The balance sheet cannot look like this:

Assets		Liabilities	
Cash	7,800	Debt to Bank	1,000
Used Truck	3,000	Equity	10,000
Total	10,800	Total	11,000

Something is obviously wrong, because this balance sheet does not balance. There must be an offsetting entry. It certainly should not be a reduction of liabilities (because the amount of the bank loan is unchanged) or an increase in value of the truck. Perhaps one could view the services as an asset something like the truck, but that does not make much sense, because the services are simply gone. One could perhaps argue that no balance sheet should be created until the payment to the truck driver is offset by whatever the driver earns during the rest of the day, but that cannot be correct either, because the balance sheet should balance after every transaction, not just at the end of a sequence of transactions. By process of elimination, the only possible solution is to reduce "owner's equity" by the payment:

Assets		Liabilities	
Cash	7,800	Debt to Bank	1,000
Used Truck	3,000	Equity	9,800
Total	10,800	Total	10,800

Second, the $500 payment for the services rendered:

Assets		Liabilities	
Cash	8,300	Debt to Bank	1,000
Used Truck	3,000	Equity	10,300
Total	11,300	Total	11,300

Admittedly, these two balance sheets are not very helpful in showing the relationship between the balance sheet and the income statement. What is needed is a segregation of income items within the equity account so that the permanent investment and the transient changes are shown separately. Thus, the following balance sheet at the end of the period is much more illuminating:

Assets		Liabilities	
Cash	8,300	Debt to Bank	1,000
Used Truck	3,000	Equity	
		Original Capital	10,000
		Earnings	300
Total	11,300	Total	11,300

The important point at present is that profit and loss items are reflected on the balance sheet as changes in owner's equity.

The balance sheet is a static concept showing the status of a business at a particular instant in time, while the income statement describes the results of operations over some period of time: daily, monthly, quarterly, or annually. In a sense, the balance sheet is a snapshot, and the income statement is a motion picture. The income statement also serves as the bridge between the balance sheet at the beginning of the period and the balance sheet at the end of the period, because positive income items (revenues) increase owner's equity while negative income items (expenses) reduce it. Most investors and creditors look first at the bottom line of the income statement when evaluating financial statements, because the income statement reflects the operations of the business. The balance sheet usually plays a lesser role in financial analysis.

The concept of profit and loss and accounting periods rests on additional fundamental postulates. First, accounting assumes the continuing existence and activity of the business enterprise as a going concern. In other words, it is assumed that the business will be around for an indefinite number of future accounting periods. If a business is in such dire straits that its continued existence is unlikely, a totally different set of accounting principles must be adopted. Second, each business must adopt a fiscal or accounting period and must report the results of operations for that period as a separate accounting unit. The unit usually chosen is a year—either a **calendar year** or a **fiscal year**. (A fiscal year is a reporting period that the business chooses that ends on a date other than December 31 and may vary somewhat in length from a period of precisely 12 months.) Third, in determining the results of operations during an accounting period, some kind of logical relationship must be created between the revenues and expenses that are taken into account in determining profit or loss for that period. The principle usually followed is that costs allocable to the creation of revenue should be matched with that revenue. Other costs arising from the passage of time are allocated to the accounting period on the basis of that time and not the time of receipt. Fourth, some principles must be established as to when revenue is realized. Usually, the rule that is adopted is that revenues are realized when the business becomes unconditionally entitled to their receipt, not when payment is received. In the case of a contract for the sale of goods, for example, revenue may be realized when the goods are shipped, not when the contract was entered into or when payment is made. As a corollary, property of the business that may have appreciated in market value does not give rise to revenue until the gain in value is realized by sale or disposition of the property.

This concept is known as **accrual accounting**, and most businesses follow it. Indeed, most businesses of any size are required to use accrual accounting even though **cash basis accounting** might seem simpler. Most individuals use cash basis accounting for tax purposes (even if they do not know it). Accrual accounting, however, tends to give investors and creditors a better sense of the financial health of a business.

* * *

NOTES

(1) Turning to the partnership financial statements for the AB Software Store, how would the partners' capital accounts look if the store had spent $10,000 rather than $8,000 on advertising in the year in question without any increase in sales? How would they look if both A and B had drawn $5,000 each out of the business at the end of the year in question? If the partnership had lost $6,000 rather than shown a profit of $60,000?

(2) A contributed $100,000 in capital and agreed to lend the partnership an additional $25,000, presumably because the store was successful. He therefore has the status of both partner and creditor. What are his rights as against other general creditors with respect to his loan if the partnership goes under? *See* UPA § 40; RUPA § 807.

(3) In actual operation, a small business such as the AB Software Store would likely use its "cash flow" as a measure of its success or failure. Accounting for cash flow differs from traditional accounting in that it considers only transactions that involve "dollars in" and "dollars out." Traditional accounting, as set forth above, includes some expenses that do not reduce the amount of available cash of the business. An example is the item "depreciation" in AB Software's financial statements. When assets are purchased by a business, they are usually recorded in the accounting records at their purchase price ("historical cost") with no subsequent adjustment for variations in market value, but with an annual charge for "depreciation" to reflect the gradual "wearing out" or "using up" of the asset. *See* ROBERT W. HAMILTON AND RICHARD A. BOOTH, BUSINESS BASICS FOR LAW STUDENTS: ESSENTIAL CONCEPTS AND APPLICATIONS § 6.11 (4th ed. 2006), for a fuller discussion. The AB Software Store has adopted this practice and has deducted from its earnings $5,000 for depreciation of its fixtures and equipment. Obviously, there was no payment of $5,000 to anyone involved in this transaction. Hence, if everything else were equal, cash flow of the AB Software Store for the first year will be $5,000 higher than its reported earnings.

There are many items, however, that do not affect earnings but that have the opposite effect of reducing cash flow. An obvious example is the repayment of a debt. Most businesses prepare "cash flow" financial statements for internal purposes and to make sure that there will be cash available when foreseeable payments become due. In modern financial analysis, there is usually more emphasis on analysis of cash flow than on accounting earnings.

Assume that the AB Software Store decides to liquidate and wind up after one year—all of the assets are sold, the proceeds are used to discharge debts, and the balance is distributed to the partners. Given the conventions described in this note, can one determine from the balance sheet how much will be available for distribution to A and B?

2. SHARING OF PROFITS AND LOSSES

In the absence of an explicit agreement, how are profits and losses shared? *See* UPA § 18(a); RUPA § 401(b). Does it make any difference if the partners contributed unequal amounts of capital? In a word, "no"; *see* Dunn v. Summerville, 669 S.W.2d 319, 319 (Tex. 1984).

Profits of a business may be divided by agreement in numerous possible ways:

(a) The partners may share on a flat percentage basis without regard to any other factor. Profit sharing ratios for each partner may be established in the partnership agreement itself. They may also be established by issuing "partnership units" to each partner and determining the profit-or loss-sharing ratio for each partner by dividing the number of units owned by that partner by the total number of units outstanding. In this way, if new partners are added, dilution of existing interests occurs automatically without any need to amend the agreement; if old partners depart without new ones being added, the remaining interests are also automatically concentrated. Partnership units also permit the creation of incentive options or unit appreciation rights that permit successful partners to increase their percentage interest in the firm.

(b) Partners may be entitled to a fixed weekly or monthly "salary." This payment may be treated as a "cost" and subtracted before the "profit" is computed for division on some other basis, or it may be considered an advance to be credited against the amount the partner is otherwise entitled to after division of the profit. In the latter case, the agreement should consider the responsibility of the partner receiving a "salary" if the "salary" exceeds the actual profit allocable to him or her during any period.

(c) The partners may share on a percentage basis, with the percentages recomputed each year on the basis of the average amount invested in the business during the year by each partner. This type of arrangement is appropriate when the business is largely dependent on capital for income generation.

(d) The partners may share on a percentage basis, with the percentages recomputed each year on the basis of total income, the sales or billings by each partner, time devoted to the business, or on the basis of some other factor.

(e) In large partnerships, each partner may be entitled to a fixed percentage applied against perhaps 80 percent of the income. A committee of senior partners will allocate the remaining 20 percent among the junior partners as a form of incentive compensation on the basis of productivity, billings, or some other factor. Usually committee members are not themselves eligible to share in the "incentive pie."

(f) The agreement may be intentionally silent on the division of profits so that each year the partners can work out the division of profits by agreement. In larger firms, a committee or a single managing partner may have the responsibility of making the division of profits.

It is not uncommon in informal ventures for the parties to agree on a sharing of the profits but not discuss the sharing of losses. There is often some judicial sympathy for the unfortunate investor who is unexpectedly caught in a losing venture with the threat of personal liability for the venture's obligations incurred by others. In these cases, a court may accept the argument that the absence of an express agreement to share losses indicates that no partnership was ever created in the first place. *See, e.g.*, FDIC v. Claycomb, 945 F.2d 853, 858–59 (5th Cir. 1991); Grimmett v. Higginbotham, 907 S.W.2d 1, 2–3 (Tex. App. 1994). Many cases, however, recognize that an express agreement to share losses is not essential for the existence of a partnership—a result that is consistent with the language of UPA §§ 6–7 and RUPA § 202. *See, e.g.*, Parks v. Riverside Ins. Co., 308 F.2d 175, 180–81 (10th Cir. 1962).

KESSLER V. ANTINORA

Superior Court of New Jersey, Appellate Division, 1995.
653 A.2d 579.

KING, P.J.A.D.

I

Plaintiff Robert H. Kessler and defendant Richard Antinora entered into a written agreement for the purpose of building and selling a single-family residence on a lot in Wayne in Passaic County. The concept of the agreement seemed simple: Kessler was to provide the money and Antinora was to act as general contractor. Profits would be divided—60% to Kessler, 40% to Antinora—after Kessler was repaid. No thought was given to losses. The venture lost money. Kessler sued Antinora to recover 40% of his financial losses or $65,742. The Law Division judge ruled in

Kessler's favor on summary judgment. The judge denied Antinora's cross-motion for summary judgment of dismissal. We disagree, reverse the judgment in Kessler's favor, and order judgment in Antinora's favor.

II

On April 15, 1987 Kessler and Antinora executed a seven-page written agreement titled "JOINT VENTURE PARTNERSHIP AGREEMENT." The agreement contemplated a single venture: buying a lot in Wayne and building and selling a residence on it. Under the agreement Kessler agreed to "provide all necessary funds to purchase land and construct a one-family dwelling and disburse all funds to pay bills." Antinora agreed to "actually construct the dwelling and be the general contractor of the job."

The agreement provided for distribution of the proceeds of the venture:

> 9.   *Distribution.* Upon or about completion of the dwelling it shall be placed for sale. Upon sale of same, and after deducting all monies expended by Robert Kessler plus [interest] at prime plus one point and/or including interest or any funds borrowed for the project, not to exceed prime plus one point, engineering fees, architectural fees, legal fees, broker fees, if any, and any other costs connected with the project, the parties, Robert Kessler and Richard Antinora, shall divide the net profits as follows: * * *

Robert Kessler—sixty (60%) percent

Richard Antinora—forty (40%) percent

The agreement was silent about losses. There was no provision to compensate Antinora for any services other than the 40% profit clause.

Both parties complied with the agreement. Kessler provided the funds; Antinora supervised and delivered the finished house. This took over three years. Meanwhile, the real estate market soured. The house sold on September 1, 1991 for $420,000. The cost incurred in building and selling the house was $498,917.

Kessler was repaid all but $78,917 of the money he advanced pursuant to the contract. He also claimed unreimbursed interest of $85,440 for his self-characterized "loan" to the partnership. This claim for interest is disputed as to amount. Kessler thus claimed a total loss of $164,357. He sought and obtained his summary judgment in the Law Division for 40% of this amount, or $65,742.80. No amount was presented on the value of Antinora's services over the three-year period as general contractor.

Antinora contended that the agreement was basically for a joint venture, silent as to losses, and that both parties risked and lost their unrecovered contributions—Kessler's money and Antinora's labor. The Law Division judge disagreed and found that statutory partnership law governed. The judge ruled that *N.J.S.A.* § 42:1–18a required each partner to "contribute towards the losses, whether of capital or otherwise, sustained by the partnership according to his share in the profits." The judge ruled that Antinora was liable for 40% of Kessler's monetary losses and inferentially rejected any recognition of Antinora's "in kind" loss.

III

We conclude that New Jersey's allegedly applicable section of the Uniform Partnership Law, *N.J.S.A.* § 42:1–18a, does not control here because of the specific terms of the agreement between the parties. The pertinent statutory section states:

> 42:1–18. Rights and duties of partners
>
> The rights and duties of the partners in relation to the partnership shall be determined, *subject to any agreement between them*, by the following rules:
>
> a.   Each partner shall be repaid his contributions, whether by way of capital or advances to the partnership property and share equally in the profits and surplus remaining after all liabilities, including those to partners, are satisfied; and must contribute towards the losses, whether of capital or otherwise, sustained by the partnership according to his share in the profits.
>
> * * *

[*N.J.S.A.* § 42:1–18a] (emphasis added).

We find the agreement controlling over the statute. The agreement said that upon sale of the house "and after deducting all monies expended by Robert Kessler plus interest," fees, and other costs the "parties [Kessler and Antinora] shall divide net profits" 60% and 40%. We conclude that the agreement evinced a clear intent that Kessler would be repaid his investment from the sale of the house only, not by Antinora. There is no suggestion in the agreement that any of Kessler's risked and lost money would be repaid in part by Antinora. Nor is there any suggestion that Antinora's risked labor would be repaid in part by Kessler.

We find particularly persuasive the reasoning of the California Supreme Court in *Kovacik v. Reed*, 49 Cal. 2d 166, 315 P.2d 314 (1957). There the parties orally agreed to participate in a kitchen remodeling venture for Sears Roebuck & Company. Kovacik agreed to invest $10,000 in the venture and Reed agreed to become the job estimator and supervisor. They agreed to share the profits on a 50–50 basis. Possible losses were not discussed. Despite their efforts, the venture was unsuccessful and Kovacik sued Reed to recover one-half the money losses he endured. Kovacik prevailed in the trial court and recovered $4,340, or one-half the net monetary loss of $8,680.

The California Supreme Court acknowledged the general rule of partnership law that in the absence of an agreement, "the law presumes that partners and joint adventurers intended to participate equally in the profits and losses of the common enterprise, irrespective of any inequality in the amounts each contributed to the capital employed in the venture, with the losses being shared by them in the same proportions as they share the profits." *Id.*, 315 P.2d at 315–16, citing *Cal.Corp.Code* § 15018, which is identical to *N.J.S.A.* § 4[2]:1–18.

The California court then observed that this "general rule" did not obtain where one party contributed the money and the other the labor, stating:

> However, it appears that in the cases in which the above stated general rule has been applied, each of the parties had contributed capital consisting of either money or land or other tangible property, or else was to receive compensation for services rendered to the common undertaking which was to be paid before computation of the profits or losses. Where, however, as in the present case, one partner or joint adventurer contributes the money capital as against the other's skill and labor, all the cases cited, and which our research has discovered, hold that neither party is liable to the other for contribution for any loss sustained. Thus, upon loss of the money the party who contributed it is not entitled to recover any part of it from the party who contributed only services.

[*Id.* at 316.]

The rationale which the California decision and the earlier cited cases adopted was where one party contributes money and the other services, in the event of a loss, each loses his own capital—one in the form of money, the other in labor. *Ibid.* A corollary view was that the parties have implicitly agreed, by their conduct and contract, to share profits and that their contributions of money and sweat equity have been valued in an equal ratio. Thus, upon the loss of both some money and labor, the loss falls upon each proportionately without any legal recourse. Thus, Kovacik lost $8,680 of his $10,000 while Reed lost all of his labor.

Likewise, in the case before us, Kessler lost some of his money— $65,472, plus disputed interest, but Antinora lost all of the value of his labor on the three-year project. * * *

     * * *

We conclude that the "JOINT VENTURE PARTNERSHIP AGREEMENT" here did contemplate repayment to Kessler of his investment but only from the proceeds of the sale of the house, not from his coventurer Antinora. This is what the parties said, the only truly reliable evidence of what they intended. Our interpretation of the agreement between the parties accords with the result reached under the common-law cases discussed, and with our overall sense of fairness. Each party shoulders a loss, one in determinative dollars; the other in labor, difficult, if not impossible, to quantify. The parties did not think about losses in casting their agreement and any attempt by the law now to reconstruct their then non-existent intent on the subject would be speculative.

Reversed for entry of summary judgment for the defendant Antinora.

NOTES

(1) Is the ruling in *Kessler* consistent with UPA § 18(a)? Why was Kessler's argument rejected? *See also* RUPA § 401(b) (following the rule of UPA § 18(a)).

(2) Consider the following modified set of facts: Kessler and Antinora agree that Kessler will contribute $200,000 to cover the expenses of construction of the home. They also agree that Antinora will oversee the construction of the home, but he will not be responsible for contributing any capital. Finally, they agree that profits will be split 50/50, but no agreement is reached about losses.

Assume that the house takes one year to build. Because of a downturn in the market, the house only sells for $125,000. Kessler takes the $125,000 as partial reimbursement for his $200,000 capital contribution. He then claims that Antinora must reimburse him for one-half of his $75,000 loss.

How should the court resolve this dispute? If UPA § 18(a) was applied literally, who would prevail? *See also* RUPA § 401(b). Do you think this is what the parties intended? Would it make a difference if Antinora received an agreed-upon salary for his services in overseeing the construction of the home? *See* UPA § 18(f); RUPA § 401(h).

(3) How could the parties in *Kessler* have avoided their dispute? Consider the following passage from the comment to RUPA § 401:

> The default rules apply, as does UPA Section 18(a), where one or more of the partners contribute no capital, although there is case law to the contrary. *See, e.g., Kovacik v. Reed*, 49 Cal.2d 166, 315 P.2d 314 (1957); *Becker v. Killarney*, 177 Ill. App. 3d 793, [532] N.E.2d [931] (1988). It may seem unfair that the contributor of services, who contributes little or no capital, should be obligated to contribute toward the capital loss of the large contributor who contributed no services. In entering a partnership with such a capital structure, the partners should foresee that application of the default rule may bring about unusual results and take advantage of their power to vary by agreement the allocation of capital losses.

Id. § 401 cmt. 3.

(4) The *Kessler* opinion references a "joint venture." What is a "joint venture?" In *United States v. Standard Oil Co.*, 155 F. Supp. 121 (S.D.N.Y. 1957), the court observed:

> Precise definition of a joint venture is difficult. The cases are of little help since they are generally restricted to their own peculiar facts. * * *
>
> * * * As a general rule joint ventures are thought of in relation to a specific venture, a single undertaking, although the undertaking need not be one susceptible of immediate accomplishment. It is in the nature of a partnership limited to a particular venture, not general in operation or duration. It has been variously defined as an association to carry out a single business enterprise for profit; a common enterprise for mutual benefit; a combination of property, efforts, skill and judgment in a common undertaking. Joint control and management of the property and authority to act each for the other are usual characteristics along with the incurring of joint obligations and the enjoyment of joint rights. An agreement to share joint profits is essential to the creation of a joint venture. The profit accruing must be joint and not several; each must have an equitable interest in the profits themselves. But such an agreement in and of itself is not determinative. The joint sharing of losses is also commonly regarded as essential.

Id. at 148.

There is a good deal of older case law suggesting that a joint venture is distinct from a general partnership in some respect. The modern view rejects this separate characterization and treats a joint venture simply as a general partnership that has a limited purpose. Under the modern view, therefore, general partnership rules govern the formation and operation of joint ventures. *See, e.g.*, Hooper v. Yoder, 737 P.2d 852, 857 n.4 (Colo. 1987) ("A joint venture is a partnership formed for a limited purpose. * * * The substantive law of partnership applies to joint ventures as well as partnerships."); RUPA § 202 cmt. 2 ("Relationships that are called 'joint ventures' are partnerships if they otherwise fit the definition of a partnership.").

3. LIABILITY TO THIRD PARTIES

a. Liability of the Partnership

With respect to the partnership's liability in contract, you have already learned that a partnership is liable for contracts entered into on its behalf by partners with actual or apparent authority. *See* UPA § 9; RUPA § 301. With respect to the partnership's liability in tort, UPA § 13 reflects agency principles by providing that a partnership is liable to third parties for "any wrongful act or omission of any partner acting in the ordinary course of the business of the partnership or with the authority of his co-partners." UPA § 14 also provides that a partnership is liable in certain circumstances if a partner misapplies money or property of a third person. RUPA § 305 generally follows these UPA provisions.

b. Liability of the Partners

A defining characteristic of the general partnership is that each partner has unlimited personal liability for the obligations of the partnership. UPA provides that partners have "joint and several" liability for all partnership obligations under §§ 13–14 (essentially tort obligations) and "joint" liability for all other partnership obligations (essentially contractual obligations). *See* UPA § 15. Joint and several liability permits a plaintiff to sue one or more of the partners without having to sue them all. In contrast, joint liability requires a plaintiff to join all of the partners as defendants in litigation. This joinder requirement may create serious practical enforcement problems when process cannot be readily served on some partners. Thus, as between a partnership's tort and contract liabilities, UPA makes it substantially easier to sue a partner for the tort obligations of the firm.

RUPA eliminates the reference to joint liability and instead provides that partners are jointly and severally liable for all obligations of the partnership. *See* RUPA § 306(a). Although RUPA allows a creditor to sue the partnership and one or more of the partners in a single action, *see id.* § 307(b), a judgment creditor is first required to exhaust partnership assets (with certain exceptions) before proceeding directly against a partner's individual assets. *See id.* § 307(d). This exhaustion requirement is an important change from UPA. It was suggested by an ABA committee who stated that the new requirement "would respect the concept of the partnership as an entity and would provide that the partners are more in the nature of guarantors than principal debtors on every partnership debt." UPA Revision Subcommittee of the Committee on Partnerships and Unincorporated Business Organizations, *Should the Uniform Partnership Act Be Revised?*, 43 BUS. LAW. 121, 143 (1987). According to the committee, "this result would be most consistent with general business expectations today." *Id.*

Paragraphs (a), (b) and (c) of RUPA § 307 deal with procedural requirements for suits brought by or against partnerships. These provisions clearly strengthen the view that a partnership is an entity separate from the partners. As mentioned in Chapter 3, Section B(3), UPA did not address how partnerships could sue or be sued. In response, many states developed rules quite similar to those now set forth in RUPA § 307. These RUPA provisions, therefore, are largely consistent with what many states have already done.

PROBLEM

Assume that the XYZ Real Estate Company is formed in a state that has adopted RUPA § 307. XYZ owns seven different rental properties. Your client, a bank, is considering making a loan to XYZ so that XYZ can perform substantial repair and renovation work on its properties. The bank knows that X, a partner in XYZ, is independently wealthy and it is relying on X to pay off the loan if XYZ is unable to do so. What provisions should you include in the loan agreements to ensure that your client is able to collect directly and immediately from X in the event of a default? Indeed, while you are at it, would it not be a good idea to revise the bank's form loan documents to include such provisions whenever a partnership is the borrower? *See* RUPA § 307(c), (d).

ROACH V. MEAD

Supreme Court of Oregon, 1986.
722 P.2d 1229.

Before PETERSON, C.J., and LENT, LINDE, CAMPBELL, CARSON and JONES, JJ.

JONES, JUSTICE.

* * * At trial, defendant, David J. Berentson, moved for a directed verdict, contending that he was not vicariously liable for the negligent acts of his partner, Kenneth E. Mead, because the negligent acts were outside the scope of the partnership's business. * * * The trial court denied the motion[ ], and the jury found defendant liable for $20,000 damages * * *. The Court of Appeals held that defendant attorney was vicariously liable for his former partner's negligence * * *. We affirm the Court of Appeals.

* * *

Mead, defendant's former law partner, first represented plaintiff in December 1974 on a traffic charge and later represented plaintiff on several occasions. On November 1, 1979, Mead and defendant formed a law partnership. Mead continued to advise plaintiff on other traffic charges and on business dealings. Defendant prepared plaintiff's income tax returns.

In June 1980, plaintiff sold his meter repair business for $50,000. On November 25, 1980, plaintiff asked for Mead's advice on investing $20,000 in proceeds from the sale. Plaintiff testified that Mead told plaintiff that "he would take [the money] at 15 percent. So, I let him have it. * * * I trusted him and felt he would look out for me." Plaintiff considered Mead's advice to be legal advice; he testified that otherwise he would not have consulted an attorney.

After plaintiff agreed to the loan, Mead executed a promissory note for $20,000 payable on or before November 25, 1982, at 15 percent interest. Mead said that he would be receiving a large sum of money with which he would repay plaintiff. Mead offered to secure the loan with a second mortgage on his house, and plaintiff replied that he should do "whatever you think is best." Mead did not secure the loan.

On May 1, 1981, Mead went to plaintiff's home and requested a $1,500 loan, telling plaintiff he was in financial trouble but "had big money coming in." Plaintiff agreed to the loan and Mead added the $1,500 to the amount due on the promissory note. Mead did not repay any money to plaintiff and later was declared bankrupt.[1]

Plaintiff sued defendant's partnership for negligence, alleging that the partnership failed to disclose the conflicting interests of plaintiff and Mead, to advise plaintiff to seek independent legal advice, to inform plaintiff of the risks involved in an unsecured loan, and to advise plaintiff that the loan would not be legally enforceable because the rate of interest was usurious. * * *

    * * *

I.   Vicarious Liability

Plaintiff contends that Mead negligently advised him about the loan and that defendant should be vicariously liable for Mead's negligent legal advice. Defendant, while conceding that Mead was negligent, argues that the transaction between plaintiff and Mead was a personal loan outside the scope of the partnership, and that the evidence did not prove that soliciting personal loans was within Mead's express, implied or apparent authority as defendant's law partner.

[The Court quotes UPA §§ 9(1), 9(2), 9(4), 13, and 15(a).]

Liability of partners for the acts of co-partners is based on a principal-agent relationship between the partners and the partnership. "Partners are jointly and severally liable for the tortious acts of other partners if they have authorized those acts or if the wrongful acts are committed 'in the ordinary course of the business of the partnership.' [UPA §§ 13, 15]" *Wheeler v. Green,* 286 Or. 99, 126, 593 P.2d 777 (1979). The issue in this case is whether Mead's failure to advise plaintiff on the legal consequences of the loan was "in the ordinary course of the business of the partnership."

---

[1]   On January 18, 1983, this court accepted Mead's resignation from the bar. He stated that he had chosen not to contest disciplinary charges alleging that he had "borrowed $45,000 from a client, that he misrepresented the priority of the security given for the loan and that he subsequently forged a satisfaction of the mortgage given as security." 43 Or.St.B.Bull., June 1983, at 42. Mead was convicted of theft by deception because of the loan referred to in the disciplinary charges. *Id.*

In *Croisant v. Watrud,* 248 Or. 234, 432 P.2d 799 (1967), this court confronted a similar issue of the vicarious liability of a partnership for the wrongful acts of a partner. In *Croisant,* the client of an accountant sued the accounting partnership, claiming damages for the accountant's breach of trust. The accountant collected income from the client's property and then made unauthorized payments to the client's husband from the money. The defendant partnership contended that the collection services were personal dealings of the accountant with the client and not part of the partnership's business. This court held:

> If a third person reasonably believes that the services he has requested of a member of an accounting partnership is undertaken as a part of the partnership business, the partnership should be bound for a breach of trust incident to that employment even though those engaged in the practice of accountancy would regard as unusual the performance of such services [collecting and disbursing funds] by an accounting firm. 248 Or. at 242, 432 P.2d 799.

The court stated that the reasonableness of the third person's belief that "the service he seeks is within the domain of the profession is a question which must be answered upon the basis of the facts in the particular case." *Id.* at 243, 432 P.2d 799.

Defendant contends that *Croisant* may be distinguished from the case at bar because in *Croisant* "the misconduct occurred in the course of * * * activities which the court held could reasonably be viewed as within the scope of the accounting firm's business," while in this case "[t]here was no evidence that the act of an attorney in taking a personal loan from a client could reasonably be viewed as part of the business of a law firm." However, defendant admits that "the evidence most favorable to Plaintiff was simply that Plaintiff thought Mead was giving him investment advice and that the giving of advice regarding legal aspects of loans and investments in general is a normal part of law practice." Defendant thus concedes the validity of plaintiff's argument that plaintiff reasonably believed that investment advice was within the scope of the partnership's business; plaintiff does not contend that soliciting loans from clients was partnership business.

In the case at bar, the jury determined that plaintiff reasonably believed that the partnership's legal services included investment advice. We agree with the Court of Appeals that:

> * * * There is expert and other testimony from which the jury could have found that plaintiff relied on Mead for legal advice concerning the loan, that a lawyer seeking a loan from a client would be negligent if the lawyer did not tell the client to get independent legal advice and that a lawyer advising a client about this particular loan would seek to secure it and would

warn the client of the risks involved in providing a usurious interest rate. 76 Or.App. at 85, 709 P.2d 246.

The Court of Appeals' rationale is buttressed by our decisions in bar disciplinary proceedings concerning loans from clients to lawyers. * * *

When a lawyer borrows money from a client, this court requires that the lawyer advise the client about the legal aspects of the loan. Mead's failure to advise plaintiff to seek independent legal advice, that loans usually should be secured and the debtor's financial status checked, and that the rate of interest was usurious were all failures of Mead as a lawyer advising his client. Because these failures occurred within the scope of the legal partnership, responsibility for Mead's negligence was properly charged to defendant as Mead's law partner.[2] The trial court did not err in submitting the negligence issue to the jury. * * *

The Court of Appeals is affirmed.

NOTES

(1) In *Roach*, what differences are there, if any, between the $20,000 loan on which liability was found and the $1,500 loan, on which it was not?

(2) There were several cases during the 1980s in which liability was imposed on the partnership or copartners in situations similar to *Roach v. Mead. See* Stephen E. Kalish, *When a Law Firm Member Borrows From a Client—The Law Firm's Responsibility: A Professional Model Replaces a Club Model*, 37 KAN. L. REV. 107 (1988).

(3) Rule 1.8 of the Model Rules of Professional Conduct states the following:

(a) A lawyer shall not enter into a business transaction with a client or knowingly acquire an ownership, possessory, security or other pecuniary interest adverse to a client unless:

(1) the transaction and terms on which the lawyer acquires the interest are fair and reasonable to the client and are fully disclosed and transmitted in writing to the client in a manner which can be reasonably understood by the client;

(2) the client is advised in writing of the desirability of seeking and is given a reasonable opportunity to seek the advice of independent counsel in the transaction; and

(3) the client gives informed consent, in a writing signed by the client, to the essential terms of the transaction and the lawyer's role in the transaction, including whether the lawyer is representing the client in the transaction.

---

[2] The jury found defendant not liable for the additional $1,500 loan, presumably because it determined that the loan was personal and that giving legal advice concerning the loan was not within the scope of the partnership's business.

Is a law firm liable for malpractice if a partner fails to obtain the written consent required by Rule 1.8(a)(3) for a personal loan from a client?

(4) What principles determine the liability of a partner for the negligence or incompetence of an employee (e.g., a secretary or a staff attorney employed by a law firm)?

(5) In *Fanaras Enterprises, Inc. v. Doane*, 666 N.E.2d 1003 (1996), Fanaras had entered into a retainer arrangement with Doane, an attorney. Fanaras alleged that, pursuant to the arrangement, Doane was paid fees of $25,000 per quarter "in return for full, total and immediate access to Mr. Doane's legal advice * * * so that [Fanaras] would always receive devoted priority service from Attorney Doane." *Id.* at 1004–05. While this arrangement continued, Fanaras also loaned Doane over $400,000, an amount that was to be repaid with 11% interest "as soon as [Doane] obtained sufficient funds by way of selling [two properties he owned] or by way of obtaining a mortgage loan against either or both of those properties." *Id.* at 1004.

Doane borrowed approximately $1,500,000 by placing mortgages against the two properties. He then diverted the funds, defaulted on the mortgages, and declared personal bankruptcy. *See id.* at 1005. Fanaras recovered nothing from the properties or from Doane. In an effort to collect from Doane's malpractice insurer, Fanaras sued Doane alleging that Doane was negligent in failing to advise Fanaras "to seek independent legal advice and/or to secure the loans with a mortgage," and that Fanaras "relied on Attorney Doane, at all times, to protect [his] interests in connection with these loans, and [Doane] failed to do that." *Id.* Doane's liability insurer intervened and successfully moved for summary judgment. The court affirmed:

> The fact that the plaintiff paid Doane a substantial retainer "in return for full, total, and immediate access to Mr. Doane's legal advice * * * so that Fanaras Enterprises, Inc., would always receive devoted priority service from Attorney Doane," * * * is of no consequence. That arrangement clearly contemplated the plaintiff's right to Doane's prompt legal advice *on request*. Nowhere * * * is there the slightest suggestion that the plaintiff, through Fanaras or otherwise, requested Doane's advice or assistance with respect to the loans to Doane and obtaining security for their repayment, or with respect to managing the plaintiff's money. To the contrary, the clear implication of the affidavit is that Fanaras did not seek such advice or assistance but merely "relied" on Doane to protect him. That reliance may or may not have been reasonable, but it did not establish an attorney-client relationship or legal malpractice with respect to the loans. It is not enough that, with respect to other matters, the parties were in an attorney-client relationship.

Id. at 1006. Three Justices dissented:

I believe that in light of the materials the plaintiff has presented, it may well be able to prove at trial that Doane owed it a duty as an attorney in respect to the loans Doane obtained from it.
* * *

* * * If Doane had been advising Fanaras about Fanaras's dealings with a building owner for whom Fanaras was doing construction work, and that building owner, in Doane's earshot, had solicited a business loan from Fanaras, a jury would surely have been warranted in finding that the "devoted priority" service, for which Fanaras was paying such a high price, extended—even without an explicit request—to Doane's advising Fanaras about any legal aspects of the loan. Similarly here, the jury might have concluded that Fanaras had put itself in Doane's hands, as far as legal advice went, and that it was a violation of the relationship (if not an attorney-client relationship, then what?) for Doane neither to have advised Fanaras of the need to obtain some security nor, because Doane was now in a conflict of interest situation, to seek outside counsel. Nor would a finding of a conflict somehow preclude a finding of an attorney-client relationship. Much more likely, the conflict was itself a potential breach of Doane's duty, and it would be brazen for Doane to urge that, because of the conflict, there was no relationship on which Fanaras might rely.

Id. at 1006–07. Is the result reached in *Doane* consistent with *Roach v. Mead*?

(6) It is perhaps unnecessary to point out that there is a difference between a lawyer warning a client that a proposed business transaction with third persons is risky or inappropriate, and the lawyer engaging in a direct business transaction with a client. What happens, however, if the direct business advice is poor? For example, the value of a proposed options contract increases dramatically but the client declined to invest on the advice of the lawyer. Can the client then sue the attorney for bad advice or for advice that is beyond the competence of a lawyer to give? If the lawyer fails to warn the client about the risk of options and significant losses are incurred, might the lawyer be liable on the theory that attorneys of ordinary competence would have warned the client under such circumstances?

4. INDEMNIFICATION AND CONTRIBUTION

UPA § 18(b) and RUPA § 401(c) provide that, in the absence of a contrary agreement, a partnership must indemnify a partner for payments made and liabilities incurred by the partner in the ordinary course of the partnership business. Thus, while an individual partner may have to pay the entirety of a partnership obligation to a third party, indemnification provides a mechanism for payment of that obligation to be shared among the partners.

In an ongoing partnership, an indemnification payment reduces the partnership's profits just like any other partnership payment. As a result, each partner of a profitable venture "suffers" from indemnification in proportion to his profit share. On dissolution, a partnership's obligation to indemnify is paid out of partnership assets like any other partnership obligation. If the partnership has insufficient assets to pay indemnification or other partnership obligations, partners must contribute to make up the shortfall in accordance with their loss shares. *See* UPA §§ 18(a), 40(b), 40(d); RUPA §§ 401(b), 807(b), 807(c). Thus, indemnification is an obligation of a partnership, while contribution is an obligation of a partner.

As between partners and outside creditors, therefore, an individual partner has unlimited personal liability for the obligations of the partnership. *See* UPA §§ 13–15; RUPA § 306(a). An outside creditor, in other words, may collect the entirety of a partnership obligation from any partner under UPA, and from any partner under RUPA if the requirements of RUPA § 307(d) have been met. As between the partners themselves, however, each partner is only responsible for his share of the partnership obligation. If one partner pays off a partnership obligation, he is entitled to indemnification from the partnership. If the partnership lacks the funds to indemnify the partner, the partners are required to contribute according to their loss shares.

E. FIDUCIARY DUTIES

1. THE COMMON LAW

MEINHARD V. SALMON
Court of Appeals of New York, 1928.
164 N.E. 545.

CARDOZO, C.J.

On April 10, 1902, Louisa M. Gerry leased to the defendant Walter J. Salmon the premises known as the Hotel Bristol at the northwest corner of Forty-Second street and Fifth avenue in the city of New York. The lease was for a term of 20 years, commencing May 1, 1902, and ending April 30, 1922. The lessee undertook to change the hotel building for use as shops and offices at a cost of $200,000. Alterations and additions were to be accretions to the land.

Salmon, while in course of treaty with the lessor as to the execution of the lease, was in course of treaty with Meinhard, the plaintiff, for the necessary funds. The result was a joint venture with terms embodied in a writing. Meinhard was to pay to Salmon half of the moneys requisite to reconstruct, alter, manage, and operate the property. Salmon was to pay to Meinhard 40 [percent] of the net profits for the first five years of the lease and 50 [percent] for the years thereafter. If there were losses, each party was to bear them equally. Salmon, however, was to have sole power to "manage, lease, underlet and operate" the building. There were to be certain pre-emptive rights for each in the contingency of death.

The two were coadventurers, subject to fiduciary duties akin to those of partners. King v. Barnes, 109 N.Y. 267, 16 N.E. 332. As to this we are all agreed. The heavier weight of duty rested, however, upon Salmon. He was a coadventurer with Meinhard, but he was manager as well. During the early years of the enterprise, the building, reconstructed, was operated at a loss. If the relation had then ended, Meinhard as well as Salmon would have carried a heavy burden. Later the profits became large with the result that for each of the investors there came a rich return. For each the venture had its phases of fair weather and of foul. The two were in it jointly, for better or for worse.

When the lease was near its end, Elbridge T. Gerry had become the owner of the reversion. He owned much other property in the neighborhood, one lot adjoining the Bristol building on Fifth avenue and four lots on Forty-Second street. He had a plan to lease the entire tract for a long term to some one who would destroy the buildings then existing and put up another in their place. In the latter part of 1921, he submitted such a project to several capitalists and dealers. He was unable to carry it through with any of them. Then, in January, 1922, with less than four months of the lease to run, he approached the defendant Salmon. The result was a new lease to the Midpoint Realty Company, which is owned and controlled by Salmon, a lease covering the whole tract, and involving a huge outlay. The term is to be 20 years, but successive covenants for renewal will extend it to a maximum of 80 years at the will of either party. The existing buildings may remain unchanged for seven years. They are then to be torn down, and a new building to cost $3,000,000 is to be placed upon the site. The rental, which under the Bristol lease was only $55,000, is to be from $350,000 to $475,000 for the properties so combined. Salmon personally guaranteed the performance by the lessee of the covenants of the new lease until such time as the new building had been completed and fully paid for.

The lease between Gerry and the Midpoint Realty Company was signed and delivered on January 25, 1922. Salmon had not told Meinhard anything about it. Whatever his motive may have been, he had kept the negotiations to himself. Meinhard was not informed even of the bare existence of a project. The first that he knew of it was in February, when the lease was an accomplished fact. He then made demand on the defendants that the lease be held in trust as an asset of the venture, making offer upon the trial to share the personal obligations incidental to the guaranty. The demand was followed by refusal, and later by this suit. A referee gave judgment for the plaintiff, limiting the plaintiff's interest in the lease, however, to 25 [percent]. The limitation was on the theory that the plaintiff's equity was to be restricted to one-half of so much of the value of the lease as was contributed or represented by the occupation of the Bristol site. Upon cross-appeals to the Appellate Division, the judgment was modified so as to enlarge the equitable interest to one-half of the whole lease. With this enlargement of plaintiff's interest, there went, of course, a corresponding enlargement of his attendant obligations. The case is now here on an appeal by the defendants.

Joint adventurers, like copartners, owe to one another, while the enterprise continues, the duty of the finest loyalty. Many forms of conduct permissible in a workaday world for those acting at arm's length are forbidden to those bound by fiduciary ties. A trustee is held to something stricter than the morals of the market place. Not honesty alone, but the punctilio of an honor the most sensitive, is then the standard of behavior. As to this there has developed a tradition that is unbending and inveterate. Uncompromising rigidity has been the attitude of courts of equity when petitioned to undermine the rule of undivided loyalty by the "disintegrating erosion" of particular exceptions. Wendt v. Fischer, 243 N.Y. 439, 444, 154 N.E. 303. Only thus has the level of conduct for fiduciaries been kept at a level higher than that trodden by the crowd. It will not consciously be lowered by any judgment of this court.

* * * To the eye of an observer, Salmon held the lease as owner in his own right, for himself and no one else. In fact he held it as a fiduciary, for himself and another, sharers in a common venture. If this fact had been proclaimed, if the lease by its terms had run in favor of a partnership, Mr. Gerry, we may fairly assume, would have laid before the partners, and not merely before one of them, his plan of reconstruction. The pre-emptive privilege, or, better, the pre-emptive opportunity, that was thus an incident of the enterprise, Salmon appropriated to himself in secrecy and silence. He might have warned Meinhard that the plan had been submitted, and that either would be free to compete for the award. If he had done this, we do not need to say whether he would have been under a duty, if successful in the competition, to hold the lease so acquired for the benefit of a venture then about to end, and thus prolong by indirection its responsibilities and duties. The trouble about his conduct is that he excluded his coadventurer from any chance to compete, from any chance to enjoy the opportunity for benefit that had come to him alone by virtue of his agency. This chance, if nothing more, he was under a duty to concede. The price of its denial is an extension of the trust at the option and for the benefit of the one whom he excluded.

No answer is it to say that the chance would have been of little value even if seasonably offered. Such a calculus of probabilities is beyond the science of the chancery. * * *

We have no thought to hold that Salmon was guilty of a conscious purpose to defraud. Very likely he assumed in all good faith that with the approaching end of the venture he might ignore his coadventurer and take the extension for himself. He had given to the enterprise time and labor as well as money. He had made it a success. Meinhard, who had given money but neither time nor labor, had already been richly paid. There might seem to be something grasping in his insistence upon more. Such recriminations are not unusual when coadventurers fall out. They are not without their force if conduct is to be judged by the common standards of competitors. That is not to say that they have pertinency here. Salmon had put himself in a position in which thought of self was to be renounced, however hard the abnegation. He was much more than a coadventurer. He was a managing coadventurer. For him and for those like him the rule of undivided loyalty is relentless and supreme. Wendt v. Fischer, supra, Munson v. Syracuse, etc., R.R. Co., 103 N.Y. 58, 74, 8 N.E. 355. A different question would be here if there were lacking any nexus of relation between the business conducted by the manager and the opportunity brought to him as an incident of management. For this problem, as for most, there are distinctions of degree. If Salmon had received from Gerry a proposition to lease a building at a location far removed, he might have held for himself the privilege thus acquired, or so we shall assume. Here the subject-matter of the new lease was an extension and enlargement of the subject-matter of the old one. A managing coadventurer appropriating the benefit of such a lease without warning to his partner might fairly expect to be reproached with conduct that was underhanded, or lacking, to say the least, in reasonable candor, if the partner were to surprise him in the act of signing the new instrument. Conduct subject to that reproach does not receive from equity a healing benediction.

A question remains as to the form and extent of the equitable interest to be allotted to the plaintiff. The trust as declared has been held to attach to the lease which was in the name of the defendant corporation. We think it ought to attach at the option of the defendant Salmon to the shares of stock which were owned by him or were under his control. The difference may be important if the lessee shall wish to execute an assignment of the lease, as it ought to be free to do with the consent of the lessor. On the other hand, an equal division of the shares might lead to other hardships. It might take away from Salmon the power of control and management which under the plan of the joint venture he was to have from first to last. The number of shares to be allotted to the plaintiff should, therefore, be reduced to such an extent as may be necessary to preserve to the defendant Salmon the expected measure of dominion. To that end an extra share should be added to his half.

Subject to this adjustment, we agree with the Appellate Division that the plaintiff's equitable interest is to be measured by the value of half of the entire lease, and not merely by half of some undivided part. A single building covers the whole area. Physical division is impracticable along the lines of the Bristol site, the keystone of the whole. Division of interests and burdens is equally impracticable. Salmon, as tenant under the new lease, or as guarantor of the performance of the tenant's obligations, might well protest if Meinhard, claiming an equitable interest, had offered to assume a liability not equal to Salmon's, but only half as great. He might justly insist that the lease must be accepted by his coadventurer in such form as it had been given, and not constructively divided into imaginary fragments. What must be yielded to the one may be demanded by the other. The lease as it has been executed is single and entire. If confusion has resulted from the union of adjoining parcels, the trustee who consented to the union must bear the inconvenience.

* * *

The judgment should be modified by providing that at the option of the defendant Salmon there may be substituted for a trust attaching to the lease a trust attaching to the shares of stock, with the result that one-half of such shares together with one additional share will in that event be allotted to the defendant Salmon and the other shares to the plaintiff, and as so modified the judgment should be affirmed with costs.

ANDREWS, J. (dissenting).

* * *

Were this a general partnership between Mr. Salmon and Mr. Meinhard, I should have little doubt as to the correctness of this result, assuming the new lease to be an offshoot of the old. Such a situation involves questions of trust and confidence to a high degree; it involves questions of good will; many other considerations. As has been said, rarely if ever may one partner without the knowledge of the other acquire for himself the renewal of a lease held by the firm, even if the new lease is to begin after the firm is dissolved. Warning of such an intent, if he is managing partner, may not be sufficient to prevent the application of this rule.

We have here a different situation governed by less drastic principles. I assume that where parties engage in a joint enterprise each owes to the other the duty of the utmost good faith in all that relates to their common venture. Within its scope they stand in a fiduciary relationship. I assume prima facie that even as between joint adventurers one may not secretly obtain a renewal of the lease of property actually used in the joint adventure where the possibility of renewal is expressly or impliedly involved in the enterprise. I assume also that Mr. Meinhard had an equitable interest in the Bristol Hotel lease. Further, that an expectancy of renewal inhered in that lease. Two questions then arise. Under his contract did he share in that expectancy? And if so, did that expectancy mature into a graft of the original lease? To both questions my answer is "No." * * *

What then was the scope of the adventure into which the two men entered? It is to be remembered that before their contract was signed Mr. Salmon had obtained the lease of the Bristol property. Very likely the matter had been earlier discussed between them. The $5,000 advance by Mr. Meinhard indicates that fact. But it has been held that the written contract defines their rights and duties. Having the lease, Mr. Salmon assigns no interest in it to Mr. Meinhard. He is to manage the property. It is for him to decide what alterations shall be made and to fix the rents. But for 20 years from May 1, 1902, Salmon is to make all advances from his own funds and Meinhard is to pay him personally on demand one-half of all expenses incurred and all losses sustained "during the full term of said lease," and during the same period Salmon is to pay him a part of the net profits. There was no joint capital provided.

It seems to me that the venture so inaugurated had in view a limited object and was to end at a limited time. There was no intent to expand it into a far greater undertaking lasting for many years. The design was to exploit a particular lease. Doubtless in it Mr. Meinhard had an equitable interest, but in it alone. This interest terminated when the joint adventure terminated. There was no intent that for the benefit of both any advantage should be taken of the chance of renewal—that the adventure should be continued beyond that date. Mr. Salmon has done all he promised to do in return for Mr. Meinhard's undertaking when he distributed profits up to May 1, 1922. Suppose this lease, nonassignable without the consent of the lessor, had contained a renewal option. Could Mr. Meinhard have exercised it? Could he have insisted that Mr. Salmon do so? Had Mr. Salmon done so could he insist that the agreement to share losses still existed, or could Mr. Meinhard have claimed that the joint adventure was still to continue for 20 or 80 years? I do not think so. The adventure by its express terms ended on May 1, 1922. The contract by its language and by its whole import excluded the idea that the tenant's expectancy was to subsist for the benefit of the plaintiff. On that date whatever there was left of value in the lease reverted to Mr. Salmon, as it would had the lease been for thirty years instead of twenty. Any equity which Mr. Meinhard possessed was in the particular lease itself, not in any possibility of renewal. There was nothing unfair in Mr. Salmon's conduct.

     * * *

The judgment of the courts below should be reversed and a new trial ordered, with costs in all courts to abide the event.

POUND, CRANE, and LEHMAN, JJ., concur with CARDOZO, C.J., * * *

ANDREWS, J., dissents in opinion in which KELLOGG and O'BRIEN, JJ., concur.

NOTES

(1) How does Judge Cardozo describe the relationship between partners? Is that an appropriate way to view the relationship? *Cf.* Crim Truck & Tractor Co. v. Navistar Int'l Transp. Corp., 823 S.W.2d 591, 594 (Tex. 1992) (noting that a fiduciary duty imposes an "onerous burden that requires a party to place the interest of the other party before his own").

(2) What did Salmon do wrong? Could Salmon have avoided the result by disclosing the renewal opportunity to Meinhard and by giving Meinhard a chance to deal directly with Gerry? What else might have been done to avoid this dispute?

(3) Does it matter that the court describes the relationship between Meinhard and Salmon as a joint venture rather than a general partnership? *See* Chapter 3, Section D(2) (discussing a joint venture in the "Notes" following *Kessler*).

(4) Is the *Meinhard* notion of fiduciary duty affected by distrust between the partners? In *Johnson v. Peckham*, 120 S.W.2d 786 (Tex. 1938), strained relations had developed between two partners and a suit for an accounting and dissolution was pending in a court. Peckham agreed to purchase Johnson's interests in two oil leases that constituted the partnership property for $1,500. Shortly after this transaction was completed, Peckham resold the leases for $10,500. *See id.* at 786. Based on a showing that negotiations for this resale had begun prior to the time Peckham purchased Johnson's interests, Peckham was required to share the profitable resale with Johnson. A judgment for $3,750 (one-half of $10,500, minus $1,500) was entered, with the court quoting the ringing language of Justice Cardozo in *Meinhard v. Salmon. See Peckham*, 120 S.W.2d at 788.

2. STATUTORY DEVELOPMENTS AND THE ROLE OF CONTRACT

UPA § 21 is the only provision in UPA that refers to a partner's "fiduciary" duty. Does § 21 incorporate the broad fiduciary duty of *Meinhard*? An ABA Committee, commenting on this section, stated that while it "is often cited as establishing a broad fiduciary duty, in fact, as presently worded, [it] is basically merely an anti-theft provision." UPA Revision Subcommittee of the Committee on Partnerships and Unincorporated Business Organizations, *Should the Uniform Partnership Act Be Revised?*, 43 BUS. LAW. 121, 151 (1987). Many partnership cases, however, cite *Meinhard* and § 21 as establishing a broad fiduciary duty among partners.

RUPA approaches the fiduciary duty issue very differently than UPA. Consider carefully RUPA § 404, particularly the word "only" in § 404(a) and the phrase "is limited to" in § 404(b). Section 404(a) limits the fiduciary duties of partners to those of loyalty and care, while § 404(b) and § 404(c) define the scope of those duties.

RUPA § 404(d) imposes an "obligation of good faith and fair dealing" upon partners when discharging duties and exercising rights. The comment indicates that the obligation is a contractual concept that is imposed on the partners because of the consensual nature of a partnership. The comment further states that the meaning of good faith and fair dealing "is not firmly fixed under present law," although good faith "clearly suggests a subjective element" while fair dealing "implies an objective component." *Id.* § 404 cmt. 4.

RUPA § 404(e) indicates that a partner does not violate a duty or obligation "merely because the partner's conduct furthers the partner's own interest." According to the comment, "[a] partner as such is not a trustee and is not held to the same standards as a trustee," and subsection (e) "makes clear that a partner's conduct is not deemed to be improper merely because it serves the partner's own individual interest." *Id.* § 404 cmt. 4; *see also id.* (noting that subsection (e) "underscores the partner's rights as an owner and principal in the enterprise, which must always be balanced against his duties and obligations as an agent and fiduciary").

Section 404(f) of RUPA states that "[a] partner may lend money to and transact other business with the partnership, and as to each loan or transaction the rights and obligations of the partner are the same as those of a person who is not a partner, subject to other applicable law." The comment indicates that this subsection would, for example, permit a partner to purchase the assets of the partnership at a foreclosure sale, upon liquidation, or at a tax sale. *See id.* § 404 cmt. 6. This subsection, along with the other subsections of RUPA § 404, will be examined further in the materials below.

a. The Duty of Loyalty

ENEA V. SUPERIOR COURT

Court of Appeal of California, 2005.
34 Cal.Rptr.3d 513.

RUSHING, P. J.

Plaintiff Benny Enea brought this petition to set aside an order of respondent court summarily adjudicating his cause of action against his former partners, defendants William Daniels and Claudia Daniels, for breaches of fiduciary duties consisting primarily of renting partnership property to themselves at less than its fair market value. The trial court ruled that, as a matter of law, no such claim could be predicated on such conduct in the absence of an agreement requiring fair market rents. We hold that this was error; the fiduciary duties imposed on partners by operation of law unquestionably bar them from conferring such benefits upon themselves at the partnership's expense. Accordingly, we will direct respondent court to set aside its order and deny the motion.

BACKGROUND

* * * Defendants state that in 1980, they and other family members formed a general partnership known as 3-D. The partnership's sole asset was a building that had been converted from a residence into offices. Some portion of the property—apparently the greater part—has been rented since 1981 on a month-to-month basis by a law practice of which William Daniels is apparently the sole member. From time to time the property was rented on similar arrangements to others, including defendant Claudia Daniels. Plaintiff's counsel stipulated in the court below that "the partnership agreement has as its principal purpose the ownership, leasing and sale of the only partnership assets, which is the building * * *." He also stipulated that the partnership agreement contained no provision that the property "[would] be leased for fair market value." Defendants also assert, as the trial court ultimately found, that there was no evidence of any agreement to maximize rental profits.

* * *

DISCUSSION

* * *

* * * [T]he sole question presented is whether defendants were categorically entitled to lease partnership property to themselves, or associated entities (or for that matter, to anyone) at less than it could yield in the open market. Remarkably, we have found no case squarely addressing this precise question. We are satisfied, however, that the answer is a resounding "No."

* * * It is hornbook law that in forming [a partnership] the partners obligate themselves to share risks and benefits and to carry out the enterprise with the highest good faith toward one another—in short, with the loyalty and care of a fiduciary. * * * "Partnership is a fiduciary relationship, and partners may not take advantages for themselves at the expense of the partnership." (*Jones v. Wells Fargo Bank* (2003) 112 Cal.App.4th 1527, 1540, 5 Cal. Rptr. 3d 835.)

Here the facts as assumed by the parties and the trial court plainly depict defendants taking advantages for themselves from partnership property *at the expense of the partnership*. The advantage consisted of occupying partnership property at below-market rates, i.e., less than they would be required to pay to an independent landlord for equivalent premises. The cost to the partnership was the additional rent thereby rendered unavailable for collection from an independent tenant willing to pay the property's value.

* * *

* * * [Section 16404 does] not entitle defendants to rent partnership property to themselves at below-market rates. The first duty listed in the statute is "[t]o account to the partnership and hold as trustee for it *any property, profit, or benefit* derived by the partner in the conduct * * * of the partnership business or *derived from a use by the partner of partnership property* * * *." (Corp. Code, § 16404, subd. (b)(1); *see id.*, § 16401, subd. (g) ["A partner may use or possess partnership property only on behalf of the partnership"]; *see* RUPA, §§ 404(b)(1), 401(g).)

Defendants persuaded the trial court that the conduct challenged by plaintiff was authorized by section 16404, subdivision (e), which states, "A partner does not violate a duty or obligation under this chapter or under the partnership agreement merely because the partner's conduct furthers the partner's own interest." The apparent purpose of this provision, which is drawn verbatim from RUPA section 404(e), is to excuse partners from accounting for incidental benefits obtained in the course of partnership activities *without detriment to the partnership*.[3] It does not by its terms authorize the kind of conduct at issue here, which did not "merely" further defendants' own interests but did so by depriving the partnership of valuable assets, i.e., the space which would otherwise have been rented at market rates. Here, the statute entitled defendants to lease partnership property *at the same rent another tenant would have paid*. It did not empower them to occupy partnership property for their own exclusive benefit at partnership expense, in effect converting partnership assets to their own and appropriating the value it would otherwise have realized as distributable profits. Defendants' argument to the contrary seems conceptually indistinguishable from a claim that if a partnership's "primary purpose" is to purchase and hold investments, individual partners may freely pilfer its office supplies.

---

[3] The authors of [one] treatise note that this provision has received "two very different interpretations * * *, one rather narrow and the other quite broad. Under the narrow interpretation, Section 404(e) is essentially an evidentiary rule which could be paraphrased as 'the fact that a partner directly personally benefits from the partner's conduct in the partnership context does not, without more, establish a violation of the partner's duties or obligations under RUPA or the partnership agreement.' Under the broad interpretation, Section 404(e) means that partners are free to pursue their short-term, individual self-interest without notice to or the consent of the partnership, subject only to the specific restrictions contained in the Section 404(b) duty of loyalty—in effect that the pursuit of self-interest cannot be a violation of the non-fiduciary obligation of good faith and fair dealing." (Hillman et al., [The Revised Uniform Partnership Act (2004 ed.)], at p. 207.) We need not decide which of these views, if either, prevails in California. Even under the broader reading, section 16404, subdivision (e), does not authorize a partner to exploit partnership property for personal advantage at partnership expense.

Defendants also persuaded the trial court that they had no duty to collect market rents in the absence of a contract expressly requiring them to do so. This argument turns partnership law on its head. Nowhere does the law declare that partners owe each other only those duties they explicitly assume by contract. On the contrary, the fiduciary duties at issue here are *imposed by law*, and their breach sounds in tort. We have no occasion here to consider the extent to which partners might effectively limit or modify those delictual duties by an explicit agreement or whether the partnership agreement in fact required market rents by its terms. There is no suggestion that it purported to affirmatively *excuse* defendants from the delictual duty not to engage in self-dealing. Instead, their argument is predicated on the wholly untenable notion that they were entitled to do so unless the agreement explicitly declared otherwise.

Defendants also assert, and the trial court found, that the "primary purpose" of the partnership was to hold the building for appreciation and eventual sale. This premise hardly justified summary adjudication. If the partners had explicitly agreed *not* to derive market rents from the property, but to let it be used for the exclusive advantage of some of them indefinitely, there would be some basis to contend that defendants were entitled to conduct themselves as they did—or at least that plaintiff was estopped to complain. But the mere anticipation of eventual capital gains as the main economic benefit to be derived from the venture has no tendency whatsoever to entitle individual partners to divert to their own advantage benefits that would otherwise flow to the partnership.

* * *

DISPOSITION

Let a peremptory writ of mandate issue directing respondent court to vacate its order granting defendants' motion for summary adjudication of plaintiff's second cause of action, and to enter a new order denying said motion. * * *

NOTES

(1) The court finds that the defendants breached their fiduciary duties by renting partnership property to themselves at below-market rates. Would the result change if the defendants had rented partnership property to themselves at a fair market rent? *See* RUPA § 404(b), (e), (f); *see also* UPA § 21 (noting that "[e]very partner must account to the partnership for any benefit, and hold as trustee for it any profits derived by him without the consent of the other partners").

(2) UPA § 21 and RUPA § 404(b)(1) are similar provisions. UPA § 21, however, refers to the "formation, conduct, or liquidation" of the partnership, while RUPA § 404(b)(1) refers only to the "conduct and winding up" of the

partnership. Under RUPA, therefore, there is no duty of loyalty in connection with the formation of the partnership.

Does this limitation in RUPA make sense? Should negotiations related to the formation of a partnership be subject to greater scrutiny (i.e., fiduciary scrutiny) than negotiations related to the formation of a contract (e.g., a contract for employment or to purchase a new automobile)? *See* RUPA § 404 cmt. 2 ("Reference to the 'formation' of the partnership has been eliminated by RUPA because of concern that the duty of loyalty could be inappropriately extended to the pre-formation period when the parties are really negotiating at arm's length. Once a partnership is agreed to, each partner becomes a fiduciary in the 'conduct' of the business. Pre-formation negotiations are, of course, subject to the general contract obligation to deal honestly and without fraud.").

(3) Notice the phrase "is limited to" in RUPA § 404(b). This language was inserted because of "a sense that vague, broad statements of a powerful duty of loyalty cause too much uncertainty. * * * [E]ven if there are no bad holdings, overly broad judicial language has left practitioners uncertain about whether their negotiated agreement will be voided. * * * [P]racticing attorneys want to be able to reach a deal, put it down on paper and know that it will not be undone by the application of fiduciary duties." Donald J. Weidner, *The Revised Uniform Partnership Act Midstream: Major Policy Decisions*, 21 U. TOL. L. REV. 825, 856 (1990).

Not all jurisdictions, however, have limited the duty of loyalty in this manner. Another portion of the *Enea* opinion, for example, discusses the California version of RUPA § 404(b):

> * * * [Defendants'] main argument appears to be that their conduct was authorized by Corporations Code section 16404 (section 16404), which codifies the fiduciary duties of a partner under California law. The implication of such an argument is that section 16404 provides the *exclusive* statement of a partner's obligation to the partnership and to other partners. This premise would be correct if California had adopted, in its proposed form, the uniform law on which section 16404 is based. Section 404 of the Uniform Partnership Act (1997 rev.), also known as the Revised Uniform Partnership Act or RUPA, contains an explicitly exclusive enumeration of a partner's duties. After noting that a partner owes fiduciary duties of loyalty and care, the uniform Act declares that those duties are "limited to" obligations listed there. (RUPA, § 404(b), (c).) While section 16404 retains this language with respect to the duty of care, it repudiates it with respect to the duty of loyalty, stating instead that "* * * [a] partner's duty of loyalty to the partnership and the other partners *includes* all of the following: * * *" (Italics added.)
>
> The leading treatise on RUPA confirms that by altering the proposed language, the California Legislature rejected one of the

"fundamental" changes the drafters sought to bring to partnership law, i.e., "an exclusive statutory treatment of partners' fiduciary duties." (Hillman et al., The Revised Uniform Partnership Act (2004 ed.), p. 202.) The proposed uniform version "[b]y its terms * * * comprises an exclusive statement of the fiduciary duties of partners among themselves and to the partnership. The formulation is exclusive in two ways; the duties of loyalty and care are the only components of the partners' fiduciary duties, and the duties themselves are exclusively defined." (*Ibid.*, fns. omitted.) But several states, *most clearly California,* balked at the latter restriction, leaving the articulation of the duty of loyalty to traditional common law processes. "Some adopting states * * * modified the RUPA language in ways which make, or arguably make, the fiduciary duty formulation non-exclusive. [Citation.] The available California legislative history states that: '[Section 16404] establishes a *comprehensive, but not exhaustive, definition* of partnership fiduciary duties. A partner owes *at least two* duties to other partners and the partnership: a duty of loyalty and a duty of care. In addition, an obligation of good faith and fair dealing is imposed on partners.' [Citation] This reading is also supported by the drafters' conclusion in the legislative history that 'the new fiduciary duty section makes no substantive change from prior law.' [Citation.]" (*Id.,* fn. 5, quoting Senate Rules Com., Off. of Sen. Floor Analyses, 3d reading analysis of Assem. Bill No. 583 (1995–1996 Reg. Sess.) as amended Aug. 23, 1996, p. 6, some italics added.)

Enea, 34 Cal.Rptr.3d at 517–18.

(4) Might there be aspects of a duty of loyalty that are not encompassed within the three subsections of RUPA § 404(b)? If so, what are they?

(5) Doesn't RUPA § 404(e) significantly undercut § 404(b)? Can't most breaches of fiduciary duty be justified on the theory that the conduct "furthers the partner's own interest?" What function, if any, does the word "merely" in § 404(e) serve?

(6) Similarly, doesn't RUPA § 404(f) significantly undercut § 404(b)? The comment to § 404(f) indicates that the subsection is based upon § 107 of the Revised Uniform Limited Partnership Act ("RULPA"). *See* RUPA § 404 cmt. 6. In *BT-I v. Equitable Life Assurance Society*, 89 Cal.Rptr.2d 811 (Cal. Ct. App. 1999), the court indicated that § 107 does not alter a general partner's fiduciary duties:

> We cannot discern anything in the purpose of Corporations Code section 15617 [analogous to RULPA § 107] that suggests an intent to affect a general partner's fiduciary duty to limited partners. Under the prior limited partnership rule, limited partners were prohibited from making secured loans to the partnership and any collateral received could be set aside as a fraud upon creditors. Corporations Code section 15617 is identical to Uniform Limited

Partnership Act (1976) section 107, which was enacted to remove the fraudulent conveyances prohibition from the limited partnership law and leave the question to the general fraudulent conveyances statute. This change hardly sanctions Equitable's self-dealing.

Id. at 818.

(7) UPA § 20 states that partners "shall render on demand true and full information of all things affecting the partnership to any partner." RUPA § 403 expands the scope of this disclosure obligation by stating that each partner and the partnership shall furnish to a partner "without demand, any information concerning the partnership's business and affairs reasonably required for the proper exercise of the partner's rights and duties under the partnership agreement or this [Act]," and shall furnish "on demand, any other information concerning the partnership's business and affairs, except to the extent the demand or the information demanded is unreasonable or otherwise improper under the circumstances." Although *Meinhard* and other cases suggest that a partner's disclosure obligation is fiduciary in nature (i.e., a partner's fiduciary duty includes a duty to disclose information to other partners in certain circumstances), UPA § 20 does not refer to the obligation as a fiduciary one. Moreover, the use of "only" in RUPA § 404(a) clearly indicates that the disclosure obligation in RUPA § 403 is not an independent fiduciary duty.

b. The Duty of Care

BANE V. FERGUSON

United States Court of Appeals, Seventh Circuit, 1989.
890 F.2d 11.

Before POSNER, COFFEY, and KANNE, CIRCUIT JUDGES.

POSNER, CIRCUIT JUDGE.

The question presented by this appeal from the dismissal of the complaint is whether a retired partner in a law firm has either a common law or a statutory claim against the firm's managing council for acts of negligence that, by causing the firm to dissolve, terminate his retirement benefits. It is a diversity case governed by the law of Illinois, rather than a federal-question case governed by the Employee Retirement Income Security Act, 29 U.S.C. §§ 1001 *et seq.*, because ERISA excludes partners from its protections.

Charles Bane practiced corporate and public utility law as a partner in the venerable Chicago law firm of Isham, Lincoln & Beale, founded more than a century ago by Abraham Lincoln's son Robert Todd Lincoln. In August 1985 the firm adopted a noncontributory retirement plan that entitled every retiring partner to a pension, the amount depending on his earnings from the firm on the eve of retirement. The plan instrument provided that the plan, and the payments under it, would end when and if the firm dissolved without a successor entity, and also that the amount paid out in pension benefits each year could not exceed five percent of the firm's net income in the preceding year. Four months after the plan was adopted, the plaintiff retired, moved to Florida with his wife, and began drawing his pension (to continue until his wife's death if he died first) of $27,483 a year. Bane was 72 years old when he retired. So far as appears, he had, apart from social security, no significant source of income other than the pension.

Several months after Bane's retirement, Isham, Lincoln & Beale merged with Reuben & Proctor, another large and successful Chicago firm. The merger proved to be a disaster, and the merged firm was dissolved in April 1988 without a successor—whereupon the payment of pension benefits to Bane ceased and he brought this suit. The suit alleges that the defendants were the members of the firm's managing council in the period leading up to the dissolution and that they acted unreasonably in deciding to merge the firm with Reuben & Proctor, in purchasing computers and other office equipment, and in leaving the firm for greener pastures shortly before its dissolution. The suit does not allege that the defendants committed fraud, engaged in self-dealing, or deliberately sought to destroy or damage the law firm or harm the plaintiff; the charge is negligent mismanagement, not deliberate wrongdoing. The suit seeks damages, presumably the present value of the pension benefits to which the Banes would be entitled had the firm not dissolved.

* * *

Bane has four theories of liability. The first is that the defendants, by committing acts of mismanagement that resulted in the dissolution of the firm, violated the Uniform Partnership Act * * * [§ 9(3)(c)], which provides that "unless authorized by the other partners * * * one or more but less than all the partners have no authority to: Do any * * * act which would make it impossible to carry on the ordinary business of the partnership." This provision is inapplicable. Its purpose is not to make negligent partners liable to persons with whom the partnership transacts (such as Bane), but to limit the liability of the other partners for the unauthorized act of one partner. See *Hackney v. Johnson*, 601 S.W.2d 523, 525 (Tex.Civ.App.1980). The purpose in other words is to protect partners. Bane ceased to be a partner when he retired in 1985.

Nor can Bane obtain legal relief on the theory that the defendants violated a fiduciary duty to him; they had none. A partner is a fiduciary of his partners, but not of his former partners, for the withdrawal of a partner terminates the partnership as to him. *Adams v. Jarvis*, 23 Wis.2d 453, 458, 127 N.W.2d 400, 403 (1964). Bane must look elsewhere for the grounds of a fiduciary obligation running from his former partners to himself. The pension plan did not establish a trust, and even if, notwithstanding the absence of one, the plan's managers were fiduciaries of its beneficiaries (there are myriad sources of fiduciary duty besides a trust), the mismanagement was not of the plan but of the firm. There is no suggestion that the defendants failed to inform the plaintiff of his rights under the plan or miscalculated his benefits or mismanaged or misapplied funds set aside for the plan's beneficiaries; no funds *were* set aside for them. Even if the defendants were fiduciaries of the plaintiff, moreover, the business-judgment rule would shield them from liability for mere negligence in the operation of the firm, just as it would shield a corporation's directors and officers, who are fiduciaries of the shareholders. * * *

That leaves for discussion Bane's claims of breach of contract and of tort. The plan instrument expressly decrees the death of the plan upon the dissolution of the firm, and nowhere is there expressed a commitment or even an undertaking to maintain the firm in existence, whether for the sake of the plan's beneficiaries or anyone else. Contracts have implicit as well as explicit terms, see, e.g., *Wood v. Duff-Gordon*, 222 N.Y. 88, 118 N.E. 214 (1917) (Cardozo, J.), and one can imagine an argument that the plaintiff was induced to retire by an implied promise that the managing council would do everything possible to keep the firm going—that without such an implied promise he would not have retired, given his dependence on the firm's retirement plan for his income after he retired. But Bane does not make this argument and anyway it is hopeless. * * *

The last question, which is the most interesting because the most fundamental, is whether the defendants violated a duty of care to the plaintiff founded on general principles of tort law. What is the liability of the managers of a failed enterprise to persons harmed by the failure? When a large firm—whether a law firm, or a manufacturing enterprise, or a bank, or a railroad—fails, and shuts its doors, many persons besides the owners of the firm may be hurt in their pocketbooks—workers, suppliers, suppliers' workers, creditors (like Mr. Bane), and members of these persons' families. * * * We can find no precedent in Illinois law or elsewhere for imposing tort liability on careless managers for the financial consequences of the collapse of the firm to all who are hurt by that collapse. "The act of dissolution of a corporation is not in itself sufficient foundation for [a] tort action even if it results in the breach of contracts. If the dissolution is motivated by good faith judgment for the benefit of the corporation rather than personal gain of the officers, directors or shareholders, no liability attaches to the dissolution." *Swager v. Couri*, 60 Ill.App.3d 192, 196, 17 Ill.Dec. 457, 460, 376 N.E.2d 456, 459 (1978) (citations omitted). The competence, not the good faith, of the defendants is drawn in question by the complaint. And the principle of *Swager* is as applicable to a partnership as to a corporation.

* * *

We are sorry about the financial blow to the Banes but we agree with the district judge that there is no remedy under the law of Illinois.

NOTES

(1) The court rejects Bane's breach of fiduciary duty claim on the ground that he is a former partner. What if Bane was still a partner of the firm? Would his breach of fiduciary duty claim be successful? *Cf.* Brehm v. Eisner, 746 A.2d 244, 264 n.66 (Del. 2000) ("The business judgment rule has been well formulated by * * * other cases. Thus, directors' decisions will be respected by courts unless the directors are interested or lack independence relative to the decision, do not act in good faith, act in a manner that cannot be attributed to a rational business purpose or reach their decision by a grossly negligent process that includes the failure to consider all material facts reasonably available.").

(2) How would Bane's breach of fiduciary duty claim fare under RUPA § 404(c)?

(3) The pension plan involved in this case contemplated that retirement payments to former partners were to be made out of future earnings of the firm. In addition to the impermanence of such a plan (as demonstrated by Judge Posner's opinion), these plans almost invariably lead to intergenerational conflict, as younger partners in their most productive years resent losing a portion of their earnings to benefit retired partners. In many instances, productive junior partners leave firms in order to be free of unfunded retirement obligations to senior partners.

Would the result in *Bane* have been different if the plaintiff could have shown that the partnership was only dissolved to permit the existing partners to avoid their obligations under the pension plan? *Cf.* RUPA § 404(d).

(4) Law firms that provide retirement plans for their partners today generally require the beneficiaries themselves to fund the plans during their productive years. In many firms, partners are expected to provide for their own retirement entirely on their own by creation of tax-deferred Keogh or other plans that permit the accumulation of substantial retirement benefits over a career.

(5) UPA § 13, which governs the liability of a partnership based on "any wrongful act or omission of any partner acting in the ordinary course of the business of the partnership," applies only to injuries to "any person, not being a partner in the partnership." This language seems to preclude one partner from suing the partnership for another partner's mismanagement or other breach of duty. The partner's only statutory remedies would appear to be the right to seek an accounting[d] pursuant to § 22 or the right to dissolution under

---

    [d] An accounting is a judicial proceeding in which all matters pending between the partners are adjudicated. In such a proceeding, "the court (or, more commonly, an auditor, master, or referee subject to court review) conducts a comprehensive investigation of the transactions of the partnership and the partners, adjudicates their relative rights, and enters a money judgment for

§ 31. Similarly, under the common law, partners were often prevented from suing other partners for breach of duty on the ground that an accounting was the exclusive means for a partner to seek recourse (or, at a minimum, was a condition precedent to maintaining a cause of action for damages). *See generally* Sertich v. Moorman, 783 P.2d 1199, 1200–02 (Ariz. 1989) (discussing the origins of the accounting rule and its application).

RUPA § 305(a), which is derived from UPA § 13, omits the phrase "any person, not being a partner in the partnership." The intent is to "permit a partner to sue the partnership on a tort or other theory during the term of the partnership, rather than being limited to the remedies of dissolution and an accounting." RUPA § 305 cmt. In addition, § 405(b) permits a partner to maintain a variety of actions against the partnership or the other partners, including actions for breach of fiduciary duty, without the requirement of an accounting. *See id.* § 405 cmt. 2 ("Under RUPA, an accounting is not a prerequisite to the availability of the other remedies a partner may have against the partnership or the other partners.").

c.   Contractual Limitations

SINGER V. SINGER

Court of Appeals of Oklahoma, 1981.
634 P.2d 766.

BOYDSTON, JUDGE.

This appeal is from [a] * * * judgment of [the] district court declaring [that] land purchased by defendants is to be held in constructive trust for * * * Josaline Production Co., a partnership * * *. All parties to this action are related through family ties, intricate partnerships and trusts. * * *

SINGER FAMILY BUSINESS RELATIONSHIP

The Singer family formed an oil production partnership in the late 1930[s]. Through inheritance and assignments, partnership interests have been conveyed and passed down to other family members, fractionalizing the ownership.

The original partnership was called Josaline Production Co. * * *

* * *

---

or against each partner according to the balance struck." II ALAN R. BROMBERG & LARRY E. RIBSTEIN, BROMBERG AND RIBSTEIN ON PARTNERSHIP § 6.08(a), at 6:172.2 (13th ed. 2005). Because all activities related to the partnership are subject to scrutiny in an accounting, a wide variety of issues may be considered, including the partnership's profits, losses, assets, and liabilities, as well as the partners' financial rights and obligations. *See id.* § 6.08(d), at 6:196.1 to 6:196.2. At least part of the rationale for an accounting is that "no rights of the partners can be accurately determined until a balance is struck" because, in a partnership, "the participants are likely to have not only claims but also liabilities arising out of their duty to contribute toward the losses of the business." *Id.* § 6.08(c), at 6:178 to 6:179.

* * * Between 1962 and 1977 intrafamily assignments resulted in Andrea and her brother Stanley becoming partners * * *. In 1977, the parties re-drafted the partnership agreement, carefully defining duties and rights of the parties and restating the current ownership percentages.

* * *

The 1977 restated partnership agreement contained the following paragraph:

8.   *Each partner shall be free to enter into business and other transactions for his or her own separate individual account,* even though such business or other transaction may be in conflict with and/or competition with the business of this partnership. Neither the partnership nor any individual member of this partnership shall be entitled to claim or receive any part of or interest in such transactions, *it being the intention and agreement that any partner will be free to deal on his or her own account to the same extent and with the same force and effect as if he or she were not and never had been members of this partnership.* (emphasis supplied)

* * *

THE DISPUTE

On July 25, 1979, the Josaline partners held a meeting in Oklahoma City which was attended by several members of the Josaline partnership * * *. At the meeting several investment opportunities were raised, but the meeting was mainly held to discuss routine business of Josaline. One item of interest on the agenda was the possible purchase * * * of 95 acres of land in the Britton area owned by Investors Diversified Services (IDS). The proposed purchase included 45 acres of minerals and was listed for sale at a purchase price of one and one-half million dollars.

Prior to the meeting, Joe L. [Singer] requested Stanley to look into the possibility of purchasing the land through the listing realtor. At the meeting the IDS land was briefly discussed but the decision of whether to purchase was deferred.

After the meeting, defendants Stanley and Andrea formed a general partnership, Gemini Realty Company (Gemini), and on September 25, 1979, purchased the IDS land, taking title in Gemini's name without further consultation with any of the Josaline partners * * *.

Within a short time, Joe L. learned of the transaction and demanded Singer Bros. partnership be permitted to purchase 50 percent of the property. Initially, Stanley offered to give Singer Bros. 16.66 percent but withdrew the offer before it had been accepted. No other member of the

Singer family requested or was permitted to participate and this suit resulted.

* * *

III

* * * Josaline's contention [is] that by reason of the fiduciary aspects of partnership it is entitled to participate in the purchase of the IDS land * * *. We would agree with Josaline's contention except for paragraph 8 of the partnership contract.

We find the defendants had a contract right to do precisely what they did, namely, compete with the partners of Josaline and with Josaline itself "as if there never had been a partnership." Because of paragraph 8, the fact that the land is in an area of partnership interest does not preclude intra-partnership competition. A special area of interest is just another way of labeling and describing an investment area where competition is ordinarily not permitted between partners, absent agreement. Josaline contracted away its right to expect a noncompetitive fiduciary relationship with any of its partners.

We find paragraph 8 is designed to allow and is uniquely drafted to promote spirited, if not outright predatory competition between the partners. Its strong wording leaves no doubt in our minds that its drafters intended to effect such a result. This is reinforced by the fact [that] the partners repeated the same clause in two successive contracts. We construe it to legitimize and extend free competition between the partners to partnership prospects and opportunities, including the Britton area of interest and the IDS land.

From a fiduciary aspect, the permissible boundaries of intra-partnership competition, under paragraph 8, are limited only after the threshold of actual partnership acquisition has been crossed. Had Stanley and Andrea pirated an existing partnership asset or used partnership funds or encumbered Josaline financially, our decision would be different.

* * *

IV

* * * We hereby reverse and remand to [the] trial court with instructions to vacate the judgment rendered below and order judgment be rendered in favor of defendants. * * *

NOTES

(1) Is the result in *Singer* correct under UPA? *See* UPA § 21(1).

(2) Is the result in *Singer* correct under RUPA? *See* RUPA §§ 103(b), 404(b).

(3) Should we allow partners to limit or eliminate fiduciary duties by contract (e.g., in a partnership agreement)?

(4) Delaware has adopted RUPA. Delaware's version of RUPA § 103(b), however, omits subsections (b)(3) and (b)(4)—indicating that the duties of loyalty and care can be limited or eliminated as the partners see fit. *See* DEL. STAT. tit. 6, § 15–103(b). The statute further states that "[a] partnership agreement may provide for the limitation or elimination of any and all liabilities for breach of contract and breach of duties (including fiduciary duties) of a partner or other person to a partnership or to another partner * * *; provided, that a partnership agreement may not limit or eliminate liability for any act or omission that constitutes a bad faith violation of the implied contractual covenant of good faith and fair dealing." *Id.* § 15–103(f). Delaware has similar provisions in its limited partnership and limited liability company statutes.

3. DUTIES WHEN LEAVING A PARTNERSHIP

MEEHAN V. SHAUGHNESSY

Supreme Judicial Court of Massachusetts, 1989.
535 N.E.2d 1255.

HENNESSEY, CHIEF JUSTICE.

The plaintiffs, James F. Meehan (Meehan) and Leo V. Boyle (Boyle), were partners of the law firm, Parker, Coulter, Daley & White (Parker Coulter). After Meehan and Boyle terminated their relationship with Parker Coulter to start their own firm, they commenced this action both to recover amounts they claim the defendants, their former partners, owed them under the partnership agreement, and to obtain a declaration as to amounts they owed the defendants for work done at Parker Coulter on cases they removed to their new firm. The defendants (hereinafter collectively Parker Coulter) counterclaimed that Meehan and Boyle violated their fiduciary duties, breached the partnership agreement, and tortiously interfered with their advantageous business and contractual relationships. As grounds for these claims, Parker Coulter asserted that Meehan and Boyle engaged in improper conduct in withdrawing cases and clients from the firm, and in inducing employees to join the new firm of Meehan, Boyle & Cohen, P.C. (MBC). * * *

After a jury-waived trial, a Superior Court judge rejected all of Parker Coulter's claims for relief, and found that Meehan and Boyle were entitled to recover amounts owed to them under the partnership agreement. The judge also found, based on the partnership agreement and a quantum meruit theory, that Parker Coulter was entitled to recover from Meehan and Boyle for time billed and expenses incurred on the cases Meehan and Boyle removed to their own firm. Parker Coulter appealed from the judgment, and we granted direct appellate review.

* * *

* * * Parker, Coulter, Daley & White is a large partnership which specializes in litigation on behalf of both defendants and plaintiffs. Meehan joined the firm in 1959, and became a partner in 1963; his practice focuses primarily on complex tort litigation, such as product liability and aviation defense work. Boyle joined Parker Coulter in 1971, and became a partner in 1980; he has concentrated on plaintiffs' work. Both have developed outstanding reputations as trial lawyers in the Commonwealth. Meehan and Boyle each were active in the management of Parker Coulter. They each served, for example, on the partnership's executive committee and, as members of this committee, were responsible for considering and making policy recommendations to the general partnership. Boyle was also in charge of the "plaintiffs department" within the firm, which managed approximately 350 cases. At the time of their leaving, Meehan's interest in the partnership was 6% and Boyle's interest was 4.8%.

Meehan and Boyle had become dissatisfied at Parker Coulter. * * * On July 1, Meehan and Boyle decided to leave Parker Coulter and form their own partnership.

Having decided to establish a new firm, Meehan and Boyle then focused on whom they would invite to join them. The two spoke with [several attorneys, including Cohen, a junior partner, and Schafer, Black, and Fitzgerald, associates at the firm, about joining them in MBC. All four ultimately agreed to join MBC].

* * *

During July and the following months, Meehan, Boyle, and Cohen made arrangements for their new practice apart from seeking associates. They began to look for office space and retained an architect. In early fall, a lease was executed on behalf of MBC in the name of MBC Realty Trust. They also retained an attorney to advise them on the formation of the new firm.

* * *

Toward the end of November, Boyle prepared form letters to send to clients and referring attorneys as soon as Parker Coulter was notified of the separation. He also drafted a form for the clients to return to him at his home address authorizing him to remove cases to MBC. An outside agency typed these materials on Parker Coulter's letterhead. Schafer prepared similar letters and authorization forms.

While they were planning their departure, from July to approximately December, Meehan, Boyle, Cohen, Schafer, Black, and Fitzgerald all continued to work full schedules. They settled cases appropriately, made reasonable efforts to avoid continuances, tried cases, and worked on discovery. Each generally maintained his or her usual standard of performance.

Meehan and Boyle had originally intended to give notice to Parker Coulter on December 1, 1984. Rumors of their leaving, however, began to circulate before then. During the period from July to early fall, different Parker Coulter partners approached Meehan individually on three separate occasions and asked him if the rumors about his leaving were true. On each occasion, Meehan denied that he was leaving. On November 30, 1984, a partner, Maurice F. Shaughnessy (Shaughnessy), approached Boyle and asked him whether Meehan and Boyle intended to leave the firm. Shaughnessy interpreted Boyle's evasive response as an affirmation of the rumors. Meehan and Boyle then decided to distribute their notice that afternoon, which stated, as their proposed date for leaving, December 31, 1984. A notice was left on the desk of each partner. When Meehan, Boyle, and Cohen gave their notice, the atmosphere at Parker Coulter became "tense, emotional and unpleasant, if not adversarial."

On December 3, the Parker Coulter partners appointed a separation committee and decided to communicate with "important sources of business" to tell them of the separation and of Parker Coulter's desire to continue representing them. Meehan and Boyle asked their partners for financial information about the firm, discussed cases and clients with them, and stated that they intended to communicate with clients and referring attorneys on the cases in which they were involved. Sometime during the week of December 3, the partners sent Boyle a list of cases and requested that he identify the cases he intended to take with him.

Boyle had begun to make telephone calls to referring attorneys on Saturday morning, December 1. He had spoken with three referring attorneys by that date and told them of his departure from Parker Coulter and his wish to continue handling their cases. On December 3, he mailed his previously typed letters and authorization forms, and by the end of the first two weeks of December he had spoken with a majority of referring attorneys, and had obtained authorizations from a majority of clients whose cases he planned to remove to MBC.

Although the partners previously were aware of Boyle's intention to communicate with clients, they did not become aware of the extent of his communications until December 12 or 13. Boyle did not provide his partners with the list they requested of cases he intended to remove until December 17. Throughout December, Meehan, Boyle, and Schafer continued to communicate with referring attorneys on cases they were currently handling to discuss authorizing their transfer to MBC. On December 19, 1984, one of the partners accepted on behalf of Parker Coulter the December 31 departure date and waived the three-month notice period provided for by the partnership agreement. * * *

MBC removed a number of cases from Parker Coulter. Of the roughly 350 contingent fee cases pending at Parker Coulter in 1984, Boyle, Schafer, and Meehan removed approximately 142 to MBC. * * * A provision in the partnership agreement in effect at the separation provided that a voluntarily retiring partner, upon the payment of a "fair charge," could remove "any matter in which the partnership had been representing a client who came to the firm through the personal effort or connection of the retiring partner," subject to the right of the client to stay with the firm. Approximately thirty-nine of the 142 contingent fee cases removed to MBC came to Parker Coulter at least in part through the personal efforts or connections of Parker Coulter attorneys other than [the MBC attorneys]. In all the cases removed to MBC, however, MBC attorneys had direct, existing relationships with the clients. In all the removed cases, MBC attorneys communicated with the referring attorney or with the client directly by telephone or letter. In each case, the client signed an authorization.

* * *

Based on these findings, the judge determined that the MBC attorneys did not manipulate cases, or handle them differently as a result of their decision to leave Parker Coulter. He also determined that Parker Coulter failed to prove that the clients whose cases were removed did not freely choose to have MBC represent them. Consequently, he concluded that Meehan and Boyle neither violated the partnership agreement nor breached the fiduciary duty they owed to their partners. In addition, the judge also found that Meehan and Boyle did not tortiously interfere with Parker Coulter's relations with clients or employees. * * *

* * *

We now consider Parker Coulter's claims of wrongdoing. Parker Coulter claims that the judge erred in finding that [Meehan and Boyle] fulfilled their fiduciary duties to the former partnership. In particular, Parker Coulter argues that these attorneys breached their duties * * * by secretly competing with the partnership, and * * * by unfairly acquiring from clients and referring attorneys consent to withdraw cases to MBC. * * *

It is well settled that partners owe each other a fiduciary duty of "the utmost good faith and loyalty." *Cardullo v. Landau*, 329 Mass. 5, 8, 105 N.E.2d 843 (1952). As a fiduciary, a partner must consider his or her partners' welfare, and refrain from acting for purely private gain. Partners thus "may not act out of avarice, expediency or self-interest in derogation of their duty of loyalty." *Donahue v. Rodd Electrotype Co. of New England, Inc.*, 367 Mass. 578, 593, 328 N.E.2d 505 (1975). Meehan and Boyle owed their copartners at Parker Coulter a duty of the utmost good faith and loyalty, and were obliged to consider their copartners' welfare, and not merely their own.

* * *

Parker Coulter next argues that the judge's findings compel the conclusion that Meehan and Boyle breached their fiduciary duty not to compete with their partners by secretly setting up a new firm during their tenure at Parker Coulter. We disagree. We have stated that fiduciaries may plan to compete with the entity to which they owe allegiance, "provided that in the course of such arrangements they [do] not otherwise act in violation of their fiduciary duties." *Chelsea Indus. v. Gaffney*, 389 Mass. 1, 10, 11–12, 449 N.E.2d 320 (1983). Here, the judge found that Meehan and Boyle made certain logistical arrangements for the establishment of MBC. These arrangements included executing a lease for MBC's office, preparing lists of clients expected to leave Parker Coulter for MBC, and obtaining financing on the basis of these lists. We believe these logistical arrangements to establish a physical plant for the new firm were permissible under *Chelsea Indus.*, especially in light of the attorneys' obligation to represent adequately any clients who might continue to retain them on their departure from Parker Coulter. * * * There was no error in the judge's determination that this conduct did not violate the partners' fiduciary duty.[14]

Lastly, Parker Coulter argues that the judge's findings compel the conclusion that Meehan and Boyle breached their fiduciary duties by unfairly acquiring consent from clients to remove cases from Parker Coulter. We agree that Meehan and Boyle, through their preparation for obtaining clients' consent, their secrecy concerning which clients they intended to take, and the substance and method of their communications with clients, obtained an unfair advantage over their former partners in breach of their fiduciary duties.

A partner has an obligation to "render on demand true and full information of all things affecting the partnership to any partner." [UPA] § 20. On three separate occasions Meehan affirmatively denied to his partners, on their demand, that he had any plans for leaving the partnership. During this period of secrecy, Meehan and Boyle made preparations for obtaining removal authorizations from clients. * * * Thus, they were "ready to move" the instant they gave notice to their partners.

On giving their notice, Meehan and Boyle continued to use their position of trust and confidence to the disadvantage of Parker Coulter. The two immediately began communicating with clients and referring

---

[14] Parker Coulter also argues that Meehan and Boyle impermissibly competed with the firm by inducing its employees to join MBC. Because Parker Coulter identifies no specific loss resulting from this claimed breach, we need not address this issue.

attorneys. Boyle delayed providing his partners with a list of clients he intended to solicit until mid-December, by which time he had obtained authorization from a majority of the clients.

Finally, the content of the letter sent to the clients was unfairly prejudicial to Parker Coulter. The ABA Committee on Ethics and Professional Responsibility, in Informal Opinion 1457 (April 29, 1980), set forth ethical standards for attorneys announcing a change in professional association.[15] Because this standard is intended primarily to protect clients, proof by Parker Coulter of a technical violation of this standard does not aid them in their claims. We will, however, look to this standard for general guidelines as to what partners are entitled to expect from each other concerning their joint clients on the division of their practice. The ethical standard provides that any notice explain to a client that he or she has the right to decide who will continue the representation. Here, the judge found that the notice did not "clearly present to the clients the choice they had between remaining at Parker Coulter or moving to the new firm." By sending a one-side announcement, on Parker Coulter letterhead, so soon after notice of their departure, Meehan and Boyle excluded their partners from effectively presenting their services as an alternative to those of Meehan and Boyle.

Meehan and Boyle could have foreseen that the news of their departure would cause a certain amount of confusion and disruption among their partners. The speed and preemptive character of their campaign to acquire clients' consent took advantage of their partners' confusion. By engaging in these preemptive tactics, Meehan and Boyle violated the duty of utmost good faith and loyalty which they owed their partners. Therefore, we conclude that the judge erred in deciding that Meehan and Boyle acted properly in acquiring consent to remove cases to MBC.

* * *

We conclude that Meehan and Boyle had the burden of proving no causal connection between their breach of duty and Parker Coulter's loss of clients. Proof of the circumstances of the preparations for obtaining

---

[15] These standards provide the following guidelines for notice to clients:

(a) the notice is mailed; (b) the notice is sent only to persons with whom the lawyer had an active lawyer-client relationship immediately before the change in the lawyer's professional association; (c) the notice is clearly related to open and pending matters for which the lawyer had direct professional responsibility to the client immediately before the change; (d) the notice is sent promptly after the change; (e) the notice does not urge the client to sever a relationship with the lawyer's former firm and does not recommend the lawyer's employment (although it indicates the lawyer's willingness to continue his responsibility for the matters); (f) the notice makes it clear that the client has the right to decide who will complete or continue the matters; and (g) the notice is brief, dignified, and not disparaging of the lawyer's former firm.

See also ABA Committee on Ethics and Professional Responsibility Informal Opinion 1466 (Feb. 12, 1981) (extending Informal Opinion 1457 to departing associates as well as partners).

authorizations and of the actual communications with clients was more accessible to Meehan and Boyle than to Parker Coulter. Furthermore, requiring these partners to disprove causation will encourage partners in the future to disclose seasonably and fully any plans to remove cases. This disclosure will allow the partnership and the departing partner an equal opportunity to present to clients the option of continuing with the partnership or retaining the departing partner individually.[16]

We remand the case to the Superior Court for findings consistent with our conclusion that the MBC attorneys bear the burden of proof. * * *

To guide the judge on remand in his reexamination of the record and his subsidiary findings, we briefly outline factors relevant to determining whether a client freely chose MBC and, thus, whether the MBC attorneys met their burden of disproving a causal relationship between their preemptive tactics and the removal of the case. We note at the outset that the partnership agreement's specific terms offer no direct assistance in resolving this issue. It is true that the partnership agreement provides that a departing partner has the right to remove any case which came to the partnership through his or her personal efforts or connections. Resorting to this provision alone to determine which cases were properly removed, however, is inappropriate. The partnership agreement states that the right to remove is subject to the client's right freely to choose who will continue handling his or her case. Thus, the parties expressly bargained with each other that they would allow a client a free choice. To give effect, therefore, to the entire agreement of the parties before us, there must be some examination of a client's reasons for choosing to retain MBC.

Although the record contains no evidence as to the actual preference of a particular client, expressed and unaffected by the MBC attorneys' improper communications, the record is replete with circumstantial evidence bearing on this issue. Circumstantial factors relevant to whether a client freely exercised his or her right to choose include the following: (1) who was responsible for initially attracting the client to the firm; (2) who managed the case at the firm; (3) how sophisticated the client was and whether the client made the decision with full knowledge; and (4) what was the reputation and skill of the removing attorneys. Therefore, the judge is to reexamine the record and his subsidiary findings in light of the factors we have identified, and to reach a conclusion as to whether Meehan and Boyle have met their burden of proof on each of the removed cases. With the burden of proof on Meehan and Boyle, Parker Coulter will prevail if the evidence is in balance.

---

[16] As between the attorneys, a mutual letter, from both the partnership and the departing partner, outlining the separation plans and the clients' right to choose, would be an appropriate means of opening the discussion between the attorneys and their clients concerning the clients' choice of continuing representation.

In those cases, if any, where the judge concludes, in accordance with the above analysis, that Meehan and Boyle have met their burden, we resolve the parties' dispute over fees solely under the partnership agreement. Under the agreement's terms, as we have interpreted them, Meehan and Boyle owe a fair charge to their former partnership for its "services to and expenditures for" the clients in these matters. Meehan and Boyle are entitled to their combined 10.8% partnership share of this amount, and their former partners are entitled to the remainder. We agree with the judge that a "fair charge" on a removed case consists of the firm's unreimbursed expenses plus the rate billed per hour by members of the firm multiplied by the hours expended on the case. In fixing this hourly rate, the firm made a determination that the time charged was reasonable and fair compensation for the services rendered. We conclude, therefore, that, in accordance with the partnership agreement, Meehan and Boyle must reimburse their former partnership for time billed and expenses incurred at that firm on all cases which were fairly removed. We further conclude that, under the agreement, Meehan and Boyle have the right to retain all fees generated by these cases in excess of the fair charge.

We now address the correct remedy in those cases, if any, which the judge determines Meehan and Boyle unfairly removed. In light of a conclusion that Meehan and Boyle have failed to prove that certain clients would not have preferred to stay with Parker Coulter, granting Parker Coulter merely a fair charge on these cases pursuant to the partnership agreement would not make it whole. We turn, therefore, to [UPA § 21]. Section 21 * * * provides: "Every partner must account to the partnership for any benefit, and hold as trustee for it any profits derived by him without the consent of the other partners from any transaction connected with the formation, conduct or liquidation of the partnership * * *." We have consistently applied this statute, and held that a partner must account for any profits which flow from a breach of fiduciary duty. * * *

Meehan and Boyle breached the duty they owed to Parker Coulter. If the judge determines that, as a result of this breach, certain clients left the firm, Meehan and Boyle must account to the partnership for any profits they receive on these cases * * * in addition to paying the partnership a fair charge on these cases pursuant to the agreement. * * * Meehan's and Boyle's former partners are thus entitled to their portion of the fair charge on each of the unfairly removed cases (89.2%), and to that amount of profit from an unfairly removed case which they would have enjoyed had the MBC attorneys handled the case at Parker Coulter (89.2%).

* * *

NOTES

(1) Did Meehan and Boyle breach their fiduciary duties by secretly setting up a new firm during their tenure at Parker Coulter? What if, in the months before their departure, Meehan and Boyle's normal working hours were spent 70% on Parker Coulter business and 30% on setting up their new firm? What about the fact that Meehan and Boyle recruited three associates to leave the firm before announcing their intention to depart?

(2) Did Meehan and Boyle breach their fiduciary duties in their communications with firm clients? If so, how?

(3) If RUPA governed this dispute, would the result be different? *See* RUPA §§ 403(c), 404.

PROBLEM

Alice is a partner and is the head of the Trusts & Estates section at Zeta Law Firm. Bert is the only other partner in the section. The section employs three associates, two accountants, and two paralegals.

On June 19, Alice and Bert inform Zeta's managing partner that they have accepted offers to join Competitor Law Firm. The managing partner asks Alice and Bert to not discuss their departure with any of the associates in the Trusts & Estates section, and Alice and Bert agree. On June 24, Alice and Bert send Competitor Law Firm a memo listing the names of the personnel in Zeta's Trusts & Estates section, their respective salaries and bonuses, their annual billable hours, and the rate at which Zeta billed out these employees to clients. The memo includes other information about the attorneys, including the colleges and law schools they attended and their bar admissions. The memo was prepared by Bert in April before Alice and Bert announced that they were leaving. Bert indicates that the memo was prepared in anticipation of discussions with prospective firms. Both Alice and Bert state that the recruitment of certain associates and support personnel was discussed with different firms (including Competitor Law Firm) in the months before they announced their departure, as Alice and Bert were considering various firm affiliations.

In late June, while Alice and Bert are still partners at Zeta, Competitor Law Firm interviews four Zeta Trusts & Estates employees that Alice had indicated she was interested in bringing over with her—two associates, an accountant, and a paralegal. On June 27, Alice and Bert submit their written resignations to Zeta, and in early July, they leave the firm. On July 11, Competitor Law Firm makes offers to all four Zeta employees, and all four accept.

Have Alice and Bert breached their fiduciary duties to Zeta?

F. OWNERSHIP INTERESTS AND TRANSFERABILITY

1. PARTNERSHIP PROPERTY

As previously discussed in Chapter 3, Section B(3), UPA generally adopts an aggregate theory of partnership. If that aggregate theory were strictly applied, a partnership could not own property itself. Instead, what we would think of as partnership property would be held, as a legal matter, by individual partners as tenants in common or joint tenants.

Despite this conceptual problem, UPA effectively treats partnership property as if it were owned by the partnership itself. UPA accomplishes this by stating, in § 25(1), that "[a] partner is co-owner with his partners of specific partnership property holding as a tenant in partnership." Having established this "tenancy in partnership" form of ownership, UPA then proceeds to negate the rights normally associated with individual ownership. A partner has no right to possess partnership property for non-partnership purposes (§ 25(2)(a)); a partner may not assign his interest in partnership property (§ 25(2)(b)); a partner's right in partnership property is not subject to attachment or execution on a claim against the partner (§ 25(2)(c)); on the death of a partner, his right in partnership property vests in the surviving partners (§ 25(2)(d)); and a partner's right in partnership property is not subject to dower, curtesy, or allowances to widows, heirs, or next of kin (§ 25(2)(e)). Interestingly, with respect to real estate, UPA § 8(3) states rather directly (and seemingly contrary to an aggregate view) that "[a]ny estate in real property may be acquired in the partnership name." The net result of these provisions is that the partnership, rather than the partners, is effectively treated as the owner of partnership property.

RUPA avoids the conceptual problems and related complexity associated with the UPA approach. RUPA recognizes the partnership as an entity (§ 201(a)) and provides, in a conceptually consistent manner, that "[p]roperty acquired by a partnership is property of the partnership and not of the partners individually." *Id.* § 203. Similarly, § 501 provides that "[a] partner is not a co-owner of partnership property and has no interest in partnership property which can be transferred, either voluntarily or involuntarily."

NOTES

(1) It can be difficult to determine whether property has been contributed to a partnership or whether it remains the personal property of an individual partner. UPA § 8 and RUPA § 204 provide rules for determining when property is considered to be partnership property.

(2) UPA § 10 provides special rules that govern the transfer of the partnership's real property. RUPA § 302 contains similar rules, although it is broader than UPA § 10 in that it also governs the transfer of some of the partnership's personal property.

2.   TRANSFERRING A PARTNERSHIP INTEREST

RAPOPORT V. 55 PERRY CO.

Supreme Court of New York, Appellate Division, 1975.
376 N.Y.S.2d 147.

TILZER, JUSTICE.

In 1969, Simon, Genia and Ury Rapoport entered into a partnership agreement with Morton, Jerome and Burton Parnes, forming the partnership known as 55 Perry Company. Pursuant to the agreement, each of the families owned 50% of the partnership interests. In December of 1974 Simon and Genia Rapoport assigned a 10% interest of their share in the partnership to their adult children, Daniel and Kalia. The Parnes defendants were advised of the assignment and an amended partnership certificate was filed in the County Clerk's Office indicating the addition of Daniel and Kalia as partners. However, when the plaintiffs, thereafter, requested the Parnes defendants to execute an amended partnership agreement to reflect the above changes in the partnership, the Parnes refused, taking the position that the partnership agreement did not permit the introduction of new partners without consent of all the existing partners. Thereafter, the plaintiffs Rapoport brought this action seeking a declaration that Simon and Genia Rapoport had an absolute right to assign their interests to their adult children without consent of the defendants and that such assignment was authorized pursuant to Paragraph 12 of the partnership agreement. The plaintiffs further sought to have Daniel and Kalia be declared partners in 55 Perry Company and have their names entered upon the books of the partnership as partners. The defendants Parnes interposed an answer, taking the position that the partnership agreement did not permit admission of additional partners without consent of all the existing partners and that the filing of the amended certificate of partnership was unauthorized. After joinder of issue plaintiffs moved for summary judgment and although the defendants did not cross-move for similar relief, such was, nevertheless, requested in their answering papers.

On the motion for summary judgment both parties agreed that there were no issues of fact and that there was only a question of the interpretation of the written documents which should be disposed of as a matter of law by the Court. Nevertheless, the Court below found that the agreement was ambiguous and that there was a triable issue with respect to the intent of the parties. We disagree and conclude that the agreement is without ambiguity and that pursuant to the terms of the agreement and of the Partnership Law, consent of the Parnes defendants was required in order to admit Daniel Rapoport and Kalia Shalleck to the partnership.

Plaintiffs, in support of their contention that they have an absolute right to assign their interests in the partnership to their adult children and that the children must be admitted to the partnership as partners rely on Paragraph 12 of the partnership agreement which provides as follows:

> "No partner or partners shall have the authority to transfer, sell * * * assign or in any way dispose of the partnership realty and/or personalty and shall not have the authority to sell, transfer, assign * * * his or their share in this firm, nor enter into any agreement as a result of which any person shall become interested with him in this firm, unless the same is agreed to in writing by a majority of the partners as determined by the percentage of ownership * * *, except for members of his immediate family who have attained majority, in which case no such consent shall be required."

As indicated, plaintiffs argue that the above provision expressly authorizes entry of their adult children into the partnership. Defendants, on the other hand, maintain that Paragraph 12 provides only for the right of a partner to assign or transfer a share of the profits in the partnership. We agree with that construction of the agreement.

A reading of the partnership agreement indicates that the parties intended to observe the differences, as set forth in the Partnership Law, between assignees of a partnership interest and the admission into the partnership itself of new partners. The Partnership Law provides that subject to any contrary agreement between the partners, "(n)o person can become a member of a partnership without the consent of all the partners." (Partnership Law § 40(7)). Partnership Law § 53 provides that an assignee of an interest in the partnership is not entitled "to interfere in the management or administration of the partnership business" but is merely entitled to receive "the profits to which the assigning partner would otherwise be entitled." (Partnership Law § 53(1)). Additionally, Partnership Law § 50 indicates the differences between the rights of an assignee and a new partner. That section states that the "property rights of a partner are (a) his rights in specific partnership property, (b) his interest in the partnership, and (c) his right to participate in the management." On the other hand, as already indicated above, an assignee is excluded in the absence of agreement from interfering in the management of the partnership business and from access to the partnership books and information about partnership transactions. (Partnership Law § 53).

The effect, therefore, of the various provisions of the Partnership Law, above discussed, is that unless the parties have agreed otherwise, a person cannot become a member of a partnership without consent of all the partners whereas an assignment of a partnership interest may be made without consent, but the assignee is entitled only to receive the profits of the assigning partner. And, as already stated, the partnership agreement herein clearly took cognizance of the differences between an assignment of an interest in the partnership as compared to the full rights of a partner as set forth in Partnership Law § 50. Paragraph 12 of the agreement by its language has reference to Partnership Law § 53 dealing with an "assignment of partner's interest." It (Paragraph 12) refers to assignments, encumbrances and agreements "as a result of which any person shall become interested with (the assignor) in this firm." That paragraph does not contain language with respect to admitting a partner to the partnership with all rights to participate in the management of its affairs. Moreover, interpretation of Paragraph 12 in this manner is consistent with other provisions of the partnership agreement. For example, in Paragraph 15 of the agreement, the following is provided:

> "In the event of the death of any partner the business of this firm shall continue with the heir, or distributee providing he has reached majority, or fiduciary of the deceased partner having the right to succeed the deceased partner with the same rights and privileges and the same obligations, pursuant to all of the terms hereof."

In that paragraph, therefore, there is specific provision to succeed to all the privileges and obligations of a partner—language which is completely absent from Paragraph 12.

Accordingly, it appears that contrary to plaintiffs' contention that Paragraph 12 was intended to give the parties the right to transfer a full partnership interest to adult children, without consent of all other partners, (an agreement which would vary the rights otherwise existing pursuant to Partnership Law § 40(7)) that paragraph was instead intended to limit a partner with respect to his right to assign a partnership interest as provided for under Partnership Law § 53 (i.e., the right to profits)—to the extent of prohibiting such assignments without consent of other partners except to children of the existing partners who have reached majority. Therefore, it must be concluded that pursuant to the terms of the partnership agreement, the plaintiffs could not transfer a full partnership interest to their children and that the children only have the rights as assignees to receive a share of the partnership income and profits of their assignors.

Accordingly, the order entered July 16, 1975 should be modified on the law to grant summary judgment in favor of the defendants to the extent of declaring that the partnership agreement does not permit entry into the partnership of new partners, including adult children of the partners who have reached their majority, without consent of all the partners; that the plaintiffs, pursuant to the terms of the agreement, had the right to assign their interests to their adult children but that such children, i.e., Daniel Rapoport and Kalia Shalleck, have not become partners but only have the rights of assignees to receive a share of the partnership income and profits of their assignors; that the amended partnership certificate filed with the County Clerk's Office on or about January 14, 1975 indicating the additional partners, i.e., Daniel Rapoport and Kalia Shalleck, was improper and should be restated to eliminate those names as partners, and as so modified the order is affirmed without costs or disbursements.

NUNEZ, JUSTICE (dissenting).

I agree with Special Term that the written partnership agreement providing for the assignment of partners' shares to members of their immediate families without the consent of the other partners is ambiguous and that there is a triable issue as to intent. The agreement being ambiguous, construction is a mixed question of law and fact and resolution thereof to determine the parties' intent should await a trial. Summary judgment was properly denied both parties. I would affirm.

NOTES

(1) Assume that there was no partnership agreement in *Rapoport*. Would the Rapoports have been able to make their adult children into full partners without the Parnes' consent? *See* UPA §§ 18(g), 24–27; RUPA §§ 101(9), 401(i), 502–503. Does this result make sense for a general partnership?

(2) Assume that there was no partnership agreement in *Rapoport*. Would the Rapoports have been able to transfer the right to receive partnership distributions to their adult children without the Parnes' consent? *See* UPA §§ 26–27; RUPA §§ 502–503.

(3) According to the Rapoports, how did Paragraph 12 of the partnership agreement change the statutory default rules? According to the Parnes, how did Paragraph 12 of the partnership agreement change the statutory default rules?

(4) What is a "charging order?" *See* UPA § 28; RUPA § 504. What must an individual creditor do to obtain such an order? What rights or powers does a creditor get with a charging order? J. Gordon Gose, *The Charging Order Under the Uniform Partnership Act*, 28 WASH. L. REV. 1, 15–18 (1953), describes the relationship between creditor, debtor, and partnership as follows:

> First, the charging order may enjoin the members of the partnership from making further disbursements of any kind to the

debtor partner, except such payments as may be permissible under a legal exemption right properly asserted by the debtor.

Second, the charging order may formally require the members of the partnership to pay to the creditor any amounts which it would otherwise pay to the debtor partner, exclusive of any amounts payable to the latter under a properly asserted legal exemption right.

Third, the appointment of a receiver is not indispensable to the collection of the claim out of the debtor partner's share. A receiver should be appointed only where he has some useful function to serve such as the maintenance of a lawsuit, the conduct of a sale or the representation of competing creditors of the debtor partner. It may be that even in such a case, no receiver is necessary since there is no insuperable reason why these services cannot be obtained by some other method. * * *

Fourth, the debtor's interest should be sold if, and only if, the court is convinced that the creditor's claim will not be satisfied with reasonable expedition by the less drastic process of diverting the debtor's income from the partnership to the payment of the debt.[51] Even in the case of a wholly solvent partnership, the creditor's claim may be so large in relation to the current income of the debtor from the firm as to require sale as the only alternative to long delay in payment.

(5) The ability of a *partnership* creditor to proceed against the *individual* property of a partner typically requires naming and serving the partner as a defendant in the suit, obtaining a judgment against the partnership and the partner, and possibly exhausting the assets of the partnership. *See* Chapter 3, Section D(3). If these steps are taken, the partner's individual property may be subject to execution, attachment, or other process. The ability of an *individual* creditor to proceed against *partnership* property, however, is sharply circumscribed. *See* UPA § 25(2)(c); RUPA § 501. Why are partnership creditors seeking to recover from individual assets treated differently from individual creditors seeking to recover from partnership assets?

(6) When a partnership or a partner is insolvent, UPA § 40(h) and (i) establish the "jingle rule" (also known as the "dual priorities" rule) for priority of payment: individual creditors have priority with regard to individual property and partnership creditors have priority with regard to partnership property. For many years, the federal Bankruptcy Code followed the same pattern.

---

[51] There is actually no authority whatsoever as to when a sale should be ordered. Necessarily the order must fall in the area of those "which the circumstances of the case require." The apparent situations in which sale would be necessary are those in which, owing to the size of the claim or the absence of current liquid income, an order to pay over the debtor partner's share of current income and other moneys would not be effective.

The most serious criticism of the jingle rule was that partnership creditors consider the net worth of both the partnership and the individual partners in deciding to extend credit to the partnership, and they should not therefore be subordinated to individual creditors with respect to individual assets. Based in part on this criticism, the Bankruptcy Code was changed in 1978 to essentially provide that partnership creditors have priority as to partnership property and equivalence with individual creditors as to individual property. *See* 11 U.S.C. § 723(c). RUPA does not seek to define the priorities between partnership and individual creditors—effectively leaving the matter to the federal Bankruptcy Code. *See* RUPA § 807 cmt. 2 ("Under Section 723(c) of the Bankruptcy Code, and under RUPA, partnership creditors share pro rata with the partners' individual creditors in the assets of the partners' estates.").

G. DISSOCIATION AND DISSOLUTION

The dissociation and dissolution provisions of UPA and RUPA differ significantly from each other and were a principal area of controversy in the drafting of RUPA. These provisions are the most complicated sections in both of these statutes. The cases and materials in the balance of this Section primarily deal with UPA. The changes made by RUPA are described at the end of the Section.

1. DISSOLUTION UNDER UPA

In UPA § 29, "dissolution" is defined as "the change in the relation of the partners caused by any partner ceasing to be associated in the carrying on * * * of the business." This definition of the word "dissolution" differs considerably from the lay understanding of that word. It refers to a change in the personal relationships among partners within the partnership and has nothing to do with the disposition of assets or the closing down and selling of the business. Put differently, "dissolution" refers to a change in the composition of the partners themselves, while "winding up" or "liquidation" refers to the process of selling off the partnership's assets, paying off creditors, and settling up profits and losses between the partners. As you will learn, in some circumstances, dissolution causes the winding up of the partnership. In other circumstances, however, it does not. Thus, it is helpful to keep the concepts separate in your mind (i.e., dissolution on the one hand, and winding up/liquidation on the other). *Cf. id.* § 30 (indicating that a partnership is not "terminated" upon dissolution and is instead continued "until the winding up of partnership affairs is completed").

Under UPA, many of the issues associated with partnership dissolution turn on whether the partnership is "at-will" or "term," and on what might be described as whether the act of dissolution is "rightful" or "wrongful." An at-will partnership is one where the partners have not specified any definite term or particular undertaking for the partnership.

See id. § 31(1)(b). It is the default form of partnership under UPA. A term partnership is the converse—it is a partnership where the partners have agreed, explicitly or implicitly, that the partnership shall have a definite term or particular undertaking. *See id.* § 31(1)(a).

For some acts of dissolution, UPA suggests that the act is rightful—it is "[w]ithout violation of the agreement between the partners." *Id.* § 31(1). Such acts include the following: (1) the termination of the definite term or particular undertaking in a term partnership; (2) the express will of any partner in an at-will partnership; (3) the express will of all of the partners who have not assigned their interests or had them subject to a charging order; and (4) the expulsion of any partner from the business bona fide in accordance with a power conferred by the partnership agreement. *See id.* UPA also specifies an act of dissolution that is, in effect, wrongful—it is "[i]n contravention of the agreement between the partners." *Id.* § 31(2). That act is when dissolution is caused by the express will of any partner at any time where the circumstances do not permit dissolution under any other provision of § 31. *See id.* For example, when a partner decides to withdraw from a term partnership before the end of the term, that act of dissolution (the "express will of any partner") typically falls under § 31(2) and is considered wrongful. UPA provides four other grounds for dissolution that are not explicitly designated as rightful or wrongful: (1) any event which makes it unlawful for the business of the partnership to be carried on or for the members to carry it on in partnership; (2) the death of any partner; (3) the bankruptcy of any partner or the partnership; and (4) a decree of court under § 32. *See id.* § 31(3)–(6). Acts of dissolution that are considered wrongful subject the dissolving partner to damages and other penalties. *See id.* § 38(2) (specifying the consequences "[w]hen dissolution is caused in contravention of the partnership agreement").

NOTES

(1) Can you explain why UPA § 29 indicates that dissolution is caused by any partner "ceasing to be associated in" the partnership? Does a technical dissolution also occur when one or more new partners are admitted but no existing partner withdraws? *See id.* § 41(1).

(2) With respect to a term partnership, what is a "definite term or particular undertaking?" *See id.* § 31(1). Is a partnership to construct an office building a term partnership? Is a partnership to operate a linen supply business a term partnership? *See* RUPA § 101 cmt.

(3) As mentioned, a term partnership can be premised on an explicit or implicit agreement between the partners. In *Page v. Page*, 359 P.2d 41 (Cal. 1961), the Supreme Court of California observed:

> Viewing this evidence most favorably for defendant, it proves
> only that the partners expected to meet current expenses from

current income and to recoup their investment if the business were successful.

Defendant contends that such an expectation is sufficient to create a partnership for a term under the rule of Owen v. Cohen, 19 Cal.2d 147, 150, 119 P.2d 713. In that case we held that when a partner advances a sum of money to a partnership with the understanding that the amount contributed was to be a loan to the partnership and was to be repaid as soon as feasible from the prospective profits of the business, the partnership is for the term reasonably required to repay the loan. It is true that Owen v. Cohen, supra, and other cases hold that partners may impliedly agree to continue in business until a certain sum of money is earned, or one or more partners recoup their investments, or until certain debts are paid, or until certain property could be disposed of on favorable terms. In each of these cases, however, the implied agreement found support in the evidence.

* * *

In the instant case, however, defendant failed to prove any facts from which an agreement to continue the partnership for a term may be implied. The understanding to which defendant testified was no more than a common hope that the partnership earnings would pay for all the necessary expenses. Such a hope does not establish even by implication a "definite term or particular undertaking" as required by section 15031, subdivision (1)(b) of the Corporations Code. All partnerships are ordinarily entered into with the hope that they will be profitable, but that alone does not make them all partnerships for a term and obligate the partners to continue in the partnerships until all of the losses over a period of many years have been recovered.

Id. at 43–44.

COLLINS V. LEWIS

Court of Civil Appeals of Texas, 1955.
283 S.W.2d 258.

HAMBLEN, CHIEF JUSTICE.

This suit was instituted in the District Court of Harris County by the appellants, who, as the owners of a fifty percent (50%) interest in a partnership known as the L-C Cafeteria, sought a receivership of the partnership business, a judicial dissolution of the partnership, and foreclosure of a mortgage upon appellees' interest in the partnership assets. Appellees denied appellants' right to the relief sought, and filed a cross-action for damages for breach of contract in the event dissolution should be decreed. Appellants' petition for receivership having been denied after a hearing before the court, trial of the issues of dissolution and foreclosure, and of appellees' cross-action, proceeded before the court and a jury. At the conclusion of such trial, the jury, in response to special issues submitted, returned a verdict upon which the trial court entered judgment denying all relief sought by appellants.

The facts are substantially as follows:

In the latter part of 1948 appellee John L. Lewis obtained a commitment conditioned upon adequate financial backing from the Brown-Bellows-Smith Corporation for a lease on the basement space under the then projected San Jacinto Building for the purpose of constructing and operating a large cafeteria therein. Lewis contacted appellant Carr P. Collins, a resident of Dallas, proposing that he (Lewis) would furnish the lease, the experience and management ability for the operation of the cafeteria, and Collins would furnish the money; that all revenue of the business, except for an agreed salary to Lewis, would be applied to the repayment of such money, and that thereafter all profits would be divided equally between Lewis and Collins. These negotiations * * * culminated in the execution between the building owners, as lessors, and Lewis and Collins, as lessees, of a lease upon such basement space for a term of 30 years. Thereafter Lewis and Collins entered into a partnership agreement to endure throughout the term of the lease contract. This agreement is in part evidenced by a formal contract between the parties, but both litigants concede that the complete agreement is ascertainable only from the verbal understandings and exchanges of letters between the principals. It appears to be undisputed that originally a corporation had been contemplated, and that the change to a partnership was made to gain the advantages which such a relationship enjoys under the internal revenue laws. The substance of the agreement was that Collins was to furnish all of the funds necessary to build, equip, and open the cafeteria for business. Lewis was to plan and supervise such construction, and, after opening for business, to manage the operation of the cafeteria. As a part of this undertaking, he guaranteed that moneys advanced by Collins would be repaid at the rate of at least $30,000, plus interest, in the first year of operation, and $60,000 per year, plus interest, thereafter, upon default of which Lewis would surrender his interest to Collins. In addition Lewis guaranteed Collins against loss to the extent of $100,000. * * *

Immediately after the lease agreement had been executed Lewis began the preparation of detailed plans and specifications for the cafeteria. Initially Lewis had estimated, and had represented to Collins, that the cost of completing the cafeteria ready for operation would be approximately $300,000. Due to delays on the part of the building owners in completing the building, and delays in procuring the equipment deemed necessary to opening the cafeteria for business, the actual opening did not occur until September 18, 1952, some 2 ½ years after the lease had been executed. * * * It likewise appears that the actual costs incurred during that period greatly exceeded the amount previously estimated by Lewis to be necessary. The cause of such increase is disputed by the litigants. Appellants contend that it was brought about largely by the extravagance and mismanagement of appellee Lewis. Appellees contend that it resulted from inflation, increased labor and material costs, caused by the Korean War, and unanticipated but necessary expenses. Whatever may have been the reason, it clearly appears that Collins, while expressing concern over the increasing cost, and urging the ~~employment of~~ every possible economy, continued to advance funds and pay expenses, which, by the date of opening for business, had exceeded $600,000.

Collins' concern over the mounting costs of the cafeteria appears to have been considerably augmented by the fact that after opening for business the cafeteria showed expenses considerably in excess of receipts. Upon being informed, shortly after the cafeteria had opened for business, that there existed incurred but unpaid items of cost over and above those theretofore paid, Collins made demand upon Lewis that the cafeteria be placed immediately upon a profitable basis, failing which he (Collins) would advance no more funds for any purpose. There followed an exchange of recriminatory correspondence between the parties, Collins on the one hand charging Lewis with extravagant mismanagement, and Lewis on the other hand charging Collins with unauthorized interference with the management of the business. Futile attempts were made by Lewis to obtain financial backing to buy Collins' interest in the business. Numerous threats were made by Collins to cause Lewis to lose his interest in the business entirely. This suit was filed by Collins in January of 1953.

The involved factual background of this litigation was presented to the jury in a trial which extended over five weeks * * *. At the conclusion of the evidence 23 special issues of fact were submitted to the jury. The controlling issues of fact, as to which a dispute existed, were resolved by the jury in their answers to Issues 1 to 5, inclusive, in which they found that Lewis was competent to manage the business of the L-C Cafeteria; that there is not a reasonable expectation of profit under the continued management of Lewis; that but for the conduct of Collins there would be a reasonable expectation of profit under the continued management of Lewis; that such conduct on the part of Collins was not that of a reasonably prudent person acting under the same or similar circumstances; and that such conduct on the part of Collins materially decreased the earnings of the cafeteria during the first year of its operation. * * * [W]e conclude not only that there is ample support for the findings of the jury which we consider to be controlling, but further that upon the entire record, including such findings, the trial court entered the only proper judgment under the law, and that * * * judgment must be in all things affirmed. * * *

As we understand appellants' position * * * they contend that there is no such thing as an indissoluble partnership; that it is not controlling or even important, in so far as the right to a dissolution is concerned, as to which of the partners is right or wrong in their disputes; and finally, that whenever it is made to appear that the partners are in hopeless disagreement concerning a partnership which has no reasonable expectation of profit, the legal right to dissolution exists. In support of these contentions appellants cite numerous authorities, all of which have been carefully examined. We do not undertake to individually distinguish the authorities cited for the reason that in no case cited by appellants does a situation analogous to that here present exist, namely, that the very facts upon which appellants predicate their right to a dissolution have been found by the jury to have been brought about by appellant Collins' own conduct, in violation of his own contractual obligations.

We agree with appellants' premise that there is no such thing as an indissoluble partnership only in the sense that there always exists the power, as opposed to the right, of dissolution. But legal right to dissolution rests in equity, as does the right to relief from the provisions of any legal contract. The jury finding that there is not a reasonable expectation of profit from the L-C Cafeteria under the continued management of Lewis * * * must be read in connection with their findings that Lewis is competent to manage the business of L-C Cafeteria, and that but for the conduct of Collins there would be a reasonable expectation of profit therefrom. In our view those are the controlling findings upon the issue of dissolution. It was Collins' obligation to furnish the money; Lewis' to furnish the management, guaranteeing a stated minimum repayment of the money. The jury has found that he was competent, and could reasonably have performed his obligation but for the conduct of Collins. We know of no rule which grants Collins, under such circumstances, the right to dissolution of the partnership. The rule is stated in Karrick v. Hannaman, 168 U.S. 328, 18 S.Ct. 135, 138, 42 L.Ed. 484, as follows: "A court of equity, doubtless, will not assist the partner breaking his contract to procure a dissolution of the partnership, because, upon familiar principles, a partner who has not fully and fairly performed the partnership agreement on his part has no standing in a court of equity to enforce any rights under the agreement." It seems to this Court that the proposition rests upon maxims of equity, too fundamental in our jurisprudence to require quotation.

The basic agreement between Lewis and Collins provided that Collins would furnish money in an amount sufficient to defray the cost of building, equipping and opening the L-C Cafeteria for operation. As a part of the agreement between Lewis and Collins, Lewis executed, and delivered to Collins, a mortgage upon Lewis' interest in the partnership "until the indebtedness incurred by the said Carr P. Collins * * * has been paid in full out of income derived from the said L-C Cafeteria, Houston, Texas."

* * *

Collins' right to foreclose [the mortgage on Lewis' interest] depends upon whether or not Lewis has met his basic obligation of repayment at the rate agreed upon. Appellees contend, we think correctly, that he has, in the following manner: the evidence shows that Collins advanced a total of $636,720 for the purpose of building, equipping and opening the cafeteria for business. The proof also shows that Lewis contended that the actual cost exceeded that amount by over $30,000. The litigants differed in regard to such excess, it being Collins' contention that it represented operating expense rather than cost of building, equipping and opening the cafeteria. The jury heard the conflicting proof relative to these contentions, and resolved the question by their answer to Special Issue 20, whereby they found that the minimum cost of building, equipping and opening the cafeteria for operation amounted to $697,603.36. Under the basic agreement of the partners, therefore, this excess was properly Collins' obligation. Upon the refusal of Collins to pay it, Lewis paid it out of earnings of the business during the first year of its operation. Thus it clearly appears that Lewis met his obligation, and the trial court properly denied foreclosure of the mortgage.

In their brief, appellants repeatedly complain that they should not be forced to endure a continuing partnership wherein there is no reasonable expectation of profit, which they say is the effect of the trial court's judgment. The proper and equitable solution of the differences which arise between partners is never an easy problem, especially where the relationship is as involved as this present one. We do not think it can properly be said, however, that the judgment of the trial court denying appellants the dissolution which they seek forces them to endure a partnership wherein there is no reasonable expectation of profit. We have already pointed out the ever present inherent power, as opposed to the legal right, of any partner to terminate the relationship. Pursuit of that course presents the problem of possible liability for such damages as flow from the breach of contract. The alternative course available to appellants seems clearly legible in the verdict of the jury, whose services in that connection were invoked by appellants.

Judgment affirmed.

NOTES

(1) The *Collins* case arose before Texas enacted its version of UPA. Nevertheless, the principles and the result are largely the same under UPA.

For the remainder of these notes, assume that UPA applied to the *Collins* dispute.

(2) Collins sought judicial dissolution of the partnership under grounds that were presumably similar to the provisions of UPA § 32(1). Why did the court refuse to grant his request?

(3) What does the *Collins* court mean when it states that "there always exists the power, as opposed to the right, of dissolution," and when it similarly references "the ever present inherent power, as opposed to the legal right, of any partner to terminate the relationship?" *See* UPA § 31(1)(b), (2).

(4) Why does it matter if a partnership is at-will or for a term? *See* UPA §§ 31, 38. How would you characterize the partnership in *Collins*?

(5) Should Collins have attempted to dissolve the partnership under UPA § 31(1)–(2)?

(6) Should Lewis have attempted to dissolve the partnership under UPA § 32(1)?

(7) Is UPA § 38(2) applicable to court-ordered dissolutions under § 32(1)(c) or (d)?

DREIFUERST V. DREIFUERST

Court of Appeals of Wisconsin, 1979.
280 N.W.2d 335.

BROWN, PRESIDING JUDGE.

The plaintiffs and the defendant, all brothers, formed a partnership. The partnership operated two feed mills, one located at St. Cloud, Wisconsin and one located at Elkhart Lake, Wisconsin. There were no written Articles of Partnership governing this partnership.

On October 4, 1975, the plaintiffs served the defendant with a notice of dissolution and wind-up of the partnership. The action for dissolution and wind-up was commenced on January 27, 1976. The dissolution complaint alleged that the plaintiffs elected to dissolve the partnership. There was no allegation of fault, expulsion or contravention of an alleged agreement as grounds for dissolution. The parties were unable, however, to agree to a winding-up of the partnership.

Hearings on the dissolution were held on October 18, 1976 and March 4, 1977. Testimony was presented regarding the value of the partnership assets and each partner's equity. At the March 4, 1977 hearing, the defendant requested that the partnership be sold pursuant to sec. 178.33(1), Stats. [UPA § 38(1)], and that the court allow a sale, at which time the partners would bid on the entire property. By such sale, the plaintiffs could continue to run the business under a new partnership, and the defendant's partnership equity could be satisfied in cash.

On February 20, 1978, the trial court, by written decision, denied the defendant's request for a sale and instead divided the partnership assets in-kind according to the valuation presented by the plaintiffs. The plaintiffs were given the physical assets from the Elkhart Lake mill, and the defendant was given the physical assets from the St. Cloud mill. The defendant appeals this order and judgment dividing the assets in-kind.

Under sec. 178.25(1), Stats. [UPA § 29], a partnership is dissolved when any partner ceases to be associated in the carrying on of the business. The partnership is not terminated, but continues, until the winding-up of [the] partnership is complete. Sec. 178.25(2), Stats. [UPA § 30]. The action started by the plaintiffs, in this case, was an action for dissolution and wind-up. * * * The sole question in this case is whether, in the absence of a written agreement to the contrary, a partner, upon dissolution and wind-up of the partnership, can force a sale of the partnership assets.

At the outset, we note, and the parties agree, that the appellant was not in contravention of the partnership agreement since there was no partnership agreement. The partnership was a partnership at will. They also agree there was no written agreement governing distribution of partnership assets upon dissolution and wind-up. The dispute, in this case, is over the authority of the trial court to order in-kind distribution in the absence of any agreement of the partners.

Sec. 178.33(1), Stats. [UPA § 38(1)], provides:

> When dissolution is caused in any way, except in contravention of the partnership agreement, each partner, as against his copartners and all persons claiming through them in respect to their interests in the partnership, *unless otherwise agreed*, may have the partnership property applied to discharge its liabilities, and the surplus applied to pay *in cash* the net amount owing to the respective partners. [Emphasis supplied].

The appellant contends this statute grants him the right to force a sale of the partnership assets in order to obtain his fair share of the partnership assets in cash upon dissolution. He claims that in the absence of an agreement of the partners to in-kind distribution, the trial court had no authority to distribute the assets in-kind. He is entitled to an in-cash settlement after judicial sale.

The respondents contend the statute does not entitle the appellant to force a sale and grants the trial court the power to distribute the assets in-kind if in-kind distribution is equitably possible and doesn't jeopardize the rights of creditors.

We do not believe that the statute can be read in any way to permit in-kind distribution unless the partners agree to in-kind distribution or unless there is a partnership agreement calling for in-kind distribution at the time of dissolution and wind-up.

A partnership at will is a partnership which has no definite term or particular undertaking and can rightfully be dissolved by the express will of any partner. In the present case, the respondents wanted to dissolve the partnership. This being a partnership at will, they could rightfully dissolve this partnership with or without the consent of the appellant. In addition, the respondents have never claimed the appellant was in violation of any partnership agreement. Therefore, neither the appellant nor the respondents have wrongfully dissolved the partnership.

Unless otherwise agreed, partners who have not wrongfully dissolved a partnership have a right to wind up the partnership. Sec. 178.32, Stats. [UPA § 37]. Winding-up is the process of settling partnership affairs after dissolution. Winding-up is often called liquidation and involves reducing the assets to cash to pay creditors and distribute to partners the value of their respective interests. Thus, lawful dissolution (or dissolution which is caused in any way except in contravention of the partnership agreement) gives each partner the right to have the business liquidated and his share of the surplus paid *in cash*. In-kind distribution is permissible only in very limited circumstances. If the partnership agreement permits in-kind distribution upon dissolution or wind-up or if, at any time prior to wind-up, all partners agree to in-kind distribution, the court may order in-kind distribution. While at least one court has permitted in-kind distribution, absent an agreement by all partners, *Rinke v. Rinke*, 330 Mich. 615, 48 N.W.2d 201 (1951), the court's holding in that case was limited. In *Rinke*, the court stated:

> The decree of the trial court provided for dividing the assets of the partnerships rather than for the sale thereof and the distribution of cash proceeds. Appellants insist that such method of procedure is erroneous and [not] contemplated by the uniform partnership act. Attention is directed to Section 38 of said act[.] Construing together pertinent provisions of the statute leads to the conclusion that it was not the intention of the legislature in the enactment of the Uniform Partnership Act to impose a mandatory requirement that, under all circumstances, the assets of a dissolved partnership shall be sold and the money received therefor divided among those entitled to it, particularly so, as in the case at bar, where there are no debts to be paid from the proceeds. *The situation disclosed by the record in the present case is somewhat unusual in that no one other than the former partners is interested in the assets of the businesses. In view of this situation and of the nature of the assets,* we think that the trial court was correct in apportioning them to the parties. There

is no showing that appellants have been prejudiced thereby. [Emphasis supplied.] 330 Mich. at 628, 48 N.W.2d at 207.

The Michigan court's holding was limited to situations where: (1) there were no creditors to be paid from the proceeds, (2) ordering a sale would be senseless since no one other than the partners would be interested in the assets of the business, and (3) an in-kind distribution was fair to all partners.

That is not the case here. There was no showing that there were no creditors who would be paid from the proceeds, nor was there a showing that no one other than the partners would be interested in the assets. These factors are important if an in-kind distribution is to be allowed. Section 178.33(1) and § 38 of the Uniform Partnership Act are intended to protect creditors as well as partners. In-kind distributions may affect a creditor's right to collect the debt owed since the assets of the partnership, as a whole, may be worth more than the assets once divided up. Thus, the creditor's ability to collect from the individual partners may be jeopardized. Secondly, if others are interested in the assets, a sale provides a more accurate means of establishing the market value of the assets and, thus, better assuring each partner his share in the value of the assets. Where only the partners are interested in the assets, a fair value can be determined without the necessity of a sale. The sale would be merely the partners bidding with each other without any competition. This process could be accomplished through negotiations or at trial with the court as a final arbitrator of the value of the assets. With these policy considerations in mind, we think the Michigan court's holding in *Rinke* was limited to the facts of that case. Those facts not being present in this case, we do not feel an in-kind distribution in this case was proper.

However, even assuming the respondents in this case can show that there are no creditors to be paid, no one other than the partners are interested in the assets, and in-kind distribution would be fair to all partners, we cannot read § 38 of the Uniform Partnership Act or sec. 178.33(1), Stats. (the Wisconsin equivalent) as permitting an in-kind distribution under any circumstances, unless all partners agree. The statute and § 38 of the Uniform Partnership Act are quite clear that if a partner may force liquidation, he is entitled to his share of the partnership assets, after creditors are paid *in cash*. To the extent that *Rinke v. Rinke, supra,* creates an exception to cash distribution, we decline to adopt that exception. We, therefore, must hold the trial court erred in ordering an in-kind distribution of the assets of the partnership.

The last question that arises is whether the appellant can force an actual sale of the assets or whether the trial court can determine the fair market value of the assets and order the respondents to pay the appellant in cash an amount equal to his share in the assets.

As discussed above, a sale is the best means of determining the true fair market value of the assets. Generally, liquidation envisions some form of sale. Since the statutes provide that, unless otherwise agreed, any partner who has not wrongfully dissolved the partnership has the right to wind up the partnership and force liquidation, he likewise has a right to force a sale, unless otherwise agreed. While judicial sales in some instances may cause economic hardships, these hardships can be avoided by the use of partnership agreements.

Judgment reversed and cause remanded for further proceedings not inconsistent with this opinion.

NOTES

(1) Did the plaintiffs have the right to dissolve the partnership? If so, on what ground? *See* UPA § 31.

(2) UPA § 37 discusses who has the right to wind up a partnership. Unless otherwise agreed, that right is given to the partners who have not wrongfully dissolved the partnership, or the legal representative of the last surviving, non-bankrupt partner. Upon cause shown, however, any partner, his legal representative, or his assignee may obtain winding up by the court.

(3) When a partnership is wound up, the assets of the partnership are typically sold and the proceeds are distributed according to the scheme provided by UPA § 40: (1) non-partner creditors are paid; (2) partner creditors are paid; (3) partner capital contributions are returned; and (4) any remaining monies are split between the partners in proportion to their profit shares. *See id.* § 40(b), (c). If the proceeds from the partnership's assets are insufficient to pay the partnership's liabilities (1–3 above), the partners must contribute in proportion to their loss shares. *See id.* §§ 18(a), 40(d). Consider the following example:

> * * * [L]et us assume that three partners contributed $10,000, $5000, and $2000, respectively, to capitalize Partnership X and agreed to share profits equally. Let us also assume that upon dissolution of the partnership only $5000 remained after paying all creditors * * *. Since each partner is entitled to repayment of his capital, Partnership X has a loss of $12,000, *i.e.* the $17,000 representing the sum of the capital due each partner less the $5000 remaining after payment of all obligations other than those owed the partners as partners. Dividing the $12,000 loss between the partners in proportion to their share of the profits, *i.e.* one-third each, would result in each partner owing $4000 to the partnership. And, once this $4000 is offset against the sums due from the partners as reflected by their respective capital accounts, the partner who initially paid $10,000 in capital would have a positive balance of $6000 in his capital account. The one who paid $5000 would have a positive balance of $1000, while the one who paid $2000 would have a negative balance of $2000. Thus, the partner

with the negative balance would be obligated to pay $2000 to the partnership to remove his capital account from its negative position.

Farnsworth v. Deaver, 147 S.W.3d 662, 664–65 (Tex. App. 2004).

(4) The trial court in *Dreifuerst* wound up the partnership business by giving the Elkhart Lake mill to the plaintiffs and the St. Cloud mill to the defendant. Why was that objectionable to the defendant as a statutory matter? *See* UPA § 38(1). Why might that have been objectionable to the defendant as an economic matter?

(5) The defendant argued for (and the appellate court in *Dreifuerst* ultimately ordered) the sale of the partnership assets and the distribution to the partners of any cash remaining after the satisfaction of creditors. Why was that objectionable to the plaintiffs?

(6) As *Rinke* demonstrates, *Dreifuerst's* view of UPA § 38(1) is not universally held. In *Creel v. Lilly*, 729 A.2d 385 (Md. 1999), the court refused to order liquidation after a partner's death caused the dissolution of the partnership:

> * * * [W]hile winding up has often traditionally been regarded as synonymous with liquidation, this "fire sale" of assets has been viewed by many courts and commentators as a harsh and destructive measure. Consequently, to avoid the drastic result of a forced liquidation, many courts have adopted judicial alternatives to this potentially harmful measure. *See Fortugno v. Hudson Manure Company,* 51 N.J.Super. 482, 144 A.2d 207, 219 (App.Div.1958) (court approved an alternative proposal to the complete liquidation of the partnership, stating that it "recogniz[ed] that a forced sale of the partnership will destroy a great part of the value of the business * * *.").

> * * *

> * * * There have been several cases in other jurisdictions * * * where * * * the court elected another option under UPA instead of a "fire sale" of all the partnership assets to ensure that the deceased partner's estate received its fair share of the partnership. These jurisdictions have recognized the unfairness and harshness of a compelled liquidation and found other judicially acceptable means of winding up a partnership under UPA, such as ordering an in-kind distribution of the assets or allowing the remaining partners to buy out the withdrawing partner's share of the partnership.

> * * *

> We hold that Maryland's UPA does not grant the estate of a deceased partner the right to demand liquidation of a partnership * * *. Winding up is not always synonymous with liquidation, which can be a harsh and unnecessary measure towards arriving at the true value of the business. A preferred method in a good faith winding up is the one used in this case—the payment to the

deceased partner's estate of its proportionate share of the partnership. Thus, we further hold that where the surviving partners have in good faith wound up the business and the deceased partner's estate is provided with an accurate accounting allowing for payment of a proportionate share of the business, then a forced sale of all partnership assets is generally unwarranted. * * *

Id. at 392–93, 403. Do you agree with the rationale of *Dreifuerst* or *Creel*?

(7) Can partners avoid the result in *Dreifuerst* (the forced liquidation of the partnership) with appropriate planning? How? *See* UPA § 38(1).

(8) When a partnership business continues after dissolution, UPA provides default rules for a number of issues that may arise. For example:

(a) A partnership continues after dissolution because a partner chooses not to exercise his liquidation right under § 38(1). What is the departing partner entitled to? *See* UPA § 42 (addressing partner retirement or death and allowing the partner or the partner's representative to receive the value of his partnership interest at the date of dissolution plus either (a) interest on that amount until it is paid or (b) his share of the partnership profits between the date of dissolution and the date that he is paid for his partnership interest).

(b) What are the rights of creditors of the old partnership with respect to the assets of the continuing business? *See id.* § 41 (providing generally that creditors of the dissolved partnership are also creditors of the continuing partnership).

(c) In view of the agency that exists between partners, what must a retiring partner do to avoid liability for post-dissolution partnership obligations? *See id.* § 35(1)(b) (providing generally that creditors must have knowledge or notice of the dissolution, but also indicating that, with respect to creditors who had not extended credit to the partnership before dissolution, it is sufficient to advertise the fact of dissolution in a newspaper of general circulation in every place where the partnership regularly does business); *see also id.* § 3 (defining "knowledge" and "notice"). A retiring partner is, of course, still liable for pre-dissolution partnership obligations. *See id.* § 36(1) (stating that the dissolution "does not of itself discharge the existing liability of any partner").

(d) If a creditor knows that a partner has retired, but the creditor chooses to deal with the successor partnership, does that release the retired partner from pre-dissolution partnership obligations? *See id.* § 36(2) (requiring an agreement to release the partner between the partner, the partnership creditor, and the successor partnership, but stating that such an agreement "may be inferred from the course of dealing between the creditor having knowledge of the dissolution and the * * * partnership continuing the business").

(e) Is a newly admitted partner responsible for partnership obligations that arose before his admission? *See id.* § 17 (providing, in a somewhat awkward manner, that the newly admitted partner is not liable for such obligations because, although the partner "is liable * * * as though he had been a partner when such obligations were incurred," the liability "shall be satisfied only out of partnership property").

NOTE ON CONTINUATION AGREEMENTS

A drafter of a continuation agreement must resolve several basic questions that are not unlike the problems faced by a drafter of share transfer restrictions in closely held corporations. *See* Chapter 8, Section B. Generally, fair treatment of the withdrawing interest is the ultimate aim. There is often an element of Russian roulette in drafting these provisions, however, as clauses are usually reciprocal and it cannot be determined in advance which partner will be the first to withdraw. Among the issues to be considered are the following:

(1) A determination must be made as to the types of dissolution which trigger the clause. The most common provision covers death or retirement, but it may also cover other types of dissolution, such as expulsion or bankruptcy.

(2) What is to happen to the withdrawing interest? There are several alternatives that have widely varying income tax consequences. The other partners may simply purchase the interest. They may arrange to have the interest purchased by an acceptable third person. The partnership may purchase the interest. The assets of the partnership may be sold as a unit to the remaining partners who are to continue the business. As another option, the outgoing interest may continue to share in future earnings on a more or less permanent basis.

(3) Is the disposition of the withdrawing interest to be optional or mandatory from the standpoint of the remaining partners? In other words, may the remaining partners elect to liquidate the partnership, ignoring the provision in the agreement?

(4) How much is the withdrawing interest to receive? Valuation is usually a complex task, and the best method depends on the nature of the business. For example, the appraisal of each asset by an independent appraiser may be the most appropriate method in a real estate partnership. This method, however, may be hopelessly inadequate in a law firm where most of the assets are represented by contingent work in progress.

The following list of suggestions cover the most popular valuation techniques: a fixed sum; book value, perhaps with supplemental appraisals; appraisal; capitalization of earnings in the past; a fraction of future earnings over a specified period of time; negotiation after the fact; a right of first refusal to meet the best offer obtainable elsewhere by the withdrawing interest; or a sum based on a fraction of the partner's income from the partnership during the previous year or an average of several years.

(5) Should the withdrawing partner's share be subject to a minority or marketability discount? A minority discount decreases the value of an ownership interest in a business on the basis that a minority ownership stake, by definition, lacks control. A marketability discount decreases the value of an ownership interest (controlling or minority) in a closely held business on the basis that such an interest, because of the lack of an established market, is less liquid than an ownership interest in a comparable publicly traded business. In short, the rationale for applying discounts is that purchasers will pay less for a minority ownership interest in a partnership because that interest lacks both control and, relative to a publicly traded interest, liquidity. *Compare* Halpern v. Goldstein & Halpern, C.P.A., 795 N.Y.S.2d 599, 601 (App. Div. 2005) (applying a 20% minority discount) *with* Marengo v. Bowen, No. M2000–02379–COA–R3–CV, 2002 WL 1484437, at *5 (Tenn. Ct. App. July 12, 2002) (refusing to apply a minority or marketability discount).

(6) Is the payment to be made in a lump sum, or over time?

(7) How will the partnership raise the cash to meet the required payments (life insurance, borrowing, funds generated by the business's regular operations)?

(8) May the withdrawing interest compete with the partnership? If not, how much of the consideration is to be allocated to the covenant not to compete?

(9) Should the withdrawing interest have the power to inspect books and records or to demand an audit?

PROBLEM

Art and Bob are brothers. They form a partnership to engage in a linen supply business with Art as the managing partner. Each brother contributes approximately $43,000 for the purchase of land, machinery, and linen needed to begin the business. Additional linen and machinery necessary for the day-to-day operation of the business is provided by a separate corporation that is wholly owned by Art. That corporation has also loaned $47,000 to the partnership and it holds a demand note evidencing the loan.

For the first eight years of the partnership, the business consistently loses money. In the ninth year of operation, however, the partnership begins to turn a profit. In fact, the future of the partnership looks bright because an Air Force base has recently been established in the vicinity (and persons on the base, one should assume, need linens). Nevertheless, Art wishes to dissolve the partnership.

Can Art dissolve the partnership? Does Bob have any rights in this situation?

BOHATCH V. BUTLER & BINION

Supreme Court of Texas, 1998.
977 S.W.2d 543.

ENOCH, JUSTICE, delivered the opinion of the Court, in which GONZALEZ, OWEN, BAKER, and HANKINSON, JUSTICES, join.

Partnerships exist by the agreement of the partners; partners have no duty to remain partners. The issue in this case is whether we should create an exception to this rule by holding that a partnership has a duty not to expel a partner for reporting suspected overbilling by another partner. The trial court rendered judgment for Colette Bohatch on her breach of fiduciary duty claim against Butler & Binion and several of its partners (collectively, "the firm"). The court of appeals held that there was no evidence that the firm breached a fiduciary duty and reversed the trial court's tort judgment; however, the court of appeals found evidence of a breach of the partnership agreement and rendered judgment for Bohatch on this ground. 905 S.W.2d 597. We affirm the court of appeals' judgment.

I. Facts

Bohatch became an associate in the Washington, D.C., office of Butler & Binion in 1986 after working for several years as Deputy Assistant General Counsel at the Federal Energy Regulatory Commission. John McDonald, the managing partner of the office, and Richard Powers, a partner, were the only other attorneys in the Washington office. The office did work for Pennzoil almost exclusively.

Bohatch was made partner in February 1990. She then began receiving internal firm reports showing the number of hours each attorney worked, billed, and collected. From her review of these reports, Bohatch became concerned that McDonald was overbilling Pennzoil and discussed the matter with Powers. Together they reviewed and copied portions of McDonald's time diary. Bohatch's review of McDonald's time entries increased her concern.

On July 15, 1990, Bohatch met with Louis Paine, the firm's managing partner, to report her concern that McDonald was overbilling Pennzoil. Paine said he would investigate. Later that day, Bohatch told Powers about her conversation with Paine.

The following day, McDonald met with Bohatch and informed her that Pennzoil was not satisfied with her work and wanted her work to be supervised. Bohatch testified that this was the first time she had ever heard criticism of her work for Pennzoil.

The next day, Bohatch repeated her concerns to Paine and to R. Hayden Burns and Marion E. McDaniel, two other members of the firm's management committee, in a telephone conversation. Over the next month, Paine and Burns investigated Bohatch's complaint. They reviewed the Pennzoil bills and supporting computer print-outs for those bills. They then discussed the allegations with Pennzoil in-house counsel John Chapman, the firm's primary contact with Pennzoil. Chapman, who had a long-standing relationship with McDonald, responded that Pennzoil was satisfied that the bills were reasonable.

In August, Paine met with Bohatch and told her that the firm's investigation revealed no basis for her contentions. He added that she should begin looking for other employment, but that the firm would continue to provide her a monthly draw, insurance coverage, office space, and a secretary. After this meeting, Bohatch received no further work assignments from the firm.

In January 1991, the firm denied Bohatch a year-end partnership distribution for 1990 and reduced her tentative distribution share for 1991 to zero. In June, the firm paid Bohatch her monthly draw and told her that this draw would be her last. Finally, in August, the firm gave Bohatch until November to vacate her office.

By September, Bohatch had found new employment. She filed this suit on October 18, 1991, and the firm voted formally to expel her from the partnership three days later, October 21, 1991.

The trial court granted partial summary judgment for the firm on Bohatch's wrongful discharge claim, and also on her breach of fiduciary duty and breach of the duty of good faith and fair dealing claims for any conduct occurring after October 21, 1991 (the date Bohatch was formally expelled from the firm). The trial court denied the firm's summary judgment motion on Bohatch's breach of fiduciary duty and breach of the duty of good faith and fair dealing claims for conduct occurring before October 21, 1991. The breach of fiduciary duty claim and a breach of contract claim were tried to a jury. The jury found that the firm breached the partnership agreement and its fiduciary duty. It awarded Bohatch $57,000 for past lost wages, $250,000 for past mental anguish, $4,000,000 total in punitive damages (this amount was apportioned against several defendants), and attorney's fees. The trial court rendered judgment for Bohatch in the amounts found by the jury, except it disallowed attorney's fees because the judgment was based in tort. After suggesting remittitur, which Bohatch accepted, the trial court reduced the punitive damages to around $237,000.

All parties appealed. The court of appeals held that the firm's only duty to Bohatch was not to expel her in bad faith. The court of appeals stated that " '[b]ad faith' in this context means only that partners cannot expel another partner for self-gain." Finding no evidence that the firm expelled Bohatch for self-gain, the court concluded that Bohatch could not recover for breach of fiduciary duty. However, the court concluded that the firm breached the partnership agreement when it reduced Bohatch's tentative partnership distribution for 1991 to zero without notice, and when it terminated her draw three months before she left. The court concluded that Bohatch was entitled to recover $35,000 in lost earnings for 1991 but none for 1990, and no mental anguish damages. Accordingly, the court rendered judgment for Bohatch for $35,000 plus $225,000 in attorney's fees.

II.   Breach of Fiduciary Duty

We have long recognized as a matter of common law that "[t]he relationship between * * * partners * * * is fiduciary in character, and imposes upon all the participants the obligation of loyalty to the joint concern and of the utmost good faith, fairness, and honesty in their dealings with each other with respect to matters pertaining to the enterprise." *Fitz-Gerald v. Hull*, 150 Tex. 39, 237 S.W.2d 256, 264 (1951) (quotation omitted). Yet, partners have no obligation to remain partners; "at the heart of the partnership concept is the principle that partners may choose with whom they wish to be associated." *Gelder Med. Group v. Webber*, 41 N.Y.2d 680, 394 N.Y.S.2d 867, 870–71, 363 N.E.2d 573, 577 (1977). The issue presented, one of first impression, is whether the fiduciary relationship between and among partners creates an exception to the at-will nature of partnerships; that is, in this case, whether it gives rise to a duty not to expel a partner who reports suspected overbilling by another partner.

At the outset, we note that no party questions that the obligations of lawyers licensed to practice in the District of Columbia—including McDonald and Bohatch—were prescribed by the District of Columbia Code of Professional Responsibility in effect in 1990, and that in all other respects Texas law applies. Further, neither statutory nor contract law principles answer the question of whether the firm owed Bohatch a duty not to expel her. The Texas Uniform Partnership Act * * * addresses expulsion of a partner only in the context of dissolution of the partnership. *See id.* §§ 31, 38. In this case, as provided by the partnership agreement, Bohatch's expulsion did not dissolve the partnership. Additionally, the new Texas Revised Partnership Act does not have retroactive effect and thus does not apply. Finally, the partnership agreement contemplates expulsion of a partner and prescribes procedures to be followed, but it does not specify or limit the grounds for expulsion. Thus, while Bohatch's claim that she was expelled in an *improper way* is governed by the partnership agreement, her claim that she was expelled for an *improper reason* is not. Therefore, we look to the common law to find the principles governing Bohatch's claim that the firm breached a duty when it expelled her.

Courts in other states have held that a partnership may expel a partner for purely business reasons. Further, courts recognize that a law firm can expel a partner to protect relationships both within the firm and with clients. Finally, many courts have held that a partnership can expel a partner without breaching any duty in order to resolve a "fundamental schism."

The fiduciary duty that partners owe one another does not encompass a duty to remain partners or else answer in tort damages. Nonetheless, Bohatch and several distinguished legal scholars urge this Court to recognize that public policy requires a limited duty to remain partners—i.e., a partnership must retain a whistleblower partner. They argue that such an extension of a partner's fiduciary duty is necessary because permitting a law firm to retaliate against a partner who in good faith reports suspected overbilling would discourage compliance with rules of professional conduct and thereby hurt clients.

While this argument is not without some force, we must reject it. A partnership exists solely because the partners choose to place personal confidence and trust in one another. *See Holman* [*v. Coie*, 522 P.2d 515, 524 (Wash. Ct. App. 1974)] ("The foundation of a professional relationship is personal confidence and trust."). Just as a partner can be expelled, without a breach of any common law duty, over disagreements about firm policy or to resolve some other "fundamental schism," a partner can be expelled for accusing another partner of overbilling without subjecting the partnership to tort damages. Such charges, whether true or not, may have a profound effect on the personal confidence and trust essential to the partner relationship. Once such charges are made, partners may find it impossible to continue to work together to their mutual benefit and the benefit of their clients.

* * * The threat of tort liability for expulsion would tend to force partners to remain in untenable circumstance[s]—suspicious of and angry with each other—to their own detriment and that of their clients whose matters are neglected by lawyers distracted with intra-firm frictions.

* * *

We emphasize that our refusal to create an exception to the at-will nature of partnerships in no way obviates the ethical duties of lawyers. Such duties sometimes necessitate difficult decisions, as when a lawyer suspects overbilling by a colleague. The fact that the ethical duty to report may create an irreparable schism between partners neither excuses failure to report nor transforms expulsion as a means of resolving that schism into a tort.

We hold that the firm did not owe Bohatch a duty not to expel her for reporting suspected overbilling by another partner.

III. Breach of the Partnership Agreement

The court of appeals concluded that the firm breached the partnership agreement by reducing Bohatch's tentative distribution for

1991 to zero without the requisite notice. The firm contests this finding on the ground that the management committee had the right to set tentative and year-end bonuses. However, the partnership agreement guarantees a monthly draw of $7,500 per month regardless of the tentative distribution. Moreover, the firm's right to reduce the bonus was contingent upon providing proper notice to Bohatch. The firm does not dispute that it did not give Bohatch notice that the firm was reducing her tentative distribution. Accordingly, the court of appeals did not err in finding the firm liable for breach of the partnership agreement. Moreover, because Bohatch's damages sound in contract, and because she sought attorney's fees at trial under section 38.001(8) of the Texas Civil Practice and Remedies Code, we affirm the court of appeals' award of Bohatch's attorney's fees. * * *

We affirm the court of appeals' judgment. * * *

HECHT, JUSTICE, concurring in the judgment.

The Court holds that partners in a law firm have no common-law liability for expelling one of their number for accusing another of unethical conduct. The dissent argues that partners in a law firm are liable for such conduct. Both views are unqualified; neither concedes or even considers whether "always" and "never" are separated by any distance. I think they must be. * * *

* * * I have trouble justifying a 500-partner firm's expulsion of a partner for reporting overbilling of a client that saves the firm not only from ethical complaints but from liability to the client. But I cannot see how a five-partner firm can legitimately survive one partner's accusations that another is unethical. Between two such extreme examples I see a lot of ground.

This case does not force a choice between diametrically opposite views. Here, the report of unethical conduct, though made in good faith, was incorrect. That fact is significant to me because I think a law firm can always expel a partner for bad judgment, whether it relates to the representation of clients or the relationships with other partners, and whether it is in good faith. I would hold that Butler & Binion did not breach its fiduciary duty by expelling Colette Bohatch because she made a good-faith but nevertheless extremely serious charge against a senior partner that threatened the firm's relationship with an important client, her charge proved groundless, and her relationship with her partners was destroyed in the process. I cannot, however, extrapolate from this case, as the Court does, that no law firm can ever be liable for expelling a partner for reporting unethical conduct. Accordingly, I concur only in the Court's judgment.

* * *

No court has considered whether expulsion of a partner from a law firm for reporting unethical conduct is a breach of fiduciary duty. Several courts have concluded that expulsion to remedy a fundamental schism in a professional firm is not a breach of fiduciary duty. There is hardly a schism more fundamental than that caused by one partner's accusing another of unethical conduct. If a partner can be expelled because of disagreements over nothing more significant than firm policy and abrasive personal conduct, as cases have held, surely a partner can be expelled for accusing another partner of something as serious as unethical conduct. Once such charges are raised, I find it hard to imagine how partners could continue to work together to their mutual benefit and the benefit of their clients. The trust essential to the relationship would have been destroyed. Indeed, I should think that a lawyer who was unable to convince his or her partners to rectify the unethical conduct of another would choose to withdraw from the firm rather than continue in association with lawyers who did not adhere to high ethical standards.

But I am troubled by the arguments of the distinguished amici curiae that permitting a law firm to retaliate against a partner for reporting unethical behavior would discourage compliance with rules of conduct, hurt clients, and contravene public policy. Their arguments have force, but they do not explain how a relationship of trust necessary for both the existence of the firm and the representation of its clients can survive such serious accusations by one partner against another. [As the majority observes, the] threat of liability for expulsion would tend to force partners to remain in untenable circumstances—suspicious of and angry with each other—to their own detriment and that of their clients whose matters are neglected by lawyers distracted with intra-firm frictions. If "at the heart of the partnership concept is the principle that partners may choose with whom they wish to be associated," *Gelder*, 394 N.Y.S.2d at 870–871, 363 N.E.2d at 577, surely partners are not obliged to continue to associate with someone who has accused one of them of unethical conduct.

* * * Pennzoil's conclusion that Butler & Binion's fees were reasonable, reached after being made aware of Bohatch's concerns that McDonald's time was overstated, establishes that Butler & Binion did not collect excessive fees from Pennzoil. A fee that a client as sophisticated as Pennzoil considers reasonable is not clearly excessive simply because a lawyer believes it could have been less. Bohatch's argument that Pennzoil had other reasons not to complain of Butler & Binion's bills is simply beside the point. Whatever its motivations, Pennzoil found the bills reasonable, thereby establishing that McDonald had not overbilled in violation of ethical rules. * * *

Bohatch's real concern was not that fees to Pennzoil were excessive—she had never even seen the bills and had no idea what the fees, or fee arrangements, were—but that McDonald was misrepresenting the number of hours he worked. The District of Columbia Code of Professional Responsibility at the time also prohibited lawyers from engaging in "conduct involving dishonesty, fraud, deceit or misrepresentation." *Id.* DR 1–102(A)(4). But there is no evidence that McDonald actually engaged in such conduct. At most, Bohatch showed only that McDonald kept sloppy time records, not that he deceived his partners or clients. Neither his partners nor his major client accused McDonald of dishonesty, even after reviewing his bills and time records. * * *

* * *

Butler & Binion's expulsion of Bohatch did not discourage ethical conduct; it discouraged errors of judgment, which ought to be discouraged. Butler & Binion did not violate its fiduciary duty to Bohatch.

* * *

* * * I would not hold that being correct is enough, only that being incorrect precludes recovery, at least in these circumstances. My criticism of the Court is not that another bright-line rule—one based on whether a report was correct—would be better, but that no bright-line rule should be adopted when the full ramifications of so broad a rule have not been adequately considered. It should come as no surprise to anyone that a lawyer can be fired for being incorrect, albeit in good faith. A lawyer can always be terminated for being incorrect about legal matters. It is, after all, a lawyer's judgment that is important, not her sincerity. Bohatch's charges were not merely an innocent mistake. They caused the expenditure of a significant amount of time in investigation, the report of possible overbilling to one of the firm's major clients, potentially jeopardizing that relationship, and an impossible strain on three lawyers working together on the same business for the same client in a small but important office of the firm.

Without offering a solution to the problems the amici raise, the Court adopts an absolute rule: a law firm that expels a partner for reporting ethics violations has no liability to the partner under any circumstances. The rule is ill-advised, particularly when it is far broader than necessary to address Bohatch's claims.

* * *

SPECTOR, J., joined by PHILLIPS, CHIEF JUSTICE, dissenting.

[W]hat's the use you learning to do right when it's troublesome to do right and ain't no trouble to do wrong, and the wages is just the same?— *The Adventures of Huckleberry Finn*

The issue in this appeal is whether law partners violate a fiduciary duty by retaliating against one partner for questioning the billing practices of another partner. I would hold that partners violate their fiduciary duty to one another by punishing compliance with the Disciplinary Rules of Professional Conduct. Accordingly, I dissent.

* * *

* * * I would hold that in this case the law partners violated their fiduciary duty by retaliating against a fellow partner who made a good-faith effort to alert her partners to the possible overbilling of a client.

* * * The duty to prevent overbilling and other misconduct exists for the protection of the client. Even if a report turns out to be mistaken or a client ultimately consents to the behavior in question, as in this case, retaliation against a partner who tries in good faith to correct or report perceived misconduct virtually assures that others will not take these appropriate steps in the future. * * *

* * * The Court's writing in this case sends an inappropriate signal to lawyers and to the public that the rules of professional responsibility are subordinate to a law firm's other interests. Under the majority opinion's vision for the legal profession, the wages would not even be the same for "doing right"; they diminish considerably and leave an attorney who acts ethically and in good faith without recourse. Accordingly, I respectfully dissent.

NOTES

(1) Assume that you are a junior partner in a large law firm. You discover that the senior partner with whom you work may be doing legal work "on the side" in his own name and not turning the fees over to the firm. Should you take the matter to the managing partner or a member of the management committee? Might you then suffer the same fate as Colette Bohatch? On the other hand, if you do nothing and the misconduct later comes to light, might you be blamed for failing to report the misconduct and, perhaps, expelled for that reason?

(2) Although *Bohatch* primarily addresses the fiduciary duties between partners, the case provides an opportunity to explore related dissolution issues as well. For example, consider the following:

(a) UPA § 31(1)(d) and § 38(1) both contemplate that an expulsion must be "bona fide." What does "bona fide" mean in this context? That the other partners have "cause" to expel the partner? That expulsion was not for self-gain, even if they didn't have "cause?" Is it significant that RUPA § 601(3) and § 601(4) omit this phrase? Consider the following:

> Plaintiffs also challenge the expulsion on the basis that there was substantial evidence that it was not bona fide, or in good faith, and contend such a requirement should be implied.

[UPA § 31(1)(d)] states: "Dissolution is caused: (1) * * * (d) By the expulsion of any partner from the business bona fide in accordance with such a power conferred by the agreement between the partners; * * *" The partnership agreement here at issue merely states that a partner may be expelled by majority vote of the executive committee with no provisions for cause, reasons, notice or hearing. "Bona fide" is defined as: "In or with good faith; honestly, openly, and sincerely; without deceit or fraud." Black's Law Dictionary 223 (4th ed. 1951).

Undoubtedly, the general rule of law is that the partners in their dealings with each other must exercise good faith. * * * However, the personal relationships between partners to which the terms "bona fide" and "good faith" relate are those which have a bearing upon the business aspects or property of the partnership and prohibit a partner, to-wit, a fiduciary, from taking any personal advantage touching those subjects. Plaintiffs' claims do not relate to the business aspects or property rights of this partnership. There is no evidence [that] the purpose of the severance was to gain any business or property advantage to the remaining partners. Consequently, in that context, there has been no showing of breach of the duty of good faith toward plaintiffs.

Holman v. Coie, 522 P.2d 515, 523 (Wash. Ct. App. 1974); *see also* Winston & Strawn v. Nosal, 664 N.E.2d 239, 243–47 (Ill. App. Ct. 1996) (concluding that a triable issue of fact was present on a partner's claim that his expulsion violated the duty of good faith and fair dealing because, even though the law firm claimed that the partner was expelled under the partnership agreement "because his interest * * * was incompatible with the interests and resources of the firm, and because he had engaged in 'disturbing' conduct," the evidence raised an inference that the partner was expelled "solely because he persisted in invoking rights belonging to him under the partnership agreement [to inspect the firm's books and records in an effort to investigate self-dealing by the executive committee] and that the reasons advanced by the firm were pretextual"); Paula J. Dalley, *The Law of Partner Expulsions: Fiduciary Duty and Good Faith*, 21 CARDOZO L. REV. 181, 185–86 (1999).

(b) The *Bohatch* majority notes that "as provided by the partnership agreement, Bohatch's expulsion did not dissolve the partnership." Is that statement correct from an aggregate view of the partnership? The prevailing view under UPA is that dissolution cannot be avoided by agreement. *See, e.g.*, Finkelstein v. Security Props., Inc., 888 P.2d 161, 166 n.6 (Wash. Ct. App. 1995) ("The statutes allow for agreements dissolving a partnership, but not agreements circumventing the legal dissolution caused by any of the circumstances listed in [UPA § 31]. Section 31 of the Uniform Partnership Act * * * is apparently not intended to be alterable by agreement of the partners."). An agreement purporting to avoid dissolution will likely be construed as an agreement to avoid winding up and to instead continue the business as a new partnership.

(c) May a partner be expelled if there is no express expulsion power in the partnership agreement? *See* UPA § 31(1)(d). In an at-will partnership, a majority of the partners might reach the same result by voluntarily dissolving the partnership and immediately reconstituting a new partnership under the same name, but without the partner whose presence is no longer desired. Is there any risk to this strategy? What if the partnership is for a term?

(d) Assume that a law firm's partnership agreement does not contain an express provision authorizing expulsion, but it does provide that the agreement may be amended by a majority vote. May a law firm amend its partnership agreement to include an expulsion clause and then immediately apply it to expel a specific partner?

(3) As *Bohatch* suggests, whistleblowers (those who report questionable practices both in-house and to other authorities) are not afforded much protection under partnership statutes or the common law. Although Bohatch received compensation arising from the firm's breach of the partnership agreement, the court found that the partnership owed her no fiduciary duties in the situation.

In publicly traded companies, Congress has given some protection to whistleblowers in a provision of the Sarbanes-Oxley Act of 2002. The statute requires the audit committee of the board of directors to set up procedures for handling complaints by whistleblowers within the company.[e] Sections 806 and 1107 of the Act, reproduced below, provide further protection for whistleblowers by making it illegal to retaliate against or to harass people who assist in an investigation of the company's violations of securities laws or other federal provisions:

> No [publicly traded company] or any officer, employee * * * or agent of such company, may discharge, demote, suspend, threaten, harass, or in any other manner discriminate against an employee * * * because of any lawful act done by the employee * * * to provide information * * * or otherwise assist in an investigation regarding any conduct which the employee reasonably believes constitutes a violation of * * * any rule or regulation of the Securities and Exchange Commission, or any provision of Federal law relating to fraud against shareholders * * *.

> Whoever knowingly, with the intent to retaliate, takes any action harmful to any person, including interference with the lawful employment or livelihood of any person, for providing to a law enforcement officer any truthful information relating to the

---

e   Public Law 107–204, Section 301(4), amending Section 10A of the Securities Exchange Act of 1934, (15 U.S.C. Section 78f), provides that public company audit committees must establish procedures for: (A) the receipt, retention, and treatment of complaints received by the issuer regarding accounting, internal accounting controls, or auditing matters; and (B) the confidential, anonymous submission by employees of the issuer of concerns regarding questionable accounting matters.

commission or possible commission of any Federal offense, shall be fined * * * or imprisoned not more than 10 years, or both.

2. DISSOCIATION AND DISSOLUTION UNDER RUPA

As discussed, the technical definition of "dissolution" set forth in UPA may be traced to the view that a partnership was an aggregate of the partners. By the time of the development of RUPA, it had become clear that the entity theory of the partnership was accepted and that a new approach towards dissolution was warranted. An influential article by Professor Larry Ribstein (*A Statutory Approach to Partner Dissociation*, 65 WASH. U. L.Q. 357 (1987)) not only added the word "dissociation" to the partnership lexicon, but also pointed out that dissociation, or "cessation of partner status," was an event that was independent of the question of whether the business should be "dissolved" and wound up. In other words, it should be possible for a partner to leave the partnership (i.e., to "dissociate" from the partnership) without affecting the partnership itself. RUPA adopts this approach.

The major features of the dissociation and dissolution provisions of RUPA are as follows:

(1) Among other events, the death, withdrawal, bankruptcy, or expulsion of a partner results in a "dissociation" of the partner from the partnership. *See* RUPA § 601. Some of these events were broadened from similar provisions relating to "dissolution" under UPA, such as an expansion of the grounds for expelling partners. *See id.* § 601(4) (allowing expulsion in certain circumstances without authorization in the partnership agreement); *see also id.* § 601(5) (providing for expulsion by judicial order).

(2) The basic distinction between "rightful" and "wrongful" dissociation is retained in RUPA. *See id.* § 602. The list of wrongful dissociation events, however, has been expanded. *See id.* § 602(b).

(3) A partnership continues in existence despite the dissociation of a partner. It may continue in existence indefinitely with the dissociated partner becoming entitled to the value of his partnership interest in cash under article 7, *see id.* §§ 701–705, or it may be dissolved and wound up under article 8. *See id.* §§ 801–807.

(4) Dissolution and winding up are required only in the limited circumstances set forth in § 801. Two provisions are of particular importance: (a) in an at-will partnership, any partner who dissociates by his express will may compel dissolution and winding up; and (b) in a term partnership, if one partner dissociates wrongfully (or if a dissociation occurs because of a partner's death or otherwise under § 601(6)–(10)), dissolution and winding up of the partnership occurs only if, within 90 days after the dissociation, one-half of the remaining partners agree to

wind up the partnership. Once an event requiring dissolution and winding up occurs, the partnership is to be wound up unless all of the partners (including any dissociated partner other than a wrongfully dissociating partner) agree otherwise. *See id.* § 802.

(5) If a partner dissociates, but the partnership business is not dissolved and wound up, the partner is entitled to receive the "buyout price." *Id.* § 701(a). This price is defined in § 701(b). If the dissociation was wrongful, damages may offset the buyout price, *see id.* § 701(c), and the payment may be deferred until the expiration of the term or completion of the undertaking, "unless the partner establishes to the satisfaction of the court that earlier payment will not cause undue hardship to the business of the partnership." *Id.* § 701(h). A deferred payment "must be adequately secured and bear interest." *Id.* Significantly, unlike UPA, RUPA does not impose a "loss of goodwill" penalty when valuing a wrongfully dissociating partner's interest. *See id.* §§ 602(c) & cmt. 3, 701 cmt. 3; *see also* UPA § 38(2)(c)(ii) (stating that "in ascertaining the value of the partner's interest the value of the good-will of the business shall not be considered").

(6) RUPA does not continue the UPA § 42 election that permitted, in certain circumstances, a former partner in a partnership that did not wind up to take either a share of post-dissolution profits or interest on the value of his partnership stake until the value of that stake was paid to him. Under RUPA § 701(b), a dissociated partner is entitled only to interest on the amount to be paid from the date of dissociation to the date of payment. *See also id.* § 701 cmt. 3 ("The UPA Section 42 option of electing a share of the profits in lieu of interest has been eliminated.").

(7) A dissociated partner has apparent authority to bind the partnership for a period of time, *see id.* § 702, and he may be liable for post-dissociation partnership liabilities incurred within two years after the dissociation. *See id.* § 703. Either a dissociated partner or the partnership may file a public statement of dissociation to limit this apparent authority and potential liability. *See id.* § 704.

(8) As mentioned, a partnership "is dissolved" and its business must be wound up if any of the events listed in RUPA § 801 occurs. After dissolution, the partnership continues in existence for the purpose of winding up. *See id.* § 802(a). The apparent authority of partners to bind the partnership continues after dissolution, *see id.* § 804, but any partner who has not wrongfully dissociated may file a public statement of dissolution to give notice that the partnership is in the winding up process. *See id.* § 805.

(9) Section 807 describes the final settlement of partnership accounts upon winding up. Partnership assets must be applied to the discharge of partnership liabilities, and if the assets are insufficient, individual partners are required to contribute in accordance with their respective

loss shares. Thus, partners with negative balances in their accounts are required to restore those balances to zero to ensure that all partners receive the amounts in their accounts. Any excess assets remaining are distributable to the partners in accordance with their profit shares.

SAINT ALPHONSUS DIVERSIFIED CARE, INC. v. MRI ASSOCIATES, LLP

Supreme Court of Idaho, 2009.
224 P.3d 1068.

EISMANN, CHIEF JUSTICE.

This is an appeal from a judgment against a general partner for wrongful dissociation * * *. We vacate the judgment and remand this case for further proceedings.

I. BACKGROUND

Doctors of Magnetic Resonance, Inc.; Saint Alphonsus Diversified Care, Inc.; Mednow, Inc.; and HCA of Idaho, Inc., formed a general partnership named MRI Associates (MRIA). The parties executed a written partnership agreement that was effective on April 26, 1985. The purpose of the partnership was to acquire and operate diagnostic and therapeutic devices, equipment, and accessories, beginning with a magnetic resonance imaging (MRI) scanner; to acquire related buildings and other facilities; and to transact all business matters incident to such activities. * * *

On February 24, 2004, Saint Alphonsus Diversified Care, Inc. gave notice to MRIA that it would dissociate from the partnership effective on April 1, 2004, and on October 18, 2004, it filed this lawsuit seeking a judicial determination of the amount it was entitled to receive for its interest in MRIA. MRIA responded by filing a multi-count counterclaim against Saint Alphonsus [which included wrongful dissociation, breach of fiduciary duty, and other claims].

* * *

III. ANALYSIS

A. Did the District Court Err in Holding that St. Alphonsus Wrongfully Dissociated from MRIA?

St. Alphonsus dissociated from MRIA on April 1, 2004. [The dissociation was apparently motivated by the desire of St. Alphonsus to compete with the partnership.] MRIA included in its counterclaim a cause of action for wrongful dissociation alleged under two theories: (a) the dissociation breached an express provision of the partnership agreement and (b) the partnership agreement had a definite term and the dissociation occurred prior to the expiration of that term. MRIA and St. Alphonsus both filed motions for partial summary judgment on that cause of action. The district court granted MRIA's motion for summary judgment, holding that St. Alphonsus's dissociation was wrongful because it breached an express provision of the partnership agreement. The court did not discuss the alternative theory that the dissociation occurred prior to the expiration of the definite term of the partnership. St. Alphonsus contends the district court erred in granting the partial summary judgment.

"A partner who wrongfully dissociates is liable to the partnership and to the other partners for damages caused by the dissociation." [RUPA § 602(c)]. A partner's dissociation is wrongful if "[i]t is in breach of an express provision of the partnership agreement." [RUPA § 602(b)(1)]. Whether there is an express provision in the partnership agreement that was breached by the dissociation is an issue of law over which we will exercise free review. * * *

* * *

The relevant provision of the partnership agreement is as follows:

ARTICLE 6

WITHDRAWAL OF HOSPITAL PARTNER

6.1 *Conditions for withdrawal.* Any Hospital Partner may withdraw from the Partnership at any time if, in a Hospital Partner's reasonable judgment, continued participation in this Partnership: (i) jeopardizes the tax-exempt status of such Hospital Partner or its parent or their subsidiaries; or (ii) jeopardizes medicare/medicaid or insurance reimbursements or participations; (iii) if the business activities of the Partnership are contrary to the ethical principles of the Roman Catholic Church as designated from time to time; or (iv) is or may be in violation of any local, state or federal laws, rules or regulations. In the event that a Hospital Partner withdraws, such Hospital Partner's interest in the Partnership shall terminate on the date of withdrawal, and that interest, including, without limitation, the Hospital Partner's vote on the Board of Partners and its interest in the Partnership management fee, shall be reallocated among the remaining Hospital Partners. (If there are no remaining Hospital Partners, the reallocation shall be among the remaining Partners). Unless otherwise agreed, the withdrawing Hospital Partner shall only be entitled to receive for its interest in the Partnership an amount: which is equal to the balance in such Hospital Partner's capital account at the time of withdrawal.

* * *

When deciding whether St. Alphonsus's dissociation was wrongful, the district court considered only the first sentence in section 6.1 of the agreement. It concluded that the words "Any Hospital Partner may withdraw from the Partnership at any time if" followed by four defined circumstances was an express provision limiting the circumstances under which St. Alphonsus could rightfully dissociate. The court reasoned as follows:

> When reading contract terms, the Court must apply the ordinary and plain meaning to the words used. The word "if" is commonly defined as "a: in the event that, b: allowing that, c: on the assumption that, d: on condition that." Substituting one of these definitions into the contract language, section 6.1 allows the Hospital Partners to withdraw *on the condition that* one of the listed events occurs. In the reverse, if one of the four reasons is not present, the Hospital Partners *may not* withdraw from the partnership rightfully. In the Court's view, the use of "only" before "if" would be redundant in this context. The section, "Conditions for Withdrawal" lends further support to the Court's finding that "if" was expressly conditional language. (Emphases in original; citation and footnote omitted.)

The district court picked one definition of the word "if" ("on condition that") and concluded that section 6.1 established the conditions that must exist before a hospital partner could withdraw from the partnership without breaching the agreement. Another definition rejected by the court would also be consistent with the context. The sentence could be read to state that the hospital partner may withdraw *in the event that* one of the listed events occurs. For example, the second sentence of the section begins, "In the event that a Hospital Partner withdraws * * *" It would not change the meaning to substitute "If" for "In the event that." The district court found some support for its interpretation by the section title, "Conditions for Withdrawal." However, the word "conditions" is synonymous with "circumstances." *Roget's II: The New Thesaurus* 164 (Houghton Mifflin Co.1988). With "if" and "conditions" given these alternative meanings, the section is not an *express* provision limiting the circumstances under which St. Alphonsus could withdraw without breaching the partnership agreement.

With these meanings, the section would provide that St. Alphonsus could withdraw from the partnership in the event that any of four circumstances occurred. To conclude it prohibited withdrawal unless one of those four circumstances occurred, one would have to apply the maxim *expressio unius est exclusio alterius* (the expression of one thing is the exclusion of another). "When certain persons or things are specified in a law, contract, or will, an intention to exclude all others from its operation may be inferred." *Black's Law Dictionary* 581 (6th ed.1990). Application of the maxim is not mandatory. However, even if that maxim were applied to *infer* that these four circumstances were exclusive, that would not be an *express* provision limiting the circumstances in which St. Alphonsus could rightfully dissociate.

* * *

[RUPA § 602(b)(1)] provides that a dissociation is wrongful if it is "in breach of an express provision of the partnership agreement." The statute does not simply provide that dissociation is wrongful if it is in breach of the partnership agreement, or if it is in breach of a provision in the partnership agreement. It is only wrongful if it breaches an *express* provision of the partnership agreement. We have defined the word "express" as follows: "Black's Law Dictionary defines 'express' as, '[c]lear; definite; explicit; plain; direct; unmistakable; not dubious or ambiguous. Declared in terms; set forth in words. Directly and distinctly stated. Made known distinctly and explicitly, and not left to inference. 'Express' means 'manifested by direct and appropriate language.'" *Sweeney v. Otter,* 804 P.2d 308, 313 (1990) (citations omitted). Because the provision limiting the right to withdraw rightfully must be an express provision, any doubt as to the meaning of the provision at issue must be resolved in favor of not limiting the right to withdraw. The provision of the partnership agreement at issue does not contain any prohibitive language. For example, it does not state that a hospital partner *shall not* withdraw from the partnership *except* under the specified circumstances. Likewise, it does not state that a hospital partner may *only* withdraw from the partnership under the specified circumstances. We hold that the provision is not an express provision limiting the right to dissociate rightfully.

St. Alphonsus was clearly prejudiced by the district court's determination that it had wrongfully dissociated from the partnership. * * * In this case, the court's erroneous instructions regarding wrongful dissociation were prejudicial in two respects. First, the court instructed the jury that St. Alphonsus had wrongfully dissociated, and the jury need only determine the amount of damages proximately caused by such wrongful dissociation. In the special verdict, the jury found that MRIA had been damaged by that wrongful dissociation. The jury awarded damages [$36.3 million], which were not separated by cause of action. Second, instructing the jury at the beginning of the trial that "the Court has already determined as a matter of law" that St. Alphonsus had breached the partnership agreement when it dissociated and instructing the jury at the conclusion of the evidence that the "facts are not in dispute" that St. Alphonsus's dissociation "has been determined by the Court to be a wrongful dissociation" could have affected the jury's determination on MRIA's other causes of action.

* * *

IV. CONCLUSION

We vacate the judgment and verdict and remand this case for further proceedings that are consistent with this opinion. * * *

NOTES

(1) Did St. Alphonsus have the power to dissociate? If so, why did it matter whether its dissociation was rightful or wrongful? *See* RUPA §§ 601–603, 701, 801.

(2) If section 6.1 of the partnership agreement did not expressly limit a partner's right to dissociate, what was the purpose of specifying the "conditions for withdrawal" in that section? Is it relevant that UPA was the partnership law in effect in Idaho at the time the parties entered into the agreement?

(3) In *Horizon/CMS Healthcare Corp. v. Southern Oaks Health Care, Inc.*, 732 So. 2d 1156, 1159–61 (Fla. Dist. Ct. App. 1999), Southern Oaks asserted that it was entitled to lost future profits because Horizon had wrongfully dissolved the partnership. The court rejected the claim:

> * * * Under RUPA, it is clear that wrongful *dissociation* triggers liability for lost future profits. *See* [RUPA § 602(c)]. However, RUPA does *not* contain a similar provision for dissolution; RUPA does not refer to the dissolutions as rightful or wrongful. [RUPA § 801], "Events causing dissolution and winding up of partnership business," outlines the events causing dissolution without any provision for liability for damages. * * *
>
> Certainly the law predating RUPA allowed for recovery of lost profits upon the wrongful dissolution of a partnership. However, RUPA brought significant changes to partnership law, among which was the adoption of the term "dissociation." Although the term is undefined in RUPA, dissociation appears to have taken the place of "dissolution" as that word was used pre-RUPA. "Dissolution" under RUPA has a different meaning, although the term is undefined in RUPA. It follows that the pre-RUPA cases providing for future damages upon wrongful dissolution are no longer applicable to a partnership dissolution. In other words a "wrongful dissolution" referred to in the pre-RUPA case law is now, under RUPA, known as "wrongful dissociation." Simply stated, under [RUPA § 602], only when a partner *dissociates* and the dissociation is wrongful can the remaining partners sue for damages. * * *

PROBLEM

How would the dissociation and dissolution issues in the following cases be resolved under RUPA: (1) *Collins v. Lewis*; (2) *Dreifuerst v. Dreifuerst*; (3) *Bohatch v. Butler & Binion*?

CHAPTER 4

THE DEVELOPMENT OF CORPORATION LAW IN THE UNITED STATES: JURISDICTIONAL COMPETITION

■ ■ ■

In England the power to award corporate charters was first assumed by the Crown and later by Parliament. In the American colonies, during the pre-revolutionary period, colonial legislatures granted some corporate charters under the presumed authority of the British Parliament. For many years, this power was exercised sparingly, usually limited to ventures of a public or quasi-public nature. Charters often contained numerous restrictions. Perhaps as a result of the English heritage (which often combined corporate charters with grants of monopoly power), corporations were viewed with suspicion and mistrust.

Following independence and the adoption of the federal Constitution, state legislatures continued to grant corporate charters, many of them for banks. After the War of 1812, the number of corporate charters increased rapidly; in addition to banks, corporations were formed to construct canals and turnpikes. Many of these early charters granted special privileges in the form of monopolies or exclusive franchises. Intensive industrial development began in about 1825. The corporation proved to be an ideal instrument for this development because it could raise large amounts of capital from numerous investors and provide centralized direction of large industrial concerns.

The federal government incorporated the Bank of the United States by statute in 1791. However, doubt continued to exist as to the general power of the federal government to create corporations for general economic purposes, and as a result states continued to form business corporations. Even today, with the power of the federal government to create corporations firmly established, that power is rarely exercised and then only for predominantly public purposes. The formation of business corporations in the United States is firmly in the hands of the states, as is control over the relationships between the investors and the managers of business organizations. As the Supreme Court has noted, "[c]orporations are creatures of state law, and investors commit their funds to corporate directors on the understanding that, except where federal law *expressly* requires certain responsibilities of directors with respect to stockholders, state law will govern the internal affairs of the corporation." Santa Fe Industries v. Green, 430 U.S. 462, 479 (1977) (quoting Cort v. Ash, 422 U.S. 66, 84 (1975)); Business Roundtable v. S.E.C., 905 F.2d 406 (D.C.Cir.1990).

Originally, state legislatures approved each individual corporate charter. Approval of a charter was a political act, involving lobbying, political influence, campaign contributions, and sometimes worse. The first general incorporation statutes permitting businesses to incorporate by action of an administrative agency without specific legislative approval were adopted in Pennsylvania in 1836 and in Connecticut in 1840. This innovation quickly became popular so that by 1859 twenty-five out of the then existing thirty-eight states and territories had enacted general incorporation statutes. By 1890, all states had adopted general incorporation statutes.

The enactment of general and unlimited corporation statutes by New Jersey and other states, followed by Delaware's enactment of its General Corporation Law in 1899, touched off a vigorous jurisdictional competition for corporate charters among the states. This race is vividly described in the following excerpt.

LOUIS K. LIGGETT CO. v. LEE

Supreme Court of the United States, 1933.
288 U.S. 517, 548–65.

MR. JUSTICE BRANDEIS, dissenting. * * *

* * * The prevalence of the corporation in America has led men of this generation to act, at times, as if the privilege of doing business in corporate form were inherent in the citizen; and has led them to accept the evils attendant upon the free and unrestricted use of the corporate mechanism as if these evils were the inescapable price of civilized life, and, hence, to be borne with resignation. Throughout the greater part of our history a different view prevailed. Although the value of this instrumentality in commerce and industry was fully recognized, incorporation for business was commonly denied long after it had been freely granted for religious, educational, and charitable purposes. It was denied because of fear. Fear of encroachment upon the liberties and opportunities of the individual. Fear of the subjection of labor to capital. Fear of monopoly. Fear that the absorption of capital by corporations, and their perpetual life, might bring evils similar to those which attended mortmain. There was a sense of some insidious menace inherent in large aggregations of capital, particularly when held by corporations. So at first the corporate privilege was granted sparingly; and only when the grant seemed necessary in order to procure for the community some specific benefit otherwise unattainable. The later enactment of general incorporation laws does not signify that the apprehension of corporate domination had been overcome. The desire for

business expansion created an irresistible demand for more charters; and it was believed that under general laws embodying safeguards of universal application the scandals and favoritism incident to special incorporation could be avoided. The general laws, which long embodied severe restrictions upon size and upon the scope of corporate activity, were, in part, an expression of the desire for equality of opportunity.

(a) Limitation upon the amount of the authorized capital of business corporations was long universal. The maximum limit frequently varied with the kinds of business to be carried on, being dependent apparently upon the supposed requirements of the efficient unit. Although the statutory limits were changed from time to time, this principle of limitation was long retained. Thus in New York the limit was at first $100,000 for some businesses and as little as $50,000 for others. Until 1881 the maximum for business corporations in New York was $2,000,000; and until 1890, $5,000,000. In Massachusetts the limit was at first $200,000 for some businesses and as little as $5,000 for others. Until 1871 the maximum for mechanical and manufacturing corporations was $500,000; and until 1899, $1,000,000. The limit of $1,000,000 was retained for some businesses until 1903.

In many other states, including the leading ones in some industries, the removal of the limitations upon size was more recent. Pennsylvania did not remove the limits until 1905. * * * Michigan did not remove the maximum limit until 1921. * * * Missouri did not remove its maximum limit until 1927. Texas still has such a limit for certain corporations.

(b) Limitations upon the scope of a business corporation's powers and activity were also long universal. At first, corporations could be formed under the general laws only for a limited number of purposes—usually those which required a relatively large fixed capital, like transportation, banking and insurance, and mechanical, mining, and manufacturing enterprises. Permission to incorporate for "any lawful purpose" was not common until 1875; and until that time the duration of corporate franchises was generally limited to a period of 20, 30, or 50 years. All, or a majority, of the incorporators or directors, or both, were required to be residents of the incorporating state. The powers which the corporation might exercise in carrying out its purposes were sparingly conferred and strictly construed. Severe limitations were imposed on the amount of indebtedness, bonded or otherwise. The power to hold stock in other corporations was not conferred or implied. The holding company was impossible.

(c) The removal by the leading industrial states of the limitations upon the size and powers of business corporations appears to have been due, not to their conviction that maintenance of the restrictions was undesirable in itself, but to the conviction that it was futile to insist upon them; because local restriction would be circumvented by foreign incorporation. Indeed, local restriction seemed worse than futile. Lesser states, eager for the revenue derived from the traffic in charters, had removed safeguards from their own incorporation laws.[34] Companies were early formed to provide charters for corporations in states where the cost was lowest and the laws least restrictive.[35] The states joined in advertising their wares.[36] The race was one not of diligence but of laxity. Incorporation under such laws was possible; and the great industrial States yielded in order not to lose wholly the prospect of the revenue and the control incident to domestic incorporation.

---

[34] The traffic in charters quickly became widespread. In 1894 Cook on Stock and Stockholders (3d Ed.) Vol. II, pp. 1604, 1605, thus described the situation: "New Jersey is a favorite state for incorporations. Her laws seem to be framed with a special view to attracting incorporation fees and business fees from her sister states and especially from New York, across the river. She has largely succeeded in doing so, and now runs the state government very largely on revenues derived from New York enterprises." * * *

In 1906 John S. Parker thus described the practice, in his volume Where and How—A Corporation Handbook (2d Ed.) p. 4:

Many years ago the corporation laws of New Jersey were so framed as to invite the incorporation of companies by persons residing in other states and countries. The liberality and facility with which corporations could there be formed were extensively advertised, and a great volume of incorporation swept into that state. * * *

The policy of New Jersey proved profitable to the state, and soon legislatures of other states began active competition. * * *

Delaware and Maine also revised their laws, taking the New Jersey act as a model, but with lower organization fees and annual taxes. Arizona and South Dakota also adopted liberal corporation laws, and contenting themselves with the incorporation fees, require no annual state taxes whatever.

West Virginia for many years has been popular with incorporators, but in 1901, in the face of the growing competition of other states, the legislature increased the rate of annual taxes. And West Virginia thus lost her popularity. See Conyngton and Bennett, Corporation Procedure (Rev.Ed.1927), p. 712. On the other hand, too drastic price cutting was also unprofitable. The bargain prices in Arizona and South Dakota attracted wild cat corporations. Investors became wary of corporations organized under the laws of Arizona or South Dakota and both states fell in disrepute among them and consequently among incorporators. See Conyngton on Corporate Organizations (1913) c. 5.

[35] Thus, in its pamphlet "Business Corporations Under the Laws of Maine" (1903), the Corporation Trust Company enumerated among the advantages of the Maine laws: The comparatively low organization fees and annual taxes; the absence of restrictions upon capital stock or corporate indebtedness; the authority to issue stock for services as well as property, with the judgment of the directors as to their value conclusive; and, significantly enough, "the method of taxation, which bases the annual tax upon the stock issued, does not necessitate inquiry into or report upon the intimate affairs of the corporation." * * * See, also, the Red Book on Arizona Corporation Laws (1908), published by the Incorporating Company of Arizona, especially page 5:

The remoteness of Arizona from the Eastern and Southern States has in a measure delayed the promulgation of the generousness of its laws. New Jersey, Delaware and West Virginia have become widely known as incorporating states. More recently Arizona, [South] Dakota, New Mexico and Nevada have come into more or less prominence by the passage of laws with liberal features.

[36] Thus, in an official pamphlet containing the corporation laws of Delaware (1901), the secretary of state wrote in the preface: "It is believed that no state has on its statute books more complete and liberal laws than these"; and the outstanding advantages were then enumerated. * * * See, also, "The General Corporation Act of New Jersey" (1898), edited by J.B. Dill, issued by the secretary of state: "Since 1875 it has been the announced and settled policy of New Jersey to attract incorporated capital to the State. * * *" P. xvii.

The history of the changes made by New York is illustrative. The New York revision of 1890, which eliminated the maximum limitation on authorized capital, and permitted intercorporate stockholding in a limited class of cases, was passed after a migration of incorporation from New York, attracted by the more liberal incorporation laws of New Jersey. But the changes made by New York in 1890 were not sufficient to stem the tide. In 1892, the Governor of New York approved a special charter for the General Electric Company, modeled upon the New Jersey act, on the ground that otherwise the enterprise would secure a New Jersey charter. Later in the same year the New York corporation law was again revised, allowing the holding of stock in other corporations. But the New Jersey law still continued to be more attractive to incorporators. By specifically providing that corporations might be formed in New Jersey to do all their business elsewhere, the state made its policy unmistakably clear. Of the seven largest trusts existing in 1904, with an aggregate capitalization of over two and a half billion dollars, all were organized under New Jersey law; and three of these were formed in 1899. During the first seven months of that year, 1336 corporations were organized under the laws of New Jersey, with an aggregate authorized capital of over two billion dollars. The Comptroller of New York, in his annual report for 1899, complained that "our tax list reflects little of the great wave of organization that has swept over the country during the past year and to which this state contributed more capital than any other state in the Union." "It is time," he declared, "that great corporations having their actual headquarters in this State and a nominal office elsewhere, doing nearly all of their business within our borders, should be brought within the jurisdiction of this State not only as to matters of taxation but in respect to other and equally important affairs." In 1901 the New York corporation law was again revised. * * *

Able, discerning scholars have pictured for us the economic and social results of thus removing all limitations upon the size and activities of business corporations and of vesting in their managers vast powers once exercised by stockholders—results not designed by the states and long unsuspected. They show that size alone gives to giant corporations a social significance not attached ordinarily to smaller units of private enterprise. Through size, corporations, once merely an efficient tool employed by individuals in the conduct of private business have become an institution—an institution which has brought such concentration of economic power that so-called private corporations are sometimes able to dominate the state. The typical business corporation of the last century, owned by a small group of individuals, managed by their owners, and limited in size by their personal wealth, is being supplanted by huge concerns in which the lives of tens or hundreds of thousands of employees and the property of tens or hundreds of thousands of investors are subjected, through the corporate mechanism, to the control of a few men. Ownership has been separated from control; and this separation has removed many of the checks which formerly operated to curb the misuse of wealth and power. And, as ownership of the shares is becoming continually more dispersed, the power which formerly accompanied ownership is becoming increasingly concentrated in the hands of a few. The changes thereby wrought in the lives of the workers, of the owners and of the general public are so fundamental and far-reaching as to lead these scholars to compare the evolving "corporate system" with the feudal system; and to lead other men of insight and experience to assert that this "master institution of civilised life" is committing it to the rule of a plutocracy. * * *

In the twentieth and twenty-first centuries, Delaware in particular has maintained a hospitable climate for corporations. The success of this small state in attracting and retaining corporation business has been the subject of considerable scholarly interest and debate.

NOTES

(1) The importance of the law of the state of incorporation (in addition to such mundane matters as differences in franchise taxes) is greatly enhanced by the so-called "internal affairs rule," which provides that foreign courts should apply the law of the state of incorporation to issues relating to the internal affairs of a foreign corporation. See MBCA § 15.05(c); Restatement of Conflict of Laws (2d) § 302.

(2) California is the principal state that has sought to apply specific provisions of its corporation statutes to corporations formed in other states but whose principal business activities are in California. California Corporations Code § 2115 requires corporations with "specified minimum contacts" in California to comply with designated provisions of the California statute: among others, sections dealing with cumulative voting, limitations on distributions, inspection rights of shareholders, and dissenters' rights. The section is not applicable to corporations with shares listed on national securities exchanges or NASDAQ. The constitutionality of this approach has not been definitively resolved. See Wilson v. Louisiana-Pacific Resources, Inc., 187 Cal.Rptr. 852 (Cal.App.1982) (upholding the imposition of the California cumulative voting provisions upon a Utah corporation that was subject to § 2115); Valtz v. Penta Inv. Corp., 188 Cal.Rptr. 922 (Cal.App.1983) (applying the California shareholders' inspection statute to a foreign corporation). But see State Farm Mut. Auto Ins. Co. v. Superior Court, 8 Cal.Rptr.3d 56 (Cal.App.2003) (questioning the validity of the holding in *Wilson* following the broad acceptance of the internal affairs doctrine over the two decades after *Wilson* was decided); VantagePoint Venture Partners 1996 v. Examen, Inc., 871 A.2d 1108 (Del. 2005) (refusing to apply § 2115 and California law to allow a class vote by preferred shares on a proposed merger involving Examen, a Delaware corporation: "[W]e hold Delaware's well-established choice of law rules and the federal constitution mandated that Examen's internal affairs, and in particular, VantagePoint's voting rights, be adjudicated exclusively in accordance with the law of its state of

incorporation, in this case, the law of Delaware."). For a further discussion of litigation with respect to § 2115 and similar statutes, see Norwood P. Beveridge Jr., The Internal Affairs Doctrine: The Proper Law of a Corporation, 44 Bus. Law 693, 702–09 (1989).

(3) According to the Delaware Corporate Law website, Delaware is the state of incorporation for "more than half" of all U.S. publicly traded companies and 64% of the companies on Fortune Magazine's list of the 500 largest companies in the United States. See http://corplaw.delaware.gov/eng/facts_myths.shtml (last visited Jan. 18, 2014).

(4) In 1999, the Chief Justice of the Delaware Supreme Court, E. Norman Veasey, stated that a major reason for the success of the Delaware General Corporation Law was the "transformation of the archaic Judicial Branch structure and judicial selection method that existed at the end of the Nineteenth Century to a modern judicial selection system which, together with a modern corporation law, propelled the Delaware bench and bar to international prominence." E. Norman Veasey, The Drama of Judicial Branch Change in this Century, 17 Delaware Lawyer (Winter 1999–2000), at 4–5. He described the current role of the State of Delaware in the corporation world as follows:

> * * * [D]epoliticizing the Judiciary attract[ed] to the Bench quality people whose focus is likely to be on service and scholarship. This may well be the central reason why Delaware has attracted over 300,000 corporations, including more than half of the Fortune 500 and half of the New York Stock Exchange corporations. It has also attracted some of the finest lawyers in America to our Bar. The role of the Judiciary complements the outstanding work of the Bar, the General Assembly and the Secretary of State's office.

(5) The high quality of the Delaware judiciary in corporate matters does not entirely explain Delaware's spectacular success in the incorporation business. Writing in 1976, Professor Seligman suggested that the advantage of Delaware lies "not [in] her statute alone, but rather [in] the manner in which her judiciary interprets it." Joel Seligman, A Brief History of Delaware's General Corporation Law of 1899, 1 Del.J.Corp.Law 249, 284 (1976). In reaching this conclusion, Professor Seligman relied primarily on an earlier article by Professor William L. Cary, a former chairman of the SEC, who, after reviewing a number of Delaware decisions, concluded that "there is no public policy left in Delaware corporate law except the objective of raising revenue. * * * Consciously or unconsciously, fiduciary standards and standards of fairness generally have been relaxed. In general, the judicial decisions can best be reconciled on the basis of a desire to foster incorporation in Delaware." William L. Cary, Federalism and Corporate Law: Reflections Upon Delaware, 83 Yale L.J. 663, 670, 684 (1974). Professor Cary attributed this attitude to the relationship between the Delaware bench, bar, and state government:

> What is striking about the membership of the court in the last 23 years is that almost all the justices were drawn from the group

responsible for the 1967 revision of the corporation law. In fact, two of them were members of the Commission. A majority of the justices practiced law in the firms which represent the important corporations registered in Delaware. * * * Three left the bench, two of them to return to leading firms in Delaware, and one to become Governor. With the exception of Justice Carey, who served from 1945 on the bench in various roles, all but two of the justices have been directly involved in major political positions in the state. The three chief justices have been chronologically (1) Attorney General, (2) Secretary of State and Governor, and (3) the Democratic candidate for Attorney General. Two other justices were Chairman of the State Planning Commission and attorney for the Delaware Senate. The whole process is reminiscent of musical chairs. In such a small state as Delaware, with a population of 548,000 and a bar of 733, of whom 423 are in private practice, we have in microcosm the ultimate example of the relationship between politics, the bar, and the judiciary. There is certainly nothing "wrong" or surprising about these relationships. Yet it is clear that Delaware may be characterized as a tight little club in which the corporate bar cites unreported decisions before the courts in which they practice. Thus major participation in state politics and in the leading firms inevitably would align the Delaware judiciary solidly with Delaware legislative policy. Indeed, as outstanding members of the bar, they may have contributed to its formulation before they became judges, and at any rate, might be disloyal to their state to pursue any other course.

Id. at 690–92.

This was harsh criticism, and it is not surprising that defenders of the Delaware General Corporation Law reacted sharply and with outrage. E.g., S. Samuel Arsht, Reply to Professor Cary, 31 Bus.Law. 1113 (1976):

Professor Cary premises his advocacy of a Federal Corporate Minimum Standards Act upon the alleged deficiencies of state law, particularly focusing upon Delaware, its statutes, bench and bar. I submit that Professor Cary's analysis of the Delaware experience is biased, unscholarly and wholly unfair. If his articles had to measure up to the required standards of an SEC disclosure document, they would be found woefully deficient.

(6) Ralph Winter, Government and the Corporation 9 (1978):

Rejecting full federal chartering as "politically unrealistic," Cary calls for federal minimum-standards legislation. He claims this legislation, designed to "raise" the standards of management conduct, would increase public confidence—and investment—in American corporations. This last claim, it is absolutely critical to note, is not that an overriding social goal is sacrificed by state law but that Delaware is preventing *private* parties from optimizing their *private* arrangements.

With all due respect to Cary and to the almost universal academic support for his position, it is implausible on its face. The plausible argument runs in exactly the opposite direction. (1) If Delaware permits corporate management to profit at the expense of shareholders and other states do not, then earnings of Delaware corporations must be less than earnings of comparable corporations chartered in other states; therefore, shares in the Delaware corporations must trade at lower prices. (2) Corporations with lower earnings will be at a disadvantage in raising debt or equity capital. (3) Corporations at a disadvantage in the capital market will be at a disadvantage in the product market, and their share price will decline, thereby increasing chances of a takeover that would replace management. To avoid this result, corporations must seek legal systems more attractive to capital. (4) States desiring corporate charters will thus try to provide legal systems that optimize the shareholder-corporation relation. * * *

(7) Whatever the merits of Professor Cary's complaints about the "cozy" relationship between the Delaware judiciary, the Bar, and the legislature in the 1970s, it is clear that the Delaware judiciary is highly regarded today. The Delaware Chancery Court, the trial court in which most corporation issues are litigated, is a specialized business and corporation court that is the envy of other states.[a] This court sits without a jury and handles local equity matters as well as major commercial disputes. Corporations often prefer to litigate issues in Delaware rather than elsewhere because of the knowledge, expertise, sophistication, and experience of the Chancellor and the four Vice Chancellors on corporate matters.

(8) Efforts to explain the success of Delaware have become virtually a cottage industry for corporate theorists. For example, it has been suggested that Delaware is successful because it reduces regulatory costs through limiting network externalities,[b] because of its "regulatory responsiveness,"[c] or because of the superiority of its Court of Chancery.[d] Another explanation is the advantage provided by the large developed body of case law in Delaware.[e] A less generous explanation is the apparent dependence of Delaware legislators on corporate and corporate-related campaign contributions, which assures that

---

[a]   Several states have created specialized business courts modeled roughly after the Delaware Chancery Court. The trend towards such courts "is in its inception but is gaining strength." Report of Ad Hoc Committee on Business Courts, Business Courts: Towards a More Efficient Judiciary, 52 Bus. Law. 947, 960 (1997). This report indicates that three states (New York, Illinois, and North Carolina) have established business courts since 1992, and that studies are underway in at least six additional states.

[b]   Marcel Kahan and Michael Klausner, Standardization and Innovation in Corporate Contracting (or "The Economics of Boilerplate"), 83 Va.L.Rev. 713, 763–74 (1997).

[c]   Roberta Romano, The Genius of American Corporate Law 38 (1993).

[d]   Curtis Alva, Delaware and the Market for Corporate Charters: History and Agency, 15 Del.J.Corp.Law 885, 918 (1990).

[e]   Stephen J. Massey, Chancellor Allen's Jurisprudence and the Theory of Corporate Law, 17 Del.J.Corp.L. 683, 702 n. 79 (1992); Henry G. Manne, The Judiciary and Free Markets, 21 Harv. J.L. & Pub. Pol'y 11, 18 (1997).

they will quickly address corporate needs. It has also been suggested that the willingness of Delaware judges to engage in corporate lawmaking explains Delaware's success.[f] Finally, a partial explanation lies in the efficiency of the Delaware courts in considering and resolving significant corporate litigation.[g]

(9) The Delaware Corporate Law website provides its own explanation for the state's "dominance in business formation." It cites the Delaware statute, the courts, the case law, the legal tradition, and the quality of the Secretary of State's Office. See http://corplaw.delaware.gov/eng/why_delaware. shtml (last visited Jan. 18, 2014).

(10) While it is clear that Delaware competes vigorously to maintain its dominant position in the jurisdictional competition for corporate charters, it is less clear how effective other states have been at competing with Delaware. For the view that "Delaware's dominant position in the incorporations market is far stronger and more secure than has been previously recognized," and that "structural features of the market for corporate law * * * make it unprofitable for other small states to challenge Delaware's position," see Bebchuk and Hamdani, Vigorous Race or Leisurely Walk: Reconsidering the Debate on State Competition Over Corporate Charters, 112 Yale L.J. 553 (2002). Professors Bebchuk and Hamdani point out that small states like South Dakota could cut taxes by half if they could capture the sort of revenues that Delaware garners from its incorporation business. Nonetheless, Bebchuk and Hamdani argue that "network and learning externalities" make it difficult for other states to compete with Delaware. By this the authors mean that corporations find Delaware incorporation valuable precisely because other corporations locate there. As more and more corporations choose to incorporate in Delaware, Delaware incorporations become increasingly valuable and other states find it increasingly difficult to compete.

(11) Several event studies were conducted in the 1980s to try to determine the effect of management discretion to choose the state of incorporation and thus the law that governs the corporation. The studies concluded that the choice benefited shareholders, but some criticized the studies for placing too much import on the change in stock price after reincorporation and failing to

---

[f] Jill E. Fisch, The Peculiar Role of the Delaware Courts in the Competition for Corporate Charters, 68 Cincinnati L.Rev. 1061 (2000). The author states: "The article concludes that Delaware lawmaking offers Delaware corporations a variety of benefits, including flexibility, responsiveness, insulation from undue political influence, and transparency. These benefits increase Delaware's ability to adjust its corporate law to changes in the business world."

[g] See Mark J. Loewenstein, Delaware As Demon: Twenty–Five Years After Professor Cary's Polemic, 71 U.Colo.L.Rev. 497, 505 (2000):

Regardless of the provisions of the corporate code, Delaware's superior judiciary would persist and provide a good reason to incorporate in Delaware. The Delaware Chancery Court * * * hears 500 business-related cases a year. The Chancery Court resolves those cases promptly, and its decisions are rarely appealed. Only five percent of its decisions are appealed to the state Supreme Court—Delaware has no intermediate appellate court—and in those appeals the Supreme Court upholds the Chancery Court in seventy-five percent of the cases. If a case is appealed to the Supreme Court, that court generally renders a decision in about thirty days from submission. Thus, litigants know that Delaware will provide a prompt resolution of their dispute, and corporate managers might well value this in deciding where to incorporate.

account for other possible explanations for the change. Responding to such criticism, Professor Robert Daines used a different methodology to test the economic effects on corporations of reincorporating in Delaware. Professor Daines compared the "Tobin's Q" of companies incorporated in Delaware with the Tobin's Q of companies not incorporated in Delaware. Tobin's Q measures the relationship between the market value of a company's stock and the book value of the company's assets. Tobin's Q is a widely used measure of the value of a company's assets as they are presently deployed. The greater the difference between the market value of the firm's stock and the book value of the assets, the more efficiently management is deploying those assets. Professor Daines found that Delaware companies had a higher Tobin's Q than other companies, even after controlling for a wide range of other factors. This implies that incorporating in Delaware allows for a more efficient deployment of a firm's assets. Robert Daines, Does Delaware Improve Firm Value?, 62 J. Fin. Econ. 525 (2001).

(12) Professor Roberta Romano examined the diffusion of corporate law innovations—such as limits on director liability and takeover regulation—and concluded that changes in corporate law are produced via a dynamic process in which states initially experiment with various approaches to solving a perceived problem. After this experimentation period, a majority settles on one formula. The result is "substantial uniformity across the states." Roberta Romano, The States as a Laboratory: Legal Innovation and State Competition For Corporate Charters, 23 Yale J. on Reg. 209, 246 (2006). She described the relationship between federalism and corporate law innovation as follows:

> The development of corporate law has been left to the states with sporadic federal intervention: the New Deal laws regulating the issuance of securities, the terms of cash takeover bids, and most recently, audit committees and executive loans. Federalism has succeeded in this domain because the states have sorted out amongst themselves who has exclusive jurisdiction over corporate law to minimize conflict by adopting an "internal affairs" jurisdictional rule in which the governing choice of law rule is the corporation's statutory domicile. This contrasts with other potential conflict rules, such as physical domicile (the corporate law conflicts rule in most of continental Europe) or the domicile of the buyer or seller of a firm's securities (U.S. states' securities law conflicts rule). The latter conflicts rule would subject firms operating across state lines to multiple legal regimes in the absence of federal regulation.

* * *

> The states' agreement on the internal affairs jurisdictional rule has had important consequences for the development of corporate law. The ease of selecting a domicile whose exclusive jurisdiction is legally recognized has resulted in considerable experimentation and innovation in corporate law, as states have sought to retain locally-domiciled firms by offering up-to-date codes to meet changing

business conditions. The output of this competition has been, for the most part, welfare-enhancing. This contention may be best illustrated by the fact that consumers of corporate law—investors, managers, and their lobbying organizations—have not advocated replacing the states' authority with either the federal government, or purely private contracts and self-regulating organizations, despite some academic support for both of those alternatives. In this regard, the production of corporate law stands as an exemplar of the advantage of a federal system: State competition for incorporations has spurred an innovative legal process that is responsive to a rapidly changing business environment to the benefit of firms and their investors.

Id. at 210–11.

(13) In their 1932 seminal work on the corporation, Adolph Berle and Gardiner Means discussed what the authors perceived to be the social and economic problems generated by the separation of ownership and control in the modern publicly held corporation. At the heart of Berle and Means' account of the corporation's role in society was their statistical work in which they made two famous claims. First, they claimed that the top 200 corporations in America were vastly larger and controlled far more wealth than all other companies. This top 200, according to Berle and Means' data, controlled almost 50% of U.S. corporate wealth and 38% of the nation's business assets. Compounding this concentration of economic power was the fact that the top managers of these firms owned only a very small fraction of the shares in these firms, but controlled all of their assets. From this observation sprang the famous notion of the "problem" of "the separation of ownership and control" of the modern public corporation.

Berle and Means' ultimate empirical observations were that:

The rise of the modern corporation has brought a concentration of economic power which can compete on equal terms with the modern state. * * * Where its own interests are concerned, it even attempts to dominate the state. The future may see the economic organism, now typified by the corporation, not only on an equal plane with the state, but possibly even superseding it as the dominant form of social organization.[h]

The corporation never approached being the political and economic monolith that Berle and Means feared for the simple reason that competition, in product markets, labor markets, and, above all, capital markets, imposed serious constraints on the freedom of managers and other corporate actors to pursue their own, selfish ends at the expense of investors. Competition imposes rigorous discipline, including the ultimate sanction of bankruptcy, on firms that pursue their own interests at the expense of their investors.

Berle and Means' concern about the concentration of economic and political power in the hands of managers can be found in current discussions of

---

[h]   Berle and Means, The Modern Corporation and Private Property, at 313.

corporate regulation, with some commentators worrying that management wields undue influence over the kind of legislation that is passed and uses this influence to entrench its own power. The regulation of the market for corporate control has been cited as one area in which managers have been able to use their power to protect their authority.

(14) To some extent, corporate law rules are likely to reflect societal attitudes about the larger role of corporations within society. See Marco Pagano & Paolo Volpin, The Political Economy of Finance, Oxford Rev. Econ. Pol'y, Vol. 17, no. 4 (2001). (Chart shows the different perspectives on corporate governance that distinguish Anglo-American corporate governance systems from corporate governance systems in continental Europe and Asia.):

Differences in Perspectives on Corporate Governance: Preferences of Senior Managers about Corporate Objectives						
Survey question	**Possible Answers**	**Japan**	**Germany**	**France**	**USA**	**UK**
(1) Whose Company is it?	All stakeholders	97.1	82.7	78	24.4	29.5
	The shareholders	2.9	17.3	22	75.6	70.5
(1) No. of respondents:		68	110	50	82	78
(2) Which is more important?	Job Security	97.1	59.1	60.4	10.8	10.7
	Dividends	2.9	40.9	39.6	89.2	89.3
(2) No. of respondents:		68	105	68	83	75

DOLE FOOD COMPANY, INC. PROXY STATEMENT
June 8, 2001.

PROPOSAL NO. 3

REINCORPORATION IN DELAWARE

INTRODUCTION

For the reasons set forth below, the Board believes that it is in the best interests of Dole and its stockholders to change the state of incorporation of Dole from Hawaii to Delaware (the "Proposed Reincorporation"). * * *

The Proposed Reincorporation will be effected by merging Dole-Hawaii into a new Delaware corporation that is a wholly-owned subsidiary of Dole-Hawaii (the "Merger"). Upon completion of the Merger, Dole-Hawaii, as a corporate entity, will cease to exist and Dole-Delaware will succeed to the assets and liabilities of Dole-Hawaii and will continue to operate the business of Dole under its current name, Dole Food Company, Inc.

NO CHANGE IN THE CORPORATE NAME, BOARD MEMBERS, BUSINESS, MANAGEMENT, CAPITALIZATION, BOARD OF DIRECTORS STRUCTURE, EMPLOYEE BENEFIT PLANS OR LOCATION OF PRINCIPAL FACILITIES OF DOLE WILL OCCUR AS A RESULT OF THE PROPOSED REINCORPORATION.

Dole-Hawaii Common Stock is listed for trading on the New York Stock Exchange and the Pacific Exchange and, after the Merger, Dole-Delaware Common Stock will be traded on the New York Stock Exchange and the Pacific Exchange under the same symbol ("DOL") as the shares of Dole-Hawaii Common Stock are currently traded. There will be no interruption in the trading of Dole's Common Stock as a result of the Merger. * * * The Proposed Reincorporation includes the implementation of a new certificate of incorporation and by-laws for Dole-Delaware (the "Delaware Charter" and "Delaware By-Laws") to replace the current articles of association and by-laws of Dole-Hawaii (the "Hawaii Charter" and "Hawaii By-Laws"). As a Delaware corporation, Dole-Delaware will be subject to the Delaware General Corporation Law (the "Delaware Law"). Dole-Hawaii is subject to the corporation laws of Hawaii. Differences between the Delaware Charter and By-Laws, on the one hand, and the Hawaii Charter and By-Laws, on the other hand, must be viewed in the context of the differences between the Delaware Law and the corporation law of Hawaii. * * *

PRINCIPAL REASONS FOR THE REINCORPORATION PROPOSAL

For many years, Delaware has followed a policy of encouraging incorporation in that state and, in furtherance of that policy, has been a leader in adopting, construing, and implementing comprehensive, flexible corporate laws responsive to the legal and business needs of corporations organized under its laws. Many corporations have initially chosen Delaware, or chosen to reincorporate in Delaware, in a manner similar to that proposed by Dole. The Board of Directors believes that the principal reasons for considering such a reincorporation are:

- the development in Delaware over the last century of a well-established body of case law construing the Delaware General Corporation Law, which provides businesses with a greater measure of predictability than exist in any other jurisdiction; the certainty afforded by the well-established principles of corporate governance under the Delaware Law are of benefit to Dole and its stockholders and should increase Dole's ability to attract and retain outstanding directors and officers;

- the Delaware Law itself, which is generally acknowledged to be the most advanced and flexible corporate statute in the country;

- the Delaware Court of Chancery, which brings to its handling of complex corporate issues a level of experience, a speed of decision and a degree of sophistication and understanding unmatched by any other court in the country, and the Delaware Supreme Court, the only appeals court, which is highly regarded and currently consists primarily of former Vice Chancellors and corporate practitioners; and

- the Delaware General Assembly, which each year considers and adopts statutory amendments that have been proposed by the Corporation Law Section of the Delaware bar to meet changing business needs.

The Proposed Reincorporation will effect only a change in the legal domicile of Dole and other changes of a legal nature. The material changes are described in this Proxy Statement. The Proposed Reincorporation will NOT result in any change in the name, business, management, capitalization, board of directors structure, fiscal year, assets, liabilities or location of the principal facilities of Dole. The directors elected at the Annual Meeting to serve on the Board of Dole-Hawaii will become the directors of Dole-Delaware. * * *

NOTES

(1) Beginning in the 1960s and early 1970s, there has been a trend toward the gradual expansion of federal law at the expense of state law. These earlier expansions were largely based on broad construction of antifraud concepts in the Securities Exchange Act of 1934 and Rule 10b–5 promulgated thereunder, but this trend had stabilized by the mid-1970s. In the early 1980s, another movement toward federalization of state corporation law developed from the conservative "law and economics" movement's theory that a national market for "corporate control" of publicly held corporations existed with which states were powerless to interfere. The United States Supreme Court abruptly dismantled this theory in CTS Corp. v. Dynamics Corp. of America, 481 U.S. 69 (1987). Justice Powell's majority opinion strongly restated the traditional role of states in the regulation of state-created publicly held corporations:

> We think the Court of Appeals failed to appreciate the significance, for Commerce Clause analysis, of the fact that state regulation of corporate governance is regulation of entities whose very existence and attributes are a product of state law. * * *

> * * * Every State in this country has enacted laws regulating corporate governance. By prohibiting certain transactions, and regulating others, such laws necessarily affect certain aspects of interstate commerce. This necessarily is true with respect to corporations with shareholders in States other than the State of incorporation. Large corporations that are listed on national exchanges, or even regional exchanges, will have shareholders in

many States and shares that are traded frequently. The markets that facilitate this national and international participation in ownership of corporations are essential for providing capital not only for new enterprises but also for established companies that need to expand their businesses. This beneficial free market system depends at its core upon the fact that a corporation—except in the rarest situations—is organized under, and governed by, the law of a single jurisdiction, traditionally the corporate law of the State of its incorporation.

These regulatory laws may affect directly a variety of corporate transactions. Mergers are a typical example. In view of the substantial effect that a merger may have on the shareholders' interests in a corporation, many States require supermajority votes to approve mergers. By requiring a greater vote for mergers than is required for other transactions, these laws make it more difficult for corporations to merge. State laws also may provide for "dissenters' rights" under which minority shareholders who disagree with corporate decisions to take particular actions are entitled to sell their shares to the corporation at fair market value. See * * * [MBCA § 13.02]. By requiring the corporation to purchase the shares of dissenting shareholders, these laws may inhibit a corporation from engaging in the specified transactions.[12]

It thus is an accepted part of the business landscape in this country for States to create corporations, to prescribe their powers, and to define the rights that are acquired by purchasing their shares. A State has an interest in promoting stable relationships among parties involved in the corporations it charters, as well as in ensuring that investors in such corporations have an effective voice in corporate affairs.

481 U.S. at 89–91.

(2) More recently, some of the provisions of the Sarbanes-Oxley Act of 2002 override traditional state law. For example, executive compensation, which typically is the province of state law, is affected by Sarbanes-Oxley in a couple of ways. First, section 1103 gives the Securities and Exchange Commission the power to seek a freeze of "extraordinary payments" made to

---

[12] Numerous other common regulations may affect both nonresident and resident shareholders of a corporation. Specified votes may be required for the sale of all of the corporation's assets. See * * * [MBCA § 12.02]. The election of directors may be staggered over a period of years to prevent abrupt changes in management. See * * * [MBCA § 8.06]. Various classes of stock may be created with differences in voting rights as to dividends and on liquidation. See * * * [MBCA § 6.01(c)]. Provisions may be made for cumulative voting. See * * * [MBCA § 7.28]. Corporations may adopt restrictions on payment of dividends to ensure that specified ratios of assets to liabilities are maintained for the benefit of the holders of corporate bonds or notes. See * * * [MBCA § 6.40 (noting that a corporation's articles of incorporation can restrict payment of dividends)]. Where the shares of a corporation are held in States other than that of incorporation, actions taken pursuant to these and similar provisions of state law will affect all shareholders alike wherever they reside or are domiciled. * * *

corporate officers and directors during the course of an SEC investigation into possible securities law violations. If the officer or director is charged with violating a securities law, the funds can be frozen until the conclusion of legal proceedings. Second, section 304 requires CEOs and CFOs to reimburse the company for any bonus or equity-based compensation or profits received from the sale of securities during the 12-month period after the first publication of a financial statement that later turned out to be erroneous and had to be restated. This provision was inserted in the statute as a response to the widespread public perception that corporate officers manipulated their companies' financial statements in order to trigger incentive-based executive compensation agreements or to make insider trading profits. Also, Sarbanes-Oxley increases the SEC's power to bar people from serving as officers or directors of public companies. Prior to the passage of the Act, in order to bar somebody from serving as an officer or director, the SEC had to make a showing that the person demonstrated "substantial unfitness" to serve as an officer or director. Over time, this provision had been interpreted to mean that the SEC had to show "egregious misconduct" or that a person had engaged in "repeated violations of securities laws." Now, the SEC need only show that a person is "unfit" (rather than substantially unfit), and the SEC can bar people from serving as officers and directors for misconduct that falls far short of being egregious or recidivist.

The nature and scope of fiduciary duties has long been the province of state law, and Sarbanes-Oxley does not change this. However, section 307 of the Act, which contains significant new provisions regulating the conduct of corporate lawyers (another area that traditionally has been the province of state law), requires the SEC to develop rules of professional conduct for lawyers of public companies. The rules that the SEC develops must require lawyers to report "evidence of a material violation of the securities laws, or breach of fiduciary duty or similar violation" by a public company or any of its agents, to the general counsel or the CEO of the company. If this person does not respond "appropriately," the lawyer is required to report the evidence to the audit committee of the board of directors, or to some other committee of the board that is comprised solely of independent directors.

(3) In 2010, the Dodd-Frank Wall Street Reform and Consumer Protection Act was signed into law. The Act was enacted in response to the financial crisis of 2008, and it implements sweeping changes in the way the financial sector is regulated and monitored. Like the Sarbanes-Oxley Act, Dodd-Frank also affects executive compensation issues in publicly traded firms (see §§ 951–957). For example, Dodd-Frank directs the SEC to promulgate regulations that: (a) give shareholders the right to participate in a non-binding vote on executive compensation at least once every 3 years (the so-called "say-on-pay" provision); (b) require compensation committees to be comprised only of independent directors; (c) require such committees to select compensation consultants, legal counsel, or other advisors only after taking into consideration independence standards established by the SEC; (d) provide for enhanced compensation disclosures, such as the relationship of

the compensation actually paid to executives versus the company's financial performance; and (e) require companies subject to SEC regulation to create policies to recover executive incentive-based compensation if such compensation was based on inaccurate financial statements or financial statements that did not comply with reporting requirements. Aside from executive compensation, the SEC under Dodd-Frank is also authorized to promulgate rules allowing certain shareholders proxy access to nominate directors (see § 971).

CHAPTER 5

THE FORMATION OF A CLOSELY HELD CORPORATION

■ ■ ■

This Chapter assumes that a decision has been made to form a corporation, and the issues are how, where, and, most importantly, what happens if things are not done correctly.

A. WHERE TO INCORPORATE

Selection of the state of incorporation involves an appraisal of two factors: (a) a dollars-and-cents analysis of the relative cost of incorporating, or qualifying as a foreign corporation, under the statutes of the states under consideration, and (b) a consideration of the advantages and disadvantages of the substantive corporation laws of these states. As a practical matter, the choice usually comes down to the jurisdiction where the business is to be conducted or Delaware, the most popular outside jurisdiction.

If the corporation is closely held and its business is to be conducted largely or entirely within a single state, local incorporation is almost always to be preferred. The cost of forming a Delaware corporation and qualifying it to transact business in another state will be greater than forming a local corporation in that state to begin with. In addition, the cost of operating a local business through a Delaware corporation qualified to transact business in the state will almost certainly be greater than the cost of operating a local corporation. Income and franchise taxes are usually the same for both domestic and qualified foreign corporations, but again the Delaware taxes must be added. In 1991, the Delaware franchise taxes were increased significantly, thereby reducing the attractiveness of that state for small out-of-state corporations. Another disadvantage of Delaware incorporation is the possibility of being forced to defend a suit in that distant state rather than where the corporation has its principal place of business. The Delaware General Corporation Law may offer some flexibility not available in other states given that § 342 and § 351 of the statute permit a corporation with thirty or fewer shareholders to be managed directly by the shareholders. Many states, however, have adopted § 7.32 of the MBCA, which also permits non-traditional management arrangements.

B. HOW TO INCORPORATE

How should one go about forming a corporation? At one time, this probably involved the employment of an attorney familiar with the incorporation process of the selected state. Today, many states accept corporate filings electronically, and a number of internet companies offer to provide, for a fee, incorporation services for any state.

Many internet companies promise to file the corporate documents with the Secretary of State on-line, and serve as a registered agent for the corporation. Others offer assured filing within 24 hours. All accept credit cards for payment. The official website of the state of Delaware's Division of Corporations[a] offers a variety of services, including "Same Day" and even "2-Hour" processing of corporate filings.[b] Whether or not all this is a bargain, or even if it results in the formation of a corporation that meets the needs of the founders, obviously depends on a variety of factors. If the corporation involves issues of any complexity, or there is any possibility whatsoever of disagreements arising among the founders of the corporation (or their heirs), it will almost certainly be necessary to utilize the services of an attorney to assure that the documents accord with the needs of the investors.

Assume that you are an attorney "just starting out," and are asked to draft specialized provisions for a corporation to be formed. There are significant issues that must be addressed. The first is what substantive provisions should be reduced to writing, and whether these provisions should be placed in the articles of incorporation, the bylaws, or a shareholders' agreement. The modern trend is to limit the articles of incorporation to provisions required by law to appear in that public document. The other substantive provisions are placed in documents such as the bylaws or a shareholders' agreement that are not filed of public record.

In forming a corporation, there is always a danger of overlooking some obvious matter or using "boilerplate" language that may have been suitable for the last corporation but is egregiously inappropriate for this corporation. Many corporations may be stamped from a single mold and be perfectly satisfactory, but some cannot. Depending on such matters as the nature of the business, the agreements among the shareholders, and their mutual degree of trust and confidence, a considerable amount of individualized drafting may be necessary. Read MBCA §§ 2.01–2.03, 2.05–2.06, 7.32.

The formal requirements for filing of documents are set forth in MBCA Chapter 1, particularly §§ 1.20–1.25. These minimal requirements

---

[a]   http://corp.delaware.gov/index.shtml (last visited Jan. 18, 2014).

[b]   A complete list of current fees is available at http://corp.delaware.gov/Aug11Fee.pdf (last visited Jan. 18, 2014).

are similar to those adopted by most states, and the trend is towards limiting the procedures for forming a corporation to those specified in the MBCA. Generally, the trend in most states is towards the simplification of the process of incorporation wherever possible, and incorporation by postcard or electronic filing is feasible in many states.

Consider again MBCA §§ 1.20, 2.02. Would the following document, submitted to the Secretary of State with the appropriate fee (a) be accepted for filing under the MBCA, and (b) result in the formation of a corporation?

ARTICLES OF INCORPORATION

1. The name of the corporation is AB Software Store, Inc.

2. The corporation is authorized to issue 1,000 shares of stock.

3. The street address of the corporation's registered office is 125 Main Street, City of _____, State of _____ and the name of the corporation's registered agent at that address is Robert B_____.

4. The name and address of the incorporator is Robert B_____, 125 Main Street, City of _____, State of _____.

> /s/ Robert B_____

> Robert B_____, Incorporator.

———

Whatever minor technical defects may exist in this form, incorporation under the MBCA appears to be a very simple process that hardly requires the services of an attorney (if a "plain vanilla" corporation such as that described above is desired).c This apparent simplicity is somewhat deceptive since articles of incorporation usually will have to contain express provisions on additional topics if the desires of the interested parties are to be fully carried out. Consider, for example, MBCA § 6.01 in the situation where it is contemplated that the corporation will issue shares of stock of more than one class. If it is contemplated that the corporation may have a significant number of shareholders, careful consideration should also be given to limiting the liability of directors [MBCA § 2.02(b)(4), discussed in Chapter 10] and adjusting the scope of the right of directors and officers to indemnification [MBCA §§ 2.02(b)(5), 8.50–8.59, discussed in Chapter 15]. The Official Comment to MBCA § 2.02 contains a list of provisions "that may be

---

c Also, it should be obvious that modern articles of incorporation provide relatively little useful information to third persons about the owners of the corporation, its assets, or the nature of its business. For example, the incorporator, "Robert B_____," might be an attorney, an employee of a law firm, or an employee of a corporation service company. Somewhat more meaningful information may sometimes be obtained from other filed documents. See for example, MBCA § 16.21.

elected only in the articles of incorporation" and a shorter list of provisions "that may be elected either in the articles of incorporation or in the bylaws."

NOTES

(1) So far as formal requirements for filing are concerned, the Committee on Corporate Laws in 1997 amended Chapter 1 of the MBCA to authorize electronic filing of documents as a guide for the adoption of such procedures by states. Among the numerous technical changes made by these amendments are definitions of the concepts of "delivery," "electronic transmission," and "signature." MBCA §§ 1.40(5), (7C), (22A). At the same time, the Committee recognized that the development of reliable and inexpensive copying machines made unnecessary the filing requirement that a copy of a document accompany the document itself. These are innovative provisions that probably will be widely followed in the future. Older requirements, such as that documents be acknowledged or verified before a notary public and his or her acknowledgement and notarial seal be attached, also serve little real purpose as a practical matter, and may gradually disappear.

(2) The processing of filed documents by the Secretary of State under the MBCA is described in § 1.25, a section that was also significantly amended in 1997. The date the existence of the corporation begins is described in § 2.03, as is the legal effect of the decision by the Secretary of State to file the document. Chapter 1 of the MBCA does not reflect a very expansive approach to the powers of the office of Secretary of State. For example, the Secretary of State may not prescribe a mandatory form for articles of incorporation (§ 1.21(b)), his filing duty is expressly defined as "ministerial" (§ 1.25(d)), and he is expressly commanded to file a document if it "satisfies the requirements of section 1.20" (§ 1.25(a)).

This restrictive view of the powers of the Secretary of State rests on the experience of attorneys in a number of states where the office of Secretary of State viewed its powers broadly, purported to adopt rules or regulations in addition to the requirements of the corporation statute,[d] and often conducted wide-ranging review of the propriety of specific provisions of documents filed with it. One can envision the frustration of an attorney who, after negotiating a complex provision for inclusion in a proposed articles of incorporation (or other document), is faced with the task of persuading a relatively low-level employee in the office of the Secretary of State that the provision is consistent with the Secretary of State's view of the meaning of the corporation statute. Of course, the office of Secretary of State has considerable political "clout" in the legislatures of most states, and therefore, these provisions may not be accepted in some states.

---

[d]   In this connection, consider also MBCA § 1.30. Contrast this narrow grant of authority with § 139 of the 1969 Model Act, which granted the secretary of state the power and authority "reasonably necessary to enable him to administer this Act efficiently and to perform the duties therein imposed upon him."

(3) *Names.* Consider, for example, the requirement that the corporation have a name, and the requirements relating to that name in MBCA §§ 2.02(a)(1), 4.01. Consider also MBCA §§ 4.02, 4.03.

(a) The critical language in § 4.01(b) is that a corporate name "must be distinguishable upon the records of the secretary of state" from other corporate names. Earlier versions of the MBCA required that a corporate name "not be the same as, or deceptively similar to, the name" of an existing corporation. MBCA (1969) § 8. Many secretaries of state construed this or other similar language to require a determination whether the proposed name constituted unfair competition with existing corporations. The Official Comment to § 4.01 states that "confusion in an absolute or linguistic sense is the appropriate test under the Model Act, not the competitive relationship between the corporations, which is the test for fraud or unfair competition." In enforcing whatever statutory standard is applicable, the secretary of state "simply maintains an alphabetical list of 'official' corporate names as they appear from corporate records and decides * * * by comparing the proposed name with those on the list." Official Comment to § 4.01. Today, this list is usually maintained electronically, and in some states, may be accessible to the public.

(b) Is the current test a desirable one for determining name availability? The "distinguishable upon the records of the secretary of state" language was taken from § 102(a)(1) of the Delaware General Corporation Law. In Trans-Americas Airlines, Inc. v. Kenton, 491 A.2d 1139 (Del.1985), Transamerica Corporation, the nationally-known conglomerate, had long associated the name "Transamerica" with the activities of a wholly owned subsidiary named "Trans International Airlines, Inc.," which operated a worldwide air charter service. This association took the form of national advertising by Transamerica and using the word "Transamerica" on many of the airplanes operated by the subsidiary. Trans International Airlines, Inc. was permitted by the Delaware Secretary of State to change its name to "Transamerica Airlines, Inc." An entirely unrelated corporation named "Trans-Americas Airlines, Inc." complained to the Secretary of State and filed suit after the Secretary of State refused to revoke the registration of the name "Transamerica Airlines, Inc." The Delaware Supreme Court accepted the lower court's conclusion that " 'Transamerica Airlines, Inc.' is distinguishable from the name 'Trans-Americas Airlines, Inc.,' on the records of the [Secretary of State]," and held that the statute did not authorize the Secretary of State to reject a name on the ground that it was "confusingly similar" to a name or names already in use.

(c) Because of the widespread adoption of earlier versions of the Model Act, the statutes of many states today contain a "deceptively similar" standard (though sometimes phrased in different words) that makes it clear that prevention of unfair competition is at least partially the objective of corporate name regulation. The extent to which secretaries of state actually attempt to police against unfair competition apparently varies widely from state to state. Many secretaries of state have also evolved "house rules" about name availability that may lead to rather peculiar results.

(d) What purposes are served by "reserved names" (MBCA § 4.02) and "registered names" (MBCA § 4.03)?

(4) *Duration.* MBCA § 3.02 automatically grants every corporation "perpetual duration" unless its articles of incorporation provide otherwise. Earlier versions of the Model Act required that the articles of incorporation affirmatively set forth "[t]he period of duration, which may be perpetual." MBCA (1969) § 54(b); see also id. § 4(a). Some state corporation acts today contain provisions similar to the 1969 Act. Since almost all corporations elected perpetual status under these provisions, MBCA § 3.02 does not reflect a significant change. Why might a corporation with less than a perpetual duration ever be created?

(5) *Purposes.* Historically, a great deal of importance was attached to the statement of purposes in the articles of incorporation. It "is undoubtedly the most important part of the corporate charter, for this clause, together with the general act under which it is drawn, is the true measure of the powers of the corporation." Louis S. Berkoff, The Object Clause in Corporate Articles, 4 Wis.L.Rev. 424 (1928). During the nineteenth and early twentieth centuries, corporations were formed for a specific "purpose" that had to be "fully stated;" general purpose and multiple purpose clauses were not accepted in many states. As a result, a great deal of litigation involved the question of whether a corporation had exceeded its purposes in some transaction. See the discussion of *ultra vires* in Section C of this Chapter. This problem has just about disappeared under modern statutes. See MBCA § 3.01(a). Indeed, the disappearance of litigation over the scope of purpose clauses is one of the more visible and sensible changes in corporation law in the last half-century.

(a) The first step in this development was recognition that a corporation may list multiple purposes without any limitation on the number of purposes specified and without any obligation that the corporation actually pursue all the purposes contained in its articles. The result was that form books were developed that contained hundreds of possible purpose clauses.

Such clauses were generally drafted on the theory that they should be as broad as possible when describing some line or kind of business. Since the number of purposes was unlimited, furthermore, it was possible to string together a large number of such clauses to produce articles of incorporation that were impressively long, and unreadable. Purpose clauses in this era often ran pages in length but usually gave little or no information as to what precise business the corporation actually planned to engage in.

(b) The next step, quite logically, was to eliminate the excessive verbiage of purposes clauses by permitting incorporation "for the transaction of any lawful business," or similar language that did not require specification of particular lines or kinds of business. These clauses, however, were not quickly accepted; their use did not become widespread until the second half of the twentieth century. The 1969 Model Act permitted this streamlined language (which, after all, did little more than what a long statement of specific purposes did), but it continued to require an affirmative statement of the purposes of the corporation in the articles of incorporation "which may be stated to be, or to include, the transaction of any or all lawful business for which corporations may be incorporated under this Act." MBCA (1969) § 54(c).

(c) Why might articles of incorporation today ever include a narrow purposes clause? There are several possible explanations: (1) some types of corporations may be engaged in businesses subject to state regulation that permit incorporation under general business statutes (see MBCA § 3.01(b)), but require limitations on certain types of corporate activities; (2) some persons may be uncomfortable with the complete lack of useful information about the purpose of the corporation permitted by the MBCA, preferring that some description of the principal business of the corporation appear in the articles of incorporation (without restricting the corporation to that business); and (3) in closely held corporations, a limited purposes clause may be used where one or more persons interested in the corporation (but not controlling its affairs) wish to restrict the lines of business the corporation may enter. Other justifications may exist as well.

(6) *Powers.* Historically, one often encountered provisions in articles of incorporation that dealt with corporate "powers" as well as corporate "purposes." The distinction between "powers" and "purposes" is not self-evident; it can best be appreciated by comparing the list of "general powers" in MBCA § 3.02 with a "purpose" such as operating a software store. The distinction between "purposes" and "powers" certainly was not understood by many practitioners, since articles of incorporation clauses dealing with "powers" were often indiscriminately mixed in with "purposes." A useful psychological device that aids in distinguishing "powers" from "purposes" is mentally to precede each statement with the phrase "to engage in the business of * * *," and then to use the present participle form of the applicable verb. Thus, instead of saying, "The purpose for which the corporation is organized is to operate a software store," say "The purpose for which the corporation is organized is *to engage in the business of* operating a software store." By transposing the verb form from the infinitive to the present participle form, the distinction between powers such as "to sue and be sued" and purposes such as "to operate a software store" becomes accentuated.

(a) Is it necessary or desirable to make any references to corporate powers in modern articles of incorporation? Consider MBCA § 2.02(c). Most attorneys agree that it is preferable to take this subsection at face value, at least in states where the statutory powers are sufficiently broad to encompass various acts that raised *ultra vires* problems in an earlier era, such as the power of a corporation to enter into a general partnership or to guarantee the debts of customers or third persons.

(b) Today, all statutes contain a list of general powers analogous to those found in MBCA § 3.02. In addition, provisions relating to specific powers may be "tucked away" in substantive provisions themselves. See, e.g., MBCA § 8.51. Section 3.02 contains several changes from earlier versions of similar sections in earlier Model Acts. Perhaps most important is the addition of the introductory phrase, "has *the same powers as an individual* to do all things necessary or convenient to carry out its business and affairs" (emphasis added).

MBCA § 3.02 begins with the phrase "[u]nless its articles of incorporation provide otherwise." Why might it be desirable to preclude a corporation from exercising specific powers? Consider, for example, § 3.02(15), which according to the Official Comment was included in addition to § 3.02(13) to permit "contributions for purposes that may not be charitable, such as for political purposes or to influence elections." Might an investor wish to preclude such contributions? What other kinds of restrictions on powers might a cautious investor wish to impose on a corporation in which he or she is making a significant investment as a minority shareholder?

(7) *Registered office and registered agent.* The designation of a registered office and registered agent, and the statutory provisions relating thereto (see MBCA §§ 5.01–5.04), are designed to ensure that every corporation has publicly stated a current place where it may be found for purposes of service of process, tax notices, and the like. Often a corporation designates its principal business office as its registered office. In such a case, the registered agent usually is a corporate officer or employee. The principal disadvantage of this is the possibility that legal documents or communications may be mixed in with routine business mail or advertisements and not receive the attention they deserve. For this reason, many attorneys suggest that they be designated as a registered agent and their office be designated as the registered office. Corporation service companies also routinely provide registered offices and registered agents for a fee.

(8) *"Initial directors" and "incorporators."* Under earlier versions of the Model Act, the organization of the corporation was accomplished by "initial directors" named in the articles of incorporation; the "incorporators" executed the articles of incorporation but did not meet. MBCA (1969) § 57. A number of states, however, provided that the incorporators were to complete the organization of the corporation, and therefore did not require that initial directors be named in the articles of incorporation. MBCA § 2.05 in effect gives the drafter of articles of incorporation an option as to how the organization of the corporation is to be completed. Factors that might be considered in this regard include (a) will it be necessary for shareholders to meet shortly after the formation of the corporation to elect permanent directors and conduct other business, and (b) do the real parties in interest desire anonymity?

Should an attorney serve as incorporator or initial director? In most states, it is clear that no liability attaches to the role of incorporator; the same may not necessarily be true of the position of director, which, as discussed in a later Chapter, carries with it certain fiduciary duties and potential liabilities. Some cautious attorneys refuse as a matter of principle to serve as directors of corporations, though there is no ethical objection to doing so.

(9) *The number of incorporators, directors or shareholders.* Blackstone noted that "Three make a corporation." Until mid-century, statutes required that there be at least three incorporators and three directors. Further, there were often residency requirements, shareholding requirements, and the like. So far as incorporators are concerned, the trend is clearly to reduce the minimum number to one and to allow corporations or other artificial entities to serve as incorporators; all but a handful of states now follow the Model Act in this regard. Of course, in view of the limited role of incorporators, this result is probably reasonable.

What about a minimum number of shareholders and directors? There apparently has never been in recent history a requirement that a corporation have at least three shareholders. A North Carolina case that appears to have so held, Park Terrace v. Phoenix Indem. Co., 91 S.E.2d 584 (N.C.1956), was promptly overruled by statute. Assuming this is so, what then about directors? See MBCA § 8.03(a). Some states still require a board of at least three directors, though a number of these states permit a corporation with one or two shareholders to reduce the size of the board to the number of shareholders.

(10) *Initial Capital.* One interesting aspect of the articles of incorporation set forth above is that there is no reference to dollars: no dollar figure is associated with the shares of stock (i.e., no minimum issuance price is established) and no minimum capitalization of the corporation is set forth.

(a) The matter of the issuance price for shares is discussed in Chapter 7 and discussion of that issue is deferred until then.

(b) Shouldn't a new corporation be required to have at least some minimum amount of capital before it is launched into the business world? Until relatively recently, there was such a requirement in most states. Prior to 1969, the Model Act prohibited a corporation from transacting any business or incurring any indebtedness "until there has been paid in for the issuance of shares consideration of the value of at least one thousand dollars." MBCA (1966) § 51. The articles of incorporation also had to contain a recitation to the same effect. Id. § 48(g). These provisions have largely disappeared in the United States.

It is probably true that in most states there was never a serious attempt to enforce these minimum capitalization requirements by holding up the certificate of incorporation, though some states did require the submission of an affidavit or certificate that the required amount had been contributed. Much more important was the question whether initial or subsequent directors who acquiesced to the conduct of business before the minimum capital was in fact paid in might be personally liable either for the minimum capital, or more dangerously, for all debts of the corporation incurred before the required capital was paid in. The Model Act (MBCA (1966 Ed.) § 43(e)) minimized the potential impact of the minimum capitalization requirement by providing that directors who assent to the commencement of business are "jointly and severally liable to the corporation for such part of one thousand dollars as shall not have been received before commencing business, but such liability shall be terminated when the corporation has actually received one thousand dollars as consideration for the issuance of shares." Not all states followed this provision. In Tri-State Developers, Inc. v. Moore, 343 S.W.2d 812 (Ky.1961), for example, a corporation began business with $500 rather than the required minimum of $1,000. The court upheld a judgment for $10,180.34 under such a statute. Kentucky eliminated entirely the minimum capital requirement in 1972. See Ky.B.C.A. § 271B.2–020 (1989).

Do you think that it was sensible to eliminate all minimum capital requirements? Considering today's prices and today's conditions, shouldn't the move be in the opposite direction? Or is this simply an illustration of the race of laxity?

———

What happens after the articles of incorporation are filed? See MBCA §§ 2.05–2.06. In addition to preparing and filing the articles of incorporation, attorneys usually handle other details in connection with the formation of a corporation. They may:

(1) Prepare the corporate bylaws;

(2) Prepare the notice calling the meeting of the initial board of directors, minutes of this meeting, and waivers of notice if necessary;

(3) Obtain a corporate seal and minute book for the corporation;

(4) Obtain blank certificates for the shares of stock, arrange for their printing or typing, and ensure that they are properly issued;

(5) Arrange for the opening of the corporate bank account;

(6) Prepare employment contracts, voting trusts, shareholder agreements, share transfer restrictions, and other special arrangements which are to be entered into with respect to the corporation and its shares;

(7) Obtain taxpayer identification numbers, occupancy certificates, and other governmental permits or consents to the operation of the business; and

(8) Evaluate whether the corporation should file an S corporation election, assuming that election is available.

Where there are to be several shareholders, consideration should be given to the manner of governance of the corporation after it is formed. There are numerous "boilerplate" forms for articles of incorporation and bylaws. But these forms create a corporation that may not be well suited for a closely held corporation with multiple shareholders. A carefully crafted shareholders' agreement may be necessary to provide appropriate protections for shareholders both in terms of participation in management and the power to "exit" in case of controversy. In some cases, these appropriate provisions may be effective if they are placed in the bylaws or articles of incorporation, but it is a mistake to assume that participants in a corporation automatically have the same freedom as partners in a partnership or members in an LLC to structure the form of governance in any manner they wish. The traditional rule was that the governance structure set forth in the corporation statute was mandatory—even a corporation with a single shareholder was required to have a board of directors, officers, meetings, and so forth. The gradual erosion of this rule is described in Chapter 8, Section A.

MBCA § 7.32 was added to the MBCA in 1991. This section represents a new approach toward the problem of governance in corporations with a few shareholders. In addition to § 7.32, most states have adopted some provisions designed to ameliorate to some extent the traditional rules of corporate management when applied to small corporations. In deciding what form of governance should be adopted for such a corporation, care must be taken to work within the confines of provisions authorized in the specific state, since failing to do so runs the risk that the manner of governance selected may later be held invalid.

Different considerations apply if the corporation contemplates that it will make a public offering of its shares after its formation. During the 1990s, many internet and "high-tech" companies were formed with the specific contemplation of receiving funds from venture capital firms and later "going public" through a public offering. These corporations included in their articles of incorporation provisions authorizing the issue of senior classes of securities and other provisions appropriate for a publicly-held corporation, e.g., proxy voting, registration of securities ownership, and similar matters.

In more traditional businesses, it is relatively uncommon for a newly formed business to contemplate an initial public offering shortly after its formation. More likely, a corporation will operate as a closely held entity for several years before reaching a position that it might decide to "go public." When that decision is made, specialized securities counsel must be retained to assure that the offering is in compliance with the requirements of the federal Securities Act of 1933. This may involve amendments to articles of incorporation and bylaws as well as a full review of pre-offering transactions and arrangements between the corporation and its shareholders to determine whether disclosure of, or offers to rescind, specific prior transactions may be necessary.

———

SAMPLE MINUTES OF ORGANIZATIONAL MEETING OF DIRECTORS

(Please consult the Statutory Supplement)

NOTES

(1) Under the MBCA, there may be only one initial director or one incorporator who organizes the corporation. Where only a single person is acting, much of the "playacting" flavor of these minutes should disappear and a simpler formulation followed, e.g., "The director of the corporation determines that * * *."

(2) Most of the miscellaneous matters relating to the launching of a new corporation are accomplished at a meeting of the incorporators or initial directors. The attorney will normally draft the minutes of this meeting. In some circumstances, it may be necessary to have a meeting of the shareholders to elect permanent directors; the attorney normally drafts the minutes of this meeting also.

(3) It is not necessary to actually hold meetings of incorporators, directors, or shareholders. See MBCA §§ 2.05, 7.04, 8.21. Similar provisions appear in all corporation statutes. Thus, a consent signed by all the incorporators, directors, or shareholders is effective as a legal matter. If the consent procedure is not utilized (as may be the case, for example, where one individual is absent, or where the number of persons involved is large), it is generally desirable to actually hold a meeting, using the minutes as a form of script.

––––––––

The bylaws of a corporation constitute the internal set of operating rules for the corporation. See MBCA § 2.06. They are usually prepared by the attorney who oversees the formation of the corporation. Numerous sample bylaws are available in form books; corporation service and internet companies also provide sample sets of bylaws as part of their services in connection with the formation of a corporation. Bylaws may vary from a brief one or two page document to elaborate provisions covering all aspects of corporate management and operation.

SAMPLE BYLAWS

(Please consult the Statutory Supplement)

NOTE

Lawyers typically use checklists when preparing documents such as bylaws or articles of incorporation in order to make sure that they do not omit any important provisions. A checklist for the bylaw provisions pertaining to directors would normally include the following: (1) number and qualifications; (2) increase or decrease in number; (3) resignation and removal; (4) filling vacancies; (5) powers and duties; (6) meetings of directors; (7) committees; (8) compensation and indemnification. What other sorts of information might such a checklist contain?

C. THE DECLINE OF THE DOCTRINE OF *ULTRA VIRES*

A classic English case presents the doctrine of *ultra vires* in its full rigor and glory. In Ashbury Railway Carriage & Iron Co. v. Riche, 33 L.T.R. 450, 1875 WL 13580 (1875), the charter of a corporation authorized it to "make and sell, or lend on hire * * * all kinds of railway plant, fittings, machinery, and rolling-stock; [and] to carry on the business of mechanical engineers and general contractors * * *." The corporation entered into contracts with one Riche to purchase a concession to construct and operate a railway line in Belgium. Riche was apparently to construct the railroad line, and the corporation was to raise the necessary capital. After partial performance, the corporation repudiated the contract. The House of Lords concluded that the corporation was not liable to Riche because owning and operating a railway line was *ultra vires*. Lord Chancellor Cairns declared:

> In a case such as that which your Lordships have now to deal with, it is not a question whether the contract sued upon involves that which is *malum prohibitum* or *malum in se*, or is a contract contrary to public policy, and illegal in itself. I assume the contract in itself to be perfectly legal, to have nothing in it obnoxious to the doctrine involved in the expressions which I have used. The question is not as to the legality of the contract; the question is as to the competency and power of the company to make the contract. Now, I am clearly of opinion that this contract was entirely, as I have said, beyond the objects in the memorandum of association. If so, it was thereby placed beyond the powers of the company to make the contract. If so, my Lords, it is not a question whether the contract ever was ratified or was not ratified. If it was a contract void at its beginning, it was void because the company could not make the contract. If every shareholder of the company had been in the room, and every shareholder of the company had said, "That is a contract which we desire to make, which we authorize the directors to make, to which we sanction the placing the seal of the company," the case would not have stood in any different position from that in which it stands now. The shareholders would thereby, by unanimous consent, have been attempting to do the very thing which, by the Act of Parliament, they were prohibited from doing.

Several things may be noted about this case. First, while it involves a purposes clause that is narrower than the activities actually engaged in by the corporation, the activities themselves were not inherently unlawful or beyond the powers of corporations generally. At the time, British law apparently did not permit corporations to amend their memoranda of association so that a new corporation would have to have been formed to operate the Belgian railroad. Presumably, however, nothing prevented that from being done with the same membership and management. Modern practice in drafting articles of incorporation greatly reduces but does not eliminate the possibility that similar problems will arise in the future. Second, the result of the case hardly seems reasonable or fair. After entering into what appears to be an entirely reasonable business contract, and presumably receiving benefits thereunder, the corporation is permitted to avoid the contract on the basis of a defense that was entirely within its power to correct. Third, the argument that corporations simply are unable to commit *ultra vires* acts threatens to be very unsettling. It might be used, for example, to set aside completed transactions, including sales of goods and land, which the corporation now regrets. It also would appear to be a handy defense for the corporation to avoid liability to injured plaintiffs in tort cases. Thus, almost from the first, *ultra vires* was viewed as a doctrine that generally produced undesirable results.

Some courts avoided the *ultra vires* doctrine by construing purposes clauses broadly and finding implied purposes from the language used. A famous example is the conclusion by the United States Supreme Court that a railway company might engage in the business of leasing and running a seaside resort hotel. Jacksonville M.P. Ry. & Nav. Co. v. Hooper, 160 U.S. 514 (1896). Other doctrines that have found acceptance include estoppel, unjust enrichment, quasi-contract, and waiver. In particular, these doctrines were applied to ensure that completed transactions would not be disturbed, and to permit tort claimants to recover for injuries suffered as a consequence of the corporation's conduct of an *ultra vires* business. *Ultra vires* continued to be applied, however, in connection with executory agreements and, when all is said and done, the doctrine was an undesirable one, involving harsh and erratic consequences.

One superficially plausible justification for the doctrine arises from the fact that articles of incorporation are on public file; it seems reasonable to argue that one is charged with notice of whatever unexpected provision might appear in public documents. From a business standpoint, that argument is unrealistic: it assumes people will check articles of incorporation when in fact they do not, and that when they do check the articles, they will make business judgments based on a reading of what often is essentially boilerplate legalese.

711 KINGS HIGHWAY CORP. V. F.I.M.'S MARINE REPAIR SERV., INC.

Supreme Court of New York, 1966.
273 N.Y.S.2d 299.

VICTOR L. ANFUSO, JUSTICE.

Defendant corporation moves pursuant to CPLR 3211, subdiv. [a], par. 7 for judgment dismissing the complaint for legal insufficiency or in the alternative for summary judgment pursuant to CPLR 3212.

The verified complaint alleges that on or about April 20, 1965, the plaintiff, owner of premises known as 711–715 Kings Highway in the County of Kings, City of New York, entered into a written lease agreement with defendant whereby plaintiff leased the aforesaid premises to defendant for a period of 15 years commencing July 1, 1966; that with the exception of a security deposit of $5,000 paid by defendant to plaintiff pursuant to the lease agreement, which sum plaintiff now tenders or offers to return to defendant, the lease remains wholly executory; that under the terms of the lease the demised premises were to be used as a motion picture theatre; that the purposes for which the defendant corporation was formed were restricted generally to marine activities including marine repairs and the building and equipment of boats and vessels, as set forth in the certificate of incorporation; that the execution of the subject lease calling for defendant's use of the demised premises as a motion picture theatre, and the conduct and operation of a motion picture theatre business for profit by the defendant are acts which fall completely outside the scope of the powers and authority conferred by the defendant's corporate charter, thereby rendering invalid the lease agreement entered into by the parties. The complaint then prays for a declaratory judgment declaring the lease to be invalid or in the alternative for rescission, and further, that the defendant be enjoined from performing, or exercising any rights, under the lease.

In the opinion of the court, Section 203 of the New York Business Corporation Law embraces the situation presented by the factual allegations of the complaint and requires a dismissal of the complaint for failure to state a cause of action. This section provides as follows:

> That no act of a corporation and no transfer of property to or by a corporation, otherwise lawful, shall be invalid by reason of the fact that the corporation was without capacity or power to do such act or engage in such transfer except that such lack of capacity or power may be asserted (1) in an action brought by a shareholder to enjoin a corporate act or (2) in an action by or in the right of a corporation against an incumbent or former officer or director of the corporation or (3) in an action or special proceeding brought by the Attorney General.

It is undisputed that the present case does not fall within the stated exceptions contained in Section 203. It is accordingly clear from the language of the statutory provision hereinabove referred to that there is no substance to plaintiff's argument, in opposition to the instant motion, which is predicated on a want of corporate power to do an act or enter into an agreement beyond the express or implied powers of the corporation conferred by the corporate charter.

Neither is there merit to the plaintiff's contention that Section 203 applies only where ultra vires is raised as a defense. Notwithstanding the fact that this section is entitled "Defense of ultra vires" it seems that except in the three stated situations set forth in the section, which are not applicable to the instant case, ultra vires may not be invoked as a sword in support of a cause of action any more than it can be utilized as a defense. To hold otherwise would render meaningless those provisions in Section 203 which permit ultra vires to be invoked in support of the actions or proceedings set forth as exceptions to the general language of this section.

Finally plaintiff's contention that the ultra vires doctrine still applies fully to executory contracts must be rejected. By virtue of Section 203 the doctrine may not be invoked even though the contract which is claimed to be ultra vires is executory, as in the instant case.

Accordingly the defendant's motion for judgment dismissing the complaint for insufficiency is granted. * * *

NOTES

(1) Consider MBCA § 3.04. Does this give the court the needed flexibility to protect legitimate and reasonable business relationships on the one hand, while safeguarding shareholders who may have relied on a narrow purposes clause as protection against undesired business expansion on the other?

(2) Don't MBCA § 3.04(b)(1) and (c) give shareholders greater rights to set aside executory transactions than the corporation itself? Might not a corporation, having entered into a disadvantageous *ultra vires* transaction, enlist a shareholder to intervene and seek the cancellation of the contract? Of course, if it is advantageous for the corporation to avoid a transaction, it probably will also be advantageous from the standpoint of the shareholder since it will increase the value of his shares.

(3) In Cucchi v. New York City Off-Track Betting Corp., 818 F.Supp. 647, 657–58 (S.D.N.Y.1993), plaintiff contended that she had been fired as an employee of defendant in violation of the statutory provisions regulating the defendant, and that therefore her firing was *ultra vires*. This argument was rejected by the court on the ground that the doctrine of *ultra vires* as embodied in § 203 could be invoked only by a shareholder or by the state through its attorney-general, and not by an employee.

SULLIVAN V. HAMMER

Court of Chancery of Delaware, 1990.
1990 WL 114223.

HARTNETT, VICE CHANCELLOR:

I

On April 25, 1989, defendant Occidental Petroleum Corporation ("Occidental") mailed to its stockholders a Proxy Statement for the Company's 1989 annual meeting, which reported that a Special Committee of Occidental had approved a proposal to provide financial support for The Armand Hammer Museum of Art and Cultural Center ("the Museum"). The Museum is to be located adjacent to and be physically integrated with Occidental's Los Angeles headquarters building, the Occidental Petroleum Center. Dr. Armand Hammer, who is over 90 years old, is the founder and Chairman of the Board of Occidental.

The Proxy Statement referred to the financial support that Occidental would provide to the Museum, including: (a) funding construction costs estimated at approximately $50 million and granting the Museum a 30-year rent-free lease in the Occidental Petroleum Center; (b) funding an annuity for the Museum, at an estimated after-tax cost of $24 million; and (c) granting the Museum an option to purchase the Museum complex and the Occidental Petroleum Center at the end of the 30-year lease term for $55 million, their estimated fair market value at that time.

The Proxy Statement also set forth a description of Dr. Hammer's employment agreements, including a provision for Occidental to contribute to the Armand Hammer Foundation a lump sum approximating seven times Dr. Hammer's aggregate compensation during the year prior to his death. These disclosures had appeared in Occidental's public filings for several years.

Plaintiffs filed this action asserting class and derivative claims on May 9, 1989. The complaint alleges * * * that Occidental's expenditures and commitments with respect to the Museum and its obligations to the Armand Hammer Foundation pursuant to Dr. Hammer's employment contract constitute a gift and waste of corporate assets * * * [and] that Dr. Hammer had breached his duty of loyalty by causing Occidental to make these expenditures for his personal benefit. The complaint sought injunctive, declaratory, rescissory and other equitable relief.

On May 9, 1989, plaintiffs' counsel accepted defendants' invitation to enter into settlement discussions and between May 24, 1989 and June 3, 1989, met to discuss a possible settlement. As a condition of entering into and continuing these discussions, plaintiffs' counsel demanded and were provided with documents relating to the Museum and Occidental's charitable contributions, among other matters. * * *

On June 3, 1989, subject to plaintiffs' right to pursue additional discovery to confirm the fairness and adequacy of the settlement, the parties entered into a written Memorandum of Understanding setting forth the general terms of a proposed settlement of the litigation and providing for the negotiations of a formal Stipulation of Settlement to be executed within thirty days for submission to this Court for approval. * * *

On August 4, 1989, a Special Committee of Occidental's Board of Directors retained former Chancellor Grover C. Brown of the law firm of Morris, James, Hitchens & Williams as its independent counsel to review the merits of the actions taken by the Board of Occidental and to advise the members of the Special Committee with respect to any financial support to be given by Occidental to the Museum. On October 6, 1989, Occidental's Board of Directors delegated to the Special Committee the additional authority to approve or disapprove the proposed settlement agreement in this action after consulting with and considering the advice of its independent counsel.

The Special Committee reexamined the proposal for the financial support by Occidental to the Museum. Also, through its independent counsel, the Special Committee met with and discussed possible settlement of the litigation * * *. The Special Committee subsequently, and for the first time, formally approved the challenged charitable contributions. Furthermore, the Special Committee was advised by its special counsel regarding the litigation[ ] and determined that, in its opinion, it was in the best interests of Occidental to agree to the proposed settlement presented in this action.

* * * Counsel for plaintiffs also engaged in further negotiations with the defendants, the Special Committee and its counsel on the aspects of the settlement. Plaintiffs' counsel asserted that he evaluated or reevaluated the challenged transactions, the relative strength of plaintiffs' complaint, the activities of the Special Committee and the claims made by * * * various others opposing settlement of this litigation.

On January 24, 1990, counsel for all the parties in this action presented to the Court a fully executed Stipulation and Agreement of Compromise, Settlement and Release ("the Stipulation of Settlement"). The Court then directed that, solely for settlement purposes, this action would be maintained as a stockholder derivative action and as a class action by plaintiffs, as representatives of the Class * * *.

II

* * * The proposed Settlement, inter alia, provides:

(1) [T]he Museum building shall be named the "Occidental Petroleum Cultural Center Building" with the name displayed appropriately on the building.

(2) Occidental shall be treated as a corporate sponsor by the Museum for as long as the Museum occupies the building.

(3) Occidental's contribution of the building shall be recognized by the Museum in public references to the facility.

(4) Three of Occidental's directors shall serve on the Museum's Board (or no less than one-third of the total Museum Board) with Occidental having the option to designate a fourth director.

(5) [T]here shall be an immediate loan of substantially all of the art collections of Dr. Hammer to the Museum and there shall be an actual transfer of ownership of the collections upon Dr. Hammer's death or the commencement of operation of the Museum whichever later occurs.

(6) All future charitable contributions by Occidental to any Hammer-affiliated charities shall be limited by the size of the dividends paid to Occidental's common stockholders. At current dividend levels, Occidental's annual contributions to Hammer-affiliated charities pursuant to this limitation could not exceed approximately 3 cents per share.

(7) Any amounts Occidental pays for construction of the Museum in excess of $50 million and any amounts paid to the Foundation upon Dr. Hammer's death must be charged against the agreed ceiling on limitations to Hammer-affiliated charities.

(8) Occidental's expenditures for the Museum construction shall not exceed $50 million, except that an additional $10 million may be expended through December 31, 1990 but only if such additional expenditures do not enlarge the scope of construction and if such expenditures are approved by the Special Committee. Amounts in excess of $50 million must be charged against the limitation on donations to Hammer-affiliated charities.

(9) Occidental shall be entitled to receive 50% of any consideration received in excess of a $55 million option price for the Museum property or 50% of any consideration the Museum receives from the assignment or transfer of its option or lease to a third party. * * *

* * * The settlement in the Court's opinion leaves much to be desired.

The Court's role in reviewing the proposed Settlement, however, is quite restricted. If the Court was a stockholder of Occidental it might vote for new directors, if it was on the Board it might vote for new management and if it was a member of the Special Committee it might vote against the Museum project. But its options are limited in reviewing a proposed settlement to applying Delaware law to the facts adduced in the record and then determining in its business judgment whether, on balance, the settlement is reasonable.

Delaware law clearly favors the voluntary settlement of litigation. It is neither necessary nor desirable for the Court to try the case or to decide any of the issues on the merits prior to determining whether a settlement should be approved. Rather, the Court must look to the facts and circumstances upon which the claim is based, and the possible defenses thereto, and must then exercise its own business judgment and determine the overall reasonableness of the settlement. In short, it is the function of the Court to decide whether the proposed settlement is fair and reasonable in light of the factual and legal circumstances of the case.

The factors to be considered in the Court's review are:

(1) the probable validity of the claims, (2) the apparent difficulties in enforcing the claims through the courts, (3) the collectibility of any judgment recovered, (4) the delay, expense and trouble of litigation, (5) the amount of the compromise as compared with the amount and collectibility of the judgment, and (6) the views of the parties involved, pro and con.

Polk v. Good, [*Del. Supr., 507 A.2d 531, 536 (1986)*] (citations omitted). * * *

The Court must therefore consider the benefit to the class and whether the benefit is reasonable when compared to the range of potential recovery.

IV

The potential for ultimate success on the merits here is, realistically, very poor. The business judgment rule, as consistently reiterated by the Delaware Supreme Court, stands as an almost impenetrable barrier to the plaintiffs.

The business judgment rule "is a presumption that in making a business decision the directors of a corporation acted on an informed basis, in good faith and in the honest belief that the action taken was in the best interests of the company." *Aronson v. Lewis, Del. Supr., 473 A.2d 805, 812 (1984)*. The presumption, which protects a board-approved transaction, can be overturned only if a plaintiff can show that a majority of the directors expected to derive personal financial benefit from the transaction, that they lacked independence, that they were grossly negligent in failing to inform themselves, or that the decision of the Board was so irrational that it could not have been the reasonable exercise of the business judgment of the Board.

The plaintiffs have not shown any facts which would show that the directors have any self-interest in the transaction either from a personal financial interest or from a motive for entrenchment in office. Nor is there any evidence in the record showing that the members of the Special Committee are in fact dominated by Dr. Hammer or anyone else.

The record also shows that the directors and the Special Committee gave due consideration to the transaction.

It is therefore highly probable that, in deciding a motion to dismiss or for summary judgment or after trial, this Court would find that the decisions of the directors are entitled to the presumption of propriety afforded by the business judgment rule. * * *

This Court, therefore, must review the claims of plaintiffs against a presumption that the acts of the directors are valid.

VI

This Court's role in reviewing the gift by Occidental Petroleum Corporation to the Museum is also severely limited.

The test of whether a corporation may make a charitable gift is its reasonableness.

It is clear that the Museum qualifies as a charity. From the present record it is also clear that the present gift (as now limited) is within the range of reasonableness.

It is therefore reasonably probable that plaintiffs would also fail to prevail on this claim.

VII

Against this background of weakness of plaintiffs' claims, the Court must weigh the consideration being received by the class.

While the consideration to be received by the class is speculative, I find, on balance, in the exercise of my business judgment, that it is adequate to support the settlement.

Plaintiffs' claim that "the proposed settlement: (1) reinforces and assures Occidental's identification with and meaningful participation in the affairs of the Museum; (2) reinforces and protects the charitable nature and consequences of Occidental's gifts by securing prompt delivery and irrevocable transfer of the art collections to the Museum; (3) imposes meaningful controls upon the total construction costs that Occidental will pay, which have already forced the reduction of the construction budget by $19.4 million; (4) places meaningful restrictions upon Occidental's future charitable donations to Hammer-affiliated entities and avoids increases in posthumous payments to the Foundation or any other designated recipient after Dr. Hammer's death; (5) restores to Occidental an equitable portion of any appreciation of the properties in the event the

Museum exercises its option and disposes of the properties or transfers its option for value; and (6) guarantees that the art collections will continue to be located in the Los Angeles area and remain available for the enjoyment of the American public rather than dissipated into private collections or sold abroad." Obviously the value of these benefits is speculative.

Plaintiffs * * * submitted an affidavit of Kenneth A. Budenstein of Duff & Phelps Financial Consulting Co. in which it is claimed that the monetary value of having the Museum Building called the "Occidental Petroleum Cultural Center Building" is approximately $10 million.

Although the Court views this estimate with a good deal of skepticism, * * * it seems clear that Occidental will receive good will from the gift and will be able to utilize the adjacent Museum in the promotion of its business purposes.

I therefore find that the benefit to the stockholders of Occidental is sufficient to support the settlement and is adequate, if only barely so, when compared to the weakness of plaintiffs' claims.

In summary, the settlement is approved.

NOTES

(1) Is there risk in broadly authorizing corporate powers in statutes such as MBCA § 3.02 without any kind of restriction or limitation? Or does the holding in *Sullivan v. Hammer* itself provide a suitable restriction?

(2) Charitable contributions by corporations, particularly publicly held corporations, have been the subject of some criticism. Are you impressed by the argument that the function of business corporations is profit, and that charitable contributions are inconsistent with that function since they involve gifts of corporate assets? What about the argument that shareholders, rather than corporate management, should be permitted to decide which charities to support since that choice is essentially a personal rather than a business-related one? Should a distinction be drawn between charitable contributions that may benefit the corporation directly (e.g., General Motors making contributions to support hospitals in areas close to General Motors plants), and more general contributions (e.g., to Harvard University)? For a thoughtful discussion of these issues, see Melvin Aron Eisenberg, Corporate Conduct that Does Not Maximize Shareholder Gain: Legal Conduct, Ethical Conduct, the Penumbra Effect, Reciprocity, the Prisoner's Dilemma, Sheep's Clothing, Social Conduct, and Disclosure, 28 Stetson L.Rev. 1 (1998).

(3) In Citizens United v. Federal Election Commission, 558 U.S. 310 (2010), the Supreme Court concluded that "the Government may not suppress political speech on the basis of the speaker's corporate identity." According to the court, "[n]o sufficient governmental interest justifies limits on the political speech of nonprofit or for-profit corporations." Does MBCA § 3.02(15) authorize political expenditures by a corporation?

PROBLEM

The board of directors of Acme Corporation votes to pay a pension to the widow of the former president of the company. Has the board committed an *ultra vires* act? See MBCA §§ 3.01, 3.02(12)–(13), 3.04.

D. PREMATURE COMMENCEMENT OF BUSINESS

1. PROMOTERS

The term "promoter" includes a "person who, acting alone or in conjunction with one or more other persons, directly or indirectly takes initiative in founding and organizing the business or enterprise of an issuer."[e] A promoter is often referred to as the "founder" or "organizer" of an enterprise. The formation of a business enterprise largely involves business rather than legal problems. If the new business needs a plant, the promoter must locate one and rent or buy it. If a key person is essential for the success of the venture, the promoter must negotiate an employment contract with him. If a distributive network for the business product or a source of raw materials is necessary, the promoter must make the arrangements. In any event, capital must be raised, either through the sale of equity interests in the business, or through loans, or commonly, a combination of both.

One important aspect of the promoter relationship is that the promoter owes significant fiduciary duties to other participants in the venture. The scope of these duties is described in Post v. United States, 407 F.2d 319, 328 (D.C.Cir.1968), as follows:

> By elementary legal principles, promoters stand in a fiduciary relationship exacting good faith in their intracompany activities and demanding adherence to a high standard of honesty and frankness. Not the lesser of the promoter's manifold responsibilities outlaw secret profit-making and command the dedication of corporate funds to corporate purposes. And it cannot be doubted that promoters of stock corporations who employ the mails in deceitful violation of their fiduciary obligations may incur the full condemnation of the law.

In *Post*, defendants were convicted of conspiracy and mail fraud stemming from their promotion of a country club in the Washington metropolitan area. The court upheld the following jury instruction as an accurate statement of both what a promoter does and what his fiduciary duty entails:

---

[e] According to S.E.C. Rule 405, 17 C.F.R. § 230.405, the term "promoter" also includes a person "who, in connection with the founding and organizing of the business or enterprise of an issuer, directly or indirectly receives in consideration of services or property, or both services and property, 10 percent or more of any class of securities of the issuer or 10 percent or more of the proceeds from the sale of any class of such securities."

The jury are instructed that a promoter is a person who sets in motion machinery that brings about the incorporation and organization of a corporation, brings together the persons interested in the enterprise to be conducted by the corporation, aids in inducing persons to become members of the corporation, and in procuring from them membership fees to carry out purposes set forth in the corporation's articles of incorporation. If from the evidence in this case the jury should find beyond a reasonable doubt that the defendants were promoters of Lakewood Country Club, Inc., then you are instructed that the defendants stood in a fiduciary relation to both the corporation as a separate legal entity and the members, including those persons who it was to be anticipated would make application to and would become members in Lakewood Country Club, Inc. Such a fiduciary relationship on the part of the defendants, should you find them to be the promoters of the Lakewood Country Club, Inc., required that they exercise the utmost good faith in their relations with the corporation and the members, including fully advising the corporation and members and persons who it was to be anticipated would become members, of any interest which the defendants had that would in any way affect the corporation, the members and anticipated members. Such a full disclosure requirement, if you should find the defendants to be promoters, would obligate them to faithfully make known all facts which might have influenced prospective members in deciding whether or not to purchase memberships. And this full disclosure would include the duty to refrain from misrepresenting any material facts, as well as the duty to make known any personal interest the defendants had in any transaction relating to the country club enterprise.

Also you are instructed that if you should find beyond a reasonable doubt that the defendants were promoters of the Lakewood Country Club, Inc., and that the funds obtained by them from members of the club corporation to accomplish the purposes of the corporation were used by them for the club's benefit, they were properly used. On the other hand, if you should find beyond a reasonable doubt that the defendants were the promoters of the club corporation, and that they had intentionally converted those funds to their own personal use, such would be a fraud on the members of the club corporation, since such funds were in the nature of trust funds as to which the defendants had a fiduciary obligation. And in that connection you are further instructed that for promoters to knowingly use their fiduciary position to obtain secret profits at the expense of the corporation of its members would not only be a breach of that fiduciary duty but an act of fraud.

407 F.2d 319, 328 n.51.

NOTES

(1) *Post v. United States* is unusual in that it involved a criminal prosecution of a promoter; most reported promoter cases involve civil suits brought against the promoter by injured parties. In *Post*, however, civil suits against the promoters were foreclosed because the promoters voluntarily agreed to relinquish control of the Lakewood Country Club project in exchange for a general release from civil liability. Presumably, representatives of the Club agreed to this settlement because prospects of recovering the converted funds from the promoters were not good.

(2) If a subsequent investor has dealt directly with the promoter in connection with the investment, there is little doubt that the promoter is liable for common law fraud in the event of misrepresentation. An additional federal remedy for fraud, or for mere nondisclosure of a material fact, may be available under Rule 10b–5. See Chapter 14. A Rule 10b–5 case must be brought in the federal courts. The rule is applicable only if the fraud or nondisclosure is "in connection with the purchase or sale of a security" and the transaction involves use of a "telephone or other interstate means of communication or any other interstate facility."

(3) In addition to subsequent investors in the enterprise, who else may attack transactions between a promoter and the corporation on the ground the transaction violates the promoter's fiduciary duty? At least the following possibilities exist:

(a) *General creditors of the corporation or their representatives, usually trustees in bankruptcy or receivers.* These suits are based on a theory that the promoters converted corporate assets to their own use and thereby defrauded creditors. See, e.g., Frick v. Howard, 126 N.W.2d 619 (Wis.1964).

(b) *Co-promoters.* It is clear that a promoter is in a fiduciary relationship with his or her co-promoters. See Geving v. Fitzpatrick, 371 N.E.2d 1228 (Ill.App.1978). Co-promoters may be viewed as partners in a venture to create the business. However, if the venture is incorporated, complications may arise from the substitution of corporate relationships for partnership relationships.

(c) *The corporation.* The corporation itself may bring suit against its promoters after it has come under the control of subsequent investors or other persons.

(4) In recent years, litigation involving promoters' fraud has declined. This is partly due to Rule 10b–5 and partly due to enhanced enforcement of a different federal statute, the Securities Act of 1933, which makes it unlawful to use means of interstate commerce or the mails to sell publicly a security

unless a registration statement has been filed with the S.E.C. setting forth required information.

STANLEY J. HOW & ASSOC., INC. V. BOSS

United States District Court, Southern District of Iowa, 1963.
222 F. Supp. 936.

[This was an action to recover on a contract for the performance of architectural services. The plaintiff, Stanley J. How & Associates, Inc., alleged that it had performed the required services and was entitled to a fee of $38,250, of which it had received only $14,500. It seeks to collect the difference from Boss, a promoter of a corporation. The pertinent parts of the contract (with italics added) are as follows:

This agreement made as of the twentieth (20th) day of April in the year Nineteen Hundred and Sixty-One by and between *Boss Hotels Company, Inc. hereinafter called the Owner,* and Stanley J. How and Associates, Inc. hereinafter called the Architect * * *.

The Owner agrees to pay the Architect for such services a fee of six (6) percent of the construction cost of the Project, with other payments and reimbursements as hereinafter provided.

The Owner and the Architect each binds himself, his partners, successors, legal representatives and assigns to the other party to this Agreement and to the partners, successors, legal representatives and assigns of such other party in respect to all covenants of this Agreement.

Except as above, neither the Owner nor the Architect shall assign, sublet or transfer his interest in this Agreement without written consent of the other.

IN WITNESS WHEREOF the parties hereto have made and executed this Agreement the day and year first above written.

Owner: /s/ Edw. A. Boss   Architect:

By: Edwin A. Boss, agent for a   Stanley J. How and Associates,
Minnesota corporation to be   Inc.
formed who will be the obligor.
                                        /s/ Stanley J. How

This contract was the Standard Form of Agreement between Owner and Architect printed by the American Institute of Architects. The blanks were originally filled in by a representative of the plaintiff; as originally prepared, the signature clause as well as the caption referred to "Boss Hotels Co., Inc." as the "Owner." However, when the contract was presented to Boss, he erased the words "Boss Hotels Co., Inc." and inserted the language "By: Edwin A. Boss, agent for a Minnesota corporation to be formed who will be the obligor." He then asked Mr. How, "Is this all right?" or "Is this acceptable, this manner of signing?" or words to that effect. How said "Yes," and the contracts were then signed by defendant and Stanley J. How. Defendant apparently caused an Iowa corporation named Minneapolis-Hunter Hotel Co. to be formed to construct the project. The checks sent to plaintiff for partial payments under the contract bore the name of this corporation. The project was ultimately abandoned after a substantial amount of architectural work had been performed under the contract.]

HANSON, DISTRICT JUDGE.

* * * To what extent [the Minneapolis-Hunter Hotel Co.] actually came into being is not clear in the record. No corporate charter, by-laws, or resolutions were offered into evidence. At any rate, if this new corporation exists, there are no assets in it to pay the amount due on the contract.

There really is not much debate as to what the law is on the questions raised. Both parties [cite] King Features Syndicate, Dept. of Hearst Corp. International News Service Division v. Courrier, 43 N.W.2d 718, for the proposition that a promoter, though he may assume to act on behalf of the projected corporation and not for himself, will be personally liable on his contract unless the other party agreed to look to some other person or fund for payment. * * *

[The court then summarizes Comment b to Section 326 of the Restatement of Agency. This comment, as revised in the Restatement (Second) of Agency, reads:

b. *Promoters.* The classic illustration of the rule stated in this Section is the promoter. When a promoter makes an agreement with another on behalf of a corporation to be formed, the following alternatives may represent the intent of the parties:

(1) They may understand that the other party is making a revocable offer to the nonexistent corporation which will result in a contract if the corporation is formed and accepts the offer prior to withdrawal. * * *

(2) They may understand that the other party is making an irrevocable offer for a limited time. Consideration to support the promise to keep the offer open can be found in an express or limited promise by the promoter to organize the corporation and use his best efforts to cause it to accept the offer.

(3) They may agree to a present contract by which the promoter is bound, but with an agreement that his liability terminates if the corporation is formed and manifests its

willingness to become a party. There can be no ratification by the newly formed corporation, since it was not in existence when the agreement was made.

(4) They may agree to a present contract on which, even though the corporation becomes a party, the promoter remains liable either primarily or as surety for the performance of the corporation's obligation.

Which one of these possible alternatives, or variants thereof, is intended is a matter of interpretation on the facts of the individual case.]

[The third] possible interpretation is not very important in this case because a novation was not pleaded or argued. * * *

In the present case, the contract was signed: "Edwin A. Boss, agent for a Minnesota corporation to be formed who will be the obligor." The defendant argues that this is an agreement that the new corporation is solely liable. The problem here is what is the import of the words "who will be the obligor." It says nothing about the present obligor. The words "will be" connote something which will take place in the future. * * *

About the closest case to the present in terms of signature is O'Rorke v. Geary, 207 Pa. 240, 56 A. 541, where the contract was signed "D.J. Geary for a bridge company to be organized and incorporated as party of the second part." The payments were to be made monthly and work was to be done before it was possible for the corporation to make the payments. The court held the promoter personally liable. * * *

* * * [T]his is a situation where the parties used ambiguous words to describe their intentions. To resolve this ambiguity, it is helpful to resort to the usual rules of interpretation of ambiguous contracts. * * *

Mr. How's testimony and his business record * * * show that he did not intend that the new corporation was the sole obligor on the contract. He stated that he believed Boss Hotel[s] Co., Inc. or Boss Hotels was liable on the contract. This is not inconsistent with thinking Mr. Boss was liable on the contract, but it is inconsistent with intending that the new corporation was to be solely liable on the contract. Promoters other than the one signing the contract may be liable on the contract also. In this case, Boss Hotel[s] Co., Inc. was not made a party but this does show a reason why Mr. How might state that he felt Boss Hotel[s] Co., Inc. was liable on the contract. The oral testimony on this point was only generally to the effect that the parties agreed that the contract was all right as written, but did tend to support the conclusion that Mr. Boss was intended to be the present obligor on the contract. * * *

It might well be that the parties were thinking about an understanding such as the [third] type wherein there would be a future novation. However, the defendant didn't feel this was the situation. He did not plead or argue novation or agreement to that effect. Therefore, the only issue was whether the contract was a continuing offer to the then nonexistent corporation or was an agreement that Mr. Boss was a present obligor. While the agreement was not completely clear, the words "who will be the obligor," are not enough to offset the rule that the person signing for the nonexistent corporation is normally to be personally liable. This is especially true when considered in light of other circumstances of this case and would be true even without the inference that the law puts on this situation. * * *

The defendant argues that a practical construction has been put on the contract to the effect the plaintiff agreed to look solely to the credit of the new corporation. For this construction, the defendant relies upon the fact that the two checks which were given to Mr. [How] carried the letterhead of the new corporation and were signed by Edwin Hunter. * * * This would be an attempt to penalize the plaintiff for being patient and not demanding strict compliance. The court feels there was no waiver of rights and none was pleaded. * * *

In this case, the defendant was the principal promoter, acting for himself personally and as President of Boss Hotels, Inc. The promoters abandoned their purpose of forming the corporation. This would make the promoter liable to the plaintiff unless the contract be construed to mean: (1) that the plaintiff agreed to look solely to the new corporation for payment, and (2) that the promoter did not have any duty toward the plaintiff to form the corporation and give the corporation the opportunity to assume and pay the liability. * * *

At the time the specifications and drawings were completed, the amount owed the plaintiff was 75% of 6% of $850,000.00 (the reasonable cost estimate). This would amount to $38,250.00. $14,500.00 of this amount has been paid leaving an amount of $23,750.00 due to the plaintiff.

Accordingly the court concludes that the plaintiff, Stanley J. How & Associates, Inc., should have and recover judgment against the defendant, Edwin A. Boss, in the sum of $23,750.00, with interest and costs and, accordingly, a judgment will be entered. * * *

NOTES

(1) A promoter and a third party may reach agreement on the basic terms of a deal but may intend only that the third party make an offer that the corporation may or may not accept once it is formed. When performance is to begin after the corporation is organized, it may be difficult to determine whether the parties intended an offer or a contract. There is one circumstance, however, where it is apparent that a contract, rather than an offer, is intended. When performance begins before the corporation is formed, it is clear that the parties intended an immediate contract.

(2) If a promoter and a third party agree to a contract before the corporation is formed, several related questions are typically raised: (1) Is the promoter personally liable on the pre-incorporation contract? (2) Is the corporation, once formed, liable on the contract? (3) If the corporation is liable, is the promoter released from liability on the contract?

With respect to the first question, *Stanley J. How* states the general rule: a promoter is personally liable on a pre-incorporation contract. There is an exception if the third party who contracted with the promoter knew that the corporation was not in existence at the time of the contract, but nevertheless agreed, expressly or impliedly, to look solely to the corporation for performance.

(3) In the absence of an express agreement to look solely to the corporation for performance, it is often difficult to predict whether a court will find an implied agreement. For example, in Goodman v. Darden, Doman & Stafford Associates, 670 P.2d 648, 651–52 (Wash. 1983), a promoter (Goodman) signed a contract as president of a corporation "in formation." When the contract was breached, the court held the promoter liable to the third party (DDS):

> The mere signing of a contract with a corporation "in formation" does not suffice to show an agreement to look solely to the corporation. * * * The fact that DDS knew of the corporation's nonexistence is not dispositive in any way of its intent. The rule is that the contracting party may know of the nonexistence of the corporation *but nevertheless* may agree to look solely to the corporation. The fact that a contracting party knows that the corporation is nonexistent does not indicate any agreement to release the promoter. To the contrary, such knowledge alone would seem to indicate that the members of DDS intended to make Goodman a party to the contract. They could not hold the corporation, a nonexistent entity, responsible and of course they would expect to have recourse against someone (Goodman) if default occurred.

By contrast, in Company Stores Development Corp. v. Pottery Warehouse, Inc., 733 S.W.2d 886, 888 (Tenn. App. 1987), the court released a promoter from liability on a lease signed by the promoter as president of a corporation to be formed. The court held:

> [T]he stipulations of fact establish the plaintiff intended to look solely to [the corporation] for satisfaction of the obligation arising under the lease at the time of execution. At the time the lease was signed, plaintiff was aware of the nonexistence of the corporate entity and did not require [the promoter] to sign the agreement in an individual capacity but as president of a future corporate entity. The lease imputes no intention on the part of [the promoter] to be bound personally.

(4) Is it not a fair inference from the circumstances surrounding the execution of the contract in *Stanley J. How* that both parties probably contemplated that the architect was to look solely to some corporation for payment, that neither party thought that Boss was to be *personally* liable and that, therefore, the holding of the court in effect gives the plaintiff an unjustified windfall?

(5) Presumably, it would have been entirely feasible for Boss to have formed a new corporation or LLC to construct the project under the laws of either Minnesota or Iowa. If he had done so, and thereafter the contract had been entered into in the name of the new corporation or LLC, the possibility of a successful suit by the architect against Boss personally would have been very slight. The fact that cases involving promoter liability on contracts continue to arise suggests that many promoters do not have legal advice in the early stages of the promotion, since presumably an attorney would insist that basic rights and obligations be expressed reasonably clearly, and that some provision should be made for obvious contingencies such as a total failure of the promotion. An attorney representing the promoter would normally recommend that a corporation or an LLC be formed and that all contracts be taken in the name of that entity exclusively. The attorney should also recommend that the agreement expressly provide that the third party should look only to the entity for payment. Of course, counsel for the third party would doubtless recommend that the promoter expressly assume personal responsibility for performance of the contract.

(6) With respect to the corporation's liability (question (2) in note (2) above), a corporation, once formed, is liable on a pre-incorporation contract only if it "adopts" the contract. Adoption can be express (e.g., a board resolution) or implied (e.g., accepting the benefits of the contract). Technically, a corporation cannot "ratify" a promoter's contract because ratification requires a principal to be in existence at the time of the contract's formation. See Restatement (Second) of Agency §§ 84, 86(1) (1958); Restatement (Third) of Agency § 4.04(1) (2006). Whereas ratification retroactively validates a contract from the moment the contract was formed, adoption makes a corporation a party to a contract only from the moment of adoption.

(7) With respect to the promoter's liability after adoption by the corporation (question (3) in note (2) above), adoption does not, absent a novation, end the promoter's liability. See, e.g., Jacobson v. Stern, 605 P.2d 198, 201 (Nev. 1980) ("[L]iability of the corporation by adoption does not, absent a novation, end the liability of the promoter to the third party. * * * Where there is a valid express or implied novation, the corporation is substituted for the promoter as a party to the contract in all respects, and the promoter is divested of his rights and released of his liabilities."); Illinois Controls, Inc. v. Langham, 639 N.E.2d 771, 781 (Ohio 1994) ("[M]ere adoption of the contract by the corporation will not relieve promoters from liability in the absence of a subsequent novation. This view is founded upon 'the well-settled principle of the law of contracts that a party to a contract cannot

relieve himself from its obligations by the substitution of another person, without the consent of [the] other party.'" (quoting Ballantine, Manual of Corporation Law & Practice 163 (1930))). In this context, a novation would require an explicit or implicit agreement between the third party and the promoter that the promoter will be released from liability upon the corporation's adoption of the contract.

(8) 2 Williston on Contracts § 306, at 431 (3d ed. 1959) states that "it seems more nearly to correspond with the intentions of the parties to suggest that when the corporation assents to the contract, it assents to take the place of the promoter—a change of parties to which the other side of the contract assented in advance." Is that true? If this inference were adopted, might promoters facing an unwanted pre-formation contractual liability form a corporation with nominal assets and arrange to have that corporation adopt the contract?

(9) Section 326 of the Restatement (Second) of Agency and § 6.04 of the Restatement (Third) of Agency both reflect the general rule that a promoter is personally liable on a pre-incorporation contract when there is knowledge that the corporation has not been formed. Consider also §§ 329–331 of the Second Restatement and §§ 6.10, 7.01 of the Third Restatement. Do they suggest alternative grounds for holding the promoter liable if he misleads a third party into believing that a corporation has been formed (e.g., the promoter executes a contract in the name of a not-yet-formed corporation, but without including the phrase "a corporation to be formed")?

(10) A "head count" of the numerous cases involving the personal liability of promoters would doubtless show that a majority of the cases hold the defendant-promoter personally liable on one theory or another.

2. DEFECTIVE INCORPORATION

ROBERTSON V. LEVY
Court of Appeals, District of Columbia, 1964.
197 A.2d 443.

HOOD, CHIEF JUDGE.

On December 22, 1961, Martin G. Robertson and Eugene M. Levy entered into an agreement whereby Levy was to form a corporation, Penn Ave. Record Shack, Inc., which was to purchase Robertson's business. Levy submitted articles of incorporation to the Superintendent of Corporations on December 27, 1961, but no certificate of incorporation was issued at this time. Pursuant to the contract an assignment of lease was entered into on December 31, 1961, between Robertson and Levy, the latter acting as president of Penn Ave. Record Shack, Inc. On January 2, 1962, the articles of incorporation were rejected by the Superintendent of Corporations but on the same day Levy began to operate the business under the name Penn Ave. Record Shack, Inc. Robertson executed a bill of sale to Penn Ave. Record Shack, Inc. on January 8, 1962, disposing of the assets of his business to that "corporation" and receiving in return a note providing for installment payments signed "Penn Ave. Record Shack, Inc. by Eugene M. Levy, President." The certificate of incorporation was issued on January 17, 1962. One payment was made on the note. The exact date when the payment was made cannot be clearly determined from the record, but presumably it was made after the certificate of incorporation was issued. Penn Ave. Record Shack, Inc. ceased doing business in June 1962 and is presently without assets. Robertson sued Levy for the balance due on the note as well as for additional expenses incurred in settling the lease arrangement with the original lessor. In holding for the defendant the trial court found that [§ 139 of the 1950 Model Act],[f] relied upon by Robertson, did not apply and further that Robertson was estopped to deny the existence of the corporation.

The case presents the following issues on appeal: Whether the president of an "association" which filed its articles of incorporation, which were first rejected but later accepted, can be held personally liable on an obligation entered into by the "association" before the certificate of incorporation has been issued, or whether the creditor is "estopped" from denying the existence of the "corporation" because, after the certificate of incorporation was issued, he accepted the first installment payment on the note.

The Business Corporation Act of the District of Columbia, Code 1961, is patterned after the Model Business Corporation Act which is largely based on the Illinois Business Corporation Act of 1933. On this appeal, we are concerned with an interpretation of [§§ 50 and 139 of the 1950 Model Act].[g] Several states have substantially enacted the Model Act, but only a few have enacted both sections similar to those under consideration. A search of the case law in each of these jurisdictions, as well as in our own jurisdiction, convinces us that these particular sections of the corporation acts have never been the subject of a reported decision.

For a full understanding of the problems raised, some historical grounding is not only illuminative but necessary. In early common law times private corporations were looked upon with distrust and disfavor. This distrust of the corporate form for private enterprise was eventually overcome by the enactment of statutes which set forth certain prerequisites before the status was achieved, and by court decisions

---

[f]   § 139.   Unauthorized Assumption of Corporate Powers

All persons who assume to act as a corporation without authority so to do shall be jointly and severally liable for all debts and liabilities incurred or arising as a result thereof.

[g]   § 50.   Effect of issuance of incorporation.

Upon the issuance of the certificate of incorporation, the corporate existence shall begin, and such certificate of incorporation shall be conclusive evidence that all conditions precedent required to be performed by the incorporators have been complied with and that the corporation has been incorporated under this chapter, except as against the [state] in a proceeding to cancel or revoke the certificate of incorporation.

which eliminated other stumbling blocks. Problems soon arose, however, where there was substantial compliance with the prerequisites of the statute, but not complete formal compliance. Thus the concepts of de jure corporations, de facto corporations, and of "corporations by estoppel" came into being.

Taking each of these in turn, a de jure corporation results when there has been conformity with the mandatory conditions precedent (as opposed to merely directive conditions) established by the statute. A de jure corporation is not subject to direct or collateral attack either by the state in a *quo warranto* proceeding or by any other person.

A de facto corporation is one which has been defectively incorporated and thus is not de jure. The Supreme Court has stated that the requisites for a corporation de facto are: (1) A valid law under which such a corporation can be lawfully organized; (2) An attempt to organize thereunder; (3) Actual user of the corporate franchise. Good faith in claiming to be and in doing business as a corporation is often added as a further condition. A de facto corporation is recognized for all purposes except where there is a direct attack by the state in a *quo warranto* proceeding. The concept of de facto corporation has been roundly criticized.[6]

Cases continued to arise, however, where the corporation was not de jure, where it was not de facto because of failure to comply with one of the four requirements above, but where the courts, lacking some clear standard or guideline, were willing to decide on the equities of the case. Thus another concept arose, the so-called "corporation by estoppel." This term was a complete misnomer. There was no corporation, the acts of the associates having failed even to colorably fulfill the statutory requirements; there was no estoppel in the pure sense of the word because generally there was no holding out followed by reliance on the part of the other party. Apparently estoppel can arise whether or not a de facto corporation has come into existence. Estoppel problems arose where the certificate of incorporation had been issued as well as where it had not been issued, and under the following general conditions: where the "association" sues a third party and the third party is estopped from denying that the plaintiff is a corporation; where a third party sues the "association" as a corporation and the "association" is precluded from denying that it was a corporation; where a third party sues the "association" and the members of that association cannot deny its existence as a corporation where they participated in holding it out as a corporation; where a third party sues the individuals behind the "association" but is estopped from denying the existence of the

---

[6]   Ballantine § 20 ("a baffling and discouraging maze,"); Stevens, Corporations, pp. 135–6 (1949) ("inaccurate and confusing,"); Frey, Legal Analysis and the De Facto Doctrine, 100 U.Pa.L.Rev. 1153, 1180 (1952) ("legal conceptualism at its worst").

"corporation"; where either a third party, or the "association" is estopped from denying the corporate existence because of prior pleadings.

One of the reasons for enacting modern corporation statutes was to eliminate problems inherent in the de jure, de facto and estoppel concepts. * * *

The first portion of [§ 50] sets forth a *sine qua non* regarding compliance. No longer must the courts inquire into the equities of a case to determine whether there has been "colorable compliance" with the statute. The corporation comes into existence only when the certificate has been issued. Before the certificate issues, there is no corporation de jure, de facto or by estoppel. * * *

The authorities which have considered the problem are unanimous in their belief that [MBCA (1950) §§ 50 and 139] have put to rest de facto corporations and corporations by estoppel. Thus the Comment to [§ 50], * * * after noting that de jure incorporation is complete when the certificate is issued, states that:

> Since it is unlikely that any steps short of securing a certificate of incorporation would be held to constitute apparent compliance, the possibility that a de facto corporation could exist under such a provision is remote.[h]

Similarly, Professor Hornstein in his work on Corporate Law and Practice (1959) observes at § 29 that: "Statutes in almost half the jurisdictions have virtually eliminated the distinction between de jure and de facto corporations [citing § 139 of the Model Act]." * * *

The portion of [§ 50] which states that the certificate of incorporation will be "conclusive evidence" that all conditions precedent have been performed eliminates the problems of estoppel and de facto corporations once the certificate has been issued. The existence of the corporation is conclusive evidence against all who deal with it. Under [§ 139], if an individual or group of individuals assumes to act as a corporation before the certificate of incorporation has been issued, joint and several liability attaches. We hold, therefore, that the impact of these sections, when considered together, is to eliminate the concepts of estoppel and de facto corporateness under the Business Corporation Act of the District of Columbia. It is immaterial whether the third person believed he was dealing with a corporation or whether he intended to deal with a

---

[h] The comment to § 56 of the 1969 MBCA (identical to § 50 of the 1950 Act) was even more unambiguous: "Under the unequivocal provisions of the Model Act, any steps short of securing a certificate of incorporation would not constitute apparent compliance. Therefore a de facto corporation cannot exist under the Model Act." The comment to § 146 of the 1969 MBCA (identical to § 139 of the 1950 Act) added: "Abolition of the concept of de facto incorporation, which at best was fuzzy, is a sound result. No reason exists for its continuance under general corporate laws, where the process of acquiring de jure incorporation is both simple and clear. The vestigial appendage should be removed."

corporation.[14] The certificate of incorporation provides the cut off point; before it is issued, the individuals, and not the corporation, are liable.

Turning to the facts of this case, Penn Ave. Record Shack, Inc. was not a corporation when the original agreement was entered into, when the lease was assigned, when Levy took over Robertson's business, when operations began under the Penn Ave. Record Shack, Inc. name, or when the bill of sale was executed. Only on January 17 did Penn Ave. Record Shack, Inc. become a corporation. Levy is subject to personal liability because, before this date, he assumed to act as a corporation without any authority so to do. Nor is Robertson estopped from denying the existence of the corporation because after the certificate was issued he accepted one payment on the note. An individual who incurs statutory liability on an obligation under [§ 139] because he has acted without authority, is not relieved of that liability where, at a later time, the corporation does come into existence by complying with [§ 50]. Subsequent partial payment by the corporation does not remove this liability.

The judgment appealed from is reversed with instructions to enter judgment against the appellee on the note and for damages proved to have been incurred by appellant for breach of the lease.

Reversed with instructions.

NOTES

(1) If Robertson "admitted intending to deal with a corporation" (see footnote 14), why was he permitted to recover from Levy individually? Why does the court hold that shareholders are personally liable until the certificate of incorporation is issued?

(2) Under the version of the Model Act cited in *Robertson*, all persons "who assume to act as a corporation without authority" shall be jointly and severally liable for any debts incurred. Does this language encompass active participants as well as inactive investors? In Timberline Equipment Co. v. Davenport, 514 P.2d 1109, 1113–14 (Or. 1973), the court stated the following:

> We conclude that the category of "persons who assume to act as a corporation" does not include those whose only connection with the organization is as an investor. On the other hand, the restriction of liability to those who personally incurred the obligation sued upon cannot be based upon logic or the realities of business practice. When several people carry on the activities of a defectively organized corporation, chance frequently will dictate which of the several active principals directly incurs a certain obligation or whether an employee, rather than an active principal, personally incurs the obligation.

---

[14] In the present case, Robertson admitted intending to deal with a corporation.

We are of the opinion that the phrase, "persons who assume to act as a corporation," should be interpreted to include those persons who have an investment in the organization and who actively participate in the policy and operational decisions of the organization. Liability should not necessarily be restricted to the person who personally incurred the obligation.

(3) In Cantor v. Sunshine Greenery, Inc., 398 A.2d 571 (N.J.Super.1979), the plaintiff sued William J. Brunetti on a lease Brunetti had signed in the name of Sunshine Greenery, Inc. on December 16, 1974. Brunetti and Sharyn N. Sansoni signed a certificate of incorporation (equivalent to articles of incorporation) on December 3, and mailed it to the Secretary of State on the same date with a check for the filing fee. For some unexplained reason, the document was not officially filed by the Secretary of State until December 18, 1974, two days after the execution of the lease. The court held that Sunshine Greenery, Inc. was a de facto corporation and that Brunetti was not personally liable:

> In view of the late filing, Sunshine Greenery, Inc. was not a *de jure* corporation on December 16, 1974 when the lease was signed. Nevertheless, there is ample evidence of the fact that it was a *de facto* corporation in that there was a *bona fide* attempt to organize the corporation some time before the consummation of the contract and there was an actual exercise of the corporate powers by the negotiations with plaintiffs and the execution of the contract involved in this litigation.

Can you see factual differences between *Cantor* and *Robertson* that might justify, on policy grounds, the difference in result? Another possible basis for reconciling the two cases is the difference in statutory provisions in the District of Columbia and New Jersey. As indicated in *Robertson,* the critical provisions in the District of Columbia were drawn directly from §§ 50 and 139 of the 1950 Model Act. New Jersey was not a Model Act state.

(4) In Cranson v. International Business Machines Corp., 200 A.2d 33 (Md.1964), Cranson was not held personally liable for the debts of his defectively incorporated association, the Real Estate Service Bureau. Cranson had agreed to invest in the Real Estate Service Bureau and to become an officer and a director of the new company. Cranson and his fellow investors hired a lawyer who assured them that the corporation had been formed under the laws of Maryland. Cranson paid for and received stock certificates, and the company set up bank accounts and maintained corporate books and records. Unknown to Cranson, due to an oversight on the part of the attorney, the certificate of incorporation was not filed with the Secretary of State until approximately seven months after the certificate had been prepared and signed. By that time, the business had purchased eight typewriters from IBM on credit. The court held that because IBM dealt with the Bureau as if it were a corporation and relied on its credit rather than that of Cranson, it was "estopped to deny the corporate existence of the Bureau."

The court in *Cranson* distinguished between the doctrine of de facto corporation and the doctrine of corporation by estoppel. The court observed that both doctrines are applied to protect officers and shareholders of defectively incorporated associations. The doctrine of de facto corporation is applied to cases where elements show: (1) the existence of law authorizing incorporation; (2) an effort in good faith to incorporate under the existing law; and (3) actual use or exercise of corporate powers. In contrast, the doctrine of estoppel to deny the corporate existence is applied where the person seeking to hold the officer or shareholder personally liable has contracted with the association in a manner that recognizes and admits its existence as a corporation.

The court observed that, while some cases assimilate these two doctrines, they are not dependent upon one another. Where the three elements of a de facto corporation are found, there exists an entity which is a corporation de jure against all persons but the state. The estoppel theory, however, is only applied to the facts of each case and may be invoked even where there is no corporation de facto. For example, even though a requirement for a de facto corporation was arguably missing in *Cranson* (i.e., a seven-month delay in filing may not have constituted a good faith effort to incorporate), this did not preclude the court from applying the estoppel doctrine.

(5) The sections relied upon by the *Robertson* court (§ 50 and § 139 of the 1950 Model Act) are now found in substance at §§ 2.03–2.04 of the current MBCA. How does § 2.03 differ from § 50? How does § 2.04 differ from § 139? Is § 2.04 consistent with the *Timberline* holding above?

(6) How would *Robertson*, *Cantor*, and *Cranson* come out under MBCA § 2.04?

(7) Do §§ 2.03–2.04 of the current MBCA eliminate the de facto corporation and corporation by estoppel doctrines in Model Act jurisdictions? Please consider the Official Comment to MBCA § 2.04.

(8) Delaware is not a Model Act jurisdiction. Unlike MBCA § 2.03, the DGCL has no provision indicating that filing is "conclusive proof" of incorporation. Compare DGCL §§ 105–106. Further, the DGCL has no provision like MBCA § 2.04. It is, therefore, not surprising that Delaware accepts the de facto corporation doctrine. See, e.g., Trustees of Peninsula Annual Conference v. Spencer, 183 A.2d 588 (Del. Ch. 1962).

DGCL § 329(a) preserves certain variants of the estoppel doctrine. It indicates that neither a purported corporation, nor a third party with whom it deals, should be able to avoid contracts based on defects in the incorporation process. The section does not address, however, the *Cranson* scenario where the doctrine of estoppel to deny the corporation's existence is applied against a third party who knowingly deals with a corporation, but who then seeks to hold an officer or shareholder personally liable for the obligation. It seems likely that a Delaware court would accept an estoppel argument in this context.

FRONTIER REFINING COMPANY V. KUNKEL'S, INC.

Supreme Court of Wyoming, 1965.
407 P.2d 880.

JUSTICE GRAY delivered the opinion of the Court.

Plaintiff Frontier Refining Company commenced an action against Kunkel's, Inc., as a partnership, and George Fairfield, Clifford D. Kunkel and Harlan Beach, as members thereof, to recover a balance claimed due on an open account. By its amended complaint, Frontier alleged that the individual defendants by oral agreement were associated in the business of operating a service station and truck terminal in Cheyenne, Wyoming, as a partnership under the name of Kunkel's, Inc., and were indebted to plaintiff in the sum of $6,732.32 for gasoline sold by plaintiff to said partnership. The defendant Kunkel was never served and the action proceeded against the defendants Fairfield and Beach. Both denied that any partnership was ever created between the individual defendants; denied that they were ever associated in the operation of any business with the defendant Kunkel under the name of Kunkel's, Inc.; and affirmatively alleged that the defendant Kunkel operated the business as an individual. Upon trial, the court found that the business known as Kunkel's, Inc., was not a partnership composed of the individual defendants; found generally for the defendants; and judgment was entered dismissing the action. Frontier appeals from the judgment. Hereafter we shall refer to the individual defendants by their last names.

* * * [I]t is Frontier's position that when this occurs the parties are individually liable as partners for the debts incurred in the business venture. To support its position Frontier cites, among other authorities, the general rule set forth in 68 C.J.S. Partnership § 40, p. 462, which states:

> * * * In most jurisdictions the rule is * * * to the effect that, where two or more persons hold themselves out as a corporation, or permit an association of which they are incorporators, stockholders, or members to be so held out, when there is no corporation either de jure or de facto, they will all be liable individually as partners for its debts and on contracts entered into either by themselves or by others as agents of the pretended corporation and in its name * * *.

* * * Nevertheless, as an initial approach to the problem here, we have been somewhat bothered as to whether or not such rule, which was laid down independently of statute, affords the remedy which Frontier seeks to pursue. A statutory remedy relating to the matter was in effect at the time the business transactions here took place. Section 17–36.122, W.S.1957, provides as follows:

All persons who assume to act as a corporation without authority so to do shall be jointly and severally liable for all debts and liabilities incurred or arising as a result thereof.

* * * In order that the basis for the conclusion reached be understood, it is necessary to relate the evidence in some detail. In this connection, however, we might point out that much of the testimony upon which appellant relies was in conflict with the evidence favorable to the defendants. * * *

With respect to the facts, the record discloses that Frontier was a refiner and distributor of petroleum products. About the middle of May 1962 Kunkel became interested in taking over a filling station and truck stop in Cheyenne, Wyoming, owned by Frontier and which was then under lease to one "Woody" Griffitt. Such lease, however, was about to be terminated. Kunkel talked with B. L. Warren, zone manager of Frontier, and advised Warren that he had no money to finance the venture but was acquainted with Fairfield and would talk with Fairfield to see "if he could raise the money." Kunkel then went to the Gas Hills area in Wyoming where Fairfield in association with Beach was engaged in a mining venture, and according to the testimony of Fairfield the approach of Kunkel was to obtain a loan. Fairfield declined and there was then some conversation with respect to the formation of a corporation. Fairfield advised Kunkel that if he and Beach went in on the venture it would have to be on that basis. Apparently very little was said concerning the details of the formation of the corporation except that it would be Kunkel's responsibility to see that the business was incorporated—which was not even attempted—and Kunkel was not to "open the door" unless that had been done. It was understood also that Kunkel would manage the business of the corporation and in order to get it started Fairfield and Beach would purchase the equipment from Griffitt and would then take stock for their investment. Each defendant was to receive one-third of the stock of the corporation.

A short time later Fairfield came to Cheyenne and looked over the station. Warren, Frontier's employee, testified that this was about June 1, 1962; that he talked with Fairfield at that time; that he was told by Fairfield that the business would be a corporation; and that he was also told "Cliff [Kunkel] would be able to go on it." However, Fairfield testified that he did not see Warren at that time and had never said anything to Warren about a proposed corporation. Neither is there evidence that Beach ever discussed such matters with anyone. In this connection, however, Warren on May 28, 1962, by written memorandum advised Frontier that the business was to be incorporated under the name of "Kunkel's Incorporated" and would be financed by Fairfield and Beach and that both would be officers of the corporation. Warren also submitted with the memorandum a financial statement of Kunkel, which he said was not to be considered that of the corporation. No financial statement of Fairfield or Beach was ever obtained or submitted to Frontier.

Also, on June 1, 1962, Frontier entered into a sublease agreement for the station with "CLIFFORD D. KUNKEL DBA KUNKEL'S INC.," as sublessee, which was to become effective on June 12, 1962. Other agreements were entered into in the same manner and with one exception the agreements were signed "C. D. Kunkel" without reference to the purported corporate name or any corporate capacity. The exception was the "Distributor's Contract" which set forth the conditions relating to the purchase and sale of petroleum products. Here the name "Kunkel's, Inc." preceded the signature. Right here we might also point out Fairfield's testimony to the effect that he never saw these agreements until sometime in November 1962, and that he had not previously discussed with Kunkel the negotiation of such agreements.

Soon after the agreements were made, Kunkel, unknown to Fairfield or Beach, took over the station and commenced doing business. The first sale of gasoline by Frontier to the station was made on June 13, 1962, and was billed "Clifford D. Kunkel dba Kunkel Inc." Subsequent sales were billed in the same manner. Some thirty days after the initial sale Frontier discovered that through error the products purchased by the station were not paid for at the time of delivery as had been provided in the "Distributor's Contract," and an indebtedness in excess of $5,000 accrued during that period.

It is also in evidence that Fairfield and Beach put some $11,000 into the venture, but the exact dates that these payments were made cannot be ascertained from the record. However, the testimony of Fairfield tends to show that two of the checks aggregating the sum of $10,000 to be used for the purchase of the inventory and equipment from Griffitt were made subsequent to the time that Kunkel opened the station. With respect to all of these payments Fairfield testified that he was not aware of Kunkel's failure at that time to incorporate the business and there is no evidence that he was aware of the indebtedness that had accrued during the thirty-day period. Fairfield also denied the testimony of Warren that Fairfield, when the delinquency was called to his attention, gave assurances that the account would be paid.

* * * However, the foregoing, when carefully analyzed, lends sufficient support to the trial court's conclusion that the facts here were such that individual liability could not be imposed upon Fairfield and Beach on the theory that they were partners in the venture under general rules of law relating to a purported corporation.

In the first instance the trial court was entitled to infer that Kunkel was the sole source of the information given to Frontier concerning a proposed corporation under the name of Kunkel's, Inc., and that neither Fairfield nor Beach, expressly or impliedly, authorized Kunkel to make such representations or to enter into contracts with Frontier in the name of "Kunkel's, Inc." Such fact would lend substantial support to a conclusion that neither Fairfield nor Beach held themselves out as a corporation, an essential element under the general rule advanced by Frontier.

Another inference that could readily be drawn was that the indebtedness was not incurred in the name of a pretended corporation. At the outset of the business relations between Frontier and the venture in question, Frontier with full knowledge that a corporation had not yet been formed chose to transact its business with Kunkel as an individual. * * * Now, after extending credit by mistake, it attempts to explain that the reason its business transactions were entered into with Kunkel as an individual was the lack of a corporate entity with which to contract. Such explanation would hardly prevent the trial court from concluding that Frontier did not extend credit or intend to extend credit to "Kunkel's, Inc.," and that Frontier was content to look only to Kunkel for performance of its agreements. It has been determined that a creditor, under such circumstances, will be held to his bargain. *Guilford Builders Supply Company v. Reynolds, 249 N.C. 612, 107 S.E.2d 80, 83.* * * *

It appears to us also that Frontier's position is inconsistent. When it became obvious that the business operated by Kunkel was insolvent, Frontier obtained from him a chattel mortgage naming "Clifford D. Kunkel, individually and doing business as Kunkel's, Inc." as mortgagor and signed simply as "C. D. Kunkel." The mortgage disclosed on its face that it was not executed in the name of or on behalf of a corporation, pretended or otherwise. It covered the equipment used in the station and was given to secure the indebtedness owing Frontier. Subsequently Fairfield, claiming to own such equipment, took possession of it. Thereupon Frontier, in a companion case, brought an action in replevin to recover possession of the property in order that its mortgage might be foreclosed. With respect to this proceeding the trial court found that the mortgage was valid and entered judgment for Frontier. That judgment has now become final, no appeal having been taken by either of the parties. As a consequence, Frontier is in this position. In this appeal it is protesting the finding of the trial court that there was no partnership composed of the individual defendants. Yet, in the companion case—consolidated for trial with this case—it accepts the fruits of a judgment which carries with it an inherent finding by the trial court that Kunkel, as an individual, was Frontier's debtor and the owner of the property pledged to secure such debt. To permit Frontier to disavow such judgment to the extent of imposing liability upon Fairfield and Beach under the general rule advanced by Frontier, would be unconscionable. Imposition by the courts of the general rules relating to a defective corporation are subject to equitable principles, *Loverin v. McLaughlin, 161 Ill. 417, 44 N.E. 99, 105;* and we think the statement in the opinion of the Supreme

Court of Iowa, *Schumacher v. Sumner Telephone Co., 161 Iowa 326, 142 N.W. 1034, 1038, Ann.Cas.1916A, 201*—a case presenting a much closer question than does the case here—is quite pertinent. There the court said:

> * * * To recover, appellant must bring himself clearly within the benefit of some established rule or principle of the law, and in this we think he has failed. There is very little shown to commend his demand against the appellees to equitable consideration, and the court ought not to go out of its way to discover grounds for compelling payment of his claim by parties who did not contract the debt, who had no knowledge of its existence until suit was begun thereon, who gave no authority to Robish to borrow money on their account, and where the lender did not part with his money relying upon their conduct or credit. * * *

Finding no error in the proceedings, we affirm the judgment.

Affirmed.

NOTES

(1) *Kunkel's* illustrates the risk of entering into a business relationship without double-checking to make sure that a proper filing has been made with the relevant authorities. Here the risk was that the investors would be treated as partners. On what basis did the defendants in this case avoid personal liability?

(2) In light of the fact that the business suffered losses and that somebody had to bear them, which party was in the best position to shoulder the losses as between the creditors and the outside investors? Is this issue best decided on a case-by-case basis or as a matter of general policy?

CHAPTER 6

DISREGARD OF THE CORPORATE ENTITY

■ ■ ■

A. THE COMMON LAW DOCTRINE OF PIERCING THE CORPORATE VEIL

BARTLE V. HOME OWNERS CO-OP.

Court of Appeals of New York, 1955.
127 N.E.2d 832.

FROESSEL, JUDGE.

Plaintiff, as trustee in bankruptcy of Westerlea Builders, Inc., has by means of this litigation attempted to hold defendant liable for the contract debts of Westerlea, defendant's wholly owned subsidiary. Defendant, as a co-operative corporation composed mostly of veterans, was organized in July, 1947, for the purpose of providing low-cost housing for its members. Unable to secure a contractor to undertake construction of the housing planned, Westerlea was organized for that purpose on June 5, 1948. With building costs running considerably higher than anticipated, Westerlea, as it proceeded with construction on some 26 houses, found itself in a difficult financial situation. On January 24, 1949, the creditors, pursuant to an extension agreement, took over the construction responsibilities. Nearly four years later, in October, 1952, Westerlea was adjudicated as bankrupt. Meanwhile, defendant had contributed to Westerlea not only its original capital of $25,000 but additional sums amounting to $25,639.38.

Plaintiff's principal contention on this appeal is that the courts below erred in refusing to "pierce the corporate veil" of Westerlea's corporate existence; as subordinate grounds for recovery he urged that the defendant equitably pledged its assets toward the satisfaction of the debts of the bankrupt's creditors, and that the doctrine of unjust enrichment should apply.

The trial court made detailed findings of fact which have been unanimously affirmed by the Appellate Division, 285 App.Div. 1113, 140 N.Y.S.2d 512, which are clearly supported by the evidence, and by which we are bound. It found that while the defendant, as owner of the stock of Westerlea, controlled its affairs, the outward indicia of these two separate corporations was at all times maintained during the period in which the creditors extended credit; that the creditors were in no wise misled; that

213

there was no fraud; and that the defendant performed no act causing injury to the creditors of Westerlea by depletion of assets or otherwise. The trial court also held that the creditors were estopped by the extension agreement from disputing the separate corporate identities.

We agree with the courts below. The law permits the incorporation of a business for the very purpose of escaping personal liability. Generally speaking, the doctrine of "piercing the corporate veil" is invoked "to prevent fraud or to achieve equity," International Aircraft Trading Co. v. Manufacturers Trust Co., 297 N.Y. 285, 292, 79 N.E.2d 249, 252. But in the instant case there has been neither fraud, misrepresentation nor illegality. Defendant's purpose in placing its construction operation into a separate corporation was clearly within the limits of our public policy.

The judgment appealed from should be affirmed, without costs.

VAN VOORHIS, JUDGE (dissenting).

The judgment of the Appellate Division should be reversed on the law, as it seems to me, and plaintiff should have judgment declaring defendant to be liable for the debts of the bankrupt, Westerlea Builders, Inc., and that defendant holds its real property subject to the claims of creditors of Westerlea. Not only is Westerlea a wholly owned subsidiary of defendant, Home Owners, having the same directors and management, but also and of primary importance, business was done on such a basis that Westerlea could not make a profit. Home Owners owned a residential subdivision; Westerlea was organized as a building corporation to erect homes for stockholders of Home Owners upon lots in this tract. Home Owners arranged with Westerlea for the construction of houses and then would sell the lots on which such houses had been erected to Home Owners' stockholders—at prices fixed by Home Owners' price policy committee in such amounts as to make no allowance for profit by Westerlea. The object was to benefit Home Owners' stockholders by enabling them to obtain their houses at cost, with no builder's profit.

The consequence is that described by Latty, Subsidiaries and Affiliated Corporations at pages 138–139: "The subsidiaries had, to begin with, nothing, made nothing, and could only end up with nothing. It is not surprising that the parent was held liable in each case." And again: "This set-up is often, though not necessarily, found in combination with a scheme whereby the corporation cannot possibly make profits (or can at the most make only nominal profits), and whereby all the net income in the course of the corporation's business is drained off as operating charges of one sort or another. The presence of this additional factor should remove any doubt that may remain as to the right of the creditor of the corporation not to be limited to the corporate assets for the satisfaction of his debt."

In the present instance, Westerlea was organized with a small capital supplied by Home Owners, which soon became exhausted. Thereafter, it had no funds and could acquire none over and beyond the actual cost of the houses which it was building for stockholders of Home Owners. Those stockholders obtained the entire benefit of Westerlea's operations by obtaining these houses at cost. Not only was Westerlea allowed no opportunity to make money, but it was placed in a position such that if its business were successful and times remained good, it would break even, otherwise it would inevitably become insolvent. The stockholders of Home Owners became the beneficiaries of its insolvency. This benefit to the stockholders of Home Owners was analogous to dividends, at least it was something of value which was obtained by them from Home Owners by virtue of their stock ownership. Under the circumstances, this benefit to its stockholders was a benefit to Home Owners as a corporation.

It follows that Westerlea was merely an agent of Home Owners to construct houses at cost for Home Owners stockholders, and therefore Home Owners is rendered liable for Westerlea's indebtedness.

CONWAY, C.J., and DESMOND, DYE, FULD and BURKE, JJ., concur with FROESSEL, J.

VAN VOORHIS, J., dissents in an opinion.

DEWITT TRUCK BROKERS V. W. RAY FLEMMING FRUIT CO.

United States Court of Appeals, Fourth Circuit, 1976.
540 F.2d 681.

Before RUSSELL and WIDENER, CIRCUIT JUDGES, and THOMSEN, SENIOR DISTRICT JUDGE.

DONALD RUSSELL, CIRCUIT JUDGE:

In this action on debt, the plaintiff seeks, by piercing the corporate veil under the law of South Carolina, to impose individual liability on the president of the indebted corporation individually.[1] The District Court, making findings of fact which may be overturned only if clearly erroneous, pierced the corporate veil and imposed individual liability. The individual defendant appeals. We affirm.

At the outset, it is recognized that a corporation is an entity, separate and distinct from its officers and stockholders, and that its debts are not the individual indebtedness of its stockholders. This is expressed in the presumption that the corporation and its stockholders are separate and distinct. And this oft-stated principle is equally applicable, whether the corporation has many or only one stockholder. But this concept of separate entity is merely a legal theory, "introduced for purposes of

---

[1]   The corporate defendant, it is conceded, is not responsive to judgment.

convenience and to subserve the ends of justice," and the courts "decline to recognize [it] whenever recognition of the corporate form would extend the principle of incorporation 'beyond its legitimate purposes and [would] produce injustices or inequitable consequences.'" Krivo Industrial Supp. Co. v. National Distill. & Chem. Corp. (5th Cir.1973), 483 F.2d 1098, 1106. Accordingly, "in an appropriate case and in furtherance of the ends of justice," the corporate veil will be pierced and the corporation and its stockholders "will be treated as identical." 18 Am.Juris.2d at 559.

This power to pierce the corporate veil, though, is to be exercised "reluctantly" and "cautiously" and the burden of establishing a basis for the disregard of the corporate fiction rests on the party asserting such claim. Coryell v. Phipps (5th Cir.1942), 128 F.2d 702, 704, aff., 317 U.S. 406, 63 S.Ct. 291, 87 L.Ed. 363 (1943).

The circumstances which have been considered significant by the courts in actions to disregard the corporate fiction have been "rarely articulated with any clarity." Swanson v. Levy (9th Cir.1975), 509 F.2d 859, 861–2. Perhaps this is true because the circumstances "necessarily vary according to the circumstances of each case," and every case where the issue is raised is to be regarded as *sui generis,* [to] * * * be decided in accordance with its own underlying facts." Since the issue is thus one of fact, its resolution "is particularly within the province of the trial court" and such resolution will be regarded as "presumptively correct and [will] be left undisturbed on appeal unless it is clearly erroneous."

Contrary to the basic contention of the defendant, however, proof of plain fraud is not a necessary element in a finding to disregard the corporate entity. * * * [E]qually as well settled * * * is the rule that the mere fact that all or almost all of the corporate stock is owned by one individual or a few individuals, will not afford sufficient grounds for disregarding corporateness. But when substantial ownership of all the stock of a corporation in a single individual is combined with other factors clearly supporting disregard of the corporate fiction on grounds of fundamental equity and fairness, courts have experienced "little difficulty" and have shown no hesitancy in applying what is described as the "alter ego" or "instrumentality" theory in order to cast aside the corporate shield and to fasten liability on the individual stockholder. Iron City S. & G. Div. of McDonough Co. v. West Fork Tow. Corp., [N.D.W.Va.1969] 298 F.Supp. at 1098.

But, in applying the "instrumentality" or "alter ego" doctrine, the courts are concerned with reality and not form, with how the corporation operated and the individual defendant's relationship to that operation. * * * [T]he authorities have indicated certain facts which are to be given substantial weight in this connection. One fact which all the authorities consider significant in the inquiry, and particularly so in the case of the one-man or closely-held corporation, is whether the corporation was grossly undercapitalized for the purposes of the corporate undertaking. Mull v. Colt Co. (S.D.N.Y.1962), 31 F.R.D. 154, 163; Automotriz Del Golfo De Cal. v. Resnick (1957), 47 Cal.2d 792, 306 P.2d 1, 63 A.L.R.2d 1042, 1048, with annotation.[13] And, "[t]he obligation to provide adequate capital begins with incorporation and is a continuing obligation thereafter * * * during the corporation's operations." Other factors that are emphasized in the application of the doctrine are failure to observe corporate formalities,[14] non-payment of dividends, the insolvency of the debtor corporation at the time, siphoning of funds of the corporation by the dominant stockholder, non-functioning of other officers or directors, absence of corporate records, and the fact that the corporation is merely a facade for the operations of the dominant stockholder or stockholders. The conclusion to disregard the corporate entity may not, however, rest on a single factor, whether undercapitalization, disregard of [the] corporation's formalities, or what-not, but must involve a number of such factors; in addition, it must present an element of injustice or fundamental unfairness. * * *

If these factors, which were deemed significant in other cases concerned with this same issue, are given consideration here, the finding of the District Court that the corporate entity should be disregarded was not clearly erroneous. Certainly the [W. Ray Flemming Fruit Company] was, in practice at least, a close, one-man corporation from the very beginning. Its incorporators were the defendant Flemming, his wife and

---

[13] * * * In *Mull,* supra, 31 F.R.D. at 163, the Court quoted from Ballentine, Corporations, 303 (rev. ed. 1946):

> * * * It is coming to be recognized as the policy of the law that shareholders should in good faith put at the risk of the business unencumbered capital reasonably adequate for its prospective liabilities. If the capital is illusory or trifling compared with the business to be done and the risks of loss, this is a ground for denying the separate entity privilege.

In Note, Disregard of the Corporate Entity: Contract Claims, 28 Ohio S.L.J. 441 (1967), the author argues that undercapitalization as a factor in determining whether to pierce the corporate veil should be inapplicable in contract cases; cf., however, Note, Limited Liability: A Definite Judicial Standard for the Inadequate Capitalization Problem, 47 Temple L.Q. 32 (1974). The reasoning is that when one extends credit or makes any other contractual arrangement with a corporation, it is to be assumed [that] he acquaints himself with the corporation's capitalization and contracts on such basis, and not on the individual credit of the dominant stockholder. In this case, however, that reasoning would be inapplicable, since the plaintiff did not rely on the corporation's capitalization but received an assurance from Flemming of personal liability.

[14] House of Koscot Dev. Corp. v. American Line Cosmetics, Inc. (5th Cir.1972), 468 F.2d 64, 66–7 ("* * * Turner ignored normal corporate formalities * * *"); Lakota Girl Scout C., Inc. v. Havey Fund-Rais. Man., Inc. (8th Cir.1975), 519 F.2d 634, 638 ("* * * corporate formalities [were] not followed * * *"). While disregard of corporate formalities is a circumstance to be considered, it is generally held to be insufficient in itself, without some other facts, to support a piercing of the corporate veil.

Cf., Zubik v. Zubik (3d Cir.1967), 384 F.2d 267, 271, cert. denied, 390 U.S. 988, 88 S.Ct. 1183, 19 L.Ed.2d 1291 (1968), n. 4, where the Court stated that "[i]n the context of an attempt by an outside party to pierce the corporate veil of such a closely-held corporation, the informalities are considered of little consequence." * * *

See, however, Harrison v. Puga (1971), 4 Wash.App. 52, 480 P.2d 247, 254, where the Court said that if the defendants disregarded the corporate formalities, they could hardly complain if the court did likewise.

his attorney. It began in 1962 with a capitalization of 5,000 shares, issued for a consideration of one dollar each. In some manner which Flemming never made entirely clear, approximately 2,000 shares were retired. At the times involved here Flemming owned approximately 90% of the corporation's outstanding stock, according to his own testimony, though this was not verified by any stock records. Flemming was obscure on who the other stockholders were and how much stock these other stockholders owned, giving at different times conflicting statements as to who owned stock and how much. His testimony on who were the officers and directors was hardly more direct. He testified that the corporation did have one other director, Ed Bernstein, a resident of New York. It is significant, however, that, whether Bernstein was nominally a director or not, there were no corporate records of a real directors' meeting in all the years of the corporation's existence and Flemming conceded this to be true. Flemming countered this by testifying that Bernstein traveled a great deal and that his contacts with Bernstein were generally by telephone. The evidence indicates rather clearly that Bernstein was * * * "nothing more than [a figurehead]," who had "attended no directors' meeting," and even more crucial, never received any fee or reimbursement of expenses or salary of any kind from the corporation.

The District Court found, also, that the corporation never had a stockholders' meeting. * * * It is thus clear that corporate formalities, even rudimentary formalities, were not observed by the defendant.

Beyond the absence of any observance of corporate formalities is the purely personal matter in which the corporation was operated. No stockholder or officer of the corporation other than Flemming ever received any salary, dividend, or fee from the corporation, or, for that matter, apparently exercised any voice in its operation or decisions. In all the years of the corporation's existence, Flemming was the sole beneficiary of its operations and its continued existence was for his exclusive benefit. During these years, he was receiving from $15,000 to $25,000 each year from a corporation, which, during most of the time, was showing no profit and apparently had no working capital. Moreover, the payments to Flemming were authorized under no resolution of the board of directors of the corporation, as recorded in any minutes of a board meeting. Actually, it would seem that Flemming's withdrawals varied with what could be taken out of the corporation at the moment: If this amount were $15,000, that was Flemming's withdrawal; if it were $25,000 that was his withdrawal. * * *

That the corporation was undercapitalized, if indeed it were not without any real capital, seems obvious. Its original stated "risk capital" had long since been reduced to approximately $3,000 by a reduction in the outstanding capital, or at least this would seem to be inferable from the record, and even this, it seems fair to conclude, had been seemingly exhausted by a long succession of years when the corporation operated at no profit. The inability of the corporation to pay a dividend is persuasive proof of this want of capital. In fact, the defendant Flemming makes no effort to refute the evidence of want of any capital reserves on the part of the corporation. It appears patent that the corporation was actually operating at all times involved here on someone else's capital. This conclusion follows from a consideration of the manner in which Flemming operated in the name of the corporation during the year when plaintiff's indebtedness was incurred.

The corporation was engaged in the business of a commission agent, selling fruit produce for the account of growers of farm products such as peaches and watermelons in the Edgefield, South Carolina, area. It never purported to own such products; * * * it (always acting through Flemming) sold the products as agent for the growers. Under the arrangement with the growers, it was to remit to the growers the full sale price, less any transportation costs incurred in transporting the products from the growers' farm or warehouse to the purchaser and its sales commission. An integral part of these collections was * * * represented by the plaintiff's transportation charges. Accordingly, during the period involved here, the corporation had as operating funds seemingly only its commissions and the amount of the plaintiff's transportation charges, for which the corporation had claimed credit in its settlement with its growers. At the time, however, Flemming was withdrawing funds from the corporation at the rate of at least $15,000 per year; and doing this, even though he must have known that the corporation could only do this by withholding payment of the transportation charges due the plaintiff, which in the accounting with the growers Flemming represented had been paid the plaintiff. And, it is of some interest that the amount due the plaintiff for transportation costs was approximately the same as the $15,000 minimum annual salary the defendant testified he was paid by the corporation. Were the opinion of the District Court herein to be reversed, Flemming would be permitted to retain substantial sums from the operations of the corporation without having any real capital in the undertaking, risking nothing of his own and using as operating capital what he had collected as due the plaintiff. Certainly, equity and fundamental justice support individual liability of Flemming for plaintiff's charges, payment for which he asserted in his accounting with the growers that he had paid and for which he took credit on such accounting. This case patently presents a blending of the very factors which courts have regarded as justifying a disregard of the corporate entity in furtherance of basic and fundamental fairness.

Finally, it should not be overlooked that at some point during the period when this indebtedness was being incurred—whether at the beginning or at a short time later is not clear in the record—the plaintiff became concerned about former delays in receipt of payment for its charges and, to allay that concern, Flemming stated to the plaintiff, according to the latter's testimony as credited by the District Court, that "he (i.e., Flemming) would take care of [the charges] personally, if the corporation failed to do so * * *." On this assurance, the plaintiff contended that it continued to haul for the defendant. The existence of this promise by Flemming is not disputed. * * * This assurance was given for the obvious purpose of promoting the *individual* advantage of Flemming. This follows because the only person who could profit from the continued operation of the corporation was Flemming. When one, who is the sole beneficiary of a corporation's operations and who dominates it, as did Flemming in this case, induces a creditor to extend credit to the corporation on such an assurance as given here, that fact has been considered by many authorities [to be a] sufficient basis for piercing the corporate veil. Weisser v. Mursam Shoe Corporation (2d Cir.1942), 127 F.2d 344, 145 A.L.R. 467. The only argument against this view is bottomed on the statute of frauds. But reliance on such statute is often regarded as without merit in a case where the promise or assurance is given "at the time or before the debt is created," for in that case the promise is original and without the statute. Goldsmith v. Erwin (4th Cir.1950), 183 F.2d 432, 435–6, 20 A.L.R.2d 240, with annotation. A number of courts, including South Carolina, however, have gone further and have held that, where the promisor owns substantially all the stock of the corporation and seeks by his promise to serve his personal pecuniary advantage, the question whether such promise is "within the statute of frauds" is a fact question to be resolved by the trial court and this is true whether the promise was made before the debt was incurred or during the time it was being incurred. Amer. Wholesale Corp. v. Mauldin (1924), 128 S.C. 241, 244–5, 122 S.E. 576. This is that type of case and may well have been resolved on this issue.

For the reasons stated, we conclude that the findings of the District Court herein are not clearly erroneous and the judgment of the District Court is

AFFIRMED.

NOTES

(1) One should not let the talismanic phrase, "piercing the corporate veil," obscure reality. The issue in piercing the corporate veil cases is whether a shareholder should be held personally liable for a corporate obligation. The decision to "pierce" in *DeWitt* does not mean that the Fruit Company was no longer a corporation. It remains in business; its name remains in the records of the Secretary of State; it has the privilege of filing federal and state income tax returns, and so forth. Further, it does not necessarily mean that *all* of the shareholders are personally liable for *all* of the obligations of the corporation. While DeWitt may be able to "pierce," other creditors may not; Fleming may be held personally liable on a "piercing" theory but the other shareholders (if

there in fact were any) may continue to be protected by the shield of limited liability. Basically, the piercing issue involves the precise question of whether a specific shareholder is personally liable for a specific corporate obligation, and the court's conclusion uses "piercing the corporate veil" as a justification to impose or refuse to impose liability in that specific context.

(2) The rhetoric and reasoning in *DeWitt* is typical of many "piercing the corporate veil" cases: long on rhetoric and contradictory general principles but short on reasoning. Indeed, perhaps in no other area are courts more prone to decide real life disputes by characterization, epithet, and metaphor: "alter ego," "instrumentality," "sham," "subterfuge," or "tool," to select a few. Various terms are often combined in artful phraseology. See, e.g., Philip L. Blumberg et al., The Law of Corporate Groups: Procedural Law 8 (2d ed.1983) ("This is jurisprudence by metaphor or epithet. It does not contribute to legal understanding because it is an intellectual construct, divorced from business realities. * * * Courts state that the corporate entity is to be disregarded because the corporation is, for example, a mere 'alter ego.' But they do not inform us why this is so, except in very broad terms that provide little general guidance. As a result, we are faced with hundreds of decisions that are irreconcilable and not entirely comprehensible. Few areas of the law have been so sharply criticized by commentators."); Frank H. Easterbrook and Daniel R. Fischel, Limited Liability and the Corporation, 52 U.Chi.L.Rev. 89 (1985) ("'Piercing' seems to happen freakishly. Like lightning, it is rare, severe, and unprincipled. There is a consensus that the whole area of limited liability, and conversely of piercing the corporate veil, is among the most confusing in corporate law."); Stephen Bainbridge, Abolishing Veil Piercing, 26 J.Corp.Law 479 (2001) (noting that veil-piercing is "rare, unprincipled, and arbitrary," and stating that "[j]udicial opinions in this area tend to open with vague generalities and close with conclusory statements, with little or no concrete analysis in between."); id. ("There simply are no bright-line rules for deciding when courts will pierce the corporate veil.").

Courts, however, often appear unconcerned by the vagueness of the doctrines they are formulating. One court observed that a "guiding concept behind * * * veil piercing cases is the need for the court to 'avoid an over-rigid preoccupation with questions of structure * * * and [to] apply the preexisting and overarching principle that liability is imposed to reach an equitable result.'" Litchfield Asset Management Corp. v. Howell, 799 A.2d 298, 312 (Conn.App.2002).

The vagueness of the articulated legal standards for piercing the corporate veil presents significant challenges for corporate lawyers required to advise clients in an area of understandably great concern to them, as personal liability may well be involved. The rules are not getting any clearer. In Great Neck Plaza v. Le Peep Restaurants, 37 P.3d 485 (Colo.App.2001), the court articulated a ten-factor test for determining whether to pierce the corporate veil. The court also indicated that it may consider only "certain factors," and it may consider factors other than the ten listed ones. The court did not specify which, if any, of the factors was essential, or whether any factors were more or less important than others. Id. at 490.

(3) Despite the vagueness of the language in many veil piercing opinions, there are very few cases in which the corporate veil is actually pierced. Courts appear to be rather reluctant to disregard the corporate form.

Even in the parent-subsidiary context, courts generally take the view that a parent corporation possesses a separate existence and is treated separately from a subsidiary unless there are circumstances clearly involving fraud, manifest unfairness, or misconduct. Courts are aware that over-utilization of their equitable power to pierce the corporate veil would make the corporate form useless: "any court must start from the general rule that the corporate entity should be recognized and upheld, unless specific, unusual circumstances call for an exception. * * * Care should be taken on all occasions to avoid making 'the entire theory of the corporate entity useless.'" Koch v. First Union Corporation, 2002 WL 372939 (Pa.Com.Pl.2002).

(4) Statistically speaking, piercing the corporate veil is entirely a phenomenon of closely held corporations, and predominantly one-person corporations. The corporate form is simply never pierced to impose liability against shareholders in a publicly traded corporation. Robert B. Thompson, The Limits of Liability in the New Limited Liability Entities, 32 Wake Forest L.Rev. 1, 9–10 (1997):

> * * * among the 1600 reported cases of piercing the veil, there was no case in which shareholders of a publicly held corporation were held liable. After additional analysis of that data base, I can make a broader statement. Piercing occurs only within corporate groups or in close corporations with fewer than ten shareholders. None of the close corporations in which piercing occurred had more than nine shareholders.
>
> * * * Those who are only passive investors, as the shareholders of a large corporation, will be insulated from the liability of the enterprise, while those who take a more active role in the business are subject to liability.

(5) Several cases involving contractual liability accept the argument that a third party who knowingly and voluntarily agrees to deal with a marginally financed corporation—without requesting assurances from the shareholders personally—cannot hold the shareholders liable. In O'Hazza v. Executive Credit Corp., 431 S.E.2d 318, 323 (Va.1993), for example, the court stated:

> [T]he record does not show that ECC was the victim of fraud, of any type, perpetrated by the O'Hazzas or by anyone else. Hughes had been involved with the corporation on at least 10 previous deals. * * * Hughes knew the financial situation of the corporation prior to advancing Guy O'Hazza the money for the hotel project. Hughes was a voluntary creditor who had the knowledge and opportunity to investigate the corporation before he agreed to loan the funds. We agree with the O'Hazzas' position that ECC "knowingly made a

risky loan to a corporation on shaky financial footing with the hope
of making a profit."

See also Consumer's Co-op. of Walworth County v. Olsen, 419 N.W.2d 211
(Wis.1988) (rejecting a piercing claim when a sophisticated creditor continued
to extend credit despite delinquencies in payment in violation of its own
internal policies with respect to the extension of credit).

(6) Is it sound to argue that (a) public policy requires attention to be paid
to corporate formalities, and (b) disregarding the corporate entity where
formalities have been ignored furthers this policy? Similarly, may one argue
that a shareholder should be liable because he is not permitted first to ignore
the rules of corporate behavior and then to claim the advantage of the
corporate shield?

(7) Observing that the law of piercing the corporate veil is confused is
not the same thing as saying that the corporate veil should never be pierced.
The veil should only be pierced with good reason, and sometimes there are
good reasons. The entire universe of piercing cases might be explained as a
judicial effort to remedy one of the following three problems.

First, piercing the corporate veil is used as a tool of statutory
interpretation in the sense that piercing is done to bring corporate actors'
behavior into conformity with a particular statutory scheme, such as social
security or state unemployment compensation. For example, the corporate
form may be ignored to accomplish a particular legislative goal with respect
to a government benefit program that distinguishes between owners and
employees.

Second, courts pierce to remedy what appears to be fraudulent conduct
that does not meet the strict elements of common law fraud. Specifically,
piercing is used as a remedy for "constructive fraud" in the contractual
context. Simply put, if a court becomes convinced that a shareholder has, by
words or actions, led a counterparty to a contract to believe that an obligation
is a personal liability rather than (or in addition to) a corporate debt, then
courts sometimes will use a piercing theory to impose liability on the
individual shareholder rather than a fraud theory.

Third, courts pierce to promote accepted "bankruptcy values." In
particular, courts will disregard the corporate form to prevent fraudulent
conveyances and preferential transfers. The goal of corporate bankruptcy law
is to maximize the value of an insolvent company for the benefit of all of the
creditors. An important element in accomplishing this goal is to resolve the
collective action problem facing a corporation's creditors, who in the absence
of such rules as the automatic stay (which prevents creditors from grabbing
the assets of a company after it has filed for bankruptcy) have incentives to
race for relief to get a jump on other creditors. Similarly, bankruptcy law
strives to achieve an orderly disposition of the debtor's assets, either through
corporate reorganization or liquidation. One way that bankruptcy law
achieves these goals is by preventing shareholders from transferring
corporate assets to themselves or to particular favored creditors in times of

acute economic stress. This result is accomplished in the context of a formal bankruptcy proceeding by invoking the doctrine of equitable subordination, as well as by the bankruptcy trustee's power to avoid and set aside preferential transfers and fraudulent conveyances. Outside of bankruptcy (and sometimes in the context of bankruptcy proceedings as well), the goal of eliminating opportunism by companies in financial distress is accomplished by disregarding the corporate form through piercing.

All of the piercing cases may be explained as an effort to accomplish one of these three goals: (1) achieving the purposes of a particular regulatory or statutory scheme; (2) avoiding fraud or misrepresentation by shareholders trying to obtain credit; and (3) promoting the bankruptcy value of eliminating favoritism among claimants to the cash flows of a firm. As you read the remaining cases in this Chapter, try to determine whether the outcomes can be explained on one of these three bases.

BAATZ V. ARROW BAR

Supreme Court of South Dakota, 1990.
452 N.W.2d 138.

SABERS, JUSTICE.

Kenny and Peggy Baatz (Baatz), appeal from [a] summary judgment dismissing Edmond, LaVella, and Jacquette Neuroth, as individual defendants in this action. * * * Kenny and Peggy were seriously injured in 1982 when Roland McBride crossed the center line of a Sioux Falls street with his automobile and struck them while they were riding on a motorcycle. McBride was uninsured at the time of the accident and apparently is judgment proof.

Baatz alleges that Arrow Bar served alcoholic beverages to McBride prior to the accident while he was already intoxicated. Baatz commenced this action in 1984, claiming that Arrow Bar's negligence in serving alcoholic beverages to McBride contributed to the injuries they sustained in the accident. Baatz supports his claim against Arrow Bar with the affidavit of Jimmy Larson. Larson says he knew McBride and observed him being served alcoholic beverages in the Arrow Bar during the afternoon prior to the accident, while McBride was intoxicated. * * *

Edmond and LaVella Neuroth formed the Arrow Bar, Inc. in May 1980. During the next two years they contributed $50,000 to the corporation pursuant to a stock subscription agreement. The corporation purchased the Arrow Bar business in June 1980 for $155,000 with a $5,000 down payment. Edmond and LaVella executed a promissory note personally guaranteeing payment of the $150,000 balance. In 1983 the corporation obtained bank financing in the amount of $145,000 to pay off the purchase agreement. Edmond and LaVella again personally guaranteed payment of the corporate debt. Edmond is the president of the corporation, and Jacquette Neuroth serves as the manager of the business. Based on the enactment of SDCL 35–4–78 and 35–11–1 and advice of counsel, the corporation did not maintain dram shop liability insurance at the time of the injuries to Kenny and Peggy.[a]

In 1987 the trial court entered summary judgment in favor of Arrow Bar and the individual defendants. Baatz appealed that judgment and we reversed and remanded to the trial court for trial. * * * Shortly before the trial date, Edmond, LaVella, and Jacquette moved for and obtained summary judgment dismissing them as individual defendants. Baatz appeals. We affirm.

Arrow Bar was dismissed / re instated / individual named as were Dropped

A trial court may grant summary judgment only when there are no genuine issues of material fact. * * * When determining whether a genuine issue of material fact exists, the evidence must be viewed most favorably to the non-moving party and reasonable doubts are to be resolved against the moving party. Groseth Int'l, Inc. v. Tenneco, Inc., 410 N.W.2d 159 (S.D.1987). * * *

Baatz claims that even if Arrow Bar, Inc. is the licensee, the corporate veil should be pierced, leaving the Neuroths, as the shareholders of the corporation, individually liable. A corporation shall be considered a separate legal entity until there is sufficient reason to the contrary. Mobridge Community Indus., Inc. v. Toure, Ltd., 273 N.W.2d 128 (S.D.1978). When continued recognition of a corporation as a separate legal entity would "produce injustices and inequitable consequences," then a court has sufficient reason to pierce the corporate veil. Farmers Feed & Seed, Inc. v. Magnum Enter., Inc., 344 N.W.2d 699, 701 (S.D.1984). Factors that indicate injustices and inequitable consequences and allow a court to pierce the corporate veil are:

1) fraudulent representation by corporation directors;

2) undercapitalization;

3) failure to observe corporate formalities;

4) absence of corporate records;

---

[a] Section 35–4–78(2) makes it a misdemeanor for any licensed bar to sell an alcoholic beverage to "any person who is obviously intoxicated at the time." In Walz v. City of Hudson, 327 N.W.2d 120 (S.D.1982), the Court held that this section created a private cause of action for persons injured by patrons who were sold alcoholic beverages in violation of this section. In 1985, the South Dakota Legislature attempted to overrule *Walz* by (1) adding a sentence to 35–4–78(2) stating that "no licensee is civilly liable to any injured person * * * for any injury suffered * * * because of the intoxication of any person due to the sale of any alcoholic beverage in violation of the provisions of this section," and (2) adding 35–11–1 which made a formal legislative finding that "the consumption of alcoholic beverages, rather than the serving of alcoholic beverages, is the proximate cause of any injury inflicted upon another by an intoxicated person" and therefore "abrogated" the *Walz* holding. Apparently, while this legislation was pending, the attorney recommended that the Arrow Bar not obtain dram shop insurance even though the Baatz law suit had been filed in 1984. However, in Baatz v. Arrow Bar, 426 N.W.2d 298 (1988), the South Dakota Supreme Court held that the attempted abrogation was invalid both retrospectively and prospectively. The court's opinion does not make clear how the attorney's recommendation not to purchase dram shop insurance presumably in 1985 affected the Baatz litigation filed in 1984 for injuries that occurred in 1982.

5) payment by the corporation of individual obligations; or

6) use of the corporation to promote fraud, injustice, or illegalities.

When the court deems it appropriate to pierce the corporate veil, the corporation and its stockholders will be treated identically.

Baatz advances several arguments to support his claim that the corporate veil of Arrow Bar, Inc. should be pierced, but fails to support them with facts, or misconstrues the facts.

First, Baatz claims that since Edmond and LaVella personally guaranteed corporate obligations, they should also be personally liable to Baatz. However, the personal guarantee of a loan is a contractual agreement and cannot be enlarged to impose tort liability. Moreover, the personal guarantee creates individual liability for a corporate obligation, the opposite of (factor 5), above. As such, it supports, rather than detracts from, recognition of the corporate entity.

Baatz also argues that the corporation is simply the alter ego of the Neuroths, and, in accord with Loving Saviour Church v. United States, 556 F.Supp. 688 (D.S.D.1983), aff'd, 728 F.2d 1085 (8th Cir.1984), the corporate veil should be pierced. Baatz' discussion of the law is adequate, but he fails to present evidence that would support a decision in his favor in accordance with that law. When an individual treats a corporation "as an instrumentality through which he [is] conducting his personal business," a court may disregard the corporate entity. Larson v. Western Underwriters, Inc., 77 S.D. 157, 163, 87 N.W.2d 883, 886 (1958). Baatz fails to demonstrate how the Neuroths were transacting personal business through the corporation. In fact, the evidence indicates the Neuroths treated the corporation separately from their individual affairs.

Baatz next argues that the corporation is undercapitalized. Shareholders must equip a corporation with a reasonable amount of capital for the nature of the business involved. See Curtis v. Feurhelm, 335 N.W.2d 575 (S.D.1983). Baatz claims the corporation was started with only $5,000 in borrowed capital, but does not explain how that amount failed to equip the corporation with a reasonable amount of capital. In addition, Baatz fails to consider the personal guarantees to pay off the purchase contract in the amount of $150,000, and the $50,000 stock subscription agreement. There simply is no evidence that the corporation's capital in whatever amount was inadequate for the operation of the business. Normally questions relating to individual shareholder liability resulting from corporate undercapitalization should not be reached until the primary question of corporate liability is determined. Questions depending in part upon other determinations are not normally ready for summary judgment. However, simply asserting that the corporation is undercapitalized does not make it so. Without some evidence of the inadequacy of the capital, Baatz fails to present specific facts demonstrating a genuine issue of material fact.

Finally, Baatz argues that Arrow Bar, Inc. failed to observe corporate formalities because none of the business' signs or advertising indicated that the business was a corporation. Baatz cites SDCL 47–2–36 as requiring the name of any corporation to contain the word corporation, company, incorporated, or limited, or an abbreviation for such a word. In spite of Baatz' contentions, the corporation is in compliance with the statute because its corporate name—Arrow Bar, Inc.—includes the abbreviation of the word incorporated. Furthermore, the "mere failure upon occasion to follow all the forms prescribed by law for the conduct of corporate activities will not justify" disregarding the corporate entity. Larson, supra, 77 S.D. at 164, 87 N.W.2d at 887 (quoting P.S. & A. Realties, Inc. v. Lodge Gate Forest, Inc., 205 Misc. 245, 254, 127 N.Y.S.2d 315, 324 (1954)). Even if the corporation is improperly using its name, that alone is not a sufficient reason to pierce the corporate veil. This is especially so where, as here, there is no relationship between the claimed defect and the resulting harm.

In addition, the record is void of any evidence which would support imposition of individual liability by piercing the corporate veil under any of the other factors listed above in 1), 4) or 6).

In summary, Baatz fails to present specific facts that would allow the trial court to find the existence of a genuine issue of material fact. There is no indication that any of the Neuroths personally served an alcoholic beverage to McBride on the day of the accident. Nor is there any evidence indicating that the Neuroths treated the corporation in any way that would produce the injustices and inequitable consequences necessary to justify piercing the corporate veil. In fact, the only evidence offered is otherwise. Therefore, we affirm summary judgment dismissing the Neuroths as individual defendants.

WUEST, C.J., and MORGAN and MILLER, JJ., concur.

HENDERSON, JUSTICE (dissenting).

This corporation has no separate existence. It is the instrumentality of three shareholders, officers, and employees. Here, the corporate fiction should be disregarded. * * *

A corporate shield was here created to escape the holding of this Court relating to an individual's liability in a dram shop action. * * * As a result of this holding, the message is now clear: Incorporate, mortgage the assets of a liquor corporation to your friendly banker, and proceed with carefree entrepreneuring.

In both of these briefs, the parties argue, all in all, about the facts. One may reasonably conclude that there exists questions of fact. * * *

[The] Baatzes had their case thrown out of court when many facts were in dispute. I am reminded of the old lawyer, before a jury, who expressed his woe of corporations. He cried out to the jury: "A corporation haveth no soul and its hind end you can kicketh not." * * *

Peggy Baatz, a young mother, lost her left leg; she wears an artificial limb; Kenny Baatz, a young father, has had most of his left foot amputated; he has been unable to work since this tragic accident. Peggy uses a cane. Kenny uses crutches. Years have gone by since they were injured and their lives have been torn asunder.

Uninsured motorist was drunk, and had a reputation of being a habitual drunkard; Arrow Bar had a reputation of serving intoxicated persons. (Supported by depositions on file). An eyewitness saw uninsured motorist in an extremely intoxicated condition, shortly before the accident, being served by Arrow Bar. * * * This evidence must be viewed most favorably to the nonmoving party. American Indian Agr. Credit Consortium, Inc. v. Ft. Pierre Livestock, Inc., 379 N.W.2d 318 (S.D.1985). A police officer testified, by deposition, that uninsured motorist was in a drunken stupor while at the Arrow Bar.

* * * Arrow Bar, Inc. is being used to justify any wrongs perpetrated by the incorporators in their individual capacity. Conclusion: Fraud is perpetrated upon the public. At a deposition of Edmond Neuroth (filed in this record), this "President" of "the corporation" was asked why the Neuroth family incorporated. His answer: "Upon advice of counsel, as a shield against individual liability." The corporation was undercapitalized (Neuroths borrowed $5,000 in capital). * * * In Loving Saviour Church, it was held that a chiropractor could not use a church to escape income taxes; here, a corporation conceived in undercapitalization as "a shield," in the words of "the President," should not be used as an artifice to avoid the intent of SDCL 35–4–78(2). * * *

Therefore, I respectfully dissent.

NOTES

(1) Tort cases involving the "piercing" doctrine have a different flavor than contract cases. Unlike tort creditors, contract creditors can decline to deal with a business unless they are satisfied that the entity is creditworthy. If the creditor perceives significant risk, she can decline to deal with the corporation, require personal guarantees from investors or others, or charge a sufficiently high rate of interest to compensate for the risk. Consider Robert W. Hamilton, The Corporate Entity, 49 Tex.L.Rev. 979, 983–85 (1971):

> Secondly, a major consideration in determining whether the shareholders or the third party should bear the loss is whether the third party dealt voluntarily with the corporation or whether he is an involuntary creditor, typically a tort claimant. In the contracts context, the plaintiff has the opportunity to negotiate with the

corporation or to walk away from any deal. In dealing with the corporation, contract creditors should be aware that the corporation lacks substance. In the absence of some sort of deception, the creditor more or less assumed the risk of loss when he dealt with a "shell"; if he was concerned, he should have insisted that some solvent third person guarantee the performance by the corporation. In tort cases, on the other hand, there is usually no element of voluntary dealing, and the question is whether it is reasonable for businessmen to transfer a risk of loss or injury to members of the general public through the device of conducting business in the name of a corporation that may be marginally financed. The issues of public policy raised by tort claims bear little relationship to the issues raised by a contract claim. It is astonishing to find that this fundamental distinction is only dimly perceived by many courts, which indiscriminately cite and purport to apply tort precedents in contract cases and vice versa.

(2) Robert B. Thompson, Piercing the Corporate Veil: An Empirical Study, 76 Cornell L.Rev. 1036 (1991), examined 1,583 cases involving the piercing the corporate veil doctrine decided before 1985. The conclusions reached from this massive survey include the following:

- The corporate veil was pierced in about 40 percent of the reported cases. This percentage remained stable over more than four decades, was about the same in state and federal courts, and variations from state to state did not appear to be statistically significant.

- 779 cases in the survey involved contract claims and 226 involved tort claims.[b] The corporate veil was pierced in 327 of the contracts cases (42 percent) and 70 of the torts cases (31 percent).

- Undercapitalization was a factor in 19 percent of the contracts cases in which the corporate veil was pierced (61 of 327), but was a factor in only 13 percent of the tort cases in which piercing occurred (9 of 70). A failure to follow corporate formalities was cited in 20 percent of the contracts cases and 11 percent of the torts cases.

See also Peter B. Oh, Veil-Piercing, 89 Tex.L.Rev. 81, 99 (2010) (indicating that undercapitalization appears in only a small fraction of veil-piercing cases and its mention is correlated with a modest rate of veil piercing).

(3) As discussed in Chapter 5, most state corporation statutes today do not require any minimum amount of capital. It is literally possible today to form a corporation with one cent or one dollar of capital. Of course, to actually form a corporation with essentially zero capital to engage in a risky business would appear to be extremely dangerous in light of the rhetoric in

---

[b]   The remaining cases were classified as "criminal" or "statute" cases.

many piercing cases about "inadequate capital." In *Baatz*, for example, the corporation began with $5,000 in cash and some personal guarantees, which the majority held was sufficient to avoid the inadequate capitalization argument. However, should that really be the test? The cash plus the personal guarantees was sufficient to permit the Neuroths to purchase the Arrow Bar, but certainly not sufficient to cover possible unexpected liabilities, let alone the serious injuries to the members of the Baatz family. If the test should be some amount of "free" capital sufficient to cover unexpected liabilities, the question becomes how much? Is the problem in *Baatz* the conscious decision not to purchase dram shop insurance? Might there be malpractice on the part of the attorney who recommended that the purchase of such insurance was unnecessary?

RADASZEWSKI V. TELECOM CORP.

United States Court of Appeals, Eighth Circuit, 1992.
981 F.2d 305.

Before RICHARD S. ARNOLD, CHIEF JUDGE, HEANEY, SENIOR CIRCUIT JUDGE, and MAGILL, CIRCUIT JUDGE.

RICHARD S. ARNOLD, CHIEF JUDGE.

This is an action for personal injuries filed on behalf of Konrad Radaszewski, who was seriously injured in an automobile accident on August 21, 1984. Radaszewski, who was on a motorcycle, was struck by a truck driven by an employee of Contrux, Inc. The question presented on this appeal is whether the District Court had jurisdiction over the person of Telecom Corporation, which is the corporate parent of Contrux. This question depends, in turn, on whether, under Missouri law, Radaszewski can "pierce the corporate veil," and hold Telecom liable for the conduct of its subsidiary, Contrux, and Contrux's driver. The District Court held that it lacked jurisdiction. We agree, though for different reasons.

In general, someone injured by the conduct of a corporation or one of its employees can look only to the assets of the employee or of the employer corporation for recovery. The shareholders of the corporation, including, if there is one, its parent corporation, are not responsible. This is a conscious decision made by the law of every state to encourage business in the corporate form. Obviously the decision has its costs. Some injuries are going to go unredressed because of the insolvency of the corporate defendant immediately involved, even when its shareholders have plenty of money. To the general rule, though, there are exceptions. There are instances in which an injured person may "pierce the corporate veil," that is, reach the assets of one or more of the shareholders of the corporation whose conduct has created liability. In the present case, the plaintiff seeks to hold Telecom Corporation liable for the conduct of an employee of its wholly owned subsidiary, Contrux, Inc.

Under Missouri law, a plaintiff in this position needs to show three things. The leading case is *Collet v. American National Stores, Inc.,* 708 S.W.2d 273 (Mo.App.1986). The Missouri Court of Appeals had this to say:

> A tripartite test has been developed for analysis of the question. To "pierce the corporate veil," one must show:
>
> (1) Control, not mere majority or complete stock control, but complete domination, not only of finances, but of policy and business practice in respect to the transaction attacked so that the corporate entity as to this transaction had at the time no separate mind, will or existence of its own; and
>
> (2) Such control must have been used by the defendant to commit fraud or wrong, to perpetrate the violation of a statutory or other positive legal duty, or dishonest and unjust act in contravention of plaintiff's legal rights; and
>
> (3) The aforesaid control and breach of duty must proximately cause the injury or unjust loss complained of.

Id. at 284.

It is common ground among all parties that Telecom, as such, has had no contact with Missouri. If it is subject to jurisdiction over its person in Missouri courts, it is only because of the conduct of Contrux, its subsidiary. So the issue of jurisdiction over the person depends on whether the corporate veil of Contrux can be pierced to bring Telecom into the case. As it happens, this is also the question upon which Telecom's substantive liability depends. (We assume for present purposes that Contrux is liable—this has not yet been proved.) * * *

Undercapitalizing a subsidiary, which we take to mean creating it and putting it in business without a reasonably sufficient supply of money, has become a sort of proxy under Missouri law for the second *Collet* element. On the prior appeal, for example, we said that "Missouri courts will disregard the existence of a corporate entity that is operated while undercapitalized." 891 F.2d at 674. *Collet, supra,* 708 S.W.2d at 286–87. The reason, we think, is not because undercapitalization, in and of itself, is unlawful (though it may be for some purposes), but rather because the creation of an undercapitalized subsidiary justifies an inference that the parent is either deliberately or recklessly creating a business that will not be able to pay its bills or satisfy judgments against it. This point has been made clear by the Supreme Court of Missouri. In *May Department Stores Co. v. Union Electric Light & Power Co.,* 341 Mo. 299, 327, 107 S.W.2d 41, 55 (1937), the Court found an improper purpose in a case where a corporation was "operating it without sufficient funds to meet obligations to those who must deal with it." Similarly, in *Consolidated Sun Ray, Inc. v. Oppenstein,* 335 F.2d 801 (8th Cir.1964), we said: "Making a corporation a supplemental part of an economic unit and operating it without sufficient funds to meet obligations to those who must deal with it would be circumstantial evidence tending to show either an improper purpose or reckless disregard of the rights of others." *Id.* at 806–07.

Here, the District Court held, and we assume, that Contrux was undercapitalized in the accounting sense. Most of the money contributed to its operation by Telecom was in the form of loans, not equity, and when Contrux first went into business, Telecom did not pay for all of the stock that was issued to it. This is a classic instance of watered stock, of putting a corporation into business without sufficient equity investment. Telecom in effect concedes that Contrux's balance sheet was anemic, and that, from the point of view of generally accepted accounting principles, Contrux was inadequately capitalized. Telecom says, however, that this doesn't matter, because Contrux had $11,000,000 worth of liability insurance available to pay judgments like the one that Radaszewski hopes to obtain. No one can say, therefore, the argument runs, that Telecom was improperly motivated in setting up Contrux, in the sense of either knowingly or recklessly establishing it without the ability of pay tort judgments.

In fact, Contrux did have $1,000,000 in basic liability coverage, plus $10,000,000 in excess coverage. This coverage was bound on March 1, 1984, about five and one-half months before the accident involving Radaszewski. Unhappily, Contrux's [excess liability] insurance carrier became insolvent two years after the accident and is now in receivership. (This record does not show the financial status of the receivership. We thus do not know whether any money would ever be available from the insurance company to pay a judgment in favor of Radaszewski, if he obtains one.) But this insurance, Telecom points out, was sufficient to satisfy federal financial-responsibility requirements. Under 49 C.F.R. § 387, motor carriers must maintain "financial reserves (e.g., insurance policies or surety bonds) sufficient to satisfy liability amounts set forth in this subpart covering public liability." 49 C.F.R. § 387.5. It is undisputed that the amount of insurance maintained by Contrux exceeded federal requirements, and that Contrux, at all times during its operations, was considered financially responsible by the relevant federal agency, the Interstate Commerce Commission.

The District Court rejected this argument. Undercapitalization is undercapitalization, it reasoned, regardless of insurance. The Court said: "The federal regulation does not speak to what constitutes a properly capitalized motor carrier company. Rather, the regulation speaks to what constitutes an appropriate level of *financial responsibility*." *Konrad Radaszewski v. Contrux, Inc.*, No. 88–0445–CV–W–1 (W.D.Mo. Oct. 26, 1990), slip op. 7 n. 6 (emphasis in original). This distinction escapes us.

The whole purpose of asking whether a subsidiary is "properly capitalized," is precisely to determine its "financial responsibility." If the subsidiary is financially responsible, whether by means of insurance or otherwise, the policy behind the second part of the *Collet* test is met. Insurance meets this policy just as well, perhaps even better, than a healthy balance sheet. * * *

The doctrine of limited liability is intended precisely to protect a parent corporation whose subsidiary goes broke. That is the whole purpose of the doctrine, and those who have the right to decide such questions, that is, legislatures, believe that the doctrine, on the whole, is socially reasonable and useful. We think that the doctrine would largely be destroyed if a parent corporation could be held liable simply on the basis of errors in business judgment. Something more than that should be shown, and *Collet* requires something more than that. In our view, this record is devoid of facts to show that "something more." * * *

We * * * affirm the judgment of the District Court dismissing the complaint for want of jurisdiction, but modify that judgment to provide that it is with prejudice as to Radaszewski's complaint against Telecom.

HEANEY, SENIOR CIRCUIT JUDGE, dissenting.

I respectfully dissent. * * * In my view, Contrux's liability insurance is a relevant factor to be considered, but a fact finder after a trial might well find that this factor alone does not require a verdict for the defendant. * * *

NOTES

(1) Do you agree that the piercing doctrine should not apply in a tort case if the corporation has acquired liability insurance against the risk—even if, under the circumstances, the plaintiff is unable to recover under that insurance? Do you think that this should be a categorical rule or are there any exceptions?

(2) What exactly does "undercapitalization" mean? If a corporation is adequately capitalized when it is formed, but thereafter suffers operating losses, is it then undercapitalized? If so, does that mean that the shareholders must infuse additional capital into the corporation or suffer the possible application of the piercing the corporate veil doctrine? For negative answers, see Consumer's Co-op. of Walworth County v. Olsen, 419 N.W.2d 211, 218–19 (Wis.1988); CNC Service Center, Inc. v. CNC Service Center, 753 F.Supp. 1427 (N.D.Ill.1991).

(3) Should shareholder loans to an otherwise undercapitalized business count as capital? Should it make any difference if the shareholders plan to have the corporation repay those loans or whether they plan to leave the funds in the corporation indefinitely? In O'Hazza v. Executive Credit Corp., 431 S.E.2d 318 (Va.1993), the Court concluded that a corporation was

adequately capitalized when the shareholders contributed $10,000 in initial capital and then loaned the corporation approximately $140,000 "without expectation of repayment." See also Arnold v. Phillips, 117 F.2d 497, 501–02 (5th Cir.1941) (distinction made between loans before the enterprise was launched and loans thereafter to keep the business afloat).

(4) In Minton v. Cavaney, 364 P.2d 473 (Cal.1961), Cavaney, an attorney, duly incorporated the Seminole Hot Springs Corporation, a corporation that thereafter leased and operated a public swimming pool. No stock was ever issued by the corporation and no capital was ever invested. Cavaney served as a director, secretary, and treasurer of Seminole; the corporate records were stored in his office. Cavaney testified on deposition that he was only a "temporary" or "accommodation" director and officer, but there was also testimony that he expected to receive a portion of the corporation's stock. During the first year of the swimming pool's operation, the plaintiffs' daughter drowned. Cavaney died sometime thereafter. The plaintiffs obtained a $10,000 default judgment against Seminole and, because that corporation had no assets, sought to hold Cavaney's estate personally liable on the judgment.

The court concluded that Cavaney's estate could be held personally liable on the plaintiffs' claim on a theory of alter ego, but his estate was allowed to relitigate the issues of Seminole's negligence and the amount of damages since Cavaney was not a party to the original proceeding. The court rejected Cavaney's claim that he should not be liable because he was merely a temporary or accommodation director with the understanding that he would not exercise any of the duties of a director: "A person may not in this manner divorce the responsibilities of a director from the statutory duties and powers of that office." 364 P.2d at 476. This and similar cases illustrate the dangers of an attorney agreeing to serve even briefly as a director or officer of a corporation created by the attorney.

(5) *Minton v. Cavaney* is cited in California for the proposition that inadequate initial capitalization alone is sufficient to pierce the corporate veil. Similarly, in Slottow v. American Cas. Co., 10 F.3d 1355, 1360 (9th Cir.1993), the court stated: "FNT's initial capitalization of $500,000 was woefully inadequate for a corporation that handled trust agreements of the magnitude involved here. The investors claimed damages in the range of $10,000,000; * * * Under California law, inadequate capitalization of a subsidiary may alone be a basis for holding the parent corporation liable * * *." But see Associated Vendors, Inc. v. Oakland Meat Co., 26 Cal. Rptr. 806, 816 (Cal. App. 1962) (noting that "[e]vidence of inadequate capitalization is, at best, merely a factor to be considered by the trial court in deciding whether or not to pierce the corporate veil"); Paul Steelman, Ltd. v. Omni Realty Partners, 885 P.2d 549, 550 (Nev.1994) ("Although undercapitalization is one criterion considered by courts in deciding whether to set aside the corporate barrier to shareholder liability for corporate debts, it is usually an insufficient ground, of itself, for disregarding the corporate entity in the absence of fraud or injustice to the aggrieved party.").

FLETCHER V. ATEX, INC.

United States Court of Appeals, Second Circuit, 1995.
68 F.3d 1451.

Before: KEARSE, CALABRESI, and CABRANES, CIRCUIT JUDGES.

JOSE A. CABRANES, CIRCUIT JUDGE:

* * * The plaintiffs-appellants filed suit against Atex, Inc. ("Atex") and its parent, Eastman Kodak Company ("Kodak"), to recover for repetitive stress injuries that they claim were caused by their use of computer keyboards manufactured by Atex. * * * [A summary judgment was entered dismissing Kodak as a defendant and plaintiffs appeal.]

* * * From 1981 until December 1992, Atex was a wholly-owned subsidiary of Kodak. In 1987, Atex's name was changed to Electronic Pre-Press Systems, Inc., ("EPPS"), but its name was changed back to Atex in 1990. In December 1992, Atex sold substantially all of its assets to an independent third party and again changed its name to 805 Middlesex Corp., which holds the proceeds from the sale. Kodak continues to be the sole shareholder of 805 Middlesex Corp. * * *

The district court correctly noted that "[u]nder New York choice of law principles, '[t]he law of the state of incorporation determines when the corporate form will be disregarded and liability will be imposed on shareholders.'" * * * Because Atex was a Delaware corporation, Delaware law determines whether the corporate veil can be pierced in this instance.

Delaware law permits a court to pierce the corporate veil of a company "where there is fraud or where [it] is in fact a mere instrumentality or alter ego of its owner." Geyer v. Ingersoll Publications Co., 621 A.2d 784, 793 (Del.Ch.1992). Although the Delaware Supreme Court has never explicitly adopted an alter ego theory of parent liability for its subsidiaries, lower Delaware courts have applied the doctrine on several occasions, as has the United States District Court for the District of Delaware. * * * [U]nder an alter ego theory, there is no requirement of a showing of fraud. To prevail on an alter ego claim under Delaware law, a plaintiff must show (1) that the parent and the subsidiary "operated as a single economic entity" and (2) that an "overall element of injustice or unfairness * * * [is] present." Harper v. Delaware Valley Broadcasters, Inc., 743 F.Supp. 1076, 1085 (D.Del.1990), aff'd, 932 F.2d 959 (3d Cir.1991) (internal quotation marks omitted).

To prevail on an alter ego theory of liability, a plaintiff must show that the two corporations " 'operated as a single economic entity such that it would be inequitable * * * to uphold a legal distinction between them.'" * * * Among the factors to be considered in determining whether a subsidiary and parent operate as a "single economic entity" are:

[W]hether the corporation was adequately capitalized for the corporate undertaking; whether the corporation was solvent; whether dividends were paid, corporate records kept, officers and directors functioned properly, and other corporate formalities were observed; whether the dominant shareholder siphoned corporate funds; and whether, in general, the corporation simply functioned as a facade for the dominant shareholder.

Harco Nat'l Ins. Co. v. Green Farms, Inc., No. CIV.A. 1331, 1989 WL 110537, at *4 (Del.Ch. Sept. 19, 1989) (quoting United States v. Golden Acres, Inc., 702 F.Supp. 1097, 1104 (D.Del.1988)). As noted above, a showing of fraud or wrongdoing is not necessary under an alter ego theory, but the plaintiff must demonstrate an overall element of injustice or unfairness. Harco, 1989 WL 110537, at *5.

A plaintiff seeking to persuade a Delaware court to disregard the corporate structure faces "a difficult task." Harco, 1989 WL 110537, at *4. Courts have made it clear that "[t]he legal entity of a corporation will not be disturbed until sufficient reason appears." Id. Although the question of domination is generally one of fact, courts have granted motions to dismiss as well as motions for summary judgment in favor of defendant parent companies where there has been a lack of sufficient evidence to place the alter ego issue in dispute. See, e.g., Akzona, Inc. v. Du Pont, 607 F.Supp. 227, 237 (D.Del.1984) (rejecting plaintiffs' alter ego theory of liability on a motion to dismiss). * * *

Kodak has shown that Atex followed corporate formalities, and the plaintiffs have offered no evidence to the contrary. Significantly, the plaintiffs have not challenged Kodak's assertions that Atex's board of directors held regular meetings, that minutes from those meetings were routinely prepared and maintained in corporate minute books, that appropriate financial records and other files were maintained by Atex, that Atex filed its own tax returns and paid its own taxes, and that Atex had its own employees and management executives who were responsible for the corporation's day-to-day business. The plaintiffs' primary arguments regarding domination concern (1) the defendant's use of a cash management system; (2) Kodak's exertion of control over Atex's major expenditures, stock sales, and the sale of Atex's assets to a third party; (3) Kodak's "dominating presence" on Atex's board of directors; (4) descriptions of the relationship between Atex and Kodak in the corporations' advertising, promotional literature, and annual reports; and (5) Atex's assignment of one of its former officer's mortgage to Kodak in order to close Atex's asset-purchase agreement with a third party. The plaintiffs argue that each of these raises a genuine issue of material fact about Kodak's domination of Atex, and that the district court therefore erred in granting summary judgment to Kodak on the plaintiffs' alter ego theory. We find that the district court correctly held that, in light of the undisputed factors of independence cited by Kodak, "the elements identified by the plaintiffs * * * [were] insufficient as a matter of law to establish the degree of domination necessary to disregard Atex's corporate identity."

First, the district court correctly held that "Atex's participation in Kodak's cash management system is consistent with sound business practice and does not show undue domination or control." The parties do not dispute the mechanics of Kodak's cash management system. Essentially, all of Kodak's domestic subsidiaries participate in the system and maintain zero-balance bank accounts. All funds transferred from the subsidiary accounts are recorded as credits to the subsidiary, and when a subsidiary is in need of funds, a transfer is made. At all times, a strict accounting is kept of each subsidiary's funds.

Courts have generally declined to find alter ego liability based on a parent corporation's use of a cash management system. See, e.g., In re Acushnet River & New Bedford Harbor Proceedings, 675 F.Supp. 22, 34 (D.Mass.1987) (Without "considerably more," "a centralized cash management system * * * where the accounting records always reflect the indebtedness of one entity to another, is not the equivalent of intermingling funds" and is insufficient to justify disregarding the corporate form.); United States v. Bliss, 108 F.R.D. 127, 132 (E.D.Mo.1985) (cash management system indicative of the "usual parent-subsidiary relationship"); Japan Petroleum Co. (Nigeria) v. Ashland Oil Inc., 456 F.Supp. 831, 838, 846 (D.Del.1978) (finding segregation of subsidiary's accounts within parent's cash management system to be "a function of administrative convenience and economy, rather than a manifestation of control"). The plaintiffs offer no facts to support their speculation that Kodak's centralized cash management system was actually a "complete commingling" of funds or a means by which Kodak sought to "siphon[ ] all of Atex's revenues into its own account."

Second, the district court correctly concluded that it could find no domination based on the plaintiffs' evidence that Kodak's approval was required for Atex's real estate leases, major capital expenditures, negotiations for a sale of minority stock ownership to IBM, or the fact that Kodak played a significant role in the ultimate sale of Atex's assets to a third party. Again, the parties do not dispute that Kodak required Atex to seek its approval and/or participation for the above transactions. However, this evidence, viewed in the light most favorable to the plaintiffs, does not raise an issue of material fact about whether the two corporations constituted "a single economic entity." Indeed, this type of conduct is typical of a majority shareholder or parent corporation. See Phoenix Canada Oil Co. v. Texaco, 842 F.2d 1466, 1476 (3d Cir.1988) (declining to pierce the corporate veil where subsidiary required to secure approval from parent for "large investments and acquisitions or disposals of major assets"), cert. denied, 488 U.S. 908, 109 S.Ct. 259, 102 L.Ed.2d 247 (1988); Akzona v. Du Pont, 607 F.Supp. 227, at 237 (D.Del.1984) (same, where parent approval required for expenditures exceeding $850,000); Japan Petrol., 456 F.Supp. at 843 (finding no parent liability where parent approval required for expenditures exceeding $250,000). In Akzona, the Delaware district court noted that a parent's "general executive responsibilities" for its subsidiary's operations included approval over major policy decisions and guaranteeing bank loans, and that that type of oversight was insufficient to demonstrate domination and control. Akzona, 607 F.Supp. at 238 (internal quotation marks omitted). Similarly, the district court in the instant case properly found that the presence of Kodak employees at periodic meetings with Atex's chief financial officer and comptroller to be "entirely appropriate." 861 F.Supp. at 245 (citing Akzona, 607 F.Supp. at 238); see Acushnet, 675 F.Supp. at 34 ("The quarterly and annual reports made [to the parent] do not represent an untoward intrusion by the owner into the corporate enterprise. The right of shareholders to remain informed is similarly recognized in many public and closely held corporations").

The plaintiffs' third argument, that Kodak dominated the Atex board of directors, also fails. Although a number of Kodak employees have sat on the Atex board, it is undisputed that between 1981 and 1988, only one director of Atex was also a director of Kodak. Between 1989 and 1992, Atex and Kodak had no directors in common. Parents and subsidiaries frequently have overlapping boards of directors while maintaining separate business operations. In Japan Petroleum, the Delaware district court held that the fact that a parent and a subsidiary have common officers and directors does not necessarily demonstrate that the parent corporation dominates the activities of the subsidiary. 456 F.Supp. at 841; see Scott-Douglas Corp. v. Greyhound Corp., 304 A.2d 309, 314 (Del.Super.Ct.1973) (same). Since the overlap is negligible here, we find this evidence to be entirely insufficient to raise a question of fact on the issue of domination.

Fourth, the district court properly rejected the plaintiffs' argument that the descriptions of the relationship between Atex and Kodak and the presence of the Kodak logo in Atex's promotional literature justify piercing the corporate veil. The plaintiffs point to several statements in both Kodak's and Atex's literature to evidence Kodak's domination of its subsidiary. For example, plaintiffs refer to (1) a promotional pamphlet produced by EPPS (a/k/a Atex) describing Atex as a business unit of EPPS and noting that EPPS was an "agent" of Kodak; (2) a document produced by Atex entitled "An Introduction to Atex Systems," which describes a "merger" between Kodak and Atex; (3) a statement in Kodak's 1985 and 1986 annual reports describing Atex as a "recent acquisition[ ]" and a "subsidiar[y] * * * combined in a new division"; and (4) a statement in an Atex/EPPS document, "Setting Up TPE 6000 on the Sun 3

Workstation," describing Atex as "an unincorporated division of Electronic Pre-Press Systems, Inc., a Kodak company." They also refer generally to the fact that Atex's paperwork and packaging materials frequently displayed the Kodak logo.

It is clear from the record that Atex never merged with Kodak or operated as a Kodak division. The plaintiffs offer no evidence to the contrary, apart from these statements in Atex and Kodak documents that they claim are indicative of the true relationship between the two companies. Viewed in the light most favorable to the plaintiffs, these statements and the use of the Kodak logo are not evidence that the two companies operated as a "single economic entity." See Coleman v. Corning Glass Works, 619 F.Supp. 950, 956 (W.D.N.Y.1985) (upholding corporate form despite "loose language" in annual report about "merger" and parent's reference to subsidiary as a "division"), aff'd, 818 F.2d 874 (1987); Japan Petrol., 456 F.Supp. at 846 (noting that representations made by parent in its annual reports that subsidiary serves as an agent "may result from public relations motives or an attempt at simplification"); American Trading & Prod. Corp. v. Fischbach & Moore, Inc., 311 F.Supp. 412, 416 (N.D.Ill.1970) ("boastful" advertising and consideration of subsidiaries as "family" do not prove that corporate identities were ignored). * * *

Finally, even if the plaintiffs did raise a factual question about Kodak's domination of Atex, summary judgment would still be appropriate because the plaintiffs offer no evidence * * * of an "overall element of injustice or unfairness" that would result from respecting the two companies' corporate separateness. * * *

NOTES

(1) Large publicly held corporations usually have numerous wholly owned subsidiaries. The number of subsidiaries of a single major company such as ExxonMobil Corporation may easily run into the hundreds. Subsidiaries are created to function in separate geographic areas, to operate businesses acquired by the parent corporation that are not closely related to the principal business, to provide services to other subsidiaries, and, generally, to operate in business areas in which the corporate management believes the business may be run most efficiently by a separately organized corporation. In many instances, a corporation acquires one or more subsidiaries almost by accident in a transaction to obtain some desired business. The opinion in *Atex* does not indicate how Kodak happened to acquire a wholly owned subsidiary that was involved in the manufacture of computer keyboards, but it might easily have occurred as part of Kodak's interest in the computer business or as the result of an acquisition of an unrelated business that happened to own Atex.

(2) Frank H. Easterbrook and Daniel R. Fischel, The Economic Structure of Corporate Law 57 (1991):

[Parent corporations should not always] be liable for the debts of those in which they hold stock. Far from it. Such general liability would give unaffiliated firms a competitive advantage. Think of the taxicab business. Taxi firms may incorporate each cab or put just a few cabs in a firm. If courts routinely pierced this arrangement and put the assets of the full venture at risk for the accidents of each cab, then "true" single-cab firms would have lower costs of operation because they alone could cut off liability. That would create a perverse incentive because, as we have emphasized, larger firms are apt to carry more insurance. Potential victims of torts would not gain from a legal rule that promoted corporate disintegration. As a result, courts properly disregard the corporate form only when the corporate arrangement has increased risks over what they would be if firms generally were organized as separate ventures.

(3) In contrast to Easterbrook & Fischel, consider Philip I. Blumberg, The Multinational Challenge to Corporation Law: The Search for a New Corporate Personality viii (1993):

> Under traditional law, the fragmentation of an integrated business among a number of affiliated companies as a matter of legal form * * * achieves legal consequences of great importance. In sanctioning this result, the traditional law ignores the fact that despite the legal restructuring, only one business is involved—a business being conducted collectively by interlinked companies under common ownership and control.

Blumberg's basic thesis—extended over seven volumes entitled "The Law of Corporate Groups"—is that a parent corporation with numerous subsidiaries should be viewed as a single economic enterprise for liability and other purposes. Do you agree? Despite Professor Blumberg's efforts to develop a "law" applicable to all corporate groups, judicial decisions lend scant support to his thesis in the liability area.

(4) A parent corporation may operate a business either as a separate subsidiary or as a division or department of the parent corporation itself. If the business is operated as a division or department, there is no legal separation between the parent and the business, and the parent is personally liable for the obligations of that business. If it is operated as a subsidiary, on the other hand, there is legal separation and the parent probably will not be liable for the subsidiary's obligations. The managerial differences between a subsidiary and a division are not as clear as might be thought, since a "division" can be set up with a board of directors and other "corporate" characteristics. Usually, the limitation of parental liability is not the dominant factor in a decision to conduct a specific business in the form of a subsidiary rather than a division. More important is the perceived benefit by the parent in terms of operational efficiency, e.g., to give the managers of a subsidiary in an unrelated business a greater degree of independence or to have outsiders on the subsidiary's board of directors. However, where the subsidiary's business seems unduly risky (or is of a type for which it is

difficult to assess the risk), the element of limited liability may become a factor. And no matter why the subsidiary was originally incorporated, when unexpected potential or actual liabilities arise, it is quite likely that the parent corporation may seek to avoid direct responsibility by relying on the separate existence of the subsidiary. The plaintiffs in turn usually argue that the subsidiary's corporate veil should be pierced in order to impose liability directly on the parent.[c]

(5) Many subsidiaries of large publicly held corporations are themselves immense businesses, with sales and assets in the billions of dollars, and profits in the millions of dollars. They have their own work force, their own managers, and their own board of directors (usually comprised of executives of the subsidiary and the parent corporation and, sometimes, individuals not affiliated with either). Large subsidiaries are almost certain to have almost complete operational freedom in their day-to-day activities. However, they are subject to control by the parent corporation in non-operational areas similar to areas in which Atex was subject to direct control by Kodak; these areas of control may be justified by economic or legal considerations:

(a) A parent corporation must file a consolidated income tax return including its subsidiaries, and accounting rules require that published financial statements consolidate the operations of all wholly and majority-owned subsidiaries. Uniform accounting principles and practices for all subsidiaries are therefore highly desirable. Accounting personnel may be provided by the parent to do all the bookkeeping for each subsidiary, for which a charge usually is imposed by the parent.

(b) Routine legal services are likely to be provided by the parent for all subsidiaries, although subsidiaries may be authorized to hire local counsel in areas in which the parent has no other operations.

(c) Subsidiaries usually are not permitted to borrow money from banks or third parties. The parent corporation is able to borrow larger amounts of money on more favorable terms than any subsidiary so that central financing of major capital improvements is sensible from an economic standpoint. Such a policy also permits the parent corporation to allocate capital funds among its various subsidiaries so as to maximize the overall return of the enterprise.

---

[c] Piercing arguments may be made for other reasons as well. A plaintiff may seek to add the parent corporation as a defendant (even though the subsidiary is clearly able to respond in damages) if exemplary damages are being sought on the theory that such damages may be larger if the assets of the parent are considered along with those of the subsidiary. Piercing arguments also arose in the wake of the stranding of the Exxon Valdez in Alaska where the issue was the proper interpretation of excess liability insurance policies issued by Lloyds of London. It turned out that the Exxon Valdez was owned and operated by a wholly owned Exxon subsidiary, Exxon Shipping Company. While Exxon did not attempt to limit its own responsibility for the costs of the Exxon Valdez disaster to Alaska residents, it did argue strenuously that Exxon Shipping Company was a separate insured for purposes of the Lloyds' policies; the insurers, in turn, attempted to pierce the corporate veil and claimed that there was only a single insured. This issue, which involved hundreds of millions of dollars of insurance coverage, was ultimately settled following a jury verdict favorable to Exxon in Houston, Texas.

(d) Employees may transfer or be transferred from one subsidiary to another, or to or from the parent. In order to facilitate these transfers, the parent corporation typically creates common pension, profit sharing, and retirement plans for all employees of both parent and subsidiaries; it also may establish salary scales so that transfers are simplified and inter-corporate competition for salaries and "perks" eliminated. Employees may be regularly "lent," "borrowed," or "assigned" on a temporary basis to or by the various corporations that make up the corporate family. The advantage of having easy transferability of employees within the corporate family is particularly apparent with respect to specialists since it avoids each subsidiary having to employ its own.

(e) Cash concentration systems similar to that described in the principal case permit the corporation to receive a higher return on excess funds than would be possible if each subsidiary maintained its own separate banking accounts. It also makes sure that idle funds are not left in non-interest bearing accounts even for a brief period. Cash concentration systems function in a manner very similar to a bank, with the parent and its various subsidiaries being its customers.

(f) Because large corporations usually have internal legal staffs, the documentation with respect to separate subsidiaries is usually maintained with a care and fastidiousness to detail that is unusual in a corporation with human shareholders. Minutes, consents, waivers, and so forth are routinely generated in great detail. Rules exist in some corporate families about careful identification of which "hat" each employee is wearing when he or she takes specific actions. Companies also may have policies limiting the use of corporate stationery. Despite these efforts, however, there usually can be found extemporaneous comments or statements that blur the legal existence between parent and subsidiary. The incidents described in the principal case are fairly typical in this regard.

(6) A choice of law issue often arises in piercing cases since states may develop different rules with respect to the piercing doctrine. Consider, for example, a Delaware corporation that transacts all of its business in Illinois; its shares are owned by Illinois residents, and the decision to incorporate in Delaware was based on the perceived benefits of Delaware law. Assume further that this corporation either breaches a contract or commits a tortious act in Illinois that injures citizens of Illinois who bring suit in an Illinois court, naming both the corporation and its shareholders as co-defendants. Should the court apply Illinois or Delaware "veil piercing" principles in determining the liability of the shareholders?

There is a plausible argument that Delaware law should apply, since the relationship of shareholders to their corporation may be viewed as a matter of "internal affairs" of the corporation to be governed by the law of the state of incorporation. For example, under section 307 of the Restatement (Second) of Conflict of Laws, "the local law of the state of incorporation will be applied to determine the existence and extent of a shareholder's liability to the corporation for assessments or contributions *and to its creditors for corporate debts*" (emphasis added). What about corporations organized under the laws of a foreign government? See Sarah Haan, Federalizing the Foreign Corporate Form, 85 St. John's L.Rev. 925 (2011) (observing that courts apply the law of the jurisdiction of incorporation to U.S firms, but not to foreign firms, and arguing that since national interests are more important than state interests in this context, federal law rather than state law should apply in this setting).

(7) Choice of law issues in torts cases apparently involve different considerations than those involved in contracts cases. In § 145 of the Restatement (Second) of Conflict of Laws, it is suggested that the local law of the state that has the "most significant relationship to the occurrence and the parties" should apply in a torts case. Is not § 145 fundamentally inconsistent with § 307 in this area? If, in the above-stated hypothetical, suit is brought in Illinois against the Delaware corporation on an automobile accident that occurred in Illinois, should not § 145 of the Second Restatement "trump" § 307 and the "internal affairs" rule, and require the application of Illinois piercing principles? Would it make any difference if Illinois veil-piercing law gives no indication that it views torts cases differently from contracts cases?

(8) In Harco National Insurance Co. v. Green Farms, Inc., 1989 WL 110537, at *6 (Del.Ch.1989), the court stated that "[p]ersuading a Delaware court to disregard the corporate entity is a difficult task." In LaSalle National Bank v. Perelman, 82 F.Supp.2d 279, 295 (D.Del.2000), the court added that "[i]n order to prevail on a claim to pierce the corporate veil and hold the corporation's shareholders liable, a plaintiff must prove that the corporate form causes fraud or similar injustice. * * * Absent a showing of fraud or that a subsidiary is in fact the mere alter ego of the parent, a common central management alone is not a proper basis for disregarding the separate corporate existence."

B. THE PIERCING DOCTRINE IN FEDERAL/STATE RELATIONS

UNITED STATES V. BESTFOODS
Supreme Court of the United States, 1998.
524 U.S. 51.

JUSTICE SOUTER delivered the opinion of the Court.

The United States brought this action for the costs of cleaning up industrial waste generated by a chemical plant. The issue before us, under the Comprehensive Environmental Response, Compensation, and Liability Act of 1980 (CERCLA), 94 Stat. 2767, as amended, 42 U.S.C. § 9601 et seq., is whether a parent corporation that actively participated in, and exercised control over, the operations of a subsidiary may, without more, be held liable as an operator of a polluting facility owned or operated by the subsidiary. We answer no, unless the corporate veil may be pierced. But a corporate parent that actively participated in, and exercised control over the operations of the facility itself, may be held directly liable in its own right as an operator of the facility.

I

In 1980, CERCLA was enacted in response to the serious environmental and health risks posed by industrial pollution. * * * "As its name implies, CERCLA is a comprehensive statute that grants the President broad power to command government agencies and private parties to clean up hazardous waste sites." * * * If it satisfies certain statutory conditions, the United States may, for instance, use the "Hazardous Substance Superfund" to finance cleanup efforts, see 42 U.S.C. §§ 9601(11), 9604, which it may then replenish by suits brought under § 107 of the Act against, among others, "any person who at the time of disposal of any hazardous substance owned or operated any facility." 42 U.S.C. § 9607(a)(2). So, those actually "responsible for any damage, environmental harm, or injury from chemical poisons may be tagged with the cost of their actions," S.Rep. No. 96–848, pp. 6119 (1980).[1] The term "person" is defined in CERCLA to include corporations and other business organizations, see 42 U.S.C. § 9601(21), and the term "facility" enjoys a broad and detailed definition as well, see § 9601(9).[2] The phrase "owner or operator" is defined only by tautology, however, as "any person owning or operating" a facility, § 9601(20)(A)(ii), and it is this bit of circularity that prompts our review. Cf. Exxon Corp. v. Hunt, supra, at 363, 106 S.Ct., at 1109 (CERCLA, "unfortunately, is not a model of legislative draftsmanship").

II

In 1957, Ott Chemical Co. (Ott I) began manufacturing chemicals at a plant near Muskegon, Michigan, and its intentional and unintentional dumping of hazardous substances significantly polluted the soil and ground water at the site. In 1965, respondent CPC International Inc.[3] incorporated a wholly owned subsidiary to buy Ott I's assets in exchange for CPC stock. The new company, also dubbed Ott Chemical Co. (Ott II),

---

[1] "CERCLA * * * imposes the costs of the cleanup on those responsible for the contamination." Pennsylvania v. Union Gas Co., 491 U.S. 1, 7 (1989). "The remedy that Congress felt it needed in CERCLA is sweeping: everyone who is potentially responsible for hazardous-waste contamination may be forced to contribute to the costs of cleanup." Id., at 21 (plurality opinion of Brennan, J.).

[2] "The term 'facility' means (A) any building, structure, installation, equipment, pipe or pipeline (including any pipe into a sewer or publicly owned treatment works), well, pit, pond, lagoon, impoundment, ditch, landfill, storage container, motor vehicle, rolling stock, or aircraft, or (B) any site or area where a hazardous substance has been deposited, stored, disposed of, or placed, or otherwise come to be located; but does not include any consumer product in consumer use or any vessel."

[3] CPC has recently changed its name to Bestfoods. Consistently with the briefs and the opinions below, we use the name CPC herein.

continued chemical manufacturing at the site, and continued to pollute its surroundings. CPC kept the managers of Ott I, including its founder, president, and principal shareholder, Arnold Ott, on board as officers of Ott II. Arnold Ott and several other Ott II officers and directors were also given positions at CPC, and they performed duties for both corporations.

In 1972, CPC sold Ott II to Story Chemical Company, which operated the Muskegon plant until its bankruptcy in 1977. Shortly thereafter, when respondent Michigan Department of Natural Resources (MDNR) examined the site for environmental damage, it found the land littered with thousands of leaking and even exploding drums of waste, and the soil and water saturated with noxious chemicals. MDNR sought a buyer for the property who would be willing to contribute toward its cleanup, and after extensive negotiations, respondent Aerojet-General Corp. arranged for transfer of the site from the Story bankruptcy trustee in 1977. Aerojet created a wholly owned California subsidiary, Cordova Chemical Company (Cordova/California), to purchase the property, and Cordova/California in turn created a wholly owned Michigan subsidiary, Cordova Chemical Company of Michigan (Cordova/Michigan), which manufactured chemicals at the site until 1986.[5]

By 1981, the federal Environmental Protection Agency had undertaken to see the site cleaned up, and its long-term remedial plan called for expenditures well into the tens of millions of dollars. To recover some of that money, the United States filed this action under § 107 in 1989, naming five defendants as responsible parties: CPC, Aerojet, Cordova/California, Cordova/Michigan, and Arnold Ott.[6] (By that time, Ott I and Ott II were defunct.) After the parties (and MDNR) had launched a flurry of contribution claims, counterclaims, and cross-claims, the District Court consolidated the cases for trial in three phases: liability, remedy, and insurance coverage.

So far, only the first phase has been completed; in 1991, the District Court held a 15-day bench trial on the issue of liability. Because the parties stipulated that the Muskegon plant was a "facility" within the meaning of 42 U.S.C. § 9601(9), that hazardous substances had been released at the facility, and that the United States had incurred reimbursable response costs to clean up the site, the trial focused on the issues of whether CPC and Aerojet, as the parent corporations of Ott II and the Cordova companies, had "owned or operated" the facility within the meaning of § 107(a)(2).

---

[5] Cordova/California and MDNR entered into a contract under which Cordova/California agreed to undertake certain cleanup actions, and MDNR agreed to share in the funding of those actions and to indemnify Cordova/California for various expenses. The Michigan Court of Appeals has held that this agreement requires MDNR to indemnify Aerojet and its Cordova subsidiaries for any CERCLA liability that they may incur in connection with their activities at the Muskegon facility.

[6] Arnold Ott settled out of court with the Government on the eve of trial.

The District Court said that operator liability may attach to a parent corporation both directly, when the parent itself operates the facility, and indirectly, when the corporate veil can be pierced under state law. See CPC Int'l, Inc. v. Aerojet-General Corp., 777 F.Supp. 549, 572 (W.D.Mich.1991).

The court explained that, while CERCLA imposes direct liability in situations in which the corporate veil cannot be pierced under traditional concepts of corporate law, "the statute and its legislative history do not suggest that CERCLA rejects entirely the crucial limits to liability that are inherent to corporate law." Id., at 573. As the District Court put it, "a parent corporation is directly liable under section 107(a)(2) as an operator only when it has exerted power or influence over its subsidiary by actively participating in and exercising control over the subsidiary's business during a period of disposal of hazardous waste. A parent's actual participation in and control over a subsidiary's functions and decision-making creates 'operator' liability under CERCLA; a parent's mere oversight of a subsidiary's business in a manner appropriate and consistent with the investment relationship between a parent and its wholly owned subsidiary does not."

Applying that test to the facts of this case, the District Court held both CPC and Aerojet liable under § 107(a)(2) as operators. As to CPC, the court found it particularly telling that CPC selected Ott II's board of directors and populated its executive ranks with CPC officials, and that a CPC official, G.R.D. Williams, played a significant role in shaping Ott II's environmental compliance policy.

After a divided panel of the Court of Appeals for the Sixth Circuit reversed in part, United States v. Cordova/Michigan, 59 F.3d 584, that court granted rehearing en banc and vacated the panel decision, 67 F.3d 586 (1995).

This time, 7 judges to 6, the court again reversed the District Court in part. 113 F.3d 572 (1997). The majority remarked on the possibility that a parent company might be held directly liable as an operator of a facility owned by its subsidiary: "At least conceivably, a parent might independently operate the facility in the stead of its subsidiary; or, as a sort of joint venturer, actually operate the facility alongside its subsidiary." Id., at 579. But the court refused to go any further and rejected the District Court's analysis with the explanation "that where a parent corporation is sought to be held liable as an operator pursuant to 42 U.S.C. § 9607(a)(2) based upon the extent of its control of its subsidiary which owns the facility, the parent will be liable only when the requirements necessary to pierce the corporate veil [under state law] are met. In other words, * * * whether the parent will be liable as an operator depends upon whether the degree to which it controls its subsidiary and the extent and manner of its involvement with the facility, amount to the abuse of the corporate form that will warrant piercing the corporate veil and disregarding the separate corporate entities of the parent and subsidiary." Id., at 580.

Applying Michigan veil-piercing law, the Court of Appeals decided that * * * CPC was [not] liable for controlling the actions of its subsidiaries, since the parent and subsidiary corporations maintained separate personalities and the [parent] did not utilize the subsidiary corporate form to perpetrate fraud or subvert justice.

We granted certiorari, 522 U.S. 1024 (1997), to resolve a conflict among the Circuits over the extent to which parent corporations may be held liable under CERCLA for operating facilities ostensibly under the control of their subsidiaries.[8] We now vacate and remand.

III

It is a general principle of corporate law deeply "ingrained in our economic and legal systems" that a parent corporation (so-called because of control through ownership of another corporation's stock) is not liable for the acts of its subsidiaries. Douglas & Shanks, Insulation from Liability Through Subsidiary Corporations, 39 Yale L.J. 193 (1929) (hereinafter Douglas); see also Berkey v. Third Ave. R. Co., 244 N.Y. 84, 85, 155 N.E. 58 (1926) (Cardozo, J.); 1 W. Fletcher, Cyclopedia of Law of Private Corporations § 33, p. 568 (rev. ed. 1990) ("Neither does the mere fact that there exists a parent-subsidiary relationship between two corporations make the one liable for the torts of its affiliate"); Horton, Liability of Corporation for Torts of Subsidiary, 7 A.L.R.3d 1343, 1349 (1966) ("Ordinarily, a corporation which chooses to facilitate the operation of its business by employment of another corporation as a subsidiary will not be penalized by a judicial determination of liability for the legal obligations of the subsidiary") * * *. Thus it is hornbook law that "the exercise of the 'control' which stock ownership gives to the stockholders * * * will not create liability beyond the assets of the subsidiary. That 'control' includes the election of directors, the making of by-laws * * * and the doing of all other acts incident to the legal status of stockholders. Nor

---

[8]   Compare United States v. Cordova/Michigan, 113 F.3d 572, 580 (C.A.6 1997) (case below) (parent may be held liable for controlling affairs of subsidiary only when the corporate veil can be pierced), and Joslyn Mfg. Co. v. T.L. James & Co., 893 F.2d 80, 82–83 (C.A.5 1990) (same), cert. denied, 498 U.S. 1108 (1991) (but cf. Riverside Market Dev. Corp. v. International Bldg. Prods., Inc., 931 F.2d 327, 330 (C.A.5) (parent companies that actually participate in the wrongful conduct cannot hide behind the corporate veil, and can be held directly liable without veil-piercing, cert. denied, 502 U.S. 1004 (1991)), with United States v. Kayser-Roth Corp., 910 F.2d 24, 27 (C.A.1 1990) (parent actively involved in the affairs of its subsidiary may be held directly liable as an operator of the facility, regardless of whether the corporate veil can be pierced), cert. denied, 498 U.S. 1084 (1991), Schiavone v. Pearce, 79 F.3d 248, 254–255 (C.A.2 1996) (same), Lansford-Coaldale Joint Water Auth. v. Tonolli Corp., 4 F.3d 1209, 1220–1225 (C.A.3 1993) (same), Jacksonville Elec. Auth. v. Bernuth Corp., 996 F.2d 1107, 1110 (C.A.11 1993) (same), and Nurad, Inc. v. William E. Hooper & Sons Co., 966 F.2d 837, 842 (C.A.4) (parent having authority to control subsidiary is liable as an operator, even if it did not exercise that authority), cert. denied, 506 U.S. 940 (1992).

will a duplication of some or all of the directors or executive officers be fatal." Douglas 196 (footnotes omitted). Although this respect for corporate distinctions when the subsidiary is a polluter has been severely criticized in the literature, see, e.g., Note, Liability of Parent Corporations for Hazardous Waste Cleanup and Damages, 99 Harv.L.Rev. 986 (1986), nothing in CERCLA purports to reject this bedrock principle, and against this venerable common-law backdrop, the congressional silence is audible. Cf. Edmonds v. Compagnie Generale Transatlantique, 443 U.S. 256, 266– 267 (1979) ("silence is most eloquent, for such reticence while contemplating an important and controversial change in existing law is unlikely"). The Government has indeed made no claim that a corporate parent is liable as an owner or an operator under § 107 simply because its subsidiary is subject to liability for owning or operating a polluting facility.

But there is an equally fundamental principle of corporate law, applicable to the parent-subsidiary relationship as well as generally, that the corporate veil may be pierced and the shareholder held liable for the corporation's conduct when, inter alia, the corporate form would otherwise be misused to accomplish certain wrongful purposes, most notably fraud, on the shareholder's behalf. See, e.g., Anderson v. Abbott, supra, at 362 ("there are occasions when the limited liability sought to be obtained through the corporation will be qualified or denied"); P. Blumberg, Law of Corporate Groups: Tort, Contract, and Other Common Law Problems in the Substantive Law of Parent and Subsidiary Corporations §§ 6.01–6.06 (1987 and 1996 Supp.) (discussing the law of veil piercing in the parent-subsidiary context). Nothing in CERCLA purports to rewrite this well-settled rule, either. CERCLA is thus like many another congressional enactment in giving no indication "that the entire corpus of state corporation law is to be replaced simply because a plaintiff's cause of action is based upon a federal statute," Burks v. Lasker, 441 U.S. 471, 478 (1979), and the failure of the statute to speak to a matter as fundamental as the liability implications of corporate ownership demands application of the rule that "[i]n order to abrogate a common-law principle, the statute must speak directly to the question addressed by the common law," United States v. Texas, 507 U.S. 529, 534 (1993) (internal quotation marks omitted). The Court of Appeals was accordingly correct in holding that when (but only when) the corporate veil may be pierced,[9] may a parent corporation be charged with derivative CERCLA liability for its subsidiary's actions.[10]

---

[9] There is significant disagreement among courts and commentators over whether, in enforcing CERCLA's indirect liability, courts should borrow state law, or instead apply a federal common law of veil piercing. Compare, e.g., U.S. v. Cordova Chemical Co. of Michigan, 113 F.3d 572, at 584–585 (6th Cir.1997) (Merritt, J., concurring in part and dissenting in part)(arguing that federal common law should apply); Brotherhood of Locomotive Engineers v. Springfield Terminal Ry. Co., 210 F.3d 18 (1st Cir.2000) (federal common law of piercing should apply to claimed violation of the Railway Labor Act); Lansford-Coaldale Joint Water Auth. v. Tonolli

IV

A

If the act rested liability entirely on ownership of a polluting facility, this opinion might end here; but CERCLA liability may turn on operation as well as ownership, and nothing in the statute's terms bars a parent corporation from direct liability for its own actions in operating a facility owned by its subsidiary. As Justice (then-Professor) Douglas noted almost 70 years ago, derivative liability cases are to be distinguished from those in which "the alleged wrong can seemingly be traced to the parent through the conduit of its own personnel and management" and "the parent is directly a participant in the wrong complained of." Douglas 207, 208. In such instances, the parent is directly liable for its own actions. See H. Henn & J. Alexander, Laws of Corporations 347 (3d ed. 1983) (hereinafter Henn & Alexander) ("Apart from corporation law principles, a shareholder, whether a natural person or a corporation, may be liable on the ground that such shareholder's activity resulted in the liability"). The fact that a corporate subsidiary happens to own a polluting facility operated by its parent does nothing, then, to displace the rule that the parent "corporation is [itself] responsible for the wrongs committed by its agents in the course of its business," Mine Workers v. Coronado Coal Co., 259 U.S. 344, 395 (1922), and whereas the rules of veil-piercing limit derivative liability for the actions of another corporation, CERCLA's "operator" provision is concerned primarily with direct liability for one's own actions. See, e.g., Sidney S. Arst Co. v. Pipefitters Welfare Ed. Fund, 25 F.3d 417, 420 (C.A.7 1994) ("the direct, personal liability provided by CERCLA is distinct from the derivative liability that results from

---

Corp., 4 F.3d, at 1225 ("given the federal interest in uniformity in the application of CERCLA, it is federal common law, and not state law, which governs when corporate veil-piercing is justified under CERCLA"), and Aronovsky & Fuller, Liability of Parent Corporations for Hazardous Substance Releases under CERCLA, 24 U.S.F.L.Rev. 421, 455 (1990) ("CERCLA enforcement should not be hampered by subordination of its goals to varying state law rules of alter ego theory"), with, e.g., 113 F.3d, at 580 ("Whether the circumstances in this case warrant a piercing of the corporate veil will be determined by state law"), and Dennis, Liability of Officers, Directors and Stockholders under CERCLA: The Case for Adopting State Law, 36 Vill.L.Rev. 1367 (1991) (arguing that state law should apply). Cf. * * * Note, Piercing the Corporate Law Veil: The Alter Ego Doctrine Under Federal Common Law, 95 Harv.L.Rev. 853 (1982) (arguing that federal common law need not mirror state law, because "federal common law should look to federal statutory policy rather than to state corporate law when deciding whether to pierce the corporate veil"). Since none of the parties challenges the Sixth Circuit's holding that CPC and Aerojet incurred no derivative liability, the question is not presented in this case, and we do not address it further.

[10] Some courts and commentators have suggested that this indirect, veil-piercing approach can subject a parent corporation to liability only as an owner, and not as an operator. See, e.g., Lansford-Coaldale Joint Water Auth. v. Tonolli Corp., supra, at 1220; Oswald, Bifurcation of the Owner and Operator Analysis under CERCLA, 72 Wash. U.L.Q. 223, 281–282 (1994) (hereinafter Oswald). We think it is otherwise, however. If a subsidiary that operates, but does not own, a facility is so pervasively controlled by its parent for a sufficiently improper purpose to warrant veil piercing, the parent may be held derivatively liable for the subsidiary's acts as an operator.

piercing the corporate veil") (internal quotation marks omitted). It is this direct liability that is properly seen as being at issue here.

Under the plain language of the statute, any person who operates a polluting facility is directly liable for the costs of cleaning up the pollution. This is so regardless of whether that person is the facility's owner, the owner's parent corporation or business partner, or even a saboteur who sneaks into the facility at night to discharge its poisons out of malice. If any such act of operating a corporate subsidiary's facility is done on behalf of a parent corporation, the existence of the parent-subsidiary relationship under state corporate law is simply irrelevant to the issue of direct liability. See Riverside Market Dev. Corp. v. International Bldg. Prods., Inc., 931 F.2d 327, 330 (C.A.5) ("CERCLA prevents individuals from hiding behind the corporate shield when, as 'operators,' they themselves actually participate in the wrongful conduct prohibited by the Act"); United States v. Kayser-Roth Corp., 910 F.2d 24, 26 (C.A.1 1990) ("a person who is an operator of a facility is not protected from liability by the legal structure of ownership").[12]

This much is easy to say; the difficulty comes in defining actions sufficient to constitute direct parental "operation." Here of course we may again rue the uselessness of CERCLA's definition of a facility's "operator" as "any person * * * operating" the facility, which leaves us to do the best we can to give the term its "ordinary or natural meaning." Bailey v. United States, 516 U.S. 137, 145 (1995) (internal quotation marks omitted). In a mechanical sense, to "operate" ordinarily means "[t]o control the functioning of; run: operate a sewing machine." American Heritage Dictionary 1268 (3d ed. 1992); see also Webster's New International Dictionary 1707 (2d ed. 1958) ("to work; as, to operate a machine"). And in the organizational sense more obviously intended by CERCLA, the word ordinarily means "[t]o conduct the affairs of; manage: operate a business." American Heritage Dictionary, supra, at 1268; see also Webster's New International Dictionary, supra, at 1707 ("to manage"). So, under CERCLA, an operator is simply someone who directs the workings of, manages, or conducts the affairs of a facility. To sharpen the definition for purposes of CERCLA's concern with environmental contamination, an operator must manage, direct, or conduct operations specifically related to pollution, that is, operations having to do with the leakage or disposal of hazardous waste, or decisions about compliance with environmental regulations.

---

[12] See Oswald 257 ("There are * * * instances * * * in which the parent has not sufficiently overstepped the bounds of corporate separateness to warrant piercing, yet is involved enough in the facility's activities that it should be held liable as an operator. Imagine, for example, a parent who strictly observed corporate formalities, avoided intertwining officers and directors, and adequately capitalized its subsidiary, yet provided active, daily supervision and control over hazardous waste disposal activities of the subsidiary. Such a parent should not escape liability just because its activities do not justify a piercing of the subsidiary's veil").

B

With this understanding, we are satisfied that the Court of Appeals correctly rejected the District Court's analysis of direct liability. But we also think that the appeals court erred in limiting direct liability under the statute to a parent's sole or joint venture operation, so as to eliminate any possible finding that CPC is liable as an operator on the facts of this case.

1

By emphasizing that "CPC is directly liable under section 107(a)(2) as an operator because CPC actively participated in and exerted significant control over Ott II's business and decision-making," 777 F.Supp., at 574, the District Court applied the "actual control" test of whether the parent "actually operated the business of its subsidiary," as several Circuits have employed it, see, e.g., United States v. Kayser-Roth Corp., supra, at 27 (operator liability "requires active involvement in the affairs of the subsidiary"); Jacksonville Elec. Auth. v. Bernuth Corp., 996 F.2d 1107, 1110 (C.A.11 1993) (parent is liable if it "actually exercised control over, or was otherwise intimately involved in the operations of, the [subsidiary] corporation immediately responsible for the operation of the facility").

The well-taken objection to the actual control test, however, is its fusion of direct and indirect liability; the test is administered by asking a question about the relationship between the two corporations (an issue going to indirect liability) instead of a question about the parent's interaction with the subsidiary's facility (the source of any direct liability). If, however, direct liability for the parent's operation of the facility is to be kept distinct from derivative liability for the subsidiary's own operation, the focus of the enquiry must necessarily be different under the two tests. "The question is not whether the parent operates the subsidiary, but rather whether it operates the facility, and that operation is evidenced by participation in the activities of the facility, not the subsidiary. Control of the subsidiary, if extensive enough, gives rise to indirect liability under piercing doctrine, not direct liability under the statutory language." Oswald 269; see also Schiavone v. Pearce, 79 F.3d 248, 254 (C.A.2 1996) ("Any liabilities [the parent] may have as an operator, then, stem directly from its control over the plant"). The District Court was therefore mistaken to rest its analysis on CPC's relationship with Ott II, premising liability on little more than "CPC's 100-percent ownership of Ott II" and "CPC's active participation in, and at times majority control over, Ott II's board of directors." 777 F.Supp., at 575. The analysis should instead have rested on the relationship between CPC and the Muskegon facility itself.

In addition to (and perhaps as a reflection of) the erroneous focus on the relationship between CPC and Ott II, even those findings of the

District Court that might be taken to speak to the extent of CPC's activity at the facility itself are flawed, for the District Court wrongly assumed that the actions of the joint officers and directors are necessarily attributable to CPC. The District Court emphasized the facts that CPC placed its own high-level officials on Ott II's board of directors and in key management positions at Ott II, and that those individuals made major policy decisions and conducted day-to-day operations at the facility: "Although Ott II corporate officers set the day-to-day operating policies for the company without any need to obtain formal approval from CPC, CPC actively participated in this decision-making because high-ranking CPC officers served in Ott II management positions." Id., at 559; see also id., at 575 (relying on "CPC's involvement in major decision-making and day-to-day operations through CPC officials who served within Ott II management, including the positions of president and chief executive officer," and on "the conduct of CPC officials with respect to Ott II affairs, particularly Arnold Ott"); id., at 558 ("CPC actively participated in, and at times controlled, the policy-making decisions of its subsidiary thorough its representation on the Ott II board of directors" * * * [and] "through representation in the highest levels of the subsidiary's management"). In imposing direct liability on these grounds, the District Court failed to recognize that "it is entirely appropriate for directors of a parent corporation to serve as directors of its subsidiary, and that fact alone may not serve to expose the parent corporation to liability for its subsidiary's acts." American Protein Corp. v. AB Volvo, 844 F.2d 56, 57(C.A.2), cert. denied, 488 U.S. 852 (1988).

This recognition that the corporate personalities remain distinct has its corollary in the "well established principle [of corporate law] that directors and officers holding positions with a parent and its subsidiary can and do 'change hats' to represent the two corporations separately, despite their common ownership." Lusk v. Foxmeyer Health Corp., 129 F.3d 773, 779 (C.A.5 1997). Since courts generally presume "that the directors are wearing their 'subsidiary hats' and not their 'parent hats' when acting for the subsidiary," P. Blumberg, Law of Corporate Groups: Procedural Problems in the Law of Parent and Subsidiary Corporations § 1.02.1, at 12 (1983), it cannot be enough to establish liability here that dual officers and directors made policy decisions and supervised activities at the facility. The Government would have to show that, despite the general presumption to the contrary, the officers and directors were acting in their capacities as CPC officers and directors, and not as Ott II officers and directors, when they committed those acts.[13] The District

---

[13] We do not attempt to recite the ways in which the Government could show that dual officers or directors were in fact acting on behalf of the parent. Here, it is prudent to say only that the presumption that an act is taken on behalf of the corporation for whom the officer claims to act is strongest when the act is perfectly consistent with the norms of corporate behavior, but wanes as the distance from those accepted norms approaches the point of action by a dual officer plainly contrary to the interests of the subsidiary yet nonetheless advantageous to the parent.

Court made no such enquiry here, however, disregarding entirely this time-honored common law rule.

In sum, the District Court's focus on the relationship between parent and subsidiary (rather than parent and facility), combined with its automatic attribution of the actions of dual officers and directors to the corporate parent, erroneously, even if unintentionally, treated CERCLA as though it displaced or fundamentally altered common law standards of limited liability. Indeed, if the evidence of common corporate personnel acting at management and directorial levels were enough to support a finding of a parent corporation's direct operator liability under CERCLA, then the possibility of resorting to veil piercing to establish indirect, derivative liability for the subsidiary's violations would be academic. There would in essence be a relaxed, CERCLA-specific rule of derivative liability that would banish traditional standards and expectations from the law of CERCLA liability. But, as we have said, such a rule does not arise from congressional silence, and CERCLA's silence is dispositive.

2

We accordingly agree with the Court of Appeals that a participation-and-control test looking to the parent's supervision over the subsidiary, especially one that assumes that dual officers always act on behalf of the parent, cannot be used to identify operation of a facility resulting in direct parental liability. Nonetheless, a return to the ordinary meaning of the word "operate" in the organizational sense will indicate why we think that the Sixth Circuit stopped short when it confined its examples of direct parental operation to exclusive or joint ventures, and declined to find at least the possibility of direct operation by CPC in this case.

In our enquiry into the meaning Congress presumably had in mind when it used the verb "to operate," we recognized that the statute obviously meant something more than mere mechanical activation of pumps and valves, and must be read to contemplate "operation" as including the exercise of direction over the facility's activities. The Court of Appeals recognized this by indicating that a parent can be held directly liable when the parent operates the facility in the stead of its subsidiary or alongside the subsidiary in some sort of a joint venture. We anticipated a further possibility above, however, when we observed that a dual officer or director might depart so far from the norms of parental influence exercised through dual office holding as to serve the parent, even when ostensibly acting on behalf of the subsidiary in operating the facility. Yet another possibility, suggested by the facts of this case, is that an agent of the parent with no hat to wear but the parent's hat might manage or direct activities at the facility.

Identifying such an occurrence calls for line-drawing yet again, since the acts of direct operation that give rise to parental liability must necessarily be distinguished from the interference that stems from the normal relationship between parent and subsidiary. Again, norms of corporate behavior (undisturbed by any CERCLA provision) are crucial reference points. Just as we may look to such norms in identifying the limits of the presumption that a dual officeholder acts in his ostensible capacity, so here we may refer to them in distinguishing a parental officer's oversight of a subsidiary from such an officer's control over the operation of the subsidiary's facility. "[A]ctivities that involve the facility but which are consistent with the parent's investor status, such as monitoring of the subsidiary's performance, supervision of the subsidiary's finance and capital budget decisions, and articulation of general policies and procedures, should not give rise to direct liability." Oswald 282. The critical question is whether, in degree and detail, actions directed to the facility by an agent of the parent alone are eccentric under accepted norms of parental oversight of a subsidiary's facility.

There is, in fact, some evidence that CPC engaged in just this type and degree of activity at the Muskegon plant. The District Court's opinion speaks of an agent of CPC alone, who played a conspicuous part in dealing with the toxic risks emanating from the operation of the plant. G.R.D. Williams worked only for CPC; he was not an employee, officer, or director of Ott II, and thus, his actions were of necessity taken only on behalf of CPC. The District Court found that "CPC became directly involved in environmental and regulatory matters through the work of * * * Williams, CPC's governmental and environmental affairs director. Williams * * * became heavily involved in environmental issues at Ott II." 777 F.Supp., at 561. He "actively participated in and exerted control over a variety of Ott II environmental matters," and he "issued directives regarding Ott II's responses to regulatory inquiries," id., at 575.

We think that these findings are enough to raise an issue of CPC's operation of the facility through Williams's actions, though we would draw no ultimate conclusion from these findings at this point. Not only would we be deciding in the first instance an issue on which the trial and appellate courts did not focus, but the very fact that the District Court did not see the case as we do suggests that there may be still more to be known about Williams's activities. Indeed, even as the factual findings stand, the trial court offered little in the way of concrete detail for its conclusions about Williams's role in Ott II's environmental affairs, and the parties vigorously dispute the extent of Williams's involvement. Prudence thus counsels us to remand, on the theory of direct operation set out here, for reevaluation of Williams's role, and of the role of any other CPC agent who might be said to have had a part in operating the Muskegon facility.[14]

---

[14] There are some passages in the District Court's opinion that might suggest that, without reference to Williams, some of Ott II's actions in operating the facility were in fact dictated by, and thus taken on behalf of, CPC. * * *

V

The judgment of the Court of Appeals for the Sixth Circuit is vacated, and the case is remanded with instructions to return it to the District Court for further proceedings consistent with this opinion.

NOTES

(1) This significant opinion resolved complex and long-standing disputes among the circuits as to the proper interpretation of CERCLA. Might the Court's analysis of "operator" have relevance in establishing piercing liability in a "run of the mill" case involving individual rather than corporate shareholders? What might a shareholder who is an individual do that would involve "operating" a business that is beyond the normal activities of a shareholder? Can an individual who is also the president and chief executive officer of a corporation ever be an "operator" of the business? Or are these questions moot because such activity would be grounds for piercing the corporate veil in any event? For a case holding that a corporate officer can be personally liable under provisions of state environmental law assigning liability to "any person creating a condition or maintaining a facility or condition that reasonably could be expected to create a source of pollution to waters of state," see BEC Corporation v. Department of Environmental Protection, 775 A.2d 928 (Conn.2001).

(2) The question of whether piercing in CERCLA cases should be governed by federal or state law was not resolved. The issue of whether the parent company "owned" or "operated" the site where environmental damage occurred should clearly be decided under federal law construing those terms because the terms are contained in CERCLA. Only in analyzing the question of whether a parent should be held liable under a veil-piercing theory does the issue of state law versus federal law arise. Since CERCLA does not specifically mention piercing the corporate veil, and instead creates a separate liability regime for parent corporations, is there any reason not to apply state piercing law in CERCLA cases? What federal statutory policy, if any, might be involved in these cases?

(3) Piercing issues also pertain to employment discrimination arising under title VII of the Civil Rights Act of 1964. The supervisor whose action is the cause for complaint may be on the payroll of the parent while the employee is on the payroll of the subsidiary. In Garcia v. Elf Atochem North America, 28 F.3d 446 (5th Cir.1994) (abrogated on other grounds by Oncale v. Sundowner Offshore Services, 523 U.S. 75 (1998)), the court stated that the test was whether the parent and subsidiary were part of a "single, integrated enterprise," and there was a four-fold test for this determination: "(1) interrelation of operations, (2) centralized control of labor relations, (3) common management, and (4) common ownership or financial control." See also Gabriele v. Cole Nat'l Corp., 78 F.Supp.2d 61, 65 (N.D.N.Y.1999). Is this simply another way of describing traditional tests for piercing the corporate veil? If not, is it more stringent or less stringent than those tests?

STARK V. FLEMMING

United States Court of Appeals, Ninth Circuit, 1960.
283 F.2d 410.

[The Secretary of Health, Education and Welfare ruled that Mrs. Stark was not entitled to old-age benefits because, in part, she lacked a bona fide employment status and had not been paid wages. The District Court affirmed, 181 F.Supp. 539 (N.D.Cal.1959).]

PER CURIAM.

* * * Appellant placed her assets—a farm and a duplex house—in a newly organized corporation. Then she began to draw $400 per month as salary. The Secretary has found the corporation was a sham. There is no doubt that the corporation was set up to qualify appellant in a short time for social security payments.

But here there seems to have been proper adherence to the normal corporate routines. And it is difficult to understand how the corporate arrangement would not have to be respected by others than the Secretary. And we think he must respect it, too.

Congress could have provided that the motivation to obtain social security by organizing a corporation would defeat the end. It did not.

The Secretary is justified in taking exception to the amount paid Mrs. Stark for her services by which she sought to qualify herself for the maximum amount of social security payments. The salary left little or nothing for a return on capital, and the capital was substantial.

So, we think the Secretary is entitled to make an objective reappraisal of the salary to determine what would have been a reasonable salary for Mrs. Stark for the services she performed. One legitimate approach would be: What would a commercial farm agency in the vicinity of the farm have charged? And what would a rental agency in the vicinity of the duplex have charged for the same service? And perhaps, she might be allowed slightly more than such agencies. It is not for us to review such determinations within reasonable limits. When the Secretary determines a reasonable salary, then the amount of social security payments can be readily computed.

We, therefore, hold that the district court's judgment should be vacated and that the case should go back through the district court for direction to the Secretary to reevaluate the case on an approach consistent with what we have indicated herein.

Reversed.

ROCCOGRANDI V. UNEMPLOYMENT COMP. BD. OF REVIEW

Superior Court of Pennsylvania, 1962.
178 A.2d 786.

MONTGOMERY, JUDGE.

The appellants are all members of a family who are involved in the wrecking business together. Each owns 40 shares of stock in the company which has 205 outstanding shares, and all three are officers of the company. The officers of the company, during periods of insufficient work to employ all the members of the family, hold a meeting and by majority vote decide which members shall be "laid off." It was decided by majority vote of all the stockholders that the appellants would be "laid off" because it was their respective turns. Immediately thereafter claims for unemployment compensation benefits were filed by the three appellants. The Bureau of Employment Security denied the claims on the grounds that the appellants were self-employed. Upon appeal the referee reversed the bureau and held the appellants to be entitled to benefits. The Board of Review reversed the referee's decision, holding that the appellants had sufficient control to lay themselves off and that they did just that. Therefore the appellants were self-employed and must be denied eligibility for benefits under section 402(h) and section 402(b)(1) of the law, 43 P.S. § 802(b)(1), (h).

This case is ruled by De Priest Unemployment Compensation Case, 196 Pa.Super. 612, 177 A.2d 20, in which this Court held that the corporate entity may be ignored in determining whether the claimants, in fact, were "unemployed" under the act, or were self-employed persons whose business merely proved to be unremunerative during the period for which the claim for benefits was made.

Decisions affirmed.

NOTES

(1) Do the questions raised by these two cases relate to the nature of corporateness, or do they merely involve an interpretation of the federal Social Security Act or the Pennsylvania Unemployment Compensation Act? If the former, is the question the same as in the traditional piercing cases? In other words, are the courts trying to accomplish something in these two cases that is different from what the courts are trying to accomplish in other piercing cases?

(2) In connection with Stark v. Flemming, compare the basically inconsistent decision in Vogel v. Sullivan, 735 F.Supp. 1353 (N.D.Ill.1990) (plaintiff may not transmute self-employment income into salary simply by incorporating his apartment house).

(3) State unemployment compensation statutes provide an exemption from contributions for employers who employ less than a minimum number of

employees, often eight. May an employer avoid liability under these statutes by splitting his business among several different corporations so that each corporation has less than the minimum number of employees? See State v. Dallas Liquor Warehouse No. 4, 217 S.W.2d 654 (Tex.1949).

C. "REVERSE" PIERCING

CARGILL, INC. v. HEDGE
Supreme Court of Minnesota, 1985.
375 N.W.2d 477.

SIMONNET, JUSTICE.

Do the owner-occupants of a farm, by placing their land in a family farm corporation, lose their homestead exemption from judgment creditors? The trial court and the court of appeals said no. We agree and affirm.

On October 24, 1973, defendant-respondent Sam Hedge and his wife Annette entered into a contract for deed for the purchase of a 160-acre farm. On March 1, 1974, the Hedges assigned their vendees' interest to Hedge Farm, Inc., a Minnesota corporation qualified as a family farm corporation under Minn. Stat. § 500.24, subd. 1(c) (1973), and took possession. Between 1976 and 1979, Sam Hedge purchased farm supplies and services on account from plaintiff-appellant Cargill, Inc., totaling about $17,000. Apparently not until 1980, however, after Cargill had started suit on the account, did it become aware of the Hedges' corporation. Eventually, pursuant to a confession of judgment, judgment was entered in favor of Cargill and against Sam Hedge and Hedge Farms, Inc., for $12,707.08.

An execution sale was held on July 15, 1982, with Cargill as the successful bidder. Shortly before the 1-year redemption period expired, the district court, on motion of the judgment debtor, enjoined further proceedings on the execution, tolled the redemption period, and allowed Annette to join the proceedings as an intervenor. Subsequently, the trial court ruled that the Hedges had a right to exempt from the execution 80 acres constituting their homestead. The court of appeals affirmed, ruling that Annette Hedge, as sole shareholder of Hedge Farm, Inc., had an "equitable interest" in the corporate property, and that this interest, coupled with the Hedges' occupancy, satisfied the homestead statute. The court implied that it was willing to reach the same result by "piercing the corporate veil." *Cargill, Inc. v. Hedge*, 358 N.W.2d 490 (Minn. Ct. App. 1984). We granted Cargills' petition for further review.

The right to a homestead exemption from execution is a constitutional right. Minn. Const. art. 1, § 12. This right exempts from seizure or sale "the house owned and occupied by the debtor as his dwelling place, together with the land upon which it is situated," Minn. Stat. § 510.01 (1984); in rural areas, 80 acres may be exempted, Minn. Stat. § 510.02 (1984). Clearly, a corporation, an artificial entity needing no dwelling, is not entitled to a homestead exemption. *E.g., Sugg v. Pollard*, 184 N.C. 494, 115 S.E. 153 (1922). If there is to be a homestead exemption here, it must be one personal to the Hedges, notwithstanding the existence of their corporation.

Annette Hedge is the sole stockholder of Hedge Farm, Inc. The court of appeals felt that this gave Annette an "equitable interest" in the property which, together with occupancy, constituted the kind of ownership which would allow the Hedges to assert a homestead exemption in the corporate property. But if Annette is the sole "owner" of the farm, there is no need to assert any homestead exemption because Annette is not a debtor. In any event, the "equitable interest" rationale seems to us conceptually ill-adapted to resolving the issue of creditors' rights we have here, especially since the relationship of a shareholder to a corporation is also implicated. We decline to adopt any equitable interest theory.

We do think, however, that the approach of a reverse pierce of the corporate veil may be used. In *Roepke v. Western National Mutual Insurance Co.*, 302 N.W.2d 350 (Minn. 1981), we disregarded the corporate entity to further the purposes of the No-Fault Act. Although title to six motor vehicles was in a corporation, in *Roepke* we nevertheless treated the vehicles as if they had been owned by the deceased, sole shareholder of the corporation, so that the decedent could be deemed an "insured" under the no-fault policy for the purpose of survivors' benefits. It seemed unfair to deprive the business owner of no-fault coverage he would have had if he had operated as a sole proprietorship. We stressed that the decedent had been president and sole stockholder of the corporation, that all six vehicles were used as family vehicles, and that no one in the family owned any other vehicles. Later, in *Kuennen v. Citizens Security Mutual Insurance Co.*, 330 N.W.2d 886 (Minn. 1983), we made clear that policy reasons for a pierce do not alone justify disregarding the corporate entity. We refused a reverse pierce in *Kuennen*, where the decedent held only 51% of the stock and used only two of the four corporate vehicles for family use. Thus the degree of identity between the individual and his or her corporation, the extent to which the corporation is an alter ego, is important. Also important is whether others, such as a creditor or other shareholders, would be harmed by a pierce.

Here there is a close identity between the Hedges and their corporation. While the Hedges maintained some of the corporate formalities, such as keeping corporate minutes, filing corporate tax returns, and dealing with the Production Credit Association as a corporation, realistically, as the trial court found, they operated the farm as their own. They had no lease with the corporation and paid no rent. The farmhouse was their family home. Annette Hedge owned all the stock. Mr. and Mrs. Hedge and their daughters were the corporate directors with Sam Hedge as president, Patricia as vice-president, and Annette as secretary-treasurer. None of the officers received any salary. The corporation was as much an alter ego for the Hedges as Mr. Roepke's corporation was for him.

In this case, too, we have strong policy reasons for a reverse pierce, much stronger than in *Roepke*, namely, furtherance of the purpose of the homestead exemption. * * *

One of the features of a corporation is limiting creditor liability to the corporate assets. We are aware of the danger of a debtor being able to raise or lower his corporate shield, depending on which position best protects his property. Consequently, a reverse pierce should be permitted in only the most carefully limited circumstances. This is such a case, and we so hold. Disregarding the entity Hedge Farm, Inc., we treat the Hedge farm as if owned by Sam and Annette Hedge as vendees under their contract for deed. As a co-vendee, Sam Hedge, the debtor, is entitled to claim a homestead exemption in 80 acres of his farm, and the creditors' execution sale of the exempted 80 acres is void.

Affirmed.

KELLEY, J., took no part in the consideration or decision of this case.

NOTES

(1) Gregory S. Crespi, The Reverse Pierce Doctrine: Applying Appropriate Standards, 16 J. Corp. L. 33, 36–37 (1990):

> [The traditional piercing the corporate veil jurisprudence] is almost wholly irrelevant to the interesting and diverse set of situations that are collectively referred to by the cases and commentary as involving a "reverse pierce" of the corporate veil. In a reverse pierce claim, either a corporate insider or a person with a claim against a corporate insider is attempting to have the insider and the corporate entity treated as a single person for some purpose. * * * [R]everse pierce claims implicate different policies and require a different analytical framework from the more routine corporate creditor veil-piercing attempts.

Crespi's analysis indicates, however, that reverse piercing claims have been met with skepticism and outright rejection by many courts. If the plaintiffs can rely on the corporate form to escape personal liability from creditors, and also rely on reverse piercing to keep the corporation's assets out of the grasp of creditors, is there any way for creditors to protect themselves?

(2) Workers' Compensation statutes provide an administrative remedy for injured employees and prohibit suits brought against the "employer" of

the injured employee. However, suits against third parties whose negligence contributed to the injury are not barred. In Sims v. Western Waste Industries ("WWI"), 918 S.W.2d 682 (Tex.App.1996), an injured employee of a subsidiary corporation sued the parent corporation of his employer, alleging that the parent was involved in the design, manufacture, and marketing of the truck involved in the employee's accident. The parent filed a motion for summary judgment arguing that it was the alter ego of the employer and therefore protected by the statutory bar against suits brought against the employer. A summary judgment in favor of the parent corporation was reversed:

> We are not persuaded that the legislature ever intended parent corporations, who deliberately chose to establish a subsidiary corporation, to be allowed to assert immunity under the Texas Workers' Compensation Act by reverse piercing of the corporate veil they themselves established. WWI has accepted the benefits of establishing a subsidiary corporation in Texas and will not be allowed to disregard that entity now that it is to their gain to do so. We hold that Texas law does not permit a parent corporation to assert the alter ego theory of piercing the corporate veil of their subsidiary and thereby assert Workers' Compensation immunity as a defense to a suit by the subsidiary's employee. Point of error one is sustained. We reverse the judgment of the trial court and remand for trial.

918 S.W.2d at 686. Accord Reboy v. Cozzi Iron & Metal, Inc., 9 F.3d 1303, 1308, n. 9 (7th Cir.1993), where the court stated: "Moreover we agree with the district court and the Reboys that Cozzi's defensive use of the 'piercing the corporate veil' doctrine may simply be inappropriate under Indiana law. There are no cases in Indiana allowing the doctrine to be used to gain immunity under the Worker's Compensation Act. Moreover, the defensive use of the 'piercing the corporate veil' doctrine in the employment context has been addressed and soundly rejected in at least one other circuit. See Boggs v. Blue Diamond Coal Co., 590 F.2d 655, 662 (6th Cir.1979)."

(3) Some courts have rejected the doctrine of reverse piercing. One concern is that reverse piercing elevates the claims of one set of creditors (the individual creditors of the shareholder) above the claims of another set of creditors (the creditors of the corporation). Another concern is that reverse piercing circumvents normal debt collection practices and procedures, such as obtaining execution against a shareholder's interest in the company.

PEPPER v. LITTON

Supreme Court of the United States, 1939.
308 U.S. 295.

[Pepper sued the Dixie Splint Coal Company for an accounting of royalties due Pepper under a lease. While this case was pending, Litton, the sole shareholder of Dixie Splint, caused Dixie Splint to confess a judgment in favor of Litton based on alleged claims for back salary. After

[handwritten: — Litton got Back salary · confessed judgment]

Pepper obtained a judgment, Litton caused execution to be issued on his judgment; Litton purchased the corporate assets at the resulting sale, and then caused Dixie Splint to file a voluntary petition in bankruptcy. The trustee in bankruptcy brought suit in state court to have the judgment obtained by Litton set aside and the execution sale quashed; the trustee lost. Smith v. Litton, 188 S.E. 214 (Va.1936). Litton then filed a claim in the bankruptcy court based on the portion of the judgment not satisfied by the proceeds of the execution sale. The District Court disallowed Litton's claim in its entirety and directed that the trustee should recover for the benefit of the bankrupt's estate the property purchased by Litton at the execution sale. The Court of Appeals reversed on the ground that the state court decision was res judicata.]

MR. JUSTICE DOUGLAS, delivered the opinion of the Court.

This case presents the question of the power of the bankruptcy court to disallow either as a secured or as a general or unsecured claim a judgment obtained by the dominant and controlling stockholder of the bankrupt corporation on alleged salary claims. * * *

The findings of the District Court, amply supported by the evidence, reveal a scheme to defraud creditors reminiscent of some of the evils with which 13 Eliz. c. 5 was designed to cope. But for the use of a so-called "one-man" or family corporation, Dixie Splint Coal Company, of which respondent was the dominant and controlling stockholder, that scheme followed an ancient pattern. * * *

In the first place, res judicata did not prevent the District Court from examining into the Litton judgment and disallowing or subordinating it as a claim. * * *

In the second place, even though we assume that the alleged salary claim on which the Litton judgment was based was not fictitious but actually existed, we are of the opinion that the District Court properly disallowed or subordinated it.

Courts of bankruptcy are constituted by §§ 1 and 2 of the bankruptcy act, 30 Stat. 544, 11 U.S.C.A. §§ 1(8), 11, and by the latter section are invested "with such jurisdiction at law and in equity as will enable them to exercise original jurisdiction in bankruptcy proceedings." Consequently this Court has held that for many purposes "courts of bankruptcy are essentially courts of equity, and their proceedings inherently proceedings in equity". Local Loan Co. v. Hunt, 292 U.S. 234, 240, 54 S.Ct. 695, 697, 78 L.Ed. 1230, 93 A.L.R. 195. * * *

That equitable power also exists in passing on claims presented by an officer, director, or stockholder in the bankruptcy proceedings of his corporation. The mere fact that an officer, director, or stockholder has a claim against his bankrupt corporation or that he has reduced that claim to judgment does not mean that the bankruptcy court must accord it *pari* *passu* treatment with the claims of other creditors. Its disallowance or subordination may be necessitated by certain cardinal principles of equity jurisprudence. A director is a fiduciary. Twin-Lick Oil Company v. Marbury, 91 U.S. 587, 588, 23 L.Ed. 328. So is a dominant or controlling stockholder or group of stockholders. Southern Pacific Company v. Bogert, 250 U.S. 483, 492, 39 S.Ct. 533, 537, 63 L.Ed. 1099. Their powers are powers in trust. See Jackson v. Ludeling, 21 Wall. 616, 624, 22 L.Ed. 492. Their dealings with the corporation are subjected to rigorous scrutiny and where any of their contracts or engagements with the corporation is challenged the burden is on the director or stockholder not only to prove the good faith of the transaction but also to show its inherent fairness from the viewpoint of the corporation and those interested therein. Geddes v. Anaconda Copper Mining Company, 254 U.S. 590, 599, 41 S.Ct. 209, 212, 65 L.Ed. 425. The essence of the test is whether or not under all the circumstances the transaction carries the earmarks of an arm's length bargain. If it does not, equity will set it aside. While normally that fiduciary obligation is enforceable directly by the corporation, or through a stockholder's derivative action, it is, in the event of bankruptcy of the corporation, enforceable by the trustee. For that standard of fiduciary obligation is designed for the protection of the entire community of interests in the corporation—creditors as well as stockholders. * * *

Though disallowance of such claims will be ordered where they are fictitious or a sham, these cases do not turn on the existence or nonexistence of the debt. Rather they involve simply the question of order of payment. At times equity has ordered disallowance or subordination by disregarding the corporate entity. That is to say, it has treated the debtor-corporation simply as a part of the stockholder's own enterprise, consistently with the course of conduct of the stockholder. But in that situation as well as in the others to which we have referred, a sufficient consideration may be simply the violation of rules of fair play and good conscience by the claimant; a breach of the fiduciary standards of conduct which he owes the corporation, its stockholders and creditors. * * *

On such a test the action of the District Court in disallowing or subordinating Litton's claim was clearly correct. Litton allowed his salary claims to lie dormant for years and sought to enforce them only when his debtor corporation was in financial difficulty. Then he used them so that the rights of another creditor were impaired. * * * Litton, though a fiduciary, was enabled by astute legal maneuvering to acquire most of the assets of the bankrupt not for cash or other consideration of value to creditors but for bookkeeping entries representing at best merely Litton's appraisal of the worth of Litton's services over the years.

This alone would be a sufficient basis for the exercise by the District Court of its equitable powers in disallowing the Litton claim. But when there is added the existence of a "planned and fraudulent scheme," as found by the District Court, the necessity of equitable relief against that fraud becomes insistent. No matter how technically legal each step in that scheme may have been, once its basic nature was uncovered it was the duty of the bankruptcy court in the exercise of its equity jurisdiction to undo it. Otherwise, the fiduciary duties of dominant or management stockholders would go for naught; exploitation would become a substitute for justice; and equity would be perverted as an instrument for approving what it was designed to thwart. * * *

In view of these considerations we do not have occasion to determine the legitimacy of the "one-man" corporation as a bulwark against the claims of creditors.[28]

Accordingly the judgment of the Circuit Court of Appeals is reversed and that of the District Court is affirmed.

Reversed.

NOTES

(1) The doctrine applied in Pepper v. Litton is usually referred to as the "Deep Rock" doctrine, after the name of a corporation involved in an earlier case. Could the court have "pierced the corporate veil" of Dixie Splint Coal Co. and avoided Litton's claim on the theory that one cannot owe a debt to oneself? If the latter approach had been followed, Litton might have become personally liable for Dixie Splint's debts. What tests should the court use in determining whether to pierce or to subordinate? Is it simply a matter of relative degrees of bad faith or improper conduct? The absence of reasonably objective tests in this area has led to considerable confusion and some inconsistency in results.

(2) Section 510(c) of the Bankruptcy Act of 1978, 11 U.S.C.A. § 510(c), provides that "* * * after notice and a hearing, the Court may * * * under principles of equitable subordination, subordinate for purposes of distribution all or part of an allowed claim to all or part of another allowed claim or all or part of an allowed interest to all or part of another allowed interest * * *." H.R.Rep. No. 595, 95th Cong., 1st Sess., at 359 (1977) states that "[t]his section [was] intended to codify case law, such as Pepper v. Litton * * *."

(3) Substantive consolidation "is an equitable doctrine that permits a bankruptcy court, in appropriate circumstances, to disregard the legal separateness of a debtor and a related but distinct legal entity, which may or

---

[28] On this point the District Court said: "An examination of the facts disclosed here shows the history of a deliberate and carefully planned attempt on the part of Scott Litton and Dixie Splint Coal Company to avoid the payment of a just debt. I speak of Litton and Dixie Splint Coal Company because they are in reality the same. In all the experience of the law, there has never been a more prolific breeder of fraud than the one-man corporation. It is a favorite device for the escape of personal liability. This case illustrates another frequent use of this fiction of corporate entity, whereby the owner of the corporation, through his complete control over it, undertakes to gather to himself all of its assets to the exclusion of its creditors."

may not itself be a debtor in bankruptcy, and to merge their respective assets and liabilities for bankruptcy purposes. * * * Substantive consolidation is analogous to * * * piercing the corporate veil." Judith Elkin, Lifting the Veil and Finding the Pot of Gold: Piercing the Corporate Veil and Substantive Consolidation in the United States, 6 Dispute Resolution International, 132, 137–38 (2012).

D. SUCCESSOR LIABILITY

What happens to a corporate liability when the company is acquired by another firm? What happens to a corporate liability when a company simply ceases doing business? Courts are split on the issue of whether it is fair to impose liability on a successor company. Courts sometimes impose such liability on successor corporations in order to impose liability on the party who is better able to bear it (possibly through insurance), or who is the only plausible defendant to compensate an injured plaintiff, or to protect the good name and reputation of the preceding company, or to prevent fraud.

Courts that decline to impose successor liability argue that the doctrine is inappropriate because it fails to respect the corporate forms of the companies involved, and that it is unfair because it holds a corporation liable for an obligation that was not its fault. Courts also argue that imposing liability will not deter misbehavior because the compensation paid is not from the wrongdoer, but from an innocent party. The courts argue that when mergers and other financial arrangement are made, finality is necessary in order to permit the free transferability of assets. Obviously, corporations will be reluctant to make acquisitions if there is significant uncertainty about their contingent liability for the debts and other obligations of the companies they acquire.

From a policy perspective, the imposition of successor liability is difficult because it has both significant potential costs and significant potential benefits. The imposition of successor liability makes it more difficult to transfer assets. The free transferability of assets is important to the creditors of the company being acquired; after all, they want to transform the assets of the business into cash so that their claims can be paid. On the other hand, there is always the risk that corporate assets will be sold for less than fair consideration, or that, once the assets are sold, the cash will disappear into the hands of the corporation's shareholders.

NISSEN CORP. V. MILLER
Court of Appeals of Maryland, 1991.
594 A.2d 564.

CHASANOW, J.

On January 31, 1981, Frederick B. Brandt (Brandt) purchased from Atlantic Fitness Products (Atlantic) a treadmill that was designed, manufactured, and marketed by American Tredex Corporation (American Tredex). Later the same year, on July 31, Nissen Corporation (Nissen) entered into an asset purchase agreement with American Tredex. Pursuant to that agreement, Nissen purchased the trade name, patents, inventory and other assets of American Tredex. Nissen also assumed some of American Tredex's obligations and liabilities, but the contract expressly excluded assumption of liability for injuries arising from any product previously sold by American Tredex. The contract contemplated the continuation of the selling corporation, American Tredex, for five years and that during that period American Tredex would be known by a new name, AT Corporation.

* * *

Over five years after his purchase of the treadmill, on October 18, 1986, Brandt was injured while trying to adjust the running treadmill. More than a year later, on December 31, 1987, American Tredex (then known as AT Corporation) was administratively dissolved. Brandt and his wife filed suit on September 1, 1988, against American Tredex, AT Corporation, Nissen, and Atlantic, seeking damages for negligence, strict liability, breach of express and implied warranties, and loss of consortium. Atlantic cross-claimed against Nissen for indemnity and contribution. Nissen filed a motion for summary judgment, which was granted. * * * Brandt and Atlantic appealed to the Court of Special Appeals. In Miller v. Nissen Corp., 83 Md.App. 448, 575 A.2d 758 (1990), the Court of Special Appeals reversed the trial court. We granted Nissen's petition for writ of certiorari on the issue of whether it, as a successor to American Tredex, is liable to Brandt for his injuries.

The issue in the instant case is whether this Court should adopt the general rule of nonliability of successor corporations, with its four well-recognized traditional exceptions, or whether we should add a fifth exception for "continuity of enterprise."

The general or traditional rule of corporate successor liability has been stated by many cases and treatises:

> [A] corporation which acquires all or part of the assets of another corporation does not acquire the liabilities and debts of the predecessor, unless: (1) there is an express or implied agreement to assume the liabilities; (2) the transaction amounts to a consolidation or merger; (3) the successor entity is a mere

continuation or reincarnation of the predecessor entity; or (4) the transaction was fraudulent, not made in good faith, or made without sufficient consideration. Thus, the general rule is one of successor nonliability, subject to four "traditional" exceptions * * *

1 American Law of Products Liability 3d § 7.1, at 10–12 (Travers, rev. ed. 1990).* * *

* * * All parties agree that this Court should adopt the general rule of nonliability of a successor corporation, with its four traditional exceptions. Brandt and Atlantic (Respondents) contend we should also adopt the more liberal "continuity of enterprise" theory as a fifth exception in products liability cases. * * *

Respondents would only be entitled to recover if we expand the traditional "mere continuation" or continuity of entity exception and add the "continuity of enterprise" exception to the general rule of nonliability of corporate successors. The mere continuation or continuity of entity exception applies where "there is a continuation of directors and management, shareholder interest and, in some cases, inadequate consideration. The gravamen of the traditional 'mere continuation' exception is the continuation of the corporate entity rather than continuation of the business operation." 1 Frumer & Friedman, supra, at 2.06[2][c], at 2–182 to 2–183 (emphasis in original, footnote omitted). * * * This exception focuses on the continuation of management and ownership. In contrast, the continuity of enterprise theory focuses on continuation of the business operation or enterprise where there is no continuation in ownership. * * *

Respondents do not contend that Nissen is a "mere continuation" of American Tredex or that the sale of assets in the instant case falls within any of the traditional exceptions to the rule of nonliability of corporate successors, nor would the record support such an argument. Only if we expand the traditional exceptions to include a "continuity of enterprise" exception would Brandt be entitled to proceed against Nissen.

Brandt urges that we adopt the continuity of enterprise theory because it "is limited, proper and pertinent to the rights of a consumer who has suffered a personal injury for which some entity must be held responsible." He argues that "courts have logically prevented the evasion of liability by any part of the manufacturing and selling chain" and that, in recognition of this public policy, we should "not allow a major corporation to purchase only the benefits in an asset purchase transaction while denying its attendant liabilities to the consuming public, particularly where the successor corporation has held itself out to the public as the sponsor of the injury-causing entity." Atlantic further argues that the traditional rule evolved to protect the rights of creditors and shareholders in the corporate context and is inapplicable in the case of products liability plaintiffs and that "[a] corporation contemplating not only the acquisition of the assets of another corporation, but also the continuation of the basic enterprise of that corporation must accept the burdens as well as the benefits of such a transaction." Atlantic contends that, because Nissen enjoyed American Tredex's goodwill and held itself out as the effective continuation of American Tredex, selling replacement parts, performing some contracts, retaining some employees, honoring existing 90-day warranties, and servicing customer accounts, it should bear the burden of American Tredex's liability for defective products.

Nissen counters that it was not part of the "manufacturing and selling chain"; it merely purchased American Tredex's assets. That transaction was fully negotiated, including the requirement that the predecessor corporation continue in existence after the sale, presumably so that it would be subject to suit in cases such as this. The price Nissen paid for the business was based on the total contract, including the provision that the predecessor retain all liability for injuries caused by defective products sold by it before the asset purchase. Nissen argues that we should adhere to "[t]he longstanding general rule and its well-defined limited exceptions" because they "have functioned well to balance the rights of creditors and successor corporations by preserving traditional principles of corporate law and promoting the free alienability of business assets while maintaining adequate protection for the interests of consumers and creditors from fraudulent and unjust corporate transactions." Nissen urges that the expansion of the traditional rule that Respondents propose would impose liability not only upon "a major corporation * * * where the successor corporation has held itself out to the public as the sponsor of the injury causing entity," but also upon the small corporation that purchases assets and carries on a business but abandons its predecessor's defective, injury-causing designs or practices.

* * * Respondents argue that public policy demands that we accept the continuity of enterprise doctrine because, as stated by Brandt in his brief, "some entity must be held responsible" where "a consumer * * * has suffered a personal injury." In *Phipps*, however, we clarified the basis for our adoption of strict products liability:

> [T]he theory of strict liability is not a radical departure from traditional tort concepts. Despite the use of the term "strict liability" the seller is not an insurer, as absolute liability is not imposed on the seller for any injury resulting from the use of his product. Proof of a defect in the product at the time it leaves the control of the seller implies fault on the part of the seller sufficient to justify imposing liability for injuries caused by the product. * * *

* * * It is clear from our decisions that inherent in our recognition of strict products liability is the concept that sellers who place defective and

unreasonably dangerous products on the market are at fault when a user is injured by that activity and should bear responsibility. A corporate successor is not a seller and bears no blame in bringing the product and the user together. It seems patently unfair to require such a party to bear the cost of unassumed and uncontemplated products liability claims primarily because it is still in business and is perceived as a "deep pocket."

Respondent Atlantic argues that, because Nissen reaped the benefits of the goodwill of American Tredex, it would be unfair to permit it to escape the burden of paying American Tredex's tort liabilities. This argument lacks merit. It overlooks the fact that, if American Tredex products do cause injuries, Nissen will suffer a resultant loss in the value of the goodwill it purchased.

Although Brandt contends that we should "not allow a major corporation to purchase only the benefits in an asset purchase transaction while denying its attendant liabilities to the consuming public," he overlooks the fact that the remedy he seeks for this "injustice" may be unfairly broad. Were we to adopt continuity of enterprise, not only would liability be imposed upon "a major corporation," but it would also be imposed upon the small business operation which may not be in a position to spread the risk or insure against it. * * *

Brandt also complains that he was not "alerted to internal corporate changes which would prevent the protection properly due to a consumer of a product." We cannot accept the proposition implied by this argument that consumers retain products in reliance upon their ability to sue a certain entity if a problem develops with the product. Brandt was notified of the sale of American Tredex. Had he realized that he would not be able to sue the successor if he was injured, we doubt that he would have scrapped his treadmill and purchased a new one. Nissen did more than was required of it by providing the needed replacement parts at Brandt's request. The fact that Nissen maintained a network to service American Tredex customers and, in fact, furnished parts to Brandt for his treadmill does not give rise to successor liability. Furthermore, we should not penalize Nissen for retaining a few of American Tredex's employees or for assuming some of American Tredex's commitments. All of these actions on Nissen's part have important societal value. While we recognize the societal value of permitting consumers to recover from those responsible when they are injured by a product, Nissen is not one of those responsible for Brandt's injuries.

The Restatement (Second) of Torts § 402A, upon which Maryland strict liability in tort law is based, Phipps, 278 Md. at 353, 363 A.2d at 963, does not contemplate imposition of liability upon successor corporations. * * * As was noted by the Third Circuit in *Polius*:

[T]he Restatement reaffirms the notion of a causal relationship between the defendant's acts and the plaintiff's injury—a concept that is fundamental to tort law. The corporate successor theories espoused by Michigan and California brush aside this bedrock requirement and impose liability on entities which in fact had no connection with the acts causing injury.

Even the wholesaler or retailer who sells a defective product has some causal connection with the plaintiff's injury. The same cannot be said of the owner of a new business who manufactures an improved, defect-free, version of a product in a facility purchased from his predecessor * * *. Under the continuity of enterprise theory, a new owner who continues his predecessor's operations may be liable if he manufactures some but not all of a number of items. If the new owner continues to manufacture ten items but decides not to produce one because it is too dangerous, he might nevertheless be liable for claims which his predecessor set in motion through the dangerous product.

802 F.2d at 81–82. The *Polius* court concluded that "the continuity of enterprise theory * * * proposes an ill-considered extension of liability to an entity having no causal relationship with the harm." Id. at 82.

     * * *

For the reasons set forth in this opinion, we reject the continuity of enterprise theory of successor corporate liability. Like the majority of our sister states, we adhere to the general rule of nonliability of successor corporations, with its four traditional exceptions, in products liability cases.

     ELDRIDGE, J. and HINKEL, J., dissenting:

We concur with the majority in the adoption of the general rule of non-liability of successor corporations, together with its four traditional exceptions. We would, however, adopt a fifth exception for "continuity of enterprise" with regard to defective products. Therefore, we dissent.

NOTES

(1) What is the justification for the general rule that a corporation that acquires all of the assets of another corporation generally does not assume the liabilities of the selling corporation absent an agreement to assume such liabilities, some other special facts, or fraud?

(2) What happens if a company offers viable products and services, and has a stable and productive workforce, but also has past or prospective tort liabilities in an amount greater than the total value of the firm? Commentators have observed that this situation poses extremely difficult problems. Any merger or other transfer of assets should not make the corporation's creditors worse off than they would have been if the transaction

had not occurred. On the other hand, the creditors should not be placed in a better position as a result of an acquisition or other change in control, as this would reduce the incentives of an acquirer to take over a company. See Mark J. Roe, Mergers, Acquisitions, and Tort: A Comment on the Problem of Successor Corporation Liability, 70 Va. L.Rev. 1559, 1562 (1984).

(3) When corporations decide to dissolve and distribute their assets to shareholders, issues closely related to those involved in piercing the corporate veil cases arise. When a corporation decides to wind up its business, there is always a risk that the proceeds of any asset sale will be distributed to the corporation's shareholders before the claims of all of the creditors have been satisfied. On the other hand, people running businesses want to be able to stop doing business and take their money out of the company without worrying that creditors will appear years later declaring that their claims were not paid. Similarly, when all of the assets of the corporation are sold, the lawyers for the selling corporation will normally be consulted about how (and when) the proceeds from the sale are to be distributed to shareholders. The members of the board of directors of the selling corporation should be particularly concerned that proper procedures are followed, as corporate directors will be personally liable if a corporation makes an improper distribution of its assets.

(4) The purpose of Chapter 14 of the MBCA is to provide a clear set of instructions for dissolving a corporation in such a way as to extinguish corporate liabilities. MBCA § 14.02 requires a shareholder vote for dissolution. MBCA § 14.03 provides that a corporation must file articles of dissolution after receiving shareholder authorization. The corporation is dissolved "upon the effective date of its articles of dissolution." MBCA § 14.03(b).

What is the effect of dissolution? MBCA § 14.05 states that after dissolution, the corporation may only carry on business associated with the process of winding up, and the rights and duties of shareholders and directors are not affected. In addition, suits by or against the corporation are not altered.

Section 14.06 sets forth the rules for dissolving corporations to follow in order to extinguish known claims against the dissolved corporation. The section provides that the dissolved corporation may dispose of the known claims against it by notifying its known creditors and permitting them to file a claim against the corporation. If no claim is filed by the creditor by the deadline set by the corporation (which must be at least 120 days from the date of the written notice), the claim is barred. A corporation that receives a claim from a creditor during the 120-day period can reject the claim. If the corporation rejects the claim, it is barred unless the creditor commences a proceeding within 90 days from the date of the rejection notice.

Section 14.07 deals with unknown claims against the corporation. This section requires filing a notice in a newspaper of general circulation in the county where the dissolved corporation has its principal office. The notice must describe the procedure for filing a claim against the corporation. If the dissolving corporation files this newspaper notice, unknown claims are barred unless they are brought within three years after the publication date of the notice.

CHAPTER 7

FINANCIAL MATTERS AND THE CORPORATION

■ ■ ■

A. DEBT AND EQUITY CAPITAL

Every firm needs financing in order to conduct its operations. The financing that firms use to fund their business activities is called "capital"[a] Capital may be obtained from a variety of different sources: (1) by borrowing funds; (2) by selling shares in the company; or (3) by retaining earnings of the business rather than distributing them to owners.

The critical distinction in finance is the distinction between "equity capital" and "debt." Debt is associated with the idea of borrowing. The main characteristics of debt are (1) it must be repaid at some point, (2) interest on the amount borrowed must be paid periodically, and (3) the repayment of principal and interest is not contingent on the success of the business.

"Equity," by contrast, is synonymous with "ownership" and has nothing to do with the word "equity" in its traditional historical or legal meaning. Rather, the principal characteristic of equity is that, conceptually, the value of an owner's equity in a piece of property equals the market value of that property minus the market value of the debts that are liens against that property. Equity capital is composed of contributions by the original entrepreneurs in the firm, capital contributed by subsequent investors usually in exchange for ownership interests in the business, and retained earnings of the enterprise.

Based on these fundamental characteristics of debt and equity, debt claims sometimes are referred to as "fixed claims" while equity claims are referred to as "residual claims." The terminology conveys the idea that fixed claimants (creditors) are entitled to be repaid the principal and interest owed to them on the loans they have made, while residual

---

[a] The word "capital" is a broad term that may be used in a wide variety of different contexts and has several meanings. For example, the term is used: (a) to describe the money or other consideration that a firm receives from issuing stock; (b) the amount of a firm's legally required capital (discussed in this Chapter); (c) a firm's "net worth," i.e., the amount by which a firm's assets exceed its total liabilities; (d) a firm's "capital plant," that is, the plant equipment and other long-lived physical assets that a firm uses in its operations; and (e) all of the money and property that a firm owns or uses. In this Chapter, we use the term "capital" to refer to the amount of equity and debt used by the firm to fund its business activities.

273

claimants (equity owners) have a claim on everything that is left over after the fixed claimants have been paid.

This Chapter considers primarily the raising of equity capital by corporations through the sale of its securities. It considers debt financing only to a limited extent. A word of caution at the outset is appropriate. An important federal statute, the Securities Act of 1933, 15 U.S.C.A. § 77a et seq., imposes substantial disclosure requirements on the public sale of securities using the mails or the facilities of interstate commerce. Public offerings of securities must be registered with the Securities and Exchange Commission, and failure to do so can result in criminal and civil penalties. In addition, states have statutes called "blue sky laws" that regulate the sale of securities within the specific state. These federal and state statutes are potentially applicable whenever a business seeks funds; they are not limited to large transactions or to transactions in which capital is raised with the assistance of professional underwriters. In real life, the potential applicability of these statutes must be considered whenever a firm is raising capital from third parties.

B. TYPES OF EQUITY SECURITIES

There is a recognized nomenclature for equity securities issued by corporations. The following brief discussion is essential background for those unfamiliar with this nomenclature; it also illustrates that while the language is sometimes arcane, the underlying ideas are not complicated.

1. SHARES GENERALLY

It is helpful to begin with fundamental concepts. "Shares" are defined in MBCA § 1.40(22) as the "units into which the proprietary interests in a corporation are divided." Further, a corporation may create and issue different "classes" of shares with different preferences, limitations, and relative rights. MBCA §§ 1.40(2), 6.01(a). Each class must have a "distinguishing designation," and all shares within a single class must generally have identical rights. If a corporation issues only one class of shares, they may be referred to as "common shares," "capital shares," "shares," or "stock." The various designations and rights of shares of different classes must be set forth in the articles of incorporation. MBCA § 6.01.

MBCA § 6.01(b) sets forth two fundamental rights of holders of common shares: (1) they are entitled to vote for the election of directors and on other matters coming before the shareholders, and (2) they are entitled to the net assets of the corporation (i.e., the assets remaining after making allowance for debts) upon dissolution. Section 6.01(b) permits these essential attributes of common shares to be placed in different classes of shares in whole or in part, but requires that one or more classes with these attributes must always be authorized. Section

6.03(c) adds that at least one share of each class with these basic attributes must always be outstanding—that is, issued to some person or persons.[b]

2. COMMON AND PREFERRED SHARES

If a corporation has more than one class of shares, a customary distinction is between "common" shares and "preferred" shares. These terms have commonly accepted meanings and are used almost ubiquitously.

"Common shares" are a class or classes of shares that have the fundamental rights of voting for directors and receiving the net assets of the corporation as described above. MBCA §§ 6.01(b), 6.03(c). Often these two fundamental rights are combined in a single class of "common shares," but they may also be divided among different classes of shares. Holders of common shares have non-financial rights as well: a right to inspect books and records (see MBCA § 16.02), a right to sue on behalf of the corporation (see MBCA §§ 7.40–7.47), a right to financial information (see MBCA § 16.20), and so forth.

Common shares may be defined in various ways. The United States Supreme Court identified the characteristics usually associated with common stock as: (i) the right to receive dividends contingent upon an apportionment of profits; (ii) negotiability (capable of being transferred by delivery or endorsement when the transferee takes the instrument for value, in good faith, and without notice of conflicting title claims or defenses); (iii) the ability to be pledged or hypothecated; (iv) the conferring of voting rights in proportion to the number of shares owned; and (v) the capacity to increase in value. United Housing Foundation, Inc. v. Forman, 421 U.S. 837 (1975).[c]

In a nutshell, common shares represent the residual ownership interest in the corporation. Their financial interest is open-ended in the sense that they benefit as the business prospers and the corporate assets increase.

---

[b] When a new corporation is in the process of being formed, there may be a brief period between the filing of the articles of incorporation and the organizational meeting when the issuance of shares is authorized. Thus there may be a brief period during which the corporation is in existence but no shares are issued or outstanding. The assumption is that the corporation will not enter into business transactions until after the organizational meeting is held, since prior to the organizational meeting, the corporation will not have officers to act on its behalf, will not have a bank account, and will not have any assets because no stock will have been issued. It is possible, however, for a corporation to commence business before articles of incorporation are filed or before a formal organizational meeting is held. Typically, in those cases there will be no doubt as to the persons who are to own the common shares of the corporation and who, therefore, are the shareholders. Premature commencement of business creates a risk of personal liability being imposed on shareholders for transactions entered into in the name of the corporation.

[c] This definition was set forth in a case involving the issue of whether a "share of stock" that entitled the owner to lease an apartment in a housing cooperative was a "security"; housing cooperative shares possessed virtually none of the enumerated characteristics.

"Preferred shares" are typically classes of shares with rights that are preferential to those assigned to the common shares, but limited in some way. For example, a class of preferred stock might have the right to receive a distribution of five dollars per share before the common shares become entitled to any distribution. Preferred shares are usually (but not always) non-voting. However, voting power often is assigned to preferred shares if the company misses scheduled dividend payments on its preferred stock, or if it fails to meet some other financial test. MBCA § 13.01(6) contains a partial definition of "preferred shares."

Preferred shares entitle the holders to a "priority" or "preference" in payment as against the holders of common shares. This priority or preference may be either in the payment of dividends or in the making of distributions out of the capital of a corporation, or very commonly in both. A "priority" or "preference" simply means that the holders of preferred shares are entitled to a specified distribution before anything can be paid on the common shares. For example, the dividend preference of $5 per share mentioned above means only that nothing can be paid to the holders of common shares until the preferred shareholders are first paid their $5 per share. Preferred shares are often described by reference to the amount of their dividend preference or by a percentage of the stock's par or stated value. Thus, a "$5.00 preferred" has a dividend preference of $5.00 per share, while a "5% preferred" has a dividend preference equal to five percent of the share's par value. Preferred shareholders typically have limited or "capped" rights to earnings, but that is not always the case.

The precise scope of the rights of a preferred shareholder is traditionally established by detailed provisions in the articles of incorporation creating that class of shares. These provisions are called the "preferred shareholder's contract" and may not be amended without the consent of holders of some statutorily designated fraction of the preferred shares themselves.

Funds may be distributed to common or preferred shareholders in the form of "dividends" or "distributions." If earnings of the corporation are retained by the corporation and not distributed, the value of common shares will increase but the value of preferred shares may not (since their rights are usually limited or capped).

The MBCA sets forth rules for distributions generally. The same rules apply to dividends and other sorts of distributions such as share repurchases. MBCA §§ 1.40(6), 6.40. Decisions involving whether or not to make a distribution to common shareholders, and if so, how much, are matters within the business judgment of directors. Typically, common shareholders have no legal basis for complaint if distributions or dividends on common shares are omitted over extended periods of time.

Where a corporation has only one class of shares outstanding, that class obviously consists of common shares, even though the shares may be described in the articles of incorporation as "capital stock" or simply "stock" or "shares." The MBCA consistently uses the word "shares" rather than "stock" in describing equity security interests, but the Official Comment to § 6.01 points out that "no specific designation is required by the Model Act."

Many corporations begin their life with only a modest amount of capital raised by the sale of shares. The statutes in a few states prescribe a minimum initial capitalization—often $1,000. The Model Act contained such a requirement until 1969 when it was eliminated on the grounds "that the protection sought to be achieved was illusory and that the provision served no useful purpose." Comment to MBCA (1969) § 56. The MBCA currently does not contain a minimum capital requirement.

3. SPECIAL CONTRACTUAL RIGHTS OF PUBLICLY TRADED PREFERRED SHARES

Rights and privileges usually given to publicly traded preferred shares include the following:

Cumulative Dividend Rights. The dividend preference of preferred shares may be cumulative, noncumulative, or partially cumulative. A cumulative dividend simply means that if a preferred dividend is not paid in any year, it accumulates and must be paid (along with the following years' unpaid cumulative dividends) before any dividend may be paid on the common shares in a later year. For example, if a preferred share has a $5.00 cumulative dividend preference, and that dividend is omitted in one year, not only may no dividend be paid on the common shares in that year, but also in the following year, no dividend may be paid on the common shares unless the holder of the preferred share receives $10.00 in dividends, making up for the omission in the prior year. A noncumulative dividend is not carried over from one year to the next; if no dividend is declared during the year, the preferred shareholder loses the right to receive the dividend for that year. A noncumulative dividend that is not paid during the year simply disappears. A partially cumulative dividend typically is cumulative to the extent there are earnings in the year, and noncumulative with respect to any excess dividend preference. Unpaid cumulative dividends are not debts of the corporation, but a right of priority in future distributions. Unlike interest on a debt, dividends on preferred shares may be paid only from funds that are legally available for making distributions. Many state statutes, however, liberally permit the payment of cumulative preferred dividends from various capital accounts. Typically, publicly traded preferred shares have cumulative dividend rights.

Voting. Preferred shares are usually nonvoting shares (though many exceptions exist, particularly in closely held corporations). In order to provide some protection for preferred shareholders, it is customary to provide that nonvoting preferred shares obtain a right to vote for the election of a specified number of directors if preferred dividends have been omitted for a specified period of time.

Liquidation Preferences. Preferred shares usually have a liquidation preference as well as a dividend preference. The liquidation preference is often fixed at a specified price per share, payable upon the dissolution of the corporation before anything may be paid to the common shares. Like preferred dividends, a liquidation preference is not a debt but a claim to priority if and when funds are available. The amount of the liquidation preference is usually a fixed amount so that the holders of the preferred do not share in any general appreciation in the value of the corporation's assets.

Redemption Rights. Preferred shares may be made redeemable at the option of the corporation, usually at a price fixed by the articles of incorporation at the time the class of preferred shares was created. A right to "redeem" shares simply means that the corporation has the power to buy back the redeemable shares at any time at the fixed price, and the shareholder has no choice but to accept that price. (If the shareholder refuses to turn in his certificates, the corporation simply deposits the redemption price in a bank and refuses to recognize that the shares are outstanding or that they have rights with respect to the corporation other than the right to the redemption price.) When a corporation elects to exercise the redemption privilege, it "calls" the stock for redemption. Typically, the power to call redeemable shares may be exercised only after a specified period of time has elapsed. The redemption price is usually set somewhat in excess of the amount of the share's liquidation preference. For example, preferred shares that are entitled to receive $100.00 per share on liquidation may be made redeemable at any time for $105.00 plus any unpaid cumulative dividends.

Conversion Rights. Preferred shares may be made convertible at the option of the *holder* into common shares at a fixed ratio specified in the articles of incorporation. Convertible preferred shares are attractive when the common shares are publicly traded because an active market exists for the conversion securities. A conversion privilege allows the holders of the preferred shares to obtain a part of the long-term appreciation of the corporation's assets if the holders are willing to give up their preferred rights by converting their shares into common shares. Typically, the conversion ratio is established so that the common shares must appreciate substantially in price before it is profitable to convert the preferred shares. When the price of the common shares rises above this level, the preferred shares fluctuate in price with the common shares.

Convertible shares are also usually redeemable, but typically the privilege to convert continues for a limited period of time after the call for redemption. A conversion is described as "forced" when shares are called for redemption at a time when the market value of the shares obtainable on conversion exceeds the redemption price.

Protective Provisions. Preferred shares may also have certain financial protections, such as sinking fund provisions, which require the corporation to set aside a certain amount each year to redeem a specified portion of the preferred stock issue. In addition, convertible preferred shares usually contain elaborate provisions protecting the conversion privilege from dilution in case of share dividends, share splits, or the issuance of additional common shares. The importance of these protections cannot be minimized since preferred shareholders have not fared well on arguments based on fiduciary duty and the like. See Lawrence E. Mitchell, The Puzzling Paradox of Preferred Stock (and Why We Should Care About It), 51 Bus.Law. 443, 443–44 (1996) (arguing that preferred stockholders' rights are often not recognized in judicial proceedings and that they should instead rely exclusively on their contract as a source of rights).

Of course, it is well-settled that corporations and their directors owe fiduciary duties to common shareholders. Perhaps the reason that preferred shareholders have fared so poorly when making fiduciary duty claims is that courts have no principled basis for dealing with such claims by preferred shareholders when those claims compete directly with the fiduciary claims of common shareholders. After all, both classes of claimants are competing for the same cash flows.

Participating Preferred. The preferred shares described above are nonparticipating. Nonparticipating shares are entitled to the specified dividend payment, the specified liquidation preference, and nothing more—no matter how profitable the corporation. "Participating preferred" shares are entitled to the specified dividend and, after the common shares receive a specified amount, they share with the common in additional distributions on some predetermined basis. Such shares combine some of the features of common and preferred. They are sometimes referred to as "Class A common" or by a similar designation that shows that their right to participate is open-ended and therefore they have one of the major attributes of common shares. Preferred shares that are participating in dividend distributions usually have liquidation preferences that are tied in some way to the amounts receivable by the common shares upon liquidation.

Classes of Preferred. A corporation may issue different classes of preferred shares. A corporation, for example, may issue "Class A preferred" and "Class B preferred" with different dividend rates, different rights on dissolution, and different priorities. The Class A preferred may be junior to the Class B in terms of priorities or it may be superior to or on par with the Class B. Both are "senior" securities, however, because both have preferential rights over common shares.

Series of Preferred. MBCA § 6.02(a)(2) refers to "one or more series within one or more classes." The concept of a "series within a class" arose because of problems of raising substantial amounts of capital through the issuance of preferred shares. In preferred share financing, it is often advantageous to tailor the price, dividend, and other terms of the shares to the market conditions current at the time of issue. It was inconvenient and expensive to amend the articles of a corporation with many shareholders to create a new class of preferred shares whenever a new issue was to be sold. As a result, a number of states authorized the board of directors (1) to create a "class" of preferred shares that contained no financial terms at all, (2) to carve out different "series" of shares from within that class, and (3) to designate the financial terms of each series when it was issued. Preferred shares for which the board of directors is authorized to establish terms are often called "blank shares." MBCA § 6.02 is a somewhat broader "blank shares" provision since it authorizes the board to establish "classes" as well as "series." In practice, however, there is usually no economic difference between a "class" of preferred shares and a "series within a class" of preferred shares. Both have unique financial terms, but all shares within the "class" or "series" have identical preferences, limitations, and relative rights. The Official Comment to MBCA § 6.02 states that the labels "class" and "series" are "often a matter of convenience"; it does not seem sensible to limit the power of directors merely because of historical nomenclature.

The terms of one or more "series" may also be specified in the articles of incorporation if that is desired. However, the term "series" is most widely used in connection with preferred shares whose financial terms may be established by the board of directors following procedures similar to those set forth in MBCA § 6.02.

4. CLASSES OF COMMON SHARES

Section 6.01 of the MBCA, like all state statutes, authorizes the creation of classes of common shares by appropriate provision in the articles of incorporation. Such classes may vary in terms of management, financial, or voting rights. For example, classes of nonvoting common shares, classes with multiple or fractional votes per share, classes entitled to twice the dividend of another class, classes entitled to a preference or priority in distributions to another class, and classes entitled to elect a specified number of directors are all permissible. Different classes of common shares are often designated by alphabetical reference, e.g., "Class A common shares," or sometimes by description, e.g., "nonvoting common stock." Classes of common shares are widely used as planning devices in closely held corporations (as are classes of preferred shares).

———

From the foregoing discussion, it should be clear that the precise line between "preferred" and "common" shares, at the margin at least, was always a shadowy one. There might be little or no difference, for example, between a "participating preferred" and a "Class A common" except the title. Developments during the 1970s and early 1980s also tended to blur this distinction (as well as the distinction between "debt securities" and preferred shares). Extremely high interest rates during this period led to the development of novel financing devices. This period, for example, saw the development of "flexible rate" preferred, where the amount of the dividend was tied to interest rates (or some other objective criteria), or left to the discretion of the board of directors.

Because of these developments, § 6.01 of the MBCA makes a significant philosophical break with the past by studiously avoiding the terms "preferred shares" and "common shares," and by establishing a scheme of consummate generality designed to accommodate the most innovative and ingenious creator of new classes or types of shares.

When considering classes of debt or equity securities, not too much weight should be given to the name. A class may be described as "senior preferred" and yet be subordinate to virtually all other classes of preferred shares with much more modest titles. Modern equity and debt issues often have unique or fanciful names, e.g., "senior reset preferred stock," debt exchangeable for common stock ("DECS"), or "preferred equity redemption cumulative stock" ("PERCS") that give little or no clue as to either the nature of the securities involved or their investment quality.

NOTES

(1) A corporation may create a class of *preferred* shares that is redeemable (callable) at the option of the holder. Such shares have some of the characteristics of a demand note, and are widely used as a financing device. They are not (or arguably may not be) permitted by the statutes of some states.

(2) What about creating *common* shares that are redeemable at the option of the holder? Is there any possible evil that might arise from such shares? Some states prohibit this kind of security except in specified limited circumstances. One well-known and universally accepted example of such shares are shares of "mutual funds," the issuer of which stands ready at any time to redeem shares at net asset value. Is there any reason to permit redeemable preferred stock, but to prohibit redeemable common stock?

(3) What about creating *common* shares that are callable at the option of the corporation? The great majority of states impose limitations on this type of security or prohibit them entirely. In older versions of the Model Act, a right of redemption at the corporation's option could be created only in connection with shares with preferential rights; several states authorize callable or redeemable common shares only if there is another class of common shares that is not callable or redeemable. E.g. Cal.Corp.Code § 402; N.Y.Bus.Corp.Law § 512. What possible evils might be created if the corporation had the power generally to "call" common shares at a predetermined price?

(4) Although it is very common (and universally legal) for preferred stock to be convertible into common stock, most state statutes prohibit shares with an "upstream conversion" right, that is, the right to convert common shares into preferred shares, or to convert either common or preferred shares into debt securities or interests. What possible evils might arise if shareholders generally had the power to convert their equity interests into more senior common stock or debt?

(5) The MBCA permits the creation of all types of shares referred to in the previous paragraphs without restriction or limitation. Indeed, the MBCA goes even further in some respects, permitting, for example, the creation of shares that are redeemable at the option of a third person, e.g., the holders of other classes of shares, or the creation of shares that are redeemable at a price determined in accordance with a designated formula. See MBCA § 6.01(c)(2).

Is this total freedom a good idea? It may be justified on several grounds: (1) There is no evidence of demonstrated harm caused by these types of securities in states that permit their use. (2) The rights of classes of shares are determined in part by contractual negotiation, and elimination of restrictions may be justified on the ground of "freedom of contract." (3) Essentially the same results may usually be attained by contractual commitments between investors and the corporation independent of the articles of incorporation, and there seems to be no reason why persons cannot place their commitments in the articles of incorporation if they wish. And, finally, (4) upstream conversions and similar transactions are potentially less damaging to creditors and other senior security holders than the reacquisition of shares by the corporation for cash.

C. ISSUANCE OF SHARES: HEREIN OF SUBSCRIPTIONS, PAR VALUE, AND WATERED STOCK

1. SHARE SUBSCRIPTIONS AND AGREEMENTS TO PURCHASE SECURITIES

Historically, the traditional method of raising capital for a new corporation was by public subscriptions pursuant to which persons agreed to purchase a specified number of shares contingent upon a specified amount of capital being raised. Usually these subscriptions were "pre-incorporation subscriptions" solicited before the corporation was formed; the actual formation of the corporation would occur only if a sufficient number of pre-incorporation subscriptions had been obtained to assure the success of the venture. After being formed, the corporation would make "calls" on the subscribers for them to actually pay to the corporation the amounts they promised to pay in their subscriptions. The common law of subscription agreements grappled with a number of problems arising from raising capital in this fashion, including the revocability of subscriptions before acceptance, the basis on which calls are to be made, and the remedies available to the new corporation if a subscription was not paid. These issues are now usually resolved in an unambiguous way by statute. See MBCA § 6.20. The use of pre-incorporation subscription agreements declined in importance with the development of the modern investment banking industry, which permitted large amounts of capital to be raised for a single venture on a nationwide basis.

Subscription agreements may be used to a limited extent in connection with the capitalization of a closely held business with a small number of investors. Modern practice, however, is to use simple contractual agreements to purchase securities rather than a formal subscription agreement. In the words of the annotation to MBCA (1969), "today financing by subscription is the exception." Comment to MBCA (1969) § 17.

2. AUTHORIZATION AND ISSUANCE OF COMMON SHARES UNDER THE MBCA

Assume that a corporation has been formed under the MBCA and that it desires to create only a single class of common shares. These shares, or some of them, are to be issued equally to two persons, A and B, for an aggregate consideration of $10,000 in cash or for specified property, the value of which is uncertain but probably about $10,000. How many shares should be authorized, how many shares should be issued, and what price should be established as the issue price for such shares?

Under the MBCA, the answers to these questions are simple and straightforward. Any number of shares may be issued at any price so long as the combination (number of shares x price) totals $10,000. It may be 5,000 shares each at $1 per share, 500 shares each at $10 per share, 50 shares each at $100 per share, 5 shares each at $1,000 per share, one share each at $5,000, or any combination in between. The only constraint is that the price be the same for both A and B, since they are buying the same class of shares. Also, the number of shares authorized in the corporation's articles of incorporation must, of course, be at least equal to the number of shares that the corporation plans to issue. Since it is always possible that the corporation will need more capital at a later date, the authorization of some excess shares may be sensible, and it is perfectly legal for a corporation to authorize more shares than it plans to issue. On the other hand, it may not be desirable to authorize vastly more shares than the corporation plans to issue for a couple of reasons. First, limiting the number of shares may protect minority shareholders because a majority investor may be able to issue authorized but unissued shares more easily than he can secure an amendment to the articles of incorporation increasing the authorized shares. The issuance of shares in some situations may harm the minority's interest; thus, the minority is generally provided with greater protection if the number of authorized shares is limited. Second, some states impose taxes based on authorized shares and, therefore, authorizing unnecessary shares may simply increase one's taxes. On balance, most attorneys recommend that some shares be authorized in excess of what is proposed to be issued, even if there is some additional tax cost.

3.   PAR VALUE AND STATED CAPITAL

"Par value" is an arbitrary dollar value assigned to shares of stock which, after being assigned, represents the minimum amount for which each share may be sold. Generally, there is no minimum or maximum value that must be assigned. In most states, shares may also have "no par value," which means that the board of directors will assign a value to the stock below which the shares cannot be issued.

In some states, the articles of incorporation must state the "par value" of the shares of each class (or state that the shares are issued "with no par value" or "without par value"). The remaining states, like the MBCA, either have eliminated entirely or made optional the concept of par value.[d] The current trend is toward the elimination of this concept as a historical anomaly. Par value provisions involve archaic and confusing common law concepts of legal capital and watered stock, and, in most jurisdictions that retain the par value concept, they form the basis for restrictions on dividends, corporate share repurchases, and other transactions involving a direct or indirect distribution of corporate assets to shareholders.

Consider MBCA (1969), §§ 15 (second sentence), 18, 21, 54(d). As these statutory provisions make clear, par value is established in the articles of incorporation as a fundamental part of the description of the shares. Par value is whatever amount that is designated as par value by the drafter; it may be one cent, one dollar, ten dollars, or some other

---

[d]   The Statutory Supplement contains the provisions of MBCA (1969) relating to par value. The discussion below is tied to these individual provisions, the text of which should be carefully examined. While not all states adopted the 1969 Model Act par value provisions, they are typical of these statutes and raise the basic issues that must be addressed under all state statutes that retain these concepts.

amount. Originally, par value had considerable importance because it was widely viewed as the amount for which shares would be issued: shares with a par value of $100 per share could be subscribed for at $100 per share with confidence that all other identical shares would also be issued for $100. In effect, par value originally ensured proportionality of treatment of widely dispersed shareholders, increased confidence in the resale market that the shares had real value (and were not "mere pieces of paper"), and assured the general population that corporations had in fact been capitalized as advertised by the par values of the shares they issued.

It did not take long, however, for unscrupulous promoters to turn this practice to their own advantage. In the leading case of Hospes v. Northwestern Mfg. & Car Co., 50 N.W. 1117, 1118 (Minn.1892), for example, the court summarized the allegations of the complaint as follows:

> Briefly stated, the allegations of the complaint are that on May 10, 1882, Seymour, Sabin & Co. owned property of the value of several million dollars, and a business then supposed to be profitable. That, in order to continue and enlarge this business, the parties interested in Seymour, Sabin & Co., with others, organized the car company, to which was sold the greater part of the assets of Seymour, Sabin & Co. at a valuation of $2,267,000, in payment of which there were issued to Seymour, Sabin & Co. shares of the preferred stock of the car company of the par value of $2,267,000, it being then and there agreed by both parties that this stock was in full payment of the property thus purchased. It is further alleged that the stockholders of Seymour, Sabin & Co., and the other persons who had agreed to become stockholders in the car company, were then desirous of issuing to themselves, and obtaining for their own benefit, a large amount of common stock of the car company, "without paying therefor, and without incurring any liability thereon or to pay therefor"; and for that purpose, and "in order to evade and set at naught the laws of this state," they caused Seymour, Sabin & Co. to subscribe for and agree to take common stock of the car company of the par value of $1,500,000. That Seymour, Sabin & Co. thereupon subscribed for that amount of the common stock, but never paid therefor any consideration whatever, either in money or property. That thereafter these persons caused this stock to be issued to D.M. Sabin as trustee, to be by him distributed among them. That it was so distributed without receipt by him or the car company from any one of any consideration whatever, but was given by the car company and received by these parties entirely "gratuitously." * * *

The common stock issued by the car company is a species of "watered stock" because the corporation did not receive the par value for the stock when it was issued. What should be done about this? Is there a danger that innocent creditors might rely on the fact that shares with a specified par value are outstanding and assume that the corporation has at least the specified amount of capital? The Court believed that this was a potential problem and concluded that, under some circumstances, the recipients of watered shares should be required to pay in the par value even though they had never agreed to do so. The Court, however, had some difficulty with the rationale:

> [The plaintiff] plants itself upon the so-called "trust-fund" doctrine that the capital stock of a corporation is a trust fund for the payment of its debts; its contention being that such a "bonus" issue of stock creates, in case of the subsequent insolvency of the corporation, a liability on part of the stockholder in favor of creditors to pay for it, notwithstanding his contract with the corporation to the contrary.

> This "trust fund" doctrine, commonly called the "American doctrine," has given rise to much confusion of ideas as to its real meaning, and much conflict of decision in its application. * * * The phrase that "the capital of a corporation constitutes a trust fund for the benefit of creditors" is misleading. Corporate property is not held in trust, in any proper sense of the term. A trust implies two estates or interests—one equitable and one legal; one person, as trustee, holding the legal title, while another, as the *cestui que trust,* has the beneficial interest. Absolute control and power of disposition are inconsistent with the idea of a trust. The capital of a corporation is its property. It has the whole beneficial interest in it, as well as the legal title. It may use the income and profits of it, and sell and dispose of it, the same as a natural person. It is a trustee for its creditors in the same sense and to the same extent as a natural person, but no further. * * *

> Another proposition which we think must be sound is that creditors cannot recover on the ground of contract when the corporation could not. Their right to recover in such cases must rest on the ground that the acts of the stockholders with reference to the corporate capital constitute a fraud on their rights. We have here a case where the contract between the corporation and the takers of the shares was specific that the shares should not be paid for. * * * In such a case the creditors undoubtedly may have rights superior to the corporation, but these rights cannot rest on the implication that the shareholder agreed to do something directly contrary to his real agreement,

but must be based on tort or fraud, actual or presumed. In England, since the act of 1867, there is an implied contract created by statute that "every share in any company shall be deemed and be taken to have been issued and to be held subject to the payment of the whole amount thereof in cash." This statutory contract makes every contrary contract void. Such a statute would be entirely just to all, for everyone would be advised of its provisions, and could conduct himself accordingly. And in view of the fact that "watered" and "bonus" stock is one of the greatest abuses connected with the management of modern corporations, such a law might, on grounds of public policy, be very desirable. But this is a matter for the legislature, and not for the courts. We have no such statute * * *.

It is well settled that an equity in favor of a creditor does not arise absolutely and in every case to have the holder of "bonus" stock pay for it contrary to his actual contract with the corporation. Thus, no such equity exists in favor of one whose debt was contracted prior to the issue, since he could not have trusted the company upon the faith of such stock. Handley v. Stutz, 139 U.S. 417, 11 Sup.Ct.Rep. 530. It does not exist in favor of a subsequent creditor who has dealt with the corporation with full knowledge of the arrangement by which the "bonus" stock was issued, for a man cannot be defrauded by that which he knows when he acts. It has also been held not to exist where stock has been issued and turned out at its full market value to pay corporate debts. The same has been held to be the case where an active corporation, whose original capital has been impaired, for the purpose of recuperating itself issues new stock, and sells it on the market for the best price obtainable, but for less than par, (Handley v. Stutz, supra) although it is difficult to perceive, in the absence of a statute authorizing such a thing, (of which everyone dealing with the corporation[ ] is bound to take notice,) any difference between the original stock of a new corporation and additional stock issued by a "going concern." It is difficult, if not impossible, to explain or reconcile these cases upon the "trust-fund" doctrine, or, in the light of them, to predicate the liability of the stockholder upon that doctrine. But by putting it upon the ground of fraud, and applying the old and familiar rules of law on that subject to the peculiar nature of a corporation and the relation which its stockholders bear to it and to the public, we have at once rational and logical ground on which to stand. The capital of a corporation is the basis of its credit. It is a substitute for the individual liability of those who own its stock. People deal with it and give it credit on the faith of it. They have a right to assume that it has paid in capital to the amount which it represents itself as having; and if they give it credit on the faith of that representation, and if the representation is false, it is a fraud upon them; and, in case the corporation becomes insolvent, the law, upon the plainest principles of common justice, says to the delinquent stockholder, make that representation good by paying for your stock. It certainly cannot require the invention of any new doctrine in order to enforce so familiar a rule of equity. It is the misrepresentation of fact in stating the amount of capital to be greater than it really is that is the true basis of the liability of the stockholder in such cases; and it follows that it is only those creditors who have relied, or who can fairly be presumed to have relied, upon the professed amount of capital, in whose favor the law will recognize and enforce an equity against the holders of "bonus" stock. This furnishes a rational and uniform rule, to which familiar principles are easily applied, and which frees the subject from many of the difficulties and apparent inconsistencies into which the "trust-fund" doctrine has involved it; and we think that, even when the trust-fund doctrine has been invoked, the decision in almost every well-considered case is readily referable to such a rule.

50 N.W. at 1119–21. The Court then concluded that subsequent creditors should not be required to allege and prove affirmatively that they relied on the capital represented by the bonus shares, but that lack of reliance might be a defense. In other words, the capitalization of a corporation as established by the par values of its issued shares was a public representation on which subsequent creditors might rely and compel the shareholders to make good their representation, unless the corporation could establish that the creditors extended credit knowing the represented capital was not there. Finally, the court concluded that the particular plaintiff involved in the *Hospes* case (a newly formed corporation that had bought up claims against the original car company at significant discounts) had not sufficiently alleged its own bona fides to be allowed to maintain suit.

NOTES

(1) The shares issued by the car company in *Hospes* are usually described as "bonus shares" because nothing was paid for them. "Watered shares" are technically shares issued for property worth less than their par value, while "discount shares" are shares issued for cash but less than par. All three types are usually lumped under the single phrase "watered stock." As indicated in *Hospes,* recipients of such shares are potentially liable to subsequent creditors of the corporation.

(2) The notion that funds paid in for stock constitute a "trust fund" for creditors has a strange fascination for many courts. See, e.g., Wood v.

Dummer, 30 Fed.Cas. 435, No. 17,944 (C.C.Me.1824). While most of these cases are old, the language appears in some fairly recent opinions, and it is possible that it may influence decisions in some cases. The idea that corporate capital constitutes a "trust fund" is a fiction for the reasons recognized in the quoted excerpts from *Hospes*. For a short and convincing explanation of why the "trust fund" argument is circular and indeterminate, see C. Robert Morris, Some Notes on "Reliance," 75 Minn. L.Rev. 815, 815–20 (1991).

HANEWALD V. BRYAN'S INC.

Supreme Court of North Dakota, 1988.
429 N.W.2d 414.

MESCHKE, JUSTICE.

Harold E. Hanewald appealed from that part of his judgment for $38,600 plus interest against Bryan's, Inc. which refused to impose personal liability upon Keith, Joan, and George Bryan for that insolvent corporation's debt. We reverse the ruling that Keith and Joan Bryan were not personally liable.

On July 19, 1984, Keith and Joan Bryan incorporated Bryan's, Inc. to "engage in and operate a general retail clothing, and related items, store * * *." The Certificate of Incorporation was issued by the Secretary of State on July 25, 1984. The first meeting of the board of directors elected Keith Bryan as president and Joan Bryan as secretary-treasurer of Bryan's, Inc. George Bryan was elected vice-president, appointed registered agent, and designated manager of the prospective business. The Articles of Incorporation authorized the corporation to issue "100 shares of common stock with a par value of $1,000 per share" with "total authorized capitalization [of] $100,000.00." Bryan's, Inc. issued 50 shares of stock to Keith Bryan and 50 shares of stock to Joan Bryan. The trial court found that "Bryan's, Inc. did not receive any payment, either in labor, services, money, or property, for the stock which was issued."

On August 30, 1984, Hanewald sold his dry goods store in Hazen to Bryan's, Inc. Bryan's, Inc. bought the inventory, furniture, and fixtures of the business for $60,000, and leased the building for $600 per month for a period of five years. Bryan's, Inc. paid Hanewald $55,000 in cash and gave him a promissory note for $5,000, due August 30, 1985, for the remainder of the purchase price. The $55,000 payment to Hanewald was made from a loan by the Union State Bank of Hazen to the corporation, personally guaranteed by Keith and Joan Bryan.

Bryan's, Inc. began operating the retail clothing store on September 1, 1984. The business, however, lasted only four months with an operating loss of $4,840. In late December 1984, Keith and Joan Bryan decided to close the Hazen store. Thereafter, George Bryan, with the assistance of a brother and local employees, packed and removed the remaining inventory and delivered it for resale to other stores in Montana operated by the Bryan family. Bryan's, Inc. sent a "Notice of Rescission" to Hanewald on January 3, 1985, in an attempt to avoid the lease. The corporation was involuntarily dissolved by operation of law on August 1, 1986, for failure to file its annual report with the Secretary of State.

Bryan's, Inc. did not pay the $5,000 promissory note to Hanewald, but paid off the rest of its creditors. Debts paid included the $55,000 loan from Union State Bank and a $10,000 loan from Keith and Joan Bryan. The Bryan loan had been, according to the trial court, "intended to be used for operating costs and expenses."

Hanewald sued the corporation and the Bryans for breach of the lease agreement and the promissory note, seeking to hold the Bryans personally liable. The defendants counterclaimed, alleging that Hanewald had fraudulently misrepresented the business's profitability in negotiating its sale. After a trial without a jury, the trial court entered judgment against Bryan's, Inc. for $38,600 plus interest on Hanewald's claims and ruled against the defendants on their counterclaim. The defendants have not cross appealed these rulings.

The trial court, however, refused to hold the individual defendants personally liable for the judgment against Bryan's, Inc., stating:

> Bryan's, Inc. was formed in a classic manner, the $10,000.00 loan by Keith Bryan being more than sufficient operating capital. Bryan's, Inc. paid all obligations except the obligation to Hanewald in a timely fashion, and since there was no evidence of bad faith by the Bryans, the corporate shield of Bryan's, Inc. should not be pierced.

Hanewald appealed from the refusal to hold the individual defendants personally liable.

Insofar as the judgment fails to impose personal liability upon Keith and Joan Bryan, the corporation's sole shareholders, we agree with Hanewald that the trial court erred. We base our decision on the Bryans' statutory duty to pay for shares that were issued to them by Bryan's, Inc.

Organizing a corporation to avoid personal liability is legitimate. Indeed, it is one of the primary advantages of doing business in the corporate form. However, the limited personal liability of shareholders does not come free. As this court said in *Bryan v. Northwest Beverages*, 69 N.D. 274, 285 N.W. 689, 694 (1939), "[t]he mere formation of a corporation, fixing the amount of its capital stock, and receiving a certificate of incorporation, do not create anything of value upon which the company can do business." It is the shareholders' initial capital investments which protects their personal assets from further liability in the corporate enterprise. Thus, generally, shareholders are not liable for corporate debts beyond the capital they have contributed to the corporation.

This protection for corporate shareholders was codified in the statute in effect when Bryan's, Inc. was incorporated and when this action was commenced * * *. [The Court quotes MBCA (1969) § 25, first paragraph.] This statute obligated shareholders to pay for their shares as a prerequisite for their limited personal liability.

The kinds of consideration paid for corporate shares may vary. Article XII, § 9 of the state constitution says that "[n]o corporation shall issue stock or bonds except for money, labor done, or money or property actually received; and all fictitious increase of stock or indebtedness shall be void." [The Court summarizes and quotes from MBCA (1969) § 19.] The purpose of these constitutional and statutory provisions is "to protect the public and those dealing with the corporation * * *." *Bryan v. Northwest Beverages, supra*, 285 N.W. at 694.

In this case, Bryan's, Inc. was authorized to issue 100 shares of stock each having a par value of $1,000. Keith Bryan and Joan Bryan, two of the original incorporators and members of the board of directors, were each issued 50 shares. The trial court determined that "Bryan's, Inc. did not receive any payment, either in labor, services, money, or property, for the stock which was issued." Bryans have not challenged this finding of fact on this appeal. We hold that Bryans' failure to pay for their shares in the corporation makes them personally liable under [MBCA (1969) § 25] for the corporation's debt to Hanewald.

Drafters' comments to § 25 of the Model Business Corporation Act * * * sketched the principles:

> The liability of a subscriber for the unpaid portion of his subscription and the liability of a shareholder for the unpaid balance of the full consideration for which his shares were issued are based upon contract principles. The liability of a shareholder to whom shares are issued for overvalued property or services is a breach of contract. These liabilities have not been considered to be exceptions to the absolute limited liability concept.

> Where statutes have been silent, courts have differed as to whether the cause of action on the liabilities of shareholders for unpaid consideration for shares issued or to be issued may be asserted by a creditor directly, by the corporation itself or its receiver, or by a creditor on behalf of the corporation. The Model Act is also silent on the subject for the reason that it can be better treated elsewhere. 1 Model Business Corporation Act Annotated 2d, Comment to § 25, at pp. 509–510 (1971).

This court, in *Marshall-Wells Hardware Co. v. New Era Coal Co.*, 13 N.D. 396, 100 N.W. 1084 (1904), held that creditors could directly enforce shareholders' liabilities to pay for shares held by them under statutes analogous to [MBCA (1969) § 25]. We believe that the shareholder liability created by [MBCA (1969) § 25] may likewise be enforced in a direct action by a creditor of the corporation.

Our conclusion comports with the generally recognized rule, derived from common law, that "a shareholder is liable to corporate creditors to the extent his stock has not been paid for." 18A Am.Jur.2d *Corporations* § 863 (1985). *See also, id.* at §§ 906 and 907. One commentator has observed:

> For a corporation to issue its stock as a gratuity violates the rights of existing stockholders who do not consent, and is a fraud upon subsequent subscribers, and upon subsequent creditors who deal with it on the faith of its capital stock. The former may sue to enjoin the issue of the stock, or to cancel it if it has been issued, and has not reached the hands of a bona fide purchaser; and the latter, according to the weight of authority, may compel payment by the person to whom it was issued, to such extent as may be necessary for the payment of their claims. 11 W. Fletcher, *Cyclopedia of the Law of Private Corporations* § 5202, at p. 450 (1986).

The shareholder "is liable to the extent of the difference between the par value and the amount actually paid," and "to such an extent only as may be necessary for the satisfaction of" the creditor's claim. 11 W. Fletcher, *supra,* § 5241, at pp. 550, 551.

The defendants asserted, and the trial court ruled, that the $10,000 loan from Keith and Joan Bryan to the corporation was nevertheless "more than sufficient operating capital" to run the business. However, a shareholder's loan is a debt, not an asset, of the corporation. Where, as here, a loan was repaid by the corporation to the shareholders before its operations were abandoned, the loan cannot be considered a capital contribution.[3]

We conclude that the trial court, having found that Keith and Joan Bryan had not paid for their stock, erred as a matter of law in refusing to hold them personally liable for the corporation's debt to Hanewald. The debt to Hanewald does not exceed the difference between the par value of their stock and the amount they actually paid. Therefore, we reverse in part to remand for entry of judgment holding Keith and Joan Bryan

---

[3] There are some circumstances in which a shareholder's loan to the corporation may be treated as a capital contribution. *See* 12B W. Fletcher, *Cyclopedia of the Law of Private Corporations* § 5739 (1984). In bankruptcy proceedings, for example, a shareholder's loans to his corporation can be treated as capital contributions when a corporation is deemed undercapitalized. *See Pepper v. Litton*, 308 U.S. 295, 60 S.Ct. 238, 84 L.Ed. 281 (1939). However, the result in this class of cases is an equitable subordination of the shareholder's claim to the claims of other creditors, which is consistent in principle with the result we reach today.

jointly and severally liable for the entire corporate debt to Hanewald. The judgment is otherwise affirmed.

NOTES

(1) Is the liability imposed on the Bryans based on the theories developed in the *Hospes* case, or does it arise from the force of the statutes themselves? Under MBCA (1969), is there watered stock liability if:

(a) The directors fraudulently recite that property is worth $2,000 when it is really worth only $1,000, and then issue shares with a par value of $2,000 for it?

(b) The directors reasonably and nonfraudulently recite that property is worth $1,000, but then issue shares with a par value of $2,000 for it?

As a practical matter, the last paragraph of MBCA (1969) § 19 eliminates many potential problems in this area.

(2) In most states, watered stock liability arises only in connection with the original issuance of shares. If a corporation reacquires some of its shares after they have been lawfully issued, it may resell those shares at any price it desires without giving rise to watered stock liability. The theory is that these shares remain "issued" even though they are held in the corporation's treasury and their resale at less than par does not water the corporation's stock account. These shares (called "treasury shares") have an intermediate status under most statutes. They are not viewed as "outstanding" for dividend, quorum, and voting purposes, but they are viewed as "issued" so that their "reissuance" does not violate the restrictions imposed by the par value statutes. See Brumfield v. Horn, 547 So.2d 415 (Ala.1989). There is some contrary authority. MBCA § 6.31 eliminates the concept of treasury shares (for reasons to be discussed later) and treats reacquired shares as authorized but unissued shares. However, most states still retain the concept of treasury shares.

4. ELIGIBLE AND INELIGIBLE CONSIDERATION FOR SHARES

Consider MBCA (1969) § 19. The idea that only the actual receipt of certain types of property or services by a corporation will support the issuance of shares is not technically a part of the par value structure, but it is closely aligned with it and must be taken into account whenever shares are being issued under a traditional statute.

What purpose is served by § 19? There are at least two possibilities. First, it was designed to protect creditors of the corporation who may rely on the company's capital in extending credit, as it attempts to assure that there is something "real" which can be levied against and sold. Second, it may protect other investors (who invest "real" assets such as money or property) from dilution of their interests.

What happens when shares are issued for a combination of past and future services in a jurisdiction in which it is legal to issue shares for services already provided, but not for future services? A Texas court held that all stock issued in consideration for a combination of past and future services is presumed valid unless the party challenging the validity of the consideration paid can allocate the part of the stock that was issued for past services and the part issued for future services. See Coates v. Parnassus Systems, Inc., 2002 WL 534595 (Tex.App.2002).

In some circumstances, a contract to perform services may have considerable value. If Jennifer Lawrence enters into a contract to perform in a film, the producer could presumably borrow large sums solely on the strength of Ms. Lawrence's commitment. If Ms. Lawrence is to receive a twenty-five percent interest in the corporation producing the film, can the corporation issue shares to her reflecting that interest when she signs the contract? If not, how can she be given the interest that her contract entitles her to at the outset of the filming?

Shares issued for a promissory note are also prohibited by MBCA (1969) § 19. Again it is possible to divine an intention either to protect creditors of the corporation or to protect other investors who contribute cash while the promoter puts in an uncollectible promissory note. Courts have held that if a corporation does issue shares for a promissory note in violation of this section, the corporation may nevertheless enforce the note. The corporation, however, also may be able to cancel the offending shares for failing to comply with § 19. Presumably, a note executed by John D. Rockefeller is "as good as gold," and yet shares cannot be issued to John D. in exchange for that note. On the other hand, if John D.'s note is owned by a third person, Pam Smith, may Smith be issued shares in consideration of John D.'s note?

Another problem may be raised by the language in MBCA (1969) § 19 "other property, tangible or intangible." What about claimed secret processes, formulas, conditional or contingent contract rights, "good will," capitalized research costs that have not yet led to a marketable product, and other intangible "property"? Intangibles are often not only difficult to value; their very existence may be so ephemeral as not to constitute "property" at all in the eyes of some courts, at least for purposes of § 19. There are several decisions in which this question has been raised, usually in the context of seeking to cancel shares issued in exchange for such "property."

5. PAR VALUE IN MODERN PRACTICE

The early practice of creating shares with a par value equal to the proposed issuance price long ago fell into disuse. Today, the practice most often followed is to use "nominal" par value that is one cent, ten cents, or one dollar per share when the shares are issued for several dollars or more per share. The use of no par shares—for reasons discussed below—is a distant second.[e] Under current practice, par value serves only a minor function and is in no way an indication of the price at which the shares are issued. There is, however, one significant carryover from the earlier practice: to avoid watered stock liability, the issuance price for shares of stock with par value must always be equal to or greater than par value.

Several factors caused the movement away from par value as a representation of the purchase price of shares and the development of nominal par value shares. Doubtless, concern about watered stock liability, particularly where property of uncertain value is being contributed, was a factor. If high par value shares are given in exchange for such property, arguments may later arise that the property was not worth the par value of the shares received and the recipients might be sued for the difference. Another factor was the possible loss of flexibility in pricing shares. When a secondary market for previously issued shares develops, a corporation raising capital by selling shares in effect competes with that market. A corporation issuing shares with a par value of $100 may not be able to reduce the price below that figure and may have to stop selling shares if the market price of the previously issued shares dropped below $100 per share. (At that point, interested investors can get a better price by buying previously issued shares in the secondary market than they can from the corporation which is locked into the $100 price by the par value.)

Still another factor was that nominal par shares increase corporate flexibility in making distributions in the future. Consider MBCA (1969) § 21, and its possible application to "high par," "nominal par," and "no par" alternatives when forming a corporation. Consider the following alternatives:

(i) The corporation issues 10 shares of $100 par value stock for $1,000 in cash.

(ii) The corporation issues 10 shares of $1 par value stock for $1,000 in cash.

(iii) The corporation issues 10 shares of no par value stock for $1,000 in cash.

The appropriate accounting for alternatives (i) and (ii) is as follows:

---

[e]   The fact that a case such as Hanewald v. Bryan's Inc. arose in the 1980s can be explained only on the basis that the person forming the corporation was unaware of modern practice and the dangers of placing a high par value on shares.

Alternative (i)

Assets			Liabilities	0
	Cash	1000	Capital accounts	
			Stated Capital	1000
			Capital Surplus	0
		1000		1000

Alternative (ii)

Assets			Liabilities	0
	Cash	1000	Capital accounts	
			Stated Capital	10
			Capital Surplus	990
		1000		1000

In connection with alternative (iii), MBCA (1969) § 21 provides that the entire $1,000 should be treated as stated capital unless the directors determine to allocate to capital surplus "any portion of the consideration received for the issuance of such shares." (Does "any portion" include "all"?) Not all states give the directors total freedom to allocate the proceeds from no par shares to capital surplus. Some states do not permit such allocation at all (in which case, alternative (iii) becomes identical to alternative (i)), while others permit only a partial allocation. Before 1985, Texas, for example, permitted allocation of only 25 percent of the consideration to capital surplus. Tex.Bus.Corp.Act, art. 2.17B (1980). Assuming that such a restriction is applicable, and the directors elect to classify the maximum amount possible to capital surplus, alternative (iii) becomes:

Alternative (iii)

Assets			Liabilities	0
	Cash	1000	Capital accounts	
			Stated Capital	750
			Capital Surplus	250
		1000		1000

Now, a logical question is: What difference does it make if the capital contribution is recorded as stated capital or capital surplus? Rather surprisingly, it does make a difference, which can best be appreciated if a balance sheet is drawn up after the corporation (financed as suggested in alternative (ii)) has (1) borrowed $1,000 from a bank, and (2) had two years of operations during which it has earned and accumulated an aggregate of $2,000 from its earnings. Further, for simplicity, it will be assumed that all of the assets are held by the corporation in the form of cash. The balance sheet looks like this:

Assets			Liabilities	$1,000
	Cash	$4,000	Capital accounts	
			Earned Surplus	$2,000
			Stated Capital	10
			Capital Surplus	990
		$4,000		$4,000

At this point the shareholders decide that they want to distribute to themselves some or all of the $4,000. If the balance sheet is to continue to balance, every dollar taken from the left-hand column must be reflected by the reduction of a right-hand column entry. The significance of the right-hand entries is that they in effect limit or monitor the distribution of assets from the left-hand column. The distributions permitted by a corporation are evaluated in accordance with MBCA (1969) §§ 6, 45, and 46.

Under these statutes, capitalizing a corporation with large amounts of capital surplus gives that company greater freedom and flexibility to make distributions or reacquire its own shares than if the corporation were capitalized with large amounts of stated capital. In the above examples, the corporation, no matter how capitalized, could use the $2,000 of earned surplus to reacquire shares or make a distribution to shareholders. However, the corporation capitalized solely with stated capital (alternative (i)) would be limited to that amount; the corporation created with no par shares (alternative (iii)) would have available for distribution an additional $250 of capital surplus, for total potential distributions of $2250; the corporation capitalized most flexibly (alternative (ii)) could legally distribute $2990 out of its assets (subject, however, to the general insolvency tests in the 1969 Model Act). Admittedly, this increase in flexibility does not seem to be of earthshaking significance, and indeed may raise policy questions about whether corporations should have the freedom to distribute virtually all of their capital as permitted in alternative (ii).

Where the consideration for no par shares may be allocated to capital surplus without limitation (as permitted by § 18 of MBCA (1969)), either no par or nominal par shares give the same amount of freedom. No par shares, however, failed to match the popularity and widespread use of nominal par shares. One factor that, in the past, undoubtedly encouraged the use of nominal par shares, and discouraged the use of both high par and no par shares, was the federal excise tax statute, repealed in 1965, that imposed a documentary stamp tax on issues and transfers of securities. This tax was based on "the par or face value of each certificate" of par value stock and "the actual value of each certificate" of no par stock. I.R.C. § 4301 (1954), repealed by Pub.L. No. 89–44, Tit. IV, § 401(a), 79 Stat. 148 (1965). Several states may continue to measure their taxes on a similar basis.

TED J. FIFLIS, HOMER KRIPKE, & PAUL M. FOSTER, ACCOUNTING FOR BUSINESS LAWYERS
Page 433 (4th ed. 1991).

* * * [A] prospective creditor who inspects the balance sheet of a corporation and finds a low par or stated capital and most of the net worth embodied in capital surplus should know * * * that corporation laws to some extent permit the distribution of capital surplus as well as earned surplus to stockholders, giving creditors no protection beyond the legal capital consisting of par or stated capital.

* * *

[C]reditors today do not rely upon statutory protection against shareholder distributions. Trade creditors rely instead on security interests or careful monitoring of their receivables while commercial lenders require disclosure of financial data, security interests, and contractual limitations on distributions. It is in the areas of disclosure and statutory and contractual limitations that the practitioner must understand the accounting in order to serve his clients properly. * * *

NOTES

(1) It is important to distinguish conceptually between "no par shares" in states that retain the par value structure, and shares issued in states that, like the MBCA, have eliminated par value. The issuance of "no par shares" in par value states affects the stated capital and capital surplus accounts, may create watered stock liability in certain circumstances, and may affect the distributions a corporation may lawfully make. States that have eliminated the par value structure have eliminated the watered stock concept and have also generally eliminated mandatory capital accounts. They have also established different rules relating to when distributions lawfully may be made.

(2) Of course, it is not strictly true that the MBCA has "eliminated" the concept of par value. See MBCA § 2.02(b)(2)(iv). The Official Comment explains that optional par value provisions may be of use "to corporations which are to be qualified in foreign jurisdictions in that franchise or other taxes are computed upon the basis of par value." In addition, optional par value may also be given effect "essentially as a matter of contract between the parties." Where a corporation formed in a state that has abolished par value contemplates multistate operations, lawyers usually recommend that an optional par value be adopted to minimize tax consequences if the corporation becomes subject to taxation in a state that uses par value as a measure of tax liability.

(3) Par value relates only to the original issuance of shares and has no application whatsoever to subsequent transactions in the shares themselves, which may be bought or sold at any mutually acceptable price. The role of par value is declining in other contexts as well.

D. DEBT FINANCING

"Bonds" and "debentures" are examples of long-term indebtedness that are usually referred to as "debt securities." Both involve unconditional promises to pay a stated sum in the future, and to make payments of interest periodically until then. Technically, a "debenture" is an unsecured corporate obligation while a "bond" is secured by a lien or mortgage on corporate property. However, the word "bond" is often used indiscriminately to cover both bonds and debentures.

In days of old, interest coupons reflecting the periodic obligation to pay interest were attached to each debt security. Each coupon was a promise to make a specified payment of interest on a specific date. As the date an interest payment became due approached, the owner would cut off ("clip" was the verb universally used) the interest coupon and submit it to the corporation for payment.

In recent years, novel types of debt instruments have been created, and new words have entered the common vocabulary. Zero coupon bonds, often called "zeroes," pay no interest at all; they sell at a substantial discount from face value and upon maturity the holder receives the face value. The entire difference between the original issue price and the face value represents interest payable upon the maturity of the "zero."[f] Junk bonds, widely used in takeovers, are simply below investment-grade debt instruments. Many other novel variations exist. See generally Robert W. Hamilton and Richard A. Booth, Business Basics for Law Students: Essential Concepts and Applications §§ 14.19–14.24 (4th ed. 2006).

1. THE CONCEPT OF LEVERAGE

Debt owed to third persons creates leverage. Leverage is favorable to the borrower when the borrower is able to earn more on the borrowed capital than the cost of the borrowing. The entire excess is allocable to the equity accounts of the corporation, thereby increasing the rate of return on the equity invested in the corporation. An example will make this clear. Assume that a corporation has total invested funds (capital) of $500,000. Let us consider the earnings per share on two alternative assumptions. Under Alternative A, 10% of the capital ($50,000) is borrowed on a long-term basis and the remaining 90% of the capital ($450,000) is raised by selling 45,000 shares of stock at $10.00 per share. Under Alternative B, 50% of the capital ($250,000) is borrowed on a long-term basis and the remaining 50% of the capital ($250,000) is raised by selling 25,000 shares of stock at $10.00 per share.

---

[f] For income tax purposes, however, a holder of a "zero" must include in taxable income an allocable portion of the discount even though it is not to be received until sometime in the distant future; as a result, "zeroes" are attractive investments primarily for tax-exempt or tax-deferred entities.

ALTERNATIVE A

Assumed net earnings	$10,000	$100,000	$150,000	$200,000
Interest on bonds (8% on $50,000)	$ 4,000	$ 4,000	$ 4,000	$ 4,000
Earnings allocable to common[g]	$ 6,000	$ 96,000	$146,000	$196,000
Number of shares	45,000	45,000	45,000	45,000
Earnings per share	$ 0.13	$ 2.13	$ 3.24	$ 4.36

ALTERNATIVE B

Assumed net earnings	$10,000	$100,000	$150,000	$200,000
Interest on bonds (8% on $250,000)	$20,000	$ 20,000	$ 20,000	$ 20,000
Earnings allocable to common[h]	$ 0.00	$ 80,000	$130,000	$180,000
Number of shares	25,000	25,000	25,000	25,000
Earnings per share	$ 0.00	$ 3.20	$ 5.20	$ 7.20

The interest on the bonds represents a fixed claim, i.e., the charge for obtaining the use of the $50,000 in debt capital in Alternative A and the $250,000 in debt capital in Alternative B. When earnings are low, debt service takes up most of the earnings. In the hypothetical above, if earnings drop below $20,000, Alternative B will show losses while Alternative A continues to show modest profits until earnings drop to $4,000.

Debt financing is attractive to borrowers (though not to lenders) during periods when borrowers anticipate high rates of inflation in the future because loans will ultimately be repaid with inflated dollars. Of course, savvy lenders will anticipate this and charge high interest rates which will offset, either wholly or partially, this advantage of debt financing. Leverage generally is obtained only by the use of other people's money.[i]

It is easy to see why a company's creditors prefer Alternative A over Alternative B. Under Alternative A, the bondholders are paid the interest that is owed to them in full under every one of the four scenarios. In contrast, under Alternative B, if the firm makes only $10,000, the firm will be able to pay only half of the $20,000 that it owes to the bondholders. Under this scenario, the firm will be bankrupt (if this is its only business venture), and the bondholders will get at most $0.50 on the dollar (the creditors will only receive $0.50 on the dollar if, counter-

---

[g] Computed simply by subtraction and without regard to reduction in income taxes as a result of the increased interest deduction.

[h] Computed simply by subtraction and without regard to reduction in income taxes as a result of the increased interest deduction.

[i] Some leverage may also be obtained if loans by shareholders are made on a basis other than in proportion to their shareholdings.

factually, the company's legal fees and other bankruptcy transaction costs are zero). Clearly the bondholders prefer Alternative A over Alternative B because a 100% chance of being fully repaid is superior to a 75% chance of being fully repaid and a 25% chance of being repaid at most $0.50 on the dollar. Put in the language of business, Alternative A is the alternative with lower leverage. The bonds are risk-free. Even under the worst-case scenario, the bondholders are paid in full because they are only owed $4,000 per year and the $10,000 earned under the worst-case scenario exceeds this. In contrast, under Alternative B, there is a 25% chance that the bondholders will only be paid one-half of what they are owed.

Because more was borrowed under Alternative B than under Alternative A, more is owed. And the more that is owed, the more money the business has to make to pay off its debts. It's as simple as that.

Turning now from the bondholders to the shareholders, under the assumptions in this exercise, when earnings increase above $20,000, the per share earnings under Alternative B rise much more rapidly than under Alternative A, even though the shares are otherwise identical and even though both firms have exactly the same businesses, investments, and earnings. In effect, in Alternative B, the common shareholders are getting $500,000 to work for them even though they contributed only $250,000. The cost of this borrowing is the fixed interest charge which they must meet out of their own capital if necessary. And even the fixed charge represented by the interest rate on the $250,000 is ameliorated by the tax savings resulting from the deductibility of the interest.[j] In Alternative A, the common shareholders have only $50,000 of borrowed (i.e., other people's) money to work for them. In Alternative B, the shareholders have $250,000 of borrowed money at their disposal.

The effects of debt, or leverage as it often is called, is well-understood in the real world by hedge funds, real estate syndicates, and corporate Chief Financial Officers, all of whom seek to obtain debt financing to the extent that they can manage it, and to make the smallest possible equity investment when trying to obtain capital to use in their businesses. The risk, of course, is that the income from the project may not be sufficient to cover the fixed charges, and the investors may quickly be wiped out.[k]

---

[j]   Nonparticipating preferred stock owned by third persons also creates leverage, which technically is a phenomenon of a senior, limited position rather than of debt. However, the tax advantage of debt—the deductibility of the interest—is lost if preferred stock is used, with the result that most leverage situations created today involve the issuance of debt. On the other hand, a corporation is entitled to a credit for dividends received, including dividends paid upon preferred stock.

[k]   An economist might show impatience with an example such as that set forth in the text. Assuming that both the common shares and the bonds are publicly traded (and with certain further simplifying assumptions), the economist would argue that the total value of the securities issued by the enterprise (the aggregate market value of all issued common shares plus all issued bonds) would be independent of the amount of debt in the capital structure of the enterprise. In other words, any increase in value of the common stock by reason of the corporation's capital structure would be offset by a decrease in the market price for the bonds.

Conflicts inevitably arise between the interests of fixed claimants (creditors) and the interests of residual claimants (shareholders). Notice that in both Alternatives A and B, the company's assumed net earnings are the same. Regardless of which alternative is pursued, the business will experience net earnings of either $10,000, $100,000, $150,000, or $200,000. Just to be clear, let's also make explicit the assumption that the probability of the firm experiencing any one of these four alternatives is the same—i.e., 25%. This simply means that there is a 25% chance that the firm will have net earnings of $10,000, $100,000, $150,000, and $200,000, respectively. And, of course, there is a 100% chance that the business will experience one (and only one) of these four outcomes. Now that this is clear, we can now calculate which alternative investment is preferred by bondholders and which is preferred by shareholders. This analysis permits us to see clearly the conflict between equity claimants (shareholders) and debt claimants (creditors). Specifically, we know that under Alternative A there is a 25% chance that shareholders will receive earnings per share of $0.13, $2.13, $3.24, or $4.36.

If we multiply each of these four possible outcomes by their respective probabilities, we can calculate the expected returns to shareholders of this investment. To do this, we simply multiply each possible outcome by its 25% probability and sum the result like this:

(.25 * $0.13) + (.25 * $2.13) + (.25 * $3.24) + (.25 * $4.36) = $2.47

In other words, on a risk-adjusted basis, Alternative A has an expected value to the shareholders of $2.47 per share.

In order to compare, let's now perform the same calculation for Alternative B:

(.25 * $0.00) + (.25 * $3.20) + (.25 * $5.20) + (.25 * $7.20) = $3.90

Thus, Alternative B has an expected value of $1.43 more per share than Alternative A, so shareholders clearly will prefer Alternative B to Alternative A. In contrast, as described above, the bondholders will prefer Alternative A to Alternative B because they prefer the 100 percent chance of getting repaid in full under Alternative A to the 25 percent chance of receiving only one-half ($10,000) of the amount owed them ($20,000) under Alternative B.

To further illustrate the effects of leverage, imagine a third alternative, C, in which the company manages to borrow 85% ($425,000) of the $500,000 capital it needs for the project, so that the shareholders only have to put up the remaining 15% ($75,000; 7,500 shares of stock at $10.00 per share). Even without any changes on the asset side of the

---

Even if this principle, first set forth by Miller and Modigliani, is abstractly accepted, a leveraged capital structure such as set forth in the example may benefit the common shareholders at the expense of the debtholders. Also, this relationship may not be visible to the holders of the bonds in situations where the debt is not publicly or widely held.

balance sheet (which shows what the company owns and/or has invested in), the change in expected returns is enormous. Under Alternative C, the expected value to the shareholders is a whopping $11.60 versus $2.47 and $3.90 under Alternatives A and B respectively. The bondholders, of course, like Alternative C even less than they like Alternative B. Under Alternative B, there is a 25 percent chance that the bondholders will receive only 50 cents on the dollar. Under Alternative C, however, there is a 25 percent chance that the bondholders will receive only 29 cents on the dollar.

ALTERNATIVE C

Assumed net earnings	$10,000	$100,000	$150,000	$200,000
Interest on bonds (8% on $425,000)	$34,000	$ 34,000	$ 34,000	$ 34,000
Earnings allocable to common[1]	$ 0.00	$ 66,000	$116,000	$166,000
Number of shares	7,500	7,500	7,500	7,500
Earnings per share	$ 0.00	$ 8.80	$ 15.47	$ 22.13

A sensible person might conclude that the company would be egregiously over-leveraged under Alternative C. Interestingly, both commercial banks (like Bank of America and JP Morgan Chase) and investment banks (like Goldman Sachs and Morgan Stanley) have more debt in proportion to their equity than this. These firms have about 10% of their capital structures in the form of equity, as opposed to the 15% equity in Alternative C.

Finally, let us consider which investment a firm will actually choose. The answer is that, among the vast array of alternatives that might be available, the company should, theoretically, choose the alternative that maximizes the overall value of the business, and not the one that narrowly maximizes the value of either the shareholders' investment or the bondholders' investment.

In a world of perfect information and zero transaction costs (what some call a "Coasean" world, after Nobel laureate Ronald Coase who analyzed important issues under these assumptions), the company will pursue the project that maximizes the overall value of the firm. As long as there is an alternative project that makes one group (either shareholders or bondholders) better off by more than it makes the other group worse off, the parties will engage in bargaining that will result in the company pursuing the alternative that maximizes the value of the entire enterprise. Suppose, for example, that the firm was considering Alternative A. If the shareholders found an investment that made the entire company more valuable, but imposed risk on the bondholders, the

---

[1] Computed simply by subtraction and without regard to reduction in income taxes as a result of the increased interest deduction.

shareholders could induce the bondholders to move to the riskier (but higher value) alternative by agreeing to pay the bondholders additional compensation for their increased risk. If the new investment were worth more to the shareholders than the amount of the side payment, both the shareholders and the bondholders would be better off if the side payment were made. Alternatively, the bondholders might find it worthwhile to pay the shareholders to refrain from pursuing Alternative C if another investment could be found that made the bondholders better off by more than the amount of the side payment that would have to be made to the shareholders.

2. TAX TREATMENT OF DEBT

In a C corporation, there are usually tax advantages for shareholders who are individuals to lend to the corporation a portion of their investment rather than making a contribution to capital. Interest payments on debt are deductible by the borrower whereas dividend payments on equity securities are not.[m] A loan by a shareholder to his corporation therefore reduces the double tax problem of a C corporation. On the other hand, if the shareholder is a corporation, the shareholder may prefer to receive payments in the form of dividends rather than interest because of the dividend-received deduction, even though this causes the "borrower" to lose the benefit of an interest deduction.

Because of the tax advantages of loans by individual shareholders to C corporations, there is an extensive jurisprudence as to whether debt should be reclassified as equity for tax purposes. A classic case is Slappey Drive Indus. Park v. United States, 561 F.2d 572 (5th Cir.1977), where the court stated:

> Articulating the essential difference between * * * [debt and equity] is no easy task. Generally, shareholders place their money "at the risk of the business" while lenders seek a more reliable return. That statement of course glosses over a good many considerations with which even the most inexperienced investor is abundantly familiar. A purchaser of General Motors stock may bear much less risk than a bona fide lender to a small corporation. * * *

> It is well established that shareholders may loan money to their corporations and achieve corresponding tax treatment. When making such loans they could hardly be expected to ignore their shareholder status; their motivations will not match those of potential lenders who have no underlying equity interest. The "risk of the business" standard, though, continues to provide a

---

[m] There are additional differences between interest payments and dividends. For example, dividends are taxable to the provider of capital only if the corporation has earnings and profits, while interest is taxable in any event.

backdrop for our analysis. While we should not expect a creditor-shareholder to evidence motivations and behavior conforming perfectly to those of a mere creditor, neither should we abandon the effort to determine whether the challenged transaction is in substance a contribution to capital masquerading as debt.

The Court then identified 13 factors that may be relevant in making the classification, and concluded that "[i]n the case at bar the most telling * * * factor is the corporate debtors' consistent failure to repay the debts on the due dates or to seek postponements. More generally, that failure and the corresponding absence of timely interest payments combine with * * * [the defendants'] testimony regarding the parties' view of their relationships to make clear that these transactions were in substance not at all the type arrangements for which debt treatment is appropriate." Id. at 582.

NOTES

(1) A "debt/equity ratio" is the mathematical ratio between a corporation's liabilities and the shareholders' equity. For example, a corporation with $10,000 of equity that borrows $100,000 has a debt/equity ratio of 10:1. This ratio may be calculated on an aggregate or overall liabilities basis (taking into account debts and obligations owed to persons other than shareholders) or on an "inside" basis (taking into account only debts owed to shareholders). At one time, the Internal Revenue Service proposed regulations to the effect that debt would not be viewed as "excessive" if the corporation's "outside" ratio was less than 10:1 and its "inside" ratio was less than or equal to 3:1. Is this a sensible way to create a "safe harbor" for shareholder-created debt? Would such a "safe harbor" be desirable?

(2) It was once thought that an inside debt/equity ratio of 4:1 or higher would be decisive in reclassifying the debt as equity. This ratio test, originally based on a statement in John Kelley Co. v. Commissioner, 326 U.S. 521 (1946), was generally rejected by courts in favor of the more flexible approach set forth in *Slappey Drive*.

(3) A corporation with a high debt/equity ratio is sometimes referred to as a "thin corporation."

3.　DEBT AS A PLANNING DEVICE

The advantages of debt as a planning device in closely held corporations are well-illustrated by Obre v. Alban Tractor Co., 179 A.2d 861 (Md.1962). Obre and Nelson formed a new corporation, Annel Corporation, to engage in the dirt moving and road building business. Obre agreed to contribute $65,548.10 to the corporation in cash and equipment, while Nelson agreed to contribute $10,000 in cash and equipment. The equipment values were based on an independent appraisal. The parties agreed that control was to be shared equally from the outset. Acting upon the advice of "a well-known and reputable firm of certified public accountants," the parties capitalized the corporation as follows:

Obre: $10,000 par value voting common stock
           $20,000 par value nonvoting preferred stock
           $35,548.10 unsecured promissory note

Nelson: $10,000 par value voting common stock

The venture was an economic failure, shortly ending up in a state insolvency proceeding. In this proceeding, Obre successfully claimed the right to participate as an unsecured creditor to the extent of his $35,548.10 unsecured note. The unpaid trade creditors argued that a "subordinating equity" principle required that this note be treated as equity—a capital contribution—rather than as a valid debt. The Court rejected this argument, stating that there was no showing of undercapitalization, fraud, misrepresentation, or estoppel. In deciding that Annel Corporation was not undercapitalized, the Court treated Obre's preferred stock as an equity investment so that the corporation had begun business with $40,000 of equity and only $35,548.10 of debt. The Court held that there was no showing that $40,000 of equity capital was inadequate for a business such as that of Annel Corporation. The Court also relied on the fact that Obre's "loan" to the corporation was either known to the creditors or could easily have been discovered by examining public state tax filings, by requesting a financial statement, or by obtaining a credit report.

NOTE

Why did the certified public accountants recommend that a significant portion of Obre's contribution be in the form of debt rather than simply having a preferred stock investment of $55,548.10?

E. PLANNING THE CAPITAL STRUCTURE FOR THE CLOSELY HELD CORPORATION

Attorneys are often asked to review and make recommendations about the proposed capital structure of newly formed closely held ventures. Usually, the capital structure will be an integral part of broader control considerations in which individual participants attempt to ensure their continued right to participate in the venture and the attorney reviews the entire "package" as a single unit. Tax considerations may also be of critical importance. In reviewing proposed capital structures, an attorney will generally have several basic concerns, including:

(1) Will the structure "work"; i.e., will it stand up in the event of later disagreement and possible legal attack?

(2) Will the structure actually provide the desired result? For example, a person desiring a guaranteed, unconditional periodic payment who is asked to accept preferred stock should be made aware that the directors may usually forego declaring dividends on the preferred stock if they so desire.

(3) Will the desired tax treatment be available, or more likely, is the structure created one that makes the desired tax treatment probable if not certain? In this regard, the availability of the S corporation election may be of major importance to the participants.

(4) Might the structure give rise to unexpected liabilities? The most likely sources of unexpected liabilities are the possible application of the concepts of par value and watered stock (in states that still recognize such concepts) and, possibly, the ubiquitous doctrine of piercing the corporate veil.

(5) Are the clients' financial contributions reasonably protected and fairly treated in the event of unexpected or calamitous occurrences causing the sudden and premature termination of the venture?

This is only a partial list. Depending on the circumstances, participants will usually have additional concerns about the capital structure. For example, a person planning on periodic payments for living expenses may wish to have assurance that corporate matters are handled conservatively and not in a way that may jeopardize future distributions. Other persons may wish to have a major voice in fiscal management and future plans to raise additional capital which may affect their roles in the venture. Considerations about capital structure obviously shade over into questions relating to control over the venture in general, and should be addressed as part of the broader considerations of control.

F. PUBLIC OFFERINGS

The goal for many closely held corporations is to "go public," that is, to raise substantial amounts of capital by making a public offering of their securities through the services of an underwriter. These transactions are known as initial public offerings ("IPOs").

Going public has both significant costs and significant benefits to the owners of the company. Of course, the principal benefit of going public is to raise additional capital for expansion. Many successful closely held corporations, however, can finance their growth from retained earnings or from loans from a small number of investors. However, going public often has the advantage of reducing a corporation's need to rely on bank debt. Money raised in public offerings often is used to pay down pre-existing indebtedness. Public offerings of equity enable a company to use the money for projects with a long-term time horizon.

Selling securities through a public offering also gives the existing shareholders liquidity. Shareholders who owned illiquid shares in closely held corporations often sell their shares after a public offering in order to diversify their investment portfolios. Funds acquired by a corporation in a public offering sometimes are used to make acquisitions of other companies. Also, public offerings have the benefit of enabling a company to better compete for employees, since options in publicly traded shares and other stock-based compensation can be offered to prospective employees. Companies whose shares are publicly traded also are preferred by prospective employees, customers, and suppliers, as such companies tend to be better known.

Many closely held companies feel uncomfortable with the amount of disclosure that must be made during the process of making an IPO. Companies that have engaged in conflict of interest transactions, for example, may decide not to go public because they are unwilling to disclose the details of those transactions. Similarly, prior to an IPO, management will have to "clean up its balance sheet." Some argue that this process sometimes requires companies to sacrifice long-term investments in order to meet short-term objectives.

In addition, the process of going public involves substantial legal risks. The company is strictly liable under Section 11 of the Securities Act of 1933 for material misstatements and omissions in the Registration Statement (which contains the prospectus and other documents that must be filed with the SEC before the company may make an IPO). Even after a company goes public, it must file quarterly and annual financial reports under the Securities Exchange Act and comply with strict internal accounting control measures and record-keeping requirements. Also, a publicly held company must constantly deal with analysts and outside shareholders.

Compliance with the Securities Act of 1933, 15 U.S.C.A. §§ 77a–77aa, involves the filing of a registration statement with the SEC pursuant to Section 5 of the Act. A registration statement consists of two parts: 1) a "prospectus," a document that is to be distributed to potential and actual investors; and 2) additional information that must be submitted to the SEC and is publicly available, but need not be included in the prospectus. Registration of an issue by an "unseasoned company," i.e., one whose shares are not widely traded in the public markets and who has never previously filed a registration statement under the 1933 Act, is an expensive, complex, and often messy process.

NOTES

(1) The registration statement of a company making an IPO must contain information about the dozens of items described in Schedule A of the 1933 Act; additional disclosure requirements appear in SEC Regulation S–K and on the registration statement form (Form S–1) itself. The company must also arrange to have certified financial statements prepared in accordance with Regulation S–X for the previous three years. Preparation of these financial statements by an independent auditor is often complicated by incomplete or misleading financial records. Virtually all closely held companies find that their existing financial statements must be significantly revised to meet the requirements of Regulation S–X even if they were originally prepared by an outside auditor and were believed to be entirely suitable for their own needs while privately held.

(2) From the standpoint of an attorney, securities registration is a highly specialized and complex matter. The process by which attorneys verify the accuracy and completeness of registration statements is usually referred to as a "due diligence" investigation. A sloppily prepared or incomplete registration statement may subject the attorneys to personal liability to investors as well as cause damage to their reputations if they are named as parties in a securities fraud or disciplinary proceeding.

(3) Robert W. Hamilton and Richard Booth, Corporation Finance: Cases and Materials 184–85 (3d ed. 2000):

> Once complete, the registration statement is then filed with the SEC. The SEC's Division of Corporate Finance reviews the registration statement and typically issues a lengthy comment letter specifying areas in which more disclosure or specificity is required. During the review process, a preliminary prospectus (sometimes called a "red herring") is circulated to potential investors. (A prospectus is in essence the same document as the registration statement but without the exhibits.) Securities may not be sold, however, until the registration statement becomes effective. In theory, a registration statement becomes effective automatically 20 calendar days after it is filed, but each change in the registration statement, whether in response to SEC comments or for any other reason, starts a new 20-day waiting period. When the registration statement is about to become effective, the price of the offering is sent in a final pricing amendment, and the SEC waives the new 20-day waiting period that would otherwise be required. The securities may then be sold to investors. A final prospectus must, however, be delivered to everyone who purchases the securities over the following 40 to 90 days depending on the circumstances of the offering.

(4) Section 12 of the Securities Exchange Act of 1934, 15 U.S.C.A. § 78*l*, requires every corporation that has (i) shares registered on a national securities exchange, or (ii) at least 2,000 shareholders (or 500 non-accredited

shareholders) and $10,000,000 in assets, to register that class of shares with the SEC. This requirement is technically independent of and separate from the registration requirement set forth in the Securities Act of 1933. However, almost all corporations that go through a full-scale 1933 Act registration will almost immediately become subject to this 1934 Act registration requirement. The 1934 Act registration requirement triggers a variety of continuous disclosure obligations and proxy rules, "short swing" profit recapture under § 16(b) of the 1934 Act, annual reports to shareholders, and the like. Indeed, most of the continuous disclosure requirements for publicly held corporations are imposed by the regulations under § 12 of the 1934 Act.

(5) New technological developments have had a dramatic effect on the dissemination of information about publicly traded securities. Many registered (and some unregistered) securities are now offered for sale on the internet or electronic communications networks and often touted through "chat rooms" or anonymous postings of questionable information. The traditional registration process was designed for a simpler era, and the SEC has struggled to respond to these new developments. For example, the SEC has found it necessary to increase dramatically its fraud section in order to respond to complaints of egregious misrepresentations in connection with the sale of securities. For an example of touting a small publicly traded stock, see Teenager in Stock-Fraud Case Kept $500,000 in Profits—The Line Between Proper and Improper Activity on Web Grows Increasingly Fuzzy, Wall Street Journal, Oct. 20, 2000, at C1 (describing a case of a fraudulent stock offering on the internet initially unnoticed by regulators). Additionally, several companies have offered unregistered "free stock" over the internet to investors if they will simply visit the company's web site. The purpose is to create a public market for the shares, clearly a valuable adjunct to any marginal corporation's activities. The SEC has taken a dim view of these offerings and has required full-scale registration of "free" stock issues. The cost of registration may deter many marginal issuers, although at least two companies have actually registered issues of free stock.

SECURITIES AND EXCHANGE COMM'N v. RALSTON PURINA CO.

Supreme Court of the United States, 1953.
346 U.S. 119.

MR. JUSTICE CLARK delivered the opinion of the Court.

Section [4(2)] of the Securities Act of 1933 exempts "transactions by an issuer not involving any public offering" from the registration requirements of § 5. We must decide whether Ralston Purina's offerings of treasury stock to its "key employees" are within this exemption. On a complaint brought by the Commission under § 20(b) of the Act seeking to enjoin respondent's unregistered offerings, the District Court held the exemption applicable and dismissed the suit. The Court of Appeals affirmed. The question has arisen many times since the Act was passed;

an apparent need to define the scope of the private offering exemption prompted certiorari.

Ralston Purina manufactures and distributes various feed and cereal products. Its processing and distribution facilities are scattered throughout the United States and Canada, staffed by some 7,000 employees. At least since 1911 the company has had a policy of encouraging stock ownership among its employees; more particularly, since 1942 it has made authorized but unissued common shares available to some of them. Between 1947 and 1951, the period covered by the record in this case, Ralston Purina sold nearly $2,000,000 of stock to employees without registration and in so doing made use of the mails.

In each of these years, a corporate resolution authorized the sale of common stock "to employees * * * who shall, without any solicitation by the Company or its officers or employees, inquire of any of them as to how to purchase common stock of Ralston Purina Company." A memorandum sent to branch and store managers after the resolution was adopted advised that "[t]he only employees to whom this stock will be available will be those who take the initiative and are interested in buying stock at present market prices." Among those responding to these offers were employees with the duties of artist, bakeshop foreman, chow loading foreman, clerical assistant, copywriter, electrician, stock clerk, mill office clerk, order credit trainee, production trainee, stenographer, and veterinarian. The buyers lived in over fifty widely separated communities scattered from Garland, Texas, to Nashua, New Hampshire and Visalia, California. The lowest salary bracket of those purchasing was $2,700 in 1949, $2,435 in 1950 and $3,107 in 1951. The record shows that in 1947, 234 employees bought stock, 20 in 1948, 414 in 1949, 411 in 1950, and the 1951 offer, interrupted by this litigation, produced 165 applications to purchase. No records were kept of those to whom the offers were made; the estimated number in 1951 was 500.

The company bottoms its exemption claim on the classification of all offerees as "key employees" in its organization. Its position on trial was that "A key employee * * * is not confined to an organization chart. It would include an individual who is eligible for promotion, an individual who especially influences others or who advises others, a person whom the employees look to in some special way, an individual, of course, who carries some special responsibility, who is sympathetic to management and who is ambitious and who the management feels is likely to be promoted to a greater responsibility." That an offering to all of its employees would be public is conceded.

The Securities Act nowhere defines the scope of [§ 4(2)'s] private offering exemption. Nor is the legislative history of much help in staking out its boundaries. * * *

Decisions under comparable exemptions in the English Companies Acts and state "blue sky" laws, the statutory antecedents of federal securities legislation, have made one thing clear—to be public, an offer need not be open to the whole world. In Securities and Exchange Comm. v. Sunbeam Gold Mines Co., 9 Cir., 1938, 95 F.2d 699, 701, this point was made in dealing with an offering to the stockholders of two corporations about to be merged. Judge Denman observed that:

> In its broadest meaning the term "public" distinguishes the populace at large from groups of individual members of the public segregated because of some common interest or characteristic. Yet such a distinction is inadequate for practical purposes; manifestly an offering of securities to all redheaded men, to all residents of Chicago or San Francisco, to all existing stockholders of the General Motors Corporation or the American Telephone & Telegraph Company, is no less "public," in every realistic sense of the word, than an unrestricted offering to the world at large. Such an offering, though not open to everyone who may choose to apply, is none the less "public" in character, for the means used to select the particular individuals to whom the offering is to be made bear no sensible relation to the purposes for which the selection is made. * * * To determine the distinction between "public" and "private" in any particular context, it is essential to examine the circumstances under which the distinction is sought to be established and to consider the purposes sought to be achieved by such distinction.

The courts below purported to apply this test. The District Court held, in the language of the Sunbeam decision, that "The purpose of the selection bears a 'sensible relation' to the class chosen," finding that "The sole purpose of the 'selection' is to keep part stock ownership of the business within the operating personnel of the business and to spread ownership throughout all departments and activities of the business." The Court of Appeals treated the case as involving "an offering, without solicitation, of common stock to a selected group of key employees of the issuer, most of whom are already stockholders when the offering is made, with the sole purpose of enabling them to secure a proprietary interest in the company or to increase the interest already held by them."

Exemption from the registration requirements of the Securities Act is the question. The design of the statute is to protect investors by promoting full disclosure of information thought necessary to informed investment decisions. * * * Since exempt transactions are those as to which "there is no practical need for * * * [the bill's] application," the applicability of [§ 4(2)] should turn on whether the particular class of persons affected need the protection of the Act. An offering to those who are shown to be able to fend for themselves is a transaction "not involving any public offering."

The Commission would have us go one step further and hold that "an offering to a substantial number of the public" is not exempt under [§ 4(2)]. We are advised that "whatever the special circumstances, the Commission has consistently interpreted the exemption as being inapplicable when a large number of offerees is involved." But the statute would seem to apply to a "public offering" whether to few or many. It may well be that offerings to a substantial number of persons would rarely be exempt. * * * [T]here is no warrant for superimposing a quantity limit on private offerings as a matter of statutory interpretation.

The exemption, as we construe it, does not deprive corporate employees, as a class, of the safeguards of the Act. We agree that some employee offerings may come within [§ 4(2)], e.g., one made to executive personnel who because of their position have access to the same kind of information that the act would make available in the form of a registration statement. Absent such a showing of special circumstances, employees are just as much members of the investing "public" as any of their neighbors in the community. * * *

Keeping in mind the broadly remedial purposes of federal securities legislation, imposition of the burden of proof on an issuer who would plead the exemption seems to us fair and reasonable. Agreeing, the court below thought the burden met primarily because of the respondent's purpose in singling out its key employees for stock offerings. But once it is seen that the exemption question turns on the knowledge of the offerees, the issuer's motives, laudable though they may be, fade into irrelevance. The focus of inquiry should be on the need of the offerees for the protections afforded by registration. The employees here were not shown to have access to the kind of information which registration would disclose. The obvious opportunities for pressure and imposition make it advisable that they be entitled to compliance with § 5.

Reversed.

THE CHIEF JUSTICE and MR. JUSTICE BURTON dissent.

NOTES

(1) Could Ralston Purina have avoided the impact of the holding in this case by structuring its stock sale plan in the form of a sale to a corporate officer (such as the president or a vice president) who clearly did not need the protection of the Act, and then having that officer sell shares to employees who asked about the possibility of stock purchases? In a word, the answer is "no." Section 2(11) of the 1933 Act, 15 U.S.C.A. § 77b, defines an "underwriter" to mean "any person who has purchased from an issuer with a view to, or offers or sells for an issuer in connection with, the distribution of

any security * * *." Thus, the officer becomes an "underwriter" and the suggested transaction violates § 5 of the Act.

(2) Section 2(11) of the 1933 Act also states that the term "issuer" includes "any person directly or indirectly controlling or controlled by the issuer, or any person under direct or indirect common control with the issuer." The effect of this language is to impose on controlling or controlled persons the same obligation as is imposed on issuers under the Securities Act. Thus, the sole shareholder of a successful company cannot avoid the registration requirements of the 1933 Act simply by selling shares from his personal portfolio to the public rather than arranging for the corporation to sell shares directly. However, if a major shareholder of a corporation that is going public wishes to obtain personally a portion of the capital to be raised in the offering, he may include a portion of his own holdings in the registration statement prepared on behalf of the corporation. The shares so registered would then be sold as part of the public offering. This type of transaction, known as a "secondary offering," is quite common.

(3) How can a person who acquires shares in a legitimate § 4(2) transaction ever safely resell those shares in light of the § 2(11) definition of "underwriter"? The SEC has adopted Rule 144, 17 C.F.R. § 230.144, to establish guidelines for the resale of unregistered shares (often called "restricted stock") by investors without concern that the seller may be deemed to be an "underwriter." Rule 144 basically establishes a one-year holding requirement; this Rule is complex, however, and cannot be simply summarized. Rule 144 is not exclusive, so resales in some circumstances within the one-year period may be consistent with the original nonpublic offering exemption even though they do not comply with Rule 144.

SECURITIES ACT RELEASE NO. 33–5450
39 Fed. Reg. 2353 (1974).

Background and Purpose

Section 3(a)(11) of the Securities Act of 1933 exempts "any security which is a part of an issue offered and sold only to persons resident within a single State * * * where the issuer of such security is a person resident and doing business within or, if a corporation, incorporated by and doing business within, such State." [This section] * * * was intended to allow issuers with localized operations to sell securities as part of a plan of local financing. Congress apparently believed that a company whose operations are restricted to one area should be able to raise money from investors in the immediate vicinity without having to register the securities with a federal agency. In theory, the investors would be protected both by their proximity to the issuer and by state regulation. Rule 147 reflects this Congressional intent and is limited in its application to transactions where state regulation will be most effective. The Commission has consistently taken the position that the exemption applies only to local financing provided by local investors for local companies. To satisfy the exemption, the entire issue must be offered and sold exclusively to residents of the state in which the issuer is resident and doing business. An offer or sale of part of the issue to a single non-resident will destroy the exemption for the entire issue.

Certain basic questions have arisen in connection with interpreting section 3(a)(11). They are:

1.   What transactions does the section cover;

2.   What is "part of an issue" for purposes of the section;

3.   When is a person "resident within" a state or territory for purposes of the section; and

4.   What does "doing business within" mean in the context of the section?

The courts and the Commission have addressed themselves to these questions in the context of different fact situations, and some general guidelines have been developed. Certain guidelines were set forth by the Commission in Securities Act Release No. 4434 and, in part, are reflected in Rule 147. However, in certain aspects, as pointed out below, the rule differs from past interpretations.

The Transaction Concept

Although the intrastate offering exemption is contained in section 3 of the Act, which section is phrased in terms of exempt "securities" rather than "transactions," the legislative history and Commission and judicial interpretations indicate that the exemption covers only specific transactions and not the securities themselves. Rule 147 reflects this interpretation.

The "Part of an Issue" Concept

The determination of what constitutes "part of an issue" for purposes of the exemption, i.e. what should be "integrated," has traditionally been dependent on the facts involved in each case. * * * [The Commission refers to the same factors that are discussed in Rule 502 of Regulation D. Please consult the Statutory Supplement.]

The "Person Resident Within" Concept

The object of the section 3(a)(11) exemption—i.e., to restrict the offering to persons within the same locality as the issuer who are, by reason of their proximity, likely to be familiar with the issuer and protected by the state law governing the issuer—is best-served by interpreting the residence requirement narrowly. In addition, the determination of whether all parts of the issue have been sold only to residents can be made only after the securities have "come to rest" within the state or territory. Rule 147 retains these concepts, but provides more objective standards for determining when a person is considered a resident within a state for purposes of the rule and when securities have come to rest within a state.

The "Doing Business Within" Requirement

Because the primary purpose of the intrastate exemption was to allow an essentially local business to raise money within the state where the investors would be likely to be familiar with the business and with the management, the doing business requirement has traditionally been viewed strictly. First, not only should the business be located within the state, but the principal or predominant business must be carried on there. Second, substantially all of the proceeds of the offering must be put to use within the local area.

Rule 147 reinforces these requirements by providing specific percentage amounts of business that must be conducted within the state, and of proceeds from the offering that must be spent in connection with such business. In addition, the rule requires that the principal office of the issuer be within the state. * * *

[The text of Rule 147 itself is omitted.]

NOTE

The combination of *Ralston Purina* and the narrow Rule 147 construction of the § 3(a)(11) exemption obviously complicates the raising of capital by small businesses that can ill-afford the cost of a full-scale Form S–1 registration. As a result, it was widely believed that the registration process had a negative impact on capital-raising by small businesses. In 1980, Congress enacted legislation designed to minimize this impact. In 1982, the SEC adopted Regulation D, a series of limited offering exemptions predominantly for small businesses. In 1992, it adopted a series of additional amendments to its regulations pursuant to its so-called "Small Business Initiative."

SECURITIES ACT RELEASE NO. 33–6389
47 Fed. Reg. 11251 (1982).

* * *

Regulation D is the product of the Commission's evaluation of the impact of its rules and regulations on the ability of small businesses to raise capital. This study has revealed a particular concern that the registration requirements and the exemptive scheme of the Securities Act impose disproportionate restraints on small issuers. * * *

Coincident with the Commission's small business program, Congress enacted the Small Business Investment Incentive Act of 1980 (the "Incentive Act") [94 Stat. 2275 (codified in scattered sections of 15 U.S.C.A.)]. The Incentive Act included three changes to the Securities

Act: the addition of an exemption in Section 4(6) for offers and sales solely to accredited investors,[n] the increase in the ceiling of Section 3(b) from $2,000,000 to $5,000,000,[o] and the addition of Section 19(c) which, among other things, authorized "the development of a uniform exemption from registration for small issuers which can be agreed upon among several States or between the States and the Federal Government." * * *

SECURITIES WITHOUT REGISTRATION UNDER THE SECURITIES ACT OF 1933 (REGULATION D)
17 C.F.R. § 230.501 et seq.

(Please consult the Statutory Supplement)

NOTES

(1) Rule 508 of Regulation D was added in 1989, SEC Rel. No. 33–6825, 54 Fed.Reg. 11369 (1989), to "alleviate the draconian consequences of an innocent and insignificant defect in perfecting an exemption from registration." Stanley Keller, Securities Exemptions: The Saga of a Substantial Compliance Defense, Insights, Vol. 3, No. 8, p. 11 (Aug. 1989) (noting that the substantial compliance test in Rule 508 will not create a significant change in practice). See also Carl W. Schneider, A Substantial Compliance ("I & I") Defense and Other Changes are Added to SEC Regulation D, 44 Bus.Law. 1207 (1989).

(2) The SEC's 1992 "Small Business Initiative" involved a series of new regulations and rule amendments designed to ease the regulatory burdens imposed on small businesses. SEC Rel. Nos. 33–6949, 34–30968, 39–30968, 57 Fed. Reg. 36,442 (1992). The principal changes made by this initiative are:

(a) *Regulation A.* The oldest and at one time the most widely used "small business" regulation adopted by the SEC under § 3(b) is Regulation A (affectionately known as "Reg. A" by securities lawyers). 17 C.F.R. § 230.251, et seq. While technically an exemption under § 3(b), it actually involves a somewhat streamlined registration process at the regional offices of the SEC. See generally Harvey Frank, The Processing

---

[n] Section 4(6) (now § 4(a)(5)) provides an exemption for "transactions involving offers or sales by an issuer solely to one or more accredited investors, if the aggregate offering price of an issue of securities offered in reliance on this paragraph does not exceed [$5,000,000], if there is no advertising or public solicitation in connection with the transaction by the issuer or anyone acting on the issuer's behalf, and if the issuer files such notice with the Commission as the Commission shall prescribe."

[o] Section 3(b) (now § 3(b)(1)) provides:

The Commission may from time to time by its rules and regulations, and subject to such terms and conditions as may be prescribed therein, add any class of securities to the securities exempted as provided in this section, if it finds that the enforcement of this title with respect to such securities is not necessary in the public interest and for the protection of investors by reason of the small amount involved or the limited character of the public offering; but no issue of securities shall be exempted under this subsection where the aggregate amount at which such issue is offered to the public exceeds $5,000,000.

of Small Issues of Securities Under Regulation A, 1962 Duke L.J. 507. The late 1980s saw a significant reduction in Reg. A filings: from $408 million in 1981 to $34 million in 1991. The principal reasons for this decline were the $1.5 million ceiling on Reg. A issues and the cost of the Reg. A qualification process itself. The 1992 Small Business Initiative made several changes to make Reg. A more attractive: the ceiling was increased to $5 million, the information required to be disclosed was simplified and integrated to some extent with the uniform filings proposed by the North American Securities Administrators Association (NASAA) under state blue sky laws, and the information was permitted to be presented in a question-and-answer format. The SEC also simplified reporting requirements under the Securities Exchange Act of 1934 for small businesses with revenue of less than $25 million for each of two consecutive years.

(b) *Testing the Waters.* Rule 254, 17 C.F.R. § 230.254(a), permits a potential Reg. A user to publish or deliver to prospective purchasers a written document to determine whether there is investor interest in the contemplated offering. This document may be distributed without any review by the central offices of the SEC; basically the only requirement is that a copy be filed with an appropriate regional office and include the name and telephone number of a person able to answer possible questions about the document. Testing the waters permits a potential issuer to defer investing funds in the Reg. A process until after it has a pretty good idea that the offer will be successful.

(c) *Rule 504.* Perhaps the most important change was the amendment of Rule 504 of Regulation D so as to permit offerings by non-reporting issuers of up to $1 million essentially with no registration requirement at all (except for continued application of broad antifraud provisions). This change required similar action to be taken at the state level if it was to be implemented in fact.

See Rutherford B. Campbell, Jr., Blue Sky Laws and Recent Congressional Preemption Failure, 22 J.Corp.L. 175, 181–85 (1997) (evaluating the small offering exemptions offered by the SEC and noting that they meet both the needs of small issuers to raise capital effectively and the needs of the investors by providing fraud protection).

(3) "Crowdfunding" is the process of raising money via the internet for a variety of endeavors—from social causes to new business ventures. The SEC and other regulators have long been suspicious of crowdfunding because it is difficult to regulate, and because it is easy to defraud gullible people on the internet. In 2012, a year in which many in Congress were facing tough reelection fights in a weak economy characterized by chronic high unemployment, Congress passed a new statute, the Jumpstart Our Business Startups Act (the "JOBS Act"). The JOBS Act was passed ostensibly to enable more crowdfunding of businesses in an effort to "jumpstart" the economy and relieve unemployment.

Proponents of the JOBS Act claimed that the statute would liberalize the SEC's strict rules over the capital-raising process by enabling crowdfunding of public and private sales of securities, and even financing for new start-up companies. The SEC was given the power to oversee the implementation of the JOBS Act and to develop the regulations necessary for crowdfunding to occur on a significant scale.

On October 24, 2013, the SEC proposed new rules for those seeking to raise money from investors through crowdfunding. Pursuant to these rules, companies can raise money from investors without complying with the onerous registration requirements generally imposed under Section 5 of the Securities Act of 1933. Highlights of the proposed rules include the following:

- Issuers may not raise more than $1 million in any 12-month period.

- Individuals with annual income or net worth less than $100,000 cannot invest more than the greater of $2,000 or 5 percent of annual income or net worth in crowdfunding ventures in a 12-month period.

- Individuals with annual income or net worth of $100,000 or more cannot invest more than 10 percent of annual income or net worth in crowdfunding ventures in a 12-month period.

- Crowdfunding can only be done by registered broker-dealer firms or through a "funding portal" that is registered with the SEC.

- Those raising money via crowdfunding are not permitted to solicit investors, offer investment advice, or compensate employees on a commission basis.

- Those raising money via crowdfunding must file a disclosure document with the SEC (21 days or more before the first sale), and must file annual reports with the SEC.

- As more money is raised, more disclosure is required. For example, if a company seeks to raise $100,000 or less, it must disclose its financial statements and income tax returns for the most recently completed year. Those seeking to attract between $100,000 and $500,000 must furnish the SEC and investors with financial statements reviewed by an independent accountant. If the crowdfunding effort is aimed at raising more than $500,000, the company seeking the money must hire an outside auditor and file audited financial statements.

SMITH V. GROSS

United States Court of Appeals, Ninth Circuit, 1979.
604 F.2d 639.

Before CARTER and GOODWIN, CIRCUIT JUDGES, and WATERS, DISTRICT JUDGE.

PER CURIAM:

Gerald and Mary Smith appeal from the district court's judgment dismissing their action against the defendants. The Smiths brought suit against Gross, Gaddie, and the two corporate defendants for violation of the federal securities laws. The district court dismissed the suit without prejudice for lack of subject matter jurisdiction on the ground that there was no security involved in the transactions between the parties. * * *

We reverse. The transaction between the parties involved an investment contract.[p] * * *

* * *

Facts

The following statement of facts is taken from the Smiths' amended complaint and Gerald Smith's affidavit. Seller Gross, in a promotional newsletter, solicited buyer-investors to raise earthworms in order to help Gross reach his quotas of selling earthworms to fishermen. In the newsletter, buyers were promised that the seller's growing instructions would enable buyers to have a profitable farm, that the time involved would be similar to raising a garden, that the earthworms double in quantity every sixty days, and that the seller would buy back all bait size worms produced by buyers at $2.25 per pound. After responding to the newsletter, the Smiths were told by Gross that very little work was required, that success was guaranteed by the agreement to repurchase the Smiths' production, and that Gross needed the Smiths' help in the common enterprise of supplying worms for the bait industry. The Smiths alleged that they would not have purchased the worms without Gross' promise to repurchase the Smiths' production at $2.25 per pound. The Smiths were assured that they need not be worried about the market for worms because Gross would handle the marketing.

The Smiths alleged that, contrary to Gross' representations, worms multiply at a maximum of eight rather than 64 times per year, and that they could achieve the promised profits only if the multiplication rate was as fast as represented and Gross purchased the Smiths' production at $2.25 per pound. They also alleged that $2.25 is greater than the true market price and that Gross could pay that price only by selling the

---

[p] Section 2(a)(1) of the Securities Act of 1933 defines "security." If the interest sold to the plaintiffs is an "investment contract," the defendants have sold a security. If that security was not registered under the Securities Act of 1933, the plaintiffs have the statutory right to rescind the transaction under § 12.

worms to new worm farmers at inflated prices. The price at which Gross sold the worms to worm farmers was ten times in excess of the true market value. There is little market for worms in the Phoenix area. * * *

Investment Contract

The Smiths contend that the transactions between the parties involved an investment contract type of security. In SEC v. W.J. Howey Co., 328 U.S. 293, 301, 66 S.Ct. 1100, 1104, 90 L.Ed. 1244 (1946), the Supreme Court set out the conditions for an investment contract: "[t]he test is whether the scheme involves [1] an investment of money [2] in a common enterprise [3] with profits to come solely from the efforts of others." This court in SEC v. Glenn W. Turner Enterprises, Inc., 474 F.2d 476, 482 (9th Cir.), cert. denied, 414 U.S. 821, 94 S.Ct. 117, 38 L.Ed.2d 53 (1973), held that despite the Supreme Court's use of the word "solely," the third element of the *Howey* test is "whether the efforts made by those other than the investor are the undeniably significant ones, those essential managerial efforts which affect the failure or success of the enterprise." The *Turner* court defined a common enterprise as "one in which the fortunes of the investor are interwoven with and dependent upon the efforts and success of those seeking the investment or of third parties." Id. at 482 n. 7.

We find this case virtually identical with Miller v. Central Chinchilla Group, Inc., 494 F.2d 414 (8th Cir.1974). In *Miller,* the defendants entered into contracts under which they sold chinchillas to the plaintiffs with the promise to repurchase the offspring. The plaintiffs were told that it was simple to breed chinchillas according to the defendants' instructions and that the venture would be highly profitable. The plaintiffs alleged that the chinchillas were difficult to raise and had a high mortality rate, and that the defendants could return the promised profits only if they repurchased the offspring and sold them to other prospective chinchilla raisers at an inflated price.

The *Miller* court focused on two features in holding that there was an investment contract: (1) the defendants persuaded the plaintiffs to invest by representing that the efforts required of them would be very minimal; and (2) that if the plaintiffs diligently exerted themselves, they still would not gain the promised profits because those profits could be achieved only if the defendants secured additional investors at the inflated prices. 494 F.2d at 417. Both of these features are present in the instant case. We find *Miller* to be persuasive and consistent with *Turner.*

The defendants argue that *Miller* is distinguishable on the ground that there the contract prohibited buyers from reselling to anyone other than the sellers; whereas here the buyers were free to resell to anyone they wanted to. The defendants contend that this distinguishing feature shows that the agreement was not a common enterprise.

The defendants' argument is without merit. There was a common enterprise as required by *Turner*. The Smiths alleged that, although they were free under the terms of the contract to sell their production anywhere they wished, they could have received the promised profits only if the defendants repurchased above the market price, and that the defendants could have repurchased above the market price only if the defendants secured additional investors at inflated prices. Thus, the fortune of the Smiths was interwoven with and dependent upon the efforts and success of the defendants.

We also find that here, as in *Miller,* the third element of an investment contract set forth in *Turner*—that the efforts of those other than the investor are the undeniably significant ones—was present here. The *Miller* court noted that the plaintiffs there had been assured by the sellers that the effort needed to raise chinchillas was minimal. The significant effort necessary for success in the endeavor was that of the seller in procuring new investors who would purchase the chinchillas at inflated prices. Here, the Smiths alleged that they were promised that the effort necessary to raise worms was minimal and they alleged that they could not receive the promised income unless the defendants purchased their harvest.

We find the analysis in *Miller* persuasive and hold that the Smiths alleged facts that, if true, were sufficient to establish an investment contract.

The defendants contend that the agreement between the parties was analogous to a franchise agreement. Franchise agreements are not securities. See, e.g., Bitter v. Hoby's International, Inc., 498 F.2d 183 (9th Cir.1974). This argument is not persuasive. The franchise cases are distinguishable. In *Bitter* this court focused on the fact that a franchisee independently determines his own success. Here, according to the Smiths' allegations, the only market in the Phoenix area for their production was the guaranteed right to resell to the sellers, and, thus, the Smiths were not solely responsible for their own success. We also note that the ultimate buyers in *Bitter* were the consuming public and not as here the offering party.

The facts as alleged in the Smiths' amended complaint and affidavit establish that an investment contract existed. * * * The judgment of the district court is reversed.

NOTES

(1) The legal approach taken in this case permits a large number of ingenious investment schemes to be attacked successfully under the securities laws. Many of these investments are at best marginal and at worst fraudulent, although some entirely legitimate ones become ensnared in the broad definition of "security." The leading case is unquestionably SEC v. W.J.

Howey Co., cited in the Court's opinion. Basically, this case involved the sale of plots of citrus acreage; purchases were made in narrow strips of land arranged so that each contained a single row of 48 trees. The cultivation, harvesting, and marketing of the crop were largely centrally provided through service contracts with the seller of the land; the seller was also heavily involved in citrus production on adjoining land. The Supreme Court held that this arrangement constituted a "security" and thereby established the legal principle applied in *Smith*.

(2) The broad definition of "security" set forth in this line of cases may seem necessary in order to protect investors in marginal, nontraditional schemes. The SEC, in particular, has long argued for a broad and expansive definition, but courts have not always accepted this position. As stated by Professor John C. Coffee: "The SEC has generally looked at any kind of unorthodox instrument or syndicate and tried to see whether or not investors need protection. Courts have been more doctrinal and formal." Quoted in Karen Donovan, SEC Defines "Securities" Expansively, National Law Journal, Mar. 31, 1997, B1, at B2. The case law involves several interesting issues:

(a) Is the solicitation of a settlement proposal, which "caps" the liability of "names" previously involved in insurance syndicates promulgated by Lloyd's of London in the United States, an offering of a "security"? For a negative answer, see Allen v. Lloyd's of London, 94 F.3d 923 (4th Cir.1996).

(b) Is a "Ponzi scheme"[q] in which the Foundation for New Era Philanthropy Inc. solicited donations from wealthy individuals, churches, foundations, and educational institutions on the basis of a promise to double their money in six months a sale of securities? For an affirmative answer, see SEC v. Bennett, 904 F.Supp. 435 (E.D.Pa.1995).

(c) Is the sale of existing life insurance policies on the lives of HIV-positive individuals to investors (in order to permit the insureds to receive a portion of the face value of their policies during their lifetimes) a sale of securities? For a negative answer, see SEC v. Life Partners, Inc., 102 F.3d 587 (D.C.Cir.1996) (one judge dissenting).

(d) Is a "pyramid scheme"[r] in which much of the sales efforts to resell interests are made by investors in the enterprise a sale of securities to those investors? For a negative answer in a criminal prosecution, see United States v. Holtzclaw, 950 F.Supp. 1306 (S.D.W.Va.1997) (investors did not rely solely or primarily on the efforts of others).

(3) In Landreth Timber Co. v. Landreth, 471 U.S. 681 (1985), the Supreme Court rejected the so-called "sale of business doctrine" and held that

---

q   A Ponzi scheme is "a fraudulent investment scheme in which money contributed by later investors generates artificially high dividends for the original investors, whose example attracts even larger investments." Black's Law Dictionary [Second Pocket Edition] 536, col. 1 (2001).

r   A familiar pyramid scheme is the chain letter. A pyramid scheme is "a property-distribution scheme in which a participant pays for the chance to receive compensation for introducing new persons to the scheme, as well as for when those new persons themselves introduce participants." Black's Law Dictionary, ibid., at 574, col. 2.

the sale of all or a majority of the shares of a closely held corporation constituted the sale of a "security" subject to the federal securities acts. The principal argument of the court was a literal one based on the language of § 2(a)(1). This holding makes available the protections of the antifraud provisions of the securities acts to all sales of closely held shares (assuming that the facilities of interstate commerce are used).

G. ISSUANCE OF SHARES BY A GOING CONCERN: PREEMPTIVE RIGHTS, DILUTION, AND RECAPITALIZATIONS

STOKES V. CONTINENTAL TRUST CO. OF CITY OF NEW YORK
Court of Appeals of New York, 1906.
78 N.E. 1090.

This action was brought by a stockholder to compel his corporation to issue to him at par such a proportion of an increase made in its capital stock as the number of shares held by him before such increase bore to the number of all the shares originally issued, and in case such additional shares could not be delivered to him for his damages in the premises. The defendant is a domestic banking corporation in the city of New York, organized in 1890, with a capital stock of $500,000, consisting of 5,000 shares of the par value of $100 each. The plaintiff was one of the original stockholders, and still owns all the stock issued to him at the date of organization, together with enough more acquired since to make 221 shares in all. On the 29th of January, 1902, the defendant had a surplus of $1,048,450.94, which made the book value of the stock at that time $309.69 per share. On the 2d of January, 1902, Blair & Co., a strong and influential firm of private bankers in the city of New York, made the following proposition to the defendant: "If your stockholders at the special meeting to be called for January 29th, 1902, vote to increase your capital stock from $500,000 to $1,000,000 you may deliver the additional stock to us as soon as issued at $450 per share ($100 par value) for ourselves and our associates, it being understood that we may nominate ten of the 21 trustees to be elected at the adjourned annual meeting of stockholders." The directors of the defendant promptly met and duly authorized a special meeting of the stockholders to be called to meet on January 29, 1902, for the purpose of voting upon the proposed increase of stock and the acceptance of the offer to purchase the same. Upon due notice a meeting of the stockholders was held accordingly, more than a majority attending either in person or by proxy. A resolution to increase the stock was adopted by the vote of 4,197 shares, all that were cast. Thereupon the plaintiff demanded from the defendant the right to subscribe for 221 shares of the new stock at par, and offered to pay immediately for the same, which demand was refused. A resolution directing a sale to Blair &

Co. at $450 a share was then adopted by a vote of 3,596 shares to 241. The plaintiff voted for the first resolution, but against the last, and before the adoption of the latter he protested against the proposed sale of his proportionate share of the stock, and again demanded the right to subscribe and pay for the same, but the demand was refused. On the 30th day of January, 1902, the stock was increased, and on the same day was sold to Blair & Co. at the price named, although the plaintiff formerly renewed his demand for 221 shares of the new stock at par, and tendered payment therefor, but it was refused upon the ground that the stock had already been issued to Blair & Co. Owing in part to the offer of Blair & Co. which had become known to the public, the market price of the stock had increased from $450 a share in September, 1901, to $550 in January, 1902, and at the time of the trial, in April, 1904, it was worth $700 per share. Prior to the special meeting of the stockholders, by authority of the board of directors, a circular letter was sent to each stockholder, including the plaintiff, giving notice of the proposition made by Blair & Co. and recommending that it be accepted. Thereupon the plaintiff notified the defendant that he wished to subscribe for his proportionate share of the new stock, if issued, and at no time did he waive his right to subscribe for the same. Before the special meeting, he had not been definitely notified by the defendant that he could not receive his proportionate part of the increase, but was informed that his proposition would "be taken under consideration." After finding these facts in substance, the trial court found, as conclusions of law, that the plaintiff had the right to subscribe for such proportion of the increase, as his holdings bore to all the stock before the increase was made; that the stockholders, directors, and officers of the defendant had no power to deprive him of that right, and that he was entitled to recover the difference between the market value of 221 shares on the 30th of January, 1902, and the par value thereof, or the sum of $99,450, together with interest from said date. The judgment entered accordingly was reversed by the Appellate Division, and the plaintiff appealed to this court, giving the usual stipulation for judgment absolute in case the order of reversal should be affirmed.

VANN, J. (after stating the facts). * * * Thus the question presented for decision is whether according to the facts found the plaintiff had the legal right to subscribe for and take the same number of shares of the new stock that he held of the old? The subject is not regulated by statute, and the question presented has never been directly passed upon by this court, and only to a limited extent has it been considered by courts in this state. * * *

If the right claimed by the plaintiff was a right of property belonging to him as a stockholder, he could not be deprived of it by the joint action of the other stockholders, and of all the directors and officers of the corporation. What is the nature of the right acquired by a stockholder through the ownership of shares of stock? What rights can he assert against the will of a majority of the stockholders, and all the officers and directors? While he does not own and cannot dispose of any specific property of the corporation, yet he and his associates own the corporation itself, its charter, franchises, and all rights conferred thereby, including the right to increase the stock. He has an inherent right to his proportionate share of any dividend declared, or of any surplus arising upon dissolution, and he can prevent waste or misappropriation of the property of the corporation by those in control. Finally, he has the right to vote for directors and upon all propositions subject by law to the control of the stockholders, and this is his supreme right and main protection. Stockholders have no direct voice in transacting the corporate business, but through their right to vote they can select those to whom the law [entrusts] the power of management and control. * * * This right to vote for directors, and upon propositions to increase the stock or mortgage the assets, is about all the power the stockholder has. So long as the management is honest, within the corporate powers, and involves no waste, the stockholders cannot interfere, even if the administration is feeble and unsatisfactory, but must correct such evils through their power to elect other directors. Hence, the power of the individual stockholder to vote in proportion to the number of his shares is vital, and cannot be cut off or curtailed by the action of all the other stockholders, even with the co-operation of the directors and officers.

In the case before us the new stock came into existence through the exercise of a right belonging wholly to the stockholders. As the right to increase the stock belonged to them, the stock when increased belonged to them also, as it was issued for money and not for property or for some purpose other than the sale thereof for money. By the increase of stock the voting power of the plaintiff was reduced one-half, and while he consented to the increase he did not consent to the disposition of the new stock by a sale thereof to Blair & Co. at less than its market value, nor by sale to any person in any way except by an allotment to the stockholders. * * * The plaintiff had power, before the increase of stock, to vote on 221 shares of stock, out of a total of 5,000, at any meeting held by the stockholders for any purpose. By the action of the majority, taken against his will and protest, he now has only one-half the voting power that he had before, because the number of shares has been doubled while he still owns but 221. This touches him as a stockholder in such a way as to deprive him of a right of property. Blair & Co. acquired virtual control, while he and the other stockholders lost it. We are not discussing equities, but legal rights, for this is an action at law, and the plaintiff was deprived of a strictly legal right. If the result gives him an advantage over other stockholders, it is because he stood upon his legal rights, while they did not. The question is what were his legal rights, not what his profit may be under the sale to Blair & Co., but what it might have been if the new stock had been issued to him in proportion to his holding of the old.

The other stockholders could give their property to Blair & Co., but they could not give his. * * *

We are thus led to lay down the rule that a stockholder has an inherent right to a proportionate share of new stock issued for money only and not to purchase property for the purposes of the corporation or to effect a consolidation, and while he can waive that right, he cannot be deprived of it without his consent except when the stock is issued at a fixed price not less than par, and he is given the right to take at that price in proportion to his holding, or in some other equitable way that will enable him to protect his interest by acting on his own judgment and using his own resources. This rule is just to all and tends to prevent the tyranny of majorities which needs restraint, as well as virtual attempts to blackmail by small minorities which should be prevented. * * *

[The court concluded that the plaintiff's damages should have been measured by the difference between the $450 sale price and the $550 market value of the shares rather than the difference between par value and market value of the shares.]

The order appealed from should be reversed and the judgment of the trial court modified by reducing the damages from the sum of $99,450, with interest from January 30, 1902, to the sum of $22,100, with interest from that date, and by striking out the extra allowance of costs, and as thus modified the judgment of the trial court is affirmed, without costs in this court or in the Appellate Division to either party.

HAIGHT, J. (dissenting). [Opinion omitted.]

CULLEN, C.J., and WERNER and HISCOCK, JJ., concur with VANN, J.; WILLARD BARLETT, J., concurs with HAIGHT, J.; O'BRIEN, J., absent.

NOTES

(1) The common law preemptive right discussed in *Stokes* is now embodied in state statutes, of which there is considerable diversity. See MBCA § 6.30, which provides standard terms on an elective basis to codify many aspects of the preemptive right.

(2) It is now generally accepted that the preemptive right is not an inherent aspect of the ownership of shares but a right that may be granted or withheld by the articles of incorporation. The MBCA adopts an "opt in" clause: under § 6.30(a), no preemptive right exists unless provision for it is expressly made. As a result, a "plain vanilla" corporation whose articles of incorporation contain the statutory minima will not have preemptive rights. Would not the converse (i.e., that a corporation has preemptive rights unless expressly denied in the articles of incorporation) be preferable? Several states have adopted an "opt out" rather than an "opt in" provision.

(3) If a corporation elects preemptive rights, should that right extend to shares issued as compensation to directors or officers? See MBCA

§ 6.30(b)(3)(i) and (ii). Does that not tend to frustrate the purpose of preemptive rights whenever one shareholder is an officer of the corporation and others are not? Why should shares "sold otherwise than for money" not be subject to preemptive rights? See MBCA § 6.30(b)(3)(iv). What is the justification for excluding shares issued within six months of the formation of the corporation? See MBCA § 6.30(b)(3)(iii). What about shares that are offered preemptively, but not purchased? May they be sold entirely free of such rights in the future? See MBCA § 6.30(b)(6).

KATZOWITZ V. SIDLER

Court of Appeals of New York, 1969.
249 N.E.2d 359.

KEATING, JUDGE.

Isador Katzowitz is a director and stockholder of a close corporation. Two other persons, Jacob Sidler and Max Lasker, own the remaining securities and, with Katzowitz, comprise Sulburn Holding Corp.'s board of directors. Sulburn was organized in 1955 to supply propane gas to three other corporations controlled by these men. Sulburn's certificate of incorporation authorized it to issue 1,000 shares of no par value stock for which the incorporators established a $100 selling price. Katzowitz, Sidler and Lasker each invested $500 and received five shares of the corporation's stock.

The three men had been jointly engaged in several corporate ventures for more than 25 years. In this period they had always been equal partners and received identical compensation from the corporations they controlled. Though all the corporations controlled by these three men prospered, disenchantment with their inter-personal relationship flared into the open in 1956. At this time, Sidler and Lasker joined forces to oust Katzowitz from any role in managing the corporations. * * *

Before the issue could be tried, the three men entered into a stipulation in 1959 whereby Katzowitz withdrew from active participation in the day-to-day operations of the business. The agreement provided that he would remain on the boards of all the corporations, and each board would be limited to three members composed of the three stockholders or their designees. Katzowitz was to receive the same compensation and other fringe benefits which the controlled corporations paid Lasker and Sidler. The stipulation also provided that Katzowitz, Sidler and Lasker were "equal stockholders and each of said parties now owns the same number of shares of stock in each of the defendant corporations and that such shares of stock shall continue to be in full force and effect and unaffected by this stipulation, except as hereby otherwise expressly provided." The stipulation contained no other provision affecting equal stock interests.

The business relationship established by the stipulation was fully complied with. Sidler and Lasker, however, were still interested in disassociating themselves from Katzowitz. * * *

In December of 1961 Sulburn was indebted to each stockholder to the extent of $2,500 for fees and commissions earned up until September, 1961. Instead of paying this debt, Sidler and Lasker wanted Sulburn to loan the money to another corporation which all three men controlled. Sidler and Lasker called a meeting of the board of directors to propose that additional securities be offered at $100 per share to substitute for the money owed to the directors. The notice of meeting for October 30, 1961 had on its agenda "a proposition that the corporation issue common stock of its unissued common capital stock, *the total par value [of] which shall equal the total sum of the fees and commissions now owing by the corporation to its * * * directors.*" (Emphasis added.) Katzowitz made it quite clear at the meeting that he would not invest any additional funds in Sulburn in order for it to make a loan to this other corporation. The only resolution passed at the meeting was that the corporation would pay the sum of $2,500 to each director.

With full knowledge that Katzowitz expected to be paid his fees and commissions and that he did not want to participate in any new stock issuance, the other two directors called a special meeting of the board on December 1, 1961. The only item on the agenda for this special meeting was the issuance of 75 shares of the corporation's common stock at $100 per share. The offer was to be made to stockholders in "accordance with their respective preemptive rights for the purpose of acquiring additional working capital." The amount to be raised was the exact amount owed by the corporation to its shareholders. The offering price for the securities was 1/18th the book value of the stock. Only Sidler and Lasker attended the special board meeting. They approved the issuance of the 75 shares.

Notice was mailed to each stockholder that they had the right to purchase 25 shares of the corporation's stock at $100 a share. The offer was to expire on December 27, 1961. Failure to act by that date was stated to constitute a waiver. At about the same time Katzowitz received the notice, he received a check for $2,500 from the corporation for his fees and commissions. Katzowitz did not exercise his option to buy the additional shares. Sidler and Lasker purchased their full complement, 25 shares each. This purchase by Sidler and Lasker caused an immediate dilution of the book value of the outstanding securities.

On August 25, 1962 the principal asset of Sulburn, a tractor trailer truck, was destroyed. On August 31, 1962 the directors unanimously voted to dissolve the corporation. Upon dissolution, Sidler and Lasker each received $18,885.52 but Katzowitz only received $3,147.59.

The plaintiff instituted a declaratory judgment action to establish his right to the proportional interest in the assets of Sulburn in liquidation less the $5,000 which Sidler and Lasker used to purchase their shares in December, 1961.

Special Term (Westchester County) found the book value of the corporation's securities on the day the stock was offered at $100 to be worth $1,800. The court also found that "the individual defendants * * * decided that in lieu of taking that sum in cash [the commissions and fees due the stockholders], they preferred to add to their investment by having the corporate defendant make available and offer each stockholder an additional twenty-five shares of unissued stock." The court reasoned that Katzowitz waived his right to purchase the stock or object to its sale to Lasker and Sidler by failing to exercise his preemptive right and found his protest at the time of dissolution untimely.

* * * On the substantive legal issues and findings of fact, the Appellate Division [two Justices dissenting, 29 App.Div.2d 955, 289 N.Y.S.2d 324] was in agreement with Special Term. The majority agreed that the book value of the corporation's stock at the time of the stock offering was $1,800. The Appellate Division reasoned, however, that showing a disparity between book value and offering price was insufficient without also showing fraud or overreaching. Disparity in price by itself was not enough to prove fraud. The Appellate Division also found that the plaintiff had waived his right to object to his recovery in dissolution by failing to either exercise his pre-emptive rights or take steps to prevent the sale of the stock.

The concept of pre-emptive rights was fashioned by the judiciary to safeguard two distinct interests of stockholders—the right to protection against dilution of their equity in the corporation and protection against dilution of their proportionate voting control. (Ballantine, Corporations [rev. ed., 1946], § 209.) After early decisions (Gray v. Portland Bank, 3 Mass. 364; Stokes v. Continental Trust Co., 186 N.Y. 285, 78 N.E. 1090, 12 L.R.A., N.S., 969), legislation fixed the right enunciated with respect to proportionate voting but left to the judiciary the role of protecting existing shareholders from the dilution of their equity (e.g., Stock Corporation Law, § 39, now Business Corporation Law, Consol.Laws, c. 4, § 622; see Drinker, The Preemptive Right of Shareholders to Subscribe to New Shares, 43 Harv.L.Rev. 586; Alexander Hamilton Frey, Shareholders' Pre-emptive Rights, 38 Yale L.J. 563).

It is clear that directors of a corporation have no discretion in the choice of those to whom the earnings and assets of the corporation should be distributed. Directors, being fiduciaries of the corporation, must, in issuing new stock, treat existing shareholders fairly. Though there is very little statutory control over the price which a corporation must receive for new shares the power to determine price must be exercised for the benefit of the corporation and in the interest of all the stockholders.

Issuing stock for less than fair value can injure existing shareholders by diluting their interest in the corporation's surplus, in current and future earnings and in the assets upon liquidation. Normally, a stockholder is protected from the loss of his equity from dilution, even though the stock is being offered at less than fair value, because the shareholder receives rights which he may either exercise or sell. If he exercises, he has protected his interest and, if not, he can sell the rights, thereby compensating himself for the dilution of his remaining shares in the equity of the corporation.[2]

When new shares are issued, however, at prices far below fair value in a close corporation or a corporation with only a limited market for its shares, existing stockholders, who do not want to invest or do not have the capacity to invest additional funds, can have their equity interest in the corporation diluted to the vanishing point.

The protection afforded by stock rights is illusory in close corporations. Even if a buyer could be found for the rights, they would have to be sold at an inadequate price because of the nature of a close corporation. Outsiders are normally discouraged from acquiring minority interests after a close corporation has been organized. Certainly a stockholder in a close corporation is at a total loss to safeguard his equity from dilution if no rights are offered and he does not want to invest additional funds.

Though it is difficult to determine fair value for a corporation's securities and courts are therefore reluctant to get into the thicket, when the issuing price is shown to be markedly below book value in a close corporation and when the remaining shareholder-directors benefit from the issuance, a case for judicial relief has been established. In that instance, the corporation's directors must show that the issuing price falls within some range which can be justified on the basis of valid business reasons. If no such showing is made by the directors, there is no reason for the judiciary to abdicate its function to a majority of the board or stockholders who have not seen fit to come forward and justify the propriety of diverting property from the corporation and allow the issuance of securities to become an oppressive device permitting the dilution of the equity of dissident stockholders.

The defendant directors here make no claim that the price set was a fair one. No business justification is offered to sustain it. Admittedly, the stock was sold at less than book value. The defendants simply contend that, as long as all stockholders were given an equal opportunity to

---

[2]   There is little justification for issuing stock far below its fair value. The only reason for issuing stock below fair value exists in publicly held corporations where the problem of floating new issues through subscription is concerned. The reason advanced in this situation is that it insures the success of the issue or that it has the same psychological effect as a dividend. * * *

purchase additional shares, no stockholder can complain simply because the offering dilutes his interest in the corporation.

The defendants' argument is fallacious.

The corollary of a stockholder's right to maintain his proportionate equity in a corporation by purchasing additional shares is the right not to purchase additional shares without being confronted with dilution of his existing equity if no valid business justification exists for the dilution.

A stockholder's right not to purchase is seriously undermined if the stock offered is worth substantially more than the offering price. Any purchase at this price dilutes his interest and impairs the value of his original holding. "A corporation is not permitted to sell its stock for a legally inadequate price at least where there is objection. Plaintiff has a right to insist upon compliance with the law whether or not he cares to exercise his option. He cannot block a sale for a fair price merely because he disagrees with the wisdom of the plan but he can insist that the sale price be fixed in accordance with legal requirements." (Bennett v. Breuil Petroleum Corp., [34 Del.Ch. 6, 14–15, 99 A.2d 236, 241 (1953)]. Judicial review in this area is limited to whether under all the circumstances, including the disparity between issuing price of the stock and its true value, the nature of the corporation, the business necessity for establishing an offering price at a certain amount to facilitate raising new capital, and the ability of stockholders to sell rights, the additional offering of securities should be condemned because the directors in establishing the sale price did not fix it with reference to financial considerations with respect to the ready disposition of securities.

Here the obvious disparity in selling price and book value was calculated to force the dissident stockholder into investing additional sums. No valid business justification was advanced for the disparity in price, and the only beneficiaries of the disparity were the two director-stockholders who were eager to have additional capital in the business.

It is no answer to Katzowitz' action that he was also given a chance to purchase additional shares at this bargain rate. The price was not so much a bargain as it was a tactic, conscious or unconscious on the part of the directors, to place Katzowitz in a compromising situation. The price was so fixed to make the failure to invest costly. However, Katzowitz at the time might not have been aware of the dilution because no notice of the effect of the issuance of the new shares on the already outstanding shares was disclosed. In addition, since the stipulation entitled Katzowitz to the same compensation as Sidler and Lasker, the disparity in equity interest caused by their purchase of additional securities in 1961 did not affect stockholder income from Sulburn and, therefore, Katzowitz possibly was not aware of the effect of the stock issuance on his interest in the corporation until dissolution.

No reason exists at this time to permit Sidler and Lasker to benefit from their course of conduct. Katzowitz' delay in commencing the action did not prejudice the defendants. By permitting the defendants to recover their additional investment in Sulburn before the remaining assets of Sulburn are distributed to the stockholders upon dissolution, all the stockholders will be treated equitably. Katzowitz, therefore, should receive his aliquot share of the assets of Sulburn less the amount invested by Sidler and Lasker for their purchase of stock on December 27, 1961.

Accordingly, the order of the Appellate Division should be reversed, with costs, and judgment granted in favor of the plaintiff against the individual defendants.

BURKE, SCILEPPI, BERGAN, BREITEL and JASEN, JJ., concur with KEATING, J.

FULD, C.J., dissents and votes to affirm on the opinion at the Appellate Division.

NOTES

(1) The transaction involved in *Katzowitz* is a type of "freeze-out." A similar type of freeze-out occurs when inside shareholders pay for their additional shares by canceling debts owed to them by the corporation (representing, in effect, capital that they have already invested in the business), while outside shareholders are put to the painful choice of investing fresh capital over which they lose effective control or see their proportionate interest decline drastically. A classic example is Hyman v. Velsicol Corp., 97 N.E.2d 122 (Ill.App.1951), where an outside shareholder was given the choice of investing an additional $136,000 in order to stay even or watching his proportional interest decline from 20 percent to a fraction of one percent. What did the shareholder do? He sued, of course, but lost when the court concluded that the plan "was not an abuse of discretion" and was not "fraudulently oppressive." As in *Katzowitz,* the shareholder's preemptive right was fully protected and shares were issued at par value, arguably below "true value." However, there was some business justification for the transaction since the majority shareholders were cancelling outstanding indebtedness owed to them and the plaintiff was a former employee who was interested in a competing business.

(2) Some freeze-out cases have been brought under the theory that the plan constitutes a violation of fiduciary duties. See generally Mark K. Kessler, Elimination of Minority Interests by Cash Merger: Two Recent Cases, 30 Bus.Law. 699 (1975). Cases have also adopted the view that transactions literally complying with statutory requirements may be set aside if they do not meet a standard of "entire fairness" when they involve conflict of interest transactions. See Weinberger v. UOP, Inc., 457 A.2d 701 (Del.1983); see also Alpert v. 28 Williams St. Corp., 473 N.E.2d 19 (N.Y.1984). The modern trend seems clearly to be running in the direction of imposing a fiduciary duty on dilutive transactions such as those involved in

Katzowitz. In the words of the Mississippi Supreme Court, "[t]he traditional view that shareholders have no fiduciary duty to each other, and [that] transactions constituting 'freeze-outs' or 'squeezeouts' generally cannot be attacked as a breach of [the] duty of loyalty or good faith to each other, is outmoded." Fought v. Morris, 543 So.2d 167, 169 (Miss.1989); see also Johnston v. Wilbourn, 760 F.Supp. 578, 582 (S.D.Miss.1991). In light of this trend, it is doubtful that older cases such as the above-mentioned *Hyman v. Velsicol* would be decided the same way if they arose today. See generally F. Hodge O'Neal, Oppression of Minority Shareholders: Protecting Minority Rights, 35 Clev.St.L.Rev. 121 (1987).

LACOS LAND COMPANY V. ARDEN GROUP, INC.

Court of Chancery of Delaware, 1986.
517 A.2d 271.

ALLEN, CHANCELLOR.

This action constitutes a multi-pronged attack upon a proposed recapitalization of defendant Arden Group, Inc., authorized by a vote of Arden's shareholders at their June 10, 1986 annual meeting. The recapitalization, if effectuated, will create a new Class B Common Stock possessing ten votes per share and entitled, as a class, to elect seventy-five percent of the members of Arden's board of directors. This new stock is, pursuant to the terms of a presently pending exchange offer, available on a share-for-share basis to all holders of Arden's Class A Common Stock. It is, however, acknowledged by defendants that the new Class B Common Stock has been deliberately fashioned to be attractive mainly to defendant Briskin—Arden's principal shareholder and chief executive officer. Thus, the recapitalization is not itself a device to raise capital but rather is a technique to transfer stockholder control of the enterprise to Mr. Briskin.

Plaintiff is an Arden stockholder owning approximately 4.5% of Arden's Class A Common Stock * * *. Defendants are the members of Arden's board of directors. Pending is an application to preliminarily enjoin the issuance of Class B Common Stock * * *.

     * * *

I.

The new supervoting common stock whose issuance is sought to be enjoined will differ from Arden's other authorized class of common stock, Class A Common Stock, most importantly, in its enhanced voting power, its diminished dividend rights and in restrictions upon its transfer.

Specifically, with respect to voting rights, the recent charter amendment provides that "on every matter submitted to a vote or consent of the stockholder, every holder of Class A Common Stock shall be entitled to one vote * * * for each share * * * and every holder of Class B Common Stock shall be entitled to 10 votes * * * for each share * * *."

As to the election of directors, the restated certificate provides that Class A shares, together with the Company's preferred stock, voting as a class shall "be entitled to elect 25% of the total number of directors to be elected" rounded up to the nearest whole number. The Class B shares are entitled to vote as a separate class and to elect the remaining 75% of directors to be elected.[1]

With respect to dividend rights, Class A Common Stock will, following the initial issuance of Class B shares, have the right to receive a one-time dividend of $.30 per share; Class B shares are to have no right to participate to any extent in that cash dividend. Excepting this one-time $.30 dividend, each share of Class B stock is to be entitled to participate in all dividends declared and paid with respect to a share of Class A stock but only to the extent of 90% of such dividend.

Class B shares may be transferred only to a Permitted Transferee,[2] but under certain circumstances may be converted on a share-for-share basis into Class A stock. A transfer of Class B to a person other than a Permitted Transferee at a time when conversion to Class A would be permitted would convert the transferred stock into Class A stock. Generally, Class B stock may, at the option of the holder, be converted to Class A stock on a share-for-share basis at the earlier of (i) the third anniversary of its issuance or (ii) the death of the holder.

* * *

II.

The creation of a dual common stock structure with one class exercising effective control of the company is, of course, not a novel idea, although it is one that, thanks to its potential as an anti-takeover device, has recently emerged from the reaches of the corporation law chorus to strut its moment upon center stage where corporate drama is acted out. In this instance, the notion of employing this dual common stock structure apparently originated with defendant Briskin.

Mr. Briskin became Arden chief executive officer in 1976 at a time when the Company was apparently in a desperate condition. Its stock was then trading between $1 and $2 per share. Briskin's stewardship has

---

[1] If, on the record date for the meeting to elect directors, the Class B shares equal less than 12 1/2% of the total of Class A and Class B shares together, then Class A will continue to vote as a class in the filling of 25% of the positions to be filled but will have the right to vote in the Class B election as well, with Class B shares continuing to be entitled to ten votes per share.

[2] For a natural person Permitted Transferees include (1) the holder's spouse or any lineal descendant of a grandparent of the holder or the holder's spouse, (2) the trustee of any trust for the benefit of the holder or a Permitted Transferee, (3) charitable organizations, (4) a corporation or partnership under majority control of the holder or a Permitted Transferee and (5) the holder's estate.

apparently been active and effective. While Arden has paid no dividends since 1970, during Briskin's tenure Arden's stock price has risen steadily; currently Arden common stock is publicly trading at around $25 per share, a price somewhat higher than the range of prices at which its stock traded in the weeks prior to the announcement of the plan that is the subject matter of this litigation.

In instigating the dual common stock voting structure, Mr. Briskin was apparently not responding to any specific threat to existing policies or practices of Arden posed by a specific takeover threat. Rather, he apparently was motivated to protect his power to control Arden's business future. Such a motivation, while it may be suspect—since it may reflect not a desire to protect business policies and capabilities for the benefit of the corporation and its shareholders but rather a wish simply to retain the benefits of office—does not itself constitute a wrong. See, e.g., Unocal Corp. v. Mesa Petroleum Co., Del. Supr., 493 A.2d 946, 955 (1985).

In this instance, Briskin initially took his idea to the board of directors at its November 22, 1985 meeting. The Board established a three member committee of non-officer directors to consider the matter. Prior to the committee's first meeting, its chairman sent the other two committee members the proxy statement of another company that had adopted a dual class common stock structure, together with materials on other companies that had adopted supervoting plans and some materials relating to a report written by Professor Fischel on "Organized Exchanges and the Regulation of Dual Class Common Stock." The special committee retained neither independent counsel nor an independent financial advisor. At its first meeting, held on April 7, 1986, the chairman of this group distributed to the committee a draft report that he had previously prepared which gave approval to a supervoting stock plan. The committee reviewed this draft and suggested changes. The chairman noted the suggested changes and prepared a final three page report which was signed four days later at the committee's second, and final, meeting.

The committee's report was presented to the board at its April 22 meeting at which time the board approved the supervoting stock plan.

At that meeting the board fixed the date of the Company's annual meeting for June 10, 1986. Management of the Company prepared a proxy statement describing the proposed charter amendments authorizing the new supervoting Class B Common Stock, describing the Exchange Offer by which it was proposed that such new stock be distributed and setting out the background of, and the reasons for, this proposal.

At the June 10 annual meeting, the Arden stockholders approved the proposed certificate amendments. Of 2,303,170 shares outstanding, 1,463,155 voted in favor (64%) and 325,004 (14%) voted to reject the proposal. Of the affirmative votes, 427,347 were voted by Briskin or his family and 388,493 were voted by a trustee as directed by Arden's management. As to the preferred stock, 74.4% of the 136,359 shares outstanding voted in favor of the proposal, more than half of which were voted by a trustee as directed by Arden's management.

As a consequence of the stockholders' approval of the proposal, the Company, on June 18, 1986, distributed to all holders of its Class A Common Stock an Offering Circular offering to exchange for each share of such common stock one share of Class B Common Stock with the rights, preferences, etc. described above.

III.

Our corporation law provides great flexibility to shareholders in creating the capital structure of their firm. Differing classes of stock with differing voting rights are permissible under our law, 8 Del.C. sec. 151(a); restriction on transfers are possible, 8 Del.C. sec. 202; and charter provisions requiring the filling of certain directorates by a class of stock are, if otherwise properly adopted, valid. Thus, each of the significant characteristics of the Class B Common Stock is in principle a valid power or limitation of common stock. The primary inquiry therefore is whether the Arden shareholders have effectively exercised their will to amend the Company's restated certificate of incorporation so as to authorize the implementation of the dual class common stock structure. * * *

For the reasons that follow I conclude that plaintiff has demonstrated a reasonable probability that on final hearing it will be demonstrated that the June 10, 1986 vote of the Arden shareholders has been fundamentally and fatally flawed and that, therefore, the amendments to Arden's restated certificate of incorporation purportedly authorized by that vote are voidable. * * * I conclude provisionally on the basis of the record now available, that the June 10 vote was inappropriately affected by an explicit threat of Mr. Briskin that unless the proposed amendments were approved, he would use his power (and not simply his power qua shareholder) to block transactions that may be in the best interests of the company, if those transactions would dilute his ownership interest in Arden. I use the word threat because such a position entails, in my opinion, the potential for a breach of Mr. Briskin's duty, as the principal officer of Arden and as a member of its board of directors, to exercise corporate power unselfishly, with a view to fostering the interests of the corporation and all of its shareholders. * * *

IV.

Judging from what is stated in the proxy materials, Arden's board in recommending the charter amendments and Arden's shareholders in approving them were both placed, inappropriately, in a position that made it significantly [more] likely than it might otherwise have been that approval of the plan to effectively transfer all shareholder power to Mr. Briskin would have been given.

To a shareholder who wondered why his board of directors was recommending a plan expected to place all effective shareholder power in a single shareholder, the proxy statement gives a clear answer: Mr. Briskin is demanding it; it's not such a big deal anyway since, as a practical matter, he has great power already; and if he doesn't get these amendments, he may exercise his power to thwart corporate transactions that may be in the Company's best interests. Thus, in order for the board to be "permitted to consider" certain transactions that might threaten to reduce Mr. Briskin's control, the board approved the proposal. This story is disclosed more or less straight forwardly in the proxy solicitation materials.

As to Mr. Briskin's position, the proxy statement states:

Purpose and Effects of the Proposal

1. **Purpose**. Mr. Briskin, the Company's largest single stockholder * * * has informed the Company of his concern that certain transactions which could be determined by the Board of Directors to be in the best interests of all of the stockholders, such as the issuance of additional voting securities in connection with financings or mergers or acquisitions by the Company, might make the Company vulnerable to an unsolicited or hostile takeover attempt or to an attempt at "greenmail," and that he would not give his support to any such transactions for which his approval might be required unless steps were taken to secure his voting position in the Company.

As to the asserted fact that Mr. Briskin already really has, as a practical matter, the power to control the Company, the proxy statement says (immediately following the foregoing quoted matter):

As a practical matter, given the present stock ownership of Mr. Briskin and certain supermajority vote requirements and other provisions of the existing Certificate (see "Possible Adverse Consequences"), explicit or implicit approval of Mr. Briskin would be required for every such major transaction the Company might choose to engage in (whether or not a vote of stockholders is actually required). Similarly, it is unlikely that the Company would engage in transactions to which Mr. Briskin is opposed. Such transactions, including the issuance of additional capital stock, although dilutive of Mr. Briskin's stock ownership, could be in the best interests of stockholders other than Mr. Briskin. * * *

Thus, Arden shareholders were unmistakably told that should they fail to approve the proposed amendments, Mr. Briskin "would not give his support to any transaction [that might make the Company vulnerable to an unsolicited or hostile takeover attempt] for which his approval might be required." Using the term in the vague way which we ordinarily do, a vote in such circumstances as these could be said to be "coerced." But that label itself supplies no basis to conclude that the legal effect of the vote is impaired in any way. * * *

The determination of whether it was inappropriate for Mr. Briskin to structure the choice of Arden's shareholders (and its directors), as was done here, requires, first, a determination of which of his hats—shareholder, officer or director—Mr. Briskin was wearing when he stated his position concerning the possible withholding of his "support" for future transactions unless steps were taken "to secure his voting position." If he spoke only as a shareholder, and should have been so understood, an evaluation of the propriety of his position might be markedly different than if the "support" referred to could be or should be interpreted as involving the exercise of his power as either an officer or director of Arden.

On this point defendants' position at oral argument confirms that which the proxy language itself indicates—that, in taking this position, Mr. Briskin did not limit, and could not be understood to have limited, himself to exercising only stockholder power. Defendants have emphasized that Briskin's "practical" power derives in part from his notable success as a chief executive officer; his history of success, I was reminded, creates influence and his position confers power to initiate board consideration of important matters. Moreover, the proxy statement made clear that the approval that Briskin threatened to withhold included approval of transactions that did not require a vote of stockholders. Accordingly, the conclusion seems inescapable that, in announcing an intent to withhold support for corporate action that might entail, for instance, the issuance of stock, even if that act might be in the best interests of the corporation, unless "steps were taken to preserve his voting position," Mr. Briskin could not be understood to have been acting only as a shareholder.

As a director and as an officer, of course, Mr. Briskin has a duty to act with complete loyalty to the interests of the corporation and its shareholders. Weinberger v. UOP, Inc., Del. Supr., 457 A.2d 701 (1983); Guth v. Loft, Del. Supr., 23 Del. Ch. 255, 5 A.2d 503 (1939). His position as stated to the shareholders in the Company proxy statement seems inconsistent with that obligation. In form at least, the statement by a director and officer that he will not give his support to a corporate transaction unless steps are taken to confer a personal power or benefit, suggests an evident disregard of duty. However, the nature of the quid pro quo sought by Mr. Briskin in this case is at least consistent with a benign or selfless motive. The Class B stock he sought to have the board recommend and the stockholders approve would transfer complete control of the enterprise to him for an indefinite period, but it is a control that may not be transferred generally and so it is unlikely that Mr. Briskin was motivated to gain access to a control premium for his stock by insisting on a device of this kind as a price of his supporting certain types of future action.

* * *

Mr. Briskin's motivation in fact, however, need not be determined in order to conclude that the stockholder vote of June 10, 1986 was fatally flawed by the implied (indeed, the expressed) threats that unless the proposed amendments were authorized, he would oppose transactions "which could be determined by the Board of Directors to be in the best interests of all of the stockholders." As a corporate fiduciary, Mr. Briskin has no right to take such a position, even if benevolently motivated in doing so. Shareholders who respect Mr. Briskin's ability and performance—and who are legally entitled to his undivided loyalty—were inappropriately placed in a position in which they were told that if they refused to vote affirmatively, Mr. Briskin would not support future possible transactions that might be beneficial to the corporation. A vote of shareholders under such circumstances cannot, in the face of a timely challenge by one of the corporation's shareholders, be said, in my opinion, to satisfy the mandate of Section 242(b) of our corporation law requiring shareholder consent to charter amendments. * * *

For the foregoing reasons, plaintiff's motion shall be granted. Plaintiff shall submit a form of implementing order on notice.

NOTES

(1) Since it appears clear that Mr. Briskin was firmly in control of this corporation anyway, why did he want to effectuate this recapitalization?

(2) Can you think of any reasons for doing the proposed recapitalization that would have passed judicial scrutiny? If so, was Mr. Briskin being punished for his honesty?

H. DISTRIBUTIONS BY A CLOSELY HELD CORPORATION

DODGE v. FORD MOTOR CO.
Supreme Court of Michigan, 1919.
170 N.W. 668.

OSTRANDER, C.J.

[Plaintiffs are minority shareholders in the Ford Motor Company. At the time, Henry Ford, president of the company, owned 58 percent of the outstanding capital stock.]

* * *

The cause came on for hearing in open court on the 21st of May, 1917. A large volume of testimony was taken, with the result that a decree was entered December 5, 1917, in and by which it is decreed that within 30 days from the entry thereof the directors of the Ford Motor Company declare a dividend upon all of the shares of stock in an amount equivalent to one-half of, and payable out of, the accumulated cash surplus of said Ford Motor Company, on hand at the close of the fiscal year ending July 31, 1916, less the aggregate amount of the special dividends declared and paid after the filing of the bill and during the year ending July 31, 1917; the amount to be declared being $19,275,385.96.
* * *

* * *

When plaintiffs made their complaint and demand for further dividends, the Ford Motor Company had concluded its most prosperous year of business. The demand for its cars at the price of the preceding year continued. It could make and could market in the year beginning August 1, 1916, more than 500,000 cars. Sales of parts and repairs would necessarily increase. The cost of materials was likely to advance, and perhaps the price of labor; but it reasonably might have expected a profit for the year of upwards of $60,000,000. It had assets of more than $132,000,000, a surplus of almost $112,000,000, and its cash on hand and municipal bonds were nearly $54,000,000. Its total liabilities, including capital stock, was a little over $20,000,000. It had declared no special dividend during the business year except the October, 1915, dividend. It had been the practice, under similar circumstances, to declare larger dividends. Considering only these facts, a refusal to declare and pay further dividends appears to be not an exercise of discretion on the part of the directors, but an arbitrary refusal to do what the circumstances required to be done. These facts and others call upon the directors to justify their action, or failure or refusal to act. In justification, the defendants have offered testimony tending to prove, and which does prove, the following facts: It had been the policy of the corporation for a considerable time to annually reduce the selling price of cars, while keeping up, or improving, their quality. As early as in June, 1915, a general plan for the expansion of the productive capacity of the concern by a practical duplication of its plant had been talked over by the executive officers and directors and agreed upon; not all of the details having been settled, and no formal action of directors having been taken. The erection of a smelter was considered, and engineering and other data in connection therewith secured. In consequence, it was determined not to reduce the selling price of cars for the year beginning August 1, 1915, but to maintain the price and to accumulate a large surplus to pay for the proposed expansion of plant and equipment, and perhaps to build a plant for smelting ore. It is hoped, by Mr. Ford, that eventually, 1,000,000 cars will be annually produced. The contemplated changes will permit the increased output.

The plan, as affecting the profits of the business for the year beginning August 1, 1916, and thereafter, calls for a reduction in the selling price of the cars. It is true that this price might be at any time increased, but the plan called for the reduction in price of $80 a car. The capacity of the plant, without the additions thereto voted to be made (without a part of them at least), would produce more than 600,000 cars annually. This number, and more, could have been sold for $440 instead of $360, a difference in the return for capital, labor, and materials employed of at least $48,000,000. In short, the plan does not call for and is not intended to produce immediately a more profitable business, but a less profitable one; not only less profitable than formerly, but less profitable than it is admitted it might be made. The apparent immediate effect will be to diminish the value of shares and the returns to shareholders.

It is the contention of plaintiffs that the apparent effect of the plan is intended to be the continued and continuing effect of it, and that it is deliberately proposed, not of record and not by official corporate declaration, but nevertheless proposed, to continue the corporation henceforth as a semi-eleemosynary institution and not as a business institution. In support of this contention, they point to the attitude and to the expressions of Mr. Henry Ford.

Mr. Henry Ford is the dominant force in the business of the Ford Motor Company. No plan of operations could be adopted unless he consented, and no board of directors can be elected whom he does not favor. One of the directors of the company has no stock. One share was assigned to him to qualify him for the position, but it is not claimed that he owns it. A business, one of the largest in the world, and one of the most profitable, has been built up. It employs many men, at good pay.

"My ambition," said Mr. Ford, "is to employ still more men, to spread the benefits of this industrial system to the greatest possible number, to help them build up their lives and their homes. To do this we are putting the greatest share of our profits back in the business."

"With regard to dividends, the company paid sixty percent on its capitalization of two million dollars, or $1,200,000, leaving $58,000,000 to reinvest for the growth of the company. This is Mr. Ford's policy at present, and it is understood that the other stockholders cheerfully accede to this plan."

He had made up his mind in the summer of 1916 that no dividends other than the regular dividends should be paid, "for the present."

"Q. For how long? Had you fixed in your mind anytime in the future, when you were going to pay? A. No.

"Q. That was indefinite in the future? A. That was indefinite; yes, sir."

The record, and especially the testimony of Mr. Ford, convinces that he has to some extent the attitude towards shareholders of one who has dispensed and distributed to them large gains and that they should be content to take what he chooses to give. His testimony creates the impression, also, that he thinks the Ford Motor Company has made too much money, has had too large profits, and that, although large profits might be still earned, a sharing of them with the public, by reducing the price of the output of the company, ought to be undertaken. We have no doubt that certain sentiments, philanthropic and altruistic, creditable to Mr. Ford, had large influence in determining the policy to be pursued by the Ford Motor Company—the policy which has been herein referred to.

* * * There should be no confusion (of which there is evidence) of the duties which Mr. Ford conceives that he and the stockholders owe to the general public and the duties which in law he and his codirectors owe to protesting, minority stockholders. A business corporation is organized and carried on primarily for the profit of the stockholders. The powers of the directors are to be employed for that end. The discretion of directors is to be exercised in the choice of means to attain that end, and does not extend to a change in the end itself, to the reduction of profits, or to the nondistribution of profits among stockholders in order to devote them to other purposes.

There is committed to the discretion of directors, a discretion to be exercised in good faith, the infinite details of business, including the wages which shall be paid to employees, the number of hours they shall work, the conditions under which labor shall be carried on, and the price for which products shall be offered to the public.

It is said by appellants that the motives of the board members are not material and will not be inquired into by the court so long as their acts are within their lawful powers. As we have pointed out, and the proposition does not require argument to sustain it, it is not within the lawful powers of a board of directors to shape and conduct the affairs of a corporation for the merely incidental benefit of shareholders and for the primary purpose of benefiting others, and no one will contend that, if the avowed purpose of the defendant directors was to sacrifice the interests of shareholders, it would not be the duty of the courts to interfere.

We are not, however, persuaded that we should interfere with the proposed expansion of the business of the Ford Motor Company. In view of the fact that the selling price of products may be increased at any time, the ultimate results of the larger business cannot be certainly estimated. The judges are not business experts. It is recognized that plans must often be made for a long future, for expected competition, for a continuing as well as an immediately profitable venture. The experience of the Ford Motor Company is evidence of capable management of its affairs. It may be noticed incidentally, that it took from the public the money required for the execution of its plan, and that the very considerable salaries paid to Mr. Ford and to certain executive officers and employees were not diminished. We are not satisfied that the alleged motives of the directors, in so far as they are reflected in the conduct of the business, menace the interests of shareholders. It is enough to say, perhaps, that the court of equity is at all times open to complaining shareholders having a just grievance.

Assuming the general plan and policy of expansion and the details of it to have been sufficiently, formally, approved at the October and November, 1917, meetings of directors, and assuming further that the plan and policy and the details agreed upon were for the best ultimate interest of the company and therefore of its shareholders, what does it amount to in justification of a refusal to declare and pay a special dividend or dividends? The Ford Motor Company was able to estimate with nicety its income and profit. It could sell more cars than it could make. Having ascertained what it would cost to produce a car and to sell it, the profit upon each car depended upon the selling price. That being fixed, the yearly income and profit was determinable, and, within slight variations, was certain. * * *

Defendants say, and it is true, that a considerable cash balance must be at all times carried by such a concern. But, as has been stated, there was a large daily, weekly, monthly, receipt of cash. The output was practically continuous and was continuously, and within a few days, turned into cash. Moreover, the contemplated expenditures were not to be immediately made. The large sum appropriated for the smelter plant was payable over a considerable period of time. So that, without going further, it would appear that, accepting and approving the plan of the directors, it was their duty to distribute on or near the 1st of August, 1916, a very large sum of money to stockholders.

In reaching this conclusion, we do not ignore, but recognize, the validity of the proposition that plaintiffs have from the beginning profited by, if they have not lately, officially, participated in, the general policy of expansion pursued by this corporation. We do not lose sight of the fact that it had been, upon an occasion, agreeable to the plaintiffs to increase the capital stock to $100,000,000 by a stock dividend of $98,000,000. These things go only to answer other contentions now made by plaintiffs, and do not and cannot operate to estop them to demand proper dividends upon the stock they own. It is obvious that an annual dividend of 60 percent, upon $2,000,000 or $1,200,000, is the equivalent of a very small dividend upon $100,000,000, or more.

The decree of the court below fixing and determining the specific amount to be distributed to stockholders is affirmed. * * *

STEERE, FELLOWS, STONE, and BROOKE, JJ., concurred with OSTRANDER, J.

MOORE, J. * * * I do not agree with all that is said by [JUSTICE OSTRANDER] in his discussion of the question of dividends. I do agree with him in his conclusion that the accumulation of so large a surplus establishes the fact that there has been an arbitrary refusal to distribute funds that ought to have been distributed to the stockholders as dividends. I therefore agree with the conclusion reached by him upon that phase of the case.

BIRD, C.J., and KUHN, J., concurred with MOORE, J.

NOTES

(1) It is rare for a court to order a corporation to pay a dividend. The traditional approach to the issue has been described as follows:

There is no essential dispute as to the principles of law involved. If an adequate corporate surplus is available for the purpose, directors may not withhold the declaration of dividends in bad faith. But the mere existence of an adequate corporate surplus is not sufficient to invoke court action to compel such a dividend. There must also be bad faith on the part of the directors.

There are no infallible distinguishing ear-marks of bad faith. The following facts are relevant to the issue of bad faith and are admissible in evidence: Intense hostility of the controlling faction against the minority; exclusion of the minority from employment by the corporation; high salaries, or bonuses or corporate loans made to the officers in control; the fact that the majority group may be subject to high personal income taxes if substantial dividends are paid; the existence of a desire by the controlling directors to acquire the minority stock interests as cheaply as possible. But if they are not motivating causes they do not constitute "bad faith" as a matter of law.

The essential test of bad faith is to determine whether the policy of the directors is dictated by their personal interests rather than the corporate welfare. Directors are fiduciaries. Their cestui que trust are the corporation and the stockholders as a body. Circumstances such as those above mentioned and any other significant factors, appraised in the light of the financial condition and requirements of the corporation, will determine the conclusion as to whether the directors have or have not been animated by personal, as distinct from corporate, considerations.

The court is not concerned with the direction which the exercise of the judgment of the Board of Directors may take, provided only that such exercise of judgment be made in good faith. It is axiomatic that the court will not substitute its judgment for that of the Board of Directors.

Gottfried v. Gottfried, 73 N.Y.S.2d 692, 695 (Sup. Ct. 1947). In *Dodge*, the court affirmed the lower court's order that Ford Motor Company declare a dividend. Can this result be explained under the traditional framework described in *Gottfried*?

(2) Today, challenges to a corporation's dividend policy are often brought as "shareholder oppression" actions. These actions are discussed at length in Chapter 13, Section B.

ROBERT W. HAMILTON, BUSINESS ORGANIZATIONS: UNINCORPORATED BUSINESSES AND CLOSELY HELD CORPORATIONS
Pages 304–05 (1997).[s]

Superficially, a purchase by a corporation of its own shares may not be thought of as involving a distribution at all. It may appear to be the purchase of an asset rather than the making of a distribution. That analysis, however, confuses transactions in which the corporation repurchases *its own stock* and transactions in which it purchases stock *issued by another corporation*. The former is a distribution, the latter is an investment.

When a corporation buys back its own stock, it does not receive anything of value in the hands of the corporation. The remaining shareholders continue to own 100 percent of the corporate assets (now reduced by the amount of the payment used to reacquire the shares). A

---

[s] Reprinted with permission of Aspen Law & Business/Panel Publishers, a division of Aspen Publishers, Inc.

corporation cannot treat stock in itself that it has purchased as an asset any more than it can treat its authorized but unissued stock as an asset. One cannot own 10 percent of oneself and have one's total worth be 110 percent of the value of one's assets. This point is so fundamental that it may be [worthwhile] to re-read the last few sentences.

Stock issued by another corporation is entirely different. That does not create the same circularity problem. Shares of corporation B have value based on the assets owned by corporation B; if shares of corporation B are purchased by corporation A they are an asset in the hands of corporation A.

The fact that a repurchase of shares constitutes a distribution can be most easily appreciated by considering a proportionate repurchase of stock by the corporation from each shareholder. Assume that three persons each own 100 shares of stock in a corporation, its entire outstanding stock. The shareholders decide that each of them will sell 10 shares back to the corporation for $100 per share, or a total of $1,000 each. When the transaction is completed, each shareholder continues to own one-third of the corporation (now represented by 90 shares rather than 100 shares), the corporation is $3,000 poorer and the shareholders are each $1,000 richer. Clearly, there has been a distribution even though the transaction was cast in the form of a repurchase of stock rather than a direct distribution of assets by the corporation. * * *

Under most state statutes, the 30 shares reacquired by the corporation in the previous example are called *treasury shares*. Treasury shares are viewed as being held by the corporation in a sort of twilight zone until they are either retired permanently or resold to someone else in the future. Treasury shares are not an asset of the corporation even though they are salable and may be sold at some later time. Exactly the same thing can be said of every share of authorized but unissued stock.

Assume that the corporation in the example described above decides to resell the treasury shares to X (a nonshareholder) for $3,000. The interests of each of the three original shareholders have been diluted: There are now four shareholders owning shares in the ratio 90:90:90:30. The corporation could have paid the original shareholders a cash dividend of $1,000 each and then sold 33 shares of authorized but unissued stock to X for $3,000 with * * * the same economic result. (In this variation, the shares are owned 100:100:100:33 rather than 90:90:90:30; the percentage ownership interest, however, is as a practical matter identical.)

A repurchase of shares by the corporation is a distribution even if the corporation purchases only shares owned by one shareholder rather than proportionately from each shareholder. Such a transaction is a disproportionate distribution (i.e., one not shared proportionately by all shareholders). The corporation has made a distribution to a single shareholder equal to the purchase price it paid for the shares. This transaction is not all bad from the standpoint of the other shareholders, however, since it simultaneously increases their percentage interest in the corporation. For example, if the corporation with three shareholders in the above example repurchased all 100 shares owned by shareholder *A* for $10,000, the interests of shareholders *B* and *C* in the corporation are both increased from 33.3 percent to 50 percent. The assets of the corporation are reduced by the $10,000 purchase price paid to shareholder *A* to eliminate his or her interest in the corporation. Whether or not this is a "winner" for *A* or for *B* and *C* depends on the value of the assets in the corporation before the share repurchase.

NOTES

(1) Consider the situation where one shareholder in a closely held corporation wishes to leave the enterprise and the other shareholders are willing to purchase her shares. The price may be established either by negotiation or by prior agreement. How should the transaction be structured? Should the remaining shareholders each purchase their proportional number of shares? Should the corporation purchase the departing shares? Does it make any economic difference which way the transaction is structured?

A redemption of shares by the corporation also provides tax benefits. From the standpoint of the departing shareholder, there is no difference: a redemption of shares is treated as a sale or exchange of the shares giving rise to short or long-term capital gain or loss equal to the difference between the redemption price of the shares and the shareholder's basis.[t] But what about the tax position of the other shareholders if the corporation is a C corporation with earnings and profits? If the corporation distributed the redemption price to the other shareholders in order for them to purchase the shares, there would clearly have been a taxable dividend. In Holsey v. Commissioner, 258 F.2d 865 (3d Cir.1958), the court held in this kind of situation that the remaining shareholders could not be taxed on the increase in wealth until the gain was realized by a sale of the shares.[u] One situation in which a tax will be imposed on the non-redeeming shareholders is where they are obligated by contract to purchase the stock of the retiring shareholder. If the corporation redeems the stock, its payment discharges a personal obligation of each non-redeeming shareholder and is a constructive dividend to him.[v] Thus, a disproportionate redemption of stock permits the distribution of earnings of a C corporation to shareholders at a minimum tax cost.

---

[t]   Exceptions to the statement in the text exist. For example, if the sale is "essentially equivalent to a dividend," the redemption is treated as a dividend giving rise to ordinary income rather than as a sale or exchange giving rise to a capital gain or loss.

[u]   The Internal Revenue Service acquiesced in this result. Rev.Rul. 58–614, 1958–2 C.B. 920. See generally William J. Rands, Closely Held Corporations: Federal Tax Consequences of Stock Transfer Restrictions, 7 J.Corp.Law 449, 456–57 (1982).

[v]   An example is Sullivan v. United States, 363 F.2d 724, 729 (8th Cir.1966), cert. denied, 387 U.S. 905 (1967). Such a transaction is a constructive dividend to the remaining shareholders for exactly the same reason that use of corporate funds to pay a valid debt of a shareholder is a constructive dividend to that shareholder.

direct the operation and management" of certain theatres. Such shareholder could be removed as manager only by arbitration among the shareholders. The Court stated:

> By virtue of these provisions the management of all theatres leased or operated by Trenton or any subsidiary is vested in Keith, without approval of the directors, and this management may not be changed by the directors but only [by arbitration]. The directors may neither select nor discharge the manager, to whom the supervision and direction of the management and operation of the theatres is delegated with full authority and power. Thus, the powers of the directors over the management of its theatres, the principal business of the corporation, were completely sterilized. Such restrictions and limitations upon the powers of the directors are clearly in violation of section 27 of the General Corporation Law of this State and the New Jersey statute. * * *

> We think these restrictions and limitations went far beyond the agreement in Clark v. Dodge. We are not confronted with a slight impingement or innocuous variance from the statutory norm, but rather with the deprivation of all the powers of the board insofar as the selection and supervision of the management of the corporation's theatres, including the manner and policy of their operation, are concerned. * * *

(3) Precisely what is the status of the rule of the *McQuade* case following these two decisions?

GALLER V. GALLER

Supreme Court of Illinois, 1964.
203 N.E.2d 577.

UNDERWOOD, JUSTICE.

Plaintiff, Emma Galler, sued in equity for an accounting and for specific performance of an agreement made in July, 1955, between plaintiff and her husband, of one part, and defendants, Isadore A. Galler and his wife, Rose, of the other. Defendants appealed from a decree of the superior court of Cook County granting the relief prayed. The First District Appellate Court reversed the decree and denied specific performance * * *. That decision is appealed here on a certificate of importance.

There is no substantial dispute as to the facts in this case. From 1919 to 1924, Benjamin and Isadore Galler, brothers, were equal partners in the Galler Drug Company, a wholesale drug concern. In 1924 the business was incorporated under the Illinois Business Corporation Act, each owning one half of the outstanding 220 shares of stock. * * *

In March, 1954, Benjamin and Isadore, on the advice of their accountant, decided to enter into an agreement for the financial protection of their immediate families and to assure their families, after the death of either brother, equal control of the corporation. In June, 1954, while the agreement was in the process of preparation by an attorney-associate of the accountant, Benjamin suffered a heart attack. Although he resumed his business duties some months later, he was again stricken in February, 1955, and thereafter was unable to return to work. During his brother's illness, Isadore asked the accountant to have the shareholders' agreement put in final form in order to protect Benjamin's wife, and this was done by another attorney employed in the accountant's office. On a Saturday night in July, 1955, the accountant brought the agreement to Benjamin's home, and 6 copies of it were executed there by the two brothers and their wives. * * * It appears from the evidence that some months after the agreement was signed, the defendants Isadore and Rose Galler and their son, the defendant, Aaron Galler sought to have the agreements destroyed. The evidence is undisputed that defendants had decided prior to Benjamin's death they would not honor the agreement, but never disclosed their intention to plaintiff or her husband.

On July 21, 1956, Benjamin executed an instrument creating a trust naming his wife as trustee. The trust covered, among other things, the 104 shares of Galler Drug Company stock and the stock certificates were endorsed by Benjamin and delivered to Emma.[a] When Emma presented the certificates to defendants for transfer into her name as trustee, they sought to have Emma abandon the 1955 agreement or enter into some kind of a noninterference agreement as a price for the transfer of the shares. Finally, in September, 1956, after Emma had refused to abandon the shareholders' agreement, she did agree to permit defendant Aaron to become president for one year and agreed that she would not interfere with the business during that year. The stock was then reissued in her name as trustee. During the year 1957 while Benjamin was still alive [Benjamin died in December 1957], Emma tried many times to arrange a meeting with Isadore to discuss business matters but he refused to see her.

Shortly after Benjamin's death, Emma went to the office and demanded [that] the terms of the 1955 agreement be carried out. Isadore told her that anything she had to say could be said to Aaron, who then told her that his father would not abide by the agreement. He offered a modification of the agreement by proposing the salary continuation payment but without her becoming a director. When Emma refused to

---

[a] In 1945, twelve shares of the 220 outstanding shares of the company were sold to an employee. As a result, each brother owned one-half of the remaining 208 shares. By the time of the superior court's decree in 1962, however, the employee had sold the shares back to the Galler families and there were no outstanding minority shareholder interests.

modify the agreement and sought enforcement of its terms, defendants refused and this suit followed.

During the last few years of Benjamin's life both brothers drew an annual salary of $42,000. Aaron, whose salary was $15,000 as manager of the warehouse prior to September, 1956, has since the time that Emma agreed to his acting as president, drawn an annual salary of $20,000. In 1957, 1958, and 1959, a $40,000 annual dividend was paid. Plaintiff has received her proportionate share of the dividend.

The July, 1955, agreement in question here, entered into between Benjamin, Emma, Isadore and Rose, recites that Benjamin and Isadore each own 47 1/2% of the issued and outstanding shares of the Galler Drug Company, an Illinois corporation, and that Benjamin and Isadore desired to provide income for the support and maintenance of their immediate families. No reference is made to the shares [sold to the employee]. The essential features of the contested portions of the agreement are substantially as set forth in the opinion of the Appellate Court: (2) that the bylaws of the corporation will be amended to provide for a board of four directors; that the necessary quorum shall be three directors; and that no directors' meeting shall be held without giving ten days notice to all directors. (3) The shareholders will cast their votes for the above named persons (Isadore, Rose, Benjamin and Emma) as directors at said special meeting and at any other meeting held for the purpose of electing directors. (4, 5) In the event of the death of either brother his wife shall have the right to nominate a director in place of the decedent. (6) Certain annual dividends will be declared by the corporation. The dividend shall be $50,000 payable out of the accumulated earned surplus in excess of $500,000. If 50% of the annual net profits after taxes exceeds the minimum $50,000, then the directors shall have discretion to declare a dividend up to 50% of the annual net profits. If the net profits are less than $50,000, nevertheless the minimum $50,000 annual dividend shall be declared, providing the $500,000 surplus is maintained. Earned surplus is defined. (9) The certificates evidencing the said shares of Benjamin Galler and Isadore Galler shall bear a legend that the shares are subject to the terms of this agreement. (10) A salary continuation agreement shall be entered into by the corporation which shall authorize the corporation upon the death of Benjamin Galler or Isadore Galler, or both, to pay a sum equal to twice the salary of such officer, payable monthly over a five-year period. Said sum shall be paid to the widow during her widowhood, but should be paid to such widow's children if the widow remarries within the five-year period. (11, 12) The parties to this agreement further agree and hereby grant to the corporation the authority to purchase, in the event of the death of either Benjamin or Isadore, so much of the stock of Galler Drug Company held by the estate as is necessary to provide sufficient funds to pay the federal estate tax, the Illinois inheritance tax and other administrative expenses of the estate. If as a result of such purchase from the estate of the decedent the amount of dividends to be received by the heirs is reduced, the parties shall nevertheless vote for directors so as to give the estate and heirs the same representation as before (2 directors out of 4, even though they own less stock), and also that the corporation pay an additional benefit payment equal to the diminution of the dividends. In the event either Benjamin or Isadore decides to sell his shares he is required to offer them first to the remaining shareholders and then to the corporation at book value, according each six months to accept the offer.

The Appellate Court found the 1955 agreement void because "the undue duration, stated purpose and substantial disregard of the provisions of the Corporation Act outweigh any considerations which might call for divisibility" and held that "the public policy of this state demands voiding this entire agreement."

While the conduct of defendants towards plaintiff was clearly inequitable, the basically controlling factor is the absence of an objecting minority interest, together with the absence of public detriment. * * *

At this juncture it should be emphasized that we deal here with a so-called close corporation. * * * Moreover, it should be recognized that shareholder agreements similar to that in question here are often, as a practical consideration, quite necessary for the protection of those financially interested in the close corporation. While the shareholder of a public-issue corporation may readily sell his shares on the open market should management fail to use, in his opinion, sound business judgment, his counterpart of the close corporation often has a large total of his entire capital invested in the business and has no ready market for his shares should he desire to sell. He feels, understandably, that he is more than a mere investor and that his voice should be heard concerning all corporate activity. Without a shareholder agreement, specifically enforceable by the courts, insuring him a modicum of control, a large minority shareholder might find himself at the mercy of an oppressive or unknowledgeable majority. Moreover, as in the case at bar, the shareholders of a close corporation are often also the directors and officers thereof. With substantial shareholding interests abiding in each member of the board of directors, it is often quite impossible to secure, as in the large public-issue corporation, independent board judgment free from personal motivations concerning corporate policy. For these and other reasons too voluminous to enumerate here, often the only sound basis for protection is afforded by a lengthy, detailed shareholder agreement securing the rights and obligations of all concerned. * * *

* * * [T]here has been a definite, albeit inarticulate, trend toward eventual judicial treatment of the close corporation as *sui generis*. Several shareholder-director agreements that have technically "violated" the letter of the Business Corporation Act have nevertheless been upheld in

the light of the existing practical circumstances, i.e., no apparent public injury, the absence of a complaining minority interest, and no apparent prejudice to creditors. However, we have thus far not attempted to limit these decisions as applicable only to close corporations and have seemingly implied that general considerations regarding judicial supervision of all corporate behavior apply.

The practical result of this series of cases, while liberally giving legal efficacy to particular agreements in special circumstances notwithstanding literal "violations" of statutory corporate law, has been to inject much doubt and uncertainty into the thinking of the bench and corporate bar of Illinois concerning shareholder agreements.

It is therefore necessary, we feel, to discuss the instant case with the problems peculiar to the close corporation particularly in mind.

It would admittedly facilitate judicial supervision of corporate behavior if a strict adherence to the provisions of the Business Corporation Act were required in all cases without regard to the practical exigencies peculiar to the close corporation. However, courts have long ago quite realistically, we feel, relaxed their attitudes concerning statutory compliance when dealing with close corporate behavior, permitting "slight deviations" from corporate "norms" in order to give legal efficacy to common business practice. See e.g., Clark v. Dodge * * *

Again, "As the parties to the action are the complete owners of the corporation, there is no reason why the exercise of the power and discretion of the directors cannot be controlled by valid agreement between themselves, provided that the interests of creditors are not affected." Clark v. Dodge, 199 N.E. 641, 643, quoting from Kassel v. Empire Tinware Co., 178 App.Div. 176, 180, 164 N.Y.S. 1033, 1035. * * *

Perhaps, as has been vociferously advanced, a separate comprehensive statutory scheme governing the close corporation would best serve here. Some states have enacted legislation dealing specifically with the close corporation.

At any rate, however, the courts can no longer fail to expressly distinguish between the close and public-issue corporation when confronted with problems relating to either. What we do here is to illuminate this problem—before the bench, corporate bar, and the legislature, in the context of a particular fact situation. To do less would be to shirk our responsibility, to do more would, perhaps be to invade the province of the legislative branch.

We now, in the light of the foregoing, turn to specific provisions of the 1955 agreement.

The Appellate Court correctly found many of the contractual provisions free from serious objection, and we need not prolong this opinion with a discussion of them here. That court did, however, find difficulties in the stated purpose of the agreement as it relates to its duration, the election of certain persons to specific offices for a number of years, the requirement for the mandatory declaration of stated dividends (which the Appellate Court held invalid), and the salary continuation agreement.

Since the question as to the duration of the agreement is a principal source of controversy, we shall consider it first. The parties provided no specific termination date, and while the agreement concludes with a paragraph that its terms "shall be binding upon and shall inure to the benefits of" the legal representatives, heirs and assigns of the parties, this clause is, we believe, intended to be operative only as long as one of the parties is living. It further provides that it shall be so construed as to carry out its purposes, and we believe these must be determined from a consideration of the agreement as a whole. Thus viewed, a fair construction is that its purposes were accomplished at the death of the survivor of the parties. While these life spans are not precisely ascertainable, and the Appellate Court noted Emma Galler's life expectancy at her husband's death was 26.9 years, we are aware of no statutory or public policy provision against stockholder's agreements which would invalidate this agreement on that ground. * * *

The clause that provides for the election of certain persons to specified offices for a period of years likewise does not require invalidation. In Kantzler v. Benzinger, 214 Ill. 589, 73 N.E. 874, this court upheld an agreement entered into by all the stockholders providing that certain parties would be elected to the offices of the corporation for a fixed period. In Faulds v. Yates, 57 Ill. 416, we upheld a similar agreement among the majority stockholders of a corporation, notwithstanding the existence of a minority which was not before the court complaining thereof.

We turn next to a consideration of the effect of the stated purpose of the agreement upon its validity. The pertinent provision is: "The said Benjamin A. Galler and Isadore A. Galler desire to provide income for the support and maintenance of their immediate families." Obviously, there is no evil inherent in a contract entered into for the reason that the persons originating the terms desired to so arrange their property as to provide post-death support for those dependent upon them. Nor does the fact that the subject property is corporate stock alter the situation so long as there exists no detriment to minority stock interests, creditors or other public injury. It is, however, contended by defendants that the methods provided by the agreement for implementation of the stated purpose are, as a whole, violative of the Business Corporation Act to such an extent as to render it void *in toto*.

The terms of the dividend agreement require a minimum annual dividend of $50,000, but this duty is limited by the subsequent provision that it shall be operative only so long as an earned surplus of $500,000 is maintained. It may be noted that in 1958, the year prior to commencement of this litigation, the corporation's net earnings after taxes amounted to $202,759 while its earned surplus was $1,543,270, and this was increased in 1958 to $1,680,079 while earnings were $172,964. The minimum earned surplus requirement is designed for the protection of the corporation and its creditors, and we take no exception to the contractual dividend requirements as thus restricted.

The salary continuation agreement is a common feature, in one form or another, of corporate executive employment. It requires that the widow should receive a total benefit, payable monthly over a five-year period, aggregating twice the amount paid her deceased husband in one year. This requirement was likewise limited for the protection of the corporation by being contingent upon the payments being income tax-deductible by the corporation. The charge made in those cases which have considered the validity of payments to the widow of an officer and shareholder in a corporation is that a gift of its property by a noncharitable corporation is in violation of the rights of its shareholders and *ultra vires*. Since there are no shareholders here other than the parties to the contract, this objection is not here applicable, and its effect, as limited, upon the corporation is not so prejudicial as to require its invalidation.

[We conclude] that the agreement, under the circumstances here present, is not vulnerable to the attack made on it * * *.

Accordingly, the judgment of the Appellate Court is reversed * * *. The cause is remanded to the circuit court of Cook County with directions to proceed in accordance herewith.

NOTES

(1) Like *Donahue* (see Chapter 13, Section B), *Galler* has had a significant impact on the development of close corporation law. Its call for special legislative treatment of closely held corporations has led to statutory developments in most states. These statutes permit closely held corporations to depart dramatically in specified circumstances from the traditional statutory scheme governing shareholders, directors, and officers. As a result, it is possible—by appropriate planning—to create corporations that vary widely from the traditional statutory scheme envisioned in *McQuade*. It is important, however, to follow whatever statutory scheme has been adopted in the specific state, since a deviation may risk invalidation of the entire arrangement. Many states have adopted more than one of the following alternative approaches.

(2) *Modification of the Statutory Scheme by Provisions in the Articles of Incorporation.* The statutes of many states permit the authority normally placed in the board of directors to be vested in other persons or organizations by including an appropriate provision in the articles of incorporation (or, in some instances, in the bylaws). Many of these statutes also provide that if managerial authority is vested in persons or organizations other than the board of directors, those persons or organizations then have the duties, responsibilities, and liabilities of directors.

(3) *Integrated Close Corporation Statutes.* Several states have followed the suggestion made by Justice Underwood in *Galler* and have enacted special close corporation statutes. While these statutes vary from state to state, they share one common characteristic: they are all integrated "opt in" statutes that may be elected by a corporation that meets the statutory definition of a close corporation.

(a) The election to take advantage of the integrated close corporation statute is usually evidenced by a provision in the corporation's articles of incorporation which simply states that "[t]his corporation is a statutory close corporation."

(b) The statutory definition usually involves a numerical limit on the number of shareholders (Delaware's maximum is 30); this type of definition obviously creates problems when a corporation grows so large that the number of shareholders exceeds the limit, though that apparently rarely occurs as a practical matter.

(c) DGCL §§ 341–356, enacted in 1967, is a fairly typical close corporation statute, though a number of states have subsequently added novel features. With respect to the role of the board of directors, § 350 broadly validates agreements that restrict the discretion of directors in ways that might be invalid under a *McQuade*-like analysis; § 351 authorizes a corporation to dispense entirely with a board of directors and to provide for direct management by shareholders; and § 354 validates written agreements among shareholders that "treat the corporation as if it were a partnership." Section 352 provides for the judicial appointment of a "custodian" if the corporation is threatened with irreparable injury or deadlock. Section 353 provides for the judicial appointment of a provisional director "if the directors are so divided respecting the management of the corporation's business and affairs that the votes required for action by the board of directors cannot be obtained with the consequence that the business and affairs of the corporation can no longer be conducted to the advantage of the stockholders generally." Section 355 authorizes close corporations to adopt a provision "granting to any stockholder, or to the holders of any specified number or percentage of shares of any class of stock, an option to have the corporation dissolved at will or upon the occurrence of any specified event or contingency."

(d) Some close corporation statutes permit a corporation to dispense with bylaws, annual meetings, and other formal requirements imposed on corporations generally. Some statutes add for good measure that the exercise of any of the powers granted to statutory close corporations "is not a ground for imposing personal liability on the shareholders for liabilities of the corporation," or provisions to the same effect.

(e) These integrated close corporation statutes, where available, do not appear to be widely used. See, e.g., Tara Wortman, *Unlocking Lock-in: Limited Liability Companies and the Key to Underutilization of Close Corporation Statutes*, 70 N.Y.U. L. REV. 1362, 1362 (1995) (estimating that approximately 5% of closely held corporations nationwide elect statutory close corporation status). To the extent this data is reliable, two conclusions might be drawn: (a) close corporation statutes may not be really needed, or (b) attorneys are very cautious about trying new and untested devices. There also may be uncertainty about whether potential liability for breach of fiduciary duties might be increased by election of statutory close corporation status.

(4) *Authorization of Shareholder Agreements.* MBCA § 7.32, which was added to the Model Act in 1992, was designed to be the ultimate solution to the close corporation management problem. The Official Comment states that it "rejects the older line of cases" epitomized by Long Park, Inc. v. Trenton-New Brunswick Theatres Co., "adds an important element of predictability currently absent from the Model Act," and "affords participants in closely held corporations greater contractual freedom to tailor the rules of their enterprise." See particularly § 7.32(a)(1), (b). When § 7.32 was approved, the Committee on Corporate Laws also withdrew a "Model Close Corporation Supplement" that was based on the Delaware model with refinements; this supplement generally had not been enacted in states that used the MBCA as the basis for revisions of their corporation statutes. The withdrawal decision was also partially based on the belief of members of the Committee that relatively few corporations actually elected statutory close corporation status in states where that election was available.

ZION V. KURTZ

Court of Appeals of New York, 1980.
405 N.E.2d 681.

MEYER, JUDGE.

On these appeals we conclude that when all of the stockholders of a Delaware corporation agree that, except as specified in their agreement, no "business or activities" of the corporation shall be conducted without the consent of a minority stockholder, the agreement is, as between the original parties to it, enforceable even though all formal steps required by the statute have not been taken. We hold further that the agreement made by the parties to this action was violated when the corporation

entered into two agreements without the minority stockholder's consent.
* * *

[Harold Kurtz formed a Delaware corporation, Lombard-Wall Group, Inc. ("Group"). Group acquired all of the stock of Lombard-Wall Incorporated ("LBW") in a complex transaction in which Abraham Zion made available assets that were used as security for a loan to finance the acquisition. As part of the transaction, Zion acquired all of the Class A stock of Group while Kurtz continued to own all of the Class B stock. Zion and Kurtz also executed a shareholders' agreement, which provided in § 3.01(a) that without the consent of the holders of the Class A stock, Group would not "engage in any business or activities of any kind, directly or indirectly, whether through any Subsidiary or by way of a loan, guarantee or otherwise, other than the acquisition and ownership of the stock of LBW as contemplated by this Agreement * * *." The articles of incorporation of Group did not refer to this veto power. Group's board of directors approved two agreements over the objection of Zion. Zion brought suit to cancel the two agreements as violating the shareholders' agreement.]

The stockholders' agreement expressly provided that it should be "governed by and construed and enforced in accordance with the laws of the State of Delaware as to matters governed by the General Corporation Law of that State," and that is the generally accepted choice-of-law rule with respect to such "internal affairs" as the relationship between shareholders and directors. Subdivision (a) of section 141 of the General Corporation Law of Delaware provides that the business and affairs of a corporation organized under that law "shall be managed by a board of directors, except as may be otherwise provided in this chapter or in its certificate of incorporation." Included in the chapter referred to are provisions relating to close corporations, which explicitly state that a written agreement between the holders of a majority of such a corporation's stock "is not invalid, as between the parties to the agreement, on the ground that it so relates to the conduct of the business and affairs of the corporation as to restrict or interfere with the discretion or powers of the board of directors" (§ 350) * * *.

Clear from those provisions is the fact that the public policy of Delaware does not proscribe a provision such as that contained in the shareholders' agreement here in issue even though it takes all management functions away from the directors. Folk, in his work on the Delaware Corporation Law, states concerning section 350 that "Although some decisions outside Delaware have sustained 'reasonable' restrictions upon director discretion contained in stockholder agreements, the theory of § 350 is to declare unequivocally, as a matter of public policy, that stockholder agreements of this character are not invalid," that section 351 "recognizes a special subclass of close corporations which operate by direct stockholder management," and with respect to section 354 that it "should be liberally construed to authorize all sorts of internal agreements and arrangements which are not affirmatively improper or, more particularly, injurious to third parties."

Defendants argue, however, that Group was not incorporated as a close corporation and the stockholders' agreement provision was never incorporated in its certificate. The answer is that any Delaware corporation can elect to become a close corporation by filing an appropriate certificate of amendment (Del.General Corporation Law, § 344) and by such amendment approved by the holders of all of its outstanding stock may include in its certificate provisions restricting directors' authority (ibid., § 351). Here, not only did defendant Kurtz agree in paragraph 8.05(b) of the stockholders' agreement to "without further consideration, do, execute and deliver, or cause to be done, executed and delivered, all such further acts, things and instruments as may be reasonably required more effectively to evidence and give effect to the provisions and the intent and purposes of this Agreement," but also as part of the transaction by which the * * * guarantee was made and Zion became a Group stockholder, defendant Kurtz, while he was still the sole stockholder and sole director of Group, executed a consent to the various parts of the transaction under which he was "authorized and empowered to execute and deliver, or cause to be executed and delivered, all such other and further instruments and documents and take, or cause to be taken, all such other and further action as he may deem necessary, appropriate or desirable to implement and give effect to the Stockholders Agreement and the transactions provided for therein." Since there are no intervening rights of third persons, the agreement requires nothing that is not permitted by statute, and all of the stockholders of the corporation assented to it, the certificate of incorporation may be ordered reformed, by requiring Kurtz to file the appropriate amendments, or more directly he may be held estopped to rely upon the absence of those amendments from the corporate charter.[3]

The result thus reached accords with the weight of authority which textwriter F. Hodge O'Neal tells us sustains agreements made by all shareholders dealing with matters normally within the province of the directors, even though the shareholders could have, but had not, provided similarly by charter or by-law provision sanctioned by statute. Moreover, though we have not yet had occasion to construe subdivision (b) of section

---

[3] The fallacy of the dissent is that it converts a shield into a sword. The notice devices on which the concept of the dissent turns are wholly unnecessary to protect the original parties, who may be presumed to have known what they agreed to. To protect an original party who has not been hurt (indeed, has expressly agreed to the limitation he is being protected against and affirmatively covenanted to see to it that all necessary steps to validate the agreement were taken) because a third party without notice could have been hurt had he been involved can only be characterized as a perversion of the liberal legislative purpose demonstrated by the Delaware statutes quoted in the text above.

620 of the Business Corporation Law,[4] which did not become effective until September 1, 1963, it is worthy of note that in adopting that provision the Legislature had before it the Revisers' Comment that: "Paragraph (b) expands the ruling in Clark v. Dodge, 269 N.Y. 410, 199 N.E. 637 [641] (1936), and, to the extent therein provided, overrules Long Park, Inc. v. Trenton-New Brunswick Theatres Co., 297 N.Y. 174, 77 N.E.2d 633 (1948); Manson v. Curtis, 223 N.Y. 313, 119 N.E. 559 (1919) and McQuade v. Stoneham, 263 N.Y. 323, 189 N.E. 234 (1934)." Thus it is clear that no New York public policy stands in the way of our application of the Delaware statute and decisional law above referred to * * *.

For the foregoing reasons the order of the Appellate Division should be modified, as above indicated.

GABRIELLI, JUDGE (dissenting in part).

* * * I conclude that the agreement requiring plaintiff's consent was invalid under well-established public policies. * * * [It was] an illegal attempt by shareholders to deprive the board of directors of its inherent authority to exercise its discretion in managing the affairs of the corporation. * * * I would, [therefore,] reverse the determination of the Appellate Division with respect to plaintiff's * * * cause of action and hold that plaintiff cannot maintain a suit based upon defendants' failure to obtain his consent prior to executing the disputed * * * agreements.

It is beyond dispute that shareholder agreements such as the one relied upon by plaintiff in this case are, as a general rule, void as against public policy. Section 3.01 of the agreement, as interpreted both by plaintiff and by a majority of this court, would have precluded the board of directors of Group from taking any action on behalf of the corporation without first obtaining plaintiff's consent. This contractual provision, if enforced, would effectively shift the authority to manage every aspect of corporate affairs from the board to plaintiff, a minority shareholder who has no fiduciary obligations with respect to either the corporation or its other shareholders. * * *

Under the statutes of Delaware, the State in which Group was incorporated, the authority to manage the affairs of a corporation is vested solely in its board of directors (Del.General Corporation Law, § 141, subd. [a]). The same is true under the applicable New York statutes (Business Corporation Law, § 701). Significantly, in both States,

---

[4] That provision reads: "(b) A provision in the certificate of incorporation otherwise prohibited by law because it improperly restricts the board in its management of the business of the corporation, or improperly transfers to one or more shareholders or to one or more persons or corporations to be selected by him or them, all or any part of such management otherwise within the authority of the board under this chapter, shall nevertheless be valid: (1) If all the incorporators or holders of record of all outstanding shares, whether or not having voting power, have authorized such provision in the certificate of incorporation or an amendment thereof; and (2) If, subsequent to the adoption of such provision, shares are transferred or issued only to persons who had knowledge or notice thereof or consented in writing to such provision."

the courts have declined to give effect to agreements which purport to vary the statutory rule by transferring effective control of the corporation to a third party other than the board of directors. The common-law rule in Delaware was aptly stated in Abercrombie v. Davies, 35 Del.Ch. at p. 611, 123 A.2d at p. 899, supra: "So long as the corporate form is used as presently provided by our statutes this Court cannot give legal sanction to agreements which have the effect of removing from directors in a very substantial way their duty to use their own best judgment on management matters."

True, the common-law rule has been modified somewhat in recent years to account for the business needs of the so-called "close corporation." The courts of our State, for example, have been willing to enforce shareholder agreements where the incursion on the board's authority was insubstantial (Clark v. Dodge, 269 N.Y. 410, 199 N.E. 641) or where the illegal provisions were severable from the otherwise legal provisions which the shareholder sought to enforce. Neither the courts of our State nor the courts of Delaware, however, have gone so far as to hold that an agreement among shareholders such as the agreement in this case, which purported to "sterilize" the board of directors by completely depriving it of its discretionary authority, can be regarded as legal and enforceable. To the contrary, the common-law rule applicable to both closely and publicly held corporations continues to treat agreements to deprive the board of directors of substantial authority as contrary to public policy.

Indeed, there heretofore has been little need for the courts to modify the general common-law rule against "sterilizing" boards of directors to accommodate the needs of closely held corporations. This is because the Legislatures of many States, including New York and Delaware, have enacted laws which enable the shareholders of closely held corporations to restrict the powers of the board of directors if they comply with certain statutory prerequisites (Del.General Corporation Law, §§ 350, 351; Business Corporation Law, § 620, subd. [b]). The majority apparently construes these statutes as indications that the public policies of the enacting States no longer proscribe the type of agreement at issue here in cases involving closely held corporations. Hence, the majority concludes that there is no bar to the enforcement of the shareholder agreement in this case, even though the statutory requirements for close corporations were not fulfilled. I cannot agree.

Under Delaware law, as the majority notes, the shareholders of a close corporation are free to enter into private, binding agreements among themselves to restrict the powers of their board of directors (Del.General Corporation Law, § 350). The same appears to be true under the present New York statutes (Business Corporation Law, § 620, subd. [b]). Both the Delaware and the New York statutory schemes, however, contemplate that such variations from the corporate norm will be recorded on the face of the certificate of incorporation (Del.General Corporation Law, § 351; Business Corporation Law, § 620, subd. [b]). New York additionally requires that the existence of a substantial restriction on the powers of the board "shall be noted conspicuously on the face or back of every certificate for shares issued by [the] corporation" (Business Corporation Law, § 620, subd. [g]). Significantly, in both Delaware and New York, a provision in the certificate of incorporation restricting the discretion of the board has the effect of shifting liability for any mismanagement from the directors to the managing shareholders (Del.General Corporation Law, § 351, subds. [2]–[3]; Business Corporation Law, § 620, subd. [f]).

In my view, these statutory provisions are not merely directory, but rather are evidence of a clear legislative intention to permit deviations from the statutory norms for corporations only under controlled conditions. In enacting these statutes, which are tailored for "close corporations," the Legislatures of Delaware and New York were apparently attempting to accommodate the needs of those who wished to take advantage of the limited liability inherent in the corporate format, but who also wished to retain the internal management structure of a partnership. At the same time, however, the Legislatures were obviously mindful of the danger to the public that exists whenever shareholders privately agree among themselves to shift control of corporate management from independent directors to the shareholders, who are not necessarily bound by the fiduciary obligations imposed upon the board. In order to protect potential purchasers of shares and perhaps even potential creditors of the corporation, the Legislatures of Delaware and New York imposed specific strictures upon incorporated businesses managed by shareholders, the most significant of which is the requirement that restrictions on the statutory powers of the board of directors be evidenced in the certificate of incorporation. This requirement is an essential component of the statutory scheme because it ensures that potential purchasers of an interest in the corporation will have at least record notice that the corporation is being managed in an unorthodox fashion. Absent an appropriate notice provision in the certificate, there can be no assurance that an unsuspecting purchaser, not privy to the private shareholder agreement, will not be drawn into an investment that he might otherwise choose to avoid.

Since I regard the statutory requirements discussed above as essentially prophylactic in nature, I cannot subscribe to the notion that the agreement in this case should be enforced merely because there has been no showing that the interests of innocent third parties have actually been impaired. As is apparent from the design of the relevant statutes, the public policies of our own State as well as those of the State of Delaware remain opposed to shareholder agreements to "sterilize" the board of directors unless notice of the agreement is provided in the certificate of incorporation. Where such notice is provided, the public policy objections to the agreement are effectively eliminated and there is no further reason to preclude enforcement. On the other hand, where, as here, the shareholders have entered into a private agreement to "sterilize" the board of directors and have failed to comply with the simple statutory prerequisites for "close corporations," the agreement must be deemed void and unenforceable in light of the inherent potential for fraud against the public. Indeed, since it is this very potential for public harm which renders these agreements unlawful, the mere fortuity that no one was actually harmed, if that be the case, cannot be the controlling factor in determining whether the agreement is legally enforceable. For the same reason, the illegality in the instant agreement cannot be cured retroactively, as the majority suggests, by requiring defendants to file the appropriate amendments to the certificate of incorporation. And, of course, it is elementary that a party to an agreement cannot be estopped from asserting its invalidity when the agreement is prohibited by law or is contrary to public policy.

By its holding today, the majority has, in effect, rendered inoperative both the language and the underlying purpose of the relevant Delaware and New York statutes governing "close corporations." According to the majority's reasoning, the only requirements for upholding an otherwise unlawful shareholder agreement which concededly deprives the directors of all discretionary authority are that all of the shareholders concur in the agreement and that no "intervening rights of third persons" exist at the time enforcement of the agreement is sought. The statutes in question also recognize these factors as conditions precedent to the enforcement of shareholder agreements to "sterilize" a corporate board of directors. But the laws of both jurisdictions go further, requiring in each case that the "close corporation" give notice of its unorthodox management structure through its filed certificate of incorporation. The obvious purpose of such a requirement is to prevent harm to the public before it occurs. If, as the majority's holding suggests, this requirement of notice to the public through the certificate of incorporation is without legal effect unless and until a third party's interests have actually been impaired, then the prophylactic purposes of the statutes governing "close corporations" would effectively be defeated. It is this aspect of the majority's ruling that I find most difficult to accept.

For all of the foregoing reasons, I must respectfully dissent and cast my vote to modify the order of the Appellate Division by directing dismissal of plaintiff's first cause of action.

JASEN, JONES and FUCHSBERG, JJ., concur with MEYER, J.

GABRIELLI, J., dissents in part and votes to modify in a separate opinion in which COOKE, C.J., and WACHTLER, J., concur.

NOTES

(1) Why should a court reach out like this and apply a Delaware statute when it is clear on the face of the statute that it is not applicable? Obviously, the majority was swayed by its belief that the application of close corporation statutes and the enforcement of shareholder agreements was desirable from a policy standpoint. If the result in *Zion* is accepted, what is left of the *McQuade* principle in states with close corporation statutes? Dubin v. Muchnick, 438 N.Y.S.2d 920, 922 (Sup.1981) states that *Zion* has "apparently swept all of the earlier authorities into the realm of legal history."

(2) In Nixon v. Blackwell, 626 A.2d 1366 (Del.1993), the Delaware Supreme Court refused to apply the Delaware close corporation statute to a nonelecting close corporation, stating that the statute "is a narrowly constructed statute which applies only to a corporation which is designated as a 'close corporation' in its certificate of incorporation, and which fulfills other requirements [set forth by the statute]." Further, it is improper to apply special provisions to a nonelecting Delaware close corporation "because the provisions of [the Delaware statute] relating to close corporations and other statutory schemes preempt the field in their respective areas." 626 A.2d at 1380. Is it not clear from these statements that the Delaware courts would reject entirely the rationale of *Zion*? Since that case is at least nominally an application of Delaware law, what is left of the holding of the principal case?

MATTER OF AUER V. DRESSEL

Court of Appeals of New York, 1954.
118 N.E.2d 590.

DESMOND, JUDGE.

This article 78 of the Civil Practice Act proceeding was brought by class A stockholders of appellant R. Hoe & Co., Inc., for an order in the nature of mandamus to compel the president of Hoe to comply with a positive duty imposed on him by the corporation's by-laws. Section 2 of article I of those by-laws says that "It shall be the duty of the President to call a special meeting whenever requested in writing so to do, by stockholders owning a majority of the capital stock entitled to vote at such meeting." On October 16, 1953, petitioners submitted to the president written requests for a special meeting of class A stockholders, which writings were signed in the names of the holders of record of slightly more than 55% of the class A stock. The president failed to call the meeting and, after waiting a week, the petitioners brought the present proceeding. The answer of the corporation and its president was not forthcoming until October 28, 1953, and it contained, in response to the petition's allegation that the demand was by more than a majority of class A stockholders, only a denial that the corporation and the president had any knowledge or information sufficient to form a belief as to the stockholding of those who had signed the requests. Since the president, when he filed that answer, had had before him for at least ten days the signed requests themselves, his denial that he had any information sufficient for a belief as to the adequacy of the number of signatures was obviously perfunctory and raised no issue whatever. There was no discretion in this corporate officer as to whether or not to call a meeting when a demand therefor was put before him by owners of the required number of shares. The important right of stockholders to have such meetings called will be of little practical value if corporate management can ignore the requests, force the stockholders to commence legal proceedings, and then, by purely formal denials, put the stockholders to lengthy and expensive litigation, to establish facts as to stockholdings which are peculiarly within the knowledge of the corporate officers. In such a situation, Special Term did the correct thing in disposing of the matter summarily, as commanded by section 1295 of the Civil Practice Act.

The petition was opposed on the further alleged ground that none of the four purposes for which petitioners wished the meeting called was a proper one for such a class A stockholders' meeting. Those four stated purposes were these: (A) to vote, upon a resolution indorsing the administration of petitioner Joseph L. Auer, who had been removed as president by the directors, and demanding that he be reinstated as such president; (B) voting upon a proposal to amend the charter and by-laws to provide that vacancies on the board of directors, arising from the removal of a director by stockholders or by resignation of a director against whom charges have been preferred, may be filled, for the unexpired term, by the stockholders only of the class theretofore represented by the director so removed or so resigned; (C) voting upon a proposal that the stockholders hear certain charges preferred, in the requests, against four of the directors, determine whether the conduct of such directors or any of them was inimical to the corporation and, if so, to vote upon their removal and vote for the election of their successors; and (D) voting upon a proposal to amend the by-laws so as to provide that half of the total number of directors in office and, in any event, not less than one-third of the whole authorized number of directors constitute a quorum of the directors.

The Hoe certificate of incorporation provides for eleven directors, of whom the class A stockholders, more than a majority of whom join in this petition, elect nine and the common stockholders elect two. The obvious purpose of the meeting here sought to be called (aside from the endorsement and reinstatement of former president Auer) is to hear charges against four of the class A directors, to remove them if the charges be proven, to amend the by-laws so that the successor directors be elected by the class A stockholders, and further to amend the by-laws so that an effective quorum of directors will be made up of no fewer than half of the directors in office and no fewer than one third of the whole authorized number of directors. No reason appears why the class A stockholders should not be allowed to vote on any or all of those proposals.

The stockholders, by expressing their approval of Mr. Auer's conduct as president and their demand that he be put back in that office, will not be able, directly, to effect that change in officers, but there is nothing invalid in their so expressing themselves and thus putting on notice the directors who will stand for election at the annual meeting. As to purpose (B), that is, amending the charter and by-laws to authorize the stockholders to fill vacancies as to class A directors who have been removed on charges or who have resigned, it seems to be settled law that the stockholders who are empowered to elect directors have the inherent power to remove them for cause, In re Koch, 257 N.Y. 318, 321, 322, 178 N.E. 545, 546. Of course, as the Koch case points out, there must be the service of specific charges, adequate notice and full opportunity of meeting the accusations, but there is no present showing of any lack of any of those in this instance. Since these particular stockholders have the right to elect nine directors and to remove them on proven charges, it is not inappropriate that they should use their further power to amend the by-laws to elect the successors of such directors as shall be removed after hearing, or who shall resign pending hearing. Quite pertinent at this point is Rogers v. Hill, 289 U.S. 582, 589, which made light of an argument that stockholders, by giving power to the directors to make by-laws, had lost their own power to make them; quoting a New Jersey case, In re Griffing Iron Co., 41 A. 931, the United States Supreme Court said: "'It would be preposterous to leave the real owners of the corporate property at the mercy of their agents, and the law has not done so.'" Such a change in the bylaws, dealing with class A directors only, has no effect on the voting rights of the common stockholders, which rights have to do with the selection of the remaining two directors only. True, the certificate of incorporation authorizes the board of directors to remove any director on charges, but we do not consider that provision as an abdication by the stockholders of their own traditional, inherent power to remove their own directors. Rather, it provides an additional method. Were that not so, the stockholders might find themselves without effective remedy in a case where a majority of the directors were accused of wrongdoing and, obviously, would be unwilling to remove themselves from office.

We fail to see, in the proposal to allow class A stockholders to fill vacancies as to class A directors, any impairment or any violation of paragraph (h) of article Third of the certificate of incorporation, which says that class A stock has exclusive voting rights with respect to all matters "other than the election of directors." That negative language should not be taken to mean that class A stockholders, who have an absolute right to elect nine of these eleven directors, cannot amend their by-laws to guarantee a similar right, in the class A stockholders and to the exclusion of common stockholders, to fill vacancies in the class A group of directors.

There is urged upon us the impracticability and unfairness of constituting the numerous stockholders a tribunal to hear charges made by themselves, and the incongruity of letting the stockholders hear and pass on those charges by proxy. Such questions are really not before us at all on this appeal. The charges here are not, on their face, frivolous or inconsequential, and all that we are holding as to the charges is that a meeting may be held to deal with them. Any director illegally removed can have his remedy in the courts.

The order should be affirmed, with costs, and the Special Term directed forthwith to make an order in the same form as the Appellate Division order with appropriate changes of dates.

VAN VOORHIS, JUDGE (dissenting).

* * * An examination of the request for a special meeting by these stockholders indicates that none of the proposals could be voted upon legally at the projected meeting. The purposes of the meeting are listed as A, B, C and D. Purpose A is described as "Voting upon a resolution endorsing the administration of Joseph L. Auer, as President of the corporation, and demanding his immediate reinstatement as President." For the stockholders to vote on this proposition would be an idle gesture, since it is provided by section 27 of the General Corporation Law, Consol.Laws, c. 23, that "The business of a corporation shall be managed by its board of directors." The directors of Hoe have been elected by the stockholders for stated terms which have not expired, and it is their function and not that of the stockholders to appoint the officers of the corporation.

Purpose B of the special meeting is to vote upon a proposal to amend the certificate and the by-laws so as to provide "that vacancies on the Board of Directors arising from the removal of a director by stockholders or by resignation of a director against whom charges have been preferred may be filled, for the unexpired term, only by the stockholders of the class theretofore represented by the director so removed." This proposal is interwoven with the next one (C), which is about to be discussed, which is to remove four directors from office before the expiration of their terms in order to alter the control of the corporation. Proposal B must be read in the context that the certificate of incorporation provides for eleven directors, of whom the class A stockholders elect nine and the common stockholders two. So long as any class A shares are outstanding, the voting rights with respect to all matters "other than the election of directors" are vested exclusively in the holders of class A stock, with one exception now irrelevant. This means that the common stockholders are entitled to participate directly in the election of two directors, who, in turn, are authorized by the certificate to vote to fill vacancies occurring among the directors elected by the class A shareholders. This proposed amendment would deprive the directors elected by the common stockholders of the power to participate in filling the vacancies which petitioners hope to create among the class A directors, four of whom they seek to remove by proposal C which is about to be discussed. Such an alteration would impair the existing right of the common stockholders to participate in filling vacancies upon the board of directors and could not be legally adopted at this meeting demanded by petitioners from which the common stockholders are excluded. * * *

Purpose C of the special meeting is to vote "upon a proposal that the Stockholders (1) hear the charges preferred against Harry K. Barr, William L. Canady, Neil P. Cullom and Edwin L. Munzert, and their answers thereto; (2) determine whether such conduct on their part or on the part of any of them was inimical to the best interest of R. Hoe & Co., Inc., and if so (3) vote upon the removal of said persons or any of them as directors of R. Hoe & Co., Inc., for such conduct, and (4) vote for the election of directors to fill any vacancies on the Board of Directors which the Stockholders may be authorized to fill." By means of this proposal, it is sought to change the control of the corporation and to accomplish what A could not achieve, viz., remove the existing president and reappoint Mr. Joseph L. Auer as president of the corporation. Neither the language nor the policy of the corporation law subjects directors to recall by the stockholders before their terms of office have expired, merely for the reason that the stockholders wish to change the policy of the corporation. In People ex rel. Manice v. Powell, 201 N.Y. 194, 201, 94 N.E. 634, 637, this court said that "It would be somewhat startling to the business world if we definitely announced that the directors of a corporation were mere [employees] and that the stockholders of the corporation have the power to convene from time to time and remove at will any or all of the directors, although their respective terms of office have not expired." Fraud or breach of fiduciary duty must be shown, Matter of Koch, 257 N.Y. 318, 178 N.E. 545. In that event, directors may be removed from office before expiration of term by an action brought under subdivision 4 of section 60 of the General Corporation Law. In addition to such procedure, paragraph Fourteenth of the certificate of incorporation states: "Any director of the corporation may at any time be removed for cause as such director by resolution adopted by a majority of the whole number of directors then in office, provided that such director, prior to his removal, shall have received a copy of the charges against him and shall have had an opportunity to be heard thereon by the board. The By-Laws may provide the manner of presentation of the charges and of the hearing thereon."

Petitioners have instituted this proceeding on the theory that although no power is conferred upon the stockholders by the certificate or the by-laws to remove directors before the expiration of their terms, with or without cause, power to do so for cause is inherent in them as the body authorized to elect the directors, citing Matter of Koch, 257 N.Y. 318, 178 N.E. 545, supra. Petitioners have argued that the grant of this power to the board of directors to remove some of their number for cause after trial, does not eliminate what is asserted to be the inherent right of the stockholders to do likewise. No cases are cited in support of the latter proposition. * * * Such cases as have been cited in support of a power in the stockholders to remove directors for cause are clear in holding that such action can be taken only subject to the rule that "specific charges must be served, adequate notice must be given, and full opportunity of meeting the accusations must be afforded." Matter of Koch, 257 N.Y. 318, 322, 178 N.E. 545, 546, supra.

Although the demand by these petitioners for a special meeting contains no specification of charges against these four directors, the proxy statement, circulated by their protective committee, does describe certain charges. No point appears to be made of the circumstance that they are not contained in the demand for the meeting. Nevertheless, although this proxy statement enumerates these charges and announces that a resolution will be introduced at the special meeting to hear them, to determine whether sufficient cause exists for the removal of said persons as directors, and, if so, to remove them and to fill the resulting vacancies, the stockholders thus solicited are requested to sign proxies running to persons nominated by petitioners' protective committee. Inasmuch as this committee, with which petitioners are affiliated, has already charged in the most forceful terms that at least one of these directors has been guilty of misconduct and that "his *clique* of directors have removed Joseph L. Auer as President," it is reasonable to assume that the case of the accused directors has already been prejudged by those who will vote the proxies alleged to represent 255,658 shares of class A stock, and that the 1,200 shareholders who are claimed to have signed proxies have (whether they know it or not) voted, in effect, to remove these directors before they have been tried. The consequence is that these directors are to be adjudged guilty of fraud or breach of faith in absentia by shareholders who have neither heard nor ever will hear the evidence against them or in their behalf. Such a procedure does not conform to the requirements of Matter of Koch, supra, nor the other authorities which have been cited, and is far removed from "a law which hears before it condemns, which proceeds upon inquiry, and renders judgment only after trial." Brief by Daniel Webster in Trustees of Dartmouth Coll. v. Woodward, 4 Wheat. [U.S.] 518, 581, 4 L.Ed. 629. The charges against these directors enumerated in the proxy statement are described as having been preferred by one John Kadel and are to the effect that these four accused directors supported a resolution on July 2, 1953, that severance pay of $50,000 be granted to Mr. Auer "upon condition that he resign and that he sign an agreement not to participate, with any stockholders group or otherwise, in any action against any of the directors or officers of the Company." This money was not in fact paid to Auer. The charge based thereon against these directors is that there was a breach of trust in offering to pay $50,000 of the corporation's money in consideration of a covenant by Auer not to participate (as the minutes of the directors' meeting of July 2, 1953, actually read) in "any hostile action against the company, its officers and directors." It is not clear how this constituted actionable misconduct in view of the circumstance that none of this money actually was paid, and that there was no showing in this record [of] any misconduct on the part of these four directors which might have furnished a basis for a stockholders' derivative action by Auer against these directors. It is not so plain that these directors should be subjected to trial by stockholders, acting through proxies who are evidently prepared to oust them with or without cause that a mandamus order should, in any event, be issued to compel the calling of a special meeting for that purpose. The other charges, viz., that Mr. Cullom was paid $300 a month as rental for office space in his suite at 63 Wall Street, and that he engaged one of his personal friends and clients in connection with appraisal proceedings involving the common stock of the company for which the friend was paid $5,000 are not supplemented by further facts indicating that such conduct was hostile to the interest of the corporation.

It is not for the courts to determine which of these warring factions is pursuing the wiser policy for the corporation. If these petitioners consider that the stockholders made a mistake in the election of the present directors, they should not be permitted to correct it by recalling them before the expiration of their terms on charges of fraud or breach of fiduciary duty without a full and fair trial, which, if not conducted in court under section 60 of the General Corporation Law, is required to be held before the remaining directors under paragraph Fourteenth of the certificate of incorporation. The difficulty inherent in conducting such a trial by proxy may well have been the reason on account of which the incorporators delegated that function to the board of directors under paragraph Fourteenth of the certificate of incorporation. If it were to develop (the papers before the court do not contain evidence of such a fact) that enough of the other directors would be disqualified so that it would be impossible to obtain a quorum for the purpose, it may well be doubted that these directors could be tried before so large a number of stockholders sitting in person (if it were possible to assemble them in one place) or that they could sit in judgment by proxy. In ancient Athens evidence is said to have been heard and judgment pronounced in court by as many as 500 jurors known as ducats, but in this instance, if petitioners be correct in their figures, there are 1,200 class A stockholders who have signed requests or proxies, and these are alleged to hold only somewhat more than half of the outstanding shares. Since it would be impossible for so large a number to conduct a trial in person, they could only do so by proxy. Voting by proxy is the accepted procedure to express the will of large numbers of stockholders on questions of corporate policy within their province to determine, and it would be suitable in this instance if the certificate of incorporation had reserved to stockholders the power to recall directors without cause before expiration of term, but it is altogether unsuited to the performance of duties which partake of the nature of the judicial function, involving, as this would need to do if the accused directors are to be removed before the expiration of their terms, a decision after trial that they have been guilty of faithlessness or fraud. Section 60 of the General Corporation Law is always available for that purpose if the occasion requires.

The final proposal to be voted on at this special meeting (D) relates simply to an amendment to the by-laws so as to provide that a quorum shall consist of not less than one half of the number of directors holding office and in no event less than one third of the authorized number of directors. Section 8 of article II of the by-laws already provides that one half of the total number of directors shall constitute a quorum; the modification that a quorum shall in no event be less than one third of the authorized number of directors was proposed in the event of the removal of the four defendant directors whom petitioners seek to eliminate.

Inasmuch as we consider that for the foregoing reasons none of the business for which the special meeting is proposed to be called could legally be transacted, this proceeding should be dismissed. * * *

The petition should be dismissed, with costs in all courts.

LEWIS, C.J., and DYE, FULD and FROESSEL, JJ., concur with DESMOND, J.

VAN VOORHIS, J., dissents in opinion in which CONWAY, J., concurs.

NOTES

(1) Unlike the earlier principal cases in this Section, this case involves a publicly held corporation: at the time of this litigation, R. Hoe & Co., Inc. had 6,000 shareholders and some 460,000 class A shares outstanding. The principal difference between a publicly held corporation and a closely held corporation from the management standpoint is that in a publicly held corporation, ownership and management are usually vested in quite different persons or groups. In a closely held corporation, the majority shareholder is likely to be the chief executive officer and possess the ability to name or remove directors virtually at will. See MBCA § 8.08. In contrast, most publicly held corporations have professional managers who in the aggregate own an insignificant fraction of the corporation's outstanding shares. Because shareholders are numerous and diffuse, the "owners" of a publicly held corporation are not a cohesive group. Indeed, the simple process of calling a shareholders' meeting involves, at the least, communicating with thousands of widely scattered shareholders. Chapter 9 discusses at length issues

relating to management and control of the publicly held corporation. The purpose of this note is to call attention to examples of provisions in state corporation statutes that are designed primarily or exclusively for the large publicly held corporation. Many other examples can be cited:

(a) Traditional corporation statutes provide that the business and affairs of a corporation shall be managed "by" the board of directors. MBCA § 8.01(b) and the statutes of many states add "or under the direction of" following the word "by" to reflect the reality that boards of directors of publicly held corporations do not actually manage the business and affairs of a corporation.

(b) MBCA § 8.09 provides that directors may be removed by judicial proceeding "if the court finds that (1) the director engaged in fraudulent conduct with respect to the corporation or its shareholders, grossly abused the position of director, or intentionally inflicted harm on the corporation; and (2) considering the director's course of conduct and the inadequacy of other available remedies, removal would be in the best interest of the corporation." If a director accused of serious misconduct stubbornly refuses to resign, removal by judicial proceeding is often simpler and less expensive than calling a shareholders' meeting to remove the director. It is possible that this provision may also be utilized by a closely held corporation which has evenly divided voting power at the shareholder level, or when action is subject to a veto by a minority shareholder.

(c) MBCA §§ 7.22–7.24 contain special rules for shareholder voting by proxy that, as a practical matter, are almost exclusively a phenomenon of publicly held corporations.

(2) Consider again the practical difficulties discussed in the dissenting opinion of holding a shareholders' meeting of R. Hoe & Co., Inc. to pass on the removal of the directors for cause. If such a meeting is to be held, how should it be structured to give even minimal "due process" to the directors threatened with removal? Do you think the conduct described in the dissenting opinion constitutes "cause" for removal?

(3) Modern statutes typically provide shareholders with the right to remove directors, with or without cause. See MBCA § 8.08; DGCL § 141(k).

B. SHAREHOLDER VOTING AND AGREEMENTS

SALGO V. MATTHEWS

Court of Civil Appeals of Texas, 1973.
497 S.W.2d 620.

GUITTARD, JUSTICE.

This equitable proceeding involves a proxy contest for control of General Electrodynamics Corporation, a Texas corporation. Stockholders Joe W. Matthews and Paul Thorp, representing the faction opposed to current management, sought the aid of the district court in requiring the president, as chairman of the stockholders' meeting, and the election inspector appointed by him, to accept certain disputed proxies, count the votes of the stockholders cast under these proxies, and declare that the candidates supported by plaintiffs had been elected directors of the corporation. We hold that the court erred in granting injunctive relief, both temporary and final, in [the] absence of any showing that plaintiffs could not have obtained adequate relief by the statutory remedy of quo warranto after the completion of the election. * * *

[The incumbent management faction was headed by Francis Salgo, the president of Electrodynamics. At the meeting, Salgo appointed Julian Meer, a well-known attorney, as election inspector. During the course of examining and tabulating proxy appointments], plaintiffs presented to defendant Meer four proxy documents purporting to have been executed in plaintiffs' favor on behalf of Pioneer Casualty Company, the registered owner of 29,934 shares of stock. Beneficial title to these shares had been transferred to Don Shepherd, who was in bankruptcy, and two of the proxy documents were signed, "Pioneer Casualty Company By Don Shepherd." Plaintiffs also presented to the inspector an order of the 126th District Court of Travis County, Texas, directing Tom I. McFarling as receiver of Pioneer Casualty Company to give Shepherd a proxy to vote these shares by giving his proxy to plaintiffs Matthews and Thorp, and plaintiffs also presented a proxy document signed by the receiver in accordance with this order. Defendant Meer refused to accept any of these proxies, and their validity is the principal matter in controversy. Defendant Meer also refused to accept two telegraphic proxies aggregating 5,000 shares from stockholders Candis and Wrobliske when plaintiff Thorp presented them to him on the afternoon of November 9. * * *

* * * [W]e hold that the inspector was not subject to judicial control in the performance of his duties because he had discretionary authority to make a preliminary determination of the validity of the proxies for the purpose of tabulating them, counting the votes, and certifying the result, although the correctness of his decision was subject to review after the election by proceeding in quo warranto. * * *

Our holding that an election inspector has discretionary authority to determine the validity of disputed proxies for the purpose of declaring the result of the election should not be interpreted as meaning that he may go beyond the corporate records in determining the identity of stockholders entitled to vote. Defendants argue that the trial court's findings establish that beneficial ownership of the 29,934 shares registered in the name of Pioneer Casualty Company was not in Pioneer's receiver or in Don Shepherd, to whom these shares had been transferred, but was vested in Shepherd's bankruptcy trustee, and, consequently, that neither the receiver nor Shepherd had the right to vote. We assume that Shepherd's trustee was the beneficial owner, but, as against the corporation and its officers, beneficial ownership does not carry with it the right to vote without having the shares transferred on the books. A bylaw of General Electrodynamics Corporation provides that stock is transferable only on its books. This bylaw indicates the strong interest of the corporation and its stockholders in determining stock ownership quickly by reference to the corporate records. If beneficial title is in dispute, that dispute cannot properly be decided by the election inspector, and neither should the losing faction be able to go into court to invalidate the election on the ground that the ownership of certain shares was not correctly shown by the corporate records. For even greater reason the election should not be interrupted or suspended while complicated questions of title to stock are litigated to final judgment.

The rule that under such a bylaw, eligibility to vote at corporate elections is determined by the corporate records rather than by the ultimate judicial decision of beneficial title of disputed shares is well sustained by authority. In re Giant Portland Cement Co., 26 Del.Ch. 32, 21 A.2d 697 (Ch.1941). This rule is in accordance with Tex.Bus.Corp.Act Ann. art. 2.27(A) (1956), V.A.T.S., which provides, "The original stock transfer books shall be prima-facie evidence as to who are the shareholders entitled * * * to vote at any meeting of shareholders." According to E. Aranow & H. Einhorn, [Proxy Contests for Corporate Control (1957) at 386], although such a statute uses the term "prima-facie," it has the effect of making stock records conclusive on the inspector. The term "prima-facie" avoids any implication that the stock record is conclusive in a suit concerning title to the stock.

The binding effect of the stock record on corporate officers does not leave a beneficial owner without remedy. He may be presumed to know that the record owner can vote the stock. The beneficial owner can protect his interest by requiring a transfer on the books or by demanding a proxy from the record owner, and if voluntary compliance is not forthcoming, relief is available by injunction or mandamus. In the present case Shepherd's trustee, the beneficial owner, made no effort to vote the shares. He sought no proxy from the receiver or the receivership court. In these circumstances neither the corporate officers nor any of the other stockholders were in a position to assert that only the trustee had the right to vote.

The question presented to the inspector was, who was entitled to act for the record owner? The shares were registered in the name of Pioneer Casualty Company, which was in receivership and had no officers to act for it. The only person entitled to act for Pioneer was its receiver under orders of the 126th district court of Travis County. The receiver, acting under such an order, gave a proxy to Shepherd to act for Pioneer, with instructions to give a further proxy to plaintiffs Matthews and Thorp, and Shepherd, acting for Pioneer in accordance with the proxy to him, gave a proxy to plaintiffs. This transaction was essentially the same as if the receiver, acting under the court's order, had given the proxy directly to plaintiffs. The recitation in the order that Shepherd was the beneficial owner is of no consequence, since the beneficial owner, whether Shepherd or his trustee, had no right under the bylaws to vote the shares as against General Electrodynamics Corporation and its officers. * * * Since the stockholder of record was Pioneer Casualty Company, and the receiver was authorized by court order to act for Pioneer, the inspector's proper course was to accept the stock record as determining that the right to vote was in Pioneer Casualty Company, and to accept the proxies given by the receiver to Shepherd and by him to plaintiffs as valid.

Defendants argue that if the inspector was authorized to go behind the stock book and recognize the voting rights of the receiver for Pioneer Casualty Company, he was authorized to go further and determine the beneficial ownership of the stock for the purpose of the election. We do not agree. The inspector was bound by the stock book to consider Pioneer Casualty Company the legal owner for the purpose of the election, but he was required to determine who could act for the record owner, just as if someone had challenged the authority of a person purporting to act as an officer of a corporate stockholder. Since Pioneer was in receivership, the inspector could consider that fact and should have treated the receiver as the authorized representative of the record owner. It is quite another matter to say that the inspector should have inquired into beneficial ownership of the stock and recognized the right of Shepherd or his trustee in bankruptcy to vote the shares. * * *

Reversed and rendered.

NOTES

(1) Underlying the holding in the principal case is the basic concept that shares are always registered in the name of a specific person on the records of the corporation. See MBCA §§ 6.25(b). The person in whose name shares are registered is called the "record holder" and may or may not be the person who is the actual owner of the shares, usually referred to as the "beneficial owner." Generally speaking, the corporation may treat the record owner as the owner of the shares for purposes such as voting, the payment of dividends or distributions, and determining to whom shares have been transferred. In *Salgo*, the record owner was a person different from the beneficial owner and the court held that the corporation must determine who has been authorized to vote the shares by the record owner. Where the record owner and the beneficial owner are different persons, it is clear, as dicta in the principal case states, that the beneficial owner can compel the record owner (by court process, if necessary) to execute a proxy appointment in the name of the beneficial owner so that the beneficial owner may vote the shares as he or she desires. The beneficial owner also has the power to compel the record owner to turn over any distributions made by the corporation and, ultimately, to re-

register the shares in the name of the beneficial owner when requested to do so. Why do some beneficial owners allow shares to be held of record by someone else, sometimes for extended periods? Shares of publicly held corporations are usually held of record by nominees or by brokerage firms ("in street name") in order to facilitate transfer.

(2) The traditional practice is to issue certificates representing shares in the name of the record owner. For an example of a share certificate, see Section B after the *Ling* case; see also MBCA § 6.25. Share certificates usually come attached to a "stub" that may be filled in when the certificate is actually issued by the corporation to a shareholder. In closely held corporations, the record of shareholders may simply consist of these stubs; in publicly held corporations, much more elaborate records may be kept by a "transfer agent," typically a commercial bank. These records, of course, reveal only the record owner, not the beneficial owner. MBCA § 6.26, and the statutes of many states, also authorize a corporation to issue uncertificated shares, i.e., shares that are not represented by certificates. This is a relatively recent innovation for closely held corporations, and it appears today that most corporations continue to prefer to issue certificated shares, although there is a slight cost savings in using uncertificated shares.

(3) Shareholder voting and entitlement to distributions are determined from the records of the corporation. It is not necessary for a record shareholder to exhibit the share certificate (in the case of certificated shares) in order to vote or receive a distribution. When a corporation conducts a vote, it must determine which shareholders are entitled to notice and to vote at the meeting. State statutes provide that the board of directors may fix a record date, or cut-off date, for determining who the shareholders of record are. See, e.g., MBCA §§ 7.07, 7.20.

Sometimes these cut-off dates can present problems, even for large publicly traded companies that, presumably, are assisted by expert counsel. In McKesson Corporation v. Derdiger, 793 A.2d 385 (Del.Ch.2002), McKesson was a large Delaware corporation whose shares traded on the New York Stock Exchange. McKesson had set May 25, 2001 as the record date for stockholders to be eligible to vote at the annual meeting, and it had announced that the annual meeting would be held on July 25, 2001. However, § 213(a) of the Delaware General Corporation Law provided that the record date cannot be set "more than 60 * * * days *before* the date of the annual meeting." McKesson's May 25 record date was 61 days before the July 25 annual meeting date. The Delaware Chancery Court reasoned that since one day before July 25 is July 24, 60 days before July 25 must be May 26, and thus, May 25 must be more than 60 days before the date of the annual meeting. The court further opined that "the Legislature includes immutable time limits in statutes to serve particular purposes and such time limits are usually strictly enforced." Despite the noncompliance, the court ultimately decided that the actions taken at the July 25 meeting were valid, but it suggested that it might not be willing to bless similar actions in future cases.

(4) Action by shareholders at a meeting requires the existence of a quorum and the approval by the requisite number of votes. See MBCA §§ 7.25–7.28. These are often viewed as mundane, technical matters, but there are a number of substantive issues that may arise.

———

Cumulative vs. Straight Voting. The workings of these two methods of voting to elect directors can be most simply described by an illustration. Let us assume a corporation with two shareholders, A with 18 shares, and B with 82 shares. Further, let us assume that there are five directors and each shareholder nominates five candidates. Directors run "at large" rather than for specific places; hence the five persons receiving the most votes are elected. If only straight voting is permitted, A may cast 18 votes for each of five candidates, and B may cast 82 votes for each of five candidates. The result, of course, is that all five of B's candidates are elected.

If cumulative voting is permitted, the number of votes that each shareholder may cast is first computed. A shareholder has a number of votes equal to the number of shares he owns multiplied by the number of board seats up for election. The shareholder is then permitted to distribute his votes as he sees fit over one or more candidates. In the example above, A is entitled to cast a total of 90 votes (18x5), and B is entitled to cast a total of 410 votes (82x5). If A casts all 90 votes for A_1, A_1 is ensured of election because B cannot divide 410 votes among five candidates in such a way as to give each candidate more than 90 votes (which would be necessary to preclude A_1's election). Obviously, the effect of cumulative voting is that it increases minority participation on the board of directors. In straight voting, the shareholder with 51 percent of the vote elects the entire board; in cumulative voting, a relatively small faction (18 percent in the above example) may obtain representation on the board. Whether this is good or bad depends on one's point of view.[b]

One undesirable aspect of cumulative voting is that it tends to be a little tricky. If a shareholder casts votes in an irrational or inefficient way, he may not get the directorships his position entitles him to; when

---

[b] Numerous arguments for and against cumulative voting have been made. Arguments in favor of such voting include: (1) it is democratic in that persons with large (but minority) holdings should have a voice in the conduct of the corporation; (2) it is desirable to have as many viewpoints as possible represented on the board of directors; and (3) the presence of a minority director may discourage conflicts of interest by management since discovery of such conflicts is considerably more likely. Arguments in opposition include: (1) the introduction of a partisan on the board is inconsistent with the notion that the board should represent all interests in the corporation; (2) a partisan director may cause disharmony which reduces the efficiency of the board; (3) a partisan director may criticize management unreasonably so as to make it less willing to take risky (but desirable) action; (4) a partisan director may leak confidential information; and (5) in practice cumulative voting is typically used to further narrow partisan goals, particularly to give an insurgent group a toehold in the corporation in an effort to obtain control. See Jeffrey N. Gordon, Institutions as Relational Investors: A New Look at Cumulative Voting, 94 Colum.L.Rev. 124 (1994).

voting cumulatively, it is relatively easy to make a mistake in spreading votes around. The most graphic illustrations of this are the cases where a majority shareholder votes in such a way that he elects only a minority of the directors. This is most likely to occur when one shareholder votes "straight" and another cumulates. For example, if A has 60 shares and B has 40, with five directors to be elected, B may nevertheless elect a majority of the board if A votes "straight" and B knows that A is doing so. The result might look like this:

A$_1$–60, A$_2$–60, A$_3$–60, A$_4$–60, A$_5$–60; B$_1$–67, B$_2$–66, B$_3$–65, B$_4$–1, B$_5$–1.

This is daring of B because he is spreading his votes over three persons when he can only be sure of electing two. If B decides to do this, and A knows that B will try to elect three persons, then A, by properly cumulating his votes, can elect four directors—in effect "stealing" one of B's.[c]

The following formula is useful in determining the number of shares needed to elect one director:

$$\frac{S}{D + 1} + 1$$

where S equals the total number of shares voting, and D equals the number of directors to be elected.[d] The analogous formula to elect n directors is:

$$\frac{nS}{D + 1} + 1$$

NOTE

In Stancil v. Bruce Stancil Refrigeration, Inc., 344 S.E.2d 789 (N.C.App.1986), all the shares of stock of a North Carolina corporation were owned by two brothers: Bruce Stancil (12,500 shares) and Howard Stancil (12,500 shares). The board of directors consisted of Bruce Stancil, Eva Stancil (Bruce's wife), and Howard Stancil. At a shareholders' meeting involving the election of directors, each brother was represented by counsel. Bruce, "without a majority vote or consent, asserted his 'right' to act as chairman of the meeting and in fact conducted the proceedings at the meeting, acting with and upon the advice and consultation of his attorney, Wiley L. Lane, Jr." Howard announced that he planned to vote cumulatively in conformity with

---

[c] The results of such an election might be as follows: A$_1$–73, A$_2$–74, A$_3$–75, A$_4$–76, A$_5$–2, B$_1$–67, B$_2$–66, B$_3$–65, B$_4$–1, B$_5$–1.

[d] A minor modification may sometimes be necessary. The first portion of the formula, S/(D+1), establishes the maximum number of shares voted for a single person which is *insufficient* to elect that person as a director. Any share, or fraction thereof, in excess of that amount will be sufficient to elect a director. The formula in the text ignores fractional shares which sometimes may lead to a one-share error. For example, where there are 100 shares voting and five directors to be elected, the first portion of the formula is 100/(5+1), or 100/6. In this example, 16 shares will not elect a director, but 17 shares will because the first part of the formula yields 16 2/3. The formula in the text yields an answer of 17 2/3.

the North Carolina statute at the time, but Bruce did not acknowledge this statement (or grant the recess the North Carolina statute provided for after such an announcement is made). Bruce nominated himself, his wife Eva, and one Sarah Barnes. Howard nominated himself, his wife Clara, and one Henry Babb. The trial court's findings and conclusions describe what happened then:

15.   The Respondent, Bruce Stancil, cast his votes for his nominees for director as follows:

Bruce Stancil	12,500 Votes
Sarah Barnes	12,500 Votes
Eva Stancil	12,500 Votes

The Petitioner, Howard K. Stancil, cast his votes for his nominees for director as follows:

Howard K. Stancil	18,750 Votes
Clara Stancil	18,750 Votes
Henry Babb	0 Votes

16.   The Respondent, Bruce Stancil, after casting 12,500 votes for each of his three nominees (totaling 37,500 votes as allowed by law), purported to cast an additional 18,750 votes against Howard Stancil and 18,750 votes against Clara Stancil.

17.   There is no provision in the North Carolina Business Corporation Act providing for the casting of shareholder votes against a nominee for director, and the purported "votes" cast by the Respondent, Bruce Stancil, subsequent to the casting of his affirmative votes totaling 37,500 for his three nominees, were void and of no lawful effect.

18.   Bruce Stancil, Sarah Barnes and Eva Stancil, all being Respondents herein and recipients of 12,500 votes each, failed, as to each of them, to receive a plurality of the votes cast, as required by G.S. 55–67(c), and were not lawfully elected as directors of the Respondent corporation.

The appellate court affirmed the trial court's conclusion as to the result of the election. Does the board of directors now consist of Howard and Clara with one vacancy? What about the possible application of a statute similar to MBCA § 8.05(e)? If you had been Wiley L. Lane, Jr., what should you have done to preserve your client's apparently dominant position on the board of directors?

HUMPHRYS V. WINOUS CO.

Supreme Court of Ohio, 1956.
133 N.E.2d 780.

BELL, JUSTICE.

It can not be disclaimed that by reason of the stock distribution of this particular corporation a classification of the three directors into three classes containing one director each effectively divests the minority shareholders of a measure of control they formerly exercised over the corporation by electing one member of the board through the expedient of cumulative voting.

The issue herein, however, is not whether a particular result was accomplished but whether, under the statutes, such a result can legally be accomplished.

Section 1701.64, Revised Code, provides, in part, as follows:

The articles or the code of regulations may provide for the term of office of all of the directors or, if classified upon the basis of the expiration of the terms of office of the directors, of each class thereof, provided that no term shall be fixed for a period of more than three years from the date of their election and until the election of their successors.

Section 1701.58, Revised Code, after providing that any shareholder may, upon giving 24 hours notice of his desire to do so, cumulate such voting power as he possesses and give one candidate as many votes as the number of directors multiplied by the number of his votes equals, then provides that "such right to vote cumulatively shall not be restricted or qualified by the articles or the code of regulations."

The Court of Appeals sustained the contention of appellees and held that, since Section 1701.58, Revised Code, was specific in character, it constituted a limitation upon the applicability of Section 1701.64, Revised Code, and that, since the classification by appellants, attempted under the authority of Section 1701.64, Revised Code, did restrict the right to vote cumulatively as specifically guaranteed by Section 1701.58, Revised Code, such classification was invalid.

[The Court notes the historical development of an interest in cumulative voting to protect the rights of minority shareholders dating back to John H. Doyle's 1893 address to the Ohio State Bar Association and the subsequent recommendation submitted to the Ohio State Bar Association by the Committee on Judicial Administration and Legal Reform.]

* * *

If we may assume that the General Assembly was motivated by the recommendation of the bar association, it is obvious that it intended to assure minority representation on a corporate board of directors by permitting cumulative voting.

The provision for classification of directors appears for the first time in Ohio as * * * part of the General Corporation Act, effective June 9, 1927. * * *

Strangely enough, however, prior to 1955, there were only two cases which discussed the effect of classification of directors on cumulative voting. In Pittsburgh Steel Co. v. Walker (Court of Common Pleas, Allegheny County, Pennsylvania, 1944), three judges said there was doubt as to the constitutionality of the staggered system, but did not pass directly on the question. In Heeps v. Byers Co. (Court of Common Pleas, Allegheny County, Pennsylvania, 1950), one judge denied a preliminary injunction against the holding of a staggered-voting election on constitutional and other grounds. The Supreme Court of Pennsylvania, in affirming the judgment of the lower court, merely denied any right to question the granting of preliminary injunctions. Cohen v. A.M. Byers Co., 363 Pa. 618, 70 A.2d 837.

But on February 1, 1955, the Circuit Court of Cook County, Illinois, decided the case of Wolfson v. Avery. The action grew out of the much-publicized battle between Sewell Avery and Louis E. Wolfson for control of the board of directors of Montgomery Ward & Company. The Wolfson group sought a declaratory judgment that a bylaw of Montgomery Ward providing for the annual election of only one-third of the nine members of the board of directors is in violation of Section 3, Article XI of the Illinois Constitution, S.H.A., which among other things, provides for cumulative voting. Since the bylaw is specifically authorized by Section 35 of the Illinois Business Corporation Act, the complaint also sought to have that portion of the statute declared unconstitutional. The Circuit Court granted the plaintiff's motion for judgment on the pleadings, declaring Section 35 of the Business Corporation Act unconstitutional.

The trial judge in the Wolfson case adopted the theory that the Constitution requires that a minority shareholder be given the right—by cumulative voting—to exercise his "maximum voting strength proportionate to his share holding." He rejected the argument that the constitutional provision merely gives minority shareholders an opportunity to have some representation on the board of directors, whether proportionate or not.

The Supreme Court of Illinois, 126 N.E.2d 701, 711, after reviewing at some length the proceedings of the constitutional convention and the publications which interpreted the constitutional provision which was ratified on July 2, 1870, concluded that "Section 35 of the Business Corporation Act, in authorizing the classification of directors, is inconsistent with the constitutional right of a stockholder to cumulate his shares through multiplying them by the 'number of directors,' and cannot be sustained."

The Illinois court, in disposing of the defendant's reliance upon the fact that a law authorizing classification was passed by the first Illinois Legislature, and that this Legislature included 13 members who had served on the Constitutional Convention, said that "that is a fact to be given some weight, but it is by no means controlling (cf. Marbury v. Madison, 1 Cranch. 137, 2 L.Ed. 60) and in this case it must yield to the evidence supplied by the constitutional debates and the contemporary accounts in the press."

* * * As distinguished from a conflict between a constitutional provision and a statutory provision as in the Wolfson case, we have here a conflict between two statutory provisions. * * *

That cumulative voting is generally accepted is evidenced by the facts that mandatory cumulative voting provisions are found in the Constitutions of 13 states and in the statutes of eight others, and that permissive cumulative voting is authorized in 18 states. Cumulative voting is provided for in [MBCA (1950) § 31], drawn by the American Bar Association, and in Section 28 of the Model Business Corporation Act, proposed by the Commissioners on Uniform State Laws. Despite the seemingly obvious conflict between classification of directors and cumulative voting, provisions for staggered elections are made in approximately 33 states. See Williams, Cumulative Voting for Directors (1951), 7; Cumulative Voting and Classification of Directors, St. John's Law Review, 83, 86.

The problem will never arise in three jurisdictions because annual election of all directors is required by statute. See Section 22, Title 10, Alabama Code; Sections 805, 2201, California Corporation Code; Section 44–109, Wyoming Compiled Statutes.

Obviously, a provision in the articles or code of regulations to the effect that a shareholder may not vote cumulatively would restrict the right given by statute and would therefore be invalid in Ohio. Similarly a provision that a shareholder could vote cumulatively only if he held a certain percentage of the corporate stock would be invalid. But the same result might easily be accomplished without running afoul of the prohibition of Section 1701.58, Revised Code.

And majority shareholders have in many instances succeeded in curtailing or eliminating cumulative voting through a number of devices. In states where the right to vote cumulatively is permissive rather than mandatory, the charters of certain corporations have been amended to replace cumulative voting with straight voting. Cumulative voting may also be circumvented by removing minority-elected directors without cause. A third method employed to prevent effective use of cumulative voting is that of reducing the number of directors.

For example, suppose in a corporation having a board of nine members a minority shareholder, by cumulating his voting power, is able to elect one member of the board. But suppose, also, at the next meeting, the code of regulations is amended to reduce the directorate from nine to seven, as permitted under Section 1701.68, Revised Code. The minority shareholder, although not deprived of his *right* to vote cumulatively, has been deprived of representation on the board just as effectively as if he had not had the right. Similar examples could be given, depending on the number of shares held by the minority and the number of directors to be elected. Can it be said that the legislative intent in enacting Section 1701.58, Revised Code, was to limit Section 1701.64, Revised Code, and not limit Section 1701.68, Revised Code, and other sections of the corporation act? We do not think so.

If effect is to be given to both enactments of the General Assembly, the guaranty provided in Section 1701.58, Revised Code, must be construed as one granting a *right* that may not be restricted or qualified rather than one *ensuring* minority representation on the board of directors.

To hold otherwise would require a complete annihilation of the provision for classification because any classification would necessarily be a restriction or qualification on the effectiveness of cumulative voting, and no corporation could ever avail itself of the privilege of classification. We do not believe the General Assembly intended any such result.

Both the Ohio State Bar Association and the General Assembly recognized that, under the law of Ohio as it existed in January 1954, the action taken here by the corporation could have been accomplished. Consequently, the bar association recommended a change in the corporation law of Ohio to the effect that any class of directors could contain not less than two directors. In commenting on the proposed change, the Corporation Law Committee of the association said: "A new provision is that the number of directors in a given class shall be not less than two. This is for the purpose of meeting the objection that has been raised to the effect that under the present law the majority shareholders may fix the number of directors at three, each director to be in a separate class so that at each annual meeting only one director is to be elected. This device would prevent the minority, even though holding 49 per cent of the shares, from electing a single director."

Subsequently, Section 1701.57, Revised Code, was enacted, supplanting former Section 1701.64, Revised Code, to require that each class of directors must consist of not less than three directors each. 126 Ohio Laws, H70, effective October 11, 1955. Thus did the General

Assembly obviate the possibility of a recurrence of the action taken by The Winous Company.

It can not be gainsaid that the action taken here effectively eliminated the minority shareholders from exercising any control over the corporation. But we are of the opinion that the throwing of an aura of uncertainty and confusion around the statutory provision for classification of directors is not required by the construction of the statutory provision for cumulative voting. We hold, therefore, that Section 1701.58, Revised Code, guarantees to minority shareholders only the right of cumulative voting and does not necessarily guarantee the effectiveness of the exercise of that right to elect minority representation on the board of directors. * * *

The judgment of the Court of Appeals is reversed and the judgment of the Court of Common Pleas is modified and, as modified, is affirmed.

Judgment reversed.

MATTHIAS, STEWART and TAFT, JJ., concur.

WEYGANDT, C.J., and HART, J., dissent.

WEYGANDT, CHIEF JUSTICE, dissents on the ground of the cogent reasoning of the Court of Appeals that "the right of a shareholder in an Ohio corporation to cumulate his vote has been provided by statute in this state for more than fifty years. The legislature in adopting the revision of the statute dealing with corporate organization in 1927, showed clearly that it intended to strengthen the cumulative voting provision by adding to existing law the provision that a corporation cannot restrict cumulative voting by its articles or code of regulations. And when in the same act the legislature, for the first time provides that there may be classification of directors when provided for by its code of regulations, it could not have been intended that the exercise of such right could be so used as to nullify the right of cumulative voting. When the minimum number of three directors is provided for, and their terms of office are for three years, one to be elected each year, the right to cumulative voting is, in such case, *completely nullified*"—an utterly futile result hardly contemplated by the emphatic language of the General Assembly in its attempt to *strengthen* the right. (Italics supplied.)

NOTES

(1) Consider MBCA §§ 7.28, 8.04. Under the MBCA, cumulative voting, like preemptive rights, is an "opt in" election to be chosen by an appropriate provision in the articles of incorporation. Most states have adopted an "opt in" provision, but some states have an "opt out" election. A handful of states make cumulative voting mandatory for all corporations—some by provision in state constitutions. The number of states with mandatory cumulative voting, however, is declining. If a corporation has opted to grant cumulative voting

under the Model Act, may it thereafter amend the articles of incorporation by less than unanimous vote to delete that requirement? See MBCA § 10.01. Section 13.02(a)(4)(iv) of MBCA (1984) granted a right of dissent and appraisal to such a shareholder; however, the 1999 amendments eliminated this right so that it now exists only if the corporation elects affirmatively to provide it.

(2) What devices are available to minimize the impact of cumulative voting where that voting is mandatory? What about creating classes of directors consisting of one director each, such as involved in the *Winous* case? See MBCA § 8.06.[e] A decision to classify the board of directors may be attacked as a breach of fiduciary duty in some circumstances if made without business justification and in the midst of a proxy campaign to elect one director. See Coalition to Advocate Pub. Util. Responsibility, Inc. v. Engels, 364 F.Supp. 1202 (D.Minn.1973). What about removal of a director elected by minority votes? See MBCA §§ 8.08, 8.09. What about "freezing out" the minority director by denying that director access to information, refusing to appoint him or her to any committees, and then holding "unofficial meetings" and "ramming through decisions * * * with little discussion"? It is reported that these tactics were used by a public corporation, Bunker-Ramo Corp., against a director elected by a dissident group. Kaufman, Directors of Bunker-Ramo Seek to Expel Unwelcome Suitor's Chief From Board, Wall St. J., March 31, 1980, at 10; see Jeffrey N. Gordon, Institutions as Relational Investors: A New Look at Cumulative Voting, 94 Colum.L.Rev. 124 (1994).

(3) Where a board is composed of three or more directors, several states permit the staggering of elections if the corporation does not have cumulative voting. Staggering a three-person board means that each director serves for three years and that only one director stands for election each year. Is there anything wrong with that? When coupled with a provision that permits removal of directors only for cause, this makes outside takeovers by share purchases or proxy fights more difficult, since the successful outsider will only be able to replace one group of directors each year. During the 1980s, a number of publicly held corporations adopted a classified board of directors, coupled with a prohibition against removal of directors without cause, as a takeover defense.

RINGLING BROS.-BARNUM & BAILEY COMBINED SHOWS V. RINGLING

Supreme Court of Delaware, 1947.
53 A.2d 441.

PEARSON, JUDGE.

The Court of Chancery was called upon to review an attempted election of directors at the 1946 annual stockholders meeting of the

---

[e] Section 8.06, as approved in 1984, limited the application of this section to boards consisting of nine or more directors. It was amended to eliminate this limitation in 1999. Do you agree that this change was desirable?

corporate defendant. The pivotal questions concern an agreement between two of the three present stockholders, and particularly the effect of this agreement with relation to the exercise of voting rights by these two stockholders. At the time of the meeting, the corporation had outstanding 1000 shares of capital stock held as follows: 315 by petitioner Edith Conway Ringling; 315 by defendant Aubrey B. Ringling Haley (individually or as executrix and legatee of a deceased husband); and 370 by defendant John Ringling North. The purpose of the meeting was to elect the entire board of seven directors. The shares could be voted cumulatively. Mrs. Ringling asserts that by virtue of the operation of an agreement between her and Mrs. Haley, the latter was bound to vote her shares for an adjournment of the meeting, or in the alternative, for a certain slate of directors. Mrs. Haley contends that she was not so bound for reason that the agreement was invalid, or at least revocable.

The two ladies entered into the agreement in 1941. * * * The agreement recites that each party was the owner "subject only to possible claims of creditors of the estates of Charles Ringling and Richard Ringling, respectively" (deceased husbands of the parties), of 300 shares of the capital stock of the defendant corporation; that in 1938 these shares had been deposited under a voting trust agreement which would terminate in 1947, or earlier, upon the elimination of certain liability of the corporation; that each party also owned 15 shares individually; that the parties had "entered into an agreement in April 1934 providing for joint action by them in matters affecting their ownership of stock and interest in" the corporate defendant; that the parties desired "to continue to act jointly in all matters relating to their stock ownership or interest in" the corporate defendant (and the other corporation). The agreement then provides as follows:

"Now, Therefore, in consideration of the mutual covenants and agreements hereinafter contained the parties hereto agree as follows:

1.   Neither party will sell any shares of stock or any voting trust certificates in either of said corporations to any other person whosoever, without first making a written offer to the other party hereto of all of the shares or voting trust certificates proposed to be sold, for the same price and upon the same terms and conditions as in such proposed sale, and allowing such other party a time of not less than 180 days from the date of such written offer within which to accept same.

2.   In exercising any voting rights to which either party may be entitled by virtue of ownership of stock or voting trust certificates held by them in either of said corporation, each party will consult and confer with the other and the parties will act jointly in exercising such voting rights in accordance with such

agreement as they may reach with respect to any matter calling for the exercise of such voting rights.

3.   In the event the parties fail to agree with respect to any matter covered by paragraph 2 above, the question in disagreement shall be submitted for arbitration to Karl D. Loos, of Washington, D.C. as arbitrator and his decision thereon shall be binding upon the parties hereto. Such arbitration shall be exercised to the end of assuring for the respective corporations good management and such participation therein by the members of the Ringling family as the experience, capacity and ability of each may warrant. The parties may at any time by written agreement designate any other individual to act as arbitrator in lieu of said Loos.

4.   Each of the parties hereto will enter into and execute such voting trust agreement or agreements and such other instruments as, from time to time they may deem advisable and as they may be advised by counsel are appropriate to effectuate the purposes and objects of this agreement.

5.   This agreement shall be in effect from the date hereof and shall continue in effect for a period of ten years unless sooner terminated by mutual agreement in writing by the parties hereto.

6.   The agreement of April 1934 is hereby terminated.

7.   This agreement shall be binding upon and inure to the benefit of the heirs, executors, administrators and assigns of the parties hereto respectively."

The Mr. Loos mentioned in the agreement is an attorney and has represented both parties since 1937, and, before and after the voting trust was terminated in late 1942, advised them with respect to the exercise of their voting rights. At the annual meetings in 1943 and the two following years, the parties voted their shares in accordance with mutual understandings arrived at as a result of discussions. In each of these years, they elected five of the seven directors. Mrs. Ringling and Mrs. Haley each had sufficient votes, independently of the other, to elect two of the seven directors. By both voting for an additional candidate, they could be sure of his election regardless of how Mr. North, the remaining stockholder, might vote.[1]

---

[1]   Each lady was entitled to cast 2205 votes (since each had the cumulative voting rights of 315 shares, and there were 7 vacancies in the directorate). The sum of the votes of both is 4410, which is sufficient to allow 882 votes for each of 5 persons. Mr. North, holding 370 shares, was entitled to cast 2590 votes, which obviously cannot be divided so as to give to more than two candidates as many as 882 votes each. It will be observed that in order for Mrs. Ringling and Mrs. Haley to be sure to elect five directors (regardless of how Mr. North might vote) they must

Some weeks before the 1946 meeting, they discussed with Mr. Loos the matter of voting for directors. They were in accord that Mrs. Ringling should cast sufficient votes to elect herself and her son; and that Mrs. Haley should elect herself and her husband; but they did not agree upon a fifth director. The day before the meeting, the discussions were continued, Mrs. Haley being represented by her husband since she could not be present because of illness. In a conversation with Mr. Loos, Mr. Haley indicated that he would make a motion for an adjournment of the meeting for sixty days, in order to give the ladies additional time to come to an agreement about their voting. On the morning of the meeting, however, he stated that because of something Mrs. Ringling had done, he would not consent to a postponement. Mrs. Ringling then made a demand upon Mr. Loos to act under the third paragraph of the agreement "to arbitrate the disagreement" between her and Mrs. Haley in connection with the manner in which the stock of the two ladies should be voted. At the opening of the meeting, Mr. Loos read the written demand and stated that he determined and directed that the stock of both ladies be voted for an adjournment of sixty days. Mrs. Ringling then made a motion for adjournment and voted for it. Mr. Haley, as proxy for his wife, and Mr. North voted against the motion. Mrs. Ringling (herself or through her attorney, it is immaterial which,) objected to the voting of Mrs. Haley's stock in any manner other than in accordance with Mr. Loos' direction. The chairman ruled that the stock could not be voted contrary to such direction, and declared the motion for adjournment had carried. Nevertheless, the meeting proceeded to the election of directors. Mrs. Ringling stated that she would continue in the meeting "but without prejudice to her position with respect to the voting of the stock and the fact that adjournment had not been taken." Mr. Loos directed Mrs. Ringling to cast her votes.

882 for Mrs. Ringling,

882 for her son, Robert, and

441 for a Mr. Dunn, who had been a member of the board for several years.

She complied. Mr. Loos directed that Mrs. Haley's votes be cast

882 for Mrs. Haley,

882 for Mr. Haley, and

441 for Mr. Dunn.

Instead of complying, Mr. Haley attempted to vote his wife's shares

1103 for Mrs. Haley, and

---

act together in the sense that their combined votes must be divided among five different candidates and at least one of the five must be voted for by both Mrs. Ringling and Mrs. Haley.

1102 for Mr. Haley.

Mr. North voted his shares

864 for a Mr. Woods,

863 for a Mr. Griffin, and

863 for Mr. North.

The chairman ruled that the five candidates proposed by Mr. Loos, together with Messrs. Woods and North, were elected. The Haley-North group disputed this ruling insofar as it declared the election of Mr. Dunn; and insisted that Mr. Griffin, instead, had been elected. A directors' meeting followed in which Mrs. Ringling participated after stating that she would do so "without prejudice to her position that the stockholders' meeting had been adjourned and that the directors' meeting was not properly held." Mr. Dunn and Mr. Griffin, although each was challenged by an opposing faction, attempted to join in voting as directors for different slates of officers. Soon after the meeting, Mrs. Ringling instituted this proceeding.

The Vice Chancellor determined that the agreement to vote in accordance with the direction of Mr. Loos was valid as a "stock pooling agreement" with lawful objects and purposes, and that it was not in violation of any public policy of this state. He held that where the arbitrator acts under the agreement and one party refuses to comply with his direction, "the Agreement constitutes the willing party * * * an implied agent possessing the irrevocable proxy of the recalcitrant party for the purpose of casting the particular vote." It was ordered that a new election be held before a master, with the direction that the master should recognize and give effect to the agreement if its terms were properly invoked.

Before taking up defendants' objections to the agreement, let us analyze particularly what it attempts to provide with respect to voting, including what functions and powers it attempts to repose in Mr. Loos, the "arbitrator." The agreement recites that the parties desired "to continue to act jointly in all matters relating to their stock ownership or interest in" the corporation. The parties agreed to consult and confer with each other in exercising their voting rights and to act jointly—that is, concertedly; unitedly; towards unified courses of action—in accordance with such agreement as they might reach. Thus, so long as the parties agree for whom or for what their shares shall be voted, the agreement provides no function for the arbitrator. His role is limited to situations where the parties fail to agree upon a course of action. In such cases, the agreement directs that "the question in disagreement shall be submitted for arbitration" to Mr. Loos "as arbitrator and his decision thereon shall be binding upon the parties." These provisions are designed to operate in aid of what appears to be a primary purpose of the parties, "to act jointly" in exercising their voting rights, by providing a means for fixing a course of action whenever they themselves might reach a stalemate.

Should the agreement be interpreted as attempting to empower the arbitrator to carry his directions into effect? Certainly there is no express delegation or grant of power to do so, either by authorizing him to vote the shares or to compel either party to vote them in accordance with his directions. The agreement expresses no other function of the arbitrator than that of deciding questions in disagreement which prevent the effectuation of the purpose "to act jointly." The power to enforce a decision does not seem a necessary or usual incident of such a function. Mr. Loos is not a party to the agreement. It does not contemplate the transfer of any shares or interest in shares to him, or that he should undertake any duties which the parties might compel him to perform. They provided that they might designate any other individual to act instead of Mr. Loos. The agreement does not attempt to make the arbitrator a trustee of an express trust. What the arbitrator is to do is for the benefit of the parties, not for his own benefit. Whether the parties accept or reject his decision is no concern of his, so far as the agreement or the surrounding circumstances reveal. We think the parties sought to bind each other, but to be bound only to each other, and not to empower the arbitrator to enforce decisions he might make.

From this conclusion, it follows necessarily that no decision of the arbitrator could ever be enforced if both parties to the agreement were unwilling that it be enforced, for the obvious reason that there would be no one to enforce it. Under the agreement, something more is required after the arbitrator has given his decision in order that it should become compulsory: at least one of the parties must determine that such decision shall be carried into effect. Thus, any "control" of the voting of the shares, which is reposed in the arbitrator, is substantially limited in action under the agreement in that it is subject to the overriding power of the parties themselves.

The agreement does not describe the undertaking of each party with respect to a decision of the arbitrator other than to provide that it "shall be binding upon the parties." It seems to us that this language, considered with relation to its context and the situations to which it is applicable, means that each party promised the other to exercise her own voting rights in accordance with the arbitrator's decision. The agreement is silent about any exercise of the voting rights of one party by the other. The language with reference to situations where the parties arrive at an understanding as to voting plainly suggests "action" by each, and "exercising" voting rights by each, rather than by one for the other. There is no intimation that this method should be different where the arbitrator's decision is to be carried into effect. Assuming that a power in each party to exercise the voting rights of the other might be a relatively more effective or convenient means of enforcing a decision of the arbitrator than would be available without the power, this would not justify implying a delegation of the power in the absence of some indication that the parties bargained for that means. The method of voting actually employed by the parties tends to show that they did not construe the agreement as creating powers to vote each other's shares; for at meetings prior to 1946 each party apparently exercised her own voting rights, and at the 1946 meeting, Mrs. Ringling, who wished to enforce the agreement, did not attempt to cast a ballot in exercise of any voting rights of Mrs. Haley. We do not find enough in the agreement or in the circumstances to justify a construction that either party was empowered to exercise voting rights of the other.

Having examined what the parties sought to provide by the agreement, we come now to defendants' contention that the voting provisions are illegal and revocable. They say that the courts of this state have definitely established the doctrine "that there can be no agreement, or any device whatsoever, by which the voting power of stock of a Delaware corporation may be irrevocably separated from the ownership of the stock, except by an agreement which complies with Section 18" of the Corporation Law, Rev.Code 1935, § 2050, and except by a proxy coupled with an interest. They * * * contend that the doctrine is derived from Section 18 itself, Rev.Code of Del.1935, § 2050. The statute reads, in part, as follows:

> Sec. 18. Voting Trusts: * * * One or more stockholders may by agreement in writing deposit capital stock of an original issue with or transfer capital stock to any person or persons, or corporation or corporations authorized to act as trustee, for the purpose of vesting in said person or persons, corporation or corporations, who may be designated Voting Trustee or Voting Trustees, the right to vote thereon for any period of time determined by such agreement, not exceeding ten years, upon the terms and conditions stated in such agreement. Such agreement may contain any other lawful provisions not inconsistent with said purpose. * * * Said Voting Trustees may vote upon the stock so issued or transferred during the period in such agreement specified; stock standing in the names of such Voting Trustees may be voted either in person or by proxy, and in voting said stock, such Voting Trustees shall incur no responsibility as stockholder, trustee or otherwise, except for their own individual malfeasance.[f]

---

[f] Omitted portions of the section provide requirements for the filing of a copy of the agreement in the principal Delaware office of the corporation, for the issuance of certificates of stock to the voting trustees, for the voting of stock where there is more than one voting trustee, and for the extension of the agreement for additional periods, not exceeding ten years each. The current Delaware voting trust statute, DGCL § 218, was amended in 1994 to eliminate the ten-

In our view, neither the cases nor the statute sustain the rule for which the defendants contend. Their sweeping formulation would impugn well-recognized means by which a shareholder may effectively confer his voting rights upon others while retaining various other rights. For example, defendants' rule would apparently not permit holders of voting stock to confer upon stockholders of another class, by the device of an amendment of the certificate of incorporation, the exclusive right to vote during periods when dividends are not paid on stock of the latter class. The broad prohibitory meaning which defendants find in Section 18 seems inconsistent with their concession that proxies coupled with an interest may be irrevocable, for the statute contains nothing about such proxies. The statute authorizes, among other things, the deposit or transfer of stock in trust for a specified purpose, namely, "vesting" in the transferee "the right to vote thereon" for a limited period; and prescribes numerous requirements in this connection. Accordingly, it seems reasonable to infer that to establish the relationship and accomplish the purpose which the statute authorizes, its requirements must be complied with. But the statute does not purport to deal with agreements whereby shareholders attempt to bind each other as to how they shall vote their shares. Various forms of such pooling agreements, as they are sometimes called, have been held valid and have been distinguished from voting trusts. We think the particular agreement before us does not violate Section 18 or constitute an attempted evasion of its requirements, and is not illegal for any other reason. Generally speaking, a shareholder may exercise wide liberality of judgment in the matter of voting, and it is not objectionable that his motives may be for personal profit, or determined by whims or caprice, so long as he violates no duty owed his fellow shareholders. The ownership of voting stock imposes no legal duty to vote at all. A group of shareholders may, without impropriety, vote their respective shares so as to obtain advantages of concerted action. They may lawfully contract with each other to vote in the future in such way as they, or a majority of their group, from time to time determine. Reasonable provisions for cases of failure of the group to reach a determination because of an even division in their ranks seem unobjectionable. The provision here for submission to the arbitrator is plainly designed as a deadlock-breaking measure, and the arbitrator's decision cannot be enforced unless at least one of the parties (entitled to cast one-half of their combined votes) is willing that it be enforced. We find the provision reasonable. It does not appear that the agreement enables the parties to take any unlawful advantage of the outside shareholder, or of any other person. It offends no rule of law or public policy of this state of which we are aware.

---

year limitation on the life of a voting trust, but it retains the requirement that a copy of the agreement be filed with the corporation.

Legal consideration for the promises of each party is supplied by the mutual promises of the other party. The undertaking to vote in accordance with the arbitrator's decision is a valid contract. The good faith of the arbitrator's action has not been challenged and, indeed, the record indicates that no such challenge could be supported. Accordingly, the failure of Mrs. Haley to exercise her voting rights in accordance with his decision was a breach of her contract. It is no extenuation of the breach that her votes were cast for two of the three candidates directed by the arbitrator. His directions to her were part of a single plan or course of action for the voting of the shares of both parties to the agreement, calculated to utilize an advantage of joint action by them which would bring about the election of an additional director. The actual voting of Mrs. Haley's shares frustrates that plan to such an extent that it should not be treated as a partial performance of her contract.

Throughout their argument, defendants make much of the fact that all votes cast at the meeting were by the registered shareholders. The Court of Chancery may, in a review of an election, reject votes of a registered shareholder where his voting of them is found to be in violation of rights of another person. It seems to us that upon the application of Mrs. Ringling, the injured party, the votes representing Mrs. Haley's shares should not be counted. Since no infirmity in Mr. North's voting has been demonstrated, his right to recognition of what he did at the meeting should be considered in granting any relief to Mrs. Ringling; for her rights arose under a contract to which Mr. North was not a party. With this in mind, we have concluded that the election should not be declared invalid, but that effect should be given to a rejection of the votes representing Mrs. Haley's shares. No other relief seems appropriate in this proceeding. Mr. North's vote against the motion for adjournment was sufficient to defeat it. With respect to the election of directors, the return of the inspectors should be corrected to show a rejection of Mrs. Haley's votes, and to declare the election of the six persons for whom Mr. North and Mrs. Ringling voted.

This leaves one vacancy in the directorate. The question of what to do about such a vacancy was not considered by the court below and has not been argued here. For this reason, and because an election of directors at the 1947 annual meeting (which presumably will be held in the near future) may make a determination of the question unimportant, we shall not decide it on this appeal. If a decision of the point appears important to the parties, any of them may apply to raise it in the Court of Chancery, after the mandate of this court is received there.

An order should be entered, directing a modification of the order of the Court of Chancery in accordance with this opinion.

NOTES

(1) Robert B. Thompson, Teaching Business Associations: Norms, Economics and Cognitive Learning, 34 Ga.L.Rev. 997, 998–99 (2000), describes the background of this famous case:

> John Ringling, the most flamboyant of five Ringling brothers, had sent the circus spiraling toward disaster by borrowing to purchase a competitor who had secured the traditional opening dates of the season at the old Madison Square Garden. The purchase unfortunately occurred on the cusp of what became the Great Depression. The ensuing financial debacle left the banks with significant control over the circus, much to the consternation of the family. It took a wonder-kid from the next generation, John Ringling North, to regain family control. His arrogance as savior, however, offended the two women who had inherited the remaining two-thirds of the stock of the circus following the death of all the members of the founding generation.

> These two controlling shareholders are the parties to [the] agreement at issue, and they worked in harmony for a short time to exclude North. It was the Great Hartford Circus Fire of 1944 that undid their alliance. The husband of one, who happened to be on the scene at the time of the fire, went to jail. The son of the other, who happened to be away at the time of the tragedy did not and apparently showed little sympathy for the plight of his co-venturer. John Ringling North saw his opening and went to jail on visiting day. The result was a defection of one shareholder, which led to the question about the agreement's enforceability.

(2) Consider MBCA § 7.31. The Official Comment states that § 7.31(b) "avoids the result reached" in *Ringling*. Does it?

NEW YORK—MCKINNEY'S BUS.CORP.LAW §§ 609, 620

(Please consult the Statutory Supplement)

NOTES

(1) A proxy appointment, like other grants of authority to an agent, is usually revocable whether or not it is stated to be irrevocable. Several situations exist, however, where courts felt it necessary to recognize irrevocable proxies. These situations were usually analyzed as those involving a "proxy coupled with an interest," a notion roughly analogous to a "power coupled with an interest" in the law of agency. The leading case is Hunt v. Rousmanier's Administrators, 21 U.S. (8 Wheat.) 174 (1823). Of course, the phrase "proxy coupled with an interest" does not help to decide anything, and at common law the whole area was one of confusion. See Proctor L. Thomas, Irrevocable Proxies, 43 Tex.L.Rev. 733 (1965). In New York, the vagueness of this test is eliminated by § 609(f), which covers the

most common kinds of "interests" that a proxy may be "coupled" with, thereby becoming irrevocable. Compare the language of MBCA § 7.22(d) with § 609 of the New York statute in this regard.

(2) In Haft v. Haft, 671 A.2d 413, 421–23 (Del.Ch.1995), Chancellor Allen held that an irrevocable proxy granted to the chief executive officer of the corporation was enforceable because of the CEO's interest in the corporation:

> Under the Delaware corporation law (§ 212(e)) an interest sufficient to support an irrevocable proxy must be either "an interest in the stock itself or an interest in the corporation generally." Do Herbert Haft's interests, other than as a secured creditor, qualify under the statute? As I now explain, in my opinion they do.
>
> * * * The language * * * ("an interest in the corporation generally") was introduced * * * to erase the implication arising from dicta in a 1933 Master's Report, which had been confirmed by this court. The report was in the case of *In re Chilson,* Del.Ch., 168 A. 82 (1933). The *Chilson* dicta was to the effect that in order to support irrevocability of a proxy, the holder had to have an interest in the stock itself. * * * [T]he enactment of new § 212(e) in 1967 * * * made it very clear that other interests (interests other than in the stock itself) could legitimately be contractually protected by the grant of an irrevocable proxy. * * *
>
> No Delaware court has been required to address this question under the language of amended Section 212. In now doing so, it is appropriate to acknowledge that the corporate law has tended to distrust and discourage the separation of the shareholder claim as equity investor (i.e., the right to enjoy distributions on stock if, as, and when declared) from the right to vote stock. For example, there was for many years a rather clear rule against the sale of a corporate vote unattached to the sale of the underlying stock. A powerful argument can be advanced that generally the congruence of the right to vote and the residual rights of ownership will tend towards efficient wealth production.
>
> A proxy is, of course, a means temporarily to split the power to vote from the residual ownership claim of the stockholder. In the vast number of instances in which proxies to vote stock are used, however, this split occasions no significant divergence between the interests of the proxy holder and the holder of the residual corporate interest because the proxy is of relatively short duration and in all events is revocable unilaterally. Thus, in effect, the grant of the proxy represented a judgment (which may be enforced through revocation) that the holder of the proxy will exercise it in the economic interest of the residual owner. A potentially inefficient split between the interests of the voter and the interests of the residual owners may, however, develop when the proxy is irrevocable. Such a holder is free from the unilateral control of the

grantor and may be expected to be inclined to exercise voting rights in a way that benefits himself. There is of course, as a general matter, nothing legally suspect in contracting parties exercising contracted-for rights in a self-interested manner.[11] Yet the exercise of voting control over corporations by persons whose interest in them is not chiefly or solely as a residual owner will create circumstances in which the corporation will be less than optimally efficient in the selection of risky investment projects. (A simple, if gross, example: the holder of an irrevocable proxy with voting control might simply refuse to elect a board that will accept the best investment projects (those with the highest risk adjusted rate of return) unless some side payment to him is arranged). The special additional costs associated with such a divorce between ownership and voting (the costs being expressed either as an otherwise unnecessary expense or as the selection of non-optimizing investment projects) will of course tend to diminish as the voter's interest becomes aligned with the residual owner's interest.

In this light, the dicta of In re Chilson may be thought to offer a means of limiting the agency costs that irrevocable proxies occasion. By recognizing only an interest in the stock itself as an interest that will support the irrevocability of a proxy, the rule of *Chilson* would eliminate a class of cases in which the incentives of the proxy holder to exploit the corporation would be greatest, that is, those in which she simply has no economic interest at all in the residual equity of the firm. Of course the Chilson rule does not entirely eliminate the inefficient incentive structure that the divorce of voting power and benefit occasions; the proxy voter/secured lender still is a creditor and thus may not be inclined to accept high-risk/high-reward projects, even if they have a positive risk-adjusted net present value. But the Chilson rule would moderate the effect. * * *

In this instance, I confess to the view that a corporation law rule allowing for the specific enforceability of an irrevocable proxy that is coupled only with the holder's interest in maintaining a salaried office seems mischievous in terms of its possible efficiency effects. But in light of the 1967 amendment to the Delaware statutory law * * * and the absence of contrary precedent, I am required to express the opinion that such an interest—the interest that Herbert Haft had and retains as the senior executive officer of Dart—is sufficient under our law to render specifically enforceable the express contract for an irrevocable proxy. * * *

---

[11] I note that this statement is subject to qualification in at least three circumstances: (1) a contract between a fiduciary and the person or entity for whom she acts (the "trust" or "corporation" etc.); (2) a contract between a fiduciary and a person who is an express beneficiary of the "trust" etc., if the contract relates to the business of the "trust" and (3) an implied obligation of good faith and fair dealing, which under certain circumstances will be found to impose a limitation on [an] arm's-length contracting party's ability to exercise legal rights in a way that deprives the other contracting party of the substance of the express bargain that the parties had reached.

(3) Consider § 609(e) of the New York statute, a provision that has no analogue in the MBCA. In Schreiber v. Carney, 447 A.2d 17, 23–26 (Del.Ch.1982), the Court was faced with a situation where a major shareholder committed itself to withdraw its opposition to a merger in exchange for a favorable loan from a participant in the merger. There was full disclosure of the arrangement to the independent shareholders, who overwhelmingly approved the proposed transaction. The Court stated:

> It is clear that the loan constituted vote-buying as that term has been defined by the courts. Vote-buying, despite its negative connotation, is simply a voting agreement supported by consideration personal to the stockholder, whereby the stockholder divorces his discretionary voting power and votes as directed by the offeror. The record clearly indicates that Texas International purchased or "removed" the obstacle of Jet Capital's opposition. Indeed, this is tacitly conceded by the defendants. However, defendants contend that the analysis of the transaction should not end here because the legality of vote-buying depends on whether its object or purpose is to defraud or in some manner disenfranchise the other stockholders. Defendants contend that because the loan did not defraud or disenfranchise any group of shareholders, but rather enfranchised the other shareholders by giving them a determinative vote in the proposed merger, it is not illegal *per se*. Defendants, in effect, contend that vote-buying is not void *per se* because the end justified the means. * * *

> The present case presents a peculiar factual setting in that the proposed vote-buying consideration was conditional upon the approval of a majority of the disinterested stockholders after a full disclosure to them of all pertinent facts and was purportedly for the best interests of all Texas International stockholders. * * *

> There are essentially two principles which appear in [the traditional vote-buying] cases. The first is that vote-buying is illegal *per se* if its object or purpose is to defraud or disenfranchise the other stockholders. A fraudulent purpose is as defined at common law, as a deceit which operates prejudicially upon the property rights of another.

> The second principle which appears in these old cases is that vote-buying is illegal *per se* as a matter of public policy; the reason being that each stockholder should be entitled to rely upon the independent judgment of his fellow stockholders. Thus, the underlying basis for this latter principle is again fraud but as viewed from a sense of duty owed by all stockholders to one another. The apparent rationale is that by requiring each stockholder to exercise his individual judgment as to all matters presented, "[t]he security of the small stockholders is found in the natural disposition of each stockholder to promote the best interests of all, in order to promote his individual interests." Cone v. Russell, 21 A. 847, 849

(1891). In essence, while self interest motivates a stockholder's vote, theoretically, it is also advancing the interests of the other stockholders. Thus, any agreement entered into for personal gain, whereby a stockholder separates his voting right from his property right was considered a fraud upon this community of interests. * * *

An automatic application of this rationale to the facts in the present case, however, would be to ignore an essential element of the transaction. The agreement in question was entered into primarily to further the interests of Texas International's other shareholders. Indeed, the shareholders, after reviewing a detailed proxy statement, voted overwhelmingly in favor of the loan agreement. Thus, the underlying rationale for the argument that vote-buying is illegal *per se,* as a matter of public policy, ceases to exist when measured against the undisputed reason for the transaction.

Moreover, the rationale that vote-buying is, as a matter of public policy, illegal *per se* is founded upon considerations of policy which are now outmoded as a necessary result of an evolving corporate environment. * * *

This is not to say, however, that vote-buying accomplished for some laudable purpose is automatically free from challenge. Because vote-buying is so easily susceptible of abuse it must be viewed as a voidable transaction subject to a test for intrinsic fairness.

The Court refused to grant summary judgment invalidating the transaction on the ground that it constituted vote-buying.

(4) The Delaware courts appear to have significantly liberalized the rules regarding vote-buying even beyond the holding in Schreiber v. Carney (where the Court declared that vote-buying was no longer illegal per-se). Hewlett v. Hewlett-Packard Company, 2002 WL 549137 (Del.Ch. Apr. 8, 2002), arose out of the hotly contested shareholder vote on the proposed merger of Hewlett-Packard Company and Compaq Computer Corporation, which, before their merger, were the second and third largest computer companies in the United States. Walter B. Hewlett opposed the merger and waged a vigorous proxy contest to defeat it. Nine days after the vote in which Hewlett-Packard's shareholders apparently had approved the merger, Walter Hewlett and a group of other merger opponents filed a lawsuit seeking a declaration that the merger was invalid because it had not been validly approved by the shareholders. One of the plaintiffs' principal claims was that Hewlett-Packard had illegally bought the votes of Deutsche Bank (which voted 17 million shares in favor of the merger) since Hewlett-Packard gave the bank a significant amount of new business when it added Deutsch Bank as a co-manager. Prior to this transaction, the proxy committee of Deutsch Bank's Asset Management Division had decided to vote against the merger. Immediately after the new arrangement was implemented, Deutsch Bank switched its votes in favor of the merger.

The Delaware Court of Chancery stated that the appropriate standard for evaluating vote-buying claims is the one articulated in Schreiber v. Carney: vote-buying is illegal *per se* if "the object or purpose is to defraud or in some way disenfranchise the other shareholders." The *Schreiber* court also stated that "because vote-buying is so easily susceptible of abuse it must be viewed as a voidable transaction subject to a test for intrinsic fairness." In *Hewlett* however, the court noted that this proposition "seems difficult to reconcile" with the Delaware legislature's "explicit validation of shareholder agreements." The court distinguished situations in which management buys votes and situations in which shareholders buy votes, stating that "[s]hareholders are free to do whatever they want with their votes, including selling them to the highest bidder." Management on the other hand, "may not use corporate assets to buy votes in a hotly contested proxy contest about an extraordinary transaction that would significantly transform the corporation unless it can be demonstrated, as it was in *Schreiber*, that management's vote-buying activity does not have a deleterious effect on the corporate franchise."

The court then denied Hewlett-Packard's motion to dismiss the plaintiffs' vote-buying claims because it found that the plaintiffs successfully alleged that Hewlett-Packard bought votes from Deutsche Bank with corporate assets, and because no steps were taken to ensure that the shareholder franchise was protected. However, the court stated that, at trial, the plaintiffs would bear the burden of presenting sufficient evidence to support a finding that Deutsche Bank was coerced by Hewlett-Packard management, and that the decision of Deutsch Bank to switch its votes was not made by Deutsch Bank for other than independent business reasons.

(5) For an argument sharply criticizing Delaware's liberal rules regarding corporate vote-buying, and asserting that vote-buying problems are likely to increase as more corporations utilize the internet and other advances in electronic communications technology, see Douglas Cole, E-Proxies for Sale? Corporate Vote-Buying in the Internet Age, 76 Wash. L. Rev. 793 (2001).

(6) DGCL § 228 permits action by shareholders without a meeting if written consents, setting forth the action taken, "shall be signed by the holders of outstanding stock having not less than the minimum number of votes that would be necessary to authorize or take such action at a meeting at which all shares entitled to vote thereon were present and voted." Contrast MBCA § 7.04 (requiring a unanimous vote). Through § 228, an aggressor who is able to obtain a majority of the outstanding voting shares may act immediately to replace the board of directors, oust incumbent management, amend bylaws, and defuse anti-takeover defenses. As noted by the Delaware Supreme Court, the "broad use [of § 228] in takeover battles, which we now observe, was not contemplated" in 1967 when this section was added to the DGCL. Allen v. Prime Computer, Inc., 540 A.2d 417, 419 (Del.1988).

(7) Should consents be subject to the same rules of revocability as an ordinary proxy? Or should consents be deemed to be "self executing" so that

once a majority has executed consents, the corporation has irrevocably acted? Or should they be analogized to voting agreements which are not revocable because they constitute contracts? In Calumet Indus., Inc. v. MacClure, 464 F.Supp. 19 (N.D.Ill.1978), the Court accepted the proxy analogy—a view that was also accepted in dictum in Allen v. Prime Computer, Inc., supra. Accepting that result, how long should a consent remain effective? In 1987, the Delaware legislature amended § 228 by adding a new subsection (c) that requires all consents to be dated. It also provides that consents are effective only if they are received within 60 days after the first-dated consent is delivered to the corporation.

(8) Effective July 1, 2000, Delaware amended its General Corporation Law to permit electronic meetings. DGCL § 211(a)(2). At such a "meeting," shareholders may use remote communication to be deemed present, to participate, and to vote at a meeting of stockholders. Voting by electronic transmission is authorized if information is submitted "from which it can be determined that the electronic transmission was authorized by the stockholder or proxy holder." Id. § 211(e). Delaware also amended its statute in several other significant respects in 2000 to recognize modern technology. It authorized written shareholder consents to be delivered electronically so long as the e-mail or telecopy is printed out before it is delivered to the corporation. Electronic notice to stockholders is permitted if the stockholder has consented to delivery of notice in that form. Notices delivered to stockholders by telecopy or e-mail are deemed given when "directed" to the proper phone number or e-mail address. Director action by unanimous consent and directors' resignations may also be made by electronic transmission. Consideration was also given to permitting meetings of directors by remote communication, but it was felt that the current practice of holding meetings by telephone conference call provided sufficient flexibility.

BROWN V. McLANAHAN

United States Court of Appeals, Fourth Circuit, 1945.
148 F.2d 703.

Before PARKER, SOPER, and DOBIE, CIRCUIT JUDGES.

DOBIE, CIRCUIT JUDGE.

This appeal from an order granting a motion to dismiss, involves the equitable rights attaching to certain voting trust certificates representing shares of preferred stock of the Baltimore Transit Company (hereinafter called the Company).

The appellant, Dorothy K. Brown (hereinafter referred to as plaintiff), as the holder of voting trust certificates representing 500 shares of the preferred stock of the Company, brought a class action against the voting trustees, the directors of the Company, the Company itself, the indenture trustee for the holders of the Company's debentures, and the debenture holders as a class (herein collectively referred to as defendants), seeking to set aside as unlawful an amendment of the Company's charter which purports to vest voting rights in the debenture holders. On oral argument before this Court, it was stated that the holders of 45,000 shares of preferred stock have indicated their approval of this suit.

The securities involved in this litigation were issued under a plan of reorganization of the United Railways and Electric Company of Baltimore, and The Maryland Electric Railways Company and Subsidiary Companies, under Section 77B of the Bankruptcy Act, 11 U.S.C.A. § 207. The plan was approved by the United States District Court for the District of Maryland.

That part of the reorganization plan relevant to the question before us may be briefly summarized.

The plan provided for the issuance of three types of securities. Debentures in the amount of $22,083,381 and 233,427 shares of preferred stock were issued to the holders of all first lien bonds on the basis of $500 principal amount of debentures, and five shares of preferred stock, par value $100 per share for each $1,000 principal amount of the bonds; 169,112 shares of new common stock, without par value, were issued to the old common stockholders and to unsecured creditors.

Under the plan of reorganization, voting rights were vested exclusively in the preferred and common stock. Each share of preferred entitled the holder to one vote on all corporate matters (except that the power to elect one director was exclusively vested in the common stock) and further, so long as any six months' installment of dividends on the preferred remained in arrears, the holders of the preferred stock held the *exclusive right* to vote for the election of all but one director. Three shares of common stock entitled the holder to one vote.

The plan also provided for the establishment of a voting trust of all the preferred and common stock of the reorganized company for a period of ten years, the maximum period permitted by Maryland law. In accordance with this provision, all the stock was issued to eight voting trustees under a voting trust agreement which was to terminate on July 1, 1945. The trustees in turn issued voting trust certificates to those entitled to distribution under the plan. Under the plan, the voting rights were to revert, on termination of the trust, to the certificate holders in proportion to the number of shares represented.

No dividends have ever been paid on the preferred stock, and pursuant to the charter provision, at all times since dividends have been in arrears, the exclusive right to elect all but one director has been vested in the preferred stock.

The eight voting trustees are also a majority of the directors of the Company, elected as such by their own vote as trustees. On June 21, 1944, *without notice of any kind to the certificate holders,* the directors passed a resolution recommending, and the voting trustees as stockholders voted to adopt, an amendment to the Company's charter.

Article VII of the Voting Trust Agreement, by authority of which the trustees purportedly acted, provides in part as follows:

> (1) Until the termination of the trusts of this instrument the entire right to vote upon or with respect to all shares of Preferred and/or Common Stock deposited, or at any time held hereunder, and the right to otherwise authorize, approve or oppose on behalf of said shares of stock any corporate action of The Baltimore Transit Company shall be vested exclusively in said Trustees; without limiting the generality or scope of the foregoing provisions such rights shall include the right to vote or act with respect to any amendment of the certificate of incorporation of the Company, the increase, reduction, classification, reclassification of its capital stock, change in the par value, preference and restrictions and qualifications of all shares, the creation of any debts or liens, any amendment to the By-Laws, the election or removal of directors, the acceptance of stock in payment of dividends as well as every other right of an absolute owner of said shares * * *

Briefly, the amendment effected several changes in voting rights. It eliminated the arrearage clause which had provided for exclusive voting rights in the preferred stock. It also granted voting rights to the holders of debentures, one vote for each $100 principal amount of the debentures, thus creating approximately 221,000 new votes eligible to be cast in all corporate matters. And, further, as of the date of termination of the voting trust agreement on July 1, 1945, the common stockholders would be deprived of their exclusive right to elect one director.

These facts are all substantially set forth in plaintiff's complaint. The complaint alleges, and for purposes of the motion to dismiss these allegations must be accepted as true, that the creation of 221,000 new votes in the debentures will dilute the voting power of the stock; that the amendment will deprive the voting trust certificate holders of their right to control the management of the Company, and the election of its directors after the expiration of the voting trust; that these voting trustees are holders of substantial amounts of debentures, either in their own right, or as officers of various banks.

Plaintiff contends that the action of the voting trustees in adopting the amendment was a breach of the fiduciary duty owed to the certificate holders and seeks fourfold relief that: (1) The amendment of June 21,

1944, be declared null and void; (2) the voting trustees be removed; (3) the voting trust be terminated; and (4) damages be allowed in the alternative.

The crux of the complaint is that the voting trustees, faced with the fact that the voting trust would shortly expire and that they would no longer be able to control the corporation, proceeded to amend its charter so that they would be able to hold on to the control by giving voting rights to the debentures (thereby enhancing the value of these debentures) which were largely owned or controlled by them or by corporations in which they were interested and to take away from the preferred stock the power of control which resided in it when dividends were in arrears. * * *

Plaintiff contends that such action on the part of the trustees was invalid for three reasons: (1) Because it was beyond the powers vested in the trustees to diminish the voting power, which they held in trust for the holders of preferred stock as well as for other stockholders and debenture holders, so that upon the termination of the trust they would not be able to return it to those from whom they had received it in the same condition in which it was received; (2) because it was an abuse of trust to use the voting power which the trustees held in trust for the benefit of preferred stockholders as well as of the debenture holders to the advantage of the latter and the detriment of the former; and (3) that it was an abuse of trust to use the voting power for their own benefit and the benefit of corporations in which they were interested and to the detriment of preferred stockholders who were beneficiaries of the trust. We think the action of the trustees was invalid for all three reasons. As to the third reason, it could well be that the evidence at the trial may show the facts to be different from the facts as alleged. There seems to be no dispute as to the facts to which the first and second reasons apply.

As to the first and second reasons, we think it perfectly clear that it was not intended by the voting trust agreement to vest the trustees with power either to impair the voting power of the preferred stock which they held in trust or to use the power for the benefit of the debenture holders and to the detriment of the holders of preferred stock. It is true that the power to amend the charter for proper purposes was conferred upon them; but at the time of the creation of the voting trust it was not permissible under the law to vest voting power in the debenture holders. An amendment of the law made it legal to do this; but it could not have been intended at the time of the creation of the voting trust that the trustees should exercise the voting power in a way which the law did not then recognize and which would result in taking from the holders of stock a part of the very power which they had conferred upon the trustees to be held in trust for their benefit. It is elementary that a trustee may not exercise powers granted in a way that is detrimental to the *cestuis que trustent*; nor may one who is trustee for different classes favor one class at the expense of another. Such an exercise of power is in derogation of the trust and may not be upheld, even though the thing done be within the scope of powers granted to the trustees in general terms. It is well settled that the depositaries of the power to vote stock are trustees in the equitable sense, Henry L. Doherty & Co. v. Rice, C.C., 186 F. 204, 214, and a voting trust is a trust in the accepted equitable view. * * *

Defendants strongly urge that the real beneficiaries here and now are the debenture holders and not the certificate holders. Such cases as Mackin v. Nicollet Hotel, 8 Cir., 25 F.2d 783, and Clark v. Foster, 98 Wash. 241, 167 P. 908, are cited for the proposition that it is the existence of a voting trust, in many cases restricting the powers of the stockholder, that attracts lending by bondholders. Assuming the correctness of this contention, we still find no such situation here. This plan of reorganization was an attempt to salvage utility companies sinking in the quagmire of bankruptcy. These debenture holders accepted, in lieu of their old obligations, two kinds of property, ownership of the company and a creditor's lien. Ownership control, for purposes of judicious management, was placed in the hands of trustees. When the debenture holders sold their ultimate rights to stock ownership with its attendant control of the Company's affairs, they retained only their creditor's lien. We are not at liberty here to distort the established rules of property and to find that by some process of corporate alchemy the legal ownership of the Company has been transmuted into evidence of debt.

The sale of the voting trust certificates by the original holders vested all equitable rights in their transferees and we cannot say that one might sell the equitable rights in preferred stock to a bona fide purchaser, and subsequently by indirection, impair or destroy the inherent equitable property in those certificates, to the benefit of the original seller. Meinhard v. Salmon, 249 N.Y. 458, 464, 164 N.E. 545. * * *

We are of the opinion, and so hold, that the action taken by these trustees was beyond the limit of their authority. The motion to dismiss should therefore have been denied.

The judgment of the District Court will be reversed and the cause remanded for further proceedings in accordance with the views herein expressed. The amendment to the charter of June 21, 1944 should be declared void, but what further relief should be granted upon the complaint is a matter resting in the sound discretion of the District Court.

Reversed and remanded.

NOTES

(1) Consider MBCA § 7.30. An earlier version of the Delaware voting trust statute, DGCL § 218, is set forth in *Ringling*. It is important to recognize that the procedural requirements with respect to the creation of a voting trust—particularly the filing of a copy of the voting trust agreement

with the corporation—is essential for its validity. This rule is a reflection of the fact that the early attitude of courts towards voting trusts was unfavorable, and mistrust may still continue to some extent in some states. The comment of Mr. Justice Douglas (in a nonjudicial context) that a voting trust is "little more than a vehicle for corporate kidnapping," William O. Douglas, Democracy and Finance 43 (1940), is a clear reflection of this early attitude. The Securities and Exchange Commission has historically opposed the use of voting trusts, and the New York Stock Exchange refuses to list voting stock where there exists a voting trust, irrevocable proxy, or any similar arrangement to which the company or any of its officers or directors is a party, either directly or indirectly.

(2) There has been some recognition that a voting trust should be viewed as simply another control mechanism that may in certain situations be abused, but that is generally no more subject to criticism than other control devices. This perspective is most clearly set forth in Oceanic Exploration Co. v. Grynberg, 428 A.2d 1, 7–8 (Del.1981). Most voting trust statutes, like § 7.30 of the MBCA, mandate a ten-year life span for voting trusts. Compare this section with § 7.31, which has no maximum period for the existence of a voting agreement. In 1994, Delaware amended its voting trust statute to eliminate the ten-year provision, perhaps a further recognition that the early attitude towards voting trusts was misplaced.

(3) If creditors do not trust a dominant shareholder, they may insist that controlling shares be placed in a voting trust as a condition to the extension of credit. The most spectacular illustration of this involved creditors of Trans World Airlines, Inc., who required Howard Hughes to place his 75 percent stock interest into a voting trust as a condition to financing TWA's purchase of jumbo jets. After the trust was created, Hughes had no voice in TWA management. Hughes later agreed to sell the shares of TWA in the voting trust, and this sale took place when TWA was near its historic high in price. Mr. Hughes received a check for over $550,000,000 from the sale. See John McDonald, Howard Hughes's Biggest Surprise, Fortune, July 1, 1966, at 119–20.

(4) Regulatory agencies may insist that voting control of a regulated corporation be placed in a voting trust as a condition for permitting private parties to acquire the regulated corporation or, more commonly, the parent corporation of a regulated corporation. For example, some state insurance commissions permit transfers of control of regulated insurance companies if the shares are placed in an irrevocable voting trust with acceptable trustees.

(5) In Hall v. Staha, 800 S.W.2d 396 (Ark.1990), Hatfield and Staha formed a Delaware limited partnership, MED-MAX Associates Limited Partnership, and transferred their stock in Dunhall Pharmaceuticals, Inc., a profitable seller of pharmaceuticals, to the limited partnership. The limited partnership also obtained Dunhall shares from a number of other shareholders in exchange for limited partnership interests. MED-MAX ultimately acquired 50.5 percent of the Dunhall stock. While Hatfield and Staha were the general partners, there was no disclosure of the identity of

the limited partners. The Court held that MED-MAX was an illegal voting trust since it was a "secret, uncontrolled, combination of stockholders formed to acquire voting control of a corporation to the possible detriment of the nonparticipating stockholders." The votes cast by MED-MAX at a shareholders' meeting were invalidated. Is there any reason why a limited partnership cannot be a voting trust?

LEHRMAN v. COHEN

Supreme Court of Delaware, 1966.
222 A.2d 800.

HERRMANN, JUSTICE.

The primary problem presented on this appeal involves the applicability of the Delaware Voting Trust Statute. Other questions involve the legality of stock having voting power but no dividend or liquidation rights except repayment of par value, and an alleged unlawful delegation of directorial duties and powers.

These are the material facts:

Giant Food Inc. (hereinafter the "Company") was incorporated in Delaware in 1935 by the defendant N.M. Cohen and Samuel Lehrman, deceased father of the plaintiff Jacob Lehrman. From its inception, the Company was controlled by the Cohen and Lehrman families, each of which owned equal quantities of the voting stock, designated Class AC (held by the Cohen family) and Class AL (held by the Lehrman family) common stock. The two classes of stock have cumulative voting rights and each is entitled to elect two members of the Company's four-member board of directors.

Over the years, as may have been expected, there were differences of opinion between the Cohen and Lehrman families as to operating policies of the Company. Samuel Lehrman died in 1949; each of his children inherited part of his stock in the Company; but a dispute arose among the children regarding an *inter vivos* gift of certain shares made to the plaintiff by his father shortly before his death. To eliminate the Lehrman family dispute and its possible disruption of the affairs of the Company, an arrangement was made which settled the dispute and permitted the plaintiff to acquire all of the outstanding Class AL stock, thereby vesting in him voting power equal to that held by the Cohen family. The arrangement involved [a] repurchase by the Company of the stock held by the plaintiff's brothers and sister, their relinquishment of any claim to the stock gift, and an equalizing surrender of certain stock by the Cohens to the Company for retirement. An essential part of the arrangement, upon the insistence of the Cohens, was the establishment of a fifth directorship to obviate the risk of deadlock which would have continued if the equal division of voting power between AL and AC stock were continued.

To implement the arrangement, on December 31, 1949, the Company's certificate of incorporation was amended, *inter alia,* to create a third class of voting stock, designated Class AD common stock, entitled to elect the fifth director. Article Fourth of the amendment to the certificate of incorporation provided for the issuance of one share of Class AD stock, having a par value of $10 and the following rights and powers:

> The holder of Class AD common stock shall be entitled to all of the rights and privileges pertaining to common stock without any limitations, prohibitions, restrictions or qualifications except that the holder of said Class AD stock shall not be entitled to receive any dividends declared and paid by the corporation, shall not be entitled to share in the distribution of assets of the corporation upon liquidation or dissolution either partial or final, except to the extent of the par value of said Class AD common stock, and in the election of Directors shall have the right to vote for and elect one of the five Directors hereinafter provided for.

> The corporation shall have the right, at any time, to redeem and call in the Class AD stock by paying to the holder thereof the par value of said stock, provided however, that such redemption or call shall be authorized and directed by the affirmative vote of four of the five Directors hereinafter provided for.[2]

By resolution of the board of directors, the share of Class AD stock was issued forthwith to the defendant Joseph B. Danzansky, who had served as counsel to the Company since 1944. All corporate action regarding the creation and the issuance of the Class AD stock was accomplished by the unanimous vote of the AC and AL stockholders and of the board of directors. In April 1950, pursuant to the arrangement, Danzansky voted his share of AD stock to elect himself as the Company's fifth director; and he served as such until the institution of this action in 1964. During that entire period, the AC and AL stock have been voted to elect two directors each. From 1950 through 1964, Danzansky regularly attended board meetings, raised and discussed general items of business, and voted on all issues as they came before the board. He was not obliged to break any deadlock among the directors prior to October 1, 1964 because no such deadlock arose before that date.

Beginning in December 1959, 200,000 shares of non-voting common stock of the Company were sold in a public issue for over $3,000,000.

---

[2] Article Fourth of the amendment also co-related the Class AL and the Class AC common stock as follows:

"The holders of Class AL common stock shall be entitled to all of the rights and privileges pertaining to common stock without any limitations, prohibitions, restrictions, or qualifications except that the holder or holders of said Class AL common stock, in the election of Directors, shall have the right to vote for and elect two of the five Directors hereinafter provided for."

Each prospectus published in connection with the public issue contained the following statement:

> Common Stock AD is not a participating stock, and the only purpose for the provision and issuance of such stock is to prevent a deadlock in case the Directors elected by the Common Stock AC and the Directors elected by the Common Stock AL cannot reach an agreement.

Similarly, a letter on behalf of the Company to the Commissioner of Internal Revenue, dated July 15, 1959, contained the following statement:

> As can be seen from the enclosed certified copy of the stock provisions of the certificate of Incorporation, as amended, the Class AD common stock is not a participating stock, the only purpose for the provision and issuance of such a stock being to prevent a deadlock in case the AC and AL Directors cannot reach an agreement.

From the outset and until October 1, 1964, the defendant N.M. Cohen was president of the Company. On that date, a resolution was adopted at the Company's annual stockholders' meeting to give Danzansky a fifteen year executive employment contract at an annual salary of $67,600, and options for 25,000 shares of the non-voting common stock of the Company. The AC and AD stock were voted in favor and the AL stock was voted against the resolution. At a directors meeting held the same day, Danzansky was elected president of the Company by a 3–2 vote, the two AL directors voting in opposition. On December 11, 1964, Danzansky resigned as director and voted his share of AD stock to elect as the fifth director Millard F. West, Jr., a former AL director and investment banker whose firm was one of the underwriters of the public issue of the Company's stock. The newly constituted board ratified the election of Danzansky as president; and, on January 27, 1965, after the commencement of this action and after a review and report by a committee consisting of the new AD director and one AL director, Danzansky's employment contract was approved and adopted with certain modifications.

The plaintiff brought this action on December 11, 1964, basing it upon two claims: The First Claim charges that the creation, issuance, and voting of the one share of Class AD stock resulted in an arrangement illegal under the law of this State for the reasons hereinafter set forth. The Second Claim, addressed to the events of October 1, 1964, charges that the election of Danzansky as president of the Company and his employment contract violated the terms of the 1959 deadlock-breaking arrangement, as made between the holders of the AC and AL stock, and constituted breaches of contract and fiduciary duty. The plaintiff and the defendants filed cross-motions for summary judgment as to the First Claim. The Court of Chancery, after considering the contentions now before us and discussed infra, granted summary judgment in favor of the defendants and denied the plaintiff's motion for summary judgment. The plaintiff appeals.

I.

The plaintiff's primary contention is that the Class AD stock arrangement is, in substance and effect, a voting trust; that, as such, it is illegal because not limited to a ten year period as required by the Voting Trust Statute. The defendants deny that the AD stock arrangement constitutes a disguised voting trust; but they concede that if it is, the arrangement is illegal for violation of the Statute. Thus, issue is clearly joined on the point.

The criteria of a voting trust under our decisions have been summarized by this Court in Abercrombie v. Davies, 36 Del.Ch. 371, 130 A.2d 338 (1957). The tests there set forth, accepted by both sides of this cause as being applicable, are as follows: (1) the voting rights of the stock are separated from the other attributes of ownership; (2) the voting rights granted are intended to be irrevocable for a definite period of time; and (3) the principal purpose[4] of the grant of voting rights is to acquire voting control of the corporation.

Adopting and applying these tests, the plaintiff says, as to the first element, that the AD arrangement provides for a divorcement of voting rights from beneficial ownership of the AC and AL stock; that the creation and issuance of the share of AD stock is tantamount to a pooling by the AC and AL stockholders of a portion of their voting stock and giving it to a trustee, in the person of the AD stockholder, to vote for the election of the fifth director; that after the creation of the AD stock, the AC and AL stockholders each hold but 40% of the voting power, and the AD stockholder holds the controlling balance of 20%; that the AD stock has no property rights except the right to a return of the $10 paid as the par value; and that, therefore, there has been a transfer of the voting rights devoid of any participating property rights. So runs the argument of the plaintiff in support of his contention that the first of the *Abercrombie* criteria for a voting trust is met.

The contention is unacceptable. The AD arrangement did not separate the voting rights of the AC or the AL stock from the other attributes of ownership of those classes of stock. Each AC and AL stockholder retains complete control over the voting of his stock; each can vote his stock directly; no AL or AC stockholder is divested of his right to vote his stock as he sees fit; no AL or AC stock can be voted against the shareholder's wishes; and the AL and AC stock continue to elect two directors each.

---

[4] It is noteworthy, in this connection, that in Abercrombie, this Court distinguished between purpose and motive, stating that it considered only purpose to be material (130 A.2d 338, 341).

The AD stock arrangement, as we view it, became a part of the capitalization of the Company. The fact that there is but a single share, or that the par value is nominal, is of no legal significance; the one share and the $10 par value might have been multiplied many times over, with the same consequence. It is true that the creation of the separate class of AD stock may have diluted the voting *power* which had previously existed in the AC and AL stock—the usual consequence when additional voting stock is created—but the creation of the new class did not divest and separate the voting *rights* which remain vested in each AC and AL shareholder, together with the other attributes of the ownership of that stock. The fallacy of the plaintiff's position lies in his premise that since the voting power of the AC and AL stock was reduced by the creation of the AD stock, the percentage of reduction became the *res* of a voting trust. In any recapitalization involving the creation of additional voting stock, the voting power of the previously existing stock is diminished; but a voting trust is not necessarily the result.

Since the holders of the Class AC and Class AL stock of the Company did not separate the voting rights from the other attributes of ownership of those classes when they created the Class AD stock, the first *Abercrombie* test of a voting trust is not met.

This conclusion disposes of the second and third *Abercrombie* tests * * *.

In the final analysis, the essence of the question raised by the plaintiff in this connection is this: Is the substance and purpose of the AD stock arrangement sufficiently close to the substance and purpose of § 218 to warrant its being subjected to the restrictions and conditions imposed by that Statute? The answer is negative not only for the reasons above stated, but also because § 218 regulates trusts and pooling agreements amounting to trusts, not other and different types of arrangements and undertakings possible among stockholders. Compare Ringling Bros.-Barnum & Bailey Combined Shows Inc. v. Ringling, 29 Del.Ch. 610, 53 A.2d 441 (1947); Abercrombie v. Davies, supra. The AD stock arrangement is neither a trust nor a pooling agreement.

We hold, therefore, that the Class AD stock arrangement is not controlled by the Voting Trust Statute.

II.

The plaintiff's second point is that even if the Class AD stock arrangement is not a voting trust in substance and effect, the AD stock is illegal, nevertheless, because the creation of a class of stock having voting rights only, and lacking any substantial participating proprietary interest in the corporation, violates the public policy of this State as declared in § 218.

The fallacy of this argument is twofold: First, it is more accurate to say that what the law has disfavored, and what the public policy underlying the Voting Trust Statute means to control, is the separation of the vote from the stock—not from the stock ownership. Clearly, the AD stock arrangement is not violative of that public policy. Secondly, there is nothing in § 218, either expressed or implied, which requires that all stock of a Delaware corporation must have both voting rights and proprietary interests. Indeed, public policy to the contrary seems clearly expressed by 8 Del.C. § 151(a) which authorizes, in very broad terms, such voting powers and participating rights as may be stated in the certificate of incorporation. Non-voting stock is specifically authorized by § 151(a); and in the light thereof, consistency does not permit the conclusion, urged by the plaintiff, that the present public policy of this State condemns the separation of voting rights from beneficial stock ownership.

We conclude that the plaintiff's contention in this regard cannot withstand the force and effect of § 151(a). In our view, that Statute permits the creation of stock having voting rights only, as well as stock having property rights only. The voting powers and the participating rights of the Class AD stock being specified in the Company's certificate of incorporation, we are of the opinion that the Class AD stock is legal by virtue of § 151(a). * * *

We are told that if the AD stock arrangement is allowed thus to stand, our Voting Trust Statute will become a "dead letter" because it will be possible to evade and circumvent its purpose simply by issuing a class of non-participating voting stock, as was done here. We have three negative reactions to this argument:

First, it presupposes a divestiture of the voting rights of the AC and AL stock—an untenable supposition as has been stated. Secondly, it fails to take into account the main purpose of a Voting Trust Statute: to avoid secret, uncontrolled combinations of stockholders formed to acquire voting control of the corporation to the possible detriment of non-participating shareholders. It may not be said that the AD stock arrangement contravenes that purpose. Finally on this point, if we misconceive the legislative intent, and if the AD stock arrangement in this case reveals a loophole in § 218 which should be plugged, it is for the General Assembly to accomplish—not for us to attempt by interstitial judicial legislation.

III.

The plaintiff advances yet another reason for invalidating the AD stock. The essence of this argument is that the only function of that class of stock is to break directorial deadlocks; that the issuance of the AD stock is merely a technical device to permit that result; that, as such, it is illegal because it permits the AC and AL directors of the Company to delegate their statutory duties to the AD director as an arbitrator.

We see nothing inherently wrong or contrary to the public policy of this State, as plaintiff seems to suggest, about a device, otherwise lawful, designed by the stockholders of a corporation to break deadlocks of directors. The plaintiff says in this connection, that if public policy sanctioned such device, our General Corporation Law would provide for it. The fallacy of this argument lies in the assumption that legislative silence is a dependable indicator of public policy. We know of no reason, either under our statutes or our decisions, which would prevent the stockholders of a Delaware corporation from protecting themselves and their corporation, by a plan otherwise lawful, against the paralyzing and often fatal consequences of a stalemate in the directorate of the corporation. We hold, therefore, that the AD stock arrangement had a proper purpose.

As to the means adopted for the accomplishment of that purpose, we find the AD stock arrangement valid by virtue of § 141(a) of the Delaware Corporation Law which provides:

> The business of every corporation organized under the provisions of this chapter shall be managed by a board of directors, except as hereinafter or in its certificate of incorporation otherwise provided.

The AD stock arrangement was created by the unanimous action of the stockholders of the Company by amendment to the certificate of incorporation. The stockholders thereby provided how the business of the corporation is to be managed, as is their privilege and right under § 141(a). It was this stockholder action which delegated to the AD director whatever powers and duties he possesses; they were not delegated to him by his fellow directors, either out of their own powers and duties, or otherwise.

It is settled, of course, as a general principle, that directors may not delegate their duty to manage the corporate enterprise. But there is no conflict with that principle where, as here, the delegation of duty, if any, is made not by the directors but by stockholder action under § 141(a), via the certificate of incorporation.

In our judgment, therefore, the AD stock arrangement is not invalid on the ground that it permits the AC and AL directors of the Company to delegate their statutory duties to the AD director.

On this point, the plaintiff relies mainly upon the Chancery Court decision in Abercrombie v. Davies, 35 Del.Ch. 599, 611, 123 A.2d 893 (1956). There, in considering an agreement requiring all eight directors to submit a disputed question to an arbitrator if seven were unable to agree, the Chancery Court stated that legal sanction may not be accorded to an agreement, at least when made by less than all the stockholders, which takes from the board of directors the power of determining substantial management policy. The plaintiff's reliance is misplaced, because, *inter alia,* the *Abercrombie* arrangement was not created by the certificate of incorporation, within the authority of § 141(a). * * *

Our conclusions upon these questions make it unnecessary to discuss the defendants' contentions that the plaintiff's action is barred by the principles of estoppel, laches, acquiescence and ratification.

Finding no error in the judgment below, it is affirmed.

NOTE

Cases support the ability of Delaware corporations to create unusual share voting patterns. For example:

(a) Providence and Worcester Co. v. Baker, 378 A.2d 121 (Del.1977). The corporation's certificate of incorporation provided that a shareholder was entitled to (i) one vote per share for each share he owned up to fifty shares and (ii) one vote for every twenty shares he owned in excess of fifty, but (iii) no shareholder might vote more than one fourth of all the outstanding shares. The Court upheld this voting arrangement under the Delaware statute. These voting restrictions, it should be noted, did not limit the power of persons to cast large numbers of votes by proxy, but rather limited the voting power of individual owners of shares. Would this voting arrangement be upheld under the last sentence of MBCA § 6.01(a)?

(b) Williams v. Geier, 671 A.2d 1368 (Del.1996). This case upheld a "tenure voting" plan by a 3–2 vote. Under this plan each share of common stock of Cincinnati Milacron, Inc. on the date the plan was implemented became entitled to 10 votes. However, if a share was sold or transferred thereafter, its voting power was immediately reduced to one vote per share; if the new holder retained the share for three years, it resumed being entitled to 10 votes per share. A family group owned more than 50 percent of Milacron, a publicly held corporation, but only three of the ten directors were associated with the family group. The stated reasons for recommending this plan was to (a) provide current and longer-term shareholders with a greater voice in the company, (b) permit the issuance of additional shares of common stock with minimal dilution of voting rights, and (c) discourage takeovers. Tenure voting clearly benefits a controlling family group in this situation, since it not only discourages takeovers but also deters transfers of shares by individual members of that group.

LING AND CO. v. TRINITY SAV. AND LOAN ASS'N

Supreme Court of Texas, 1972.
482 S.W.2d 841.

REAVLEY, JUSTICE.

Trinity Savings and Loan Association sued Bruce W. Bowman for the balance owed on a promissory note and also to foreclose on a certificate for 1500 shares of Class A Common Stock in Ling & Company, Inc. pledged by Bowman to secure payment of the note. Ling & Company was made a party to the suit by Trinity Savings and Loan because of Ling & Company's insistence that the transfer of its stock was subject to restrictions that were unfulfilled. Bowman did not appear and has not appealed from the judgment against him. The trial court entered summary judgment in favor of Trinity Savings and Loan, against the contentions of Ling & Company, foreclosing the security interest in the stock and ordering it sold. The court of civil appeals affirmed. We reverse the judgments and remand the case to the trial court.

The objection to the foreclosure and public sale of this stock is based upon restrictions imposed upon the transfer of the stock by the articles of incorporation of Ling & Company. It is conceded that no offer of sale has been made to the other holders of this class of stock and that the approval of the pledge of the stock has not been obtained from the New York Stock Exchange. It is the position of Trinity Savings and Loan that all of the restrictions upon the transfer of any interest in this stock are invalid and of no effect. This has been the holding of the courts below.

The face and back of the stock certificate are reproduced and attached to this opinion.

The restrictions appear in Article Four of the Ling & Company articles of incorporation, as amended and filed with the Secretary of State in 1968. Section D requires the holder to obtain written approval of the New York Stock Exchange prior to the sale or encumbrance of the stock if, at the time, Ling & Company is a member corporation of the Exchange. Then Section E(4) prevents the sale of the stock without first affording the corporation the opportunity to buy and, if it fails to purchase, giving that opportunity to all holders of the same class of stock. The method of computation of the price, based upon the corporate books, is provided in this section of the articles.

The court of civil appeals struck down the restrictions for [two] reasons: the lack of conspicuous notice thereof on the stock certificate, [and] the unreasonableness of the restrictions * * *.

Conspicuousness

The Texas Business Corporation Act as amended in 1957, V.A.T.S.Bus.Corp.Act, art. 2.22, subd. A, provides that a corporation may impose restrictions on the transfer of its stock if they are "expressly set forth in the articles of incorporation * * * and * * * copied at length or in summary form on the face or so copied on the back and referred to on the face of each certificate * * *." Article 2.19, subd. F, enacted by the Legislature at the same time, permits the incorporation by reference on the face or back of the certificate of the provision of the articles of incorporation which restricts the transfer of the stock. The court of civil appeals objected to the general reference to the articles of incorporation and the failure to print the full conditions imposed upon the transfer of the shares. However, reference is made on the face of the certificate to the restrictions described on the reverse side; the notice on the reverse side refers to the particular article of the articles of incorporation as restricting the transfer or encumbrance and requiring "the holder hereof to grant options to purchase the shares represented hereby first to the Corporation and then pro rata to the other holders of the Class A Common Stock * * *." We hold that the content of the certificate complies with the requirements of the Texas Business Corporation Act.

There remains the requirement of the Texas [Uniform Commercial] Code that the restriction or reference thereto on the certificate must be conspicuous. Sec. [8–204] requires that a restriction on transferability be "noted conspicuously on the security." Sec. [1–201(10)] defines "conspicuous" and makes the determination a question of law for the court to decide. It is provided that a conspicuous term is so written as to be noticed by a reasonable person. Examples of conspicuous matter are given there as a "printed heading in capitals * * * [or] larger or other contrasting type or color." This means that something must appear on the face of the certificate to attract the attention of a reasonable person when he looks at it. 1 Anderson, Uniform Commercial Code 87 (2nd ed. 1970). The line of print on the face of the Ling & Company certificate does not stand out and cannot be considered conspicuous.

Our holding that the restriction is not noted conspicuously on the certificate does not entitle Trinity Savings and Loan to a summary judgment under this record. Sec. [8–204] provides that the restriction is effective against a person with actual knowledge of it. The record does not establish conclusively that Trinity Savings and Loan lacked knowledge of the restriction on January 28, 1969, the date the record indicates when Bowman executed an assignment of this stock to Trinity Savings and Loan.

Reasonableness

Art. 2.22, subd. A of the Texas Business Corporation Act provides that a corporation may impose restrictions on disposition of its stock if the restrictions "do not unreasonably restrain or prohibit transferability." The court of civil appeals has held that the restrictions on the transferability of this stock are unreasonable for two reasons: because of the required approval of the New York Stock Exchange and because of successive options to purchase given the corporation and the other holders of the same class of stock.

Ling & Company in its brief states that it was a brokerage house member of the New York Stock Exchange at an earlier time and that Rule 315 of the Exchange required approval of any sale or pledge of the stock. Under these circumstances, we must disagree with the court of civil appeals holding that this provision of article 4D of the articles of incorporation is "arbitrary, capricious, and unreasonable." Nothing appears in the summary judgment proof on this matter, and the mere provision in the article is no cause for vitiating the restrictions as a matter of law.

It was also held by the intermediate court that it is unreasonable to require a shareholder to notify all other record holders of Class A Common Stock of his intent to sell and to give the other holders a ten day option to buy. The record does not reveal the number of holders of this class of stock; we only know that there are more than twenty. We find nothing unusual or oppressive in these first option provisions. See 2 O'Neal, Close Corporations, § 7.13 (1971). Conceivably the number of stockholders might be so great as to make the burden too heavy upon the stockholder who wishes to sell and, at the same time, dispel any justification for contending that there exists a reasonable corporate purpose in restricting the ownership. But there is no showing of that nature in this summary judgment record. * * *

The summary judgment proof does not justify the holding that restrictions on the transfer of this stock were ineffective as to Trinity Savings and Loan Association. The judgment below is reversed and the cause is remanded to the trial court.

DANIEL, J., concurs in result.

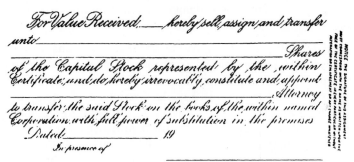

NOTICE: The shares represented by this certificate are subject to all the terms, conditions and provisions of the Articles of Incorporation of the Corporation, as the same may be amended from time to time, which Articles are incorporated herein by reference as though fully set forth herein. Copies of the Articles of Incorporation may be obtained from the Secretary of State of the State of Texas or upon written request therefor from the Secretary of the Corporation. Reference is specifically made to the provisions of Article Four of the Articles of Incorporation which set forth the designations, preferences, limitations and relative rights of the shares of each class of capital stock authorized to be issued, which deny pre-emptive rights, prohibit cumulative voting, restrict the transfer, sale, assignment, pledge, hypothecation or encumbrance of any of the shares represented hereby under certain conditions, and which under certain conditions require the holder hereof to grant options to purchase the shares represented hereby first to the Corporation and then pro rata to the other holders of the Class A Common Stock, all as set forth in said Article Four. Reference is also specifically made to the provisions of Article Nine which vests the power to adopt, alter, amend or repeal the by-laws in the Board of Directors except to the extent such power may be modified or divested by action of shareholders representing a majority of the holders of the Class A Common Stock.

[A5775]

NOTES

(1) The traditional view is that share transfer restrictions constitute a restraint on alienation, and therefore are strictly construed. This attitude is changing. One case, for example, has described this attitude as "anachronistic." Bruns v. Rennebohm Drug Stores, Inc., 442 N.W.2d 591, 596 (Wis.App.1989). Nevertheless, because of this historic approach, it is important to specify clearly and unambiguously the essential attributes of

the restrictions. This should include such matters as whether the purchase is optional or mandatory, the persons who may or must purchase the shares and the sequence in which they may purchase, the manner in which the price is to be determined, the time periods during which persons may decide whether or not to purchase (if an option), and the events (e.g., proposed sale, death, bankruptcy, family gift, etc.) which trigger the restriction.

(2) Share transfer restrictions essentially constitute contractual obligations that limit the power of owners to freely transfer their shares. There are several different justifications for imposing share transfer restrictions, and the type of restriction imposed may depend on the objective. Consider MBCA § 6.27. What kinds of "status" are referred to in subsection (c)(1)? The Official Comment refers to election of close corporation status under an integrated close corporation statute, subchapter S, or "entitlement to a program or eligibility for a privilege administered by governmental agencies or national securities exchanges." Presumably, the share transfer restriction involved in *Ling* was of the latter type, designed to allow the New York Stock Exchange to police ownership interests in member firms. MBCA § 6.27(c)(3) also refers to "other reasonable purpose[s]," which presumably includes provisions designed to enable owners in closely held corporations to remain close, i.e., to select the persons with whom they will be associated in business, and to permit withdrawing participants to liquidate their investments on some reasonable basis.

(3) A variety of possible share transfer restrictions are described in MBCA § 6.27(d). In closely held corporations, the two most common types of restrictions are option agreements (see subsection (d)(1)) and buy-sell agreements (see subsection (d)(2)). An option does not guarantee the shareholder a specified price, whereas a buy-sell agreement does. The restrictions described in subsections (d)(3) and (d)(4) are potentially more onerous since they may prohibit all transfers to anyone at any price; it will be noted that they are valid only if the prohibition "is not manifestly unreasonable." Does it follow that (d)(1) and (d)(2) restrictions are valid even if they are "manifestly unreasonable?"

(4) Some share transfer restrictions in closely held corporations are phrased as rights of first refusal, giving the corporation or the shareholders an opportunity to meet the best price the shareholder has been able to obtain from outsiders. Does this kind of restraint "chill" the interest of outsiders in making offers for shares? Does such a provision give any real protection to a minority shareholder in a closely held corporation who wishes to exit the company?

(5) Couldn't most, if not all, of the problems faced by minority shareholders in closely held corporations be solved if minority shareholders demanded a "buy-sell agreement?" Such agreements, if properly drafted, enable shareholders to require either the corporation or their fellow shareholders to buy out their equity interest in the corporation at some mutually-agreed-upon price, upon the occurrence of some mutually-agreed-upon triggering event. Certainly such agreements appear to solve the "freeze-

out" and lack of liquidity problems that minority shareholders in closely held corporations often face. See Chapter 13, Section B. At a minimum, lawyers counseling investors who are about to become minority shareholders in a closely held corporation should insist that their clients at least consider seeking the protections afforded by buy-sell agreements.

(6) When drafting a buy-sell agreement, determining the method of valuation is extremely important. There are several alternative approaches the parties can choose. The shareholders can retain an outside expert to appraise the value of the company's stock. This has the advantage of involving a neutral third party. The parties may want to determine ex ante how the appraiser will be selected to prevent charges of bias. One drawback is the high cost associated with retaining professional appraisers. The shareholders may choose to refer to the corporation's book value. This method has the advantage of being relatively straightforward, although the book value of the company may not accurately reflect its value as a going concern. Another option is for the parties to set a value for the shares, subject to periodic reevaluation.

(7) Buy-sell agreements that are triggered by the death of a shareholder may raise serious estate tax problems for the decedent's estate. The stock is likely to be the principal asset in the estate and have considerable (but uncertain) value. The critical question is whether the amount received pursuant to the buy-sell agreement determines the value of the stock for estate tax purposes. Prior to 1990, this issue was largely governed by case law, but today it is addressed by § 2703 of the Internal Revenue Code. Section 2703 indicates that the value of property shall be determined without regard to a buy-sell agreement unless the agreement (1) "is a bona fide business arrangement"; (2) "is not a device to transfer such property to members of the decedent's family for less than full and adequate consideration in money or money's worth"; and (3) has terms "comparable to similar arrangements entered into by persons in an arms' length transaction." If these requirements are not met, it is quite possible that the Internal Revenue Service may seek a valuation for estate tax purposes considerably higher than the amount actually received by the estate as payment for the shares.

(8) Consider the restrictions on corporate repurchases. MBCA § 6.40 governs distributions by corporations. Such distributions may take the form of dividend payments, as well as repurchases or other acquisitions by the corporation of its own shares of stock. See Chapter 7, Section I. Might these provisions require a corporation to refuse to repurchase shares pursuant to a buy-sell agreement? If so, a carefully prepared estate plan may go awry.

(9) Many cases hold that a share transfer restriction is valid even though it compels a shareholder to sell shares at an arbitrary price that may not reflect the real value of the shares. See, e.g., Unigroup, Inc. v. O'Rourke Storage & Transfer Co., 980 F.2d 1217 (8th Cir.1992)(book value); In re Estate of Mather, 189 A.2d 586 (Pa.1963) (price of $1 per share upheld despite contention that shares were worth $1,060 per share); Allen v. Biltmore Tissue Corp., 141 N.E.2d 812 (N.Y.1957) (repurchase at original

price issued). Reasons for this result include: (1) judicial reluctance to upset an agreement reached by the parties; (2) the lack of an easily ascertainable value for stock in a closely held corporation; and (3) the possibility that the sale price might have benefitted the selling shareholder had the corporation performed poorly.

C. ACTION BY DIRECTORS AND OFFICERS

IN THE MATTER OF DRIVE-IN DEVELOPMENT CORP.

United States Court of Appeals, Seventh Circuit, 1966.
371 F.2d 215.

SWYGERT, CIRCUIT JUDGE.

The principal question in this appeal relates to the circumstances which may bind a corporation to a guaranty of the obligations of a related corporation when it is contended that the corporate officer who executed the guaranty had no authority to do so. The facts giving rise to the question underlie a claim filed by the National Boulevard Bank of Chicago in an arrangement proceeding under chapter XI of the Bankruptcy Act, 11 U.S.C.A. §§ 701–799, in which the Drive In Development Corporation ["Drive In"] was the debtor. National Boulevard's claim was disallowed by the referee, whose decision was confirmed by the district court.

Drive In was one of four subsidiary companies controlled by Tastee Freez Industries, Inc., a holding company that conducted no business of its own. * * *

[The officers of Drive In executed a guarantee of payment to induce National Boulevard Bank to make a loan to Drive In's parent corporation. The guarantee was executed by Maranz on behalf of Drive In as "Chairman," and Dick attested to its execution as secretary. National Boulevard requested a copy of the authorizing resolution of the board of directors of Drive In. A copy, certified by Dick with the corporate seal affixed, was duly delivered. No such resolution, however, was contained in Drive In's corporate minute book, and the directors' testimony left it uncertain as to whether any such resolution had ever been considered or approved at a directors' meeting. National Boulevard advanced substantial sums under the guaranty.]

Turning to the merits of the objections to National Boulevard's claim, the referee found that Drive In's minute book did not show that a resolution authorizing Maranz to sign the guaranty was adopted by the directors and that Dick could not recall a specific directors' meeting at which such a resolution was approved. From these findings, the referee concluded that Maranz, who signed the guaranty on behalf of Drive In, had no authority, "either actual or implied or apparent," to bind Drive In.

This conclusion was erroneous. Drive In was estopped to deny Maranz' express authority to sign the guaranty because of the certified copy of a resolution of Drive In's board of directors purporting to grant such authority furnished to the bank by Dick, whether or not such a resolution was in fact formally adopted. Dick was the secretary of the corporation. Generally, it is the duty of the secretary to keep the corporate records and to make proper entries of the actions and resolutions of the directors. Therefore it was within the authority of Dick to certify that a resolution such as challenged here was adopted. Statements made by an officer or agent in the course of a transaction in which the corporation is engaged and which are within the scope of his authority are binding upon the corporation. Consequently Drive In was estopped to deny the representation made by Dick in the certificate forwarded to National Boulevard, in the absence of actual or constructive knowledge on the part of the bank that the representation was untrue. * * *

The objectors argue that since William Schneider, a vice president of National Boulevard, requested Dick to furnish the certified copy of a resolution granting authority to execute the guaranty, and since Hugh Driscoll, another vice president of National Boulevard, was also a director of Tastee Freez and was familiar with the organization of the subsidiaries, the bank was somehow in a position to know that no resolution had in fact been adopted by Drive In's board of directors. These facts, however, fall far short of proving such knowledge on the part of National Boulevard.

* * * Although intercorporate contracts of guaranty do not usually occur in the regular course of commercial business, here the interrelationship of Tastee Freez and its subsidiaries presented a situation in which the guaranty was not so unusual as would ordinarily obtain. Furthermore, the realities of modern corporate business practices do not contemplate that those who deal with officers or agents acting for a corporation should be required to go behind the representations of those who have authority to speak for the corporation and who verify the authority of those who presume to act for the corporation. * * *

The order of the district court confirming the referee's order is reversed in part and affirmed in part.

NOTES

(1) What if the third person really should know that the directors could not have adopted the resolution being certified by the secretary on the date specified? In Keystone Leasing Corp. v. Peoples Protective Life Ins. Co., 514 F.Supp. 841 (E.D.N.Y.1981), the Court refused to grant the third person the benefit of the estoppel principle set forth in *Drive In* where the third person "must have been aware" that the transaction had not been authorized by the board of directors.

(2) The estoppel recognized in this case is based on the authority of the secretary of the corporation to execute documents and affix the corporate seal. If a document is appropriately executed and sealed by the corporate secretary, third parties without specific knowledge about the actions taken may rely with confidence on the document. It is obviously sensible for such parties to accept documents at their face value and not inquire into the details of their approval and execution.

LEE V. JENKINS BROS.

United States Court of Appeals, Second Circuit, 1959.
268 F.2d 357.

MEDINA, CIRCUIT JUDGE. * * *

[In 1919, the Crane Company agreed to sell its Bridgeport, Connecticut plant to a New Jersey Corporation, Jenkins Brothers. Jenkins Brothers felt it needed to employ competent personnel, and sought to employ Lee, the business manager of Crane Company. Yardley, the President of Jenkins Brothers and a substantial stockholder, met with Lee at a hotel on June 1, 1920, and sought to entice him to join Jenkins Brothers. Also present was a vice president and his wife, though at the time of the trial in October 1957, only Lee was alive to describe the conversation.]

First, Lee testified:

> As far as the pension that I had earned with Crane Company he said the company [Jenkins Brothers] would pay that pension (and) if they didn't or, if anything came up, he would assume the liability himself, he would guarantee payment of the pension; and in consideration of that promise I agreed to go to work for Jenkins [Brothers] on June 1, 1920.

> The amount of the pension referred to by Mr. Yardley was a maximum of $1500 a year and that would be paid me when I reached the age of 60 years; regardless of what happened in the meantime, if I were with the company or not, I would be given a credit for those 13 years of service with the maximum pension of $1500.

Later Lee put it this way:

> Mr. Farnham Yardley said that Jenkins would assume the obligation for my credit pension record with Crane Company and, if anything happened and they did not pay it, he would guarantee it himself.

> Mr. Yardley's words were 'regardless of what happens, you will get that pension if you join our company.'

Finally, Lee summarized his position:

> My claim is that the company through the chairman of the board of directors and the president, promised me credit for my 13 years of service with Crane Company, regardless of what happened I would receive a pension at the age of 60, not to exceed $1,500 a year. If I was discharged in 1921 or 1922 or left I would still get that pension. That is what I am asking for.

This agreement was never reduced to writing.

Lee's prospects with Jenkins turned out to be just about as bright as he had hoped. He subsequently became vice president and general manager in charge of manufacturing and a director of the company. At that time he was receiving a salary of $25,000 from Jenkins, $8,000 more from an affiliate, plus an annual 10 percent bonus. In 1945, however, after 25 years with Jenkins, Lee was discharged at the age of 55 * * *.

In the discussion which follows we assume *arguendo* that there was evidence sufficient to support a finding that Yardley orally agreed on behalf of the corporation that Lee would be paid at the age of 60 a pension not to exceed $1500, and that Yardley's words "regardless of what happens" were, as Lee contends, to be interpreted as meaning that Lee would receive this pension even if he were not working for Jenkins at the time the pension became payable. Jenkins asserts that Yardley had no authority to bind it to such an "extraordinary" contract, express, implied, or apparent and the trial court so found. There is nothing in the proofs submitted by Lee to warrant any finding of actual authority in Yardley. The Certificate of Incorporation and By-Laws of Jenkins are not in evidence nor was any course of conduct shown as between the corporation and Yardley. Accordingly, on the phase of the case now under discussion, we are dealing only with apparent authority. * * *

The ascertainment of the Connecticut law on this critical question of Yardley's apparent authority is a far from simple task. The Connecticut cases have not yet quite come to grips with the question. Hence, it is necessary to consult the "general" law on the subject, on the assumption that, if a general rule can be found, Connecticut would follow it. * * *

Our question on this phase of the case then boils itself down to the following: can it be said as a matter of law that Yardley as president, chairman of the board, substantial stockholder and trustee and son-in-law of the estate of the major stockholder, had no power in the presence of the company's most interested vice president to secure for a "reasonable" length of time badly needed key personnel by promising an experienced local executive a life pension to commence in 30 years at the age of 60, even if Lee were not then working for the corporation, when the maximum liability to Jenkins under such a pension was $1500 per year.

A survey of the law on the authority of corporate officers does not reveal a completely consistent pattern. For the most part the courts perhaps have taken a rather restrictive view on the extent of powers of corporate officials, but the dissatisfaction with such an approach has been manifested in a variety of exceptions such as ratification, estoppel, and promissory estoppel. * * *

The rule most widely cited is that the president only has authority to bind his company by acts arising in the usual and regular course of business but not for contracts of an "extraordinary" nature. The substance of such a rule lies in the content of the term "extraordinary" which is subject to a broad range of interpretation.

The growth and development of this rule occurred during the late nineteenth and early twentieth centuries when the potentialities of the corporate form of enterprise were just being realized. As the corporation became a more common vehicle for the conduct of business it became increasingly evident that many corporations, particularly small closely held ones, did not normally function in the formal ritualistic manner hitherto envisaged. While the boards of directors still nominally controlled corporate affairs, in reality officers and managers frequently ran the business with little, if any, board supervision. The natural consequence of such a development was that third parties commonly relied on the authority of such officials in almost all the multifarious transactions in which corporations engaged. The pace of modern business life was too swift to insist on the approval by the board of directors of every transaction that was in any way "unusual."

The judicial recognition given to these developments has varied considerably. Whether termed "apparent authority" or an "estoppel" to deny authority, many courts have noted the injustice caused by the practice of permitting corporations to act commonly through their executives and then allowing them to disclaim an agreement as beyond the authority of the contracting officer, when the contract no longer suited its convenience. Other courts, however, continued to cling to the past with little attempt to discuss the unconscionable results obtained or the doctrine of apparent authority. Such restrictive views have been generally condemned by the commentators.

The summary of holdings pro and con in general on the subject of what are and what are not "extraordinary" agreements is inconclusive at best * * *. But the pattern becomes more distinct when we turn to the more limited area of employment contracts.

It is generally settled that the president as part of the regular course of business has authority to hire and discharge employees and fix their compensation. In so doing he may agree to hire them for a specific number of years if the term selected is deemed reasonable. But employment contracts for life or on a "permanent" basis are generally regarded as "extraordinary" and beyond the authority of any corporate executive if the only consideration for the promise is the employee's promise to work for that period. Jenkins would have us analogize the pension agreement involved herein to these generally condemned lifetime employment contracts because it extends over a long period of time, is of indefinite duration, and involves an indefinite liability on the part of the corporation.

It is not surprising that lifetime employment contracts have met with substantial hostility in the courts, for these contracts are often oral, uncorroborated, vague in important details and highly improbable. Accordingly, the courts have erected a veritable array of obstacles to their enforcement. They have been construed as terminable at will, too indefinite to enforce, *ultra vires,* lacking in mutuality or consideration, abandoned or breached by subsequent acts, and the supporting evidence deemed insufficient to go to the jury, as well as made without proper authority.

Where reasons have been given to support the conclusion that lifetime employments are "extraordinary," and hence made without authority, a scrutiny of these reasons may be helpful for their bearing on the analogous field of pension agreements. It is said that: they unduly restrict the power of the shareholders and future boards of directors on questions of managerial policy; they subject the corporation to an inordinately substantial amount of liability; they run for long and indefinite periods of time. Of these reasons the only one applicable to pension agreements is that they run for long and indefinite periods of time. There the likeness stops. Future director or shareholder control is in no way impeded; the amount of liability is not disproportionate; the agreement was not only not unreasonable but beneficial and necessary to the corporation; and pension contracts are commonly used fringe benefits in employment contracts. Moreover, unlike the case with life employment contracts, courts have often gone out of their way to find pension promises binding and definite even when labeled gratuitous by the employer. The consideration given to the employee involved is not at all dependent on profits or sales, nor does it involve some other variable suggesting director discretion.

In this case Lee was hired at a starting salary of $4,000 per year plus a contemplated pension of $1500 per year in thirty years. Had Lee been hired at a starting salary of $10,000 per year the cost to the corporation over the long run would have been substantially greater, yet no one could plausibly contend that such an employment contract was beyond Yardley's authority.

The cases on executive authority to make pension agreements are few. In West v. Hunt Foods, Inc., 1951, 225 P.2d 978, the most recent case on the subject, a nonsuit was reversed on the theory that the jury might have decided in plaintiff's favor either upon the basis of authority in the president and vice-president to make the promise of a pension or on the basis of a promissory estoppel. In Langer v. Superior Steel Corp., 1935, 178 A. 490, authority was found lacking in the president, who acted in direct violation of a directors' resolution, to promise a pension for life in return for past services. His apparent authority was not discussed. In Plowman v. Indian Refining Co., D.C.E.D.Ill.1937, 20 F.Supp. 1, the vice president was found to lack authority gratuitously to promise 18 employees life pensions at half wages. * * *

Apparent authority is essentially a question of fact. It depends not only on the nature of the contract involved, but the officer negotiating it, the corporation's usual manner of conducting business, the size of the corporation and the number of its stockholders, the circumstances that give rise to the contract, the reasonableness of the contract, the amounts involved, and who the contracting third party is, to list a few but not all of the relevant factors. In certain instances a given contract may be so important to the welfare of the corporation that outsiders would naturally suppose that only the board of directors (or even the shareholders) could properly handle it. It is in this light that the "ordinary course of business" rule should be given its content. Beyond such "extraordinary" acts, whether or not apparent authority exists is simply a matter of fact.

Accordingly, we hold that, assuming there was sufficient proof of the making of the pension agreement, Connecticut, in the particular circumstances of this case, would probably take the view that reasonable men could differ on the subject of whether or not Yardley had apparent authority to make the contract, and that the trial court erred in deciding the question as a matter of law. We do not think Connecticut would adopt any hard and fast rule against apparent authority to make pension agreements generally, on the theory that they were in the same category as lifetime employment contracts. * * *

NOTES

(1) The American Law Institute, Principles of Corporate Governance: Analysis and Recommendations § 3.01 cmt. d:

In general, questions concerning the authority of senior executives are normally special issues of agency law, and, as in agency law, the major relevant concepts are those of actual and apparent authority. When an agent is an executive of a corporation, the application of both these concepts often rests on the executive's formal position. Actual authority may rest on formal position, because in the absence of a formal job description the role an executive is expected to play may depend in part on the role customarily played by executives holding the position in question. Apparent authority may rest on formal position, because third parties frequently do not have notice of an executive's actual authority, and may reasonably depend on the authority customarily vested in executives holding the position in question.

The law on the apparent authority of executives other than the president is not well-developed (except for special rules relating to the corporation's secretary). In contrast, there are a great number of cases concerning the apparent authority of a president by virtue of that position. Although the rules on this issue have varied in the past, the accepted modern rule is that (unless restricted by a corporate standard that the third person has reason to know) the president has apparent authority by virtue of that position to take actions in the ordinary course of business, but not extraordinary actions.

The difficulty, of course, lies in drawing a line between what is ordinary and what is extraordinary. Any attempt at precision in drawing this line would almost certainly be futile, because the issue is highly dependent on the context in which it arises, and the types of business transactions that may arise are endlessly variable. Nevertheless, certain boundaries can be identified. To begin with, some matters, such as the declaration of dividends, are required by statute to be decided by the board. Typically, the statutes also enumerate certain matters that the board cannot delegate to a committee. By parity of reasoning, it would normally not be within the authority of the president or other senior executives to take binding action on these matters.

Beyond these boundaries, among the elements to be taken into account for purposes of determining what constitutes an "extraordinary" action, which would normally be outside the apparent authority of senior executives, are the economic magnitude of the action in relation to corporate assets and earnings, the extent of risk involved, the time span of the action's effect, and the cost of reversing the action. Examples of the kinds of actions that would normally be "extraordinary" include the creation or retirement of long-term or other significant debt, the reacquisition of significant amounts of equity, significant capital investments, business combinations including those effected for cash, the disposition of significant businesses, entry into important new lines of business, significant acquisitions of stock in other corporations, and actions that would foreseeably expose the corporation to significant litigation or significant new regulatory problems. A useful generalization is that decisions that would make a significant change in the structure of the business enterprise, or the structure of control over the enterprise, are extraordinary corporate actions, and therefore are normally outside the apparent authority of senior executives.

(2) Consider MBCA §§ 8.01, 8.41. The management of the business and affairs of a corporation ordinarily rests with the board of directors. The president and other officers perform functions set forth in the bylaws or prescribed by the board. As *Lee* illustrates, the line between actions that require board approval and actions that officers are authorized to perform on their own is often unclear.

(3) MBCA § 8.40(a) states that a corporation will have "the officers described in its bylaws or appointed by the board of directors in accordance with the bylaws." The only officer that a corporation is required to have is a secretary who is responsible for preparing minutes and for maintaining and authenticating the records of the company. See MBCA §§ 1.40(20), 8.40(c). This is a departure from earlier versions of the Model Act and most state corporation acts, which require a corporation to have certain officers, usually the president, the secretary, and the treasurer. The Official Comment to § 8.40 suggests that "[e]xperience has shown * * * that little purpose is served by a statutory requirement that there be certain offices, and statutory requirements may sometimes create problems of apparent authority or confusion with nonstatutory offices the corporation desires to create."

(4) Presumably, the chief executive officer of a small corporation, no matter what her formal title, will be required to take a number of actions on her own authority. For example, who is to hire secretaries, order needed equipment and supplies, and the like? Where does one go to find the basis of authority? Often the primary source is the bylaws of the corporation, which usually describe the roles and responsibilities of the principal officers. James R. Burkhard, Proposed Model Bylaws to be Used with the Revised Model Business Corporation Act (1984), 46 Bus.Law. 189, 225–26 (1990), suggests the following descriptions of the roles of the president, secretary, and treasurer:

§ 4.4   President.

> The president shall be the principal executive officer of the corporation and, subject to the control of the board of directors, shall in general supervise and control all of the business and affairs of the corporation. He shall, when present, preside at all meetings of the shareholders and of the board of directors. He may sign, with the secretary or any other proper officer of the corporation thereunto authorized by the board of directors, certificates for shares of the corporation and deeds, mortgages, bonds, contracts, or other instruments which the board of directors has authorized to be executed, except in cases where the signing and execution thereof shall be expressly delegated by the board of directors or by these bylaws to some other officer or agent of the corporation, or shall be required by law to be otherwise signed or executed; and in general shall perform all duties incident to the office of president and such other duties as may be prescribed by the board of directors from time to time. * * *

§ 4.6   The Secretary.

The secretary shall: (a) keep the minutes of the proceedings of the shareholders and of the board of directors in one or more books provided for that purpose; (b) see that all notices are duly given in accordance with the provisions of these bylaws or as required by law; (c) be custodian of the corporate records and of any seal of the corporation and if there is a seal of the corporation, see that it is affixed to all documents the execution of which on behalf of the corporation under its seal is duly authorized; (d) when requested or required, authenticate any records of the corporation; (e) keep a register of the post office address of each shareholder which shall be furnished to the secretary by such shareholder; (f) sign with the president, or a vice-president, certificates for shares of the corporation, the issuance of which shall have been authorized by resolution of the board of directors; (g) have general charge of the stock transfer books of the corporation; and (h) in general perform all duties incident to the office of secretary and such other duties as from time to time may be assigned to him by the president or by the board of directors. * * *

§ 4.7   The Treasurer.

The treasurer shall: (a) have charge and custody of and be responsible for all funds and securities of the corporation; (b) receive and give receipts for moneys due and payable to the corporation from any source whatsoever, and deposit all such moneys in the name of the corporation in such banks, trust companies, or other depositories as shall be selected by the board of directors; and (c) in general perform all of the duties incident to the office of treasurer and such other duties as from time to time may be assigned to him by the president or by the board of directors. If required by the board of directors, the treasurer shall give a bond for the faithful discharge of his duties in such sum and with such surety or sureties as the board of directors shall determine. * * *

PROBLEM

The president of Acme Corporation hires an attorney to bring a breach of contract action on the corporation's behalf. Acme's articles and bylaws are silent on whether the president has authority to institute litigation for the company. Does the president have authority to take this action?

CHAPTER 9

MANAGEMENT AND CONTROL OF THE PUBLICLY HELD CORPORATION

■ ■ ■

A.   CORPORATE GOVERNANCE IN THE 21st CENTURY

"Corporate governance" is the term used to describe the rules, norms, institutions, and mechanisms by which corporations are governed. The purpose of corporate governance is to persuade, induce, compel, and otherwise motivate corporate managers to keep the promises they make to investors.

1.   BUSINESS FAILURES AND CORPORATE SCANDALS

Attention galvanized around the issue of corporate governance in the late 1990s and the early part of the 21st century because of what appeared to be a tsunami of major business failures and corporate scandals. In particular, accounting irregularities and apparent lapses in oversight by boards of directors focused attention on the failure of the modern public corporation to control its agents. Trust in the way that public companies presented their financial results to investors reached record lows as over 112 telecom companies were required to restate downward prior earnings even though public accounting firms had previously given clean bills of health to virtually all of them. Particularly unnerving were the collapses of corporate giants such as Adelphia, which had hidden $2.3 billion in "off-balance sheet" debt, and Worldcom, Inc., which overstated its profits by $3.85 billion by treating a number of expense items as capital investments rather than as expenses. At the time, this was the largest restatement of income ever announced by an American corporation. It turned out that this was merely the first of a sequence of profit restatements and fraud charges against Worldcom and other telecommunication companies.

Many other public companies were racked by accounting scandals. The list included not only companies like Global Crossing, which was associated with the technology boom, but also old-line manufacturers and conglomerates such as Tyco International, Inc., Berlin Metals, Computer Associates, Dynegy, HomeStore, Livent, PNC Financial, Reliant Resources, Sunbeam, Waste Management, and others.

No scandal rocked the comfortable world of pubic company boards and management more than Enron—the iconic corporate governance failure of the twentieth century. Throughout the late 1990s, Enron was considered one of the country's most innovative companies—a new-economy maverick that forsook musty, old industries with their cumbersome hard assets in favor of the freewheeling world of e-commerce. The company continued to build power plants and operate gas lines, but it became better known for its unique trading businesses. Besides buying and selling gas and electricity futures, it created whole new markets for such oddball "commodities" as broadcast time for advertisers, weather futures, and Internet bandwidth.

C. WILLIAM THOMAS, THE RISE AND FALL OF ENRON

J. of Accountancy 41–45, 47–48 (April 2002).

* * * The Enron case is a dream for academics who conduct research and teach. For those currently or formerly involved with the company, such as creditors, auditors, the SEC and accounting regulators, it's a nightmare. * * *

In 1985, after federal deregulation of natural gas pipelines, Enron was born from the merger of Houston Natural Gas and InterNorth, a Nebraska pipeline company. In the process of the merger, Enron incurred massive debt and, as the result of deregulation, no longer had exclusive rights to its pipelines. In order to survive, the company had to come up with a new and innovative business strategy to generate profits and cash flow. Kenneth Lay, CEO, hired McKinsey & Co. to assist in developing Enron's business strategy. It assigned a young consultant named Jeffrey Skilling to the engagement. Skilling, who had a background in banking and asset and liability management, proposed a revolutionary solution to Enron's credit, cash and profit woes in the gas pipeline business: create a "gas bank" in which Enron would buy gas from a network of suppliers and sell it to a network of consumers, contractually guaranteeing both the supply and the price, charging fees for the transactions and assuming the associated risks. Thanks to the young consultant, the company created both a new product and a new paradigm for the industry—the energy derivative.

Lay was so impressed with Skilling's genius that he created a new division in 1990 called Enron Finance Corp. and hired Skilling to run it. Under Skilling's leadership, Enron Finance Corp. soon dominated the market for natural gas contracts, with more contacts, more access to supplies and more customers than any of its competitors. * * *

Skilling began to change the corporate culture of Enron to match the company's transformed image as a trading business. He set out on a quest to hire the best and brightest traders, recruiting associates from the top MBA schools in the country and competing with the largest and most prestigious investment banks for talent. In exchange for grueling schedules, Enron pampered its associates with a long list of corporate perks, including concierge services and a company gym. Skilling rewarded production with merit-based bonuses that had no cap, permitting traders to "eat what they killed."

One of Skilling's earliest hires in 1990 was Andrew Fastow, a 29-year-old Kellogg MBA who had been working on leveraged buyouts and other complicated deals at Continental Illinois Bank in Chicago. * * * Fastow moved swiftly through the ranks and was promoted to chief financial officer in 1998. As Skilling oversaw the building of the company's vast trading operation, Fastow oversaw its financing by ever more complicated means.

As Enron's reputation with the outside world grew, the internal culture apparently began to take a darker tone. Skilling instituted the performance review committee (PRC), which became known as the harshest employee-ranking system in the country. It was known as the "360-degree review" based on the values of Enron—respect, integrity, communication and excellence (RICE). However, associates came to feel that the only real performance measure was the amount of profits they could produce. In order to achieve top ratings, everyone in the organization became instantly motivated to "do deals" and post earnings. Employees were regularly rated on a scale of 1 to 5, with 5s usually being fired within six months. The lower an employee's PRC score, the closer he or she got to Skilling, and the higher the score, the closer he or she got to being shown the door. Skilling's division was known for replacing up to 15% of its workforce every year. Fierce internal competition prevailed and immediate gratification was prized above long-term potential. Paranoia flourished and trading contracts began to contain highly restrictive confidentiality clauses. Secrecy became the order of the day for many of the company's trading contracts, as well as its disclosures. * * *

* * * In January 2000 Enron announced an ambitious plan to build a high-speed broadband telecommunications network and to trade network capacity, or bandwidth, in the same way it traded electricity or natural gas. In July of that year Enron and Blockbuster announced a deal to provide video on demand to customers throughout the world via high-speed Internet lines. As Enron poured hundreds of millions into broadband with very little return, Wall Street rewarded the strategy with as much as $40 on the stock price—a factor that would have to be discounted later when the broadband bubble burst. In August 2000 Enron's stock hit an all-time high of $90.56, and the company was being touted by Fortune and other business publications as one of the most admired and innovative companies in the world. * * *

Enron incorporated "mark-to-market accounting" for the energy trading business in the mid-1990s and used it on an unprecedented scale for its trading transactions. Under mark-to-market rules, whenever companies have outstanding energy-related or other derivative contracts (either assets or liabilities) on their balance sheets at the end of a particular quarter, they must adjust them to fair market value, booking unrealized gains or losses to the income statement of the period. A difficulty with application of these rules in accounting for long-term futures contracts in commodities such as gas is that there are often no quoted prices upon which to base valuations. Companies having these types of derivative instruments are free to develop and use discretionary valuation models based on their own assumptions and methods. * * *

In order to satisfy Moody's and Standard & Poor's credit rating agencies, Enron had to make sure the company's leverage ratios were within acceptable ranges. Fastow continually lobbied the ratings agencies to raise Enron's credit rating, apparently to no avail. That notwithstanding, there were other ways to lower the company's debt ratio. Reducing hard assets while earning increasing paper profits served to increase Enron's return on assets (ROA) and reduce its debt-to-total-assets ratio, making the company more attractive to credit rating agencies and investors.

Enron, like many other companies, used "special purpose entities" (SPEs) to access capital or hedge risk. By using SPEs such as limited partnerships with outside parties, a company is permitted to increase leverage and ROA without having to report debt on its balance sheet. The company contributes hard assets and related debt to an SPE in exchange for an interest. The SPE then borrows large sums of money from a financial institution to purchase assets or conduct other business without the debt or assets showing up on the company's financial statements. The company can also sell leveraged assets to the SPE and book a profit. To avoid classification of the SPE as a subsidiary (thereby forcing the entity to include the SPE's financial position and results of operations in its financial statements), FASB guidelines require that only 3% of the SPE be owned by an outside investor.

Under Fastow's leadership, Enron took the use of SPEs to new heights of complexity and sophistication, capitalizing them with not only a variety of hard assets and liabilities, but also extremely complex derivative financial instruments, its own restricted stock, rights to acquire its stock and related liabilities. As its financial dealings became more complicated, the company apparently also used SPEs to "park" troubled assets that were falling in value, such as certain overseas energy facilities, the broadband operation or stock in companies that had been spun off to the public. Transferring these assets to SPEs meant their losses would be kept off Enron's books. To compensate partnership investors for downside risk, Enron promised issuance of additional shares of its stock. As the value of the assets in these partnerships fell, Enron began to incur larger and larger obligations to issue its own stock later down the road. Compounding the problem toward the end was the precipitous fall in the value of Enron stock. Enron conducted business through thousands of SPEs. The most controversial of them were LJM Cayman LP and LJM2 Co-Investment LP, run by Fastow himself. From 1999 through July 2001, these entities paid Fastow more than $30 million in management fees, far more than his Enron salary, supposedly with the approval of top management and Enron's board of directors. In turn, the LJM partnerships invested in another group of SPEs, known as the Raptor vehicles, which were designed in part to hedge an Enron investment in a bankrupt broadband company, Rhythm NetConnections. As part of the capitalization of the Raptor entities, Enron issued common stock in exchange for a note receivable of $1.2 billion. Enron increased notes receivable and shareholders' equity to reflect this transaction, which appears to violate generally accepted accounting principles. Additionally, Enron failed to consolidate the LJM and Raptor SPEs into their financial statements when subsequent information revealed they should have been consolidated. * * *

A very confusing footnote in Enron's 2000 financial statements described the above transactions. Douglas Carmichael, the Wollman Distinguished Professor of Accounting at Baruch College in New York City, told the Wall Street Journal in November of 2001 that most people would be hard pressed to understand the effects of these disclosures on the financial statements, casting doubt on both the quality of the company's earnings as well as the business purpose of the transaction. By April 2001 other skeptics arrived on the scene. A number of analysts questioned the lack of transparency of Enron's disclosures. One analyst was quoted as saying, "The notes just don't make sense, and we read notes for a living." Skilling was very quick to reply with arrogant comments and, in one case, even called an analyst a derogatory name. What Skilling and Fastow apparently underestimated was that, because of such actions, the market was beginning to perceive the company with greater and greater skepticism, thus eroding its trust and the company's reputation. * * * In February 2001 Lay announced his retirement and named Skilling president and CEO of Enron. In February Skilling held the company's annual conference with analysts, bragging that the stock (then valued around $80) should be trading at around $126 per share.

In March Enron and Blockbuster announced the cancellation of their video-on-demand deal. By that time the stock had fallen to the mid-$60s. Throughout the spring and summer, risky deals Enron had made in underperforming investments of various kinds began to unravel, causing it to suffer a huge cash shortfall. Senior management, which had been voting with its feet since August 2000, selling Enron stock in the bull market, continued to exit, collectively hundreds of millions of dollars richer for the experience. On August 14, just six months after being named CEO, Skilling himself resigned, citing "personal reasons." The stock price slipped below $40 that week and, except for a brief recovery in early October after the sale of Portland General, continued its slide to below $30 a share.

Also in August, in an internal memorandum to Lay, a company vice-president, Sherron Watkins, described her reservations about the lack of disclosure of the substance of the related party transactions with the SPEs run by Fastow. She concluded the memo by stating her fear that the company might "implode under a series of accounting scandals." Lay notified the company's attorneys, Vinson & Elkins, as well as the audit partner at Enron's auditing firm, Arthur Andersen LLP, so the matter could be investigated further. The proverbial "ship" of Enron had struck the iceberg that would eventually sink it.

On October 16 Enron announced its first quarterly loss in more than four years after taking charges of $1 billion on poorly performing businesses. The company terminated the Raptor hedging arrangements which, if they had continued, would have resulted in its issuing 58 million Enron shares to offset the company's private equity losses, severely diluting earnings. It also disclosed the reversal of the $1.2 billion entry to assets and equities it had made as a result of dealings with these arrangements. It was this disclosure that got the SEC's attention.

On October 17 the company announced it had changed plan administrators for its employees' 401(k) pension plan, thus by law locking their investments for a period of 30 days and preventing workers from selling their Enron stock. The company contends this decision had in fact been made months earlier. However true that might be, the timing of the decision certainly has raised suspicions.

On October 22 Enron announced the SEC was looking into the related party transactions between Enron and the partnerships owned by Fastow, who was fired two days later. On November 8 Enron announced a restatement of its financial statements back to 1997 to reflect consolidation of the SPEs it had omitted, as well as to book Andersen's recommended adjustments from those years, which the company had previously "deemed immaterial." This restatement resulted in another $591 million in losses over the four years as well as an additional $628 million in liabilities as of the end of 2000. The equity markets immediately reacted to the restatement, driving the stock price to less than $10 a share. One analyst's report stated the company had burned through $5 billion in cash in 50 days.

A merger agreement with smaller cross-town competitor Dynegy was announced on November 9, but rescinded by Dynegy on November 28 on the basis of Enron's lack of full disclosure of its off-balance-sheet debt, downgrading Enron's rating to junk status. On November 30 the stock closed at an astonishing 26 cents a share. The company filed for bankruptcy protection on December 2. * * *

Unquestionably, the Enron implosion has wreaked more havoc on the accounting profession than any other case in U.S. history. Critics in the media, Congress and elsewhere are calling into question not only the adequacy of U.S. disclosure practices but also the integrity of the independent audit process. The general public still questions how CPA firms can maintain audit independence while at the same time engaging in consulting work, often for fees that dwarf those of the audit. Companies that deal in special purpose entities and complex financial instruments similar to Enron's have suffered significant declines in their stock prices. The scandal threatens to undermine confidence in financial markets in the United States and abroad. * * *

In a characteristic move, the SEC and the public accounting profession have been among the first to respond to the Enron crisis. Unfortunately, and sadly reminiscent of financial disasters in the 1970s and 1980s, this response will likely be viewed by investors, creditors, lawmakers and employees of Enron as "too little, too late." * * *

The CEOs of the Big Five accounting firms made a joint statement on December 4 committing to develop improved guidance on disclosure of related party transactions, SPEs and market risks for derivatives including energy contracts for the 2001 reporting period. In addition, the Big Five called for modernization of the financial reporting system in the United States to make it more timely and relevant, including more nonfinancial information on entity performance. They also vowed to streamline the accounting standard-setting process to make it more responsive to the rapid changes that occur in a technology-driven economy. * * *

The impact of Enron [was] felt at the highest levels of government as legislators engage in endless debate and accusation, quarreling over the influence of money in politics. The GAO has requested that the White House disclose documents concerning appointments to President George W. Bush's Task Force on Energy, chaired by Vice-President Dick Cheney, former CEO of Halliburton. The White House has refused, and the GAO has filed suit, the first of its kind in history. Congressional investigations are expected to continue well into 2002 and beyond. Lawmakers are expected to investigate not only disclosure practices at Enron, but for all public companies, concerning SPEs, related party transactions and use of "mark-to-market" accounting. * * *

* * * [S]ome of the classic risk factors associated with management fraud outlined in SAS no. 82 are evident in the Enron case. Those include management characteristics, industry conditions and operating characteristics of the company. Although written five years [before

Enron's bankruptcy filing], the list almost looks as if it was excerpted from Enron's case:

- Unduly aggressive earnings targets and management bonus compensation based on those targets.

- Excessive interest by management in maintaining stock price or earnings trend through the use of unusually aggressive accounting practices.

- Management setting unduly aggressive financial targets and expectations for operating personnel.

- Inability to generate sufficient cash flow from operations while reporting earnings and earnings growth.

- Assets, liabilities, revenues or expenses based on significant estimates that involve unusually subjective judgments such as * * * reliability of financial instruments.

- Significant related party transactions.

* * * The Enron story has produced many victims, the most tragic of which is a former vice-chairman of the company who committed suicide, apparently in connection with his role in the scandal. Another 4,500 individuals have seen their careers ended abruptly by the reckless acts of a few. Enron's core values of respect, integrity, communication and excellence stand in satirical contrast to allegations now being made public. * * *

2. THE RESPONSE TO THE BUSINESS FAILURES AND CORPORATE SCANDALS

The numerous events involving fraud and misconduct described in the previous Section shocked and angered both the business community and ordinary investors. Investors began to bail out of securities holdings, and a sharp decline in securities prices followed. The attitude of investors was well reflected in comments by Tom Sticke, Chairman of the California Chamber of Commerce: "Until we see a CEO and a General Counsel march off to jail together—for a long, uncomfortable non-country club sentence—capitalism is at risk because people are losing confidence."[a]

The response of the market to these events was quite predictable: securities values dropped precipitously. The Dow Jones Industrial Average declined from above 11,000 to under 10,000, and then dropped to

---

[a] Abraham C. Reich and Michelle T. Wirtner, What Do You Do When Confronted with Fraud? Business Law Today, September/October 2002, at 39. See also the comments of Jonathan Wiseman, Efforts to Restrict Retirement Funds Lose Steam, Wash. Post, Aug. 7, 2002, p. 1, col. 3, stating that the disclosures "initially fueled a wave of indignation among lawmakers in Washington and solemn vows to protect" their constituents in the future.

about 4,000 when the full magnitude and extent of corporate misconduct became known. While Enron was the largest and most visible collapse, it was only the first in a combination of events that cumulatively led to a major crisis in corporate governance beginning in July 2002. This crisis atmosphere was augmented by a report issued by the American Bar Association Task Force on Corporate Responsibility in July 2002. The conclusions in this report were stark:

> * * * [T]he system of corporate governance at many public companies has failed dramatically. It is a clear failure of corporate responsibility, for example, if a corporation belatedly and precipitously discloses that the equity on its balance sheet has been overstated by billions of dollars. It is a clear failure of corporate responsibility if employees whose retirement [accounts] are heavily invested in the corporation's stock are assured by management of the corporation's financial prospects and then discover that the value of that stock has promptly vanished as a result of earnings misstatements and self-dealing by corporate officers. It is a clear failure of corporate responsibility if executive officers aware of potential accounting irregularities sell millions of dollars of stock to public investors who are unaware of such information.[b]

President George W. Bush had taken office in January 2001. His first response to the corporate governance crisis was dismissive: the problems arose, he said, because of "a few bad apples" but the economy was still "fundamentally sound." However, this approach had little traction as the economy continued to decline and bad news continued to make headlines. He then changed course dramatically and announced that he would address the current problems when legislation that was then being considered was presented to him for signature. He stated that "[a]t this moment, America's greatest economic need is higher ethical standards, standards enforced by strict laws and upheld by responsible business leaders." He added, "[I]f you're a CEO and you think you can fudge the books in order to make yourselves look better, we're going to find you, we're going to arrest you and we're going to hold you to account."

3. THE SARBANES-OXLEY ACT

The only legislation that was in the Congressional pipeline that dealt directly with corporate governance problems was the Sarbanes-Oxley bill—a proposed statute that had been rather hastily cobbled together by Senator Paul Sarbanes of Maryland, with the addition of some provisions developed by Congressman Michael Oxley of Ohio. This bill included ideas and proposals that had been discussed from time to time prior to

---

[b] See James Cheek III, et al., Am.Bar Ass'n, Preliminary Report of the American Bar Association Task Force on Corporate Responsibility, 1–7 (2002).

the corporate governance crisis, but had not been seriously considered or studied by corporate scholars. Indeed, until the governance crisis became acute in 2002, enactment of Sarbanes-Oxley seemed quite improbable.[c]

However, in 2002, matters were moving far too fast for affected businesses to gear up and consider, let alone significantly affect, the provisions of this proposed legislation. Congressman Oxley introduced his draft bill in the House of Representatives. One day was allocated for the House's consideration of the proposed bill, and there was no discussion of the impact of the various provisions on state law and practice. The Senate version, modified by Senator Sarbanes, was debated at some length, but the political environment changed dramatically when the WorldCom scandal was announced on June 26, 2002. There was a media frenzy over WorldCom, the declining stock market, the high profile accounting frauds, and the numerous business failures in the middle of an election year. A lobbyist for the Chamber of Commerce (which was opposing the Senate bill) described the situation by saying that "when the WorldCom scandal hit, it became to me, a bit of a—a very different attitude and atmosphere, if not a political tsunami," and we quickly decided that "an unconditional surrender was inevitable."

President Bush announced that he planned to sign the Sarbanes-Oxley bill as soon as it was presented to him. Professor John Coffee wryly commented: "I don't think he [Bush] can claim credit at all. * * * [The Republicans] resisted it until they saw a tidal wave forming. They had the good judgment not to stand in the way of a Tsunami." President Bush signed the new legislation on July 30, 2002, the day after it was presented to him. Predictably he put the best possible "spin" on recent events. He attempted to overcome the very common impression that he valued "big corporations over ordinary Americans," and "strongly" challenged "the perception that his administration was too close to big business." He also criticized the excesses of the previous few years, commenting that corporate corruption had offended "the conscience of our nation." He later added that there was to be "[n]o more easy money for corporate criminals. Just hard time."

The Sarbanes-Oxley Act makes dramatic changes in the legal responsibilities of audit committees, the regulation of the accounting profession, and the relationship between corporations and their auditors. Significant provisions of the Act will be discussed here and in the following Section.

---

[c] David S. Hizenrath, et al., How Congress Rode a "Storm" to Corporate Reform, Wash.Post, July 28, 2002, at A1, chronicles the sequence of events surrounding the creation and enactment of Sarbanes-Oxley. He notes that "the collaboration between Sarbanes and Oxley resulted in few changes to Sarbanes's original bill." He added, "few people gave Sarbanes much chance of bringing his bill to the Senate floor, much less passing it into law," but the disclosures of WorldCom's accounting misstatements had renewed "public anger over corporate misdeeds that had faded somewhat following Enron's collapse."

The statute creates a new independent regulatory entity, the Public Company Accounting Oversight Board (PCAOB), consisting of five members to oversee the auditing of publicly traded companies. Under Sarbanes-Oxley, the SEC appoints the chair and other members of the PCAOB, after consultation with the Chairman of the Board of Governors of the Federal Reserve System and the Secretary of the Treasury. The PCAOB is funded by fees assessed against public companies and is broadly charged with responsibility for regulating the accounting profession.

Section 202 of Sarbanes-Oxley imposes significant new responsibilities on audit committees. All audit services must be pre-approved by corporate management and the company's audit committee. Section 201(a) of Sarbanes-Oxley goes significantly beyond the requirements of prior law by making it unlawful for accounting firms that audit public companies simultaneously to provide the company with a variety of non-audit services: book-keeping, services related to accounting records and financial statements, financial information systems design and implementation, fairness opinions, management or human resource functions, legal services, and expert services unrelated to the audit.

In essence, Sarbanes-Oxley requires accounting firms to contract for services with the audit committees of the boards of directors of the companies they propose to audit rather than with management. This major change in the relationship between auditors and audit clients is effectuated by Section 301 of Sarbanes-Oxley, which provides that the audit committee of each issuer "shall be directly responsible for the appointment, compensation, and oversight of the work of any registered public accounting firm employed by [the] issuer (including resolution of disagreements between management and the auditor regarding financial reporting)."

The power of audit committees is bolstered by provisions in Sarbanes-Oxley that require any accounting firm performing an audit of a public company to timely report to the audit committee: (1) all critical accounting policies and practices; (2) all alternative treatments of financial information within GAAP that have been discussed with management, the "ramifications" of the use of such alternative disclosures and treatments, and the treatment preferred by the accounting firm; and (3) other material written communications between the registered public accounting firm and management of the issuer.[d]

Sarbanes-Oxley also requires the audit committee to set up procedures for handling complaints by "whistleblowers" within the

---

[d] Public Law 107–204, Section 204, amending Section 10A of the Securities Exchange Act of 1934, (15 U.S.C. Section 78j–1).

company,[e] and to engage independent legal counsel and other advisors where necessary to carry out its duties.[f]

Perhaps the best-known provisions of Sarbanes-Oxley are the rules relating to "Corporate Responsibility for Financial Reports." These rules require the principal executive officer (CEO), and the principal financial officer (CFO) of each public company to certify that he/she has reviewed each quarterly or annual report filed with the SEC, that to his or her knowledge the report does not contain any material false statements or omissions, and that it fairly presents, in all material respects, the financial condition and results of operations of the company for the period being reported. CEOs and CFOs also must certify that they have evaluated the effectiveness of the company's internal controls and have presented their conclusions about the effectiveness of such controls.[g] Knowingly false certifications may be punished by fines of up to $1 million and imprisonment not exceeding ten years.[h]

Other provisions of Sarbanes-Oxley are designed to restore the integrity of the public company audit process. They make it unlawful for any person to fraudulently influence, coerce, manipulate, or to mislead any accountant performing an audit of the company's financial statements for the purpose of rendering the financial statements materially misleading.[i] Audit firms also are forbidden to perform audit services for a public company if the company's chief executive officer, controller, chief financial officer, chief accounting officer, or similarly situated corporate official has been employed by the accounting firm and participated in the audit of the company during the one-year period prior to the initiation of the audit.[j]

---

[e] Public Law 107–204, Section 301(4), amending Section 10A of the Securities Exchange Act of 1934, (15 U.S.C. Section 78f), provides that public company audit committees must establish procedures for:

(A) the receipt, retention, and treatment of complaints received by the issuer regarding accounting, internal accounting controls, or auditing matters; and

(B) the confidential, anonymous submission by employees of the issuer of concerns regarding questionable accounting or auditing matters.

Section 806 of the Act provides further protection for whistleblowers by making it illegal to retaliate against or to harass people who assist in an investigation of the company's violations of securities laws.

[f] Public Law 107–204, Section 301(5), amending Section 10A of the Securities Exchange Act of 1934, (15 U.S.C. Section 78f).

[g] Public Law 107–204, Section 302.

[h] Public Law 107–204, Section 906(c)(1), amending Chapter 63 of Title 18, by inserting new material after existing Section 1349. Willful violations are punished even more severely than knowing violations. See Section 906(c)(2), punishing willful violations with fines of up to $5 million and/or 20 years of imprisonment.

[i] Public Law 107–204, Section 303(a).

[j] Public Law 107–204, Section 206, amending Section 10A of the Securities Exchange Act of 1934, (15 U.S.C. Section 78j–1).

4. ANALYSIS OF THE PROVISIONS OF THE SARBANES-OXLEY ACT

From the outset, Sarbanes-Oxley was criticized by corporate governance experts. One commentator described the Act as a "sparsely worded law [that] is both poorly written and hastily put together so there's little to go on when it comes to interpreting some of its murkier provisions." Another commentator asserted that the Act is "a telling example of the law of unintended consequences. It will have wide-ranging effects on securities, derivative and other (private) shareholder lawsuits." Other commentators generally tended to dismiss the legislation on the grounds (1) that it was unnecessary, (2) that the changes it made were at best only incremental, (3) that on balance it was undesirable because it would impose significant new costs on U.S. firms, or (4) that it was probably unnecessary because modern markets were liquid and quite capable of responding adequately to fraud on their own without additional regulation. Professor Larry Ribstein opined that the Act "represents a hasty, panicked reaction of an electorate looking for an easy fix to the apparent 'problem' that stock prices go down as well as up. Whether or not the Act has provided some short-term relief, in the long run regulatory responses to corporate frauds are unlikely to be more effective in preventing future frauds than existing regulation has been in preventing the current problem, and have a significant chance of imposing substantial costs * * *."

In an important article, Professor Roberta Romano reviewed the major provisions of Sarbanes-Oxley and evaluated their desirability from a policy standpoint, emphasizing the extent to which the provisions of the Act conflicted with the best research in finance, economics, and other relevant social sciences.[k] Professor Romano's analysis of the costs involved with the implementation of Sarbanes-Oxley found the following:

1. Section 301 of Sarbanes-Oxley requires all listed companies to have audit committees composed entirely of independent directors (these persons may not accept any "consulting, advisory or other compensatory fee" nor be an "affiliated person" of the issuer or a subsidiary). There must also be disclosure of whether individual directors are "financial experts," and if none, why there are none. Under Sarbanes-Oxley, shareholders do not have the power to hire or fire an outside auditor since such authority is vested solely in the audit committee. These provisions have increased the cost of the audit function since state law permits the full board to grant or retract delegated authority and to select auditors; Sarbanes-Oxley does not. In addition, state law does not mandate the composition of the board of directors or committees, while Sarbanes-Oxley does. State law also does not define what constitutes "independence,"

---

[k] Roberta Romano, The Sarbanes-Oxley Act and the Making of Quack Corporate Governance, 114 Yale L.J. 1521 (2005).

while Sarbanes-Oxley does. Professor Romano suggests that these requirements of Sarbanes-Oxley go "far beyond" existing corporate law and increase auditing costs.

2.   Since 1999, stock exchanges have had listing standards that require audit committees to be comprised of independent directors, but they permit the appointment of non-independent directors and exempt small businesses from the listing requirements. Sarbanes-Oxley does not permit such appointments or exemptions, thereby increasing costs.

3.   Many studies in economics and finance show that independent boards of directors do not improve corporate performance. Boards with too many independent persons may actually have a negative impact on performance. As mentioned, Sarbanes-Oxley requires all members of the audit committee of the board of directors to be independent.

4.   Section 201 of Sarbanes-Oxley prohibits accounting firms from providing a wide variety of specified non-audit services to firms that they audit. This provision, Professor Romano observes, is in effect a Congressional judgment as to what services the board or shareholders should purchase from the auditor. However there is no evidence that audits were ever compromised as a result of the provision of non-audit services.

5.   Section 402(a) of Sarbanes-Oxley prohibits corporations from arranging or extending credit to executive officers or directors (with narrow exceptions). This blanket prohibition appears to forbid standard compensation practices that are clearly desirable in specific situations: advancing indemnification expenses, the purchase of split-life insurance policies (the company advances funds for the premiums and is repaid out of the policy's later payout following retirement or death), the cashless exercise of stock options under incentive compensation plans, and the like. Professor Romano points out that while state law on such payments varies, no state absolutely forbids such payments. Moreover, the prohibition in Sarbanes-Oxley may be easily evaded by the simple (but generally undesirable) strategy of increasing compensation levels of officers and executives to cover desired expenses. Studies suggest that the blanket prohibition against executive loans was "self-evidently a public policy error."

6.   Section 302 of Sarbanes-Oxley requires the CEO and CFO to certify that the company's periodic reports do not contain any material misstatements or omissions and "fairly present" the firm's financial condition and results of operations. This is a substantive corporate governance mandate imposing significant responsibility on the certifying officer for establishing and maintaining internal controls and evaluating their effectiveness. Another provision of Sarbanes-Oxley, section 906, establishes criminal penalties for a knowing violation of a similar certification requirement. Professor Romano observes that studies into

certification requirements are inconsistent and that "[t]here is a need for considerably more research in order to draw strong inferences."

7. Perhaps the most central concern by companies subject to Sarbanes-Oxley is section 404. This section requires companies to include in their annual reports an acknowledgement of management's obligation to establish internal controls and procedures for financial disclosure. These reports must also contain an assessment by management of the adequacy and effectiveness of both the internal controls and the reporting procedures. In addition, the independent auditor's report on internal control over financial reporting must include the auditor's opinion on (1) whether management's assessment is fairly stated in all material respects, and (2) the effectiveness of the company's internal control over financial reporting. These requirements are relatively new and were not extensively discussed during the enactment process that led to Sarbanes-Oxley.

The ultimate conclusion of Professor Romano's exhaustive analysis is that the Sarbanes-Oxley provisions were poorly conceived and ineffective as an original matter, and should be treated as default provisions under which smaller companies would be free to opt out by shareholder vote.

Beginning in 2004, several of the largest American corporations reported significant costs in complying with the various provisions of Sarbanes-Oxley. The audit costs imposed by the PCAOB alone on such corporations were estimated to be as much as two million dollars a year. For smaller firms, audit costs had increased by 30% or more over the pre-Sarbanes-Oxley period. Perhaps more significantly, the cost of compliance with other new corporate governance provisions imposed by Sarbanes-Oxley for publicly held companies had increased by 100% or more. Furthermore, many of these extra costs did not appear to improve the effectiveness of the statute itself.

A 2004 survey of projected expenditures to meet the internal control provisions of Sarbanes-Oxley indicated that companies with annual revenues over $5 billion were projecting annual external consulting, software, and additional audit fees of $2.8 million, while companies with annual revenues under $25 million were projecting additional costs in the range of $220,000 per year. The new attestation requirements of section 404 were estimated to have created an additional 38 percent increase in costs.

Faced with the costs of complying with Sarbanes-Oxley, a number of large publicly held corporations, particularly foreign firms with shares traded in the U.S., have considered possible ways to avoid Sarbanes-Oxley by deregistering as an "issuer" under sections 3 and 12 of the Securities Exchange Act of 1934. This requires the number of investors to be reduced to less than 300, a result which may be achieved by a reverse stock split or by other devices. In a reverse stock split, the corporation announces a reclassification of its issued shares, e.g., each certificate for a specified number of old shares or a multiple thereof can be exchanged for one new share, or a multiple thereof. All certificates for less than the specified number of old shares have no continuing value in the corporation, but they may be exchanged for cash of a specified amount per share. After the transaction, the number of outstanding shares has been greatly reduced.[1]

The SEC provided small companies with market capitalizations under $75 million until July 2007 to comply with section 404's internal control requirements. In 2005, the SEC chartered the Advisory Committee on Small Public Companies to assess the impact of corporate governance regulatory requirements (and of Sarbanes-Oxley in particular) on small companies, and to make suggestions for improvement. The Committee concluded that Sarbanes-Oxley disproportionately burdened smaller companies, and recommended creating a new system of scaled regulation for microcap and smallcap companies. The recommendations have been applauded by some[m] and derided by others.[n]

The best empirical evidence suggests that no justification existed for the principal corporate governance mandates in Sarbanes-Oxley, and that these mandates will not benefit investors. However, their enactment can be very readily explained by the confluence of significant events in 2002— the Enron scandal, the collapse of Global Crossing, Adelphia Communications, Tyco International, WorldCom, etc., plus a very substantial decline in securities prices that led to widespread losses for investors.

5. THE FINANCIAL CRISIS OF 2007–2010

The subprime mortgage crisis compelled the American executive and legislature to drastically reconsider the role of the SEC and financial regulation in general. Two ardent supporters of regulation lamented that "[t]he natural superiority of the U.S. model for securities regulation is no longer an article of faith, and the credibility of the SEC as a financial regulatory has never been lower." John Coffee and Hillary Sale, Redesigning the SEC: Does the Treasury Have A Better Idea?, 95 Va. L. Rev. 707, 708 (2009).

Most accounts of the crisis start by describing the rapid inflation of a bubble in the U.S. housing market. The housing market in 2008 was propelled by a sudden increase in the availability of mortgage funds to borrowers, regardless of their creditworthiness. This bubble was caused

---

[1]   This device, which permits the corporation to terminate its registration under the Securities Acts, is often referred to as "going black."

[m]   See Bob Greifeld, It's Time to Pull up Our SOX, Wall St. J., Mar. 6, 2006, at A14.

[n]   See Arthur Levitt, Jr., A Misguided Exemption, Wall St. J., Jan. 27, 2006, at A8.

by a relaxation in lending standards that was fueled by the general recognition that big banks underwriting mortgage-backed securities were willing to buy portfolios of mortgage loans to bundle up and sell in asset-backed securitization deals without any serious investigation of the underlying collateral.

The evidence is clear that between 2001 and 2006, an extraordinary increase occurred in the supply of mortgage funds, with much of this increased supply being channeled into poorer communities in which previously there had been a high denial rate on mortgage loan applications. With an increased supply of mortgage credit, housing prices rose rapidly, as new buyers entered the market. But at the same time, a corresponding increase in mortgage debt relative to income levels in these same communities made these loans precarious.

Initially the companies affected were those directly involved in home construction and mortgage lending, such as Northern Rock and Countrywide Financial. Over 100 mortgage lenders went bankrupt during 2007 and 2008. However, the crisis eventually affected many major institutions, and by the end of 2008, several had failed, were acquired under duress, or were subject to government takeover. These included Lehman Brothers, Merrill Lynch, Fannie Mae, Freddie Mac, and AIG.

After nearly eight years favoring the deregulation of the financial industry, the Bush administration aggressively interceded in the private markets in the fall of 2008 to quell panic and to stabilize the nation's leading financial institutions. The dramatic change in regulatory policy began in earnest when the venerable investment bank Bear Stearns, badly damaged by the subprime-mortgage crisis, sold itself to JPMorgan Chase in a fire sale in March 2008.

By September 2008, the escalation of the global financial crisis prompted President Bush and Secretary of the Treasury Henry Paulson to push for passage of a House bill that authorized the Secretary of the Treasury to spend $700 billion to buy "toxic" mortgage-backed securities from banks and other financial institutions. The proposed bailout came hard on the heels of the government's decision to bail out and recapitalize Fannie Mae and Freddie Mac, the home mortgage giants devastated by the subprime mortgage crisis, and the de facto nationalization of insurance behemoth American International Group (AIG), which had issued $440 billion in credit-default swaps insuring the repayment of mortgage-backed securities and other debt. Originally procured by investors to guarantee the repayment of bonds in case the issuer defaulted, credit-default swaps became a popular vehicle for hedge funds and other traders betting on how close a firm was to insolvency.

In 1998, Brooksley Born, then chair of the Commodity Futures Trading Commission (CFTC), had warned that the explosion of the financial derivatives market allowed traders "to take positions that may threaten our regulatory markets, or, indeed, our economy, without the knowledge of any federal regulatory authority." Her colleagues on the Working Group on Financial Markets—Alan Greenspan, chair of the Federal Reserve, SEC chair Arthur Levitt Jr., and U.S. Treasury Secretary Robert Rubin—voiced "grave concerns" about her proposal to regulate the financial derivatives market. Deputy Treasury Secretary Lawrence Summers criticized her for "casting a shadow of regulatory uncertainty over an otherwise thriving market," and Congress passed a law in 2000 that exempted swaps from oversight by the CFTC and the SEC. As discussed further below, the massive but unregulated swaps markets only aggravated the downward pressure on financial institutions already burdened by subprime mortgage-backed securities.

President Bush attempted to arouse national support for the bailout bill in a televised address on September 24, 2008, warning Americans that the bailout was necessary to prevent a widespread collapse of the national economy. On the same day, presidential candidates Barack Obama and John McCain issued a joint public statement in support of the bailout bill. Despite their efforts, the U.S. House of Representatives initially rejected the proposal 228 to 205 on September 29. A number of members of Congress cited significant resistance to the bill from their constituents, who were outraged that the measure appeared to unfairly enrich the same executives who may have caused the financial crisis in the first place. Bloomberg News reported that the top five Wall Street investment banks paid their senior executives more than $5 billion in the five years before Lehman Brothers filed for bankruptcy. Critics of the bill also claimed that the broad powers it gave the Treasury Secretary created a conflict of interest for Paulson, who had served for seven years as the chair and CEO of Goldman Sachs, then the biggest investment bank on Wall Street.

After the bill's defeat in the House, the Dow Jones Industrial Average dropped by nearly 800 points, its largest single-day loss in history. In response, the Senate incorporated the substance of the defeated House bill as an amendment to an existing bill from the House, H.R. 1424, and passed what became the Emergency Economic Stabilization Act[o] on October 1 by a vote of seventy-four to twenty-five. On Friday, October 3, the House passed the bill 263 to 171; President Bush signed it into law a few hours later.

In his testimony before the U.S. Senate, Paulson claimed that the bill would stabilize the economy, improve liquidity in the credit markets, and stimulate investor confidence. In fact, the Act failed to spark the hoped-for rebound in the stock market; on Monday, October 6, the Dow Jones dropped more than 350 points and fell below 10,000 for the first time in four years.

---

    [o]   Pub. L. No. 110–343, Div. A., enacted Oct. 3, 2008 (originally proposed as H.R. 3997).

Critics of the Act argued that Congress delegated to the Secretary of the Treasury an unconstitutionally broad amount of power. The statute authorized the Secretary to "immediately provide authority and facilities that the Secretary of the Treasury can use to restore liquidity and stability to the financial system of the United States," and granted the Secretary the power to "purchase * * * troubled assets from any financial institution, on such terms and conditions as determined by the Secretary." This language implied that the powers granted to the Treasury were discretionary, rather than limited, enumerated powers. Although the Act created the Financial Stability Oversight Board (FSOB) to ensure that all policies implemented under the Act protected taxpayers and were in the nation's economic interest, it only granted the FSOB the power to make recommendations to the Secretary.

Even before the Act was enacted, other regulatory agencies took action to resuscitate ailing companies and to combat the plunging stock market. In September 2008, the SEC banned short selling on 799 financial stocks with exposure to risky mortgage-backed securities and other distressed assets. The temporary ban was passed in response to allegations that traders had illegally spread misinformation in order to drive down the shares of financial firms that they had already sold short. When the thirteen-day ban was lifted on October 9, Morgan Stanley's stock plummeted 26 percent in a day, which prompted many financial sector officials to press the SEC to extend the ban. However, 24 percent of the companies on the SEC's protected list experienced increases after the ban was lifted, and 20 percent saw no change at all.

Meanwhile, the Federal Reserve Board and others worked to create an electronic trading platform for the $55 trillion credit-default swap market. The value of a swap or other financial derivative contract depends in part on the counterparty's solvency and its ability to honor its obligations. AIG's inability to honor its credit-default swap commitments led to the U.S. government having to pump more than $123 billion into AIG in exchange for voting preferred stock. The effort to create an electronic trading market for derivatives rested on the premise that greater transparency around the pricing of derivatives would reduce short selling while bringing structure and stability to this heretofore "dark market." In October 2008, the Chicago Mercantile Exchange announced its plan to join with hedge fund Citadel Investment Group to establish an electronic trading platform and clearinghouse for credit-default swaps. Meanwhile, the SEC, CFTC, and Federal Reserve Bank of New York fought over who should oversee the swaps market if Congress, as expected, authorized greater regulation of these speculative instruments.

In September 2008, the Federal Reserve, with Paulson's urging and Wall Street's cooperation, waived the normal review process and opportunity for public comment and approved in a matter of days a major overhaul of the structure of two leading investment banks, Goldman Sachs and Morgan Stanley. Both firms announced on September 21 that they would become commercial bank holding companies subject to permanent on-site regulation by the Federal Reserve. The transition of these major companies from the regulatory supervision of the SEC to the Fed reflects public and governmental recognition of the SEC's failures during the crisis.

After Lehman Brothers declared bankruptcy and Bank of America acquired Merrill Lynch, Goldman and Morgan Stanley were the last two major independent investment banks in the United States. Their decision to become regulated bank holding companies marked the end of an era and instantly altered the landscape of modern Wall Street.

The Federal Reserve immediately extended credit to the firms' broker-dealer subsidiaries and sent the message that it would not allow these powerhouses to go under. As bank-holding companies, Goldman and Morgan Stanley can tap the Fed's so-called discount window, and more of their client accounts are covered by the Federal Deposit Insurance Corporation (FDIC). In exchange, the firms subjected themselves to greater government scrutiny that could limit their ability to engage in potentially risky but lucrative strategies, such as borrowing heavily to make securities trades.

In early October 2008, the Federal Reserve announced its intention to start lending directly to nonfinancial firms by buying up short-term corporate debt (commercial paper) for the first time since the Great Depression. On October 14, President Bush announced that the Treasury Department would spend up to $250 billion of the $700 billion authorized by the bailout law to buy nonvoting senior preferred shares in the nation's commercial banks. Secretary Paulson had summoned the CEOs of the nine largest U.S. banks to the Treasury Department on October 13 and told them in no uncertain terms that they had no choice but to accept $125 billion in government funds in exchange for preferred stock "for their own good and that of the country." As part of the deal, the banks were required to limit executive compensation and to agree not to increase dividends to their common shareholders. President Bush promised that "government's role will be limited and temporary" and that the partial nationalization of the nation's banks, which was patterned after Britain's purchase of equity stakes in its major banks, was a short-term move. The FDIC also temporarily guaranteed most new debt issued by insured banks and expanded the government insurance to cover all non-interest-bearing accounts in an effort to stall cash withdrawals by small businesses.

The apparent loser in all this is the SEC. Paulson had recommended that many of the SEC's policy-making powers be transferred to a newly created agency and that the SEC be relegated to primarily an enforcement role. Paulson also suggested that the SEC be merged with the CFTC, commenting in a press release that "the realities of the current marketplace * * * make it increasingly difficult to rationalize a separate regulatory regime" for securities and futures products. At a minimum, transfer of regulatory control over the largest investment banks to the Federal Reserve seemed destined to reducing the power of the SEC to regulate the securities brokerage industry.

In September 2008, presidential candidate and Senator John McCain accused SEC Chair Christopher Cox, a fellow Republican who had served in Congress with McCain for seventeen years, of "betray[ing] the public trust" and stated that if "I were president today, I would fire him." Critics faulted the SEC for reducing investment banks' net capital requirements in 2004 and suggested that this decision had contributed to the subprime-mortgage crisis.

In fact, some commentators place partial blame for the 2008 financial meltdown with deregulatory measures taken by the SEC, particularly those that placed some categories of derivatives and some firms beyond effective regulation. Well before the financial crisis crested, the President's Working Group on Financial Markets issued a "Policy Statement on Financial Market Developments" in March 2008 that identified five "principal underlying causes of the turmoil in financial markets":

1) a breakdown in underwriting standards for subprime mortgages;

2) a significant erosion of market discipline by those involved in the securitization process, including originators, underwriters, credit rating agencies, and global investors, related in part to failures to provide or obtain adequate risk disclosures;

3) flaws in credit rating agencies' assessment of subprime residential mortgages;

4) risk management weaknesses at some large U.S. and European financial institutions; and

5) regulatory policies, including capital and disclosure requirements, that failed to mitigate risk management weaknesses.

Professor John Coffee argues that although the President's Working Group was correct in noting the connection between the decline of discipline in the mortgage loan origination market and a similar laxity among underwriters in the capital markets, the study largely ignored the direction of the causality. In retrospect, irresponsible lending in the mortgage market appears to have been a direct response to the capital markets' increasingly insatiable demand for financial assets to securitize. If underwriters were willing to rush deeply flawed asset-backed securitizations to the market, mortgage loan originators had no rational reason to resist them.

Professor Richard Mendales has suggested that the SEC contributed to this problem by softening its disclosure and due diligence standards for asset-backed securitizations.[p] Coffee agrees that failures in regulatory oversight by the SEC have played a greater causal role in the debacle than has been generally emphasized.[q]

In the wake of the financial crisis, almost all agree that the SEC is in need of serious reform. Recent discussions about reforming the SEC tout the superiority of "principles" as a basis for regulatory reform over "rules-based" regulation. Some stress that quick change to a principles-oriented system is vital to maintaining global competitiveness. Coffee contends that our current system maintains a subtler balance between the two than had generally been recognized, and that without rules and enforcement, the system would decline in ways that business would actually find unpalatable.

Far from an ideal model, the SEC has repeatedly found itself underequipped to deal with even the most glaring enforcement priorities. For example, the SEC recently examined its own failure to investigate past allegations of wrongdoing by Bernard Madoff, who was recently sentenced to 150 years in prison for perpetrating a $50 billion Ponzi scheme. Christopher Cox, former SEC chairman, admitted that although credible and specific allegations regarding Madoff's financial wrongdoing were repeatedly brought to the attention of the SEC, they were never recommended for enforcement action.

NOTES

(1) The United States, at the beginning of 2008, had five major investment banks that were not owned by a large commercial bank: Merrill Lynch, Goldman Sachs, Morgan Stanley, Lehman Brothers, and Bear Stearns. By late fall of 2008, all of these investment banks had either failed or abandoned their status as independent investment banks. Bear Stearns and Merrill Lynch had been forced (at the brink of insolvency) to merge with larger commercial banks in transactions orchestrated by banking regulators. Lehman Brothers had filed for bankruptcy. Goldman Sachs and Morgan Stanley had converted into bank holding companies under pressure from the Federal Reserve Bank, thus moving from SEC to Federal Reserve supervision.

(2) The subprime mortgage crisis and subsequent failure of many American banks has renewed academic interest in corporate governance and regulatory matters and spawned a substantial body of academic literature.

---

[p]   Richard E. Mendales, Collateralized Explosive Devices: Why Securities Regulation Failed to Prevent the CDO Meltdown, and How to Fix It, 2009 U. Ill. L. Rev. 1359.

[q]   Coffee, 95 VA. L. REV. 707, 734.

the nature of corporations, and of the duties owed by directors, equates the duty of directors with the duty to maximize profits of the firm for the benefit of shareholders.

This model of the public corporation is highly coherent and offers several alternative arguments to support the legitimacy of corporate power in our democracy. The first argument in favor of the property concept is political and normative. It is premised on the conclusionary notion that shareholders "own" the corporation, and asserts that to admit the propriety of non-profit maximizing behavior is to approve agents spending other people's money in pursuit of their own, perhaps eccentric, views of the public good. * * *

The second rationale for the property model is that the model, and action consistent with it, maximize wealth creation. This rationale asserts that the purpose of business corporations is the creation of wealth, nothing else. It asserts that business corporations are not formed to assist in self-realization through social interaction; they are not formed to create jobs or to provide tax revenues; they are not formed to endow university departments or to pursue knowledge. All of these other things—job creation, tax payments, research, and social interaction—desirable as they may be, are said to be side effects of the pursuit of profit for the residual owners of the firm.

This argument asserts that the creation of more wealth should always be the corporation's objective, regardless of who benefits. The sovereign's taxing and regulatory power can then address questions of social costs and re-distribution of wealth. * * *

[T]he last quarter of the nineteenth century saw the emergence of social forces that would oppose the conception of business corporations as simply the property of contracting stockholders. The scale and scope of the modern integrated business enterprise that emerged in the late nineteenth century required distinctive professional management skills and huge capital investments that often necessitated risk sharing through dispersed stock ownership. National securities markets emerged and stockholders gradually came to look less like flesh and blood owners and more like investors who could slip in or out of a particular stock almost costlessly. These new giant business corporations came to seem to some people like independent entities, with purposes, duties, and loyalties of their own; purposes that might diverge in some respect from shareholder wealth maximization. * * *

One would think that whether the corporation law endorses the property conception or the social entity conception would have important consequences. * * * [But] for the fifty years preceding that contentious decade [the 1980s], we did not share agreement on the legal nature of the public business corporation and that failure did not seem especially problematic.

The law "papered over" the conflict in our conception of the corporation by invoking a murky distinction between long-term profit maximization and short-term profit maximization. Corporate expenditures which at first blush did not seem to be profit maximizing, could be squared with the property conception of the corporation by recognizing that they might redound to the long-term benefit of the corporation and its shareholders. Thus, without purporting to abandon the idea that directors ultimately owe loyalty only to stockholders and their financial interests, the law was able to approve reasonable corporate expenditures for charitable or social welfare purposes or other actions that did not maximize current profit. * * *

DANIEL R. FISCHEL, THE CORPORATE GOVERNANCE MOVEMENT

35 Vand.L.Rev. 1259, 1268–70 (1982).

It has become fashionable to argue that the pursuit of profit maximization by corporations is at variance with the public interest. Proponents of this argument, however, face the insuperable problem of defining what the public interest is, and when the pursuit of profit maximization should be sacrificed for these ends. As Harold Demsetz has remarked, centuries of philosophers and economists have tried and failed to provide any workable definition of "the fair price," "the just wage," or "fair competition," let alone what constitutes "the good society."[29] * * *

Although potential conflict exists between profit maximization and pursuit of other goals, far more consistency is present between the two than generally assumed. A successful business venture provides jobs to workers and goods and services that consumers want to buy. While these benefits may not appear to be particularly dramatic, they should not be underestimated, as the tens of thousands of workers in distressed industries who have had to give back concessions previously won or have lost their jobs outright will readily attest. Much the same is true in other areas. * * * Frequently this harmony of interests exists, but is difficult to perceive. Firms that close plants to move to different geographical areas commonly are accused, for example, of lacking a sense of responsibility to affected workers and the community as a whole. The difficulty with this argument is that it ignores the presumably greater benefits that will accrue to workers and the community in the new locale where the firm can operate more profitably. A firm that causes dislocations by moving a plant is behaving no more "unethically" than a firm that causes dislocations by, say, inventing a new technology that causes competitors to go out of business.

---

[29] Demsetz, Social Responsibility in the Enterprise Economy, 10 Sw.U.L.Rev. 1, 1 (1978).

I do not mean to suggest that profit maximization will always lead to the socially optimal result. In those situations in which externalities are present—pollution is the most common example—a firm may impose costs on others without providing compensation. But even this situation is misunderstood. If a firm dumps pollutants in a stream, the firm imposes costs on the users of the stream that may exceed the benefits to the firm. It does not follow, however, that pollution is immoral behavior which should be halted. Consider the reciprocal case in which the firm does not pollute because of concern for users of the stream and instead relies on a more expensive method of disposing wastes. In this situation, the users of the stream impose costs on the firm's investors, employees, and consumers that may exceed the benefits to users of the stream. Neither polluting nor failing to pollute is *a priori* the "ethically" or "morally" correct course of action. * * *

NOTE

The United Nations has taken steps toward regulating transnational corporations by developing the Norms on the Responsibilities of Transnational Corporations and Other Business Enterprises with Regard to Human Rights. The Norms make transnational corporations responsible for protecting human rights within their spheres of influence and activities. Among the enumerated rights and obligations are the right to non-discriminatory treatment; certain workers' rights such as the right to collective bargaining and prohibitions on child labor; and obligations to protect the environment. Many Western countries opposed the promulgation of the Norms, and in 2005, any further attempts to ratify the Norms were abandoned. For an in-depth discussion of the Norms, see Larry Cata Backer, Multinational Corporations, Transnational Law: The United Nations' Norms on the Responsibilities of Transnational Corporations as a Harbinger of Corporate Social Responsibility in International Law, 37 Colum. Hum. Rts. L. Rev. 287 (2006).

THE AMERICAN LAW INSTITUTE, PRINCIPLES OF CORPORATE GOVERNANCE: ANALYSIS & RECOMMENDATIONS

§ 2.01   The Objective and Conduct of the Corporation

(a) Subject to the provisions of Subsection (b) and § 6.02 (Action of Directors That Has the Foreseeable Effect of Blocking Unsolicited Tender Offers), a corporation should have as its objective the conduct of business activities with a view to enhancing corporate profit and shareholder gain.

(b) Even if corporate profit and shareholder gain are not thereby enhanced, the corporation, in the conduct of its business:

(1) Is obliged, to the same extent as a natural person, to act within the boundaries set by law;

(2) May take into account ethical considerations that are reasonably regarded as appropriate to the responsible conduct of business; and

(3) May devote a reasonable amount of resources to public welfare, humanitarian, educational, and philanthropic purposes.

NOTE

Many transactions (such as charitable contributions) that provide no direct benefit to the corporation may be justified on the theory that the directors are maximizing the "long term" profits of the business. While doubtless many such actions do in fact benefit the corporation on a long term basis, the problem is that practically any expenditure can be justified by this argument, and its acceptance virtually means that "anything goes" so far as the use of corporate assets is concerned. Does § 2.01(b) adequately channel the power to enter into non-profit-maximizing transactions? For a careful examination of this section see Melvin Aron Eisenberg, Corporate Conduct that Does Not Maximize Shareholder Gain: Legal Conduct, Ethical Conduct, the Penumbra Effect, Reciprocity, the Prisoner's Dilemma, Sheep's Clothing, Social Conduct, and Disclosure, 28 Stetson L.Rev. 1 (1998). For a criticism of many aspects of the ALI's *Principles of Corporate Governance,* see Douglas M. Branson, Corporate Governance (1993). Consider also Henry Hansmann and Reinier Kraakman, The End of History for Corporate Law, 89 Geo. L.J. 439, 441–42 (2001) (arguing that there is convergence on a consensus that the best means to this end of pursuing aggregate social welfare is to make corporate managers strongly accountable to shareholder interests and, at least in direct terms, only to those interests).

ILLINOIS BUSINESS CORPORATION ACT
805 ILCS 5/8.85.

5/8.85 Discharge of Duties—Considerations

In discharging the duties of their respective positions, the board of directors, committees of the board, individual directors and individual officers may, in considering the best long term and short term interests of the corporation, consider the effects of any action (including without limitation, action which may involve or relate to a change or potential change in control of the corporation) upon employees, suppliers and customers of the corporation or its subsidiaries, communities in which offices or other establishments of the corporation or its subsidiaries are located, and all other pertinent factors.

PENNSYLVANIA BUSINESS CORPORATION LAW

15 Pa. Stat. § 1715.

§ 1715   Exercise of Powers Generally

(a) General rule.—In discharging the duties of their respective positions, the board of directors, committees of the board and individual directors of a business corporation may, in considering the best interests of the corporation, consider to the extent they deem appropriate:

(1) The effects of any action upon any or all groups affected by such action, including shareholders, employees, suppliers, customers and creditors of the corporation, and upon communities in which offices or other establishments of the corporation are located.

(2) The short-term and long-term interests of the corporation, including benefits that may accrue to the corporation from its long-term plans and the possibility that these interests may be best served by the continued independence of the corporation.

(3) The resources, intent and conduct (past, stated and potential) of any person seeking to acquire control of the corporation.

(4) All other pertinent factors.

(b) Consideration of interests and factors.—The board of directors, committees of the board and individual directors shall not be required, in considering the best interests of the corporation or the effects of any action, to regard any corporate interest or the interests of any particular group affected by such action as a dominant or controlling interest or factor. * * *

NOTES

(1) These sorts of statutes, generally known as "other constituency" or "alternative constituency" statutes, have been extremely popular. Most states have adopted similar statutes, which vary considerably in language. This phenomenon is "[o]ne of the most remarkable but least remarked developments in corporation law in many years." James J. Hanks, Jr., Non-Stockholder Constituency Statutes: An Idea Whose Time Should Never Have Come, Insights, Vol. 3, No. 12, at 20 (Dec. 1989). While considerable law review commentary has been devoted to these statutes, they have been surprisingly non-controversial at the state level; indeed, they have been enacted almost routinely with little or no attention paid to the fact that they may dramatically change the basic ground rules of corporate governance. Their genesis, however, is clear: they were enacted in response to the fear of takeovers during the 1980s. As described by Hanks, "Opponents of hostile takeovers apparently felt that by giving directors a wider range of factors upon which to base a rejection of a takeover offer, they would help protect the directors from liability and thus encourage them to resist takeover offers." Id.

(2) Many comments about constituency statutes are very negative. For example, Lynda J. Oswald: Shareholders v. Stakeholders: Evaluating Corporate Constituency Statutes Under the Takings Clause, 24 J.Corp.L. 1, 2 (1998): "[T]hese constituency statutes blur the lines of corporate control and ownership and create a class of managers whose decisions are utterly discretionary and unfettered by the normal (albeit) weak constraints imposed by traditional corporate law doctrine."

(3) Committee on Corporate Laws, Other Constituencies Statutes: Potential for Confusion, 45 Bus. Law. 2253, 2269 (1990):

> The Committee believes that the better interpretation of these [constituency] statutes, and one that avoids such consequences [i.e., creating conflicts of duty for directors and undermining the effectiveness of the system that has made the corporation an efficient device for the creation of jobs and wealth], is that they confirm what the common law has been: directors may take into account the interests of other constituencies but only as and to the extent that the directors are acting in the best interests, long as well as short term, of the shareholders and the corporation. * * *

C. SHAREHOLDERS

1. IN GENERAL

JOSEPH A. LIVINGSTON, THE AMERICAN STOCKHOLDER
Pages 60–61, 67 (1958).

Here's a natural question: If a stockholder is not satisfied with a company's management, why should he start a proxy fight, why should he sue, why shouldn't he just sell his stock and be done with it?

Answer: That is what most stockholders do.

It is the easiest, cheapest, and, from many points of view, the most practical way to express stockholder dissatisfaction with a management, a company, or an industry.

The right to sell is a vote. And the stock market—Wall Street—is the polling booth. If the price of a stock goes up, it registers stockholder-investor-satisfaction. If it goes down, it registers dissatisfaction in the market place. * * *

This right to sell stock—to vote for or against a management—in the market place—is different from a vote at a stockholders' meeting. When a stockholder votes against a slate of directors, he is exercising his right as a stockholder, as an owner. He hopes to change the management and improve the company. But a stockholder who sells says to hell with it. He is not going to reform the company. He is not an owner trying to increase the value of his property. He says, in effect, "Include me out." * * *

Thus, the market-place vote has power. It is a positive warning, a financial warning, to an incumbent management, of stockholder dissatisfaction. It lets the officers know that dissatisfaction has got beyond the discussion stage. The "big boys" are selling. So, the management might bestir itself—make changes—to strengthen the company's position. For that reason, selling stock is not an entirely empty gesture. True, the big investors do not fight for a change; they do not stay with the company that is retrogressing. But their leave-taking has an effect.

DANIEL R. FISCHEL, EFFICIENT CAPITAL MARKET THEORY, THE MARKET FOR CORPORATE CONTROL, AND THE REGULATION OF CASH TENDER OFFERS

57 Tex.L.Rev. 1, 3–5, 8–9 (1978).

* * * [I]f a publicly traded company is poorly or less than optimally managed, the price of its securities will reflect this fact accurately and promptly. That a capital market is efficient, however, does not imply that there is a similarly efficient mechanism whereby control shifts from less capable managers to others who can manage corporate assets more profitably. The market for corporate control, so called by Henry Manne in his ground-breaking work on the subject,[13] must perform that function in our economic system.

The lower the market price of the securities compared to what it would be with better management, the more attractive the firm is to outsiders with the ability to take the firm over. * * *

One of the basic themes of corporation law is the significance for shareholders of the modern corporation's separation of ownership and control. In their famous work on this subject, Professors Berle and Means assumed that managers do not seek to maximize what is most important to shareholders—appreciation of the shareholders' underlying investment.

Berle and Means failed to recognize, however, that unity of ownership and control is not a necessary condition of efficient performance of a firm. If the owner of a wholly owned firm is its manager, he will make operating decisions that maximize his utility. After the owner-manager sells equity in the firm to raise capital, however, his incentive to search out new profitable ventures diminishes because he now bears only a fraction of the losses resulting from less profitable investments. The agency relationship between shareholders and

---

[13] E.g., Manne, Cash Tender Offers for Shares—A Reply to Chairman Cohen, 1967 Duke L.J. 231; Manne, Mergers and the Market for Corporate Control, 73 J.Pol.Econ. 110 (1965).

managers inevitably calls into question the identity of the agent's decisions with decisions that would maximize the welfare of shareholders.

Various market mechanisms exist, however, to minimize this divergence of interests between managers and shareholders. * * * The market for corporate control and the threat of cash tender offers in particular are of great importance in creating incentives for management to maximize the welfare of shareholders. Theoretically, shareholders may oust poor management on their own initiative, but the costs to individual shareholders of monitoring management performance and campaigning for its defeat in shareholder elections when performance is poor are prohibitive. On the other hand, inefficient performance by management is reflected in share price thus making the corporation a likely candidate for a takeover bid. Since a successful takeover bid often results in the displacement of current management, managers have a strong incentive to operate efficiently and keep share prices high.

NOTE

If Fischel and others are correct about the operation of the market for corporate control, is corporate social responsibility even possible?

2.   THE GROWTH OF INSTITUTIONAL INVESTORS

RICHARD H. KOPPES, CORPORATE GOVERNANCE: INSTITUTIONAL INVESTORS, NOW IN CONTROL OF MORE THAN HALF THE SHARES OF U.S. CORPORATIONS, DEMAND MORE ACCOUNTABILITY

The National Law Journal, April 14, 1997, p. B5.

Nothing has so defined the revolution of corporate governance over the last 20 years as the rise of institutional investors. This key group has become a powerful force in corporate America. As activists, institutional investors have set the standards and terms for the corporate governance reform movement and are changing the face of American business.

Aging baby boomers have fueled the increase in public and private funds from approximately $2 trillion in 1986 to more than $5 trillion today—accounting for a sizable portion of all institutional investments.

While patterns of share ownership in the United States are almost always changing in one way or another, the 1990s marked a watershed: For the first time on record, institutional investors controlled more than half the shares in American corporations. By contrast, as recently as 40 years ago, these institutions together held less than 10 percent of the outstanding shares. Progressive institutionalization has been the dominant ongoing change in U.S. share ownership.

This change in ownership structure has had a number of important consequences over time. Many institutional investors have such large holdings that they have become permanent, long-term shareowners of major corporations. As buy-and-hold players, institutional investors have become the patient capital of companies. As a result they have an economic interest in using corporate governance to improve performance.

And as the size of their holdings has grown, institutional investors have discovered ownership rights. The practice of simply selling shares in disgust has given way to the realization that taking an active role as an owner makes economic sense.

NOTES

(1) The principal kinds of institutional investors are (a) pension funds created by corporate employers, by states and cities for their employees, and by universities, churches, and foundations; (b) mutual funds (and other types of investment companies) that offer opportunities to invest in broad portfolios of securities; (c) insurance companies, both life and casualty; (d) foundations; (e) university and charitable endowments; (f) banks investing trust funds; (g) brokerage firms; and (h) a variety of investment vehicles for sophisticated investors, many in the form of limited partnerships.

(2) The growth of institutional investors described by Mr. Koppes is graphically revealed by statistics. In 1953, individual investors held 90 percent of all outstanding shares listed on the New York Stock Exchange, while institutional investors held less than 10 percent. Cf. Carolyn Kay Brancato & Stephen Rabimov, Conference Bd., The 2008 Institutional Investment Report: Trends in Institutional Investor Assets and Equity Ownership of U.S. Corporations 20 (2008) (Table 10) (noting, based on values of total outstanding equity from the Board of Governors of the Federal Reserve System, that institutional investors accounted for just 6.1 percent of equity ownership in 1950). By 2006, individual stock ownership had fallen to approximately 30 percent of U.S. equities. Mutual funds alone are estimated to hold approximately 27 percent of U.S. equities, and public pension funds are estimated to account for 10 percent or more of the total U.S. equity market. See id. at 22 (Table 13); Report of the Task Force of the ABA Section of Business Law Corporate Governance Committee on Delineation of Governance Roles and Responsibilities, 65 Bus. Law. 107, 135 (2009). The data is even more dramatic for equity ownership in the largest publicly traded U.S. companies. According to a recent study, in 2008 institutional investors owned 76.9 percent of the largest 1,000 U.S. companies. See Brancato & Rabimov at 27 (Table 19). Corporations may have to pay more attention to corporate governance issues in the years to come, if only because the growth of institutional holdings has resulted in more demanding and sophisticated shareholders. By virtue of the size and concentration of their holdings, institutional investors are the antithesis of the small, dispersed, relatively powerless, and rationally apathetic shareholders described by Berle and Means in 1932. To the extent that shareholdings are concentrated among

a smaller group of shareholders, the collective action problem can be overcome by institutional investors.

(3) Institutional investors almost always have fiduciary duties to persons other than the issuers of the portfolio securities in which they invest. For example, pension funds have a duty to the employees covered by the fund to maximize the funds available for retirement benefits. These duties to third parties are construed by some institutional investors as requiring that they strive to maximize the gain to the institutional investor even though the gain is on a short-term basis. This short-horizon investment philosophy, when being applied by a relatively small number of shareholders who collectively may own more than 50 percent of the outstanding securities issued by the largest domestic corporations, is itself a source of concern. However, as suggested by Mr. Koppes, many institutional investors, particularly employee retirement plans, do not adopt a policy of short-term maximization of gains, but view themselves instead as permanent investors in individual companies.

MICHAEL B. DORFF, SOFTENING PHARAOH'S HEART: HARNESSING ALTRUISTIC THEORY AND BEHAVIORAL LAW AND ECONOMICS TO REIN IN EXECUTIVE SALARIES
51 Buff.L.Rev. 811, 834–36 (2003).

The free market school has also argued that institutional investors will eventually solve problems—such as those with executive compensation—that stem from the split between ownership and control in public corporations. Unlike most other types of shareholders, institutional investors, such as mutual funds, private and public pension funds, banks, and insurance companies, typically own large amounts of stock. These entities possess the potential to reunify ownership and control. Institutional investors may own large enough blocks of a company's stock to exercise real control, especially if they act in concert. Moreover, concentrated stock ownership may mean that the rewards that come from close monitoring of corporate activities outweigh the associated costs. As a result, institutional investors should possess a strong incentive to oppose any attempt by the CEO to act contrary to the shareholders' interests.

Unfortunately, this theory has often not borne out well in practice, in part because of two popular investment strategies, diversification and indexing. Most institutional investors diversify their holdings to reduce risk exposure. Dividing investments among many different companies limits the consequences of a disaster suffered by any single corporation. But by limiting their investments in any one company, institutional investors also sharply reduce their incentive to monitor any particular corporation's management.

Many institutional investors now also employ indexing for part or all of their equity investments. Indexing involves buying stock in all of the companies in a particular sector index or in the market as a whole, often weighted according to market capitalization. Academic studies have asserted that in the long-term, the vast majority of investors who choose individual stocks will underperform the relevant market index. An additional advantage of indexing is that it eliminates the need for expensive research on individual corporations. In other words, institutional investors who practice indexing need not monitor corporate behavior and, therefore, will not want to bear the expense of an active role in managing the corporation.

Another reason institutional investors may not prove an effective panacea is that institutional investors often have close ties to the corporations in which they invest. Institutional investors include private and public pension funds, mutual funds, insurance companies, and banks. With the exception of public pension funds, all of these entities may seek business from the same companies whose stock they own. * * *

NOTES

(1) Despite the potential obstacles to institutional investor activism identified by Professor Dorff, some institutional investors, particularly those controlled by unions or public sector pension funds such as CalPers, the nation's largest public pension fund with assets totaling $277.2 billion as of October 31, 2013, have increasingly participated in corporate governance in recent years. Less clear is whether activism on the part of these sorts of institutional investors has improved firm performance. Professor Roberta Romano has argued that institutional investors have focused on reforms that have not been demonstrated to improve performance, such as limiting executive compensation and altering the structure of the board. Roberta Romano, Less Is More: Making Institutional Investor Activism a Valuable Mechanism of Corporate Governance, 18 Yale J. on Reg. 174 (2001).

(2) One kind of institutional investor may have a greater impact on firm performance than others. Recently some have found evidence that activism on the part of hedge funds notably improves firm performance. See Mark Hulbert, A Good Word for Hedge Fund Activism, N.Y. Times, Feb. 18, 2007, at Section 3. Lucian Bebchuk, Alon Brav, and Wei Jiang conducted a comprehensive empirical investigation into the role of activist shareholders, particularly hedge funds. After studying approximately 2,000 interventions by activist hedge funds during the period 1994–2007, they concluded that interventions are followed by improved operating performance during the five-year period following the interventions. According to the authors, these improvements in long-term performance are present also when focusing on the two subsets of activist interventions that are most resisted and criticized: (a) interventions that lower or constrain long-term investments by enhancing leverage, beefing up shareholder payouts, or reducing investments, and (b)

adversarial interventions employing hostile tactics. See Lucian Bebchuk, Alon Brav, and Wei Jiang, The Long Term Effects of Hedge Fund Activism, July 2013 Working Paper, available at http://ssrn.com/abstract=2291577.

(3) Institutional investors are also actively involved in persuading public companies to scale back on their arsenal of takeover defenses in order to make changes in control, which generally result in target company shareholders realizing a significant premium for their shares. Takeovers are discussed in detail in Chapter 16.

D. DIRECTORS

MYLES L. MACE, DIRECTORS: MYTH AND REALITY
Pages 178–81 (1971).

[D]irectors at regular meetings where there is no crisis demanding immediate action perform only two basic functions:

(a) They provide advice and counsel to management. They may be a sounding board from which a variety of views on * * * difficult questions may be obtained. The views of a director with expertise in an area such as law or finance may be given greater weight with respect to questions arising within his or her area of expertise.

(b) They provide discipline to management, who must appear before them and present information and defend business decisions. Even though the board may not question the management's conclusion, the mere fact that it is a possibility requires an organization of thoughts and points of view and a careful review of [the] work of subordinates. The mere fact that a difficult question might be asked ensures that the chief executive officer will prepare carefully for his appearance before the board.

ROBERT W. HAMILTON, RELIANCE AND LIABILITY STANDARDS FOR OUTSIDE DIRECTORS
24 Wake Forest L.Rev. 5, 9–12 (1989).

Modern boards of directors have practically nothing to do with the day-to-day business of the corporation. Publicly held corporations are immense economic entities. * * * The internal organization of such large economic entities necessarily involves complex hierarchical structures in which successively higher levels of management are given increasingly broad discretion and responsibility. Indeed, starting at the lowest level of corporate management, such as shop foreman or a similar position, successive layers of broader responsibility can be traced up through several levels of management. By following this process through to its logical conclusion, the highest level reached still would be below the level of the board of directors.

* * *

Corporate headquarters itself has a hierarchical structure. At the highest levels are a series of executive managers, usually organized on a functional rather than a product basis, who have ultimate authority over broad areas of corporate activities. They have titles, such as "chief legal officer," "chief operations officer," "chief financial officer," and "chief accounting officer," that bear no relationship to the traditional corporate officers of "President," "Secretary," or "Treasurer" referred to in older state corporation statutes. At the ultimate apex is an individual referred to almost universally as the chief executive officer (the "CEO") who has responsibility for the enterprise as a whole. The CEO may have additional titles and roles, such as "President" or "Chairman of the Board of Directors," but many CEOs do not. The CEO has responsibility for the management team that directs the enterprise. If, for example, he loses confidence in the chief financial officer, the CEO must replace him and find a more satisfactory one. In theory, the CEO has power to call the shots in the corporate bureaucracy on narrow issues as well as broad ones, where and when he wishes. Of course, the CEO, as the head of a large bureaucratic organization, cannot hope to run details of the business operations; if he is to be effective, authority over details must be delegated to subordinates, and the CEO must concentrate on the broadest issues relating to the corporation.[17]

Because the CEO has ultimate responsibility for the success or failure of the business, he—and quite possibly he alone—will make the final decision on whether to embark upon a radical change in business strategy that may lead to the loss of his or her job if the change turns out to be disastrous. He may decide, for example, to close fifteen plants in order to redirect the primary emphasis of the corporation, or to develop a new product such as a state-of-the-art airplane or modern computer that will strain the economic resources of the entire entity and may well be unsuccessful; "betting the company" is the slang phrase that describes such fundamental and risky decisions. Such decisions may or may not be reviewed by the board of directors before they are implemented, but it is almost certain that if the CEO wishes to embark on such a course of

---

[17] The effect of this delegation of details has been characterized as follows:

[P]ower—having great influence, force, and authority—is slipping through the chief executive's hands, and has been for some time. * * * Now a chief executive hardly ever "runs" anything. * * * Chief executives, many management gurus agree, are less powerful today than they were 10 or 15 years ago. The most significant reason is that their task is much bigger. It's one thing to manage a single operation well. It's another thing to decide that you're no longer in a certain business, to change, cut back, and deal with foreign competition. The agenda has been greatly expanded. * * *

John A. Byrne and Laurie Baum, The Limits of Power, Bus. Wk., October 23, 1987, 33–34.

action, the board of directors will acquiesce in that decision despite the reservations of many, or even all, members.[18]

Where then does the board of directors fit in? * * * [I]t is somewhere above the CEO, and floating off to one side. Its principal source of power is a cataclysmic one: If it loses confidence in the CEO, it can compel his resignation and the installation of a successor. Obviously, such a power is an extreme one with wide-reaching implications upon the management of the business and is used only rarely and in extreme circumstances. Furthermore, it is not exercised easily. Because of the manner of their selection and the nature of their working relationships with the CEO, directors tend to give the CEO the benefit of the doubt. * * *

NOTES

(1) Section 3.02(a) of the ALI's Principles of Corporate Governance (1994) lists five mandatory functions of a board of a publicly held corporation:

(1) Select, regularly evaluate, fix the compensation of, and, where appropriate, replace the principal senior executives;

(2) Oversee the conduct of the corporation's business to evaluate whether the business is being properly managed;

(3) Review and, where appropriate, approve the corporation's financial objectives and major corporate plans and activities;

(4) Review and, where appropriate, approve major changes in, and determinations of other major questions of choice respecting, the appropriate auditing and accounting principles and practices to be used in the preparation of the corporation's financial statements;

(5) Perform such other functions as are prescribed by law, or assigned to the board under a standard of the corporation.

Section 3.02(b) lists seven additional functions that "a board of directors also has power" to perform, including initiation of corporate plans, changes in accounting principles, providing advice and counsel to senior executives, and so forth.

(2) A leading source of principles of good corporate practice is the Corporate Directors Guidebook, prepared and published by the Committee on Corporate Laws, Section of Business Law, American Bar Association. The backbone of the modern view of corporate governance is based on basic concepts: a substantial majority of members of a board of directors should be "independent of management," and the critical oversight committees—audit, compensation, and nominating—should be staffed entirely by "independent" or "nonmanagement" directors. Today the New York Stock Exchange and the NASDAQ require a majority of board members to meet their definitions of independence, and require all members of audit committees to meet the

---

[18] A vote on an issue of the nature described in the text is, in effect, a vote of confidence on the stewardship of the CEO. * * *

criteria for director independence set forth in the Sarbanes-Oxley Act. In light of the growing importance of independent directors, the American Bar Association has published a manual to help independent directors understand the legal and governance issues they face. Bruce F. Davis, Independent Director's Guidebook (2007).

(3) The corporate scandals of recent years have raised the personal stakes for corporate directors. In 2005, eleven WorldCom directors settled a shareholder class action suit for $20 million, or 20 percent of their aggregate net worth, rather than relying on D & O insurance. See Daniel Akst, Fining the Directors Misses the Mark, N.Y. Times, Aug. 21, 2005, at Section 3 p.6. That same year former Enron directors agreed to pay $13 million of their own money to settle a shareholder suit arising from the company's demise. Some argue that increasing the personal risks associated with serving on a corporate board will make it difficult to staff boards with knowledgeable, competent directors. See The Directors' Cut, Wall St. J., Jan. 13, 2005, at A12; Jonathan D. Glater, A Big New Worry For Corporate Directors, N.Y. Times, Jan. 6, 2005, at C1. For an opposing view, see Lucian Bebchuk, What's $13 Million Among Friends?, N.Y. Times, Jan. 17, 2005, at A17.

JONATHAN R. MACEY, CORPORATE GOVERNANCE: PROMISES MADE, PROMISES BROKEN
Pages 52–85 (2010).

* * * The prevailing theory among policy-makers in the U.S. is that increasing the quantity and improving the quality of board oversight is the key to improving corporate governance. Thus, the response of policy-makers to the public concern about the Enron-era wave of corporate scandals was simultaneously to blame the Enron board of directors, and to exhort future boards to perform more and better oversight of corporate managers. Courts similarly have emphasized that board composition is an important factor in determining how much deference to give corporate decisions made with board approval. Reliance on the ability of future boards to out-perform the Enron board are at the heart of the post-Enron corporate governance environment, as reflected in the new rules promulgated for public companies by the National Association of Securities Dealers, the New York Stock Exchange, and by Congress in the Sarbanes-Oxley Act. * * *

It is well understood that corporate boards of directors have a dual role in corporate governance. They are simultaneously supposed to serve as advisors to senior officers about management issues and as monitors of management. Simply put, directors are supposed to serve both a management function and monitoring function. However, the policy implications of the existence of this dual role are not well understood. In particular, the issue of whether it is possible for board members to serve in both of these roles has not been thoroughly explored. * * * It is unreasonable to expect directors to perform both of these functions because there is a fundamental and irreconcilable conflict between the monitoring function and the management function. * * *

Board members also face collective action problems in decision-making that make it * * * difficult for individual board members to challenge management or otherwise to act independently. Where a CEO makes a proposal to a group of board members, the first board member to raise questions or to disagree with management bears the greatest risk of being branded uncooperative or non-collegial. With this in mind, even when a board member disagrees with management, he has an incentive to remain quiet, hoping that another board member will speak first, thereby relieving the pressure on the remaining board members. Famed corporate gadfly Warren Buffett captured the problem well in a 2002 letter to shareholders of his company, Berkshire Hathaway. Note that Mr. Buffett uses the term "boardroom atmosphere" when he refers to the social norms that permeate the boardroom. Consistent with the analysis here, Mr. Buffett suggests that breaching these norms simply is not done be well-mannered people:

> Why have intelligent and decent directors failed so miserably? The answer lies not in inadequate laws—it's always been clear that directors are obligated to represent the interests of shareholders—but rather in what I'd call "boardroom atmosphere." It's almost impossible, for example, in a boardroom populated by well-mannered people, to raise the question of whether the CEO should be replaced. It's equally awkward to question a proposed acquisition that has been endorsed by the CEO, particularly when his inside staff and outside advisors are present and unanimously support his decision. (They wouldn't be in the room if they didn't.) Finally, when the compensation committee—armed, as always, with support from a high-paid consultant—reports on a megagrant of options to the CEO, it would be like belching at the dinner table for a director to suggest that the committee reconsider.[s] * * *

[Four problems make it difficult for boards of directors to be effective monitors of corporate management]:

(a) the existence of cognitive biases and information asymmetries that make boards susceptible to capture by management and constrain the capacity and effectiveness of boards to monitor and control managerial conduct;

(b) the inability of outside investors to distinguish objective boards from captured boards;

(c) the nature and limitations of the collegial model that defines the scope of acceptable board conduct;

---

[s]   http://www.berkshirehathaway.com/letters/2002pdf.pdf.

(d) the dominance of a collegial model of board behavior that appears to dominate the alternative adversarial model of board conduct, despite the fact that the prevailing norms of collegiality undermine the capacity of boards of directors to serve as effective monitors of managerial pathologies. * * *

Enron

When Enron declared bankruptcy on December 2, 2001, it was ranked as the seventh largest publicly traded company in the United States. * * * [T]he company went from being Fortune Magazine's Year 2000 pick for America's best-managed company to bankruptcy in less than a year! * * * [I]n 2000, the year before the company collapsed, Enron's board of directors was identified by "Chief Executive" magazine as among the best boards of any U.S. corporation. * * *

The most important corporate governance lesson to be learned from Enron is that it is unwise to place too much trust and reliance on a company's board of directors. Unfortunately, it appears that this lesson has not been learned. Commentators have been virtually unanimous in criticizing the poor performance of the Enron board. Echoing the typical views expressed, one law professor observed that "as the Enron board starkly demonstrated, boards often fail to live up to our expectations, and ineffectual boards cast doubt on the entire corporate governance system."

These sorts of observations are of interest for two reasons. First, the recognition that boards often fail to live up to expectations should, one would hope, inexorably lead investors to wonder whether it is sensible to continue to rely on a demonstrably faulty corporate governance institution. Yet analysis that concludes with palliatives such as "[b]oards of directors should not simply rubber-stamp management's decisions and certainly should not fall asleep at the wheel" do not provide any concrete guidance about how we might structure a corporate governance system on which investors could justifiably rely.

Second, the observation that the Enron board was "ineffectual" is of great interest due to the timing of the observation. Accurate though the observation may now be, the fact that the commentators did not begin to describe the Enron board as ineffectual until after the complete collapse of the company speaks volumes. That it was not until after the conviction of the CFO and the indictment of the President and the CEO that commentators routinely began to describe the Enron board in such terms signals that investors are not served by such ex post descriptions. One wonders where these astute observers were before the crash of the company, when their prognostications about the deficiencies in Enron's corporate governance might have actually done some good for investors.

Far from being the target of suspicion before the company collapse, the Enron board was widely lauded as a shining example of good corporate governance. The company had 14 directors, 12 of which were outsiders. The board included luminaries like Norman Blake, CEO and Chairman of Comdisco and Secretary General of the United States Olympic Committee, Wendy Gramm, former Chairman of the Commodities Futures Trading Commission, Robert Jaedicke, former Dean of Stanford's Graduate School of Business and former chair of the department of accounting at Stanford's business school, and Johan Wakeham, former U.K. Secretary of State for Energy and Leader of the Houses of Commons and Lords. Enron directors were also directors in a combined total of almost fifty other public companies. Thus, if the Enron board was defective, a whole passel of other companies are certainly infected with defective directors.

In addition to being highly independent and populated with luminaries from the corporate and academic world, the board met frequently. For example, in an attempt at crisis management, the board met almost daily from the moment that the company began to experience severe problems in October 2001 until the company filed its petition for bankruptcy protection on December 2, 2001.

The organization and structure of the Enron board was also viewed as a paradigm of good corporate governance. As one commentator put it, "the [Enron] board had all of the committees one would hope to see, including an executive committee, finance committee, audit and compliance committee, compensation committee, and nominating and corporate governance committee."

The Enron audit committee, the committee universally acknowledged as playing the central role in monitoring, "had a model charter and was chaired by a former accounting professor who had served as the Dean of the Stanford Graduate School of Business." Even more impressive was the fact that investigators found that all of the members of the audit committee save one had extensive familiarity with complex accounting principles. Two members of the committee, Professor Jaedicke and Lord Wakeham, had formal accounting training and professional experience in accounting.

In a show of independence that surpassed the then-existing standards of conduct for audit committees, the Enron audit committee received regular presentation[s] on Enron's financial statements, accounting practices and audit results from the company's outside auditors. The audit committee chair would report on the presentations to the full Enron board after the audit committee had received these presentations outside of the presence of management.

Consistent with best corporate governance practices and as mentioned above, the members of the audit committee, the compensation committee, and the nominating committee all were comprised of outside directors unaffiliated with management. Indeed, one of the great ironies of the myriad new corporate governance rules passed by courts, legislatures, administrative agencies, and stock exchanges in response to the collapse of Enron is that Enron itself met or exceeded the higher standards ostensibly promulgated to prevent future "Enrons." Oddly, if Enron survived to this day, it would not have to change its corporate governance structure at all in order to conform to the new rules.

For this reason, even commentators who claim that the Enron board performed poorly must acknowledge that "by all appearances Enron's board looked great." Indeed, Enron would be considered now, as it was then, a model of corporate governance. * * * [T]he Enron board was not only a model of professionalism, it also was a model of board capture by management. Only a capture hypothesis can explain the complete trust in management reflected in the board's acquiescence to the now-infamous related party transactions that ultimately played the pivotal role in Enron's demise. For example, Enron's annual reports (which are filed with the SEC on Form 10–K) showed that Enron closed deals with three thousand related entities in 1999 and 2000 alone. Hundreds of these transactions were with Enron-affiliates that operated out of post office boxes in the Cayman Islands. The Enron board acquiesced in high risk accounting practices, inappropriate conflict-of-interest activities and undisclosed off-the-books transactions. It also approved executive compensation packages that were, at least in retrospect, clearly excessive in light of the companies poor performance.

The most heralded governance failures of the Enron board were its decisions, on three separate occasions, to waive the company's code of conduct in order to allow Enron CFO Andrew Fastow to organize and manage limited partnerships, called special purpose entities, designed to do business with Enron. The transactions that Fastow envisioned and conducted involved the purchase and sale of assets to and from Enron by these special purpose entities in which Fastow had interests. A waiver was required because the company's code of conduct prohibited Enron employees from obtaining any personal financial gain from any company doing business with Enron, but Fastow made millions in profits as a result of these transactions. The conflict of interest was so palpable that Benjamin Neuhausen posed the following unanswerable question to his Arthur Anderson colleague David Duncan, "[w]hy would any director in his or her right mind ever approve such a scheme?"

Of course the corporate governance failures of the Enron board did not end with the approval of these inappropriate transactions. After approving the deals, the Enron board failed to monitor the terms of the deals between these entities and Enron, to manage the compensation that Fastow received from running these limited partnerships, or to determine whether appropriate internal controls were in place to regulate the business being done between Enron and the businesses controlled by Fastow.

While the Enron board had a wealth of information about Enron at its disposal, and unfettered capacity to demand more, the information actually received by the board was confined exclusively to that information supplied to it by management. This is the reality for most boards of directors. Indeed, board members typically do not have any other source of information about management other than management itself.

In the case of Enron, it appears that management often decided not to supply the board with information it requested. For example, in October of 2000, Enron board member Charles LeMaistre, who at the time was the chair of the board's compensation committee, attempted to obtain information about Andrew Fastow's compensation from the special purpose entities he controlled that were doing business with Enron. Mr. LeMaistre ultimately testified to a Senate subcommittee investigating the collapse of Enron that he wanted information about Andrew Fastow's compensation, but did not want to start office gossip about Fastow. Thus, he asked Mary Joyce, the Enron senior officer in charge of compensation, to provide him with information on the outside incomes of all of Enron's senior officers. LeMaistre made two requests for this information. The information was never supplied to him despite these requests. Rather than move the issue to a confrontation, Mr. LeMaistre "let the matter drop."

A year later, the board was still wholly uninformed about Mr. Fastow's compensation, despite the fact that the SEC had commenced an inquiry into Enron's relationships with these special purpose entities and into the accounting treatment of the transactions between Enron and the entities. The board remained uninformed until October of 2001 when a Wall Street Journal article entitled "Enron CFO's Partnership Had Millions in Profit," alleging that Mr. Fastow had received more than $7 million in compensation from the Enron-related special purpose entities he controlled appeared.

Generally speaking, management's control of the flow of information to the board of directors creates a dynamic in which management is able to capture its board of directors by controlling the nature of the information available to directors when making decisions. In the extensive literature on the economic theory of regulation, it is widely known that well-organized special interest groups with limited resources can influence political outcomes by controlling the flow of information to legislatures and to voters. Senior managers in public companies have interests and agendas parallel to the interests and agendas of special interest groups in the realm of politics. Senior managers have an interest in influencing the selection of projects, the compensation of managers, and the choice of strategies. The ability of managers to control the flow of information to the board of directors greatly facilitates their ability to achieve their private objectives, often at the expense of investors. This dynamic goes a long way towards explaining the fact that Enron's apparently sophisticated and engaged board indicated that "they were as surprised as anyone by the company's collapse."

Less than a week after former Enron Corp. chairman Kenneth L. Lay was convicted of fraud by a jury in Houston, Texas, Charles Walker, a long-time director of Enron, told The Washington Post that he was still unable to believe that Lay actually knew about the fraudulent accounting practices that caused the Company's collapse in 2001. He also expressed his disbelief of the claim that Lay had lied to conceal the true financial condition of Enron. Walker even expressed continued confidence in Mr. Lay's integrity, saying, "I'm convinced he didn't know what was going on. * * * I just can't bear the picture of him going off to jail."

The board of directors of Enron provides a vivid example of the following point: even those boards that appear from the outside to be independent, professional and highly qualified are susceptible to board capture. Worse, directors tend to be judged only in retrospect. The directors of Enron, though lauded before its collapse, are now viewed as bad directors not because of any particular misdeeds of the group, but rather because the company on whose board they served collapsed so publicly and ignominiously.

As mentioned, strengthening the independence and oversight provided by directors of publicly traded companies is the primary solution offered to avoid the occurrence of future "Enrons." This response is misguided for three reasons. First, the proposed solution fails to appreciate the fact that improving board independence may weaken the capacity of boards to do what they are actually good at—providing managerial support to senior officers. Second, the appeal for more independence unjustifiably and inexplicably assumes that it is indeed possible for those in charge of their selection to identify directors who will reliably think and act independently of management after they have become directors. Finally, the assumption that directors can be relied upon to prevent future "Enrons" creates a false sense of security in unwitting investors who believe that this truly is the case.

When Enron collapsed dozens of other companies were faced with the interesting dilemma of what to do with the Enron directors who were simultaneously serving on their boards of directors. Some Enron directors like Wendy Gramm, who sat on the Invesco Mutual Fund board, and Robert Jaedicke, who sat on the California Water Service board, took matters into their own hands by resigning from these boards as soon as Enron collapsed.

Labor unions went after the remaining Enron directors with varying degrees of success. The AFL-CIO Investment Fund launched a campaign against all former Enron board members who served on other boards. The labor union announced that "the colossal failure of these directors to protect shareholder interests in the Enron case disqualified them from being re-nominated to any future public board service. * * * In cases in which the board re-nominated those directors, we urged shareholders to vote no."

In 2002 Enron director Frank Savage was re-elected to the boards of Lockheed Martin Corporation and Qualcomm Corporation over the objections of shareholder activists including the AFL-CIO and other labor groups. The campaign to remove Savage from the Lockheed Martin board convinced only 28 percent of Lockheed Martin shareholders to withhold their votes. Savage thus remained a valuable member of Lockheed Martin's board long after Enron's collapse, although he did resign from the Qualcomm board voluntarily in 2004 at the age of 65.

While the vast majority of Enron board members resigned or were removed from the other boards on which they served, some companies vigorously defended their Enron directors. A spokesperson for Lockheed was reported by the New York Times to have said that former Enron director Frank Savage "is a valued director with a long and distinguished association with the company." Similarly, Enron board member Norman P. Blake Jr., the former chairman of Comdisco Inc., remained on the board of Owens Corning after Enron's collapse. The Washington Post reported that Owens Corning responded to inquiries about Mr. Blake's board service by observing that "[o]ur board reviews our director's independence and effectiveness as a part of good governance practices. Mr. Blake has capably met the requirements."

E. PROXY REGULATION AND DISCLOSURE REQUIREMENTS

1. SCOPE OF REGULATION

SECURITIES EXCHANGE ACT OF 1934 §§ 14(a), 12(a), 12(g)
15 U.S.C.A. §§ 78n, 78l.

Proxies

Section 14. (a)(1) It shall be unlawful for any person, by the use of the mails or by any means or instrumentality of interstate commerce or of any facility of a national securities exchange or otherwise, in contravention of such rules and regulations as the Commission may prescribe as necessary or appropriate in the public interest or for the protection of investors, to solicit or to permit the use of his name to solicit any proxy or consent or authorization in respect of any security (other than an exempted security) registered pursuant to section 12 of this title.

Registration Requirements for Securities

Section 12. (a) It shall be unlawful for any member, broker, or dealer to effect any transaction in any security (other than an exempted security) on a national securities exchange unless a registration is effective as to such security for such exchange in accordance with the provisions of this title and the rules and regulations thereunder. * * *

(g)(1) Every issuer which is engaged in interstate commerce, or in a business affecting interstate commerce, or whose securities are traded by use of the mails or any means or instrumentality of interstate commerce shall—

(A) within 120 days after the last day of its first fiscal year ended on which the issuer has total assets exceeding $10,000,000 and a class of equity security (other than an exempted security) held of record by either—

(i) 2,000 persons, or

(ii) 500 persons who are not accredited investors (as such term is defined by the Commission), * * *

register such security by filing with the Commission a registration statement * * *.

* * *

(4) Registration of any class of security pursuant to this subsection shall be terminated ninety days, or such shorter period as the Commission may determine, after the issuer files a certification with the Commission that the number of holders of record of such class of security is reduced to less than 300 persons * * *.

(5) For the purposes of this subsection the term "class" shall include all securities of an issuer which are of substantially similar character and the holders of which enjoy substantially similar rights and privileges. * * *

NOTES

(1) The SEC has adopted the following regulations under § 12(g):

§ 240.12g–1 Exemption from section 12(g).

An issuer shall be exempt from the requirement to register any class of equity securities pursuant to section 12(g)(1) if on the last day of its most recent fiscal year the issuer had total assets not exceeding $10 million * * *

§ 240.12g–4 Certifications of termination of registration under section 12(g).

(a) Termination of registration of a class of securities under section 12(g) of the Act shall take effect 90 days * * * after the issuer certifies to the Commission * * * that the class of securities is held of record by:

(1) Less than 300 persons; or

(2) Less than 500 persons, where the total assets of the issuer have not exceeded $10 million on the last day of each of the issuer's most recent three fiscal years. * * *

17 C.F.R. §§ 240.12g–1, 240.12g–4.

(2) A corporation that is required to register a securities issue under § 12 is subject to a significant degree of regulation under various sections of the Securities Exchange Act of 1934 in addition to the regulation of proxy solicitations. Many of these sections are discussed below and in the following Chapters. When considering federally imposed requirements under the 1934 Act it is important to ascertain whether the requirements are applicable only to corporations required to register under § 12, or whether they are more broadly applicable to all corporations using the mails or the facilities of interstate commerce.

(3) Registration of the publicly held securities of an issuer under § 12 of the 1934 Act should be distinguished from the registration of an issue for its public distribution under the 1933 Act. Registration under § 12 of the 1934 Act involves the submission of information about the issuer, its organization, its finances, its securities, and similar matters. There is also a requirement for the periodic revision of information; these periodic reports are colloquially referred to as 8–K and 10–K reports. Historically, registration of an issue under the 1933 Act for sale to the public was considered more onerous and difficult than supplying information for registration under § 12. The emphasis on full disclosure at the time an issue is sold publicly under the 1933 Act is partly an historical accident, and a more rational system would doubtless emphasize issuer registration and periodic full disclosure rather than full disclosure only when the issuer wishes to sell securities. In 1982, the SEC achieved essentially this result by regulation through its integrated disclosure program, SEC Rel. No. 33–6383, AS Rel. No. 306, 47 Fed.Reg. 11380 (1982). The general effect of this program is to permit issuers that have filed reports under the 1934 Act for more than three years to incorporate by reference this information in its 1933 Act filing, thereby greatly simplifying the registration process under that Act.

(4) In 1988, the SEC promulgated Rule 19c–4, which prohibited national securities exchanges from listing for trading the securities of corporations that created weighted or unequal voting classifications for classes of common shares, the so-called "one share/one vote" principle. In Business Roundtable v. S.E.C., 905 F.2d 406, 410–11 (D.C.Cir.1990), the Court invalidated this rule on the ground that it exceeded the power granted to the Commission by § 14 of the Securities Exchange Act:

* * * [A]lthough § 14(a) broadly bars use of the mails (and other means) "to solicit * * * any proxy" in contravention of Commission rules and regulations, it is not seriously disputed that Congress's central concern was with disclosure. See J.I. Case Co. v. Borak, 377 U.S. 426, 431, 84 S.Ct. 1555, 1559, 12 L.Ed.2d 423 (1964) ("The purpose of § 14(a) is to prevent management or others from obtaining authorization for corporate action by means of deceptive or inadequate disclosure in proxy solicitation"); see also Santa Fe Industries, Inc. v. Green, 430 U.S. 462, 477–78, 97 S.Ct. 1292, 1302–04, 51 L.Ed.2d 480 (1977) (emphasizing Exchange Act's philosophy of full disclosure and dismissing the fairness of the terms of the transaction as "at most a tangential concern of the statute" once full and fair disclosure has occurred). * * *

That proxy regulation bears almost exclusively on disclosure stems as a matter of necessity from the nature of proxies. Proxy solicitations are, after all, only communications with potential absentee voters. The goal of federal proxy regulation was to improve those communications and thereby to enable proxy voters to control the corporation as effectively as they might have by attending a shareholder meeting. Id. See also S.Rep. No. 1455, 73d Cong., 2d Sess. 74 (1934); Sheldon E. Bernstein and Henry G. Fischer, The Regulation of the Solicitation of Proxies: Some Reflections on Corporate Democracy, 7 U.Chi.L.Rev. 226, 227–28 (1940).

We do not mean to be taken as saying that disclosure is necessarily the sole subject of § 14. See Louis Loss, Fundamentals of Securities Regulation 452–53 (1988) (asserting that § 14 is not limited to ensuring disclosure), quoted in Final Rule, 53 Fed.Reg. at 26,391 n. 163; * * * For example, the Commission's Rule 14a–4(b)(2) requires a proxy to provide some mechanism for a security holder to withhold authority to vote for each nominee individually. * * * It thus bars a kind of electoral tying arrangement, and may be supportable as a control over management's power to set the voting agenda, or, slightly more broadly, voting procedures. * * * But while Rule 14a–4(b)(2) may lie in a murky area between substance and procedure, Rule 19c–4 much more directly interferes with the substance of what the shareholders may enact. It prohibits certain reallocations of voting power and certain capital structures, even if approved by a shareholder vote subject to full disclosure and the most exacting procedural rules.

2. PROXY FORMS, PROXY STATEMENTS, AND ANNUAL REPORTS

The comprehensive federal proxy regulations provide the basic structure for whatever corporate democracy exists in the modern public corporation. The import of these rather lengthy and detailed regulations is difficult to summarize. Further, the sequence in which they are set forth by the SEC is not very logical. It is simpler to discuss them by subject matter rather than numerically even though the result is skipping around the numbers. Most of these regulations are discussed in this Chapter while Chapter 16 addresses proxy fights. The mere listing of the principal areas discussed in this Chapter gives an indication of the scope and importance of these regulations:

(a) The regulations relating to the form of proxy, the proxy statement, and annual reports are discussed immediately below;

(b) The regulation prohibiting false and misleading statements in connection with proxies is discussed in Part (3) of this Section of this Chapter;

(c) The regulation requiring the inclusion of certain shareholder proposals in the proxy solicitation is discussed in Part (4) of this Section of this Chapter; and

(d) The regulation requiring communications to be mailed to securities holders in certain circumstances is discussed in Part (5) of this Section of this Chapter.

a.   Form of Proxy. Rule 14a–4 of the proxy regulations contains specific requirements as to the form of proxy documents. The purpose of this rule is to ensure that shareholders have the option to vote to approve or disapprove issues submitted to them, and to vote for or against the directors proposed by the persons soliciting the proxy, usually management. Broad grants of discretionary power to the nominee are prohibited subject to certain exceptions; for example, generally a proxy may not confer power to vote for a person as a director unless he is named in the proxy statement as a nominee. However, a proxy may confer discretion to vote for a person not named to replace a bona fide nominee who is unable to serve or for good cause will not serve. Similarly, a proxy must be for a specified meeting, and undated or post-dated proxies are prohibited (Rule 14a–10).

Generally, it is difficult to given an accurate description of these disclosure documents. The following is an example of a routine proxy that meets SEC requirements.

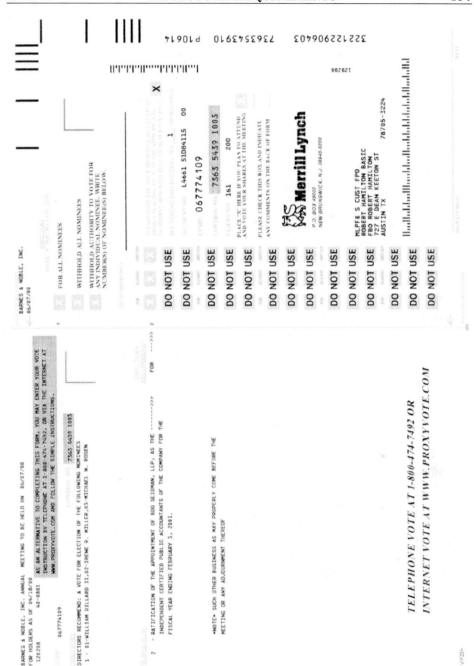

VOTING INSTRUCTIONS

TO OUR CLIENTS:

WE HAVE BEEN REQUESTED TO FORWARD TO YOU THE ENCLOSED PROXY MATERIAL RELATIVE TO SECURITIES HELD BY US IN YOUR ACCOUNT BUT NOT REGISTERED IN YOUR NAME. SUCH SECURITIES CAN BE VOTED ONLY BY US AS THE HOLDER OF RECORD. WE SHALL BE PLEASED TO VOTE YOUR SECURITIES IN ACCORDANCE WITH YOUR WISHES, IF YOU WILL EXECUTE THE FORM AND RETURN IT TO US PROMPTLY IN THE ENCLOSED BUSINESS REPLY ENVELOPE. IT IS UNDERSTOOD THAT, IF YOU SIGN WITHOUT OTHERWISE MARKING THE FORM, THE SECURITIES WILL BE VOTED AS RECOMMENDED BY THE BOARD OF DIRECTORS ON ALL MATTERS TO BE CONSIDERED AT THE MEETING.

FOR THIS MEETING, THE EXTENT OF OUR AUTHORITY TO VOTE YOUR SECURITIES IN THE ABSENCE OF YOUR INSTRUCTIONS CAN BE DETERMINED BY REFERRING TO THE APPLICABLE VOTING INSTRUCTION NUMBER INDICATED ON THE FACE OF YOUR FORM.

VOTING INSTRUCTION NUMBER 1 -
WE URGE YOU TO SEND IN YOUR INSTRUCTIONS SO THAT WE MAY VOTE YOUR SECURITIES IN ACCORDANCE WITH YOUR WISHES. HOWEVER, THE RULES OF THE NEW YORK STOCK EXCHANGE PROVIDE THAT IF INSTRUCTIONS ARE NOT RECEIVED FROM YOU PRIOR TO THE ISSUANCE OF THE FIRST VOTE, <u>THE PROXY MAY BE GIVEN AT DISCRETION BY THE HOLDER OF RECORD OF THE SECURITIES</u> (ON THE TENTH DAY, IF THE PROXY MATERIAL WAS MAILED AT LEAST 15 DAYS PRIOR TO THE MEETING DATE; ON THE FIFTEENTH DAY IF PROXY MATERIAL WAS MAILED 25 DAYS OR MORE PRIOR TO THE MEETING DATE). IF YOU ARE UNABLE TO COMMUNICATE WITH US BY SUCH DATE, WE WILL NEVERTHELESS FOLLOW YOUR INSTRUCTIONS, EVEN IF OUR DISCRETIONARY VOTE HAS ALREADY BEEN GIVEN, PROVIDED YOUR INSTRUCTIONS ARE RECEIVED PRIOR TO THE MEETING DATE.

VOTING INSTRUCTION NUMBER 2 -
WE WISH TO CALL YOUR ATTENTION TO THE FACT THAT, UNDER THE RULES OF THE NEW YORK STOCK EXCHANGE, <u>WE CANNOT VOTE YOUR SECURITIES ON ONE OR MORE OF THE MATTERS TO BE ACTED UPON AT THE MEETING WITHOUT YOUR SPECIFIC VOTING INSTRUCTIONS.</u>

IF WE DO NOT HEAR FROM YOU PRIOR TO THE ISSUANCE OF THE FIRST VOTE, <u>WE MAY VOTE YOUR SECURITIES IN OUR DISCRETION TO THE EXTENT PERMITTED BY THE RULES OF THE EXCHANGE</u> (ON THE TENTH DAY, IF THE PROXY MATERIAL WAS MAILED AT LEAST 15 DAYS PRIOR TO THE MEETING DATE; ON THE FIFTEENTH DAY IF THE PROXY MATERIAL WAS MAILED 25 DAYS OR MORE PRIOR TO THE MEETING DATE). IF YOU ARE UNABLE TO COMMUNICATE WITH US BY SUCH DATE, WE WILL NEVERTHELESS FOLLOW YOUR VOTING INSTRUCTIONS, EVEN IF OUR DISCRETIONARY VOTE HAS ALREADY BEEN GIVEN, PROVIDED YOUR INSTRUCTIONS ARE RECEIVED PRIOR TO THE MEETING DATE.

VOTING INSTRUCTION NUMBER 3 -
IN ORDER FOR YOUR SECURITIES TO BE REPRESENTED AT THE MEETING, <u>IT WILL BE NECESSARY FOR US TO HAVE YOUR SPECIFIC VOTING INSTRUCTIONS.</u> PLEASE DATE, SIGN AND RETURN YOUR VOTING INSTRUCTIONS TO US PROMPTLY IN THE RETURN ENVELOPE PROVIDED.

VOTING INSTRUCTION NUMBER 4 REMINDER - WE HAVE PREVIOUSLY SENT YOU PROXY SOLICITING MATERIAL PERTAINING TO THE MEETING OF SHAREHOLDERS OF THE COMPANY INDICATED.

ACCORDING TO OUR LATEST RECORDS, WE HAVE NOT AS YET RECEIVED YOUR VOTING INSTRUCTION ON THE MATTERS TO BE CONSIDERED AT THIS MEETING AND THE COMPANY HAS REQUESTED US TO COMMUNICATE WITH YOU IN AN ENDEAVOR TO HAVE YOUR SECURITIES VOTED.

THE VOTING INSTRUCTIONS REQUEST PERTAINS TO SECURITIES CARRIED BY US IN YOUR ACCOUNT BUT NOT REGISTERED IN YOUR NAME. SUCH SECURITIES CAN BE VOTED ONLY BY US AS THE HOLDER OF RECORD OF THE SECURITIES.
PLEASE DATE, SIGN AND RETURN YOUR VOTING INSTRUCTIONS TO US PROMPTLY IN THE RETURN ENVELOPE PROVIDED.

SHOULD YOU WISH TO ATTEND THE MEETING AND <u>VOTE</u> IN PERSON, PLEASE CHECK THE BOX ON THE FRONT OF THE FORM FOR THIS PURPOSE. A LEGAL PROXY COVERING YOUR SECURITIES WILL BE ISSUED TO YOU.

b. Proxy Statements. Rule 14a–3 requires that a proxy solicitation be accompanied by a proxy statement containing the information set forth in Schedule 14A, 17 C.F.R. § 240.14a–101. However, for several items, Schedule 14A in turn refers to two more general regulations applicable to public disclosures: Regulation S–X (relating to financial data) and Regulation S–K (relating to nonfinancial data). The type of information required depends of course to some extent on the type of issue to be presented to the shareholders for their vote. The following are the disclosure requirements relating to the annual selection of an independent public accountant:

Item 9. Independent public accountants. If the solicitation is made on behalf of the registrant and relates to: (1) The annual (or special meeting in lieu of annual) meeting of security holders at which directors are to be elected, or a solicitation of consents or authorizations in lieu of such meeting or (2) the election, approval or ratification of the registrant's accountant, furnish the following information describing the registrant's relationship with its independent public accountant:

(a) The name of the principal accountant selected or being recommended to security holders for election, approval or ratification for the current year. If no accountant has been selected or recommended, so state and briefly describe the reasons therefor.

(b) The name of the principal accountant for the fiscal year most recently completed if different from the accountant selected or recommended for the current year or if no accountant has yet been selected or recommended for the current year.

(c) The proxy statement shall indicate: (1) Whether or not representatives of the principal accountant for the current year and for the most recently completed fiscal year are expected to be present at the security holders' meeting, (2) whether or not they will have the opportunity to make a statement if they desire to do so, and (3) whether or not such representatives are expected to be available to respond to appropriate questions.

(d) If during the registrant's two most recent fiscal years or any subsequent interim period, (1) an independent accountant who was previously engaged as the principal accountant to audit the registrant's financial statements, or an independent accountant on whom the principal accountant expressed reliance in its report regarding a significant subsidiary, has resigned (or indicated it has declined to stand for re-election after the completion of the current audit) or was dismissed, or (2) a new independent accountant has been engaged as either the principal accountant to audit the registrant's financial statements or as an independent accountant on whom the principal accountant has expressed or is expected to express reliance in its report regarding a significant subsidiary, then, notwithstanding any

previous disclosure, provide the information required by Item
304(a) of Regulation S–K (§ 229.304 of this chapter).[t]

Schedule 14A, Item 9, 17 C.F.R. § 240.14a–101. The information in the
proxy statement must be "clearly presented." Rule 14a–5. Furthermore,
there is a procedure by which preliminary copies of certain proxy
statements and soliciting material must be submitted to the SEC for
review. Prior to 1992, preliminary review was required of virtually all
such material, but the October 22, 1992 amendments narrowed sharply
the SEC's program of making preliminary reviews of proxy documents.
Proxy statements must be submitted for preliminary review only if out-of-
the-ordinary matters are to be considered. Rule 14a–6. Copies of the
definitive documents must be filed with the SEC when they are
distributed to shareholders.

In 2006, the SEC adopted changes to disclosure requirements that
will compel companies to provide information about executive and
director compensation, related person transactions, and security
ownership of officers and directors in their proxy statements and periodic
reports. SEC Rel. No. 33–8732A, 71 Fed. Reg. 53,158 (2006). The
amendments require that the information be written in "plain English" to
make it comprehensible to the average investor. For example, the
disclosures must use the active voice, use short sentences, avoid legalese,
and use everyday words.

In early 2007, the SEC adopted new rules allowing the electronic
dissemination of proxy materials. An issuer can satisfy the SEC's delivery
requirements by posting a copy of its proxy on its website and notifying
shareholders of the proxy's electronic availability. The issuer must mail
or email the Notice of Internet Availability of Proxy Materials at least 40
days before the shareholder meeting. SEC Rel. No. 34–55146, 72 Fed.
Reg. 4148 (2007). This "notice and access" approach may help reduce costs
associated with proxy solicitation.

In August 2009, new amendments to the Delaware General
Corporation Law (DGCL) took effect that may be catalysts for proposals
by activist stockholders in upcoming proxy seasons. The amendments
may result in stockholders having greater access to companies' proxy
statements and rights to expense reimbursement for proxy solicitations
with respect to director elections. Section 112 of the DGCL permits, but
does not require, a Delaware corporation to adopt bylaw provisions that
require director nominations by stockholders to be included in the
corporation's proxy statements. Section 113 permits, but does not require,
a Delaware corporation to adopt bylaw provisions that could require the

---

[t]   Item 304 of Regulation S–K applies only when there has been a change in or
disagreement with the independent public accountant within the prior two most recent fiscal
years. Item 304 is composed of four densely packed pages of instructions relating to various
aspects of the reasons for the change and the nature of the disagreement.

corporation to reimburse proxy-solicitation expenses incurred by a stockholder in connection with an election of directors. Stockholder activism regarding such bylaw amendments likely will not be limited to corporations domiciled in Delaware because the laws of many other states are silent on the topic and, arguably, permit corporations to adopt such amendments. See Catherine L. Beck and Scott Towers, Change To Delaware General Corporation Law May Enliven 2010 Proxy Season, Ballard Spahr LLP, April 27, 2009.

c. Annual Reports. Rule 14a–3 provides that if a solicitation is by management and relates to an annual meeting at which directors are to be elected, the solicitation must be accompanied or preceded by an annual report containing the financial information and other material described in the rule. 17 C.F.R. § 240.14a–3(b). Many state incorporation statutes do not require the distribution of even such minimal information to shareholders; see, however, MBCA § 16.20. The SEC has long recognized that the annual report is an effective means of communication between management and security holders. In part this was because annual reports are generally readable and avoid legalistic and technical terminology. In its integration of filings under the various securities acts, the SEC broadened the information required to be included in annual reports. It is not practical to provide an example of an annual report, but they are widely available; indeed many issuers treat the annual report as a modest advertising device, using flashy covers and high quality paper and printing, and offering to mail copies free to any person who asks.

d. Management's Discussion of Financial Condition and Results of Operations. 2 Loss & Seligman, Securities Regulation 668 (3d ed. 1989) states that "[o]ften the most important textual disclosure item" in the annual report is formally known as "Management's Discussion and Analysis of Financial Condition and Results of Operations," usually shortened to "MD & A." Codified as Item 303 of Regulation S–K, it is to consist of a discussion of the registrant's "financial condition, changes in financial condition and results of operations," specifically with respect to liquidity and capital resources. It "also shall provide such other information that the registrant believes to be necessary to an understanding of its financial condition, changes in financial condition and results of operations." 17 C.F.R. § 229.303(a). In the promulgating release, the purpose of the MD & A is somewhat fancifully stated as "giv[ing] the investor an opportunity to look at the company through the eyes of management by providing both a short-and long-term analysis of the business of the company." Concept Release on Management's Discussion and Analysis of Financial Condition and Operations, Sec.Act Rel. 33–6711 (April 17, 1987), at 3. Item 303 must be responded to not only in the annual report, but also whenever financial information must be made public.

In order to appreciate the MD & A and the problems it creates for issuers, a brief discussion of the SEC's approach toward the disclosure of forward-looking information is helpful. See generally Edmund W. Kitch, The Theory and Practice of Securities Disclosure, 61 Brook.L.Rev. 763 (1995). Historically, the SEC insisted that financial disclosures be limited to historical facts. "Conjecture and speculations as to the future are left by the Act to the investor on the theory that he is as competent as anyone to predict the future from the given facts." Harry Heller, Disclosure Requirements Under Federal Securities Regulation, 16 Bus.Law. 300, 307 & n.31 (1961). This position that full disclosure should be limited to "hard"—that is readily verifiable—historical data and that projections or predictions were "soft"—that is, unverifiable—and therefore inherently misleading—permitted easy administration by the SEC but was unrealistic: investors generally are interested in future predictions rather than past events, investors are certainly less able to make reliable predictions about the future from past data than knowledgeable management, and undue emphasis on historical data leads to long and unreadable prospectuses and proxy statements. See Homer Kripke, The SEC and Corporate Disclosure: Regulation in Search of a Purpose (1979).

The SEC decided to permit projections of financial data, discussion of management objectives and goals for future performance, and the assumptions underlying such statements, ("forward looking statements") only after considerable soul-searching and a study by an advisory committee, SEC Rel. No. 33–5993, 43 Fed.Reg. 53251 (1978). In 1979, the SEC adopted a "safe harbor" rule (Rule 175) that provided that such statements would not be deemed false or misleading unless they were "made or reaffirmed without a reasonable basis or [were] disclosed other than in good faith." 17 C.F.R. §§ 230.175, 240.3b–6. The Private Securities Litigation Reform Act of 1995 enacted a new section 21E to the Securities Exchange Act of 1934 providing a much broader and more secure "safe harbor" provision while preserving Rule 3b–6. See Edward A. Fallone, Section 10(b) and the Vagaries of Federal Common Law: The Merits of Codifying the Private Cause of Action Under a Structuralist Approach, 1997 U.Ill.L.Rev. 71, 86 (explaining that statements qualifying for the safe harbor cannot give rise to private liability if either of two tests is met: no private liability may be imposed for forward-looking statements made without actual knowledge that the statements were false or misleading and no private liability may be imposed if the forward-looking statement is identified as such when made and is accompanied by meaningful cautionary language identifying important factors that could prevent the statement from becoming accurate); Jeanne Calderon and Rachel Kowal, Safe Harbors: Historical and Current Approaches to Future Forecasting, 22 J.Corp.L. 661 (1997). Rather paradoxically, this section does not appear to have had the intended effect since its enactment. Item 10(b) of Regulation S–K encourages but does not require the use of "management's projections of future economic performance" in other financial information filed with the SEC and sets forth extensive guidelines for the use and presentation of projections. 17 C.F.R. § 229.10(b).

The MD & A requirements in effect often mandate a discussion of forward-looking information in annual reports and other financial documents filed with the SEC. The following administrative proceeding deals with compliance with Item 303 in two SEC periodic disclosure documents, Forms 10–K and 10–Q, but the decision is "the" SEC statement as to the interpretation of the MD & A requirement.

IN THE MATTER OF CATERPILLAR, INC.
Administrative Proceeding File No. 3–7692.
SEC Rel. No. 34–30532 (1992).

The Commission deems it appropriate and in the public interest that public administrative proceedings be instituted pursuant to Section 21C of the Securities Exchange Act of 1934 ("Exchange Act") to determine whether Caterpillar Inc. ("Caterpillar") has failed to comply with Section 13(a) of the Exchange Act and Rules 13a–1 and 13a–13 promulgated under the Exchange Act in connection with reports on Form 10–K and Form 10–Q filed with the Commission. Accordingly, such proceedings are hereby instituted.

In anticipation of the institution of these administrative proceedings, Caterpillar has submitted an Offer of Settlement for the purpose of disposing of the issue raised in these proceedings. * * *

On the basis of this Order and the Respondent's Offer of Settlement, the Commission finds the following: * * *

This matter involves Caterpillar's failure in its Form 10–K for the year ended December 31, 1989, and its Form 10–Q for the first quarter of 1990, to comply with Item 303 of Regulation S–K, Management's Discussion and Analysis of Financial Conditions and Results of Operations ("MD & A"). Specifically, the MD & A rules required Caterpillar to disclose information about the 1989 earnings of Caterpillar Brasil, S.A. ("CBSA"), its wholly owned Brazilian subsidiary, and uncertainties about CBSA's 1990 earnings.

1. CBSA's 1989 Results

Caterpillar has had a Brazilian subsidiary since the 1950's. Nineteen eighty-nine was an exceptionally profitable year for CBSA. That year, without accounting for the effect of integration, CBSA accounted for some 23 percent of Caterpillar's net profits of $497 million, although its revenues represented only 5 percent of the parent company's revenues. In 1989, CBSA's operating profit was in line with prior years but a number of nonoperating items contributed to greater than usual overall profit.

Those items included currency translation gains, export subsidies, interest income, and Brazilian tax loss carryforwards. Many of these gains were caused by the hyperinflation in Brazil in 1989 and the fact that the dollar-cruzado exchange rate lagged behind inflation.

CBSA's financial results were presented on a consolidated basis with the remainder of Caterpillar's operations. Thus, the impact of CBSA's operations on Caterpillar's overall results was not apparent from the face of Caterpillar's financial statements or the notes thereto.

2.   Management's View of CBSA

Caterpillar was and is a highly integrated organization. Its various divisions and subsidiaries were, and are, very interdependent. As a consequence, Caterpillar typically viewed and managed the organization on a consolidated basis. While unadjusted profit numbers for subsidiaries and divisions were available to management, they were not viewed by management as reliable indicators of that subsidiary's or division's contribution to the consolidated enterprise. The various divisions and subsidiaries were not viewed as profit centers but rather as cost centers. Profit and results of operations were managed on a consolidated basis. Because of that management perspective, the profit contribution of each subsidiary or division has not historically been used as a basis for personnel, product sourcing or disclosure decisions.

In January of 1990, accounting department personnel began to separately analyze CBSA's 1989 results compared with its 1990 forecast. In the process of that analysis, the various components of CBSA's results were aggregated. The result of that analysis was conveyed to top management and then to the board. By the middle of February 1990—i.e., at least two weeks before Caterpillar filed its 1989 Form 10–K— Caterpillar's top management had recognized that, to adequately understand Caterpillar's 1990 forecast, it was necessary to understand CBSA's 1990 forecast. Management also recognized that CBSA's future performance was exceptionally difficult to predict—particularly in light of anticipated sweeping economic reforms to be instituted by a new administration in Brazil—and that there were substantial uncertainties [regarding] whether CBSA would repeat its exceptional 1989 earnings in 1990.

The board of directors was told in February 1990 that Brazil was "volatile" and that "the impact of Brazil is so significant to reduced 1990 projected results, [management] felt it was necessary to explain it [to the directors] in some detail."

Minutes of the February 1990 board meeting include the following about Brazil:

> [Management] commented on results of operations in Brazil because of the significant [negative] impact they will have on

overall results for 1990. Beginning in February 1990 and continuing through the rest of the year management departed from this usual practice of viewing the company as a whole and provided projections to the board of directors which separated out the impact of Brazil.

During the interim between the February board meeting and the next board meeting, held on April 11, 1990, a new administration took office in Brazil. Fernando Collor de Mello, who had been elected president of Brazil in December 1989, was inaugurated on March 15, 1990, "putting an end," as one Brazilian business journal put it, "to weeks of intense speculation as to what economic measures he will actually announce." Collor immediately instituted sweeping economic and monetary changes in an effort to bring Brazil's hyperinflation under control. * * *

When the Caterpillar board met on April 11, management gave presentations in which it discussed, among other things, the likely negative effects the Collor plan would have on CBSA's sales and profits:

At our last meeting, we reviewed the impact that [CBSA] is expected to have on our 1990 results * * *. Brazil is volatile and difficult to predict. Their recently announced economic reforms have made the situation even more uncertain.

The impact of these reforms is not at all clear, so we have made no attempt to change the forecast. However, it's difficult to see any short-term positives, so there is considerable risk that Brazil's new economic plan could bring additional pressure on our 1990 profit.

[Management] * * * also noted * * * that the profit in Brazil will be substantially lower than in 1989.

Throughout April and May of 1990 Caterpillar continued to monitor the events in Brazil and their effects on CBSA, including the consequences of the Collor plan on Caterpillar. * * * However, after a review of April and May results, the company concluded the new economic policies would cause CBSA to suffer significant losses in 1990. It also concluded that those losses would not likely be balanced by gains in other parts of the world and consolidated results would be lower than originally anticipated.

At 8:00 a.m. on Monday, June 25, 1990, before the beginning of trading, the company voluntarily issued a press release explaining that the anticipated results for 1990 would be substantially lower than previously projected. * * *

3.   Preparation and Review of Caterpillar's Periodic Reports

The MD & A sections of the 1989 10–K and 10–Q for the first quarter of 1990 were drafted by employees in Caterpillar's accounting department.[2] Prior to the issuance of those reports, the language of the MD & A was reviewed by the Controller, Financial Vice President, Treasurer, and the company's legal, economic, and public affairs departments. After that, the language of the MD & A was reviewed by the top officers of the Company.

The board of directors reviewed the final draft of the 1989 Form 10–K, including the MD & A, at the February 1990 board meeting. At that time, the board, including top management, who were members of the board, received a written opinion of the company's independent auditor that the financial statements complied with the rules and regulations of the Commission, and also an opinion of the company's General Counsel that the Form 10–K complied with all the rules and regulations of the Commission.

In rendering their opinion on the financial statements contained in Caterpillar's 1989 Form 10–K, the auditor had reviewed the disclosure set forth in the MD & A for inconsistencies with the financial statements but did not opine on the MD & A. The General Counsel was aware of management's concerns regarding Brazil, however, he disregarded management's statements about Brazil when reviewing and opining upon the MD & A disclosure regarding Brazil.

4.   Caterpillar's Disclosure Regarding CBSA

Neither the 1989 Form 10–K nor the first quarter 1990 Form 10–Q indicated the extent to which CBSA had affected Caterpillar's bottom line in 1989, nor did they indicate that a decline in CBSA's future results could have a material adverse effect on Caterpillar's bottom line in 1990.[4]
* * *

---

[2]   The same employees also drafted portions of management's presentations regarding Brazil [for] the February and April 1990 meetings of the board of directors.

[4]   The 1989 Form 10–K contained the following statements about Brazil:

Sales Outside the United States

Dealer machine sales rose in most selling areas, with demand especially strong in Europe, Brazil, Australia, and the Far East.

Latin America

Sales rose 14% in 1989, the sixth consecutive year of improvement. The biggest gain was in Brazil, where very high inflation rates increased demand for hard goods, including earth moving equipment. (Given the extraordinarily high rate of inflation in Brazil, many contractors preferred to own hard assets, such as equipment, rather than depreciating cruzados.) Toward year-end, however, sales growth in Brazil moderated as interest rates rose.

Outlook

Latin American countries continue to be plagued with debt problems. However, debt rescheduling; stable profitable commodity prices; and increased privatization should help business in some countries. Sales in Brazil, however, could be hurt by post-election policies which will likely aim at curbing inflation.

The Form 10–Q for the first quarter of 1990 contained the following statements about Brazil:

Demand also rose in a number of Latin American countries. In Brazil, demand increased over one year ago despite the uncertainty of the Brazilian economy.

Nothing in the MD & A section of the 1989 Form 10–K suggested the disproportionate impact of CBSA's profits on Caterpillar's 1989 overall profitability. Similarly, the 1989 Form 10–K and the Form 10–Q for the first quarter of 1990 did not adequately mention management's uncertainty about CBSA's 1990 performance.

II. Applicable Law

* * * *A. Management's Discussion and Analysis as Required by Item 303 of Regulation S–K*

For reports on Form 10–K, Item 303(a) requires the registrant to discuss the liquidity, capital resources, and results of operations of the registrant and to "provide such other information that the registrant believes to be necessary to an understanding of its financial condition, changes in financial condition and results of operations." Item 303(a) also specifically requires

> [W]here in the registrant's judgment a discussion of segment information or of other subdivisions of the registrant's business would be appropriate to an understanding of such business, the discussion shall focus on each relevant, reportable segment or other subdivision of the business and on the registrant as a whole.

In discussing results of operations the registrant is to "[d]escribe any unusual or infrequent events or transactions * * * that materially affected the amount of reported income from continuing operations and in each case, indicate the extent to which income was so affected." Item 303(a)(3)(i). Furthermore, the registrant is to describe other significant components of revenues or expenses that should be described to allow a reader of the company's financial statements to understand the registrant's results of operations. Id.

As a separate component of the discussion of results of operations, the registrant is to discuss "any known trends or uncertainties that have had or that the registrant reasonably expects will have a material favorable or unfavorable impact on net sales or revenues or income from continuing operations." Item 303(a)(3)(ii). "The discussion and analysis shall focus specifically on material events and uncertainties known to management that would cause reported financial information not to be necessarily indicative of future operating results." Instruction 3 to Item 303(a). Registrants are instructed to discuss both new matters which will have an impact on future results, and matters which have previously had

---

The company hasn't changed its outlook from what was stated in its 1989 annual report.

Caterpillar Chairman George Schaefer said:

First-quarter sales were somewhat stronger than anticipated. Nevertheless, the company continues to be concerned about tight monetary policies in major industrial countries; the recent weakening of the Japanese yen; and the uncertainty of the economic situation in Brazil.

an impact on reported operations but which are not expected to have an impact on future operations. Id.

For interim reports such as a Form 10–Q, Item 303(b) requires a discussion and analysis of the results of operations to enable the reader to assess material changes in financial condition and results of operations that have occurred since the end of the preceding fiscal year. Item 303(b). Discussions of material changes in results of operations must identify any significant elements of the registrant's income or loss from continuing operations which do not arise from or are not necessarily representative of the registrant's business. Instruction 4 to Item 303(b).

B. The MD & A Release

In 1989, the Commission determined that additional interpretive guidance was needed regarding a number of areas of MD & A disclosure and published an interpretive release. Release Nos. 33–6835, 34–26831, IC–16961, FR–36 (May 18, 1989) (hereafter "MD & A Release"). Drawing on earlier releases, the MD & A Release noted the underlying rationale for requiring MD & A disclosure and management's core responsibility in providing that disclosure: The MD & A is needed because, without such a narrative explanation, a company's financial statements and accompanying footnotes may be insufficient for an investor to judge the quality of earnings and the likelihood that past performance is indicative of future performance. MD & A is intended to give the investor an opportunity to look at the company through the eyes of management by providing both a short and long-term analysis of the business of the company.

MD & A Release Par. III.A (quoting Securities Act Release No. 6771 (April 24, 1987)). It is management's responsibility in the MD & A to identify and address those key variables and other qualitative and quantitative factors which are peculiar to and necessary for an understanding and evaluation of the company.[6] MD & A Release Par. III.A (quoting Securities Act Release No. 6349 (September 28, 1981)). The MD & A Release further notes,

> The MD & A requirements are intentionally flexible and general. Because no two registrants are identical, good MD & A disclosure for one registrant is not necessarily good * * * for another. The same is true for MD & A disclosure of the same registrant in different years.

MD & A Release Par. IV.

As to prospective information, the MD & A Release sets forth the following test for determining when disclosure is required:

---

[6] Although an auditor or other third party may review the MD & A section of a periodic report, the substance of the S–K Item 303 disclosure is the responsibility of management.

Where a trend, demand, commitment, event or uncertainty is known, management must make two assessments:

(1) Is the known trend, demand, commitment, event or uncertainty likely to come to fruition? If management determines that it is not reasonably likely to occur, no disclosure is required.

(2) If management cannot make that determination, it must evaluate objectively the consequences of the known trend, demand, commitment, event or uncertainty, on the assumption that it will come to fruition.

Disclosure is then required unless management determines that a material effect on the registrant's financial condition or results of operations is not reasonably likely to occur.

MD & A Release Par. III.B. Where the test for disclosure is met, "MD & A disclosure of the effects [of the uncertainty,] quantified to the extent reasonably practicable, [is] required."[7] Id. * * *

C. Analysis

Regulation S–K requires disclosure of information necessary to understand the registrant's financial statements. Item 303(a); MD & A Release Par. III.A. Caterpillar's failure to include required information about CBSA in the MD & A left investors with an incomplete picture of Caterpillar's financial condition and results of operations and denied them the opportunity to see the company "through the eyes of management." MD & A Release Par. IV.

Specifically, by failing (i) in its Annual Report on Form 10–K for the year ended December 31, 1989 to provide an adequate discussion and analysis of the impact of CBSA on its 1989 results of operations as contained in its financial statements, and (ii) to adequately disclose in its 1989 Form 10–K and in its Quarterly Report on Form 10–Q for the first quarter of 1990 known uncertainties reasonably likely to have a material effect on Caterpillar's future results of operations, due to CBSA's questionable ability to repeat its 1989 performance, Caterpillar violated

---

[7]   The Commission has noted:

"Both required disclosure regarding the future impact of presently known trends, events or uncertainties and optional forward-looking information may involve some prediction or projection. The distinction between the two rests with the nature of the prediction required. Required disclosure is based on currently known trends, events, and uncertainties that are reasonably expected to have material effects * * *. In contrast, optional forward-looking disclosure involves anticipating a future trend or event or anticipating a less predictable impact of a known event, trend or uncertainty."

Securities Act Release No. 6711 (April 24, 1987) (final paragraph of Part III); MD & A Release P III.B. (text at n.21).

Section 13(a) of the Exchange Act and Rules 13a–1 and 13a–13 thereunder.[8] * * *

Given the magnitude of CBSA's contribution to Caterpillar's overall earnings, disclosure of the extent of that contribution was required under the MD & A provisions of Regulation S–K since CBSA's earnings materially affected Caterpillar's reported income from continuing operations. See, Item 303(a)(3)(i). Furthermore, the MD & A should have discussed various factors which contributed to CBSA's earnings including currency translation gains, export subsidies, interest income, and Brazilian tax loss carryforwards since such items were significant components of CBSA's revenues that should have been identified and addressed in order for a reader of the company's financial statements to understand Caterpillar's results of operations. * * *

By the time of the February 14, 1990, board meeting—two weeks before Caterpillar's Form 10–K for 1989 was filed—management could not conclude that lower earnings from CBSA were not reasonably likely to occur, nor could management conclude that a material effect on Caterpillar's results of operations was not reasonably likely to occur due to CBSA's lower earnings. It was at that meeting that management told the company's directors "the impact of Brazil is so significant to reduced 1990 projected results, * * * it was necessary to explain it [to the directors] in some detail."

By the end of the first quarter of 1990, before Caterpillar's Form 10–Q for the first quarter of 1990 was filed, management had concluded that "the profit in Brazil will be substantially lower than in 1989." Therefore, it became even more apparent that management could not conclude that lower earnings from CBSA were not reasonably likely to occur, nor could management conclude that a material effect on Caterpillar's results of operations was not reasonably likely to occur due to CBSA's lower earnings. Thus, discussion of the uncertainties surrounding CBSA's earnings, and possible material future impact on Caterpillar's overall financial condition and results of operations was required. * * *

Caterpillar's MD & A disclosure was deficient in two respects. First, Caterpillar's Annual Report on Form 10–K for the year ended December 31, 1989 should have discussed the impact of CBSA on Caterpillar's overall results of operations. Second, both the Annual Report on Form 10–K for 1989 and the Quarterly Report on Form 10–Q for the first quarter of 1990 should have discussed the future uncertainties regarding CBSA's operations, the possible risk of Caterpillar having materially lower earnings as a result of that risk and, to the extent reasonably practicable, quantified the impact of such risk. MD & A Release Par.III.B. The MD & A disclosure in the 1989 Form 10–K and the Form 10–Q for

---

[8]   During the time period in question, Caterpillar did not have adequate procedures in place designed to ensure compliance with the MD & A requirements.

the first quarter of 1990 failed to adequately disclose the risk of lower earnings and did not attempt to quantify the impact of lower earnings from CBSA on Caterpillar. * * *

NOTE

Edmund W. Kitch, The Theory and Practice of Securities Disclosure, 61 Brook.L.Rev. 763, 807–19 (1995):

> The Commission has not been pleased with issuer compliance with Item 303. In Release 33–6835, issued in May 1989, the Commission reported that the staff had undertaken "a special review of the MD & A disclosures to assess the adequacy of disclosure practices and to identify any common areas of deficiencies." Of the 218 registrants reviewed, 206 received letters of comment, many of which related to more than one report. * * * The Commission treated this high level of deficiency as a problem of lack of understanding by registrants, and proceeded to discuss what disclosure was required and to give examples of adequate disclosure. * * * As it turned out the Commission had had enough of preaching. It was time for a test case, and the object of the test case turned out to be the Caterpillar Corporation. * * *

Professor Kitch also pointed out that the SEC's analysis of the economic importance of the Brazil operations to Caterpillar was less than complete. The issue was not whether the profitability of the operations of Caterpillar in Brazil had declined, but whether the overall profitability of Caterpillar had declined as a result. It was quite possible, he suggests, that the company could have made the forecast of 1990 earnings it did in good faith and did not learn until later that its other operations would not offset the negative events in Brazil. His strongest criticism, however, was directed at the reliance by the SEC on management's communications with the board of directors. He argues that SEC reliance on these discussions in litigation over proxy deficiencies will lead management's communications to become guarded or non-existent, withholding important information from the board and preventing effective board governance.

3. FALSE OR MISLEADING STATEMENTS IN CONNECTION WITH PROXY SOLICITATIONS

REGULATION 14A. SOLICITATION OF PROXIES
17 C.F.R. § 240.14a–9.

§ 240.14a–9 FALSE OR MISLEADING STATEMENTS

(a) No solicitation subject to this regulation shall be made by means of any proxy statement, form of proxy, notice of meeting or other communication, written or oral, containing any statement which, at the time and in the light of the circumstances under which it is made, is false or misleading with respect to any material fact, or which omits to state any material fact necessary in order to make the statements therein not false or misleading or necessary to correct any statement in any earlier communication with respect to the solicitation of a proxy for the same meeting or subject matter which has become false or misleading.

(b) The fact that a proxy statement, form of proxy or other soliciting material has been filed with or examined by the Commission shall not be deemed a finding by the Commission that such material is accurate or complete or not false or misleading, or that the Commission has passed upon the merits of or approved any statement contained therein or any matter to be acted upon by security holders. No representation contrary to the foregoing shall be made.

* * *

Note: The following are some examples of what, depending upon particular facts and circumstances, may be misleading within the meaning of this section.

(a) Predictions as to specific future market values.

(b) Material which directly or indirectly impugns character, integrity or personal reputation, or directly or indirectly makes charges concerning improper, illegal or immoral conduct or associations, without factual foundation.

(c) Failure to so identify a proxy statement, form of proxy and other soliciting material as to clearly distinguish it from the soliciting material of any other person or persons soliciting for the same meeting or subject matter.

(d) Claims made prior to a meeting regarding the results of a solicitation.

NOTES

(1) Is this provision a restatement of common law principles or is it broader? In a pre-1964 case, Bresnick v. Home Title Guar. Co., 175 F.Supp. 723 (S.D.N.Y.1959), the Court stated that the test at common law "is not compliance with the technical rules, but rather whether the proxy soliciting material was so tainted with fraud that an inequitable result was accomplished." 175 F.Supp. at 725.

(2) The note to Rule 14a–9 formerly included, as examples of potentially misleading statements, "predictions as to specific future market values, earnings, or dividends," and was changed to its present form in July 1979 to reflect the SEC policy with respect to forward-looking statements described briefly in the prior Section. SEC Rel. No. 34–15944, 44 Fed.Reg. 38810 (1979).

TSC INDUS., INC. V. NORTHWAY, INC.

Supreme Court of the United States, 1976.
426 U.S. 438.

JUSTICE MARSHALL delivered the opinion of the Court.

The proxy rules promulgated by the Securities and Exchange Commission under the Securities Exchange Act of 1934 bar the use of proxy statements that are false or misleading with respect to the presentation or omission of material facts. We are called upon to consider the definition of a material fact under those rules, and the appropriateness of resolving the question of materiality by summary judgment in this case.

I

The dispute in this case centers on the acquisition of petitioner TSC Industries, Inc., by petitioner National Industries, Inc. In February 1969 National acquired 34% of TSC's voting securities by purchase from Charles E. Schmidt and his family. Schmidt, who had been TSC's founder and principal shareholder, promptly resigned along with his son from TSC's board of directors. Thereafter, five National nominees were placed on TSC's board; and Stanley R. Yarmuth, National's president and chief executive officer, became chairman of the TSC board, and Charles F. Simonelli, National's executive vice president, became chairman of the TSC executive committee. On October 16, 1969, the TSC board, with the attending National nominees abstaining, approved a proposal to liquidate and sell all of TSC's assets to National. * * * On November 12, 1969, TSC and National issued a joint proxy statement to their shareholders, recommending approval of the proposal. The proxy solicitation was successful, * * * and the exchange of shares was effected.

This is an action brought by respondent Northway, a TSC shareholder, against TSC and National, claiming that their joint proxy statement was incomplete and materially misleading in violation of § 14(a) of the Securities Exchange Act of 1934, and Rules 14a–3 and 14a–9, promulgated thereunder. The basis of Northway's claim under Rule 14a–3 is that TSC and National failed to state in the proxy statement that the transfer of the Schmidt interests in TSC to National had given National control of TSC. The Rule 14a–9 claim, insofar as it concerns us, is that TSC and National omitted from the proxy statement material facts relating to the degree of National's control over TSC and the favorability of the terms of the proposal to TSC shareholders.

* * * [T]he Court of Appeals reversed the District Court's denial of summary judgment to Northway on its Rule 14a–9 claims, holding that certain omissions of fact were material as a matter of law. 512 F.2d 324 (1975).

We granted certiorari because the standard applied by the Court of Appeals in resolving the question of materiality appeared to conflict with the standard applied by other Courts of Appeals. 423 U.S. 820, 96 S.Ct. 33, 46 L.Ed.2d 37 (1975). We now hold that the Court of Appeals erred in ordering that partial summary judgment be granted to Northway.

II

A

As we have noted on more than one occasion, § 14(a) of the Securities Exchange Act "was intended to promote 'the free exercise of the voting rights of stockholders' by ensuring that proxies would be solicited with 'explanation to the stockholder of the real nature of the questions for which authority to cast his vote is sought.'" Mills v. Electric Auto-Lite Co., 396 U.S. 375, 381, 90 S.Ct. 616, 620, 24 L.Ed.2d 593 (1970). See also J.I. Case Co. v. Borak, 377 U.S. 426, 431, 84 S.Ct. 1555, 1559, 12 L.Ed.2d 423 (1964). In Borak, the Court held that § 14(a)'s broad remedial purposes required recognition under § 27 of the Securities Exchange Act, of an implied private right of action for violations of the provision. And in Mills, we attempted to clarify to some extent the elements of a private cause of action for violation of § 14(a). In a suit challenging the sufficiency under § 14(a) and Rule 14a–9 of a proxy statement soliciting votes in favor of a merger, we held that there was no need to demonstrate that the alleged defect in the proxy statement actually had a decisive effect on the voting. So long as the misstatement or omission was material, the causal relation between violation and injury is sufficiently established, we concluded, if "the proxy solicitation itself * * * was an essential link in the accomplishment of the transaction." 396 U.S., at 385, 90 S.Ct., at 622. After Mills, then, the content given to the notion of materiality assumes heightened significance.[7]

B

The question of materiality, it is universally agreed, is an objective one, involving the significance of an omitted or misrepresented fact to a reasonable investor. Variations in the formulation of a general test of materiality occur in the articulation of just how significant a fact must be or, put another way, how certain it must be that the fact would affect a reasonable investor's judgment.

The Court of Appeals in this case concluded that material facts include "all facts which a reasonable shareholder might consider important." 512 F.2d, at 330 (emphasis added). This formulation of the test of materiality has been explicitly rejected by at least two courts as

---

[7] Our cases have not considered, and we have no occasion in this case to consider, what showing of culpability is required to establish the liability under § 14(a) of a corporation issuing a materially misleading proxy statement, or of a person involved in the preparation of a materially misleading proxy statement. See Ernst & Ernst v. Hochfelder, 425 U.S. 185, 209 n. 28, 96 S.Ct. 1375, 1388, 47 L.Ed.2d 668 (1976).

setting too low a threshold for the imposition of liability under Rule 14a–9. * * *

C

In formulating a standard of materiality under Rule 14a–9, we are guided, of course, by the recognition in *Borak* and *Mills* of the Rule's broad remedial purpose. That purpose is not merely to ensure by judicial means that the transaction, when judged by its real terms, is fair and otherwise adequate, but to ensure disclosures by corporate management in order to enable the shareholders to make an informed choice. As an abstract proposition, the most desirable role for a court in a suit of this sort, coming after the consummation of the proposed transaction, would perhaps be to determine whether in fact the proposal would have been favored by the shareholders and consummated in the absence of any misstatement or omission. But as we recognized in *Mills*, such matters are not subject to determination with certainty. Doubts as to the critical nature of information misstated or omitted will be commonplace. And particularly in view of the prophylactic purpose of the Rule and the fact that the content of the proxy statement is within management's control, it is appropriate that these doubts be resolved in favor of those the statute is designed to protect.

We are aware, however, that the disclosure policy embodied in the proxy regulations is not without limit. Some information is of such dubious significance that insistence on its disclosure may accomplish more harm than good. The potential liability for a Rule 14a–9 violation can be great indeed, and if the standard of materiality is unnecessarily low, not only may the corporation and its management be subjected to liability for insignificant omissions or misstatements, but also management's fear of exposing itself to substantial liability may cause it simply to bury the shareholders in an avalanche of trivial information—a result that is hardly conducive to informed decisionmaking. Precisely these dangers are presented, we think, by the definition of a material fact adopted by the Court of Appeals in this case—a fact which a reasonable shareholder *might* consider important. We agree with Judge Friendly, speaking for the Court of Appeals in *Gerstle,* that the "might" formulation is "too suggestive of mere possibility, however unlikely." 478 F.2d, at 1302.

The general standard of materiality that we think best comports with the policies of Rule 14a–9 is as follows: An omitted fact is material if there is a substantial likelihood that a reasonable shareholder would consider it important in deciding how to vote. This standard is fully consistent with *Mills* general description of materiality as a requirement that "the defect have a significant *propensity* to affect the voting process." It does not require proof of a substantial likelihood that disclosure of the omitted fact would have caused the reasonable investor to change his vote. What the standard does contemplate is a showing of a substantial likelihood that, under all the circumstances, the omitted fact would have assumed actual significance in the deliberations of the reasonable shareholder. Put another way, there must be a substantial likelihood that the disclosure of the omitted fact would have been viewed by the reasonable investor as having significantly altered the "total mix" of information made available.[10]

D

The issue of materiality may be characterized as a mixed question of law and fact, involving as it does the application of a legal standard to a particular set of facts. In considering whether summary judgment on the issue is appropriate, we must bear in mind that the underlying objective facts, which will often be free from dispute, are merely the starting point for the ultimate determination of materiality. The determination requires delicate assessments of the inferences a "reasonable shareholder" would draw from a given set of facts and the significance of those inferences to him, and these assessments are peculiarly ones for the trier of fact. Only if the established omissions are "so obviously important to an investor, that reasonable minds cannot differ on the question of materiality" is the ultimate issue of materiality appropriately resolved "as a matter of law" by summary judgment. * * *

[In Part III of its opinion the Court conducts a careful reexamination of the facts and concludes that none of the claimed omissions were material.]

IV

In summary, none of the omissions claimed to have been in violation of Rule 14a–9 were, so far as the record reveals, materially misleading as a matter of law, and Northway was not entitled to partial summary judgment. The judgment of the Court of Appeals is reversed, and the case is remanded for further proceedings consistent with this opinion.

It is so ordered.

JUSTICE STEVENS took no part in the consideration or decision of this case.

---

[10] In defining materiality under Rule 14a–9, we are, of course, giving content to a rule promulgated by the SEC pursuant to broad statutory authority to promote "the public interest" and "the protection of investors." Cf. Ernst & Ernst v. Hochfelder, 425 U.S., at 212–214, 96 S.Ct., at 1390–1391. Under these circumstances, the SEC's view of the proper balance between the need to insure adequate disclosure and the need to avoid the adverse consequences of setting too low a threshold for civil liability is entitled to consideration. The standard we adopt is supported by the SEC.

NOTE

Shidler v. All American Life & Fin. Corp., 775 F.2d 917 (8th Cir.1985), involved a proxy statement for a merger that included a statement that under Iowa law the transaction required the approval of two-thirds of all classes of shares, common and preferred, voting together in a single election. This statement turned out to be incorrect since the Iowa Supreme Court later concluded that Iowa law required a two-thirds vote of each class of shares, voting separately. Shidler v. All American Life & Fin. Corp., 298 N.W.2d 318 (Iowa 1980). This result, however, could hardly have been predicted with certainty since the issue was a novel one under Iowa law. In holding that no claim for relief under Rule 14a–9 was stated, the Court concluded that Rule 14a–9 did not impose strict liability, and that the lower court's conclusion that the corporation and its directors were not negligent in including the incorrect statement was not "clearly erroneous." The Court held, however, that a claim might be stated under Iowa law for damages for conversion or breach of contract. See also Nelson v. All American Life & Fin. Corp., 889 F.2d 141 (8th Cir.1989).

VIRGINIA BANKSHARES, INC. V. SANDBERG

Supreme Court of the United States, 1991.
501 U.S. 1083.

JUSTICE SOUTER delivered the opinion of the Court.

* * * The questions before us are whether a statement couched in conclusory or qualitative terms purporting to explain directors' reasons for recommending certain corporate action can be materially misleading within the meaning of Rule 14a–9, and whether causation of damages compensable under § 14(a) can be shown by a member of a class of minority shareholders whose votes are not required by law or corporate bylaw to authorize the corporate action subject to the proxy solicitation. We hold that knowingly false statements of reason may be actionable even though conclusory in form, but that respondents have failed to demonstrate the equitable basis required to extend the § 14(a) private action to such shareholders when any indication of congressional intent to do so is lacking.

I

In December 1986, First American Bankshares, Inc., (FABI), a bank holding company, began a "freeze-out" merger,[u] in which the First American Bank of Virginia (Bank) eventually merged into Virginia Bankshares, Inc., (VBI), a wholly owned subsidiary of FABI. VBI owned

---

[u] In a "freeze-out" merger, minority shareholders (who do not have the power to block the merger with their votes) are required to accept cash in a specified amount for their shares and have no right to a continuing ownership interest in the combined entity. However, if dissatisfied with the offered price, minority shareholders have the statutory right of dissent-and-appraisal that permits them, if they follow prescribed procedures, to have a judicial appraisal of the value of their shares and be paid that appraised value.

85% of the Bank's shares, the remaining 15% being in the hands of some 2,000 minority shareholders. FABI hired the investment banking firm of Keefe, Bruyette & Woods (KBW) to give an opinion on the appropriate price for shares of the minority holders, who would lose their interests in the Bank as a result of the merger. Based on market quotations and unverified information from FABI, KBW gave the Bank's executive committee an opinion that $42 a share would be a fair price for the minority stock. The executive committee approved the merger proposal at that price, and the full board followed suit.

Although Virginia law required only that such a merger proposal be submitted to a vote at a shareholders' meeting, and that the meeting be preceded by circulation of a statement of information to the shareholders, the directors nevertheless solicited proxies for voting on the proposal at the annual meeting set for April 21, 1987.[3] In their solicitation, the directors urged the proposal's adoption and stated they had approved the plan because of its opportunity for the minority shareholders to achieve a "high" value, which they elsewhere described as a "fair" price, for their stock.

Although most minority shareholders gave the proxies requested, respondent Sandberg did not, and after approval of the merger, she sought damages in the United States District Court for the Eastern District of Virginia from VBI, FABI, and the directors of the Bank. She pleaded two counts, one for soliciting proxies in violation of § 14(a) and Rule 14a–9, and the other for breaching fiduciary duties owed to the minority shareholders under state law. Under the first count, Sandberg alleged, among other things, that the directors had not believed that the price offered was high or that the terms of the merger were fair, but had recommended the merger only because they believed they had no alternative if they wished to remain on the board. At trial, Sandberg invoked language from this Court's opinion in *Mills v. Electric Auto-Lite Co.*, 396 U.S. 375, 385, 90 S.Ct. 616, 622, 24 L.Ed.2d 593 (1970), to obtain an instruction that the jury could find for her without a showing of her own reliance on the alleged misstatements, so long as they were material and the proxy solicitation was an "essential link" in the merger process.

The jury's verdicts were for Sandberg on both counts, after finding violations of Rule 14a–9 by all defendants and a breach of fiduciary duties by the Bank's directors. The jury awarded Sandberg $18 a share, having found that she would have received $60 if her stock had been valued adequately. * * *

On appeal, the United States Court of Appeals for the Fourth Circuit affirmed * * *, holding that certain statements in the proxy solicitation

---

[3]   Had the directors chosen to issue a statement instead of a proxy solicitation, they would have been subject to an SEC antifraud provision analogous to Rule 14a–9. See 17 CFR 240.14c–6 (1990).

were materially misleading for purposes of the Rule, and that respondents could maintain their action even though their votes had not been needed to effectuate the merger. 891 F.2d 1112 (1989).[4] We granted certiorari because of the importance of the issues presented. 495 U.S. 903, 110 S.Ct. 1921, 109 L.Ed.2d 285 (1990).

II

The Court of Appeals affirmed petitioners' liability for two statements found to have been materially misleading in violation of § 14(a) of the Act, one of which was that "The Plan of Merger has been approved by the Board of Directors because it provides an opportunity for the Bank's public shareholders to achieve a high value for their shares." Petitioners argue that statements of opinion or belief incorporating indefinite and unverifiable expressions cannot be actionable as misstatements of material fact within the meaning of Rule 14a–9, and that such a declaration of opinion or belief should never be actionable when placed in a proxy solicitation incorporating statements of fact sufficient to enable readers to draw their own, independent conclusions.

A

We consider first the actionability per se of statements of reasons, opinion or belief. Because such a statement by definition purports to express what is consciously on the speaker's mind, we interpret the jury verdict as finding that the directors' statements of belief and opinion were made with knowledge that the directors did not hold the beliefs or opinions expressed, and we confine our discussion to statements so made. That such statements may be materially significant raises no serious question. * * *

B

1

But, assuming materiality, the question remains whether statements of reasons, opinions, or beliefs are statements "with respect to * * * material fact[s]" so as to fall within the strictures of the Rule. * * *

* * * [D]irectors' statements of reasons or belief * * * are factual in two senses: as statements that the directors do act for the reasons given or hold the belief stated and as statements about the subject matter of the reason or belief expressed. In neither sense does the proof or disproof of such statements * * * [permit the plaintiff] to manufacture claims of hypothetical action, unconstrained by independent evidence. Reasons for directors' recommendations or statements of belief are * * * characteristically matters of corporate record subject to documentation, to

---

4   The Court of Appeals reversed the District Court, however, on its refusal to certify a class of all minority shareholders in Sandberg's action. Consequently, it ruled that petitioners were liable to all of the Bank's former minority shareholders for $18 per share. 891 F.2d, at 1119.

be supported or attacked by evidence of historical fact outside a plaintiff's control. Such evidence would include not only corporate minutes and other statements of the directors themselves, but circumstantial evidence bearing on the facts that would reasonably underlie the reasons claimed and the honesty of any statement that those reasons are the basis for a recommendation or other action, a point that becomes especially clear when the reasons or beliefs go to valuations in dollars and cents.

It is no answer to argue, as petitioners do, that the quoted statement on which liability was predicated did not express a reason in dollars and cents, but focused instead on the "indefinite and unverifiable" term, "high" value, much like the similar claim that the merger's terms were "fair" to shareholders.[6] The objection ignores the fact that such conclusory terms in a commercial context are reasonably understood to rest on a factual basis that justifies them as accurate, the absence of which renders them misleading. Provable facts either furnish good reasons to make a conclusory commercial judgment, or they count against it, and expressions of such judgments can be uttered with knowledge of truth or falsity just like more definite statements, and defended or attacked through the orthodox evidentiary process that either substantiates their underlying justifications or tends to disprove their existence. In addressing the analogous issue in an action for misrepresentation, the court in *Day v. Avery*, 179 U.S.App.D.C. 63, 548 F.2d 1018 (1976), for example, held that a statement by the executive committee of a law firm that no partner would be any "worse off" solely because of an impending merger could be found to be a material misrepresentation. Id., at 70–72, 548 F.2d at 1025–1027. Cf. *Vulcan Metals Co. v. Simmons Mfg. Co.*, 248 F. 853, 856 (C.A.2 1918) (L. Hand, J.) ("An opinion is a fact * * * [w]hen the parties are so situated that the buyer may reasonably rely upon the expression of the seller's opinion, it is no excuse to give a false one."). In this case, whether $42 was "high," and the proposal "fair" to the minority shareholders depended on whether provable facts about the Bank's assets, and about actual and potential levels of operation, substantiated a value that was above, below, or more or less at the $42 figure, when assessed in accordance with recognized methods of valuation.

---

[6] Petitioners are also wrong to argue that construing the statute to allow recovery for a misleading statement that the merger was "fair" to the minority shareholders is tantamount to assuming federal authority to bar corporate transactions thought to be unfair to some group of shareholders. It is, of course, true that we said in *Santa Fe Industries, Inc. v. Green*, 430 U.S. 462, 479, 97 S.Ct. 1292, 1304, 51 L.Ed.2d 480 (1977), that " '[c]orporations are creatures of state law, and investors commit their funds to corporate directors on the understanding that, except where federal law *expressly* requires certain responsibilities of directors with respect to stockholders, state law will govern the internal affairs of the corporation,' " quoting *Cort v. Ash*, 422 U.S. 66, 84, 95 S.Ct. 2080, 2091, 45 L.Ed.2d 26 (1975). But § 14(a) does impose responsibility for false and misleading proxy statements. Although a corporate transaction's "fairness" is not, as such, a federal concern, a proxy statement's claim of fairness presupposes a factual integrity that federal law is expressly concerned to preserve.

Respondents adduced evidence for just such facts in proving that the statement was misleading about its subject matter and a false expression of the directors' reasons. Whereas the proxy statement described the $42 price as offering a premium above both book value and market price, the evidence indicated that a calculation of the book figure based on the appreciated value of the Bank's real estate holdings eliminated any such premium. The evidence on the significance of market price showed that KBW had conceded that the market was closed, thin and dominated by FABI, facts omitted from the statement. There was, indeed, evidence of a "going concern" value for the Bank in excess of $60 per share of common stock, another fact never disclosed. However conclusory the directors' statement may have been, then, it was open to attack by garden-variety evidence, subject neither to a plaintiff's control nor ready manufacture, and there was no undue risk of open-ended liability or uncontrollable litigation in allowing respondents the opportunity for recovery on the allegation that it was misleading to call $42 "high." * * *

2

Under § 14(a), then, a plaintiff is permitted to prove a specific statement of reason knowingly false or misleadingly incomplete, even when stated in conclusory terms. In reaching this conclusion, we have considered statements of reasons of the sort exemplified here, which misstate the speaker's reasons and also mislead about the stated subject matter (e.g., the value of the shares). A statement of belief may be open to objection only in the former respect, however, solely as a misstatement of the psychological fact of the speaker's belief in what he says. In this case, for example, the Court of Appeals alluded to just such limited falsity in observing that "the jury was certainly justified in believing that the directors did not believe a merger at $42 per share was in the minority stockholders' interest but, rather, that they voted as they did for other reasons, e.g., retaining their seats on the board." 891 F.2d, at 1121.

The question arises, then, whether disbelief, or undisclosed belief or motivation, standing alone, should be a sufficient basis to sustain an action under § 14(a), absent proof by the sort of objective evidence described above that the statement also expressly or impliedly asserted something false or misleading about its subject matter. We think that proof of mere disbelief or belief undisclosed should not suffice for liability under § 14(a), and if nothing more had been required or proven in this case we would reverse for that reason. * * *

C

Petitioners' fall-back position assumes the same relationship between a conclusory judgment and its underlying facts that we described in Part II–B–1, supra. Thus, citing *Radol v. Thomas*, 534 F.Supp. 1302, 1315, 1316 (S.D.Ohio 1982), petitioners argue that even if conclusory statements of reason or belief can be actionable under § 14(a), we should confine liability to instances where the proxy material fails to disclose the offending statement's factual basis. There would be no justification for holding the shareholders entitled to judicial relief, that is, when they were given evidence that a stated reason for a proxy recommendation was misleading, and an opportunity to draw that conclusion themselves.

The answer to this argument rests on the difference between a merely misleading statement and one that is materially so. While a misleading statement will not always lose its deceptive edge simply by joinder with others that are true, the true statements may discredit the other one so obviously that the risk of real deception drops to nil. Since liability under § 14(a) must rest not only on deceptiveness but materiality as well (i.e., it has to be significant enough to be important to a reasonable investor deciding how to vote), petitioners are on perfectly firm ground insofar as they argue that publishing accurate facts in a proxy statement can render a misleading proposition too unimportant to ground liability.

But not every mixture with the true will neutralize the deceptive. If it would take a financial analyst to spot the tension between the one and the other, whatever is misleading will remain materially so, and liability should follow. *Gerstle v. Gamble-Skogmo, Inc.*, 478 F.2d 1281, 1297 (C.A.2 1973) ("[I]t is not sufficient that overtones might have been picked up by the sensitive antennae of investment analysts"). * * * The point of a proxy statement, after all, should be to inform, not to challenge the reader's critical wits. Only when the inconsistency would exhaust the misleading conclusion's capacity to influence the reasonable shareholder would a § 14(a) action fail on the element of materiality.

Suffice it to say that the evidence invoked by petitioners in the instant case fell short of compelling the jury to find the facial materiality of the misleading statement neutralized. The directors claim, for example, to have made an explanatory disclosure of further reasons for their recommendation when they said they would keep their seats following the merger, but they failed to mention what at least one of them admitted in testimony, that they would have had no expectation of doing so without supporting the proposal.[7] And although the proxy statement did speak factually about the merger price in describing it as higher than share prices in recent sales, it failed even to mention the closed market dominated by FABI. None of these disclosures that the directors point to

---

[7] Petitioners fail to dissuade us from recognizing the significance of omissions such as this by arguing that we effectively require them to accuse themselves of breach of fiduciary duty. Subjection to liability for misleading others does not raise a duty of self-accusation; it enforces a duty to refrain from misleading. We have no occasion to decide whether the directors were obligated to state the reasons for their support of the merger proposal here, but there can be no question that the statement they did make carried with it no option to deceive. Cf. Berg v. First American Bankshares, Inc., 254 U.S.App.D.C. 198, 205, 796 F.2d 489, 496 (1986)("Once the proxy statement purported to disclose the factors considered * * *, there was an obligation to portray them accurately.").

was, then, anything more than a half-truth, and the record shows that another fact statement they invoke was arguably even worse. The claim that the merger price exceeded book value was controverted, as we have seen already, by evidence of a higher book value than the directors conceded, reflecting appreciation in the Bank's real estate portfolio. Finally, the solicitation omitted any mention of the Bank's value as a going concern at more than $60 a share, as against the merger price of $42. There was, in sum, no more of a compelling case for the statement's immateriality than for its accuracy.

III

The second issue before us, left open in *Mills v. Electric Auto-Lite Co.*, is whether causation of damages compensable through the implied private right of action under § 14(a) can be demonstrated by a member of a class of minority shareholders whose votes are not required by law or corporate bylaw to authorize the transaction giving rise to the claim. *J.I. Case Co. v. Borak*, 377 U.S. 426, 84 S.Ct. 1555, 12 L.Ed.2d 423 (1964), did not itself address the requisites of causation, as such, or define the class of plaintiffs eligible to sue under § 14(a). But its general holding, that a private cause of action was available to some shareholder class, acquired greater clarity with a more definite concept of causation in *Mills*, where we addressed the sufficiency of proof that misstatements in a proxy solicitation were responsible for damages claimed from the merger subject to complaint.

* * * The *Mills* Court avoided the evidentiary morass that would have followed from requiring individualized proof that enough minority shareholders had relied upon the misstatements to swing the vote [by holding] that causation of damages by a material proxy misstatement could be established by showing that minority proxies necessary and sufficient to authorize the corporate acts had been given in accordance with the tenor of the solicitation[.] [The] Court described such a causal relationship by calling the proxy solicitation an "essential link in the accomplishment of the transaction." In the case before it, the Court found the solicitation essential, as contrasted with one addressed to a class of minority shareholders without votes required by law or by-law to authorize the action proposed, and left it for another day to decide whether such a minority shareholder could demonstrate causation.

In this case, respondents address *Mills'* open question by proffering two theories that the proxy solicitation addressed to them was an "essential link" under the *Mills* causation test.[9] They argue, first, that a

---

[9]   Citing the decision in Schlick v. Penn-Dixie Cement Corp., 507 F.2d 374, 382–383 (C.A.2 1974), petitioners characterize respondents' proffered theories as examples of so-called "sue facts" and "shame facts" theories. "A 'sue fact' is, in general, a fact which is material to a sue decision. A 'sue decision' is a decision by a shareholder whether or not to institute a representative or derivative suit alleging a state-law cause of action." Gelb, Rule 10b–5 and Santa Fe—Herein of Sue Facts, Shame Facts, and Other Matters, 87 W.Va.L.Rev. 189, 198, and

link existed and was essential simply because VBI and FABI would have been unwilling to proceed with the merger without the approval manifested by the minority shareholders' proxies, which would not have been obtained without the solicitation's express misstatements and misleading omissions. On this reasoning, the causal connection would depend on a desire to avoid bad shareholder or public relations, and the essential character of the causal link would stem not from the enforceable terms of the parties' corporate relationship, but from one party's apprehension of the ill will of the other.

In the alternative, respondents argue that the proxy statement was an essential link between the directors' proposal and the merger because it was the means to satisfy a state statutory requirement of minority shareholder approval, as a condition for saving the merger from voidability resulting from a conflict of interest on the part of one of the Bank's directors, Jack Beddow, who voted in favor of the merger while also serving as a director of FABI. Under the terms of [MBCA § 8.31(a)], minority approval after disclosure of the material facts about the transaction and the director's interest was one of three avenues to insulate the merger from later attack for conflict, the two others being ratification by the Bank's directors after like disclosure, and proof that the merger was fair to the corporation. On this theory, causation would depend on the use of the proxy statement for the purpose of obtaining votes sufficient to bar a minority shareholder from commencing proceedings to declare the merger void.[10]

Although respondents have proffered each of these theories as establishing a chain of causal connection in which the proxy statement is claimed to have been an "essential link," neither theory presents the proxy solicitation as essential in the sense of *Mills*' causal sequence, in which the solicitation links a directors' proposal with the votes legally required to authorize the action proposed. As a consequence, each theory would, if adopted, extend the scope of *Borak* actions beyond the ambit of *Mills*, and expand the class of plaintiffs entitled to bring *Borak* actions to

---

n. 52 (1985), quoting Borden, "Sue Fact" Rule Mandates Disclosure to Avoid Litigation in State Courts, 10 SEC § 82, pp. 201, 204–205 (1982). See also Note, Causation and Liability in Private Actions for Proxy Violations, 80 Yale L.J. 107, 116 (1970) (discussing theories of causation). "Shame facts" are said to be facts which, had they been disclosed, would have "shamed" management into abandoning a proposed transaction.

[10] The District Court and Court of Appeals have grounded causation on a further theory, that Virginia law required a solicitation of proxies even from minority shareholders as a condition of consummating the merger. While the provisions of [MBCA § 11.04(a), (d), (e)] are said to have required the Bank to solicit minority proxies, they actually compelled no more than submission of the merger to a vote at a shareholders' meeting, [MBCA § 11.04(e)], preceded by issuance of an informational statement, [MBCA § 11.04(d)]. There was thus no need under this statute to solicit proxies, although it is undisputed that the proxy solicitation sufficed to satisfy the statutory obligation to provide a statement of relevant information. On this theory causation would depend on the use of the proxy statement to satisfy a statutory obligation, even though a proxy solicitation was not, as such, required. In this Court, respondents have disclaimed reliance on any such theory.

include shareholders whose initial authorization of the transaction prompting the proxy solicitation is unnecessary.

Assessing the legitimacy of any such extension or expansion calls for the application of some fundamental principles governing recognition of a right of action implied by a federal statute, the first of which was not, in fact, the considered focus of the *Borak* opinion. The rule that has emerged in the years since *Borak* and *Mills* came down is that recognition of any private right of action for violating a federal statute must ultimately rest on congressional intent to provide a private remedy, *Touche Ross & Co. v. Redington*, 442 U.S. 560, 575, 99 S.Ct. 2479, 2488–2489, 61 L.Ed.2d 82 (1979). From this the corollary follows, that the breadth of the right once recognized should not, as a general matter, grow beyond the scope congressionally intended.

This rule and corollary present respondents with a serious obstacle, for we can find no manifestation of intent to recognize a cause of action (or class of plaintiffs) as broad as respondents' theory of causation would entail. At first blush, it might seem otherwise, for the *Borak* Court certainly did not ignore the matter of intent. Its opinion adverted to the statutory object of "protection of investors" as animating Congress' intent to provide judicial relief where "necessary," *Borak*, 377 U.S., at 432, 84 S.Ct., at 1559–1560, and it quoted evidence for that intent from House and Senate Committee Reports, id., at 431–32, 84 S.Ct., at 1559–1560. *Borak*'s probe of the congressional mind, however, never focused squarely on private rights of action, as distinct from the substantive objects of the legislation, and one member of the *Borak* Court later characterized the "implication" of the private right of action as resting modestly on the Act's "exclusively procedural provision affording access to a federal forum." *Bivens v. Six Unknown Fed. Narcotics Agents*, 403 U.S. 388, 403, n. 4, 91 S.Ct. 1999, 2008, n. 4, 29 L.Ed.2d 619 (1971) (Harlan, J., concurring in judgment) (internal quotation marks omitted). In fact, the importance of enquiring specifically into intent to authorize a private cause of action became clear only later, see *Cort v. Ash*, 422 U.S., at 78, 95 S.Ct., at 2087–2088, and only later still, in *Touche Ross*, was this intent accorded primacy among the considerations that might be thought to bear on any decision to recognize a private remedy. There, in dealing with a claimed private right under § 17(a) of the Act, we explained that the "central inquiry remains whether Congress intended to create, either expressly or by implication, a private cause of action." 442 U.S., at 575–576, 99 S.Ct., at 2489.

Looking to the Act's text and legislative history mindful of this heightened concern reveals little that would help toward understanding the intended scope of any private right. According to the House report, Congress meant to promote the "free exercise" of stockholders' voting rights, H.R.Rep. No. 1383, 73d Cong., 2d Sess., 14 (1934), and protect "[f]air corporate suffrage," id., at 13, from abuses exemplified by proxy solicitations that concealed what the Senate report called the "real nature" of the issues to be settled by the subsequent votes, S.Rep. No. 792, 73d Cong., 2d Sess., 12 (1934). While it is true that these reports, like the language of the Act itself, carry the clear message that Congress meant to protect investors from misinformation that rendered them unwitting agents of self-inflicted damage, it is just as true that Congress was reticent with indications of how far this protection might depend on self-help by private action. The response to this reticence may be, of course, to claim that § 14(a) cannot be enforced effectively for the sake of its intended beneficiaries without their participation as private litigants. *Borak*, supra, 377 U.S., at 432, 84 S.Ct., at 1559–1560. But the force of this argument for inferred congressional intent depends on the degree of need perceived by Congress, and we would have trouble inferring any congressional urgency to depend on implied private actions to deter violations of § 14(a), when Congress expressly provided private rights of action in §§ 9(e), 16(b) and 18(a) of the same Act.[11]

The congressional silence that is thus a serious obstacle to the expansion of cognizable *Borak* causation is not, however, a necessarily insurmountable barrier. This is not the first effort in recent years to expand the scope of an action originally inferred from the Act without "conclusive guidance" from Congress, and we may look to that earlier case for the proper response to such a plea for expansion. There, we accepted the proposition that where a legal structure of private statutory rights has developed without clear indications of congressional intent, the contours of that structure need not be frozen absolutely when the result would be demonstrably inequitable to a class of would-be plaintiffs with claims comparable to those previously recognized. Faced in that case with such a claim for equality in rounding out the scope of an implied private statutory right of action, we looked to policy reasons for deciding where the outer limits of the right should lie. We may do no less here, in the face of respondents' pleas for a private remedy to place them on the same footing as shareholders with votes necessary for initial corporate action.

A

[We reject] respondents' first theory, that a desire to avoid minority shareholders' ill will should suffice to justify recognizing the requisite causality of a proxy statement needed to garner that minority support.

* * * [If this were accepted, causation] would turn on inferences about what the corporate directors would have thought and done without the

---

[11] The object of our [inquiry] does not extend further to question the holding of either *J.I. Case Co. v. Borak*, 377 U.S. 426, 84 S.Ct. 1555, 12 L.Ed.2d 423 (1964), or *Mills v. Electric Auto-Lite Co.*, 396 U.S. 375, 90 S.Ct. 616, 24 L.Ed.2d 593 (1970) at this date, any more than we have done so in the past, see *Touche Ross & Co. v. Redington*, 442 U.S. 560, 577, 99 S.Ct. 2479, 2489–2490, 61 L.Ed.2d 82 (1979). Our point is simply to recognize the hurdle facing any litigant who urges us to enlarge the scope of the action beyond the point reached in *Mills*.

minority shareholder approval unneeded to authorize action. A subsequently dissatisfied minority shareholder would have virtual license to allege that managerial timidity would have doomed corporate action but for the ostensible approval induced by a misleading statement, and opposing claims of hypothetical diffidence and hypothetical boldness on the part of directors would probably provide enough depositions in the usual case to preclude any judicial resolution short of the credibility judgments that can only come after trial. Reliable evidence would seldom exist. Directors would understand the prudence of making a few statements about plans to proceed even without minority endorsement, and discovery would be a quest for recollections of oral conversations at odds with the official pronouncements, in hopes of finding support for ex post facto guesses about how much heat the directors would have stood in the absence of minority approval. The issues would be hazy, their litigation protracted, and their resolution unreliable. Given a choice, we would reject any theory of causation that raised such prospects, and we reject this one.[12]

B

The theory of causal necessity derived from the requirements of Virginia law dealing with postmerger ratification seeks to identify the essential character of the proxy solicitation from its function in obtaining the minority approval that would preclude a minority suit attacking the merger. Since the link is said to be a step in the process of barring a class of shareholders from resort to a state remedy otherwise available, this theory of causation rests upon the proposition of policy that § 14(a) should provide a federal remedy whenever a false or misleading proxy statement results in the loss under state law of a shareholder plaintiff's state remedy for the enforcement of a state right. Respondents agree with the suggestions of counsel for the SEC and FDIC that causation be recognized, for example, when a minority shareholder has been induced by a misleading proxy statement to forfeit a state-law right to an appraisal remedy by voting to approve a transaction, cf. *Swanson v. American Consumers Industries, Inc.*, 475 F.2d 516, 520–521 (C.A.7 1973), or when such a shareholder has been deterred from obtaining an order enjoining a damaging transaction by a proxy solicitation that misrepresents the facts on which an injunction could properly have been

---

[12] In parting company from us on this point, Justice Kennedy emphasizes that respondents in this particular case substantiated a plausible claim that petitioners would not have proceeded without minority approval. FABI's attempted freeze-out merger of a Maryland subsidiary had failed a year before the events in question when the subsidiary's directors rejected the proposal because of inadequate share price, and there was evidence of FABI's desire to avoid any renewal of adverse comment. The issue before us, however, is whether to recognize a theory of causation generally, and our decision against doing so rests on our apprehension that the ensuing litigation would be exemplified by cases far less tractable than this. Respondents' burden to justify recognition of causation beyond the scope of Mills must be addressed not by emphasizing the instant case but by confronting the risk inherent in the cases that could be expected to be characteristic if the causal theory were adopted.

issued. Respondents claim that in this case a predicate for recognizing just such a causal link exists in [MBCA §§ 8.61(b)(2), 8.63], which sets the conditions under which the merger may be insulated from suit by a minority shareholder seeking to void it on account of Beddow's conflict.

This case does not, however, require us to decide whether § 14(a) provides a cause of action for lost state remedies, since there is no indication in the law or facts before us that the proxy solicitation resulted in any such loss. The contrary appears to be the case. Assuming the soundness of respondents' characterization of the proxy statement as materially misleading, the very terms of the Virginia statute indicate that a favorable minority vote induced by the solicitation would not suffice to render the merger invulnerable to later attack on the ground of the conflict. The statute bars a shareholder from seeking to avoid a transaction tainted by a director's conflict if, inter alia, the minority shareholders ratified the transaction following disclosure of the material facts of the transaction and the conflict. [MBCA §§ 8.60, 8.63]. Assuming that the material facts about the merger and Beddow's interests were not accurately disclosed, the minority votes were inadequate to ratify the merger under state law, and there was no loss of state remedy to connect the proxy solicitation with harm to minority shareholders irredressable under state law.[13] Nor is there a claim here that the statement misled respondents into entertaining a false belief that they had no chance to upset the merger, until the time for bringing suit had run out.

The judgment of the Court of Appeals is reversed.

It is so ordered.

JUSTICE SCALIA, concurring in part and concurring in the judgment.

I

As I understand the Court's opinion, the statement "In the opinion of the Directors, this is a high value for the shares" would produce liability if in fact it was not a high value and the Directors knew that. It would not produce liability if in fact it was not a high value but the Directors honestly believed otherwise. The statement "The Directors voted to accept the proposal because they believe it offers a high value" would not produce liability if in fact the Directors' genuine motive was quite different—except that it would produce liability if the proposal in fact did not offer a high value and the Directors knew that.

I agree with all of this. However, not every sentence that has the word "opinion" in it, or that refers to motivation for Directors' actions, leads us into this psychic thicket. Sometimes such a sentence actually

---

[13] In his opinion dissenting on this point, Justice Kennedy suggests that materiality under Virginia law might be defined differently from the materiality standard of our own cases, resulting in a denial of state remedy even when a solicitation was materially misleading under federal law. Respondents, however, present nothing to suggest that this might be so.

represents facts as facts rather than opinions—and in that event no more need be done than apply the normal rules for § 14(a) liability. I think that is the situation here. In my view, the statement at issue in this case is most fairly read as affirming *separately* both the fact of the Directors' opinion *and* the accuracy of the facts upon which the opinion was assertedly based. It reads as follows:

> The Plan of Merger has been approved by the Board of Directors because it provides an opportunity for the Bank's public shareholders to achieve a high value for their shares. App. to Pet. for Cert. 53a.

Had it read "because *in their estimation* it provides an opportunity, etc." it would have set forth nothing but an opinion. As written, however, it asserts both that the Board of Directors acted for a particular reason *and* that that reason is correct. * * *

If the present case were to proceed, therefore, I think the normal § 14(a) principles governing misrepresentation of fact would apply.

II

I recognize that the Court's disallowance (in Part II–B–2) of an action for misrepresentation of belief is entirely contrary to the modern law of torts, as authorities cited by the Court make plain. I have no problem with departing from modern tort law in this regard, because I think the federal cause of action at issue here was never enacted by Congress, and hence the more narrow we make it (within the bounds of rationality) the more faithful we are to our task. * * *

JUSTICE STEVENS, with whom JUSTICE MARSHALL joins, concurring in part and dissenting in part.

While I agree in substance with Parts I and II of the Court's opinion, I do not agree with the reasoning in Part III. * * *

The case before us today involves a merger that has been found by a jury to be unfair, not fair. The interest in providing a remedy to the injured minority shareholders therefore is stronger, not weaker, than in *Mills*. The interest in avoiding speculative controversy about the actual importance of the proxy solicitation is the same as in *Mills*. Moreover, as in *Mills*, these matters can be taken into account at the remedy stage in appropriate cases. Accordingly, I do not believe that it constitutes an unwarranted extension of the rationale of *Mills* to conclude that because management found it necessary—whether for "legal or practical reasons"—to solicit proxies from minority shareholders to obtain their approval of the merger, that solicitation "was an essential link in the accomplishment of the transaction." In my opinion, shareholders may bring an action for damages under § 14(a) of the Securities Exchange Act of 1934, whenever materially false or misleading statements are made in proxy statements. That the solicitation of proxies is not required by law or by the bylaws of a corporation does not authorize corporate officers, once they have decided for whatever reason to solicit proxies, to avoid the constraints of the statute. I would therefore affirm the judgment of the Court of Appeals.

JUSTICE KENNEDY, with whom JUSTICE MARSHALL, JUSTICE BLACKMUN, and JUSTICE STEVENS join, concurring in part and dissenting in part.

I am in general agreement with Parts I and II of the majority opinion, but do not agree with the views expressed in Part III regarding the proof of causation required to establish a violation of § 14(a). With respect, I dissent from Part III of the Court's opinion. * * *

II

A

The severe limits the Court places upon possible proof of nonvoting causation in a § 14(a) private action are justified neither by our precedents nor any case in the courts of appeals. These limits are said to flow from a shift in our approach to implied causes of action that has occurred since we recognized the § 14(a) implied private action in J.I. Case Co. v. Borak, 377 U.S. 426, 84 S.Ct. 1555, 12 L.Ed.2d 423 (1964).

I acknowledge that we should exercise caution in creating implied private rights of action and that we must respect the primacy of congressional intent in that inquiry. Where an implied cause of action is well accepted by our own cases and has become an established part of the securities laws, however, we should enforce it as a meaningful remedy unless we are to eliminate it altogether. As the Court phrases it, we must consider the causation question in light of the underlying "policy reasons for deciding where the outer limits of the right should lie."

According to the Court, acceptance of non-voting causation theories would "extend the scope of *Borak* actions beyond the ambit of *Mills*." But *Mills* did not purport to limit the scope of *Borak* actions, and some courts have applied nonvoting causation theories to *Borak* actions for at least the past 25 years.

To the extent the Court's analysis considers the purposes underlying § 14(a), it does so with the avowed aim to limit the cause of action and with undue emphasis upon fears of "speculative claims and procedural intractability." The result is a sort of guerrilla warfare to restrict a well-established implied right of action. If the analysis adopted by the Court today is any guide, Congress and those charged with enforcement of the securities laws stand forewarned that unresolved questions concerning the scope of those causes of action are likely to be answered by the Court in favor of defendants.

B

The Court seems to assume * * * that Sandberg bears a special burden to demonstrate causation because the public shareholders held only 15 percent of the Bank's stock. Justice Stevens is right to reject this theory. Here, First American Bankshares, Inc. (FABI) and Virginia Bankshares, Inc. (VBI) retained the option to back out of the transaction if dissatisfied with the reaction of the minority shareholders, or if concerned that the merger would result in liability for violation of duties to the minority shareholders. The merger agreement was conditioned upon approval by two-thirds of the shareholders, App. 463, and VBI could have voted its shares against the merger if it so decided. To this extent, the Court's distinction between cases where the "minority" shareholders could have voted down the transaction and those where causation must be proved by nonvoting theories is suspect. Minority shareholders are identified only by a post hoc inquiry. The real question ought to be whether an injury was shown by the effect the nondisclosure had on the entire merger process, including the period before votes are cast.

The Court's distinction presumes that a majority shareholder will vote in favor of management's proposal even if proxy disclosure suggests that the transaction is unfair to minority shareholders or that the board of directors or majority shareholder are in breach of fiduciary duties to the minority. If the majority shareholder votes against the transaction in order to comply with its state law duties, or out of fear of liability, or upon concluding that the transaction will injure the reputation of the business, this ought not to be characterized as nonvoting causation. Of course, when the majority shareholder dominates the voting process, as was the case here, it may prefer to avoid the embarrassment of voting against its own proposal and so may cancel the meeting of shareholders at which the vote was to have been taken. For practical purposes, the result is the same: because of full disclosure the transaction does not go forward and the resulting injury to minority shareholders is avoided. The Court's distinction between voting and nonvoting causation does not create clear legal categories. * * *

There is no authority whatsoever for limiting § 14(a) to protecting those minority shareholders whose numerical strength could permit them to vote down a proposal. One of Section 14(a)'s "chief purposes is 'the protection of investors.' " *J.I. Case Co. v. Borak*, 377 U.S., at 432, 1559–1560. Those who lack the strength to vote down a proposal have all the more need of disclosure. The voting process involves not only casting ballots but also the formulation and withdrawal of proposals, the minority's right to block a vote through court action or the threat of adverse consequences, or the negotiation of an increase in price. The proxy rules support this deliberative process. These practicalities can result in causation sufficient to support recovery.

The facts in the case before us prove this point. Sandberg argues that had all the material facts been disclosed, FABI or the Bank likely would have withdrawn or revised the merger proposal. The evidence in the record, and more that might be available upon remand, meets any reasonable requirement of specific and nonspeculative proof.

FABI wanted a "friendly transaction" with a price viewed as "so high that any reasonable shareholder will accept it." Management expressed concern that the transaction result in "no loss of support for the bank out in the community, which was important." Although FABI had the votes to push through any proposal, it wanted a favorable response from the minority shareholders. Because of the "human element involved in a transaction of this nature," FABI attempted to "show those minority shareholders that [it was] being fair."

The theory that FABI would not have pursued the transaction if full disclosure had been provided and the shareholders had realized the inadequacy of the price is supported not only by the trial testimony but also by notes of the meeting of the Bank's board which approved the merger. The inquiry into causation can proceed not by "opposing claims of hypothetical diffidence and hypothetical boldness," but through an examination of evidence of the same type the Court finds acceptable in its determination that directors' statements of reasons can lead to liability. Discussion at the board meeting focused upon matters such as "how to keep PR afloat" and "how to prevent adverse reac[tion]/perception," demonstrating the directors' concern that an unpopular merger proposal could injure the Bank.

Only a year or so before the Virginia merger, FABI had failed in an almost identical transaction, an attempt to freeze out the minority shareholders of its Maryland subsidiary. FABI retained Keefe, Bruyette & Woods (KBW) for that transaction as well, and KBW had given an opinion that FABI's price was fair. The subsidiary's board of directors then retained its own adviser and concluded that the price offered by FABI was inadequate. The Maryland transaction failed when the directors of the Maryland bank refused to proceed; and this was despite the minority's inability to outvote FABI if it had pressed on with the deal.

In the Virginia transaction, FABI again decided to retain KBW. Beddow, who sat on the boards of both FABI and the Bank, discouraged the Bank from hiring its own financial adviser, out of fear that the Maryland experience would be repeated if the Bank received independent advice. Directors of the Bank testified they would not have voted to approve the transaction if the price had been demonstrated unfair to the minority. Further, approval by the Bank's board of directors was facilitated by FABI's representation that the transaction also would be approved by the minority shareholders.

These facts alone suffice to support a finding of causation, but here Sandberg might have had yet more evidence to link the nondisclosure with completion of the merger. FABI executive Robert Altman and Bank Chairman Drewer met on the day before the shareholders meeting when the vote was taken. Notes produced by petitioners suggested that Drewer, who had received some shareholder objections to the $42 price, considered postponing the meeting and obtaining independent advice on valuation. Altman persuaded him to go forward without any of these cautionary measures. This information, which was produced in the course of discovery, was kept from the jury on grounds of privilege. Sandberg attacked the privilege ruling on five grounds in the Court of Appeals. In light of its ruling in favor of Sandberg, however, the panel had no occasion to consider the admissibility of this evidence.

Though I would not require a shareholder to present such evidence of causation, this case itself demonstrates that nonvoting causation theories are quite plausible where the misstatement or omission is material and the damage sustained by minority shareholders is serious. As Professor Loss summarized the holdings of a "substantial number of cases," even if the minority cannot alone vote down a transaction, minority stockholders will be in a better position to protect their interests with full disclosure and * * * an unfavorable minority vote might influence the majority to modify or reconsider the transaction in question. In [*Schlick v. Penn-Dixie Cement Corp.*, 507 F.2d 374, 384 (C.A.2 1974),] where the stockholders had no appraisal rights under state law because the stock was listed on the New York Stock Exchange, the court advanced two additional considerations: (1) the *market* would be informed; and (2) even "a rapacious controlling management" might modify the terms of a merger because it would not want to "hang its dirty linen out on the line and thereby expose itself to suit or Securities Commission or other action—in terms of reputation and future takeovers." L. Loss, Fundamentals of Securities Regulation at 1119–1120 (footnote omitted).

I conclude that causation is more than plausible; it is likely, even where the public shareholders cannot vote down management's proposal. Causation is established where the proxy statement is an essential link in completing the transaction, even if the minority lacks sufficient votes to defeat a proposal of management. * * *

NOTES

(1) Do you agree that a statement that an offer price is higher than "book value" is misleading because the statement would not be true if a recalculated book value—based on current market values for real estate rather than historical cost—was used? Would it be misleading if the disclosure made clear that the comparison was being made with book value "calculated in the traditional manner and without regard to current real estate values?" Would an average investor understand that distinction? Or

would the proxy statement have to say what the recalculated book value was if "book value" is referred to at all? After this decision, could the SEC amend Rule 14a–9 to make it applicable to proxy solicitations that are not "essential" to the transaction in the sense used by Justice Souter? Or does that require an amendment to § 14(a) of the Securities Exchange Act of 1934?

(2) What do you think of Justice Scalia's approach toward cases involving implied causes of action that because "the federal cause of action at issue here was never enacted by Congress, * * * the more narrow we make it (within the bounds of rationality) the more faithful we are to our task"? What is "the task" that Justice Scalia refers to?

(3) If the protection of Rule 14a–9 is removed from minority shareholders by *Virginia Bankshares*, can any statement, no matter how outrageously wrong, be made by management?

(4) One question left open in Justice Souter's opinion is whether a different rule should be applicable if minority shareholders induced to vote in favor of a proposal because of false statements thereby lose state remedies, such as the right of dissent and appraisal or the right to serve as a derivative plaintiff. Two decisions holding that *Virginia Bankshares* does not extend that far are Howing Co. v. Nationwide Corp., 972 F.2d 700 (6th Cir.1992), cert. denied 507 U.S. 1004 (1993), and Wilson v. Great American Indus., Inc., 979 F.2d 924 (2d Cir.1992). But see Roosevelt v. E.I. Du Pont de Nemours & Co., 958 F.2d 416 (D.C.Cir.1992); Scattergood v. Perelman, 945 F.2d 618 (3d Cir.1991). For an analysis of these issues, see Scott Jordan, Loss of State Claims as a Basis for Rule 10b–5 and 14a–9 Actions: The Impact of *Virginia Bankshares*, 49 Bus.Law. 295 (1993); Note, Virginia Bankshares v. Sandberg: Should Minority Approval be Required by Law or Corporate Bylaw? 37 Ariz.L.Rev. 913 (1995).

4. SHAREHOLDER PROPOSALS

REGULATION 14A. SOLICITATION OF PROXIES (RULE 14a–8)
17 C.F.R. § 240.14a–8.

(Please consult the Statutory Supplement)

NOTES

(1) Rule 14a–8 has long been viewed by the SEC as a potentially important element of corporate democracy since it in effect permits individual shareholders to place proposals before the body of shareholders through the corporation's proxy statement. Is this right of ballot access based on state law or is it federally created? See Jill E. Fisch, From Legitimacy to Logic: Reconstructing Proxy Regulation, 46 Vand.L.Rev. 1129, 1143–48 (1993):

> Many of the restrictions in Rule 14a–8 appear both sensible and within the SEC's power to impose. Few commentators would argue with the propriety of permitting management to exclude proposals

that are false and misleading or that call for the corporation to violate state or federal law. Only the first basis for exclusion, however, which requires that the proposal deal with a matter that is a proper subject for shareholder action under state law, is strictly true to the SEC's original premise that proper subject is determined by state law.

Moreover, many of the bases for exclusion are not grounded directly in state law. * * * Rule 14a–8[b](1) imposes minimum ownership requirements and holding period qualifications upon shareholders who seek inclusion of a proposal under Rule 14a–8. No uniform state or common-law principle requires that a shareholder hold one percent or [two] thousand dollars worth of a corporation's stock for a minimum of one year before making a motion at a shareholders' meeting. No state law bars a shareholder from making the same motion or proposal in successive years, yet Rule 14a–8[i](12) limits a shareholder's ability to do so. Additionally, state law does not restrict shareholders to dealing with issues concerning more than five percent of the corporation's total assets or extraordinary business matters. The SEC, however, has imposed these limits on shareholder democracy.

Many of the restrictions imposed by the proxy rules can be attributed to a pragmatic effort by the SEC to limit the number of shareholder proposals and to restrict use of the proxy statement to issues of general importance to shareholders. Although such limits may be desirable, they have no foundation in state or common-law restrictions regarding proper subjects to be raised at a shareholders' meeting. The SEC's authority to impose these restrictions on the use of the proxy mechanism is therefore unclear.

Apart from pragmatic concerns, the SEC's restrictions appear to stem primarily from the general principle that state law vests management, rather than shareholders, with the authority to run the corporation. State corporation statutes generally provide that the corporation shall be managed by or under the direction of the board of directors. This common provision suggests that a shareholder proposal affecting the management of the corporation's affairs may improperly interfere with the board's authority.

The absence of modern judicial decisions voiding shareholder action on the basis of these statutes suggests that their limitation on shareholder activity is, at best, minimal. Additionally, it would seem that framing the proposal as a shareholder recommendation rather than an attempt to bind the board would address any limitation the statutes impose. * * *

Accordingly, both in determining appropriate criteria for excluding shareholder proposals and in applying those criteria, the SEC does not replicate passively the annual meeting process by applying state law principles, but creates a federal common law as to what constitutes a proper subject for shareholder action.

(2) A major source of shareholder proposals has been the members of the Interfaith Center on Corporate Responsibility, a loose organization of nearly 250 Protestant and Roman Catholic denominations, religious communities, agencies, pension funds,[v] healthcare systems, dioceses, and a few individuals. In 1997, nearly one hundred ICCR-member religious investors sponsored 191 resolutions to 137 companies. Examples include: requesting RJR Nabisco "to adopt a policy ending Joe Camel ads anywhere in the world by the end of 1997"; requesting Anheuser Busch to "revise existing company educational materials and develop all future materials to include in a prominent fashion the definition of moderate drinking found in the Dietary Guidelines * * *"; requesting General Electric to "no longer seek new nuclear fuel sales abroad, and instead, promote the sale of safer, lower-risk, energy-efficient alternate generating systems to foreign markets"; and requesting more than 40 companies to endorse the CERES Principles for Public Environmental Accountability. However, many proposals also relate to traditional corporate governance concerns, for example: proposals to Coca-Cola and four other companies to create a Nominating Committee of the board of directors consisting entirely of independent directors; to Texaco and four other companies to declassify the election of directors so that all directors are elected annually; and to more than a dozen companies to make formal review of executive compensation policies. The Corporate Examiner, Vol. 25, No. 7–8, at 8–10, 14 (1997).

(3) The construction of 14a–8(i) in the context of social responsibility issues has a considerable history. The original attitude of the SEC was to permit proposals of this nature to be excluded, but the courts disagreed. The leading case involved an attempt in 1968 by an organization called the Medical Committee for Human Rights to require Dow Chemical Company to include the following "resolution" in its proxy statement:

> RESOLVED, that the shareholders of the Dow Chemical Company request the Board of Directors, in accordance with the laws of the State of Delaware, and the Composite Certificate of Incorporation of the Dow Chemical Company, to adopt a resolution setting forth an amendment to the Composite Certificate of Incorporation of the Dow Chemical Company that napalm shall not be sold to any buyer unless that buyer gives reasonable assurance that the substance will not be used on or against human beings.

The letter concluded with the following statement:

> Finally, we wish to note that our objections to the sale of this product [are] primarily based on the concerns for human life inherent in our organization's credo. However, we are further

---

[v] Before 1992, Rule 14a–8 was widely used by institutional investors to raise economic issues with individual corporations, often with a considerable degree of success. Today, most of these issues are raised by institutional investors directly with the targeted issuer.

informed by our investment advisers that this product is also bad for our company's business as it is being used in the Vietnamese War. It is now clear from company statements and press reports that it is increasingly hard to recruit the highly intelligent, well-motivated, young college men so important for company growth. There is, as well, an adverse impact on our global business, which our advisers indicate, suffers as a result of the public reaction to this product.

In Medical Comm. for Human Rights v. SEC, 432 F.2d 659 (D.C.Cir.1970), vacated as moot 404 U.S. 403 (1972), the Court did not hold that this proposal was includable, but strongly intimated that it was, and that Rule 14a–8 was an important mechanism for shareholder democracy and control of management. The Supreme Court appeal, incidentally, became moot after the corporation voluntarily submitted the Medical Committee proposal to its shareholders, where it received the support of less than three percent of the shares voting on the issue.

(4) In SEC Rel. No. 34–12999, 41 Fed. Reg. 52,994, 52,998 (1976), the SEC announced a major change in policy with respect to its view of "ordinary business operations":

> [T]he term "ordinary business operations" has been deemed on occasion to include certain matters which have significant policy, economic or other implications inherent in them. For instance, a proposal that a utility company not construct a proposed nuclear power plant has in the past been considered excludable * * *. In retrospect, however, it seems apparent that the economic and safety considerations attendant to nuclear power plants are of such magnitude that a determination whether to construct one is not an "ordinary" business matter. Accordingly proposals of that nature, as well as others that have major implications, will in the future be considered beyond the realm of an issuer's ordinary business operations, and future interpretive letters of the Commission's staff will reflect that view.

> * * * [W]here proposals involve business matters that are mundane in nature and do not involve any substantial policy or other considerations, the subparagraph may be relied upon to omit them.

Following the 1976 release, the SEC required a number of corporations to include proposals reporting on their compliance with the requirements of equal opportunity and affirmative action. Generally, the SEC considered whether the subject of the reporting related to "day-to-day" employment matters (in which event the proposal was excludable as relating to "ordinary business matters") or whether it raised significant policy considerations.

(5) In March 1991, the SEC's position with respect to employment matters again changed significantly. This new policy was set forth most

explicitly in a "no action letter"[w] addressed to Cracker Barrel Old Country Store, Inc. relating to a proposal that Cracker Barrel be required to establish a policy not to discriminate against homosexuals. 1992 WL 289095 (Oct. 13, 1992):

> As a general rule, the staff views proposals directed at a company's employment policies and practices with respect to its non-executive workforce to be uniquely matters relating to the conduct of the company's ordinary business operations. Examples of the categories of proposals that have been deemed to be excludable on this basis are: employee health benefits, general compensation issues not focused on senior executives, management of the workplace, employee supervision, labor-management relations, employee hiring and firing, conditions of employment and employee training and motivation.

> Notwithstanding the general view that employment matters concerning the workforce of the company are excludable as matters involving the conduct of day-to-day business, exceptions have been made in some cases where a proponent based an employment-related proposal on "social policy" concerns. In recent years, however, the line between includable and excludable employment-related proposals based on social policy considerations has become increasingly difficult to draw. The distinctions recognized by the staff are characterized by many as tenuous, without substance and effectively nullifying the application of the ordinary business exclusion to employment related proposals.

> The Division has reconsidered the application of Rule 14a–8[i](7) to employment-related proposals in light of these concerns and the staff's experience with these proposals in recent years. As a result, the Division has determined that the fact that a shareholder proposal concerning a company's employment policies and practices for the general workforce is tied to a social issue will no longer be viewed as removing the proposal from the realm of ordinary business operations of the registrant. Rather, determinations with respect to any such proposals are properly governed by the employment-based nature of the proposal.

> * * * [The Division distinguished these "social policy proposals" from proposals relating to the compensation of senior executives and directors, asserting that the latter were inherently outside the scope of "ordinary business of the corporation" as they involved the relationships between shareholders and management.]

Efforts by labor unions to enjoin the implementation of this revised policy relating to employment-related proposals failed essentially on

---

[w]   A "no action" letter is a letter sent by SEC staff to a corporation stating that "it will not recommend any enforcement action to the Commission if the proposal is omitted." The legal status of such a letter is discussed in the following text.

procedural grounds. In 1997, the SEC proposed to reverse its *Cracker Barrel* interpretation:

> The Cracker Barrel interpretation has been controversial since it was announced. While the reasons for adopting the Cracker Barrel interpretation continue to have some validity, as well as significant support in the corporate community,[72] we believe that reversal of the position is warranted in light of the broader package of reforms proposed today. Reversal will require companies to include proposals in their proxy materials that some shareholders believe are important to companies and fellow shareholders. In place of the 1992 position, the Division would return to its approach to such proposals prevailing before it adopted the position. That is, employment-related proposals focusing on significant social policy issues could not automatically be excluded under the "ordinary business" exclusion.
>
> Under this proposal, the "bright line" approach for employment-related proposals established by the Cracker Barrel position would be replaced by the case-by-case analysis that prevailed previously. Return to a case-by-case approach should redress the concerns of shareholders interested in submitting for a vote by fellow shareholders employment-related proposals raising significant social issues. While this would be a change in the Commission's interpretation of the rule, we nonetheless request your comments on whether we should reverse the Cracker Barrel interpretation. * * *

Proposed Rule: Amendments to Rules on Shareholder Proposals, SEC Rel. No. 34–39093 (September 25, 1997), at 9–10. The reversal was approved in Exchange Act Rel. 40018 (May 21, 1998). See Patricia R. Uhlenbrock, Note, Roll Out the Barrel: The SEC Reverses Its Stance on Employment-Related Shareholder Proposals Under Rule 14a–8—Again, 25 Del.J.Corp.L. 277, 308 (2000) (arguing that the 1998 reversal has not yet provided a meaningful standard for guidance in an important area of the law and that state law should step in to fill the void).

TIAA-CREF, a large institutional investor which manages pension funds for teachers and college professors, decided to use Rule 14a–8 to try to control what it regarded as the excessive use of stock options as compensation for corporate employees. On October 26, 2001, TIAA-CREF proposed that Synopsys, Inc. include in its proxy solicitation the following proposal:

> RESOLVED: That the shareholders request that the Board of Directors submit all equity compensation plans (other than those that would not result in material potential dilution) to shareholders for approval.

---

[72] In response to the Questionnaire, 91% of companies favored excluding employment-related shareholder proposals raising significant social policy issues under the Cracker Barrel interpretation. Eighty-six percent of shareholders thought such proposals should be included.

The Staff of the Securities and Exchange Commission, Division of Corporate Finance, ruled initially that Synopsys could properly exclude the TIAA-CREF proposal on the grounds that it concerned "ordinary business operations." The Staff based its decision on the fact that the Synopsys stock option plan covered not only senior executive officers and directors, but the entire workforce of the company, and thus related to general employee compensation matters, excludable under SEC Rule 14a–8(i)(7).

TIAA-CREF appealed within the SEC, arguing that their proposal raised fundamental issues of substantial importance, and not ordinary business issues. TIAA-CREF argued that the explosion in the use of stock options had dramatically transformed the compensation structure of U.S. corporations and the relationship between equity owners and employees. At many companies, the value of options granted to executives and employees constituted a significant fraction of earnings and revenues thereby causing serious dilution to shareholders.

On July 12, 2002, the SEC's Division of Corporate Finance reversed the earlier decision of its staff, noting that "the public debate regarding shareholder approval of equity compensation plans has become significant in recent months. Consequently, in view of the widespread public debate regarding shareholder approval of equity compensation plans we are modifying our treatment of proposals relating to this topic." From now on, a public company may not rely on the rule's "ordinary business" provision to omit the following proposals from its proxy statement: "any proposal that focuses on equity compensation plans that potentially would result in material dilution to existing shareholders, regardless of who participates in the plan."

RAUCHMAN v. MOBIL CORP.

United States Court of Appeals, Sixth Circuit, 1984.
739 F.2d 205.

Before ENGEL and KEITH, CIRCUIT JUDGES, and WEICK, SENIOR CIRCUIT JUDGE.

ENGEL, CIRCUIT JUDGE.

The principal issue in this appeal is whether defendant Mobil Corporation properly refused to include in its proxy statement a proposal which would amend Mobil's bylaws to prevent a citizen of an OPEC country from sitting on Mobil's board of directors. The plaintiff's claim is premised upon the existence of an implied private cause of action under section 14(a) of the Securities Exchange Act, and upon Rule 14a–8 promulgated thereunder. Rauchman asserts that Mobil was required to include the proposal in the corporation's proxy statement for the 1982 annual meeting.

Plaintiff in the instant case argues that the directors are acting for reasons unrelated to the financial interest and welfare of the Cubs. However, we are not satisfied that the motives assigned to Philip K. Wrigley, and through him to the other directors, are contrary to the best interests of the corporation and the stockholders. For example, it appears to us that the effect on the surrounding neighborhood might well be considered by a director who was considering the patrons who would or would not attend the games if the park were in a poor neighborhood. Furthermore, the long run interest of the corporation in its property value at Wrigley Field might demand all efforts to keep the neighborhood from deteriorating. By these thoughts we do not mean to say that we have decided that the decision of the directors was a correct one. That is beyond our jurisdiction and ability. We are merely saying that the decision is one properly before directors and the motives alleged in the amended complaint showed no fraud, illegality or conflict of interest in their making of that decision.

While all the courts do not insist that one or more of the three elements must be present for a stockholder's derivative action to lie, nevertheless we feel that unless the conduct of the defendants at least borders on one of the elements, the courts should not interfere. The trial court in the instant case acted properly in dismissing plaintiff's amended complaint.

We feel that plaintiff's amended complaint was also defective in failing to allege damage to the corporation. * * *

There is no allegation that the night games played by the other nineteen teams enhanced their financial position or that the profits, if any, of those teams were directly related to the number of night games scheduled. There is an allegation that the installation of lights and scheduling of night games in Wrigley Field would have resulted in large amounts of additional revenues and incomes from increased attendance and related sources of income. Further, the cost of installation of lights, funds for which are allegedly readily available by financing, would be more than offset and recaptured by increased revenues. However, no allegation is made that there will be a net benefit to the corporation from such action, considering all increased costs.

Plaintiff claims that the losses of defendant corporation are due to poor attendance at home games. However, it appears from the amended complaint, taken as a whole, that factors other than attendance affect the net earnings or losses. For example, in 1962, attendance at home and road games decreased appreciably as compared with 1961, and yet the loss from direct baseball operation and of the whole corporation was considerably less.

The record shows that plaintiff did not feel he could allege that the increased revenues would be sufficient to cure the corporate deficit. The only cost plaintiff was at all concerned with was that of installation of lights. No mention was made of operation and maintenance of the lights or other possible increases in operating costs of night games and we cannot speculate as to what other factors might influence the increase or decrease of profits if the Cubs were to play night home games. * * *

Finally, we do not agree with plaintiff's contention that failure to follow the example of the other major league clubs in scheduling night games constituted negligence. Plaintiff made no allegation that these teams' night schedules were profitable or that the purpose for which night baseball had been undertaken was fulfilled. Furthermore, it cannot be said that directors, even those of corporations that are losing money, must follow the lead of the other corporations in the field. Directors are elected for their business capabilities and judgment and the courts cannot require them to forego their judgment because of the decisions of directors of other companies. Courts may not decide these questions in the absence of a clear showing of dereliction of duty on the part of the specific directors and mere failure to "follow the crowd" is not such a dereliction.

For the foregoing reasons the order of dismissal entered by the trial court is affirmed.

Affirmed.

NOTES

(1) It is easy to say that corporate directors have a fiduciary duty of care. A perennial problem in corporate law has been articulating that duty with a sufficient level of precision to provide an effective guide for directors and for the lawyers who advise them. Consider MBCA § 8.30(a). The language of this section was revised in 1998. Prior to that time, § 8.30(a) read as follows:

(a) A director shall discharge his duties as a director, including his duties as a member of a committee:

(1) in good faith;

(2) with the care an ordinarily prudent person in a like position would exercise under similar circumstances; and

(3) in a manner he reasonably believes to be in the best interests of the corporation.

This simple section was by far the most contentious issue that arose during the 1984 recodification, and at the time was marked for reconsideration. Why was paragraph (a)(2) of old § 8.30 so controversial? Should not directors always act as "ordinarily prudent persons" when making decisions with respect to their corporation? The Official Comment to the present section explains the reason for the change:

The use of the phrase "ordinarily prudent person" in a basic guideline for director conduct, suggesting caution or circumspection vis-à-vis danger or risk, has long been problematic given the fact that risk-taking decisions are central to the directors' role. When coupled with the exercise of "care," the prior text had a familiar resonance long associated with the field of tort law. * * * The further coupling with the verb "shall discharge" added to the inference that former section 8.30(a)'s standard of conduct involved a negligence standard, with resultant confusion.

Clearly, "risk taking is central to the directors' role" when making decisions on behalf of the corporation. What then is wrong with a "negligence standard" or "the ordinarily prudent person" test in this context? Aren't the risks involved in director-made decisions usually different from ordinary negligence? Consider, for example, the question whether an electronics company should invest the bulk of its resources in a novel computer language; that is presumably a high-risk decision that may have either spectacular or disastrous consequences. Can such a decision be judged on an "ordinarily prudent person" standard? On the other hand, don't we also want some degree of preliminary investigation and consideration by directors before the making of such decisions?

(2) Revised MBCA § 8.30(b) requires directors, "when becoming informed in connection with their decision-making function or devoting attention to their oversight function," to exercise the care "that a person in a like position would reasonably believe appropriate under similar circumstances." There are two fundamentally important insights about corporate law packed into this short statutory provision. First, "Section 8.30 sets forth the standards of conduct for directors by focusing on the manner in which directors perform their duties, not the correctness of the decisions made." Id. § 8.30 cmt. Does that make sense? Second, the legal regime that governs directors operates when directors are performing two functions that are separate and distinct from one another. What are the two directorial functions described in MBCA § 8.30(b)? Which of these functions was involved in Shlensky v. Wrigley?

(3) The Official Comment to revised § 8.30(a) states that it "establishes the basic standards of conduct for all directors. Its command is to be understood as peremptory—its obligations are to be observed by every director—and at the core of the subsection's mandate is the requirement that, when performing directors' duties, a director shall act in good faith coupled with conduct reasonably believed to be in the best interests of the corporation. This mandate governs all aspects of directors' duties: the duty of care, the duty to become informed, the duty of inquiry, the duty of informed judgment, the duty of attention, the duty of disclosure, the duty of loyalty, the duty of fair dealing and, finally, the broad concept of fiduciary duty that the courts often use as a frame of reference when evaluating a director's conduct."

(4) Consider also the revised MBCA § 8.31. Should there be a different test for the imposition of liability on directors than for determining whether appropriate care was exercised? The Official Comment to this section describes the relationship between new MBCA §§ 8.30 and 8.31 as follows:

> Section 8.30(b)'s standard of conduct is frequently referred to as a director's duty of care. * * * Although some decisions turn out to be unwise or the result of a mistake of judgment, it is not reasonable to reexamine an unsuccessful decision with the benefit of hindsight. * * * Therefore, as a general rule, a director is not exposed to personal liability for injury or damage caused by an unwise decision. * * * [A] director[, however,] can be held liable for misfeasance or nonfeasance in performing the duties of a director.

(5) The American Law Institute, Principles of Corporate Governance: Analysis and Recommendations, § 4.01:

> (a) A director or officer has a duty to the corporation to perform the director's or officer's functions in good faith, in a manner that he or she reasonably believes to be in the best interests of the corporation, and with the care that an ordinarily prudent person would reasonably be expected to exercise in a like position and under similar circumstances. This Subsection (a) is subject to the provisions of Subsection (c) (the business judgment rule) where applicable. * * *

> (c) A director or officer who makes a business judgment in good faith fulfills the duty under this Section if the director or officer:

> > (1) is not interested in the subject of the business judgment;

> > (2) is informed with respect to the subject of the business judgment to the extent the director or officer reasonably believes to be appropriate under the circumstances; and

> > (3) rationally believes that the business judgment is in the best interests of the corporation.

Does this reach essentially the same result as the revised MBCA provisions discussed in the previous note?

(6) Section 4.01(d) of the Principles of Corporate Governance reads as follows:

> (d) A person challenging the conduct of a director or officer under this Section has the burden of proving a breach of the duty of care, including the inapplicability of the provisions as to the fulfillment of duty under Subsection (b) or (c), and, in a damage action, the burden of proving that the breach was the legal cause of damage suffered by the corporation.

Section 7.18 of the Principles states that "legal cause" of loss exists where the plaintiff proves "that (i) satisfaction of the applicable standard would have been a substantial factor in averting the loss, and (ii) the likelihood of injury would have been foreseeable to an ordinarily prudent person in like position to that of the defendant and in similar circumstances. It is not a defense to liability in such cases that damage to the corporation would not have resulted but for the acts or omissions of other individuals."

(7) The justification for the "business judgment rule" is set forth by Charles Hansen, The ALI Corporate Governance Project: Of the Duty of Due Care and the Business Judgment Rule, 41 Bus.Law. 1237, 1238–42, 1247 (1986):

> The foundation stone of the American law of corporate governance is currently enunciated in the holdings (not the dicta) of the leading corporate law states: there must be a minimum of interference by the courts in internal corporate affairs. Except in the egregious case of bad judgment or when there is evidence of bad faith, courts have made no attempt to second-guess directors on the substantive soundness of decisions reached. * * *

> * * * Under [the business judgment rule], as long as a director acts in good faith and with due care in the process sense, the director will not be found liable even though the decision itself was not that of the "ordinarily prudent person." The process due care test will be met if the director takes appropriate steps to become informed. Thus, the description of the duty in section 4.01(a) [of the ALI Corporate Governance Project] as "the care that an ordinarily prudent person would reasonably be expected to exercise in a like position and under similar circumstances" is misleading.

> * * * *Cramer v. General Telephone & Electronics Corp.,* [582 F.2d 259, 274 (3d Cir.1978)], for example, states the appropriate principle of law: "Absent bad faith or some other corrupt motive, directors are normally not liable to the corporation for mistakes of judgment. * * *"

> * * * [U]nder corporate law, the standard of due care is met if two tests are satisfied: (i) due care must be used in "ascertaining relevant facts and law before making the decision," and (ii) the decision must be made after reasonable deliberation. * * * Thus, the due care standard in corporate law is applied to the decision-making process and not to its result. * * *

> The one possible exception to applying the standard of due care to process, rather than to content or result, concerns egregious conduct. * * *

SMITH V. VAN GORKOM

Supreme Court of Delaware, 1985.
488 A.2d 858.

Before HERRMANN, C.J., and McNEILLY, HORSEY, MOORE and CHRISTIE, JJ., constituting the Court en banc.

HORSEY, JUSTICE (for the majority):

This appeal from the Court of Chancery involves a class action brought by shareholders of the defendant Trans Union Corporation ("Trans Union" or "the Company"), originally seeking rescission of a cash-out merger of Trans Union into the defendant New T Company ("New T"), a wholly-owned subsidiary of the defendant, Marmon Group, Inc. ("Marmon"). Alternate relief in the form of damages is sought against the defendant members of the Board of Directors of Trans Union * * *.

Following trial, the former Chancellor granted judgment for the defendant directors by unreported letter opinion dated July 6, 1982. Judgment was based on [the finding] that the Board of Directors had acted in an informed manner so as to be entitled to protection of the business judgment rule in approving the cash-out merger * * *. The plaintiffs appeal.

Speaking for the majority of the Court, we conclude that [the ruling] of the Court of Chancery [is] clearly erroneous. Therefore, we reverse and direct that judgment be entered in favor of the plaintiffs and against the defendant directors for the fair value of the plaintiffs' stockholdings in Trans Union, in accordance with Weinberger v. UOP, Inc., Del.Supr., 457 A.2d 701 (1983).[3]

We hold * * * that the Board's decision, reached September 20, 1980, to approve the proposed cash-out merger was not the product of an informed business judgment * * *.

I.

The nature of this case requires a detailed factual statement. The following facts are essentially uncontradicted:

–A–

Trans Union was a publicly-traded, diversified holding company, the principal earnings of which were generated by its railcar leasing business. During the period here involved, the Company had a cash flow of hundreds of millions of dollars annually. However, the Company had difficulty in generating sufficient taxable income to offset increasingly

---

[3] It has been stipulated that plaintiffs sue on behalf of a class consisting of 10,537 shareholders (out of a total of 12,844) and that the class owned 12,734,404 out of 13,357,758 shares of Trans Union outstanding.

large investment tax credits (ITCs).[a] Accelerated depreciation deductions had decreased available taxable income against which to offset accumulating ITCs. The Company took these deductions, despite their effect on usable ITCs, because the rental price in the railcar leasing market had already impounded the purported tax savings.

In the late 1970's, together with other capital-intensive firms, Trans Union lobbied in Congress to have ITCs refundable in cash to firms which could not fully utilize the credit. During the summer of 1980, defendant Jerome W. Van Gorkom, Trans Union's Chairman and Chief Executive Officer, testified and lobbied in Congress for refundability of ITCs and against further accelerated depreciation. By the end of August, Van Gorkom was convinced that Congress would neither accept the refundability concept nor curtail further accelerated depreciation.

Beginning in the late 1960's, and continuing through the 1970's, Trans Union pursued a program of acquiring small companies in order to increase available taxable income. In July 1980, Trans Union Management prepared the annual revision of the Company's Five Year Forecast. This report was presented to the Board of Directors at its July, 1980 meeting. The report projected an annual income growth of about 20%. The report also concluded that Trans Union would have about $195 million in spare cash between 1980 and 1985, "with the surplus growing rapidly from 1982 onward." The report referred to the ITC situation as a "nagging problem" and, given that problem, the leasing company "would still appear to be constrained to a tax breakeven." The report then listed four alternative uses of the projected 1982–1985 equity surplus: (1) stock repurchase; (2) dividend increases; (3) a major acquisition program; and (4) combinations of the above. The sale of Trans Union was not among the alternatives. The report emphasized that, despite the overall surplus, the operation of the Company would consume all available equity for the next several years, and concluded: "As a result, we have sufficient time to fully develop our course of action."

–B–

On August 27, 1980, Van Gorkom met with Senior Management of Trans Union. Van Gorkom reported on his lobbying efforts in Washington and his desire to find a solution to the tax credit problem more permanent than a continued program of acquisitions. Various alternatives were suggested and discussed preliminarily, including the sale of Trans Union to a company with a large amount of taxable income.

---

[a] Investment tax credits are subsidies (since repealed) equal to a portion of the cost of depreciable personal property designed to induce taxpayers to invest in that property, thereby stimulating business demand for capital goods. See generally Allaire Urban Karzon and Charles H. Coffin, 1982 Extension of the At-Risk Concept to the Investment Tax Credit: A Shotgun Approach to the Tax Shelter Problem, 1982 Duke L.J. 847.

Donald Romans, Chief Financial Officer of Trans Union, stated that his department had done a "very brief bit of work on the possibility of a leveraged buy-out."[b] This work had been prompted by a media article which Romans had seen regarding a leveraged buy-out by management. The work consisted of a "preliminary study" of the cash which could be generated by the Company if it participated in a leveraged buy-out. As Romans stated, this analysis "was very first and rough cut at seeing whether a cash flow would support what might be considered a high price for this type of transaction."

On September 5, at another Senior Management meeting which Van Gorkom attended, Romans again brought up the idea of a leveraged buy-out as a "possible strategic alternative" to the Company's acquisition program. Romans and Bruce S. Chelberg, President and Chief Operating Officer of Trans Union, had been working on the matter in preparation for the meeting. According to Romans: They did not "come up" with a price for the Company. They merely "ran the numbers" at $50 a share and at $60 a share with the "rough form" of their cash figures at the time. Their "figures indicated that $50 would be very easy to do but $60 would be very difficult to do under those figures." This work did not purport to establish a fair price for either the Company or 100% of the stock. It was intended to determine the cash flow needed to service the debt that would "probably" be incurred in a leveraged buyout, based on "rough calculations" without "any benefit of experts to identify what the limits were to that, and so forth." These computations were not considered extensive and no conclusion was reached.

At this meeting, Van Gorkom stated that he would be willing to take $55 per share for his own 75,000 shares. He vetoed the suggestion of a leveraged buy-out by Management, however, as involving a potential conflict of interest for Management. Van Gorkom, a certified public accountant and lawyer, had been an officer of Trans Union for 24 years, its Chief Executive Officer for more than 17 years, and Chairman of its Board for 2 years. It is noteworthy in this connection that he was then approaching 65 years of age and mandatory retirement.

For several days following the September 5 meeting, Van Gorkom pondered the idea of a sale. He had participated in many acquisitions as a manager and director of Trans Union and as a director of other companies. He was familiar with acquisition procedures, valuation methods, and negotiations; and he privately considered the pros and cons of whether Trans Union should seek a privately or publicly-held purchaser.

---

[b] A "leveraged buy-out" of a corporation is a sale of the corporation in which at least part of the purchase price is obtained through debt assumed by the corporation.

Van Gorkom decided to meet with Jay A. Pritzker, a well-known corporate takeover specialist and a social acquaintance. However, rather than approaching Pritzker simply to determine his interest in acquiring Trans Union, Van Gorkom assembled a proposed per share price for sale of the Company and a financing structure by which to accomplish the sale. Van Gorkom did so without consulting either his Board or any members of Senior Management except one: Carl Peterson, Trans Union's Controller. Telling Peterson that he wanted no other person on his staff to know what he was doing, but without telling him why, Van Gorkom directed Peterson to calculate the feasibility of a leveraged buy-out at an assumed price per share of $55. Apart from the Company's historic stock market price,[5] and Van Gorkom's long association with Trans Union, the record is devoid of any competent evidence that $55 represented the per share intrinsic value of the Company.

Having thus chosen the $55 figure, based solely on the availability of a leveraged buy-out, Van Gorkom multiplied the price per share by the number of shares outstanding to reach a total value of the Company of $690 million. Van Gorkom told Peterson to use this $690 million figure and to assume a $200 million equity contribution by the buyer. Based on these assumptions, Van Gorkom directed Peterson to determine whether the debt portion of the purchase price could be paid off in five years or less if financed by Trans Union's cash flow as projected in the Five Year Forecast, and by the sale of certain weaker divisions identified in a study done for Trans Union by the Boston Consulting Group ("BCG study"). Peterson reported that, of the purchase price, approximately $50–80 million would remain outstanding after five years. Van Gorkom was disappointed, but decided to meet with Pritzker nevertheless.

Van Gorkom arranged a meeting with Pritzker at the latter's home on Saturday, September 13, 1980. Van Gorkom prefaced his presentation by stating to Pritzker: "Now as far as you are concerned, I can, I think, show how you can pay a substantial premium over the present stock price and pay off most of the loan in the first five years. * * * If you could pay $55 for this Company, here is a way in which I think it can be financed."

Van Gorkom then reviewed with Pritzker his calculations based upon his proposed price of $55 per share. Although Pritzker mentioned $50 as a more attractive figure, no other price was mentioned. However, Van Gorkom stated that to be sure that $55 was the best price obtainable, Trans Union should be free to accept any better offer. Pritzker demurred, stating that his organization would serve as a "stalking horse" for an "auction contest" only if Trans Union would permit Pritzker to buy

---

[5]   The common stock of Trans Union was traded on the New York Stock Exchange. Over the five year period from 1975 through 1979, Trans Union's stock had traded within a range of a high of $39 1/2 and a low of $24 1/4. Its high and low range for 1980 through September 19 (the last trading day before announcement of the merger) was $38 1/4–$29 1/2.

1,750,000 shares of Trans Union stock at market price which Pritzker could then sell to any higher bidder. After further discussion on this point, Pritzker told Van Gorkom that he would give him a more definite reaction soon.

On Monday, September 15, Pritzker advised Van Gorkom that he was interested in the $55 cash-out merger proposal and requested more information on Trans Union. Van Gorkom agreed to meet privately with Pritzker, accompanied by Peterson, Chelberg, and Michael Carpenter, Trans Union's consultant from the Boston Consulting Group. The meetings took place on September 16 and 17. Van Gorkom was "astounded that events were moving with such amazing rapidity."

On Thursday, September 18, Van Gorkom met again with Pritzker. At that time, Van Gorkom knew that Pritzker intended to make a cash-out merger offer at Van Gorkom's proposed $55 per share. Pritzker instructed his attorney, a merger and acquisition specialist, to begin drafting merger documents. There was no further discussion of the $55 price. However, the number of shares of Trans Union's treasury stock to be offered to Pritzker was negotiated down to one million shares; the price was set at $38—75 cents above the per share price at the close of the market on September 19. At this point, Pritzker insisted that the Trans Union Board act on his merger proposal within the next three days, stating to Van Gorkom: "We have to have a decision by no later than Sunday [evening, September 21] before the opening of the English stock exchange on Monday morning." Pritzker's lawyer was then instructed to draft the merger documents, to be reviewed by Van Gorkom's lawyer, "sometimes with discussion and sometimes not, in the haste to get it finished."

On Friday, September 19, Van Gorkom, Chelberg, and Pritzker consulted with Trans Union's lead bank regarding the financing of Pritzker's purchase of Trans Union. The bank indicated that it could form a syndicate of banks that would finance the transaction. On the same day, Van Gorkom retained James Brennan, Esquire, to advise Trans Union on the legal aspects of the merger. Van Gorkom did not consult with William Browder, a Vice-President and director of Trans Union and former head of its legal department, or with William Moore, then the head of Trans Union's legal staff.

On Friday, September 19, Van Gorkom called a special meeting of the Trans Union Board for noon the following day. He also called a meeting of the Company's Senior Management to convene at 11:00 a.m., prior to the meeting of the Board. No one, except Chelberg and Peterson, was told the purpose of the meetings. Van Gorkom did not invite Trans Union's investment banker, Salomon Brothers or its Chicago-based partner, to attend.

Of those present at the Senior Management meeting on September 20, only Chelberg and Peterson had prior knowledge of Pritzker's offer. Van Gorkom disclosed the offer and described its terms, but he furnished no copies of the proposed Merger Agreement. Romans announced that his department had done a second study which showed that, for a leveraged buy-out, the price range for Trans Union stock was between $55 and $65 per share. Van Gorkom neither saw the study nor asked Romans to make it available for the Board meeting.

Senior Management's reaction to the Pritzker proposal was completely negative. No member of Management, except Chelberg and Peterson, supported the proposal. Romans objected to the price as being too low;[6] he was critical of the timing and suggested that consideration should be given to the adverse tax consequences of an all-cash deal for low-basis shareholders; and he took the position that the agreement to sell Pritzker one million newly-issued shares at market price would inhibit other offers, as would the prohibitions against soliciting bids and furnishing inside information to other bidders. Romans argued that the Pritzker proposal was a "lock up" and amounted to "an agreed merger as opposed to an offer." Nevertheless, Van Gorkom proceeded to the Board meeting as scheduled without further delay.

Ten directors served on the Trans Union Board, five inside (defendants Bonser, O'Boyle, Browder, Chelberg, and Van Gorkom) and five outside (defendants Wallis, Johnson, Lanterman, Morgan and Reneker). All directors were present at the meeting, except O'Boyle who was ill. Of the outside directors, four were corporate chief executive officers and one was the former Dean of the University of Chicago Business School. None was an investment banker or trained financial analyst. All members of the Board were well informed about the Company and its operations as a going concern. They were familiar with the current financial condition of the Company, as well as operating and earnings projections reported in the recent Five Year Forecast. The Board generally received regular and detailed reports and was kept abreast of the accumulated investment tax credit and accelerated depreciation problem.

Van Gorkom began the Special Meeting of the Board with a twenty-minute oral presentation. Copies of the proposed Merger Agreement were delivered too late for study before or during the meeting.[7] He reviewed

---

[6] Van Gorkom asked Romans to express his opinion as to the $55 price. Romans stated that he "thought the price was too low in relation to what he could derive for the company in a cash sale, particularly one which enabled us to realize the values of certain subsidiaries and independent entities."

[7] The record is not clear as to the terms of the Merger Agreement. The Agreement, as originally presented to the Board on September 20, was never produced by defendants despite demands by the plaintiffs. Nor is it clear that the directors were given an opportunity to study

the Company's ITC and depreciation problems and the efforts theretofore made to solve them. He discussed his initial meeting with Pritzker and his motivation in arranging that meeting. Van Gorkom did not disclose to the Board, however, the methodology by which he alone had arrived at the $55 figure, or the fact that he first proposed the $55 price in his negotiations with Pritzker.

Van Gorkom outlined the terms of the Pritzker offer as follows: Pritzker would pay $55 in cash for all outstanding shares of Trans Union stock upon completion of which Trans Union would be merged into New T Company, a subsidiary wholly-owned by Pritzker and formed to implement the merger; for a period of 90 days, Trans Union could receive, but could not actively solicit, competing offers; the offer had to be acted on by the next evening, Sunday, September 21; Trans Union could only furnish to competing bidders published information, and not proprietary information; the offer was subject to Pritzker obtaining the necessary financing by October 10, 1980; if the financing contingency were met or waived by Pritzker, Trans Union was required to sell to Pritzker one million newly-issued shares of Trans Union at $38 per share.

Van Gorkom took the position that putting Trans Union "up for auction" through a 90-day market test would validate a decision by the Board that $55 was a fair price. He told the Board that the "free market will have an opportunity to judge whether $55 is a fair price." Van Gorkom framed the decision before the Board not as whether $55 per share was the highest price that could be obtained, but as whether the $55 price was a fair price that the stockholders should be given the opportunity to accept or reject.[8]

Attorney Brennan advised the members of the Board that they might be sued if they failed to accept the offer and that a fairness opinion was not required as a matter of law.

Romans attended the meeting as chief financial officer of the Company. He told the Board that he had not been involved in the negotiations with Pritzker and knew nothing about the merger proposal until the morning of the meeting; that his studies did not indicate either a fair price for the stock or a valuation of the Company; that he did not see his role as directly addressing the fairness issue; and that he and his people "were trying to search for ways to justify a price in connection with such a [leveraged buy-out] transaction, rather than to say what the shares are worth." Romans testified:

---

the Merger Agreement before voting on it. All that can be said is that Brennan had the Agreement before him during the meeting.

[8]   In Van Gorkom's words: The "real decision" is whether to "let the stockholders decide it" which is "all you are being asked to decide today."

I told the Board that the study ran the numbers at 50 and 60, and then the subsequent study at 55 and 65, and that was not the same thing as saying that I have a valuation of the company at X dollars. But it was a way—a first step towards reaching that conclusion.

Romans told the Board that, in his opinion, $55 was "in the range of a fair price," but "at the beginning of the range."

Chelberg, Trans Union's President, supported Van Gorkom's presentation and representations. He testified that he "participated to make sure that the Board members collectively were clear on the details of the agreement or offer from Pritzker;" that he "participated in the discussion with Mr. Brennan, inquiring of him about the necessity for valuation opinions in spite of the way in which this particular offer was couched;" and that he was otherwise actively involved in supporting the positions being taken by Van Gorkom before the Board about "the necessity to act immediately on this offer," and about "the adequacy of the $55 and the question of how that would be tested."

The Board meeting of September 20 lasted about two hours. Based solely upon Van Gorkom's oral presentation, Chelberg's supporting representations, Romans' oral statement, Brennan's legal advice, and their knowledge of the market history of the Company's stock,[9] the directors approved the proposed Merger Agreement. * * *

The Merger Agreement was executed by Van Gorkom during the evening of September 20 at a formal social event that he hosted for the opening of the Chicago Lyric Opera. Neither he nor any other director read the agreement prior to its signing and delivery to Pritzker. * * *

[Following the approval of the Pritzker proposal, Trans Union retained Salomon Brothers to actively seek other possible offers. This search produced two other possible purchasers, one at $60 per share and the other at $2 to $5 above the $55 price. However, one potential bidder withdrew when Pritzker refused to rescind its merger agreement with Trans Union and the other withdrew when an executive in an important Trans Union subsidiary declined to join the buying group. Van Gorkom made no effort to assist either of these potential offerors and may have affirmatively discouraged them.]

On December 19, this litigation was commenced and, within four weeks, the plaintiffs had deposed eight of the ten directors of Trans

---

[9]   The Trial Court stated the premium relationship of the $55 price to the market history of the Company's stock as follows:

* * * [T]he merger price offered to the stockholders of Trans Union represented a premium of 62% over the average of the high and low prices at which Trans Union stock had traded in 1980, a premium of 48% over the last closing price, and a premium of 39% over the highest price at which the stock of Trans Union had traded any time during the prior six years.

Union, including Van Gorkom, Chelberg and Romans, its Chief Financial Officer. On January 21, Management's Proxy Statement for the February 10 shareholder meeting was mailed to Trans Union's stockholders. On January 26, Trans Union's Board met and, after a lengthy meeting, voted to proceed with the Pritzker merger. The Board also approved for mailing, "on or about January 27," a Supplement to its Proxy Statement. The Supplement purportedly set forth all information relevant to the Pritzker Merger Agreement, which had not been divulged in the first Proxy Statement. * * *

On February 10, the stockholders of Trans Union approved the Pritzker merger proposal. Of the outstanding shares, 69.9% were voted in favor of the merger; 7.25% were voted against the merger; and 22.85% were not voted.

II.

We turn to the issue of the application of the business judgment rule to the September 20 meeting of the Board.

The Court of Chancery concluded from the evidence that the Board of Directors' approval of the Pritzker merger proposal fell within the protection of the business judgment rule. The Court found that the Board had given sufficient time and attention to the transaction, since the directors had considered the Pritzker proposal on three different occasions, on September 20, and on October 8, 1980 and finally on January 26, 1981. On that basis, the Court reasoned that the Board had acquired, over the four-month period, sufficient information to reach an informed business judgment on the cash-out merger proposal. The Court ruled:

> * * * that given the market value of Trans Union's stock, the business acumen of the members of the board of Trans Union, the substantial premium over market offered by the Pritzkers and the ultimate effect on the merger price provided by the prospect of other bids for the stock in question, that the board of directors of Trans Union did not act recklessly or improvidently in determining on a course of action which they believed to be in the best interest of the stockholders of Trans Union. * * *

* * * [W]e conclude that the Court's ultimate finding that the Board's conduct was not "reckless or imprudent" is contrary to the record and not the product of a logical and deductive reasoning process.

* * * [The Court reviews the Delaware law relating to the duty of care and the business judgment rule and concludes that "the proper standard for determining whether a business judgment is an informed one in Delaware is predicated upon concepts of gross negligence."]

III.

* * * The issue of whether the directors reached an informed decision to "sell" the Company on September 20, 1980 must be determined only upon the basis of the information then reasonably available to the directors and relevant to their decision to accept the Pritzker merger proposal. This is not to say that the directors were precluded from altering their original plan of action, had they done so in an informed manner. What we do say is that the question of whether the directors reached an informed business judgment in agreeing to sell the Company, pursuant to the terms of the September 20 Agreement presents, in reality, two questions: (A) whether the directors reached an informed business judgment on September 20, 1980; and (B) if they did not, whether the directors' actions taken subsequent to September 20 were adequate to cure any infirmity in their action taken on September 20. We first consider the directors' September 20 action in terms of their reaching an informed business judgment.

–A–

On the record before us, we must conclude that the Board of Directors did not reach an informed business judgment on September 20, 1980 in voting to "sell" the Company for $55 per share pursuant to the Pritzker cash-out merger proposal. * * * [The Court stated that a simple comparison of the current market price of Trans Union with the $55 offer was not an informed business judgment because there had been no study of the "intrinsic value" of Trans Union as a going concern, no valuation study, and no attempt to document the $55 price as a measure of the fair value of Trans Union as a going concern. The Court specifically criticized the failure of directors to request a valuation based on the cash flow of Trans Union.]

We do not imply that an outside valuation study is essential to support an informed business judgment; nor do we state that fairness opinions by independent investment bankers are required as a matter of law. Often insiders familiar with the business of a going concern are in a better position than are outsiders to gather relevant information; and under appropriate circumstances, such directors may be fully protected in relying in good faith upon the valuation reports of their management. See 8 Del.C. § 141(e).

Here, the record establishes that the Board did not request its Chief Financial Officer, Romans, to make any valuation study or review of the proposal to determine the adequacy of $55 per share for sale of the Company. On the record before us: The Board rested on Romans' elicited response that the $55 figure was within a "fair price range" within the context of a leveraged buy-out. No director sought any further information from Romans. No director asked him why he put $55 at the bottom of his range. No director asked Romans for any details as to his study, the reason why it had been undertaken or its depth. No director asked to see the study; and no director asked Romans whether Trans Union's finance department could do a fairness study within the remaining 36-hour period available under the Pritzker offer. * * *

The record also establishes that the Board accepted without scrutiny Van Gorkom's representation as to the fairness of the $55 price per share for sale of the Company—a subject that the Board had never previously considered. The Board thereby failed to discover that Van Gorkom had suggested the $55 price to Pritzker and, most crucially, that Van Gorkom had arrived at the $55 figure based on calculations designed solely to determine the feasibility of a leveraged buy-out.[19] No questions were raised either as to the tax implications of a cash-out merger or how the price for the one million share option granted Pritzker was calculated.

We do not say that the Board of Directors was not entitled to give some credence to Van Gorkom's representation that $55 was an adequate or fair price. Under § 141(e), the directors were entitled to rely upon their chairman's opinion of value and adequacy, provided that such opinion was reached on a sound basis. Here, the issue is whether the directors informed themselves as to all information that was reasonably available to them. Had they done so, they would have learned of the source and derivation of the $55 price and could not reasonably have relied thereupon in good faith. * * *

Thus, the record compels the conclusion that on September 20 the Board lacked valuation information adequate to reach an informed business judgment as to the fairness of $55 per share for sale of the Company. * * *

(2)

* * * [The court concludes in this portion of the opinion that there was not a "post-September 20 market test" of the $55 price sufficient to confirm the reasonableness of the board's decision.]

(3)

* * * [In this portion of the opinion, the court rejects the argument that the Board's "collective experience and sophistication" was a sufficient

---

[19] As of September 20 the directors did not know: that Van Gorkom had arrived at the $55 figure alone, and subjectively, as the figure to be used by Controller Peterson in creating a feasible structure for a leveraged buy-out by a prospective purchaser; that Van Gorkom had not sought advice, information or assistance from either inside or outside Trans Union directors as to the value of the Company as an entity or the fair price per share for 100% of its stock; that Van Gorkom had not consulted with the Company's investment bankers or other financial analysts; that Van Gorkom had not consulted with or confided in any officer or director of the Company except Chelberg; and that Van Gorkom had deliberately chosen to ignore the advice and opinion of the members of his Senior Management group regarding the adequacy of the $55 price.

basis for finding that it reached its September 20 decision with informed, reasonable deliberation.][21]

(4)

Part of the defense is based on a claim that the directors relied on legal advice rendered at the September 20 meeting by James Brennan, Esquire, who was present at Van Gorkom's request. Unfortunately, Brennan did not appear and testify at trial even though his firm participated in the defense of this action. There is no contemporaneous evidence of the advice given by Brennan on September 20, only the later deposition and trial testimony of certain directors as to their recollections or understanding of what was said at the meeting. Since counsel did not testify, and the advice attributed to Brennan is hearsay received by the Trial Court over the plaintiffs' objections, we consider it only in the context of the directors' present claims. In fairness to counsel, we make no findings that the advice attributed to him was in fact given. We focus solely on the efficacy of the defendants' claims, made months and years later, in an effort to extricate themselves from liability.

Several defendants testified that Brennan advised them that Delaware law did not require a fairness opinion or an outside valuation of the Company before the Board could act on the Pritzker proposal. If given, the advice was correct. However, that did not end the matter. Unless the directors had before them adequate information regarding the intrinsic value of the Company, upon which a proper exercise of business judgment could be made, mere advice of this type is meaningless; and, given this record of the defendants' failures, it constitutes no defense here.[22] * * *

We conclude that Trans Union's Board was grossly negligent in that it failed to act with informed reasonable deliberation in agreeing to the Pritzker merger proposal on September 20; and we further conclude that the Trial Court erred as a matter of law in failing to address that question before determining whether the directors' later conduct was sufficient to cure its initial error. * * *

---

[21] Trans Union's five "inside" directors had backgrounds in law and accounting, 116 years of collective employment by the Company and 68 years of combined experience on its Board. Trans Union's five "outside" directors included four chief executives of major corporations and an economist who was a former dean of a major school of business and chancellor of a university. The "outside" directors had 78 years of combined experience as chief executive officers of major corporations and 50 years of cumulative experience as directors of Trans Union. Thus, defendants argue that the Board was eminently qualified to reach an informed judgment on the proposed "sale" of Trans Union notwithstanding their lack of any advance notice of the proposal, the shortness of their deliberation, and their determination not to consult with their investment banker or to obtain a fairness opinion.

[22] Nonetheless, we are satisfied that in an appropriate factual context a proper exercise of business judgment may include, as one of its aspects, reasonable reliance upon the advice of counsel. This is wholly outside the statutory protections of 8 Del.C. § 141(e) involving reliance upon reports of officers, certain experts and books and records of the company.

IV.

Whether the directors of Trans Union should be treated as one or individually in terms of invoking the protection of the business judgment rule and the applicability of 8 Del.C. § 141(c) are questions which were not originally addressed by the parties in their briefing of this case. This resulted in a supplemental briefing and a second rehearing en banc on two basic questions: (a) whether one or more of the directors were deprived of the protection of the business judgment rule by evidence of an absence of good faith; and (b) whether one or more of the outside directors were entitled to invoke the protection of 8 Del.C. § 141(e) by evidence of a reasonable, good faith reliance on "reports," including legal advice, rendered the Board by certain inside directors and the Board's special counsel, Brennan.

The parties' response, including reargument, has led the majority of the Court to conclude: (1) that since all of the defendant directors, outside as well as inside, take a unified position, we are required to treat all of the directors as one as to whether they are entitled to the protection of the business judgment rule; and (2) that considerations of good faith, including the presumption that the directors acted in good faith, are irrelevant in determining the threshold issue of whether the directors as a Board exercised an informed business judgment. For the same reason, we must reject defense counsel's *ad hominem* argument for affirmance: that reversal may result in a multi-million dollar class award against the defendants for having made an allegedly uninformed business judgment in a transaction not involving any personal gain, self-dealing or claim of bad faith.[c]

In their brief, the defendants similarly mistake the business judgment rule's application to this case by erroneously invoking presumptions of good faith and "wide discretion":

> This is a case in which plaintiff challenged the exercise of business judgment by an independent Board of Directors. There were no allegations and no proof of fraud, bad faith, or self-dealing by the directors. * * *

> The business judgment rule, which was properly applied by the Chancellor, allows directors wide discretion in the matter of valuation and affords room for honest differences of opinion. In

---

[c]   In the petition for rehearing that was ultimately denied in this case, the Court quotes the beginning of the oral argument made by counsel for the individual defendants as follows:

COUNSEL: I'll make the argument on behalf of the nine individual defendants against whom the plaintiffs seek more than $100,000,000 in damages. That is the ultimate issue in this case, whether or not nine honest, experienced businessmen should be subject to damages in a case where—

At this point counsel was interrupted by the Court with a question and never returned to the beginning point.

order to prevail, plaintiffs had the heavy burden of proving that the merger price was so grossly inadequate as to display itself as a badge of fraud. That is a burden which plaintiffs have not met.

However, plaintiffs have not claimed, nor did the Trial Court decide, that $55 was a grossly inadequate price per share for sale of the Company. That being so, the presumption that a board's judgment as to adequacy of price represents an honest exercise of business judgment (absent proof that the sale price was grossly inadequate) is irrelevant to the threshold question of whether an informed judgment was reached.

* * * We hold, therefore, that the Trial Court committed reversible error in applying the business judgment rule in favor of the director defendants in this case.

On remand, the Court of Chancery shall conduct an evidentiary hearing to determine the fair value of the shares represented by the plaintiffs' class, based on the intrinsic value of Trans Union on September 20, 1980. * * * Thereafter, an award of damages may be entered to the extent that the fair value of Trans Union exceeds $55 per share. * * *

REVERSED and REMANDED for proceedings consistent herewith.

McNEILLY, JUSTICE, dissenting:

The majority opinion reads like an advocate's closing address to a hostile jury. And I say that not lightly. Throughout the opinion great emphasis is directed only to the negative, with nothing more than lip service granted the positive aspects of this case. In my opinion Chancellor Marvel (retired) should have been affirmed. The Chancellor's opinion was the product of well reasoned conclusions, based upon a sound deductive process, clearly supported by the evidence and entitled to deference in this appeal. Because of my diametrical opposition to all evidentiary conclusions of the majority, I respectfully dissent.

It would serve no useful purpose, particularly at this late date, for me to dissent at great length. I restrain myself from doing so, but feel compelled to at least point out what I consider to be the most glaring deficiencies in the majority opinion. The majority has spoken and has effectively said that Trans Union's Directors have been the victims of a "fast shuffle" by Van Gorkom and Pritzker. That is the beginning of the majority's comedy of errors. The first and most important error made is the majority's assessment of the directors' knowledge of the affairs of Trans Union and their combined ability to act in this situation under the protection of the business judgment rule.

Trans Union's Board of Directors consisted of ten men, five of whom were "inside" directors and five of whom were "outside" directors. The "inside" directors were Van Gorkom, Chelberg, Bonser, William B. Browder, Senior Vice-President-Law, and Thomas P. O'Boyle, Senior

Vice-President-Administration. At the time the merger was proposed the inside five directors had collectively been employed by the Company for 116 years and had 68 years of combined experience as directors. The "outside" directors were A.W. Wallis, William B. Johnson, Joseph B. Lanterman, Graham J. Morgan and Robert W. Reneker. With the exception of Wallis, these were all chief executive officers of Chicago based corporations that were at least as large as Trans Union. The five "outside" directors had 78 years of combined experience as chief executive officers, and 53 years cumulative service as Trans Union directors.

The inside directors wear their badge of expertise in the corporate affairs of Trans Union on their sleeves. But what about the outsiders? Dr. Wallis is or was an economist and math statistician, a professor of economics at Yale University, dean of the graduate school of business at the University of Chicago, and Chancellor of the University of Rochester. Dr. Wallis had been on the Board of Trans Union since 1962. He also was on the Board of Bausch & Lomb, Kodak, Metropolitan Life Insurance Company, Standard Oil and others.

William B. Johnson is a University of Pennsylvania law graduate, President of Railway Express until 1966, Chairman and Chief Executive of I.C. Industries Holding Company, and member of Trans Union's Board since 1968.

Joseph Lanterman, a Certified Public Accountant, is or was President and Chief Executive of American Steel, on the Board of International Harvester, Peoples Energy, Illinois Bell Telephone, Harris Bank and Trust Company, Kemper Insurance Company and a director of Trans Union for four years.

Graham Morgan is a chemist, was Chairman and Chief Executive Officer of U.S. Gypsum, and in the 17 and 18 years prior to the Trans Union transaction had been involved in 31 or 32 corporate takeovers.

Robert Reneker attended University of Chicago and Harvard Business Schools. He was President and Chief Executive of Swift and Company, director of Trans Union since 1971, and member of the Boards of seven other corporations including U.S. Gypsum and the Chicago Tribune.

Directors of this caliber are not ordinarily taken in by a "fast shuffle". I submit they were not taken into this multi-million dollar corporate transaction without being fully informed and aware of the state of the art as it pertained to the entire corporate panorama of Trans Union. True, even directors such as these, with their business acumen, interest and expertise, can go astray. I do not believe that to be the case here. These men knew Trans Union like the back of their hands and were more than well qualified to make on the spot informed business judgments concerning the affairs of Trans Union including a 100% sale of the corporation. Lest we forget, the corporate world of then and now operates on what is so aptly referred to as "the fast track". These men were at the time an integral part of that world, all professional business men, not intellectual figureheads. * * *

NOTES

(1) The response of the corporate bar to *Van Gorkom* was one of shocked incredulity. "The Delaware Supreme Court * * * exploded a bomb. Stated minimally, the Court * * * pierced the Business Judgment Rule and imposed liability on independent (even eminent) outside directors of Trans Union Corporation * * * because (roughly) the Court thought they had not been careful enough, and had not enquired enough, before deciding to accept and recommend to Trans Union's shareholders a cash-out merger at a per share price that was less than the 'intrinsic value' of the shares. * * * The corporate bar generally views the decision as atrocious and predicts the most dire consequences as directors come to realize how exposed they have become." Bayless Manning, in a newsletter to his clients. Professor Richard Buxbaum, in a CLE newsletter for California Bar subscribers, headlined his analysis of the case "Summer Lightning Out of Delaware." Subsequent commentary also has not been kind to this decision, though some have found a silver lining. "[W]hile on a professional level, I'd be inclined to endorse Dan Fischel's assessment of *Van Gorkom* as the worst case in corporate law history, I have to say that I think it was an important political and social success. * * * *Van Gorkom* exploded on the world of corporate directors. People most definitely took notice of its stern message. From an ex-ante perspective, it almost certainly has had a positive effect on corporate governance." Former Chancellor William Allen, Symposium on the Next Century of Corporate Law, 25 Del. J. Corp. L. 70 (2000). Almost 20 years after the decision, a lawyer who regularly advises corporate directors observed "I have never been in a boardroom where I couldn't get a director's attention by saying 'Remember Van Gorkom.'" Remark of Ira Millstein, at a Roundtable on "The Legacy of Smith v. Van Gorkom," 24 Directors and Boards 28 (2000).

(2) Leo Herzel and Leo Katz argue that the court's decision "seems misguided and Trans Union's actions entirely proper." Both Van Gorkom and the board knew a good deal when they saw one. Further, the only effect of the decision will be to create more formalism and transaction costs (lawyers, investment bankers, accountants) for a board when executing a deal. Leo Herzel & Leo Katz, Smith v. Van Gorkom: The Business of Judging Business Judgment, 41 Bus.Law. 1187, 1188–89, 1191 (1986).

(3) The response of the Delaware legislature to Smith v. Van Gorkom was both swift and decisive. A new paragraph (7) was promptly added to § 102(b) of the Delaware General Corporation Law.

DEL. GEN. CORP. LAW
§ 102(b)(7).

§ 102   CONTENTS OF CERTIFICATE OF INCORPORATION

* * * (b) In addition to the matters required to be set forth in the certificate of incorporation by subsection (a) of this section, the certificate of incorporation may also contain any or all of the following matters: * * *

(7) A provision eliminating or limiting the personal liability of a director to the corporation or its stockholders for monetary damages for breach of fiduciary duty as a director, provided that such provision shall not eliminate or limit the liability of a director (i) [f]or any breach of the director's duty of loyalty to the corporation or its stockholders, (ii) for acts or omissions not in good faith or which involve intentional misconduct or a knowing violation of law, (iii) under section 174 of this title,[d] or (iv) for any transaction from which the director derived an improper personal benefit. No such provision shall eliminate or limit the liability of a director for any act or omission occurring prior to the date when such provision becomes effective. * * *

NOTES

(1) Consider also MBCA § 2.02(b)(4), a subsection added in 1990. Nearly every state has adopted a statute similar either to this section or to DGCL § 102(b)(7). These statutory provisions have since become known as "raincoat" provisions because of the protections they provide to corporate directors.

(2) The Official Comment to § 2.02(b)(4) states:

Developments in the mid- and late 1980s highlighted the need to permit reasonable protection of directors from exposure to personal liability, in addition to indemnification, so that directors would not be discouraged from fully and freely carrying out their duties, including responsible entrepreneurial risk-taking. These developments included increased costs and reduced availability of director and officer liability insurance, the decision of the Delaware Supreme Court in *Smith v. Van Gorkom* * * *, and the resulting reluctance of qualified individuals to serve as directors.

So long as any such liability-limitation provision does not extend to liability to third parties, shareholders should be permitted—except when important societal values are at stake—to decide how to allocate the economic risk of the directors' conduct between the corporation and the directors. * * * In addition, it follows the path of

---

[d] Section 174 refers to the liability of directors for unlawful dividends, stock repurchases, or redemptions.

virtually all the states that have adopted charter option statutes and is applicable only to money damages and not to equitable relief.

(3) Cede & Co. v. Technicolor, Inc., 634 A.2d 345 (Del.1993), involved a merger negotiated in 1982 (three years before Smith v. Van Gorkom was decided) under circumstances roughly comparable to those that occurred in *Van Gorkom*. In a suit brought by an individual shareholder, the Court of Chancery refused to impose personal liability on the directors, despite a finding of gross negligence, unless the plaintiff could establish not only that it suffered a loss but also that the loss was caused by the grossly negligent conduct of the directors. The rule of *Van Gorkom* would lead to "draconian results," Chancellor Allen stated, unless modified to require this proof of causation. The Delaware Supreme Court reversed, holding that to require the plaintiff to show a causal connection between the defendants' gross negligence and the damage or loss suffered by the plaintiff "would lead to most unfortunate results, detrimental to goals of heightened and enlightened standards for corporate governance of Delaware corporations." Once the controlling principles of *Van Gorkom* become applicable and the requirements of the business judgment rule are not met, the defendants may avoid liability only if they can establish the entire fairness of the transaction. Tort principles of causation or proximate cause "have no place in a business judgment rule standard of review analysis." Subsequently, Chancellor Allen concluded that no liability existed because the transaction was in all respects fair to shareholders and this opinion was promptly affirmed. 663 A.2d 1134 (Del.Ch.1994), aff'd, 663 A.2d 1156 (Del.1995). The Technicolor decision has been criticized by scholars and practitioners for its use of an "entire fairness" standard to evaluate directors' conduct in a duty of care case.

(4) The issue of how the "raincoat" provisions contained in section 102(b)(7) work from a mechanical perspective has been the subject of considerable controversy in Delaware. Understandably, when directors are sued, they want to know precisely when they can invoke the protections promised by the statute: "[T]he usefulness of director protection statutes turns in large measure upon the ability of directors to rely upon charter provisions adopted in accordance with these statutes in the context of motions to dismiss filed at the outset of litigation and before discovery. Requiring directors to defend such litigation beyond the motion to dismiss stage eviscerates the protection provided by director protection statutes and thus undermines the policy behind the statutes." Stephen A. Radin, Director Protection Statutes After Malpiede and Emerald Partners, Business and Securities Litigator (February 2002).

(5) For differing perspectives on the benefits and drawbacks of the corporate governance principles articulated in Smith v. Van Gorkom, see Mark Roe, Corporate Law's Limits, 31 J. Legal Studies 233 (2002); Lawrence A. Hamermesh, Why I Do Not Teach *Van Gorkom*, 34 Ga.L.Rev. 477 (2000); Jonathan R. Macey, Smith v. Van Gorkom: Insights About CEO's, Corporate Law Rules, and the Jurisdictional Competition for Corporate Charters, 96 Nw. U. L. Rev. 607 (2002); David Rosenberg, Making Sense of Good Faith in

Delaware Corporate Fiduciary Law: A Contractarian Approach, 29 Del. J. Corp. L. 491 (2004).

IN RE CAREMARK INTERN. INC. DERIVATIVE LITIGATION
Court of Chancery of Delaware, 1996.
698 A.2d 959.

[Caremark was a substantial, publicly held corporation with shares traded on the New York Stock Exchange. It was involved in two main health care business areas: (1) patient care and (2) managed care services. Its patient care business (which accounted for the majority of its revenues) involved alternative site health care services, including infusion therapy, growth hormone therapy, HIV/AIDS-related treatments and hemophilia therapy. Its managed care services included prescription drug programs and the operation of multi-specialty group practices. Caremark had approximately 7,000 employees and ninety branch operations. It also had a decentralized management structure.

A substantial part of the revenues generated by Caremark's businesses was derived from third-party payments, insurers, and Medicare and Medicaid reimbursement programs. The latter source of payments was subject to the terms of the Anti-Referral Payments Law ("ARPL"), 42 U.S.C.A. § 1395nn (1989), a federal statute that prohibits health care providers from paying any form of remuneration to induce the referral of Medicare or Medicaid patients. From its inception, Caremark entered into a variety of agreements with hospitals, physicians, and health care providers for advice and services, as well as distribution agreements with drug suppliers. Caremark also entered into contracts for services (e.g., consultation agreements and research grants) with physicians—at least some of whom prescribed or recommended services or products that Caremark provided to Medicare recipients and other patients. Such contracts were not prohibited by ARPL but they raised a possibility of unlawful "kickbacks." Caremark repeatedly stated that it was not in violation of ARPL, although it also stated that there was a scarcity of court decisions interpreting ARPL and that there was uncertainty concerning Caremark's interpretation of the law.

In August 1991, the HHS Office of the Inspector General ("OIG") initiated an investigation of Caremark. Caremark was served with a subpoena requiring the production of documents, including Quality Service Agreements ("QSAs") between Caremark and physicians. Under the QSAs, Caremark appears to have paid physicians fees for monitoring patients under Caremark's care, including Medicare and Medicaid recipients. Apparently those physicians monitoring patients were sometimes referring physicians, which raised ARPL concerns. In March 1992, the Department of Justice ("DOJ") joined the OIG investigation and separate investigations were commenced by several additional federal and state agencies.

In 1994, Caremark was charged in an indictment with multiple felonies. It began settlement negotiations with federal and state government entities in May 1995. In return for a guilty plea to a single count of mail fraud by the corporation, the payment of a criminal fine, substantial civil damages, and an agreement to cooperate with further federal investigations on matters relating to the OIG investigation, the government entities agreed to negotiate a settlement that would permit Caremark to continue participating in Medicare and Medicaid programs. On June 15, 1995, Caremark's board approved a settlement ("Government Settlement Agreement") with the DOJ, OIG, other federal agencies, and related state agencies in all fifty states and the District of Columbia.

In all, Caremark paid approximately $250 million to settle the claims against it. No senior officers or directors of Caremark were charged with wrongdoing in the Government Settlement Agreement or in any of the prior indictments. Subsequently, Caremark also agreed to make reimbursements to various private and public parties.

The present derivative suit was filed in 1994, seeking to recover on behalf of the company damages for all losses suffered by Caremark. The defendants were the individual members of the board of directors of Caremark. A proposed settlement was negotiated and a hearing held on its terms following notice to shareholders. The proposed settlement did not require any monetary payment or relinquishment of stock options by the defendants. Rather, the principal provisions of the settlement required Caremark (1) to take steps to assure that no future violations of ARPL occurred, (2) to advise patients in writing of any financial relationship between Caremark and a health care professional or provider who made the referral, and (3) to create a Compliance and Ethics Committee composed of four directors, including two non-management directors, to monitor future conduct.

The opinion below dealt with the motion to approve the proposed settlement as fair and reasonable.]

ALLEN, CHANCELLOR.

* * * A motion of this type requires the court to assess the strengths and weaknesses of the claims asserted in light of the discovery record and to evaluate the fairness and adequacy of the consideration offered to the corporation in exchange for the release of all claims made or arising from the facts alleged. The ultimate issue then is whether the proposed settlement appears to be fair to the corporation and its absent shareholders. * * * Legally, evaluation of the central claim made entails consideration of the legal standard governing a board of directors'

obligation to supervise or monitor corporate performance. For the reasons set forth below I conclude * * * that there is a very low probability that it would be determined that the directors of Caremark breached any duty to appropriately monitor and supervise the enterprise. Indeed the record tends to show an active consideration by Caremark management and its Board of the Caremark structures and programs that ultimately led to the company's indictment and to the large financial losses incurred in the settlement of those claims.[e] It does not tend to show knowing or intentional violation of law. Neither the fact that the Board, although advised by lawyers and accountants, did not accurately predict the severe consequences to the company that would ultimately follow from the deployment by the company of the strategies and practices that ultimately led to this liability, nor the scale of the liability, gives rise to an inference of breach of any duty imposed by corporation law upon the directors of Caremark. * * *

A. Principles Governing Settlements of Derivative Claims. As noted at the outset of this opinion, this Court is now required to exercise an informed judgment whether the proposed settlement is fair and reasonable in the light of all relevant factors. Polk v. Good, Del.Supr., 507 A.2d 531 (1986). On an application of this kind, this Court attempts to protect the best interests of the corporation and its absent shareholders all of whom will be barred from future litigation on these claims if the settlement is approved. The parties proposing the settlement bear the burden of persuading the court that it is in fact fair and reasonable. Fins v. Pearlman, Del.Supr., 424 A.2d 305 (1980).

B. Directors' Duties to Monitor Corporate Operations. The complaint charges the director defendants with breach of their duty of attention or care in connection with the on-going operation of the corporation's business. The claim is that the directors allowed a situation to develop and continue which exposed the corporation to enormous legal liability and that in so doing they violated a duty to be active monitors of corporate performance. The complaint thus does not charge either director self-dealing or the more difficult loyalty-type problems arising from cases of suspect director motivation, such as entrenchment or sale of control contexts.[14] The theory here advanced is possibly the most difficult

---

[e] For example, an omitted portion of Chancellor Allen's opinion states: "As early as 1989, Caremark's predecessor issued an internal 'Guide to Contractual Relationships' * * * to govern its employees in entering into contracts with physicians and hospitals. The Guide tended to be reviewed annually by lawyers and updated. Each version of the Guide stated as Caremark's and its predecessor's policy that no payments would be made in exchange for or to induce patient referrals. * * *"

[14] See Weinberger v. UOP, Inc., Del.Supr., 457 A.2d 701, 711 (1983) (entire fairness test when financial conflict of interest involved); Unitrin, Inc. v. American General Corp., Del.Supr., 651 A.2d 1361, 1372 (1995) (intermediate standard of review when "defensive" acts taken); Paramount Communications, Inc. v. QVC Network, Del.Supr., 637 A.2d 34, 45 (1994) (intermediate test when corporate control transferred).

theory in corporation law upon which a plaintiff might hope to win a judgment. * * *

1. *Potential liability for directoral decisions:* Director liability for a breach of the duty to exercise appropriate attention may, in theory, arise in two distinct contexts. First, such liability may be said to follow from a board decision that results in a loss because that decision was ill advised or "negligent". Second, liability to the corporation for a loss may be said to arise from an unconsidered failure of the board to act in circumstances in which due attention would, arguably, have prevented the loss. See generally Veasey & Seitz, The Business Judgment Rule in the Revised Model Act, 63 Texas L.Rev. 1483 (1985). The first class of cases will typically be subject to review under the director-protective business judgment rule, assuming the decision made was the product of a process that was either deliberately considered in good faith or was otherwise rational. See Aronson v. Lewis, Del.Supr., 473 A.2d 805 (1984); Gagliardi v. TriFoods Int'l, Inc., Del.Ch., 683 A.2d 1049 (1996). What should be understood, but may not widely be understood by courts or commentators who are not often required to face such questions,[15] is that compliance with a director's duty of care can never appropriately be judicially determined by reference to the content of the board decision that leads to a corporate loss, apart from consideration of the good faith or rationality of the process employed. That is, whether a judge or jury considering the matter after the fact, believes a decision substantively wrong, or degrees of wrong extending through "stupid" to "egregious" or "irrational," provides no ground for director liability, so long as the court determines that the process employed was either rational or employed in a good faith effort to advance corporate interests. To employ a different rule—one that permitted an "objective" evaluation of the decision—would expose directors to substantive second guessing by ill-equipped judges or juries, which would, in the long-run, be injurious to investor interests.[16] Thus, the business judgment rule is process oriented and informed by a deep respect for all good faith board decisions.

---

[15] See American Law Institute, Principles of Corporate Governance § 4.01(c) (to qualify for business judgment treatment a director must "rationally" believe that the decision is in the best interests of the corporation).

[16] The vocabulary of negligence while often employed, e.g., Aronson v. Lewis, Del.Supr., 473 A.2d 805 (1984) is not well-suited to judicial review of board attentiveness, see, e.g. Joy v. North, 692 F.2d 880, 885–6 (2d Cir.1982), especially if one attempts to look to the substance of the decision as any evidence of possible "negligence." Where review of board functioning is involved, courts leave behind as a relevant point of reference the decisions of the hypothetical "reasonable person", who typically supplies the test for negligence liability. It is doubtful that we want business men and women to be encouraged to make decisions as hypothetical persons of *ordinary* judgment and prudence might. The corporate form gets its utility in large part from its ability to allow diversified investors to accept greater investment risk. If those in charge of the corporation are to be adjudged personally liable for losses on the basis of a substantive judgment based upon what * * * persons of ordinary or average judgment and average risk assessment talent regard as "prudent," "sensible," or even "rational," such persons will have a strong incentive at the margin to authorize less risky investment projects.

Indeed, one wonders on what moral basis might shareholders attack a good faith business decision of a director as "unreasonable" or "irrational." Where a director in fact exercises a good faith effort to be informed and to exercise appropriate judgment, he or she should be deemed to satisfy fully the duty of attention. If the shareholders thought themselves entitled to some other quality of judgment than such a director produces in the good faith exercise of the powers of office, then the shareholders should have elected other directors. Judge Learned Hand made the point rather better than can I. In speaking of the passive director defendant Mr. Andrews in Barnes v. Andrews, Judge Hand said:

> True, he was not very suited by experience for the job he had undertaken, but I cannot hold him on that account. After all it is the same corporation that chose him that now seeks to charge him * * *. Directors are not specialists like lawyers or doctors * * *. They are the general advisors of the business and if they faithfully give such ability as they have to their charge, it would not be lawful to hold them liable. Must a director guarantee that his judgment is good? Can a shareholder call him to account for deficiencies that their votes assured him did not disqualify him for his office? While he may not have been the Cromwell for that Civil War, Andrews did not engage to play any such role. [298 F. 614, 618 (S.D.N.Y.1924)].

In this formulation Learned Hand correctly identifies, in my opinion, the core element of any corporate law duty of care inquiry: whether there was good faith effort to be informed and exercise judgment.

2. Liability for failure to monitor: The second class of cases in which director liability for inattention is theoretically possible entail circumstances in which a loss eventuates not from a decision but, from unconsidered inaction. Most of the decisions that a corporation, acting through its human agents, makes are, of course, not the subject of director attention. Legally, the board itself will be required only to authorize the most significant corporate acts or transactions: mergers, changes in capital structure, fundamental changes in business, appointment and compensation of the CEO, etc. As the facts of this case graphically demonstrate, ordinary business decisions that are made by officers and employees deeper in the interior of the organization can, however, vitally affect the welfare of the corporation and its ability to achieve its various strategic and financial goals. * * * [W]hat is the board's responsibility with respect to the organization and monitoring of the enterprise to assure that the corporation functions within the law to achieve its purposes?

Modernly this question has been given special importance by an increasing tendency, especially under federal law, to employ the criminal law to assure corporate compliance with external legal requirements, including environmental, financial, employee and product safety as well as assorted other health and safety regulations. In 1991, pursuant to the Sentencing Reform Act of 1984,[21] the United States Sentencing Commission adopted Organizational Sentencing Guidelines which impact importantly on the prospective effect these criminal sanctions might have on business corporations. The Guidelines set forth a uniform sentencing structure for organizations to be sentenced for violation of federal criminal statutes and provide for penalties that equal or often massively exceed those previously imposed on corporations.[22] The Guidelines offer powerful incentives for corporations today to have in place compliance programs to detect violations of law, promptly to report violations to appropriate public officials when discovered, and to take prompt, voluntary remedial efforts.

In 1963, the Delaware Supreme Court in Graham v. Allis-Chalmers Mfg. Co.,[23] addressed the question of potential liability of board members for losses experienced by the corporation as a result of the corporation having violated the anti-trust laws of the United States. There was no claim in that case that the directors knew about the behavior of subordinate employees of the corporation that had resulted in the liability. Rather, as in this case, the claim asserted was that the directors ought to have known of it and if they had known they would have been under a duty to bring the corporation into compliance with the law and thus save the corporation from the loss. The Delaware Supreme Court concluded that, under the facts as they appeared, there was no basis to find that the directors had breached a duty to be informed of the ongoing operations of the firm. In notably colorful terms, the court stated that "absent cause for suspicion there is no duty upon the directors to install and operate a corporate system of espionage to ferret out wrongdoing which they have no reason to suspect exists."[24] The Court found that there were no grounds for suspicion in that case and, thus, concluded that the directors were blamelessly unaware of the conduct leading to the corporate liability.[25]

How does one generalize this holding today? Can it be said today that, absent some ground giving rise to suspicion of violation of law, that corporate directors have no duty to assure that a corporate information gathering and reporting systems exists which represents a good faith

---

[21] Pub.L. 98–473, Title II, § 212(a)(2)(1984); 18 U.S.C.A. §§ 3551–3656.

[22] See United States Sentencing Commission, Guidelines Manual, Chapter 8 (U.S. Government Printing Office November 1994).

[23] Del.Supr., 41 Del.Ch. 78, 188 A.2d 125 (1963).

[24] Id. at 130.

[25] Recently, the *Graham* standard was applied by the Delaware Chancery in a case involving Baxter. In re Baxter International, Inc. Shareholders Litig., Del.Ch., 654 A.2d 1268, 1270 (1995).

attempt to provide senior management and the Board with information respecting material acts, events or conditions within the corporation, including compliance with applicable statutes and regulations? I certainly do not believe so. I doubt that such a broad generalization of the *Graham* holding would have been accepted by the Supreme Court in 1963. The case can be more narrowly interpreted as standing for the proposition that, absent grounds to suspect deception, neither corporate boards nor senior officers can be charged with wrongdoing simply for assuming the integrity of employees and the honesty of their dealings on the company's behalf.

A broader interpretation of Graham v. Allis-Chalmers—that it means that a corporate board has no responsibility to assure that appropriate information and reporting systems are established by management— would not, in any event, be accepted by the Delaware Supreme Court in 1996, in my opinion. In stating the basis for this view, I start with the recognition that in recent years the Delaware Supreme Court has made it clear—especially in its jurisprudence concerning takeovers, from Smith v. Van Gorkom through Paramount Communications v. QVC[26]—the seriousness with which the corporation law views the role of the corporate board. Secondly, I note the elementary fact that relevant and timely information is an essential predicate for satisfaction of the board's supervisory and monitoring role under Section 141 of the Delaware General Corporation Law. Thirdly, I note the potential impact of the federal organizational sentencing guidelines on any business organization. Any rational person attempting in good faith to meet an organizational governance responsibility would be bound to take into account this development and the enhanced penalties and the opportunities for reduced sanctions that it offers.

In light of these developments, it would, in my opinion, be a mistake to conclude that our Supreme Court's statement in *Graham* concerning "espionage" means that corporate boards may satisfy their obligation to be reasonably informed concerning the corporation, without assuring themselves that information and reporting systems exist in the organization that are reasonably designed to provide to senior management and to the board itself timely, accurate information sufficient to allow management and the board, each within its scope, to reach informed judgments concerning both the corporation's compliance with law and its business performance.

Obviously the level of detail that is appropriate for such an information system is a question of business judgment. And obviously too, no rationally designed information and reporting system will remove the possibility that the corporation will violate laws or regulations, or that

---

[26] Smith v. Van Gorkom, Del.Supr., 488 A.2d 858 (1985); Paramount Communications v. QVC Network, Del.Supr., 637 A.2d 34 (1994).

senior officers or directors may nevertheless sometimes be misled or otherwise fail reasonably to detect acts material to the corporation's compliance with the law. But it is important that the board exercise a good faith judgment that the corporation's information and reporting system is in concept and design adequate to assure the board that appropriate information will come to its attention in a timely manner as a matter of ordinary operations, so that it may satisfy its responsibility.

Thus, I am of the view that a director's obligation includes a duty to attempt in good faith to assure that a corporate information and reporting system, which the board concludes is adequate, exists, and that failure to do so under some circumstances may, in theory at least, render a director liable for losses caused by non-compliance with applicable legal standards.[27] I now turn to an analysis of the claims asserted with this concept of the directors duty of care, as a duty satisfied in part by assurance of adequate information flows to the board, in mind.

III. ANALYSIS OF THIRD AMENDED COMPLAINT AND SETTLEMENT

A.   The Claims

On balance, after reviewing an extensive record in this case, including numerous documents and three depositions, I conclude that this settlement is fair and reasonable. In light of the fact that the Caremark Board already has a functioning committee charged with overseeing corporate compliance, the changes in corporate practice that are presented as consideration for the settlement do not impress one as very significant. Nonetheless, that consideration appears fully adequate to support dismissal of the derivative claims of director fault asserted, because those claims find no substantial evidentiary support in the record and quite likely were susceptible to a motion to dismiss in all events.[28]

In order to show that the Caremark directors breached their duty of care by failing adequately to control Caremark's employees, plaintiffs would have to show either (1) that the directors knew or (2) should have known that violations of law were occurring and, in either event, (3) that the directors took no steps in a good faith effort to prevent or remedy that situation, and (4) that such failure proximately resulted in the losses

---

[27] Any action seeking recovery for losses would logically entail a judicial determination of proximate cause, since, for reasons that I take to be obvious, it could never be assumed that an adequate information system would be a system that would prevent all losses. I need not touch upon the burden allocation with respect to a proximate cause issue in such a suit. See Cede & Co. v. Technicolor, Inc., Del.Supr., 636 A.2d 956 (1994); Cinerama, Inc. v. Technicolor, Inc., Del.Ch., 663 A.2d 1134 (1994), aff'd, Del.Supr., 663 A.2d 1156 (1995). Moreover, questions of waiver of liability under certificate provisions authorized by 8 Del.C. § 102(b)(7) may also be faced.

[28] See In re Baxter International, Inc. Shareholders Litig., Del.Ch., 654 A.2d 1268, 1270 (1995). A claim in some respects similar to that here made was dismissed. The court relied, in part, on the fact that the Baxter certificate of incorporation contained a provision as authorized by section 102(b)(7) of the Delaware General Corporation Law, waiving director liability for due care violations. That fact was thought to require pre-suit demand on the board in that case.

complained of, although under Cede & Co. v. Technicolor, Inc., Del.Supr., 636 A.2d 956 (1994) this last element may be thought to constitute an affirmative defense.

1. **Knowing violation of statute:** Concerning the possibility that the Caremark directors knew of violations of law, none of the documents submitted for review, nor any of the deposition transcripts appear to provide evidence of it. Certainly the Board understood that the company had entered into a variety of contracts with physicians, researchers, and health care providers and it was understood that some of these contracts were with persons who had prescribed treatments that Caremark participated in providing. The board was informed that the company's reimbursement for patient care was frequently from government funded sources and that such services were subject to the ARPL. But the Board appears to have been informed by experts that the company's practices while contestable, were lawful. There is no evidence that reliance on such reports was not reasonable. Thus, this case presents no occasion to apply a principle to the effect that knowingly causing the corporation to violate a criminal statute constitutes a breach of a director's fiduciary duty. See Roth v. Robertson, N.Y.Sup.Ct., 64 Misc. 343, 118 N.Y.S. 351 (1909); Miller v. American Tel. & Tel. Co., 507 F.2d 759 (3d Cir.1974). It is not clear that the Board knew the detail found, for example, in the indictments arising from the Company's payments. But, of course, the duty to act in good faith to be informed cannot be thought to require directors to possess detailed information about all aspects of the operation of the enterprise. Such a requirement would simply be inconsistent with the scale and scope of efficient organization size in this technological age.

2. **Failure to monitor:** Since it does appear that the Board was to some extent unaware of the activities that led to liability, I turn to a consideration of the other potential avenue to director liability that the pleadings take: director inattention or "negligence." Generally where a claim of directorial liability for corporate loss is predicated upon ignorance of liability creating activities within the corporation, as in *Graham* or in this case, in my opinion only a sustained or systematic failure of the board to exercise oversight—such as an utter failure to attempt to assure a reasonable information and reporting system exits— will establish the lack of good faith that is a necessary condition to liability. Such a test of liability—lack of good faith as evidenced by sustained or systematic failure of a director to exercise reasonable oversight—is quite high. But, a demanding test of liability in the oversight context is probably beneficial to corporate shareholders as a class, as it is in the board decision context, since it makes board service by qualified persons more likely, while continuing to act as a stimulus to good faith performance of duty by such directors.

Here the record supplies essentially no evidence that the director defendants were guilty of a sustained failure to exercise their oversight function. To the contrary, insofar as I am able to tell on this record, the corporation's information systems appear to have represented a good faith attempt to be informed of relevant facts. If the directors did not know the specifics of the activities that lead to the indictments, they cannot be faulted.

The liability that eventuated in this instance was huge. But the fact that it resulted from a violation of criminal law alone does not create a breach of fiduciary duty by directors. The record at this stage does not support the conclusion that the defendants either lacked good faith in the exercise of their monitoring responsibilities or conscientiously permitted a known violation of law by the corporation to occur. The claims asserted against them must be viewed at this stage as extremely weak. * * *

B.   *The Consideration For Release of Claim*

The proposed settlement provides very modest benefits. Under the settlement agreement, plaintiffs have been given express assurances that Caremark will have a more centralized, active supervisory system in the future. Specifically, the settlement mandates duties to be performed by the newly named Compliance and Ethics Committee on an ongoing basis and increases the responsibility for monitoring compliance with the law at the lower levels of management. In adopting the resolutions required under the settlement, Caremark has further clarified its policies concerning the prohibition of providing remuneration for referrals. These appear to be positive consequences of the settlement of the claims brought by the plaintiffs, even if they are not highly significant. Nonetheless, given the weakness of the plaintiffs' claims the proposed settlement appears to be an adequate, reasonable, and beneficial outcome for all of the parties. Thus, the proposed settlement will be approved. * * *

[Chancellor Allen finally considered the request of the plaintiff's attorneys for an award of attorneys' fees for negotiating the settlement. He stated:] "In awarding attorneys' fees, this Court considers an array of relevant factors, * * * [including], most importantly, the financial value of the benefit that the lawyers work produced; the strength of the claims (because substantial settlement value may sometimes be produced even though the litigation added little value—i.e., perhaps any lawyer could have settled this claim for this substantial value or more); the amount of complexity of the legal services; the fee customarily charged for such services; and the contingent nature of the undertaking. In this case no factor points to a substantial fee, other than the amount and sophistication of the lawyer services required. There is only a modest substantive benefit produced; in the particular circumstances of the government activity there was realistically a very slight contingency faced by the attorneys at the time they expended time. The services rendered required a high degree of sophistication and expertise. I am told that at normal hourly billing rates approximately $710,000 of time was expended by the attorneys. * * * In these circumstances, I conclude that an award of a fee determined by reference to the time expended at normal hourly rates plus a premium of 15% of that amount to reflect the limited degree of real contingency in the undertaking, is fair. Thus I will award a fee of $816,000 plus $53,000 of expenses advanced by counsel."[30]

NOTES

(1) The *Caremark* opinion brought into focus the responsibility of the board of directors to monitor corporate operations. The collapse of Enron Corporation in November 2001, followed shortly thereafter by a spate of cases also involving inappropriate management conduct in other corporations, provide classic illustrations of the potential consequences of a failure by a board of directors to monitor the performance of management as contemplated in Chancellor Allen's classic opinion. Because of these developments, the responsibility of directors to monitor managers is receiving renewed attention by regulators, academics, and lawyers. See Note, Earnings Management, the SEC and Corporate Governance: Director Liability Arising From the Audit Committee Report, 102 Colum.L.Rev. 168 (2002). *Caremark* is the leading case describing and defining this oversight responsibility, and Enron Corporation is the principal example of the consequences of a virtually total failure to monitor managers.

(2) Post-*Caremark* decisions indicate that shareholder litigation against directors and officers continues to be a tough road. For example, in Salsitz v. Nasser, 208 F.R.D. 589 (E.D.Mich.2002), the directors of the Ford Motor Company were sued for making three unfortunate business decisions. One was the decision to install inadequate tires for Ford Explorers. A second was the decision to put an ignition system in a location which sometimes caused the motor to quit unexpectedly or the ignition system to fail. The third decision related to the excessive purchases of palladium, a precious metal, that led Ford to take costly write-downs when the excess palladium was resold. A motion by the defendants to dismiss for failure to state a claim was granted.

(3) There are two older cases in which liability was imposed on directors for failure to pay attention or for breach of the duty to be informed with respect to the business of the corporation.

In Bates v. Dresser, 251 U.S. 524 (1920), a bank president who was also a director was held personally liable for the amount stolen by Coleman, a young bookkeeper at the bank. The president was made aware of the missing

---

[30] The court has been informed by letter of counsel that after the fairness of the proposed settlement had been submitted to the court, Caremark was involved in a merger in which its stock was canceled and the holders of its stock became entitled to shares of stock of the acquiring corporation. * * *

deposits. He was further told that Coleman was the likely culprit. Even with these warnings, the president did nothing. The other directors were not held liable, since they reasonably relied on bank examinations and the president.

In Francis v. United Jersey Bank, 432 A.2d 814 (N.J.1981), the sons of the founder of a corporation, an "insurance reinsurance" business, siphoned large sums of money from the corporation in the form of "shareholder loans" and other improper payments to family members. As a result of these transactions, the corporation became insolvent; the bankruptcy trustee brought suit against Mrs. Pritchard, the widow of the founder for more than $10,000,000, representing funds transferred unlawfully from the firm to the family members while she was a director of the company. Mrs. Pritchard literally did nothing in her role as a director. Instead, she began to drink heavily after her husband's death and had nothing to do with direction of the business. The court found that Mrs. Pritchard was grossly negligent in her duties as a director. Most importantly, the court found that Mrs. Pritchard's negligence was a proximate cause of the misappropriations by her two co-director sons.

(4) The judicial ground of director liability may be shifting in a post-Enron, Tyco, and WorldCom world. Courts, especially in Delaware, seem more receptive to suits which charge breach of good faith and loyalty by board members. Such claims are troubling to board members because a breach of good faith voids exculpation clauses such as those permitted by section 102(b)(7) of the DGCL. Exculpation clauses shield directors and officers from personal liability for decisions made on the job. Without such protection, personal liability can be astronomical. For a look into this shifting ground of director liability, see In re Abbott Laboratories Derivative S'holders Litig., 293 F.3d 378 (7th Cir.2002) (holding that the Abbott board, because of their inattention to costly problems, breached their duty of good faith, which thus barred the application of the exculpation provision); In re Walt Disney Co. Derivative Litig., 825 A.2d 275 (Del.Ch.2003) (evidence that Disney's board breached its duty of good faith by consciously and deliberately ignoring its responsibilities barred the application of the exculpation provision); Guttman v. Huang, 823 A.2d 492 (Del.Ch.2003).

(5) In the wake of the financial crisis of 2007 and 2008, which threatened to bring the U.S. economy (along with the economies of many other countries) to its knees, federal regulators have moved decisively into the business of holding corporations responsible for performing adequate oversight and monitoring of their activities. On September 19, 2013, Wall Street mega-bank JPMorgan Chase agreed to pay a total of $920 million in fines and to admit wrongdoing to settle charges by the SEC, the Board of Governors of the Federal Reserve System, the Comptroller of the Currency, and the Financial Conduct Authority of the U.K. The bank was charged with lacking effective internal controls to detect and prevent its traders from fraudulently overvaluing investments to conceal hundreds of millions of dollars in trading losses. The SEC's lawsuit against JPMorgan faulted the bank's internal controls for failing to ensure that the company's traders were properly

valuing their investments, and faulted the bank's senior management for failing to inform the audit committee of the severe breakdowns in the internal controls associated with the bank's investing activities.

According to the SEC's order instituting a settled administrative proceeding against JPMorgan, the Sarbanes-Oxley Act of 2002 established important requirements for public companies and their management regarding corporate governance and disclosure. Public companies such as JPMorgan are required to create and maintain internal controls that provide investors with reasonable assurances that the company's financial statements are reliable, and to ensure that senior management shares important information with key internal decisionmakers, such as the board of directors. JPMorgan failed to adhere to these requirements, and consequently misstated its financial results in public filings for the first quarter of 2012. According to the SEC's order, after the portfolio began to significantly decline in value in late April 2012, JPMorgan commissioned several internal reviews to assess, among other matters, the effectiveness of the internal controls in the firm's chief investment office (CIO). From these reviews, senior management learned that the valuation control group within the CIO—whose function was to detect and prevent trader mismarking—was woefully ineffective and insufficiently independent from the traders it was supposed to police. As JPMorgan senior management learned additional troubling facts about the state of affairs in the CIO, they failed to timely escalate and share that information with the firm's audit committee.

The facts that JPMorgan has admitted in settling the SEC's enforcement action include, among others, the following:

- The trading losses occurred against a backdrop of woefully deficient accounting controls in the CIO, including spreadsheet miscalculations that caused large valuation errors and the use of subjective valuation techniques that made it easier for the traders to mismark the CIO portfolio.

- JPMorgan senior management personally rewrote the CIO's valuation control policies before the firm filed with the SEC its first quarter report for 2012 in order to address the many deficiencies in existing policies.

- By late April 2012, JPMorgan senior management knew that the firm's Investment Banking unit used far more conservative prices when valuing the same kind of derivatives held in the CIO portfolio, and that applying the Investment Bank valuations would have led to approximately $750 million in additional losses for the CIO in the first quarter of 2012.

- External counterparties who traded with the CIO had valued certain positions in the CIO book at $500 million less than the CIO traders did, precipitating large collateral calls against JPMorgan.

- As a result of the findings of certain internal reviews of the CIO, some executives expressed reservations about signing sub-certifications supporting the CEO and CFO certifications required under the Sarbanes-Oxley Act.

- Senior management failed to adequately update the audit committee on these and other important facts concerning the CIO before the firm filed its first quarter report for 2012.

- Deprived of access to these facts, the audit committee was hindered in its ability to discharge its obligations to oversee management on behalf of shareholders and to ensure the accuracy of the firm's financial statements.

SEC Press Release 2013–187, JPMorgan Chase Agrees to Pay $200 Million and Admits Wrongdoing to Settle SEC Charges: Firm Must Pay $920 Million in Total Penalties in Global Settlement (Sept. 19, 2013).

STONE V. RITTER
Supreme Court of Delaware, 2006.
911 A.2d 362.

Before STEELE, C.J., HOLLAND, BERGER, JACOBS, and RIDGELY, J.J., constituting the Court en Banc.

HOLLAND, JUSTICE.

[AmSouth Bancorporation (AmSouth) and a subsidiary paid $40 million in fines and $10 million in civil penalties arising from the failure of bank employees to file reports required under the Bank Secrecy Act (BSA) and anti-money laundering (AML) regulations. Plaintiff shareholders filed a derivative suit without making a demand on the company's board of directors, alleging demand futility. The shareholders claimed that AmSouth directors breached their fiduciary duty of oversight. The Chancery Court dismissed the derivative complaint.]

* * * [T]he plaintiffs concede that "[t]he standards for determining demand futility in the absence of a business decision" are set forth in *Rales v. Blasband*. To excuse demand under *Rales*, "a court must determine whether or not the particularized factual allegations of a derivative stockholder complaint create a reasonable doubt that, as of the time the complaint is filed, the board of directors could have properly exercised its independent and disinterested business judgment in responding to a demand." The plaintiffs attempt to satisfy the *Rales* test in this proceeding by asserting that the incumbent defendant directors "face a substantial likelihood of liability" that renders them "personally interested in the outcome of the decision on whether to pursue the claims asserted in the complaint," and are therefore not disinterested or independent.

Critical to this demand excused argument is the fact that the directors' potential personal liability depends upon whether or not their conduct can be exculpated by the section 102(b)(7) provision contained in the AmSouth certificate of incorporation. Such a provision can exculpate directors from monetary liability for a breach of the duty of care, but not for conduct that is not in good faith or a breach of the duty of loyalty. * * *

It is important * * * to clarify a doctrinal issue that is critical to understanding fiduciary liability under *Caremark* as we construe that case. The phraseology used in *Caremark* and that we employ here—describing the lack of good faith as a "necessary condition to liability"—is deliberate. The purpose of that formulation is to communicate that a failure to act in good faith is not conduct that results, *ipso facto*, in the direct imposition of fiduciary liability. The failure to act in good faith may result in liability because the requirement to act in good faith "is a subsidiary element[,]" i.e., a condition, "of the fundamental duty of loyalty." It follows that because a showing of bad faith conduct * * * is essential to establish director oversight liability, the fiduciary duty violated by that conduct is the duty of loyalty.

This view of a failure to act in good faith results in two additional doctrinal consequences. First, although good faith may be described colloquially as part of a "triad" of fiduciary duties that includes the duties of care and loyalty, the obligation to act in good faith does not establish an independent fiduciary duty that stands on the same footing as the duties of care and loyalty. Only the latter two duties, where violated, may directly result in liability, whereas a failure to act in good faith may do so, but indirectly. The second doctrinal consequence is that the fiduciary duty of loyalty is not limited to cases involving a financial or other cognizable fiduciary conflict of interest. It also encompasses cases where the fiduciary fails to act in good faith. * * *

We hold that *Caremark* articulates the necessary conditions predicate for director oversight liability: (a) the directors utterly failed to implement any reporting or information system or controls; *or* (b) having implemented such a system or controls, consciously failed to monitor or oversee its operations thus disabling themselves from being informed of risks or problems requiring their attention. In either case, imposition of liability requires a showing that the directors knew that they were not discharging their fiduciary obligations. Where directors fail to act in the face of a known duty to act, thereby demonstrating a conscious disregard for their responsibilities, they breach their duty of loyalty by failing to discharge that fiduciary obligation in good faith.

The plaintiffs contend that demand is excused under Rule 23.1 because AmSouth's directors breached their oversight duty and, as a result, face a "substantial likelihood of liability" as a result of their "utter failure" to act in good faith to put into place policies and procedures to ensure compliance with BSA and AML obligations. The Court of Chancery found that the plaintiffs did not plead the existence of "red flags"—"facts showing that the board ever was aware that AmSouth's internal controls were inadequate, that these inadequacies would result in illegal activity, and that the board chose to do nothing about problems it allegedly knew existed." In dismissing the derivative complaint in this action, the Court of Chancery concluded:

> This case is not about a board's failure to carefully consider a material corporate decision that was presented to the board. This is a case where information was not reaching the board because of ineffective internal controls. * * *

This Court reviews *de novo* a Court of Chancery's decision to dismiss a derivative suit under Rule 23.1.

Reasonable Reporting System Existed

The KPMG Report evaluated the various components of AmSouth's longstanding BSA/AML compliance program. The KPMG Report reflects that AmSouth's Board dedicated considerable resources to the BSA/AML compliance program and put into place numerous procedures and systems to attempt to ensure compliance. According to KPMG, the program's various components exhibited between a low and high degree of compliance with applicable laws and regulations. * * *

The KPMG Report reflects that the directors not only discharged their oversight responsibility to establish an information and reporting system, but also proved that the system was designed to permit the directors to periodically monitor AmSouth's compliance with BSA and AML regulations. For example, as KPMG noted in 2004, AmSouth's designated BSA Officer "has made annual high-level presentations to the Board of Directors in each of the last five years." Further, the Board's Audit and Community Responsibility Committee (the "Audit Committee") oversaw AmSouth's BSA/AML compliance program on a quarterly basis. The KPMG Report states that "the BSA Officer presents BSA/AML training to the Board of Directors annually," and the "Corporate Security training is also presented to the Board of Directors."

The KPMG Report shows that AmSouth's Board at various times enacted written policies and procedures designed to ensure compliance with the BSA and AML regulations. * * *

* * * KPMG's findings reflect that the Board received and approved relevant policies and procedures, delegated to certain employees and departments the responsibility for filing [suspicious activity reports] and monitoring compliance, and exercised oversight by relying on periodic reports from them. Although there ultimately may have been failures by

employees to report deficiencies to the Board, there is no basis for an oversight claim seeking to hold the directors personally liable for such failures by the employees. * * *

* * * In the absence of red flags, good faith in the context of oversight must be measured by the directors' actions "to assure a reasonable information and reporting system exists" and not by second-guessing after the occurrence of employee conduct that results in an unintended adverse outcome. Accordingly, we hold that the Court of Chancery properly applied *Caremark* and dismissed the plaintiffs' derivative complaint for failure to excuse demand by alleging particularized facts that created reason to doubt whether the directors had acted in good faith in exercising their oversight responsibilities.

NOTES

(1) In affirming the Chancery Court's decision in *Stone*, the Delaware Supreme Court affirmed that *Caremark* is the law in Delaware. *Stone* also puts to rest the question whether directors have a duty of good faith that is separate from their other fiduciary duties. The Court found that good faith is not a distinct duty but is rather a component of the duty of loyalty.

(2) After *Stone*, plaintiffs seeking to hold directors liable for failure to monitor will have to show that "(a) the directors utterly failed to implement any reporting or information system or controls; *or* (b) having implemented such a system or controls, consciously failed to monitor or oversee its operations thus disabling themselves from being informed of risks or problems." Does the Court in *Stone* set the bar too high for proving director oversight liability?

M<small>ALONE</small> v. B<small>RINCAT</small>
Supreme Court of Delaware, 1998.
722 A.2d 5.

H<small>OLLAND</small>, J<small>USTICE</small> (en banc).

Doran Malone, Joseph P. Danielle, and Adrienne M. Danielle, the plaintiffs-appellants, filed this individual and class action in the Court of Chancery. The complaint alleged that the directors of Mercury Finance Company ("Mercury"), a Delaware corporation, breached their fiduciary duty of disclosure. * * * The complaint also alleged that the defendant-appellee, KPMG Peat Marwick LLP ("KPMG") aided and abetted the Mercury directors' breaches of fiduciary duty. The Court of Chancery dismissed the complaint with prejudice pursuant to Chancery Rule 12(b)(6) for failure to state a claim upon which relief may be granted.

The complaint alleged that the director defendants intentionally overstated the financial condition of Mercury on repeated occasions throughout a four-year period in disclosures to Mercury's shareholders.

Plaintiffs contend that the complaint states a claim upon which relief can be granted for a breach of the fiduciary duty of disclosure. Plaintiffs also contend that, because the director defendants breached their fiduciary duty of disclosure to the Mercury shareholders, the Court of Chancery erroneously dismissed the aiding and abetting claim against KPMG.

This Court has concluded that the Court of Chancery properly granted the defendants' motions to dismiss the complaint. That dismissal, however, should have been without prejudice. Plaintiffs are entitled to file an amended complaint. Therefore, the judgment of the Court of Chancery is affirmed in part, reversed in part, and remanded for further proceedings consistent with this opinion. * * *

Mercury is a publicly-traded company engaged primarily in purchasing installment sales contracts from automobile dealers and providing short-term installment loans directly to consumers. This action was filed on behalf of the named plaintiffs and all persons (excluding defendants) who owned common stock of Mercury from 1993 through the present and their successors in interest, heirs and assigns (the "putative class"). The complaint alleged that the directors "knowingly and intentionally breached their fiduciary duty of disclosure because the SEC filings made by the directors and every communication from the company to the shareholders since 1994 was materially false" and that "as a direct result of the false disclosures * * * the Company has lost all or virtually all of its value (about $2 billion)." The complaint also alleged that KPMG knowingly participated in the directors' breaches of their fiduciary duty of disclosure.

According to plaintiffs, since 1994, the director defendants caused Mercury to disseminate information containing overstatements of Mercury's earnings, financial performance and shareholders' equity. Mercury's earnings for 1996 were actually only $56.7 million, or $.33 a share, rather than the $120.7 million, or $.70 a share, as reported by the director defendants. * * * [Similar false statements, though smaller in absolute amounts, were also alleged for each of the years 1993–1995.] Shareholders' equity on December 31, 1996 was disclosed by the director defendants as $353 million, but was only $263 million or less. The complaint alleged that all of the foregoing inaccurate information was included or referenced in virtually every filing Mercury made with the SEC and every communication Mercury's directors made to the shareholders during this period of time.

Having alleged these violations of fiduciary duty, which (if true) are egregious, plaintiffs alleged that as "a direct result of [these] false disclosures * * * the company has lost all or virtually all its value (about $2 billion)," and seeks class action status to pursue damages against the directors and KPMG for the individual plaintiffs and common stockholders. The individual director defendants filed a motion to dismiss, contending that they owed no fiduciary duty of disclosure under the circumstances alleged in the complaint. KPMG also filed a motion to dismiss the aiding and abetting claim asserted against it.

After briefing and oral argument, the Court of Chancery granted both of the motions to dismiss with prejudice. The Court of Chancery held that directors have no fiduciary duty of disclosure under Delaware law in the absence of a request for shareholder action. In so holding, the Court stated:

> The federal securities laws ensure the timely release of accurate information into the marketplace. The federal power to regulate should not be duplicated or impliedly usurped by Delaware. When a shareholder is damaged merely as a result of the release of inaccurate information into the marketplace, unconnected with any Delaware corporate governance issue, that shareholder must seek a remedy under federal law. [1997 WL 697940, at *2 (Oct. 30, 1997).]

We disagree, and although we hold that the Complaint as drafted should have been dismissed, our rationale is different. * * *

This Court has held that a board of directors is under a fiduciary duty to disclose material information when seeking shareholder action:[5]

> It is well-established that the duty of disclosure "represents nothing more than the well-recognized proposition that directors of Delaware corporations are under a fiduciary duty to disclose fully and fairly all material information within the board's control when it seeks shareholder action."[6]

The majority of opinions from the Court of Chancery have held that there may be a cause of action for disclosure violations only where directors seek shareholder action. The present appeal requires this Court to decide whether a director's fiduciary duty arising out of misdisclosure is implicated in the absence of a request for shareholder action. We hold that directors who knowingly disseminate false information that results in corporate injury or damage to an individual stockholder violate their

---

[5] See Loudon v. Archer-Daniels-Midland Co., Del.Supr., 700 A.2d 135, 137–38 (1997) ("* * * Delaware law of the fiduciary duties of directors * * * establishes a general duty to disclose to stockholders all material information reasonably available when seeking stockholder action. * * * But there is no per se doctrine imposing liability * * *."); Arnold v. Society for Savings Bancorp, Inc., Del.Supr., 650 A.2d 1270, 1277 (1994) (a fiduciary disclosure obligation "attaches to proxy statements and any other disclosures in contemplation of shareholder action."); Stroud v. Grace, Del.Supr., 606 A.2d 75, 84 (1992) ("directors of Delaware corporations are under a fiduciary duty to disclose fully and fairly all material information within the board's control when it seeks shareholder action.").

[6] Zirn v. VLI Corp., Del.Supr., 681 A.2d 1050, 1056 (1996) (quoting Stroud v. Grace, 606 A.2d at 84 (emphasis added)).

fiduciary duty, and may be held accountable in a manner appropriate to the circumstances.

An underlying premise for the imposition of fiduciary duties is a separation of legal control from beneficial ownership. Equitable principles act in those circumstances to protect the beneficiaries who are not in a position to protect themselves. See McMahon v. New Castle Associates, Del. Ch., 532 A.2d 601, 604 (1987). One of the fundamental tenets of Delaware corporate law provides for a separation of control and ownership. The board of directors has the legal responsibility to manage the business of a corporation for the benefit of its shareholder owners. 8 Del. C. § 141(a). Accordingly, fiduciary duties are imposed on the directors of Delaware corporations to regulate their conduct when they discharge that function. Mills Acquisition Co. v. Macmillan, Inc., Del.Supr., 559 A.2d 1261, 1280 (1989).

The directors of Delaware corporations stand in a fiduciary relationship not only to the stockholders but also to the corporations upon whose boards they serve. The director's fiduciary duty to both the corporation and its shareholders has been characterized by this Court as a triad: due care, good faith, and loyalty. Cede & Co. v. Technicolor, Inc., Del.Supr., 634 A.2d 345, 361 (1993). That tripartite fiduciary duty does not operate intermittently but is the constant compass by which all director actions for the corporation and interactions with its shareholders must be guided.

Although the fiduciary duty of a Delaware director is unremitting, the exact course of conduct that must be charted to properly discharge that responsibility will change in the specific context of the action the director is taking with regard to either the corporation or its shareholders. Mills Acquisition Co. v. Macmillan, Inc., 559 A.2d at 1280. This Court has endeavored to provide the directors with clear signal beacons and brightly lined-channel markers as they navigate with due care, good faith, and loyalty on behalf of a Delaware corporation and its shareholders.[15] This Court has also endeavored to mark the safe harbors clearly.

The shareholder constituents of a Delaware corporation are entitled to rely upon their elected directors to discharge their fiduciary duties at all times. Whenever directors communicate publicly or directly with shareholders about the corporation's affairs, with or without a request for shareholder action, directors have a fiduciary duty to shareholders to

---

[15] See, e.g., Unocal Corp. v. Mesa Petroleum Co., Del.Supr., 493 A.2d 946, 954 (1985) (directors have an "enhanced duty" in the context of a threatened takeover because of the "omnipresent specter that a board may be acting primarily in its own interests, rather than those of the corporation and its shareholders * * *."); Revlon, Inc. v. MacAndrews Forbes Holdings, Inc., Del.Supr., 506 A.2d 173, 182 (1986) (when sale of the company becomes inevitable, the director's duties are "significantly altered").

exercise due care, good faith and loyalty. It follows a fortiori that when directors communicate publicly or directly with shareholders about corporate matters the sine qua non of directors' fiduciary duty to shareholders is honesty.[17]

According to the appellants, the focus of the fiduciary duty of disclosure is to protect shareholders as the "beneficiaries" of all material information disseminated by the directors. The duty of disclosure is, and always has been, a specific application of the general fiduciary duty owed by directors. The duty of disclosure obligates directors to provide the stockholders with accurate and complete information material to a transaction or other corporate event that is being presented to them for action.

The issue in this case is not whether Mercury's directors breached their duty of disclosure. It is whether they breached their more general fiduciary duty of loyalty and good faith by knowingly disseminating to the stockholders false information about the financial condition of the company. The directors' fiduciary duties include the duty to deal with their stockholders honestly.

Shareholders are entitled to rely upon the truthfulness of all information disseminated to them by the directors they elect to manage the corporate enterprise. Delaware directors disseminate information in at least three contexts: public statements made to the market, including shareholders; statements informing shareholders about the affairs of the corporation without a request for shareholder action; and, statements to shareholders in conjunction with a request for shareholder action. Inaccurate information in these contexts may be the result of a violation of the fiduciary duties of care, loyalty or good faith. We will examine the remedies that are available to shareholders for misrepresentations in each of these three contexts by the directors of a Delaware corporation. * * *

In the absence of a request for stockholder action, the Delaware General Corporation Law does not require directors to provide shareholders with information concerning the finances or affairs of the corporation. Even when shareholder action is sought, the provisions in the General Corporation Law requiring notice to the shareholders of the proposed action do not require the directors to convey substantive information beyond a statutory minimum. Consequently, in the context of a request for shareholder action, the protection afforded by Delaware law

---

[17] Marhart, Inc. v. Calmat Co., Del. Ch., CA. No. 11820, Berger, V.C., 1992 WL 212587 (Apr. 22, 1992), slip op. at 6 (reported in 18 Del. J. Corp. L. 330 (1992)) ("Delaware directors are fiduciaries and are held to a high standard of conduct * * *. It is entirely consistent with this settled principle of law that fiduciaries, who undertake the responsibility of informing shareholders about corporate affairs, be required to do so honestly.").

is a judicially recognized equitable cause of action by shareholders against directors.

The fiduciary duty of directors in connection with disclosure violations in Delaware jurisprudence was restated in Lynch v. Vickers Energy Corp., Del.Supr., 383 A.2d 278 (1978). In *Lynch*, this Court held that, in making a tender offer to acquire the stock of the minority stockholders, a majority stockholder "owed a fiduciary duty * * * which required 'complete candor' in disclosing fully 'all the facts and circumstances surrounding the' tender offer."[21] In *Stroud v. Grace,* we noted that the language of our jurisprudence should be clarified to the extent that "candor" requires no more than the duty to disclose all material facts when seeking stockholder action.[22] * * *

The duty of directors to observe proper disclosure requirements derives from the combination of the fiduciary duties of care, loyalty and good faith. The plaintiffs contend that, because directors' fiduciary responsibilities are not "intermittent duties," there is no reason why the duty of disclosure should not be implicated in every public communication by a corporate board of directors. The directors of a Delaware corporation are required to disclose fully and fairly all material information within the board's control when it seeks shareholder action. When the directors disseminate information to stockholders when no stockholder action is sought, the fiduciary duties of care, loyalty and good faith apply. Dissemination of false information could violate one or more of those duties.

An action for a breach of fiduciary duty arising out of disclosure violations in connection with a request for stockholder action does not include the elements of reliance, causation and actual quantifiable monetary damages. Instead, such actions require the challenged disclosure to have a connection to the request for shareholder action. The essential inquiry in such an action is whether the alleged omission or misrepresentation is material. Stroud v. Grace, 606 A.2d at 85. Materiality is determined with respect to the shareholder action being sought.

The directors' duty to disclose all available material information in connection with a request for shareholder action must be balanced

___

[21] Lynch v. Vickers Energy Corp., Del.Supr., 383 A.2d 278, 279 (1977) quoting Lynch v. Vickers Energy Corp., Del. Ch., 351 A.2d 570, 573 (1976); accord Shell Petroleum, Inc. v. Smith, Del.Supr., 606 A.2d 112, 114–15 (1992) (majority stockholder bears burden of showing full disclosure of all facts within its knowledge that are material to stockholder action). The fiduciary duty of disclosure is also applicable to directors of a Delaware corporation, In re Anderson, Clayton Shareholders Litig., Del. Ch., 519 A.2d 680, 688–90 (1986); Smith v. Van Gorkom, Del. Supr., 488 A.2d 858, 890 (1985) and to less-than-majority shareholders who control or affirmatively attempt to mandate the destiny of the corporation. In re Tri-Star Pictures, Inc. Litig., 634 A.2d at 328–29.

[22] Stroud v. Grace, 606 A.2d at 84.

against its concomitant duty to protect the corporate enterprise, in particular, by keeping certain financial information confidential. Stroud v. Grace, 606 A.2d at 89. Directors are required to provide shareholders with all information that is material to the action being requested and to provide a balanced, truthful account of all matters disclosed in the communications with shareholders.[31] Accordingly, directors have definitive guidance in discharging their fiduciary duty by an analysis of the factual circumstances relating to the specific shareholder action being requested and an inquiry into the potential for deception or misinformation.[32] * * *

When corporate directors impart information they must comport with the obligations imposed by both the Delaware law and the federal statutes and regulations of the United States Securities and Exchange Commission * * *. Historically, federal law has regulated disclosures by corporate directors into the general interstate market. This Court has noted that "in observing its congressional mandate the SEC has adopted a 'basic philosophy of disclosure.' "[35] Accordingly, this Court has held that there is "no legitimate basis to create a new cause of action which would replicate, by state decisional law, the provisions of * * * the 1934 Act." Arnold v. Society for Savings Bancorp, Inc., Del.Supr., 678 A.2d 533, 539 (1996). In deference to the panoply of federal protections that are available to investors in connection with the purchase or sale of securities of Delaware corporations, this Court has decided not to recognize a state common law cause of action against the directors of Delaware corporations for "fraud on the market." Here, it is to be noted, the claim appears to be made by those who did not sell and, therefore, would not implicate federal securities laws which relate to the purchase or sale of securities.

The historic roles played by state and federal law in regulating corporate disclosures have been not only compatible but complementary. That symbiotic relationship has been perpetuated by the recently enacted federal Securities Litigation Uniform Standards Act of 1998.[39] Although that statute by its terms does not apply to this case, the new statute will

---

[31] Zirn v. VLI Corp., 681 A.2d at 1056. In *Zirn II,* this Court held, "in addition to the traditional duty to disclose all facts material to the proffered transaction, directors are under a fiduciary obligation to avoid misleading partial disclosures. The law of partial disclosure is likewise clear: Once defendants travel down the road of partial disclosure they have an obligation to provide the stockholders with an accurate, full and fair characterization of those historic events." [internal quotations omitted].

[32] See Zirn v. VLI Corp., 681 A.2d at 1062 ("a good faith erroneous judgment as to the proper scope or content of required disclosure implicates the duty of care rather than the duty of loyalty."); Arnold v. Society for Savings Bancorp, 650 A.2d at 1287–88 & n. 36.

[35] Stroud v. Grace, Del.Supr., 606 A.2d 75, 86 (1992). See, e.g., Randall S. Thomas & Catherine T. Dixon, Aranow & Einhorn on Proxy Contests for Corporation Control, § 21.02 (3d ed.1998).

[39] Securities Litigation Uniform Standards Act of 1998, Pub.L. No. 105–353, 112 Stat. 3227 (1998).

require securities class actions involving the purchase or sale of nationally traded securities, based upon false or misleading statements, to be brought exclusively in federal court under federal law. The 1998 Act, however, contains two important exceptions: the first provides that an "exclusively derivative action brought by one or more shareholders on behalf of a corporation" is not preempted; the second preserves the availability of state court class actions, where state law already provides that corporate directors have fiduciary disclosure obligations to shareholders.[41] These exceptions have become known as the "Delaware carve-outs."

We need not decide at this time, however, whether this new Act will have any effect on this litigation if plaintiffs elect to replead. See Section (c) of the Act:

> (c) Applicability.—The amendments made by this section shall not affect or apply to any action commenced before and pending on the date of enactment of this Act.

* * * Delaware law also protects shareholders who receive false communications from directors even in the absence of a request for shareholder action. When the directors are not seeking shareholder action, but are deliberately misinforming shareholders about the business of the corporation, either directly or by a public statement, there is a violation of fiduciary duty. That violation may result in a derivative claim on behalf of the corporation or a cause of action for damages. See Zirn v. VLI Corp., 681 A.2d at 1060–61. There may also be a basis for equitable relief to remedy the violation.

Here the complaint alleges (if true) an egregious violation of fiduciary duty by the directors in knowingly disseminating materially false information. Then it alleges that the corporation lost about $2 billion in value as a result. Then it merely claims that the action is brought on behalf of the named plaintiffs and the putative class. It is a non sequitur rather than a syllogism.

The allegation in paragraph 3 that the false disclosures resulted in the corporation losing virtually all its equity seems obliquely to claim an injury to the corporation. The plaintiffs, however, never expressly assert a derivative claim on behalf of the corporation or allege compliance with Court of Chancery Rule 23.1, which requires pre-suit demand or cognizable and particularized allegations that demand is excused.[44] If the

---

[41] See, e.g., Zirn v. VLI Corp., 621 A.2d 773; Zirn v. VLI Corp., 681 A.2d at 1060–61. See also Michael A. Perino, Fraud and Federalism: Preempting Private State Securities Fraud Causes of Action, 50 Stan. L.Rev. 273 (1998).

[44] It seems that plaintiffs have attempted to allege the basis for demand excusal by the very nature of the central claim that the directors knowingly misstated the company's financial condition, thus seemingly taking this case out of the business judgment rule because all the directors are alleged to be implicated in the wrongdoing.

plaintiffs intend to assert a derivative claim, they should be permitted to replead to assert such a claim and any damage or equitable remedy sought on behalf of the corporation.[46] Likewise, the plaintiffs should have the opportunity to replead to assert any individual cause of action and articulate a remedy that is appropriate on behalf of the named plaintiffs individually, or a properly recognizable class consistent with Court of Chancery Rule 23, and our decision in Gaffin.[47]

The Court of Chancery properly dismissed the complaint before it against the individual director defendants, in the absence of well-pleaded allegations stating a derivative, class or individual cause of action and properly assertable remedy. Without a well-pleaded allegation in the complaint for a breach of fiduciary duty, there can be no claim for aiding and abetting such a breach. Accordingly, the plaintiffs' aiding and abetting claim against KPMG was also properly dismissed.

Nevertheless, we disagree with the Court of Chancery's holding that such a claim cannot be articulated on these facts. The plaintiffs should have been permitted to amend their complaint, if possible, to state a properly cognizable cause of action against the individual defendants and KPMG. Consequently, the Court of Chancery should have dismissed the complaint without prejudice.

The judgment of the Court of Chancery to dismiss the complaint is affirmed. The judgment to dismiss the complaint with prejudice is reversed. This matter is remanded for further proceedings in accordance with this opinion.

NOTES

(1) *Caremark* and *Malone* broaden to some extent long-accepted obligations of directors of publicly held Delaware corporations. Should these obligations be extended to closely held corporations as well? See Mary Siegel, Fiduciary Myths in Close Corporate Law, 29 Del. J. Corp. L. 377 (2004).

(2) Is it appropriate for Delaware courts to impose new obligations on these types of directors? Should that not be the role of the Delaware legislature? Professor Jill Fisch comments that "[a] substantial portion of Delaware's corporate law is made by the courts, but the Delaware courts make law in a manner traditionally associated with legislative rather than judicial lawmaking." She concludes that "Delaware's unusual lawmaking structure enhances firm value and perhaps explains the widespread

---

[46] We express no opinion whether equitable remedies such as injunctive relief, judicial removal of directors or disqualification from directorship could be asserted here. No such equitable relief has been sought in the current complaint. See Randall S. Thomas & Catherine T. Dixon, Aranow & Einhorn on Proxy Contests for Corporate Control, § 19.01 (3d ed.1998).

[47] Gaffin v. Teledyne, Inc., 611 A.2d 467, 474 (1992) ("A class action may not be maintained in a purely common law or equitable fraud case since individual questions of law or fact, particularly as to the element of justifiable reliance, will inevitably predominate over common questions of law or fact.").

preference for Delaware incorporation." Jill E. Fisch, The Peculiar Role of the Delaware Courts in the Competition for Corporate Charters, 68 U. Cincinnati L. Rev. 1061, 1071, 1081 (2000).

(3) In *Malone,* the Delaware Supreme Court stated that it has "endeavored to provide the directors with clear signal beacons and brightly lined-channel markers as they navigate with due care, good faith, and loyalty * * *." Has the court succeeded? One of the issues that remains open after *Malone* is what the standard will be for showing that nondisclosures in the absence of a request for shareholder action are material. Another important issue is how the liability shield in section 102(b)(7) will operate in the context of a violation of the disclosure requirements in Delaware, particularly when the false or misleading disclosures arise outside of the context of a request for shareholder action. See Note, Fiduciary Duties and Disclosure Obligations: Resolving Questions After Malone v. Brincat, 26 Del. J. Corp. L. 563 (2001).

CHAPTER 11

DUTY OF LOYALTY AND CONFLICT OF INTEREST

▪ ▪ ▪

A. SELF-DEALING

MARCIANO v. NAKASH
Supreme Court of Delaware, 1987.
535 A.2d 400.

Before HORSEY, MOORE and WALSH, JJ.

WALSH, JUSTICE.

This is an appeal from a decision of the Court of Chancery which validated a claim in liquidation of Gasoline, Ltd. ("Gasoline"), a Delaware corporation, placed in custodial status pursuant to 8 *Del.C.* § 226 by reason of a deadlock among its board of directors. Fifty percent of Gasoline is owned by Ari, Joe, and Ralph Nakash (the "Nakashes") and fifty percent by Georges, Maurice, Armand and Paul Marciano (the "Marcianos"). The Vice Chancellor ruled that $2.5 million in loans made by the Nakashes faction to Gasoline were valid and enforceable debts of the corporation, notwithstanding their origin in self-dealing transactions. The Marcianos argue that the disputed debt is voidable as a matter of law but, in any event, the Nakashes failed to meet their burden of establishing full fairness. We conclude that the Vice Chancellor applied the proper standard for review of self-dealing transactions and the finding of full fairness is supported by the record. Accordingly, we affirm.
* * *

The parties agree that the loans made by the Nakashes to Gasoline were interested transactions. The Nakashes as officers of Gasoline executed the various documents which supported the loans and at the same time guaranteed those loans extended through their wholly owned entities. It is also not disputed that, given the control deadlock, the questioned transactions did not receive majority approval of Gasoline's directors or shareholders. The Marcianos argue that the loan transaction is voidable at the option of the corporation notwithstanding its fairness or the good faith of its participants. A review of this contention, rejected by the Court of Chancery, requires analysis of the concept of director self-dealing under Delaware law.

It is a long-established principle of Delaware corporate law that the fiduciary relationship between directors and the corporation imposes fundamental limitations on the extent to which a director may benefit from dealings with the corporation he serves. *Guth v. Loft, Inc.,* Del.Supr., 5 A.2d 503 (1939). Thus, the "voting [for] and taking" of compensation may be deemed "constructively fraudulent" in the absence of shareholder ratification, or statutory or bylaw authorization. *Cahall v. Lofland,* Del.Ch., 114 A. 224, 232 (1921). Perhaps the strongest condemnation of interested director conduct appears in *Potter v. Sanitary Co. of America,* Del.Ch., 194 A. 87 (1937), a decision which the Marcianos advance as definitive of the rule of per se voidability. In *Potter* the Court of Chancery characterized transactions between corporations having common directors and officers "constructively fraudulent," absent shareholder ratification.

Support can also be found for the per se rule of voidability in this Court's decision in *Kerbs v. California Eastern Airways Inc.,* Del.Supr., 90 A.2d 652 (1952). The *Kerbs* court, in considering the validity of a profit sharing plan, ruled that the self-interest of the directors who voted on the plan caused the transaction to be voidable. The court concluded that the profit sharing plan was voidable based on the common law rule that the vote of an interested director will not be counted in determining whether the challenged action received the affirmative vote of a majority of the board of directors. *Id.* at 658 (*citing Bovay v. H.M. Byllesby & Co.,* Del.Supr., 38 A.2d 808 (1944)).

The principle of per se voidability for interested transactions, which is sometimes characterized as the common law rule, was significantly ameliorated by the 1967 enactment of Section 144 of the Delaware General Corporation Law.[a] The Marcianos argue that section 144(a) provides the only basis for immunizing self-interested transactions and since none of the statute's component tests are satisfied the stricture of the common law per se rule applies. The Vice Chancellor agreed that the disputed loans did not withstand a section 144(a) analysis but ruled that the common law rule did not invalidate transactions determined to be intrinsically fair. We agree that section 144(a) does not provide the only validation standard for interested transactions.

It overstates the common law rule to conclude that relationship, alone, is the controlling factor in interested transactions. Although the application of the per se voidability rule in early Delaware cases resulted in the invalidation of interested transactions, the result was not dictated simply by a tainted relationship. Thus in *Potter,* the Court, while adopting the rule of voidability, emphasized that interested transactions should be subject to close scrutiny. Where the undisputed evidence tended to show that the transaction would advance the personal interests of the

---

[a] Please consult the Statutory Supplement.

directors at the expense of stockholders, the stockholders, upon discovery, are entitled to disavow the transaction.

Further, the court examined the motives of the defendant directors and the effect the transaction had on the corporation and its shareholders.

In other Delaware cases, decided before the enactment of section 144, interested director transactions were deemed voidable only after an examination of the fairness of a particular transaction *vis-a-vis* the nonparticipating shareholders and a determination of whether the disputed conduct received the approval of a noninterested majority of directors or shareholders. *Keenan v. Eshleman,* Del.Supr., 2 A.2d 904, 908 (1938); *Blish v. Thompson Automatic Arms Corp.,* Del.Supr., 64 A.2d 581, 602 (1948). The latter test is now crystallized in the ratification criteria of section 144(a), although the nonquorum restriction of *Kerbs* has been superceded by the language of subparagraph (b) of section 144.

The Marcianos view compliance with section 144 as the sole basis for avoiding the per se rule of voidability. The Court of Chancery rejected this contention and we agree that it is not consonant with Delaware corporate law. This Court in *Fliegler v. Lawrence,* Del.Supr., 361 A.2d 218 (1976), a post-section 144 decision, refused to view section 144 as either completely preemptive of the common law duty of director fidelity or as constituting a grant of broad immunity. As we stated in *Fliegler:* "It merely removes an 'interested director' cloud when its terms are met and provides against invalidation of an agreement 'solely' because such a director or officer is involved." *Id.* at 222. In *Fliegler* this Court applied a two-tiered analysis: application of section 144 coupled with an intrinsic fairness test.

If section 144 validation of interested director transactions is not deemed exclusive, as *Fliegler* clearly holds, the continued viability of the intrinsic fairness test is mandated not only by fact situations, such as here present, where shareholder deadlock prevents ratification but also where shareholder control by interested directors precludes independent review. Indeed, if an independent committee of the board, contemplated by section 144(a)(1) is unavailable, the sole forum for demonstrating intrinsic fairness may be a judicial one. In such situations the intrinsic fairness test furnishes the substantive standard against which the evidential burden of the interested directors is applied. * * *

This case illustrates the limitation inherent in viewing section 144 as the touchstone for testing interested director transactions. Because of the shareholder deadlock, even if the Nakashes had attempted to invoke section 144, it was realistically unavailable. The ratification process contemplated by section 144 presupposes the functioning of corporate constituencies capable of providing assents. Just as the statute cannot "sanction unfairness" neither can it invalidate fairness if, upon judicial review, the transaction withstands close scrutiny of its intrinsic elements.[3]

[The Marcianos claimed that the Nakashes had not proved that the costs of the loans were fair to the corporation and also that some of the proceeds of the loans had been used to pay invoices from companies controlled by the Nakashes. The Court held, however, that the Chancellor's conclusion that the terms of the loans met the "intrinsic fairness standard" was supported by the record and was the product of a logical deductive process. The Court concluded that the possible misuse of the proceeds of the loans should be litigated in a derivative proceeding brought by the Marcianos which was then pending.]

We hold, therefore, that the Court of Chancery properly applied the intrinsic fairness test in determining the validity of the interested director transactions and its finding of full fairness is clearly supported by the record. Accordingly, the decision is AFFIRMED.

NOTES

(1) The Sarbanes-Oxley Act, passed in response to Enron and other corporate scandals, contains a provision entitled "Enhanced Conflict of Interest Provisions" that imposes prohibitions on personal loans to corporate executives. The provision, section 402 of Sarbanes-Oxley, makes it unlawful for any public company to extend credit or to arrange for the extension of credit in the form of a personal loan to any director or executive officer of the company. There are a variety of narrow exceptions for such things as extensions of credit associated with the use of credit cards (presumably to permit corporate entertainment to continue unabated), and loans that are part of the ordinary business of the issuer made on terms no more favorable than those offered to the public. Wouldn't the SOX prohibition apply to loans such as the one made in Marciano v. Nakash? In light of this, do you agree with the SOX provision outlawing such loans to public companies?

(2) Consider the general problem of a director who enters into a business transaction with the corporation—for example, the purchase of a business or other assets from, or the sale of assets to, the corporation. In any such transaction there is an obvious risk that the deal will be skewed in favor of the director and will correspondingly harm the corporation or prevent the corporation from obtaining the full benefit of the deal. This risk is increased as the interested director's influence over other board members increases,

---

[3] Although in this case none of the curative steps afforded under section 144(a) were available because of the director-shareholder deadlock, a non-disclosing director seeking to remove the cloud of interestedness would appear to have the same burden under section 144(a)(3), as under prior case law, of proving the intrinsic fairness of a questioned transaction which had been approved or ratified by the directors or shareholders. Folk, *The Delaware General Corp. Law: A Commentary and Analysis,* 86 (1972). On the other hand, approval by fully-informed disinterested directors under section 144(a)(1), or disinterested stockholders under section 144(a)(2), permits invocation of the business judgment rule and limits judicial review to issues of gift or waste with the burden of proof upon the party attacking the transaction.

such as where the interested director has sufficient voting power to enable him or her to elect or remove a majority of the directors. What position should the law take with respect to such transactions?

The position taken during the last part of the nineteenth century was that all transactions involving conflicts of interest were voidable at the insistence of the corporation or its shareholders without regard to the fairness or unfairness of the transaction. This absolute position has now been entirely rejected, for reasons that should be clear from the facts and reasoning in *Marciano*: many such transactions are beneficial to the corporation and are entered into by the director to assist, rather than to harm, the corporation. As such, the old rule of automatic voidability was extremely over-inclusive, as it voided many transactions that benefitted the corporation. In addition, it was thought that requiring the board of directors to utilize certain mandated proper procedures for vetting conflict of interest transactions would make it possible for courts to evaluate the legitimacy of director conflict of interest deals on a case-by-case basis. The challenge, of course, is determining what tests should be applied to sort out the harmful transactions from the harmless or desirable ones. Several possible tests have received some degree of modern judicial approval in the absence of a statute:

(a) Such a transaction is voidable if it is not approved or ratified by a disinterested majority of the directors or by the shareholders without regard to its fairness;

(b) Such a transaction is *not* voidable if the interested director can show that the transaction is fair to the corporation;

(c) Such a transaction is voidable if the plaintiff shows that the transaction is unfair to the corporation;

(d) Such a transaction is voidable only if the plaintiff shows that the transaction constitutes fraud, waste, or serious overreaching;

(e) Such a transaction is *not* voidable if it has been approved or ratified by a disinterested majority of the directors, and no further inquiry need be made into its fairness;

(f) Such a transaction is *not* voidable if it has been approved or ratified by a majority of the disinterested shareholders and no further inquiry need be made into its fairness;

(g) Such a transaction is always voidable if the vote of the interested director is necessary to approve the transaction or his presence is necessary to form a quorum;

(h) Such a transaction is always voidable if the interested director participates in the decisionmaking process, urging approval of the transaction, but does not vote.

These alternatives are not mutually exclusive, since some relate to the *procedures* by which the transaction was approved while others (particularly (b), (c), and (d)) relate to the *substance*—the effect of the transaction on the corporation—and it is possible to combine them. For example, one might establish a rule that such a transaction is voidable if it is unfair (alternative (c)) or constitutes waste (alternative (d)), but the disinterested shareholders may ratify the transaction (alternative (f)). Would that rule be desirable? Or, one might establish the rule that a transaction that is voidable under alternative (a) may not be voidable if the director can establish fairness (alternative (b)). Would that rule be desirable? Of course, at the extreme, there probably is no reason to consider setting aside a transaction approved by *all* of the shareholders, no matter how damaging to the corporation, although one can imagine situations involving injury to creditors or senior interests.

(3) While many transactions between directors and their corporation have been held to be valid in the absence of a controlling statute, considerable confusion exists in the case law as to the precise procedures required in order to validate such transactions. If one examines the results of cases (as contrasted with statements in the opinions), the following comments reflect most of the decisions:

(a) If the court believes that the transaction is fair to the corporation, it will be upheld;

(b) If the court believes that the transaction involves fraud, undue overreaching, or waste of corporate assets (e.g., a director using corporate assets for personal purposes without paying for them), the transaction will be set aside; and

(c) If the court believes that the transaction does not involve fraud, undue overreaching, or waste of corporate assets, but is not convinced that the transaction is fair, the transaction will be upheld only where the interested director can convincingly show that the transaction was approved (or ratified) by a truly disinterested majority of the board of directors without participation by the interested director, or by a majority of the disinterested shareholders after full disclosure of all relevant facts.

(4) The most notorious example of a board of directors approving a conflict of interest transaction was the decision of Enron Corporation's board to approve conflict-laden transactions between Enron and a variety of partnerships and other special purpose entities (SPEs) controlled by the company's Chief Financial Officer, Andrew Fastow. Enron was an Oregon corporation, and Oregon has a statutory provision (ORS § 60.361) similar to DGCL § 144. Even if the directors could show that they were disinterested, if they were not fully informed, they would need to show that the transactions were fair to Enron. Despite clear conflicts of interest, the U.S. Senate Subcommittee on Investigations found that:

> The Enron Board of Directors approved an unprecedented arrangement allowing Enron's Chief Financial Officer to establish and operate the LJM private equity funds which transacted business with Enron and profited at Enron's expense. The Board exercised inadequate oversight of LJM transaction and

compensation controls and failed to protect Enron shareholders from unfair dealing.

The Enron Board's decision to waive the company's code of conduct and allow its Chief Financial Officer (CFO) Andrew Fastow to establish and operate off-the-books entities designed to transact business with Enron was also highly unusual and disturbing. This arrangement allowed inappropriate conflict of interest transactions as well as accounting and related party disclosure problems, due to the dual role of Mr. Fastow as a senior officer at Enron and an equity holder and general manager of the new entities. Nevertheless, with little debate or independent inquiry, the Enron Board approved three code of conduct waivers enabling Mr. Fastow to establish three private equity funds in 1999 and 2000, known as LJM1, LJM2 and LJM3 (the initials "LJM" referred to Mr. Fastow's wife and children).

The Enron Board approved code of conduct waivers for Mr. Fastow knowing that the LJM partnerships were designed to transact business primarily with Enron, and controls would be needed to ensure the LJM transactions and Mr. Fastow's compensation were fair to Enron. The Board failed, however, to make sure the controls were effective, to monitor the fairness of the transactions, or to monitor Mr. Fastow's LJM-related compensation. The result was that the LJM partnerships realized hundreds of millions of dollars in profits at Enron's expense.

Enron's code of conduct for its employees expressly prohibited Enron employees from obtaining personal financial gain from a company doing business with Enron.

Report of the Permanent Subcommittee on Investigations of the Committee on Governmental Affairs, United States Senate, The Role of the Board of Directors in Enron's Collapse (July 8, 2002).

(5) The treatment of conflict of interest transactions is now controlled by statute. Virtually all states have statutes dealing with such transactions. Most of these statutes are similar in structure to DGCL § 144, although there are significant variations in language.

(6) In December 1988, the Committee on Corporate Laws approved a new treatment of conflict of interest transactions, now codified as §§ 8.60–8.63 of the MBCA. The new Subchapter F, as it is usually called, is a much more ambitious undertaking than earlier conflict of interest statutes. This new treatment of conflict of interest transactions has not been widely adopted. A further reconsideration of Subchapter F by the Committee on Corporate Laws is likely.

(7) Under Subchapter F, a conflict of interest transaction is not voidable by the corporation if (a) it has been approved by disinterested directors or shareholders, or (b) the interested director establishes the fairness of the

transaction. Subchapter F is also designed to create a series of "bright-line" principles that increase predictability and enhance practical administrability.

(8) Abstractly, self-dealing transactions have two attributes that make a substantial degree of judicial oversight desirable: (1) they are voluntary transactions on the part of the self-dealing director and (2) they provide an opportunity for direct pecuniary enrichment at the expense of the corporation by the self-dealing director. Indeed, most commentary on directors' duties recognizes that breaches of the duty of loyalty raise serious problems that merit continuing judicial scrutiny. For example, in Kenneth E. Scott, Corporation Law and the American Law Institute Corporate Governance Project, 35 Stan.L.Rev. 927 (1983), the author urged (long before the Trans Union case) that liability for violations of the duty of care should be entirely eliminated, but that judicial vigilance over violations of the duty of loyalty should be vigorously encouraged. Does Subchapter F go against the grain of this analysis by withdrawing (or appearing to withdraw) all judicial scrutiny from conflict of interest cases, relying instead on the vote of "qualified directors" to protect the corporation and minority shareholders against overreaching transactions?

IN RE EL PASO CORP. SHAREHOLDER LITIGATION
Delaware Court of Chancery, 2012.
41 A.3d 432.

STRINE, CHANCELLOR.

Stockholder plaintiffs seek a preliminary injunction to enjoin a merger between El Paso Corporation and Kinder Morgan, Inc. (the "Merger"). The chief executive officer of El Paso, a public company, undertook sole responsibility for negotiating the sale of El Paso to Kinder Morgan in the Merger. Kinder Morgan intended to keep El Paso's pipeline business and sell off El Paso's exploration and production, or "E&P," business to finance the purchase. The CEO did not disclose to the El Paso board of directors (the "Board") his interest in working with other El Paso managers in making a bid to buy the E&P business from Kinder Morgan. He kept that motive secret, negotiated the Merger, and then approached Kinder Morgan's CEO on two occasions to try to interest him in the idea. In other words, when El Paso's CEO was supposed to be getting the maximum price from Kinder Morgan, he actually had an interest in not doing that.

This undisclosed conflict of interest [was] compounded [by] the [fact] that the Board and management of El Paso relied in part on advice given by a financial advisor, Goldman, Sachs & Co., which owned 19% of Kinder Morgan (a $4 billion investment) and controlled two Kinder Morgan board seats. Although Goldman's conflict was known, inadequate efforts to cabin its role were made. When a second investment bank was brought in to address Goldman's economic incentive for a deal with, and on terms that favored, Kinder Morgan, Goldman continued to intervene and advise El Paso on strategic alternatives, and with its friends in El Paso management, was able to achieve a remarkable feat: giving the new investment bank an incentive to favor the Merger by making sure that this bank only got paid if El Paso adopted the strategic option of selling to Kinder Morgan. In other words, the conflict-cleansing bank only got paid if the option Goldman's financial incentives gave it a reason to prefer was the one chosen. On top of this, the lead Goldman banker advising El Paso did not disclose that he personally owned approximately $340,000 of stock in Kinder Morgan.

The record is filled with debatable negotiating and tactical choices made by El Paso fiduciaries and advisors. Absent a conflict of interest, these debatable choices could be seen as the sort of reasonable, if arguable, ones that must be made in a world of uncertainty. After discovery, however, these choices now must be viewed more skeptically, as the key negotiator on behalf of the Board and a powerfully influential financial advisor each had financial motives adverse to the best interests of El Paso's stockholders. In the case of the CEO, he was the one who made most of the important tactical choices, and he never surfaced his own conflict of interest. In the case of Goldman, it claimed to step out of the process while failing to do so completely and while playing a key role in distorting the economic incentives of the bank that came in to ensure that Goldman's conflict did not taint the Board's deliberations. This behavior makes it difficult to conclude that the Board's less than aggressive negotiating strategy and its failure to test Kinder Morgan's bid actively in the market through even a quiet, soft market check were not compromised by the conflicting financial incentives of these key players.

The record thus persuades me that the plaintiffs have a reasonable likelihood of success in proving that the Merger was tainted by disloyalty. Because, however, there is no other bid on the table and the stockholders of El Paso, as the seller, have a choice whether to turn down the Merger themselves, the balance of harms counsels against a preliminary injunction. Although the pursuit of a monetary damages award may not be likely to promise full relief, the record does not instill in me the confidence to deny, by grant of an injunction, El Paso's stockholders from accepting a transaction that they may find desirable in current market conditions, despite the disturbing behavior that led to its final terms.

The plaintiffs are stockholders of El Paso and seek to enjoin a vote on a proposed Merger with Kinder Morgan that offers El Paso a combination of cash, stock, and warrants * * * At the time of signing, the Merger consideration was worth $26.87 per share, and has appreciated [to] $30.37 per share, or a 47.8% premium over El Paso's stock price because Kinder Morgan's stock has grown in value. In order to obtain a preliminary injunction, the plaintiffs must demonstrate: (1) a reasonable probability of success on the merits; (2) that they will suffer irreparable harm if an injunction does not issue; and (3) that the balance of the equities favors the issuance of an injunction.

The Merger resulted from a non-public overture that Kinder Morgan made in the wake of El Paso's public announcement that it would spin off its E&P business. El Paso is an energy company composed of two main business segments: a pipeline business, which transports natural gas throughout the United States, and the E&P business, which looks for and exploits opportunities to drill and produce oil and natural gas. The market had reacted favorably to the May 24, 2011 announcement of the spin-off, and El Paso's stock price had risen, although El Paso believed that its stock price would rise further when the spin-off was actually effected. El Paso understood that Kinder Morgan was trying to preempt any competition by other bidders for what would be the separate pipeline business, which is the business Kinder Morgan wanted to buy, by making a bid before El Paso divided into two companies.

The first time after the spin-off announcement that Kinder Morgan expressed its interest in acquiring El Paso was on August 30, 2011, when Kinder Morgan offered El Paso $25.50 per share in cash and stock. The El Paso Board fended this off * * *. On September 9, 2011, Kinder Morgan threatened to go public with its interest in buying El Paso. Rather than seeing this as a chance to force Kinder Morgan into an expensive public struggle, the Board entered into negotiations with Kinder Morgan. The Board looked to its longtime advisor Goldman Sachs (which as noted owns 19% of Kinder Morgan, fills two seats on the Kinder Morgan board under a voting agreement with Kinder Morgan's CEO and controlling stockholder, Rich Kinder, and is part of the control group which collectively holds 78.4% of the voting power of Kinder Morgan stock), and a new advisor, Morgan Stanley & Co., LLC, for financial and tactical advice in making that decision and for developing its negotiating strategy. On September 16, 2011, El Paso asked Kinder Morgan for a bid of $28 per share in cash and stock, deploying the company's CEO, Doug Foshee, as its sole negotiator. Foshee reached an agreement in principle with Rich Kinder two days later on a deal at $27.55 per share in cash and stock, subject to due diligence by Kinder Morgan.

[One week later,] Kinder said "oops, we made a mistake. We relied on a bullish set of analyst projections in order to make our bid. Our bad. * * *"

* * * Instead of telling Kinder where to put his drilling equipment, Foshee backed down. In a downward spiral, El Paso ended up taking a package that was valued at $26.87 as of signing on October 16, 2011, comprised of $25.91 in cash and stock, and a warrant with a strike price of $40—some $13 above Kinder Morgan's then-current stock price of $26.89 per share. * * *

Still, the deal was at a substantial premium to market, and the Board was advised by Morgan Stanley (and also by the analyses of Goldman—which had, and continued to, advise El Paso on the spin-off of the E&P business) that the offer was more attractive in the immediate term than doing the spin-off and had less execution risk, because Kinder Morgan had agreed to a great deal of closing certainty. Thus, the Board approved the Merger.

On October 16, 2011, the parties entered into the "Merger Agreement." The Merger Agreement contains a commitment from El Paso to assist Kinder Morgan in the sale of the E&P business, which Kinder Morgan hoped could be accomplished before the closing of the Merger. The Merger Agreement also contains a "no-shop" provision preventing El Paso from affirmatively soliciting higher bids, but gives the Board a fiduciary out in the event it receives a "Superior Proposal" from a third party for more than 50% of El Paso's equity securities or consolidated assets. These measures preclude El Paso from abandoning the Merger in order to pursue a sale of the E&P assets because the E&P assets make up less than 50% of El Paso's consolidated assets. By contrast, El Paso could terminate the Merger Agreement to pursue a sale of the pipeline business (which makes up more than 50% of the company's consolidated assets), but Kinder Morgan has a right to match any such Superior Proposal.

In the event that the Board accepts a Superior Proposal, El Paso must pay a $650 million termination fee to Kinder Morgan. In terms of the overall deal size, the termination fee represents 3.1% of the equity value and 1.69% of the enterprise value of El Paso as implied by the Merger Agreement. Thus, to buy just the pipeline business, an interloper would have to pay a termination fee that was, say, 5.1% of the equity value and 2.5% of the enterprise value of El Paso's pipeline business, assuming it comprised around 60.3% of El Paso's equity value and 67% of El Paso's enterprise value at the time of signing.

Despite the premium to market, the plaintiffs contend that the Merger is tainted by the selfish motivations of both Doug Foshee and Goldman Sachs. As the plaintiffs point out, there were numerous decisions made by the El Paso Board during the process that could be seen as questionable. These include:

- The failure of the Board to shop El Paso as a whole or its two key divisions separately to any other bidder after Kinder Morgan made its initial overture, despite knowing that Kinder Morgan was hoping to preempt competition by bidding for the whole company, and despite knowing that although there would be a number of bidders for the company's two key divisions if marketed separately, there was unlikely to be any rival to Kinder Morgan willing to purchase El Paso as a whole;

- The failure of the Board to reject Kinder Morgan's initial overtures and force it to go public and face the market pressure to raise its offer to a level where it could prevail in a hostile takeover bid;

- Charging Foshee with handling all negotiations with Kinder Morgan without any presence or close supervision by an independent director or legal advisor;

- Allowing Kinder Morgan (a supposedly tough, potential hostile bidder) to renege on an agreement in principle to pay cash and stock equal to $27.55 entered into on September 18, 2011 (a package that would likely be worth $31.76 today assuming current market prices) * * *

- Signing on to deal protection measures that would effectively preclude a post-signing market check for bids for the separate divisions because of the limited fiduciary out, which precludes the Board from accepting a topping bid for the E&P business, and which makes the emergence of a topping bid for the pipeline business difficult because of the $650 million termination fee and Kinder Morgan's matching rights; and

- Eventually agreeing to a deal that only provided El Paso stockholders with cash and stock equal to $25.91 in value (excluding the warrant), far less than the $27.55 previously agreed to by Kinder Morgan.

* * *

* * * [W]hen there is a reason to conclude that debatable tactical decisions were motivated not by a principled evaluation of the risks and benefits to the company's stockholders, but by a fiduciary's consideration of his own financial or other personal self-interests, then [the board has breached its fiduciary duties to shareholders]. * * * [T]he potential sale of a corporation has enormous implications for corporate managers and advisors, and a range of human motivations, including but by no means limited to greed, can inspire fiduciaries and their advisors to be less than faithful to their contextual duty to pursue the best value for the company's stockholders.

* * * [D]efendants begrudgingly concede that El Paso's longstanding financial advisor, Goldman, had a "potential conflict" because: (1) it owned approximately 19%, or $4 billion worth, of Kinder Morgan stock; (2) it controlled two of Kinder Morgan's board seats; (3) it had placed two senior Goldman principals on the Kinder Morgan board who thus owed Kinder Morgan fiduciary duties; and (4) the lead Goldman banker working for El Paso, Steve Daniel, personally owned approximately $340,000 of Kinder Morgan stock. But, the defendants argue that Goldman was walled off from giving strategic advice about the Kinder

Morgan bid early in the process and another top-tier bank, Morgan Stanley, came in and gave unconflicted advice.

* * * [T]he record developed in expedited discovery belies their argument that there is no reason to question the motives behind the decisions made by El Paso in negotiating the Merger Agreement. Although it is true that measures were taken to cabin Goldman's conflict (for example, Goldman formally set up an internal "Chinese wall" between the Goldman advisors to El Paso and the Goldman representatives responsible for the firm's Kinder Morgan investment) * * * those efforts were not effective. Goldman still played an important role in advising the Board by suggesting that the Board should avoid causing Kinder Morgan to go hostile and by presenting information about the value of pursuing the spin-off instead of the Kinder Morgan deal. * * *

Goldman was not out of the picture entirely, as El Paso management only thought it was necessary to limit Goldman's involvement in the Kinder Morgan side of the advisory work. Goldman continued its role as primary financial advisor to El Paso for the spin-off, and was asked to continue to provide financial updates to the Board that would enable the El Paso directors to compare the spin-off to the Merger.

The fact that Goldman continued to have its hands in the dough of the spin-off is important, because the Board was assessing the attractiveness of the Merger relative to the attractiveness of the spin-off. That was critical because the Board, at the recommendation of Foshee, Goldman, and Morgan Stanley, decided not to risk Kinder Morgan going hostile and not to do any test of the market with other possible buyers of El Paso as a whole, or of either or both of its two key business segments separately.

Thus, the Board was down to two strategic options: the spin-off or a sale to Kinder Morgan. Therefore, because Goldman stayed involved as the lead advisor on the spinoff, it was in a position to continue to exert influence over the Merger. The record suggests that there were questionable aspects to Goldman's valuation of the spin-off and its continued revision downward that could be seen as suspicious in light of Goldman's huge financial interest in Kinder Morgan.

Heightening these suspicions is the fact that Goldman's lead banker failed to disclose his own personal ownership of approximately $340,000 in Kinder Morgan stock, a very troubling failure that tends to undercut the credibility of his testimony and of the strategic advice he gave.

Even worse, Goldman tainted the cleansing effect of Morgan Stanley. Goldman clung to its previously obtained contract to make it the exclusive advisor on the spin-off and which promised Goldman $25 million in fees if the spin-off was completed. Despite the reality that Morgan Stanley was retained to address Goldman's bias toward a suboptimally priced deal with Kinder Morgan and thus Morgan Stanley's work in evaluating whether the spin-off was a more valuable option was critical to its integrity enforcing role, Goldman refused to concede that Morgan Stanley should be paid anything if the spin-off, rather than the Merger, was consummated. Goldman's friends in El Paso management—and that is what they seem to have been—easily gave in to Goldman. This resulted in an incentive structure like this for Morgan Stanley:

- Approve a deal with Kinder Morgan (the entity of which Goldman owned 19%)—get $35 million; or

- Counsel the Board to go with the spin-off or to pursue another option—get zilch, nada, zero.

This makes more questionable some of the tactical advice given by Morgan Stanley and some of its valuation advice, which can be viewed as stretching to make Kinder Morgan's offers more favorable than other available options. Then, despite saying that it did not advise on the Merger—a claim that the record does not bear out in large measure—Goldman asked for a $20 million fee for its work on the Merger. Of course, by the same logic it used to shut out Morgan Stanley from receiving any fee for the spin-off, Goldman should have been foreclosed from getting fees for working on the Merger when it supposedly was walled off from advising on that deal. But, Goldman's affectionate clients, more wed to Goldman than to logical consistency, quickly assented to this demand.

Worst of all was that the supposedly well-motivated and expert CEO entrusted with all the key price negotiations kept from the Board his interest in pursuing a management buy-out of the Company's E&P business. Knowing that Kinder Morgan intended to sell the E&P business in order to finance its overall purchase of El Paso, Foshee spoke with fellow El Paso manager Brent Smolik, the head of the E&P business, about approaching Kinder Morgan with a management bid for the E&P assets. The record does not make clear exactly when the idea of an MBO first occurred to Foshee, but an email exchange between Smolik and John Sult (the CFO of El Paso) suggests that Smolik and Foshee were discussing the MBO opportunity while Foshee was negotiating the Merger terms with Rich Kinder. Rather than disclose that he was contemplating an MBO to the Board, Foshee kept this information to himself, and even told Smolik that he wanted to discuss the MBO "as late [in the process] as possible." After the Merger price was finally set and the Merger Agreement entered into, Foshee went to Rich Kinder not once, but twice, to try to get Kinder interested in letting El Paso management bid. Although Kinder did not embrace Foshee's idea of an El Paso management-led buyout of the E&P business, the reality is that Foshee was interested in being a buyer of a key part of El Paso at the same time he was charged with getting the highest possible price as a seller of that same asset. At no time did Foshee come clean to his board about his self-interest, and he never sought permission from the Board before twice going to the CEO of the company's negotiating adversary.

At a time when Foshee's and the Board's duty was to squeeze the last drop of the lemon out for El Paso's stockholders, Foshee had a motive to keep juice in the lemon that he could use to make a financial Collins for himself and his fellow managers interested in pursuing an MBO of the E&P business. The defendants defend this by calling Foshee's actions and motivations immaterial and frivolous.

It may turn out after trial that Foshee is the type of person who entertains and then dismisses multi-billion dollar transactions at whim. Perhaps his interest in an MBO was really more of a passing fancy, a casual thought that he could have mentioned to Kinder over canapés and forgotten about the next day.

It could be.

Or it could be that Foshee is a very smart man, and very financially savvy. He did not tell anyone but his management confreres that he was contemplating an MBO because he knew that would have posed all kinds of questions about the negotiations with Kinder Morgan and how they were to be conducted. Thus, he decided to keep quiet about it and approach his negotiating counterpart Rich Kinder late in the process— after the basic deal terms were set—to maximize the chance that Kinder would be receptive. * * *

The concealed motives of Foshee, the concealed financial interest of Goldman's lead banker in Kinder Morgan, Goldman's continued influence over the Board's assessment of the spin-off, and the distortion of Morgan Stanley's incentives that arose as a result of El Paso management's acquiescence to its Goldman friends' demands leave me persuaded that the plaintiffs have a reasonable probability of success on a claim that the Merger is tainted by breaches of fiduciary duty. * * * Likewise, as mentioned, there are odd aspects to some of the financial analyses presented, which seem to go some way to making the Kinder Morgan bid look more favorable in comparison to other options than perhaps a more consistent approach to valuation would have done. The failure to use the emergence of Kinder Morgan as a bidder to do a soft test of the market for El Paso's attractive business units is, of course, relevant * * * particularly when questions of loyalty exist. And that failure was compounded by a deal protection package that (1) precluded termination of the Merger Agreement if a favorable bid for the E&P business emerged; and (2) made it very expensive for a bidder for the pipeline business to make an offer because of the $650 million termination fee and Kinder Morgan's matching rights. This is important because it was clear that the most valuable alternative to the Merger other than the announced spin-off was likely a sale of El Paso's two main businesses to separate buyers * * * or a sale of one business while retaining the other as a standalone public company (a twist on the spin-off).

Perhaps most troubling is that Foshee's velvet glove negotiating strategy—which involved proffering counter-offers at levels below the level he was authorized by the Board to advance—can now be viewed as having been influenced by an improper motive. Rather than having only the best interests of El Paso's stockholders in mind, Foshee had something else important on his mind—his interest in working with some of his fellow managers on a bid for the E&P business, which had been valued between $6 billion and $10 billion at various times by Goldman during 2011. That sort of deal would allow him to monetize a large part of his company-specific investment in El Paso, while permitting him the chance to continue to participate in managing key assets he knew and for another equity pop in the future. That goal, however, gave him an incentive different from maximizing what Kinder Morgan would pay El Paso, because the more Kinder Morgan had to pay El Paso, the more it might want for the E&P assets. And as mentioned, the bloodier the negotiation, the more Foshee risked having Kinder not wish to deal with him.

When anyone conceals his self-interest—as both Foshee and Goldman banker Steve Daniel did—it is far harder to credit that person's assertion that that self-interest did not influence his actions. That is particularly true when a court is reviewing the actions of businessmen and investment bankers. People like Foshee and Daniel get paid the big money because they are masters of economic incentives, and keenly aware of them at all times.

For similar reasons, the court is not swayed by Goldman's assertions that it was not influenced by its own economic incentives to maximize its $4 billion investment in Kinder Morgan by steering El Paso towards a deal with Kinder Morgan at a suboptimal price. Why? Goldman's claim that it was capable of putting aside its $4 billion investment in Kinder Morgan when advising El Paso on its strategic options is hard to square with the record evidence demonstrating the lengths to which Goldman would go to secure an advisory fee of $20 million from El Paso—a fraction of the dollar size of its Kinder Morgan investment—in connection with the Merger. For starters, * * * earlier in the deal process, Goldman had Lloyd Blankfein, its CEO and Chairman, give Foshee a personal, obsequious phone call to thank him for El Paso's retention of Goldman over the years and to try to secure a continuing role in working for El Paso during the pendency of the Kinder Morgan bid despite what Goldman deemed an "appearance of conflict." And despite now claiming that it was not a key strategic advisor in the Kinder Morgan deal, Goldman sought credit as an advisor in the press release announcing the

Merger, a move at self-promotion its rival Morgan Stanley called Goldman "at its most shameless." * * *

* * * Foshee knew that he was discussing and considering an MBO of the E&P business when he was negotiating price terms with Kinder Morgan, but he did not disclose that fact. He did not even disclose his discussions with Kinder about an MBO after the deal was baked to the Board.

This kind of furtive behavior engenders legitimate concern and distrust. Given that there are numerous debatable tactical choices that now seem to have been made in large measure based on Foshee's advice and with important influence from Goldman, I believe that the plaintiffs have a probability of showing that more faithful, unconflicted parties could have secured a better price from Kinder Morgan.

The question is what to do about it.

The El Paso stockholders arguably have much to gain by seeing this Merger proceed. No one can tell what would have happened had unconflicted parties negotiated the Merger. That is beyond the capacity of humans.

The price being offered by Kinder Morgan is one that reasonable El Paso stockholders might find very attractive. But it nags, of course, that it is not all that it might have been had things been done the way they should have been. The absence of a pre-signing market check also grates, when the decision not to explore the market and do a safe, friendly deal rather than stretch for value or push Kinder Morgan into a public, hostile fight might have been influenced by selfish considerations, rather than the desire to strike the best risk-reward balance for El Paso's stockholders.

* * *

Here, although the plaintiffs do not have the basis for claiming irreparable injury that exists when the plaintiff is a bidder, the adequacy of monetary damages as a remedy to them as stockholders is not apparent. By way of example, the difference in value of Kinder Morgan's original agreement in principle bid of $27.55 in cash and stock and the one agreed to of $26.87 equaled approximately $534 million in value as of the time of signing, even giving full value to Morgan Stanley's less than certain estimate of the value of the warrant component.

On this record, it appears unlikely that the independent directors of El Paso—who are protected by an exculpatory charter provision—could be held liable in monetary damages for their actions. Although they should have been more keen to Goldman's conflict, they were given reason to believe that that conflict had been addressed by the hiring of Morgan Stanley and by cabining Goldman's role. The extent to which the independent directors understood the perverse incentives created for Morgan Stanley by Goldman and El Paso management by the terms of Morgan Stanley's engagement is not spelled out in the record and is the type of issue that independent directors tend to look to advisors to address. Most important, the independent directors' reliance upon Foshee seems to have been made in good faith. From the standpoint of the independent directors, Foshee seems to have been well positioned as a large holder of El Paso stock and as a trusted executive to get the best deal for El Paso's stockholders. The independent directors were not trusted with the information that Foshee (and El Paso managers like Sult and Smolik) were mulling over a bid to Kinder Morgan for the E&P assets.

Although Foshee is a wealthy man, it is unlikely that he would be good for a verdict of more than half a billion dollars. And although Goldman has been named as an aider and abettor and it has substantial, some might say even government-insured, financial resources, it is difficult to prove an aiding and abetting claim. Given that Goldman's largest conflict was surfaced fully and addressed, albeit in incomplete and inadequate ways, whether the plaintiffs could ultimately prove Goldman liable for any shortfall is, at best, doubtful, despite Daniel's troubling individual failure of disclosure.

Nor do I find any basis to conclude that Kinder Morgan is likely to be found culpable as an aider and abettor. It bargained hard, as it was entitled to do. From its perspective, it appeared that steps were taken by El Paso and Goldman to address Goldman's conflict of interest. * * *

For present purposes, therefore, I am willing to accept that the plaintiffs have shown that there is a likelihood of irreparable injury if the Merger is not enjoined. That raises the hardest question, which is whether the threat of irreparable injury justifies an injunction in light of the risks that an injunction itself would present to the stockholders of El Paso.

At oral argument * * * upon questioning by the court, the plaintiffs clarified that they would be willing to accept the traditional injunctive relief of preventing the stockholders from voting on the Merger.

But the plaintiffs' understandable reluctance in their papers to deny the El Paso stockholders the ultimate chance to take the deal with Kinder Morgan despite the troubling behavior in the record is one that I share. * * * I share the plaintiffs' frustration that the traditional tools of equity may not provide the kind of fine instrument that enables optimal protection of stockholders in this context.

The kind of troubling behavior exemplified here can result in substantial wealth shifts from stockholders to insiders that are hard for the litigation system to police if stockholders continue to display a reluctance to ever turn down a premium-generating deal when that is presented. The negotiation process and deal dance present ample opportunities for insiders to forge deals that, while "good" for stockholders, are not "as good" as they could have been, and then * * * put the stockholders to a Hobson's choice. * * *

Fundamentally, the plaintiffs say that I can issue a preliminary injunction that allows El Paso a free option. It can shop any or all of itself, terminate the Merger Agreement without paying the break fee, and do what it wishes until the injunction expires. If something it likes comes along, El Paso should be able to take it, cost free. But if nothing does, then the injunction will expire and Kinder Morgan would somehow—by judicial compulsion, I assume—be forced to close, despite the pervasive breach of fundamental provisions of the Merger Agreement, including the one requiring El Paso to help Kinder Morgan to sell for itself the same assets the plaintiffs seek to have El Paso market. If my assumption about judicial compulsion is right, the plaintiffs do not seek a traditional negative injunction, but rather mandatory relief that can only be granted after a trial and a careful evaluation of Kinder Morgan's legitimate interests. If the plaintiffs do not view the injunction as one involving the court compelling Kinder Morgan to close upon the injunction's expiration if the El Paso stockholders approve the Merger, then the plaintiffs are asking me to enter an injunction that, to my view, would likely relieve Kinder Morgan of any obligation to close because its contractual rights would have been materially breached.

Given that the El Paso stockholders are well positioned to turn down the Kinder Morgan price if they do not like it, I am not persuaded that I should deprive them of the chance to make that decision for themselves. Although an after-the-fact monetary damages claim against the defendants is not a perfect tool, it has some value as a remedial instrument, and the likely prospect of a damages trial is no doubt unpleasant to Foshee, other El Paso managers who might be added as defendants, and to Goldman. And, of course, the defendants themselves should be mindful of the reality that in the period of truncated, expedited discovery, troubling facts arose about the interests of certain key players in this M&A drama. After full discovery, it would hardly be unprecedented for additional troubling information to emerge, given the suspicious instances of non-disclosure that have already been surfaced.

For now, however, I reluctantly deny the plaintiffs' motion for a preliminary injunction, concluding that the El Paso stockholders should not be deprived of the chance to decide for themselves about the Merger, despite the disturbing nature of some of the behavior leading to its terms.

IT IS SO ORDERED.

NOTES

(1) Shortly after this decision, the parties settled. According to the Notice of Settlement, "[i]n consideration for the full and final settlement and dismissal with prejudice of the Delaware Consolidated Action, and the release * * * of any and all Claims against the Defendant[s], El Paso has agreed to pay or cause to be paid $110,000,000 in cash into an interest-bearing escrow account for the benefit of the Class as provided in the Settlement Stipulation." As part of the settlement, Goldman Sachs agreed to forego its $20 million advisory fee. This was the first time in Goldman's history that the firm agreed to forego such a fee.

(2) The Delaware Court of Chancery approved the settlement terms as fair and reasonable in December 2012. In the settlement hearing, Chancellor Strine remarked: "I think it's a very substantial achievement for the class [as] there is clearly a sizeable and tangible benefit that was produced only because of the litigation." Do you agree? As Ronald Barusch observed on a Wall Street Journal blog: "[T]he settlement will probably amount to about 11¢ per share. Strine valued the merger consideration at $30.37 per share. So the settlement works out to be about 0.4% of the merger consideration. That is pretty close to a rounding error in the world of negotiating M&A exchange ratios."

(3) "In evaluating the $20 million give-up of Goldman's fee, one might also want to look at the value of the alleged conflicting interest challenged in the lawsuit. Goldman owned 19% of Kinder at the same time it was advising El Paso on selling itself to Kinder. Strine valued that investment at $4 billion. But what is more interesting is that El Paso shares were trading at $25.88 on October 14, 2011[—]the trading day before the El Paso deal was announced. Deal Journal reported in June of [2012] that Goldman sold 36.7 million shares (or about 27% of Goldman's stake in Kinder) for $31.88, or an aggregate of $220 million more than the pre-El Paso value—more than ten times the fee given up. And Kinder's shares are currently trading at around $35.80. There is no indication that the alleged Goldman conflict in any way contributed to this market gain. Nevertheless, it is a frame of reference for evaluating how painful the Goldman contribution * * * to the settlement is." Ronald Barusch, Dealpolitik: El Paso Case Sends Warning, but Bark is Worse than Bite (Sept. 9, 2012), http://blogs.wsj.com/deals/2012/09/11/deal politik-el-paso-case-sends-warning-but-bark-is-worse-than-bite/.

(4) Another way to evaluate the costs and benefits of the Goldman settlement is to balance the cost, the $20 million lost fee plus legal expenses, against the benefit, which is the difference between what Goldman indirectly paid for El Paso and the higher price that it would have had to pay if it had not engaged in the shenanigans described by Chancellor (later Chief Justice) Strine.

(5) Something of a bright spot in the ethical mess that was the El Paso-Kinder Morgan merger was that one of El Paso's law firms, the New York firm of Wachtell, Lipton, Rosen and Katz, apparently advised El Paso not to

hire Goldman Sachs as a financial adviser on the $25.91-a-share offer because of the conflicting interests that Goldman faced in the transaction. According to Stuart Grant, one of the lead attorneys for the plaintiffs, "[Wachtell] told the El Paso folks that given Goldman's conflict problems in the Kinder deal, it would be a really stupid thing to do." Jeff Feeley, El Paso's Lawyers at Wachtell Opposed Using Goldman, Lawyers Say, Reuters, Mar. 8, 2012.

(6) The plaintiffs' sizable legal fees and expenses were of course paid from the settlement fund. According to a Notice to Shareholders, the plaintiffs' lawyers disclosed that they would request an award of $800,000 in expenses and 24 percent of the settlement, which translates into a total of $27.2 million.

B. EXECUTIVE COMPENSATION AND THE WASTE DOCTRINE

HELLER V. BOYLAN
Supreme Court of New York, 1941.
29 N.Y.S.2d 653.

[Only the portions of this opinion dealing with the incentive compensation plan are included.]

COLLINS, JUSTICE.

In this derivative action 7 out of a total of 62,000 stockholders—holding under 1,000 out of a total of 5,074,076 shares—of the American Tobacco Company, seek recovery for the corporation from the Company's directors for alleged improper payments to certain of the Company's officers.

The suit derives from an incentive compensation by-law of the Company, known as Article XII, virtually unanimously adopted by the stockholders in March, 1912. Thereunder 10 percent of the annual profits over the earnings of the corresponding properties in 1910 are to be distributed, 2 1/2 percent to the president and 1 1/2 percent to each of the five vice-presidents "in addition to the fixed salary of each of said officers."

The profits, and consequently the bonuses, undulated with the years; but at all times they were quite lush. By virtue of this by-law, the officers have received from and including 1929 to and including 1939—in addition to $3,784,999.69 in salaries—bonuses aggregating $11,672,920.27, or total compensation during that eleven-year period of $15,457,919.69. The president alone, George W. Hill, Sr., received $592,370 in 1929; $1,010,508 in 1930; $1,051,570 in 1931; $825,537.49 in 1932. The other payments to him during such period were obese, the thinnest being

$137,042.65, in 1938, and the average around $400,000. The other officers likewise received handsome compensation though not as huge.

The plaintiffs maintain that these large bonus payments bore no relation to the value of the services for which they were given, that, consequently, they were in reality a gift in part, and that the majority stockholders committed waste and spoliation in thus giving away corporate property against the protest of the minority. Rogers v. Hill, 289 U.S. 582, 590–592, 53 S.Ct. 731, 77 L.Ed. 1385, 88 A.L.R. 744.

The validity of the by-law * * * has been sustained. Rogers v. Hill, supra. Nor do plaintiffs impugn the principle of incentive compensation. * * * That the Company has been singularly prosperous is indubitable. Its growth has been prodigious, its record for earnings is an enviable one, the management has been extraordinarily efficient, and the stockholders, as well as the officers, have been the beneficiaries of this immensely capable organization. The Company has made money even in direful times. Its capital investment is $265,000,000. It produces more than 200,000,000 cigarettes a day. In 1939 the Company's sales amounted to $262,416,000, its most popular brand—"Lucky Strike"—yielding $218,542,749. The Company is one of the world's giant industrial enterprises. Its activities are farflung, if not worldwide. Nevertheless, charge the plaintiffs, the payments to the officers have become "so large as in substance and effect to amount to spoliation or waste of corporate property." Rogers v. Hill, supra. * * *

[In] Rogers v. Hill, 289 U.S. 582, 53 S.Ct. 731, 735, 77 L.Ed. 1385, 88 A.L.R. 744, Butler, J., for the unanimous Court, enunciated the principle: * * *

> It follows from what has been shown that when adopted the by-law was valid. But plaintiff alleges that the measure of compensation fixed by it is not now equitable or fair. And he prays that the court fix and determine the fair and reasonable compensation of the individual defendants, respectively, for each of the years in question. * * * The * * * payments that plaintiff by this suit seeks to have restored to the company are the payments made to the individual defendants under the by-law.

> We come to consider whether these amounts are subject to examination and revision in the District Court. As the amounts payable depend upon the gains of the business, the specified percentages are not per se unreasonable. The by-law was adopted in 1912 by an almost unanimous vote of the shares represented at the annual meeting and presumably the stockholders supporting the measure acted in good faith and according to their best judgment. The tabular statement in the margin shows the payments to individual defendants under the by-law. Plaintiff does not complain of any made prior to 1921.

Regard is to be had to the enormous increase of the company's profits in recent years. The 2 1/2 percent yielded President Hill $447,870.30 in 1929 and $842,507.72 in 1930. The 1 1/2 percent yielded to each of the vice presidents, Neiley and Riggio, $115,141.86 in 1929 and $409,495.25 in 1930 and for these years payments under the by-law were in addition to the cash credits and fixed salaries shown in the statement. * * *

[T]he payments under the by-law have by reason of increase of profits become so large as to warrant investigation in equity in the interest of the company. Much weight is to be given to the action of the stockholders, and the by-law is supported by the presumption of regularity and continuity. But the rule prescribed by it cannot, against the protest of a shareholder, be used to justify payments of sums as salaries so large as in substance and effect to amount to spoliation or waste of corporate property. The dissenting opinion of Judge Swan indicates the applicable rule: 'If a bonus payment has no relation to the value of services for which it is given, it is in reality a gift in part, and the majority stockholders have no power to give away corporate property against the protest of the minority.' 60 F.2d 109, 113. The facts alleged by plaintiff are sufficient to require that the District Court, upon a consideration of all the relevant facts brought forward by the parties, determine whether and to what extent payments to the individual defendants under the by-laws constitute misuse and waste of the money of the corporation [citing cases].

Following Rogers' victory in the Supreme Court, and before the "investigation in equity" was launched, negotiations for adjustment were started. These eventuated in a settlement, from which the Company benefited—at the time of the settlement in July, 1933—by $6,200,000 and a further saving of about $2,250,000 by March, 1940. Many more millions were saved—inasmuch as the settlement reduced the bonus base and the employee's stock subscription plan was revised. In addition, Rogers was paid a fee of $525,000, the net being $263,000, and the income tax thereon exhausting the remaining $262,000. Thus ended the Rogers campaign.

But the echoes therefrom persisted. Seven stockholders, including three of the plaintiffs in this action (Heller, Wile and Mandelkor), and represented by most of the attorneys who appear for the plaintiffs here, assailed the settlement and sought to have it cancelled on the ground that the huge fee to Rogers was in the nature of a bribe. * * *

The Perplexities of the Case

Quite obviously, this case carries a number of perplexities. A few of them will be noted:

1.   The general reluctance of the Courts to interfere with the internal management of a corporation. Pragmatism by the Courts—interference or meddling with free and lawful enterprise honestly conducted—is repugnant to our concept of government. Of course the hesitancy is overcome if fraud or bad faith or over-reaching appears—if the fiduciaries have been faithless to their trust.

2.   Though this is a derivative stockholders' action, only 7 out of 62,000 stockholders have joined the onslaught; these 7 holding less than 1,000 out of a total of 5,074,076 shares of the Company. This factor, though significant, bears only on the equities; it is by no means decisive. Tyranny over the minority by the majority is abhorrent and will not be tolerated. The majority cannot, save by due legal process, make that which is illegal, legal, nor can it confiscate the company's assets or dispense them as unearned bounties. Majority rule does not license subjugation or immunize spoliation. The possession of power does not authorize or excuse its abuse. Power is not a franchise to do wrong. The majority cannot any more than the minority violate the law with impunity.

3.   This case differs from most stockholders suits in that in those cases it is the conduct of directors which forms the basis of the complaint, whereas here not only is the by-law a creature of the stockholders, but on at least two other occasions, one in April, 1933, and again in April, 1940, the stockholders, by almost unanimous vote, ratified many of the payments involved in this suit. To be sure, "the majority stockholders have no power to give away corporate property against the protest of the minority." Rogers v. Hill, supra [60 F.2d 114].

4.   The fact that the by-law has been in existence since 1912 and has been held valid.

5.   The embarrassment which some of the defendants might experience in refunding even a part of what they received, especially since taxes were paid thereon.

6.   The language of finality contained in paragraph 4 of the by-law.[b]

7.   The paucity of apposite precedents.

Let it be emphasized, however, that the above are alluded to only as difficulties; they enter into the equities, but do not constitute a bar. * * *

---

[b]   Paragraph 4 reads as follows:

The declaration of the Treasurer as to the amount of net profits for the year and the sum due anyone hereunder shall be binding and conclusive on all parties, and no one claiming hereunder shall have the right to question the said declaration, or to any examination of the books or accounts of the Company, and nothing herein contained shall give any incumbent of any office any right to claim to continue therein, or any other right except as herein specifically expressed.

Now, even a high-bracketer would deem [the stipends involved in this case] munificent. To the person of moderate income they would be princely—perhaps as something unattainable; to the wage-earner ekeing out an existence, they would be fabulous, and the unemployed might regard them as fantastic, if not criminal. To others they would seem immoral, inexcusably unequal, and an indictment of our economic system. The opinion of Judge Swan has been unfairly paraphrased as announcing that "no man can be worth $1,000,000 a year". * * *

At the stockholders meeting on April 3, 1941, a holder of 80 shares of common stock—who thought the compensation grandiose—offered a resolution to restrict the president's bonus to a maximum of $100,000 and to impose other limitations. But the resolution was defeated by 2,193,418 votes to 74,571. * * *

Let it be boldly marked that the particular business before this Court is not the revamping of the social or economic order—*justiciable* disputes confront it. * * *

Here, the plaintiffs proffered no testimony whatever in support of their charge of waste. The figures, they reason, speak for themselves, and the defendants must justify them. The figures do speak, but just what do they say as a matter of equity? They are immense, staggeringly so. Even so, is that enough to compel the substitution of the Court's judgment for that of the stockholders? Larger compensation has been judicially approved. * * *

Assuming, arguendo, that the compensation should be revised, what yardstick is to be employed? Who or what is to supply the measuring-rod? The conscience of equity? Equity is but another name for human being temporarily judicially robed. He is not omnipotent or omniscient. Can equity be so arrogant as to hold that it knows more about managing this corporation than its stockholders?

Yes, the Court possesses the *power* to prune these payments, but openness forces the confession that the pruning would be synthetic and artificial rather than analytic or scientific. Whether or not it would be fair and just, is highly dubious. Yet, merely because the problem is perplexing is no reason for eschewing it. It is not timidity, however, which perturbs me. It is finding a rational or just gauge for revising these figures were I inclined to do so. No blueprints are furnished. The elements to be weighed are incalculable; the imponderables, manifold. To act out of whimsy or caprice or arbitrariness would be more than inexact—it would be the precise antithesis of justice; it would be a farce.

If comparisons are to be made, with whose compensation are they to be made—executives? Those connected with the motion picture industry? Radio artists? Justices of the Supreme Court of the United States? The President of the United States? Manifestly, the material at hand is not of adequate plasticity for fashioning into a pattern or standard. Many instances of positive underpayment will come to mind, just as instances of apparent rank overpayment abound. Haplessly, intrinsic worth is not always the criterion. A classic might perhaps produce trifling compensation for its author, whereas a popular novel might yield a titanic fortune. Merit is not always commensurately rewarded, whilst mediocrity sometimes unjustly brings incredibly lavish returns. Nothing is so divergent and contentious and inexplicable as values.

Courts are ill-equipped to solve or even to grapple with these entangled economic problems. Indeed, their solution is not within the juridical province. Courts are concerned that corporations be honestly and fairly operated by its directors, with the observance of the formal requirements of the law; but what is reasonable compensation for its officers is primarily for the stockholders. This does not mean that fiduciaries are to commit waste, or misuse or abuse trust property, with impunity. A just cause will find the Courts at guard and implemented to grant redress. But the stockholder must project a less amorphous plaint than is here presented.

* * * I find for the defendants. Yet it does not follow that I affirmatively approve these huge payments. It means that I cannot by any reliable standard find them to be waste or spoliation; it means that I find no valid ground for disapproving what the great majority of stockholders have approved. In the circumstances, if a ceiling for these bonuses is to be erected, the stockholders who built and are responsible for the present structure must be the architects. Finally, it is not amiss to accent the antiseptic policy stressed by Judge Liebell in Winkelman et al. v. General Motors Corporation, D.C.S.D.N.Y. decided August 14, 1940, 39 F.Supp. 826, that: "The duty of the director executives participating in the bonus seems plain—they should be the first to consider unselfishly whether under all the circumstances their bonus allowances are fair and reasonable".

NOTE

What do you think of the fact that the named plaintiff in the prior case, a Mr. Rogers, received what the court called a "huge fee" in the settlement when none of the other shareholders received any such fee?

WILDERMAN V. WILDERMAN

Court of Chancery of Delaware, 1974.
315 A.2d 610.

MARVEL, VICE CHANCELLOR:

Eleanor M. Wilderman, the plaintiff in this action, sues in her own right and in her capacity as a stockholder with an interest in one-half of the issued and outstanding stock of the defendant Marble Craft Company, Inc. She primarily seeks a ruling to the effect that the defendant Joseph M. Wilderman (the president of the corporate defendant and her former husband) for the fiscal years ending March 31, from 1971 through 1973, caused excessive and unauthorized payments to be made to himself out of earnings of the corporate defendant and that such payments, made in the form of unearned and unauthorized salary and bonuses, must accordingly be returned to the treasury of Marble Craft Company.

Plaintiff asks that upon the Court-ordered return of such excessive payments to the corporate treasury that they be treated as corporate profits and required to be distributed as dividends, thereby opening the way to plaintiff to share in the net corporate profits as a stockholder with a 50% equity in her corporation. Plaintiff also asks that appropriate adjustments be made in the corporate defendant's pension plan so as to reflect the return to the corporate treasury of amounts found to be excessive compensation received by the defendant for the fiscal years in question. Also sought is an injunction against disbursement by the individual defendant of moneys from corporate funds or the transfer by such defendant of corporate assets without the approval of the board of directors of the corporation. Finally, plaintiff seeks an order directing the continuance of the business of the corporate defendant under a custodian as provided for under the provisions of 8 Del.C. § 226.

Marble Craft is engaged in the business of installing ceramic tile and marble facings in residences and commercial buildings, such business having been organized by the individual parties to this action some fifteen years ago, being originally operated from the family home. Defendant's initial knowledge of the tile business was gained while working briefly for his father-in-law prior to going into business with his former wife, and there is no doubt but that defendant has been the major force in the business of the corporate defendant inasmuch as he has done most of the estimating, supervising and business getting for the corporation, working up to sixty hours or more per week on corporate business. Plaintiff, on the other hand, has been primarily a bookkeeper for the business, although there is no doubt but that plaintiff is fully versed in the tile business, her father having started such a business in 1929. Significantly, in the beginning of the enterprise the parties' respective compensation was not entirely disparate, as it is now, defendant having initially drawn $125 a week compared to plaintiff's $75.

The business proved successful as a family venture, and in 1961 it was incorporated under the name of Marble Craft Company, Inc., its authorized capital shares consisting of one hundred shares of stock being issued to plaintiff and defendant as joint tenants in exchange for the assets of the business. By-laws providing for the election of two directors were adopted, and the parties, as the duly elected directors, thereupon chose themselves to fill the designated corporate offices, defendant being elected president and the plaintiff vice president, secretary, and treasurer.

The controversy here involved primarily centers around the amount of compensation which defendant has caused to be paid to himself for the fiscal years 1971, 1972 and 1973, compensation which had its origin in a policy[2] designed to avoid corporate taxation by paying out the net corporate profits of Marble Craft Company in the form of executive compensation before the end of each taxable year, thus avoiding double taxation. Accordingly, dividends attributable to corporate profits have never been formally paid until ordered by the Court in the course of this litigation. Such policy of avoiding dividend payments initially worked to the advantage of both parties and their two children, the financial advantage to plaintiff in the plan having been virtually destroyed by the parties' separation and divorce. Thus, following the breakup of the home, plaintiff was largely excluded from the benefits enuring to defendant as a result of the large amounts he proceeded to pay himself. Asserting his authority as the chief executive officer of the corporate defendant, defendant caused the amount of compensation to be paid to him to be increased from $25,000 in 1963 to $60,000 in 1970, the last year for which salary payments to defendant are not questioned, such salary having concededly been authorized by corporate resolution. Next, despite the pendency of this action defendant paid himself a bonus of $71,738.71 in addition to a flat salary of $20,800 for the fiscal year 1971, the salary being based on an authorized draw of $400 per week, this being the first year after marital differences arose in which defendant could not point to at least tacit corporate authorization as to the full amount of his compensation. For the fiscal year 1972 defendant paid himself total compensation of $35,000, a year in which corporate profits were substantially lower than those of the previous year due to a building trades strike, and for the fiscal year ending March 31, 1973, defendant caused payment to himself of total compensation in the amount of $86,893.40. During this same period plaintiff received the annual sum of $7,800 for her services to the corporation.

On June 26, 1972, in an effort to work out some accommodation between the parties, a custodian was appointed by order of this Court as provided for by 8 Del.C. § 226(a)(2). However, the deadlock between the parties persisted, and on March 29, 1973, the defendant having caused

---

[2] This policy, however, encountered the opposition of the Internal Revenue Service which reduced the deduction allowable to Marble Craft for salary paid to defendant from $30,000 to $20,000 for 1965, from $30,000 to $25,000 for 1966, and from $60,000 to $40,000 for 1970. Presumably the effect of this action was twofold (1) the amount of disallowance was taxed as income to the corporation, and (2) the amount of disallowance less the tax due thereon became a de facto dividend.

the sum of $86,893.40[3] to be paid to himself as compensation for such fiscal year, an order was entered, on the recommendation of the custodian, which stipulated that such payment was without prejudice to the right to contest defendant's compensation in excess of his authorized salary of $20,800. Also authorized and paid on the custodian's recommendation was a dividend of $20,000 to be divided equally between plaintiff and defendant.

The authority to compensate corporate officers is normally vested in the board of directors, 8 Del.C. § 122(5), and the compensating of corporate officers is usually a matter of contract. * * * By early April 1971 the management of Marble Craft was clearly deadlocked with its owner-managers in complete disagreement as to the amount of compensation to be paid the defendant, the payment of anything above a $400 weekly salary being opposed by plaintiff. Therefore, the only amount agreed upon by the board and hence the only authorized payment to Mr. Wilderman for the fiscal years 1971, 1972 and 1973 would appear to have been at the rate of $20,800 per year, or $400 per week, and that additional compensation received by him for the years in question must find its authorization in the theory of quantum meruit.

Turning from the issue of corporate authorization of defendant's salary to the issue of the reasonableness of the compensation paid Mr. Wilderman, plaintiff contends that the compensation paid to defendant for the years in question was unreasonable, plaintiff arguing that although courts are hesitant to inquire into the reasonableness of executive compensation when it is fixed by a disinterested board, the standard for fixing executive compensation is obviously more strict when it is fixed by the recipient himself. And where, as in the case at bar, the recipient's vote as a director was necessary to the fixing of the amount of his compensation, then the burden of showing the reasonableness of such compensation clearly falls upon its recipient. This is so, of course, because of the fiduciary position which directors hold towards their corporation and its stockholders.

As to the facts to be considered in reaching a determination of the question as to whether or not defendant has met the burden he must carry there is little authority in Delaware. In Hall v. Isaacs, [37 Del.Ch. 530, 146 A.2d 602 (1958), affirmed in part 39 Del.Ch. 244, 163 A.2d 288 (1960)] the Court was of the view that evidence of what other executives similarly situated received was relevant, and in Meiselman v. Eberstadt, [39 Del.Ch. 563, 170 A.2d 720 (1961)] the ability of the executive was considered. Other factors which have been judicially recognized elsewhere are whether or not the Internal Revenue Service has allowed the corporation to deduct the amount of salary alleged to be unreasonable.

---

[3] Based on an authorized salary of $35,000 per annum plus 15% of gross receipts in excess of $300,000, a formula which was operative through the fiscal year 1970.

Other relevant factors are whether the salary bears a reasonable relation to the success of the corporation, the amount previously received as salary, whether increases in salary are geared to increases in the value of services rendered, and the amount of the challenged salary compared to other salaries paid by the employer. See 2 Washington and Rothschild, Compensating the Corporate Executive, 848–873 (3rd Ed.1962). Dr. Seligman, an expert, testified that on the basis of a financial analysis of Marble Craft and its present earnings that reasonable compensation for defendant would range between $25,000 and $35,000. It also appears that the Internal Revenue Service proposes to permit Marble Craft a deduction of $52,000 for defendant's 1971 compensation of $92,538.

On the present record I am not convinced that defendant has discharged his burden as to the reasonableness of amounts he has drawn for all of the years in question. * * * Thus, while for the fiscal years 1971, 1972 and 1973 Mr. Wilderman was technically entitled to be compensated for his services in the amount of only $20,800, I am of the opinion that in light of the nature of defendant's services to the corporation, which appear to have been important to its success, that he is entitled to compensation in the amount of $45,000 for the fiscal year 1971 and the same amount for fiscal 1973. Defendant's compensation of $35,000 for the fiscal year ending 1972 will be left undisturbed. Accordingly, he will be ordered to return $47,538 in excess compensation to the corporate treasury for fiscal 1971 and $41,893.40 for fiscal 1973, both amounts with interest.

Additionally, because payments to the Marble Craft pension fund have been tied to defendant's compensation for the years in question, defendant will be directed to repay to the defendant Marble Craft excessive payments to such fund in the same ratio as the refunds of his excessive compensation. * * *

An appropriate order may be submitted on notice.

NOTE

Other courts have agreed with the basic principles of *Wilderman* that where one party in effect sets his own compensation, he then has the burden of establishing its fundamental fairness. Lynch v. Patterson, 701 P.2d 1126 (Wyo.1985); Giannotti v. Hamway, 387 S.E.2d 725 (Va.1990).

BREHM V. EISNER

Supreme Court of Delaware, 2000.
746 A.2d 244.

VEASEY, CHIEF JUSTICE. [In this shareholder derivative action, the Court of Chancery dismissed Plaintiffs' Complaint which stated that the

Board of Directors had breached its fiduciary duty. This court affirms the decision as set forth in the following opinion.]

The claims before us are that: (a) the board of directors of The Walt Disney Company ("Disney") as it was constituted in 1995 (the "Old Board") breached its fiduciary duty in approving an extravagant and wasteful Employment Agreement of Michael S. Ovitz as president of Disney; (b) the Disney board of directors as it was constituted in 1996 (the "New Board") breached its fiduciary duty in agreeing to a non-fault termination of the Ovitz Employment Agreement, a decision that was extravagant and wasteful; and (c) the directors were not disinterested and independent.

This is potentially a very troubling case on the merits. On the one hand, it appears from the Complaint that: (a) the compensation and termination payout for Ovitz were exceedingly lucrative, if not luxurious, compared to Ovitz' value to the Company; and (b) the processes of the boards of directors in dealing with the approval and termination of the Ovitz Employment Agreement were casual, if not sloppy and perfunctory. On the other hand, the Complaint is so inartfully drafted that it was properly dismissed under our pleading standards for derivative suits. * * * Therefore, both as to the processes of the two Boards and the waste test, this is a close case.

A. The 1995 Ovitz Employment Agreement

By an agreement dated October 1, 1995, Disney hired Ovitz as its president. * * * Although he lacked experience managing a diversified public company, other companies with entertainment operations had been interested in hiring him for high-level executive positions. The Employment Agreement was unilaterally negotiated by [Disney Chairman and CEO Michael] Eisner and approved by the Old Board. Their judgment was that Ovitz was a valuable person to hire as president of Disney, and they agreed ultimately with Eisner's recommendation in awarding him an extraordinarily lucrative contract.

Ovitz' Employment Agreement had an initial term of five years and required that Ovitz "devote his full time and best efforts exclusively to the Company," with exceptions for volunteer work, service on the board of another company, and managing his passive investments. In return, Disney agreed to give Ovitz a base salary of $1 million per year, a discretionary bonus, and two sets of stock options (the "A" options and the "B" options) that collectively would enable Ovitz to purchase 5 million shares of Disney common stock.

[A termination clause in the employment agreement provided that if Ovitz left Disney's employment and it was not his fault, he would receive a compensation package. A lump sum of $10 million plus his remaining salary and an amount representing the probable unpaid installments of the bonus would be awarded if he left before 2002. Things did not work out well and 14 months later the arrangement was terminated on a non-fault basis, and Ovitz left with about $140 million as consolation.] * * *

The Complaint * * * alleges that the Old Board failed properly to inform itself about the total costs and incentives of the Ovitz Employment Agreement, especially the severance package. This is the key allegation related to this issue on appeal. Specifically, plaintiffs allege that the Board failed to realize that the contract gave Ovitz an incentive to find a way to exit the Company via a non-fault termination as soon as possible because doing so would permit him to earn more than he could by fulfilling his contract. The Complaint alleges, however, that the Old Board had been advised by a corporate compensation expert, Graef Crystal, in connection with its decision to approve the Ovitz Employment Agreement. Two public statements by Crystal form the basis of the allegation that the Old Board failed to consider the incentives and the total cost of the severance provisions.* * *

* * * [One] article appears first to paraphrase Crystal: "With no one expecting failure, the sleeper clauses in Ovitz's contract seemed innocuous, Crystal says, explaining that no one added up the total cost of the severance package." The article then quotes Crystal as saying that the amount of Ovitz' severance was "shocking" and that "nobody quantified this and I wish we had." One of the charging paragraphs of the Complaint concludes:

> 57. As has been conceded by Graef Crystal, the executive compensation consultant who advised the Old Board with respect to the Ovitz Employment Agreement, the Old Board never considered the costs that would be incurred by Disney in the event Ovitz was terminated from the Company for a reason other than cause prior to the natural expiration of the Ovitz Employment Agreement.

B. The New Board's Actions in Approving the Non-Fault Termination

Soon after Ovitz began work, problems surfaced and the situation continued to deteriorate during the first year of his employment. * * * The Complaint uses these reports to suggest that the New Board had reason to believe that Ovitz' performance and lack of commitment met the gross negligence or malfeasance standards of the termination-for-cause provisions of the contract.

The deteriorating situation, according to the Complaint, led Ovitz to begin seeking alternative employment and to send Eisner a letter in September 1996 that the Complaint paraphrases as stating his dissatisfaction with his role and expressing his desire to leave the Company.* * *

On December 11, 1996, Eisner and Ovitz agreed to arrange for Ovitz to leave Disney on the non-fault basis provided for in the 1995 Employment Agreement. Eisner then "caused" the New Board "to rubber-stamp his decision (by 'mutual consent')." This decision was implemented by a December 27, 1996 letter to Ovitz from defendant Sanford M. Litvack, an officer and director of Disney. That letter stated:

"This will confirm the terms of your agreement with the Company as follows:

1. The Term of your employment under your existing Employment Agreement with The Walt Disney Company will end at the close of business today * * *.

2. This letter will for all purposes of the Employment Agreement be treated as a 'Non-Fault Termination.' By our mutual agreement, the total amount payable to you under your Employment Agreement, including the amount payable under Section 11(c) in the event of a 'Non-Fault Termination,' is $38,888,230.77, net of withholding required by law or authorized by you * * *.

3. This letter will further confirm that the option to purchase 3,000,000 shares of the Company's Common Stock granted to you pursuant to Option A described in your Employment Agreement will vest as of today and will expire in accordance with its terms on September 30, 2002."

Although the non-fault termination left Ovitz with what essentially was a very lucrative severance agreement, it is important to note that Ovitz and Disney had negotiated for that severance payment at the time they initially contracted in 1995, and in the end the payout to Ovitz did not exceed the 1995 contractual benefits. * * *

The Complaint charges the New Board with waste, computing the value of the severance package agreed to by the Board at over $140 million, consisting of cash payments of about $39 million and the value of the immediately vesting "A" options of over $101 million. * * *

The allegation of waste is based on the inference most favorable to plaintiffs that Disney owed Ovitz nothing, either because he had resigned (de facto) or because he was unarguably subject to firing for cause. These allegations must be juxtaposed with the presumption that the New Board exercised its business judgment in deciding how to resolve the potentially litigable issues of whether Ovitz had actually resigned or had definitely breached his contract. * * *

Principles of Corporation Law Compared with Good Corporate Governance Practices

All good corporate governance practices include compliance with statutory law and case law establishing fiduciary duties. But the law of corporate fiduciary duties and remedies for violation of those duties are distinct from the aspirational goals of ideal corporate governance practices. Aspirational ideals of good corporate governance practices for boards of directors that go beyond the minimal legal requirements of the corporation law are highly desirable, often tend to benefit stockholders, sometimes reduce litigation and can usually help directors avoid liability. But they are not required by the corporation law and do not define standards of liability. * * *

* * * The sole issue that this Court must determine is whether the particularized facts alleged in this Complaint provide a reason to believe that the conduct of the Old Board in 1995 and the New Board in 1996 constituted a violation of their fiduciary duties.

Independence of the Disney Board

* * * Plaintiffs' allegation that Eisner was interested in maximizing his compensation at the expense of Disney and its shareholders cannot reasonably be inferred from the facts alleged in Plaintiffs' amended complaint. At all times material to this litigation, Eisner owned several million options to purchase Disney stock. Therefore, it would not be in Eisner's economic interest to cause the Company to issue millions of additional options unnecessarily and at considerable cost. Such a gesture would not, as Plaintiffs suggest, "maximize" Eisner's own compensation package. Rather, it would dilute the value of Eisner's own very substantial holdings. * * * Nothing alleged by Plaintiffs generates a reasonable inference that Eisner would benefit personally from allowing Ovitz to leave Disney without good cause. * * *

Analytical Framework for the Informational Component of Directorial Decisionmaking

* * * The question is whether the trial court's formulation is consistent with our objective test of reasonableness, the test of materiality and concepts of gross negligence. We agree with the Court of Chancery that the standard for judging the informational component of the directors' decisionmaking does not mean that the Board must be informed of every fact. The Board is responsible for considering only material facts that are reasonably available, not those that are immaterial or out of the Board's reasonable reach. * * *

Plaintiffs' Contention that the Old Board Violated the Process Duty of Care in Approving the Ovitz Employment Agreement

Certainly in this case the economic exposure of the corporation to the payout scenarios of the Ovitz contract was material, particularly given its large size, for purposes of the directors' decisionmaking process. And those dollar exposure numbers were reasonably available because the logical inference from plaintiffs' allegations is that Crystal or the New Board could have calculated the numbers. Thus, the objective tests of reasonable availability and materiality were satisfied by this Complaint. But that is not the end of the inquiry for liability purposes.

The fact that Crystal did not quantify the potential severance benefits to Ovitz for terminating early without cause (under the terms of the Employment Agreement) does not create a reasonable inference that the Board failed to consider the potential cost to Disney in the event that they decided to terminate Ovitz without cause. But, even if the Board did fail to calculate the potential cost to Disney, I nevertheless think that this allegation fails to create a reasonable doubt that the former Board exercised due care. * * * Merely because Crystal now regrets not having calculated the package is not reason enough to overturn the judgment of the Board then. It is the essence of the business judgment rule that a court will not apply 20/20 hindsight to second guess a board's decision, except "in rare cases [where] a transaction may be so egregious on its face that the board approval cannot meet the test of business judgment." Because the Board's reliance on Crystal and his decision not to fully calculate the amount of severance lack "egregiousness," this is not that rare case. I think it a correct statement of law that the duty of care is still fulfilled even if a Board does not know the exact amount of a severance payout but nonetheless is fully informed about the manner in which such a payout would be calculated. A board is not required to be informed of every fact, but rather is required to be reasonably informed. * * *

The Complaint, fairly construed, admits that the directors were advised by Crystal as an expert and that they relied on his expertise. Accordingly, the question here is whether the directors are to be "fully protected" (i.e., not held liable) on the basis that they relied in good faith on a qualified expert under Section 141(e) of the Delaware General Corporation Law.[51] The Old Board is entitled to the presumption that it exercised proper business judgment, including proper reliance on the expert.

---

[51] Section 141(e) provides: A member of the board of directors, or a member of any committee designated by the board of directors, shall, in the performance of such member's duties, be fully protected in relying in good faith upon the records of the corporation and upon such information, opinions, reports or statements presented to the corporation by any of the corporation's officers or employees, or committees of the board of directors, or by any other person as to matters the member reasonably believes are within such other person's professional or expert competence and who has been selected with reasonable care by or on behalf of the corporation. 8 Del. C. § 141(e).

Although the Court of Chancery did not expressly predicate its decision on Section 141(e), Crystal is presumed to be an expert on whom the Board was entitled to rely in good faith under Section 141(e) in order to be "fully protected." Plaintiffs must rebut the presumption that the directors properly exercised their business judgment, including their good faith reliance on Crystal's expertise. * * *

To survive a Rule 23.1 motion to dismiss in a due care case where an expert has advised the board in its decisionmaking process, the complaint must allege particularized facts (not conclusions) that, if proved, would show, for example, that: (a) the directors did not in fact rely on the expert; (b) their reliance was not in good faith; (c) they did not reasonably believe that the expert's advice was within the expert's professional competence; (d) the expert was not selected with reasonable care by or on behalf of the corporation, and the faulty selection process was attributable to the directors; (e) the subject matter (in this case the cost calculation) that was material and reasonably available was so obvious that the board's failure to consider it was grossly negligent regardless of the expert's advice or lack of advice; or (f) that the decision of the Board was so unconscionable as to constitute waste or fraud.

Plaintiffs' Contention that the Old Board Violated "Substantive Due Care" Requirements and Committed Waste Ab Initio with Ovitz' Employment Agreement

* * * Plaintiffs' principal theory is that the 1995 Ovitz Employment Agreement was a "wasteful transaction for Disney ab initio" because it was structured to "incentivize" Ovitz to seek an early non-fault termination. The Court of Chancery correctly dismissed this theory as failing to meet the stringent requirements of the waste test, i.e., " 'an exchange that is so one sided that no business person of ordinary, sound judgment could conclude that the corporation has received adequate consideration.' " Moreover, the Court concluded that a board's decision on executive compensation is entitled to great deference. It is the essence of business judgment for a board to determine if "a 'particular individual warrant[s] large amounts of money, whether in the form of current salary or severance provisions.' "

Specifically, the Court of Chancery inferred from a reading of the Complaint that the Board determined it had to offer an expensive compensation package to attract Ovitz and that they determined he would be valuable to the Company. The Court also concluded that the vesting schedule of the options actually was a disincentive for Ovitz to leave Disney. * * *

* * * We agree with the analysis of the Court of Chancery that the size and structure of executive compensation are inherently matters of judgment. As former Chancellor Allen stated in Vogelstein:

* * * Roughly, a waste entails an exchange of corporate assets for consideration so disproportionately small as to lie beyond the range at which any reasonable person might be willing to trade. * * * If, however, there is any substantial consideration received by the corporation, and if there is a good faith judgment that in the circumstances the transaction is worthwhile, there should be no finding of waste, even if the fact finder would conclude ex post that the transaction was unreasonably risky. * * *

To be sure, there are outer limits, but they are confined to unconscionable cases where directors irrationally squander or give away corporate assets. Here, however, we find no error in the decision of the Court of Chancery on the waste test.

As for the plaintiffs' contention that the directors failed to exercise "substantive due care," we should note that such a concept is foreign to the business judgment rule. Courts do not measure, weigh or quantify directors' judgments. We do not even decide if they are reasonable in this context. Due care in the decisionmaking context is process due care only. Irrationality is the outer limit of the business judgment rule. Irrationality may be the functional equivalent of the waste test or it may tend to show that the decision is not made in good faith, which is a key ingredient of the business judgment rule.

Plaintiffs' Contention that the New Board Committed Waste in Its Decision That Ovitz' Contract Should be Terminated on a "Non-Fault" Basis

* * * The terms of the Employment Agreement limit "good cause" for terminating Ovitz's employment to gross negligence or malfeasance, or a voluntary resignation without the consent of the Company. * * * None of Plaintiffs' allegations rise to the level of gross negligence or malfeasance. * * *

* * * But the Complaint fails on its face to meet the waste test because it does not allege with particularity facts tending to show that no reasonable business person would have made the decision that the New Board made under these circumstances. * * *

IN RE WALT DISNEY CO. DERIVATIVE LITIGATION (BREHM V. EISNER)

Supreme Court of Delaware, 2006.
906 A.2d 27.

Before STEELE, C.J., HOLLAND, BERGER, JACOBS, and RIDGELEY, J.J., constituting the Court en Banc.

JACOBS, JUSTICE.

[After this court remanded the case to the Court of Chancery and granted plaintiffs leave to replead in Brehm v. Eisner, 746 A.2d 244 (Del.

2000), the plaintiffs filed their second amended complaint in January 2002. In August 2005, the Court of Chancery entered judgment in favor of all defendants. This court affirms the decision.]

The appellants * * * challenge the Chancellor's determination that although the compensation committee's decision-making process fell far short of corporate governance "best practices," the committee members breached no duty of care in considering and approving the [No Fault Termination (NFT)] terms of the [Ovitz Employment Agreement (OEA)]. That conclusion is reversible error, the appellants claim, because the record establishes that the compensation committee members did not properly inform themselves of the material facts and, hence, were grossly negligent in approving the NFT provisions of the OEA. * * *

* * * In a "best case" scenario, all committee members would have received, before or at the committee's first meeting on September 26, 1995, a spreadsheet or similar document prepared by (or with the assistance of) a compensation expert (in this case, Graef Crystal). Making different, alternative assumptions, the spreadsheet would disclose the amounts that Ovitz could receive under the OEA in each circumstance that might foreseeably arise. One variable in that matrix of possibilities would be the cost to Disney of a non-fault termination for each of the five years of the initial term of the OEA. The contents of the spreadsheet would be explained to the committee members, either by the expert who prepared it or by a fellow committee member similarly knowledgeable about the subject. * * *

Had that scenario been followed, there would be no dispute (and no basis for litigation) over what information was furnished to the committee members or when it was furnished. Regrettably, the committee's informational and decisionmaking process used here was not so tidy. * * *

The Disney compensation committee met twice: on September 26 and October 16, 1995. The minutes of the September 26 meeting reflect that the committee approved the terms of the OEA (at that time embodied in the form of a letter agreement), except for the option grants, which were not approved until October 16—after the Disney stock incentive plan had been amended to provide for those options. At the September 26 meeting, the compensation committee considered a "term sheet" which, in summarizing the material terms of the OEA, relevantly disclosed that in the event of a non-fault termination, Ovitz would receive: (i) the present value of his salary ($1 million per year) for the balance of the contract term, (ii) the present value of his annual bonus payments (computed at $7.5 million) for the balance of the contract term, (iii) a $10 million termination fee, and (iv) the acceleration of his options for 3 million shares, which would become immediately exercisable at market price.

* * * [T]he issue may be framed as whether the compensation committee members knew, at the time they approved the OEA, that the

value of the option component of the severance package could reach the $92 million order of magnitude if they terminated Ovitz without cause after one year. The evidentiary record shows that the committee members were so informed. * * *

The compensation committee members derived their information about the potential magnitude of an NFT payout from two sources. The first was the value of the "benchmark" options previously granted to Eisner and Wells and the valuations by Watson of the proposed Ovitz options. * * *

The committee's second source of information was the amount of "downside protection" that Ovitz was demanding. Ovitz required financial protection from the risk of leaving a very lucrative and secure position at CAA, of which he was a controlling partner, to join a publicly held corporation to which Ovitz was a stranger, and that had a very different culture and an environment which prevented him from completely controlling his destiny. The committee members knew that by leaving CAA and coming to Disney, Ovitz would be sacrificing "booked" CAA commissions of $150 to $200 million—an amount that Ovitz demanded as protection against the risk that his employment relationship with Disney might not work out. * * *

The OEA was specifically structured to compensate Ovitz for walking away from $150 million to $200 million of anticipated commissions from CAA over the five-year OEA contract term. This meant that if Ovitz was terminated without cause, the earlier in the contract term the termination occurred the larger the severance amount would be to replace the lost commissions. * * *

* * * [T]he appellants contend that [directors] Poitier and Lozano did not review the spreadsheets generated by Watson at the September 26 meeting. The short answer is that even if Poitier and Lozano did not review the spreadsheets themselves, Russell and Watson adequately informed them of the spreadsheets' contents. * * *

For these reasons, we uphold the Chancellor's determination that the compensation committee members did not breach their fiduciary duty of care in approving the OEA.

(e) HOLDING THAT THE REMAINING DISNEY DIRECTORS DID NOT FAIL TO EXERCISE DUE CARE IN APPROVING THE HIRING OF OVITZ AS THE PRESIDENT OF DISNEY

The Court of Chancery held that the business judgment rule presumptions protected the decisions of the compensation committee and the remaining Disney directors, not only because they had acted with due care but also because they had not acted in bad faith. That latter ruling, the appellants claim, was reversible error because the Chancellor formulated and then applied an incorrect definition of bad faith.

In its Opinion the Court of Chancery defined bad faith as follows:

Upon long and careful consideration, I am of the opinion that the concept of *intentional dereliction of duty*, a *conscious disregard for one's responsibilities*, is an appropriate (although not the only) standard for determining whether fiduciaries have acted in good faith. Deliberate indifference and inaction *in the face of a duty to act* is, in my mind, conduct that is clearly disloyal to the corporation. It is the epitome of faithless conduct.

* * * This case * * * is one in which the duty to act in good faith has played a prominent role, yet to date is not a well-developed area of our corporate fiduciary law. * * * [T]he duty to act in good faith is * * * up to this point relatively uncharted. Because of the increased recognition of the importance of good faith, some conceptual guidance to the corporate community may be helpful. * * *

The precise question is whether the Chancellor's articulated standard for bad faith corporate fiduciary conduct—intentional dereliction of duty, a conscious disregard for one's responsibilities—is legally correct. In approaching that question, we note that the Chancellor characterized that definition as "*an* appropriate (*although not the only*) standard for determining whether fiduciaries have acted in good faith." That observation is accurate and helpful, because as a matter of simple logic, at least three different categories of fiduciary behavior are candidates for the "bad faith" pejorative label.

The first category involves so-called "subjective bad faith," that is, fiduciary conduct motivated by an actual intent to do harm. * * * We need not dwell further on this category, because no such conduct is claimed to have occurred, or did occur, in this case.

The second category of conduct, which is at the opposite end of the spectrum, involves lack of due care—that is, fiduciary action taken solely by reason of gross negligence and without any malevolent intent. In this case, appellants assert claims of gross negligence to establish breaches not only of director due care but also of the directors' duty to act in good faith. Although the Chancellor found, and we agree, that the appellants failed to establish gross negligence, to afford guidance we address the issue of whether gross negligence (including a failure to inform one's self of available material facts), without more, can also constitute bad faith. The answer is clearly no.

* * * Both our legislative history and our common law jurisprudence distinguish sharply between the duties to exercise due care and to act in good faith, and highly significant consequences flow from that distinction.

The Delaware General Assembly has addressed the distinction between bad faith and a failure to exercise due care (*i.e.*, gross negligence) in two separate contexts. The first is Section 102(b)(7) of the DGCL, which authorizes Delaware corporations, by a provision in the certificate of incorporation, to exculpate their directors from monetary damage liability for a breach of the duty of care. That exculpatory provision affords significant protection to directors of Delaware corporations. The statute carves out several exceptions, however, including most relevantly, "for acts or omissions not in good faith * * *." Thus, a corporation can exculpate its directors from monetary liability for a breach of the duty of care, but not for conduct that is not in good faith. To adopt a definition of bad faith that would cause a violation of the duty of care automatically to become an act or omission "not in good faith," would eviscerate the protections accorded to directors by the General Assembly's adoption of Section 102(b)(7).

A second legislative recognition of the distinction between fiduciary conduct that is grossly negligent and conduct that is not in good faith, is Delaware's indemnification statute, found at 8 *Del. C.* § 145. To oversimplify, subsections (a) and (b) of that statute permit a corporation to indemnify (*inter alia*) any person who is or was a director, officer, employee or agent of the corporation against expenses (including attorneys' fees), judgments, fines and amounts paid in settlement of specified actions, suits or proceedings, where (among other things): (i) that person is, was, or is threatened to be made a party to that action, suit or proceeding, and (ii) that person "acted in good faith and in a manner the person reasonably believed to be in or not opposed to the best interests of the corporation. . . . " Thus, under Delaware statutory law a director or officer of a corporation can be indemnified for liability (and litigation expenses) incurred by reason of a violation of the duty of care, but not for a violation of the duty to act in good faith. * * *

That leaves the third category of fiduciary conduct. * * * This third category is what the Chancellor's definition of bad faith—intentional dereliction of duty, a conscious disregard for one's responsibilities—is intended to capture. The question is whether such misconduct is properly treated as a non-exculpable, non-indemnifiable violation of the fiduciary duty to act in good faith. In our view it must be, for at least two reasons.

First, the universe of fiduciary misconduct is not limited to either disloyalty in the classic sense (*i.e.*, preferring the adverse self-interest of the fiduciary or of a related person to the interest of the corporation) or gross negligence. Cases have arisen where corporate directors have no conflicting self-interest in a decision, yet engage in misconduct that is more culpable than simple inattention or failure to be informed of all facts material to the decision. To protect the interests of the corporation and its shareholders, fiduciary conduct of this kind, which does not involve disloyalty (as traditionally defined) but is qualitatively more culpable than gross negligence, should be proscribed. * * *

Second, the legislature has also recognized this intermediate category of fiduciary misconduct, which ranks between conduct involving subjective bad faith and gross negligence. Section 102(b)(7)(ii) of the DGCL expressly denies money damage exculpation for "acts or omissions not in good faith or which involve intentional misconduct or a knowing violation of law." By its very terms that provision distinguishes between "intentional misconduct" and a "knowing violation of law" (both examples of subjective bad faith) on the one hand, and "acts * * * not in good faith," on the other. Because the statute exculpates directors only for conduct amounting to gross negligence, the statutory denial of exculpation for "acts * * * not in good faith" must encompass the intermediate category of misconduct captured by the Chancellor's definition of bad faith.

For these reasons, we uphold the Court of Chancery's definition as a legally appropriate, although not the exclusive, definition of fiduciary bad faith. * * *

The appellants' final claim is that even if the approval of the OEA was protected by the business judgment rule presumptions, the payment of the severance amount to Ovitz constituted waste. This claim is rooted in the doctrine that a plaintiff who fails to rebut the business judgment rule presumptions is not entitled to any remedy unless the transaction constitutes waste. * * *

To recover on a claim of corporate waste, the plaintiffs must shoulder the burden of proving that the exchange was "so one sided that no business person of ordinary, sound judgment could conclude that the corporation has received adequate consideration." A claim of waste will arise only in the rare, "unconscionable case where directors irrationally squander or give away corporate assets." This onerous standard for waste is a corollary of the proposition that where business judgment presumptions are applicable, the board's decision will be upheld unless it cannot be "attributed to any rational business purpose."

The claim that the payment of the NFT amount to Ovitz, without more, constituted waste is meritless on its face, because at the time the NFT amounts were paid, Disney was contractually obligated to pay them. The payment of a contractually obligated amount cannot constitute waste, unless the contractual obligation is itself wasteful. Accordingly, the proper focus of a waste analysis must be whether the amounts required to be paid in the event of an NFT were wasteful *ex ante*.

Appellants claim that the NFT provisions of the OEA were wasteful because they incentivized Ovitz to perform poorly in order to obtain payment of the NFT provisions. The Chancellor found that the record did not support that contention. * * *

That ruling is erroneous, the appellants argue, because the NFT provisions of the OEA were wasteful in their very design. Specifically, the

OEA gave Ovitz every incentive to leave the Company before serving out the full term of his contract. The appellants urge that although the OEA may have induced Ovitz to join Disney as President, no contractual safeguards were in place to retain him in that position. In essence, appellants claim that the NFT provisions of the OEA created an irrational incentive for Ovitz to get himself fired.

That claim does not come close to satisfying the high hurdle required to establish waste. The approval of the NFT provisions in the OEA had a rational business purpose: to induce Ovitz to leave CAA, at what would otherwise be a considerable cost to him, in order to join Disney. * * * Ovitz had no control over whether or not he would be fired, either with or without cause. To suggest that at the time he entered into the OEA Ovitz would engineer an early departure at the cost of his extraordinary reputation in the entertainment industry and his historical friendship with Eisner, is not only fanciful but also without proof in the record. Indeed, the Chancellor found that it was "patently unreasonable to assume that Ovitz intended to perform just poorly enough to be fired quickly, but not so poorly that he could be terminated for cause."

We agree. Because the appellants have failed to show that the approval of the NFT terms of the OEA was not a rational business decision, their waste claim must fail.

NOTES

(1) U.S. executives earn many times what line workers do in total remuneration. According to the most recent available analysis, which is for the year 2012, the top 200 chief executives at public companies with $1 billion or more in revenues received significant pay increases. Equilar Inc., the executive compensation analysis firm, reported the median 2012 pay package at $15.1 million, which represents an increase of 16 percent over 2011. In general, executive pay is about 450 times the average pay of production workers. The presidents and CEOs of the very largest companies far outrun these figures, however, and are light-years distant from the ordinary wage earner. For example, Michael Duke, the CEO of Walmart, made $17.6 million in 2012, while the average employee of the company made only $22,100. Tim Cook of Apple made a whopping $378 million in 2012, while the average pay at Apple was $60,400. Jamie Dimon of JPMorgan Chase made $23.1 million in 2012, versus the average employee salary of $52,200. In other words, the CEOs of these companies made, respectively, 796 times, 6258 times, and 442 times the salary of the average worker. Similarly, Rex Tillerson, the CEO of Exxon Mobil, made $25.2 million in 2012, and while this is 278 times the salary of the average worker, the average Exxon Mobil worker makes a healthy $90,600. Does the huge difference between CEO incomes and workers' salaries seem so bad when the average worker's salary is high enough to provide a solid standard of living?

(2) Bonuses tied to company performance and the exercise of stock options following increases in share prices account for both the massive increases in executive compensation as well as the difference in CEO compensation and average salaries.

(3) There is general acceptance today of the idea that compensation of CEOs should be performance based—i.e., executive compensation should be tied to improvements in shareholder wealth. The most common devices are grants of stock options and sales of restricted stock to executives at favorable prices. Both apparently link the level of executive compensation directly with the share price. The examples given above of extremely high levels of compensation are all based on significant increases in the market value of stock. However, several well-known devices permit recipients of options or restricted stock to indirectly obtain their current value immediately and without regard to the subsequent performance of the stock. For example, a recipient of restricted stock options may immediately thereafter sell shares from his portfolio, or may exercise options granted previously and sell the stock so obtained.

(4) Executive compensation has long been the target of regulatory action:

(a) *Disclosure of Executive Compensation.* In October 1992, the SEC adopted major amendments to its rules governing disclosure of executive compensation. SEC Rel. No. 33–6962, 57 Fed. Reg. 48,126 (Oct. 16, 1992); rev'd SEC Rel. No. 33–7032, 58 Fed.Reg. 63010–01 (Nov. 29, 1993).

(b) *Revenue Reconciliation Act of 1993.* This Act added new § 162(m) to the Internal Revenue Code, disallowing corporate deductions for executive compensation for 1994 and later years to the extent that the compensation for an executive exceeds $1 million per year.

Certainly § 162(m) has had an effect on current compensation practices. Long-term compensation plans have been modified so that they are based on "performance goals" that comply with § 162(m) and the regulations; compensation arrangements have been shifted toward deferred compensation plans; and the membership of compensation committees have been revised to make sure that the members are all "outside" directors as defined in the regulations. However, not all companies have made these adjustments. Since the only effect of noncompliance with § 162(m) is the disallowance of a portion of a corporate deduction, many corporations have simply continued to pay executives in excess of $1 million per year and foregone the tax deduction, even though that increases somewhat their total tax bills.

(5) Criticism of executive compensation continues into the 21st century. The Enron scandal and the collapse of many of the nation's leading banking institutions in the financial crisis of 2007–2010 convinced many Americans that pay is not always linked to performance. For example, Kenneth Lay received more than $8 million in 2000, less than a year before Enron's collapse. Some scholars have argued that public disapproval, whether reaching the level of "outrage" or not, has served to limit executive pay packages, or at least led executives to disguise what they are actually paid.

See Lucian Bebchuk & Jesse Fried, Pay Without Performance: The Unfulfilled Promise of Executive Compensation 64–70 (2004); see also Paul Krugman, For Richer, N.Y. Times, Oct. 20, 2002, at E62.

(6) Other commentators argue that pay reflects performance, and that high CEO salaries are necessary to retain executives who might otherwise bolt for jobs in private equity. See, e.g., John E. Core, Wayne R. Guay, & Randall S. Thomas, Is U.S. CEO Compensation Inefficient Pay Without Performance?, 103 Mich. L. Rev. 1142, 1144 (2005) (reviewing Bebchuk & Fried, supra, and expressing doubt that Bebchuk and Fried have shown there are systematic failures in U.S. executive compensation); Bengt Holmstrom, Pay Without Performance and the Managerial Power Hypothesis: A Comment, 30 J. Corp. L. 703, 704 (2005) (attributing some of the recent rise in executive pay to increased demand for executive talent while also noting peculiarities of the executive labor market).

(7) Some suggest that banks have been excessively rewarding their employees at shareholders' expense. Eric Dash, Ailing Banks Favor Salaries Over Shareholders, N.Y. Times, Jan. 27, 2010. The reporters found that those banks that received TARP money have cut back on dividends but not on employee compensation: "[r]oughly 90 cents out of every dollar that these banks earned in 2009—and sometimes more—is going toward employee salaries, bonuses and benefits, according to company filings." Bank of America recently doubled the share of earnings that it sets aside for employees, even though it was forced to cut its quarterly dividend to a penny as a condition of its second government bailout. Shareholder advocates have long claimed that Wall Street pay works in favor of management and employees rather than shareholders. Have recent government bailouts aggravated this problem by incentivizing managers to take bigger risks for higher bonuses?

(8) On January 23, 2014, the New York Times reported: "A year after an embarrassing trading blowup * * * JPMorgan's board voted this week to increase [company CEO and Board Chairman Jamie] Dimon's annual compensation for 2013, hashing out the pay package after a series of meetings that turned heated at times. * * * The raise * * * follows a move by the board last year to slash Mr. Dimon's compensation by half, to $11.5 million." The New York Times also observed that:

> JPMorgan's directors may have decided that Mr. Dimon, as his peers may, should get a raise, but to ordinary Americans—and possibly to regulators—the decision to increase his compensation may seem curious given the banner penalties that federal authorities have extracted from the bank. It is not unheard-of for chief executives to lose their jobs when their companies have been battered by regulators.
>
> But a crucial difference is that JPMorgan's legal travails have not threatened the bank financially. While steep legal fees did weigh on the bank's bottom line, JPMorgan still reported annual 2013 profits

of $17.9 billion. And while other bank chief executives stumbled during the financial crisis, Mr. Dimon never did, emerging from the wreckage even more powerful.

Mr. Dimon's star has risen more recently as he took on a critical role in negotiating both the bank's $13 billion settlement with government authorities over its sale of mortgage-backed securities in the years before the financial crisis and the $2 billion settlement over accusations that the bank turned a blind eye to signs of fraud surrounding Bernard Madoff.

Jessica Silver-Greenberg and Susanne Craig, Fined Billions, JPMorgan Chase Will Give Dimon a Raise, N.Y. Times, Jan. 23, 2014.

C. CONTROLLING SHAREHOLDER CONFLICTS OF INTEREST

SINCLAIR OIL CORP. V. LEVIEN

Supreme Court of Delaware, 1971.
280 A.2d 717.

WOLCOTT, CHIEF JUSTICE.

This is an appeal by the defendant, Sinclair Oil Corporation (hereafter Sinclair), from an order of the Court of Chancery, 261 A.2d 911 in a derivative action requiring Sinclair to account for damages sustained by its subsidiary, Sinclair Venezuelan Oil Company (hereafter Sinven), organized by Sinclair for the purpose of operating in Venezuela, as a result of dividends paid by Sinven, the denial to Sinven of industrial development, and a breach of contract between Sinclair's wholly-owned subsidiary, Sinclair International Oil Company, and Sinven.

Sinclair, operating primarily as a holding company, is in the business of exploring for oil and of producing and marketing crude oil and oil products. At all times relevant to this litigation, it owned about 97% of Sinven's stock. The plaintiff owns about 3000 of 120,000 publicly held shares of Sinven. Sinven, incorporated in 1922, has been engaged in petroleum operations primarily in Venezuela and since 1959 has operated exclusively in Venezuela.

Sinclair nominates all members of Sinven's board of directors. The Chancellor found as a fact that the directors were not independent of Sinclair. Almost without exception, they were officers, directors, or employees of corporations in the Sinclair complex. By reason of Sinclair's domination, it is clear that Sinclair owed Sinven a fiduciary duty. Sinclair concedes this.

The Chancellor held that because of Sinclair's fiduciary duty and its control over Sinven, its relationship with Sinven must meet the test of intrinsic fairness. The standard of intrinsic fairness involves both a high degree of fairness and a shift in the burden of proof. Under this standard the burden is on Sinclair to prove, subject to careful judicial scrutiny, that its transactions with Sinven were objectively fair. Guth v. Loft, Inc., 23 Del.Ch. 255, 5 A.2d 503 (1939).

Sinclair argues that the transactions between it and Sinven should be tested, not by the test of intrinsic fairness with the accompanying shift of the burden of proof, but by the business judgment rule under which a court will not interfere with the judgment of a board of directors unless there is a showing of gross and palpable overreaching. Meyerson v. El Paso Natural Gas Co., 246 A.2d 789 (Del.Ch.1967). A board of directors enjoys a presumption of sound business judgment, and its decisions will not be disturbed if they can be attributed to any rational business purpose. A court under such circumstances will not substitute its own notions of what is or is not sound business judgment.

We think, however, that Sinclair's argument in this respect is misconceived. When the situation involves a parent and a subsidiary, with the parent controlling the transaction and fixing the terms, the test of intrinsic fairness, with its resulting shifting of the burden of proof, is applied. The basic situation for the application of the rule is the one in which the parent has received a benefit to the exclusion and at the expense of the subsidiary.

Recently, this court dealt with the question of fairness in parent-subsidiary dealings in Getty Oil Co. v. Skelly Oil Co., [267 A.2d 883 (Del.Sup.) 1970]. In that case, both parent and subsidiary were in the business of refining and marketing crude oil and crude oil products. The Oil Import Board ruled that the subsidiary, because it was controlled by the parent, was no longer entitled to a separate allocation of imported crude oil. The subsidiary then contended that it had a right to share the quota of crude oil allotted to the parent. We ruled that the business judgment standard should be applied to determine this contention. Although the subsidiary suffered a loss through the administration of the oil import quotas, the parent gained nothing. The parent's quota was derived solely from its own past use. The past use of the subsidiary did not cause an increase in the parent's quota. Nor did the parent usurp a quota of the subsidiary. Since the parent received nothing from the subsidiary to the exclusion of the minority stockholders of the subsidiary, there was no self-dealing. Therefore, the business judgment standard was properly applied.

A parent does indeed owe a fiduciary duty to its subsidiary when there are parent-subsidiary dealings. However, this alone will not evoke the intrinsic fairness standard. This standard will be applied only when the fiduciary duty is accompanied by self-dealing — the situation when a parent is on both sides of a transaction with its subsidiary. Self-dealing occurs when the parent, by virtue of its causes the subsidiary to act in such a way that the parent receives something from the subsidiary to the exclusion of, and detriment to, the minority stockholders of the subsidiary.

We turn now to the facts. The plaintiff argues that, from 1960 through 1966, Sinclair caused Sinven to pay out such excessive dividends that the industrial development of Sinven was effectively prevented, and it became in reality a corporation in dissolution.

From 1960 through 1966, Sinven paid out $108,000,000 in dividends ($38,000,000 in excess of Sinven's earnings during the same period). The Chancellor held that Sinclair caused these dividends to be paid during a period when it had a need for large amounts of cash. Although the dividends paid exceeded earnings, the plaintiff concedes that the payments were made in compliance with 8 Del.C. § 170, authorizing payment of dividends out of surplus or net profits. However, the plaintiff attacks these dividends on the ground that they resulted from an improper motive—Sinclair's need for cash. The Chancellor, applying the intrinsic fairness standard, held that Sinclair did not sustain its burden of proving that these dividends were intrinsically fair to the minority stockholders of Sinven.

Since it is admitted that the dividends were paid in strict compliance with 8 Del.C. §170, the alleged excessiveness of the payments alone would not state a cause of action. Nevertheless, compliance with the applicable statute may not, under all circumstances, justify all dividend payments. If a plaintiff can meet his burden of proving that a dividend cannot be grounded on any reasonable business objective, then the courts can and will interfere with the board's decision to pay the dividend.

Sinclair contends *that* it is improper to apply the intrinsic fairness standard to dividend payments even when the board which voted for the dividends is completely dominated. In support of this contention, Sinclair relies heavily [on] American District Telegraph Co. [ADT] v. Grinnell Corp., (N.Y.Sup. [19]69) aff'd. 33 A.D.2d 769, 306 N.Y.S.2d 209 (1969). Plaintiffs were [minori]ty stockholders of ADT, a subsidiary of Grinnell. The plaintiffs ally [contended that] Grinnell, realizing that it would soon have to sell its ADT stock[, cau]sed ADT to pay excessive divide[nds. B]ecause the dividend payments conformed with applicable statutory [provisions,] the cour[t he]ld the plaintiffs could not prove an abuse of discretion, the cour[t found that] the complaint did not state a cause of action. Other decis[ions] [see]m to support Sinclair's contention. In Metropolitan Casualt[y Co. of N.Y.]m v. First State Bank of Temple, 54 S.W.2d 358 (Tex.Civ.App.193[1] [rev'd] on other grounds, 79 S.W.2d 835 (Sup.Ct.1935), the cour[t did] not void a declaration o[f divi]dend[s because] a majority of interested directors does interested in and benefit[ted] because all directors, by necessity, are [divi]dend declaration.

We do not accept the argument that the intrinsic fairness test can never be applied to a dividend declaration by a dominated board, although a dividend declaration by a dominated board will not inevitably demand the application of the intrinsic fairness standard. Moskowitz v. Bantrell, 41 Del.Ch. 177, 190 A.2d 749 (Del.Supr.1963). If such a dividend is in essence self-dealing by the parent, then the intrinsic fairness standard is the proper standard. For example, suppose a parent dominates a subsidiary and its board of directors. The subsidiary has outstanding two classes of stock, X and Y. Class X is owned by the parent and Class Y is owned by minority stockholders of the subsidiary. If the subsidiary, at the direction of the parent, declares a dividend on its Class X stock only, this might well be self-dealing by the parent. It would be receiving something from the subsidiary to the exclusion of and detrimental to its minority stockholders. This self-dealing, coupled with the parent's fiduciary duty, would make intrinsic fairness the proper standard by which to evaluate the dividend payments.

Consequently it must be determined whether the dividend payments by Sinven were, in essence, self-dealing by Sinclair. The dividends resulted in great sums of money being transferred from Sinven to Sinclair. However, a proportionate share of this money was received by the minority shareholders of Sinven. Sinclair received nothing from Sinven to the exclusion of its minority stockholders. As such, these dividends were not self-dealing. We hold therefore that the Chancellor erred in applying the intrinsic fairness test as to these dividend payments. The business judgment standard should have been applied.

We conclude that the facts demonstrate that the dividend payments complied with the business judgment standard and with 8 Del.C. § 170. The motives for causing the declaration of dividends are immaterial unless the plaintiff can show that the dividend payments resulted from improper motives and amounted to waste. The plaintiff contends only that the dividend payments drained Sinven of cash to such an extent that it was prevented from expanding.

The plaintiff proved no business opportunities which came to Sinven independently and which Sinclair either took to itself or denied to Sinven. As a matter of fact, with two minor exceptions which resulted in losses, all of Sinven's operations have been conducted in Venezuela, and Sinclair had a policy of exploiting its oil properties located in different countries by subsidiaries located in the particular countries.

From 1960 to 1966 Sinclair purchased or developed oil fields in Alaska, Canada, Paraguay, and other places around the world. The plaintiff contends that these were all opportunities which could have been taken by Sinven. The Chancellor concluded that Sinclair had not proved that its denial of expansion opportunities to Sinven was intrinsically fair. He based this conclusion on the following findings of fact. Sinclair made no real effort to expand Sinven. The excessive dividends paid by Sinven resulted in so great a cash drain as to effectively deny to Sinven any ability to expand. During this same period Sinclair actively pursued a company-wide policy of developing through its subsidiaries new sources of revenue, but Sinven was not permitted to participate and was confined in its activities to Venezuela.

However, the plaintiff could point to no opportunities which came to Sinven. Therefore, Sinclair usurped no business opportunity belonging to Sinven. Since Sinclair received nothing from Sinven to the exclusion of and detriment to Sinven's minority stockholders, there was no self-dealing. Therefore, business judgment is the proper standard by which to evaluate Sinclair's expansion policies.

Since there is no proof of self-dealing on the part of Sinclair, it follows that the expansion policy of Sinclair and the methods used to achieve the desired result must, as far as Sinclair's treatment of Sinven is concerned, be tested by the standards of the business judgment rule. Accordingly, Sinclair's decision, absent fraud or gross overreaching, to achieve expansion through the medium of its subsidiaries, other than Sinven, must be upheld.

Even if Sinclair was wrong in developing these opportunities as it did, the question arises, with which subsidiaries should these opportunities have been shared? No evidence indicates a unique need or ability of Sinven to develop these opportunities. The decision of which subsidiaries would be used to implement Sinclair's expansion policy was one of business judgment with which a court will not interfere absent a showing of gross and palpable overreaching. No such showing has been made here.

Next, Sinclair argues that the Chancellor committed error when he held it liable to Sinven for breach of contract.

In 1961 Sinclair created Sinclair International Oil Company (hereafter International), a wholly owned subsidiary used for the purpose of coordinating all of Sinclair's foreign operations. All crude purchases by Sinclair were made thereafter through International.

On September 28, 1961, Sinclair caused Sinven to contract with International whereby Sinven agreed to sell all of its crude oil and refined products to International at specified prices. The contract provided for minimum and maximum quantities and prices. The plaintiff contends that Sinclair caused this contract to be breached in two respects. Although the contract called for payment on receipt, International's payments lagged as much as 30 days after receipt. Also, the contract required International to purchase at least a fixed minimum amount of crude and refined products from Sinven. International did not comply with this requirement.

Clearly, Sinclair's act of contracting with its dominated subsidiary was self-dealing. Under the contract Sinclair received the products produced by Sinven, and of course the minority shareholders of Sinven were not able to share in the receipt of these products. If the contract was breached, then Sinclair received these products to the detriment of Sinven's minority shareholders. We agree with the Chancellor's finding that the contract was breached by Sinclair, both as to the time of payments and the amounts purchased.

Although a parent need not bind itself by a contract with its dominated subsidiary, Sinclair chose to operate in this manner. As Sinclair has received the benefits of this contract, so must it comply with the contractual duties.

Under the intrinsic fairness standard, Sinclair must prove that its causing Sinven not to enforce the contract was intrinsically fair to the minority shareholders of Sinven. Sinclair has failed to meet this burden. Late payments were clearly breaches for which Sinven should have sought and received adequate damages. As to the quantities purchased, Sinclair argues that it purchased all the products produced by Sinven. This, however, does not satisfy the standard of intrinsic fairness. Sinclair has failed to prove that Sinven could not possibly have produced or someway have obtained the contract minimums. As such, Sinclair must account on this claim.

Finally, Sinclair argues that the Chancellor committed error in refusing to allow it a credit or setoff of all benefits provided by it to Sinven with respect to all the alleged damages. The Chancellor held that setoff should be allowed on specific transactions, e.g., benefits to Sinven under the contract with International, but denied an overall setoff against all damages claimed. We agree with the Chancellor, although the point may well be moot in view of our holding that Sinclair is not required to account for the alleged excessiveness of the dividend payments.

We will therefore reverse that part of the Chancellor's order that requires Sinclair to account to Sinven for damages sustained as a result of dividends paid between 1960 and 1966, and by reason of the denial to Sinven of expansion during that period. We will affirm the remaining portion of that order and remand the cause for further proceedings.

NOTES

(1) Difficult issues can arise in a number of contexts whenever there are minority shareholders in a corporate subsidiary. For example, the Internal Revenue Code permits a corporation to file a "consolidated return" with subsidiaries that are at least 80 percent owned. The effect of consolidation is that a single return is filed covering the income or loss of all the corporations as a group, and the result may be that a valuable tax loss owned by a subsidiary may be utilized to offset income of the parent or of other

subsidiaries within the group. Today, problems created by consolidated returns within parent/subsidiary groups are usually handled by formal written agreements, known as tax allocation or tax sharing agreements. These agreements typically provide that the parent corporation will compensate the subsidiary in cash for the net tax benefits actually obtained by the parent as a result of the consolidation. For a case involving such an agreement (after the subsidiary was sold by the parent to an outside third party), see Summit Nat'l Life Ins. Co. v. Cargill, Inc., 807 F.Supp. 363 (E.D.Pa.1992), aff'd, 981 F.2d 1248 (3d Cir.1992).

(2) Problems such as those involved in the principal case can be avoided by the elimination of the minority shareholders. How can this be done? A negotiated buyout? What if the minority is unwilling to sell at a reasonable price? Could Sinclair create a wholly owned subsidiary, "X Corporation," transfer its holdings of Sinven to it, and then merge Sinven into X Corporation, requiring the minority shareholders to accept cash rather than X Corporation stock? See MBCA §§ 11.02(c)(3), 11.04. What protection does the minority have? See MBCA § 13.02(a) and, generally, MBCA ch. 13.

WEINBERGER V. UOP, INC.

Supreme Court of Delaware, 1983.
457 A.2d 701.

Before HERRMANN, C.J., MCNEILLY, QUILLEN, HORSEY and MOORE, JJ., constituting the Court en Banc.

MOORE, JUSTICE:

This post-trial appeal was reheard en banc from a decision of the Court of Chancery. It was brought by the class action plaintiff below, a former shareholder of UOP, Inc., who challenged the elimination of UOP's minority shareholders by a cash-out merger between UOP and its majority owner, The Signal Companies, Inc. * * * [T]he defendants in this action were Signal, UOP, [and] certain officers and directors of those companies * * *. The present Chancellor held that the terms of the merger were fair to the plaintiff and the other minority shareholders of UOP. Accordingly, he entered judgment in favor of the defendants.

Numerous points were raised by the parties, but we address only the following questions presented by the trial court's opinion:

(1) The plaintiff's duty to plead sufficient facts demonstrating the unfairness of the challenged merger;

(2) The burden of proof upon the parties where the merger has been approved by the purportedly informed vote of a majority of the minority shareholders;

(3) The fairness of the merger in terms of adequacy of the defendants' disclosures to the minority shareholders;

(4) The fairness of the merger in terms of adequacy of the price paid for the minority shares and the remedy appropriate to that issue; and

(5) The continued force and effect of Singer v. Magnavox Co., Del.Supr., 380 A.2d 969, 980 (1977), and its progeny. * * *

I.

The facts found by the trial court, pertinent to the issues before us, are supported by the record, and we draw from them as set out in the Chancellor's opinion.

Signal is a diversified, technically based company operating through various subsidiaries. Its stock is publicly traded on the New York, Philadelphia and Pacific Stock Exchanges. UOP, formerly known as Universal Oil Products Company, was a diversified industrial company engaged in various lines of business, including petroleum and petrochemical services and related products, construction, fabricated metal products, transportation equipment products, chemicals and plastics, and other products and services including land development, lumber products and waste disposal. Its stock was publicly held and listed on the New York Stock Exchange.

In 1974 Signal sold one of its wholly-owned subsidiaries for $420,000,000 in cash. See Gimbel v. Signal Companies, Inc., Del.Ch., 316 A.2d 599, aff'd, Del.Supr., 316 A.2d 619 (1974). While looking to invest this cash surplus, Signal became interested in UOP as a possible acquisition. Friendly negotiations ensued, and Signal proposed to acquire a controlling interest in UOP at a price of $19 per share. UOP's representatives sought $25 per share. In the arm's length bargaining that followed, an understanding was reached whereby Signal agreed to purchase from UOP 1,500,000 shares of UOP's authorized but unissued stock at $21 per share.

This purchase was contingent upon Signal making a successful cash tender offer for 4,300,000 publicly held shares of UOP, also at a price of $21 per share. This combined method of acquisition permitted Signal to acquire 5,800,000 shares of stock, representing 50.5% of UOP's outstanding shares. The UOP board of directors advised the company's shareholders that it had no objection to Signal's tender offer at that price. Immediately before the announcement of the tender offer, UOP's common stock had been trading on the New York Stock Exchange at a fraction under $14 per share.

The negotiations between Signal and UOP occurred during April 1975, and the resulting tender offer was greatly oversubscribed. However, Signal limited its total purchase of the tendered shares so that, when coupled with the stock bought from UOP, it had achieved its goal of becoming a 50.5% shareholder of UOP.

Although UOP's board consisted of thirteen directors, Signal nominated and elected only six. Of these, five were either directors or employees of Signal. The sixth, a partner in the banking firm of Lazard Freres & Co., had been one of Signal's representatives in the negotiations and bargaining with UOP concerning the tender offer and purchase price of the UOP shares.

However, the president and chief executive officer of UOP retired during 1975, and Signal caused him to be replaced by James V. Crawford, a long-time employee and senior executive vice president of one of Signal's wholly-owned subsidiaries. Crawford succeeded his predecessor on UOP's board of directors and also was made a director of Signal.

By the end of 1977 Signal basically was unsuccessful in finding other suitable investment candidates for its excess cash, and by February 1978 considered that it had no other realistic acquisitions available to it on a friendly basis. Once again its attention turned to UOP.

The trial court found that at the instigation of certain Signal management personnel, including William W. Walkup, its board chairman, and Forrest N. Shumway, its president, a feasibility study was made concerning the possible acquisition of the balance of UOP's outstanding shares. This study was performed by two Signal officers, Charles S. Arledge, vice president (director of planning), and Andrew J. Chitiea, senior vice president (chief financial officer). Messrs. Walkup, Shumway, Arledge and Chitiea were all directors of UOP in addition to their membership on the Signal board.

Arledge and Chitiea concluded that it would be a good investment for Signal to acquire the remaining 49.5% of UOP shares at any price up to $24 each. Their report was discussed between Walkup and Shumway who, along with Arledge, Chitiea and Brewster L. Arms, internal counsel for Signal, constituted Signal's senior management. In particular, they talked about the proper price to be paid if the acquisition was pursued, purportedly keeping in mind that as UOP's majority shareholder, Signal owed a fiduciary responsibility to both its own stockholders as well as to UOP's minority. It was ultimately agreed that a meeting of Signal's executive committee would be called to propose that Signal acquire the remaining outstanding stock of UOP through a cash-out merger in the range of $20 to $21 per share.

The executive committee meeting was set for February 28, 1978. As a courtesy, UOP's president, Crawford, was invited to attend, although he was not a member of Signal's executive committee. On his arrival, and prior to the meeting, Crawford was asked to meet privately with Walkup and Shumway. He was then told of Signal's plan to acquire full ownership of UOP and was asked for his reaction to the proposed price range of $20 to $21 per share. Crawford said he thought such a price would be "generous," and that it was certainly one which should be submitted to

UOP's minority shareholders for their ultimate consideration. He stated, however, that Signal's 100% ownership could cause internal problems at UOP. He believed that employees would have to be given some assurance of their future place in a fully-owned Signal subsidiary. Otherwise, he feared the departure of essential personnel. Also, many of UOP's key employees had stock option incentive programs which would be wiped out by a merger. Crawford therefore urged that some adjustment would have to be made, such as providing a comparable incentive in Signal's shares, if after the merger he was to maintain his quality of personnel and efficiency at UOP.

Thus, Crawford voiced no objection to the $20 to $21 price range, nor did he suggest that Signal should consider paying more than $21 per share for the minority interests. Later, at the executive committee meeting the same factors were discussed, with Crawford repeating the position he earlier took with Walkup and Shumway. Also considered was the 1975 tender offer and the fact that it had been greatly oversubscribed at $21 per share. For many reasons, Signal's management concluded that the acquisition of UOP's minority shares provided the solution to a number of its business problems.

Thus, it was the consensus that a price of $20 to $21 per share would be fair to both Signal and the minority shareholders of UOP. Signal's executive committee authorized its management "to negotiate" with UOP "for a cash acquisition of the minority ownership in UOP, Inc., with the intention of presenting a proposal to [Signal's] board of directors * * * on March 6, 1978." Immediately after this February 28, 1978 meeting, Signal issued a press release stating:

> The Signal Companies, Inc. and UOP, Inc. are conducting negotiations for the acquisition for cash by Signal of the 49.5 percent of UOP which it does not presently own, announced Forrest N. Shumway, president and chief executive officer of Signal, and James V. Crawford, UOP president.

> Price and other terms of the proposed transaction have not yet been finalized and would be subject to approval of the boards of directors of Signal and UOP, scheduled to meet early next week, the stockholders of UOP and certain federal agencies.

The announcement also referred to the fact that the closing price of UOP's common stock on that day was $14.50 per share.

Two days later, on March 2, 1978, Signal issued a second press release stating that its management would recommend a price in the range of $20 to $21 per share for UOP's 49.5% minority interest. This announcement referred to Signal's earlier statement that "negotiations" were being conducted for the acquisition of the minority shares.

Between Tuesday, February 28, 1978 and Monday, March 6, 1978, a total of four business days, Crawford spoke by telephone with all of UOP's non-Signal, i.e., outside, directors. Also during that period, Crawford retained Lehman Brothers to render a fairness opinion as to the price offered the minority for its stock. He gave two reasons for this choice. First, the time schedule between the announcement and the board meetings was short (by then only three business days) and since Lehman Brothers had been acting as UOP's investment banker for many years, Crawford felt that it would be in the best position to respond on such brief notice. Second, James W. Glanville, a long-time director of UOP and a partner in Lehman Brothers, had acted as a financial advisor to UOP for many years. Crawford believed that Glanville's familiarity with UOP, as a member of its board, would also be of assistance in enabling Lehman Brothers to render a fairness opinion within the existing time constraints.

Crawford telephoned Glanville, who gave his assurance that Lehman Brothers had no conflicts that would prevent it from accepting the task. Glanville's immediate personal reaction was that a price of $20 to $21 would certainly be fair, since it represented almost a 50% premium over UOP's market price. Glanville sought a $250,000 fee for Lehman Brothers' services, but Crawford thought this too much. After further discussions Glanville finally agreed that Lehman Brothers would render its fairness opinion for $150,000.

During this period Crawford also had several telephone contacts with Signal officials. In only one of them, however, was the price of the shares discussed. In a conversation with Walkup, Crawford advised that as a result of his communications with UOP's non-Signal directors, it was his feeling that the price would have to be the top of the proposed range, or $21 per share, if the approval of UOP's outside directors was to be obtained. But again, he did not seek any price higher than $21.

Glanville assembled a three-man Lehman Brothers team to do the work on the fairness opinion. These persons examined relevant documents and information concerning UOP, including its annual reports and its Securities and Exchange Commission filings from 1973 through 1976, as well as its audited financial statements for 1977, its interim reports to shareholders, and its recent and historical market prices and trading volumes. In addition, on Friday, March 3, 1978, two members of the Lehman Brothers team flew to UOP's headquarters in Des Plaines, Illinois, to perform a "due diligence" visit, during the course of which they interviewed Crawford as well as UOP's general counsel, its chief financial officer, and other key executives and personnel.

As a result, the Lehman Brothers team concluded that "the price of either $20 or $21 would be a fair price for the remaining shares of UOP." They telephoned this impression to Glanville, who was spending the weekend in Vermont.

On Monday morning, March 6, 1978, Glanville and the senior member of the Lehman Brothers team flew to Des Plaines to attend the scheduled UOP directors meeting. Glanville looked over the assembled information during the flight. The two had with them the draft of a "fairness opinion letter" in which the price had been left blank. Either during or immediately prior to the directors' meeting, the two-page "fairness opinion letter" was typed in final form and the price of $21 per share was inserted.

On March 6, 1978, both the Signal and UOP boards were convened to consider the proposed merger. Telephone communications were maintained between the two meetings. Walkup, Signal's board chairman, and also a UOP director, attended UOP's meeting with Crawford in order to present Signal's position and answer any questions that UOP's non-Signal directors might have. Arledge and Chitiea, along with Signal's other designees on UOP's board, participated by conference telephone. All of UOP's outside directors attended the meeting either in person or by conference telephone.

First, Signal's board unanimously adopted a resolution authorizing Signal to propose to UOP a cash merger of $21 per share as outlined in a certain merger agreement and other supporting documents. This proposal required that the merger be approved by a majority of UOP's outstanding minority shares voting at the stockholders meeting at which the merger would be considered, and that the minority shares voting in favor of the merger, when coupled with Signal's 50.5% interest would have to comprise at least two-thirds of all UOP shares. Otherwise the proposed merger would be deemed disapproved.

UOP's board then considered the proposal. Copies of the agreement were delivered to the directors in attendance, and other copies had been forwarded earlier to the directors participating by telephone. They also had before them UOP financial data for 1974–1977, UOP's most recent financial statements, market price information, and budget projections for 1978. In addition they had Lehman Brothers' hurriedly prepared fairness opinion letter finding the price of $21 to be fair. Glanville, the Lehman Brothers partner, and UOP director, commented on the information that had gone into preparation of the letter. * * *

After consideration of Signal's proposal, Walkup and Crawford left the meeting to permit a free and uninhibited exchange between UOP's non-Signal directors. Upon their return a resolution to accept Signal's offer was then proposed and adopted. While Signal's men on UOP's board participated in various aspects of the meeting, they abstained from voting. However, the minutes show that each of them "if voting would have voted yes."

On March 7, 1978, UOP sent a letter to its shareholders advising them of the action taken by UOP's board with respect to Signal's offer.

This document pointed out, among other things, that on February 28, 1978 "both companies had announced negotiations were being conducted."

Despite the swift board action of the two companies, the merger was not submitted to UOP's shareholders until their annual meeting on May 26, 1978. In the notice of that meeting and proxy statement sent to shareholders in May, UOP's management and board urged that the merger be approved. The proxy statement also advised:

> The price was determined after *discussions* between James V. Crawford, a director of Signal and Chief Executive Officer of UOP, and officers of Signal which took place during meetings on February 28, 1978, and in the course of several subsequent telephone conversations. (Emphasis added.)

In the original draft of the proxy statement the word "negotiations" had been used rather than "discussions." However, when the Securities and Exchange Commission sought details of the "negotiations" as part of its review of these materials, the term was deleted and the word "discussions" was substituted. The proxy statement indicated that the vote of UOP's board in approving the merger had been unanimous. It also advised the shareholders that Lehman Brothers had given its opinion that the merger price of $21 per share was fair to UOP's minority. However, it did not disclose the hurried method by which this conclusion was reached.

As of the record date of UOP's annual meeting, there were 11,488,302 shares of UOP common stock outstanding, 5,688,302 of which were owned by the minority. At the meeting only 56%, or 3,208,652, of the minority shares were voted. Of these, 2,953,812, or 51.9% of the total minority, voted for the merger, and 254,840 voted against it. When Signal's stock was added to the minority shares voting in favor, a total of 76.2% of UOP's outstanding shares approved the merger while only 2.2% opposed it.

By its terms the merger became effective on May 26, 1978, and each share of UOP's stock held by the minority was automatically converted into a right to receive $21 cash.

II.

A.

A primary issue mandating reversal is the preparation by two UOP directors, Arledge and Chitiea, of their feasibility study for the exclusive use and benefit of Signal. This document was of obvious significance to both Signal and UOP. Using UOP data, it described the advantages to Signal of ousting the minority at a price range of $21–$24 per share. Mr. Arledge, one of the authors, outlined the benefits to Signal:[6]

---

[6] The parentheses indicate certain handwritten comments of Mr. Arledge.

Purpose of the Merger

(1) Provides an outstanding investment opportunity for Signal— (Better than any recent acquisition we have seen).

(2) Increases Signal's earnings.

(3) Facilitates the flow of resources between Signal and its subsidiaries. (Big factor works both ways).

(4) Provides cost savings potential for Signal and UOP.

(5) Improves the percentage of Signal's 'operating earnings' as opposed to 'holding company earnings.'

(6) Simplifies the understanding of Signal.

(7) Facilitates technological exchange among Signal's subsidiaries.

(8) Eliminates potential conflicts of interest.

Having written those words, solely for the use of Signal, it is clear from the record that neither Arledge nor Chitiea shared this report with their fellow directors of UOP. We are satisfied that no one else did either. This conduct hardly meets the fiduciary standards applicable to such a transaction. * * *

The Arledge-Chitiea report speaks for itself in supporting the Chancellor's finding that a price of up to $24 was a "good investment" for Signal. It shows that a return on the investment at $21 would be 15.7% versus 15.5% at $24 per share. This was a difference of only two-tenths of one percent, while it meant over $17,000,000 to the minority. Under such circumstances, paying UOP's minority shareholders $24 would have had relatively little long-term effect on Signal, and the Chancellor's findings concerning the benefit to Signal, even at a price of $24, were obviously correct.

Certainly, this was a matter of material significance to UOP and its shareholders. Since the study was prepared by two UOP directors, using UOP information for the exclusive benefit of Signal, and nothing whatever was done to disclose it to the outside UOP directors or the minority shareholders, a question of breach of fiduciary duty arises. This problem occurs because there were common Signal-UOP directors participating, at least to some extent, in the UOP board's decision-making processes without full disclosure of the conflicts they faced.[7]

---

[7] Although perfection is not possible, or expected, the result here could have been entirely different if UOP had appointed an independent negotiating committee of its outside directors to deal with Signal at arm's length. See, e.g., Harriman v. E.I. Du Pont de Nemours & Co., 411 F.Supp. 133 (D.Del.1975). Since fairness in this context can be equated to conduct by a theoretical, wholly independent, board of directors acting upon the matter before them, it is unfortunate that this course apparently was neither considered nor pursued. Johnston v. Greene, Del.Supr., 121 A.2d 919, 925 (1956). Particularly in a parent-subsidiary context, a showing that

B.

In assessing this situation, the Court of Chancery was required to:

> [E]xamine what information defendants had and to measure it against what they gave to the minority stockholders, in a context in which 'complete candor' is required. In other words, the limited function of the Court was to determine whether defendants had disclosed all information in their possession germane to the transaction in issue. And by 'germane' we mean, for present purposes, information such as a reasonable shareholder would consider important in deciding whether to sell or retain stock.

> * * * Completeness, not adequacy, is both the norm and the mandate under present circumstances.

Lynch v. Vickers Energy Corp., Del.Supr., 383 A.2d 278, 281 (1977) (*Lynch I*). This is merely stating in another way the long-existing principle of Delaware law that these Signal designated directors on UOP's board still owed UOP and its shareholders an uncompromising duty of loyalty. The classic language of Guth v. Loft, Inc., Del.Supr., 5 A.2d 503, 510 (1939), requires no embellishment:

> A public policy, existing through the years, and derived from a profound knowledge of human characteristics and motives, has established a rule that demands of a corporate officer or director, peremptorily and inexorably, the most scrupulous observance of his duty, not only affirmatively to protect the interests of the corporation committed to his charge, but also to refrain from doing anything that would work injury to the corporation, or to deprive it of profit or advantage which his skill and ability might properly bring to it, or to enable it to make in the reasonable and lawful exercise of its powers. The rule that requires an undivided and unselfish loyalty to the corporation demands that there shall be no conflict between duty and self-interest.

Given the absence of any attempt to structure this transaction on an arm's length basis, Signal cannot escape the effects of the conflicts it faced, particularly when its designees on UOP's board did not totally abstain from participation in the matter. There is no "safe harbor" for such divided loyalties in Delaware. When directors of a Delaware corporation are on both sides of a transaction, they are required to demonstrate their utmost good faith and the most scrupulous inherent fairness of the bargain. Gottlieb v. Heyden Chemical Corp., Del.Supr., 91 A.2d 57, 57–58 (1952). The requirement of fairness is unflinching in its

---

the action taken was as though each of the contending parties had in fact exerted its bargaining power against the other at arm's length is strong evidence that the transaction meets the test of fairness. Getty Oil Co. v. Skelly Oil Co., Del.Supr., 267 A.2d 883, 886 (1970).

demand that where one stands on both sides of a transaction, he has the burden of establishing its entire fairness, sufficient to pass the test of careful scrutiny by the courts. Sterling v. Mayflower Hotel Corp., Del.Super., 93 A.2d 107, 110 (1952).

There is no dilution of this obligation where one holds dual or multiple directorships, as in a parent-subsidiary context. Levien v. Sinclair Oil Corp., Del.Ch., 261 A.2d 911, 915 (1969). Thus, individuals who act in a dual capacity as directors of two corporations, one of whom is parent and the other subsidiary, owe the same duty of good management to both corporations, and in the absence of an independent negotiating structure (see note 7, supra), or the directors' total abstention from any participation in the matter, this duty is to be exercised in light of what is best for both companies. Warshaw v. Calhoun, Del.Supr., 221 A.2d 487, 492 (1966). The record demonstrates that Signal has not met this obligation.

C.

The concept of fairness has two basic aspects: fair dealing and fair price. The former embraces questions of when the transaction was timed, how it was initiated, structured, negotiated, disclosed to the directors, and how the approvals of the directors and the stockholders were obtained. The latter aspect of fairness relates to the economic and financial considerations of the proposed merger, including all relevant factors: assets, market value, earnings, future prospects, and any other elements that affect the intrinsic or inherent value of a company's stock. Moore, The "Interested" Director or Officer Transaction, 4 Del.J.Corp.L. 674, 676 (1979). See Tri-Continental Corp. v. Battye, Del.Supr., 74 A.2d 71, 72 (1950); 8 Del.C. § 262(h). However, the test for fairness is not a bifurcated one as between fair dealing and price. All aspects of the issue must be examined as a whole since the question is one of entire fairness. However, in a non-fraudulent transaction we recognize that price may be the preponderant consideration outweighing other features of the merger. Here, we address the two basic aspects of fairness separately because we find reversible error as to both.

D.

Part of fair dealing is the obvious duty of candor required by *Lynch I,* supra. Moreover, one possessing superior knowledge may not mislead any stockholder by use of corporate information to which the latter is not privy. Lank v. Steiner, Del.Supr., 224 A.2d 242, 244 (1966). Delaware has long imposed this duty even upon persons who are not corporate officers or directors, but who nonetheless are privy to matters of interest or significance to their company. Brophy v. Cities Service Co., Del.Ch., 70 A.2d 5, 7 (1949). With the well-established Delaware law on the subject, and the Court of Chancery's findings of fact here, it is inevitable that the obvious conflicts posed by Arledge and Chitiea's preparation of their "feasibility study," derived from UOP information, for the sole use and benefit of Signal, cannot pass muster.

The Arledge-Chitiea report is but one aspect of the element of fair dealing. How did this merger evolve? It is clear that it was entirely initiated by Signal. The serious time constraints under which the principals acted were all set by Signal. It had not found a suitable outlet for its excess cash and considered UOP a desirable investment, particularly since it was now in a position to acquire the whole company for itself. For whatever reasons, and they were only Signal's, the entire transaction was presented to and approved by UOP's board within four business days. Standing alone, this is not necessarily indicative of any lack of fairness by a majority shareholder. It was what occurred, or more properly, what did not occur, during this brief period that makes the time constraints imposed by Signal relevant to the issue of fairness.

The structure of the transaction, again, was Signal's doing. So far as negotiations were concerned, it is clear that they were modest at best. Crawford, Signal's man at UOP, never really talked price with Signal, except to accede to its management's statements on the subject, and to convey to Signal the UOP outside directors' view that as between the $20–$21 range under consideration, it would have to be $21. The latter is not a surprising outcome, but hardly arm's length negotiations. Only the protection of benefits for UOP's key employees and the issue of Lehman Brothers' fee approached any concept of bargaining.

As we have noted, the matter of disclosure to the UOP directors was wholly flawed by the conflicts of interest raised by the Arledge-Chitiea report. All of those conflicts were resolved by Signal in its own favor without divulging any aspect of them to UOP.

This cannot but undermine a conclusion that this merger meets any reasonable test of fairness. The outside UOP directors lacked one material piece of information generated by two of their colleagues, but shared only with Signal. True, the UOP board had the Lehman Brothers' fairness opinion, but that firm has been blamed by the plaintiff for the hurried task it performed, when more properly the responsibility for this lies with Signal. There was no disclosure of the circumstances surrounding the rather cursory preparation of the Lehman Brothers' fairness opinion. Instead, the impression was given UOP's minority that a careful study had been made, when in fact speed was the hallmark, and Mr. Glanville, Lehman's partner in charge of the matter, and also a UOP director, having spent the weekend in Vermont, brought a draft of the "fairness opinion letter" to the UOP directors' meeting on March 6, 1978 with the price left blank. We can only conclude from the record that the rush imposed on Lehman Brothers by Signal's timetable contributed to the difficulties under which this investment banking firm attempted to perform its responsibilities. Yet, none of this was disclosed to UOP's minority.

Finally, the minority stockholders were denied the critical information that Signal considered a price of $24 to be a good investment. Since this would have meant over $17,000,000 more to the minority, we cannot conclude that the shareholder vote was an informed one. Under the circumstances, an approval by a majority of the minority was meaningless. Lynch I, 383 A.2d at 279, 281.

Given these particulars and the Delaware law on the subject, the record does not establish that this transaction satisfies any reasonable concept of fair dealing, and the Chancellor's findings in that regard must be reversed.

Turning to the matter of price, plaintiff also challenges its fairness. His evidence was that on the date the merger was approved the stock was worth at least $26 per share. In support, he offered the testimony of a chartered investment analyst who used two basic approaches to valuation: a comparative analysis of the premium paid over market in ten other tender offer-merger combinations, and a discounted cash flow analysis.

In this breach of fiduciary duty case, the Chancellor perceived that the approach to valuation was the same as that in an appraisal proceeding. Consistent with precedent, he rejected plaintiff's method of proof and accepted defendants' evidence of value as being in accord with practice under prior case law. This means that the so-called "Delaware block" or weighted average method was employed wherein the elements of value, i.e., assets, market price, earnings, etc., were assigned a particular weight and the resulting amounts added to determine the value per share. This procedure has been in use for decades. See In re General Realty & Utilities Corp., Del.Ch., 52 A.2d 6, 14–15 (1947). However, to the extent it excludes other generally accepted techniques used in the financial community and the courts, it is now clearly outmoded. It is time we recognize this in appraisal and other stock valuation proceedings and bring our law current on the subject.

While the Chancellor rejected plaintiff's discounted cash flow method of valuing UOP's stock, as not corresponding with "either logic or the existing law," it is significant that this was essentially the focus, i.e., earnings potential of UOP, of Messrs. Arledge and Chitiea in their evaluation of the merger. Accordingly, the standard "Delaware block" or weighted average method of valuation, formerly employed in appraisal and other stock valuation cases, shall no longer exclusively control such proceedings. We believe that a more liberal approach must include proof of value by any techniques or methods which are generally considered acceptable in the financial community and otherwise admissible in court, subject only to our interpretation of 8 Del.C. § 262(h), infra. This will obviate the very structured and mechanistic procedure that has heretofore governed such matters. See Jacques Coe & Co. v. Minneapolis-Moline Co., Del.Ch., 75 A.2d 244, 247 (1950); Tri-Continental Corp. v. Battye, Del.Ch., 66 A.2d 910, 917–18 (1949).

Fair price obviously requires consideration of all relevant factors involving the value of a company. * * *

Although the Chancellor received the plaintiff's evidence, his opinion indicates that the use of it was precluded because of past Delaware practice. While we do not suggest a monetary result one way or the other, we do think the plaintiff's evidence should be part of the factual mix and weighed as such. Until the $21 price is measured on remand by the valuation standards mandated by Delaware law, there can be no finding at the present stage of these proceedings that the price is fair. Given the lack of any candid disclosure of the material facts surrounding establishment of the $21 price, the majority of the minority vote, approving the merger, is meaningless.

The plaintiff has not sought an appraisal, but rescissory damages of the type contemplated by Lynch v. Vickers Energy Corp., Del., 429 A.2d 497, 505–06 (1981) (*Lynch II*).[c] In view of the approach to valuation that we announce today, we see no basis in our law for *Lynch II*'s exclusive monetary formula for relief. On remand the plaintiff will be permitted to test the fairness of the $21 price by the standards we herein establish, in conformity with the principle applicable to an appraisal—that fair value be determined by taking "into account all relevant factors" [see 8 Del.C. § 262(h)]. In our view this includes the elements of rescissory damages if the Chancellor considers them susceptible of proof and a remedy appropriate to all the issues of fairness before him. To the extent that Lynch II, 429 A.2d at 505–06, purports to limit the Chancellor's discretion to a single remedial formula for monetary damages in a cash-out merger, it is overruled.

While a plaintiff's monetary remedy ordinarily should be confined to the more liberalized appraisal proceeding herein established, we do not intend any limitation on the historic powers of the Chancellor to grant such other relief as the facts of a particular case may dictate. The appraisal remedy we approve may not be adequate in certain cases, particularly where fraud, misrepresentation, self-dealing, deliberate

---

[c] Rescissory damages are defined in *Lynch* as "damages which are the monetary equivalent of rescission and which will, in effect, equal the increment in value that [the defendant] enjoyed as a result of acquiring and holding the * * * stock in issue. That is consistent with the basis for liability which is the law of the case, and it is a norm applied when the equitable remedy of rescission is impractical." 429 A.2d at 501. When calculating rescissory damages, the principle of mitigation of damages is inapplicable, i.e., damages are not reduced by amounts the plaintiff could have saved by making an investment in the security in question at some later time. However, damages are reduced by any amount received by the plaintiff in connection with the wrongful transaction that gave rise to the right to rescissory damages. Id. at 505–06.

waste of corporate assets, or gross and palpable overreaching are involved. Cole v. National Cash Credit Association, Del.Ch., 156 A. 183, 187 (1931). Under such circumstances, the Chancellor's powers are complete to fashion any form of equitable and monetary relief as may be appropriate, including rescissory damages. Since it is apparent that this long completed transaction is too involved to undo, and in view of the Chancellor's discretion, the award, if any, should be in the form of monetary damages based upon entire fairness standards, i.e., fair dealing and fair price.

Obviously, there are other litigants, like the plaintiff, who abjured an appraisal and whose rights to challenge the element of fair value must be preserved.[8] Accordingly, the quasi-appraisal remedy we grant the plaintiff here will apply only to: (1) this case; (2) any case now pending on appeal to this Court; (3) any case now pending in the Court of Chancery which has not yet been appealed but which may be eligible for direct appeal to this Court; (4) any case challenging a cash-out merger, the effective date of which is on or before February 1, 1983; and (5) any proposed merger to be presented at a shareholders' meeting, the notification of which is mailed to the stockholders on or before February 23, 1983. Thereafter, the provisions of 8 Del.C. § 262, as herein construed, respecting the scope of an appraisal and the means for perfecting the same, shall govern the financial remedy available to minority shareholders in a cash-out merger. Thus, we return to the well established principles of Stauffer v. Standard Brands Inc., Del.Supr., 187 A.2d 78 (1962) and David J. Greene & Co. v. Schenley Industries, Inc., Del.Ch., 281 A.2d 30 (1971), mandating a stockholder's recourse to the basic remedy of an appraisal.

III.

Finally, we address the matter of business purpose. The defendants contend that the purpose of this merger was not a proper subject of inquiry by the trial court. The plaintiff says that no valid purpose existed—the entire transaction was a mere subterfuge designed to eliminate the minority. The Chancellor ruled otherwise, but in so doing he clearly circumscribed the thrust and effect of *Singer*. This has led to the thoroughly sound observation that the business purpose test "may be * * * virtually interpreted out of existence, as it was in *Weinberger*."

The requirement of a business purpose is new to our law of mergers and was a departure from prior case law. In view of the fairness test which has long been applicable to parent-subsidiary mergers, Sterling v. Mayflower Hotel Corp., Del.Supr., 93 A.2d 107, 109–10 (1952), the expanded appraisal remedy now available to shareholders, and the broad discretion of the Chancellor to fashion such relief as the facts of a given

---

[8]   Under 8 Del.C. § 262(a), (d) & (e), a stockholder is required to act within certain time periods to perfect the right to an appraisal.

case may dictate, we do not believe that any additional meaningful protection is afforded minority shareholders by the business purpose requirement of the trilogy of *Singer, Tanzer* [v. International General Industries, Inc., 379 A.2d 1121 (Del.1977)], [Roland International Corp. v.] *Najjar* [407 A.2d 1032 (Del.1979)], and their progeny. Accordingly, such requirement shall no longer be of any force or effect.

The judgment of the Court of Chancery, finding both the circumstances of the merger and the price paid the minority shareholders to be fair, is reversed. The matter is remanded for further proceedings consistent herewith. Upon remand the plaintiff's post-trial motion to enlarge the class should be granted. * * *

REVERSED AND REMANDED.

NOTES

(1) In a "cash out" merger, a parent corporation owning more than 50 percent of the stock of a subsidiary corporation may compel the minority shareholders of the subsidiary to accept cash for their shares in an amount determined by the parent, subject, however, to the appraisal rights provided in Chapter 13 of the MBCA. The process by which this is accomplished is a merger in which minority shareholders in the subsidiary corporation are required to accept cash rather than shares in the continuing corporation, as permitted by § 11.02(c)(3) of the MBCA. In the modern law of corporations, it is important to recognize that a "merger" is not limited to the intuitive notion of two independent corporations agreeing to fuse together with shareholders of both corporations having a continuing interest in the fused enterprise.

(2) Generally, scholars have been skeptical of the traditional appraisal remedy, citing at least five problems: (1) The shareholders must litigate with the corporation as to the fair value issue; the corporation usually has extensive resources and intimate knowledge of where the skeletons are while the shareholder does not. (2) The shareholder receives nothing until the litigation establishing fair value, including appeals, is exhausted; as a result, he or she may receive nothing for five years or so (while a person accepting the transaction receives immediate payment), and an ultimate award of statutory interest is not likely to be viewed as adequate compensation for the loss of the use of the proceeds for a long period. (3) The shareholder must bear his or her own litigation expenses, which may be substantial, particularly if asset valuations are involved. (4) The method of valuation routinely used in most states, the "Delaware block" approach discussed in *Weinberger*, may not yield a valuation that is realistic. (5) The payment of interest on the award is discretionary with the court, so that no interest at all may be awarded, or interest may be calculated on a simple interest basis rather than on a compound interest basis, as occurred, for example, in In the Matter of the Appraisal of Shell Oil Co., 607 A.2d 1213 (Del.1992). See, e.g., Jesse Fried & Mira Ganor, Agency Costs of Venture Capitalist Control in Startups, 81 N.Y.U. L.Rev. 967 (2006) ("[T]he shortcomings of the appraisal

remedy are widely known. Commentators have long recognized that appraisal is a remedy that few shareholders will seek under any circumstance."); Guhan Subramanian, Fixing Freezeouts, 115 Yale L.J. 2 (2005) ("[I]t is well accepted among academic commentators and practitioners that appraisal is a weak remedy compared to entire fairness review.").

(3) In an interesting study by Charles Korsmo & Minor Myers, the authors examined 141 appraisal proceedings over a six-year period. They found that appraisal rights were exercised in one percent to six percent of public transactions each year. Out of the 141 proceedings, 92 settled; in those that went to trial, the parties seeking appraisal were successful in obtaining additional money. In the 40 cases where both the merger premium and the court's finding were disclosed, appraisal litigation generated a median award of 50.2 percent over the buyout price.

This paper casts significant doubt on the notion that appraisal is a useless remedy. As the authors observe:

> Appraisal * * * differs from standard fiduciary class actions in important ways. In appraisal, there are no class actions. The only shareholders who can press appraisal claims are those who have affirmatively opted-in to the litigation. Also, there is no provision for allowing the attorneys' fees to be paid by the defendant. The only way that the plaintiff's attorney gets paid in appraisal is if the plaintiff decides to pay. * * * The result is a set of incentives that should attract litigation only when a shareholder actually believes the claim is worth the cost of bringing it. * * * Our thought was that appraisal litigation ought to appear more meritorious than standard fiduciary duty class actions in mergers.

The authors also found that appraisal actions targeted deals with lower prices. By contrast, the only thing that accounted for which transactions attracted fiduciary class actions was the size of the transaction, not the premium. Charles R. Korsmo & Minor Myers, The Law and Economics of Merger Litigation: Do the Merits Matter in Shareholder Appraisal? (June 14, 2013 draft).

(4) It has become customary in Delaware cash-out transactions to structure the procedure so that (a) "independent" directors of the subsidiary negotiate the terms of the transaction with representatives of the parent, and (b) approval of the transaction is conditional upon an affirmative vote of a majority of the minority shareholders. One consequence is that it has become standard practice to place outside persons on the board of directors of subsidiaries that have publicly-held minority shares. Cases discussing these procedural requirements include Rosenblatt v. Getty Oil Co., 493 A.2d 929 (Del.1985).

(5) The reason to have an independent committee when negotiating a cash-out transaction is to replicate arm's-length bargaining and thereby shift the burden of proof in a shareholder suit to the plaintiff. In many cases, this allocation of the burden of proof is outcome determinative. In Kahn v. Lynch

Communication Systems, Inc., 638 A.2d 1110 (Del.1994), a properly constituted and appropriately functioning special committee was created, but the defendants were not able to show that the bargaining process replicated a truly arm's-length process. Hence the burden of proof on fairness did not shift to the plaintiff. On remand, the defendants were able to persuade the court that there had been full disclosure and the price was entirely fair so that the transaction was upheld. The Supreme Court accepted this conclusion. Kahn v. Lynch Communication Systems, Inc., 669 A.2d 79 (Del.1995). In Kahn v. Tremont Corporation, 694 A.2d 422 (Del.1997), the Court held (in an unusual 2–1–2 decision) that the burden did not shift where the chairman of the independent committee had close associations with the corporation and in fact dominated the negotiation process, while the other two members of the committee were passive. As a result, arm's-length bargaining was not replicated.

(6) In all of these cases, the Delaware courts have emphasized the importance of full disclosure to the minority shareholders, and have not hesitated to enjoin cash-out transactions when such disclosure was lacking. E.g., Joseph v. Shell Oil Co., 482 A.2d 335 (Del.Ch.1984), holding affirmed in connected case, Selfe v. Joseph, 501 A.2d 409 (Del.1985). Similarly, the Delaware courts have set aside transactions where there appears to have been manipulation of the transaction to minimize the financial rights of minority shareholders (e.g., Rabkin v. Philip A. Hunt Chem. Corp., 498 A.2d 1099 (Del.1985)), or the use of unfair or abusive tactics (e.g., Sealy Mattress Co. of N.J. v. Sealy, Inc., 532 A.2d 1324, 1335 (Del.Ch.1987)).

(7) Decisions since *Weinberger* have made it easier for plaintiffs to bring cases using the entire fairness test. In Cede & Co. v. Technicolor, 634 A.2d 345 (Del. 1993), the Delaware Supreme Court held that unfair dealing is compensable even in the absence of an unfair price. The Court of Chancery had found the board of directors had breached its duty of care but dismissed the suit because plaintiffs had not proven an injury resulting from the breach. In rejecting the Chancellor's proximate cause test, the Delaware Supreme Court suggested that unfair dealing alone could be a compensable harm, thus expanding the kinds of harm that fall under the procedural prong of the entire fairness test. In In re Tri-Star Pictures, Inc., Litig., 634 A.2d 319 (Del. 1993), shareholders challenged a transaction that gave Coca-Cola an eighty percent interest in Tri-Star in exchange for Coca-Cola's Entertainment Sector. The Court confronted the difficulty minority shareholders can face in gaining standing because their injuries often sound like derivative claims rather than individualized harms. In *Tri-Star*, the Court found that dilution of voting power, equity dilution, and interference with a shareholder's right to cast an informed vote supported individual causes of action against a controlling shareholder when only minority shareholders were harmed.

(8) A "fairness opinion," such as the one provided by Lehman Brothers in connection with the UOP buyout, is now standard operating procedure in transactions involving corporate control and cash-out transactions. Such an opinion states that the price is "fair from a financial point of view," and

thereby provides assurance to the directors. Valuation of a minority interest in a large corporation is subjective to some extent in many circumstances, and there is a good chance that independent valuations of the same business might vary considerably. Hence, it is certainly not a coincidence that the overwhelming bulk of fairness opinions come in very close to the figure desired by the board of directors authorizing the opinion. There apparently has been no recent example of liability being imposed on an investment banker for an inaccurate fairness opinion.

(9) Rule 13e–3, 17 C.F.R. § 240.13e–3, promulgated under the Securities Exchange Act of 1934, is applicable to "going private" transactions which involve the solicitation of public shareholders in cash-out transactions. This rule and the accompanying schedules require the issuer or affiliate to make extensive disclosures in considerable detail about the source of any fairness opinion, the relationship between the preparer of the opinion and the issuer, and the analyses underlying the opinion, including specific values or ranges of values derived from such analyses. These disclosure requirements probably result in considerably greater care being taken in the preparation of a fairness opinion. The SEC staff also requires similar disclosures in connection with outside opinions or appraisals obtained in connection with control transactions that do not involve the elimination of public shareholders, and which therefore are not subject to Rule 13e–3.

D. CORPORATE OPPORTUNITY

NORTHEAST HARBOR GOLF CLUB, INC. V. HARRIS

Supreme Judicial Court of Maine, 1995.
661 A.2d 1146.

Before WATHEN, C.J., and ROBERTS, GLASSMAN, DANA, and LIPEZ, JJ.

ROBERTS, JUSTICE.

Northeast Harbor Golf Club, Inc., appeals from a judgment entered in the Superior Court (Hancock County, Atwood, J.) following a nonjury trial. The Club maintains that the trial court erred in finding that Nancy Harris did not breach her fiduciary duty as president of the Club by purchasing and developing property abutting the golf course. Because we today adopt principles different from those applied by the trial court in determining that Harris's activities did not constitute a breach of the corporate opportunity doctrine, we vacate the judgment.

I.

The Facts

Nancy Harris was the president of the Northeast Harbor Golf Club, a Maine corporation, from 1971 until she was asked to resign in 1990. The Club also had a board of directors that was responsible for making or approving significant policy decisions. The Club's only major asset was a golf course in Mount Desert. During Harris's tenure as president, the board occasionally discussed the possibility of developing some of the Club's real estate in order to raise money. Although Harris was generally in favor of tasteful development, the board always "shied away" from that type of activity.

In 1979, Robert Suminsby informed Harris that he was the listing broker for the Gilpin property, which comprised three noncontiguous parcels located among the fairways of the golf course. The property included an unused right-of-way on which the Club's parking lot and clubhouse were located. It was also encumbered by an easement in favor of the Club allowing foot traffic from the green of one hole to the next tee. Suminsby testified that he contacted Harris because she was the president of the Club and he believed that the Club would be interested in buying the property in order to prevent development.

Harris immediately agreed to purchase the Gilpin property in her own name for the asking price of $45,000. She did not disclose her plans to purchase the property to the Club's board prior to the purchase. She informed the board at its annual August meeting that she had purchased the property, that she intended to hold it in her own name, and that the Club would be "protected." The board took no action in response to the Harris purchase. She testified that at the time of the purchase she had no plans to develop the property and that no such plans took shape until 1988.

In 1984, while playing golf with the postmaster of Northeast Harbor, Harris learned that a parcel of land owned by the heirs of the Smallidge family might be available for purchase. The Smallidge parcel was surrounded on three sides by the golf course and on the fourth side by a house lot. It had no access to the road. With the ultimate goal of acquiring the property, Harris instructed her lawyer to locate the Smallidge heirs. Harris testified that she told a number of individual board members about her attempt to acquire the Smallidge parcel. At a board meeting in August 1985, Harris formally disclosed to the board that she had purchased the Smallidge property.[1] The minutes of that meeting show that she told the board she had no present plans to develop the Smallidge parcel. Harris testified that at the time of the purchase of the Smallidge property she nonetheless thought it might be nice to have some houses there. Again, the board took no formal action as a result of Harris's purchase. Harris acquired the Smallidge property from ten heirs, paying a total of $60,000. In 1990, Harris paid $275,000 for the lot and building separating the Smallidge parcel from the road in order to gain access to the otherwise landlocked parcel.

---

[1] In fact, it appears that Harris did not take title to the property until October 26, 1985. She had only signed a purchase and sale agreement at the time of the August board meeting.

The trial court expressly found that the Club would have been unable to purchase either the Gilpin or Smallidge properties for itself, relying on testimony that the Club continually experienced financial difficulties, operated annually at a deficit, and depended on contributions from the directors to pay its bills. On the other hand, there was evidence that the Club had occasionally engaged in successful fund-raising, including a two-year period shortly after the Gilpin purchase during which the Club raised $115,000. The Club had $90,000 in a capital investment fund at the time of the Smallidge purchase.

In 1987 or 1988, Harris divided the real estate into 41 small lots, 14 on the Smallidge property and 27 on the Gilpin property. Apparently as part of her estate plan, Harris conveyed noncontiguous lots among the 41 to her children and retained others for herself. In 1991, Harris and her children exchanged deeds to reassemble the small lots into larger parcels. At the time the Club filed this suit, the property was divided into 11 lots, some owned by Harris and others by her children who are also defendants in this case. Harris estimated the value of all the real estate at the time of the trial to be $1,550,000.

In 1988, Harris, who was still president of the Club, and her children began the process of obtaining approval for a five-lot subdivision known as Bushwood on the lower Gilpin property. Even when the board learned of the proposed subdivision, a majority failed to take any action. A group of directors formed a separate organization in order to oppose the subdivision on the basis that it violated the local zoning ordinance. After Harris's resignation as president, the Club also sought unsuccessfully to challenge the subdivision. See Northeast Harbor Golf Club, Inc. v. Town of Mount Desert, 618 A.2d 225 (Me.1992). Plans of Harris and her family for development of the other parcels are unclear, but the local zoning ordinance would permit construction of up to 11 houses on the land as currently divided.

After Harris's plans to develop Bushwood became apparent, the board grew increasingly divided concerning the propriety of development near the golf course. At least two directors, Henri Agnese and Nick Ludington, testified that they trusted Harris to act in the best interests of the Club and that they had no problem with the development plans for Bushwood. Other directors disagreed.

In particular, John Schafer, a Washington, D.C., lawyer and long-time member of the board, took issue with Harris's conduct. He testified that he had relied on Harris's representations at the time she acquired the properties that she would not develop them. According to Schafer, matters came to a head in August 1990 when a number of directors concluded that Harris's development plans irreconcilably conflicted with the Club's interests. As a result, Schafer and two other directors asked Harris to resign as president. In April 1991, after a substantial change in the board's membership, the board authorized the instant lawsuit against Harris for the breach of her fiduciary duty to act in the best interests of the corporation. The board simultaneously resolved that the proposed housing development was contrary to the best interests of the corporation.

The Club filed a complaint against Harris, her sons John and Shepard, and her daughter-in-law Melissa Harris. As amended, the complaint alleged that during her term as president Harris breached her fiduciary duty by purchasing the lots without providing notice and an opportunity for the Club to purchase the property and by subdividing the lots for future development. The Club sought an injunction to prevent development and also sought to impose a constructive trust on the property in question for the benefit of the Club.

The trial court found that Harris had not usurped a corporate opportunity because the acquisition of real estate was not in the Club's line of business. Moreover, it found that the corporation lacked the financial ability to purchase the real estate at issue. Finally, the court placed great emphasis on Harris's good faith. It noted her long and dedicated history of service to the Club, her personal oversight of the Club's growth, and her frequent financial contributions to the Club. The court found that her development activities were "generally * * * compatible with the corporation's business." This appeal followed.

II.

The Corporate Opportunity Doctrine

Corporate officers and directors bear a duty of loyalty to the corporations they serve. As Justice Cardozo explained the fiduciary duty in Meinhard v. Salmon, 249 N.Y. 458, 164 N.E. 545, 546 (1928): * * * Maine has embraced this "unbending and inveterate" tradition. Corporate fiduciaries in Maine must discharge their duties in good faith with a view toward furthering the interests of the corporation. They must disclose and not withhold relevant information concerning any potential conflict of interest with the corporation, and they must refrain from using their position, influence, or knowledge of the affairs of the corporation to gain personal advantage. See Rosenthal v. Rosenthal, 543 A.2d 348, 352 (Me.1988); 13–A M.R.S.A. § 716 (Supp.1994).

Despite the general acceptance of the proposition that corporate fiduciaries owe a duty of loyalty to their corporations, there has been much confusion about the specific extent of that duty when, as here, it is contended that a fiduciary takes for herself a corporate opportunity. See, e.g., Victor Brudney & Robert C. Clark, A New Look at Corporate Opportunities, 94 Harv.L.Rev. 998, 998 (1981) ("Not only are the common formulations vague, but the courts have articulated no theory that would serve as a blueprint for constructing meaningful rules."). This case requires us for the first time to define the scope of the corporate opportunity doctrine in Maine.

Various courts have embraced different versions of the corporate opportunity doctrine. The test applied by the trial court and embraced by Harris is generally known as the "line of business" test. The seminal case applying the line of business test is Guth v. Loft, Inc., 5 A.2d 503 (Del.1939). In Guth, the Delaware Supreme Court adopted an intensely factual test stated in general terms as follows:

> [I]f there is presented to a corporate officer or director a business opportunity which the corporation is financially able to undertake, is, from its nature, in the line of the corporation's business and is of practical advantage to it, is one in which the corporation has an interest or a reasonable expectancy, and, by embracing the opportunity, the self-interest of the officer or director will be brought into conflict with that of his corporation, the law will not permit him to seize the opportunity for himself.

Id. at 511. The "real issue" under this test is whether the opportunity "was so closely associated with the existing business activities * * * as to bring the transaction within that class of cases where the acquisition of the property would throw the corporate officer purchasing it into competition with his company." Id. at 513. The Delaware court described that inquiry as "a factual question to be decided by reasonable inferences from objective facts." Id.

The line of business test suffers from some significant weaknesses. First, the question whether a particular activity is within a corporation's line of business is conceptually difficult to answer. The facts of the instant case demonstrate that difficulty. The Club is in the business of running a golf course. It is not in the business of developing real estate. In the traditional sense, therefore, the trial court correctly observed that the opportunity in this case was not a corporate opportunity within the meaning of the Guth test. Nevertheless, the record would support a finding that the Club had made the policy judgment that development of surrounding real estate was detrimental to the best interests of the Club. The acquisition of land adjacent to the golf course for the purpose of preventing future development would have enhanced the ability of the Club to implement that policy. The record also shows that the Club had occasionally considered reversing that policy and expanding its operations to include the development of surrounding real estate. Harris's activities effectively foreclosed the Club from pursuing that option with respect to prime locations adjacent to the golf course.

Second, the Guth test includes as an element the financial ability of the corporation to take advantage of the opportunity. The court in this case relied on the Club's supposed financial incapacity as a basis for excusing Harris's conduct. Often, the injection of financial ability into the equation will unduly favor the inside director or executive who has command of the facts relating to the finances of the corporation. Reliance on financial ability will also act as a disincentive to corporate executives to solve corporate financing and other problems. In addition, the Club could have prevented development without spending $275,000 to acquire the property Harris needed to obtain access to the road.

The Massachusetts Supreme Judicial Court adopted a different test in Durfee v. Durfee & Canning, Inc., 323 Mass. 187, 80 N.E.2d 522 (1948). The Durfee test has since come to be known as the "fairness test." According to Durfee, the

> true basis of governing doctrine rests on the unfairness in the particular circumstances of a director, whose relation to the corporation is fiduciary, taking advantage of an opportunity [for her personal profit] when the interest of the corporation justly call[s] for protection. This calls for application of ethical standards of what is fair and equitable * * * in particular sets of facts.

Id. at 529 (quoting Ballantine on Corporations 204–05 (rev. ed. 1946)). As with the Guth test, the Durfee test calls for a broad-ranging, intensely factual inquiry. The Durfee test suffers even more than the Guth test from a lack of principled content. It provides little or no practical guidance to the corporate officer or director seeking to measure her obligations.

The Minnesota Supreme Court elected "to combine the 'line of business' test with the 'fairness' test." Miller v. Miller, 301 Minn. 207, 222 N.W.2d 71, 81 (1974). It engaged in a two-step analysis, first determining whether a particular opportunity was within the corporation's line of business, then scrutinizing "the equitable considerations existing prior to, at the time of, and following the officer's acquisition." Id. The Miller court hoped by adopting this approach "to ameliorate the often-expressed criticism that the [corporate opportunity] doctrine is vague and subjects today's corporate management to the danger of unpredictable liability." Id. In fact, the test adopted in Miller merely piles the uncertainty and vagueness of the fairness test on top of the weaknesses in the line of business test.

Despite the weaknesses of each of these approaches to the corporate opportunity doctrine, they nonetheless rest on a single fundamental policy. At bottom, the corporate opportunity doctrine recognizes that a corporate fiduciary should not serve both corporate and personal interests at the same time. As we observed in Camden Land Co. v. Lewis, 101 Me. 78, 97, 63 A. 523, 531 (1905), corporate fiduciaries "owe their whole duty to the corporation, and they are not to be permitted to act when duty conflicts with interest. They cannot serve themselves and the corporation at the same time." The various formulations of the test are merely attempts to moderate the potentially harsh consequences of strict adherence to that policy. It is important to preserve some ability for corporate fiduciaries to pursue personal business interests that present no real threat to their duty of loyalty.

III.

The American Law Institute Approach

In an attempt to protect the duty of loyalty while at the same time providing long-needed clarity and guidance for corporate decisionmakers, the American Law Institute has offered the most recently developed version of the corporate opportunity doctrine. PRINCIPLES OF CORPORATE GOVERNANCE § 5.05 (May 13, 1992), provides as follows:

§ 5.05   Taking of Corporate Opportunities by Directors or Senior Executives

(a) General Rule. A director [§ 1.13] or senior executive [§ 1.33] may not take advantage of a corporate opportunity unless:

> (1) The director or senior executive first offers the corporate opportunity to the corporation and makes disclosure concerning the conflict of interest [§ 1.14(a)] and the corporate opportunity [§ 1.14(b)];

> (2) The corporate opportunity is rejected by the corporation; and

> (3) Either:

> > (A) The rejection of the opportunity is fair to the corporation;

> > (B) The opportunity is rejected in advance, following such disclosure, by disinterested directors [§ 1.15], or, in the case of a senior executive who is not a director, by a disinterested superior, in a manner that satisfies the standards of the business judgment rule [§ 4.01(c)]; or

> > (C) The rejection is authorized in advance or ratified, following such disclosure, by disinterested shareholders [§ 1.16], and the rejection is not equivalent to a waste of corporate assets [§ 1.42].

(b) Definition of a Corporate Opportunity. For purposes of this Section, a corporate opportunity means:

> (1) Any opportunity to engage in a business activity of which a director or senior executive becomes aware, either:

> > (A) In connection with the performance of functions as a director or senior executive, or under circumstances that should reasonably lead the director or senior

executive to believe that the person offering the opportunity expects it to be offered to the corporation; or

(B) Through the use of corporate information or property, if the resulting opportunity is one that the director or senior executive should reasonably be expected to believe would be of interest to the corporation; or

(2) Any opportunity to engage in a business activity of which a senior executive becomes aware and knows is closely related to a business in which the corporation is engaged or expects to engage.

(c) Burden of Proof. A party who challenges the taking of a corporate opportunity has the burden of proof, except that if such party establishes that the requirements of Subsection (a)(3)(B) or (C) are not met, the director or the senior executive has the burden of proving that the rejection and the taking of the opportunity were fair to the corporation.

(d) Ratification of Defective Disclosure. A good faith but defective disclosure of the facts concerning the corporate opportunity may be cured if at any time (but no later than a reasonable time after suit is filed challenging the taking of the corporate opportunity) the original rejection of the corporate opportunity is ratified, following the required disclosure, by the board, the shareholders, or the corporate decisionmaker who initially approved the rejection of the corporate opportunity, or such decisionmaker's successor.

(e) Special Rule Concerning Delayed Offering of Corporate Opportunities. Relief based solely on failure to first offer an opportunity to the corporation under Subsection (a)(1) is not available if: (1) such failure resulted from a good faith belief that the business activity did not constitute a corporate opportunity, and (2) not later than a reasonable time after suit is filed challenging the taking of the corporate opportunity, the corporate opportunity is to the extent possible offered to the corporation and rejected in a manner that satisfies the standards of Subsection (a).

The central feature of the ALI test is the strict requirement of full disclosure prior to taking advantage of any corporate opportunity. Id., § 5.05(a)(1). "If the opportunity is not offered to the corporation, the director or senior executive will not have satisfied § 5.05(a)." Id., cmt. to § 5.05(a). The corporation must then formally reject the opportunity. Id., § 505(a)(2). The ALI test is discussed at length and ultimately applied by the Oregon Supreme Court in Klinicki v. Lundgren, 298 Or. 662, 695 P.2d 906 (1985). As Klinicki describes the test, "full disclosure to the appropriate corporate body is * * * an absolute condition precedent to the validity of any forthcoming rejection as well as to the availability to the director or principal senior executive of the defense of fairness." Id. at 920. A "good faith but defective disclosure" by the corporate officer may be ratified after the fact only by an affirmative vote of the disinterested directors or shareholders. Principles of Corporate Governance § 5.05(d).

The ALI test defines "corporate opportunity" broadly. It includes opportunities "closely related to a business in which the corporation is engaged." Id., § 5.05(b). It also encompasses any opportunities that accrue to the fiduciary as a result of her position within the corporation. Id. This concept is most clearly illustrated by the testimony of Suminsby, the listing broker for the Gilpin property, which, if believed by the factfinder, would support a finding that the Gilpin property was offered to Harris specifically in her capacity as president of the Club. If the factfinder reached that conclusion, then at least the opportunity to acquire the Gilpin property would be a corporate opportunity. The state of the record concerning the Smallidge purchase precludes us from intimating any opinion whether that too would be a corporate opportunity.

Under the ALI standard, once the Club shows that the opportunity is a corporate opportunity, it must show either that Harris did not offer the opportunity to the Club or that the Club did not reject it properly. If the Club shows that the board did not reject the opportunity by a vote of the disinterested directors after full disclosure, then Harris may defend her actions on the basis that the taking of the opportunity was fair to the corporation. Id., § 5.05(c). If Harris failed to offer the opportunity at all, however, then she may not defend on the basis that the failure to offer the opportunity was fair. Id., cmt. to § 5.05(c).

The Klinicki court viewed the ALI test as an opportunity to bring some clarity to a murky area of the law. Klinicki, 695 P.2d at 915. We agree, and today we follow the ALI test. The disclosure-oriented approach provides a clear procedure whereby a corporate officer may insulate herself through prompt and complete disclosure from the possibility of a legal challenge. The requirement of disclosure recognizes the paramount importance of the corporate fiduciary's duty of loyalty. At the same time it protects the fiduciary's ability pursuant to the proper procedure to pursue her own business ventures free from the possibility of a lawsuit.

The importance of disclosure is familiar to the law of corporations in Maine. Pursuant to 13–A M.R.S.A. § 717 (1981), a corporate officer or director may enter into a transaction with the corporation in which she has a personal or adverse interest only if she discloses her interest in the transaction and secures ratification by a majority of the disinterested directors or shareholders.[2] * * * Like the ALI rule, section 717 was designed to "eliminate the inequities and uncertainties caused by the existing rules." Model Business Corp. Act § 41, ¶ 2, at 844 (1971).

IV.

Conclusion

The question remains how our adoption of the rule affects the result in the instant case. The trial court made a number of factual findings based on an extensive record.[3] The court made those findings, however, in the light of legal principles that are different from the principles that we today announce. Similarly, the parties did not have the opportunity to develop the record in this case with knowledge of the applicable legal standard. In these circumstances, fairness requires that we remand the case for further proceedings. Those further proceedings may include, at the trial court's discretion, the taking of further evidence. * * *

Judgment vacated [and remanded] for further proceedings consistent with the opinion herein.

All concurring.

NOTES

(1) On a subsequent appeal, Northeast Harbor Golf Club v. Harris, 725 A.2d 1018 (Me.1999), the Maine Supreme Court held that while Harris had usurped corporate opportunities, the 6-year Maine statute of limitations had run on the bulk of Ms. Harris' acquisitions. The doctrine of laches was applied with respect to one small tract, and these two doctrines together barred entirely the Club's recovery. In the principal case, the Supreme Court of Maine rejects the traditional notion that an executive can usurp a corporate opportunity if it is shown that the corporation is financially unable to pursue the opportunity itself. What reasons does the court give for doing this? Is the rationale unique to the facts of this case? While most courts refuse to allow financial inability to justify the pursuit of a corporate opportunity by a fiduciary, Delaware has affirmed the view that in order to plead usurpation of corporate opportunity, "the plaintiff must plead (*inter alia*) facts that demonstrate that the company had the financial means to take advantage of the alleged opportunity." Gibralt Capital Corp. v. Smith, 2001 WL 647837 (Del.Ch. May. 9, 2001).

---

[2] Unlike the ALI rule, 13–A M.R.S.A. § 717(1)(C) permits the director to defend on the ground of fairness even in the absence of disclosure. We are not troubled by this difference because the nature of the transactions covered by section 717 is such that the board will necessarily be aware of the transaction. It may therefore act to protect the interests of the corporation even if it is not aware of the interest of the fiduciary. In the case of a usurpation of a corporate opportunity, the corporation is defenseless unless the director discloses.

[3] Harris raised the defense of laches and the statute of limitations but the court made no findings on those issues. We do not intimate what result the application of either doctrine would produce in this case. * * *

(2) The complicating factor of the corporate opportunity doctrine is that its application cannot be determined by simple hard and fast rules. Rather, it requires a particularized analysis of the circumstances. As a result, courts may readily disagree whether a specific opportunity should be viewed as a corporate opportunity. Section 5.05 seems to be a reasonable effort to encapsulate tests for this difficult, fact-sensitive area.

(3) The earliest test for corporate opportunities has been described as the "interest or expectancy" test. Professor Richard A. Epstein analyzes this test in the context of a contractual approach toward corporation law in Contract and Trust in Corporate Law: The Case of Corporate Opportunity, 21 Del.J.Corp.L. 5, 14–15 (1996).

(4) The most widely cited common law test is the "seminal" holding in Guth v. Loft, discussed in the principal case. In addition to the criticisms of this test in the principal opinion, Professor Pat Chew complains that it is much too favorable to the corporation. Professor Chew argues strongly that the corporate opportunity doctrine is warped in favor of the corporation and that, as a result, it is a serious "restraint on individuals' freedom to compete [which] is contrary to society's long-standing goal of promoting competition." Pat K. Chew, Competing Interests in the Corporate Opportunity Doctrine, 67 N.C.L.Rev. 435, 456–58 (1989).

Not surprisingly, a significant number of corporate opportunity cases arise in Delaware. While *Guth* is always cited as the controlling case, Delaware courts have in fact moved towards the fairness test both in holding and in dicta. In Johnston v. Greene, 121 A.2d 919, 923 (Del.Supr.1956), for example, the court stated that the test in every corporate opportunity case was "whether or not the director had appropriated something to himself *that in all fairness should belong to his corporation*" (emphasis added). This language was quoted approvingly in a recent Delaware corporate opportunity case, Broz v. Cellular Information Systems, Inc., 673 A.2d 148 (Del. 1996), which added that *Guth* provided "guidelines * * * in balancing the equities."

(5) One of the allegations in a derivative suit against Martha Stewart and other corporate officers and directors of Martha Stewart Living Omnimedia was usurpation of a corporate opportunity. The complaint alleged that Stewart and other officers had usurped a corporate opportunity by selling shares of their stock. The judge used the test in *Broz* to dismiss the allegation:

> [A] corporate officer or director may not take a business opportunity for his own if: (1) the corporation is financially able to exploit the opportunity; (2) the opportunity is within the corporation's line of business; (3) the corporation has an interest or expectancy in the opportunity; and (4) by taking the opportunity for his own, the corporate fiduciary will thereby be placed in a position [inimical] to his duties to the corporation. Broz, 673 A.2d at 155.

In short, the stock was not in the corporation's line of business, the corporation did not have an interest or expectancy in the stock, and the sale of stock did not make Stewart and others inimical to the corporation. See Beam v. Stewart, 833 A.2d 961, 972 (Del.Ch.2003).

(6) May a corporation renounce an opportunity voluntarily in order to enable an officer, director, or shareholder to take advantage of the opportunity? In 2000, Delaware added § 122(17) to the DGCL that expressly authorizes such a renunciation. While such a renunciation when minority shareholders exist would seem clearly to implicate fiduciary duties, a renunciation before any minority interests are created presumably would not.

(7) Despite much judicial and academic discussion, many argue that the corporate opportunity doctrine is still a source of confusion. As Professor Eric Talley observes: "[R]epeated endeavors by litigants, judges, and legal scholars to clarify the doctrine have generated a panoply of tests, variations, and hybrids. But the end product of this collective effort appears—by virtually all accounts—more tautologous than diagnostic, replete with exceptions and indecipherable distinctions that provide little guidance either to theorists or to practitioners." Professor Talley proposes a "normative account of the [corporate opportunity doctrine] that emerges from the economic theory of contract." Eric Talley, Turning Service Opportunities to Gold: A Strategic Analysis of the Corporate Opportunity Doctrine, 108 Yale L.J. 277 (1998).

CHAPTER 12

SHAREHOLDER DERIVATIVE LAWSUITS

■ ■ ■

GALL v. EXXON CORP.

United States District Court, Southern District of New York, 1976.
418 F. Supp. 508.

ROBERT L. CARTER, DISTRICT JUDGE.

Defendants have moved, pursuant to Rule 56, F.R.Civ.P., for summary judgment dismissing plaintiff's complaint on the grounds that the Special Committee on Litigation ("Special Committee"), acting as the Board of Directors of Exxon Corporation ("Exxon"), has determined in the good faith exercise of its sound business judgment that it is contrary to the interests of Exxon to institute suit on the basis of any matters raised in plaintiff's complaint. Defendants' motion is hereby denied without prejudice to its renewal after plaintiff has conducted relevant discovery. * * *

Plaintiff's complaint arises out of the alleged payment by Exxon Corporation of some $59 million in corporate funds as bribes or political payments, which were improperly contributed to Italian political parties and others during the period 1963–1974, in order to secure special political favors as well as other allegedly illegal commitments. * * *

On September 24, 1975, Exxon's Board of Directors unanimously resolved, pursuant to Article III, Section 1, of Exxon's By-Laws to establish a Special Committee on Litigation, composed of Exxon directors Jack F. Bennett, Richard P. Dobson and Edward G. Harness,[2] and refer to the Special Committee for the determination of Exxon's action the matters raised in this and several other pending actions relating to the Italian expenditures. * * *

On January 23, 1976, after an investigation of approximately four months, including interviews with over 100 witnesses, the Special Committee issued the "Determination and Report of the Special

---

[2] * * * According to the affidavits submitted, each of the members of the Special Committee has confirmed that he has not been in any way connected or involved with the matters relating to the Italian expenditures referred to in this action or in the other related actions and none has been named as a defendant in any of the pending actions. Indeed, none of the members of the Committee was elected to the Exxon Board until long after the Italian expenditures complained of were terminated and Exxon had taken steps to ensure that such expenditures would not be resumed.

Committee on Litigation" ("Report"), an 82-page document summarizing the Committee's findings and recommendations. The facts as uncovered by the Special Committee may be briefly summarized as follows. * * *

[The Committee report described a pattern of secret payments made for various purposes between 1963 and 1972 and political contributions to Italian political parties during the same period. The secret payments, totaling about 39 million dollars, were made through secret bank accounts not reflected on the books of Exxon's Italian subsidiary, Esso Italiana. The political contributions, totaling about 20 million dollars, were channeled through newspaper and public relations firms connected with Italian political parties; these payments were reflected by fictitious invoices purportedly for services rendered. Several of the Exxon directors named as defendants in this suit were aware of the existence of at least the political payments in Italy prior to their termination in 1972. Some of the defendants had simply been advised of the existence of the payments; others, in positions of responsibility within corporate management urged that the contributions be phased out as promptly as possible. Some of the defendant-directors were also aware of the payments made through the secret bank accounts, but apparently the knowledge of these payments was more limited than the knowledge about the political contributions.]

After careful review, analysis and investigation, and with the advice and concurrence of Special Counsel,[12] the Special Committee unanimously determined on January 23, 1976, that it would be contrary to the interests of Exxon and its shareholders for Exxon, or anyone on its behalf, to institute or maintain a legal action against any present or former Exxon director or officer.[13] The Committee further resolved to direct and authorize the proper officers of Exxon and its General Counsel to oppose and seek dismissal of all shareholder derivative actions relating to payments made by or on behalf of Esso Italiana S.p.A., which had been filed against any present or former Exxon director or officer.

Discussion

There is no question that the rights sought to be vindicated in this lawsuit are those of Exxon and not those of the plaintiff suing derivatively on the corporation's behalf. Since it is the interests of the corporation which are at stake, it is the responsibility of the directors of the corporation to determine, in the first instance, whether an action should be brought on the corporation's behalf. It follows that the decision of corporate directors whether or not to assert a cause of action held by

---

[12] At its second meeting on October 29, 1975, the Special Committee appointed Justice Joseph Weintraub, former Chief Justice of the New Jersey Supreme Court, as its Special Counsel.

[13] Among the factors cited by the Special Committee in reaching its decision were the unfavorable prospects for success of the litigation, the cost of conducting the litigation, interruption of corporate business affairs and the undermining of personnel morale.

the corporation rests within the sound business judgment of the management. See, e.g., United Copper Securities Co. v. Amalgamated Copper Co., 244 U.S. 261, 263–4, 37 S.Ct. 509, 61 L.Ed. 1119 (1917).

This principle, which has come to be known as the business judgment rule, was articulated by Mr. Justice Brandeis speaking for a unanimous Court in United Copper Securities Co. v. Amalgamated Copper Co., supra, 244 U.S. at 263–64, 37 S.Ct. at 510. In that case the directors of a corporation chose not to bring an antitrust action against a third party. Mr. Justice Brandeis said:

> Whether or not a corporation shall seek to enforce in the courts a cause of action for damages is, like other business questions, ordinarily a matter of internal management, and is left to the discretion of the directors, in the absence of instruction by vote of the stockholders. Courts interfere seldom to control such discretion intra vires the corporation, except where the directors are guilty of misconduct equivalent to a breach of trust, or where they stand in a dual relation which prevents an unprejudiced exercise of judgment. * * *

It is clear that absent allegations of fraud, collusion, self-interest, dishonesty or other misconduct of a breach of trust nature, and absent allegations that the business judgment exercised was grossly unsound, the court should not at the instigation of a single shareholder interfere with the judgment of the corporate officers. * * *

In recent months, the legality and morality of foreign political contributions, bribes and other payments by American corporations has been widely debated. The issue before me for decision, however, is not whether the payments made by Esso Italiana to Italian political parties and other unauthorized payments were proper or improper. Were the court to frame the issue in this way, it would necessarily involve itself in the business decisions of every corporation, and be required to mediate between the judgment of the directors and the judgment of the shareholders with regard to particular corporate actions. As Mr. Justice Brandeis said in his concurring opinion in Ashwander v. Tennessee Valley Authority, 297 U.S. [288,] at 343, 56 S.Ct. [466,] at 481, "[i]f a stockholder could compel the officers to enforce every legal right, courts instead of chosen officers, would be the arbiters of the corporation's fate." Rather, the issue is whether the Special Committee, acting as Exxon's Board of Directors and in the sound exercise of their business judgment, may determine that a suit against any present or former director or officer would be contrary to the best interests of the corporation. * * *

Plaintiff also calls into question the disinterestedness and bona fides of the Special Committee, suggesting that the members of the Special Committee may have been personally involved in the transactions in question, or, at the least, interested in the alleged wrongdoing "in a way calculated to impair their exercise of business judgment on behalf of the corporation." Klotz v. Consolidated Edison of New York, Inc., supra, 386 F.Supp. at 581.[22]

With the foregoing in mind, I am constrained to conclude that it is premature at this stage of the lawsuit to grant summary judgment. Plaintiff must be given an opportunity to test the bona fides and independence of the Special Committee through discovery and, if necessary, at a plenary hearing. Issues of intent, motivation, and good faith are particularly inappropriate for summary disposition.

Accordingly, defendants' motion for summary judgment is hereby denied without prejudice to its renewal after plaintiff has conducted relevant discovery. * * *

NOTES

(1) *Gall* involved a decision by presumably independent directors not to pursue a derivative suit in which other directors were the ultimate target. In invoking the business judgment rule, Judge Carter relied on *United Copper Securities Co.,* a case involving a decision by directors not to sue an unrelated third party. Are these situations really comparable?

(2) The litigation committee device adopted by Exxon to seek dismissal of the Gall suit has become the standard response of publicly held corporations to derivative suits brought or threatened by shareholders which the corporation does not desire to have pursued. In effect, it transmutes a discussion of the merits of the plaintiffs' suit into a discussion of the *bona fides* of the business judgment of a special committee of the board to discontinue inconvenient litigation.

(3) The development of the independent litigation committee has produced a torrent of law review commentary. For a sampling of this literature, see Michael P. Dooley and E. Norman Veasey, The Role of the Board in Derivative Litigation: Delaware Law and the Current ALI Proposals Compared, 44 Bus.Law. 503, 521–22 (1989) (arguing for the economic and management benefits of special litigation committees); James D. Cox, Searching for the Corporation's Voice in Derivative Suit Litigation: A Critique of *Zapata* and the ALI Project, 1982 Duke L.J. 959, 960 (1982) (arguing that special litigation committees limit waste of valuable corporate

---

[22] * * * At a hearing held on February 27, 1976, plaintiff, for the first time, questioned the independence and bona fides of the members of the Special Committee. Subsequently, on March 2, 1976, plaintiff submitted to the court a statement * * * challenging defendants' assertion that the resolution of the Special Committee was made in the independent, disinterested and good faith exercise of their business judgment. Rule 56, F.R.Civ.P., requires that the moving party demonstrate, on the basis of admissible evidence adduced from persons with personal knowledge of the facts, that "there is no genuine issue as to any material fact." Where this initial showing is not made, summary judgment will be denied, even though the party opposing the motion has submitted no probative evidence to support its position or to establish that there is a genuine issue for trial.

resources); Comment, The Propriety of Judicial Deference to Corporate Boards of Directors, 96 Harv.L.Rev. 1894, 1896, 1906–08 (1983) (arguing that corporate boards produce structural biases which make dismissal much more likely). For an even stronger statement that directors have a "structural bias" in favor of dismissing all derivative litigation, see James D. Cox & Henry C. Munsinger, Bias in the Boardroom: Psychological Foundations and Legal Implications of Corporation Cohesion, 48 Law & Contemp. Probs. 83 (Summer 1985).

Many corporate lawyers reject the underlying premise of this argument, which is also not accepted by some commentators familiar with the underlying social science research. See Robert J. Haft, Business Decisions by the New Board: Behavioral Science and Corporate Law, 80 Mich.L.Rev. 1 (1981); Charles W. Murdock, Corporate Governance: The Role of Special Litigation Committees, 68 Wash.L.Rev. 79, 101–20 (1993); Renier Kraakman, Hyun Park, and Steven Shavell, When Are Shareholder Suits in Shareholder Interests?, 82 Geo.L.J. 1733 (1994) (attempts to evaluate the fundamental relationship between shareholder suits and shareholder welfare).

(4) One practical question involving the procedure followed in *Gall* is how independent must a "litigation committee" be? If you were the attorney for a plaintiff faced with the prospect of a *Gall*-type defense, might you consider naming all of the directors as defendants? Could a director without direct involvement in a transaction be sufficiently independent to satisfy the *Gall* principle, if named as a nominal defendant? Assume that the corporation appoints or elects two new directors and names them as the litigation committee. Do you have any basis for naming them as defendants? What about bringing or threatening a derivative suit claiming that a decision by an independent committee was itself a violation of fiduciary duty? Even if the prospects for success of such a suit are slim, could it be used to disqualify directors from serving on the "litigation committee"? Could the corporation appoint yet another litigation committee in order to consider dismissing that suit?

ZAPATA CORP. v. MALDONADO
Supreme Court of Delaware, 1981.
430 A.2d 779.

[The Delaware Chancery Court described the underlying controversy involved in this case as follows:

The relevant facts, construed most favorably to Maldonado, show that in 1970 Zapata's board of directors adopted a stock option plan under which certain of Zapata's officers and directors were granted options to purchase Zapata common stock at $12.15 per share. The plan provided for the exercise of the options in five separate installments, the last of which was to occur on July 14, 1974. In 1971 this plan was ratified by Zapata's stockholders. As the date for the exercise of the final options grew near, however, Zapata was planning a tender offer for 2,300,000 of its own shares. Announcement of the tender offer was expected to be made just prior to July 14, 1974, and it was predicted that the effect of the announcement would be to increase the then market price of Zapata stock from $18–$19 per share to near the tender offer price of $25 per share.

Zapata's directors, most of whom were optionees under the 1970 plan, were aware that the optionees would incur substantial additional federal income tax liability if the options were exercised after the date of the tender offer announcement and that this additional liability could be avoided if the options were exercised prior to the announcement. This was so because the amount of capital gain for federal income tax purposes to the optionees would have been an amount equal to the difference between the $12.15 option price and the price on the date of the exercise of the option: $18–$19 if the options were exercised prior to the tender offer announcement, or nearly $25 if the options were exercised immediately after the announcement.

In order to reduce the amount of federal income tax liability the optionees would incur in exercising their options, Zapata's directors accelerated the date on which the options could be exercised to July 2, 1974. On that day the optionees exercised their options and the directors requested the New York Stock Exchange to suspend trading in Zapata shares pending "an important announcement." On July 8, 1974, Zapata announced the tender offer. The market price of Zapata stock promptly rose to $24.50.

413 A.2d 1251, 1254–55.]

Before DUFFY, QUILLEN and HORSEY, JJ.

QUILLEN, JUSTICE:

This is an interlocutory appeal from an order entered on April 9, 1980, by the Court of Chancery denying appellant-defendant Zapata Corporation's (Zapata) alternative motions to dismiss the complaint or for summary judgment. The issue to be addressed has reached this Court by way of a rather convoluted path.

In June, 1975, William Maldonado, a stockholder of Zapata, instituted a derivative action in the Court of Chancery on behalf of Zapata against ten officers and/or directors of Zapata, alleging, essentially, breaches of fiduciary duty. Maldonado did not first demand that the board bring this action, stating instead such demand's futility because all directors were named as defendants and allegedly participated in the acts specified.[1] * * *

By June, 1979, four of the defendant-directors were no longer on the board, and the remaining directors appointed two new outside directors to the board. The board then created an "Independent Investigation Committee" (Committee), composed solely of the two new directors, to investigate Maldonado's actions, as well as a similar derivative action then pending in Texas, and to determine whether the corporation should continue any or all of the litigation. The Committee's determination was stated to be "final, * * * not * * * subject to review by the Board of Directors and * * * in all respects * * * binding upon the Corporation."

Following an investigation, the Committee concluded, in September, 1979, that each action should "be dismissed forthwith as their continued maintenance is inimical to the Company's best interests * * *." Consequently, Zapata moved for dismissal or summary judgment * * *.

On March 18, 1980, the Court of Chancery, in a reported opinion, the basis for the order of April 9, 1980, denied Zapata's motions, holding that Delaware law does not sanction this means of dismissal. More specifically, it held that the "business judgment" rule is not a grant of authority to dismiss derivative actions and that a stockholder has an individual right to maintain derivative actions in certain instances. Maldonado v. Flynn, Del.Ch., 413 A.2d 1251 (1980). * * * We limit our review in this interlocutory appeal to whether the Committee has the power to cause the present action to be dismissed.

We begin with an examination of the carefully considered opinion of the Vice Chancellor which states, in part, that the "business judgment" rule does not confer power "to a corporate board of directors to terminate a derivative suit," 413 A.2d at 1257. His conclusion is particularly pertinent because several federal courts, applying Delaware law, have held that the business judgment rule enables boards (or their committees) to terminate derivative suits * * *.

As the term is most commonly used, and given the disposition below, we can understand the Vice Chancellor's comment that "the business judgment rule is irrelevant to the question of whether the Committee has the authority to compel the dismissal of this suit." 413 A.2d at 1257. Corporations, existing because of legislative grace, possess authority as granted by the legislature. Directors of Delaware corporations derive their managerial decision making power, which encompasses decisions whether to initiate, or refrain from entering, litigation, from 8 Del.C.

---

[1] Court of Chancery Rule 23.1 states in part: "The complaint shall also allege with particularity the efforts, if any, made by the plaintiff to obtain the action he desires from the directors or comparable authority and the reasons for his failure to obtain the action or for not making the effort."

§ 141(a).[6] This statute is the fount of directorial powers. The "business judgment" rule is a judicial creation that presumes propriety, under certain circumstances, in a board's decision. Viewed defensively, it does not create authority. In this sense the "business judgment" rule is not relevant in corporate decision making until after a decision is made. It is generally used as a defense to an attack on the decision's soundness. The board's managerial decision making power, however, comes from § 141(a). The judicial creation and legislative grant are related because the "business judgment" rule evolved to give recognition and deference to directors' business expertise when exercising their managerial power under § 141(a).

In the case before us, although the corporation's decision to move to dismiss or for summary judgment was, literally, a decision resulting from an exercise of the directors' (as delegated to the Committee) business judgment, the question of "business judgment," in a defensive sense, would not become relevant until and unless the decision to seek termination of the derivative lawsuit was attacked as improper. This question was not reached by the Vice Chancellor because he determined that the stockholder had an individual right to maintain this derivative action.

Thus, the focus in this case is on the power to speak for the corporation as to whether the lawsuit should be continued or terminated. As we see it, this issue in the current appellate posture of this case has three aspects: the conclusions of the Court below concerning the continuing right of a stockholder to maintain a derivative action; the corporate power under Delaware law of an authorized board committee to cause dismissal of litigation instituted for the benefit of the corporation; and the role of the Court of Chancery in resolving conflicts between the stockholder and the committee.

Accordingly, we turn first to the Court of Chancery's conclusions concerning the right of a plaintiff stockholder in a derivative action. We find that its determination that a stockholder, once demand is made and refused, possesses an independent, individual right to continue a derivative suit for breaches of fiduciary duty over objection by the corporation, as an absolute rule, is erroneous. * * * McKee v. Rogers, Del.Ch. 156 A. 191 (1931), stated "as a general rule" that "a stockholder cannot be permitted * * * to invade the discretionary field committed to the judgment of the directors and sue in the corporation's behalf when the managing body refuses. This rule is a well settled one." 156 A. at 193.

---

[6]   8 Del.C. § 141(a) states:

The business and affairs of every corporation organized under this chapter shall be managed by or under the direction of a board of directors * * *.

The *McKee* rule, of course, should not be read so broadly that the board's refusal will be determinative in every instance. Board members, owing a well-established fiduciary duty to the corporation, will not be allowed to cause a derivative suit to be dismissed when it would be a breach of their fiduciary duty. Generally disputes pertaining to control of the suit arise in two contexts.

Consistent with the purpose of requiring a demand, a board decision to cause a derivative suit to be dismissed as detrimental to the company, after demand has been made and refused, will be respected unless it was wrongful.[10] See, e.g., United Copper Securities Co. v. Amalgamated Copper Co., 244 U.S. 261, 263–64, 37 S.Ct. 509, 510, 61 L.Ed. 1119, 1124 (1917). A claim of a wrongful decision not to sue is thus the first exception and the first context of dispute. Absent a wrongful refusal, the stockholder in such a situation simply lacks legal managerial power.

But it cannot be implied that, absent a wrongful board refusal, a stockholder can never have an individual right to initiate an action. For, as is stated in *McKee,* a "well settled" exception exists to the general rule.

> [A] stockholder may sue in equity in his derivative right to assert a cause of action in behalf of the corporation, *without prior demand* upon the directors to sue, when it is apparent that a demand would be futile, that the officers are under an influence that sterilizes discretion and could not be proper persons to conduct the litigation.

156 A. at 193 (emphasis added). This exception, the second context for dispute, is consistent with the Court of Chancery's statement below, that "[t]he stockholders' individual right to bring the action does not ripen, however, * * * unless he can show a demand to be futile."

These comments in *McKee* and in the opinion below make obvious sense. A demand, when required and refused (if not wrongful), terminates a stockholder's legal ability to initiate a derivative action.[12] But where demand is properly excused, the stockholder does possess the ability to initiate the action on his corporation's behalf.

These conclusions, however, do not determine the question before us. Rather, they merely bring us to the question to be decided. It is here that

---

[10] In other words, when stockholders, after making demand and having their suit rejected, attack the board's decision as improper, the board's decision falls under the "business judgment" rule and will be respected if the requirements of the rule are met. See Dent, * * * 75 Nw.U.L.Rev. at 100–01 & nn. 24–25. That situation should be distinguished from the instant case, where demand was not made, and the power of the board to seek a dismissal, due to disqualification, presents a threshold issue. For examples of what has been held to be a wrongful decision not to sue, see Stockholder Derivative Actions, 44 U.Chi.L.Rev. at 193–98. We recognize that the two contexts can overlap in practice.

[12] Even in this situation it may take litigation to determine the stockholder's lack of power, i.e., standing.

we part company with the Court below. Derivative suits enforce corporate rights and any recovery obtained goes to the corporation. "The right of a stockholder to file a bill to litigate corporate rights is, therefore, solely for the purpose of preventing injustice where it is apparent that material corporate rights would not otherwise be protected." We see no inherent reason why the "two phases" of a derivative suit, the stockholder's suit to compel the corporation to sue and the corporation's suit should automatically result in the placement in the hands of the litigating stockholder sole control of the corporate right throughout the litigation. To the contrary, it seems to us that such an inflexible rule would recognize the interest of one person or group to the exclusion of all others within the corporate entity. Thus, we reject the view of the Vice Chancellor as to the first aspect of the issue on appeal.

The question to be decided becomes: When, if at all, should an authorized board committee be permitted to cause litigation, properly initiated by a derivative stockholder in his own right, to be dismissed? As noted above, a board has the power to choose not to pursue litigation when demand is made upon it, so long as the decision is not wrongful. If the board determines that a suit would be detrimental to the company, the board's determination prevails. Even when demand is excusable, circumstances may arise when continuation of the litigation would not be in the corporation's best interests. Our inquiry is whether, under such circumstances, there is a permissible procedure under § 141(a) by which a corporation can rid itself of detrimental litigation. If there is not, a single stockholder in an extreme case might control the destiny of the entire corporation. This concern was bluntly expressed by the Ninth Circuit in Lewis v. Anderson, 615 F.2d 778, 783 (9th Cir.1979), cert. denied, 449 U.S. 869, 101 S.Ct. 206, 66 L.Ed.2d 89 (1980): "To allow one shareholder to incapacitate an entire board of directors merely by leveling charges against them gives too much leverage to dissident shareholders." But, when examining the means, including the committee mechanism examined in this case, potentials for abuse must be recognized. This takes us to the second and third aspects of the issue on appeal.

Before we pass to equitable considerations as to the mechanism at issue here, it must be clear that an independent committee possesses the corporate power to seek the termination of a derivative suit. Section 141(c) allows a board to delegate all of its authority to a committee. Accordingly, a committee with properly delegated authority would have the power to move for dismissal or summary judgment if the entire board did.

Even though demand was not made in this case and the initial decision of whether to litigate was not placed before the board, Zapata's board, it seems to us, retained all of its corporate power concerning litigation decisions. If Maldonado had made demand on the board in this case, it could have refused to bring suit. Maldonado could then have asserted that the decision not to sue was wrongful and, if correct, would have been allowed to maintain the suit. The board, however, never would have lost its statutory managerial authority. The demand requirement itself evidences that the managerial power is retained by the board. When a derivative plaintiff is allowed to bring suit after a wrongful refusal, the board's authority to choose whether to pursue the litigation is not challenged although its conclusion—reached through the exercise of that authority—is not respected since it is wrongful. Similarly, Rule 23.1, by excusing demand in certain instances, does not strip the board of its corporate power. It merely saves the plaintiff the expense and delay of making a futile demand resulting in a probable tainted exercise of that authority in a refusal by the board or in giving control of litigation to the opposing side. But the board entity remains empowered under § 141(a) to make decisions regarding corporate litigation. The problem is one of member disqualification, not the absence of power in the board.

The corporate power inquiry then focuses on whether the board, tainted by the self-interest of a majority of its members, can legally delegate its authority to a committee of two disinterested directors. We find our statute clearly requires an affirmative answer to this question. As has been noted, under an express provision of the statute, § 141(c), a committee can exercise all of the authority of the board to the extent provided in the resolution of the board. Moreover, at [least] by analogy to our statutory section on interested directors, 8 Del.C. § [144], it seems clear that the Delaware statute is designed to permit disinterested directors to act for the board.[14]

---

[14] 8 Del.C. § 144 [Interested directors; quorum] states:

(a) No contract or transaction between a corporation and 1 or more of its directors or officers, or between a corporation and any other corporation, partnership, association, or other organization in which 1 or more of its directors or officers are directors or officers, or have a financial interest, shall be void or voidable solely for this reason, or solely because the director or officer is present at or participates in the meeting of the board or committee which authorizes the contract or transaction, or solely because his or their votes are counted for such purpose, if:

(1) The material facts as to his relationship or interest and as to the contract or transaction are disclosed or are known to the board of directors or the committee, and the board or committee in good faith authorizes the contract or transaction by the affirmative votes of a majority of the disinterested directors, even though the disinterested directors be less than a quorum; or

(2) The material facts as to his relationship or interest and as to the contract or transaction are disclosed or are known to the shareholders entitled to vote thereon, and the contract or transaction is specifically approved in good faith by vote of the shareholders; or

(3) The contract or transaction is fair to the corporation as of the time it is authorized, approved or ratified, by the board of directors, a committee, or the shareholders.

(b) Common or interested directors may be counted in determining the presence of a quorum at a meeting of the board of directors or of a committee which authorizes the contract or transaction.

We do not think that the interest taint of the board majority is per se a legal bar to the delegation of the board's power to an independent committee composed of disinterested board members. The committee can properly act for the corporation to move to dismiss derivative litigation that is believed to be detrimental to the corporation's best interest.

Our focus now switches to the Court of Chancery which is faced with a stockholder assertion that a derivative suit, properly instituted, should continue for the benefit of the corporation and a corporate assertion, properly made by a board committee acting with board authority, that the same derivative suit should be dismissed as inimical to the best interests of the corporation.

At the risk of stating the obvious, the problem is relatively simple. If, on the one hand, corporations can consistently wrest bona fide derivative actions away from well-meaning derivative plaintiffs through the use of the committee mechanism, the derivative suit will lose much, if not all, of its generally-recognized effectiveness as an intra-corporate means of policing boards of directors. If, on the other hand, corporations are unable to rid themselves of meritless or harmful litigation and strike suits, the derivative action, created to benefit the corporation, will produce the opposite, unintended result. * * * It thus appears desirable to us to find a balancing point where bona fide stockholder power to bring corporate causes of action cannot be unfairly trampled on by the board of directors, but the corporation can rid itself of detrimental litigation.

As we noted, the question has been treated by other courts as one of the "business judgment" of the board committee. If a "committee, composed of independent and disinterested directors, conducted a proper review of the matters before it, considered a variety of factors and reached, in good faith, a business judgment that [the] action was not in the best interest of [the corporation]," the action must be dismissed. The issues become solely independence, good faith, and reasonable investigation. The ultimate conclusion of the committee, under that view, is not subject to judicial review.

We are not satisfied, however, that acceptance of the "business judgment" rationale at this stage of derivative litigation is a proper balancing point. While we admit an analogy with a normal case respecting board judgment, it seems to us that there is sufficient risk in the realities of a situation like the one presented in this case to justify caution beyond adherence to the theory of business judgment.

The context here is a suit against directors where demand on the board is excused. We think some tribute must be paid to the fact that the lawsuit was properly initiated. It is not a board refusal case. Moreover, this complaint was filed in June of 1975 and, while the parties undoubtedly would take differing views on the degree of litigation activity, we have to be concerned about the creation of an "Independent Investigation Committee" four years later, after the election of two new outside directors. Situations could develop where such motions could be filed after years of vigorous litigation for reasons unconnected with the merits of the lawsuit.

Moreover, notwithstanding our conviction that Delaware law entrusts the corporate power to a properly authorized committee, we must be mindful that directors are passing judgment on fellow directors in the same corporation and fellow directors, in this instance, who designated them to serve both as directors and committee members. The question naturally arises whether a "there but for the grace of God go I" empathy might not play a role. And the further question arises whether inquiry as to independence, good faith and reasonable investigation is [a] sufficient safeguard against abuse, perhaps subconscious abuse.

There is another line of exploration besides the factual context of this litigation which we find helpful. The nature of this motion finds no ready pigeonhole, as perhaps illustrated by its being set forth in the alternative. It is perhaps best considered as a hybrid summary judgment motion for dismissal because the stockholder plaintiff's standing to maintain the suit has been lost. But it does not fit neatly into a category described in Rule 12(b) of the Court of Chancery Rules nor does it correspond directly with Rule 56 since the question of genuine issues of fact on the merits of the stockholder's claim are not reached. * * *

Whether the Court of Chancery will be persuaded by the exercise of a committee power resulting in a summary motion for dismissal of a derivative action, where a demand has not been initially made, should rest, in our judgment, in the independent discretion of the Court of Chancery. We thus steer a middle course between those cases which yield to the independent business judgment of a board committee and this case as determined below which would yield to unbridled plaintiff stockholder control. In pursuit of the course, we recognize that "[t]he final substantive judgment whether a particular lawsuit should be maintained requires a balance of many factors—ethical, commercial, promotional, public relations, employee relations, fiscal as well as legal." But we are content that such factors are not "beyond the judicial reach" of the Court of Chancery which regularly and competently deals with fiduciary relationships, disposition of trust property, approval of settlements and scores of similar problems. We recognize the danger of judicial overreaching but the alternatives seem to us to be outweighed by the fresh view of a judicial outsider. Moreover, if we failed to balance all the interests involved, we would in the name of practicality and judicial economy foreclose a judicial decision on the merits. At this point, we are not convinced that is necessary or desirable.

After an objective and thorough investigation of a derivative suit, an independent committee may cause its corporation to file a pretrial motion to dismiss in the Court of Chancery. The basis of the motion is the best interests of the corporation, as determined by the committee. The motion should include a thorough written record of the investigation and its findings and recommendations. Under appropriate Court supervision, akin to proceedings on summary judgment, each side should have an opportunity to make a record on the motion. As to the limited issues presented by the motion noted below, the moving party should be prepared to meet the normal burden under Rule 56 that there is no genuine issue as to any material fact and that the moving party is entitled to dismiss as a matter of law.[15] The Court should apply a two-step test to the motion.

First, the Court should inquire into the independence and good faith of the committee and the bases supporting its conclusions. Limited discovery may be ordered to facilitate such inquiries. The corporation should have the burden of proving independence, good faith and a reasonable investigation, rather than presuming independence, good faith and reasonableness.[17] If the Court determines either that the committee is not independent or has not shown reasonable bases for its conclusions, or, if the Court is not satisfied for other reasons relating to the process, including but not limited to the good faith of the committee, the Court shall deny the corporation's motion. If, however, the Court is satisfied under Rule 56 standards that the committee was independent and showed reasonable bases for good faith findings and recommendations, the Court may proceed, in its discretion, to the next step.

The second step provides, we believe, the essential key in striking the balance between legitimate corporate claims as expressed in a derivative stockholder suit and a corporation's best interests as expressed by an independent investigating committee. The Court should determine, applying its own independent business judgment, whether the motion should be granted.[18] This means, of course, that instances could arise where a committee can establish its independence and sound bases for its good faith decisions and still have the corporation's motion denied. The

---

[15] We do not foreclose a discretionary trial of factual issues but that issue is not presented in this appeal. See Lewis v. Anderson, supra, 615 F.2d at 780. Nor do we foreclose the possibility that other motions may proceed or be joined with such a pretrial summary judgment motion to dismiss, e.g., a partial motion for summary judgment on the merits.

[17] Compare Auerbach v. Bennett, 47 N.Y.2d 619, 419 N.Y.S.2d 920, 928–29, 393 N.E.2d 994 (1979). Our approach here is analogous to and consistent with the Delaware approach to "interested director" transactions, where the directors, once the transaction is attacked, have the burden of establishing its "intrinsic fairness" to a court's careful scrutiny. See, e.g., Sterling v. Mayflower Hotel Corp., Del.Supr., 93 A.2d 107 (1952).

[18] This step shares some of the same spirit and philosophy of the statement by the Vice Chancellor: "Under our system of law, courts and not litigants should decide the merits of litigation." 413 A.2d at 1263.

second step is intended to thwart instances where corporate actions meet the criteria of step one, but the result does not appear to satisfy its spirit, or where corporate actions would simply prematurely terminate a stockholder grievance deserving of further consideration in the corporation's interest. The Court of Chancery of course must carefully consider and weigh how compelling the corporate interest in dismissal is when faced with a non-frivolous lawsuit. The Court of Chancery should, when appropriate, give special consideration to matters of law and public policy in addition to the corporation's best interests.

If the Court's independent business judgment is satisfied, the Court may proceed to grant the motion, subject, of course, to any equitable terms or conditions the Court finds necessary or desirable.

The interlocutory order of the Court of Chancery is reversed and the cause is remanded for further proceedings consistent with this opinion.

NOTE

Following this decision, several courts refused to give decisions by litigation committees the finality that appeared to be required under pre-Zapata decisions. Among these cases are Joy v. North, 692 F.2d 880 (2d Cir.1982), cert. denied sub nom. Citytrust v. Joy, 460 U.S. 1051 (1983) (nominally decided under Connecticut law); Hasan v. CleveTrust Realty Investors, 729 F.2d 372 (6th Cir.1984) (no presumption of regularity or good faith to support litigation committee decision); In Matter of Continental Illinois Sec. Litig., 732 F.2d 1302 (7th Cir.1984). While there were dissents in some of these cases, the majority opinions generally reflect skepticism about the wisdom of uncritical acceptance of the principle that plaintiffs attacking a corporate transaction should be remitted only to an attack on the independence and good faith of the litigation committee. However, the development of Delaware law was not complete.

ARONSON V. LEWIS

Supreme Court of Delaware, 1984.
473 A.2d 805.

Before McNeilly, Moore and Christie, JJ.

Moore, Justice:

In the wake of Zapata Corp. v. Maldonado, Del.Supr., 430 A.2d 779 (1981), this Court left a crucial issue unanswered: when is a stockholder's demand upon a board of directors, to redress an alleged wrong to the corporation, excused as futile prior to the filing of a derivative suit? We granted this interlocutory appeal to the defendants, Meyers Parking System, Inc. (Meyers), a Delaware corporation, and its directors, to review the Court of Chancery's denial of their motion to dismiss this action, pursuant to Chancery Rule 23.1, for the plaintiff's failure to make such a demand or otherwise demonstrate its futility. The Vice Chancellor ruled that plaintiff's allegations raised a "reasonable inference" that the directors' action was unprotected by the business judgment rule. Thus, the board could not have impartially considered and acted upon the demand. See Lewis v. Aronson, Del.Ch., 466 A.2d 375, 381 (1983).

We cannot agree with this formulation of the concept of demand futility. In our view demand can only be excused where facts are alleged with particularity which create a reasonable doubt that the directors' action was entitled to the protections of the business judgment rule. Because the plaintiff failed to make a demand, and to allege facts with particularity indicating that such demand would be futile, we reverse the Court of Chancery and remand with instructions that plaintiff be granted leave to amend the complaint. * * *

The issues of demand futility rest upon the allegations of the complaint. The plaintiff, Harry Lewis, is a stockholder of Meyers. The defendants are Meyers and its ten directors, some of whom are also company officers.

In 1979, Prudential Building Maintenance Corp. (Prudential) spun off its shares of Meyers to Prudential's stockholders. Prior thereto Meyers was a wholly owned subsidiary of Prudential. Meyers provides parking lot facilities and related services throughout the country. Its stock is actively traded over-the-counter.

This suit challenges certain transactions between Meyers and one of its directors, Leo Fink, who owns 47% of its outstanding stock. Plaintiff claims that these transactions were approved only because Fink personally selected each director and officer of Meyers.[2]

Prior to January 1, 1981, Fink had an employment agreement with Prudential which provided that upon retirement he was to become a consultant to that company for ten years. This provision became operable when Fink retired in April 1980. Thereafter, Meyers agreed with Prudential to share Fink's consulting services and reimburse Prudential for 25% of the fees paid Fink. Under this arrangement Meyers paid Prudential $48,332 in 1980 and $45,832 in 1981.

On January 1, 1981, the defendants approved an employment agreement between Meyers and Fink for a five year term with provision for automatic renewal each year thereafter, indefinitely. Meyers agreed to pay Fink $150,000 per year, plus a bonus of 5% of its pre-tax profits over $2,400,000. Fink could terminate the contract at any time, but Meyers could do so only upon six months' notice. At termination, Fink was to become a consultant to Meyers and be paid $150,000 per year for the first

---

[2] The Court of Chancery stated that Fink had been chief executive officer of Prudential prior to the spinoff and thereafter became chairman of Meyers' board.

three years, $125,000 for the next three years, and $100,000 thereafter for life. Death benefits were also included. Fink agreed to devote his best efforts and substantially his entire business time to advancing Meyers' interests. The agreement also provided that Fink's compensation was not to be affected by any inability to perform services on Meyers' behalf. Fink was 75 years old when his employment agreement with Meyers was approved by the directors. There is no claim that he was, or is, in poor health.

Additionally, the Meyers board approved and made interest-free loans to Fink totaling $225,000. These loans were unpaid and outstanding as of August 1982 when the complaint was filed. At oral argument defendants' counsel represented that these loans had been repaid in full.

The complaint charges that these transactions had "no valid business purpose," and were a "waste of corporate assets" because the amounts to be paid are "grossly excessive," that Fink performs "no or little services," and because of his "advanced age" cannot be "expected to perform any such services." The plaintiff also charges that the existence of the Prudential consulting agreement with Fink prevents him from providing his "best efforts" on Meyers' behalf. Finally, it is alleged that the loans to Fink were in reality "additional compensation" without any "consideration" or "benefit" to Meyers.

The complaint alleged that no demand had been made on the Meyers board because:

13. * * * such attempt would be futile for the following reasons:

(a) All of the directors in office are named as defendants herein and they have participated in, expressly approved and/or acquiesced in, and are personally liable for, the wrongs complained of herein.

(b) Defendant Fink, having selected each director, controls and dominates every member of the Board and every officer of Meyers.

(c) Institution of this action by present directors would require the defendant-directors to sue themselves, thereby placing the conduct of this action in hostile hands and preventing its effective prosecution.

The relief sought included the cancellation of the Meyers-Fink employment contract and an accounting by the directors, including Fink, for all damage sustained by Meyers and for all profits derived by the directors and Fink. * * *

A cardinal precept of the General Corporation Law of the State of Delaware is that directors, rather than shareholders, manage the business and affairs of the corporation. 8 Del.C. § 141(a). * * * The existence and exercise of this power carries with it certain fundamental fiduciary obligations to the corporation and its shareholders.[4] Loft, Inc. v. Guth, Del.Ch., 2 A.2d 225 (1938), aff'd, Del.Supr., 5 A.2d 503 (1939). Moreover, a stockholder is not powerless to challenge director action which results in harm to the corporation. The machinery of corporate democracy and the derivative suit are potent tools to redress the conduct of a torpid or unfaithful management. The derivative action developed in equity to enable shareholders to sue in the corporation's name where those in control of the company refused to assert a claim belonging to it. The nature of the action is two-fold. First, it is the equivalent of a suit by the shareholders to compel the corporation to sue. Second, it is a suit by the corporation, asserted by the shareholders on its behalf, against those liable to it.

By its very nature the derivative action impinges on the managerial freedom of directors.[5] Hence, the demand requirement of Chancery Rule 23.1 exists at the threshold, first to ensure that a stockholder exhausts his intracorporate remedies, and then to provide a safeguard against strike suits. Thus, by promoting this form of alternate dispute resolution, rather than immediate recourse to litigation, the demand requirement is a recognition of the fundamental precept that directors manage the business and affairs of corporations.

---

[4]   The broad question of structuring the modern corporation in order to satisfy the twin objectives of managerial freedom of action and responsibility to shareholders has been extensively debated by commentators. See, e.g., Fischel, The Corporate Governance Movement, 35 Vand.L.Rev. 1259 (1982); Dickstein, Corporate Governance and the Shareholders' Derivative Action: Rules and Remedies for Implementing the Monitoring Model, 3 Cardozo L.Rev. 627 (1982); Haft, Business Decisions by the New Board: Behavioral Science and Corporate Law, 80 Mich.L.Rev. 1 (1981); Dent, The Revolution in Corporate Governance, The Monitoring Board, and The Director's Duty of Care, 61 B.U.L.Rev. 623 (1981); Moore, Corporate Officer & Director Liability: Is Corporate Behavior Beyond the Control of Our Legal System? 16 Capital U.L.Rev. 69 (1980); Jones, Corporate Governance: Who Controls the Large Corporation? 30 Hastings L.J. 1261 (1979); Small, The Evolving Role of the Director in Corporate Governance, 30 Hastings L.J. 1353 (1979).

[5]   Like the broader question of corporate governance, the derivative suit, its value, and the methods employed by corporate boards to deal with it have received much attention by commentators. See, e.g., Brown, Shareholder Derivative Litigation and the Special Litigation Committee, 43 U.Pitt.L.Rev. 601 (1982); Coffee and Schwartz, The Survival of the Derivative Suit: An Evaluation and a Proposal for Legislative Reform, 81 Colum.L.Rev. 261 (1981); Shnell, A Procedural Treatment of Derivative Suit Dismissals by Minority Directors, 69 Calif.L.Rev. 885 (1981); Dent, The Power of Directors to Terminate Shareholder Litigation: The Death of the Derivative Suit? 75 N.W.U.L.Rev. 96 (1980); Jones, An Empirical Examination of the Incidence of Shareholder Derivative and Class Action Lawsuits, 1971–1978, 60 B.U.L.Rev. 306 (1980); Comment, The Demand and Standing Requirements in Stockholder Derivative Actions, 44 U.Chi.L.Rev. 168 (1976); Dykstra, The Revival of the Derivative Suit, 116 U.Pa.L.Rev. 74 (1967); Note, Demand on Directors and Shareholders as a Prerequisite to a Derivative Suit, 73 Harv.L.Rev. 729 (1960).

In our view the entire question of demand futility is inextricably bound to issues of business judgment and the standards of that doctrine's applicability. The business judgment rule is an acknowledgment of the managerial prerogatives of Delaware directors under Section 141(a). See Zapata Corp. v. Maldonado, 430 A.2d at 782. It is a presumption that in making a business decision the directors of a corporation acted on an informed basis, in good faith and in the honest belief that the action taken was in the best interests of the company. Kaplan v. Centex Corp., Del.Ch., 284 A.2d 119, 124 (1971); Robinson v. Pittsburgh Oil Refinery Corp., Del.Ch., 126 A. 46 (1924). Absent an abuse of discretion, that judgment will be respected by the courts. The burden is on the party challenging the decision to establish facts rebutting the presumption. See Puma v. Marriott, Del.Ch., 283 A.2d 693, 695 (1971).

The function of the business judgment rule is of paramount significance in the context of a derivative action. It comes into play in several ways—in addressing a demand, in the determination of demand futility, in efforts by independent disinterested directors to dismiss the action as inimical to the corporation's best interests, and generally, as a defense to the merits of the suit. However, in each of these circumstances there are certain common principles governing the application and operation of the rule.

First, its protections can only be claimed by disinterested directors whose conduct otherwise meets the tests of business judgment. From the standpoint of interest, this means that directors can neither appear on both sides of a transaction nor expect to derive any personal financial benefit from it in the sense of self-dealing, as opposed to a benefit which devolves upon the corporation or all stockholders generally. Sinclair Oil Corp. v. Levien, Del.Supr., 280 A.2d 717, 720 (1971); Cheff v. Mathes, Del.Supr., 199 A.2d 548, 554 (1964). See also 8 Del.C. § 144. Thus, if such director interest is present, and the transaction is not approved by a majority consisting of the disinterested directors, then the business judgment rule has no application whatever in determining demand futility.

Second, to invoke the rule's protection directors have a duty to inform themselves, prior to making a business decision, of all material information reasonably available to them. Having become so informed, they must then act with requisite care in the discharge of their duties. While the Delaware cases use a variety of terms to describe the applicable standard of care, our analysis satisfies us that under the business judgment rule director liability is predicated upon concepts of gross negligence.[6] See Veasey & Manning, Codified Standard—Safe Harbor or Uncharted Reef? 35 Bus.Law. 919, 928 (1980).

However, it should be noted that the business judgment rule operates only in the context of director action. Technically speaking, it has no role where directors have either abdicated their functions, or absent a conscious decision, failed to act.[7] But it also follows that under applicable principles, a conscious decision to refrain from acting may nonetheless be a valid exercise of business judgment and enjoy the protections of the rule.

The gap in our law, which we address today, arises from this Court's decision in *Zapata Corp. v. Maldonado.* There, the Court defined the limits of a board's managerial power granted by Section 141(a) and restricted application of the business judgment rule in a factual context similar to this action. Zapata Corp. v. Maldonado, 430 A.2d at 782–86, rev'g, Maldonado v. Flynn, Del.Ch., 413 A.2d 1251 (1980).

By way of background, this Court's review in *Zapata* was limited to whether an independent investigation committee of disinterested directors had the *power* to cause the derivative action to be dismissed. Preliminarily, it was noted in *Zapata* that "[d]irectors of Delaware corporations derive their managerial decision making power, which encompasses decisions whether to initiate, or refrain from entering, litigation, from 8 Del.C. § 141(a)." In that context, this Court observed that the business judgment rule has no relevance to corporate decision making until *after a decision has been made.* In *Zapata,* we stated that a shareholder does not possess an independent individual right to continue a derivative action. Moreover, where demand on a board has been made and refused, we apply the business judgment rule in reviewing the board's refusal to act pursuant to a stockholder's demand. Unless the business judgment rule does not protect the refusal to sue, the shareholder lacks the legal managerial power to continue the derivative action, since that power is terminated by the refusal. We also concluded

---

[6] While the Delaware cases have not been precise in articulating the standard by which the exercise of business judgment is governed, a long line of Delaware cases holds that director liability is predicated on a standard which is less exacting than simple negligence. Sinclair Oil Corp. v. Levien, Del.Supr., 280 A.2d 717, 722 (1971), rev'g, Del.Ch., 261 A.2d 911 (1969) ("fraud or gross overreaching"); Getty Oil Co. v. Skelly Oil Co., Del.Supr., 267 A.2d 883, 887 (1970), rev'g, Del.Ch., 255 A.2d 717 (1969) ("gross and palpable overreaching"); Warshaw v. Calhoun, Del.Supr., 221 A.2d 487, 492–93 (1966) ("bad faith * * * or a gross abuse of discretion"); Moskowitz v. Bantrell, Del.Supr., 190 A.2d 749, 750 (1963) ("fraud or gross abuse of discretion"); Penn Mart Realty Co. v. Becker, Del.Ch., 298 A.2d 349, 351 (1972) ("directors may breach their fiduciary duty * * * by being grossly negligent"); Kors v. Carey, Del.Ch., 158 A.2d 136, 140 (1960) ("fraud, misconduct or abuse of discretion"); Allaun v. Consolidated Oil Co., Del.Ch., 147 A. 257, 261 (1929) ("reckless indifference to or a deliberate disregard of the stockholders").

[7] Although questions of director liability in such cases have been adjudicated upon concepts of business judgment, they do not in actuality present issues of business judgment. See Arsht, Fiduciary Responsibilities of Directors, Officers & Key Employees, 4 Del.J.Corp.L. 652, 659 (1979).

that where demand is excused a shareholder possesses the ability to initiate a derivative action, but the right to prosecute it may be terminated upon the exercise of applicable standards of business judgment. The thrust of *Zapata* is that in either the demand-refused or the demand-excused case, the board still retains its Section 141(a) managerial authority to make decisions regarding corporate litigation. Moreover, the board may delegate its managerial authority to a committee of independent disinterested directors. See 8 Del.C. § 141(c). Thus, even in a demand-excused case, a board has the power to appoint a committee of one or more independent disinterested directors to determine whether the derivative action should be pursued or dismissal sought. Under *Zapata,* the Court of Chancery, in passing on a committee's motion to dismiss a derivative action in a demand excused case, must apply a two-step test. First, the court must inquire into the independence and good faith of the committee and review the reasonableness and good faith of the committee's investigation. Second, the court must apply its own independent business judgment to decide whether the motion to dismiss should be granted.

After *Zapata* numerous derivative suits were filed without prior demand upon boards of directors. The complaints in such actions all alleged that demand was excused because of board interest, approval or acquiescence in the wrongdoing. In any event, the *Zapata* demand-excused/demand-refused bifurcation, has left a crucial issue unanswered: when is demand futile and, therefore, excused? * * *

Our view is that in determining demand futility the Court of Chancery in the proper exercise of its discretion must decide whether, under the particularized facts alleged, a reasonable doubt is created that: (1) the directors are disinterested and independent and (2) the challenged transaction was otherwise the product of a valid exercise of business judgment. Hence, the Court of Chancery must make two inquiries, one into the independence and disinterestedness of the directors and the other into the substantive nature of the challenged transaction and the board's approval thereof. As to the latter inquiry the court does not assume that the transaction is a wrong to the corporation requiring corrective steps by the board. Rather, the alleged wrong is substantively reviewed against the factual background alleged in the complaint. As to the former inquiry, directorial independence and disinterestedness, the court reviews the factual allegations to decide whether they raise a reasonable doubt, as a threshold matter, that the protections of the business judgment rule are available to the board. Certainly, if this is an "interested" director transaction, such that the business judgment rule is inapplicable to the board majority approving the transaction, then the inquiry ceases. In that event futility of demand has been established by any objective or subjective standard.[8] See, e.g., Bergstein v. Texas Internat'l Co., Del.Ch., 453 A.2d 467, 471 (1982) (because five of nine directors approved stock appreciation rights plan likely to benefit them, board was interested for demand purposes and demand held futile).

However, the mere threat of personal liability for approving a questioned transaction, standing alone, is insufficient to challenge either the independence or disinterestedness of directors, although in rare cases a transaction may be so egregious on its face that board approval cannot meet the test of business judgment, and a substantial likelihood of director liability therefore exists. See Gimbel v. Signal Cos., Inc., Del.Ch., 316 A.2d 599, aff'd, Del.Supr., 316 A.2d 619 (1974). In sum the entire review is factual in nature. The Court of Chancery in the exercise of its sound discretion must be satisfied that a plaintiff has alleged facts with particularity which, taken as true, support a reasonable doubt that the challenged transaction was the product of a valid exercise of business judgment. Only in that context is demand excused. * * *

Having outlined the legal framework within which these issues are to be determined, we consider plaintiff's claims of futility here: Fink's domination and control of the directors, board approval of the Fink-Meyers employment agreement, and board hostility to the plaintiff's derivative action due to the directors' status as defendants.

Plaintiff's claim that Fink dominates and controls the Meyers' board is based on: (1) Fink's 47% ownership of Meyers' outstanding stock, and (2) that he "personally selected" each Meyers director. Plaintiff also alleges that mere approval of the employment agreement illustrates Fink's domination and control of the board. In addition, plaintiff argued on appeal that 47% stock ownership, though less than a majority, constituted control given the large number of shares outstanding, 1,245,745.

Such contentions do not support any claim under Delaware law that these directors lack independence. In Kaplan v. Centex Corp., Del.Ch., 284 A.2d 119 (1971), the Court of Chancery stated that "[s]tock ownership alone, at least when it amounts to less than a majority, is not sufficient proof of domination or control." Id. at 123. Moreover, in the demand context even proof of majority ownership of a company does not strip the directors of the presumptions of independence, and that their acts have been taken in good faith and in the best interests of the corporation.

---

[8] We recognize that drawing the line at a majority of the board may be an arguably arbitrary dividing point. Critics will charge that we are ignoring the structural bias common to corporate boards throughout America, as well as the other unseen socialization processes cutting against independent discussion and decisionmaking in the boardroom. The difficulty with structural bias in a demand futile case is simply one of establishing it in the complaint for purposes of Rule 23.1. We are satisfied that discretionary review by the Court of Chancery of complaints alleging specific facts pointing to bias on a particular board will be sufficient for determining demand futility.

There must be coupled with the allegation of control such facts as would demonstrate that through personal or other relationships the directors are beholden to the controlling person. See Mayer v. Adams, Del.Ch., 167 A.2d 729, 732, aff'd, Del.Supr., 174 A.2d 313 (1961). To date the principal decisions dealing with the issue of control or domination arose only after a full trial on the merits. Thus, they are distinguishable in the demand context unless similar particularized facts are alleged to meet the test of Chancery Rule 23.1.

The requirement of director independence inheres in the conception and rationale of the business judgment rule. The presumption of propriety that flows from an exercise of business judgment is based in part on this unyielding precept. Independence means that a director's decision is based on the corporate merits of the subject before the board rather than extraneous considerations or influences. * * *

Thus, it is not enough to charge that a director was nominated by or elected at the behest of those controlling the outcome of a corporate election. That is the usual way a person becomes a corporate director. It is the care, attention and sense of individual responsibility to the performance of one's duties, not the method of election, that generally touches on independence.

We conclude that in the demand-futile context a plaintiff charging domination and control of one or more directors must allege particularized facts manifesting "a direction of corporate conduct in such a way as to comport with the wishes or interests of the corporation (or persons) doing the controlling." Kaplan, 284 A.2d at 123. The shorthand shibboleth of "dominated and controlled directors" is insufficient. * * * [W]e stress that the plaintiff need only allege specific facts; he need not plead evidence. * * *

Here, plaintiff has not alleged any facts sufficient to support a claim of control. The personal-selection-of-directors allegation stands alone, unsupported. At best it is a conclusion devoid of factual support. The causal link between Fink's control and approval of the employment agreement is alluded to, but nowhere specified. The director's approval, alone, does not establish control, even in the face of Fink's 47% stock ownership. The claim that Fink is unlikely to perform any services under the agreement, because of his age, and his conflicting consultant work with Prudential, adds nothing to the control claim. Therefore, we cannot conclude that the complaint factually particularizes any circumstances of control and domination to overcome the presumption of board independence, and thus render the demand futile. * * *

Turning to the board's approval of the Meyers-Fink employment agreement, plaintiff's argument is simple: all of the Meyers directors are named defendants, because they approved the wasteful agreement; if plaintiff prevails on the merits all the directors will be jointly and severally liable; therefore, the directors' interests in avoiding personal liability automatically and absolutely disqualifies them from passing on a shareholder's demand.

Such allegations are conclusory at best. * * * The complaint does not allege particularized facts indicating that the agreement is a waste of corporate assets. Indeed, the complaint as now drafted may not even state a cause of action, given the directors' broad corporate power to fix the compensation of officers.

In essence, the plaintiff alleged a lack of consideration flowing from Fink to Meyers, since the employment agreement provided that compensation was not contingent on Fink's ability to perform any services. The bare assertion that Fink performed "little or no services" was plaintiff's conclusion based solely on Fink's age and the existence of the Fink-Prudential employment agreement. As for Meyers' loans to Fink, beyond the bare allegation that they were made, the complaint does not allege facts indicating the wastefulness of such arrangements. Again, the mere existence of such loans, given the broad corporate powers conferred by Delaware law, does not even state a claim.[13] * * *

Plaintiff's final argument is the incantation that demand is excused because the directors otherwise would have to sue themselves, thereby placing the conduct of the litigation in hostile hands and preventing its effective prosecution. This bootstrap argument has been made to and dismissed by other courts. Its acceptance would effectively abrogate Rule 23.1 and weaken the managerial power of directors. Unless facts are alleged with particularity to overcome the presumptions of independence and a proper exercise of business judgment, in which case the directors could not be expected to sue themselves, a bare claim of this sort raises no legally cognizable issue under Delaware corporate law. * * *

In sum, we conclude that the plaintiff has failed to allege facts with particularity indicating that the Meyers directors were tainted by interest, lacked independence, or took action contrary to Meyers' best interests in order to create a reasonable doubt as to the applicability of the business judgment rule. Only in the presence of such a reasonable doubt may a demand be deemed futile. Hence, we reverse the Court of Chancery's denial of the motion to dismiss, and remand with instructions that plaintiff be granted leave to amend his complaint to bring it into compliance with Rule 23.1 based on the principles we have announced today. * * *

REVERSED AND REMANDED.

---

[13] Plaintiff's allegation ignores 8 Del.C. § 143 which expressly authorizes interest-free loans to "any officer or employee of the corporation * * * whenever, in the judgment of the directors, such loan * * * may reasonably be expected to benefit the corporation." 8 Del.C. § 143.

NOTES

(1) Dennis J. Block & H. Adam Prussin, Termination of Derivative Suits Against Directors on Business Judgment Grounds: From *Zapata* to *Aronson*, 39 Bus.Law. 1503, 1505–06 (Aug. 1984):

> *Aronson* makes it clear that demand will almost always be required unless a majority of the Board is so directly self-interested in the challenged transaction that there is serious doubt that the business judgment rule would protect that transaction. Self-interest, for these purposes, is defined in terms of direct financial interest in the challenged transaction: the fact that a majority of directors voted to approve the transaction—and are therefore named as defendants in the action—does *not* constitute the requisite self-interest and will not excuse demand. After *Aronson* there should be relatively few demand-excused cases, and therefore relatively few cases where the *Zapata* two-step test will be applied. Thus, in run-of-the-mill cases the test actually applied will be the same under Delaware and New York law, the business judgment rule.

(2) The practical and tactical problems faced by a plaintiff under the complex Delaware structure of rules set forth in *Zapata* and *Aronson* were further complicated by four additional holdings.

(a) Spiegel v. Buntrock, 571 A.2d 767, 775 (Del.1990), holds that where a shareholder makes a demand, he thereby "tacitly acknowledges the absence of facts to support a finding of futility," thus placing his case in the hands of the board of directors under the business judgment rule. As a result of this "waiver" rule, plaintiffs today seldom make demand in Delaware, but instead litigate the issue whether demand was excused and futile. See John C. Coffee, Jr., New Myths and Old Realities: The American Law Institute Faces the Derivative Action, 48 Bus. Law. 1407, 1414 (1993).

(b) In Levine v. Smith, 591 A.2d 194 (Del.1991), a case involving General Motors' buy-out of Ross Perot, Levine made a demand on the directors which was unanimously refused. Levine then filed an amended complaint arguing that the refusal of the demand by the board of directors was not a proper exercise of business judgment. He sought the right to institute limited discovery in an effort to establish that the refusal was wrongful. The Court held that discovery should not be permitted following a refused demand, and to obtain judicial review of the claim of wrongful refusal, the plaintiff must allege particularized facts that create reasonable doubt that the refusal was a proper exercise of business judgment. In other words, judicial review of a decision rejecting a demand was subject to the same pleading standard established in *Aronson* to determine whether demand was excused.

(c) In Scattered Corporation v. Chicago Stock Exchange, 701 A.2d 70 (Del.1997), the court stated that in determining whether a demand was wrongfully refused, the plaintiff may use the "tools at hand" to obtain information about the basis of the decision. These "tools" include the statutory right of inspection of books, records, and minutes of meetings, but not discovery or production of records through a writ of mandamus.

(d) In re Walt Disney Co. Derivative Litigation, 825 A.2d 275 (Del.Ch.2003), began with a suit which claimed demand futility. The plaintiffs charged that the directors violated their duty of care and good faith by allowing the extravagant compensation package of former President Michael Ovitz. The Delaware Supreme Court did not excuse demand but they allowed the plaintiffs to amend their original complaint. The plaintiffs, in line with the court's suggestion, requested an inspection of Disney's books and records in order to find evidence of their claim. The plaintiffs were excused demand with their amended complaint in the Court of Chancery.

(3) In virtually every case in which derivative litigation has been considered by a litigation committee or by the board of directors since 1984, the determination has been that pursuit of the litigation is not in the best interest of the corporation. Does this not lend credence to the objection that there is in fact "structural bias" in this decisional process? Or should this datum be explained on the basis that virtually all derivative litigation filed today is without merit? For such a thesis, see Roberta Romano, The Shareholder Suit: Litigation without Foundation?, 7 J.L. Econ. & Org. 56 (1991); Daniel R. Fischel & Michael Bradley, The Role of Liability Rules and the Derivative Suit in Corporate Law: A Theoretical and Empirical Analysis, 71 Cornell L.Rev. 261 (1986); Richard W. Duesenberg, The Business Judgment Rule and Shareholder Derivative Suits: A View From the Inside, 60 Wash. U. L.Q. 311 (1982). Whatever the explanation, certainly one consequence of the use of litigation committees during this period is that control of derivative litigation has largely passed to the board of directors.

GORDON V. GOODYEAR

United States District Court, N.D. Illinois, 2012.
2012 WL 2885695.

AMY J. ST. EVE, DISTRICT COURT JUDGE:

FACTUAL ALLEGATIONS

* * * Plaintiff Natalie Gordon, who owns Navigant common stock, has brought this shareholder derivative suit against the Navigant Board of Directors (the "Board") and various officers. She alleges that the Board awarded "excessive executive compensation despite the fact that Navigant shareholders have seen the value of their investment plummet." * * * She further alleges that they breached their duties and financial obligations and failed to act in the best interests of Navigant and its shareholders.

Navigant is a "[specialty] consulting firm which provides dispute, investigative, economic, operational, risk management, and financial and risk advisory solutions to government agencies and companies."

Defendant Goodyear has served as Navigant's Chairman of the Board of Directors and Chief Executive Officer ("CEO"). * * * Defendant Howard has served as the President of Navigant since February 2006 and has been the Chief Operating Officer ("COO") of Navigant since 2003. Plaintiff alleges that Defendant Howard "has responsibility for the day to day management of company profitability, including compensation strategy." * * * Navigant's Board of Directors was comprised of eight Directors during the relevant time period: Goodyear, Gildehaus, Glassman, James, Pond, Skinner, Thompson, and Tipsord. Defendant Goodyear is the only Director who is also an Executive of Navigant. The other seven Directors on the Board are outside Directors. * * *

Plaintiff alleges that each of the individual Defendants owed Navigant and its shareholders fiduciary obligations of trust, loyalty, good faith and due care, "and were and are required to use their utmost ability to control and manage Navigant in a fair, just, honest and equitable manner." Given their positions as directors and/or officers of Navigant, they have a duty to act in furtherance of the best interests of Navigant and its shareholders so as to benefit all shareholders equally and not in furtherance of their personal interest or benefit. * * *

Navigant's Compensation Committee Charter (the "Charter") sets forth the duties and responsibilities of the Compensation Committee. Pursuant to the terms of the Charter, the Compensation Committee must "review and recommend to the Board compensation policies as well as approve individual executive officer compensation, intended to attract, retain and appropriately reward employees in order to motivate their performance in the achievement of the Company's business objectives and align their interests with the long-term interest of the Company's shareholders * * *." The Charter directs the Compensation Committee to consider a number of factors when assessing the incentive component of executive payment. These factors include, but are not limited to "the Company's performance and relative shareholder return, the value of similar incentive awards to chief executive officers at comparable companies, and the awards given to the Company's Chief Executive Officer in past years. * * *

Plaintiff alleges that, from January 2006 until December 2010, Navigant's share price fell from over $21 per share to $9.20 per share. Navigant posted a negative 38.1 percent shareholder return in 2010, which "capped off a three year return of negative 12.4 percent." Plaintiff alleges that Navigant significantly underperformed both the S&P 500 Total Returns Index and the "[B]usiness Services" industry performance between 2006 and 2010. Plaintiff alleges that the Board members approved pay increases and or cash bonuses for Navigant's top executive officers in 2010 "[d]espite Navigant's dismal financial results, which included a negative 38.1 percent shareholder return over the past year."

According to Plaintiff, the total 2010 combined compensation for Defendants Goodyear, Howard, Nardi and Weed totaled in excess of $4.8 million.

IV. The Shareholder Proxy

On March 16, 2011, Navigant issued and filed a Proxy Statement with the United States Securities and Exchange Commission ("SEC"). Pursuant to the Dodd-Frank Wall Street Reform and Consumer Protection Act ("Dodd-Frank Act"), in the Proxy Statement, the Board recommended that the shareholders approve the compensation that Navigant paid to its executive officers in 2010. The Proxy informed the shareholders that their vote on the compensation was non-binding on both Navigant and its Board. The Proxy, which Navigant sent to its shareholders, specifically provided:

ADVISORY VOTE ON EXECUTIVE COMPENSATION

Pursuant to recently-enacted Section 14A of the Securities Exchange Act of 1934, as amended (the "Exchange Act"), we are providing our shareholders with a vote to approve, on an advisory basis, the compensation paid to our named executive officers as disclosed in this Proxy Statement. This advisory vote on executive compensation is commonly referred to as a "say-on-pay" vote. The guiding principle of our executive compensation philosophy is "pay for performance." Our executive compensation program has been designed to reward the achievement of annual and long-term performance goals and align our named executive officers' interests with those of our shareholders, with the ultimate objective of improving long-term shareholder value. This pay for performance philosophy informs our executive compensation program design as well as the compensation committee's determination of compensation levels for each of our named executive officers.

This pay for performance philosophy guided our executive compensation decisions for 2010, as evidenced by the following:

• Base Salary—Our named executive officers received no salary increase in 2010. Based on our peer group benchmarks, as well as individual and company performance assessments for 2010, the compensation committee did not approve any salary increases for our named executive officers for 2011. As a result, the base salaries for our named executive officers have remained unchanged for the last three years.

• Annual Performance-Based Cash Bonus—Cash bonuses for our named executive officers, in the aggregate, were awarded at 37% of target for 2010, reflecting the fact that the company's financial performance during 2010 only partially met the Board's expectations with respect to revenue growth and EBITDA (and did not meet expectations with respect to net income and earnings per share), despite the company largely achieving its strategic goals for 2010. Consideration was also given to the fact that the company's stock price performance was below the average for its peer group during 2010.

• Long-Term Equity-Based Incentive Compensation—The company's overall performance for 2010 was also a significant factor in determining the value of the equity-based incentive awards granted to our named executive officers for the 2010 performance year. The value of these grants was well below the 50th percentile of our peer group and represented more than a 50% decrease from the value of the prior year's grants. These decisions resulted in a decrease, both individually and in the aggregate, in the total direct compensation to our [named executive officers] for 2010 as compared to 2009, and positioned total direct compensation in the bottom decile of our peer group. We believe these decisions demonstrate our commitment to aligning our executive compensation with performance and our shareholders' interests.

We urge you to read the section entitled "Compensation Discussion and Analysis" in this Proxy Statement for additional details on our executive compensation program, including our executive compensation philosophy and objectives and the 2010 compensation of our named executive officers. We are asking our shareholders to indicate their support for our executive compensation program by voting "FOR" the following resolution at the annual meeting:

"RESOLVED, that the company's shareholders approve, on an advisory basis, the compensation paid to the company's named executive officers, as disclosed in the Proxy Statement pursuant to the compensation disclosure rules of the Securities and Exchange Commission, including the Compensation Discussion and Analysis and the compensation tables and related narrative discussion."

The say-on-pay vote is an advisory vote only, and therefore, it will not bind the company or the Board. However, the Board and the compensation committee will consider the voting results as appropriate when making future compensation decisions for our named executive officers.

The Board and the compensation committee recommend that shareholders vote "FOR" the approval of the advisory resolution relating to the compensation paid to our named executive officers as disclosed in this Proxy Statement.

According to Plaintiff, on March 31, 2011, ISS Proxy Advisory Services ("ISS") a leading proxy advisory service, recommended that shareholders vote against the Board's executive compensation proposal. The ISS based its recommendation on a finding that "there is a misalignment of CEO pay and company stock performance."

V. The Shareholder Meeting

On April 25, 2011, Navigant held its 2011 Annual Meeting of Shareholders. At that meeting, over 55% of Navigant's voting shareholders rejected the compensation package for Navigant's executive management for fiscal year 2010. * * *

VI. Plaintiff Did Not Make a Demand on the Board

* * * [Plaintiff] did not make any demand on the Board to institute this action "because such a demand would have been [a] futile, wasteful and useless act, since the entire Board would be incapable of evaluating such a demand in a disinterested and independent manner." She alleges that a pre-suit demand is excused because "the entire Board faces a substantial likelihood of liability for breach of loyalty." Plaintiff asserts that the majority of the Board are also members of the Compensation Committee and thus incapable of evaluating a pre-suit demand in a disinterested and independent manner. She further alleges that Defendant Goodyear's principal profession is his employment as CEO of Navigant, and thus any pre-suit demand on him is excused. Because he receives and continues to receive substantial monetary compensation, Plaintiff alleges that Defendant Goodyear lacks the appropriate independence to impartially consider a demand.

* * *

Rule 23.1(b)(3) requires that a plaintiff bringing a shareholder derivative action state with particularity the following:

> (A) any effort by the plaintiff to obtain the desired action from the directors or comparable authority and, if necessary, from the shareholders or members; and (B) [t]he reasons for not obtaining the action or not making the effort.

Fed. R. Civ. P. 23.1(b)(3).

In contrast to a motion to dismiss pursuant to Rule 12(b)(6), a Rule 23.1 motion to dismiss for failure to make a demand is not intended to test the legal sufficiency of the plaintiffs' substantive claim. Rather, its purpose is to determine who is entitled, as between the corporation and its shareholders, to assert the plaintiff's underlying substantive claim on the corporation's behalf.

* * *

ANALYSIS

Plaintiff's shareholder derivative suit asserts a claim of breach of a fiduciary duty of loyalty against the Individual Defendants and unjust enrichment against Defendants Goodyear, Howard, Nardi, and Weed. As the Seventh Circuit teaches:

> A derivative suit permits a shareholder to bring an action on behalf of a corporation. A derivative suit has dual aspects: first, the stockholder's right to sue on behalf of the corporation; and second, the claim of the corporation against directors or third parties. The corporation is a necessary party to the action; without it the case cannot proceed. Although named a defendant, it is the real party in interest, the stockholder being at best the nominal plaintiff. Preconditions for a derivative action include both a valid claim on which the corporation could have sued, and that the corporation itself has refused to proceed after suitable demand, unless excused by extraordinary conditions. Because Navigant is incorporated under the laws of Delaware, Delaware law applies in determining whether a demand may be excused when shareholders file a derivative suit on behalf of a company.
> * * *

I. The Demand Requirement Under Delaware Law

Under Delaware law, "directors of a corporation and not its shareholders manage the business and affairs of the corporation, and accordingly, the directors are responsible for deciding whether to engage in derivative litigation." Given the director's role, Delaware law requires a pre-suit demand on the corporation's board of directors unless such a demand would be futile. Because directors are empowered to manage, or direct the management of, the business affairs of the corporation * * *, the right of a stockholder to prosecute a derivative suit is limited to situations where the stockholder has demanded that the directors pursue the corporate claim and they have wrongfully refused to do so or where demand is excused because the directors are incapable of making an impartial decision regarding such litigation. The demand requirement "exists to preserve the primacy of board decisionmaking regarding legal claims belonging to the corporation."

The Supreme Court of Delaware has articulated a two-prong test for determining the futility of a demand on the directors. Specifically, a demand on the board is futile where "under the particularized facts alleged, a reasonable doubt is created that (1) the directors are disinterested and independent and (2) the challenged transaction was otherwise the product of a valid exercise of business judgment." The plaintiff bears the burden of establishing the futility requirements. If a plaintiff can satisfy either prong of the Aronson test, demand is excused.

Plaintiff concedes in her Complaint that she has not made a demand on Navigant's Board of Directors as required under Delaware law. If Plaintiff has sufficiently alleged that such a demand would have been futile, the demand requirement is excused.

II. Plaintiff Has Failed to Plead Demand Futility

A. Plaintiff Has Not Met the First Prong of Aronson

Under the first prong of the Aronson test, Plaintiff must allege with particularity sufficient facts to raise a reasonable doubt that a majority of the board is disinterested or independent. A disinterested director "can neither appear on both sides of a transaction nor expect to derive any personal benefit from [the challenged transaction] in the sense of self-dealing, as opposed to a benefit which devolves upon the corporation or all stockholders generally." Further, "[a] director's independence exists when "a director's decision is based on the corporate merits of the subject before the board rather than extraneous considerations or influences." In addition, a "director * * * is not independent if the director is 'beholden' to another such that the director's decision would not be based on the merits of the subject before her."

Plaintiff has failed to meet her burden of alleging that a majority of the Directors are interested or not independent. She has alleged that only one of the eight Directors—Defendant Goodyear—personally benefitted from the Board's approval of the executive compensation. This Court has never held that one director's colorable interest in a challenged transaction is sufficient, without more, to deprive a board of the protection of the business judgment rule presumption of loyalty. The other seven Directors were outside Directors who did not hold a position with Navigant and did not receive any of the pay at issue. This is especially true because Plaintiff has not alleged that Defendant Goodyear was on the Board's Compensation Committee or played any role in setting his 2010 compensation. She also has not alleged that he dominated the Board or that he held the Board under his influence such that the majority of its members were not independent. In addition, she has not alleged that a majority of the board appeared on both sides of the transaction.

In her response, Plaintiff asserts that the Board members acted "disloyally to enhance the selfish interests of themselves and/or fellow directors." Plaintiff's Complaint, however, does not contain any * * * facts to support Plaintiff's bold assertion in her response. The Complaint also does not allege that any of the outside Directors received any personal benefit from the executive compensation decisions, nor does it assert that they took action for any selfish reasons.

Plaintiff further argues that she has met her burden under this prong of Aronson because the Defendant Directors approved the 2010 executive compensation package and thus "faced a substantial likelihood of liability for breach of loyalty for authorizing the 2010 executive compensation." Under Delaware law, "the mere threat of personal liability for approving a questioned transaction, standing alone, is insufficient to challenge either the independence or disinterestedness of directors * * *." Aronson, 473 A.2d at 815. Instead, courts will excuse the demand requirement under this prong of the Aronson test only in "rare cases" where the transaction is "so egregious on its face that board approval cannot meet the test of business judgment, and a substantial likelihood of director liability therefore exists." Aronson, 473 A.2d at 815. This is not one of the "rare cases" in which the Court will excuse the demand requirement, however, because Plaintiff has not pled that the Defendant Directors face a "substantial likelihood" of liability for breach of loyalty. Id.

Under Delaware law, the duty of loyalty requires that "the best interest of the corporation and its shareholders takes precedence over any interest possessed by a director, officer or controlling shareholder and not shared by the stockholders generally." Cede & Co., 634 A.2d at 361. "Classic examples of director self-interest in a business transaction involve either a director appearing on both sides of a transaction or a director receiving a personal benefit from a transaction not received by the shareholders generally." Id. at 361–62. The fiduciary duty of loyalty involves a "financial or other cognizable fiduciary conflict of interest," and "encompasses cases where the fiduciary fails to act in good faith." Stone v. Ritter, 911 A.2d 362, 370 (Del. 2006). Indeed, "[t]he requirement to act in good faith is a 'subsidiary element[,]' i.e., a condition, 'of the fundamental duty of loyalty.' " Id.

Plaintiff's allegations are insufficient to establish a substantial likelihood of liability for breach of a duty of loyalty on the part of the Defendant Directors. As noted above, Plaintiff's Complaint does not allege that seven of the eight members of the Board received any personal benefit from the executive compensation package or that the seven outside Directors appeared on both sides of the transaction. Furthermore, the Complaint does not include particularized allegations to support a substantial likelihood of establishing that the Directors acted in bad faith, and indeed Plaintiff has failed to argue otherwise in response to Defendants' motion.

B. Plaintiff Has Not Rebutted the Presumption of the Business Judgment Rule

The second prong of the Aronson test involves the business judgment rule. Under Delaware law, the business judgment rule is "a presumption that in making a business decision the directors of a corporation acted on an informed basis, in good faith and in the honest belief that the action taken was in the best interest of the company." Aronson, 437 A.2d at 812. Plaintiff has the burden of rebutting this presumption through particularized allegations. Id. Specifically, in order to plead demand futility under this prong of the Aronson test, Plaintiff must allege particularized facts sufficient to raise (1) a reason to doubt that the action was taken honestly and in good faith or (2) a reason to doubt that the board was adequately informed in making the decision.

The business judgment rule generally protects compensation decisions. Under Delaware law, a board's decision regarding executive compensation is "entitled to great deference." Courts' deference to directors' "business judgment is particularly broad in matters of executive compensation." Indeed, "it is the essence of business judgment for a board to determine if 'a particular individual warrant[s] large amounts of money, whether in the form of current salary or severance provisions.' "

Plaintiff contends that the Complaint sufficiently rebuts the presumption of the business judgment rule under the second prong of Aronson. In her Complaint, Plaintiff primarily relies on the negative shareholder vote to rebut the presumption. In response to the motion, Plaintiff adds additional factors and asserts that the following factors rebut the presumption: 1) the say-on-pay negative shareholder vote under Dodd-Frank; 2) the Directors' alleged violation of the company's policy of "carefully linking executive pay to company performance"; and 3) the Directors increase of compensation when the company's performance was decreasing. Even taken together, however, these factors are insufficient to meet Plaintiff's burden of rebutting the business judgment rule presumption.

1. Say-on-Pay Vote

The thrust of Plaintiff's Complaint relies on a negative vote on April 26, 2011 pursuant to the Dodd-Frank Act, in which Navigant's shareholders voted against the compensation that Navigant paid to its executives in 2010. The Dodd-Frank Act became law in July 2010. The stated purpose of the law is to "promote the financial stability of the United States by improving accountability and transparency in the financial system, to end 'too big to fail,' to protect the American taxpayer by ending bailouts, to protect consumers from abusive financial services practices, and for other purposes." Pub. L. No. 111–203, Stat. 1376 (2010). Section 951 of the Dodd-Frank Act requires publicly-traded companies to permit shareholders to vote on executive compensation at least once every three years. 15 U.S.C. § 78n–1. It specifically provides that the shareholder vote "shall not be binding on the issuer or the board of directors." Id. § 78n–1(c). Further, the vote "may not be construed": (1) as overruling a decision by such issuer or board of directors; (2) to create or imply any change to the fiduciary duties of such issuer or board of directors; (3) to create or imply any additional fiduciary duties for such issuer or board of directors; or (4) to restrict or limit the ability of shareholders to make proposals for inclusion in proxy materials related to executive compensation. Id.

The plain language of the statute makes clear that the shareholders vote is non-binding on the corporation and that it does not create or imply any change in the board members' fiduciary duties. The Proxy Statement also made this non-binding status clear. Plaintiff's Complaint almost exclusively relies on the negative shareholder vote to rebut the presumption. Plaintiff alleges the shareholder vote "is direct and probative evidence rebutting the presumption that the Navigant Board's executive compensation decisions were in the best interests of the Navigant shareholders." To the extent Plaintiff seeks to rely solely on the negative shareholder vote to rebut the business judgment rule, these allegations directly contradict the plain language of the statute. * * * Plaintiff's attempt in her Complaint to use the negative shareholder vote alone to rebut the business judgment rule and to excuse the demand requirement and permit her to pursue a breach of fiduciary [duty] claim against the directors circumvents the protections in the statute. Other courts applying Delaware law have held that negative say-on-pay votes alone do not provide a basis to permit a breach of fiduciary duty claim to survive a motion to dismiss. See Bogart, 2012 WL 2160436, at *4 ("the 64% negative vote by shareholders does not, on its own, rebut the business judgment presumption"); Intersil, 2012 WL 762319, at *5 (holding that a shareholder vote may be used as evidence for a court to determine whether a plaintiff has met the business judgment prong, but finding the vote insufficient to rebut the business judgment rule presumption where only 56% of shareholders disapproved of executive compensation package). * * *

2. Company Policy

Plaintiff next argues that she has rebutted the business judgment rule based, in part, on allegations that the Directors violated the company's policy of "carefully linking executive pay to company performance." Plaintiff asserts that it is "uncontested that the Individual Defendants formulated and awarded executive compensation in 2010 that they knew w[as] not in compliance with the Company's compensation guidelines and w[as] not in the best interests of the Company." The allegations in the Complaint, however, do not support this assertion. Indeed, Plaintiff alleges that the Compensation Committee Charter directed the Compensation Committee to "review and recommend to the Board compensation policies as well as approve individual executive officer compensation, intended to attract, retain and appropriately reward employees in order to motivate their performance in the achievement of the Company's business objectives and align their interests with the long-term interest of the Company's shareholders * * *." Furthermore, the Charter directed the Compensation Committee to consider a number of factors when assessing the incentive component of executive payment, including, but not limited to "the Company's performance and relative shareholder return, the value of similar incentive awards to chief executive officers at comparable companies, and the awards given to the Company's Chief Executive Officer in past years." The Complaint, however, focuses solely on the Company's performance and shareholder return, which is only part of the equation. The Complaint does not, for example, contain any allegations pertaining to similar incentive awards to executives in Navigant's peer group, nor does it contain any facts regarding incentive awards that Navigant paid to its executives in past years.

Moreover, the Proxy upon which Plaintiff relies further directs the Compensation Committee to look at additional factors in determining its compensation recommendations. The Proxy specifically describes other performance aspects that the Compensation Committee considered for 2010, including "net income and earnings per share," "strategic investment in core growth practice areas; senior level recruitment; and management's timely and effective response to changes in the competitive landscape." Additionally, it is the Compensation Committee's practice to consider "individual performance in the area of the company over which [the executive] has direct responsibility" and "his or her individual contributions to the company's financial and strategic performance for the year in question." Yet, the Complaint does not contain any allegations regarding these other factors. Because Plaintiff's allegations do not contain any facts regarding any of the other factors that the Committee considered in determining executive compensation, she has not established that Navigant violated company policy in awarding the executive compensation at issue in her Complaint.

3. Stock Price Decrease

Plaintiff's reliance on the decrease in Navigant's stock price also does not excuse her failure make a demand on the Board. Her allegations do not set forth an extreme situation that overrides the great deference given to the board in making executive compensation decisions. The alleged facts do not give rise to an inference that the board members must have acted in bad faith or without an honest belief in the compensation they approved.

Plaintiff has not rebutted the business judgment rule presumption based on a combination of the negative shareholder vote, Navigant's policy regarding executive pay, and Navigant's stock price. Therefore, she has failed to establish that demand is futile in this case. Accordingly, the Court dismisses her claims against all Defendants. * * *

NOTES

(1) The demand rules established in Delaware are complex and interconnected. They have been criticized on the ground that they prolong litigation by encouraging sparring over the preliminary question of whether a demand was required. Judge Easterbrook, in a concurring opinion in Starrels v. First Nat'l Bank of Chicago, 870 F.2d 1168, 1172–76 (7th Cir.1989), offers a negative assessment of the Delaware rules and argues that a rule of universal demand would be more rational. See also John C. Coffee, Jr., New Myths and Old Realities: The American Law Institute Faces the Derivative Action, 48 Bus. Law. 1407, 1414 (1993):

> Delaware's demand rule also results in a substantial amount of collateral litigation and sometimes can be a trap for the unwary. * * * [Further,] the shareholder plaintiff usually faces an unattractive choice: either (i) not make a demand and thereby accept the burden of convincing the court that seemingly respectable directors should be deemed too biased even to deserve an opportunity to respond to demand, or (ii) make demand and thereby acknowledge the applicability of the business judgment rule to the directors' decision whether or not to reject demand (and, for most practical purposes, concede the outcome of the case).

(2) Given these criticisms, it is not surprising that mandatory demand in all cases has become the cornerstone of alternative systems in other states for resolving derivative litigation in the corporate context. See, e.g., MBCA § 7.42; cf. ALI Principles § 7.03. This issue is further addressed in the notes following *Cuker*, infra.

IN RE ORACLE CORP. DERIVATIVE LITIGATION

Court of Chancery of Delaware, 2003.
824 A.2d 917.

STRINE, VICE CHANCELLOR.

[Plaintiff shareholders brought a derivative suit alleging insider trading by four members of Oracle's board of directors—Lawrence Ellison, the company's Chairman and CEO; Jeffrey Henley, the company's CFO; Donald Lucas; and Michael Boskin. In response, Oracle formed a special litigation committee (SLC) to investigate the merits of the claims and to determine whether the company should take any action. Directors Hector Garcia-Molina and Joseph Grundfest were appointed to the SLC. Both men were professors at Stanford University and had obtained their graduate degrees from Stanford. Upon conclusion of its investigation, the SLC recommended that no action be taken. Plaintiffs challenged the independence of the SLC. The Court concluded that Garcia-Molina and

Grundfest were not independent due to their affiliation with Stanford University. The portions of the opinion set forth below relate to the Vice Chancellor's discussion of how the independence of SLC members should be assessed.]

The SLC's investigation was, by any objective measure, extensive. The SLC reviewed an enormous amount of paper and electronic records. SLC counsel interviewed seventy witnesses, some of them twice. SLC members participated in several key interviews, including the interviews of the Trading Defendants. * * *

In the end, the SLC produced an extremely lengthy Report totaling 1,110 pages (excluding appendices and exhibits) that concluded that Oracle should not pursue the plaintiffs' claims against the Trading Defendants or any of the other Oracle directors serving during the 3Q FY 2001. * * *

In order to prevail on its motion to terminate the Delaware Derivative Action, the SLC must persuade me that: (1) its members were independent; (2) that they acted in good faith; and (3) that they had reasonable bases for their recommendations. * * *

[The court noted that in its report, the SLC asserted that its members were independent.]

Noticeably absent from the SLC Report was any disclosure of several significant ties between Oracle or the Trading Defendants and Stanford University, the university that employs both members of the SLC. In the Report, it was only disclosed that:

- defendant Boskin was a Stanford professor;

- the SLC members were aware that Lucas had made certain donations to Stanford; and

- among the contributions was a donation of $50,000 worth of stock that Lucas donated to Stanford Law School after Grundfest delivered a speech to a venture capital fund meeting in response to Lucas's request. It happens that Lucas's son is a partner in the fund and that approximately half the donation was allocated for use by Grundfest in his personal research.

In view of the modesty of these disclosed ties, it was with some shock that a series of other ties among Stanford, Oracle, and the Trading Defendants emerged during discovery. Although the plaintiffs have embellished these ties considerably beyond what is reasonable, the plain facts are a striking departure from the picture presented in the Report. * * *

1. Boskin

Defendant Michael J. Boskin is the T.M. Friedman Professor of Economics at Stanford University. * * *

During the 1970s, Boskin taught Grundfest when Grundfest was a Ph.D. candidate. Although Boskin was not Grundfest's advisor and although they do not socialize, the two have remained in contact over the years, speaking occasionally about matters of public policy.

Furthermore, both Boskin and Grundfest are senior fellows and steering committee members at the Stanford Institute for Economic Policy Research, which was previously defined as "SIEPR." * * *

2. Lucas

As noted in the SLC Report, the SLC members admitted knowing that Lucas was a contributor to Stanford. They also acknowledged that he had donated $50,000 to Stanford Law School in appreciation for Grundfest having given a speech at his request. About half of the proceeds were allocated for use by Grundfest in his research.

But Lucas's ties with Stanford are far, far richer than the SLC Report lets on. To begin, Lucas is a Stanford alumnus, having obtained both his undergraduate and graduate degrees there. By any measure, he has been a very loyal alumnus.

In showing that this is so, I start with a matter of some jousting between the SLC and the plaintiffs. Lucas's brother, Richard, died of cancer and by way of his will established a foundation. Lucas became Chairman of the Foundation and serves as a director along with his son, a couple of other family members, and some non-family members. A principal object of the Foundation's beneficence has been Stanford. The Richard M. Lucas Foundation has given $11.7 million to Stanford since its 1981 founding. Among its notable contributions, the Foundation funded the establishment of the Richard M. Lucas Center for Magnetic Resonance Spectroscopy and Imaging at Stanford's Medical School. Donald Lucas was a founding member and lead director of the Center. * * *

Lucas's connections with Stanford as a contributor go beyond the Foundation, however. From his own personal funds, Lucas has contributed $4.1 million to Stanford, a substantial percentage of which has been donated within the last half-decade. Notably, Lucas has, among other things, donated $424,000 to SIEPR and approximately $149,000 to Stanford Law School. Indeed, Lucas is not only a major contributor to SIEPR, he is the Chair of its Advisory Board. At SIEPR's facility at Stanford, the conference center is named the Donald L. Lucas Conference Center. * * *

3. Ellison

There can be little doubt that Ellison is a major figure in the community in which Stanford is located. The so-called Silicon Valley has generated many success stories, among the greatest of which is that of Oracle and its leader, Ellison. One of the wealthiest men in America, Ellison is a major figure in the nation's increasingly important information technology industry. Given his wealth, Ellison is also in a position to make—and, in fact, he has made—major charitable contributions.

Some of the largest of these contributions have been made through the Ellison Medical Foundation, which makes grants to universities and laboratories to support biomedical research relating to aging and infectious diseases. Ellison is the sole director of the Foundation. * * *

* * * Stanford has * * * been the beneficiary of grants from the Ellison Medical Foundation—to the tune of nearly $10 million in paid or pledged funds. * * *

During the time Ellison has been CEO of Oracle, the company itself has also made over $300,000 in donations to Stanford. Not only that, when Oracle established a generously endowed educational foundation—the Oracle Help Us Help Foundation—to help further the deployment of educational technology in schools serving disadvantaged populations, it named Stanford as the "appointing authority," which gave Stanford the right to name four of the Foundation's seven directors. * * *

Beginning in the year 2000 and continuing well into 2001—the same year that Ellison made the trades the plaintiffs contend were suspicious and the same year the SLC members were asked to join the Oracle board—Ellison and Stanford discussed a much more lucrative donation. The idea Stanford proposed for discussion was the creation of an Ellison Scholars Program modeled on the Rhodes Scholarship at Oxford. The proposed budget for Stanford's answer to Oxford: $170 million. The Ellison Scholars were to be drawn from around the world and were to come to Stanford to take a two-year interdisciplinary graduate program in economics, political science, and computer technology. During the summer between the two academic years, participants would work in internships at, among other companies, Oracle.

The SLC contends that even together, these facts regarding the ties among Oracle, the Trading Defendants, Stanford, and the SLC members do not impair the SLC's independence. In so arguing, the SLC places great weight on the fact that none of the Trading Defendants have the practical ability to deprive either Grundfest or Garcia-Molina of their current positions at Stanford. Nor, given their tenure, does Stanford itself have any practical ability to punish them for taking action adverse to Boskin, Lucas, or Ellison—each of whom, as we have seen, has contributed (in one way or another) great value to Stanford as an institution. As important, neither Garcia-Molina nor Grundfest are part of the official fundraising apparatus at Stanford; thus, it is not their on-the-job duty to be solicitous of contributors, and fundraising success does not factor into their treatment as professors. * * *

* * * According to the SLC, its members are independent unless they are essentially subservient to the Trading Defendants—*i.e.*, they are under the "domination and control" of the interested parties. * * *

But, in my view, an emphasis on "domination and control" would serve only to fetishize much-parroted language, at the cost of denuding the independence inquiry of its intellectual integrity. * * *

* * * Delaware law should not be based on a reductionist view of human nature that simplifies human motivations on the lines of the least sophisticated notions of the law and economics movement. *Homo sapiens* is not merely *homo economicus*. We may be thankful that an array of other motivations exist that influence human behavior; not all are any better than greed or avarice, think of envy, to name just one. But also think of motives like love, friendship, and collegiality, think of those among us who direct their behavior as best they can on a guiding creed or set of moral values.

Nor should our law ignore the social nature of humans. To be direct, corporate directors are generally the sort of people deeply enmeshed in social institutions. Such institutions have norms, expectations that, explicitly and implicitly, influence and channel the behavior of those who participate in their operation. Some things are "just not done," or only at a cost, which might not be so severe as a loss of position, but may involve a loss of standing in the institution. In being appropriately sensitive to this factor, our law also cannot assume—absent some proof of the point—that corporate directors are, as a general matter, persons of unusual social bravery, who operate heedless to the inhibitions that social norms generate for ordinary folk. * * *

* * * I conclude that the SLC has not met its burden to show the absence of a material factual question about its independence. I find this to be the case because the ties among the SLC, the Trading Defendants, and Stanford are so substantial that they cause reasonable doubt about the SLC's ability to impartially consider whether the Trading Defendants should face suit. * * *

As SLC members, Grundfest and Garcia-Molina were already being asked to consider whether the company should level extremely serious accusations of wrongdoing against fellow board members. As to Boskin, both SLC members faced another layer of complexity: the determination of whether to have Oracle press insider trading claims against a fellow professor at their university. * * * To accuse a fellow professor—whom one might see at the faculty club or at inter-disciplinary presentations of academic papers—of insider trading cannot be a small thing—even for the most callous of academics.

As to Boskin, Grundfest faced an even more complex challenge than Garcia-Molina. Boskin was a professor who had taught him and with whom he had maintained contact over the years. Their areas of academic interest intersected, putting Grundfest in contact if not directly with Boskin, then regularly with Boskin's colleagues. * * * Having these ties, Grundfest (I infer) would have more difficulty objectively determining whether Boskin engaged in improper insider trading than would a person who was not a fellow professor, had not been a student of Boskin, had not kept in touch with Boskin over the years, and who was not a senior fellow and steering committee member at SIEPR. * * *

The same concerns also exist as to Lucas. For Grundfest to vote to accuse Lucas of insider trading would require him to accuse SIEPR's Advisory Board Chair and major benefactor of serious wrongdoing—of conduct that violates federal securities laws. Such action would also require Grundfest to make charges against a man who recently donated $50,000 to Stanford Law School after Grundfest made a speech at his request.

And, for both Grundfest and Garcia-Molina, service on the SLC demanded that they consider whether an extremely generous and influential Stanford alumnus should be sued by Oracle for insider trading. Although they were not responsible for fundraising, as sophisticated professors they undoubtedly are aware of how important large contributors are to Stanford, and they share in the benefits that come from serving at a university with a rich endowment. A reasonable professor giving any thought to the matter would obviously consider the effect his decision might have on the University's relationship with Lucas, it being (one hopes) sensible to infer that a professor of reasonable collegiality and loyalty cares about the well-being of the institution he serves. * * *

* * * Ellison's relationship to Stanford itself contributes to my overall doubt, when heaped on top of the ties involving Boskin and Lucas. During the period when Grundfest and Garcia-Molina were being added to the Oracle board, Ellison was publicly considering making extremely large contributions to Stanford. * * *

* * * [T]he SLC contends that neither SLC member was aware of Ellison's relationship with Stanford until after the Report was completed. Thus, this relationship, in its various facets, could not have compromised their independence. Again, I find this argument from ignorance to be unavailing. An inquiry into Ellison's connections with Stanford should have been conducted before the SLC was finally formed and, at the very

least, should have been undertaken in connection with the Report. In any event, given how public Ellison was about his possible donations it is difficult not to harbor troublesome doubt about whether the SLC members were conscious of the possibility that Ellison was pondering a large contribution to Stanford. * * *

It seems to me that the connections outlined in this opinion would weigh on the mind of a reasonable special litigation committee member deciding whether to level the serious charge of insider trading against the Trading Defendants. As indicated before, this does not mean that the SLC would be less inclined to find such charges meritorious, only that the connections identified would be on the mind of the SLC members in a way that generates an unacceptable risk of bias. That is, these connections generate a reasonable doubt about the SLC's impartiality because they suggest that material considerations other than the best interests of Oracle could have influenced the SLC's inquiry and judgments.

NOTES

(1) The *Oracle* court's consideration of the social and institutional connections between SLC members and management in analyzing director independence was a departure from the traditional independence inquiry, which focused on directors' financial interests. The court emphasized the ways in which social ties can have a subconscious influence on directors' judgment. How should companies assess SLC independence going forward? Should a director's social or institutional ties be given as much weight as financial entanglements with management?

(2) The approach to assessing director independence articulated in *Oracle* has been followed by courts outside of Delaware. See, e.g., Klein v. FPL Group, Inc., 2003 WL 22768424 (S.D. Fla. Sept. 26, 2003); Demoulas v. Demoulas Super Markets, Inc., 2004 WL 1895052 (Mass. Super. Ct. Aug. 2, 2004). The rule in *Oracle* was pronounced in a case evaluating the independence of SLC members, but several courts have already applied it beyond that scope. See Official Committee of Unsecured Creditors of Integrated Health Services, Inc. v. Elkins, 2004 WL 1949290 (Del. Ch. Aug. 24, 2004) (plaintiffs alleged directors subordinated the best interests of the company to their loyalty to the former president and the court noted that domination and control are not tested by economics alone); Atlantic Coast Airlines Holdings, Inc. v. Mesa Air Group, Inc., 295 F.Supp.2d 75 (D.D.C. 2003) (examining allegations that preexisting business or social relationships rendered individuals unfit to serve as company directors).

CUKER V. MIKALAUSKAS

Supreme Court of Pennsylvania, 1997.
692 A.2d 1042.

Before FLAHERTY, C.J., and ZAPPALA, CAPPY, CASTILLE, NIGRO, and
NEWMAN, JJ.

FLAHERTY, C.J.

PECO Energy Company filed a motion for summary judgment
seeking termination of minority shareholder derivative actions. When the
motion was denied by the court of common pleas, PECO sought
extraordinary relief in this court pursuant to Pa.R.A.P. 3309. We granted
the petition, limited to the issue of "whether the 'business judgment rule'
permits the board of directors of a Pennsylvania corporation to terminate
derivative lawsuits brought by minority shareholders."

PECO is a publicly regulated utility incorporated in Pennsylvania
which sells electricity and gas to residential, commercial, and industrial
customers in Philadelphia and four surrounding counties. PECO is
required to conform to PUC regulations which govern the provision of
service to residential customers, including opening, billing, and
terminating accounts. PECO is required to report regularly to the PUC on
a wide variety of statistical and performance information regarding its
compliance with the regulations as interpreted by the PUC. Like other
utilities, PECO is required to undergo a comprehensive management
audit at the direction of the PUC approximately every ten years. The
most recent audit was conducted by Ernst & Young. The report issued in
1991 recommended changes in twenty-two areas, including criticisms and
recommendations regarding PECO's credit and collection function.

* * * [Following the PUC report, one set of minority shareholders
filed a demand on PECO (the Katzman demand)], alleging wrongdoing by
some PECO directors and officers. This Katzman demand, made in May,
1993, asserted that the delinquent officers had damaged PECO by
mismanaging the credit and collection function, particularly as to the
collection of overdue accounts. The shareholders demanded that PECO
authorize litigation against the wrongdoers to recover monetary damages
sustained by PECO. At its meeting of June 28, 1993, PECO's board
responded by creating a special litigation committee to investigate the
Katzman allegations.

Less than a month later, a second group of minority shareholders
filed a complaint against PECO officers and directors. Cuker v.
Mikalauskas, July Term, 1998, No. 3470 (C.P.Phila.). The Cuker
complaint * * * made the same allegations as those in the Katzman
demand * * *. The Cuker complaint was filed before the special litigation
committee had begun its substantive work of investigating and
evaluating the Katzman demand, so the committee's work encompassed

both the Katzman and Cuker matters. Only the twelve nondefendant members of the PECO board acted to create the special committee, which consisted of three outside directors who had never been employed by PECO and who were not named in the Katzman demand or the Cuker complaint.

The work of the special committee was aided by the law firm of Dilworth, Paxson, Kalish & Kauffman, as well as PECO's regular outside auditor, Coopers & Lybrand, selected to assist in accounting matters because Coopers was knowledgeable about the utility industry and was familiar with PECO's accounting practices. The special committee conducted an extensive investigation over many months while maintaining a separate existence from PECO and its board of directors and keeping its deliberations confidential. The special committee held its final meeting on January 26, 1994, whereupon it reached its conclusions and prepared its report.

The report of the special committee concluded that there was no evidence of bad faith, self-dealing, concealment, or other breaches of the duty of loyalty by any of the defendant officers. It also concluded that the defendant officers "exercised sound business judgment in managing the affairs of the company" and that their actions "were reasonably calculated to further the best interests of the company." The three-hundred-page report identified numerous factors underlying the conclusions of the special committee. Significant considerations included the utility's efforts before the PUC to raise electricity rates in consequence of the expense of new nuclear generating plants. Other factors were the impact of PUC regulations limiting wintertime termination of residential service and other limitations on the use of collection techniques such as terminations of overdue customers, particularly with a large population of poverty level users among PECO's customer base. These considerations were supported by PUC documents which criticized PECO for aggressive and excessive terminations in recent years. The report of the special litigation committee also described how PECO's management had been attentive to the credit and collection function, with constant efforts to improve performance in that area. According to the report, limiting the use of terminations as a collection technique was a sound business judgment, reducing antagonism between the PUC and PECO and resulting in rate increases which produced revenue far in excess of the losses attributed to nonaggressive collection tactics. The report concluded that proceeding with a derivative suit based largely on findings of the Ernst & Young audit would not be in the best interests of PECO.

When it received the report of the special litigation committee with appendices containing the documents and interviews underlying the report, the board debated the recommendations at two meetings early in 1994. The twelve nondefendant members of the PECO board voted unanimously on March 14, 1994 to reject the Katzman demand and to terminate the Cuker action.

In the Cuker action, the court of common pleas rejected PECO's motion for summary judgment. The court stated that "the 'business judgment rule' [has been] adopted in some states but never previously employed in Pennsylvania." The court held that as a matter of Pennsylvania public policy, a corporation lacks power to terminate pending derivative litigation. * * * PECO sought extraordinary relief in this court under our King's Bench powers, which we granted.

* * * [The Court concludes that the business judgment rule permits the board of directors of a Pennsylvania corporation to terminate derivative lawsuits brought by minority shareholders.] Ironically, this court has never used the term "business judgment rule" in a corporate context nor has it explicitly adopted the business judgment rule. Nevertheless a review of Pennsylvania decisions establishes that the business judgment doctrine or rule is the law of Pennsylvania. * * *

The * * * practical effect of [our] holding needs elaboration. Assuming that an independent board of directors may terminate shareholder derivative actions, what is needed is a procedural mechanism for implementation and judicial review of the board's decision. Without considering the merits of the action, a court should determine the validity of the board's decision to terminate the litigation; if that decision was made in accordance with the appropriate standards, then the court should dismiss the derivative action prior to litigation on the merits.

The business judgment rule should insulate officers and directors from judicial intervention in the absence of fraud or self-dealing, if challenged decisions were within the scope of the directors' authority, if they exercised reasonable diligence, and if they honestly and rationally believed their decisions were in the best interests of the company. It is obvious that a court must examine the circumstances surrounding the decisions in order to determine if the conditions warrant application of the business judgment rule. If they do, the court will never proceed to an examination of the merits of the challenged decisions, for that is precisely what the business judgment rule prohibits. In order to make the business judgment rule meaningful, the preliminary examination should be limited and precise so as to minimize judicial involvement when application of the business judgment rule is warranted.

To achieve these goals, a court might stay the derivative action while it determines the propriety of the board's decision. The court might order limited discovery or an evidentiary hearing to resolve issues respecting the board's decision. Factors bearing on the board's decision will include whether the board or its special litigation committee was disinterested, whether it was assisted by counsel, whether it prepared a written report, whether it was independent, whether it conducted an adequate investigation, and whether it rationally believed its decision was in the best interests of the corporation (i.e., acted in good faith). If all of these criteria are satisfied, the business judgment rule applies and the court should dismiss the action.

These considerations and procedures are all encompassed in Part VII, chapter 1 of the ALI Principles (relating to the derivative action), which provides a comprehensive mechanism to address shareholder derivative actions. A number of its provisions are implicated in the action at bar. Sections 7.02 (standing), 7.03 (the demand rule), 7.04 (procedure in derivative action), 7.05 (board authority in derivative action), 7.06 (judicial stay of derivative action), 7.07, 7.08, and 7.09 (dismissal of derivative action), 7.10 (standard of judicial review), and 7.13 (judicial procedures) are specifically applicable to this case.[3] These sections set forth guidance which is consistent with Pennsylvania law and precedent, which furthers the policies inherent in the business judgment rule, and which provides an appropriate degree of specificity to guide the trial court in controlling the proceedings in this litigation.

We specifically adopt §§ 7.02–7.10, and § 7.13 of the ALI Principles.[4] [Please consult the Statutory Supplement for the text of these sections.] * * *

[W]e adopt the specified sections of the ALI Principles, reverse the orders of the court of common pleas, and remand the matter for further proceedings consistent with this opinion.

Orders reversed and case remanded.

NOTES

(1) The ALI's Principles of Corporate Governance is not a statute intended for adoption by individual states. Rather, it is a statement of "black letter" principles followed by a plain text explanation of the operation of the "black letter" principles. In this respect it is similar to the various Restatements with which all law students are familiar. Of the various sections mentioned by the court in *Cuker*, by far the most controversial is

---

[3] ALI Principles §§ 4.01, 4.02, and 4.03 (duties of directors and officers; the business judgment rule; reliance on committees and other persons) are similar but not identical to the statutory standards found in 15 Pa.C.S. §§ 512, 513, 515, 1712, 1713, and 1715. The statutory standards, of course, control the duties of directors and the application of the business judgment rule in Pennsylvania.

[4] * * * Our adoption of these sections is not a rejection of other sections not cited. We have identified and studied the sections which apply to this case and have adopted those which appear most relevant. The entire publication, all seven parts, is a comprehensive, cohesive work more than a decade in preparation. Additional sections of the publication, particularly procedural ones due to their interlocking character, may be adopted in the future. Issues in future cases or, perhaps, further proceedings in this case might implicate additional sections of the ALI Principles. Courts of the Commonwealth are free to consider other parts of the work and utilize them if they are helpful and appear to be consistent with Pennsylvania law.

§ 7.10, which was developed and approved only after exhaustive discussion and negotiation. This section was explained as "a mechanism for judicial review of the board's power to dismiss a derivative action [which] is necessary if fiduciary duties are to remain meaningful legal obligations." Comment to § 7.10, The American Law Institute, Principles of Corporate Governance: Analysis and Recommendations. However, much of the controversy arose because of the Reporters' plain text explanation of the operation of this section:

> At the other end of the spectrum from the [simple] due care case is the case involving a substantial duty of loyalty issue, such as one, for example, when a majority of the board personally benefited from the transaction and then expanded the board's size to appoint new directors to staff a litigation committee, which later recommended dismissal of the action. Here, close judicial scrutiny of the justifications offered for dismissal is obviously appropriate. Under *Zapata*, if a majority received a pecuniary benefit, the Delaware courts would excuse demand and permit the trial court to use its own "independent business judgment." Section 7.10 avoids the use of the potentially misleading phrase "independent business judgment." Rather, § 7.10 contemplates that heightened judicial scrutiny should be reserved for a limited number of instances and that, overall, the degree of judicial scrutiny should relate to the legal standards [applicable to the conduct in question]. Thus, for example, if * * * the transaction was one in which the burden of proving fairness remained on the director or senior executive, the reviewing court should be mindful that in this instance Part V invites close judicial scrutiny. Therefore, less deference to the justifications asserted for dismissal by the board or committee would be warranted.

> Put simply, the court should review the board's or committee's determinations in a manner that is consistent with the standards of review and burdens of proof established by [other parts of these principles]. This does not mean, however, that § 7.10 specifies a uniform standard of review for all duty of loyalty cases. The closest review will be in those cases in which the defendant has the burden of proving fairness. For example, such a standard would apply in the case of a corporate opportunity when the corporate rejection of the opportunity was not by a disinterested majority of the board, with the result that * * * the defendant must prove the fairness of the defendant's conduct. Conversely, if a disinterested board had earlier rejected the corporate opportunity after appropriate disclosure, then the board's decision is protected by the business judgment rule * * * and correspondingly a motion to dismiss is to be reviewed under the similar standard * * *. An intermediate case [occurs when] a self interested transaction is approved in advance by disinterested directors or a disinterested superior, [and] the court

should determine whether the directors or senior executive "could reasonably have concluded that the transaction was fair to the corporation," even when there has been full disclosure and disinterested approval. In such a case, the standard of review * * * should be less exacting than in a case in which the defendant is required to prove the fairness of the transaction, but more searching than in a case in which the business judgment rule is applicable. * * *

* * * In some circumstances, disputed factual issues may make it necessary for the court to hold a limited evidentiary hearing, or to delay its decision for additional discovery, before it rules on the motion. However, the importance of an expedited decision should normally lead the court to constrain discovery * * * and seek an early resolution of the motion.

This formulation was bitterly attacked, particularly by members who were familiar with the Delaware structure for resolving derivative litigation, as "departing dramatically from well settled principles" established in many cases and as accepting a "litigation model" of corporate governance. Michael Dooley & E. Norman Veasey, The Role of the Board in Derivative Litigation Delaware Law and the Current ALI Proposals Compared, 44 Bus. Law. 503 (1989); Dennis J. Block, et al., Derivative Litigation: Current Law Versus the American Law Institute, 48 Bus. Law. 1443 (1993). Every suggestion of even superficial judicial review of the merits of a litigation committee decision in the "demand required" context is systematically referred to by Dooley and Veasey as "judicially intrusive review." The Block article also accuses the reporters of seeking to undermine a compromise negotiated at an earlier plenary session of the Institute. Id. at 1470, 1474. For a spirited defense, see John C. Coffee, Jr., New Myths and Old Realities: The American Law Institute Faces the Derivative Action, 48 Bus. Law. 1407 (1993). See also Carol B. Swanson, Juggling Shareholder Rights and Strike Suits in Derivative Litigation: The ALI Drops the Ball, 77 Minn. L.Rev. 1339 (1993).

(2) The Committee on Corporate Laws created its own solution to the derivative litigation issue in 1989 when it approved Subchapter D of Chapter 7 of the MBCA, §§ 7.40 et seq. The critical sections are § 7.42, relating to demand, and § 7.44 relating to the dismissal of derivative suits. The Official Comment to § 7.42 explains the demand requirement:

Section 7.42 requires a written demand on the corporation in all cases. The demand must be delivered at least 90 days before commencement of suit unless irreparable injury to the corporation would result. This approach has been adopted for two reasons. First, even though no director may be [independent], the demand will give the board of directors the opportunity to re-examine the act complained of in the light of a potential lawsuit and take corrective action. Secondly, the provision eliminates the time and expense of the litigants and the court involved in litigating the question whether demand is required. * * *

The more critical and controversial section is § 7.44, dealing with the finality of committee and/or board of directors determinations. The Official Comment elaborates upon the language of § 7.44(a):

> Section 7.44(a) requires that the determination, by the appropriate person or persons, be made "in good faith, after conducting a reasonable inquiry upon which their conclusions are based." * * * The word "inquiry"—rather than "investigation"—has been used to make it clear that the scope of the inquiry will depend upon the issues raised and the knowledge of the group making the determination with respect to those issues. In some cases, the issues may be so simple or the knowledge of the group so extensive that little additional inquiry is required. In other cases, the group may need to engage counsel and possibly other professionals to make an investigation and assist the group in its evaluation of the issues. * * *

(3) The Delaware litigation committee procedures are of course of central importance primarily because of the very large number of publicly held corporations incorporated in that state. The two alternative solutions—one put forth by the ALI, the other by the Committee on Corporate Laws—also deal with the core issue whether a court should simply defer to the business judgment of a litigation committee or board of directors, without more, or whether it should make some kind of substantive review of the apparent merits of that decision. Several state courts have had an opportunity to consider this aspect of the litigation committee device in the absence of statute with mixed results.

(a) A number of states appear to give the committee decision at least the same degree of deference that it is given in Delaware. Dennis J. Block et al., Derivative Litigation: Current Law Versus the American Law Institute, 48 Bus. Law. 1443, 1443–44, 1447 (1993), states that since 1984, "the courts both in and out of Delaware have ruled with near unanimity" that the business judgment rule is the appropriate standard of judicial review.

(b) Basically accepting the "structural bias" argument, the court in Miller v. Register & Tribune Syndicate, Inc., 336 N.W.2d 709 (Iowa 1983), held that the board of directors was unable to delegate the power to bind the corporation to an independent litigation committee if the board of directors was itself unable to act because a majority was interested in the transaction. The court suggested that a committee might be appointed by judicial order in this situation.

(c) In Alford v. Shaw, 349 S.E.2d 41 (N.C.1986), the North Carolina Supreme Court uncritically adopted the *Gall* approach in a case involving charges of fraud and self-dealing by a majority of the board of directors; defendant directors participated in the selection of new directors to serve as the special litigation committee. See Deborah DeMott, The Corporate Fox and the Shareholders' Hen House: Reflections on Alford v. Shaw, 65 N.C.L.Rev. 569 (1987). The North Carolina Supreme Court then granted a petition for rehearing, and significantly modified—indeed, virtually rejected the underlying premises of—its earlier opinion. See 358 S.E.2d 323 (N.C.1987).

(d) In Houle v. Low, 556 N.E.2d 51, 59 (Mass.1990), the Court stated that a reviewing court should determine whether the committee (i) was independent and disinterested and (ii) "reached a reasonable and principled decision." Lewis v. Boyd, 838 S.W.2d 215, 224 (Tenn.App.1992), adopted the same test.

(e) Michigan amended its corporation statute in 1989 to authorize a court to appoint one or more "disinterested persons" at the request of the corporation to make findings with respect to a derivative suit. Mich. Stat. § 450.1495. See Joel Seligman, The Disinterested Person: An Alternative Approach to Shareholder Derivative Litigation, 55 Law & Contemp. Probs. 357 (Autumn 1992). If the determination is made by incumbent directors, the burden shifts to the corporation to establish that the determination was made in good faith and the investigation was reasonable.

(f) In PSE & G Shareholder Litigation, 801 A.2d 295 (N.J.2002) the New Jersey Supreme Court decided not to follow Delaware or the Model Act. Instead, it created its own, specialized jurisprudence, despite its admitted lack of experience in dealing with these issues. First, like the North Carolina Court in Alford v. Shaw discussed above, the New Jersey court held that it would apply a single standard of review in both demand-made and demand-excused cases. The court announced that it would apply a modified business judgment rule that imposes an initial burden on the corporation to demonstrate that in deciding to reject or terminate a shareholder's suit the members of the board: (1) were independent and disinterested, (2) acted in good faith and with due care in their investigation of the shareholders' allegations, and that (3) the board's decision was reasonable. The court also noted that shareholders must be given access to corporate documents and other discovery limited to the narrow issue of what steps the directors took to inform themselves of the shareholder demand and the reasonableness of its decision. See id. at 312.

(4) Most of the concern about derivative suits, litigation committees, and the like relate to publicly held corporations. The elaborate procedures of the ALI Principles of Corporate Governance are not suitable for closely held corporations with relatively few shareholders. Section 7.01(d) of the Principles sets forth a simple and practical solution for derivative litigation within such corporations:

> In the case of a closely held corporation, the court in its discretion may treat an action raising derivative claims as a direct action, exempt it from those restrictions and defenses applicable only to derivative actions, and order an individual recovery, if it finds that to do so will not (i) unfairly expose the corporation or the defendants

to a multiplicity of actions, (ii) materially prejudice the interests of creditors of the corporation, or (iii) interfere with a fair distribution of the recovery among all interested persons.

For a case adopting this approach, see Barth v. Barth, 659 N.E.2d 559, 562–63 (Ind.1995).

CHAPTER 13

DISSENSION IN THE CLOSELY HELD CORPORATION

■ ■ ■

A. DEADLOCK

GEARING V. KELLY

Court of Appeals of New York, 1962.
182 N.E.2d 391.

PER CURIAM.

Appellants, who own 50% of the stock of the Radium Chemical Company, Inc., seek, within the provisions of section 25 of the General Corporation Law, to set aside the election of a director.

In a proceeding under that section, the court sits as a court of equity which may order a new election "as justice may require." We have concluded, as did the majority of the Appellate Division, that appellants have failed to show that justice requires a new election, in that they may not now complain of an irregularity which they themselves have caused.

Mrs. Meacham stayed away from the meeting of March 6, 1961 for the sole purpose of preventing a quorum from assembling, and intended, in that manner, to paralyze the board. There can be no doubt, and indeed it is not even suggested, that she lacked notice or any manner found it temporarily inconvenient to present herself at that particular time and place. It is certain, then, that Mrs. Meacham's absence from the noticed meeting of the board was intentional and deliberate. Much is said by appellants about a desire to protect their equal ownership of stock through equal representation on the board. It is, however, clear that such balance was voluntarily surrendered in 1955. Whether this was done in reliance on representations of Kelly, Sr., as alleged in the plenary suit, is properly a matter for that litigation, rather than the summary type of action here.

The relief sought by appellants, the ordering of a new election, would, furthermore, be of no avail to them, for Mrs. Meacham would then be required, as evidence of her good faith, to attend. Such a futile act will not be ordered.

The identity of interests of the appellants is readily apparent. Mrs. Gearing has fully indorsed and supported all of the demands and actions of her daughter, and has associated herself with the refusal to attend the directors' meeting. A court of equity need not permit Mrs. Gearing to attack actions of the board of directors which were marred through conduct of the director whom she has actively encouraged. To do so would allow a director to refuse to attend meetings, knowing that thereafter an associated stockholder could frustrate corporate action until all of their joint demands were met.

The failure of Mrs. Meacham to attend the directors' meeting, under the present circumstances, bars appellants from invoking an exercise of the equitable powers lodged in the courts under the statute.

The order appealed from should be affirmed, with costs.

FROESSEL, JUDGE (dissenting).

The bylaws of Radium Chemical Company, Inc., provided for a board of four directors, a majority of whom "shall constitute a quorum for the transaction of business." Prior to 1955 the board consisted of appellant Meacham, who had succeeded her father (appellant Gearing's late husband), respondent Kelly, Sr., and Margaret E. Lee. In 1955 Kelly, Jr., was elected to the then vacant directorship. The board continued thus until Margaret Lee offered her resignation in 1961 and, on March 6 of that year, at a meeting of the board of directors at which she and the two Kellys were present, her resignation was accepted. Thereupon the two Kellys elected Julian Hemphill, a son-in-law of Kelly, Sr., to replace Margaret Lee.

I agree with Justice Eager, who dissented in the Appellate Division, that two members of the board were insufficient to constitute a quorum in this case for the purpose of electing the new director. It necessarily follows that the election of Julian Hemphill is not merely irregular, as the majority hold, but is wholly void and must be set aside.

Section 25 of the General Corporation Law grants to the court two alternatives in a case such as this: (1) to confirm the election, or (2) to order a new election as justice may require (Matter of Faehndrich, 2 N.Y.2d 468, 474, 161 N.Y.S.2d 99, 104, 141 N.E.2d 597, 600). As we held in the case just cited, the clause "as justice may require" does not enlarge the court's power nor authorize it to grant different relief from that specified in the statute. There is no basis whatever here for the application of the doctrine of estoppel, and in no event could it reasonably be applied to the nondirector, appellant Gearing, a substantial stockholder in this corporation. The purported election is, therefore, a nullity.

This is a mere contest for control, and the court should not assist either side, each of which holds an equal interest in the corporation, particularly where, as here, petitioners were willing that director Meacham attend meetings for the purpose of transacting all the necessary business of the board, but were unwilling that she attend a meeting, the purpose of which was to strip them of every vestige of control. Appellant Meacham had surrendered nothing in 1955 when she permitted Kelly, Jr., to become a director as well as his father, for Margaret Lee was then a third director.

The statute mandates a new election and that should be ordered. It is no answer to say that the results will probably be the same. If the parties are deadlocked, whether as directors or stockholders, and choose to remain that way, they have other remedies, and I see no reason why we should help one side or the other by disregarding a bylaw that follows the statute (General Corporation Law, § 27), particularly when it results in giving the Kellys complete control of the corporation.

I would, therefore, reverse the order appealed from, and modify the order of Special Term by ordering a special election and affirming it in all other respects.

DESMOND, C.J., and FULD, VAN VOORHIS, BURKE and FOSTER, JJ., concur in Per Curiam opinion.

FROESSEL, J., dissents in an opinion in which DYE, J., concurs.

NOTE

Many state statutes relating to the filling of vacancies on the board of directors are based on the first sentence of MBCA (1969) § 38: "[a]ny vacancy occurring in the board of directors may be filled by the affirmative vote of a majority of the remaining directors though less than a quorum of the board of directors." If this statute had been in effect in New York at the time *Gearing* arose, would the Kellys need the presence of Mrs. Meacham in order to elect Hemphill? What does the clause "though less than a quorum" in § 38 modify? Compare MBCA § 8.10(a)(3). Does the language of that section resolve all possible ambiguity? Consider also the possible application of MBCA § 8.05(e) to the facts of this case.

IN RE RADOM & NEIDORFF, INC.

Court of Appeals of New York, 1954.
119 N.E.2d 563.

DESMOND, JUDGE.

Radom & Neidorff, Inc., the proposed dissolution of which is before us here, is a domestic corporation which has for many years conducted, with great success, the business of lithographing or printing musical compositions. For some thirty years prior to February 18, 1950, Henry Neidorff, now deceased, husband of respondent Anna Neidorff, and David Radom, brother-in-law of Neidorff and brother of Mrs. Neidorff, were the sole stockholders, each holding eighty shares. Henry Neidorff's will made his wife his executrix and bequeathed her the stock, so that, ever since his death, petitioner-appellant David Radom and Anna Neidorff, brother and sister, have been the sole and equal stockholders. Although brother and sister, they were unfriendly before Neidorff's death and their estrangement continues. On July 17, 1950, five months after Neidorff's death, Radom brought this proceeding, praying that the corporation be dissolved under section 103 of the General Corporation Law, Consol.Laws, c. 23, the applicable part of which is as follows:

§ 103.   *Petition in Case of Deadlock*

Unless otherwise provided in the certificate of incorporation, if a corporation has an even number of directors who are equally divided respecting the management of its affairs, or if the votes of its stockholders are so divided that they cannot elect a board of directors, the holders of one-half of the stock entitled to vote at an election of directors may present a verified petition for dissolution of the corporation as prescribed in this article.

That statute, like others in article 9 of the General Corporation Law, describes the situations in which dissolution may be petitioned for, but, as we shall show later, it does not mandate the granting of the relief in every such case.

The petition here stated to the court that the corporation is solvent and its operations successful, but that, since Henry Neidorff's death, his widow (respondent here) has refused to co-operate with petitioner as president, and that she refuses to sign his salary checks, leaving him without salary, although he has the sole burden of running the business. It was alleged, too, that, because of "unresolved disagreements" between petitioner and respondent, election of any directors, at a stockholders' meeting held for that purpose in June, 1950, had proved impossible. A schedule attached to the petition showed corporate assets consisting of machinery and supplies worth about $9,500, cash about $82,000, and no indebtedness except about $17,000 owed to petitioner (plus his salary claim). Mrs. Neidorff's answering papers alleged that, while her husband was alive, the two owners had each drawn about $25,000 per year from the corporation, that, shortly after her husband's death, petitioner had asked her to allow him alone to sign all checks, which request she refused, that he had then offered her $75,000 for her stock, and, on her rejection thereof, had threatened to have the corporation dissolved and to buy it in at a low price or, if she should be the purchaser, that he would start a competing business. She further alleged that she has not, since her husband's death, interfered with Radom's conduct of the business and has signed all corporate checks sent her by him except checks for his own salary which, she says, she declined to sign because of a stockholder's derivative suit brought by her against Radom, and still pending, charging him with enriching himself at this corporation's expense.

Because of other litigation now concluded, see Matter of Radom's Estate, 305 N.Y. 679, 112 N.E.2d 768, to which Mrs. Neidorff was not a party, but which had to do with a contest as to the ownership of the Radom stock, respondent's answering papers in this dissolution proceeding were not filed until three years after the petition was entered. From the answering papers it appears, without dispute, that for those three years, the corporation's profits before taxes had totaled about $242,000, or an annual average of about $71,000, on a gross annual business of about $250,000, and that the corporation had, in 1953, about $300,000 on deposit in banks. There are many other accusations and counteraccusations in these wordy papers, but the only material facts are undisputed: first, that these two equal stockholders dislike and distrust each other; second, that despite the feuding and backbiting, there is no stalemate or impasse as to corporate policies; third, that the corporation is not sick but flourishing; fourth, that dissolution is not necessary for the corporation or for either stockholder; and, fifth, that petitioner, though he is in an uncomfortable and disagreeable situation for which he may or may not be at fault, has no grievance cognizable by a court except as to the nonpayment of his salary, hardly a ground for dissolving the corporation.

Special Term held that these papers showed a basic and irreconcilable conflict between the two stockholders requiring dissolution, for the protection of both of them, if the petition's allegations should be proven. An order for a reference was, accordingly, made, but respondent appealed therefrom, and no hearings were held by the Referee. The Appellate Division reversed the order and dismissed the petition, pointing out, among other things, that not only have the corporation's activities not been paralyzed but that its profits have increased and its assets trebled during the pendency of this proceeding, that the failure of petitioner to receive his salary did not frustrate the corporate business and was remediable by means other than dissolution. The dismissal of the proceeding was "without prejudice, however, to the bringing of another proceeding should deadlock in fact arise in the selection of a board of directors, at a meeting of stockholders to be duly called, or if other deadlock should occur threatening impairment or in fact impairing the economic operations of the corporation." 124 N.Y.S.2d 424, 425. Petitioner then appealed to this court.

It is worthy of passing mention, at least, that respondent has, in her papers, formally offered, and repeated the offer on the argument of the appeal before us, "to have the third director named by the American Arbitration Association, any Bar Association or any recognized and respected public body."

Clearly, the dismissal of this petition was within the discretion of the Appellate Division. There is no absolute right to dissolution under such circumstances. Even when majority stockholders file a petition because of internal corporate conflicts, the order is granted only when the competing interests "are so discordant as to prevent efficient management" and the "object of its corporate existence cannot be attained." Hitch v. Hawley, 30 N.E. 401, 404. The prime inquiry is, always, as to necessity for dissolution, that is, whether judicially-imposed death "will be beneficial to the stockholders or members and not injurious to the public," General Corporation Law, § 117; Hitch v. Hawley, supra. * * * Taking everything in the petition as true, this was not such a case, and so there was no need for a reference, or for the taking of proof, under sections 106 and 113 of the General Corporation Law.

The order should be affirmed, with costs.

FULD, JUDGE (dissenting).

Section 103 of the General Corporation Law, insofar as here relevant, permits a petition for dissolution of a corporation by the holders of one half of the shares of stock entitled to vote for directors "if the votes of its stockholders are so divided that they cannot elect a board of directors." That is the precise situation in the case before us, for the petition explicitly recites that petitioner Radom and respondent Neidorff "are hopelessly deadlocked with respect to the management and operation of the corporation" and that serious disputes have developed between them with the result that "the votes of the two stockholders are so divided that they cannot elect a Board of Directors." * * *

For upwards of thirty years, petitioner Radom and Henry Neidorff, respondent's husband, shared equally in the ownership and management of Radom & Neidorff, Inc. Through all that time, their relationship was harmonious as well as profitable. Neidorff died in 1950, at which time respondent, through inheritance, acquired her present 50% stock interest in the business. Since then, all has been discord and conflict. The parties, brother and sister, are at complete loggerheads; they have been unable to elect a board of directors; dividends have neither been declared nor distributed, although the corporation has earned profits; debts of the corporation have gone unpaid, although the corporation is solvent; petitioner, who since Neidorff's death has been the sole manager of the business, has not received a penny of his salary—amounting to $25,000 a year—because respondent has refused to sign any corporate check to his order. More, petitioner's business judgment and integrity, never before questioned, have been directly attacked in the stockholder's derivative suit, instituted by respondent, charging that he has falsified the corporation's records, converted its assets and otherwise enriched himself at its expense. Negotiations looking to the purchase by one stockholder of the other's interest were begun—in an effort to end the impasse—but they, too, have failed.

In very truth, as petitioner states in his papers, "a corporation of this type, with only two stockholders in it cannot continue to operate with incessant litigation and feuding between the two stockholders, and with differences as fundamental and wholly irreconcilable as are those of Mrs. Neidorff and myself. * * * [S]ettlement of these differences cannot be effected, [and] continuance on the present basis is impossible, so that there is no alternative to judicial dissolution." Indeed, petitioner avers, in view of the unceasing discord and the fact that he has had to work without salary and advance his own money to the corporation, he does not, whether or not dissolution be granted, "propose to continue to labor in and operate this business."

It is, then, undisputed and indisputable that the stockholders are not able to elect a board of directors. In addition, it is manifest, on the facts alleged, that the Supreme Court could find that the stockholders are hopelessly deadlocked vis-à-vis the management of the corporation; that the corporation cannot long continue to function effectively or profitably under such condition; that petitioner's resignation as president and manager—which he contemplates—will be highly detrimental to the interests of both corporation and stockholders and cannot help but result in substantial loss; and that petitioner is not responsible for the deadlock that exists. In such circumstances, the requisite statutory hearing may well establish that dissolution is indispensable, the only remedy available. As the high court of New Jersey recently declared in applying to somewhat comparable facts a statute similar to section 103 of our General Corporation Law, Matter of Collins-Doan Co., 70 A.2d 159, 166, "In the case at hand, *there is a want of that community of interest essential to corporate operation.* Dissolution will serve the interests of the shareholders as well as public policy. * * * And, if the statutory authority be deemed discretionary in essence, there is no ground for withholding its affirmative exercise here, *for there is no alternative corrective remedy.* * * *" (Emphasis supplied.)

Here, too, the asserted dissension, the court could find, permits of no real or effective remedy but a section 103 dissolution. And that is confirmed by a consideration of the alternatives seemingly open to petitioner. He could remain as president and manager of the corporation, without compensation, completely at odds with his embittered sister— certainly neither a natural nor a satisfying way in which to conduct a business. Or he could carry out his present plan to quit the enterprise— and thereby risk a loss, to corporation and stockholders, far greater than that involved in terminating the business. Or he could, without quitting, set up a competing enterprise and thereby expose himself to suit for breach of fiduciary duty to the corporation. It is difficult to believe that the legislature could have intended to put one in petitioner's position to such a choice. Reason plainly indicates, and the law allows, the reasonable course of orderly dissolution pursuant to section 103.

Respondent, however, suggests that, in view of the fact that petitioner is managing the business profitably, he should continue to do so, defend against the stockholder's suit which she brought attacking his honor and integrity and himself start an action for the compensation denied him for more than three years. But, it seems self-evident, more and further litigation would only aggravate, not cure, the underlying deadlock of which petitioner complains. And, if he were to bring the suggested suit for salary due him, the question arises, whom should he sue, and who is to defend? The mere proposal that petitioner embark on a series of actions against the corporation, of which he is president and half owner, indicates the extent of the present impasse, as well as the futility of perpetuating it. The same is true of the other alternative suggested by respondent, namely, that the third of the three directors, required by section 5 of the Stock Corporation Law, Consol.Laws, c. 59, be appointed by an impartial party. The deadlock of which petitioner complains is between the stockholders, not the directors, and when stockholders are deadlocked, section 103 calls for dissolution, not arbitration. Beyond that, and even if the offer to elect an impartial director were relevant, it would still be necessary to inquire when it was made and under what circumstances. It does not justify, alone or in conjunction with the other facts, a summary dismissal of the proceeding without a hearing.

Although respondent relies on the fact that the corporation is now solvent and operating at a profit, it is manifest that, if petitioner carries out his plan to resign as president and quits the business, there may be irreparable loss, not alone to him and respondent, as the owners of the corporation, but also to the corporation's creditors. Quite apart from that, however, the sole issue under section 103 is whether there is a deadlock as to the management of the corporation, not whether business is being conducted at a profit or loss. Whether the petition should or should not be entertained surely cannot be made to turn on proof that the corporation is on the verge of ruin or insolvency.

* * * By virtue of other provisions of Article 9 of the General Corporation Law—sections 101 and 102—directors and stockholders may seek dissolution, when the corporation is insolvent, in order to prevent further loss to the owners and creditors. Section 103, however—which bears the title, *"Petition in case of deadlock"*—was designed to serve a far different purpose. As amended in 1944, upon the recommendation of the Law Revision Commission, that section provides for dissolution "if the votes of its stockholders are so divided that they cannot elect a board of directors." Nothing in the statute itself or in its legislative history suggests that a "Petition in case of deadlock" must wait until the corporation's profits have dried up and financial reverses set in. Had the commission or the legislature intended to incorporate such a qualification into section 103, it could readily have done so. The only test envisaged by

the commission, however, was that which the legislature enacted, and a court may not import any other. * * *

The order of the Appellate Division should be reversed and that at Special Term affirmed.

CONWAY, DYE and VAN VOORHIS, JJ., concur with DESMOND, J.

FULD, J., dissents in opinion in which LEWIS, C.J., and FROESSEL, J., concur.

NOTES

(1) *See* MBCA § 14.30, a statute that is typical of many state involuntary dissolution statutes. The Official Comment to this section makes it clear that the use of the word "may" in the preamble preserves a court's discretion (applied in *Radom*) "as to whether dissolution is appropriate even though grounds exist under the specific circumstances."

(2) Consider MBCA §§ 14.01–14.02, 14.20. Could a dissatisfied shareholder in a closely held corporation use these alternative dissolution provisions to avoid the limitations of § 14.30?

(3) Courts are often reluctant to dissolve profitable corporations, even if dissension has been established. The reluctance seems to be premised on the notion that dissolution will destroy the business and will cause loss of employment and other economic harm. It should be noted, however, that dissolution does not necessarily result in the termination of a business:

> In corporate involuntary dissolution cases, the courts appear to assume that a decree will result in the termination of the business. Perceiving a public interest in the continuation of profitable firms, courts understandably grant dissolution reluctantly and only after considering competing interests in preserving the firm. The concern is misplaced in this instance, and both the courts and the legislatures have misperceived the effect of a dissolution decree. In practical effect a decree is no different than the dissolution of a partnership. The entry of a decree results in the termination of a business only if both the majority and the minority shareholders desire that result. Each faction has the ability at any stage of the proceeding to insure the continued existence of the firm by buying out, or selling out to, the other faction. The business will cease only if continuing it is not in the interest of any of its shareholders [or a third party].

> The point becomes clearer if one focuses on the motives for bringing a dissolution proceeding. Except for the rare case where the petition is prompted by pique, a shareholder suing for dissolution is trying to accomplish one of three things: (1) to withdraw his investment from the firm; (2) to induce the other shareholders to sell out to him; or (3) to use the threat of dissolution to induce the other shareholders to agree to a change in the balance

of power or in the policies of the firm. All of these objectives can be accomplished without dissolution. If the petitioner wants to sell out, he is interested in receiving the highest possible price and is indifferent whether the purchase funds are raised by the other shareholders individually or by a sale of the firm's assets. If the second and third objectives motivate the suit, it is plain that the petitioner does not want dissolution at all. In all three situations, a dissolution petition is a means to another end.

* * * The court's decision to grant or to deny dissolution is significant only as it affects the relative bargaining strength of the parties; negotiations will go forward in any event. * * *

* * *

The foregoing analysis suggests that while a decision to grant or to deny dissolution will have some effect on whether the parties continue in business together, it will have no independent effect on the continued existence of the firm. If a court orders dissolution and one party wishes to continue the business, a mutually advantageous purchase of the other's interest will result. If the dissolution is denied, the majority has less incentive to settle and will reduce the amount it offers for the minority's interest, but a sale is still likely to occur eventually. In short, a decree will not result in liquidation of the firm where either party [or a third party] wishes to continue it.

J.A.C. Hetherington & Michael P. Dooley, *Illiquidity and Exploitation: A Proposed Statutory Solution to the Remaining Close Corporation Problem*, 63 VA. L. REV. 1, 27, 29–30 (1977).

(4) When a corporation is actually dissolved, the business is typically sold at a public sale. As a result, the market values the business and determines (ultimately) what a shareholder will receive for his holdings. Dissolution sales, however, may not generate a fair value for the business. Some reasons for this include the following: (1) the business may be so dependent on the skills of the majority shareholder that the majority himself is the only realistic purchaser of the business (and without competition at the public sale, the majority may be able to purchase the business for far below fair value); (2) even if the minority shareholder could run the business himself, he may not have sufficient capital to bid competitively at the sale; (3) many dissolution sales are "fire sales" in that the business assets are sold separately, usually yielding less than if the business were sold as a going concern; (4) the business "is not always operated between the appointment of the receiver or court-appointed auctioneer and the date of sale," and, as a result, "[d]uring this interim, the customers of the business may develop relationships and preferences for other vendors, often dealing a fatal blow to the corporation's ability to operate profitably"; (5) dissolution sales "usually require payment of the purchase price immediately or within a short period of time," which tends to "exclude[ ] potential purchasers from the market and

may result in lower purchase prices offered by those not excluded"; and (6) purchase prices at dissolution sales "are depressed because it is difficult to insure that the buyer will reap the benefit of the seller's goodwill." In other words, "[b]usiness management, as well as nonmanagement employees, often develop important customer contacts and special expertise," and "[t]o the extent that management expertise and customer relationships cannot be sold with the business, buyers do not receive the benefit of, nor are they willing to pay for, these important elements of goodwill." Steven C. Bahls, *Resolving Shareholder Dissension: Selection of the Appropriate Equitable Remedy*, 15 J. CORP. L. 285, 297 (1990); *see also id.* at 331 (stating that "[b]uyers generally are unwilling to pay full value for a business at a judicial sale even though it is a going concern" due to the following risks: (1) the risk of losing the management team; (2) the risk of inadequate or inaccurate financial statements; (3) the risk of post-sale competition by the seller; and (4) the risk of material adverse change before completion of the purchase).

(5) Many modern statutes authorize a court to appoint a custodian or provisional director as a remedy for deadlock. Such an appointment relieves the deadlock by either taking the board's managerial power away (custodian), or by adding a "tiebreaker" voter to the board (provisional director). This statutory flexibility allows a court to offer relief without having to dissolve the corporation. For more on custodians and provisional directors, see Section C below.

B. OPPRESSION

In a publicly held corporation, a shareholder is typically a passive investor who neither contributes labor to the corporation nor takes part in management responsibilities. A shareholder in a publicly held corporation simply invests money and hopes to receive a return on that money through dividend payments and/or sale of the company's stock at an appreciated value. By contrast, in a closely held corporation, a shareholder typically expects an active participatory role in the company, usually through employment and a meaningful role in management. A shareholder in a closely held corporation also invests money in the venture and, like all shareholders, she hopes to receive a return on that money. By definition, however, a closely held corporation lacks an active market for its stock. Absent a sale of the entire company, therefore, investment return is normally provided by employment compensation and dividends, rather than by sales of stock at an appreciated value.

Conventional corporate law norms of majority rule and centralized control can lead to serious problems for a minority investor in a closely held corporation. Traditionally, most corporate power is centralized in the hands of a board of directors. As you know, the directors set policy, elect officers, and supervise the normal operation of the corporation. Because directors are elected by shareholder vote, the board of a closely held corporation is typically controlled by the shareholder (or shareholders) holding a majority of the voting power. Through this control of the board, a majority shareholder (or majority group) has the ability to take unjustified actions that are harmful to a minority shareholder's interests. Such actions are often referred to as "freezeout" or "squeezeout" techniques that "oppress" a minority shareholder in a closely held corporation. Common freezeout techniques include the termination of a minority shareholder's employment, the refusal to declare dividends, the removal of a minority shareholder from the board of directors, and the siphoning off of corporate earnings through high compensation to the majority shareholder. This denial of financial and participatory rights is at the core of many lawsuits alleging that the majority has used her control in an abusive or "oppressive" fashion against a minority shareholder.

In a publicly held corporation, a minority shareholder can largely escape these abuses of power by selling his shares into the market and by correspondingly recovering the value of his investment. This ability to liquidate provides some protection to investors in publicly held corporations from the conduct of those in control. In a closely held corporation, however, there is no market exit. Even without a market for a company's shares, a minority shareholder could still recover the value of his investment if he could force the corporation (or the majority shareholder) to purchase his shares on demand. No state's corporation law, however, provides such a right. Without an explicit buyout provision in a stockholders' agreement or a company's organizational documents, corporate shareholders have no right to compel a redemption of their holdings.

Dissolution of a company can also provide liquidity to business owners by requiring the sale of the company and by allocating to each owner his proportionate share of the company's sale value. If a minority shareholder in a closely held corporation had the right to compel dissolution, a mechanism for recovering the value of the invested capital would exist (think about the dissolution provisions of the general partnership, for example). In the closely held corporation setting, however, a minority shareholder has no default right to dissolve a corporation by "express will" (i.e., voluntary dissolution usually requires the assent of at least a majority of the outstanding voting stock of a corporation). For an oppressed minority shareholder, therefore, voluntary dissolution rights are largely unhelpful.

A minority shareholder who is cognizant of the risks of oppressive majority conduct could seek to protect his financial and participatory rights by contract before committing his capital to the venture. As you learned in Chapter 8, shareholder agreements and buy-sell provisions are only some of the contractual tools that shareholders can use to strengthen their employment, dividend, exit, and other rights. If the majority shareholder or the corporation is unwilling to enter into protective contractual arrangements, the minority shareholder can simply refuse to invest in the company.

How should the law respond when minority shareholders fail to protect their financial and participatory rights by contract? Broadly speaking, courts have followed two different approaches. First, most jurisdictions have developed special common-law doctrines (often aided by statutes) that are designed to protect minority shareholders from oppressive majority conduct. In these jurisdictions, the protection is doctrinally articulated either as a fiduciary duty that shareholders in closely held corporations owe to one another, or as a right to dissolution (or other remedy) on the grounds of oppressive conduct by those in control.

Second, a few jurisdictions (including, notably, Delaware) have refused to develop special common-law rules to protect minority shareholders in closely held corporations. In these jurisdictions, an oppressed investor can attempt to rely on traditional legal principles for protection (e.g., traditional corporate or contract law doctrines), but no additional common-law safeguards are provided.

The materials that follow explore these approaches and doctrinal articulations in greater detail. As you read, think about which of these approaches makes sense—i.e., think about whether courts should provide shareholders in closely held corporations with a special set of protections.

DONAHUE v. RODD ELECTROTYPE CO.

Supreme Judicial Court of Massachusetts, 1975.
328 N.E.2d 505.

TAURO, CHIEF JUSTICE.

The plaintiff, Euphemia Donahue, a minority stockholder in the Rodd Electrotype Company of New England, Inc. (Rodd Electrotype), a Massachusetts corporation, brings this suit against the directors of Rodd Electrotype, Charles H. Rodd, Frederick I. Rodd and Mr. Harold E. Magnuson, against Harry C. Rodd, a former director, officer, and controlling stockholder of Rodd Electrotype and against Rodd Electrotype (hereinafter called defendants). The plaintiff seeks to rescind Rodd Electrotype's purchase of Harry Rodd's shares in Rodd Electrotype and to compel Harry Rodd "to repay to the corporation the purchase price of said shares, $36,000, together with interest from the date of purchase." The plaintiff alleges that the defendants caused the corporation to purchase the shares in violation of their fiduciary duty to her, a minority stockholder of Rodd Electrotype.

The trial judge, after hearing oral testimony, dismissed the plaintiff's bill on the merits. He found that the purchase was without prejudice to the plaintiff and implicitly found that the transaction had been carried out in good faith and with inherent fairness. The Appeals Court affirmed with costs.

* * *

The evidence may be summarized as follows: * * * [Various] stock purchases left Harry Rodd in control of Royal of New England. Early in 1955 * * * he had assumed the presidency of the company. [Rodd had also been a director, general manager, and treasurer of the company]. His 200 shares [purchased at $20 per share] gave him a dominant eighty per cent interest [there were 250 outstanding shares of the company]. Joseph Donahue, at this time, was the only minority stockholder. [Donahue owned the remaining 50 shares, which he also purchased at $20 per share. Donahue's duties were confined to operational matters within the plant. Although Donahue ultimately achieved the positions of plant superintendent and corporate vice president, he never participated in the management aspect of the business].

Subsequent events reflected Harry Rodd's dominant influence. In June, 1960 * * * the company was renamed the Rodd Electrotype Company of New England, Inc. In 1962, Charles H. Rodd, Harry Rodd's son (a defendant here), who had long been a company employee working in the plant, became corporate vice president. In 1963, he joined his father on the board of directors. In 1964, another son, Frederick I. Rodd (also a defendant), replaced Joseph Donahue as plant superintendent. By 1965, Harry Rodd had evidently decided to reduce his participation in corporate management. That year Charles Rodd succeeded him as president and general manager of Rodd Electrotype.

From 1959 to 1967, Harry Rodd pursued what may fairly be termed a gift program by which he distributed the majority of his shares equally among his two sons and his daughter, Phyllis E. Mason. Each child received thirty-nine shares. Two shares were returned to the corporate treasury in 1966.

We come now to the events of 1970 which form the grounds for the plaintiff's complaint. In May of 1970, Harry Rodd was seventy-seven years old. The record indicates that for some time he had not enjoyed the best of health and that he had undergone a number of operations. His sons wished him to retire. Mr. Rodd was not averse to this suggestion. However, he insisted that some financial arrangements be made with respect to his remaining eighty-one shares of stock. A number of conferences ensued. Harry Rodd and Charles Rodd (representing the company) negotiated terms of purchase for forty-five shares which, Charles Rodd testified, would reflect the book value and liquidating value of the shares.

A special board meeting convened on July 13, 1970. As the first order of business, Harry Rodd resigned his directorship of Rodd Electrotype. The remaining incumbent directors, Charles Rodd and Mr. Harold E. Magnuson (clerk of the company and a defendant and defense attorney in the instant suit), elected Frederick Rodd to replace his father. The three directors then authorized Rodd Electrotype's president (Charles Rodd) to execute an agreement between Harry Rodd and the company in which the company would purchase forty-five shares for $800 a share ($36,000).

The stock purchase agreement was formalized between the parties on July 13, 1970. Two days later, a sale pursuant to the July 13 agreement was consummated. At approximately the same time, Harry Rodd resigned his last corporate office, that of treasurer.

Harry Rodd completed divestiture of his Rodd Electrotype stock in the following year. As was true of his previous gifts, his later divestments gave equal representation to his children. Two shares were sold to each child on July 15, 1970, for $800 a share. Each was given ten shares in March, 1971.[7] Thus, in March, 1971, the shareholdings in Rodd Electrotype were apportioned as follows: Charles Rodd, Frederick Rodd and Phyllis Mason each held fifty-one shares; the Donahues[8] held fifty shares.

A special meeting of the stockholders of the company was held on March 30, 1971. At the meeting, Charles Rodd, company president and general manager, reported the tentative results of an audit conducted by the company auditors and reported generally on the company events of the year. For the first time, the Donahues learned that the corporation had purchased Harry Rodd's shares. According to the minutes of the meeting, following Charles Rodd's report, the Donahues raised questions about the purchase. They then voted against a resolution, ultimately adopted by the remaining stockholders, to approve Charles Rodd's report. Although the minutes of the meeting show that the stockholders unanimously voted to accept a second resolution ratifying all acts of the company president (he executed the stock purchase agreement) in the preceding year, the trial judge found, and there was evidence to support his finding, that the Donahues did not ratify the purchase of Harry Rodd's shares.

A few weeks after the meeting, the Donahues, acting through their attorney, offered their shares to the corporation on the same terms given to Harry Rodd. Mr. Harold E. Magnuson replied by letter that the

---

[7]   An inference is permissible that the "gift" of these shares was a part of the "deal" for the stock purchase.

[8]   Joseph Donahue gave his wife, the plaintiff, joint ownership of his fifty shares in 1962. In 1968, they transferred five shares to their son, Dr. Robert Donahue. On Joseph Donahue's death, the plaintiff became outright owner of the forty-five share block. This was the ownership pattern which obtained in March, 1971.

corporation would not purchase the shares and was not in a financial position to do so.[10] This suit followed.

In her argument before this court, the plaintiff has characterized the corporate purchase of Harry Rodd's shares as an unlawful distribution of corporate assets to controlling stockholders. She urges that the distribution constitutes a breach of the fiduciary duty owed by the Rodds, as controlling stockholders, to her, a minority stockholder in the enterprise, because the Rodds failed to accord her an equal opportunity to sell her shares to the corporation. The defendants reply that the stock purchase was within the powers of the corporation and met the requirements of good faith and inherent fairness imposed on a fiduciary in his dealings with the corporation. They assert that there is no right to equal opportunity in corporate stock purchases for the corporate treasury. For the reasons hereinafter noted, we agree with the plaintiff and reverse the decree of the Superior Court. However, we limit the applicability of our holding to "close corporations," as hereinafter defined. Whether the holding should apply to other corporations is left for decision in another case, on a proper record.

A. *Close Corporations.*

In previous opinions, we have alluded to the distinctive nature of the close corporation, but have never defined precisely what is meant by a close corporation. There is no single, generally accepted definition. Some commentators emphasize an "integration of ownership and management," in which the stockholders occupy most management positions. Others focus on the number of stockholders and the nature of the market for the stock. In this view, close corporations have few stockholders; there is little market for corporate stock. The Supreme Court of Illinois adopted this latter view in Galler v. Galler, 32 Ill.2d 16, 203 N.E.2d 577 (1965): "For our purposes, a close corporation is one in which the stock is held in a few hands, or in a few families, and wherein it is not at all, or only rarely, dealt in by buying or selling." We accept aspects of both definitions. We deem a close corporation to be typified by: (1) a small number of stockholders; (2) no ready market for the corporate stock; and (3) substantial majority stockholder participation in the management, direction and operations of the corporation.

As thus defined, the close corporation bears striking resemblance to a partnership. Commentators and courts have noted that the close corporation is often little more than an "incorporated" or "chartered" partnership.[12] The stockholders "clothe" their partnership "with the

---

[10] Between 1965 and 1969, the company offered to purchase the Donahue shares for amounts between $2,000 and $10,000 ($40 to $200 a share). The Donahues rejected these offers.

[12] The United States Internal Revenue Code gives substantial recognition to the fact that close corporations are often merely incorporated partnerships. The so called Subchapter S * * * enables "small business corporations," defined by the statute, to make an election which generally exempts the corporation from taxation and causes inclusion of the corporation's

benefits peculiar to a corporation, limited liability, perpetuity and the like." In essence, though, the enterprise remains one in which ownership is limited to the original parties or transferees of their stock to whom the other stockholders have agreed,[13] in which ownership and management are in the same hands, and in which the owners are quite dependent on one another for the success of the enterprise. Many close corporations are "really partnerships, between two or three people who contribute their capital, skills, experience and labor." Just as in a partnership, the relationship among the stockholders must be one of trust, confidence and absolute loyalty if the enterprise is to succeed. Close corporations with substantial assets and with more numerous stockholders are no different from smaller close corporations in this regard. All participants rely on the fidelity and abilities of those stockholders who hold office. Disloyalty and self-seeking conduct on the part of any stockholder will engender bickering, corporate stalemates, and, perhaps, efforts to achieve dissolution.

In Helms v. Duckworth, 101 U.S.App.D.C. 390, 249 F.2d 482 (1957), the United States Court of Appeals for the District of Columbia Circuit had before it a stockholders' agreement providing for the purchase of the shares of a deceased stockholder by the surviving stockholder in a small "two-man" close corporation. The court held the surviving stockholder to a duty "to deal fairly, honestly, and openly with * * * [his] fellow stockholders." Judge Burger, now Chief Justice Burger, writing for the court, emphasized the resemblance of the two-man close corporation to a partnership: "In an intimate business venture such as this, stockholders of a close corporation occupy a position similar to that of joint adventurers and partners. While courts have sometimes declared stockholders 'do not bear toward each other that same relation of trust and confidence which prevails in partnerships,' this view ignores the practical realities of the organization and functioning of a small 'two-man' corporation organized to carry on a small business enterprise in which the stockholders, directors, and managers are the same persons" (footnotes omitted).

Although the corporate form provides the above-mentioned advantages for the stockholders (limited liability, perpetuity, and so forth), it also supplies an opportunity for the majority stockholders to oppress or disadvantage minority stockholders. The minority is vulnerable to a variety of oppressive devices, termed "freezeouts," which

---

undistributed, as well as distributed, taxable income in the gross income of the stockholders for the year. This is essentially the manner in which partnership earnings are taxed.

[13] The original owners commonly impose restrictions on transfers [of] stock designed to prevent outsiders who are unacceptable to the other stockholders from acquiring an interest in the close corporation. These restrictions often take the form of agreements among the stockholders and the corporation or by-laws which give the corporation or the other stockholders a right of "first refusal" when any stockholder desires to sell his shares. In a partnership, of course, a partner cannot transfer his interest in the partnership so as to give his assignee a right to participate in the management or business affairs of the continuing partnership without the agreement of the other partners.

the majority may employ. An authoritative study of such "freeze-outs" enumerates some of the possibilities: "The squeezers [those who employ the freeze-out techniques] may refuse to declare dividends; they may drain off the corporation's earnings in the form of exorbitant salaries and bonuses to the majority shareholder-officers and perhaps to their relatives, or in the form of high rent by the corporation for property leased from majority shareholders * * *; they may deprive minority shareholders of corporate offices and of employment by the company; they may cause the corporation to sell its assets at an inadequate price to the majority shareholders * * *." F. H. O'Neal and J. Derwin, Expulsion or Oppression of Business Associates, 42 (1961). In particular, the power of the board of directors, controlled by the majority, to declare or withhold dividends and to deny the minority employment is easily converted to a device to disadvantage minority stockholders.

The minority can, of course, initiate suit against the majority and their directors. Self-serving conduct by directors is proscribed by the director's fiduciary obligation to the corporation. However, in practice, the plaintiff will find difficulty in challenging dividend or employment policies.[14] Such policies are considered to be within the judgment of the directors. This court has said: "The courts prefer not to interfere * * * with the sound financial management of the corporation by its directors, but declare as a general rule that the declaration of dividends rests within the sound discretion of the directors, refusing to interfere with their determination unless a plain abuse of discretion is made to appear." Crocker v. Waltham Watch Co., 315 Mass. 397, 402, 53 N.E.2d 230, 233 (1944). * * * Although contractual provisions in an "agreement of association and articles of organization" or in by-laws, have justified decrees in this jurisdiction ordering dividend declarations, generally, plaintiffs who seek judicial assistance against corporate dividend or employment policies do not prevail.

Thus, when these types of "freeze-outs" are attempted by the majority stockholders, the minority stockholders, cut off from all corporation-related revenues, must either suffer their losses or seek a buyer for their shares. Many minority stockholders will be unwilling or unable to wait for an alteration in majority policy. Typically, the minority stockholder in a close corporation has a substantial percentage of his personal assets invested in the corporation. The stockholder may have anticipated that his salary from his position with the corporation would be his livelihood. Thus, he cannot afford to wait passively. He must liquidate his investment in the close corporation in order to reinvest the funds in income-producing enterprises.

---

[14] It would be difficult for the plaintiff in the instant case to establish breach of a fiduciary duty *owed to the corporation*, as indicated by the finding of the trial judge.

At this point, the true plight of the minority stockholder in a close corporation becomes manifest. He cannot easily reclaim his capital. In a large public corporation, the oppressed or dissident minority stockholder could sell his stock in order to extricate some of his invested capital. By definition, this market is not available for shares in the close corporation. In a partnership, a partner who feels abused by his fellow partners may cause dissolution by his "express will * * * at any time" and recover his share of partnership assets and accumulated profits. If dissolution results in a breach of the partnership articles, the culpable partner will be liable in damages. By contrast, the stockholder in the close corporation or "incorporated partnership" may achieve dissolution and recovery of his share of the enterprise assets only by compliance with the rigorous terms of the applicable chapter of the General Laws. * * * To secure dissolution of the ordinary close corporation * * *, the stockholder, in the absence of corporate deadlock, must own at least fifty per cent of the shares or have the advantage of a favorable provision in the articles of organization. The minority stockholder, by definition lacking fifty per cent of the corporate shares, can never "authorize" the corporation to file a petition for dissolution * * * by his own vote. He will seldom have at his disposal the requisite favorable provision in the articles of organization.

Thus, in a close corporation, the minority stockholders may be trapped in a disadvantageous situation. No outsider would knowingly assume the position of the disadvantaged minority. The outsider would have the same difficulties. To cut losses, the minority stockholder may be compelled to deal with the majority. This is the capstone of the majority plan. Majority "freeze-out" schemes which withhold dividends are designed to compel the minority to relinquish stock at inadequate prices. When the minority stockholder agrees to sell out at less than fair value, the majority has won.

Because of the fundamental resemblance of the close corporation to the partnership, the trust and confidence which are essential to this scale and manner of enterprise, and the inherent danger to minority interests in the close corporation, we hold that stockholders[17] in the close corporation owe one another substantially the same fiduciary duty in the operation of the enterprise[18] that partners owe to one another. In our previous decisions, we have defined the standard of duty owed by partners to one another as the "utmost good faith and loyalty." Stockholders in close corporations must discharge their management and

---

[17] We do not limit our holding to majority stockholders. In the close corporation, the minority may do equal damage through unscrupulous and improper "sharp dealings" with an unsuspecting majority.

[18] We stress that the strict fiduciary duty which we apply to stockholders in a close corporation in this opinion governs *only* their actions relative to the operations of the enterprise and the effects of that operation on the rights and investments of other stockholders. We express no opinion as to the standard of duty applicable to transactions in the shares of the close corporation when the corporation is not a party to the transaction.

stockholder responsibilities in conformity with this strict good faith standard. They may not act out of avarice, expediency or self-interest in derogation of their duty of loyalty to the other stockholders and to the corporation.

We contrast this strict good faith standard with the somewhat less stringent standard of fiduciary duty to which directors and stockholders of all corporations must adhere in the discharge of their corporate responsibilities. Corporate directors are held to a good faith and inherent fairness standard of conduct and are not "permitted to serve two masters whose interests are antagonistic." "Their paramount duty is to the corporation, and their personal pecuniary interests are subordinate to that duty."

The more rigorous duty of partners and participants in a joint adventure, here extended to stockholders in a close corporation, was described by then Chief Judge Cardozo of the New York Court of Appeals in Meinhard v. Salmon, 249 N.Y. 458, 164 N.E. 545 (1928): "Joint adventurers, like copartners, owe to one another, while the enterprise continues, the duty of the finest loyalty. Many forms of conduct permissible in a workaday world for those acting at arm's length, are forbidden to those bound by fiduciary ties. * * * Not honesty alone, but the punctilio of an honor the most sensitive, is then the standard of behavior."

* * *

B. *Equal Opportunity in a Close Corporation.*

Under settled Massachusetts law, a domestic corporation, unless forbidden by statute, has the power to purchase its own shares. An agreement to reacquire stock "[is] enforceable, subject, at least, to the limitations that the purchase must be made in good faith and without prejudice to creditors and stockholders." Scriggins v. Thomas Dalby Co., [290 Mass. 414, 418, 19 N.E. 749 (1935);] Winchell v. Plywood Corp., [324 Mass. 171, 174–75, 85 N.E.2d 313, 315 (1949)]. When the corporation reacquiring its own stock is a close corporation, the purchase is subject to the additional requirement, in the light of our holding in this opinion, that the stockholders, who, as directors or controlling stockholders, caused the corporation to enter into the stock purchase agreement, must have acted with the utmost good faith and loyalty to the other stockholders.

To meet this test, if the stockholder whose shares were purchased was a member of the controlling group, the controlling stockholders must cause the corporation to offer each stockholder an equal opportunity to sell a ratable number of his shares to the corporation at an identical price.[24] Purchase by the corporation confers substantial benefits on the members of the controlling group whose shares were purchased. These benefits are not available to the minority stockholders if the corporation does not also offer them an opportunity to sell their shares. The controlling group may not, consistent with its strict duty to the minority, utilize its control of the corporation to obtain special advantages and disproportionate benefit from its share ownership.

The benefits conferred by the purchase are twofold: (1) provision of a market for shares; (2) access to corporate assets for personal use. By definition, there is no ready market for shares of a close corporation. The purchase creates a market for shares which previously had been unmarketable. It transforms a previously illiquid investment into a liquid one. If the close corporation purchases shares only from a member of the controlling group, the controlling stockholder can convert his shares into cash at a time when none of the other stockholders can. Consistent with its strict fiduciary duty, the controlling group may not utilize its control of the corporation to establish an exclusive market in previously unmarketable shares from which the minority stockholders are excluded.

The purchase also distributes corporate assets to the stockholder whose shares were purchased. Unless an equal opportunity is given to all stockholders, the purchase of shares from a member of the controlling group operates as a *preferential* distribution of assets. In exchange for his shares, he receives a percentage of the contributed capital and accumulated profits of the enterprise. The funds he so receives are available for his personal use. The other stockholders benefit from no such access to corporate property and cannot withdraw their shares of the corporate profits and capital in this manner unless the controlling group acquiesces. Although the purchase price for the controlling stockholder's shares may seem fair to the corporation and other stockholders under the tests established in the prior case law, the controlling stockholder whose stock has been purchased has still received a relative advantage over his fellow stockholders, inconsistent with his strict fiduciary duty—an opportunity to turn corporate funds to personal use.

The rule of equal opportunity in stock purchases by close corporations provides equal access to these benefits for all stockholders. We hold that, in any case in which the controlling stockholders have exercised their power over the corporation to deny the minority such equal opportunity, the minority shall be entitled to appropriate relief. * * *

---

[24] Of course, a close corporation may purchase shares from one stockholder without offering the others an equal opportunity if all other stockholders give advance consent to the stock purchase arrangements through acceptance of an appropriate provision in the articles of organization, the corporate by-laws, or a stockholder's agreement. Similarly, all other stockholders may ratify the purchase.

C. *Application of the Law to this Case.*

We turn now to the application of the learning set forth above to the facts of the instant case.

The strict standard of duty is plainly applicable to the stockholders in Rodd Electrotype. Rodd Electrotype is a close corporation. * * *

Through their control of these management positions and of the majority of the Rodd Electrotype stock, the Rodds effectively controlled the corporation. In testing the stock purchase from Harry Rodd against the applicable strict fiduciary standard, we treat the Rodd family as a single controlling group. We reject the defendants' contention that the Rodd family cannot be treated as a unit for this purpose. From the evidence, it is clear that the Rodd family was a close-knit one with strong community of interest. Harry Rodd had hired his sons to work in the family business, Rodd Electrotype. As he aged, he transferred portions of his stock holdings to his children. Charles Rodd and Frederick Rodd were given positions of responsibility in the business as he withdrew from active management. In these circumstances, it is realistic to assume that appreciation, gratitude, and filial devotion would prevent the younger Rodds from opposing a plan which would provide funds for their father's retirement.

Moreover, a strong motive of interest requires that the Rodds be considered a controlling group. When Charles Rodd and Frederick Rodd were called on to represent the corporation in its dealings with their father, they must have known that further advancement within the corporation and benefits would follow their father's retirement and the purchase of his stock. The corporate purchase would take only forty-five of Harry Rodd's eighty-one shares. The remaining thirty-six shares were to be divided among Harry Rodd's children in equal amounts by gift and sale.[28] Receipt of their portion of the thirty-six shares and purchase by the corporation of forty-five shares would effectively transfer full control of the corporation to Frederick Rodd and Charles Rodd, if they chose to act in concert with each other or if one of them chose to ally with his sister. Moreover, Frederick Rodd was the obvious successor to his father as director and corporate treasurer when those posts became vacant after his father's retirement. Failure to complete the corporate purchase (in other words, impeding their father's retirement plan) would have delayed, and perhaps have suspended indefinitely, the transfer of these benefits to the younger Rodds. They could not be expected to oppose their father's wishes in this matter. Although the defendants are correct when they assert that no express agreement involving a quid pro quo—subsequent

---

[28] Charles Rodd admitted in his trial testimony that the parties to the negotiations which led to the stock purchase agreement structured subsequent transactions so that each of the Rodd children would eventually own fifty-one shares of corporate stock. The plaintiff points out that this was precisely the number of shares which would permit any two of Harry Rodd's children to outvote the third child and the remaining stockholders.

stock gifts for votes from the directors—was proved, no express agreement is necessary to demonstrate the identity of interest which disciplines a controlling group acting in unison.

On its face, then, the purchase of Harry Rodd's shares by the corporation is a breach of the duty which the controlling stockholders, the Rodds, owed to the minority stockholders, the plaintiff and her son. The purchase distributed a portion of the corporate assets to Harry Rodd, a member of the controlling group, in exchange for his shares. The plaintiff and her son were not offered an equal opportunity to sell their shares to the corporation. In fact, their efforts to obtain an equal opportunity were rebuffed by the corporate representative. As the trial judge found, they did not, in any manner, ratify the transaction with Harry Rodd.

Because of the foregoing, we hold that the plaintiff is entitled to relief. Two forms of suitable relief are set out hereinafter. The judge below is to enter an appropriate judgment. The judgment may require Harry Rodd to remit $36,000 with interest at the legal rate from July 15, 1970, to Rodd Electrotype in exchange for forty-five shares of Rodd Electrotype treasury stock. This, in substance, is the specific relief requested in the plaintiff's bill of complaint. * * * In the alternative, the judgment may require Rodd Electrotype to purchase all of the plaintiff's shares for $36,000 without interest. In the circumstances of this case, we view this as the equal opportunity which the plaintiff should have received. Harry Rodd's retention of thirty-six shares, which were to be sold and given to his children within a year of the Rodd Electrotype purchase, cannot disguise the fact that the corporation acquired one hundred per cent of that portion of his holdings (forty-five shares) which he did not intend his children to own. The plaintiff is entitled to have one hundred per cent of her forty-five shares similarly purchased. * * *

So ordered.

WILKINS, JUSTICE (concurring).

I agree with much of what the Chief Justice says in support of granting relief to the plaintiff. However, I do not join in any implication (see, e.g., footnote 18 and the associated text) that the rule concerning a close corporation's purchase of a controlling stockholder's shares applies to all operations of the corporation as they affect minority stockholders. That broader issue, which is apt to arise in connection with salaries and dividend policy, is not involved in this case. The analogy to partnerships may not be a complete one.

FRANK H. EASTERBROOK & DANIEL R. FISCHEL, CLOSE CORPORATIONS AND AGENCY COSTS

38 Stan. L. Rev. 271, 297–300 (1986).

That closely held corporations are really "incorporated partnerships" is a common refrain. The participants in the venture view each other as partners; therefore, the argument runs, they should be governed by the law of partnerships. Equal sharing rules, automatic buy-out rights, and strict fiduciary duties are fundamental principles of partnership law and thus, proponents of the partnership analogy contend, should also be fundamental principles of the law of closely held corporations.

There is something to the analogy. We have conjectured elsewhere, and there is now some evidence, that participants in smaller firms who are unable to reduce risk by diversifying their investments are more likely to contract for equal sharing rules and to opt for other principles that constrain managers' discretion. Still, there are problems with pushing the analogy to partnerships too far. First, at least with respect to automatic buy-out rights, the analogy is based on a misstatement of partnership law. Although partnership law allows any partner (unless all agree otherwise in advance) to disinvest at any time and dissolve the firm, the withdrawing partner may be liable in damages for "wrongful" termination and may be able to disinvest only on disadvantageous terms. Thus [any] proposal for automatic buy-out rights in closely held corporations, although supposedly based on partnership law, actually goes well beyond existing doctrine.

Second, the assumption that participants in closely held corporations want to be governed by partnership law is itself questionable. The participants incorporated for a reason. Perhaps the reason was only limited liability or favorable tax treatment, and in all other respects they wanted to be treated like partners. But this is not the only possibility. Corporate law is different from partnership law in many ways, and the venturers may desire to preserve these differences. Partners, for example, are entitled to share equally in the profits and management of the partnership, are mutual agents for each other, have the right to veto any decisions made by the majority on matters outside the ordinary course of business, and have the right to dissolve the partnership at any time if they are willing to bear the consequences. Corporate law treats each of these differently. Proponents of the partnership analogy assume that participants in closely held corporations are knowledgeable enough to incorporate to obtain the benefits of favorable tax treatment or limited liability but ignorant of all other differences between corporate and partnership law. There is no support for this assumption once you realize that people have to jump through a lot of formal hoops (assisted by counsel) to incorporate but could become partners by accident.

The right inquiry is always what the parties would have contracted for had transaction[ ] costs been zero, not whether closely held corporations are more similar to partnerships than to publicly held corporations. The failure to recognize the limited role of analogical reasoning can have significant consequences. The court that decided *Donahue* was apparently so concerned about establishing the similarities between closely held corporations and partnerships that it never considered the possibility that its rule of equal opportunity might be inconsistent with the observed behavior of participants in both partnerships and closely held corporations. Both types of firms must provide some mechanism for dealing with retirements or terminations in situations where the firm will continue to exist. Most firms could not survive if the purchase of the interest of a retiring member required that everyone else be given the opportunity to sell out at the same price. Because the court never asked what the parties would have intended, it missed the boat.

Participants in business ventures are free to reflect their wishes explicitly in a written contract. Both partnership and corporate law enforce private decisions. When the parties do not or cannot contract explicitly, it will often be difficult to discern what they would have done if contracting were costless. This subtle inquiry is not made any simpler by asking whether closely held corporations are really partnerships. This latter focus simply puts everyone off the scent; indeed, it may be perverse because it directs attention away from the questions of why people formed the corporation and why, having done so, they did not adopt partnership-like rules by contract. Even if the parties did not consciously decide to opt out of the partnership rule, all this means is that they were asleep. What reason have we to think that if they were awake they would have selected the partnership rule?

One reason might be tax. Sometimes people pick the corporate form solely because of its tax consequences. This is not, however, a problem of drowsy investors. Whether they select the corporate form for tax reasons or for any others, the investors want to operate under the rules that maximize the expected return from the business venture. Investors who are aware of the tax consequences of the form they select are likely to be aware of other consequences; as we have emphasized, they commonly hire expert advice. A claim that people alert to the tax effects of incorporation were unaware of other effects is hard to take seriously, and when such people do not contract for the use of partnership-like rules, it is appropriate to apply corporate rules.

NOTES

(1) Why does the *Donahue* court feel that special rules are needed for shareholders in closely held corporations? Would Euphemia Donahue have

prevailed under traditional corporate law principles? In thinking about these questions, you may wish to consider the problem below.

(2) What special protection does the *Donahue* court provide to shareholders in closely held corporations?

(3) As part of its holding, the *Donahue* court analogizes a closely held corporation to a partnership. Does the partnership analogy make sense? Are the same reasons for imposing a fiduciary duty in the partnership context present in the closely held corporation setting?

(4) Is *Donahue*'s "equal opportunity" rule a good one? Did Joseph Donahue stand in the same position as Harry Rodd such that equal treatment might be warranted?

(5) Does the equal opportunity rule apply only in the context of a corporation purchasing the shares of a controlling shareholder (or a member of the controlling group of shareholders), or does the court intend for the rule to have a broader application?

(6) Courts outside of Massachusetts have also imposed a fiduciary duty between shareholders in closely held corporations. *See, e.g.*, Orchard v. Covelli, 590 F. Supp. 1548, 1556–59 (W.D. Pa. 1984); W & W Equip. Co. v. Mink, 568 N.E.2d 564, 574 (Ind. Ct. App. 1991); Evans v. Blesi, 345 N.W.2d 775, 779 (Minn. Ct. App. 1984); Fought v. Morris, 543 So. 2d 167, 170–71 (Miss. 1989); Daniels v. Thomas, Dean & Hoskins, Inc., 804 P.2d 359, 366 (Mont. 1990); Crosby v. Beam, 548 N.E.2d 217, 220 (Ohio 1989); A. Teixeira & Co. v. Teixeira, 699 A.2d 1383, 1386–87 (R.I. 1997). Most courts, however, reject the equal opportunity rule. *See, e.g.*, Toner v. Baltimore Envelope Co., 498 A.2d 642, 647–54 (Md. 1985); Delahoussaye v. Newhard, 785 S.W.2d 609, 611–12 (Mo. Ct. App. 1990). *But see* Jones v. H.F. Ahmanson & Co., 460 P.2d 464, 474–76 (Cal. 1969) (holding that majority shareholders breached their fiduciary duty by creating a market for their stock that was not made available to the minority investors).

PROBLEM

Four friends (Able, Baker, Carter, and Dee) quit their prior jobs and start ABCD, Inc., a closely held corporation. Each contributes $50,000 in capital and receives 25% of the company's shares. Each serves as an employee, officer, and director of the company. No dividends are paid, but each shareholder receives a salary and an annual bonus. After dissension arises between the investors, Able, Baker, and Carter vote (as directors) to terminate Dee's employment position as well as his officer status. Able, Baker, and Carter then vote (as shareholders) to remove Dee as a director of the company. Assume that Able, Baker, and Carter assert that their actions are necessary because of a need to trim expenses and a desire to improve the company's decision-making speed.

Dee sues Able, Baker, and Carter for breach of fiduciary duty under traditional corporate law principles. Is Dee likely to prevail?

NOTE ON EMPLOYMENT, MANAGEMENT, AND DIVIDEND EXPECTATIONS IN CLOSELY HELD CORPORATIONS

As the *Donahue* court described, oppressive conduct often involves interference with a minority shareholder's employment, management, and/or dividend expectations. Why are these expectations so important to a minority shareholder in a closely held corporation? Regarding employment, one commentator has stated the following:

> * * * In a closely held corporation, a shareholder-employee has interests in his job and stock that are often economically intertwined. Holding stock in a closely held corporation, viewed purely as an investment decision, seems almost irrational from an economic perspective. Small businesses are exceedingly risky enterprises with high failure rates. To compensate fairly for this level of risk, the expected return would also have to be disproportionately large. Moreover, many investors in small businesses invest a significant portion of their life savings in the business. This practice defeats their ability to diversify their investment portfolios and exposes them to company- and industry-specific risk. As a result, investors in closely held corporations would seem well advised to trust their capital to diversified mutual funds rather than a small corporation.

> If investors in closely held corporations are economically rational, it can only be because such investments have compensating benefits not available to investors in publicly held corporations. In many cases, a shareholder in a closely held corporation expects to receive such compensating benefits through employment. The shareholder may invest for the purpose of having a job that produces higher compensation than could be garnered through employment by third parties. Even if the employee-shareholder's compensation is no higher than his next best alternative, an investment in a closely held corporation may still be justified because the ability to keep his job may be more stable and certain. Additionally, the employee may simply derive satisfaction from working in a business that he himself takes a substantial part in managing.

> * * *

> Thus, a shareholder in a closely held corporation often has a significant investment interest in his job. He often invests for the purpose of having a job, and the salary and other benefits he receives are conceived to be part of the return on his investment. * * * After discharge, the minority is relegated to the corporation's expected returns to justify the risk of its investment capital. As discussed above, these returns are unlikely to be satisfactory on their own.

Robert A. Ragazzo, *Toward a Delaware Common Law of Closely Held Corporations*, 77 WASH. U. L.Q. 1099, 1109–10 (1999). Similarly, Professor Moll has observed:

> * * * [T]he procurement of close corporation employment, in and of itself, is often a reason for investing in a close corporation. * * * Indeed, the value of a particular close corporation job takes many forms. For example, because salaries are generally permissible from a tax standpoint if they are "reasonable" in amount, and because "reasonableness" is often viewed as a range, there is value associated with the ability to set a reasonable salary at the higher end of the range. As owners of a small company, shareholder-employees are typically able to set their own salaries for the labor they provide to the close corporation. As a consequence, it is likely that such salaries are pegged to the higher end of the range of reasonable compensation for that type of work. If salaries are bargained for, as in the case of the traditional employee, the compensation paid may be lower in the range, especially when the employee lacks leverage.
>
> In addition, as an owner of the close corporation, a shareholder-employee can typically arrange with the other owners to be named to an officer or other high-level management position. The certainty associated with the ability to name oneself to a high-level position has value, as the traditional employee usually has no direct control over whether he will be chosen for a particular position or over whether he will be hired by the business at all. * * * This ability to insure selection is valuable, especially because a high-level position is generally associated with greater salary and prestige.
>
> Finally, and relatedly, a close corporation may be founded by individuals who desire to work for themselves. Indeed, founding shareholder-employees may have left junior positions in more stable and established companies for the opportunity to run their own business and to serve as their own bosses. A close corporation position, therefore, may carry the intangible value of "being your own boss"—a value that is not present in many other employment contexts.
>
> Because close corporation employment provides these additional aspects of value, the retention of a particular close corporation job may be a vital component of a shareholder-employee's return on investment. The loss of a job, therefore, may eliminate a unique employment position that was fundamental to the shareholder-employee's decision to commit capital to the venture.

Douglas K. Moll, *Shareholder Oppression v. Employment at Will in the Close Corporation: The Investment Model Solution*, 1999 U. ILL. L. REV. 517, 548–50 (1999).

A minority shareholder's expectation of a role in management is also important to her decision to invest in a closely held corporation. Because of the absence of a market exit, a shareholder in a closely held corporation has a greater incentive to participate actively in a company's decisions in order to safeguard her investment. As Professor Moll explains:

> * * * [I]nvestors are also motivated to commit capital to a close corporation because of their desire for management participation as a director or officer of the company. Aside from the prestige and other intangibles associated with holding a director or officer position, a management role also presents an opportunity to effectively monitor the shareholder's investment.
>
> Within a close corporation, such a monitoring ability is vitally important. After all, close corporation shareholders often invest a substantial portion of their life savings in the company and, as a consequence, they need some way of protecting their investment. Unfortunately, a mere shareholder has no say in routine corporate decisionmaking. * * * Because management has the ability to make corporate decisions and has access to corporate information, however, a management role provides a direct opportunity for a shareholder to effectively participate in and monitor the company's activities. Ideally, such an opportunity allows the shareholder to try and steer the business away from investment-threatening decisions.
>
> Because of the importance of a monitoring ability in a close corporation, shareholders in such ventures expect that their investments entitle them to an active management role in the company. * * *

Douglas K. Moll, *Reasonable Expectations v. Implied-in-Fact Contracts: Is the Shareholder Oppression Doctrine Needed?*, 42 B.C. L. REV. 989, 1015–16 (2001).

Finally, with respect to the expectation of dividends, Professor Moll has written the following:

> In a public corporation, one could argue that dividend decisions do not significantly affect the value of an investor's stockholdings. After all, economic theory suggests that any decision to retain earnings within the company rather than to pay dividends will have a positive effect on the overall value of the firm—an effect which translates into an increase in the value of the company's shares. Assuming that retained funds are reinvested at the firm's cost of capital, the theory suggests that a minority shareholder of a public corporation is largely indifferent as to whether dividends are declared or not (ignoring taxes and transaction costs). If a dividend of one dollar per share is paid, a minority shareholder is enriched by one dollar per share. If that same amount is instead retained in the company, the company's value increases by one dollar per share and, correspondingly, the value of the minority's stock increases by

one dollar per share. By selling the stock, the minority can capture that increase in value. The minority's wealth, in other words, increases by one dollar per share regardless of whether a payout or reinvestment decision is made, as the dollar takes the form of either a cash dividend or of stock appreciation.

In the close corporation, of course, this theory of "dividend irrelevance" is harder to accept, as there is no liquid market that allows for the realization of capital appreciation. When funds are retained and reinvested in the company rather than paid out as dividends, the minority has little ability to capture the increased value of its shares * * *. For the minority shareholder to receive a return on investment, therefore, dividends are needed, as capital appreciation is difficult (if not impossible) to realize.

Douglas K. Moll, *Shareholder Oppression & Dividend Policy in the Close Corporation*, 60 WASH. & LEE L. REV. 841, 858–60 (2003).

WILKES V. SPRINGSIDE NURSING HOME, INC.
Supreme Judicial Court of Massachusetts, 1976.
353 N.E.2d 657.

HENNESSEY, CHIEF JUSTICE.

On August 5, 1971, the plaintiff (Wilkes) filed a bill in equity for declaratory judgment in the Probate Court for Berkshire County, naming as defendants T. Edward Quinn (Quinn), Leon L. Riche (Riche), the First Agricultural National Bank of Berkshire County and Frank Sutherland MacShane as executors under the will of Lawrence R. Connor (Connor), and the Springside Nursing Home, Inc. (Springside or the corporation). Wilkes alleged that he, Quinn, Riche and Dr. Hubert A. Pipkin (Pipkin)[4] entered into a partnership agreement in 1951, prior to the incorporation of Springside, which agreement was breached in 1967 when Wilkes's salary was terminated and he was voted out as an officer and director of the corporation. Wilkes sought, among other forms of relief, damages in the amount of the salary he would have received had he continued as a director and officer of Springside subsequent to March, 1967.

A judge of the Probate Court referred the suit to a master, who, after a lengthy hearing, issued his final report in late 1973. Wilkes's objections to the master's report were overruled after a hearing, and the master's report was confirmed in late 1974. A judgment was entered dismissing Wilkes's action on the merits. We granted direct appellate review. Mass.R.A.P. 11, 365 Mass. ___ (1974). On appeal, Wilkes argued in the alternative that (1) he should recover damages for breach of the alleged partnership agreement; and (2) he should recover damages because the defendants, as majority stockholders in Springside, breached their

---

[4] Dr. Pipkin transferred his interest in Springside to Connor in 1959 and is not a defendant in this action.

fiduciary duty to him as a minority stockholder by their action in February and March, 1967.

We conclude that the master's findings were warranted by the evidence and that his report was properly confirmed. However, we reverse so much of the judgment as dismisses Wilkes's complaint and order the entry of a judgment substantially granting the relief sought by Wilkes under the second alternative set forth above.

A summary of the pertinent facts as found by the master is set out in the following pages. It will be seen that, although the issue whether there was a breach of the fiduciary duty owed to Wilkes by the majority stockholders in Springside was not considered by the master, the master's report and the designated portions of the transcript of the evidence before him supply us with a sufficient basis for our conclusion.

In 1951 Wilkes acquired an option to purchase a building and lot located on the corner of Springside Avenue and North Street in Pittsfield, Massachusetts, the building having previously housed the Hillcrest Hospital. Though Wilkes was principally engaged in the roofing and siding business, he had gained a reputation locally for profitable dealings in real estate. Riche, an acquaintance of Wilkes, learned of the option, and interested Quinn (who was known to Wilkes through membership on the draft board in Pittsfield) and Pipkin (an acquaintance of both Wilkes and Riche) in joining Wilkes in his investment. The four men met and decided to participate jointly in the purchase of the building and lot as a real estate investment which, they believed, had good profit potential on resale or rental.

The parties later determined that the property would have its greatest potential for profit if it were operated by them as a nursing home. Wilkes consulted his attorney, who advised him that if the four men were to operate the contemplated nursing home as planned, they would be partners and would be liable for any debts incurred by the partnership and by each other. On the attorney's suggestion, and after consultation among themselves, ownership of the property was vested in Springside, a corporation organized under Massachusetts law.

Each of the four men invested $1,000 and subscribed to ten shares of $100 par value stock in Springside.[6] At the time of incorporation it was understood by all of the parties that each would be a director of Springside and each would participate actively in the management and decision making involved in operating the corporation.[7] It was, further,

---

[6] On May 2, 1955, and again on December 23, 1958, each of the four original investors paid for and was issued additional shares of $100 par value stock, eventually bringing the total number of shares owned by each to 115.

[7] Wilkes testified before the master that, when the corporate officers were elected, all four men "were * * * guaranteed directorships." Riche's understanding of the parties' intentions was that they all wanted to play a part in the management of the corporation and wanted to have

the understanding and intention of all the parties that, corporate resources permitting, each would receive money from the corporation in equal amounts as long as each assumed an active and ongoing responsibility for carrying a portion of the burdens necessary to operate the business.

The work involved in establishing and operating a nursing home was roughly apportioned, and each of the four men undertook his respective tasks.[8] Initially, Riche was elected president of Springside, Wilkes was elected treasurer, and Quinn was elected clerk.[9] Each of the four was listed in the articles of organization as a director of the corporation.

At some time in 1952, it became apparent that the operational income and cash flow from the business were sufficient to permit the four stockholders to draw money from the corporation on a regular basis. Each of the four original parties initially received $35 a week from the corporation. As time went on the weekly return to each was increased until, in 1955, it totalled $100.

In 1959, after a long illness, Pipkin sold his shares in the corporation to Connor, who was known to Wilkes, Riche and Quinn through past transactions with Springside in his capacity as president of the First Agricultural National Bank of Berkshire County. Connor received a weekly stipend from the corporation equal to that received by Wilkes, Riche and Quinn. He was elected a director of the corporation but never held any other office. He was assigned no specific area of responsibility in the operation of the nursing home but did participate in business discussions and decisions as a director and served additionally as financial adviser to the corporation.

In 1965 the stockholders decided to sell a portion of the corporate property to Quinn who, in addition to being a stockholder in Springside, possessed an interest in another corporation which desired to operate a rest home on the property. Wilkes was successful in prevailing on the other stockholders of Springside to procure a higher sale price for the property than Quinn apparently anticipated paying or desired to pay. After the sale was consummated, the relationship between Quinn and Wilkes began to deteriorate.

---

some "say" in the risks involved; that, to this end, they all would be directors; and that "unless you (were) a director and officer you could not participate in the decisions of (the) enterprise."

[8] Wilkes took charge of the repair, upkeep and maintenance of the physical plant and grounds; Riche assumed supervision over the kitchen facilities and dietary and food aspects of the home; Pipkin was to make himself available if and when medical problems arose; and Quinn dealt with the personnel and administrative aspects of the nursing home, serving informally as a managing director. Quinn further coordinated the activities of the other parties and served as a communication link among them when matters had to be discussed and decisions had to be made without a formal meeting.

[9] Riche held the office of president from 1951 to 1963; Quinn served as president from 1963 on, as clerk from 1951 to 1967, and as treasurer from 1967 on; Wilkes was treasurer from 1951 to 1967.

The bad blood between Quinn and Wilkes affected the attitudes of both Riche and Connor. As a consequence of the strained relations among the parties, Wilkes, in January of 1967, gave notice of his intention to sell his shares for an amount based on an appraisal of their value. In February of 1967 a directors' meeting was held and the board exercised its right to establish the salaries of its officers and employees.[10] A schedule of payments was established whereby Quinn was to receive a substantial weekly increase and Riche and Connor were to continue receiving $100 a week. Wilkes, however, was left off the list of those to whom a salary was to be paid. The directors also set the annual meeting of the stockholders for March, 1967.

At the annual meeting in March, Wilkes was not reelected as a director, nor was he reelected as an officer of the corporation. He was further informed that neither his services nor his presence at the nursing home was wanted by his associates.

The meetings of the directors and stockholders in early 1967, the master found, were used as a vehicle to force Wilkes out of active participation in the management and operation of the corporation and to cut off all corporate payments to him. Though the board of directors had the power to dismiss any officers or employees for misconduct or neglect of duties, there was no indication in the minutes of the board of directors' meeting of February, 1967, that the failure to establish a salary for Wilkes was based on either ground. The severance of Wilkes from the payroll resulted not from misconduct or neglect of duties, but because of the personal desire of Quinn, Riche and Connor to prevent him from continuing to receive money from the corporation. Despite a continuing deterioration in his personal relationship with his associates, Wilkes had consistently endeavored to carry on his responsibilities to the corporation in the same satisfactory manner and with the same degree of competence he had previously shown. Wilkes was at all times willing to carry on his responsibilities and participation if permitted so to do and provided that he receive his weekly stipend.

1. We turn to Wilkes's claim for damages based on a breach of the fiduciary duty owed to him by the other participants in this venture. In light of the theory underlying this claim, we do not consider it vital to our approach to this case whether the claim is governed by partnership law or the law applicable to business corporations. This is so because, as all the parties agree, Springside was at all times relevant to this action, a close corporation as we have recently defined such an entity in *Donahue v.*

---

[10] The by-laws of the corporation provided that the directors, subject to the approval of the stockholders, had the power to fix the salaries of all officers and employees. This power, however, up until February, 1967, had not been exercised formally; all payments made to the four participants in the venture had resulted from the informal but unanimous approval of all the parties concerned.

Rodd Electrotype Co. of New England, Inc., ___ Mass. ___, ___–___, 328 N.E.2d 505 (1975).

In *Donahue*, we held that "stockholders in the close corporation owe one another substantially the same fiduciary duty in the operation of the enterprise that partners owe to one another." As determined in previous decisions of this court, the standard of duty owed by partners to one another is one of "utmost good faith and loyalty." Thus, we concluded in Donahue, with regard to "their actions relative to the operations of the enterprise and the effects of that operation on the rights and investments of other stockholders," "[s]tockholders in close corporations must discharge their management and stockholder responsibilities in conformity with this strict good faith standard. They may not act out of avarice, expediency or self-interest in derogation of their duty of loyalty to the other stockholders and to the corporation."

In the *Donahue* case we recognized that one peculiar aspect of close corporations was the opportunity afforded to majority stockholders to oppress, disadvantage or "freeze out" minority stockholders. In *Donahue* itself, for example, the majority refused the minority an equal opportunity to sell a ratable number of shares to the corporation at the same price available to the majority. The net result of this refusal, we said, was that the minority could be forced to "sell out at less than fair value," since there is by definition no ready market for minority stock in a close corporation.

"Freeze outs," however, may be accomplished by the use of other devices. One such device which has proved to be particularly effective in accomplishing the purpose of the majority is to deprive minority stockholders of corporate offices and of employment with the corporation. This "freeze-out" technique has been successful because courts fairly consistently have been disinclined to interfere in those facets of internal corporate operations, such as the selection and retention or dismissal of officers, directors and employees, which essentially involve management decisions subject to the principle of majority control. As one authoritative source has said, "[M]any courts apparently feel that there is a legitimate sphere in which the controlling (directors or) shareholders can act in their own interest even if the minority suffers." F. H. O'Neal, ["Squeeze-Outs" of Minority Shareholders,] at 59 [(1975)] (footnote omitted).

The denial of employment to the minority at the hands of the majority is especially pernicious in some instances. A guaranty of employment with the corporation may have been one of the "basic reason[s] why a minority owner has invested capital in the firm." The minority stockholder typically depends on his salary as the principal return on his investment, since the "earnings of a close corporation * * * are distributed in major part in salaries, bonuses and retirement benefits."[13] Other noneconomic interests of the minority stockholder are likewise injuriously affected by barring him from corporate office. Such action severely restricts his participation in the management of the enterprise, and he is relegated to enjoying those benefits incident to his status as a stockholder. In sum, by terminating a minority stockholder's employment or by severing him from a position as an officer or director, the majority effectively frustrate the minority stockholder's purposes in entering on the corporate venture and also deny him an equal return on his investment.

The *Donahue* decision acknowledged, as a "natural outgrowth" of the case law of this Commonwealth, a strict obligation on the part of majority stockholders in a close corporation to deal with the minority with the utmost good faith and loyalty. On its face, this strict standard is applicable in the instant case. The distinction between the majority action in *Donahue* and the majority action in this case is more one of form than of substance. Nevertheless, we are concerned that untempered application of the strict good faith standard enunciated in *Donahue* to cases such as the one before us will result in the imposition of limitations on legitimate action by the controlling group in a close corporation which will unduly hamper its effectiveness in managing the corporation in the best interests of all concerned. The majority, concededly, have certain rights to what has been termed "selfish ownership" in the corporation which should be balanced against the concept of their fiduciary obligation to the minority.

Therefore, when minority stockholders in a close corporation bring suit against the majority alleging a breach of the strict good faith duty owed to them by the majority, we must carefully analyze the action taken by the controlling stockholders in the individual case. It must be asked whether the controlling group can demonstrate a legitimate business purpose for its action. In asking this question, we acknowledge the fact that the controlling group in a close corporation must have some room to maneuver in establishing the business policy of the corporation. It must have a large measure of discretion, for example, in declaring or withholding dividends, deciding whether to merge or consolidate, establishing the salaries of corporate officers, dismissing directors with or without cause, and hiring and firing corporate employees.

When an asserted business purpose for their action is advanced by the majority, however, we think it is open to minority stockholders to demonstrate that the same legitimate objective could have been achieved through an alternative course of action less harmful to the minority's interest. If called on to settle a dispute, our courts must weigh the

---

[13] We note here that the master found that Springside never declared or paid a dividend to its stockholders.

legitimate business purpose, if any, against the practicability of a less harmful alternative.

Applying this approach to the instant case it is apparent that the majority stockholders in Springside have not shown a legitimate business purpose for severing Wilkes from the payroll of the corporation or for refusing to reelect him as a salaried officer and director. The master's subsidiary findings relating to the purpose of the meetings of the directors and stockholders in February and March, 1967, are supported by the evidence. There was no showing of misconduct on Wilkes's part as a director, officer or employee of the corporation which would lead us to approve the majority action as a legitimate response to the disruptive nature of an undesirable individual bent on injuring or destroying the corporation. On the contrary, it appears that Wilkes had always accomplished his assigned share of the duties competently, and that he had never indicated an unwillingness to continue to do so.

It is an inescapable conclusion from all the evidence that the action of the majority stockholders here was a designed "freeze out" for which no legitimate business purpose has been suggested. Furthermore, we may infer that a design to pressure Wilkes into selling his shares to the corporation at a price below their value well may have been at the heart of the majority's plan.[14]

In the context of this case, several factors bear directly on the duty owed to Wilkes by his associates. At a minimum, the duty of utmost good faith and loyalty would demand that the majority consider that their action was in disregard of a long-standing policy of the stockholders that each would be a director of the corporation and that employment with the corporation would go hand in hand with stock ownership; that Wilkes was one of the four originators of the nursing home venture; and that Wilkes, like the others, had invested his capital and time for more than fifteen years with the expectation that he would continue to participate in corporate decisions. Most important is the plain fact that the cutting off of Wilkes's salary, together with the fact that the corporation never declared a dividend, assured that Wilkes would receive no return at all from the corporation.

2. The question of Wilkes's damages at the hands of the majority has not been thoroughly explored on the record before us. Wilkes, in his original complaint, sought damages in the amount of the $100 a week he believed he was entitled to from the time his salary was terminated up until the time this action was commenced. However, the record shows that, after Wilkes was severed from the corporate payroll, the schedule of salaries and payments made to the other stockholders varied from time to

---

[14] This inference arises from the fact that Connor, acting on behalf of the three controlling stockholders, offered to purchase Wilkes's shares for a price Connor admittedly would not have accepted for his own shares.

time. In addition, the duties assumed by the other stockholders after Wilkes was deprived of his share of the corporate earnings appear to have changed in significant respects.[15] Any resolution of this question must take into account whether the corporation was dissolved during the pendency of this litigation.

Therefore our order is as follows: So much of the judgment as dismisses Wilkes's complaint and awards costs to the defendants is reversed. The case is remanded to the Probate Court for Berkshire County for further proceedings concerning the issue of damages. Thereafter a judgment shall be entered declaring that Quinn, Riche and Connor breached their fiduciary duty to Wilkes as a minority stockholder in Springside, and awarding money damages therefor. Wilkes shall be allowed to recover from Riche, the estate of T. Edward Quinn and the estate of Lawrence R. Connor, ratably, according to the inequitable enrichment of each, the salary he would have received had he remained an officer and director of Springside. In considering the issue of damages the judge on remand shall take into account the extent to which any remaining corporate funds of Springside may be diverted to satisfy Wilkes's claim.

So ordered.

FRANK H. EASTERBROOK & DANIEL R. FISCHEL, CLOSE CORPORATIONS AND AGENCY COSTS

38 Stan. L. Rev. 271, 295 (1986).

Not surprisingly, courts have found the equal opportunity rule of *Donahue* impossible to administer. It is hard to imagine, for example, how closely held corporations could function under a requirement that all shareholders have an "equal opportunity" to receive salary increases and continue in office regardless of their conduct. Yet this is the logical implication of *Donahue*, which holds that the business justifications for unequal treatment are irrelevant. In light of this threat to the day-to-day functioning of closely held corporations, it was predictable that subsequent courts would either refuse to follow *Donahue* or limit its scope.

NOTES

(1) After *Wilkes*, what is the status of the *Donahue* holding that shareholders in closely held corporations owe a fiduciary duty to one another? What is the status of the "equal opportunity" rule?

---

[15] In fairness to Wilkes, who, as the master found, was at all times ready and willing to work for the corporation, it should be noted that neither the other stockholders nor their representatives may be heard to say that Wilkes's duties were performed by them and [that] Wilkes's damages should, for that reason, be diminished.

(2) Why is it relevant to the *Wilkes* court that there was "a long-standing policy of the stockholders that each would be a director of the corporation and that employment with the corporation would go hand and hand with stock ownership?" Why is it relevant that "Wilkes was one of the four originators of the nursing home venture?" In answering these questions, consider the following:

> * * * [T]he defendants argue * * * that a fiduciary duty does not arise absent evidence of a nexus between the plaintiff's investment of capital and his employment in the corporation. No doubt a nexus must be made out in cases such as the one before us. * * * The required nexus may fall short of an enforceable contract, but that does not matter. All that is required is the express, or reasonably understood, coupling of continuing employment with the employee's investment in the equity securities of the corporation where there is no active trading market for those securities. * * *

Merola v. Exergen Corp., 648 N.E.2d 1301, 1304–05 (Mass. App. Ct. 1995).

(3) What is a legitimate business purpose? Assume that Wilkes' employment was terminated under three different scenarios: (a) Wilkes was stealing from the company; (b) Wilkes and the controlling group developed an acrimonious relationship and could no longer work together; and (c) an economic recession required the firm to cut expenses. Which do you think would satisfy the legitimate business purpose standard? *Cf.* A.W. Chesterton Co. v. Chesterton, 128 F.3d 1, 7 (1st Cir. 1997) ("The Massachusetts cases make clear that a 'legitimate business purpose' must be a legitimate purpose *for the corporation*, not for the defendant shareholder.").

(4) The *Wilkes* court states that "[w]hen an asserted business purpose for their action is advanced by the majority * * * we think it is open to minority stockholders to demonstrate that the same legitimate objective could have been achieved through an alternative course of action less harmful to the minority's interest." What is meant by an "alternative course of action less harmful to the minority's interest?" Can you suggest some alternative courses of action less harmful to the minority's interest that would help Wilkes in the scenarios listed in the prior note?

(5) Why are the actions of the controlling group in *Wilkes* not protected by the business judgment rule? How does the *Wilkes* framework differ from the business judgment rule?

(6) Some courts have explicitly acknowledged that majority shareholder decisions in closely held corporations require more judicial scrutiny than conventional business judgment rule deference. *See, e.g.*, Fox v. 7L Bar Ranch Co., 645 P.2d 929, 935 (Mont. 1982) ("When it is also considered that in close corporations dividend withholding may be used by controlling shareholders to force out minority shareholders, the traditional judicial restraint in interfering with corporate dividend policy cannot be justified." (internal quotation omitted)); Exadaktilos v. Cinnaminson Realty Co., 400 A.2d 554, 561 (N.J. Super. Ct. Law Div. 1979) ("[T]he statutory language embodies a

legislative determination that freeze-out maneuvers in close corporations constitute an abuse of corporate power. Traditional principles of corporate law, such as the business judgment rule, have failed to curb this abuse. Consequently, actions of close corporations that conform with these principles cannot be immune from scrutiny.").

PROBLEM

Return to the facts of *Donahue v. Rodd Electrotype Co.* Does the *Wilkes* framework change the result in *Donahue*? As part of your analysis, consider the following:

> * * * Buy-out arrangements on contingencies such as retirement are common in closely held corporations. Such agreements provide some liquidity and ensure that the identity of the managers and the investors remains the same, reducing agency problems. * * *

> The terms of the purchase in *Donahue* were not extraordinary. The trial court found them fair. The purchase appears to have been nothing more than an attempt to facilitate the retirement of a manager who, by virtue of advancing age and poor health, could no longer contribute. The firm doubtless was the better for his retirement. * * *

Frank H. Easterbrook & Daniel R. Fischel, *Close Corporations and Agency Costs*, 38 STAN. L. REV. 271, 294–95 (1986).

MEROLA V. EXERGEN CORP.
Supreme Judicial Court of Massachusetts, 1996.
668 N.E.2d 351.

LYNCH, JUSTICE.

The plaintiff, a former vice president of Exergen Corporation (Exergen) and a former minority stockholder of that corporation, brought suit in the Superior Court against Exergen and the president and majority stockholder, Francesco Pompei, because of his termination as an officer and employee of Exergen. * * * [C]ount III (breach of fiduciary duty) alleged that the corporation was a "close corporation," and that Pompei, as the majority stockholder, violated his fiduciary obligations to the plaintiff as a minority stockholder by terminating his employment without cause.

* * *

[The trial] judge found that the corporation was a "close corporation" and that Pompei had breached his fiduciary obligations to the plaintiff by failing to give him an opportunity to become a major stockholder and by terminating his employment. She adopted the jury's advisory conclusion that he had been damaged only by the termination of employment to the extent of $50,000.

The Appeals Court affirmed the judgment as to Pompei * * *. We granted the defendants' application for further appellate review and now reverse the judgment of the Superior Court.

We summarize the facts found by the judge. Exergen was formed in May, 1980, as a corporation in the business of developing and selling infrared heat detection devices. From Exergen's inception to the date of trial, Pompei, the founder, was the majority shareholder in the corporation, as well as its president, owning over sixty per cent of the shares issued. At all relevant times, Pompei actively participated in and controlled the management of Exergen and, as the majority shareholder, had power to elect and change Exergen's board of directors.

The plaintiff began working for Exergen on a part-time basis in late 1980 while he was also employed full time by Analogic Corporation. In the course of conversations with Pompei in late 1981, and early 1982, the plaintiff was offered full-time employment with Exergen, and he understood that, if he came to work there and invested in Exergen stock, he would have the opportunity to become a major shareholder of Exergen and for continuing employment with Exergen.

As of March 1, 1982, the plaintiff resigned from Analogic and began working full time for Exergen. He also then began purchasing shares in Exergen when the company made periodic offerings to its employees. From March, 1982, through June, 1982, the plaintiff purchased 4,100 shares at $2.25 per share, for a total of $9,225. Exergen announced at the Exergen shareholders meeting in September, 1982, another option program to purchase shares at $5 per share within one year. By late 1983, the plaintiff had exercised his option to purchase an additional 1,200 shares. The plaintiff was not offered additional stock options after late 1983.

* * *

With regard to the alleged breach of fiduciary duty for terminating the plaintiff's employment with Exergen, the judge adopted the following findings by the jury: (1) the plaintiff was terminated by Pompei on April 16, 1987, and therefore did not receive continuing employment by Exergen; (2) there was no legitimate business purpose for not continuing the plaintiff's employment by Exergen; and (3) the plaintiff suffered damages in lost wages, reduced by income from other employment, in the total amount of $50,000. * * *

* * * Based on these findings, the judge ruled that, as [a] matter of law, Pompei breached a fiduciary duty to the plaintiff to honor the reasonable expectations that the plaintiff had concerning investments of

time and resources in Exergen, and awarded the plaintiff $50,000 in damages.

Breach of fiduciary duty. In *Donahue v. Rodd Electrotype Co.,* 367 Mass. 578, 593, 328 N.E.2d 505 (1975), this court recognized a fiduciary duty by a majority shareholder of "utmost good faith and loyalty" toward shareholders of a close corporation. A claim based on this duty is an equitable claim against individual stockholders. The determination whether a breach of this fiduciary duty has occurred is a matter of law for the court, as is the remedy for such breach.

We agree with the judge's conclusion that Exergen was a close corporation, and that stockholders in a close corporation owe one another a fiduciary duty of "utmost good faith and loyalty." *Donahue v. Rodd Electrotype Co., supra* at 593, 328 N.E.2d 505. We, therefore, look to see whether the plaintiff has established a breach of that duty under the principles of *Donahue.* Even in close corporations, the majority interest "must have a large measure of discretion, for example, in declaring or withholding dividends, deciding whether to merge or consolidate, establishing the salaries of corporate officers, dismissing directors with or without cause, and hiring and firing corporate employees." *Wilkes v. Springside Nursing Home, Inc.,* 370 Mass. 842, 851, 353 N.E.2d 657 (1976).

Principles of employment law permit the termination of employees at will, with or without cause excepting situations within a narrow public policy exception. However, the termination of a minority shareholder's employment may present a situation where the majority interest has breached its fiduciary duty to the minority interest. [In *Wilkes,*] the court concluded that the majority stockholders had attempted unfairly to "freeze out" a minority stockholder by terminating his employment, in part because their policy and practice was to divide the available resources of the corporation equally by way of salaries to the shareholders who all participated in the operation of the enterprise. As the investment became more profitable, the salaries were increased. The court recognized that "[t]he minority stockholder typically depends on his salary as the principal return on his investment, since the 'earnings of a close corporation * * * are distributed in major part in salaries, bonuses and retirement benefits.'" Given those facts, this court concluded that the other shareholders did not show a legitimate business purpose for terminating the minority stockholder and that the other parties acted "in disregard of a long-standing policy of the stockholders that each would be a director of the corporation and that employment with the corporation would go hand in hand with stock ownership."

Here, although the plaintiff invested in the stock of Exergen with the reasonable expectation of continued employment, there was no general policy regarding stock ownership and employment, and there was no evidence that any other stockholders had expectations of continuing employment because they purchased stock. The investment in the stock was an investment in the equity of the corporation which was not tied to employment in any formal way. The plaintiff acknowledged that he could have purchased 5,000 shares of stock while he was working part time before resigning from his position at Analogic Corporation and accepting full-time employment at Exergen. He testified that he was induced to work for Exergen with the promise that he could become a major stockholder. There was no testimony that he was ever required to buy stock as a condition of employment.

Unlike the *Wilkes* case, there was no evidence that the corporation distributed all profits to shareholders in the form of salaries. On the contrary, the perceived value of the stock increased during the time that the plaintiff was employed. The plaintiff first purchased his stock at $2.25 per share and, one year later, he purchased more for $5 per share. This indicated that there was some increase in value to the investment independent of the employment expectation. Neither was the plaintiff a founder of the business, his stock purchases were made after the business was established, and there was no suggestion that he had to purchase stock to keep his job.

The plaintiff testified that, when he sold his stock back to the corporation in 1991, he was paid $17 per share. This was a price that had been paid to other shareholders who sold their shares to the corporation at a previous date, and it is a price which, after consulting with his attorney, he concluded was a fair price. With this payment, the plaintiff realized a significant return on his capital investment independent of the salary he received as an employee.

We conclude that this is not a situation where the majority shareholder breached his fiduciary duty to a minority shareholder. "[T]he controlling group in a close corporation must have some room to maneuver in establishing the business policy of the corporation." *Wilkes v. Springside Nursing Home, Inc., supra* at 851, 353 N.E.2d 657. Although there was no legitimate business purpose for the termination of the plaintiff, neither was the termination for the financial gain of Pompei or contrary to established public policy. Not every discharge of an at-will employee of a close corporation who happens to own stock in the corporation gives rise to a successful breach of fiduciary duty claim. The plaintiff was terminated in accordance with his employment contract and fairly compensated for his stock. He failed to establish a sufficient basis for a breach of fiduciary duty claim under the principles of *Donahue v. Rodd Electrotype Co., supra*.

* * *

Judgment reversed.

NOTES

(1) In *Wilkes*, the plaintiff's employment is terminated and no legitimate business purpose is established. A breach of fiduciary duty is found. In *Merola*, the plaintiff's employment is terminated and no legitimate business purpose is established. A breach of fiduciary duty is not found. Same court, different result. Why?

(2) In general, the employment at will doctrine provides that "an employee without a contract for a fixed term [can] be fired for any reason or for no reason at all." 2 MARK A. ROTHSTEIN ET AL., EMPLOYMENT LAW § 8.1, at 226 (2d ed. 1999). The doctrine is based on the notion that employers need unimpeded flexibility to manage their workforces and to remain competitive. Over time, however, exceptions to the at-will doctrine have developed. Those exceptions can be broadly characterized as follows: "(1) breach of an express or implied promise, including representations made in employee handbooks; (2) discharge in violation of public policy; and (3) breach of the implied covenant of good faith and fair dealing." *Id.* at 227.

(3) On the relationship between oppressive majority conduct and the employment at will doctrine, Professor Moll has written the following:

> * * * [T]he proper scope of employment at will is limited to discharge-related harms suffered in an *employee* capacity. There is room, therefore, for a conception of oppression as a close corporation doctrine that focuses upon harms, whether from discharge or otherwise, suffered in a *shareholder* capacity. When harms from termination have occurred, the at-will doctrine refuses to recognize an *employment* interest in the job. The recognition of a potential *investment* interest in the job, however, is a different issue that falls outside of the legitimate coverage of the at-will rule.

> Put differently * * * oppression should be viewed as a doctrine that protects the fair value of a close corporation shareholder's investment. To the extent that employment in a close corporation may be a component of that investment, the investment model of oppression may indirectly protect the job as well. But this corporate law protection of employment should only be present when a job is proven to be part of a shareholder-employee's investment * * *.

Douglas K. Moll, *Shareholder Oppression v. Employment at Will in the Close Corporation: The Investment Model Solution*, 1999 U. ILL. L. REV. 517, 520–21.

(4) Although most oppression disputes involve a challenge to the conduct of a controlling shareholder or controlling group, the courts have also entertained claims of oppression against minority shareholders when their conduct is objectionable. Such claims typically arise when a minority shareholder possesses control in some manner, such as through a supermajority provision, over some critical issue affecting the corporation. *See, e.g.*, A.W. Chesterton Co. v. Chesterton, 128 F.3d 1, 3, 6 (1st Cir. 1997)

(concluding that a minority shareholder breached his fiduciary duty by threatening to transfer his shares in a manner that would have destroyed the S-corporation status of the company); Smith v. Atlantic Props., 422 N.E.2d 798, 799–800, 802–03 (Mass. App. Ct. 1981) (stating that a 25% minority shareholder became "an ad hoc controlling interest" as a result of an 80% supermajority provision, and finding that he breached a fiduciary duty to his fellow shareholders by refusing to vote for the declaration of dividends); *see also* Bonavita v. Corbo, 692 A.2d 119, 123–24 (N.J. Super. Ct. Ch. Div. 1996) (noting that the oppression doctrine is about "protection from the abusive exercise of *power*," and allowing a 50% shareholder to sue the other 50% shareholder (who was also the president and chief executive officer) for oppression).

IN RE KEMP & BEATLEY, INC.

Court of Appeals of New York, 1984.
473 N.E.2d 1173.

COOKE, CHIEF JUDGE.

When the majority shareholders of a close corporation award *de facto* dividends to all shareholders except a class of minority shareholders, such a policy may constitute "oppressive actions" and serve as a basis for an order made pursuant to section 1104–a of the Business Corporation Law dissolving the corporation. In the instant matter, there is sufficient evidence to support the lower courts' conclusion that the majority shareholders had altered a long-standing policy to distribute corporate earnings on the basis of stock ownership, as against petitioners only. Moreover, the courts did not abuse their discretion by concluding that dissolution was the only means by which petitioners could gain a fair return on their investment.

I

The business concern of Kemp & Beatley, incorporated under the laws of New York, designs and manufactures table linens and sundry tabletop items. The company's stock consists of 1,500 outstanding shares held by eight shareholders. Petitioner Dissin had been employed by the company for 42 years when, in June 1979, he resigned. Prior to resignation, Dissin served as vice-president and a director of Kemp & Beatley. Over the course of his employment, Dissin had acquired stock in the company and currently owns 200 shares.

Petitioner Gardstein, like Dissin, had been a long-time employee of the company. Hired in 1944, Gardstein was for the next 35 years involved in various aspects of the business including material procurement, product design, and plant management. His employment was terminated by the company in December 1980. He currently owns 105 shares of Kemp & Beatley stock.

Apparent unhappiness surrounded petitioners' leaving the employ of the company. Of particular concern was that they no longer received any distribution of the company's earnings. Petitioners considered themselves to be "frozen out" of the company; whereas it had been their experience when with the company to receive a distribution of the company's earnings according to their stockholdings, in the form of either dividends or extra compensation, that distribution was no longer forthcoming.

Gardstein and Dissin, together holding 20.33% of the company's outstanding stock, commenced the instant proceeding in June 1981, seeking dissolution of Kemp & Beatley pursuant to section 1104–a of the Business Corporation Law. Their petition alleged "fraudulent and oppressive" conduct by the company's board of directors such as to render petitioners' stock "a virtually worthless asset." Supreme Court referred the matter for a hearing, which was held in March 1982.

Upon considering the testimony of petitioners and the principals of Kemp & Beatley, the referee concluded that "the corporate management has by its policies effectively rendered petitioners' shares worthless, and * * * the only way petitioners can expect any return is by dissolution." Petitioners were found to have invested capital in the company expecting, among other things, to receive dividends or "bonuses" based upon their stock holdings. Also found was the company's "established buy-out policy" by which it would purchase the stock of employee shareholders upon their leaving its employ.

The involuntary-dissolution statute (Business Corporation Law, § 1104–a) permits dissolution when a corporation's controlling faction is found guilty of "oppressive action" toward the complaining shareholders. The referee considered oppression to arise when "those in control" of the corporation "have acted in such a manner as to defeat those expectations of the minority stockholders which formed the basis of [their] participation in the venture." The expectations of petitioners that they would not be arbitrarily excluded from gaining a return on their investment and that their stock would be purchased by the corporation upon termination of employment, were deemed defeated by prevailing corporate policies. Dissolution was recommended in the referee's report, subject to giving respondent corporation an opportunity to purchase petitioners' stock.

Supreme Court confirmed the referee's report. It, too, concluded that due to the corporation's new dividend policy petitioners had been prevented from receiving any return on their investments. Liquidation of the corporate assets was found the only means by which petitioners would receive a fair return. The court considered judicial dissolution of a corporation to be "a serious and severe remedy." Consequently, the order of dissolution was conditioned upon the corporation's being permitted to purchase petitioners' stock. The Appellate Division affirmed, without opinion.

At issue in this appeal is the scope of section 1104–a of the Business Corporation Law. Specifically, this court must determine whether the provision for involuntary dissolution when the "directors or those in control of the corporation have been guilty of * * * oppressive actions toward the complaining shareholders" was properly applied in the circumstances of this case. We hold that it was, and therefore affirm.

II

Judicially ordered dissolution of a corporation at the behest of minority interests is a remedy of relatively recent vintage in New York. Historically, this State's courts were considered divested of equity jurisdiction to order dissolution, as statutory prescriptions were deemed exclusive. Statutes permitting judicial dissolution of corporations either limited the types of corporations under their purview or restricted the parties who could petition for dissolution to the Attorney-General, or the directors, trustees, or majority shareholders of the corporation.

Minority shareholders were granted standing in the absence of statutory authority to seek dissolution of corporations when controlling shareholders engaged in certain egregious conduct. Predicated on the majority shareholders' fiduciary obligation to treat all shareholders fairly and equally, to preserve corporate assets, and to fulfill their responsibilities of corporate management with "scrupulous good faith," the courts' equitable power can be invoked when "it appears that the directors and majority shareholders 'have so palpably breached the fiduciary duty they owe to the minority shareholders that they are disqualified from exercising the exclusive discretion and the dissolution power given to them by statute.'" (*Leibert v. Clapp,* 13 N.Y.2d, at p. 317, 247 N.Y.S.2d 102, 196 N.E.2d 540, quoting Hoffman, New Horizons for the Close Corporation, 28 Brooklyn L.Rev. 1, 14.) * * *

Supplementing this principle of judicially ordered equitable dissolution of a corporation, the Legislature has shown a special solicitude toward the rights of minority shareholders of closely held corporations by enacting section 1104–a of the Business Corporation Law. That statute provides a mechanism for the holders of at least 20% of the outstanding shares of a corporation whose stock is not traded on a securities market to petition for its dissolution "under special circumstances." The circumstances that give rise to dissolution fall into two general classifications: mistreatment of complaining shareholders, or misappropriation of corporate assets by controlling shareholders, directors or officers.

Section 1104–a (subd. [a], par. [1]) describes three types of proscribed activity: "illegal", "fraudulent", and "oppressive" conduct. The first two terms are familiar words that are commonly understood at law. The last, however, does not enjoy the same certainty gained through long usage. As no definition is provided by the statute, it falls upon the courts to provide guidance.

The statutory concept of "oppressive actions" can, perhaps, best be understood by examining the characteristics of close corporations and the Legislature's general purpose in creating this involuntary-dissolution statute. It is widely understood that, in addition to supplying capital to a contemplated or ongoing enterprise and expecting a fair and equal return, parties comprising the ownership of a close corporation may expect to be actively involved in its management and operation. The small ownership cluster seeks to "contribute their capital, skills, experience and labor" toward the corporate enterprise.

As a leading commentator in the field has observed: "Unlike the typical shareholder in a publicly held corporation, who may be simply an investor or a speculator and cares nothing for the responsibilities of management, the shareholder in a close corporation is a co-owner of the business and wants the privileges and powers that go with ownership. His participation in that particular corporation is often his principal or sole source of income. As a matter of fact, providing employment for himself may have been the principal reason why he participated in organizing the corporation. He may or may not anticipate an ultimate profit from the sale of his interest, but he normally draws very little from the corporation as dividends. In his capacity as an officer or employee of the corporation, he looks to his salary for the principal return on his capital investment, because earnings of a close corporation, as is well known, are distributed in major part in salaries, bonuses and retirement benefits." (O'Neal, Close Corporations [2d ed.], § 1.07, at pp. 21–22 [n. omitted].)

Shareholders enjoy flexibility in memorializing these expectations through agreements setting forth each party's rights and obligations in corporate governance. In the absence of such an agreement, however, ultimate decision-making power respecting corporate policy will be reposed in the holders of a majority interest in the corporation. A wielding of this power by any group controlling a corporation may serve to destroy a stockholder's vital interests and expectations.

As the stock of closely held corporations generally is not readily salable, a minority shareholder at odds with management policies may be without either a voice in protecting his or her interests or any reasonable means of withdrawing his or her investment. This predicament may fairly be considered the legislative concern underlying the provision at issue in this case; inclusion of the criteria that the corporation's stock not be traded on securities markets and that the complaining shareholder be subject to oppressive actions supports this conclusion.

Defining oppressive conduct as distinct from illegality in the present context has been considered in other forums. The question has been resolved by considering oppressive actions to refer to conduct that substantially defeats the "reasonable expectations" held by minority shareholders in committing their capital to the particular enterprise. This concept is consistent with the apparent purpose underlying the provision under review. A shareholder who reasonably expected that ownership in the corporation would entitle him or her to a job, a share of corporate earnings, a place in corporate management, or some other form of security, would be oppressed in a very real sense when others in the corporation seek to defeat those expectations and there exists no effective means of salvaging the investment.

Given the nature of close corporations and the remedial purpose of the statute, this court holds that utilizing a complaining shareholder's "reasonable expectations" as a means of identifying and measuring conduct alleged to be oppressive is appropriate. A court considering a petition alleging oppressive conduct must investigate what the majority shareholders knew, or should have known, to be the petitioner's expectations in entering the particular enterprise. Majority conduct should not be deemed oppressive simply because the petitioner's subjective hopes and desires in joining the venture are not fulfilled. Disappointment alone should not necessarily be equated with oppression.

Rather, oppression should be deemed to arise only when the majority conduct substantially defeats expectations that, objectively viewed, were both reasonable under the circumstances and were central to the petitioner's decision to join the venture. It would be inappropriate, however, for us in this case to delineate the contours of the courts' consideration in determining whether directors have been guilty of oppressive conduct. As in other areas of the law, much will depend on the circumstances in the individual case.

The appropriateness of an order of dissolution is in every case vested in the sound discretion of the court considering the application. Under the terms of this statute, courts are instructed to consider both whether "liquidation of the corporation is the only feasible means" to protect the complaining shareholder's expectation of a fair return on his or her investment and whether dissolution "is reasonably necessary" to protect "the rights or interests of any substantial number of shareholders" not limited to those complaining. Implicit in this direction is that once oppressive conduct is found, consideration must be given to the totality of circumstances surrounding the current state of corporate affairs and relations to determine whether some remedy short of or other than dissolution constitutes a feasible means of satisfying both the petitioner's expectations and the rights and interests of any other substantial group of shareholders.

By invoking the statute, a petitioner has manifested his or her belief that dissolution may be the only appropriate remedy. Assuming the petitioner has set forth a prima facie case of oppressive conduct, it should be incumbent upon the parties seeking to forestall dissolution to demonstrate to the court the existence of an adequate, alternative remedy. A court has broad latitude in fashioning alternative relief, but when fulfillment of the oppressed petitioner's expectations by these means is doubtful, such as when there has been a complete deterioration of relations between the parties, a court should not hesitate to order dissolution. Every order of dissolution, however, must be conditioned upon permitting any shareholder of the corporation to elect to purchase the complaining shareholder's stock at fair value (see Business Corporation Law, § 1118).

One further observation is in order. The purpose of this involuntary dissolution statute is to provide protection to the minority shareholder whose reasonable expectations in undertaking the venture have been frustrated and who has no adequate means of recovering his or her investment. It would be contrary to this remedial purpose to permit its use by minority shareholders as merely a coercive tool. Therefore, the minority shareholder whose own acts, made in bad faith and undertaken with a view toward forcing an involuntary dissolution, give rise to the complained-of oppression should be given no quarter in the statutory protection.

III

There was sufficient evidence presented at the hearing to support the conclusion that Kemp & Beatley had a long-standing policy of awarding *de facto* dividends based on stock ownership in the form of "extra compensation bonuses." Petitioners, both of whom had extensive experience in the management of the company, testified to this effect. Moreover, both related that receipt of this compensation, whether as true dividends or disguised as "extra compensation," was a known incident to ownership of the company's stock understood by all of the company's principals. Finally, there was uncontroverted proof that this policy was changed either shortly before or shortly after petitioners' employment ended. Extra compensation was still awarded by the company. The only difference was that stock ownership was no longer a basis for the payments; it was asserted that the basis became services rendered to the corporation. It was not unreasonable for the fact finder to have determined that this change in policy amounted to nothing less than an attempt to exclude petitioners from gaining any return on their investment through the mere recharacterization of distributions of corporate income. Under the circumstances of this case, there was no error in determining that this conduct constituted oppressive action within the meaning of section 1104–a of the Business Corporation Law.[2]

Nor may it be said that Supreme Court abused its discretion in ordering Kemp & Beatley's dissolution, subject to an opportunity for a buy-out of petitioners' shares. After the referee had found that the controlling faction of the company was, in effect, attempting to "squeeze-out" petitioners by offering them no return on their investment and increasing other executive compensation, respondents, in opposing the report's confirmation, attempted only to controvert the factual basis of the report. They suggested no feasible, alternative remedy to the forced dissolution. In light of an apparent deterioration in relations between petitioners and the governing shareholders of Kemp & Beatley, it was not unreasonable for the court to have determined that a forced buy-out of petitioners' shares or liquidation of the corporation's assets was the only means by which petitioners could be guaranteed a fair return on their investments.

Accordingly, the order of the Appellate Division should be modified, with costs to petitioners-respondents, by affirming the substantive determination of that court but extending the time for exercising the option to purchase petitioners-respondents' shares to 30 days following this court's determination. * * *

NOTE ON "DE FACTO" DIVIDENDS

A dividend is a distribution of a corporation's profits to its shareholders. More precisely, a dividend is "a pro rata distribution to one or more classes of shareholders by the corporation usually out of its current or retained earnings." ROBERT W. HAMILTON & RICHARD A. BOOTH, BUSINESS BASICS FOR LAW STUDENTS: ESSENTIAL TERMS AND CONCEPTS § 12.1, at 301 (3d ed. 2002). Dividends are paid on an equivalent per-share basis to owners of the same class of stock (e.g., a corporation might declare a dividend of $1.00 per share on all shares of its Class A stock).

When calculating a corporation's taxable income, a corporation can deduct reasonable compensation paid to its employees, see I.R.C. § 162(a)(1), but it cannot deduct dividends paid to its shareholders. To decrease the amount of income tax that a company pays, therefore, a closely held corporation will often distribute profit to its shareholders in the form of employment-related compensation, rather than in the form of dividends. Many closely held corporations, in other words, distribute profit to shareholders not as "true" dividends but as "de facto" dividends—i.e., dividends disguised, for tax purposes, as employment-related compensation.

---

[2] Respondent is correct in arguing that there is no basis in the record for the referee's conclusion that the corporation had an established policy to buy-out the shares of employees when they left the company. * * * The referee's reliance on this ground is irrelevant for the purposes of this appeal, however, as Supreme Court's confirmation of the report was based solely on the principal ground for the finding of oppression, the company's failure to award dividends.

A "de facto" dividend, however, is still a dividend, and, like all dividends, it should ordinarily be paid on an equivalent per-share basis.

In theory, the compensation paid to an employee of a corporation should be no more than the reasonable value of the labor provided by the employee. When a corporation pays an employee more than the reasonable value of the employee's labor, the compensation paid actually reflects two components: (1) an amount for the value of the labor provided by the employee; and (2) an "extra" amount that represents a distribution of corporate profit to the employee—i.e., a "de facto" dividend.

NOTE ON GENERAL AND SPECIFIC REASONABLE EXPECTATIONS

When thinking about reasonable expectations, it is often useful to distinguish between what might be called "general" reasonable expectations and "specific" reasonable expectations. At its core, the shareholder oppression doctrine protects investors in closely held corporations with a set of special rules that go beyond the protections provided by traditional corporate law. Nevertheless, shareholders in closely held corporations do not lose any of the baseline protections of traditional corporate law. In a corporation, the mere status of "shareholder" entitles one to various rights including, among others, a right to receive a proportionate share of any distributed profits, a right to inspect company books and records (with a proper purpose), a right to vote on shareholder issues, and a right to be recognized as a shareholder. One can assert, therefore, that every shareholder—whether in a publicly held or closely held corporation—reasonably expects that his position as a shareholder entitles him to various rights. Whenever these status-based or "general" reasonable expectations are frustrated in a closely held corporation, oppression liability should arise.

Unlike in a publicly held corporation, shareholders in closely held corporations often expect that their investments will entitle them to employment and management benefits as well. "Specific" reasonable expectations refer to these extra rights—extra to the extent that they go beyond the rights normally associated with shareholder status in a publicly held corporation:

> * * * Unlike a status-triggered general reasonable expectation, a specific reasonable expectation is not held by every close corporation participant who can be characterized as a "shareholder." To the contrary, a specific reasonable expectation is personal in nature, as it requires proof that a close corporation majority shareholder and a particular minority shareholder reached a mutual understanding about a certain entitlement (for example, employment, management) the minority is to receive in return for its investment in the business. By safeguarding specific reasonable expectations of employment, management, or other entitlement, the oppression doctrine is offering special protection to close corporation

shareholders—"special" to the extent that public corporation shareholders do not receive similar protection.

Douglas K. Moll, *Shareholder Oppression & Dividend Policy in the Close Corporation*, 60 WASH. & LEE L. REV. 841, 857–58 (2003).

NOTES

(1) What reasonable expectations of petitioners Dissin and Gardstein were frustrated by the majority shareholders of Kemp & Beatley, Inc.? Would the petitioners have prevailed under traditional corporate law principles?

(2) The *Kemp* court orders dissolution of the company or a buyout of the petitioners' shares. How does dissolution help the petitioners? How does a buyout help the petitioners?

(3) Determining whether a shareholder-employee's compensation includes a "de facto" dividend—that is, determining whether a shareholder-employee is receiving more than the reasonable value of his labor—is a difficult task. Because the Internal Revenue Service often sues to disallow the deduction of "unreasonable" amounts of compensation, tax decisions can provide useful guidance. The tax courts have looked to various factors to guide an inquiry into the reasonableness of compensation, including the following: "(1) the type and extent of the services rendered; (2) the scarcity of qualified employees; (3) the qualifications and prior earning capacity of the employee; (4) the contributions of the employee to the business venture; (5) the net earnings of the employer; (6) the prevailing compensation paid to employees with comparable jobs; and (7) the peculiar characteristics of the employer's business." Exacto Spring Corp. v. Comm'r of Internal Revenue, 196 F.3d 833, 834 (7th Cir. 1999). Such multi-factor tests, however, are not without criticism. *Id.* at 834–35 ("It is apparent that this test, though it or variants of it (one of which has the astonishing total of 21 factors), are encountered in many cases, leaves much to be desired—being, like many other multi-factor tests, redundant, incomplete, and unclear." (citations omitted) (internal quotation omitted)). The tax courts have also applied an "independent investor" test, whose operation has been described as follows:

> * * * A corporation can be conceptualized as a contract in which the owner of assets hires a person to manage them. The owner pays the manager a salary and in exchange the manager works to increase the value of the assets that have been entrusted to his management; that increase can be expressed as a rate of return to the owner's investment. The higher the rate of return (adjusted for risk) that a manager can generate, the greater the salary he can command. If the rate of return is extremely high, it will be difficult to prove that the manager is being overpaid, for it will be implausible that if he quit if his salary was cut, and he was replaced by a lower-paid manager, the owner would be better off; it would be killing the goose that lays the golden egg. The Service's expert believed that investors in a firm like Exacto would expect a 13

percent return on their investment. Presumably they would be delighted with more. * * *

When, notwithstanding the CEO's "exorbitant" salary (as it might appear to a judge or other modestly paid official), the investors in his company are obtaining a far higher return than they had any reason to expect, his salary is presumptively reasonable.

Id. at 838–39.

(4) How does the *Kemp* reasonable expectations framework differ from the Massachusetts fiduciary duty/legitimate business purpose framework? Are the frameworks likely to produce the same results in litigated disputes? (The second problem below is helpful in exploring these questions).

(5) Thirty-nine states include "oppressive" conduct or a similar term (e.g., "unfairly prejudicial" conduct) in their dissolution statutes. *See* DOUGLAS K. MOLL & ROBERT A. RAGAZZO, THE LAW OF CLOSELY HELD CORPORATIONS § 7.01[D][1][b], at 7–76 n.192 (2010). Not surprisingly, the breach of fiduciary duty approach to protecting shareholders from oppressive conduct has developed primarily in states without a dissolution for oppression statute (e.g., Massachusetts, Ohio).

(6) Judicial decisions have articulated various definitions of oppression:

[C]ourts have developed three principal approaches to defining the statutory term. First, some courts define oppression as "burdensome, harsh and wrongful conduct, a lack of probity and fair dealing in the affairs of a company to the prejudice of some of its members, or a visible departure from the standards of fair dealing, and a violation of fair play on which every shareholder who entrusts his money to a company is entitled to rely." [Fix v. Fix Material Co., 538 S.W.2d 351, 358 (Mo. Ct. App. 1976).] Second, some courts define oppression by linking it to action that constitutes a breach of fiduciary duty. Third, many courts tie oppression to majority conduct that frustrates a minority shareholder's "reasonable expectations." Of these three approaches, the reasonable expectations standard garners the most approval. The highest courts in several states have adopted the reasonable expectations approach, and commentators have generally been in favor of the reasonable expectations standard.

DOUGLAS K. MOLL & ROBERT A. RAGAZZO, THE LAW OF CLOSELY HELD CORPORATIONS § 7.01[D][1][b][i], at 7–78 to 7–79 (2010) (footnotes omitted).

(7) Courts have repeatedly stated that a protected "reasonable expectation" is more than a shareholder's subjective wish and desire. *See, e.g., In re* Kemp & Beatley, Inc., 473 N.E.2d 1173, 1179 (N.Y. 1984) (noting that unfulfilled "subjective hopes and desires in joining the venture" are insufficient to establish a reasonable expectation, and stating that "[d]isappointment alone should not necessarily be equated with oppression");

Meiselman v. Meiselman, 307 S.E.2d 551, 563 (N.C. 1983) ("Privately held expectations which are not made known to the other participants are not 'reasonable.' "). The majority shareholder must have some level of awareness of the minority's expectation, but implicit awareness appears to suffice. *See, e.g., id.* at 563 ("In order for plaintiff's expectations to be reasonable, they must be known to or assumed by the other shareholders and concurred in by them. * * * Only expectations embodied in understandings, express or implied, among the participants should be recognized by the court.").

(8) At what time should a court measure a shareholder's reasonable expectations? The *Kemp* court refers to " 'reasonable expectations' held by minority shareholders in committing their capital to the particular enterprise," and it mentions "expectations that, objectively viewed, were * * * central to the petitioner's decision to join the venture." In Meiselman v. Meiselman, 307 S.E.2d 551, 563 (N.C. 1983), the Supreme Court of North Carolina stated the following:

> * * * These "reasonable expectations" are to be ascertained by examining the entire history of the participants' relationship. That history will include the "reasonable expectations" created at the inception of the participants' relationship; those "reasonable expectations" as altered over time; and the "reasonable expectations" which develop as the participants engage in a course of dealing in conducting the affairs of the corporation. * * *

Are there differences between the *Kemp* and *Meiselman* formulations?

(9) Can investors who receive their shares via gift or inheritance have reasonable expectations? Under the *Kemp* formulation, how are those expectations "held by minority shareholders in committing their capital to the particular enterprise?" Similarly, how are those expectations "central to the petitioner's decision to join the venture?"

PROBLEM

Able, Baker, and Carter decide to form a closely held corporation to engage in the manufacture and distribution of T-shirts. They each invest $25,000 in the company in return for a 33.3% ownership stake. They quit their prior employment to work full-time at the company, and they also serve as the company's officers and directors.

At the time of the venture's formation, Able, Baker, and Carter agree that company profits will be distributed to the shareholders as salary and other employment-related compensation. The company does well, and Able, Baker, and Carter earn substantial salaries and employment perquisites over the years—well in excess of what persons performing similar work in similar positions typically earn at comparable firms. The company pays no dividends. Ten years after the company's formation, Baker develops a severe drug addiction. He starts to miss a substantial amount of work. Moreover, when he actually comes to work, his performance is poor. Customers serviced by Baker begin complaining, and some stop doing business with the company.

At a board meeting attended by all three directors, Able and Carter vote to terminate Baker's employment and officer status due to his inadequate performance. Baker no longer receives the salary and perquisites that Able and Carter receive.

(a) Does Baker have a viable oppression claim in a jurisdiction containing a provision identical to MBCA § 14.30?

(b) Change the following fact: before Baker's termination, assume that the three investors did not earn in excess of what persons performing similar work in similar positions typically earn at comparable firms. That is, they each earned a "market" rate of salary and perquisites—but no more than a market rate of salary and perquisites—for their work in the business. Able and Carter continue to earn this market rate after Baker's termination. Does this affect Baker's oppression claim?

PROBLEM

For each scenario, assume that the minority shareholder is a founder of a closely held corporation who quit her prior employment to work full-time for the company. If the minority challenges her termination from employment under each scenario, what result under the Massachusetts fiduciary duty framework (*Donahue/Wilkes*)? Under the New York reasonable expectations framework (*Kemp*)?

(a) The minority shareholder is terminated from employment in order to effectuate a freezeout of the minority.

(b) The minority shareholder is terminated from employment as a result of the minority's incompetence and resulting inability to perform her job.

(c) The minority shareholder is terminated from employment due to an economic recession and a corresponding need to reduce company expenses.

(d) The minority shareholder is terminated from employment because her job, and only her job, can now be performed entirely by machine. The minority's job performance is superior when compared to other human beings, but use of the machine will indisputably result in greater productivity and decreased costs for the company.

(e) The minority shareholder is terminated from employment because the majority shareholder has decided to bring in a professional non-shareholder manager—a manager who can do the work of both the minority shareholder and the majority shareholder at less expense to the corporation. As a result, the majority shareholder also terminates his own employment.

NIXON V. BLACKWELL

Supreme Court of Delaware, 1993.
626 A.2d 1366.

VEASEY, CHIEF JUSTICE:

* * *

VI. NO SPECIAL RULES FOR A "CLOSELY-HELD CORPORATION" NOT QUALIFIED AS A "CLOSE CORPORATION" UNDER SUBCHAPTER XIV OF THE DELAWARE GENERAL CORPORATION LAW.

We wish to address one further matter which was raised at oral argument before this Court: Whether there should be any special, judicially-created rules to "protect" minority stockholders of closely-held Delaware corporations.

The case at bar points up the basic dilemma of minority stockholders in receiving fair value for their stock as to which there is no market and no market valuation. It is not difficult to be sympathetic, in the abstract, to a stockholder who finds himself or herself in that position. A stockholder who bargains for stock in a closely-held corporation and who pays for those shares (unlike the plaintiffs in this case who acquired their stock through gift) can make a business judgment whether to buy into such a minority position, and if so on what terms. One could bargain for definitive provisions of self-ordering permitted to a Delaware corporation through the certificate of incorporation or by-laws by reason of the provisions in 8 *Del.C.* §§ 102, 109, and 141(a). Moreover, in addition to such mechanisms, a stockholder intending to buy into a minority position in a Delaware corporation may enter into definitive stockholder agreements, and such agreements may provide for elaborate earnings tests, buy-out provisions, voting trusts, or other voting agreements. *See, e.g.,* 8 *Del.C.* § 218.

The tools of good corporate practice are designed to give a purchasing minority stockholder the opportunity to bargain for protection before parting with consideration. It would do violence to normal corporate practice and our corporation law to fashion an ad hoc ruling which would result in a court-imposed stockholder buy-out for which the parties had not contracted.

In 1967, when the Delaware General Corporation Law was significantly revised, a new Subchapter XIV entitled "Close Corporations; Special Provisions," became a part of that law for the first time. * * * Subchapter XIV is a narrowly constructed statute which applies only to a corporation which is designated as a "close corporation" in its certificate of incorporation, and which fulfills other requirements, including a limitation to 30 on the number of stockholders, that all classes of stock have to have at least one restriction on transfer, and that there be no "public offering." 8 *Del.C.* § 342. Accordingly, subchapter XIV applies only to "close corporations," as defined in section 342. "Unless a corporation elects to become a close corporation under this subchapter in the manner prescribed in this subchapter, it shall be subject in all respects to this chapter, except this subchapter." 8 *Del.C.* § 341. The corporation before the Court in this matter, is not a "close corporation." Therefore it is not governed by the provisions of Subchapter XIV.[19]

One cannot read into the situation presented in the case at bar any special relief for the minority stockholders in this closely-held, but not statutory "close corporation" because the provisions of Subchapter XIV relating to close corporations and other statutory schemes preempt the field in their respective areas. It would run counter to the spirit of the doctrine of independent legal significance,[21] and would be inappropriate judicial legislation for this Court to fashion a special judicially-created rule for minority investors when the entity does not fall within those statutes, or when there are no negotiated special provisions in the certificate of incorporation, by-laws, or stockholder agreements. The entire fairness test, correctly applied and articulated, is the proper judicial approach.

* * *

---

[19] We do not intend to imply that, if the Corporation had been a close corporation under Subchapter XIV, the result in this case would have been different.

> [S]tatutory close corporations have not found particular favor with practitioners. Practitioners have for the most part viewed the complex statutory provisions underlying the purportedly simplified operational procedures for close corporations as legal quicksand of uncertain depth and have adopted the view that the objectives sought by the subchapter are achievable for their clients with considerably less uncertainty by cloaking a conventionally created corporation with the panoply of charter provisions, transfer restrictions, by-laws, stockholders' agreements, buy-sell arrangements, irrevocable proxies, voting trusts or other contractual mechanisms which were and remain the traditional method for accomplishing the goals sought by the close corporation provisions.

David A. Drexler, Lewis S. Black, Jr., and A. Gilchrist Sparks, III, *Delaware Corporation Law and Practice* § 43.01 (1993).

[21] *See* David A. Drexler, Lewis S. Black, Jr., and A. Gilchrist Sparks, III, *Delaware Corporation Law and Practice* § 4.02 (1993):

> An important tool to practitioners in the use of the General Corporation Law is the principle of "independent legal significance." The principle holds that the validity of a transaction accomplished pursuant to a specified section or sections of the statute will be tested by the standards applicable to those sections and not by those of other provisions, even though the ultimate economic results could have been achieved through use of procedures authorized by such other provisions and even though use of such other procedures might have created different rights among those affected by the transaction.

DOUGLAS K. MOLL, MINORITY OPPRESSION & THE LIMITED LIABILITY COMPANY: LEARNING (OR NOT) FROM CLOSE CORPORATION HISTORY

40 Wake Forest L. Rev. 883, 911–16 (2005).

Despite this apparent opportunity for ex ante bargaining, it is widely recognized that close corporation investors typically fail to engage in such contracting. A number of reasons have been advanced for this failure. Because close corporation owners are frequently linked by family or other personal relationships, there is often an initial atmosphere of mutual trust that diminishes the sense that contractual protection is needed. Commentators have also argued that close corporation owners are often unsophisticated in business and legal matters such that the need for contractual protection is rarely recognized.

Even if an investor did recognize that planning for dissension was useful, barriers to effective contracting would still exist. In light of the countless ways in which oppressive conduct can occur, it is quite difficult to foresee all (if not most) of the situations that may require contractual protection. This inability to appreciate the universe of potential problems may result in incomplete contracting or, possibly, in no contracting at all. Further, the typical decision to invest in a close corporation venture is, for all intents and purposes, a decision to engage in a long-term association with other shareholders that will involve significant personal interaction in the future. Effective contracting for protection is particularly challenging in such a setting, as the parties usually seek to avoid harming their relationship during the contracting process. Indeed, a minority shareholder may be hesitant to even raise the topic of dissension because of a fear that it will damage the trust between the shareholders— trust that is critical to the operation of any small business. This hesitation may result in no planning for dissension at all.

Even if the topic of dissension is broached, a similar concern exists that any "hard feelings" created by the bargaining process will hinder the parties' abilities to work together in the future. Given this concern and the related desire to preserve as much goodwill between the shareholders as possible, a minority investor at the outset of a close corporation venture is likely to feel constrained in its ability to freely exercise any bargaining advantage that it has—i.e., constrained in its ability to fully "flex" its bargaining "muscle" against the majority shareholder. When the typical familiarity between close corporation participants is factored into the analysis, the minority shareholder is likely to feel even more constrained, as the shareholder will be concerned that fair (but hard) bargaining may harm both a business *and* a family/friendship relationship. Unlike discrete, single-interaction transactions, therefore, effective contracting in the close corporation setting is frequently hindered by relationship-oriented concerns. As a result, contractual protection for the minority shareholder is often incomplete or nonexistent.

For all of these reasons, it is rare for effective ex ante contracting to occur between close corporation investors.[112] * * *

NOTES

(1) The *Nixon* court relies heavily on principles of contract to support its refusal to create special common-law rules for minority shareholders in closely held corporations. Why might the typical minority shareholder in a closely held corporation fail to contract for protection from abusive majority conduct?

(2) Does the contract rationale apply to all "types" of minority shareholders? Consider, for example, investors who receive their shares via gift or inheritance. Are these shareholders different from the typical investor who contributes capital to the corporation in exchange for shares? *See, e.g.,* Douglas K. Moll, *Shareholder Oppression & Reasonable Expectations: Of Change, Gifts, and Inheritances in Close Corporation Disputes*, 86 MINN. L. REV. 717, 763–82 (2002) (discussing "non-investing" shareholders).

(3) The *Nixon* court notes that the corporation at issue was not a "close corporation" as defined in subchapter XIV of the Delaware General Corporation Law. *See* DGCL §§ 341–356. If the provisions of subchapter XIV did apply to a closely held corporation, would they provide protection to a minority shareholder in a classic freezeout situation? Reconsider, for example, the facts of *Wilkes v. Springside Nursing Home, Inc.* If Springside Nursing Home was a qualifying and electing "close corporation" under subchapter XIV of the Delaware General Corporation Law, what statutory protection would Wilkes have received?

(4) Do you prefer the "special rules" approach (e.g., *Wilkes*, *Kemp*) or the "no special rules" approach (e.g., *Nixon*) to the oppression problem in the closely held corporation? What is the cost of having special common-law rules? What is the cost of foregoing such rules?

GALLAGHER V. LAMBERT

Court of Appeals of New York, 1989.
549 N.E.2d 136.

BELLACOSA, JUDGE.

Plaintiff Gallagher purchased stock in the defendant close corporation with which he was employed. The purchase of his 8.5% interest was subject to a mandatory buy-back provision: if the

---

[112] It should also be noted that ex ante contracting is expensive, as it often requires the assistance of an attorney. In fact, effective ex ante contracting may require the services of multiple attorneys—one (or more) representing the majority's interests, and one (or more) representing the minority's interests. This level of expense may be prohibitive for many small businesses, especially at their inception.

employment ended for any reason before January 31, 1985, the stock would return to the corporation for book value. The corporation fired plaintiff prior to the fulcrum date, after which the buy-back price would have been higher.

We must decide whether plaintiff's dismissed causes of action, seeking the higher repurchase price based on an alleged breach of a fiduciary duty, should be reinstated. We think not and affirm, concluding that the Appellate Division did not err in dismissing these causes of action by summary judgment because there was no cognizable breach of any fiduciary duty owed to plaintiff under the plain terms of the parties' repurchase agreement.

Gallagher was employed by defendant Eastdil Realty as a mortgage broker from 1968 to 1973. Three years later, in 1976, he returned to the company as a broker, officer and director, serving additionally as president and chief executive officer of defendant's wholly owned subsidiary, Eastdil Advisors, Inc. Gallagher was at all times an employee at will. Still later, in 1981, Eastdil offered all its executive employees an opportunity to purchase stock subject to a mandatory buy-back provision, which provided that upon "voluntary resignation or other termination" prior to January 31, 1985, an employee would be required to return the stock for book value. After that date, the formula for the buy-back price was keyed to the company's earnings. Plaintiff accepted the offer and its terms.

On January 10, 1985, Gallagher was fired by Eastdil Realty. He did not and does not now contest the firing. But he demanded payment for his shares calculated on the post-January 31, 1985 buy-back formula. Eastdil refused and Gallagher sued, asserting eight causes of action. Only three claims, based on an alleged breach of fiduciary duty of good faith and fair dealing, are before us. * * *

The parties negotiated a written contract containing a common and plain buy-back provision. Plaintiff got what he bargained for—book value for his minority shares if his employment in the corporation ended before January 31, 1985. There being no basis presented for the courts to interfere with the operation and consequences of this agreement between the parties, the order of the Appellate Division granting summary judgment to defendants, dismissing the first three causes of action, should be affirmed. * * *

Earlier this year, in *Ingle v. Glamore Motor Sales,* 535 N.E.2d 1311, we expressly refrained from deciding the precise issue presented by this case. There, the challenge was directed to the at-will discharge from employment and was predicated on a claimed fiduciary obligation flowing from the shareholder relationship. * * * [W]e held that "[a] minority shareholder in a close corporation, by that status alone, who contractually agrees to the repurchase of his shares upon termination of his employment for any reason, *acquires no right from the corporation or majority shareholders against at-will discharge.*" (*Ingle v. Glamore Motor Sales,* 535 N.E.2d 1311 [emphasis added].) However, we cautioned that "[i]t is necessary * * * to appreciate and keep distinct the duty a corporation owes to a minority shareholder *as a shareholder* from any duty it might owe him as an *employee.*" *(Id.,* 535 N.E.2d 1311.)

The causes before us on this appeal are based on an alleged departure from a fiduciary duty of fair dealing existing independently of the employment and arising from the plaintiff's simultaneous relationship as a minority shareholder in the corporation. Plaintiff claims entitlement to the higher price based on a breach flowing from Eastdil's premature "bad faith" termination of his at-will employment because, he asserts, the sole purpose of the firing at that time was to acquire the stock at a contractually and temporally measured lower buy-back price formula.

The claim seeking a higher price for the shares cannot be neatly divorced, as the dissent urges, from the employment because the buy-back provision links them together as to timing and consequences. Plaintiff not only agreed to the particular buy-back formula, he helped write it and he reviewed it with his attorney during the negotiation process, before signing the agreement and purchasing the minority interest. These provisions, which require an employee shareholder to sell back stock upon severance from corporate employment, are designed to ensure that ownership of all of the stock, especially of a close corporation, stays within the control of the remaining corporate owners-employees; that is, those who will continue to contribute to its successes or failures. These agreements define the scope of the relevant fiduciary duty and supply certainty of obligation to each side. They should not be undone simply upon an allegation of unfairness. This would destroy their very purpose, which is to provide a certain formula by which to value stock in the future (*Allen v. Biltmore Tissue Corp.,* 141 N.E.2d 812). * * *

Gallagher accepted the offer to become a minority stockholder, but only for the period during which he remained an employee. The buy-back price formula was designed for the benefit of both parties precisely so that they could know their respective rights on certain dates and avoid costly and lengthy litigation on the "fair value" issue (*see, Coleman v. Taub,* 3d Cir., 638 F.2d 628, 637). Permitting these causes to survive would open the door to litigation on both the value of the stock and the date of termination, and hinder the employer from fulfilling its contractual rights under the agreement. This would frustrate the agreement and would be disruptive of the settled principles governing like agreements where parties contract between themselves in advance so that there may be reliance, predictability and definitiveness between themselves on such matters. There being no dispute that the employer had the unfettered discretion to fire plaintiff at any time, we should not redefine the precise measuring device and scope of the agreement. Defendant agreed to abide by these terms and thus fulfilled its fiduciary duty in that respect.

The dissenting opinion uses a number of rhetorical characterizations about the defendant and about what we are deciding or avoiding to decide, none of which, we believe, require response, because our holding and rationale rest on the application of fundamental contractual principles to the plain terms in the parties' own stock repurchase agreement.

Accordingly, the order of the Appellate Division should be affirmed * * *.

   * * *

KAYE, JUDGE (dissenting). By proceeding, as if inexorably, from * * * *Ingle* to *Gallagher,* the court avoids confronting plaintiff's true claims and unnecessarily weakens traditional protections afforded minority shareholders in close corporations. I therefore respectfully dissent.

I.

To begin at a point of agreement, this case is significantly different from *Ingle v. Glamore Motor Sales,* 535 N.E.2d 1311. As the majority acknowledges, this case presents "an alleged departure from a fiduciary duty of fair dealing existing independently of the employment" that was not present in *Ingle.*

In *Ingle* we reached only the corporation's duty to plaintiff as *an employee,* carving out and reserving for another day any question of the duty a corporation might owe an employee as *a shareholder,* which was not in issue. The court was careful to note that Mr. Ingle had already accepted full payment for his shares without reservation; while his complaint referred to a fiduciary duty owed him as a shareholder, the only interest he asserted in the litigation was in his job. In its succinct opinion the court took pains to emphasize at least six separate times that its concern was only with Mr. Ingle's employment, not in any sense with the duty a corporation owes to a minority shareholder, or with undervaluation of shares.

Here, plaintiff *does* question the duty the corporation owes him as a shareholder. He *does* contend that the corporation undervalued his shares and that it did not offer a fair price for his equity interest. Indeed, that is the only question he raises; he does not challenge defendant's absolute right to terminate his employment. Yet despite careful identification and recognition in *Ingle* of the different considerations such a question would present, now that the question is before us the court finds that the very same answer and the very same rationale are wholly dispositive, with no analysis of the fiduciary obligation owed plaintiff.

The court's insistence that the rationale of *Ingle* and the other at-will employment cases must be carried over—lock, stock and barrel—even to the fiduciary obligations owed minority shareholders in close corporations, plainly represents an extension of the law to a different jural relationship. I believe this is wholly unwarranted.

* * *

Before he was dismissed on January 10, 1985, plaintiff (James V. Gallagher) was an officer and director of both defendant Eastdil Realty, Inc. and its wholly owned subsidiary, Eastdil Advisers, Inc. Eastdil Realty is a closely held real estate investing banking firm. Defendant Lambert is its founder, principal shareholder and chief executive officer. The other defendants are officers and shareholders of the corporation.

* * *

In summer 1984, Gallagher received 8.5% of Eastdil's stock, becoming the third largest shareholder, and he executed an amended stockholders' agreement. The agreement continued to provide for mandatory repurchase at book value upon "voluntary resignation or other termination" of employment. But it also stipulated that after January 31, 1985, the buy-out price would be calculated by an escalating formula based on the company's earnings and the length of the shareholder's employment. According to Gallagher, the new buy-out price represented "golden handcuffs" designed to induce employees to remain on, at least until January 31, 1985.

On January 10, 1985—just 21 days before the new valuation formula became effective—Gallagher was fired and Eastdil invoked its right to repurchase his stock at book value. According to Gallagher, book value for the shares was $89,000; the price under the new valuation formula would have been around $3,000,000.

* * *

Gallagher alleges that defendants had no bona fide, business-related reason to terminate his employment when they did—assertions we must accept as true on this summary judgment motion. He charges that defendants fired him for the sole purpose of recapturing his shares at an unfairly low price and redistributing them among themselves.

These claims put in issue an aspect of the employee-shareholder relationship that we have not previously considered in our at-will employment cases. Plaintiff claims that defendants, the holders of a majority of the corporate stock, breached distinctly different duties to him by manipulating his termination so as to deprive him of the opportunity to reap the benefits of a "golden handcuffs" agreement, and for no other reason than to effect repurchase of his shares at less than their fair value. In short, plaintiff claims defendants breached two duties related to each other but conceptually unrelated to his at-will employment status: (1) a duty of good faith in the performance of the shareholders' agreement, and (2) a fiduciary obligation owed to him as a minority shareholder by the controlling shareholders to refrain from purely self-aggrandizing conduct. Neither claim is foreclosed by plaintiff's status as an at-will employee.

If plaintiff were a minority shareholder, but not an employee, defendants would be barred from acting selfishly and opportunistically, for no corporate purpose, as he alleges they did. The controlling stockholders in a close corporation stand, in relation to minority owners, in the same fiduciary position as corporate directors generally, and are held "to the extreme measure of candor, unselfishness and good faith." (*Kavanaugh v. Kavanaugh Knitting Co.*, 123 N.E. 148.) Although, without more, the courts will not interfere when parties have set the repurchase price at book value (*Allen v. Biltmore Tissue Corp.*, 141 N.E.2d 812), here plaintiff asserts there was more. The corporation agreed, commencing January 31, 1985, to pay a higher price, said to be more reflective of the true value of defendant's shares. Defendants' invocation of the pre-January 31 repurchase price was adverse to plaintiff's interests as a minority stockholder, and therefore subject to a standard of good faith under the foregoing principles.

Directors and majority shareholders may not act "for the aggrandizement or undue advantage of the fiduciary to the exclusion or detriment of the [minority] stockholders." (*Alpert v. 28 Williams St. Corp.*, 473 N.E.2d 19 [citing cases].) Nor is it considered a legitimate corporate interest if the sole purpose is reduction of the number of profit-sharers, or ultimately "to increase the individual wealth of the remaining shareholders" (*id.*, 473 N.E.2d 19). Yet that is precisely what we must assume defendants' motive was, and this court now sanctions such conduct.

Defendants' broad interpretation of the "other termination" language of the repurchase clause amounts to an assertion that plaintiff agreed to waive substantial rights he might otherwise have possessed as a minority shareholder. However, in the absence of evidence that plaintiff knowingly assented to such a waiver, I cannot agree that the general language of the clause unambiguously expresses an understanding that the option could be exploited for the sole personal gain of the controlling shareholders in derogation of their fiduciary obligations to minority shareholders. Notably, the repurchase clause contains no reference to plaintiff's at-will employment status and no reservation of defendant's right to discharge plaintiff for any reason at all.

Moreover, defendants' interpretation denies that defendants themselves had any duty of good faith in connection with the shareholders' agreement. We have said that "there is an implied covenant that neither party shall do anything which will have the effect of destroying or injuring the right of the other party to receive the fruits of the contract, which means that in every contract there exists an implied covenant of good faith and fair dealing." (*Kirke La Shelle Co. v. Armstrong Co.*, 188 N.E. 163.) This general rule does not apply to at-will employment relationships, as "it would be incongruous to say that an inference may be drawn that the employer impliedly agreed to a provision which would be destructive of his right of termination." (*Murphy v. American Home Prods. Corp.*, 448 N.E.2d 86.) It does not follow, however, that there can be no covenant of good faith implicit in the shareholders' agreement that gives rise to obligations surviving termination of the employment relationship.

Assuming plaintiff's claims about the purpose of the amendments to be true, the expectations and relationship of the parties, as structured by the shareholders' agreement, dictate an implied contractual obligation of good faith, notwithstanding that there is none in their employment relationship (*see, Wakefield v. Northern Telecom*, 769 F.2d 109 [2d Cir.]). A covenant of good faith is anomalous in the context of at-will employment because performance and entitlement to benefits are simultaneous. Termination even without cause does not operate to deprive the employee of the benefits promised in return for performance.

But the alleged "golden handcuffs" agreement is different. An implied covenant of good faith *is* necessary to enable the employee to receive the benefits promised for performance. As one court noted, "an unfettered right to avoid payment * * * creates incentives counterproductive to the purpose of the contract itself in that the better the performance by the employee, the greater the temptation to terminate." (*Wakefield v. Northern Telecom, supra,* at 112–113; Note, *Exercising Options to Repurchase Employee-Held Stock: A Question of Good Faith,* 68 Yale L.J. 773, 779 [1959].).

* * * Here, the language relied upon by defendants cannot be deemed so clear as to unambiguously constitute an agreement by plaintiff to cede the fiduciary duties owed him as a shareholder and relinquish his entitlement to a higher price for his stock solely for defendants' pecuniary benefit.

IV.

Denial of summary judgment would deprive defendants of no legitimate expectation or right, contractual or otherwise. Under the law, they remain free to terminate plaintiff's employment as agreed; they remain free to buy back his stock at book value as agreed—so long as there is a corporate purpose for their conduct. What controlling shareholders cannot do to a minority shareholder is take action against him solely for the self-aggrandizing, opportunistic purpose of themselves acquiring his shares at the low price, and they cannot do this because in the law it means something to be a shareholder, particularly a minority shareholder.

Because the majority gives no credence whatever to plaintiff's independent status as a shareholder, and because the majority now needlessly extends the at-will employment doctrine yet another notch, to diminish the long-recognized duties owed minority shareholders, I must dissent.

* * *

NOTES

(1) What is the purpose of the buy-back provision in *Gallagher*? Why does Gallagher lose?

(2) Assume that the plaintiff's employment in *Gallagher* was terminated by the company on January 30, 1985 at 11:59 p.m. (January 31, 1985 is the "fulcrum date" under the buy-back provision.) How do you think the *Gallagher* court would rule?

(3) As the dissent points out in *Gallagher*, every contract contains an implied covenant of good faith and fair dealing that "neither party shall do anything which will have the effect of destroying or injuring the right of the other party to receive the fruits of the contract." Is this argument applicable to Gallagher's situation? If so, why doesn't it prevail?

(4) In *Jordan v. Duff and Phelps, Inc.*, 815 F.2d 429 (7th Cir. 1987), Jordan was a securities analyst who, on November 16, 1983, informed his employer (Duff & Phelps) that he planned to resign. At that time, Duff & Phelps knew that the company was involved in merger negotiations, but it did not reveal that fact to Jordan. Pursuant to a Stock Restriction and Purchase Agreement, Jordan was required, upon resignation, to sell his stock back to Duff & Phelps for "adjusted book value * * * of the Shares on the December 31 which coincides with, or immediately precedes, the date of termination." Jordan worked until December 31, 1983 in order to receive the book value of the stock on that date (he received a total of $23,225 for his shares). *See id.* at 432. On January 10, 1984, a merger was announced involving Duff & Phelps that would have provided Jordan with substantially more compensation for his shares ($452,000 and an opportunity to earn an additional $194,000) had he remained an employee until that time. Jordan sued, claiming that Duff & Phelps breached a duty to disclose to him. *See id.* at 433. The trial court granted summary judgment for Duff & Phelps, but the Seventh Circuit reversed. In dissent, Judge Posner argued that because Jordan was an at-will employee, a duty to disclose was meaningless, as Duff & Phelps could have fired Jordan at any time, "even the day before the merger, for any reason—including the desire to deprive Jordan of a share of the profits." *Id.* at 437, 446–47. Judge Easterbrook, writing for the majority, disagreed:

* * * The silence of the parties may make it necessary to imply other terms—those we are confident the parties would have bargained for if they had signed a written agreement. One term implied in every written contract and therefore, we suppose, every unwritten one, is that neither party will try to take opportunistic advantage of the other.

Employment creates occasions for opportunism. A firm may fire an employee the day before his pension vests, or a salesman the day before a large commission becomes payable. Cases of this sort may present difficult questions about the reasons for the decision (was it opportunism, or was it a decline in the employee's performance?). * * * But no one * * * doubts that an *avowedly* opportunistic discharge is a breach of contract, although the employment is at-will. The element of good faith dealing implied in a contract "is not an enforceable legal duty to be nice or to behave decently in a general way." [Zick v. Verson Allsteel Press Co., 623 F. Supp. 927, 929 (N.D. Ill. 1985)]. It is not a version of the Golden Rule, to regard the interests of one's contracting partner the same way you regard your own. An employer may be thoughtless, nasty, and mistaken. Avowedly opportunistic conduct has been treated differently, however.

The stock component in Jordan's package induced him to stick around and work well. Such an inducement is effective only if the employee reaps the rewards of success as well as the penalties of failure. We do not suppose for a second that if Jordan had not resigned on November 16, the firm could have fired him on January 9 with a little note saying: "Dear Mr. Jordan: There will be a lucrative merger tomorrow. You have been a wonderful employee, but in order to keep the proceeds of the merger for ourselves, we are letting you go, effective this instant. Here is the $23,000 for your shares." Had the firm fired Jordan for this stated reason, it would have broken an implied pledge to avoid opportunistic conduct. It may well be that Duff & Phelps could have fired Jordan without the slightest judicial inquiry; it does not follow that an opportunistic discharge would have allowed Duff & Phelps to cash out the stock on the eve of its appreciation.

Id. at 438–39.

(5) Like *Gallagher*, other courts have used contract law to limit the reach of the oppression doctrine. *See, e.g., In re* Apple, 637 N.Y.S.2d 534, 535 (App. Div. 1996) (involving an agreement that "explicitly binds each shareholder to offer to sell his or her stock within 30 days after ceasing for any reason, either voluntarily or involuntarily, to be in the employ of the corporation," and concluding that the "agreement is enforceable and Peter Apple cannot be heard to argue that he had a reasonable expectation that he would be employed and would be a shareholder for life"). In the Massachusetts decision of *Evangelista v. Holland*, 537 N.E.2d 589 (Mass. App. Ct. 1989), four

brothers in the restaurant business entered into a stockholders' agreement providing that the corporation shall purchase the stock of any deceased shareholder for $75,000. At the time of the death of one of the brothers, there was evidence that his shares were worth $191,000. The discrepancy in value prompted a *Donahue* claim, which the court ultimately rejected:

> * * * The executors [of the deceased brother's estate] suggest that to require them to part with their interest in the business for so much less [$75,000] than the price offered [to another brother's children for their equivalent interest in the business— $191,000] violates the duty of good faith and loyalty owed one another by stockholders in a closely held corporation. See *Donahue v. Rodd Electrotype Co.,* 367 Mass. 578, 593–595, 328 N.E.2d 505 (1975); *Wilkes v. Springside Nursing Home, Inc.,* 370 Mass. 842, 850–851, 353 N.E.2d 657 (1976). Questions of good faith and loyalty do not arise when all the stockholders in advance enter into an agreement for the purchase of stock of a withdrawing or deceased stockholder. That the price established by a stockholders' agreement may be less than the appraised or market value is unremarkable. Such agreements may have as their purpose: the payment of a price for a decedent's stock which will benefit the corporation or surviving stockholders by not unduly burdening them; the payment of a price tied to life insurance; or fixing a price which assures the beneficiaries of the deceased stockholder of a predetermined price for stock which might have little market value. * * *

Evangelista, 537 N.E.2d at 590–93.

C. REMEDIES FOR DISSENSION

When a shareholder is successful in proving oppressive conduct, what remedy is provided? In fiduciary duty jurisdictions, there is already a large body of existing case law on traditional remedies for breach of fiduciary duty (e.g., damages, injunctions). As a result, developments in this area have largely occurred in states with involuntary dissolution statutes. In most of these states, courts are not limited to orders of dissolution; instead, courts are empowered (either by statute or by judicial decision) to offer a wide range of alternative remedies when oppressive conduct is demonstrated. The materials below will examine these remedial developments in greater detail. Although most of the materials involve oppression claims, keep in mind that the remedy discussions are broader and, in many circumstances, they will also apply to deadlock and other shareholder grounds for involuntary dissolution.

DAVIS V. SHEERIN

Court of Appeals of Texas, 1988.
754 S.W.2d 375.

DUNN, JUSTICE.

This is an appeal from portions of a trial court's judgment, in which James L. Sheerin ("appellee") was declared to own a 45% share in a corporation * * *. William H. Davis ("appellant") is the owner of the remaining 55% interest in * * * the corporation * * *.

In May of 1985, appellee brought suit individually in his own right, and as a shareholder on behalf of W.H. Davis Co., Inc., a Texas corporation ("the corporation"), against William H. Davis and Catherine L. Davis ("appellants") based on allegations of appellants' oppressive conduct toward appellee as a minority shareholder, and their breaches of fiduciary duties owed to appellee and the corporation. * * *

In 1955, William Davis and appellee incorporated a business, initially started by William Davis, in which appellant Davis owned 55% and appellee owned 45% of the corporation's stock. Appellants and appellee all served as directors and officers, with William Davis serving as president and running the day-to-day operations of the business. Appellee, unlike appellants, was not employed by the corporation. In 1960, appellee and appellant William Davis formed a partnership for the purpose of acquiring real estate.

The precipitating cause of appellee's lawsuit in 1985 was appellants' denial of appellee's right to inspect the corporate books, unless appellee produced his stock certificate. Appellants claimed that appellee had made a gift to them, in the late 1960[s], of his 45% interest. * * *

Following a six-week trial to a jury, the trial court, in addition to declaring that appellee owned a 45% interest in the corporation, the partnership, and the six tracts of land found to be partnership assets, issued the following orders and award of damages:

(1) an ordered "buy-out" by appellants of appellee's 45% of the stock in the corporation for $550,000, the fair value determined by the jury;

(2) the appointment of a receiver for the corporation;

(3) an injunction against appellants' contributing to a profit sharing plan for their benefit unless a proportionate sum is paid to appellee;

(4) a mandatory injunction for the payment of dividends in the future;

(5) an award of damages in the amount of $20,893 to appellee, individually, for appellants' willful breach of fiduciary duty in receiving informal dividends by making contributions to a profit sharing plan for their benefit to the exclusion of appellee;

(6) an award of $8,500 for costs incurred by appellee in enforcing his rights to inspect the books and $65,000 for paying the court-appointed accounting firm;

(7) an award of $192,600 to appellee, on behalf of the corporation, for recovery of corporate funds used for appellants' attorney's fees; * * * [and]

(8) An award of $10,583 for actual damages and $500 exemplary damages for breach of fiduciary duty in converting partnership assets other than the land. * * *

    * * *

In points of error one through seven, appellants challenge the court's order that they buy-out appellee's 45% interest in the corporation. Appellants' basic argument is two fold: (1) the remedy of a "buy-out" is not available to a minority shareholder under Texas law, and (2) if such a remedy were available, the facts of this case are not appropriate for, nor do the jury's findings support, the application of this remedy based on the court's determination of oppressive conduct.

The Texas Business Corporation Act does not expressly provide for the remedy of a "buy-out" for an aggrieved minority shareholder. Tex.Bus.Corp.Act. art. 7.05 (Vernon 1980) does provide for the appointment of a receiver, with the eventual possibility of liquidation, for aggrieved shareholders who can establish the existence of one of five situations, including illegal, oppressive, or fraudulent conduct by those in control.[a]

Nor do we find any Texas cases where the particular remedy of a "buy-out" has been ordered, unless provided for in a contract between the parties. But courts of other jurisdictions have recognized a "buy-out" as an appropriate remedy, even in the absence of express statutory or contractual authority. *See Alaska Plastics, Inc. v. Coppock,* 621 P.2d 270 (Alaska 1980); *Sauer v. Moffitt,* 363 N.W.2d 269 (Iowa Ct.App.1984); *McCauley v. Tom McCauley & Son, Inc.,* 104 N.M. 523, 724 P.2d 232 (Ct.App.1986) (granting the option of liquidation or "buy-out"); *In re Wiedy's Furniture Clearance Center Co.,* 108 A.D.2d 81, 487 N.Y.S.2d 901 (1985); *Delaney v. Georgia-Pacific Corp.,* 278 Or. 305, 564 P.2d 277 (1977). Alaska, Iowa, New Mexico, New York, and Oregon all have statutes that provide for liquidation as the remedy for oppressive acts, and, in the above cited cases, the courts allowed a "buy-out" as a less harsh remedy. *See* Alaska Stat. § 10.05.540(2) (1985); Iowa Code § 496A.94 (Supp.1988); N.M.Stat.Ann. § 53–16–16 (Supp.1987); N.Y.Bus.Corp.Law § 1104–a (McKinney 1986); Or.Rev.Stat. § 57.595 (1983). Other states' statutes specifically provide for a "buy-out," either as a remedy for an aggrieved

---

[a]   Director and shareholder deadlock are also situations listed under the Texas statute. *See* TEX. BUS. ORGS. CODE § 11.404 (formerly TEX. BUS. CORP. ACT art. 7.05).

minority shareholder, Conn.Gen.Stat.Ann. § 33–384 (West 1987); Ill.Rev.Stat. ch. 32, para. 12.55 (Supp.1988); Minn.Stats.Ann. § 302A.751 (West 1985); N.C.Gen.Stat. § 55–125.1 (1982); S.C.Code Ann. § 33–21–155 (Law.Co-op 1987), or as an option available to a majority shareholder to avoid a liquidation order, Cal.Corp.Code § 2000 (West Supp.1988); W.Va.Code § 31–1–134 (1988).

Both parties rely on *Patton v. Nicholas,* 279 S.W.2d 848 (1955), to support their respective arguments in favor of or against a court's authority in Texas to order a "buy-out." In that case, the court reversed an order of liquidation in a suit brought by an aggrieved minority shareholder, although it found that liquidation might be an appropriate remedy in some instances. The court made a thorough analysis of earlier decisions in Texas and in other jurisdictions, and held that "Texas courts, under their general equity powers, may in the more extreme cases of the general type of the instant one, decree liquidation and accordingly appoint a receiver." The court recognized the absence of such a remedy for a shareholder under either the old statute or the newly enacted Business Corporation Act, article 7.05, which, the court stated, reflected a preference for rehabilitation through the appointment of a receiver, as opposed to liquidation.

In describing liquidation as the "extreme or ultimate remedy," the court called for the use of lesser remedies, where such remedies were adequate to protect the interests of the aggrieved shareholders, and for "tailoring the remedy to fit the particular case." * * *

* * *

* * * As appellee points out, *Patton* has been cited as support for the proposition that most states have adopted the view that a dissolution statute[ ] does not provide the exclusive remedy for injured shareholders, and that courts have equitable powers to fashion appropriate remedies where the majority shareholders have engaged in oppressive conduct.

Appellants further argue that appellee's reliance on the New York case of *Wiedy's* is misplaced because the New York statute grants authority to fashion less harsh remedies,[1] and that Texas has no statutory authority to do so. However, based on the *Patton* holding that courts could order liquidation under their general equity powers in the absence of statutory authority, we hold that a court could order less harsh remedies under those same equity powers.

* * *

---

[1] New York Bus.Corp.Law sec. 1104–a (McKinney 1986) provides that the court shall take into consideration whether liquidation is the only feasible means and whether it is reasonably necessary for protection of shareholders' rights.

We conclude that Texas courts, under their general equity power, may decree a "buy-out" in an appropriate case where less harsh remedies are inadequate to protect the rights of the parties.

Having decided that a "buy-out" is an available remedy under the court's general equity powers, we must decide whether it was appropriate in this case. The trial court's judgment reflects that its "buy-out" order was based on the jury's finding of conspiracy to deprive appellee of his stock, on the evidence and arguments, and on its conclusion that appellants acted oppressively against appellee and would continue to do so.

* * *

Courts in states with statutes containing situations establishing causes of action for minority shareholders, similar to those allowed in the Texas statute, have held that oppressive conduct is an independent ground for relief not requiring a showing of fraud, illegality, mismanagement, wasting of assets, nor deadlock, the other grounds available for shareholders, though these factors are frequently present.

* * *

Our review of the record shows that the jury made the following findings in regards to appellants' conduct:

(1)   appellants conspired to deprive appellee of his stock ownership in the corporation;

(2)   appellants received informal dividends by making profit sharing contributions for their benefit and to the exclusion of appellee, and that this was a willful breach of fiduciary duty;

(3)   appellants wasted corporate funds by using them for their legal fees, and that this was a willful breach of fiduciary duty;

(4)   appellants did not convert appellee's stock;

(5)   appellants were not paid excessive compensation;

(6)   there was no malicious suppression of dividends;

(7)   various purchases or investments did not constitute a breach of fiduciary duty; and

(8)   appellants did not conspire to breach their fiduciary duty.

The jury also found that appellee did not make a gift of his stock to appellants, represent that he would, nor agree to do so in the future. * * *

Some of the undisputed evidence that the trial court could have also considered in its conclusion of oppressive conduct includes the following:

(1)   appellants claimed that appellee had gifted them his stock in the late 1960[s], even though the records of the corporation and income tax

returns through 1986 clearly show appellee as a 45% stockholder, and appellants and/or their son had made several attempts to purchase appellee's stock in the 1970[s] and 1980[s];

(2) a letter from the corporation's attorney, dated May 16, 1979, referred to appellant Davis' "wish to avoid declaring dividends and disburse the surplus in the form of bonuses to the officers of the corporation" and the fact that such action may result in an allegation by appellee of "fraudulent intent to deny a shareholder his right to dividends" and "would probably be characterized as a direct effort to deny a shareholder his dividends;" and

(3) appellants approved the minutes of a special meeting of the Board of Director[s] on February 7, 1986, after the filing of this lawsuit, that stated that "Mr. Sheerin's opinions or actions would have no effect on the Board's deliberations."

Even though there were findings of the absence of some of the typical "squeeze out" techniques used in closely held corporations, e.g., no malicious suppression of dividends or excessive salaries, we find that conspiring to deprive one of his ownership of stock in a corporation, especially when the corporate records clearly indicate such ownership, is more oppressive than either of those techniques. Appellant's conduct not only would substantially defeat any reasonable expectations appellee may have had * * * but would totally extinguish any such expectations.

* * *

We therefore hold that the jury's finding of conspiracy to deprive appellee of his interest in the corporation, together with the acts of willful breach of a fiduciary duty as found by the jury, and the undisputed evidence indicating that appellee would be denied any future voice in the corporation, are sufficient to support the trial court's conclusion of oppressive conduct and the likelihood that it would continue in the future.

Under the analysis set out by the *Patton* court in its determination of whether liquidation was appropriate, we must determine whether lesser remedies than a "buy-out" could adequately protect appellee's interests. In *Patton,* the court found sufficient evidence to support only the malicious suppression of dividends claim, and thus concluded that a mandatory injunction to pay reasonable dividends then and in the future was adequate, with the additional protection of the court retaining jurisdiction.

In this case, the award of damages and certain injunctions might be sufficient to remedy the willful breaches of fiduciary duty found by the jury, i.e., informal dividends to appellants by making contributions to the profit sharing plan and waste of corporate funds for legal fees. However, based on appellants' conduct denying appellee any interest or voice in the corporation, we find that these remedies are inadequate to protect appellee's interest and his rights in the corporation.

Appellants' oppressive conduct, along with their attempts to purchase appellee's stock, are indications of their desire to gain total control of the corporation. That is exactly what a "buy-out" will achieve. We disagree with appellants' suggestion that a "buy-out" is a more drastic remedy than liquidation. This is especially true in light of the fact that appellants do not challenge the jury's finding of $550,000 as the fair value of appellee's stock, which is the amount set by the trial court for the "buy-out."

* * *

Based on the facts of this case, we find that a "buy-out" was an appropriate remedy, and that the trial court did not abuse its discretion.

* * *

ROBERT B. THOMPSON, THE SHAREHOLDER'S CAUSE OF ACTION FOR OPPRESSION

48 Bus. Law. 699, 708, 718, 721–26 (1993).

* * * Oppressive conduct by the majority or controlling shareholder now is listed widely in most state dissolution statutes, and has become the principal vehicle used by legislatures, courts, and litigants to address the particular needs of close corporations. * * * [I]t is fair to say that the remedy has outgrown its dissolution origins and now is better described as a general remedy for shareholder dissension within a close corporation that only rarely results in the dissolution of a corporation. * * *

* * *

* * * The most dramatic change in legislative and judicial thinking on solutions to minority shareholder problems is reflected in the increased popularity of a buyout as a remedy for deadlock or dissension. Legislative or judicial support for this remedy now exists in half of the states, although the criteria for its use is not uniform. In some states, a statute permits the corporation or majority shareholders to buy the shares of a minority shareholder seeking involuntary dissolution. In other states, a statute authorizes courts to order buyouts as one of several possible remedies in dissolution proceedings or other litigation among shareholders. Courts also may order buyouts pursuant to their general equitable authority.

* * *

Often, a court expressly will choose a buyout over dissolution as a less harsh remedy. The recognition of the possibility of a buyout as a less drastic remedy undoubtedly has contributed to the breakdown of the traditional judicial and legislative resistance to granting relief where there is dissension among shareholders. * * *

* * *

In addition to buyouts, many corporation statutes now provide for additional remedies, such as the appointment of a custodian or provisional director. * * * Despite their widespread inclusion in statutes, these remedies are not used often. There is a cost to an additional layer of management, which would unduly burden a small enterprise, and the appointment of an outside party may not address the underlying differences among the participants.

Dissolution, buyout, and appointment of a provisional director or custodian do not exhaust the array of possible remedies for shareholder dissension. Some statutes authorize additional remedies, and sometimes courts order remedies that are not enumerated in a statute. Some corporation statutes, such as California's, North Dakota's, and Alaska's, simply authorize a court to provide any equitable relief that the court deems to be appropriate. * * *

The statutes in some states authorize courts to provide relief other than dissolution, with a nonexclusive list of possible relief. Additional remedies specifically mentioned by statute beyond those already discussed include: cancelling or altering any provision of the articles of incorporation, the by-laws, or a corporate resolution; directing or prohibiting any act of the corporation, shareholders, directors, officers, or other persons party to the action; or even providing for the sale of all the property and franchises of the corporation to a single purchaser. * * *

These remedies often are presented as alternatives to dissolution, but a court still may order a dissolution in an appropriate case. * * *

In the absence of a statute, judicial decisions reflect an increasing willingness to fashion a remedy best suited to the particular factual circumstances. Several opinions list ten or more remedies that might be appropriate. The list of remedies applied in individual cases is even longer, and includes:

1.   requiring dissolution at a future date, effective only if the parties do not resolve their differences before that time;

2.   appointing a receiver or special fiscal agent to continue the operation of the corporation until differences are resolved or until oppressive conduct ceases. This relief is similar to the appointment of a custodian. * * *

3.   retaining jurisdiction for the protection of minority shareholders;

4.   ordering an accounting for funds alleged to have been misappropriated;

5.   ordering access to corporate records;

6.   enjoining continuing acts of oppressive conduct, e.g., by reducing unjustified or excessive salary or bonus payments to controlling shareholders;

7.   requiring declaration of a dividend;

8.   defining as constructive dividends any corporate funds above a "reasonable salary" paid to the controlling shareholders and ordering the corporation to pay a shareholder discharged without cause an amount per share equal to the constructive dividend (a combination of the last two remedies listed immediately above);

9.   ordering issued stock to be cancelled or redeemed in order to achieve an equal balance of ownership or some other ownership structure fair to the shareholders;

10. permitting the minority to purchase additional shares;

11. rescinding a particular corporate act that is unfair to the minority;

12. treating a group of related corporations [as] a single entity for the purpose of determining appropriate relief;

13. awarding damages to the minority shareholder as compensation for injuries suffered by oppressive conduct; and

14. awarding punitive damages.

In many situations, the relief listed * * * is not different from that which courts traditionally have given for breach of fiduciary duty * * *. These cases illustrate that modern courts move easily back and forth between the dissolution-related remedies and the direct fiduciary duty remedies, depending on which is more appropriate in the particular factual circumstances.

NOTES

(1) In *Davis*, what "reasonable expectations" of appellee Sheerin were frustrated by the conduct of appellants?

(2) The Texas statute at issue in *Davis* did not expressly provide for a buyout remedy. Why did the court believe that it had authority to order a buyout?

(3) The Virginia Supreme Court has held that the remedy provided in the Virginia involuntary dissolution statute is exclusive. *See* Giannotti v. Hamway, 387 S.E.2d 725, 733 (Va. 1990) ("[T]he General Assembly has cloaked courts of equity with, in the words of the statute, 'full power' to liquidate in a proper case where oppressive conduct has been established. The remedy specified by the legislature, while discretionary, is 'exclusive,' and does not permit the trial court to fashion other, apparently equitable

remedies."). Most other courts disagree with this "exclusivity" conclusion. *See, e.g.*, Brenner v. Berkowitz, 634 A.2d 1019, 1033 (N.J. 1993) ("We hold that the statutory remedies of *N.J.S.A.* 14A:12–7(1) [the New Jersey dissolution for oppression and deadlock statute] are discretionary. Even when the statute is triggered, the trial court has the discretion to choose the appropriate remedies. * * * Importantly, courts are not limited to the statutory remedies, but have a wide array of equitable remedies available to them."). As between the *Davis/Brenner* courts (non-statutory alternative remedies are permissible) and the *Giannotti* court (non-statutory alternative remedies are impermissible), which approach makes more sense?

(4) A buyout of an aggrieved investor's shares at "fair value" has become the most common remedy for dissension in a closely held corporation. Why? What are the advantages of a buyout? What are the disadvantages?

(5) When an investor files a petition for dissolution on oppression or other grounds, a number of statutes permit a corporation or one or more shareholders to circumvent the dissolution petition by "electing" to purchase the petitioner's shares at "fair value." *See, e.g.*, CAL. CORP. CODE § 2000; N.Y. BUS. CORP. LAW § 1118; MBCA § 14.34. When such an election is made, the dissolution action is effectively converted into a valuation proceeding, as the oppression (or other) allegations are usually no longer at issue. These election statutes stem in large part from the notion that "the rights of the petitioning shareholder are fully protected by liquidating only the petitioner's interest and paying the fair value of his or her shares while permitting the remaining shareholders to continue the business." MBCA § 14.34 cmt.

(6) What does "fair value" mean in the dissension-related buyout context? Consider the following:

> * * * [There are] two conflicting approaches to the meaning of "fair value"—conflicting approaches that litigants still argue over today.

> The first approach equates fair value with fair market value. Under this position, a court values an oppressed minority's shares by considering what a hypothetical purchaser would pay for them. Because minority shares, by definition, lack control, a hypothetical purchaser is likely to pay less for minority shares than for shares that possess control (the "minority discount"). Moreover, because close corporation shares lack a ready market and are, as a consequence, difficult to liquidate, a hypothetical purchaser is likely to pay less for close corporation shares than for readily traded public corporation shares (the "marketability discount"). Under the fair market value interpretation of fair value, therefore, minority and marketability discounts are appropriate. * * *

> The second approach to the meaning of fair value defines fair value simply as a pro rata share of a company's overall value. If a close corporation is valued at $10 million, for example, the fair value of a 25 percent minority ownership position in that company is

worth 25 percent of the overall company value, or $2.5 million. Under this "enterprise value" approach, discounting for the shares' lack of control and lack of liquidity is inappropriate. * * *

Because the combined effect of minority and marketability discounts can reduce the value of a pro rata stake in a company by 50 percent or more, the propriety of discounts and the related debate over the meaning of fair value are issues of critical importance to close corporation investors.

Douglas K. Moll, *Shareholder Oppression & "Fair Value": Of Discounts, Dates, and Dastardly Deeds in the Close Corporation*, 54 DUKE L.J. 293, 296–97 (2004).

(7) Valuation experts usually derive minority discounts from empirical data comparing "control acquisition prices with pre-acquisition minority interest transaction prices." SHANNON P. PRATT ET AL., VALUING A BUSINESS: THE ANALYSIS AND APPRAISAL OF CLOSELY HELD COMPANIES 316 (3rd ed. 1996). That data suggests that minority discounts are usually 26%–33% off the value of controlling shares. Marketability discounts usually derive from empirical data comparing sales of illiquid securities to sales of liquid publicly traded securities. *See id.* at 334–48. "Because of these extreme contrasts between the ability to sell or hypothecate closely held minority stock as compared with publicly traded stock, empirical evidence * * * suggests that discounts for lack of marketability for minority interest closely held stocks tend to cluster in the range of 35 to 50 percent from their publicly traded counterparts." *Id.* at 334.

(8) While courts largely agree that the minority discount should be rejected in the oppression setting, *see, e.g.*, Brown v. Allied Corrugated Box Co., 154 Cal. Rptr. 170, 176 (Ct. App. 1979), less consensus exists on the propriety of the marketability discount. *Compare* Balsamides v. Protameen Chems., Inc., 734 A.2d 721, 733, 735–36, 738 (N.J. 1999) (applying a marketability discount to a buyout of the oppressor's shares by the oppressed investor), *and In re* Blake, 486 N.Y.S.2d 341, 349 (App. Div. 1985) ("A discount for lack of marketability is properly factored into the equation because the shares of a closely held corporation cannot be readily sold on a public market."), *with* Chiles v. Robertson, 767 P.2d 903, 926 (Or. Ct. App. 1989) ("We agree with the trial court's refusal to adjust the purchase price to reflect * * * marketability discounts. This is not a sale by a willing seller to a willing buyer, and defendants should not benefit from reductions in value that are based on such a sale. We require defendants to purchase plaintiffs' interests because of their breach of duty to plaintiffs. The purchase is a judicial remedy to compensate plaintiffs for the damage resulting from defendants' wrongs, not a market transaction.").

(9) When considering the meaning of fair value in the oppression context, courts frequently look to appraisal (also known as dissenters' rights) statutes and precedents for guidance. *See* Chapter 16, Section F (discussing appraisal). In every jurisdiction, shareholders have statutory rights to dissent

from specified corporate actions (usually fundamental transactions, such as mergers) and to receive the appraised fair value of their shares. (Not all appraisal statutes use the term "fair value," but the vast majority do.) MBCA § 13.02, for example, provides appraisal rights for certain mergers, share exchanges, dispositions of assets, and amendments to the articles of incorporation. Similar issues regarding the meaning of fair value and the propriety of discounts arise in the appraisal context as well. *See, e.g.,* Cavalier Oil Corp. v. Harnett, 564 A.2d 1137, 1145 (Del. 1989) (rejecting the use of minority and marketability discounts in the appraisal context).

(10) As the above materials mention, the appointment of a custodian or provisional director is often a remedial option for a court dealing with deadlock or other dissension in a closely held corporation. *See, e.g.,* MBCA § 14.32; DGCL §§ 226, 352, 353. What is the function of a custodian or provisional director? How do the positions differ? The following excerpt addresses these questions:

> When corporate participants are unable to agree on critical business decisions necessary to advance the operations of the company, a court may appoint a custodian or temporary receiver to manage the affairs of the corporation until the conflicts are resolved. The terms "custodian" and "temporary receiver" are often used interchangeably and are to be distinguished from receivers who are appointed to wind up the corporation and liquidate its assets. The custodian has the power to take over and maintain all operations of the deadlocked corporation until the parties can reach agreement and resume management of the corporation's affairs. Because the custodian is vested with the ability to exercise all of the powers of the board of directors, the custodian effectively replaces the board as the decisionmaking body of the corporation.

> Appointing a custodian is less severe than ordering dissolution. It provides the parties with the opportunity to attempt to break the deadlock themselves by giving them a sufficient cooling off period to restore their relationship. The presence of the custodian also encourages the parties to resolve their differences quickly so that the outsider may be removed from managing the business for them.

> One of the drawbacks of appointing a custodian or temporary receiver is the potential negative impact it will have on the company's relationship with its creditors, suppliers, and customers. These groups may view the appointment of the custodian as an indication that the corporation is financially troubled, and they may consequently demand greater protections or refuse to approve further extensions of credit. In a broader sense, the custodian's effectiveness is limited because businesses typically will not prosper as well in the hands of an outside custodian. Custodians in effect maintain the status quo; they are appointed to preserve the operations of the business, not to maximize its profitability.

* * *

A provisional director is a neutral third party who is appointed by the court and vested with the rights and powers of a director to vote at board meetings. The provisional director acts as a type of in-house arbitrator with the power to vote to break deadlocks. At the same time, the provisional director serves a mediating function by facilitating communication between the parties at board meetings and offering new ideas or alternatives for resolving the contested issues. In this regard, the provisional director remedy appears to share many of the same characteristics as [mediation-arbitration] as a form of dispute resolution: the provisional director listens to the parties state their positions and vent their emotions, attempts to help them reach some type of agreement and, failing that, votes to break the tie. The remedy is less severe than the appointment of a custodian or receiver who takes over the management of the business entirely. The provisional director cannot initiate actions over the objections of the other directors, nor can the provisional director shift control of the business operations away from the owners.

Various advantages are associated with the provisional director remedy. It avoids the dissolution of the corporation and enables the business to continue operating as a going concern in the hands of its current owners. Shareholders of successful companies presumably wish to restore rather than to destroy the symbiotic relationship which was once the source of mutual wealth. Like the custodian remedy, the appointment of a provisional director buys the parties some time to cool off and attempt to reestablish cooperation with each other. However, in contrast to custodianships, the provisional director remedy allows the parties to stay in charge of the company and involves less disruption to the business. Moreover, the appointment of a provisional director does not draw the same alarm from the corporation's creditors and suppliers as the appointment of a custodian or receiver.

* * *

* * * If the parties have become completely incompatible, the appointment of a provisional director may be futile and may only delay the inevitable break-up of the company. The remedy involves higher transaction costs because the parties must return to the court for more serious relief if the remedy fails. * * * However, the provisional director remedy may be problematic on more fundamental grounds. It deprives resisting shareholders of their right to veto managerial decisions by vesting in a court-appointed stranger the authority essentially to override the veto. This raises deeper questions about the extent to which courts may influence or interfere with private business and, equally important, about whether courts should be intricately involved at all in the enforcement of ongoing, personal, consensual business relationships that are fraught with friction.

Susanna M. Kim, *The Provisional Director Remedy for Corporate Deadlock: A Proposed Model Statute*, 60 WASH. & LEE L. REV. 111, 125–27, 134–37 (2003) (internal quotations omitted).

PROBLEM

Able, Baker, and Carter form a closely held corporation. They each invest the same sum of money and receive a one-third ownership interest in the firm. The three owners share an understanding that each investor is entitled to employment and to a management position with the company. Not surprisingly, therefore, Able, Baker, and Carter all work full-time for the company as employees, and they serve as the company's officers and directors as well. The company pays no dividends.

Baker earns $120,000 in his position as Chief Operating Officer of the company (comparable positions in similar companies earn between $80,000–$120,000). Able and Carter unjustifiably terminate Baker's employment and remove Baker from his officer and director positions. Baker seeks comparable employment elsewhere and, after a diligent search, he accepts his best offer: a non-officer position paying a salary of $90,000.

Ultimately, Baker brings an oppression lawsuit against Able and Carter.

(a)   How has Baker been harmed by the conduct of Able and Carter?

(b)   Assume that Baker's lawsuit is successful and that a court orders a buyout of Baker's shares by the corporation. Does the buyout fully remedy the harms that Baker has suffered?

CHAPTER 14

TRANSACTIONS IN SHARES: SECURITIES FRAUD AND SALES OF CONTROL

■ ■ ■

A. THE DEVELOPMENT OF A FEDERAL REMEDY: RULE 10b–5

The foundational rule against insider trading (and other fraudulent activities) is SEC Rule 10b–5 promulgated by the Securities and Exchange Commission pursuant to authority granted by Congress in Section 10(b) of the Securities Exchange Act of 1934. Rule 10b–5 is, by a considerable margin, the most famous rule in securities law and probably in all of business law. The notes following the statute tell the story of how the rule came to be enacted in response to a particular case of insider trading that the existing rules didn't appear to cover.

SECURITIES EXCHANGE ACT OF 1934 § 10(b)
15 U.S.C.A. § 78j.

Section 10. It shall be unlawful for any person, directly or indirectly, by the use of any means or instrumentality of interstate commerce or of the mails, or of any facility of any national securities exchange—* * *

(b) To use or employ, in connection with the purchase or sale of any security registered on a national securities exchange or any security not so registered, any manipulative or deceptive device or contrivance in contravention of such rules and regulations as the Commission may prescribe as necessary or appropriate in the public interest or for the protection of investors.

RULE 10b–5: EMPLOYMENT OF MANIPULATIVE AND DECEPTIVE DEVICES
17 C.F.R. § 240.10b–5.

It shall be unlawful for any person, directly or indirectly, by the use of any means or instrumentality of interstate commerce, or of the mails or of any facility of any national securities exchange,

(a) to employ any device, scheme, or artifice to defraud,

(b) to make any untrue statement of a material fact or to omit to state a material fact necessary in order to make the statements made, in the light of the circumstances under which they were made, not misleading, or

(c) to engage in any act, practice, or course of business which operates or would operate as a fraud or deceit upon any person, in connection with the purchase or sale of any security.

NOTES

(1) A variety of factors contributed to the original growth of Rule 10b–5. A major factor was that the state law of securities fraud was embryonic. There was little question that if A sold shares of stock to B on the basis of a misrepresentation, B could sue A for fraud under state law. Some state blue sky laws also provided a limited remedy against fraud in the sale of registered securities by issuers, but there appeared to be no practical state remedy against many perceived abuses in the markets for publicly traded securities. An early effort to bring a private action against a corporate officer who had engaged in insider trading was unsuccessful because of the lack of an affirmative misstatement by the defendant, and no duty was owed by a corporate officer to an individual shareholder. Goodwin v. Agassiz, 186 N.E. 659 (Mass.1933). Where, however, managers dealt personally with the shareholders or hid their identities by the use of intermediaries, concepts of fraud, misrepresentation, and reliance were developed that formed part of the basis of the modern state law of securities fraud and influenced developments under Rule 10b–5. This is well-illustrated by two famous cases: 1. Strong v. Repide, 213 U.S. 419 (1909) (holding for the plaintiff because a director used "special information" to buy undervalued stock from shareholders), and 2. Hotchkiss v. Fischer, 16 P.2d 531 (Kan.1932) (holding for the plaintiff shareholder because she was told to sell her stock because a dividend was not going to be declared even though the president of the company intended to declare a dividend).

(2) The first significant step in the development of Rule 10b–5 was the holding by Judge Kirkpatrick in 1947 that Rule 10b–5 could be the basis of a private suit to rescind a securities transaction. Kardon v. National Gypsum Co., 73 F.Supp. 798 (E.D.Pa.1947). The facts of this case, as set forth by Judge Kirkpatrick, were as follows:

> The plaintiffs, Morris and Eugene B. Kardon (father and son), and the defendants, Leon A. Slavin and William Slavin (brothers), owned all the capital stock of Western Board and Paper Co. and Michigan Paper Stock Co., its affiliate, each of the four holding one fourth. Western was engaged in manufacturing paper board and other paper products, having its plant located at Kalamazoo, and Michigan was a purchasing agent dealing chiefly in waste paper and similar materials for Western. All four were officers and together constituted the entire board of directors[.] * * *

> Prior to March 18, 1946, Leon Slavin had agreed for the corporation, by written instrument, considered by the parties to it to be binding,

to sell to National Gypsum, the plant and equipment of Western for the sum of $1,500,000. * * * The agreement was signed by Leon Slavin in his capacity as Executive Vice President of Western.

On March 18, 1946, the Slavins purchased all the stock of the Kardons in the two corporations, Western and Michigan, for $504,000. At that time the Kardons knew nothing whatever about the negotiations with National Gypsum, and the Slavins did not disclose any of the facts relating to them[.] * * *

Having acquired the plaintiffs' stock, the Slavins proceeded to consummate the transaction with National Gypsum. * * *

73 F.Supp. at 800.

On the critical question whether Rule 10b–5 might be used as the basis for a private cause of action in federal court, the judge simply stated that while the statute and rule "does not even provide in express terms for a remedy, * * * the existence of a remedy is implicit under general principles of the law." Id. at 802. Is this not a simple, garden-variety fraud case of little national or federal interest? Why should such litigation be in the federal courts in the absence of diversity? Rather surprisingly, various limiting doctrines for Rule 10b–5 later developed by the Supreme Court do not affect at all the availability of that rule for plaintiffs in *Kardon*-type cases, and such cases may continue to be freely brought in federal courts under the federal cause of action provided by Rule 10b–5. See, e.g., Glick v. Campagna, 613 F.2d 31 (3d Cir.1979). Indeed, one possible doctrine that might deflect many of these garden-variety fraud cases back to state court—the so-called "sale of business" doctrine—was expressly rejected by the United States Supreme Court in Landreth Timber Co. v. Landreth, 471 U.S. 681 (1985).

(3) Rule 10b–5 quickly became the provision routinely relied upon in all cases involving not only claims of improper trading by insiders, but also claims of securities fraud, deception, or trading in securities on the basis of undisclosed information in both publicly held and closely held corporations. The language of the Rule was broad, flexible, and not hedged with qualifications or limiting doctrine. Plaintiffs came to prefer the federal forum with its Rule 10b–5 precedents rather than the limited or nonexistent case law in the state courts. Rule 10b–5 flourished, and the state law tended to atrophy.

(4) Procedural advantages also encouraged the use of Rule 10b–5. The federal forum was viewed as superior for several reasons: nationwide service of process under § 27 of the Securities Exchange Act of 1934, liberal venue provisions, and generous discovery rules. The doctrine of pendent jurisdiction permits a federal court to hear both the Rule 10b–5 claim and the state claim in a single proceeding, while a state court cannot hear the Rule 10b–5 claim.

(5) The private cause of action for violations of Rule 10b–5, judicially created in Kardon v. National Gypsum Co., has received legislative recognition in federal statutes. In Musick, Peeler & Garrett v. Employers Ins. of Wausau, 508 U.S. 286, 292 (1993), the Court referred to these statutory

references and commented that "[w]e infer from these references an acknowledgment of the 10b–5 action without any further expression of legislative intent to define it."

———

Beginning in 1975, changes in the composition and philosophical orientation of the Supreme Court resulted in a significant change in approach toward Rule 10b–5. In a word, the period of unlimited growth and the use of Rule 10b–5 as a sort of universal solvent to resolve all securities problems ended. Three decisions outline the modern contours of Rule 10b–5.

Blue Chip Stamps v. Manor Drug Stores, 421 U.S. 723 (1975): In this case, the Court was faced with a claim by a person who was offered an opportunity to purchase securities but failed to do so because of materially misleading and overly pessimistic statements in the prospectus. An earlier decision by the Second Circuit, Birnbaum v. Newport Steel Corp., 193 F.2d 461 (2d Cir.), certiorari denied, 343 U.S. 956 (1952), had held that private plaintiffs in Rule 10b–5 suits should be limited to actual purchasers or sellers of securities. Over the dissent of Justices Blackmun, Douglas and Brennan—the then liberal wing of the Court—Justice Rehnquist approved of the *Birnbaum* rule in an opinion that reflected profound skepticism about the growth of Rule 10b–5. The opinion starts with a brief outline of the provisions of the Securities Act of 1933, the Securities Exchange Act of 1934, and Rule 10b–5. The Court then launched into a discussion of the scope of Rule 10b–5:

> We believe that the concern expressed for the danger of vexatious litigation which could result from a widely expanded class of plaintiffs under Rule 10b–5 is founded in something more substantial than the common complaint of the many defendants who would prefer avoiding lawsuits entirely to either settling them or trying them. These concerns have two largely separate grounds.

> The first of these concerns is that in the field of federal securities laws governing disclosure of information even a complaint which by objective standards may have very little chance of success at trial has a settlement value to the plaintiff out of any proportion to its prospect of success at trial so long as he may prevent the suit from being resolved against him by dismissal or summary judgment. * * *

> The potential for possible abuse of the liberal discovery provisions of the Federal Rules of Civil Procedure may likewise exist in this type of case to a greater extent than they do in other litigation * * * [T]o the extent that it permits a plaintiff with a largely groundless claim to simply take up the time of a number

of other people, with the right to do so representing an *in terrorem* increment of the settlement value, rather than a reasonably founded hope that the process will reveal relevant evidence, it is a social cost rather than a benefit.

Without the *Birnbaum* rule, an action under Rule 10b–5 will turn largely on which oral version of a series of occurrences the jury may decide to credit, and therefore no matter how improbable the allegations of the plaintiff, the case will be virtually impossible to dispose of prior to trial other than by settlement. * * *

The second ground for fear of vexatious litigation is based on the concern that, given the generalized contours of liability, the abolition of the *Birnbaum* rule would throw open to the trier of fact many rather hazy issues of historical fact the proof of which depended almost entirely on oral testimony. * * * The Securities and Exchange Commission, while opposing the adoption of the *Birnbaum* rule by this Court, states that it agrees with petitioners "that the effect, if any, of a deceptive practice on someone who has neither purchased nor sold securities may be more difficult to demonstrate than is the effect on a purchaser or seller." * * * The Commission suggests that in particular cases additional requirements of corroboration of testimony and more limited measure of damages would correct the dangers of an expanded class of plaintiffs.

But the very necessity, or at least the desirability, of fashioning unique rules of corroboration and damages as a correlative to the abolition of the *Birnbaum* rule suggests that the rule itself may have something to be said for it. * * *

[I]n the absence of the *Birnbaum* rule, it would be sufficient for a plaintiff to prove that he had failed to purchase or sell stock by reason of a defendant's violation of Rule 10b–5. * * * The very real risk in permitting those in respondent's position to sue under Rule 10b–5 is that the door will be open to recovery of substantial damages on the part of one who offers only his own testimony to prove that he ever consulted a prospectus of the issuer, that he paid any attention to it, or that the representations contained in it damaged him.[10] * * *

---

[10] The SEC, recognizing the necessity for limitations on nonpurchaser, nonseller plaintiffs in the absence of the *Birnbaum* rule, suggests two such limitations to mitigate the practical adverse effects flowing from abolition of the rule. First it suggests requiring some corroborative evidence in addition to oral testimony tending to show that the investment decision of a plaintiff was affected by an omission or misrepresentation. Apparently ownership of stock or receipt of a prospectus or press release would be sufficient corroborative evidence in the view of the SEC to reach the jury. We do not believe that such a requirement would adequately respond to the concerns in part underlying the *Birnbaum* rule. Ownership of stock or receipt of a prospectus

NOTES

(1) One issue discussed in *Blue Chip* was whether Rule 10b–5 might apply to transactions that also fall within express liability provisions of other federal securities laws. This issue was definitively answered in Herman & MacLean v. Huddleston, 459 U.S. 375 (1983), where the Court unanimously held that a cause of action may be maintained under Rule 10b–5 for fraudulent misrepresentations and omissions in a 1933 Act prospectus even though that conduct might also be actionable under § 11 of the 1933 Act.

(2) The *Birnbaum* principle involves a qualifying test for *plaintiffs* in Rule 10b–5 suits. As will appear below, a *defendant* may readily violate Rule 10b–5 even though it is not a purchaser or seller of securities, e.g., by influencing the market by a false press release or preparing a prospectus that contains false statements. Further, the issuer itself may be a nonselling defendant in Rule 10b–5 cases.

––––––––

Ernst & Ernst v. Hochfelder, 425 U.S. 185 (1976): In this case, the Court limited the scope of Rule 10b–5 by holding that the Rule applies only to activities that involve scienter. Later, the accounting profession was given even greater insulation from liability arising from Rule 10b–5 by the holding that it does not apply to claims based on aiding and abetting. Central Bank of Denver, N.A. v. First Interstate Bank of Denver, N.A., 511 U.S. 164 (1994). Ernst & Ernst v. Hochfelder involved a claim against an accounting firm for failing to have discovered a major fraud in a securities firm under the following circumstances:

> Petitioner, Ernst & Ernst, is an accounting firm. From 1946 through 1967 it was retained by First Securities Company of Chicago (First Securities) * * * to perform periodic audits of the firm's books and records. In connection with these audits Ernst & Ernst prepared for filing with the Securities and Exchange Commission (Commission) the annual reports required of First Securities under § 17(a) of the 1934 Act.[1] It also prepared for

––––––––

says little about whether a plaintiff's investment decision was affected by a violation of Rule 10b–5 or whether a decision was even made. Second, the SEC would limit the vicarious liability of corporate issuers to nonpurchasers and nonsellers to situations where the corporate issuer has been unjustly enriched by a violation. We have no occasion to pass upon the compatibility of this limitation with § 20(a) of the 1934 Act. We do not believe that this proposed limitation is relevant to the concerns underlying in part the *Birnbaum* rule as we have expressed them. * * *

[1]   Section 17(a) requires that securities brokers or dealers "make * * * and preserve * * * such accounts * * * books, and other records, and make such reports, as the Commission by its rules and regulations may prescribe as necessary or appropriate in the public interest or for the protection of investors." During the period relevant here, Commission Rule 17a–5, 17 CFR § 240.17a–5 (1975), required that First Securities file an annual report of its financial condition that included a certificate stating "clearly the opinion of the accountant with respect to the financial statement covered by the certificate and the accounting principles and practices reflected therein." The Rule required Ernst & Ernst to state in its certificate, *inter alia,* "whether the audit was made in accordance with generally accepted auditing standards applicable in the circumstances" and provided that nothing in the Rule should "be construed to imply authority for

First Securities responses to the financial questionnaires of the Midwest Stock Exchange (Exchange).

Respondents were customers of First Securities who invested in a fraudulent securities scheme perpetrated by Leston B. Nay, president of the firm and owner of 92% of its stock. Nay induced the respondents to invest funds in "escrow" accounts that he represented would yield a high rate of return. Respondents did so from 1942 through 1966, with the majority of the transactions occurring in the 1950s. In fact, there were no escrow accounts as Nay converted respondents' funds to his own use immediately upon receipt. These transactions were not in the customary form of dealings between First Securities and its customers. The respondents drew their personal checks payable to Nay or a designated bank for his account. No such escrow accounts were reflected on the books and records of First Securities, and none was shown on its periodic accounting to respondents in connection with their other investments. Nor were they included in First Securities' filings with the Commission or the Exchange.

This fraud came to light in 1968 when Nay committed suicide, leaving a note that described First Securities as bankrupt and the escrow accounts as "spurious." Respondents subsequently filed this action for damages against Ernst & Ernst in the United States District Court for the Northern District of Illinois under § 10(b) of the 1934 Act. The complaint charged that Nay's escrow scheme violated § 10(b) and Commission Rule 10b–5,[4] and that Ernst & Ernst had "aided and abetted" Nay's violations by its "failure" to conduct proper audits of First Securities. As revealed through discovery, respondents' cause of action rested on a theory of negligent nonfeasance. The premise was that Ernst & Ernst had failed to utilize "appropriate auditing procedures" in its audits of First Securities, thereby failing to discover internal practices of the firm said to prevent an effective audit. The practice principally relied on was Nay's rule that only he could open mail addressed to him at First Securities or addressed to First Securities to his attention, even if it arrived in his absence. Respondents contended that if Ernst & Ernst had conducted a proper audit, it would have discovered this "mail rule." The

---

the omission of any procedure which independent accountants would ordinarily employ in the course of an audit for the purpose of expressing the opinions required" by the Rule.

[4] Immediately after Nay's suicide the Commission commenced receivership proceedings against First Securities. In those proceedings all of the respondents except two asserted claims based on the fraudulent escrow accounts. These claims ultimately were allowed in SEC v. First Securities Co., 463 F.2d 981, 986 (CA7), cert. denied, 409 U.S. 880, 93 S.Ct. 85, 34 L.Ed.2d 134 (1972), where the court held that Nay's conduct violated § 10(b) and Rule 10b–5, and that First Securities was liable for Nay's fraud as an aider and abettor. The question of Ernst & Ernst's liability was not considered in that case.

existence of the rule then would have been disclosed in reports to the Exchange and to the Commission by Ernst & Ernst as an irregular procedure that prevented an effective audit. This would have led to an investigation of Nay that would have revealed the fraudulent scheme. Respondents specifically disclaimed the existence of fraud or intentional misconduct on the part of Ernst & Ernst.[5] * * *

As in *Blue Chip*, the court approached the issue of whether scienter was required as an element of a Rule 10b–5 violation in a narrow fashion:

> * * * Courts and commentators long have differed with regard to whether scienter is a necessary element of such a cause of action, or whether negligent conduct alone is sufficient. In addressing this question, we turn first to the language of § 10(b), for "[t]he starting point in every case involving construction of a statute is the language itself."

> Section 10(b) makes unlawful the use or employment of "any manipulative or deceptive device or contrivance" in contravention of Commission rules. The words "manipulative or deceptive" used in conjunction with "device or contrivance" strongly suggest that § 10(b) was intended to proscribe knowing or intentional misconduct. * * * [Their use makes] unmistakable a congressional intent to proscribe a type of conduct quite different from negligence. Use of the word "manipulative" is especially significant. It is and was virtually a term of art when used in connection with securities markets. It connotes intentional or willful conduct designed to deceive or defraud investors by controlling or artificially affecting the price of securities.* * *

> * * * The Commission contends * * * that subsections (b) and (c) of Rule 10b–5 are cast in language which—if standing alone—could encompass both intentional and negligent behavior. * * * Viewed in isolation the language of subsection (b), and arguably that of subsection (c), could be read as proscribing, respectively, any type of material misstatement or omission, and any course of conduct, that has the effect of defrauding investors, whether the wrongdoing was intentional or not.

> We note first that such a reading cannot be harmonized with the administrative history of the Rule, a history making clear that when the Commission adopted the Rule it was intended to apply

---

[5]   In their response to interrogatories in the District Court respondents conceded that they did "not accuse Ernst & Ernst of deliberate, intentional fraud," merely with "inexcusable negligence."

only to activities that involved scienter.[32] More importantly, Rule 10b–5 was adopted pursuant to authority granted the Commission under § 10(b). The rulemaking power granted to an administrative agency charged with the administration of a federal statute is not the power to make law. Rather, it is " 'the power to adopt regulations to carry into effect the will of Congress as expressed by the statute.' " Dixon v. United States, 381 U.S. 68, 74, 85 S.Ct. 1301, 1305, 14 L.Ed.2d 223, 228 (1965). Thus, despite the broad view of the Rule advanced by the Commission in this case, its scope cannot exceed the power granted the Commission by Congress under § 10(b). * * * When a statute speaks so specifically in terms of manipulation and deception, and of implementing devices and contrivances—the commonly understood terminology of intentional wrongdoing— and when its history reflects no more expansive intent, we are quite unwilling to extend the scope of the statute to negligent conduct.[33] * * *

---

[32] Apparently the Rule was a hastily drafted response to a situation clearly involving intentional misconduct. * * * See Conference on Codification of the Federal Securities Laws, 22 Bus.Law. 793, 922 (1967) (remarks of Milton Freeman, one of the rule's co-drafters). * * * There is no indication in the administrative history of the Rule that any of the subsections was intended to proscribe conduct not involving scienter. Indeed the Commission's release issued contemporaneously with the Rule explained:

"The Securities and Exchange Commission today announced the adoption of a rule prohibiting fraud by any person in connection with the purchase of securities. The previously existing rules against fraud in the purchase of securities applied only to brokers and dealers. The new rule closes a loophole in the protections against fraud administered by the Commission by prohibiting individuals or companies from buying securities if they engage in fraud in their purchase." SEC Release No. 3230 (May 21, 1942).

That same year, in its Annual Report, the Commission again stated that the purpose of the Rule was to protect investors against "fraud":

"During the fiscal year the Commission adopted Rule X–10B–5 as an additional protection to investors. The new rule prohibits fraud by any person in connection with the purchase of securities, while the previously existing rules against fraud in the purchase of securities applied only to brokers and dealers." 1942 Annual Report of the Securities Exchange Commission 10.

[33] As we find the language and history of § 10(b) dispositive of the appropriate standard of liability, there is no occasion to examine the additional considerations of "policy," set forth by the parties, that may have influenced the lawmakers in their formulation of the statute. We do note that the standard urged by respondents would significantly broaden the class of plaintiffs who may seek to impose liability upon accountants and other experts who perform services or express opinions with respect to matters under the Acts * * *.

This case, on its facts, illustrates the extreme reach of the standard urged by respondents. As investors in transactions initiated by Nay, not First Securities, they were not foreseeable users of the financial statements prepared by Ernst & Ernst. Respondents conceded that they did not rely on either these financial statements or Ernst & Ernst's certificates of opinion. The class of persons eligible to benefit from such a standard, though small in this case, could be numbered in the thousands in other cases. Acceptance of respondents' view would extend to new frontiers the "hazards" of rendering expert advice under the Acts, raising serious policy questions not yet addressed by Congress.

NOTES

(1) The question whether scienter should be required in SEC enforcement actions seeking injunctive relief was definitely resolved in Aaron v. Securities and Exch. Comm'n, 446 U.S. 680 (1980), where the Court held that scienter was a critical ingredient of all Rule 10b–5 cases.

(2) Virtually all lower courts addressing the question whether "reckless disregard" might constitute "scienter" since *Hochfelder* have concluded that a Rule 10b–5 violation may be grounded on "recklessness" or "reckless disregard of the truth" and that knowing, intentional misconduct is not a necessary ingredient of establishing liability. See, e.g., First Interstate Bank of Denver, N.A. v. Pring, 969 F.2d 891, 901 (10th Cir.1992), stating that "[t]he established rule is that recklessness is sufficient scienter for a primary violation of § 10(b) and Rule 10b–5." The Supreme Court granted certiorari in this case and reversed it on the grounds that Rule 10b–5 does not permit claims based on aiding and abetting.

————

Santa Fe Indus., Inc. v. Green, 430 U.S. 462 (1977): This case involved the question whether Rule 10b–5 could be applied to a Delaware short-form cash-out merger when the transaction was unfair to the minority shareholders but the effect of the transaction was fully disclosed.[a] The Court of Appeals held that although Rule 10b–5 clearly reaches material misrepresentations and nondisclosures in connection with the purchase or sale of securities, neither misrepresentation nor nondisclosure was an essential element of a Rule 10b–5 action. Rather, the Rule also reached "breaches of fiduciary duty by a majority against minority shareholders without any charge of misrepresentation or lack of disclosure."

The Supreme Court reversed in an opinion by Justice White:

> It is our judgment that the transaction, if carried out as alleged in the complaint, was neither deceptive nor manipulative and therefore did not violate either § 10(b) of the Act or Rule 10b–5. * * * [T]he cases do not support the proposition, adopted by the Court of Appeals below and urged by respondents here, that a breach of fiduciary duty by majority stockholders, without any deception, misrepresentation, or nondisclosure, violates the statute and the Rule.

> It is also readily apparent that the conduct alleged in the complaint was not "manipulative" within the meaning of the statute. "Manipulation" is "virtually a term of art when used in connection with securities markets." Ernst & Ernst, 425 U.S., at

---

[a] The Delaware appraisal procedure was available to dissenting shareholders on the facts of this case, but that remedy was unattractive because the case antedated by several years the *Weinberger* liberalization of the rules surrounding this state-created remedy.

199, 96 S.Ct., at 1384. The term refers generally to practices, such as wash sales, matched orders, or rigged prices, that are intended to mislead investors by artificially affecting market activity. * * * Indeed, nondisclosure is usually essential to the success of a manipulative scheme. * * * But we do not think it would have chosen this "term of art" if it had meant to bring within the scope of § 10(b) instances of corporate mismanagement such as this, in which the essence of the complaint is that shareholders were treated unfairly by a fiduciary. * * *

The language of the statute is, we think, "sufficiently clear in its context" to be dispositive here, Ernst & Ernst, 425 U.S., at 201, 96 S.Ct., at 1385; but even if it were not, there are additional considerations that weigh heavily against permitting a cause of action under Rule 10b–5 for the breach of corporate fiduciary duty alleged in this complaint. Congress did not expressly provide a private cause of action for violations of § 10(b). Although we have recognized an implied cause of action under that section in some circumstances, we have also recognized that a private cause of action under the antifraud provisions of the Securities Exchange Act should not be implied where it is "unnecessary to ensure the fulfillment of Congress' purposes" in adopting the Act. Piper v. Chris-Craft Industries, 430 U.S., at 41, 97 S.Ct., at 949 (1977). As we noted earlier, the Court repeatedly has described the "fundamental purpose" of the Act as implementing a "philosophy of full disclosure"; once full and fair disclosure has occurred, the fairness of the terms of the transaction is at most a tangential concern of the statute. As in Cort v. Ash, 422 U.S. 66, 78, 80, 95 S.Ct. 2080, 2087, 2090, 45 L.Ed.2d 26 (1975), we are reluctant to recognize a cause of action here to serve what is "at best a subsidiary purpose" of the federal legislation.

A second factor in determining whether Congress intended to create a federal cause of action in these circumstances is "whether 'the cause of action [is] one traditionally relegated to state law. * * *' " Piper v. Chris-Craft Industries, Inc., 430 U.S., at 40, 97 S.Ct., at 949, quoting Cort v. Ash, 422 U.S., at 78, 95 S.Ct., at 2087. The Delaware Legislature has supplied minority shareholders with a cause of action in the Delaware Court of Chancery to recover the fair value of shares allegedly undervalued in a short-form merger. Of course, the existence of a particular state law remedy is not dispositive of the question whether Congress meant to provide a similar federal remedy, but as in *Cort* and *Piper,* we conclude that "it is entirely appropriate in this instance to relegate respondent and others in his situation to whatever remedy is created by state law." 422 U.S., at 84, 95 S.Ct., at 2091; 430 U.S., at 41, 97 S.Ct., at 949.

* * * "Corporations are creatures of state law, and investors commit their funds to corporate directors on the understanding that, except where federal law *expressly* requires certain responsibilities of directors with respect to stockholders, state law will govern the internal affairs of the corporation." 422 U.S., at 84, 95 S.Ct., at 2091.

NOTE

The practical effect of the Supreme Court's decision in this case was to focus attention on state law as the regulator of transactions that literally followed state statutes but that were or might be unfair to defenseless interests. Six years following the decision in *Santa Fe,* the Delaware Supreme Court imposed duties of "intrinsic fairness" or "fiduciary duties" as a matter of state law to protect such interests. See Weinberger v. UOP, Inc. in Chapter 11, Section C, and the cases cited in the notes following that case.

IN RE ENRON CORPORATION SECURITIES, DERIVATIVE & ERISA LITIGATION

United States District Court, Southern District of Texas, 2002.
235 F. Supp. 2d 549.

HARMON, DISTRICT JUDGE:

The above referenced putative class action, brought on behalf of purchasers of Enron Corporation's publicly traded equity and debt securities during a proposed federal Class Period from October 19, 1998 through November 27, 2001, alleges * * * that: (1) Canadian Imperial Bank of Commerce ("CIBC"); (2) CitiGroup Inc.; (3) J.P. Morgan Chase & Co.; (4) Vinson & Elkins L.L.P.; (5) Arthur Andersen LLP; (6) Barclays PLC; (7) Credit Suisse First Boston; (8) Kirkland & Ellis; (9) Bank of America Corporation; (10) Merrill Lynch & Co.; (11) Lehman Brothers Holdings Inc.; and (12) Deutsche Bank AG, and other named Defendants, "are liable for (i) making false statements, or failing to disclose adverse facts while selling Enron securities and/or (ii) participating in a scheme to defraud and/or a course of business that operated as a fraud or deceit on purchasers of Enron's public securities during the Class Period." * * *

c.   *Central Bank* and Primary Violations

Of substantial relevance to the motions this Court now reviews is the Supreme Court's holding in a 5–4 decision in *Central Bank of Denver, N.A. v. First Interstate Bank of Denver, N.A.,* 511 U.S. 164, 114 S.Ct. 1439, 128 L.Ed.2d 119 (1994), based on the language and legislative history of the statute, that a private plaintiff may not bring an aiding and abetting claim under § 10(b) and Rule 10b–5. The high court construed the general anti-fraud provision as prohibiting only the making of a material misstatement or a material omission or the commission of a manipulative act; therefore it does not prohibit giving aid to another, who then commits a primary § 10(b) violation. It further emphasized that none of the express private causes of action in both the Securities Act of 1933 and the 1934 Exchange Act imposes liability on one who aids or abets such primary violators.

Nevertheless, the Supreme Court did not conclude that secondary actors such as lawyers, accountants, banks, and underwriters were therefore always shielded from § 10(b) and Rule 10b–5 liability:

> * * * Any person or entity, including a lawyer, accountant, or bank, who employs a manipulative device or makes a material misstatement (or omission) on which a purchaser or seller of securities relies may be liable as a primary violator under 10b–5, assuming *all* of the requirements for primary liability under Rule 10b–5 are met. * * *

The SEC proposes * * * the following rule for primary liability of a secondary party under § 10(b): "when a person, acting alone or with others, creates a misrepresentation [on which the investor-plaintiffs relied], the person can be liable as a primary violator * * * if * * * he acts with the requisite scienter. * * * Moreover it would not be necessary for a person to be the initiator of a misrepresentation in order to be a primary violator. Provided that a plaintiff can plead and prove scienter, a person can be a primary violator if he or she writes misrepresentations for inclusion in a document to be given to investors, even if the idea for those misrepresentations came from someone else." * * *

Because § 10(b) expressly delegated rule-making authority to the agency, which it exercised *inter alia* in promulgating Rule 10b–5, this Court accords considerable weight to the SEC's construction of the statute since the Court finds that construction is not arbitrary, capricious or manifestly contrary to the statute. * * * *Chevron, U.S.A., Inc. v. Natural Resources Defense Council*, 467 U.S. 837, 842–44, 104 S.Ct. 2778, 81 L.Ed.2d 694 (1984) ("considerable weight should be accorded to an executive department's construction of a statutory scheme it is entrusted to administer" * * *).

Thus * * * to survive a motion to dismiss, a complaint alleging that more than one defendant participated in a "scheme" to defraud must allege a primary violation of § 10(b) by each defendant.

1. Attorneys

The issue of attorney liability involving a duty to disclose nonmisleading information to nonclients and third parties is a thorny one, complicated by tension between the need to provide remedy to parties suffering monetary loss because of a lawyer's conduct and the attorney-client relationship with its attendant confidentiality, loyalty and zealous representation requirements and policy concerns. * * *

Pursuant to ABA Model Rule of Professional Conduct 1.2(d) an attorney "shall not counsel a client to engage, or assist a client in, conduct that the lawyer knows is criminal or fraudulent * * *, but the attorney may discuss the legal consequences of any proposed conduct and help the client make a good faith effort to determine the application of the law to that proposed conduct. However, a lawyer may not knowingly assist a client in criminal or fraudulent conduct. There is a critical distinction between presenting an analysis of legal aspects of questionable conduct and recommending the means by which a crime or fraud might be committed with impunity." * * *

This Court concludes that professionals, including lawyers and accountants, when they take the affirmative step of speaking out, whether individually or as essentially an author or co-author in a statement or report, whether identified or not, about their client's financial condition, do have a duty to third parties not in privity not to knowingly or with severe recklessness issue materially misleading statements on which they intend or have reason to expect that those third parties will rely.

2.   Accountant/Auditor

There is no accountant/client privilege analogous to that accorded to lawyers. The United States Supreme Court has held, "[b]y certifying the public reports that collectively depict a corporation's financial status, the independent auditor assumes a public responsibility transcending any employment relationship with the client. The independent public accountant performing this special function owes ultimate allegiance to the corporation's creditors and stockholders, as well as to the investing public." *United States v. Arthur Young & Co.,* 465 U.S. 805, 817–18, 104 S.Ct. 1495, 79 L.Ed.2d 826 (1984). * * *

III. Lead Plaintiff's Allegations in Consolidated Complaint

A.   The Scheme, Generally

Lead Plaintiff asserts that Defendants participated in "an enormous Ponzi scheme, the largest in history," involving illusory profits "generated by phony, non-arm's-length transactions with Enron-controlled entities and improper accounting tricks" in order to inflate Enron's reported revenues and profits, conceal its growing debts, maintain its artificially high stock prices and investment grade credit rating, as well as allow individual defendants to personally enrich themselves by looting the corporation, while continuing to raise money from public offerings of Enron or related entities' securities to sustain the scheme and to postpone the collapse of the corporation, a scenario characterized by Lead Plaintiff as "a hall of mirrors inside a house of cards." The consolidated complaint sets out an elaborate scheme of off-the-books, illicit partnerships, secretly controlled by Enron and established at times critical for requisite financial disclosures by Enron in order to conceal its actual financial status. These Enron-controlled entities typically would buy troubled assets from Enron, which Enron would have had difficulty selling in an arm's length transaction to an independent entity and which otherwise would have to be reported on Enron's balance sheet, by means of sham swaps, hedges, and transfers, to record phony profits and conceal debt on Enron's balance sheet. Lead Plaintiff further paints a picture of participation in the scheme by Enron's accountants, outside law firms, and banks, which all were the beneficiaries of such enormous fees and increasing business, as well as investment opportunities for personal enrichment, with the result that their opinions were rubber stamps that deceived investors and the public. * * *

[T]he consolidated complaint charges that Defendants caused Enron to violate GAAP (Generally Accepted Accounting Principles) and SEC rules in order to overstate Enron's assets, shareholders' equity, net income and earnings per share, and to understate its debt. Defendants also caused Enron to present materially misleading statements in Enron's financial statements (including press releases and SEC filings, such as Form 10–Qs for interim results and Form 10–Ks for annual results), which were incorporated into Registration Statements and Prospectuses (filed during the Class Period). Enron also made misrepresentations about Defendants' manipulations, all concealed by the following numerous, improper accounting ploys: not consolidating illicit SPEs (Special Purpose Entities) into Enron's financial statements to properly reflect reduced earnings and debt on Enron's balance sheet; improperly accounting for common stock issued to a related-party entity that should have been treated as a reduction in shareholders' equity, but was identified as a note receivable; improperly accounting for broadband transactions; abusing mark-to-market accounting; characterizing loans as forward contracts to conceal Enron's debt; improperly accounting for long-term contracts; failing to record required write-downs for impairment in value of Enron's investments, long-term assets, and its broadband and technology investments in a timely manner; failing to record an aggregate of $92 million in proposed audit adjustments from 1997 until the end of the Class period; failing to disclose related-party transactions; and misstating Enron's debt-to-equity ratio (measured as debt to total capitalization, a figure which rating agencies use to determine a company's credit rating) and ratio of earnings to fixed charges. Even while demonstrating the contrast between Enron's original financial statements and its restatement results, the consolidated complaint notes that many of Defendants' manipulations are not included in the restatement, such as the effects of Enron's abuse of accounting techniques.

B.   Defendant-Specific Allegations

1.   The Banks

Lead Plaintiff alleges that the banks participated in the Ponzi scheme for personal enrichment and for continuing business generating spectacular fees (such as the "long gravy train" of lucrative underwriting of Enron stock and bond offerings). Moreover, according to the complaint, once they were involved, their continued participation was also to limit their exposure to risk, salvage their financial investments, and save their reputations.

The charges against the banks are a blend of repetitive, conclusory, cookie-cutter contentions and of assertions that are unique or limited to only a few Defendants. In the former group, the consolidated complaint alleges that the banks advanced funds [to the SPEs] at key times to allow them and Enron to complete bogus transactions just before year- or quarter-end in order to create fake profits and to conceal billions of dollars of Enron debt that should have been reported on its balance sheet. Aware of Enron's financial fragility, the banks further made loans to Enron to insure its liquidity and continuing operations, while simultaneously aiding Enron in selling securities to public investors so that Enron could continue to pay down its short-term commercial paper and bank debt and keep the fraudulent Ponzi scheme afloat. The banks were central players in inflating and supporting the price of Enron stock through issuance of glowing research reports with misleading information about Enron.

JP Morgan, CitiGroup, and Credit Suisse First Boston also concealed billions of dollars in loans to Enron that were disguised as sales transactions. * * *

b.   CitiGroup

The complaint asserts that * * * CitiGroup enjoyed huge underwriting, advisory and transactional fees, interest, and commitment charges, and that some of its executives were given the opportunity to invest and did invest $15 million in LJM2 for lucrative returns. Its senior executives also allegedly interacted nearly daily with top executives at Enron, discussing its business in detail. It participated in the fraudulent course of conduct and business through loans to Enron of over $4 billion during the Class Period, helping Enron raise over $2 billion from the investing public through the sale of securities during the Class Period; it helped to structure and finance one or more of the illicit partnerships or SPEs that Enron used to inflate its earnings and conceal its debt; and it engaged in disguised loans to Enron that allowed Enron to falsify its financial situation.

CitiGroup purportedly also made false and misleading statements in the Registration Statements and Prospectuses for Enron securities sales for which it was an underwriter, including false interim and annual financial statements and statements regarding the structure of and Enron's relationship to SPEs and related parties. The complaint asserts that CitiGroup is liable for its participation as lead underwriter in the resale of the Enron zero coupon convertible notes on or after 7/18/01.

Lead Plaintiff further complains that CitiGroup issued numerous analysts' reports on Enron that contained false and misleading statements about Enron's financial condition, * * * all serving to artificially inflate the price of Enron's publicly traded securities.

2.   Law Firms

The consolidated complaint claims that Vinson & Elkins, Enron's outside general counsel during the Class Period, * * * participated in writing, reviewing, and approving Enron's SEC filings, shareholder reports and financial press releases, and in creating Chewco, JEDI, LJM1, LJM2, and nearly all the related SPEs' transactions. They knew that LJM2's principal purpose was to engage in transactions with Enron and that Enron insiders Fastow, Kopper and Glisan were operating on both sides of the transactions, to virtually insure lucrative returns for the entities' partners.

a.   Vinson & Elkins L.L.P.

Enron was Vinson & Elkins' largest client, accounting for more than 7% of the firm's revenues. Over the years more than twenty Vinson & Elkins lawyers have left the firm and joined Enron's in-house legal department.

The complaint recites a long history of alleged improprieties by Vinson & Elkins as part of the elaborate Ponzi scheme.

The complaint asserts that Vinson & Elkins participated in the negotiations for, prepared the transactions for, participated in the structuring of, and approved the illicit partnerships and the SPEs with knowledge that they were manipulative devices, not independent third parties and not valid SPEs, designed to move debt off Enron's books, inflate its earnings, and falsify Enron's reported financial results and financial condition at crucial times. Vinson & Elkins repeatedly provided "true sale"[91] and other opinions that were false and were indispensable for the sham deals to close and the fraudulent scheme to continue. * * *

Specifically, the complaint asserts that Vinson & Elkins provided advice in structuring virtually every Enron off-balance sheet transaction

---

[91] The complaint explains, "[T]rue sales opinions are letters that law firms write vouching for the fact that the business transactions meet particular legal requirements." Complaint at 404.

and prepared the transaction documents, * * * Vinson & Elkins allegedly had to know about and joined in the fraudulent Ponzi scheme because of its continuing, intimate involvement in the formation of and transactions with these blatantly fraudulent entities, created solely to cook Enron's books. * * *

The complaint * * * asserts that common to all Enron related-party disclosures, drafted and approved by Vinson & Elkins, was concealment of the following material matters known to Vinson & Elkins: (1) that the transactions were not true commercial, economic transactions comparable to those with independent third-parties; (2) the "disclosures" concealed the real substance and effect of the transactions on Enron and on its financial statements, e.g., that the transactions should have been consolidated on Enron's financial statements; and (3) they failed to disclose Fastow's actual financial interest in or compensation from the LJM partnerships. Instead the disclosures in SEC filings through the Class Period gave the impression that each transaction was fair to the company, not contrived, but made at arm's length as it would have been if made with an independent third party. In actuality the transactions, which were controlled only by Enron, Fastow or Kopper * * * were bogus, contrived to enrich individual Defendants, and, according to the special investigative committee [led by Dean William Powers], designed "to accomplish financial results, not achieve *bona fide* economic objectives or to transfer risk." * * *

The complaint points out that although [Enron employee and whistleblower] Sherron Watkins' August 2001 letter to Ken Lay represented that Vinson & Elkins had been involved in the fraud and had a clear conflict of interest, Lay still turned to top Vinson & Elkins partners to find out how to cover up the allegations. Furthermore, Vinson & Elkins despite this obvious conflict, agreed to conduct an investigation into the charges and to issue a letter or report dismissing the allegations of fraud that Vinson & Elkins knew were true. Vinson & Elkins also agreed not to "second guess" the accounting work or judgments of Arthur Andersen and to limit its inquiry to top level executives at Enron. Vinson & Elkins' review took place between August 15 and October 15, 2001.

During its investigation, according to the complaint, Vinson & Elkins only interviewed top level executives that Vinson & Elkins knew were involved in the fraud and would deny it. On October 15, 2001 the law firm issued a letter to Enron dismissing all of Sherron Watkins' allegations even though Vinson & Elkins knew they were true from its own involvement. The letter is quoted in part in the complaint:

> You requested that Vinson & Elkins L.L.P. ("V & E") conduct an investigation into certain allegations initially made on an *anonymous* basis by an employee of Enron Corp. ("Enron"). Those allegations question the propriety of Enron's accounting

treatment and public disclosures. * * * The anonymous employee later identified herself as Sherron Watkins, who met with Kenneth L. Lay, Chairman and Chief Executive Officer of Enron, for approximately one hour to express her concerns and provided him with materials to supplement her initial anonymous letter. * * *

In general, the scope of V & E's undertaking was to review the allegations raised by Ms. Watkins' anonymous letter and supplemental materials to conduct an investigation to determine whether the facts she has raised warrant further independent legal or accounting review.

In preliminary discussions with you, it was decided that our initial approach would not involve the second guessing of the accounting advice and treatment provided by AA, that there would be no detailed analysis of each and every transaction and that there would be no full scale discovery style inquiry. Instead the inquiry would be confined to a determination whether the anonymous letter and supplemental materials raised new factual information that would warrant a broader investigation. * * *

Interviews were also conducted with various Enron personnel. * * * Interviews were also conducted with David B. Duncan and Debra A. Cash, both partners with AA assigned to the Enron audit engagement. * * *

[N]one of the individuals interviewed could identify any transaction between Enron and LJM that was not reasonable from Enron's standpoint or that was contrary to Enron's best interests. * * *

The concern with adequacy of disclosures is that one can always argue in hindsight that disclosures contained in proxy solicitations, management's discussion and analysis and financial footnotes could be more detailed. In this regard, it is our understanding that Enron's practice is to provide its financial statements and disclosure statements to V & E with a relatively short time frame with which to respond with comments. * * *

The complaint recites that although Lay wanted to fire Watkins, he and Vinson & Elkins agreed that discharge would be a mistake and would lead to a wrongful termination suit, disclosing Watkins' allegations about transactions at Enron. So she was shifted to another position at Enron where she would have less exposure to information damaging to Enron.

3.   The Accountant/Auditor: Arthur Andersen LLP

Noting that an independent auditor is supposed to be the "investing public's watch dog," the complaint at 447 quotes the United States Supreme Court in *United States v. Arthur Young & Co.,* 465 U.S. 805, 817–18 (1984):

> By certifying the public reports that collectively depict a corporation's financial status, the independent auditor assumes a public responsibility transcending any employment relationship with the client. The independent public accountant performing this special function owes ultimate allegiance to the corporation's creditors and stockholders, as well as to the investing public. This "public watchdog" function demands that the accountant maintain total independence from the client at all times and requires complete fidelity to the public trust.

The complaint charges that Arthur Andersen abandoned its responsibilities to Enron investors and to the investing public and violated professional standards in perpetrating a massive accounting fraud.

The consolidated complaint maintains that Arthur Andersen was not independent of its client. Enron was Arthur Andersen's second largest client and Arthur Andersen was economically dependent on Enron, which generated approximately $50 million in fees annually for Arthur Andersen and expectations for more in the future. Indeed Arthur Andersen estimated internally that its fees for services for Enron could increase to $100 million per year. To generate even more fees, Arthur Andersen pressured, and provided incentive compensation to, its audit partners to solicit and market non-audit consulting services, which were far more lucrative, from Enron as well as other clients. David Duncan in the Houston office was earning as much as $2 million a year based largely on the level of fees he "controlled" or sold to his clients. The complaint asserts that the pressures on partners to generate more fees created a conflict of interest for auditors on the Enron engagement and were a substantial factor in Arthur Andersen's abandonment of its independence, objectivity, and integrity on the Enron financial statement audits and reviews. * * *

Arthur Andersen knew that the critical factor to increasing its fees was to maintain Enron's investment-grade credit rating, requiring a careful balance between creating outside entities to hold assets and the debt Enron was incurring to finance them and making it appear that Enron was not controlling these entities to avoid consolidation of their assets and debts into Enron's financial statements under GAAP. Aware of the risk, in a meeting [in] February 2001 about Enron's accounting issues, top level Arthur Andersen partners from the Houston and Chicago offices decided that the potential for doubling its fees to $100 million a year justified retaining Enron as a client. Furthermore when partner Carl Bass objected to and opposed the improper accounting practices used at Enron in 1999–2000, and thereby upset Enron management, top level Arthur Andersen partners removed him from his oversight role on the Enron audits.

Arthur Andersen operated its consulting services in a manner that revealed its lack of independence in audits and reviews.

Arthur Andersen was fully aware of Enron's unusually complex organization because it helped structure hundreds of complicated partnerships, many with no business purpose other than to conceal debt and losses. The number of related-party transactions was enormous, and in many Enron maintained control over the entities and deliberately and improperly did not consolidate them. Andersen knew that Enron utilized at least 600 offshore tax haven entities to shift income, minimize taxation, circumvent United States laws, and maintain secrecy. * * * Even Arthur Andersen's tax and consulting departments knew that Enron's use of such entities was excessive and that many had no business justification. * * *

A number of surviving Arthur Andersen documents reveal that Arthur Andersen knew, was concerned about, yet covered up or ignored fraudulent accounting practices by Enron. * * *

During a meeting on February 5, 2001, top Arthur Andersen executives from the Chicago headquarters participated in a teleconference with top Houston and Gulf Coast partners assigned to the Enron engagement about whether to retain Enron as a client. * * * The minutes of the meeting reflect a discussion, and therefore the participants' knowledge, of the accounting issues that ultimately caused Enron's collapse, including significant related-party transactions with LJM, the materiality of such amounts to Enron's income statement, and the amount retained "off balance sheet"; Fastow's conflict of interest in serving as CFO of Enron and LJM fund manager; Fastow's compensation for his services and participation in LJM; disclosures of transactions in the financial footnotes; Enron's mark-to-market earnings, described as "intelligent gambling"; Enron's reliance on its credit rating to maintain solvency; and Enron's aggressive transaction structuring. They decided to keep Enron as a client despite the red flags because of the potential $100 million fee they could receive, and a few weeks later Arthur Andersen issued a "clean" audit opinion on Enron's 2000 financial statements. * * *

In its audits of Enron's financial statements in 1997, Arthur Andersen identified $51 million of adjustments where the accounting was improper. Arthur Andersen knew these adjustments altogether constituted almost 50% of Enron's $105 million net income for that year and were therefore clearly material to the financial statements and needed to be made if those statements were not to be misleading.

Nevertheless, Enron informed Arthur Andersen it did not want to make those adjustments, which would radically reduce the net income that management wanted to report to the public. Arthur Andersen acquiesced in order to retain its lucrative client, and it abandoned its role as a public watch dog and violated GAAS. To justify not making such large adjustments, Arthur Andersen obfuscated the information by calculating the $51 million as an immaterial 8% of a contrived figure that it denominated as "normalized earnings," requiring no adjustment, instead of as a very material 51% of Enron's net income for 1997, which would require an adjustment. The complaint asserts that in 2001, too late for thousands of investors who lost billions of dollars because they relied on earlier years' financial statements, Enron restated its financial statements for 1997–2000 and Arthur Andersen commented that the audit reports covering the year-end financial statements for 1997–2000 "should not be relied upon."

III. Motions to Dismiss and the Court's Rulings

A.   Defendants' Common Objections

A number of Defendants argue that Lead Plaintiff's allegations that Defendants knew of the Ponzi scheme and yet poured millions of dollars into it or risked their reputations to conceal the scheme merely for fees, payments and profits, and subsequently, once caught in the scheme, shored it up in order to limit their exposure to liability and obtain what payments they could on Enron's debts to them, are inherently irrational, implausible, and/or illogical and the alleged actions are against Defendants' own self-interest. This Court notes that what may have been implausible two or three years ago is hardly so today, in light of a plethora of revelations, investigations, evidence, indictments, guilty pleas, and confessions of widespread corporate corruption and fraud by companies, auditors, brokerage houses, and banks. Lining one's pockets with gold, at the expense of investors, employees, and the public, appears too often to be a dominating ambition, and public skepticism about the market is very prevalent.

The third-party entities have objected with justification to the undifferentiated, boiler-plate allegations repetitively applied to all or many defendants or with generalized references. * * * They also criticize claims of misconduct based on what are common, legitimate business actions or practices (e.g., loans, commodity swaps, passive investments, underwriting securities offerings, regular working relationships with a company's executives, issuance of analyst reports, and desire to earn profits) that are not inherently improper or fraudulent. This Court responds that the activities must be viewed in context, i.e., within the totality of surrounding circumstances, to determine whether they are merely ordinary and legitimate acts or contrivances and deceptive devices used to defraud. * * *

B.   Section 10(b) Claims Against Defendants Individually

Rather than focusing upon deficiencies in the complaint, especially conclusory or boiler plate allegations, of which the Court agrees that there are many, the Court examines what Lead Plaintiff has specifically and successfully pled in this complaint against each Defendant to determine whether it adequately states a claim with specificity under § 10(b) and raises a strong inference of the requisite scienter that warrants denial of its motion to dismiss.

1.   Legal Standards

As a factor common to all, the Court initially finds that the scienter pleading requirement is partially satisfied by allegations of a regular pattern of related and repeated conduct involving the creation of unlawful, Enron-controlled SPEs, sale of unwanted Enron assets to these entities in clearly non-arm's length transactions and often with guarantees of no risk, in order to shift debt off Enron's balance sheet and sham profits onto its books at critical times when quarterly or year-end reports to the SEC, and by extension the public, were due, followed in many cases by the undoing of these very deals once the reports had been made. These transactions were not isolated, * * * but deliberate, repeated actions with shared characteristics that were part of an alleged common scheme through which Defendants all profited handsomely, many exorbitantly. The very pattern that is alleged undermines claims of unintentional or negligent behavior and supports allegations of intent to defraud. * * *

Moreover, Lead Plaintiff has pleaded effectively the common motive of, fixation on, and obsession with monetary gain. It has * * * alleged that extraordinary fees, interest rates, etc., were pocketed by the secondary actor Defendants, which only inflated with the expanding mirage of corporate success that they allegedly fraudulently created. * * *

Similarly, conclusory allegations asserted against all or most of the secondary actor Defendants, such as the long-term, continuous, intimate and extensive relationships with Enron and daily interaction with Enron's top executives, necessarily raise the specter of potential and unusual opportunities to learn about and take an active role in Enron's financial affairs, open access to nonpublic information about Enron, intimacy blending into complicity fueled by financial interests, and involvement in formulating, funding, drafting, and decision-making about key aspects of Enron's business, including the structuring and financing of Enron's secretly controlled partnerships with no economic purpose other than to defraud. In addition, the provision of both commercial banking and investment banking services to Enron raises the possibility of conflicts of interest and the standard mandatory in-depth credit analyses required of borrowers by lenders, etc., which should have raised red flags, are all background factors to be considered. * * *

Defendants have complained that they are being targeted for performing the normal functions of their businesses, e.g., lending money, underwriting stocks, accounting and auditing, or drafting legal documents. Obviously, regular business conduct within the bounds of the law would not support a claim of securities law violation; instead the allegations must demonstrate that they knowingly or with reckless disregard stepped outside the boundary of legitimate and professionally acceptable activities in performing material acts to defraud the public. * * *

a.   The Banks

Viewing the specific allegations together, the Court finds that plaintiff has stated a claim against Citigroup [and several other banks] as a primary violator under § 10(b) and Rule 10b–5 [because it] knowingly, or at least with severe recklessness, [made] a material misrepresentation * * * or engaged in an act, practice or course of business that operated as a fraud or deceit upon Enron investors. * * * Citigroup, through its Cayman Island subsidiary, also allegedly participated in a repeated pattern of * * * disguised large loans to Enron totaling $2.4 billion that were never disclosed on its balance sheet, through the [so-called] Delta transactions, at interest rates nearly double the normal borrowing rate, providing Citigroup with nearly $70 million annually for its participation in the Ponzi scheme.

b.   The Law Firms

Contrary to Vinson & Elkins' contention, the situation alleged in the consolidated complaint is not one in which Vinson & Elkins merely represented and kept confidential the interests of its client, which has the final authority to control the contents of the registration statement, other filing, or prospectus. Instead, the complaint alleges that the two were in league, with others, participating in a plan, with each participant making material misrepresentations or omissions or employing a device, scheme or artifice to defraud, or engaging in an act, practice or course of business that operated as a fraud, in order to establish and perpetuate a Ponzi scheme that was making them all very rich. * * *

Among the complaint's specific allegations of acts in furtherance of the scheme are * * * the firm's involvement in negotiation and structuring of the illicit partnerships and off-the-books SPEs, whose formation documentation it drafted, as well as * * * the subsequent transactions of these entities. * * * In other words, it "effected the very" deceptive devices and contrivances that were the heart of the alleged Ponzi scheme. *SEC v. U.S. Environmental,* 155 F.3d at 112. According to the allegations in the complaint, Vinson & Elkins chose to engage in illegal activity for and with its client in return for lucrative fees. Contrary to the Rules of Professional Conduct, it did not resign and thereby violated its professional principles and ethics. Nevertheless, had Vinson & Elkins remained silent publicly, the attorney/client relationship and the traditional rule of privity for suit against lawyers might protect Vinson & Elkins from liability to nonclients for such alleged actions on its client's (and its own) behalf.

But the complaint goes into great detail to demonstrate that Vinson & Elkins did not remain silent, but chose not once, but frequently, to make statements to the public about Enron's business and financial situation. Moreover in light of its alleged voluntary, essential, material, and deep involvement as a primary violator in the ongoing Ponzi scheme, Vinson & Elkins was not merely a drafter, but essentially a co-author of the documents it created for public consumption concealing its own and other participants' actions. Vinson & Elkins made the alleged fraudulent misrepresentations to potential investors, credit agencies, and banks, whose support was essential to the Ponzi scheme, and Vinson & Elkins deliberately or with severe recklessness directed those public statements toward them in order to influence those investors to purchase more securities, credit agencies to keep Enron's credit high, and banks to continue providing loans to keep the Ponzi scheme afloat. Therefore Vinson & Elkins had a duty to be accurate and truthful. Lead Plaintiff has alleged numerous inadequate disclosures by Vinson & Elkins that breached that duty.

Vinson & Elkins protests that its purported "whitewash" investigation and report in the wake of Sherron Watkins' August 1999 memorandum were not disclosed to the public until after Enron waived the attorney/client privilege and produced the report for Congressional hearings in 2002, after the Class Period ended, and thus cannot be the basis of a § 10(b) misrepresentation claim by the investors. Nevertheless the investigation and report can serve as the basis of a § 10(b) and Rule 10b–5(a) or (c) claim alleging use of a device, scheme or artifice to defraud or engagement in an act, practice or course of business that operated as a fraud in the perpetuation of the Ponzi scheme.

For these reasons the Court finds that Lead Plaintiff has stated claims under § 10(b) against Vinson & Elkins.

b.   The Accountant/Auditor: Arthur Andersen

Lead Plaintiff has alleged specific facts giving rise to a strong inference of scienter. Arthur Andersen's comprehensive accounting, auditing, and consulting services to Enron necessarily made it intimately privy to the smallest details of Enron's alleged fraudulent activity. Lead Plaintiff has described several similar prior fraudulent audits of other companies, establishing a pattern of such conduct, and the SEC's and courts' repeated imposition of penalties on Arthur Andersen and its employees, including the consent decree and injunction from the Waste Management fraud which was in effect at the time Lead Plaintiff alleges that Arthur Andersen violated § 10(b) in auditing Enron. Lead Plaintiff has also alleged details of the February 5, 2001 teleconference meeting of senior Arthur Andersen partners * * * from Chicago and Houston and the Gulf Coast when they discussed material concerns at the heart of the consolidated complaint: related-party transactions with LJM, Fastow's conflicts of interest, disclosures of transactions in financial footnotes, Enron's mark-to-market earnings, and Enron's aggressive transaction structuring, in essence the risk of continuing fraudulent accounting for Enron and retaining it as a client. They decided to continue because Enron's business was so lucrative, and a few weeks later they issued a clean audit opinion on the 2000 financial statements. Moreover, it has described e-mails and internal memoranda between and among Arthur Andersen employees * * * before the '99 financial statements were issued that reflect Arthur Andersen's knowledge and intent to continue in the fraudulent scheme. * * *

Because Lead Plaintiff has alleged numerous violations of GAAP and GAAS and pleaded facts giving rise to a strong inference of scienter, he has pleaded a securities fraud claim against Arthur Andersen.

NOTES

(1) Judge Harmon allowed the plaintiffs to use circumstantial evidence to create an inference that the defendants acted with the requisite scienter to support a cause of action for a violation of the securities laws. The circumstantial evidence used in this case was the active and intimate involvement of Enron's lawyers, accountants, and bankers in structuring the deals that misled investors and regulators. Doesn't this eviscerate the holding in Central Bank of Denver v. First Interstate Bank of Denver that the securities laws do not prohibit giving aid to another, who then commits a primary § 10(b) violation? If Judge Harmon's approach is correct, won't it always be possible to infer that advisers had knowledge of the misrepresentations and omissions of the primary actor?

(2) Note also the last two sentences in the Vinson & Elkins letter reporting on its investigation of Sherron Watkins' concerns about Enron's accounting practices: "[t]he concern with adequacy of disclosures is that one can always argue in hindsight that disclosures contained in proxy solicitations, management's discussion and analysis and financial footnotes could be more detailed. In this regard, it is our understanding that Enron's practice is to provide its financial statements and disclosure statements to V & E with a relatively short time frame with which to respond with comments." Whose interests were these sentences intended to serve?

(3) In high profile criminal proceedings, Kenneth Lay, Enron's former CEO, Jeffrey Skilling, alternately COO and CEO of Enron, and Richard Causey, Enron's Chief Accounting Officer, were charged individually and indicted by a grand jury on charges of multiple securities law violations, including violations of Rule 10b–5. Indictment in United States v. Causey, Cr. No. H–04–25 (S–2) (S.D. Tex.), filed July 7, 2004. Among other things, the three defendants were accused of misleading the public about Enron's true

financial situation right up until the company's collapse in 2001. Causey ultimately pled guilty, while Skilling and Lay were convicted by a jury in early 2006. Skilling was sentenced to 24 years and 4 months in prison for his role in the debacle, while Causey received a sentence of 5½ years. Lay's conviction was vacated after his sudden death in July 2006, prior to sentencing, from heart disease. United States v. Lay, 456 F.Supp.2d 869 (S.D. Tex. 2006).

B. INSIDER TRADING

The first statement that trading on the basis of inside information in the anonymous securities markets might violate Rule 10b–5 appeared in In the Matter of Cady, Roberts & Co., 40 SEC 907 (1961). This was an administrative proceeding by the SEC to discipline a broker who learned from a director of Curtiss-Wright Corporation that Curtiss-Wright planned to reduce its dividend and who then sold Curtiss-Wright common stock (and entered into several short sales of that stock) before the announcement of the dividend cut was made. Chairman Cary's opinion for the Commission broadly stated that insider trading violated Rule 10b–5:

> We have already noted that the anti-fraud provisions are phrased in terms of "any person" and that a special obligation has been traditionally required of corporate insiders, e.g., officers, directors and controlling stockholders. These three groups, however, do not exhaust the classes of persons upon whom there is such an obligation. Analytically, the obligation rests on two principal elements: first, the existence of a relationship giving access, directly or indirectly, to information intended to be available only for a corporate purpose and not for the personal benefit of anyone; and second, the inherent unfairness involved where a party takes advantage of such information knowing it is unavailable to those with whom he is dealing. In considering these elements under the broad language of the anti-fraud provisions we are not to be circumscribed by fine distinctions and rigid classifications. Thus our task here is to identify those persons who are in a special relationship with a company and privy to its internal affairs, and thereby suffer correlative duties in trading in its securities. Intimacy demands restraint lest the uninformed be exploited.

40 SEC at 912. Chairman Cary also rejected arguments that an insider's responsibility was limited to existing shareholders, that there was no prohibition against selling shares to members of the general public, and that Rule 10b–5 was only applicable to face-to-face transactions or cases of misrepresentation or manipulation.

While this holding received attention at the time, its full implication did not sink in for nearly eight years.

SECURITIES AND EXCHANGE COMM'N V. TEXAS GULF SULPHUR CO.

United States Court of Appeals, Second Circuit, 1968.
401 F.2d 833.

Before LUMBARD, CHIEF JUDGE, and WATERMAN, MOORE, FRIENDLY, SMITH, KAUFMAN, HAYS, ANDERSON and FEINBERG, CIRCUIT JUDGES.

WATERMAN, CIRCUIT JUDGE:

This action was commenced in the United States District Court for the Southern District of New York by the Securities and Exchange Commission (the SEC) pursuant to Sec. 21(e) of the Securities Exchange Act of 1934 (the Act), against Texas Gulf Sulphur Company (TGS) and several of its officers, directors and employees, to enjoin certain conduct by TGS and the individual defendants said to violate Section 10(b) of the Act, and Rule 10b–5 (the Rule) promulgated thereunder, and to compel the rescission by the individual defendants of securities transactions assertedly conducted contrary to law. * * *

The Factual Setting

This action derives from the exploratory activities of TGS begun in 1957 on the Canadian Shield in eastern Canada. In March of 1959, aerial geophysical surveys were conducted over more than 15,000 square miles of this area by a group led by defendant Mollison, a mining engineer and a Vice President of TGS. The group included defendant Holyk, TGS's chief geologist, defendant Clayton, an electrical engineer and geophysicist, and defendant Darke, a geologist. These operations resulted in the detection of numerous anomalies, i.e., extraordinary variations in the conductivity of rocks, one of which was on the Kidd 55 segment of land located near Timmins, Ontario.

On October 29 and 30, 1963, Clayton conducted a ground geophysical survey on the northeast portion of the Kidd 55 segment which confirmed the presence of an anomaly and indicated the necessity of diamond core drilling for further evaluation. Drilling of the initial hole, K–55–1, at the strongest part of the anomaly was commenced on November 8, and terminated on November 12 at a depth of 655 feet. Visual estimates by Holyk of the core of K–55–1 indicated an average copper content of 1.15% and an average zinc content of 8.64% over a length of 599 feet. This visual estimate convinced TGS that it was desirable to acquire the remainder of the Kidd 55 segment, and in order to facilitate this acquisition TGS President Stephens instructed the exploration group to keep the results of K–55–1 confidential and undisclosed even as to other officers, directors, and employees of TGS. The hole was concealed and a barren core was intentionally drilled off the anomaly. Meanwhile, the core of K–55–1 had been shipped to Utah for chemical assay which, when received in early December, revealed an average mineral content of 1.18% copper, 8.26% zinc, and 3.94% ounces of silver per ton over a length of 602 feet. These results were so remarkable that neither Clayton, an experienced geophysicist, nor four other TGS expert witnesses, had ever seen or heard of a comparable initial exploratory drill hole in a base metal deposit. So, the trial court concluded, "There is no doubt that the drill core of K–55–1 was unusually good and that it excited the interest and speculation of those who knew about it." [258 F.Supp.] at 282. By March 27, 1964, TGS decided that the land acquisition program had advanced to such a point that the company might well resume drilling, and drilling was resumed on March 31.

During this period, from November 12, 1963 when K–55–1 was completed, to March 31, 1964 when drilling was resumed, certain of the individual defendants[2] and persons said to have received "tips" from

---

[2] The purchases by the parties during this period were:

Date		Purchase Purchaser	Shares Number	Price	Calls Number	Price
1963						
Nov.	12	Fogarty	300	17 3/4–18		
	15	Clayton	200	17 3/4		
	15	Fogarty	700	17 5/8–7 7/8		
	15	Mollison	100	17 7/8		
	19	Fogarty	500	18 1/8		
	26	Fogarty	200	17 3/4		
	29	Holyk (Mrs.)	50	18		

Chemical Assays of Drill Core of K–55–1 Received December 9–13, 1963

Date		Purchaser	Number	Price	Number	Price
1963						
Dec.	10	Holyk (Mrs.)	100	20 3/8		
	12	Holyk (or wife)			200	21
	13	Mollison	100	21 1/8		
	30	Fogarty	200	22		
	31	Fogarty	100	23 1/4		
1964						
Jan.	6	Holyk (or wife)			100	23 5/8
	8	Murray			400	23 1/4
	24	Holyk (or wife)			200	22 1/4–22 3/8
Feb.	10	Fogarty	300	22 1/8–2 1/4		
	20	Darke	300	24 1/8		
	24	Clayton	400	23 7/8		
	24	Holyk (or wife)			200	24 1/8
	26	Holyk (or wife)			200	23 3/8
	26	Huntington	50	23 1/4		
Feb.	27	Darke (Moran as nominee)			1000	22 5/8–22 3/4
Mar.	2	Holyk (Mrs.)	200	22 3/8		
	3	Clayton	100	22 1/4		
	16	Huntington			100	22 3/8
	16	Holyk (or wife)			300	23 1/4
	17	Holyk (Mrs.)	100	23 7/8		
	23	Darke			1000	24 3/4
	26	Clayton	200	25		

Land Acquisition Completed March 27, 1964

Date		Purchaser	Number	Price	Number	Price
Mar.	30	Darke			1000	25 1/2

them, purchased TGS stock or calls[3] thereon. Prior to these transactions these persons had owned 1135 shares of TGS stock and possessed no calls; thereafter they owned a total of 8235 shares and possessed 12,300 calls.[4]

	30	Holyk (Mrs.)	100	25 7/8

Core Drilling of Kidd Segment Resumed March 31, 1964

April	1	Clayton	60	26 1/2
	1	Fogarty	400	26 1/2
	2	Clayton	100	26 7/8
	6	Fogarty	400	28 1/8–28 7/8
	8	Mollison (Mrs.)	100	28 1/8

First Press Release Issued April 12, 1964

April	15	Clayton	600	30 1/8–30 1/4

Second Press Release Issued 10:00–10:10 or 10:15 A.M., April 16, 1964

April   16 (app. 10:20 A.M.)

Coates (for family trusts)		2000	31–31 5/8

[3] A "call" is a negotiable option contract by which the bearer has the right to buy from the writer of the contract a certain number of shares of a particular stock at a fixed price on or before a certain agreed-upon date.

[4] The purchases made by "tippees" during this period were:

Date	Purchase Purchaser	Shares Number	Shares Price	Calls Number	Calls Price
Chemicals Assays of K–55–1 Received Dec. 9–13, 1963					
1963					
Dec. 30	Caskey (Darke)			300	22 1/4
1964					
Jan. 16	Westreich (Darke)	2000	21 1/4–21 3/4		
Feb. 17	Atkinson (Darke)	50	23 1/4	200	23 1/8
17	Westreich (Darke)	50	23 1/4	1000	23 1/4–23 3/8
24	Miller (Darke)			200	23 3/4
25	Miller (Darke)			300	23 3/8–23 1/2
Mar. 3	E. W. Darke (Darke)			500	22 1/2–22 5/8
17	E. W. Darke (Darke)			200	23 3/8
Land Acquisition Completed Mar. 27, 1964					
1964					
Mar. 30	Atkinson (Darke)			400	25 3/4–25 7/8
	Caskey (Darke)	100	25 7/8		
	E. W. Darke (Darke)			1000	25 3/4–25 7/8
	Miller (Darke)			200	25 1/2
	Westreich (Darke)	500	25 3/4		
30–31	Klotz (Darke)			2000	25 1/2–26 1/8

Second Press Release Issued April 16, 1964 (Reported over Dow Jones tape at 10:54 A.M.)

April   16 (from 10:31 A.M.)

Haemisegger (Coates)	1500	31 1/4–35	

In this connection, we point out that, though several of the Holyk purchases of shares and calls made between November 29, 1963 and March 30, 1964 were in the name of Mrs. Holyk or were in the names of both spouses, we have treated these purchases as if made in the name of defendant Holyk alone.

Defendant Mollison purchased 100 shares on November 15 in his name only and on April 8 100 shares were purchased in the name of Mrs. Mollison. We have made no distinction between those purchases.

Defendant Crawford ordered 300 shares about midnight on April 15 and 300 more shares the following morning, to be purchased for himself, and his wife, and these purchases are treated as having been made by the defendant Crawford.

In these particulars we have followed the lead of the court below. * * * It would be unrealistic to include any of these purchases as having been made by other than the defendants,

On February 20, 1964, also during this period, TGS issued stock options to 26 of its officers and employees whose salaries exceeded a specified amount, five of whom were the individual defendants Stephens, Fogarty, Mollison, Holyk, and Kline. Of these, only Kline was unaware of the detailed results of K–55–1, but he, too, knew that a hole containing favorable bodies of copper and zinc ore had been drilled in Timmins. At this time, neither the TGS Stock Option Committee nor its Board of Directors had been informed of the results of K–55–1, presumably because of the pending land acquisition program which required confidentiality. All of the foregoing defendants accepted the options granted them. * * *

[Texas Gulf had discovered one of the largest copper/zinc deposits in North America. As drilling explorations continued at the site to determine the size of the deposit, Texas Gulf also sought to acquire land or mineral rights in the area. Rumors leaked out that Texas Gulf had made a major mineral discovery. On April 12, Texas Gulf issued a press release downplaying the importance of the exploration activity, but issued a corrective release four days later confirming the scope of the discovery.]

During the period of drilling in Timmins, the market price of TGS stock fluctuated but steadily gained overall. On Friday, November 8, when the drilling began, the stock closed at 17 3/8; on Friday, November 15, after K–55–1 had been completed, it closed at 18. * * * By May 15, TGS stock was selling at 58 1/4.

I. The Individual Defendants

A. Introductory

Rule 10b–5, on which this action is predicated, * * * was promulgated * * * to prevent inequitable and unfair practices and to insure fairness in securities transactions generally, whether conducted face-to-face, over the counter, or on exchanges. * * * [T]he Rule is based in policy on the justifiable expectation of the securities marketplace that all investors trading on impersonal exchanges have relatively equal access to material information. The essence of the Rule is that anyone who, trading for his own account in the securities of a corporation has "access, directly or indirectly, to information intended to be available only for a corporate purpose and not for the personal benefit of anyone" may not take "advantage of such information knowing it is unavailable to those with whom he is dealing," i.e., the investing public. Matter of Cady, Roberts & Co., 40 SEC 907, 912 (1961). Insiders, as directors or management officers are, of course, by this Rule, precluded from so unfairly dealing, but the Rule is also applicable to one possessing the information who may not be strictly termed an "insider" within the meaning of Sec. 16(b) of the Act.

---

and unrealistic to include them as having been made by members of the general public receiving "tips" from insiders.

Thus, anyone in possession of material inside information must either disclose it to the investing public, or if he is disabled from disclosing it in order to protect a corporate confidence, or he chooses not to do so, must abstain from trading in or recommending the securities concerned while such inside information remains undisclosed. So, it is here no justification for insider activity that disclosure was forbidden by the legitimate corporate objective of acquiring options to purchase the land surrounding the exploration site; if the information was, as the SEC contends, material,[9] its possessors should have kept out of the market until disclosure was accomplished. Cady, Roberts, supra at 911.

B.   Material Inside Information

[The Court concludes that K–55–1 constituted "material" information, an issue now controlled by the test of TSC Industries v. Northway, supra. In the course of this discussion, the Court included observations about insider trading that are relevant today:]

An insider is not, of course, always foreclosed from investing in his own company merely because he may be more familiar with company operations than are outside investors. * * *

Nor is an insider obligated to confer upon outside investors the benefit of his superior financial or other expert analysis by disclosing his educated guesses or predictions. 3 Loss, op. cit. supra at 1463. The only regulatory objective is that access to material information be enjoyed equally, but this objective requires nothing more than the disclosure of basic facts so that outsiders may draw upon their own evaluative expertise in reaching their own investment decisions with knowledge equal to that of the insiders. * * *

The speculators and chartists of Wall and Bay Streets are also "reasonable" investors entitled to the same legal protection afforded conservative traders. * * *

Our survey of the facts found below conclusively establishes that knowledge of the results of the discovery hole, K–55–1, would have been important to a reasonable investor and might have affected the price of the stock.[12] * * *

---

[9] Congress intended by the Exchange Act to eliminate the idea that the use of inside information for personal advantage was a normal emolument of corporate office. See Sections 2 and 16 of the Act.

[12] We do not suggest that material facts must be disclosed immediately; the timing of disclosure is a matter for the business judgment of the corporate officers entrusted with the management of the corporation within the affirmative disclosure requirements promulgated by the exchanges and by the SEC. Here, a valuable corporate purpose was served by delaying the publication of the K–55–1 discovery. We do intend to convey, however, that where a corporate purpose is thus served by withholding the news of a material fact, those persons who are thus quite properly true to their corporate trust must not during the period of non-disclosure deal personally in the corporation's securities or give to outsiders confidential information not generally available to all the corporations' stockholders and to the public at large.

* * *

The core of Rule 10b–5 is the implementation of the Congressional purpose that all investors should have equal access to the rewards of participation in securities transactions. * * * The insiders here were not trading on an equal footing with the outside investors. They alone were in a position to evaluate the probability and magnitude of what seemed from the outset to be a major ore strike; they alone could invest safely, secure in the expectation that the price of TGS stock would rise substantially in the event such a major strike should materialize, but would decline little, if at all, in the event of failure, for the public, ignorant at the outset of the favorable probabilities would likewise be unaware of the unproductive exploration, and the additional exploration costs would not significantly affect TGS market prices. Such inequities based upon unequal access to knowledge should not be shrugged off as inevitable in our way of life, or in view of the congressional concern in the area, remain uncorrected.

* * *

C. When May Insiders Act?

Appellant Crawford, who ordered[17] the purchase of TGS stock shortly before the TGS April 16 official announcement, and defendant Coates, who placed orders with and communicated the news to his broker immediately after the official announcement was read at the TGS-called press conference, concede that they were in possession of material information. They contend, however, that their purchases were not proscribed purchases for the news had already been effectively disclosed. We disagree.

Crawford telephoned his orders to his Chicago broker about midnight on April 15 and again at 8:30 in the morning of the 16th, with instructions to buy at the opening of the Midwest Stock Exchange that morning. The trial court's finding that "he sought to, and did, 'beat the news,' " 258 F.Supp. at 287, is well documented by the record. The rumors of a major ore strike which had been circulated in Canada and, to a lesser extent, in New York, had been disclaimed by the TGS press release of April 12, which significantly promised the public an official detailed announcement when possibilities had ripened into actualities. The abbreviated announcement to the Canadian press at 9:40 A.M. on the 16th by the Ontario Minister of Mines and the report carried by The Northern Miner, parts of which had sporadically reached New York on the morning of the 16th through reports from Canadian affiliates to a few

---

[17] The effective protection of the public from insider exploitation of advance notice of material information requires that the time that an insider places an order, rather than the time of its ultimate execution, be determinative for Rule 10b–5 purposes. Otherwise, insiders would be able to "beat the news," cf. Fleischer, supra, 51 Va.L.Rev. at 1291, by requesting in advance that their orders be executed immediately after the dissemination of a major news release but before outsiders could act on the release. * * *

New York investment firms, are assuredly not the equivalent of the official 10–15 minute announcement which was not released to the American financial press until after 10:00 A.M. Crawford's orders had been placed before that. Before insiders may act upon material information, such information must have been effectively disclosed in a manner sufficient to insure its availability to the investing public. * * *

[A]t the minimum Coates should have waited until the news could reasonably have been expected to appear over the media of widest circulation, the Dow Jones broad tape, rather than hastening to insure an advantage to himself and his broker son-in-law.[19] * * *

Conclusion

In summary, therefore, we affirm the finding of the court below that appellants Richard H. Clayton and David M. Crawford have violated [§ 10b] and Rule 10b–5; we reverse the judgment order entered below dismissing the complaint against appellees Charles F. Fogarty, Richard H. Clayton, Richard D. Mollison, Walter Holyk, Kenneth H. Darke, Earl L. Huntington, and Francis G. Coates, as we find that they have violated [§ 10b] and Rule 10b–5. As to these eight individuals we remand so that in accordance with the agreement between the parties the Commission may notice a hearing before the court below to determine the remedies to be applied against them. We reverse the judgment order dismissing the complaint against Claude O. Stephens, Charles F. Fogarty, and Harold B. Kline as recipients of stock options, direct the district court to consider in its discretion whether to issue injunction orders against Stephens and Fogarty, and direct that an order issue rescinding the option granted Kline and that such further remedy be applied against him as may be proper by way of an order of restitution. * * *

NOTES

(1) On remand, the District Court required Darke to pay to TGS the profits which he and his tippees made on TGS stock prior to April 17, 1964, and required Holyk, Huntington, and Clayton to pay to TGS the profits which each of them made on the TGS stock prior to April 17, 1964. The order stated that the payments were to be held in escrow in an interest-bearing account for a period of five years, subject to disposition in such manner as the Court might direct upon application by the SEC or other interested person, or on the Court's own motion. At the end of the five years, any money remaining would become the property of TGS. To protect these defendants against

---

[19] The record reveals that news usually appears on the Dow Jones broad tape 2–3 minutes after the reporter completes dictation.

Here, assuming that the Dow Jones reporter left the press conference as early as possible, 10:10 A.M., the 10–15 minute release (which took at least that long to dictate) could not have appeared on the wire before 10:22, and for other reasons unknown to us did not appear until 10:54. Indeed, even the abbreviated version of the release reported by Merrill Lynch over its private wire did not appear until 10:29. Coates, however, placed his call no later than 10:20.

double liability, any private judgments against them arising out of the events of this case were to be paid from this fund. This order was affirmed in its entirety by a panel consisting of Judges Friendly, Waterman, and Hays. 446 F.2d 1301 (2d Cir.1971), cert. denied, 404 U.S. 1005 (1971).

(2) Later cases recognize that full "disgorgement" or restitution may be sought from tippees as well as from insiders themselves. See, e.g., SEC v. Lund, 570 F.Supp. 1397 (C.D.Cal.1983). Presumably, Darke's tippees could have been required to restore the profits they made if they had been named as parties in the original suit by the SEC.

(3) What kind of trading strategy should an officer or director adopt to eliminate or minimize exposure under Rule 10b–5 as applied in *TGS*? The New York Stock Exchange Listed Company Manual § 309.00, discusses this problem and offers the following analysis:

> Shareholders have indicated however that they want directors and officers to have a meaningful investment in the companies they manage. So, in the interest of promoting better shareholder relationships, some general rules under which corporate officials may properly buy or sell stock in their company may be helpful. One appropriate method of purchase might be a periodic investment program where the directors or officers make regular purchases under an established program administered by a broker and where the timing of purchases is outside the control of the individual. It would also seem appropriate for officials to buy or sell stock in their companies for a 30-day period commencing one week after the annual report has been mailed to shareholders and otherwise broadly circulated (provided, of course, that the annual report has adequately covered important corporate developments and that no new major undisclosed developments occur within that period).

> Transactions may also be appropriate under the following circumstances, provided that prior to making a purchase or sale a director or officer contacts the chief executive officer of the company to be sure there are no important developments pending which need to be made public before an insider could properly participate in the market:

> • Following a release of quarterly results, which includes adequate comment on new developments during the period. This timing of transactions might be even more appropriate where the report has been mailed to shareholders.

> • Following the wide dissemination of information on the status of the company and current results. For example, transactions may be appropriate after a proxy statement or prospectus which gives such information in connection with a merger or new financing.

> • At those times when there is relative stability in the company's operations and the market for its securities. Under these

circumstances, timing of transactions may be relatively less important. Of course such periods of relative stability will vary greatly from time to time and will also depend to a large extent on the nature of the industry or the company.

Where a development of major importance is expected to reach the appropriate time for announcement within the next few months, transactions by directors and officers should be avoided.

Corporate officials should wait until after the release of earnings, dividends, or other important developments have appeared in the press before making a purchase or sale. This permits the news to be widely disseminated and negates the inference that officials had an inside advantage. Similarly, transactions just prior to important press releases should be avoided.

In granting stock options to directors and key officers, the same philosophy that relates to purchases and sales may well apply. Where an established pattern or formula is part of a plan specifically approved by shareholders, the question of timing may not arise. In taking up an option, the timing of a purchase is not usually critical as the price is set at the time the option is granted. The reasoning relating to stock options might also apply to employee stock purchase plans in which directors and officers may be entitled to participate.

The considerations that affect director and officer transactions in stock of their own company may be pertinent to transactions in the shares of other companies with which discussions of merger, acquisition, important contracts, etc., are being considered or carried on. The same considerations apply to the families or close associates of directors and officers who are often presumed to have preferential access to information. As far as the public is concerned, they also are insiders. While this assumption may be unjustified in many cases, it is a fact of life which those in positions of leadership and responsibility cannot ignore.

Some companies have adopted policies for the guidance of their personnel relating to transactions in the company's stock, as well as other areas where conflicts of interest could arise. Such policies can be very helpful to employees who have access to important confidential information, as well as to the directors and officers.

In the final analysis, directors and officers must be guided by a sense of fairness to all segments of the investing public. * * *

DENNIS W. CARLTON & DANIEL R. FISCHEL, THE REGULATION OF INSIDER TRADING

35 Stan.L.Rev. 857, 857–58, 866, 868 (1983).

Imagine two firms, A and B, which are identical in all respects except that, in its charter, firm A prohibits the trading of its shares based on inside (nonpublic) information. The firm requires insiders (employees) to report their trades, which a special committee or an independent accounting firm then checks to ensure compliance with the charter provision. Firm B, by contrast, neither prohibits insider trading nor requires reporting. Insiders openly trade shares of firm B and regularly earn positive abnormal returns. In competitive capital markets, which charter provision will survive?

Despite the deceptive simplicity of this question, it has no obvious answer. The consensus, to the extent that any exists, appears to be that firm A's charter will survive because it eliminates various perceived harmful effects of insider trading. Thus, investors would pay less for shares in B. The managers of B, in order to maximize the value of B shares, would have to adopt a similar charter provision.

As for these harmful effects, many believe that insider trading is "unfair" and undermines public confidence in capital markets. Other critics have argued that insider trading creates perverse incentives by allowing corporate managers to profit on bad news as well as good, encourages managers to invest in risky projects, impedes corporate decisionmaking, and tempts managers to delay public disclosure of valuable information. Some also have argued that insider trading is an inefficient compensation scheme because, in effect, it compensates risk-averse managers with a benefit akin to lottery tickets. Still others have claimed that insider trading allows insiders to divert part of the firm's earnings that would otherwise go to shareholders and therefore raises the firm's cost of capital. Under this "insider trading is harmful to investors" hypothesis, competitive capital markets would force firm B to prohibit insider trading.

The difficulty with this hypothesis is that it appears to be contradicted by the actions of firms. * * *

A.   Information Effects

The social gains from efficient capital markets are well known. The more accurately prices reflect information, the better prices guide capital investment in the economy. * * *

Since the firm's shareholders value the ability to control information that flows to the stock market, they may also value insider trading because it gives the firm an additional method of communicating and controlling information. If insiders trade, the share price will move closer to what it would have been had the information been disclosed. How close will depend on the amount of "noise" surrounding the trade. The greater the ability of market participants to identify insider trading, the more information such trading will convey. * * *

Several reasons explain why communicating information through insider trading may be of value to the firm. Through insider trading, a firm can convey information it could not feasibly announce publicly because an announcement would destroy the value of the information, would be too expensive, not believable, or—owing to the uncertainty of the information—would subject the firm to massive damage liability if it turned out ex post to be incorrect. Conversely, firms also could use insider trading to limit the amount of information to be reflected in price. Controlling the number of traders who have access to information may be easier than controlling how much information gets announced over time. In other words, announcement of information need not be continuous, while trading on inside information can be. Thus, insider trading gives firms a tool either to increase or to decrease the amount of information that is contained in share prices.

NOTES

(1) In the year prior to the bankruptcy of Enron, Kenneth Lay, the Company's then-chairman, sold $70 million in stock. During the period December 1999 through the bankruptcy in December 2001, Enron insiders sold a stunning total of $1,190,479,472 in Enron stock, totaling 51% of the shares held by insiders. Bill Lerach, a partner in Milberg Weiss Bershad Hynes & Lerach, LLP, the law firm that is leading the securities litigation against Enron, described the Enron transactions as "one of the worst instances of illegal insider trading we've ever encountered." Is the existence of such trading consistent with the thesis put forward by Carlton and Fischel?

(2) An early justification for permitting insider trading appeared in a provocative book by Professor Henry G. Manne entitled "Insider Trading and the Stock Market" (1966). Professor Manne argued that insider trading is essential to the survival of our economic system because without it, in his view, truly creative, risk-taking entrepreneurs would shun the corporate world. Carlton and Fischel refer to Professor Manne's path-breaking book as "brilliant" and state that it is the "starting point for anyone interested in the subject." 35 Stan.L.Rev. at 857 n.1. Following similar economic reasoning, Carlton and Fischel also suggest that corporations may prefer to permit insiders to trade on inside information because it "allows a manager to alter his compensation package in light of new knowledge, thereby avoiding continual renegotiation," and it "provides firms with valuable information concerning prospective managers." Id. at 870–71.

(3) Many economics scholars have questioned the Manne thesis. See, e.g., Mark Klock, Mainstream Economics and the Case for Prohibiting Inside Trading, 10 Ga.St.L.J. 297 (1994). Professor Klock, an economist and not a

lawyer by training, concludes that allocational economic analysis justifies a ban on inside trading, with a possible exception based on the cost of enforcing such a ban. See also Boyd Kimball Dyer, Economic Analysis, Insider Trading, and Game Markets, 1992 Utah L.Rev. 1, 6 (1992). More recently, law and finance scholars have looked at the social consequences of insider trading by examining whether countries with capital markets that fail to enforce vigorously the applicable legal prohibitions on insider trading must pay higher capital costs. These studies show that, while passing laws that regulate insider trading don't lower the cost of capital, enforcing the laws that are on the books does improve the operation of the capital markets by lowering the costs of raising capital. See Utpal Bhattacharya and Hazem Daouk, The World Price of Insider Trading, 57 Journal of Finance 75 (2002).

(4) For an argument that some anonymous investor is inevitably harmed by insider trading, see William K.S. Wang, Trading on Material Nonpublic Information on Impersonal Stock Markets: Who is Harmed, and Who Can Sue Whom Under SEC Rule 10b–5?, 54 S.Cal.L.Rev. 1217 (1981). For a further articulation of this argument, see William K.S. Wang and Marc I. Steinberg, Insider Trading, Chs. 2–3 (1996). Professor Wang's argument that someone always loses as a result of insider trading seems logically unassailable. However, should that make trading on nonpublic information unlawful or even criminal? Should not one also consider possible benefits as an offset?

(5) Professors Carlton and Fischel respond to the intuitive argument that trading on inside information—a sure thing—is fundamentally and obviously unfair and immoral as follows:

> We have left for last the most common argument against insider trading—that it is unfair or immoral. * * *

> * * * A more powerful response to the argument that insiders profit at the expense of outsiders is that if insider trading is a desirable compensation scheme, it benefits insiders and outsiders alike. Nobody would argue seriously that salaries, options, bonuses, and other compensation devices allow insiders to profit at the expense of outsiders because these sums otherwise would have gone to shareholders. Compensating managers in this fashion increases the size of the pie, and thus outsiders as well as insiders profit from the incentives managers are given to increase the value of the firm. Insider trading does not come "at the expense of" outsiders for precisely the same reason.

> Contrary to popular sentiment with respect to insider trading, therefore, there is no tension between considerations of fairness and of efficiency. To say that insider trading is a desirable method of compensating corporate managers is to say that shareholders would voluntarily enter into contractual arrangements with insiders giving them property rights in valuable information. If insider

trading is efficient, no independent notions of fairness suggest that it should be prohibited.

Dennis W. Carlton & Daniel R. Fischel, The Regulation of Insider Trading, 35 Stan.L.Rev. 857, 880–82 (1983).

(6) Despite complaints and arguments by some law and economics scholars that insider trading is harmless and may be beneficial, the SEC has continued to enforce vigorously the prohibition against such trading. However, insider trading law is made primarily by courts, particularly the Supreme Court of the United States.

CHIARELLA V. UNITED STATES

Supreme Court of the United States, 1980.
445 U.S. 222.

JUSTICE POWELL delivered the opinion of the Court.

The question in this case is whether a person who learns from the confidential documents of one corporation that it is planning an attempt to secure control of a second corporation violates § 10(b) of the Securities Exchange Act of 1934 if he fails to disclose the impending takeover before trading in the target company's securities.

I

Petitioner is a printer by trade. In 1975 and 1976, he worked as a "markup man" in the New York composing room of Pandick Press, a financial printer. Among documents that petitioner handled were five announcements of corporate takeover bids. When these documents were delivered to the printer, the identities of the acquiring and target corporations were concealed by blank spaces or false names. The true names were sent to the printer on the night of the final printing.

The petitioner, however, was able to deduce the names of the target companies before the final printing from other information contained in the documents. Without disclosing his knowledge, petitioner purchased stock in the target companies and sold the shares immediately after the takeover attempts were made public. By this method, petitioner realized a gain of slightly more than $30,000 in the course of 14 months. Subsequently, the Securities and Exchange Commission (Commission or SEC) began an investigation of his trading activities. In May 1977, petitioner entered into a consent decree with the Commission in which he agreed to return his profits to the sellers of the shares. On the same day, he was discharged by Pandick Press.

In January 1978, petitioner was indicted on 17 counts of violating § 10(b) of the Securities Exchange Act of 1934 (1934 Act) and SEC Rule

10b–5.[5] After petitioner unsuccessfully moved to dismiss the indictment, he was brought to trial and convicted on all counts.

The Court of Appeals for the Second Circuit affirmed petitioner's conviction. 588 F.2d 1358 (1978). We granted certiorari, 441 U.S. 942, 99 S.Ct. 2158, 60 L.Ed.2d 1043 (1979), and we now reverse.

II

* * * This case concerns the legal effect of the petitioner's silence. The District Court's charge permitted the jury to convict the petitioner if it found that he willfully failed to inform sellers of target company securities that he knew of a forthcoming takeover bid that would make their shares more valuable. In order to decide whether silence in such circumstances violates § 10(b), it is necessary to review the language and legislative history of that statute as well as its interpretation by the Commission and the federal courts.

Although the starting point of our inquiry is the language of the statute, Ernst & Ernst v. Hochfelder, 425 U.S. 185, 197, 96 S.Ct. 1375, 1382, 47 L.Ed.2d 668 (1976), § 10(b) does not state whether silence may constitute a manipulative or deceptive device. Section 10(b) was designed as a catch-all clause to prevent fraudulent practices. But neither the legislative history nor the statute itself affords specific guidance for the resolution of this case. When Rule 10b–5 was promulgated in 1942, the SEC did not discuss the possibility that failure to provide information might run afoul of § 10(b).

The SEC took an important step in the development of § 10(b) when it held that a broker-dealer and his firm violated that section by selling securities on the basis of undisclosed information obtained from a director of the issuer corporation who was also a registered representative of the brokerage firm. In Cady, Roberts & Co., 40 SEC 907 (1961), the Commission decided that a corporate insider must abstain from trading in the shares of his corporation unless he has first disclosed all material inside information known to him. The obligation to disclose or abstain derives from

> [a]n affirmative duty to disclose material information[,] [which] has been traditionally imposed on corporate 'insiders,' particular officers, directors, or controlling stockholders. We * * * and the courts have consistently held that insiders must disclose material facts which are known to them by virtue of their position but which are not known to persons with whom they

---

[5] Only Rules 10b–5(a) and (c) are at issue here. Rule 10b–5(b) provides that it shall be unlawful "[t]o make any untrue statement of a material fact or to omit to state a material fact necessary in order to make the statements made, in the light of the circumstances under which they were made, not misleading." The portion of the indictment based on this provision was dismissed because the petitioner made no statements at all in connection with the purchase of stock.

deal and which, if known, would affect their investment judgment. Id., at 911.

The Commission emphasized that the duty arose from (i) the existence of a relationship affording access to inside information intended to be available only for a corporate purpose, and (ii) the unfairness of allowing a corporate insider to take advantage of that information by trading without disclosure.[8]

That the relationship between a corporate insider and the stockholders of his corporation gives rise to a disclosure obligation is not a novel twist of the law. At common law, misrepresentation made for the purpose of inducing reliance upon the false statement is fraudulent. But one who fails to disclose material information prior to the consummation of a transaction commits fraud only when he is under a duty to do so. And the duty to disclose arises when one party has information "that the other [party] is entitled to know because of a fiduciary or other similar relation of trust and confidence between them." In its *Cady, Roberts* decision, the Commission recognized a relationship of trust and confidence between the shareholders of a corporation and those insiders who have obtained confidential information by reason of their position with that corporation.[10] This relationship gives rise to a duty to disclose because of the "necessity of preventing a corporate insider from * * * [taking] unfair advantage of the uninformed minority stockholders." Speed v. Transamerica Corp., 99 F.Supp. 808, 829 (D.Del.1951).

The federal courts have found violations of § 10(b) where corporate insiders used undisclosed information for their own benefit. E.g., SEC v. Texas Gulf Sulphur Co., 401 F.2d 833 (C.A.2 1968), cert. denied, 404 U.S. 1005, 92 S.Ct. 561, 30 L.Ed.2d 558 (1971). The cases also have emphasized, in accordance with the common-law rule, that "[t]he party charged with failing to disclose market information must be under a duty

---

[8] In *Cady, Roberts*, the broker-dealer was liable under § 10(b) because it received nonpublic information from a corporate insider of the issuer. Since the insider could not use the information, neither could the partners in the brokerage firm with which he was associated. The transaction of *Cady, Roberts* involved sale of stock to persons who previously may not have been shareholders in the corporation. The Commission embraced the reasoning of Judge Learned Hand that "the director or officer assumed a fiduciary relation to the buyer by the very sale; for it would be a sorry distinction to allow him to use the advantage of his position to induce the buyer into the position of a beneficiary although he was forbidden to do so once the buyer had become one." Id., at 914, n. 23, quoting *Gratz v. Claughton*, 187 F.2d 46, 49 (CA2), cert. denied, 341 U.S. 920, 71 S.Ct. 741, 95 L.Ed. 1353 (1951).

[10] * * * The dissent of Mr. Justice Blackmun suggests that the "special facts" doctrine may be applied to find that silence constitutes fraud where one party has superior information to another. This Court has never so held. In Strong v. Repide, 213 U.S. 419, 431–434, 29 S.Ct. 521, 525, 526, 53 L.Ed. 853 (1909), this Court applied the special facts doctrine to conclude that a corporate insider had a duty to disclose to a shareholder. In that case, the majority shareholder of a corporation secretly purchased the stock of another shareholder without revealing that the corporation, under the insider's direction, was about to sell corporate assets at a price that would greatly enhance the value of the stock. The decision in Strong v. Repide was premised upon the fiduciary duty between the corporate insider and the shareholder. See Pepper v. Litton, 308 U.S. 295, 307, n. 15, 60 S.Ct. 238, 245, n. 15, 84 L.Ed. 281 (1939).

to disclose it." Frigitemp Corp. v. Financial Dynamics Fund, Inc., 524 F.2d 275, 282 (C.A.2 1975). Accordingly, a purchaser of stock who has no duty to a prospective seller because he is neither an insider nor a fiduciary has been held to have no obligation to reveal material facts. * * *

Thus, administrative and judicial interpretations have established that silence in connection with the purchase or sale of securities may operate as a fraud actionable under § 10(b) despite the absence of statutory language or legislative history specifically addressing the legality of nondisclosure. But such liability is premised upon a duty to disclose arising from a relationship of trust and confidence between parties to a transaction. Application of a duty to disclose prior to trading guarantees that corporate insiders, who have an obligation to place the shareholder's welfare before their own, will not benefit personally through fraudulent use of material nonpublic information.[12]

III

In this case, the petitioner was convicted of violating § 10(b) although he was not a corporate insider and he received no confidential information from the target company. Moreover, the "market information" upon which he relied did not concern the earning power or operations of the target company, but only the plans of the acquiring company. Petitioner's use of that information was not a fraud under § 10(b) unless he was subject to an affirmative duty to disclose it before trading. In this case, the jury instructions failed to specify any such duty. In effect, the trial court instructed the jury that petitioner owed a duty to everyone; to all sellers, indeed, to the market as a whole. The jury simply was told to decide whether petitioner used material, nonpublic information at a time when "he knew other people trading in the securities market did not have access to the same information."

The Court of Appeals affirmed the conviction by holding that "[a]nyone—corporate insider or not—who regularly receives material nonpublic information may not use that information to trade in securities without incurring an affirmative duty to disclose." Although the court said that its test would include only persons who regularly receive material nonpublic information, its rationale for that limitation is unrelated to the existence of a duty to disclose.[14] The Court of Appeals,

---

[12] "Tippees" of corporate insiders have been held liable under § 10(b) because they have a duty not to profit from the use of inside information that they know is confidential and know or should know came from a corporate insider, Shapiro v. Merrill Lynch, Pierce, Fenner & Smith, 495 F.2d 228, 237–238 (C.A.2 1974). The tippee's obligation has been viewed as arising from his role as a participant after the fact in the insider's breach of a fiduciary duty. Subcommittees of American Bar Association Section of Corporation, Banking, and Business Law, Comment Letter on Material, Non-Public Information (Oct. 15, 1973) reprinted in BNA, Securities Regulation & Law Report No. 233, at D–1, D–2 (Jan. 2, 1974).

[14] The Court of Appeals said that its "regular access to market information" test would create a workable rule embracing "those who occupy * * * strategic places in the market mechanism." 588 F.2d, at 1365. These considerations are insufficient to support a duty to

like the trial court, failed to identify a relationship between petitioner and the sellers that could give rise to a duty. Its decision thus rested solely upon its belief that the federal securities laws have "created a system providing equal access to information necessary for reasoned and intelligent investment decisions." The use by anyone of material information not generally available is fraudulent, this theory suggests, because such information gives certain buyers or sellers an unfair advantage over less informed buyers and sellers.

This reasoning suffers from two defects. First not every instance of financial unfairness constitutes fraudulent activity under § 10(b). See Santa Fe Industries, Inc. v. Green, 430 U.S. 462, 474–477, 97 S.Ct. 1292, 1301–1303, 51 L.Ed.2d 480 (1977). Second, the element required to make silence fraudulent—a duty to disclose—is absent in this case. No duty could arise from petitioner's relationship with the sellers of the target company's securities, for petitioner had no prior dealings with them. He was not their agent, he was not a fiduciary, he was not a person in whom the sellers had placed their trust and confidence. He was, in fact, a complete stranger who dealt with the sellers only through impersonal market transactions.

We cannot affirm petitioner's conviction without recognizing a general duty between all participants in market transactions to forgo actions based on material, nonpublic information. Formulation of such a broad duty, which departs radically from the established doctrine that duty arises from a specific relationship between two parties, should not be undertaken absent some explicit evidence of congressional intent.

As we have seen, no such evidence emerges from the language or legislative history of § 10(b). Moreover, neither the Congress nor the Commission ever has adopted a parity-of-information rule. * * *

We see no basis for applying such a new and different theory of liability in this case. As we have emphasized before, the 1934 Act cannot be read " 'more broadly than its language and the statutory scheme reasonably permit.' " Touche Ross & Co. v. Redington, 442 U.S. 560, 578, 99 S.Ct. 2479, 2490, 61 L.Ed.2d 82 (1979). Section 10(b) is aptly described as a catch-all provision, but what it catches must be fraud. When an

disclose. A duty arises from the relationship between parties, and not merely from one's ability to acquire information because of his position in the market.

The Court of Appeals also suggested that the acquiring corporation itself would not be a "market insider" because a tender offeror creates, rather than receives, information and takes a substantial economic risk that its offer will be unsuccessful. Again, the Court of Appeals departed from the analysis appropriate to recognition of a duty. The Court of Appeals for the Second Circuit previously held, in a manner consistent with our analysis here, that a tender offeror does not violate § 10(b) when it makes preannouncement purchases precisely because there is no relationship between the offeror and the seller: "We know of no rule of law * * * that a purchaser of stock, who was not an 'insider' and had no fiduciary relation to a prospective seller, had any obligation to reveal circumstances that might raise a seller's demands and thus abort the sale." General Time Corp. v. Talley Industries, 403 F.2d 159, 164 (1968), cert. denied, 393 U.S. 1026, 89 S.Ct. 631, 21 L.Ed.2d 570 (1969).

allegation of fraud is based upon nondisclosure, there can be no fraud absent a duty to speak. We hold that a duty to disclose under § 10(b) does not arise from the mere possession of nonpublic market information. The contrary result is without support in the legislative history of § 10(b) and would be inconsistent with the careful plan that Congress has enacted for regulation of the securities markets. Cf. Santa Fe Industries, Inc. v. Green, 430 U.S., at 479, 97 S.Ct., at 1304.[20]

IV

In its brief to this Court, the United States offers an alternative theory to support petitioner's conviction. It argues that petitioner breached a duty to the acquiring corporation when he acted upon information that he obtained by virtue of his position as an employee of a printer employed by the corporation. The breach of this duty is said to support a conviction under § 10(b) for fraud perpetrated upon both the acquiring corporation and the sellers.

We need not decide whether this theory has merit for it was not submitted to the jury. * * *

The jury instructions demonstrate that petitioner was convicted merely because of his failure to disclose material, nonpublic information to sellers from whom he bought the stock of target corporations. The jury was not instructed on the nature or elements of a duty owed by petitioner to anyone other than the sellers. Because we cannot affirm a criminal conviction on the basis of a theory not presented to the jury, we will not speculate upon whether such a duty exists, whether it has been breached, or whether such a breach constitutes a violation of § 10(b).

The judgment of the Court of Appeals is reversed.

[The separate opinions of JUSTICE STEVENS, concurring in the majority opinion and judgment, and JUSTICE BRENNAN, concurring in the judgment, are omitted].

---

[20] Mr. Justice Blackmun's dissent would establish the following standard for imposing criminal and civil liability under § 10(b) and Rule 10b–5:

"[P]ersons having access to confidential material information that is not legally available to others generally are prohibited * * * from engaging in schemes to exploit their structural information advantage through trading in affected securities."

This view is not substantially different from the Court of Appeals theory that anyone "who regularly receives material nonpublic information may not use that information to trade in securities without incurring an affirmative duty to disclose," and must be rejected for the reasons stated in Part III. Additionally, a judicial holding that certain undefined activities "generally are prohibited" by § 10(b) would raise questions whether either criminal or civil defendants would be given fair notice that they have engaged in illegal activity.

It is worth noting that this is apparently the first case in which criminal liability has been imposed upon a purchaser for § 10(b) nondisclosure. Petitioner was sentenced to a year in prison, suspended except for one month, and a five-year term of probation.

CHIEF JUSTICE BURGER, dissenting.

I believe that the jury instructions in this case properly charged a violation of § 10(b) and Rule 10b–5, and I would affirm the conviction.

I

As a general rule, neither party to an arm's length business transaction has an obligation to disclose information to the other unless the parties stand in some confidential or fiduciary relation. See Prosser, Law of Torts § 106 (2d ed.1955). This rule permits a businessman to capitalize on his experience and skill in securing and evaluating relevant information; it provides incentive for hard work, careful analysis, and astute forecasting. But the policies that underlie the rule also should limit its scope. In particular, the rule should give way when an informational advantage is obtained, not by superior experience, foresight, or industry, but by some unlawful means. * * * I would read § 10(b) and Rule 10b–5 to encompass and build on this principle: to mean that a person who has misappropriated nonpublic information has an absolute duty to disclose that information or to refrain from trading.

The language of § 10(b) and of Rule 10b–5 plainly support such a reading. By their terms, these provisions reach *any* person engaged in *any* fraudulent scheme. This broad language negates the suggestion that congressional concern was limited to trading by "corporate insiders" or to deceptive practices related to "corporate information."[1] Just as surely Congress cannot have intended one standard of fair dealing for "white collar" insiders and another for the "blue collar" level. The very language of § 10(b) and Rule 10b–5 "by repeated use of the word 'any' [was] obviously meant to be inclusive." Affiliated Ute Citizens v. United States, 406 U.S. 128, 151, 92 S.Ct. 1456, 1471, 31 L.Ed.2d 741 (1972).

The history of the statute and of the rule also supports this reading. * * *

II

The Court's opinion, as I read it, leaves open the question whether § 10(b) and Rule 10b–5 prohibit trading on misappropriated nonpublic information.[4] Instead, the Court apparently concludes that this theory of

---

[1] Academic writing in recent years has distinguished between "corporate information"— information which comes from within the corporation and reflects on expected earnings or assets—and "market information." See, e.g., Fleischer, Mundheim & Murphy, An Initial Inquiry into the Responsibility to Disclose Market Information, 121 U.Pa.L.Rev. 798, 799 (1973). It is clear that the § 10(b) and Rule 10b–5 by their terms and by their history make no such distinction. See Brudney, Insiders, Outsiders, and Informational Advantages Under the Federal Securities Laws, 93 Harv.L.Rev. 322, 329–333 (1979).

[4] There is some language in the Court's opinion to suggest that only "a relationship between petitioner and the sellers * * * could give rise to a duty [to disclose]." The Court's holding, however, is much more limited, namely that mere possession of material nonpublic information is insufficient to create a duty to disclose or to refrain from trading. Accordingly, it is my understanding that the Court has not rejected the view, advanced above, that an absolute duty to disclose or refrain arises from the very act of misappropriating nonpublic information.

the case was not submitted to the jury. In the Court's view, the instructions given the jury were premised on the erroneous notion that the mere failure to disclose nonpublic information, however acquired, is a deceptive practice. And because of this premise, the jury was not instructed that the means by which Chiarella acquired his informational advantage—by violating a duty owed to the acquiring companies—was an element of the offense.

The Court's reading of the District Court's charge is unduly restrictive. * * * In sum, the evidence shows beyond all doubt that Chiarella, working literally in the shadows of the warning signs in the printshop, misappropriated—stole to put it bluntly—valuable nonpublic information entrusted to him in the utmost confidence. He then exploited his ill-gotten informational advantage by purchasing securities in the market. In my view, such conduct plainly violates § 10(b) and Rule 10b–5. Accordingly, I would affirm the judgment of the Court of Appeals.

JUSTICE BLACKMUN, with whom JUSTICE MARSHALL joins, dissenting.

Although I agree with much of what is said in Part I of the dissenting opinion of The Chief Justice, I write separately because, in my view, it is unnecessary to rest petitioner's conviction on a "misappropriation" theory. The fact that petitioner Chiarella purloined, or, to use The Chief Justice's word, "stole," information concerning pending tender offers certainly is the most dramatic evidence that petitioner was guilty of fraud. He has conceded that he knew it was wrong, and he and his co-workers in the print shop were specifically warned by their employer that actions of this kind were improper and forbidden. But I also would find petitioner's conduct fraudulent within the meaning of § 10(b) [and] Rule 10b–5, even if he had obtained the blessing of his employer's principals before embarking on his profiteering scheme. Indeed, I think petitioner's brand of manipulative trading, with or without such approval, lies close to the heart of what the securities laws are intended to prohibit.

The Court continues to pursue a course, charted in certain recent decisions, designed to transform § 10(b) from an intentionally elastic "catchall" provision to one that catches relatively little of the misbehavior that all too often makes investment in securities a needlessly risky business for the uninitiated investor. See, e.g., Ernst & Ernst v. Hochfelder, 425 U.S. 185, 96 S.Ct. 1375, 47 L.Ed.2d 668 (1976); Blue Chip Stamps v. Manor Drug Stores, 421 U.S. 723, 95 S.Ct. 1917, 44 L.Ed.2d 539 (1975). Such confinement in this case is now achieved by imposition of a requirement of a "special relationship" akin to fiduciary duty before the statute gives rise to a duty to disclose or to abstain from trading upon material nonpublic information.[1] * * *

---

[1] The Court fails to specify whether the obligations of a special relationship must fall directly upon the person engaging in an allegedly fraudulent transaction, or whether the

Whatever the outer limits of the Rule, petitioner Chiarella's case fits neatly near the center of its analytical framework. He occupied a relationship to the takeover companies giving him intimate access to concededly material information that was sedulously guarded from public access. The information, in the words of Cady, Roberts & Co., 40 SEC, at 912, was "intended to be available only for a corporate purpose and not for the personal benefit of anyone." Petitioner, moreover, knew that the information was unavailable to those with whom he dealt. And he took full, virtually riskless advantage of this artificial information gap by selling the stocks shortly after each takeover bid was announced. By any reasonable definition, his trading was "inherent[ly] unfai[r]." This misuse of confidential information was clearly placed before the jury. Petitioner's conviction, therefore, should be upheld and I dissent from the Court's upsetting that conviction.

NOTES

(1) Would the Court's construction of Rule 10b–5 reach the following persons:

(a) The secretary or messenger who overhears snippets of conversations from his superiors, infers that a favorable development is about to occur, and buys shares of his employer?

(b) The person sitting in a restaurant who overhears conversations at the next table from which she infers that a favorable development is about to occur with respect to Acme Company, and who buys shares in Acme Company?

(c) The reporter who attends a press conference at which a favorable development is announced, and then, immediately after the conference and before the news appears on the ticker services, telephones his broker and places an order to purchase?

(d) A subtippee who believes his tippee has "connections" with employees of the corporation but is not himself employed by the corporation?

(2) Vincent Chiarella was apparently the first person against whom criminal charges were filed for violation of Rule 10b–5. The press noted at the time that he was a "blue collar" worker and commented that it seemed unfair to apply the criminal process only against persons in lower economic classes.

(3) The criminalization of insider trading reached a new level in Carpenter v. United States, 484 U.S. 19 (1987), where the court upheld a conviction under the mail and wire fraud statutes, 18 U.S.C.A. §§ 1341, 1343,[b] of Kenneth Felis and R. Foster Winans under the following circumstances:

---

derivative obligations of "tippees" that lower courts long have recognized, are encompassed by its rule.

[b]   Section 1341 provides:

In 1981, Winans became a reporter for the Wall Street Journal (the Journal) and in the summer of 1982 became one of the two writers of a daily column, "Heard on the Street." That column discussed selected stocks or groups of stocks, giving positive and negative information about those stocks and taking "a point of view with respect to investment in the stocks that it reviews." Winans regularly interviewed corporate executives to put together interesting perspectives on the stocks that would be highlighted in upcoming columns, but, at least for the columns at issue here, none contained corporate inside information or any "hold for release" information. Because of the "Heard" column's perceived quality and integrity, it had the potential of affecting the price of the stocks which it examined. The District Court concluded on the basis of testimony presented at trial that the "Heard" column "does have an impact on the market, difficult though it may be to quantify in any particular case."

The official policy and practice at the Journal was that prior to publication, the contents of the column were the Journal's confidential information. Despite the rule, with which Winans was familiar, he entered into a scheme in October 1983 with Peter Brant and petitioner Felis, both connected with the Kidder Peabody brokerage firm in New York City, to give them advance information as to the timing and contents of the "Heard" column. This permitted Brant and Felis and another conspirator, David Clark, a client of Brant, to buy or sell based on the probable impact of the column on the market. Profits were to be shared. The conspirators agreed that the scheme would not affect the journalistic purity of the "Heard" column, and the District Court did not find that the contents of any of the articles were altered to further the profit potential of petitioners' stock-trading scheme. Over a four-month period, the brokers made prepublication trades on the basis of information

---

Whoever, having devised or intending to devise any scheme or artifice to defraud, or for obtaining money or property by means of false or fraudulent pretenses, representations, or promises, or to sell, dispose of, loan, exchange, alter, give away, distribute, supply, or furnish or procure for unlawful use any counterfeit or spurious coin, obligation, security, or other article, or anything represented to be or intimated or held out to be such counterfeit or spurious article, for the purpose of executing such scheme or artifice or attempting so to do, places in any post office or authorized depository for mail matter, any matter or thing whatever to be sent or delivered by the Postal Service, or takes or receives therefrom, any such matter or thing, or knowingly causes to be delivered by mail according to the direction thereon, or at the place at which it is directed to be delivered by the person to whom it is addressed, any such matter or thing, shall be fined not more than $1,000 or imprisoned not more than five years, or both.

Section 1343 provides:

Whoever, having devised or intending to devise any scheme or artifice to defraud, or for obtaining money or property by means of false or fraudulent pretenses, representations, or promises, transmits or causes to be transmitted by means of wire, radio, or television communication in interstate or foreign commerce, any writings, signs, signals, pictures, or sounds for the purpose of executing such scheme or artifice, shall be fined not more than $1,000 or imprisoned not more than five years, or both.

given them by Winans about the contents of some 27 Heard columns. The net profits from these trades were about $690,000.

In November 1983, correlations between the "Heard" articles and trading in the Clark and Felis accounts were noted at Kidder Peabody and inquiries began. Brant and Felis denied knowing anyone at the Journal and took steps to conceal the trades. Later, the Securities and Exchange Commission began an investigation. Questions were met by denials both by the brokers at Kidder Peabody and by Winans at the Journal. As the investigation progressed, the conspirators quarreled, and on March 29, 1984, Winans and [David] Carpenter [Winans' roommate] went to the SEC and revealed the entire scheme. This indictment and a bench trial followed. Brant, who had pled guilty under a plea agreement, was a witness for the Government.

In addition, Felis and Winans were convicted of conspiracy under 18 U.S.C.A. § 371,c and Carpenter was convicted of aiding and abetting. The defendants were also charged with criminal violations of § 10(b) and Rule 10b–5 under the theory set forth in Chief Justice Burger's dissent, an issue on which the Justices were evenly divided and therefore did not address. The convictions under the mail and wire fraud statutes, however, were unanimously affirmed:

> We have little trouble in holding that the conspiracy here to trade on the Journal's confidential information is not outside the reach of the mail and wire fraud statutes, provided the other elements of the offenses are satisfied. The Journal's business information that it intended to be kept confidential was its property; the declaration to that effect in the employee manual merely removed any doubts on that score and made the finding of specific intent to defraud that much easier. Winans continued in the employ of the Journal, appropriating its confidential business information for his own use, all the while pretending to perform his duty of safeguarding it. * * * Furthermore, the District Court's conclusion that each of the petitioners acted with the required specific intent to defraud is strongly supported by the evidence.

> Lastly, we reject the submission that using the wires and the mail to print and send the Journal to its customers did not satisfy the requirement that those mediums be used to execute the scheme at issue. The courts below were quite right in observing that circulation of the "Heard" column was not only anticipated but an essential part of the scheme. Had the column not been made available to Journal customers, there would have been no effect on

---

c   Section 371 provides:

   If two or more persons conspire either to commit any offense against the United States, or to defraud the United States, or any agency thereof in any manner or for any purpose, and one or more of such persons do any act to effect the object of the conspiracy, each shall be fined not more than $10,000 or imprisoned not more than five years, or both.

stock prices and no likelihood of profiting from the information leaked by Winans.

The federal mail and wire fraud statutes, 18 U.S.C.A. §§ 1341, 1343, are widely used by federal prosecutors in white collar crime cases. A U.S. attorney has written that the mail fraud statute is "our Stradivarius, our Colt 45, our Louisville Slugger, our Cuisinart—and our true love." Jed S. Rakoff, The Federal Mail Fraud Statute (Part 1), 18 Duq. L.Rev. 771 (1980).

(4) The theory of liability set forth in Chief Justice Burger's dissenting opinion in *Chiarella* (and which evenly divided the Justices in *Carpenter*) is called the "misappropriation" theory. Basically, it provides that an insider trading violation may be based on a breach of fiduciary duty by the trader, regardless of whether that duty runs to the issuer of the securities involved or to other parties.

(5) If Chiarella is guilty under Rule 10b–5 pursuant to the misappropriation theory, have we not simply criminalized violations by employees of employer work rules? Is there any public harm to the securities markets or securities trading if Chiarella disobeys the signs posted by his employer? For a negative evaluation of *Carpenter* on the grounds that it "overcriminalizes" what should essentially be a matter for the civil law, see John C. Coffee, Jr., Hush! The Criminal Status of Confidential Information after *McNally* and *Carpenter* and the Enduring Problem of Overcriminalization, 26 Am.Crim.L.Rev. 121 (1988). For the perspective of an official of the Department of Justice on the *Carpenter* decision and background on the mail and wire fraud statutes, see Michael R. Dreeben, Insider Trading and Intangible Rights: The Redefinition of the Mail Fraud Statute, 26 Am.Crim.L.Rev. 181 (1988). See generally, Charles C. Cox & Kevin S. Fogarty, Bases of Insider Trading Law, 49 Ohio St.L.Rev. 353 (1988); Lawrence E. Mitchell, The Jurisprudence of the Misappropriation Theory and the New Insider Trading Legislation: From Fairness to Efficiency and Back, 52 Alb.L.Rev. 775 (1988).

(6) Approximately four months after *Chiarella* was decided, the SEC adopted Rule 14e–3 pursuant to §§ 14(e) and 23 of the Securities Exchange Act. SEC Rel. No. 34–17120, 45 Fed.Reg. 60410 (1980). These sections of the Exchange Act are part of the Williams Act (described in Chapter 16), relating to takeover bids and cash tender offers. The SEC release describes the purpose and scope of this rule as follows:

> The rule pertains to trading by persons in securities which may be the subject of a tender offer as well as tipping of material, nonpublic information relating to a contemplated tender offer. It should be noted that the rule applies only in the context of tender offers. * * *

II. Synopsis of Rule

* * * Rule 14e–3(a) imposes a duty of disclosure under Section 14(e) on any person who trades in securities which will be sought or are being sought in a tender offer while that person is in possession of material information which he knows or has reason to know is

nonpublic and has been acquired directly or indirectly from the offering person, from the issuer or from an officer, director, partner or employee or any other person acting on behalf of the offering person or the issuer. Since no duty to disclose would arise if a person subject to the rule does not purchase or sell or cause the purchase or sale of such securities while in possession of such information, the rule establishes a specific duty to "disclose or abstain from trading" under Section 14(e). The "disclose or abstain from trading" framework of Rule 14e–3(a) is similar to the approach taken in *Texas Gulf* and *Cady, Roberts* which the *Chiarella* Court cited with approval. In the Commission's view this framework is the least restrictive method of regulating this abusive practice. * * *

The operation of Rule 14e–3(a) may be illustrated by examples. It should be emphasized that these examples are not exclusive and do not constitute the only situations in which the duty under Rule 14e–3(a) would arise:

(1) If an offering person tells another person that the offering person will make a tender offer which information is nonpublic, the other person has acquired material, nonpublic information directly from the offering person and has a duty under Rule 14e–3(a). * * *

(3) If the offering person sends a nonpublic letter to a subject company notifying the subject company of a proposed tender offer at a specified price and upon specified terms and the management of the subject company learns the contents of the letter, the management of the subject company has acquired material, nonpublic information directly from the offering person. An individual member of such management will violate Rule 14e–3(a) if he purchases or sells or causes the purchase or sale of the securities to be sought in the tender offer.

(4) If, under the facts in the preceding example, the management of the subject company also tells other persons not affiliated with management of the letter, then those other persons have acquired material, nonpublic information indirectly from the offering person and are under a duty to disclose or abstain from trading under Rule 14e–3(a). * * *

(6) If a person steals, converts or otherwise misappropriates material, nonpublic information relating to a tender offer from an offering person, such person will have acquired the information directly from the offering person and has a duty under Rule 14e–3(a).

(7) If an offering person tells another person of his intention to make a tender offer, and such other person subsequently tells a third person that a tender offer will be made and this third person knows or has reason to know that this non-public information came

indirectly from the offering person, then this third person has a duty under Rule 14e–3(a).

45 Fed.Reg. 60410–60414. The validity of Rule 14e–3 remained in some doubt until the following decision by the Supreme Court.

UNITED STATES V. O'HAGAN

Supreme Court of the United States, 1997.
521 U.S. 642.

JUSTICE GINSBURG delivered the opinion of the Court.

This case concerns the interpretation and enforcement of § 10(b) and § 14(e) of the Securities Exchange Act of 1934, and rules made by the Securities and Exchange Commission pursuant to these provisions, Rule 10b–5 and Rule 14e–3(a). Two prime questions are presented. The first relates to the misappropriation of material, nonpublic information for securities trading; the second concerns fraudulent practices in the tender offer setting. In particular, we address and resolve these issues: (1) Is a person who trades in securities for personal profit, using confidential information misappropriated in breach of a fiduciary duty to the source of the information, guilty of violating § 10(b) and Rule 10b–5? (2) Did the Commission exceed its rulemaking authority by adopting Rule 14e–3(a), which proscribes trading on undisclosed information in the tender offer setting, even in the absence of a duty to disclose? Our answer to the first question is yes, and to the second question, viewed in the context of this case, no.

I

Respondent James Herman O'Hagan was a partner in the law firm of Dorsey & Whitney in Minneapolis, Minnesota. In July 1988, Grand Metropolitan PLC (Grand Met), a company based in London, England, retained Dorsey & Whitney as local counsel to represent Grand Met regarding a potential tender offer for the common stock of the Pillsbury Company, headquartered in Minneapolis. Both Grand Met and Dorsey & Whitney took precautions to protect the confidentiality of Grand Met's tender offer plans. O'Hagan did no work on the Grand Met representation. Dorsey & Whitney withdrew from representing Grand Met on September 9, 1988. Less than a month later, on October 4, 1988, Grand Met publicly announced its tender offer for Pillsbury stock.

On August 18, 1988, while Dorsey & Whitney was still representing Grand Met, O'Hagan began purchasing call options for Pillsbury stock. Each option gave him the right to purchase 100 shares of Pillsbury stock by a specified date in September 1988. Later in August and in September, O'Hagan made additional purchases of Pillsbury call options. By the end of September, he owned 2,500 unexpired Pillsbury options, apparently more than any other individual investor. O'Hagan also purchased, in

September 1988, some 5,000 shares of Pillsbury common stock, at a price just under $39 per share. When Grand Met announced its tender offer in October, the price of Pillsbury stock rose to nearly $60 per share. O'Hagan then sold his Pillsbury call options and common stock, making a profit of more than $4.3 million.

The Securities and Exchange Commission (SEC or Commission) initiated an investigation into O'Hagan's transactions, culminating in a 57-count indictment. The indictment alleged that O'Hagan defrauded his law firm and its client, Grand Met, by using for his own trading purposes material, nonpublic information regarding Grand Met's planned tender offer.[1] According to the indictment, O'Hagan used the profits he gained through this trading to conceal his previous embezzlement and conversion of unrelated client trust funds.[2] O'Hagan was charged with 20 counts of mail fraud, in violation of 18 U.S.C. § 1341; 17 counts of securities fraud, in violation of § 10(b) of the Securities Exchange Act of 1934, and SEC Rule 10b–5; 17 counts of fraudulent trading in connection with a tender offer, in violation of § 14(e) of the Exchange Act and SEC Rule 14e–3(a); and 3 counts of violating federal money laundering statutes, 18 U.S.C. §§ 1956(a)(1)(B)(i), 1957. A jury convicted O'Hagan on all 57 counts, and he was sentenced to a 41-month term of imprisonment.

A divided panel of the Court of Appeals for the Eighth Circuit reversed all of O'Hagan's convictions. 92 F.3d 612 (1996). Liability under § 10(b) and Rule 10b–5, the Eighth Circuit held, may not be grounded on the "misappropriation theory" of securities fraud on which the prosecution relied. The Court of Appeals also held that Rule 14e–3(a)— which prohibits trading while in possession of material, nonpublic information relating to a tender offer—exceeds the SEC's § 14(e) rulemaking authority because the rule contains no breach of fiduciary duty requirement. The Eighth Circuit further concluded that O'Hagan's mail fraud and money laundering convictions rested on violations of the securities laws, and therefore could not stand once the securities fraud convictions were reversed. Judge Fagg, dissenting, stated that he would recognize and enforce the misappropriation theory, and would hold that

---

[1] As evidence that O'Hagan traded on the basis of nonpublic information misappropriated from his law firm, the Government relied on a conversation between O'Hagan and the Dorsey & Whitney partner heading the firm's Grand Met representation. That conversation allegedly took place shortly before August 26, 1988. O'Hagan urges that the Government's evidence does not show he traded on the basis of nonpublic information. O'Hagan points to news reports on August 18 and 22, 1988, that Grand Met was interested in acquiring Pillsbury, and to an earlier, August 12, 1988, news report that Grand Met had put up its hotel chain for auction to raise funds for an acquisition. O'Hagan's challenge to the sufficiency of the evidence remains open for consideration on remand.

[2] O'Hagan was convicted of theft in state court, sentenced to 30 months' imprisonment, and fined. See State v. O'Hagan, 474 N.W.2d 613, 615, 623 (Minn.App.1991). The Supreme Court of Minnesota disbarred O'Hagan from the practice of law. See In re O'Hagan, 450 N.W.2d 571 (Minn.1990).

the SEC did not exceed its rulemaking authority when it adopted Rule 14e–3(a) without requiring proof of a breach of fiduciary duty.

Decisions of the Courts of Appeals are in conflict on the propriety of the misappropriation theory under § 10(b) and Rule 10b–5, and on the legitimacy of Rule 14e–3(a) under § 14(e). We granted certiorari, 519 U.S 1087, 117 S.Ct. 759, 136 L.Ed.2d 695 (1997), and now reverse the Eighth Circuit's judgment.

II

We address first the Court of Appeals' reversal of O'Hagan's convictions under § 10(b) and Rule 10b–5. Following the Fourth Circuit's lead, see United States v. Bryan, 58 F.3d 933, 943–959 (1995), the Eighth Circuit rejected the misappropriation theory as a basis for § 10(b) liability. We hold, in accord with several other Courts of Appeals, that criminal liability under § 10(b) may be predicated on the misappropriation theory.[4] * * *

A

* * * [Section] 10(b) of the Exchange Act * * * proscribes (1) using any deceptive device (2) in connection with the purchase or sale of securities, in contravention of rules prescribed by the Commission. The provision, as written, does not confine its coverage to deception of a purchaser or seller of securities, see United States v. Newman, 664 F.2d 12, 17 (C.A.2 1981); rather, the statute reaches any deceptive device used "in connection with the purchase or sale of any security."

Pursuant to its § 10(b) rulemaking authority, the Commission has adopted Rule 10b–5 * * *. Liability under Rule 10b–5, our precedent indicates, does not extend beyond conduct encompassed by § 10(b)'s prohibition. See Ernst & Ernst v. Hochfelder, 425 U.S. 185, 214, 96 S.Ct. 1375, 1391, 47 L.Ed.2d 668 (1976) (scope of Rule 10b–5 cannot exceed power Congress granted Commission under § 10(b)); see also Central Bank of Denver, N.A. v. First Interstate Bank of Denver, N.A., 511 U.S. 164, 173, 114 S.Ct. 1439, 1446, 128 L.Ed.2d 119 (1994) ("We have refused to allow [private] 10b–5 challenges to conduct not prohibited by the text of the statute.").

Under the "traditional" or "classical theory" of insider trading liability, § 10(b) and Rule 10b–5 are violated when a corporate insider

---

4 Twice before we have been presented with the question whether criminal liability for violation of § 10(b) may be based on a misappropriation theory. In Chiarella v. United States * * * the jury had received no misappropriation theory instructions, so we declined to address the question. In Carpenter v. United States, * * * the Court divided evenly on whether, under the circumstances of that case, convictions resting on the misappropriation theory should be affirmed. See Barbara B. Aldave, The Misappropriation Theory: Carpenter and Its Aftermath, 49 Ohio St. L.J. 373, 375 (1988) (observing that "Carpenter was, by any reckoning, an unusual case," for the information there misappropriated belonged not to a company preparing to engage in securities transactions, e.g., a bidder in a corporate acquisition, but to the Wall Street Journal).

trades in the securities of his corporation on the basis of material, nonpublic information. Trading on such information qualifies as a "deceptive device" under § 10(b), we have affirmed, because "a relationship of trust and confidence [exists] between the shareholders of a corporation and those insiders who have obtained confidential information by reason of their position with that corporation." Chiarella v. United States, 445 U.S. 222, 228, 100 S.Ct. 1108, 1114, 63 L.Ed.2d 348 (1980). That relationship, we recognized, "gives rise to a duty to disclose [or to abstain from trading] because of the 'necessity of preventing a corporate insider from * * * tak[ing] unfair advantage of * * * uninformed * * * stockholders.'" Id., at 228–229, 100 S.Ct., at 1115 (citation omitted). The classical theory applies not only to officers, directors, and other permanent insiders of a corporation, but also to attorneys, accountants, consultants, and others who temporarily become fiduciaries of a corporation. See Dirks v. SEC, 463 U.S. 646, 655, n. 14, 103 S.Ct. 3255, 3262, 77 L.Ed.2d 911 (1983).

The "misappropriation theory" holds that a person commits fraud "in connection with" a securities transaction, and thereby violates § 10(b) and Rule 10b–5, when he misappropriates confidential information for securities trading purposes, in breach of a duty owed to the source of the information. Under this theory, a fiduciary's undisclosed, self-serving use of a principal's information to purchase or sell securities, in breach of a duty of loyalty and confidentiality, defrauds the principal of the exclusive use of that information. In lieu of premising liability on a fiduciary relationship between company insider and purchaser or seller of the company's stock, the misappropriation theory premises liability on a fiduciary-turned-trader's deception of those who entrusted him with access to confidential information.

The two theories are complementary, each addressing efforts to capitalize on nonpublic information through the purchase or sale of securities. The classical theory targets a corporate insider's breach of duty to shareholders with whom the insider transacts; the misappropriation theory outlaws trading on the basis of nonpublic information by a corporate "outsider" in breach of a duty owed not to a trading party, but to the source of the information. The misappropriation theory is thus designed to "protec[t] the integrity of the securities markets against abuses by 'outsiders' to a corporation who have access to confidential information that will affect th[e] corporation's security price when revealed, but who owe no fiduciary or other duty to that corporation's shareholders." Ibid.

In this case, the indictment alleged that O'Hagan, in breach of a duty of trust and confidence he owed to his law firm, Dorsey & Whitney, and to its client, Grand Met, traded on the basis of nonpublic information regarding Grand Met's planned tender offer for Pillsbury common stock.

This conduct, the Government charged, constituted a fraudulent device in connection with the purchase and sale of securities.[5]

B

We agree with the Government that misappropriation, as just defined, satisfies § 10(b)'s requirement that chargeable conduct involve a "deceptive device or contrivance" used "in connection with" the purchase or sale of securities. We observe, first, that misappropriators, as the Government describes them, deal in deception. A fiduciary who "[pretends] loyalty to the principal while secretly converting the principal's information for personal gain," Brief for United States 17, "dupes" or defrauds the principal. See Aldave, Misappropriation: A General Theory of Liability for Trading on Nonpublic Information, 13 Hofstra L.Rev. 101, 119 (1984).

We addressed fraud of the same species in Carpenter v. United States, 484 U.S. 19, 108 S.Ct. 316, 98 L.Ed.2d 275 (1987), which involved the mail fraud statute's proscription of "any scheme or artifice to defraud," 18 U.S.C. § 1341. Affirming convictions under that statute, we said in *Carpenter* that an employee's undertaking not to reveal his employer's confidential information "became a sham" when the employee provided the information to his co-conspirators in a scheme to obtain trading profits. 484 U.S., at 27, 108 S.Ct., at 321. A company's confidential information, we recognized in *Carpenter*, qualifies as property to which the company has a right of exclusive use. The undisclosed misappropriation of such information, in violation of a fiduciary duty, the Court said in *Carpenter*, constitutes fraud akin to embezzlement—" 'the fraudulent appropriation to one's own use of the money or goods entrusted to one's care by another.' " Id., at 27, 108 S.Ct., at 317 (quoting Grin v. Shine, 187 U.S. 181, 189, 23 S.Ct. 98, 101–102, 47 L.Ed. 130 (1902)); see Aldave, 13 Hofstra L.Rev., at 119. Carpenter's discussion of the fraudulent misuse of confidential information, the Government notes, "is a particularly apt source of guidance here, because [the mail fraud statute] (like Section 10(b)) has long been held to require deception, not merely the breach of a fiduciary duty."

Deception through nondisclosure is central to the theory of liability for which the Government seeks recognition. As counsel for the Government stated in explanation of the theory at oral argument: "To satisfy the common law rule that a trustee may not use the property that [has] been entrusted [to] him, there would have to be consent. To satisfy

---

[5] The Government could not have prosecuted O'Hagan under the classical theory, for O'Hagan was not an "insider" of Pillsbury, the corporation in whose stock he traded. Although an "outsider" with respect to Pillsbury, O'Hagan had an intimate association with, and was found to have traded on confidential information from, Dorsey & Whitney, counsel to tender offeror Grand Met. Under the misappropriation theory, O'Hagan's securities trading does not escape Exchange Act sanction, as it would under the dissent's reasoning, simply because he was associated with, and gained nonpublic information from, the bidder, rather than the target.

the requirement of the Securities Act that there be no deception, there would only have to be disclosure." [S]ee generally Restatement (Second) of Agency §§ 390, 395 (1958) (agent's disclosure obligation regarding use of confidential information).[6]

The misappropriation theory advanced by the Government is consistent with Santa Fe Industries, Inc. v. Green, 430 U.S. 462, 97 S.Ct. 1292, 51 L.Ed.2d 480 (1977), a decision underscoring that § 10(b) is not an all-purpose breach of fiduciary duty ban; rather, it trains on conduct involving manipulation or deception. In contrast to the Government's allegations in this case, in *Santa Fe Industries*, all pertinent facts were disclosed by the persons charged with violating § 10(b) and Rule 10b–5; therefore, there was no deception through nondisclosure to which liability under those provisions could attach. Similarly, full disclosure forecloses liability under the misappropriation theory: Because the deception essential to the misappropriation theory involves feigning fidelity to the source of information, if the fiduciary discloses to the source that he plans to trade on the nonpublic information, there is no "deceptive device" and thus no § 10(b) violation—although the fiduciary-turned-trader may remain liable under state law for breach of a duty of loyalty.[7]

We turn next to the § 10(b) requirement that the misappropriator's deceptive use of information be "in connection with the purchase or sale of [a] security." This element is satisfied because the fiduciary's fraud is consummated, not when the fiduciary gains the confidential information, but when, without disclosure to his principal, he uses the information to purchase or sell securities. The securities transaction and the breach of duty thus coincide. This is so even though the person or entity defrauded is not the other party to the trade, but is, instead, the source of the nonpublic information. See Aldave, 13 Hofstra L.Rev., at 120 ("a fraud or deceit can be practiced on one person, with resultant harm to another person or group of persons"). A misappropriator who trades on the basis of material, nonpublic information, in short, gains his advantageous market position through deception; he deceives the source of the information and simultaneously harms members of the investing public.

The misappropriation theory targets information of a sort that misappropriators ordinarily capitalize upon to gain no-risk profits

---

[6] Under the misappropriation theory urged in this case, the disclosure obligation runs to the source of the information, here, Dorsey & Whitney and Grand Met. Chief Justice Burger, dissenting in Chiarella, advanced a broader reading of § 10(b) and Rule 10b–5; the disclosure obligation, as he envisioned it, ran to those with whom the misappropriator trades ("a person who has misappropriated nonpublic information has an absolute duty to disclose that information or to refrain from trading"). The Government does not propose that we adopt a misappropriation theory of that breadth.

[7] Where, however, a person trading on the basis of material, nonpublic information owes a duty of loyalty and confidentiality to two entities or persons—for example, a law firm and its client—but makes disclosure to only one, the trader may still be liable under the misappropriation theory.

through the purchase or sale of securities. Should a misappropriator put such information to other use, the statute's prohibition would not be implicated. The theory does not catch all conceivable forms of fraud involving confidential information; rather, it catches fraudulent means of capitalizing on such information through securities transactions.

The Government notes another limitation on the forms of fraud § 10(b) reaches: "The misappropriation theory would not * * * apply to a case in which a person defrauded a bank into giving him a loan or embezzled cash from another, and then used the proceeds of the misdeed to purchase securities." In such a case, the Government states, "the proceeds would have value to the malefactor apart from their use in a securities transaction, and the fraud would be complete as soon as the money was obtained." In other words, money can buy, if not anything, then at least many things; its misappropriation may thus be viewed as sufficiently detached from a subsequent securities transaction that § 10(b)'s "in connection with" requirement would not be met.

The dissent's charge that the misappropriation theory is incoherent because information, like funds, can be put to multiple uses misses the point. The Exchange Act was enacted in part "to insure the maintenance of fair and honest markets," and there is no question that fraudulent uses of confidential information fall within § 10(b)'s prohibition if the fraud is "in connection with" a securities transaction. It is hardly remarkable that a rule suitably applied to the fraudulent uses of certain kinds of information would be stretched beyond reason were it applied to the fraudulent use of money.

The dissent does catch the Government in overstatement. Observing that money can be used for all manner of purposes and purchases, the Government urges that confidential information of the kind at issue derives its value *only* from its utility in securities trading. See Brief for United States 10, 21 (several times emphasizing the word "only"). Substitute "ordinarily" for "only," and the Government is on the mark.[8] * * *

The misappropriation theory comports with § 10(b)'s language, which requires deception "in connection with the purchase or sale of any security," not deception of an identifiable purchaser or seller. The theory is also well-tuned to an animating purpose of the Exchange Act: to insure

---

[8] [The dissent's] evident struggle to invent other uses to which O'Hagan plausibly might have put the nonpublic information is telling. It is imaginative to suggest that a trade journal would have paid O'Hagan dollars in the millions to publish his information. Counsel for O'Hagan hypothesized, as a nontrading use, that O'Hagan could have "misappropriat[ed] this information of [his] law firm and its client, deliver[ed] it to [Pillsbury], and suggest[ed] that [Pillsbury] in the future * * * might find it very desirable to use [O'Hagan] for legal work." But Pillsbury might well have had large doubts about engaging for its legal work a lawyer who so stunningly displayed his readiness to betray a client's confidence. Nor is the Commission's theory "incoherent" or "inconsistent," for failing to inhibit use of confidential information for "personal amusement * * * in a fantasy stock trading game."

honest securities markets and thereby promote investor confidence. See 45 Fed.Reg. 60412 (1980) (trading on misappropriated information "undermines the integrity of, and investor confidence in, the securities markets"). Although informational disparity is inevitable in the securities markets, investors likely would hesitate to venture their capital in a market where trading based on misappropriated nonpublic information is unchecked by law. An investor's informational disadvantage vis-a-vis a misappropriator with material, nonpublic information stems from contrivance, not luck; it is a disadvantage that cannot be overcome with research or skill. See Brudney, Insiders, Outsiders, and Informational Advantages Under the Federal Securities Laws, 93 Harv. L.Rev. 322, 356 (1979) ("If the market is thought to be systematically populated with * * * transactors [trading on the basis of misappropriated information] some investors will refrain from dealing altogether, and others will incur costs to avoid dealing with such transactors or corruptly to overcome their unerodable informational advantages."); Aldave, 13 Hofstra L.Rev., at 122–123.

In sum, considering the inhibiting impact on market participation of trading on misappropriated information, and the congressional purposes underlying § 10(b), it makes scant sense to hold a lawyer like O'Hagan a § 10(b) violator if he works for a law firm representing the target of a tender offer, but not if he works for a law firm representing the bidder. The text of the statute requires no such result.[9] The misappropriation at issue here was properly made the subject of a § 10(b) charge because it meets the statutory requirement that there be "deceptive" conduct "in connection with" securities transactions.

C

The Court of Appeals rejected the misappropriation theory primarily on two grounds. First, as the Eighth Circuit comprehended the theory, it requires neither misrepresentation nor nondisclosure. * * * Second and "more obvious," the Court of Appeals said, the misappropriation theory is not moored to § 10(b)'s requirement that "the fraud be 'in connection with the purchase or sale of any security.'" * * * "[O]nly a breach of a duty to parties to the securities transaction," the Court of Appeals concluded, "or, at the most, to other market participants such as investors, will be sufficient to give rise to § 10(b) liability." 92 F.3d, at 618. We read the

---

[9]   As noted earlier, however, the textual requirement of deception precludes § 10(b) liability when a person trading on the basis of nonpublic information has disclosed his trading plans to, or obtained authorization from, the principal—even though such conduct may affect the securities markets in the same manner as the conduct reached by the misappropriation theory. Contrary to the dissent's suggestion, the fact that § 10(b) is only a partial antidote to the problems it was designed to alleviate does not call into question its prohibition of conduct that falls within its textual proscription. Moreover, once a disloyal agent discloses his imminent breach of duty, his principal may seek appropriate equitable relief under state law. Furthermore, in the context of a tender offer, the principal who authorizes an agent's trading on confidential information may, in the Commission's view, incur liability for an Exchange Act violation under Rule 14e–3(a).

statute and our precedent differently, and note again that § 10(b) refers to "the purchase or sale of any security," not to identifiable purchasers or sellers of securities. * * * [A discussion of earlier Supreme Court decisions is omitted].

In sum, the misappropriation theory, as we have examined and explained it in this opinion, is both consistent with the statute and with our precedent. Vital to our decision that criminal liability may be sustained under the misappropriation theory, we emphasize, are two sturdy safeguards Congress has provided regarding scienter. To establish a criminal violation of Rule 10b–5, the Government must prove that a person "willfully" violated the provision. Furthermore, a defendant may not be imprisoned for violating Rule 10b–5 if he proves that he had no knowledge of the rule.[13] O'Hagan's charge that the misappropriation theory is too indefinite to permit the imposition of criminal liability, thus fails not only because the theory is limited to those who breach a recognized duty. In addition, the statute's "requirement of the presence of culpable intent as a necessary element of the offense does much to destroy any force in the argument that application of the [statute]" in circumstances such as O'Hagan's is unjust.

III

We consider next the ground on which the Court of Appeals reversed O'Hagan's convictions for fraudulent trading in connection with a tender offer, in violation of § 14(e) of the Exchange Act and SEC Rule 14e–3(a). A sole question is before us as to these convictions: Did the Commission, as the Court of Appeals held, exceed its rulemaking authority under § 14(e) when it adopted Rule 14e–3(a) without requiring a showing that the trading at issue entailed a breach of fiduciary duty? We hold that the Commission, in this regard and to the extent relevant to this case, did not exceed its authority.

The governing statutory provision, § 14(e) of the Exchange Act, reads in relevant part:

> It shall be unlawful for any person * * * to engage in any fraudulent, deceptive, or manipulative acts or practices, in connection with any tender offer. * * * The [SEC] shall, for the purposes of this subsection, by rules and regulations define, and prescribe means reasonably designed to prevent, such acts and practices as are fraudulent, deceptive, or manipulative.

Section 14(e)'s first sentence prohibits fraudulent acts in connection with a tender offer. This self-operating proscription was one of several provisions added to the Exchange Act in 1968 by the Williams Act. The section's second sentence delegates definitional and prophylactic rulemaking authority to the Commission. Congress added this

---

[13] The statute provides no such defense to imposition of monetary fines.

rulemaking delegation to § 14(e) in 1970 amendments to the Williams Act.

Through § 14(e) and other provisions on disclosure in the Williams Act, Congress sought to ensure that shareholders "confronted by a cash tender offer for their stock [would] not be required to respond without adequate information." Rondeau v. Mosinee Paper Corp., 422 U.S. 49, 58, 95 S.Ct. 2069, 2076, 45 L.Ed.2d 12 (1975). As we recognized in Schreiber v. Burlington Northern, Inc., 472 U.S. 1, 105 S.Ct. 2458, 86 L.Ed.2d 1 (1985), Congress designed the Williams Act to make "disclosure, rather than court imposed principles of 'fairness' or 'artificiality,' * * * the preferred method of market regulation." Section 14(e), we explained, "supplements the more precise disclosure provisions found elsewhere in the Williams Act, while requiring disclosure more explicitly addressed to the tender offer context than that required by § 10(b)." [472 U.S.], at 10–11, 105 S.Ct., at 2464.

Relying on § 14(e)'s rulemaking authorization, the Commission, in 1980, promulgated Rule 14e–3(a). * * * As characterized by the Commission, Rule 14e–3(a) is a "disclose or abstain from trading" requirement. 45 Fed.Reg. 60410 (1980).[15] The Second Circuit concisely described the rule's thrust:

> "One violates Rule 14e–3(a) if he trades on the basis of material nonpublic information concerning a pending tender offer that he knows or has reason to know has been acquired 'directly or indirectly' from an insider of the offeror or issuer, or someone working on their behalf. Rule 14e–3(a) is a disclosure provision. It creates a duty in those traders who fall within its ambit to abstain or disclose, *without regard to whether the trader owes a pre-existing fiduciary duty* to respect the confidentiality of the information." United States v. Chestman, 947 F.2d 551, 557 (1991) (en banc) (emphasis added), cert. denied, 503 U.S. 1004, 112 S.Ct. 1759, 118 L.Ed.2d 422 (1992).

* * * [The Court holds that this Rule does not exceed the SEC's powers under § 14(e) of the Securities Exchange Act].

We need not resolve in this case whether the Commission's authority under § 14(e) to "define * * * such acts and practices as are fraudulent" is broader than the Commission's fraud-defining authority under § 10(b), for we agree with the United States that Rule 14e–3(a), as applied to cases of this genre, qualifies under § 14(e) as a "means reasonably designed to prevent" fraudulent trading on material, nonpublic information in the tender offer context. * * * We hold * * * that under § 14(e), the Commission may prohibit acts, not themselves fraudulent under the

---

[15] The rule thus adopts for the tender offer context a requirement resembling the one Chief Justice Burger would have adopted in Chiarella for misappropriators under § 10(b).

common law or § 10(b), if the prohibition is "reasonably designed to prevent * * * acts and practices [that] are fraudulent."[18]

Because Congress has authorized the Commission, in § 14(e), to prescribe legislative rules, we owe the Commission's judgment "more than mere deference or weight." Batterton v. Francis, 432 U.S. 416, 424–426, 97 S.Ct. 2399, 2406, 53 L.Ed.2d 448 (1977). Therefore, in determining whether Rule 14e–3(a)'s "disclose or abstain from trading" requirement is reasonably designed to prevent fraudulent acts, we must accord the Commission's assessment "controlling weight unless [it is] arbitrary, capricious, or manifestly contrary to the statute." Chevron U.S.A., Inc. v. Natural Resources Defense Council, Inc., 467 U.S. 837, 844, 104 S.Ct. 2778, 2782, 81 L.Ed.2d 694 (1984). In this case, we conclude, the Commission's assessment is none of these. * * *

IV

Based on its dispositions of the securities fraud convictions, the Court of Appeals also reversed O'Hagan's convictions, under 18 U.S.C. § 1341, for mail fraud. Reversal of the securities convictions, the Court of Appeals recognized, "d[id] not as a matter of law require that the mail fraud convictions likewise be reversed." (citing Carpenter * * *). But in this case, the Court of Appeals said, the indictment was so structured that the mail fraud charges could not be disassociated from the securities fraud charges, and absent any securities fraud, "there was no fraud upon which to base the mail fraud charges." 92 F.3d, at 627–628.

The United States urges that the Court of Appeals' position is irreconcilable with Carpenter: Just as in Carpenter, so here, the "mail fraud charges are independent of [the] securities fraud charges, even [though] both rest on the same set of facts." We need not linger over this matter, for our rulings on the securities fraud issues require that we reverse the Court of Appeals judgment on the mail fraud counts as well.[25]

O'Hagan, we note, attacked the mail fraud convictions in the Court of Appeals on alternate grounds; his other arguments, not yet addressed by the Eighth Circuit, remain open for consideration on remand.

---

[18] The Commission's power under § 10(b) is more limited. * * * Rule 10b–5 may proscribe only conduct that § 10(b) prohibits.

[25] [The dissent] finds O'Hagan's convictions on the mail fraud counts, but not on the securities fraud counts, sustainable. Under [the dissent's] view, securities traders like O'Hagan would escape SEC civil actions and federal prosecutions under legislation targeting securities fraud, only to be caught for their trading activities in the broad mail fraud net. If misappropriation theory cases could proceed only under the federal mail and wire fraud statutes, practical consequences for individual defendants might not be large; however, "proportionally more persons accused of insider trading [might] be pursued by a U.S. Attorney, and proportionally fewer by the SEC." Our decision, of course, does not rest on such enforcement policy considerations.

The judgment of the Court of Appeals for the Eighth Circuit is reversed, and the case is remanded for further proceedings consistent with this opinion.

It is so ordered.

JUSTICE SCALIA, concurring in part and dissenting in part.

I join Parts I, III, and IV of the Court's opinion. I do not agree, however, with Part II of the Court's opinion, containing its analysis of respondent's convictions under § 10(b) and Rule 10b–5.

I do not entirely agree with Justice Thomas's analysis of those convictions either, principally because it seems to me irrelevant whether the Government's theory of why respondent's acts were covered is "coherent and consistent." It is true that with respect to matters over which an agency has been accorded adjudicative authority or policymaking discretion, the agency's action must be supported by the reasons that the agency sets forth, SEC v. Chenery Corp., 318 U.S. 80, 94, 63 S.Ct. 454, 462, 87 L.Ed. 626 (1943); see also SEC v. Chenery Corp., 332 U.S. 194, 196, 67 S.Ct. 1575, 91 L.Ed. 1995 (1947), but I do not think an agency's unadorned application of the law need be, at least where (as here) no Chevron deference is being given to the agency's interpretation. In point of fact, respondent's actions either violated § 10(b) and Rule 10b–5, or they did not—regardless of the reasons the Government gave. And it is for us to decide.

While the Court's explanation of the scope of § 10(b) and Rule 10b–5 would be entirely reasonable in some other context, it does not seem to accord with the principle of lenity we apply to criminal statutes (which cannot be mitigated here by the Rule, which is no less ambiguous than the statute). * * * In light of that principle, it seems to me that the unelaborated statutory language: "[t]o use or employ in connection with the purchase or sale of any security * * * any manipulative or deceptive device or contrivance," § 10(b), must be construed to require the manipulation or deception of a party to a securities transaction.

JUSTICE THOMAS, with whom THE CHIEF JUSTICE joins, concurring in the judgment in part and dissenting in part.

Today the majority upholds respondent's convictions for violating § 10(b) of the Securities Exchange Act of 1934, and Rule 10b–5 promulgated thereunder, based upon the Securities and Exchange Commission's "misappropriation theory." Central to the majority's holding is the need to interpret § 10(b)'s requirement that a deceptive device be "use[d] or employ[ed], in connection with the purchase or sale of any security." Because the Commission's misappropriation theory fails to provide a coherent and consistent interpretation of this essential requirement for liability under § 10(b), I dissent.

The majority also sustains respondent's convictions under § 14(e) of the Securities Exchange Act, and Rule 14e–3(a) promulgated thereunder, regardless of whether respondent violated a fiduciary duty to anybody. I dissent too from that holding because, while § 14(e) does allow regulations prohibiting nonfraudulent acts as a prophylactic against certain fraudulent acts, neither the majority nor the Commission identifies any relevant underlying fraud against which Rule 14e–3(a) reasonably provides prophylaxis. With regard to the respondent's mail fraud convictions, however, I concur in the judgment of the Court.

I

I do not take issue with the majority's determination that the undisclosed misappropriation of confidential information by a fiduciary can constitute a "deceptive device" within the meaning of § 10(b). Nondisclosure where there is a pre-existing duty to disclose satisfies our definitions of fraud and deceit for purposes of the securities laws.

Unlike the majority, however, I cannot accept the Commission's interpretation of when a deceptive device is "use[d] * * * in connection with" a securities transaction. Although the Commission and the majority at points seem to suggest that any relation to a securities transaction satisfies the "in connection with" requirement of § 10(b), both ultimately reject such an overly expansive construction and require a more integral connection between the fraud and the securities transaction. The majority states, for example, that the misappropriation theory applies to undisclosed misappropriation of confidential information "for securities trading purposes," thus seeming to require a particular intent by the misappropriator in order to satisfy the "in connection with" language. * * * The Commission goes further, and argues that the misappropriation theory satisfies the "in connection with" requirement because it "depends on an inherent connection between the deceptive conduct and the purchase or sale of a security." * * *

The Commission's construction of the relevant language in § 10(b), and the incoherence of that construction, become evident as the majority attempts to describe why the fraudulent theft of information falls under the Commission's misappropriation theory, but the fraudulent theft of money does not. * * * And when the majority seeks to distinguish the embezzlement of funds from the embezzlement of information, it becomes clear that neither the Commission nor the majority has a coherent theory regarding § 10(b)'s "in connection with" requirement. * * *

NOTES

(1) Justice Thomas' dissent (only a small portion of which is reprinted above) points out logical problems in the position of the majority (and the SEC) with respect to the "in connection with" requirement. Accepting for purposes of argument that it is not entirely logical, is that a justification for

rejecting the misappropriation doctrine? Consider the consequences of rejecting that doctrine. If an attorney represents the aggressor in a takeover attempt, he does not violate Rule 10b–5 if he capitalizes on that information and buys stock (or options on stock) of the target. However, if he represents the target, he commits a serious crime if he makes the same purchases. Isn't that even more illogical? Perhaps the answer is that Rule 14e–3 should have been upheld and the misappropriation doctrine rejected? Might there be other situations in a non-takeover context in which similar irrational results would arise?

(2) During the course of the oral argument in *O'Hagan*, the Government conceded that on the facts of Carpenter v. United States, if Winans had gone to the Wall Street Journal and said, "look, you know, you're not paying me very much; I'd like to make a little bit more money by buying stock, particularly the stocks that are going to appear in my Heard on the Street column," and the Wall Street Journal had said, "that's fine," there would have been no deception of the Wall Street Journal, and no violation of Rule 10b–5. Do you agree? If not, what possible theory is available, given the language of § 10(b) and Rule 10b–5?

(3) *O'Hagan* was, of course, a major victory for the SEC. However, it did not resolve all problems. For one thing, Justice Ginsburg's opinion consistently refers to O'Hagan trading "on the basis of" insider information. The phrase preferred by the SEC is "trading while in possession of" insider information. Does Justice Ginsburg's formulation mean that a person may possess insider information but trade "on the basis of" other factors (such as the mistaken belief that the information has been released publicly) without violating Rule 10b–5? See United States v. Teicher, 987 F.2d 112, 120–21 (2d Cir.1993), where the Court held that the appropriate standard of causation was "knowing possession" of insider information at the time of the trade: "As a matter of policy then, a requirement of a causal connection between the information and the trade could frustrate attempts to distinguish between legitimate trades and those conducted in connection with inside information. * * * Unlike a loaded weapon which may stand ready but unused, material information cannot lay idle in the human brain."

(4) The SEC attempted to resolve the "use-possession" debate about whether insiders who possess but do not use non-public information are guilty of insider trading by adopting Rule 10b–5–1, SEC Rel. 34–43154 (August 24, 2000). This rule establishes the test of liability to be trading "on the basis of" material nonpublic information, a test that is satisfied if the person "was aware of the material nonpublic information when the person made the purchase or sale."

This provision attempts to clarify what constitutes trading based on material nonpublic information in insider trading cases under § 10(b). The importance of Rule 10b–5–1 from the standpoint of those subject to the insider trading prohibition cannot be overstated. Before the adoption of this Rule, there could never be complete certainty as to whether an insider's securities transaction might run afoul of Rule 10b–5.

MICHAEL KAPLAN, RULE 10b5–1 PLANS:
WHAT YOU NEED TO KNOW

Harvard Law School Forum on Corporate Governance and Financial Regulation,
http://blogs.law.harvard.edu/corpgov/2013/02/05/rule-10b5-1-plans-what-you-need-to-know/.

Rule 10b5–1 plans are back in the news. These plans are widely used by officers and directors of public companies to sell stock according to the parameters of the affirmative defense to illegal insider trading available under Rule 10b5–1, which was adopted by the SEC in 2000. Several recent Wall Street Journal articles suggest that some executives may have achieved above-market returns using the plans. These articles are reported to have drawn the interest of federal prosecutors and the SEC enforcement staff. Rule 10b5–1 plans are no strangers to controversy. An academic study published in December 2006 found that, on average, trades under 10b5–1 plans outperformed the market by about 6% after six months. The resulting scrutiny did not lead to a significant uptick in insider-trading prosecutions, but did cause many companies to revisit their executives' use of the plans. We suggested then that the potential for controversy was not by itself a reason to forego the benefits of employing 10b5–1 plans. We continue to believe that using properly designed plans is a good idea in many cases and can be at least as prudent as discretionary selling under normal insider-trading policies, with trading windows, blackouts and the like. Although regulators and the media may scrutinize trades made under 10b5–1 plans even when above board and done according to best practices, a well-thought-out and implemented 10b5–1 plan may help a company and its executives avoid or ultimately refute accusations of impropriety. * * *

Overview of 10b5–1 Plans

Under Rule 10b5–1, large stockholders, directors, officers and other insiders who regularly possess material nonpublic information (MNPI) but who nonetheless wish to buy or sell stock may establish an affirmative defense to an illegal insider trading charge by adopting a written plan to buy or sell at a time when they are not in possession of MNPI. (Companies themselves may also employ 10b5–1 plans for stock repurchases.) A 10b5–1 plan typically takes the form of a contract between the insider and his or her broker.

The plan must be entered into at a time when the insider has no MNPI about the company or its securities (even if no trades will occur until after the release of the MNPI). The plan must:

1. specify the amount, price (which may include a limit price) and specific dates of purchases or sales; or

2. include a formula or similar method for determining amount, price and date; or

3. give the broker the exclusive right to determine whether, how and when to make purchases and sales, as long as the broker does so without being aware of MNPI at the time the trades are made.

Under the first two alternatives, the 10b5–1 plan cannot give the broker any discretion as to trade dates. As a result, a plan that requests the broker to sell 1,000 shares per week would have to meet the requirements under the third alternative. On the other hand, under the second alternative, the date may be specified by indicating that trades should be made on any date on which the limit price is hit.

The affirmative defense is only available if the trade is in fact made pursuant to the preset terms of the 10b5–1 plan (unless the terms are revised at a time when the insider is not aware of any MNPI and could therefore enter into a new plan). Trades are deemed not to have been made pursuant to the plan if the insider later enters into or alters a corresponding or hedging transaction or position with respect to the securities covered by the plan (although hedging transactions could be part of the plan itself).

Guidelines for 10b5–1 Plans * * *

» **When can a plan be adopted or amended?** Because Rule 10b5–1 prohibits an insider from adopting or amending a plan while in possession of MNPI, allegations of insider trading despite the existence of a 10b5–1 plan are likely to focus on what was known at the time of plan adoption or amendment. * * *

» **Should a plan impose a waiting period before trading can begin?** Because an insider cannot have MNPI when a plan is adopted or amended, Rule 10b5–1 does not require the plan to include a waiting period before trading can begin. And importantly, including a waiting period (even a lengthy delay) will not correct the fatal flaw of adopting or amending a plan while in possession of MNPI. * * *

» **Should adoption of a plan be announced publicly?** Generally speaking, there is no requirement to publicly disclose the adoption, amendment or termination of a 10b5–1 plan. * * * That said, announcing the adoption of a 10b5–1 plan may be a useful way to head off future public relations issues, since announcing a plan's adoption prepares the market and should help investors understand the reasons for insider sales when trades are later reported. * * * If a company decides to announce the adoption of a 10b5–1 plan, we do not generally recommend disclosing plan details, other than, perhaps, the aggregate number of shares involved; this is to diminish the ability of market professionals to front-run the insider's transactions. It is unusual to announce the suspension or termination of a plan. * * *

» **Can a plan be terminated or suspended?** Unlike amending a plan, a 10b5–1 plan may legally be terminated before its predetermined end date even though the insider is in possession of MNPI (although some brokers' forms prohibit this as a contractual matter). * * *

DIRKS V. SEC

Supreme Court of the United States, 1983.
463 U.S. 646.

JUSTICE POWELL delivered the opinion of the Court.

Petitioner Raymond Dirks received material nonpublic information from "insiders" of a corporation with which he had no connection. He disclosed this information to investors who relied on it in trading in the shares of the corporation. The question is whether Dirks violated the antifraud provisions of the federal securities laws by this disclosure.

I.

In 1973, Dirks was an officer of a New York broker-dealer firm who specialized in providing investment analysis of insurance company securities to institutional investors. On March 6, Dirks received information from Ronald Secrist, a former officer of Equity Funding of America. Secrist alleged that the assets of Equity Funding, a diversified corporation primarily engaged in selling life insurance and mutual funds, were vastly overstated as the result of fraudulent corporate practices. Secrist also stated that various regulatory agencies had failed to act on similar charges made by Equity Funding employees. He urged Dirks to verify the fraud and disclose it publicly.

Dirks decided to investigate the allegations. He visited Equity Funding's headquarters in Los Angeles and interviewed several officers and employees of the corporation. The senior management denied any wrongdoing, but certain corporation employees corroborated the charges of fraud. Neither Dirks nor his firm owned or traded any Equity Funding stock, but throughout his investigation he openly discussed the information he had obtained with a number of clients and investors. Some of these persons sold their holdings of Equity Funding securities, including five investment advisers who liquidated holdings of more than $16 million.[2]

While Dirks was in Los Angeles, he was in touch regularly with William Blundell, The *Wall Street Journal*'s Los Angeles bureau chief. Dirks urged Blundell to write a story on the fraud allegations. Blundell did not believe, however, that such a massive fraud could go undetected

---

[2] Dirks received from his firm a salary plus a commission for securities transactions above a certain amount that his clients directed through his firm. But "[i]t is not clear how many of those with whom Dirks spoke promised to direct some brokerage business through [Dirks' firm] to compensate Dirks, or how many actually did so." The Boston Company Institutional Investors, Inc., promised Dirks about $25,000 in commissions, but it is unclear whether Boston actually generated any brokerage business for his firm.

and declined to write the story. He feared that publishing such damaging hearsay might be libelous.

During the two-week period in which Dirks pursued his investigation and spread word of Secrist's charges, the price of Equity Funding stock fell from $26 per share to less than $15 per share. This led the New York Stock Exchange to halt trading on March 27. Shortly thereafter California insurance authorities impounded Equity Funding's records and uncovered evidence of the fraud. Only then did the Securities and Exchange Commission (SEC) file a complaint against Equity Funding[3] and only then, on April 2, did the *Wall Street Journal* publish a front-page story based largely on information assembled by Dirks. Equity Funding immediately went into receivership.[4]

The SEC began an investigation into Dirks' role in the exposure of the fraud. After a hearing by an administrative law judge, the SEC found that Dirks had aided and abetted violations of § 17(a) of the Securities Act of 1933,[5] § 10(b) of the Securities Exchange Act of 1934, and SEC Rule 10b–5, by repeating the allegations of fraud to members of the investment community who later sold their Equity Funding stock. The SEC concluded: "Where 'tippees'—regardless of their motivation or occupation—come into possession of material 'information that they know is confidential and know or should know came from a corporate insider,' they must either publicly disclose that information or refrain from trading." Recognizing, however, that Dirks "played an important role in bringing [Equity Funding's] massive fraud to light," the SEC only censured him.

Dirks sought review in the Court of Appeals for the District of Columbia Circuit. The court entered judgment against Dirks "for the reasons stated by the Commission in its opinion." * * *

---

[3]   As early as 1971, the SEC had received allegations of fraudulent accounting practices at Equity Funding. Moreover, on March 9, 1973, an official of the California Insurance Department informed the SEC's regional office in Los Angeles of Secrist's charges of fraud. Dirks himself voluntarily presented his information at the SEC's regional office beginning on March 27.

[4]   A federal grand jury in Los Angeles subsequently returned a 105-count indictment against 22 persons, including many of Equity Funding's officers and directors. All defendants were found guilty of one or more counts, either by a plea of guilty or a conviction after trial.

[5]   Section 17(a) of the Securities Act of 1933, 15 U.S.C.A. § 77q(a) (1981), provides:

It shall be unlawful for any person in the offer or sale of any securities by the use of any means or instruments of transportation or communication in interstate commerce or by the use of the mails, directly or indirectly—

(1) to employ any device, scheme, or artifice to defraud, or

(2) to obtain money or property by means of any untrue statement of a material fact or any omission to state a material fact necessary in order to make the statements made, in the light of the circumstances under which they were made, not misleading, or

(3) to engage in any transaction, practice, or course of business which operates or would operate as a fraud or deceit upon the purchaser.

In view of the importance to the SEC and to the securities industry of the question presented by this case, we granted a writ of certiorari. 459 U.S. 1014, 103 S.Ct. 371, 74 L.Ed.2d 506 (1982). We now reverse. * * *

III.

We were explicit in *Chiarella* in saying that there can be no duty to disclose where the person who has traded on inside information "was not [the corporation's] agent, * * * was not a fiduciary, [or] was not a person in whom the sellers [of the securities] had placed their trust and confidence." 445 U.S., at 232, 100 S.Ct., at 1116. Not to require such a fiduciary relationship, we recognized, would "depar[t] radically from the established doctrine that duty arises from a specific relationship between two parties" and would amount to "recognizing a general duty between all participants in market transactions to forgo actions based on material, nonpublic information." Id., at 232, 233, 100 S.Ct., at 1116, 1117. This requirement of a specific relationship between the shareholders and the individual trading on inside information has created analytical difficulties for the SEC and courts in policing tippees who trade on inside information. Unlike insiders who have independent fiduciary duties to both the corporation and its shareholders, the typical tippee has no such relationships.[14] In view of this absence, it has been unclear how a tippee acquires the *Cady, Roberts* duty to refrain from trading on inside information.

A.

The SEC's position, as stated in its opinion in this case, is that a tippee "inherits" the *Cady, Roberts* obligation to shareholders whenever he receives inside information from an insider:

> "In tipping potential traders, Dirks breached a duty which he had assumed as a result of knowingly receiving confidential information from [Equity Funding] insiders. Tippees such as Dirks who receive non-public material information from insiders become 'subject to the same duty as [the] insiders.' Shapiro v. Merrill Lynch, Pierce, Fenner & Smith, Inc. [495 F.2d 228, 237 (C.A.2 1974) (quoting Ross v. Licht, 263 F.Supp. 395, 410 (S.D.N.Y.1967))]. Such a tippee breaches the fiduciary duty

---

[14] Under certain circumstances, such as where corporate information is revealed legitimately to an underwriter, accountant, lawyer, or consultant working for the corporation, these outsiders may become fiduciaries of the shareholders. The basis for recognizing this fiduciary duty is not simply that such persons acquire nonpublic corporate information, but rather that they have entered into a special confidential relationship in the conduct of the business of the enterprise and are given access to information solely for corporate purposes. When such a person breaches his fiduciary relationship, he may be treated more properly as a tipper than a tippee. See Shapiro v. Merrill Lynch, Pierce, Fenner & Smith, Inc., 495 F.2d 228, 237 (C.A.2 1974) (investment banker had access to material information when working on a proposed public offering for the corporation). For such a duty to be imposed, however, the corporation must expect the outsider to keep the disclosed nonpublic information confidential, and the relationship at least must imply such a duty.

which he assumes from the insider when the tippee knowingly transmits the information to someone who will probably trade on the basis thereof. * * * Presumably, Dirks' informants were entitled to disclose the [Equity Funding] fraud in order to bring it to light and its perpetrators to justice. However, Dirks— standing in their shoes—committed a breach of the fiduciary duty which he had assumed in dealing with them, when he passed the information on to traders." 21 SEC Docket, at 1410, n. 42.

This view differs little from the view that we rejected as inconsistent with congressional intent in *Chiarella*. In that case, the Court of Appeals agreed with the SEC and affirmed Chiarella's conviction, holding that " '*[a]nyone*—corporate insider or not—who regularly receives material nonpublic information may not use that information to trade in securities without incurring an affirmative duty to disclose.' " United States v. Chiarella, 588 F.2d 1358, 1365 (C.A.2 1978) (emphasis in original). Here, the SEC maintains that anyone who knowingly receives nonpublic material information from an insider has a fiduciary duty to disclose before trading.[15]

In effect, the SEC's theory of tippee liability in both cases appears rooted in the idea that the antifraud provisions require equal information among all traders. This conflicts with the principle set forth in *Chiarella* that only some persons, under some circumstances, will be barred from trading while in possession of material nonpublic information. * * * We reaffirm today that "[a] duty [to disclose] arises from the relationship between parties * * * and not merely from one's ability to acquire information because of his position in the market." 445 U.S., at 232–233, n. 14, 100 S.Ct., at 1116–17, n. 14.

Imposing a duty to disclose or abstain solely because a person knowingly receives material nonpublic information from an insider and trades on it could have an inhibiting influence on the role of market analysts, which the SEC itself recognizes is necessary to the preservation

---

[15] Apparently, the SEC believes this case differs from *Chiarella* in that Dirks' receipt of inside information from Secrist, an insider, carried Secrist's duties with it, while Chiarella received the information without the direct involvement of an insider and thus inherited no duty to disclose or abstain. The SEC fails to explain, however, why the receipt of nonpublic information from an insider automatically carries with it the fiduciary duty of the insider. As we emphasized in *Chiarella*, mere possession of nonpublic information does not give rise to a duty to disclose or abstain; only a specific relationship does that. And we do not believe that the mere receipt of information from an insider creates such a special relationship between the tippee and the corporation's shareholders.

Apparently recognizing the weakness of its argument in light of *Chiarella,* the SEC attempts to distinguish that case factually as involving not "inside" information, but rather "market" information, i.e., "information generated within the company relating to its assets or earnings." This Court drew no such distinction in *Chiarella* and, as The Chief Justice noted, "[i]t is clear that § 10(b) and Rule 10b–5 by their terms and by their history make no such distinction." 445 U.S., at 241, n. 1, 100 S.Ct., at 1121, n. 1 (dissenting opinion).

of a healthy market.[17] It is commonplace for analysts to "ferret out and analyze information," 21 SEC, at 1406,[18] and this often is done by meeting with and questioning corporate officers and others who are insiders. And information that the analysts obtain normally may be the basis for judgments as to the market worth of a corporation's securities. The analyst's judgment in this respect is made available in market letters or otherwise to clients of the firm. It is the nature of this type of information, and indeed of the markets themselves, that such information cannot be made simultaneously available to all of the corporation's stockholders or the public generally.

B.

The conclusion that recipients of inside information do not invariably acquire a duty to disclose or abstain does not mean that such tippees always are free to trade on the information. The need for a ban on some tippee trading is clear. Not only are insiders forbidden by their fiduciary relationship from personally using undisclosed corporate information to their advantage, but they may not give such information to an outsider for the same improper purpose of exploiting the information for their personal gain. * * * Similarly, the transactions of those who knowingly participate with the fiduciary in such a breach are "as forbidden" as transactions "on behalf of the trustee himself." Mosser v. Darrow, 341 U.S. 267, 272, 71 S.Ct. 680, 682 (1951). As the Court explained in *Mosser,* a contrary rule "would open up opportunities for devious dealings in the name of the others that the trustee could not conduct in his own." 341 U.S., at 271, 71 S.Ct., at 682. See SEC v. Texas Gulf Sulphur Co., 446 F.2d 1301, 1308 (CA2), cert. denied, 404 U.S. 1005, 92 S.Ct. 561 (1971). Thus, the tippee's duty to disclose or abstain is derivative from that of the insider's duty. As we noted in *Chiarella,* "[t]he tippee's obligation has

---

[17] The SEC expressly recognized that "[t]he value to the entire market of [analysts'] efforts cannot be gainsaid; market efficiency in pricing is significantly enhanced by [their] initiatives to ferret out and analyze information, and thus the analyst's work redounds to the benefit of all investors." 21 S.E.C., at 1406. The SEC asserts that analysts remain free to obtain from management corporate information for purposes of "filling in the 'interstices in analysis'. * * *" But this rule is inherently imprecise, and imprecision prevents parties from ordering their actions in accord with legal requirements. Unless the parties have some guidance as to where the line is between permissible and impermissible disclosures and uses, neither corporate insiders nor analysts can be sure when the line is crossed.

[18] On its facts, this case is the unusual one. Dirks is an analyst in a broker-dealer firm, and he did interview management in the course of his investigation. He uncovered, however, startling information that required no analysis or exercise of judgment as to its market relevance. Nonetheless, the principle at issue here extends beyond these facts. The SEC's rule— applicable without regard to any breach by an insider—could have serious ramifications on reporting by analysts of investment views.

Despite the unusualness of Dirks' "find," the central role that he played in uncovering the fraud at Equity Funding, and that analysts in general can play in revealing information that corporations may have reason to withhold from the public, is an important one. Dirks' careful investigation brought to light a massive fraud at the corporation. And until the Equity Funding fraud was exposed, the information in the trading market was grossly inaccurate. But for Dirks' efforts, the fraud might well have gone undetected longer.

been viewed as arising from his role as a participant after the fact in the insider's breach of a fiduciary duty." 445 U.S., at 230, n. 12, 100 S.Ct., at 1115, n. 12.

Thus, some tippees must assume an insider's duty to the shareholders not because they receive inside information, but rather because it has been made available to them *improperly*. And for rule 10b–5 purposes, the insider's disclosure is improper only where it would violate his *Cady, Roberts* duty. Thus, a tippee assumes a fiduciary duty to the shareholders of a corporation not to trade on material nonpublic information only when the insider has breached his fiduciary duty to the shareholders by disclosing the information to the tippee and the tippee knows or should know that there has been a breach. As Commissioner Smith perceptively observed in *Investors Management Co.*: "[T]ippee responsibility must be related back to insider responsibility by a necessary finding that the tippee knew the information was given to him in breach of a duty by a person having a special relationship to the issuer not to disclose the information * * *." 44 SEC, at 651 (concurring in the result). Tipping thus properly is viewed only as a means of indirectly violating the *Cady, Roberts* disclose-or-abstain rule.[21]

C.

In determining whether a tippee is under an obligation to disclose or abstain, it thus is necessary to determine whether the insider's "tip" constituted a breach of the insider's fiduciary duty. All disclosures of confidential corporate information are not inconsistent with the duty insiders owe to shareholders. In contrast to the extraordinary facts of this case, the more typical situation in which there will be a question whether disclosure violates the insider's *Cady, Roberts* duty is when insiders disclose information to analysts. In some situations the insider will act consistently with his fiduciary duty to shareholders, and yet release of the

---

[21] We do not suggest that knowingly trading on inside information is ever "socially desirable or even that it is devoid of moral considerations." Dooley, Enforcement of Insider Trading Restrictions, 66 Va.L.Rev. 1, 55 (1980). Nor do we imply an absence of responsibility to disclose promptly indications of illegal actions by a corporation to the proper authorities— typically the SEC and exchange authorities in cases involving securities. Depending on the circumstances, and even where permitted by law, one's trading on material nonpublic information is behavior that may fall below ethical standards of conduct. But in a statutory area of the law such as securities regulation, where legal principles of general application must be applied, there may be "significant distinctions between actual legal obligations and ethical ideals." SEC, Report of the Special Study of Securities Markets, H.R.Doc. No. 95, 88th Cong., 1st Sess., pt. 1, pp. 237–238 (1963). The SEC recognizes this. At oral argument, the following exchange took place:

"QUESTION: So, it would not have satisfied his obligation under the law to go to the SEC first?

"[SEC's counsel]: That is correct. That an insider has to observe what has come to be known as the abstain or disclosure rule. Either the information has to be disclosed to the market if it is inside information * * * or the insider must abstain."

Thus, it is clear that Rule 10b–5 does not impose any obligations simply to tell the SEC about the fraud before trading.

information may affect the market. For example, it may not be clear—either to the corporate insider or to the recipient analyst—whether the information will be viewed as material nonpublic information. Corporate officials may mistakenly think the information already has been disclosed or that it is not material enough to affect the market. Whether disclosure is a breach of duty therefore depends in large part on the purpose of the disclosure. This standard was identified by the SEC itself in *Cady, Roberts*: a purpose of the securities laws was to eliminate "use of inside information for personal advantage." 40 SEC, at 912, n. 15. Thus, the test is whether the insider personally will benefit, directly or indirectly, from his disclosure. Absent some personal gain, there has been no breach of duty to stockholders. And absent a breach by the insider, there is no derivative breach. As Commissioner Smith stated in *Investors Management Co.*: "It is important in this type of case to focus on policing insiders and what they do * * * rather than on policing information *per se* and its possession. * * *" 44 SEC, at 648 (concurring in the result).

The SEC argues that, if inside-trading liability does not exist when the information is transmitted for a proper purpose but is used for trading, it would be a rare situation when the parties could not fabricate some ostensibly legitimate business justification for transmitting the information. We think the SEC is unduly concerned. In determining whether the insider's purpose in making a particular disclosure is fraudulent, the SEC and the courts are not required to read the parties' minds. Scienter in some cases is relevant in determining whether the tipper has violated his *Cady, Roberts* duty.[23] But to determine whether the disclosure itself "deceive[s], manipulate[s], or defraud[s]" shareholders, Aaron v. SEC, 446 U.S. 680, 686, 100 S.Ct. 1945, 1950 (1980), the initial inquiry is whether there has been a breach of duty by the insider. This requires courts to focus on objective criteria, i.e., whether the insider receives a direct or indirect personal benefit from the disclosure, such as a pecuniary gain or a reputational benefit that will translate into future earnings. Cf. 40 SEC, at 912, n. 15; Brudney, Insiders, Outsiders, and Informational Advantages Under the Federal Securities Laws, 93 Harv.L.Rev. 324, 348 (1979) ("The theory * * * is that the insider, by giving the information out selectively, is in effect selling the information to its recipient for cash, reciprocal information, or other

---

[23] *Scienter*—"a mental state embracing intent to deceive, manipulate, or defraud," Ernst & Ernst v. Hochfelder, 425 U.S. 185, 193, n. 12, 96 S.Ct. 1375, 1381, n. 12 (1976)—is an independent element of a Rule 10b–5 violation. See Aaron v. SEC, 446 U.S. 680, 695, 100 S.Ct. 1945, 1955 (1980). * * * It is not enough that an insider's conduct results in harm to investors; rather, a violation may be found only where there is "intentional or willful conduct designed to deceive or defraud investors by controlling or artificially affecting the price of securities." Ernst & Ernst v. Hochfelder, supra, at 199, 96 S.Ct., at 1383. The issue in this case, however, is not whether Secrist or Dirks acted with *scienter,* but rather whether there was any deceptive or fraudulent conduct at all, i.e., whether Secrist's disclosure constituted a breach of his fiduciary duty and thereby caused injury to shareholders. Only if there was such a breach did Dirks, a tippee, acquire a fiduciary duty to disclose or abstain.

things of value for himself. * * *"). There are objective facts and circumstances that often justify such an inference. For example, there may be a relationship between the insider and the recipient that suggests a *quid pro quo* from the latter, or an intention to benefit the particular recipient. The elements of fiduciary duty and exploitation of nonpublic information also exist when an insider makes a gift of confidential information to a trading relative or friend. The tip and trade resemble trading by the insider himself followed by a gift of the profits to the recipient.

Determining whether an insider personally benefits from a particular disclosure, a question of fact, will not always be easy for courts. But it is essential, we think, to have a guiding principle for those whose daily activities must be limited and instructed by the SEC's inside-trading rules, and we believe that there must be a breach of the insider's fiduciary duty before the tippee inherits the duty to disclose or abstain. In contrast, the rule adopted by the SEC in this case would have no limiting principle.[24]

IV.

Under the inside-trading and tipping rules set forth above, we find that there was no actionable violation by Dirks. It is undisputed that Dirks himself was a stranger to Equity Funding, with no pre-existing fiduciary duty to its shareholders. He took no action, directly or indirectly, that induced the shareholders or officers of Equity Funding to repose trust or confidence in him. There was no expectation by Dirks' sources that he would keep their information in confidence. Nor did Dirks misappropriate or illegally obtain the information about Equity Funding. Unless the insiders breached their *Cady, Roberts* duty to shareholders in disclosing the nonpublic information to Dirks, he breached no duty when he passed it on to investors as well as to the *Wall Street Journal.*

It is clear that neither Secrist nor the other Equity Funding employees violated their *Cady, Roberts* duty to the corporation's shareholders by providing information to Dirks.[27] The tippers received no

---

[24] Without legal limitations, market participants are forced to rely on the reasonableness of the SEC's litigation strategy, but that can be hazardous, as the facts of this case make plain. * * *

[27] In this Court, the SEC appears to contend that an insider invariably violates a fiduciary duty to the corporation's shareholders by transmitting nonpublic corporate information to an outsider when he has reason to believe that the outsider may use it to the disadvantage of the shareholders. "Thus, regardless of any ultimate motive to bring to public attention the derelictions at Equity Funding, Secrist breached his duty to Equity Funding shareholders." Brief for Respondent 31. This perceived "duty" differs markedly from the one that the SEC identified in Cady, Roberts and that has been the basis for federal tippee-trading rules to date. In fact, the SEC did not charge Secrist with any wrongdoing, and we do not understand the SEC to have relied on any theory of a breach of duty by Secrist in finding that Dirks breached his duty to Equity Funding's shareholders. * * *

Chiarella made it explicitly clear there is no general duty to forgo market transactions "based on material, nonpublic information." 455 U.S., at 233, 100 S.Ct., at 1117. Such a duty

monetary or personal benefit for revealing Equity Funding's secrets, nor was their purpose to make a gift of valuable information to Dirks. As the facts of this case clearly indicate, the tippers were motivated by a desire to expose the fraud. In the absence of a breach of duty to shareholders by the insiders, there was no derivative breach by Dirks. Dirks therefore could not have been "a participant after the fact in [an] insider's breach of a fiduciary duty." Chiarella, 445 U.S., at 230, n. 12, 100 S.Ct., at 1115, n. 12.

V.

We conclude that Dirks, in the circumstances of this case, had no duty to abstain from use of the inside information that he obtained. The judgment of the Court of Appeals therefore is

Reversed.

JUSTICE BLACKMUN, with whom JUSTICE BRENNAN and JUSTICE MARSHALL join, dissenting. * * * [The dissenting opinion is omitted.]

NOTES

(1) Academic commentary on the "benefit" requirement imposed by *Dirks* has been generally negative: "This benefit requirement is a curious and largely unnecessary wrinkle; if there is one clear understanding in the common law of fiduciary responsibility, it is that an intent to benefit is not a necessary element." Donald Langevoort, Commentary—The Insider Trading Sanctions Act of 1984 and its Effect on Existing Law, 37 Vand.L.Rev. 1273, 1292 (1984). On the other hand, the SEC appears to have little problem in finding a "benefit" in order to meet this requirement. In United States v. Reed, 601 F.Supp. 685 (S.D.N.Y.1985), the Court refused to dismiss an indictment of a tippee who was the son of the tipper, even though there was no evidence that the father intended to benefit his son by the disclosure. See also SEC v. Gaspar, 1985 WL 521 (CBM) (S.D.N.Y.1985) (tipper received an "enhanced professional relationship" from tippee).

(2) In SEC v. Switzer, 590 F.Supp. 756 (W.D.Okla.1984), Barry Switzer, then coach of the University of Oklahoma football team, was attending his son's high school track meet when he unintentionally overheard a Mr. Platt discussing business problems. Switzer traded profitably on the information

---

would "depar[t] radically from the established doctrine that duty arises from a specific relationship between two parties."

Moreover, to constitute a violation of Rule 10b–5, there must be fraud. See Ernst & Ernst v. Hochfelder, 425 U.S. 185, 199, 96 S.Ct. 1375, 1383, 47 L.Ed.2d 668 (1976) (statutory words "manipulative," "device," and "contrivance * * * connot[e] intentional or willful conduct designed to deceive or defraud investors by controlling or artificially affecting the price of securities") (emphasis added). There is no evidence that Secrist's disclosure was intended to or did in fact "deceive or defraud" anyone. Secrist certainly intended to convey relevant information that management was unlawfully concealing, and—so far as the record shows—he believed that persuading Dirks to investigate was the best way to disclose the fraud. Other efforts had proved fruitless. Under any objective standard, Secrist received no direct or indirect personal benefit from the disclosure.

he thereby learned, but was absolved of liability under the Dirks standard since Switzer was basically an eavesdropper and the information was not disclosed by Mr. Platt for his own benefit.

(3) One important issue in insider trading law is the extent to which prosecutors can pursue remote tippees—persons who indirectly acquire partial information about developments that have not been publicly disclosed. This issue was graphically raised by the ImClone litigation in 2002. ImClone, Inc. is a publicly held pharmaceutical company, the founder of which was Dr. Samuel Waksal. ImClone's most promising drug was Erbitux, an anti-cancer drug. ImClone had filed a new drug application with the Food and Drug Administration ("FDA") that was pending. In December 2001, ImClone common stock was trading in the $60 range. On December 25, 2001, Dr. Waksal learned indirectly that the FDA had determined not to complete the review of ImClone's Erbitux application because clinical studies had not adequately established its effectiveness. Dr. Waksal learned of this decision through a conversation with an officer of Bristol-Myers Squibb, Co., who was apparently unaware that the FDA decision on Erbitux had not been formally announced. The FDA decision was not formally announced until December 28, 2001.

Almost immediately after learning of this decision, Dr. Waksal began to sell his shares of ImClone. Dr. Waksal also advised friends and his immediate family members, many of whom owned ImClone shares, that he was selling his ImClone stock but apparently did not tell them the reason. The consequence of this disclosure was that there were numerous sales of ImClone stock over the next few days. Following the formal FDA announcement on December 28, the price of ImClone common stock declined from about $60 per share to between $10 and $15 per share. Assuming that Dr. Waksal told family and friends that he was selling his ImClone shares, but did not disclose the reason why nor directly recommend that they also sell their shares, have the family members and friends that sold their ImClone shares before December 28 violated Rule 10b–5?

The loss avoided by Dr. Waksal and his family and friends exceeded $9 million. In June 2002, Dr. Waksal was arrested and charged with insider trading in connection with the sale of his own stock and providing "tips" to family and friends. Dr. Waksal subsequently pleaded guilty to six charges of insider trading, bank fraud, and perjury.

(4) One of Dr. Waksal's close friends was Ms. Martha Stewart, the CEO and Chair of Martha Stewart Omnimedia, Inc., a publicly held corporation that was widely known for its television presence and sales of home products through K-Mart. Ms. Stewart owned several thousand shares of ImClone, which she sold on December 27, 2001, one day before the announcement of the FDA decision. She strenuously argued that she had no inside information, and that her sale of ImClone shares was authorized by a standing instruction she had given to her brokers at Merrill Lynch to sell her ImClone shares if the market price dropped below $60 per share. If true, it is clear that Ms. Stewart did nothing improper.

The major problem facing Ms. Stewart was that Merrill Lynch, and the brokers involved, particularly her close friend and stockbroker, Peter Bacanovic, were unable to verify receipt of such an instruction. Bacanovic's former assistant, Douglas Faneuil, initially confirmed Ms. Stewart's story and later testified in the criminal trial against Stewart and Bacanovic. The following is the gist of Faneuil's story which contradicts Stewart's story of a prearranged agreement to sell her ImClone stock. On December 26, 2001, Martha Stewart was flying to a Mexican beach resort. While the plane was refueling in Texas on its way from New York to Cancun, Ms. Stewart called her office, and a call from Peter Bacanovic was forwarded to her. Apparently during this call Bacanovic told Ms. Stewart that ImClone shares were trading downward. Two minutes later, Merrill Lynch sold Ms. Stewart's ImClone shares. Peter Bacanovic has filed an affidavit which states:

> Stewart, however, was unreachable. She was on a private plane, on her way from Connecticut to San Antonio, Texas. As they waited for Stewart's plane to land, Bacanovic * * * and Faneuil swapped e-mails. At 1:17 p.m. Bacanovic wrote [to Faneuil] "Has news come out yet? Let me know." * * * When Stewart's plane landed at 1:30 p.m., she called her office, where her assistant had earlier noted in the message log: "Peter thinks ImClone is going to start trading downward." Almost immediately, Stewart called Bacanovic's office and 11 minutes later, the broker was selling all of Stewart's ImClone stock. Faneuil wrote: "Dear Ms. Stewart, You sold your remaining (3,928 imcl) shares at an average price of $58.43(25). As always, feel free to call me with any questions." * * *

In addition to Stewart's criminal prosecution, the SEC also filed a civil suit against Martha Stewart and Peter Bacanovic for insider trading.

In 2004, Martha Stewart and Peter Bacanovic were both convicted of criminal charges stemming from the sale of ImClone stock. Interestingly enough, none of Stewart's or Bacanovic's convictions involved charges of securities fraud. They were both convicted of making misleading statements, perjury, and conspiracy. For a more detailed account, see United States v. Stewart, 305 F.Supp.2d 368 (S.D.N.Y. 2004).

(5) Courts have readily accepted the idea set forth in footnote 14 of *Dirks* that a person may become a "temporary insider." See SEC v. Lund, 570 F.Supp. 1397 (C.D.Cal.1983) (a confidant of a corporate officer); SEC v. Musella, 578 F.Supp. 425 (S.D.N.Y.1984) (the manager of office services of Sullivan and Cromwell); SEC v. Tome, 638 F.Supp. 596 (S.D.N.Y.1986) (social friend and adviser to CEO).

(6) The opinion in *Dirks* was a victory for securities markets analysts and a defeat for the SEC. The *Dirks* opinion appeared to permit corporate executives to provide sensitive information to favored securities analysts prior to the public release of the information so long as the executives making the disclosures did not receive any personal benefit. In the 1990s, the SEC became increasing concerned about such "selective disclosure."

(7) Regulation FD, discussed in Chapter 9, Section E, provided the desired weapon against selective disclosure. Regulation FD in effect limits or prohibits selective disclosure by requiring companies and executives that provide material, non-public information to market professionals (such as securities analysts and money managers) to publish this information immediately if the disclosure was intentional, and within 24 hours if the disclosure was unintentional. A violation of Regulation FD does not give rise to liability for securities fraud but may give rise to an SEC enforcement action. Regulation FD also exempts ordinary, business-related communication between corporations and their customers or suppliers, and communications with members of the press if analysts are not present.

(8) The purpose of Regulation FD in this respect is laudable in theory since it directly relates to the policies behind the prohibition against insider trading. It raises, however, some serious practical problems. For example, it is often difficult for companies to know whether or not a particular disclosure will be viewed as "material," a term that is not defined in SEC regulations. There is also concern that corporate officials may elect not to disclose information to outsiders in order to make sure that they do not run afoul of Regulation FD. See also Goshen and Parchomovsky, On Insider Trading, Markets, and "Negative Property Rights in Information," 87 Va. L.Rev. 1229, 1270 (2002) (Regulation FD may have negative impact "on small companies with low liquidity, companies that fail to attract analysts' coverage"). The prior practice, according to Goshen and Parchomovsky, permitted analysts covering small companies to receive informational benefits or rewards in exchange for covering the company, but this practice appears to be prohibited by Regulation FD.

UNITED STATES V. CHESTMAN

United States Court of Appeals, Second Circuit, 1991.
947 F.2d 551.

Before OAKES, CHIEF JUDGE, FEINBERG, MESKILL, NEWMAN, KEARSE, CARDAMONE, WINTER, PRATT, MINER, ALTIMARI, MAHONEY and McLAUGHLIN, CIRCUIT JUDGES.

ON REHEARING EN BANC

MESKILL, CIRCUIT JUDGE, joined by CARDAMONE, PRATT, MINER and ALTIMARI, CIRCUIT JUDGES: * * *

[Ira Waldbaum was the controlling shareholder of Waldbaum, Inc., a corporation that owned a large supermarket chain. In 1986, Ira agreed to sell the corporation to A & P. Ira told his sister, Shirley Witkin, three of his children, and a nephew, about the pending sale, admonished them to keep the news quiet and confidential until after a public announcement, and offered to tender their shares, along with his controlling block, to enable them to avoid the administrative difficulties of tendering after the public announcement. Shirley nevertheless told her daughter, Susan

Loeb, who in turn told her husband, Keith Loeb. The circumstances under which these disclosures occurred are described in the dissenting opinion below. Keith Loeb telephoned Robert Chestman, a broker used by the junior members of the family, and told him that Waldbaum, Inc. was going to be sold at a "substantially higher" price than the market price. Chestman knew that Susan Loeb was a granddaughter of the Waldbaums. That morning Chestman executed several purchases of Waldbaum stock both for his own account and for the discretionary accounts of several customers, including Keith Loeb. After the SEC investigation began, Keith agreed to cooperate with the government, disgorging a profit of $25,000 and paying a $25,000 fine. Chestman was indicted and convicted on 31 counts of violation of Rule 10b–5, mail fraud, violation of Rule 14e–3(a), and one count of perjury. A panel of the Second Circuit set aside this conviction in its entirety, 903 F.2d 75 (2d Cir.1990)]. * * *

B. RULE 10b–5

Chestman's Rule 10b–5 convictions were based on the misappropriation theory, which provides that "one who misappropriates nonpublic information in breach of a fiduciary duty and trades on that information to his own advantage violates Section 10(b) and Rule 10b–5." * * * With respect to the shares Chestman purchased on behalf of Keith Loeb, Chestman was convicted of aiding and abetting Loeb's misappropriation of nonpublic information in breach of a duty Loeb owed to the Waldbaum family and to his wife Susan. As to the shares Chestman purchased for himself and his other clients, Chestman was convicted as a "tippee" of that same misappropriated information. Thus, while Chestman is the defendant in this case, the alleged misappropriator was Keith Loeb. The government agrees that Chestman's convictions cannot be sustained unless there was sufficient evidence to show that (1) Keith Loeb breached a duty owed to the Waldbaum family or Susan Loeb based on a fiduciary or similar relationship of trust and confidence, and (2) Chestman knew that Loeb had done so. We have heretofore never applied the misappropriation theory—and its predicate requirement of a fiduciary breach—in the context of family relationships. * * *

3. *Fiduciary Duties and Their Functional Equivalent*

* * * [W]e turn to our central inquiry—what constitutes a fiduciary or similar relationship of trust and confidence in the context of Rule 10b–5 criminal liability? We begin by noting two factors that do not themselves create the necessary relationship.

First, a fiduciary duty cannot be imposed unilaterally by entrusting a person with confidential information. *Walton v. Morgan Stanley & Co.*, 623 F.2d 796, 799 (2d Cir.1980) (applying Delaware law). *Walton* concerned the conduct of an investment bank, Morgan Stanley. While investigating possible takeover targets for one of its clients, Morgan

Stanley obtained unpublished material information (internal earnings reports) on a confidential basis from a prospective target, Olinkraft. After its client abandoned the planned takeover, Morgan Stanley was charged with trading in Olinkraft's stock on the basis of the confidential information. Observing that the parties had bargained at "arm's length" and that there had not been a pre-existing agreement of confidentiality between Morgan Stanley and Olinkraft, we rejected the argument that

> Morgan Stanley became a fiduciary of Olinkraft by virtue of the receipt of the confidential information * * *. [T]he fact that the information was confidential did nothing, in and of itself, to change the relationship between Morgan Stanley and Olinkraft's management. Put bluntly, although, according to the complaint, Olinkraft's management placed its confidence in Morgan Stanley not to disclose the information, Morgan Stanley owed no duty to observe that confidence.

Walton, 623 F.2d at 799. *See also Dirks*, 463 U.S. at 662 n. 22, 103 S.Ct. at 3265 n. 22 (citing *Walton* approvingly as "a case turning on the court's determination that the disclosure did not impose any fiduciary duties on the recipient of the inside information"). Reposing confidential information in another, then, does not by itself create a fiduciary relationship.

Second, marriage does not, without more, create a fiduciary relationship. " '[M]ere kinship does not of itself establish a confidential relation.' * * * Rather, the existence of a confidential relationship must be determined independently of a preexisting family relationship." *Reed*, 601 F.Supp. at 706. Although spouses certainly may by their conduct become fiduciaries, the marriage relationship alone does not impose fiduciary status. In sum, more than the gratuitous reposal of a secret to another who happens to be a family member is required to establish a fiduciary or similar relationship of trust and confidence.

We take our cues as to what *is* required to create the requisite relationship from the securities fraud precedents and the common law. *See Chiarella*, 445 U.S. at 227–30, 100 S.Ct. at 1114–16. * * * [I]t is clear that the relationships involved in this case—those between Keith and Susan Loeb and between Keith Loeb and the Waldbaum family—were not traditional fiduciary relationships.

That does not end our inquiry, however. The misappropriation theory requires us to consider not only whether there exists a fiduciary relationship but also whether there exists a "similar relationship of trust and confidence." * * *

A fiduciary relationship involves discretionary authority and dependency: One person depends on another—the fiduciary—to serve his interests. In relying on a fiduciary to act for his benefit, the beneficiary of the relation may entrust the fiduciary with custody over property of one sort or another. Because the fiduciary obtains access to this property to serve the ends of the fiduciary relationship, he becomes duty-bound not to appropriate the property for his own use. What has been said of an agent's duty of confidentiality applies with equal force to other fiduciary relations: "an agent is subject to a duty to the principal not to use or to communicate information confidentially given him by the principal or acquired by him during the course of or on account of his agency." Restatement (Second) of Agency § 395 (1958). These characteristics represent the measure of the paradigmatic fiduciary relationship. A similar relationship of trust and confidence consequently must share these qualities.

* * *

We have little trouble finding the evidence insufficient to establish a fiduciary relationship or its functional equivalent between Keith Loeb and the Waldbaum family. The government presented only two pieces of evidence on this point. The first was that Keith was an extended member of the Waldbaum family, specifically the family patriarch's (Ira Waldbaum's) "nephew-in-law." The second piece of evidence concerned Ira's discussions of the business with family members. "My children," Ira Waldbaum testified, "have always been involved with me and my family and they know we never speak about business outside of the family." His earlier testimony indicates that the "family" to which he referred were his "three children who were involved in the business."

* * * The government proffered nothing more to establish a fiduciary-like association. It did not show that Keith Loeb had been brought into the family's inner circle, whose members, it appears, discussed confidential business information either because they were kin or because they worked together with Ira Waldbaum. Keith was not an employee of Waldbaum and there was no showing that he participated in confidential communications regarding the business. The critical information was gratuitously communicated to him. The disclosure did not serve the interests of Ira Waldbaum, his children or the Waldbaum company. Nor was there any evidence that the alleged relationship was characterized by influence or reliance of any sort. Measured against the principles of fiduciary relations, the evidence does not support a finding that Keith Loeb and the Waldbaum family shared either a fiduciary relation or its functional equivalent. * * *

Keith's status as Susan's husband could not itself establish fiduciary status. Nor, absent a pre-existing fiduciary relation or an express agreement of confidentiality, could the coda—"Don't tell." * * *

In the absence of evidence of an explicit acceptance by Keith of a duty of confidentiality, the context of the disclosure takes on special import.

While acceptance may be implied, it must be implied from a pre-existing fiduciary-like relationship between the parties. * * *

In sum, because Keith owed neither Susan nor the Waldbaum family a fiduciary duty or its functional equivalent, he did not defraud them by disclosing news of the pending tender offer to Chestman. Absent a predicate act of fraud by Keith Loeb, the alleged misappropriator, Chestman could not be derivatively liable as Loeb's tippee or as an aider and abettor. Therefore, Chestman's Rule 10b–5 convictions must be reversed. * * *

Accordingly, we affirm the Rule 14e–3(a) convictions and reverse the Rule 10b–5 and mail fraud convictions. The reversal of these convictions does not warrant reconsideration of the sentence since the sentences on the Rule 10b–5 and mail fraud convictions are concurrent with the sentences in the Rule 14e–3(a) counts. * * *

WINTER, CIRCUIT JUDGE (joined by OAKES, CHIEF JUDGE, NEWMAN, KEARSE, and MCLAUGHLIN, CIRCUIT JUDGES), concurring in part and dissenting in part:

I concur in the decision to affirm Chestman's convictions under Section 14(e) of the Securities Exchange Act of 1934, and under Rule 14e–3. I respectfully dissent, however, from the reversals of his convictions under Section 10(b) and under the mail fraud statute.

* * *

* * * In the case of family-controlled corporations, family and business affairs are necessarily intertwined, and it is inevitable that from time to time normal familial interactions will lead to the revelation of confidential corporate matters to various family members. Indeed, the very nature of familial relationships may cause the disclosure of corporate matters to avoid misunderstandings among family members or suggestions that a family member is unworthy of trust.

Keith Loeb learned of the pending acquisition of Waldbaum's by A & P through precisely such interactions. His wife Susan was asked one day by her sister to take carpool responsibilities for their children. When Susan inquired as to why this was necessary, the sister was vague and said that she had to take their mother somewhere. After further inquiry, the sister flatly declined to tell Susan what was going on. Susan did not say, "Gee, confidential corporate information must be involved, and I have no right to such information." Instead, concerned about her mother's ongoing health problems, Susan made direct inquiry of her mother, who revealed that Susan's sister took her to get stock certificates to give to Ira Waldbaum for the initial phase of the A & P acquisition. The mother swore Susan to secrecy, telling Susan that the acquisition would be very profitable to the family and premature disclosure could ruin the deal. Susan then asked whether she could tell her husband Keith. Instead of saying, "No, Keith may be your husband but you are to button your lips in his presence," her mother assented but warned against disclosure to anyone else.

* * *

I have little difficulty in concluding that Chestman's convictions can be affirmed on either the *Dirks* rule or on a misappropriation theory. The disclosure of information concerning the A & P acquisition among Ira Waldbaum's extended family was the result of ordinary familial interactions that can be expected in the case of family-controlled corporations. * * * When members of a family have benefitted from the family's control of a corporation and are in a position to acquire such information in the ordinary course of family interactions, that position carries with it a duty not to disclose. * * * Such a duty is of course based on mutual understandings among family members—quite explicit in this case—and owed to the family. However, the duty originates in the corporation and is ultimately intended to protect the corporation and its public shareholders. The duty is thus also owed to the corporation, to a degree sufficient in my view to trigger the *Dirks* rule. Because trading on inside information so acquired by family members amounts to theft, the misappropriation theory also applies.

Under my colleagues' theory, the disclosure of family corporate information can be avoided only by family members extracting formal, express promises of confidentiality or by elderly mothers in poor health refusing to tell their daughters about mysterious travels. * * *

I thus believe that a family member (i) who has received or expects (e.g., through inheritance) benefits from family control of a corporation, here gifts of stock, (ii) who is in a position to learn confidential corporate information through ordinary family interactions, and (iii) who knows that under the circumstances both the corporation and the family desire confidentiality, has a duty not to use information so obtained for personal profit where the use risks disclosure. The receipt or expectation of benefits increases the interest of such family members in corporate affairs and thus increases the chance that they will learn confidential information. Disclosure in the present case occurred in the course of a discussion that included, *inter alia*, an examination of the benefits of the A & P acquisition to Susan, Keith and their children. Susan's warning to Keith about secrecy was clearly intended to protect the corporation as well as the family and clearly had originated with Ira Waldbaum. In such circumstances, Susan's saying "Don't tell" is enough for me. Not to have such a rule means that a family-controlled corporation with public shareholders is subject to greater risk of disclosure of confidential information than is a corporation that is entirely publicly owned.

I see no room for argument over whether there was sufficient evidence for the jury to find that Chestman knew Keith Loeb was violating an obligation. The record fairly brims with Chestman's consciousness that Keith Loeb was behaving improperly. * * *

MINER, CIRCUIT JUDGE, concurring:

* * * It is important to note that in the case at bar we deal with an attenuated trail of family confidences in which information was received without any assurance of confidentiality by the receiver and without any prior sharing of business information within the family. Neither Shirley Witkin nor her daughter nor her son-in-law were involved in any way in the operation of the Waldbaum business or privy to any of its past secrets. Family relationships being what they are, it makes little sense under the circumstances to imply assurances that confidentiality would be maintained. Of course, a different situation obtains where the giver of business confidences, in addition to having a family relationship with the receiver, also has a history of reposing such confidences in the receiver. *See United States v. Reed*, 601 F.Supp. 685, 712, 717 (S.D.N.Y.), *rev'd on other grounds*, 773 F.2d 477 (2d Cir.1985) (son of corporate director as receiver of non-public corporate information). Under those circumstances, the duty of confidentiality is implied from the business relationship coupled with the family one.

Finally, to further extend the concept of confidential duty would be to take the courts into an area of securities regulation not yet entered by Congress. It would give the wrong signal to prosecutors in their continuing efforts to push against existing boundaries in the prosecution of securities fraud cases. "[P]rosecutors can often claim that some confidential relationship was abused—whether between lovers, family members, longtime friends, or simply that well-known confidential relationship between bartender and drunk. Such a test inherently creates legal uncertainty and invites selective prosecutions." Coffee, *Outsider Trading, That New Crime*, Wall St.J., Nov. 14, 1990, at 16, col. 4. I would await further instructions from Congress before sailing into this unchartered area.

[The opinion of MAHONEY, CIRCUIT JUDGE, concurring in part and dissenting in part, is omitted.]

NOTE

In 2000, the SEC promulgated two important new rules: Rule 10b–5–1, intended to clarify the definition of insider trading (which we describe above), and Rule 10b–5–2, designed to provide more of a bright-line test for certain enumerated close family relationships. SEC Rel. No. 34–43154 (Aug. 24, 2000). Rule 10b–5–1 addressed conflicts among courts over whether a person can be found guilty of insider trading merely by a showing that the person traded *while in knowing possession* of insider information, or whether a showing that the person actually *used* such insider information was necessary. Rule 10b–5–1 reveals that a standard closer to "knowing possession" rather than "use" is appropriate and states that a person is guilty of insider trading when he or she makes a trade while aware of material, nonpublic information. The Rule does, however, contain a safe harbor for certain pre-planned trades where the person making the trade was not in possession of material, non-public information at the time the trade was planned.

The second new provision, Rule 10b–5–2, sets forth a non-exclusive list of three situations in which a person has a duty of trust or confidence for purposes of the misappropriation theory: (1) where a person agrees to maintain information in confidence; (2) when two people have a history, pattern, or practice of sharing confidences such that the recipient of the information knows or reasonably should know that the person communicating the material nonpublic information expects that the recipient will maintain its confidentiality; or (3) a "bright line" rule that states that a duty of trust or confidence exists when a person receives or obtains material nonpublic information from spouses, parents, children, or siblings. It may be noted that an automatic relationship of trust or confidence is not created between unmarried domestic partners, step-parents, or step-children (though such a relationship might arises under alternatives (1) or (2)).

SECURITIES AND EXCHANGE COMMISSION V. CUBAN

United States District Court, Northern District of Texas, 2009.
634 F. Supp. 2d 713.

Before FITZWATER, CHIEF JUDGE.

The dispositive question presented by defendant Mark Cuban's[d] ("Cuban's") motion to dismiss is whether plaintiff Securities and Exchange Commission ("SEC") has adequately alleged that Cuban undertook a duty of non-use of information required to establish liability under the misappropriation theory of insider trading. Concluding that it has not, the court grants Cuban's motion to dismiss, but it also allows the SEC to replead.

İ

A

This is a suit brought by the SEC against Cuban under the misappropriation theory of insider trading. The SEC alleges that, after Cuban agreed to maintain the confidentiality of material, nonpublic information concerning a planned private investment in public equity ("PIPE") offering by Mamma.com Inc. ("Mamma.com"),[1] he sold his stock in the company without first disclosing to Mamma.com that he intended

---

d   As of 2010, Mark Cuban was one of the 400 richest Americans with a net worth of $2.6 billion. The owner of the Dallas Mavericks, an NBA basketball team, Cuban was the highest-profile U.S. figure to be charged in insider trading since Martha Stewart.

1   In June 2007 Mamma.com changed its name to Copernic Inc. The court will refer to the company as Mamma.com, by which it was known at all times relevant to this litigation.

to trade on this information, thereby avoiding substantial losses when the stock price declined after the PIPE was publicly announced. The SEC maintains that Cuban is liable for violating § 17(a) of the Securities Act of 1933 ("Securities Act"), § 10(b) of the Securities Exchange Act of 1934 ("Exchange Act"), and Rule 10b–5 promulgated thereunder.[2]

According to the SEC's complaint, in March 2004 Cuban purchased 600,000 shares, or a 6.3% stake, in Mamma.com, a Canadian company that operated an Internet search engine and traded on the NASDAQ. In the spring of 2004, Mamma.com decided to raise capital through a PIPE offering. As the PIPE offering progressed toward closing, the company decided to inform Cuban, its then-largest known shareholder, of the offering and to invite him to participate. The CEO of Mamma.com spoke with Cuban by telephone.

The CEO prefaced the call by informing Cuban that he had confidential information to convey to him, and Cuban agreed that he would keep whatever information the CEO intended to share with him confidential. The CEO, in reliance on Cuban's agreement to keep the information confidential, proceeded to tell Cuban about the PIPE offering.

As Mamma.com "anticipated," Cuban reacted angrily to this news, stating that he did not like PIPE offerings because they dilute the existing shareholders. At the end of the call Cuban said: "Well, now I'm screwed. I can't sell." Two internal company emails quoted in the complaint indicate that the executive chairman of Mamma.com may have expected that Cuban would not sell his shares until after the PIPE was announced. *See* [Complaint] at ¶ 15 ("[Cuban] said he would sell his shares (recognizing that he was not able to do anything until we announce the equity)[.]"); *id.* at ¶ 20 ("[Cuban's] answers were: he would not invest, he does not want the company to make acquisitions, he will sell his shares which he can not [sic] do until after we announce.").

Several hours after they spoke by telephone, the CEO sent Cuban a follow-up email in which he provided contact information for the investment bank conducting the offering, in case Cuban wanted more information about the PIPE. Cuban then contacted the sales representative, who "supplied Cuban with additional confidential details about the PIPE." One minute after ending this call, Cuban telephoned his broker and directed the broker to sell all 600,000 of his Mamma.com shares. The broker sold a small amount of the shares during after-hours trading on June 28, 2004, and sold the remainder during regular trading hours on June 29, 2004. Cuban did not inform Mamma.com of his intention to trade on the information that he had been given in confidence

---

[2] The court will focus its discussion and analysis on § 10(b) and Rule 10b–5 because the parties agree that § 17(a) is "routinely examined * * * under the same standards" as these provisions. D. Br. 7 n. 6. *See, e.g., Landry v. All Am. Assurance Co.,* 688 F.2d 381, 386 (5th Cir.1982) ("Rule 10b–5, adopted under § 10(b) of the Securities and Exchange Act of 1934, is substantially identical to § 17(a).").

and that he had agreed to keep confidential. *See id.* at ¶ 25 ("Cuban never disclosed to Mamma.com that he was going to sell his shares prior to the public announcement of the PIPE."). After the markets had closed on June 29, 2004, Mamma.com publicly announced the PIPE offering. Trading in the company's stock opened substantially lower the next day and continued to decline in the days following. Cuban avoided losses in excess of $750,000 by selling his shares prior to the public announcement of the PIPE. After the sale, Cuban filed the required disclosure statement with the SEC and "publicly stated that he had sold his Mamma.com shares because the company was conducting a PIPE[.]" *Id.*

Based on Cuban's alleged violation of § 17(a) of the Securities Act, § 10(b) of the Exchange Act, and Rule 10b–5, the SEC seeks a permanent injunction against future violations, disgorgement of losses avoided, prejudgment interest, and imposition of a civil monetary penalty.

B

Cuban, supported by five law professors as *amici curiae,* moves to dismiss the complaint under Fed.R.Civ.P. 12(b)(6) for failure to state a claim on which relief can be granted, and under Rule 9(b) for failing to plead fraud with particularity. * * * Cuban maintains that, to establish liability for insider trading, the SEC must demonstrate that his conduct was deceptive under § 10(b), which he asserts the SEC has not done under the facts pleaded. Specifically, Cuban contends that the SEC has alleged merely that he entered into a confidentiality agreement, which is of itself insufficient to establish misappropriation theory liability because the agreement must arise in the context of a preexisting fiduciary or fiduciary-like relationship, or create a relationship that bears all the hallmarks of a traditional fiduciary relationship; the existence of a fiduciary or fiduciary-like relationship is governed exclusively by state law and, under Texas law, the facts pleaded do not demonstrate that he had such a relationship with Mamma.com; even if the court applies federal common law, the facts pleaded still fail to show such a relationship; and the SEC cannot rely on Rule 10b5–2(b)(1) to supply the requisite duty because the Rule applies only in the context of family or personal relationships, and, if the Rule does create liability in the absence of a preexisting fiduciary or fiduciary-like relationship, it exceeds the SEC's § 10(b) rulemaking authority and cannot be applied against him. * * *

III

A

* * * The law of insider trading is not based on a federal statute expressly prohibiting the practice; it has instead developed through SEC

and judicial interpretations of § 10(b)'s prohibition of "deceptive"[4] conduct and Rule 10b–5's antifraud provisions. The SEC, in *In re Cady, Roberts & Co.,* 40 S.E.C. 907, 1961 WL 60638 (1961), and the Supreme Court, in *Chiarella v. United States,* 445 U.S. 222, 227–30, 100 S.Ct. 1108, 63 L.Ed.2d 348 (1980), first recognized the "traditional" or "classical" theory of insider trading liability. Under this theory, "§ 10(b) and Rule 10b–5 are violated when a corporate insider trades in the securities of his corporation on the basis of material, nonpublic information." *United States v. O'Hagan,* 521 U.S. 642, 651–52, 117 S.Ct. 2199, 138 L.Ed.2d 724 (1997) (citing *Chiarella,* 445 U.S. at 228, 100 S.Ct. 1108). Liability is premised on the "relationship of trust and confidence between the shareholders of a corporation and those insiders who have obtained confidential information by reason of their position with that corporation." *Chiarella,* 445 U.S. at 228, 100 S.Ct. 1108. This relationship gives rise to a "duty to disclose" confidential information prior to trading. *Id.*

In *O'Hagan* the Supreme Court expanded the scope of insider trading liability by recognizing the "misappropriation theory," which had been the subject of disagreement among lower courts. "The 'misappropriation theory' holds that a person commits fraud 'in connection with' a securities transaction, and thereby violates § 10(b) and Rule 10b–5, when he misappropriates confidential information for securities trading purposes, in breach of a duty owed to the source of the information." *O'Hagan,* 521 U.S. at 652, 117 S.Ct. 2199. The "undisclosed, self-serving use of a principal's information to purchase or sell securities, in breach of a duty of loyalty and confidentiality, defrauds the principal of the exclusive use of that information." *Id.* "In lieu of premising liability on a fiduciary relationship between company insider and purchaser or seller of the company's stock, the misappropriation theory premises liability on a fiduciary-turned-trader's deception of those who entrusted him with access to confidential information." *Id.*

The two theories are complementary, each addressing efforts to capitalize on nonpublic information through the purchase or sale of securities. The classical theory targets a corporate insider's breach of duty to shareholders with whom the insider transacts; the misappropriation theory outlaws trading on the basis of nonpublic information by a corporate "outsider" in breach of a duty owed not to a trading party, but to the source of the information. *Id.* at 652–53, 117 S.Ct. 2199.

---

[4] "Manipulative," as used in § 10(b), is a narrow " 'term of art.' " *Regents of the Univ. of Ca. v. Credit Suisse First Boston (USA), Inc.,* 482 F.3d 372, 390 (5th Cir.2007) (quoting *Ernst & Ernst v. Hochfelder,* 425 U.S. 185, 199, 96 S.Ct. 1375, 47 L.Ed.2d 668 (1976)). It "refers generally to practices, such as wash sales, matched orders, or rigged prices, that are intended to mislead investors by artificially affecting market activity." *Santa Fe Indus., Inc. v. Green,* 430 U.S. 462, 476, 97 S.Ct. 1292, 51 L.Ed.2d 480 (1977).

The nature of the duty required to support misappropriation theory liability is at the heart of the present case and Cuban's motion to dismiss. In 2000 the SEC adopted Rule 10b5–2, which delineates certain circumstances that will give rise to a "duty of trust or confidence" for purposes of the misappropriation theory. Rule 10b5–2(b)(1) provides that "a 'duty of trust or confidence' exists * * * [w]henever a person agrees to maintain information in confidence[.]"

B

The SEC argues that, under Rule 10b5–2(b)(1) and the facts pleaded in the complaint, it has stated a claim on which relief can be granted. According to the SEC, Cuban is liable under the misappropriation theory based on a duty created by his agreement to keep confidential the information that Mamma.com's CEO provided him about the impending PIPE offering. It posits that Cuban breached this duty when, without disclosing to Mamma.com his intent to trade in its stock based on the information, he sold his shares in the company.

Cuban maintains that he is entitled to dismissal of this suit * * *.

IV

Because it affects the resolution of Cuban's other arguments, the court turns first to his contention that his liability under the misappropriation theory depends on the existence of a preexisting fiduciary or fiduciary-like relationship, as determined exclusively under applicable state law.

A

Cuban relies on this court's opinion in *Southwest Realty, Ltd. v. Daseke,* 1992 WL 373166, at *9–*10 (N.D.Tex. May 21, 1992) (Fitzwater, J.), to support his contention that state law regarding fiduciary and fiduciary-like relationships is the exclusive source of the predicate duty for misappropriation theory liability. He also posits that, unless the court derives the duty from state law alone, its decision will violate the general rule—applied in cases like *Santa Fe Industries, Inc. v. Green,* 430 U.S. 462, 478–80, 97 S.Ct. 1292, 51 L.Ed.2d 480 (1977)—against the creation of federal common law.

The SEC counters that no federal court has relied exclusively on state law to determine whether a duty sufficient to support misappropriation theory liability exists. It contends that were the court to adopt a state-specific standard for deriving the duty, the decision would balkanize the misappropriation theory and lead to divergent outcomes under the federal securities laws depending on the state of jurisdiction in a particular insider trading case.

B

The court rejects Cuban's contention that *Southwest Realty* compels the conclusion that the existence of a duty sufficient to support misappropriation theory liability is determined exclusively under state law. In *Southwest Realty* the court followed the conclusions of several appellate courts that "the federal securities laws themselves are not the source of a duty of disclosure. 'Rather the duty to disclose material facts arises only where there is some basis outside the securities laws, such as state law, for finding a fiduciary or other confidential relationship.'" *Sw. Realty,* 1992 WL 373166, at *10 (quoting *Fortson v. Winstead, McGuire, Sechrest & Minick,* 961 F.2d 469 (4th Cir.1992)). *Southwest Realty* did not address insider trading or the misappropriation theory, which the Supreme Court did not adopt until several years later. Thus the court had no occasion to hold that state law regarding fiduciary or similar relationships was the only source of a duty to support liability under this theory. Rather, in the factual and legal context presented, the court simply followed settled precedent that provided that the federal securities laws are not the source of a duty of disclosure, and that such a duty must be found elsewhere, such as in state law.

Moreover, although the source of a duty adequate to support insider trading liability *can* be found in state law—this certainly appears to be the case, for example, in *O'Hagan,* 521 U.S. at 652–53, 117 S.Ct. 2199 (relying on attorney's fiduciary duty to client)—it may be located elsewhere without violating the general rule against creating federal common law. The SEC can promulgate a rule that imposes such a duty, provided the rule conforms with the SEC's rulemaking powers, such as those found in § 10(b) of the Exchange Act. In doing so, the SEC does not create federal general common law. "Common law," when discussed in cases that hold there is no federal general common law, *see, e.g., O'Melveny & Myers v. FDIC,* 512 U.S. 79, 83, 114 S.Ct. 2048, 129 L.Ed.2d 67 (1994) (citing *Erie R.R. Co. v. Tompkins,* 304 U.S. 64, 78, 58 S.Ct. 817, 82 L.Ed. 1188 (1938)), means judge-made law. *See* Black's Law Dictionary 293 (8th ed.) ("The body of law derived from judicial decisions, rather than from statutes or constitutions[.]"). An agency regulation promulgated under authority conferred by Congress is not judge-made law. And in concluding below that an agreement with the proper components can establish the duty necessary to support liability under the misappropriation theory, the court is not creating federal general common law. Because all states recognize and enforce duties created by agreement, the court is essentially relying on the state law of contracts to supply the requisite duty.

Finally, for reasons the court will explain in the next section, it rejects Cuban's contention that liability under the misappropriation theory depends on the existence of a preexisting fiduciary or fiduciary-like relationship.

V

The court now considers whether, under the Supreme Court's precedents, breach of a legal duty arising by agreement can be the basis for misappropriation theory liability, and, if so, what are the essential components of the agreement.

A

In *Chiarella* the Court recognized the classical theory of insider trading and explained that because insider trading essentially involves the nondisclosure of information, it falls within § 10(b)'s requirement of deception only if there is a duty to disclose. *See Chiarella,* 445 U.S. at 231, 100 S.Ct. 1108 (reasoning that trading on material, nonpublic information is "not a fraud under § 10(b)" unless the trader is under a duty to disclose); *id.* at 228, 100 S.Ct. 1108 ("But one who fails to disclose material information prior to the consummation of a transaction commits fraud only when he is under a duty to do so."); *id.* at 235, 100 S.Ct. 1108 ("When an allegation of fraud is based upon nondisclosure, there can be no fraud absent a duty to speak."). Further, the duty is not a general one but must arise from "a specific relationship between two parties." *Id.* at 233, 100 S.Ct. 1108. *Chiarella* unequivocally rejects a "parity-of-information" principle, under which a disclosure duty would arise based on the mere possession of material, nonpublic information. *Id.*

Building on *Chiarella,* the Supreme Court concluded in *O'Hagan* that, like the classical theory, the misappropriation theory also involves deception within the meaning of § 10(b). *O'Hagan* teaches that the essence of the misappropriation theory is the trader's undisclosed use of material, nonpublic information that is the property of the source, in breach of a duty owed to the source to keep the information confidential and not to use it for personal benefit. *See O'Hagan,* 521 U.S. at 652, 117 S.Ct. 2199 ("Under this theory, a fiduciary's undisclosed, self-serving use of a principal's information to purchase or sell securities, in breach of a duty of loyalty and confidentiality, defrauds the principal of the exclusive use of that information."); *id.* at 656, 117 S.Ct. 2199 ("[T]he fiduciary's fraud is consummated, not when the fiduciary gains the confidential information, but when, without disclosure to his principal, he uses the information to purchase or sell securities."); *see also id.* at 655, 117 S.Ct. 2199 (contrasting government's allegations in *O'Hagan* with *Santa Fe* because, in *Santa Fe,* "all pertinent facts were disclosed by the persons charged with violating § 10(b) and Rule 10b–5; therefore, there was no deception through nondisclosure to which liability under those provisions could attach" (citation omitted)). Under the misappropriation theory of insider trading, the deception flows from the undisclosed, duplicitous nature of the breach. *See id.* at 653–54, 117 S.Ct. 2199 ("A fiduciary who '[pretends] loyalty to the principal while secretly converting the principal's information for personal gain' 'dupes' or defrauds the principal." (quoting Brief for United States 17)); *id.* at 655, 117 S.Ct. 2199 ("[T]he deception essential to the misappropriation theory involves feigning fidelity to the source of information[.]").

O'Hagan states unmistakably that "[d]eception through nondisclosure is central to [this] theory[.]" *Id.* at 654, 117 S.Ct. 2199. And by providing that a person can avoid misappropriation theory liability by disclosing his intention to use confidential information, it confirms that the deception inheres in the undisclosed use of information, in breach of a duty not to do so.

[F]ull disclosure forecloses liability under the misappropriation theory. * * * [I]f the fiduciary discloses to the source that he plans to trade on the nonpublic information, there is no "deceptive device" and thus no § 10(b) violation—although the fiduciary-turned-trader may remain liable under state law for breach of a duty of loyalty. *Id.* at 655, 117 S.Ct. 2199; *see also id.* at 659 n. 9, 117 S.Ct. 2199 ("[T]he textual requirement of deception precludes § 10(b) liability when a person trading on the basis of nonpublic information has disclosed his trading plans to, or obtained authorization from, the principal—even though such conduct may affect the securities markets in the same manner as the conduct reached by the misappropriation theory."). In simple terms, the misappropriator acts deceptively, not merely because he uses the source's material, nonpublic information for personal benefit, in breach of a duty not to do so, but because he does not disclose to the source that he intends to trade on or otherwise use the information.

B

In the context of the misappropriation theory, therefore, trading on the basis of material, nonpublic information cannot be deceptive unless the trader is under a legal duty to refrain from trading on or otherwise using it for personal benefit. Where the trader and the information source are in a fiduciary relationship, this obligation arises by operation of law upon the creation of the relationship. As *O'Hagan* makes clear, a fiduciary is bound to act loyally toward the principal, and as a part of the duty of loyalty, to use property that has been entrusted to him—including confidential information—to benefit only the principal and not himself. *See O'Hagan,* 521 U.S. at 652, 117 S.Ct. 2199 ("[A] fiduciary's undisclosed, self-serving use of a principal's information to purchase or sell securities, in breach of a duty of loyalty and confidentiality, defrauds the principal of the exclusive use of that information."). The deception inheres in the fiduciary's undisclosed breach of this duty. Specifically, the fiduciary deceives the principal by acting the part of a faithful agent in other respects while secretly appropriating the principal's confidential information for his own use. Because of the fiduciary's duty of loyalty, the principal has a right to expect that the fiduciary is not trading on or otherwise using the principal's confidential information. The fiduciary's duplicitous conduct confirms that expectation while the fiduciary is contemporaneously and secretly violating his duty. Thus the fiduciary's trading violates the principal's legitimate and justifiable expectation that the fiduciary is using the information only for the principal's benefit.

Because under *O'Hagan* the deception that animates the misappropriation theory involves at its core the undisclosed breach of a duty not to use another's information for personal benefit, there is no apparent reason why that duty cannot arise by agreement.[5]

Further, recognizing that a duty analogous to the fiduciary's duty of "loyalty and confidentiality" can be created by agreement fully comports with *Chiarella*'s teaching that the duty must arise out of a relationship between specific parties and not the mere possession of confidential information. The court therefore concludes that a duty sufficient to support liability under the misappropriation theory can arise by agreement absent a preexisting fiduciary or fiduciary-like relationship.

Indeed, the duty that arises by agreement can be seen as conferring a stronger footing for imposing liability for deceptive conduct than does the existence, without more, of a fiduciary or similar relationship of trust and confidence. In the context of an agreement, the misappropriator has committed to refrain from trading on material, nonpublic information. The duty is thus created by conduct that captures the person's obligation with greater acuity than does a duty that flows more generally from the nature of the parties' relationship. The misappropriator is held to terms created by his own agreement rather than to a duty triggered merely by operation of law due to his relationship with the information source.

The agreement, however, must consist of more than an express or implied promise merely to keep information confidential. It must also impose on the party who receives the information the legal duty to refrain from trading on or otherwise using the information for personal gain.

---

[5] The court disagrees with Cuban's assertion that, in *O'Hagan*, "[t]he Court [drew] a clear distinction between fiduciaries and non-fiduciaries because *only* a fiduciary would have a duty to make this disclosure and therefore can be said to have engaged in a 'deception' if he does not disclose or abstain from trading." D. Reply Br. 2–3 (citing *O'Hagan*, 521 U.S. at 655, 117 S.Ct. 2199). Although *O'Hagan* is written in terms of fiduciaries and fiduciary relationships, duties, and obligations, it is reasonable to infer that this is because *O'Hagan* was a criminal case that involved the conduct of a fiduciary. "In this case, the indictment alleged that O'Hagan, in breach of a duty of trust and confidence he owed to his law firm, Dorsey & Whitney, and to its client, Grand Met, traded on the basis of nonpublic information regarding Grand Met's planned tender offer for Pillsbury common stock. This conduct, the Government charged, constituted a fraudulent device in connection with the purchase and sale of securities." *O'Hagan*, 521 U.S. at 653, 117 S.Ct. 2199 (citation omitted). The Court may simply have intended that its opinion decide the case without injecting *dicta* to cover other circumstances in which the misappropriation theory could apply. But regardless of the reason, there is no indication in *O'Hagan* that such a fiduciary or fiduciary-like relationship is necessary—as opposed to merely sufficient—to impose the requisite duty, or is otherwise an essential element of the misappropriation theory.

With respect to confidential information, nondisclosure[6] and non-use are logically distinct. A person who receives material, nonpublic information may in fact preserve the confidentiality of that information while simultaneously using it for his own gain. Indeed, the nature of insider trading is such that one who trades on material, nonpublic information refrains from disclosing that information to the other party to the securities transaction. To do so would compromise his advantageous position. *See O'Hagan,* 521 U.S. at 656, 117 S.Ct. 2199 ("The misappropriation theory targets information of a sort that misappropriators ordinarily capitalize upon to gain no-risk profits through the purchase or sale of securities."). But although conceptually separate, both nondisclosure and non-use comprise part of the duty that arises by operation of law when a fiduciary relationship is created. Where misappropriation theory liability is predicated on an agreement, however, a person must undertake, either expressly or implicitly, both obligations. He must agree to maintain the confidentiality of the information *and* not to trade on or otherwise use it. Absent a duty not to use the information for personal benefit, there is no deception in doing so. As in the fiduciary context, the deception occurs when a person secretly trades on confidential information in violation of the source's legitimate and justifiable expectation that the recipient will not do so. *Id.* at 654, 117 S.Ct. 2199 ("Deception through nondisclosure is central to [this] theory[.]"). This expectation can be created where the source entrusts a person with confidential information in reliance on the recipient's agreement not to disclose the information and not to use it for personal gain. The expectation is not unilateral, arising merely from the source's subjective belief that the recipient will not trade on the information. It rests on the recipient's undertaking of a duty to refrain from doing so as well. *Cf. United States v. Chestman,* 947 F.2d 551, 567 (2d Cir.1991) (noting, in context of insider trading suit, that "a fiduciary duty cannot be imposed unilaterally by entrusting a person with confidential information"); *United States v. Reed,* 601 F.Supp. 685, 715 (S.D.N.Y.) (reasoning, in same context, that "[t]he mere unilateral investment of confidence by one party in the other ordinarily will not suffice to saddle the parties with the obligations and duties of a confidential relationship"), *rev'd on other grounds,* 773 F.2d 477 (2d Cir.1985). For the recipient then to exploit the information's value in the securities markets, without disclosing to the source his intent to do so, violates the source's legitimate and justifiable expectation and deceives him. In short, the recipient's agreement not to use the source's information for personal benefit, combined with his subsequent undisclosed use of the information for

---

[6]   In this respect, by "nondisclosure" the court means maintaining the confidentiality of information, not the nondisclosure of one's intention to trade on or otherwise use such information.

securities trading purposes, makes his conduct deceptive under § 10(b) and Rule 10b–5.[7]

Although the court therefore agrees with Cuban that an agreement must contain more than a promise of confidentiality, the court disagrees with his contention that, for a person to be held liable under the misappropriation theory, he must enter into an agreement that creates a relationship bearing all the hallmarks of a traditional fiduciary relationship. And the court respectfully declines to follow the case Cuban cites in support of this proposition: *United States v. Kim*, 184 F.Supp.2d 1006 (N.D.Cal.2002). *See id.* at 1011 (holding that "a similar relationship of trust and confidence must be characterized by superiority, dominance, or control"); *id.* at 1015 ("In the Court's opinion * * * an express agreement can provide the basis for misappropriation liability only if the express agreement sets forth a relationship with the hallmarks of a fiduciary relationship detailed above."). Although no court appears to have analyzed the precise question that this court examines above—i.e., the nature of an agreement that can give rise to misappropriation theory liability—some have disagreed with *Kim*'s holding that a relationship marked by factors such as superiority, dominance, or control is required. *See, e.g., SEC v. Nothern*, 598 F.Supp.2d 167, 176 (D.Mass.2009) ("[A] 'similar relationship of trust and confidence' [may] exist [ ] even in the absence of a scintilla of superiority or dominance[.]"); *SEC v. Kirch*, 263 F.Supp.2d 1144, 1150 (N.D.Ill.2003) ("[T]he 'duty of loyalty and confidentiality' owed by the outsider * * * to the person * * * who shared confidential information with him or her * * * is *not* limited to fiduciary relationships in the limited sense that requires such factors as control

---

[7] Cases decided both before and after *O'Hagan* have recognized that a duty sufficient to support misappropriation theory liability may arise by agreement. *See, e.g., SEC v. Yun*, 327 F.3d 1263, 1273 (11th Cir.2003) (stating that "[o]f course, a breach of an agreement to maintain business confidences would also suffice" to yield insider trading liability); *United States v. Falcone*, 257 F.3d 226, 234 (2d Cir.2001) (holding that "a fiduciary relationship, or its functional equivalent, exists only where there is explicit acceptance of a duty of confidentiality or where such acceptance may be implied from a similar relationship of trust and confidence between the parties" (citing *Chestman*, 947 F.2d at 567–68)); *Chestman*, 947 F.2d at 571 (reasoning that "fiduciary status" could be established by "a pre-existing fiduciary relation or an express agreement of confidentiality"); *SEC v. Nothern*, 598 F.Supp.2d 167, 175 (D.Mass.2009) (holding that SEC's allegation that person had "expressly agreed to maintain the confidentiality of * * * information is sufficient to state a claim that he had a 'similar relationship of trust and confidence' "); *SEC v. Lyon*, 529 F.Supp.2d 444, 452–53 (S.D.N.Y.2008) (holding that SEC had adequately alleged existence of predicate duty for misappropriation theory liability by pleading that purchase agreement and other materials related to PIPE offering contained confidentiality conditions and provisions, including requirements that defendants use information for sole purpose of evaluating possible investment in the offering, and discovery might reveal that defendants had explicitly accepted the conditions or that it was customary practice among participants in private placement market to be bound and abide by such provisions). Because none of these cases analyzes the nature of the agreement that is required for misappropriation theory liability, none is contrary to the court's holding today that an agreement must include both an obligation to maintain the confidentiality of the information *and* not to trade on or otherwise use it.

and dominance on the part of the fiduciary.").[8] Moreover, if an agreement has the elements necessary to conform to the principles of the misappropriation theory liability recognized in *O'Hagan,* it should not be determinative whether the agreement creates a relationship in which one party is superior to, or exercises control or dominance over, the other.

C

The conclusion that an agreement imposing duties of nondisclosure and non-use can support liability under the misappropriation theory is supported by its consistency with the purpose of the theory. The misappropriation theory "address[es] efforts to capitalize on nonpublic information through the purchase or sale of securities." *O'Hagan,* 521 U.S. at 652, 117 S.Ct. 2199. It is "designed to 'protec[t] the integrity of the securities markets against abuses by "outsiders" to a corporation who have access to confidential information that will affect th[e] corporation's security price when revealed, but who owe no fiduciary or other duty to that corporation's shareholders.'" *Id.* at 653, 117 S.Ct. 2199 (quoting Brief for United States 14). "The theory is * * * well tuned to an animating purpose of the Exchange Act: to insure honest securities markets and thereby promote investor confidence." *Id.* at 658, 117 S.Ct. 2199. "Although informational disparity is inevitable in the securities markets, investors likely would hesitate to venture their capital in a market where trading based on misappropriated nonpublic information is unchecked by law." *Id.* The goal of protecting the integrity of the securities markets and promoting investor confidence would be achieved just as effectively by enforcing duties of nondisclosure and non-use that arise by agreement as by enforcing duties that flow from the nature of the relationship between the information source and the misappropriator. In fact, the converse is also true: investors likely would hesitate to venture their capital if they knew that while a corporate outsider in a fiduciary relationship could *not* trade based on misappropriated nonpublic information, an outsider who had actually agreed with the source not to trade on such information, but was not a fiduciary, *could* do so.

VI

The court next addresses whether the SEC has adequately alleged that Cuban entered into an agreement sufficient to create the duty necessary to establish misappropriation theory liability. State common law can impose such a duty, provided Cuban entered into an express or

---

[8]   The court notes that, in an insider trading case decided by this court, Judge Lindsay relied in part on the *Kim* factors to hold that liability existed under the misappropriation theory. *See SEC v. Kornman,* 391 F.Supp.2d 477, 488–89 (N.D.Tex.2005) (Lindsay, J.). But unlike in *Kim,* Judge Lindsay was not explicitly addressing whether factors such as superiority, dominance, or control were required for liability under the misappropriation theory. Instead, he relied on *Kim* and other cases in "consider[ing] the indicia giving rise to a fiduciary or fiduciary-like relationship in the arena of securities fraud." *Id.* at 486. In other words, he assumed that such a relationship was necessary for misappropriation theory liability, and he relied on *Kim* and similar cases to determine whether such a relationship had been adequately pleaded.

implied agreement with Mamma.com not to disclose material, nonpublic information about the PIPE offering *and* not to trade on or otherwise use the information. The court concludes that the SEC's complaint is deficient in this critical respect.

Regarding the telephone call during which the alleged agreement was made, the SEC merely alleges that Cuban "agreed that he would keep whatever information the CEO intended to share with him confidential"; that in reliance on that agreement, the CEO informed him of the PIPE offering; and that Cuban expressed displeasure at this news and, at the end of the call, stated "Well, now I'm screwed. I can't sell." Compl. ¶ 14. Thus while the SEC adequately pleads that Cuban entered into a confidentiality agreement, it does not allege that he agreed, expressly or implicitly, to refrain from trading on or otherwise using for his own benefit the information the CEO was about to share. Although at one point Cuban allegedly stated that he was "screwed" because he "[could not] sell," this appears to express his belief, at least at that time, that it would be illegal for him to sell his Mamma.com shares based on the information the CEO had provided. This statement, however, cannot reasonably be understood as an agreement not to sell based on the information. Further, the complaint asserts no facts that reasonably suggest that the CEO intended to obtain from Cuban an agreement to refrain from trading on the information as opposed to an agreement merely to keep it confidential.

Nor is it sufficient that the complaint indicates that the executive chairman of Mamma.com may have expected that Cuban would not sell until the PIPE was publicly announced. *See id.* at ¶ 15 (" '[Cuban] said he would sell his shares (recognizing that he was not able to do anything until we announce the equity)[.]' " (quoting email of executive chairman to Mamma.com board)); *id.* at ¶ 20 (" '[Cuban's] answers were: he would not invest, he does not want the company to make acquisitions, he will sell his shares which he can not [sic] do until after we announce.' " (quoting second email of executive chairman to board)). Outside a fiduciary or fiduciary-like relationship, a mere unilateral expectation on the part of the information source—one that is not based on the other party's agreement to refrain from trading on the information—cannot create the predicate duty for misappropriation theory liability.

VII

Having determined that the SEC's complaint is insufficient to plead a duty arising by agreement, the court turns finally to the parties' arguments regarding whether the SEC can rely on Rule 10b5–2(b)(1) to impose the required duty.[9]

---

[9] In light of the court's conclusion on this issue, it need not address at length Cuban's contention that Rule 10b5–2(b)(1) applies only to family and other personal relationships, i.e., non-business relationships. Were the court to reach this question, however, it would join the

A

The SEC's rulemaking authority under § 10(b) is bounded by the statute's proscription of conduct that is manipulative or deceptive. The SEC cannot by rule make unlawful conduct that does not fall into one of these categories. *See O'Hagan,* 521 U.S. at 651, 117 S.Ct. 2199 ("Liability under Rule 10b–5, our precedent indicates, does not extend beyond conduct encompassed by § 10(b)'s prohibition.") (citing *Ernst & Ernst v. Hochfelder,* 425 U.S. 185, 214, 96 S.Ct. 1375, 47 L.Ed.2d 668 (1976); *Cent. Bank of Denver, N.A. v. First Interstate Bank of Denver, N.A.,* 511 U.S. 164, 173, 114 S.Ct. 1439, 128 L.Ed.2d 119 (1994)); *id.* at 655, 117 S.Ct. 2199 ("[Section] 10(b) is not an all-purpose breach of fiduciary duty ban; rather, it trains on conduct involving manipulation or deception." (citing *Santa Fe Indus.,* 430 U.S. at 473–76, 97 S.Ct. 1292)). In the context of the misappropriation theory, the SEC cannot by rule predicate liability on an agreement that lacks the necessary component of an obligation not to trade on or otherwise use confidential information for personal benefit. As the court has explained, it is the undisclosed use of such information, in breach of a duty not to use it for personal benefit, that makes the conduct deceptive under § 10(b) and Rule 10b–5.

B

In considering whether Rule 10b5–2(b)(1) can serve as the basis for misappropriation theory liability, the court first examines its plain meaning. Courts in the Fifth Circuit "interpret regulations in the same manner as statutes, looking first to the regulation's plain language. Where the language is unambiguous, [courts] do not look beyond the plain wording of the regulation to determine meaning." *Anthony v. United States,* 520 F.3d 374, 380 (5th Cir.2008). "The appropriate starting point when interpreting any statute is its plain meaning." *United States v. Elrawy,* 448 F.3d 309, 315 (5th Cir.2006) (citing *United States v. Ron Pair Enters., Inc.,* 489 U.S. 235, 242, 109 S.Ct. 1026, 103 L.Ed.2d 290 (1989)). "The plain meaning of legislation should be conclusive, except in the 'rare cases [in which] the literal application of a statute will produce a result demonstrably at odds with the intentions of its drafters.' " *Ron Pair Enters.,* 489 U.S. at 242, 109 S.Ct. 1026 (quoting *Griffin v. Oceanic Contractors, Inc.,* 458 U.S. 564, 571, 102 S.Ct. 3245, 73 L.Ed.2d 973 (1982)).

To determine "the plain meaning of the statute, the court must look to the particular statutory language at issue, as well as the language and design of the statute as a whole." *K Mart Corp. v. Cartier, Inc.,* 486 U.S. 281, 291, 108 S.Ct. 1811, 100 L.Ed.2d 313 (1988) (citing *Bethesda Hosp. Ass'n v. Bowen,* 485 U.S. 399, 403–05, 108 S.Ct. 1255, 99 L.Ed.2d 460 (1988); *Offshore Logistics, Inc. v. Tallentire,* 477 U.S. 207, 220–21, 106

---

other courts that reject such a limitation on Rule 10b5–2(b)(1)'s reach. *See, e.g., Nothern,* 598 F.Supp.2d at 174–75.

S.Ct. 2485, 91 L.Ed.2d 174 (1986)). "It is 'a cardinal principle of statutory construction' that 'a statute ought, upon the whole, to be so construed that, if it can be prevented, no clause, sentence, or word shall be superfluous, void, or insignificant.'" *TRW Inc. v. Andrews,* 534 U.S. 19, 31, 122 S.Ct. 441, 151 L.Ed.2d 339 (2001) (quoting *Duncan v. Walker,* 533 U.S. 167, 174, 121 S.Ct. 2120, 150 L.Ed.2d 251 (2001)). The court "must, if possible, construe a statute to give every word some operative effect." *Cooper Indus., Inc. v. Aviall Servs., Inc.,* 543 U.S. 157, 167, 125 S.Ct. 577, 160 L.Ed.2d 548 (2004) (citing *United States v. Nordic Vill., Inc.,* 503 U.S. 30, 35–36, 112 S.Ct. 1011, 117 L.Ed.2d 181 (1992)).

C

* * * The court concludes that, by its terms, Rule 10b5–2(b)(1) attempts to base misappropriation theory liability on an agreement that lacks an obligation not to trade on or otherwise use confidential information. The agreement specified in the Rule—"to maintain information in confidence"—relates merely to preserving the confidentiality of the information. The word "maintain" captures the obligation to keep the information in its existing state, and the modifying phrase "in confidence" indicates that the state to be preserved is its confidentiality. Nothing in Rule 10b5–2(b)(1) requires that the agreement encompass an obligation not to trade on or otherwise use the information.

That Rule 10b5–2(b)(1) relates to an agreement to preserve confidentiality is supported by the language and design of Rule 10b5–2 as a whole. It accords with the interpretation of Rule 10b5–2(b)(2) and (b)(3), which, like (b)(1), specify circumstances in which a duty of trust or confidence exists. Rule 10b5–2(b)(2) creates the duty based on a history, pattern, or practice of sharing confidences if "the recipient of the information knows or reasonably should know that the person communicating the material nonpublic information expects that the recipient will maintain its confidentiality." Rule 10b5–2(b)(3) creates a rebuttable rule that a duty of trust or confidence exists in certain enumerated family relationships, unless the person demonstrates that "he or she neither knew nor reasonably should have known that the person who was the source of the information expected that the person would keep the information confidential, because of the parties' history, pattern, or practice of sharing and maintaining confidences, and because there was no agreement or understanding to maintain the confidentiality of the information." Thus Rule 10b5–2(b)(2) and (b)(3) also base misappropriation theory liability on an undertaking, express or implied, to maintain confidentiality of information, but they do not require an undertaking not to trade on or otherwise use the information for personal benefit.

Because Rule 10b5–2(b)(1) attempts to predicate misappropriation theory liability on a mere confidentiality agreement lacking a non-use component, the SEC cannot rely on it to establish Cuban's liability under the misappropriation theory. To permit liability based on Rule 10b5–2(b)(1) would exceed the SEC's § 10(b) authority to proscribe conduct that is deceptive. *See O'Hagan,* 521 U.S. at 651, 117 S.Ct. 2199 ("Liability under Rule 10b–5, our precedent indicates, does not extend beyond conduct encompassed by § 10(b)'s prohibition."). This is because, as the court has explained, under the misappropriation theory of liability, it is the undisclosed use of confidential information for personal benefit, in breach of a duty not to do so, that constitutes the deception.

VIII

Because the SEC has failed to allege that Cuban undertook a duty to refrain from trading on information about the impending PIPE offering, and because the SEC cannot rely on the duty imposed by Rule 10b5–2(b)(1) alone, Cuban cannot be held liable under the misappropriation theory of insider trading liability, even accepting all well-pleaded facts as true and viewing them in the light most favorable to the SEC. The court therefore grants Cuban's motion to dismiss the complaint under Rule 12(b)(6).

The court will allow the SEC 30 days from the date of this memorandum opinion and order to file an amended complaint, if the SEC can allege that Cuban undertook a duty, expressly or implicitly, not to trade on or otherwise use material, nonpublic information about the PIPE offering.

> [I]n view of the consequences of dismissal on the complaint alone, and the pull to decide cases on the merits rather than on the sufficiency of pleadings, district courts often afford plaintiffs at least one opportunity to cure pleading deficiencies before dismissing a case, unless it is clear that the defects are incurable or the plaintiffs advise the court that they are unwilling or unable to amend in a manner that will avoid dismissal.

In re Am. Airlines, Inc., Privacy Litig., 370 F.Supp.2d 552, 567–68 (N.D.Tex.2005) (Fitzwater, J.) (quoting *Great Plains Trust Co. v. Morgan Stanley Dean Witter & Co.,* 313 F.3d 305, 329 (5th Cir.2002)). If the SEC cannot replead as required by today's decision, it may so inform the court, and this case will be dismissed with prejudice.

* * *

Cuban's January 14, 2009 motion to dismiss is granted. The SEC is granted 30 days from the date of this memorandum opinion and order to file an amended complaint.

SO ORDERED.

MEMORANDUM OPINION AND ORDER

In a memorandum opinion and order filed July 17, 2009, the court granted defendant Mark Cuban's ("Cuban's") motion to dismiss under Fed.R.Civ.P. 12(b)(6), but it also gave plaintiff Securities and Exchange Commission ("SEC") 30 days to file an amended complaint. The court concluded that "Cuban cannot be held liable under the misappropriation theory of insider trading liability, even accepting all well-pleaded facts as true and viewing them in the light most favorable to the SEC." "The court [allowed] the SEC 30 days from the date of th[e] memorandum opinion and order to file an amended complaint, if the SEC can allege that Cuban undertook a duty, expressly or implicitly, not to trade on or otherwise use material, nonpublic information about the PIPE offering." It stated that "[i]f the SEC cannot replead as required by today's decision, it may so inform the court, and this case will be dismissed with prejudice."

On August 12, 2009 the SEC timely filed a "Notice and Request Pursuant to the Court's July 17, 2009 Memorandum Opinion and Order." In its notice and request, the SEC "states that it does not intend to file an amended complaint and respectfully requests that the Court enter the final judgment against it to initiate the time for consideration of an appeal."

Accordingly, for the reasons stated in the court's memorandum opinion and order filed July 17, 2009, and in the absence of an amended complaint, the court grants Cuban's January 14, 2009 motion to dismiss and dismisses this action with prejudice by judgment filed today.

NOTES

(1) In October 2009, the SEC filed court papers saying it would appeal the district court's dismissal of insider trading charges against Cuban. The Court of Appeals overturned the District Court's dismissal, as it found that "[t]he allegations, taken in their entirety, provide more than a plausible basis to find that the understanding between the CEO and Cuban was that he was not to trade, [and] that it was more than a simple confidentiality agreement." S.E.C. v. Cuban, 620 F.3d 551, 557 (5th Cir. 2010).

In October 2013, a federal jury cleared Mark Cuban of the SEC's insider trading charges:

> * * * [T]he outspoken billionaire [received] a decisive victory and [dealt] a setback to the Securities and Exchange Commission's toughened enforcement stance. * * * The jury cleared Mr. Cuban * * * after deliberating less than four hours. "I am glad this happened to me," Mr. Cuban said. "I'm glad I'm able to be the person who can afford to stand up to" the SEC. * * * Speaking to reporters after the verdict, Mr. Cuban said paying his top-flight legal team to take the case to trial had cost him "far more" than it would have to settle out of court.

John Carreyrou, Mark Cuban Cleared in Insider-Trading Case: Jury Rejects SEC's Charges Related to Sale of Internet Company Stake, Wall St. J., Oct. 16, 2013.

(2) As discussed below, another big issue in insider trading cases is the ability of the government to pursue companies and individuals who supervise people engaging in illegal insider trading.

SECURITIES EXCHANGE ACT OF 1934 § 21A
15 U.S.C. § 78u–1.

Section 21A. Civil Penalties for Insider Trading

(a) AUTHORITY TO IMPOSE CIVIL PENALTIES

(1) *Judicial actions by Commission authorized.* Whenever it shall appear to the Commission that any person has violated any provision of this title or the rules or regulations thereunder by purchasing or selling a security * * * while in possession of material, nonpublic information in, or has violated any such provision by communicating such information in connection with, a transaction on or through the facilities of a national securities exchange or from or through a broker or dealer, and which is not part of a public offering by an issuer of securities other than standardized options * * * the Commission—

(A) may bring an action in a United States district court to seek, and the court shall have jurisdiction to impose, a civil penalty to be paid by the person who committed such violation; and

(B) may, subject to subsection (b)(1), bring an action in a United States district court to seek, and the court shall have jurisdiction to impose, a civil penalty to be paid by a person who, at the time of the violation, directly or indirectly controlled the person who committed such violation.

(2) *Amount of penalty for person who committed violation.* The amount of the penalty which may be imposed on the person who committed such violation shall be determined by the court in light of the facts and circumstances, but shall not exceed three times the profit gained or loss avoided as a result of such unlawful purchase, sale, or communication.

(3) *Amount of penalty for controlling person.* The amount of the penalty which may be imposed on any person who, at the time of the violation, directly or indirectly controlled the person who committed such violation, shall be determined by the court in light of the facts and circumstances, but shall not exceed the greater of $1,000,000, or three times the amount of the profit gained or loss avoided as a result of such controlled person's violation. If such controlled person's violation was a violation by communication, the profit gained or loss avoided as a result

of the violation shall, for purposes of this paragraph only, be deemed to be limited to the profit gained or loss avoided by the person or persons to whom the controlled person directed such communication.

(b) LIMITATIONS ON LIABILITY

(1) *Liability of controlling persons.* No controlling person shall be subject to a penalty under subsection (a)(1)(B) unless the Commission establishes that—

(A) such controlling person knew or recklessly disregarded the fact that such controlled person was likely to engage in the act or acts constituting the violation and failed to take appropriate steps to prevent such act or acts before they occurred; or

(B) such controlling person knowingly or recklessly failed to establish, maintain, or enforce any policy or procedure required under section 15(f) of this title[e] or section 204A of the Investment Advisers Act of 1940 and such failure substantially contributed to or permitted the occurrence of the act or acts constituting the violation.

(2) *Additional restrictions on liability.* No person shall be subject to a penalty under subsection (a) solely by reason of employing another person who is subject to a penalty under such subsection, unless such employing person is liable as a controlling person under paragraph (1) of this subsection. Section 20(a) of this title[f] shall not apply to actions under subsection (a) of this section.

* * *

NOTES

(1) Section 21A was enacted as part of the Insider Trading Sanctions Act of 1984, Pub.L.No. 98–376, 98 Stat. 1264 (ITSA). The power to impose civil penalties greatly increases the risk of insider trading, since the penalty is

---

[e] The referenced section 15(f) [now 15(g)] provides:

Every registered broker or dealer shall establish, maintain, and enforce written policies and procedures reasonably designed, taking into consideration the nature of such broker's or dealer's business, to prevent the misuse in violation of this title, or the rules or regulations thereunder, of material, nonpublic information by such broker or dealer or any person associated with such broker or dealer. The Commission, as it deems necessary or appropriate in the public interest or for the protection of investors, shall adopt rules or regulations to require specific policies or procedures reasonably designed to prevent misuse in violation of this title (or the rules or regulations thereunder) of material, nonpublic information.

[f] Section 20(a) provides:

Every person who, directly or indirectly, controls any person liable under any provision of this title or of any rule or regulation thereunder shall also be liable jointly and severally with and to the same extent as such controlled person to any person to whom such controlled person is liable * * *, unless the controlling person acted in good faith and did not directly or indirectly induce the act or acts constituting the violation or cause of action.

added to the disgorgement of profit, and the inside trader ends up much worse off than if he had never traded at all. Courts have consistently added substantial civil penalties to the disgorgement of insider trading profits.

(2) A second statute, the Insider Trading and Securities Fraud Enforcement Act of 1988, Pub.L.No. 100–704, 102 Stat. 4677 (codified in scattered sections of 15 U.S.C.) (ITSFEA) increased the criminal penalties for willful violation of the Securities Acts or regulations issued thereunder from $100,000 and five years to $1,000,000 and ten years for individuals, and a fine of up to $2,500,000 when the defendant is a "person other than a natural person." ITSFEA, § 4.

(3) The Investment Advisers Act of 1940 applies to people who accept fees for advising people, pension funds, and institutions like hedge funds on investment matters. On July 11, 2007, the SEC approved new Rule 206(4)–8 to clarify the SEC's authority to pursue fraudulent misconduct against hedge fund advisers. The Dodd-Frank Wall Street Reform and Consumer Protection Act, signed into law by President Obama on July 21, 2010, required the registration of many investment advisers to hedge funds under the Investment Advisers Act of 1940. The Investment Advisers Act vests the SEC with the authority to impose sanctions on a person who has failed reasonably to supervise others to prevent violations of securities laws, rules, and regulations.

(4) The largest financial penalty in the history of insider trading litigation is the $1.8 billion fine levied on the hedge fund SAC Capital Advisors. The settlement, which resolved the outstanding criminal and civil cases against SAC, includes an agreement that SAC will cease operating as an investment adviser and will not accept any additional funds from third-party investors. There is a separate civil case pending against Steven A. Cohen, the founder of SAC, for failure to supervise. In numerous lawsuits against individual SAC traders, government prosecutors and SEC Enforcement Division lawyers charged that SAC earned hundreds of millions of dollars illegally from 1999 to 2010 through insider trading in the stock of at least 20 public companies by SAC portfolio managers and analysts. Preet Bharara, the U.S. Attorney for the Southern District of New York, claimed that SAC "trafficked in inside information on a scale without any known precedent in the history of hedge funds."

Eight former SAC employees have been criminally charged with insider trading and most have pleaded guilty. One portfolio manager at an SAC affiliate company was accused of using illegal tips about an experimental Alzheimer's drug to net more than $276 million for his fund and others.

But the firm is not dead. SAC has billions of dollars of Steven Cohen's own money, which it will continue to invest after it shuts down its investment advisory business, which invested for outsiders. On November 7, 2013, SAC owned close to 1 million shares in Intercept Pharmaceuticals Inc. The value of these shares increased by 283% in one day after it reported the results of a successful drug trial. On this trade alone, SAC made $400 million in a single day. Many of the criminal insider trading allegations against SAC officials also were for trading in health care stocks, including insider trading based on tips about drug experiments by Wyeth, a New Jersey-based subsidiary of the pharmaceutical giant Pfizer.

SECURITIES EXCHANGE ACT OF 1934 § 20A
15 U.S.C. § 78t–1.

Section 20A. Liability to contemporaneous traders for insider trading

(a) PRIVATE RIGHTS OF ACTION BASED ON CONTEMPORANEOUS TRADING

Any person who violates any provision of this title or the rules or regulations thereunder by purchasing or selling a security while in possession of material, non-public information shall be liable in an action in any court of competent jurisdiction to any person who, contemporaneously with the purchase or sale of securities that is the subject of such violation, has purchased (where such violation is based on a sale of securities) or sold (where such violation is based on a purchase of securities) securities of the same class.

* * *

(c) JOINT AND SEVERAL LIABILITY FOR COMMUNICATING

Any person who violates any provision of this title or the rules or regulations thereunder by communicating material, nonpublic information shall be jointly and severally liable under subsection (a) with, and to the same extent as, any person or persons liable under subsection (a) to whom the communication was directed.

(d) AUTHORITY NOT TO RESTRICT OTHER EXPRESS OR IMPLIED RIGHTS OF ACTION

Nothing in this section shall be construed to limit or condition the right of any person to bring an action to enforce a requirement of this title or the availability of any cause of action implied from a provision of this title.

NOTES

(1) Prior to enactment of this section, the question whether private actions may be maintained against persons trading on inside information had arisen in a number of cases. A majority of courts, however, did not permit such suits. See Fridrich v. Bradford, 542 F.2d 307 (6th Cir.1976), cert. denied, 429 U.S. 1053 (1977) (defendants did not purchase shares from plaintiffs and their trading in no way affected the plaintiffs' decision to sell; private civil liability does not need to be coextensive with the reach of the SEC); Moss v. Morgan Stanley Inc., 719 F.2d 5 (2d Cir.1983), cert. denied sub nom. Moss v. Newman, 465 U.S. 1025 (1984) (defendants were tippees of aggressor in

proposed tender offer and traded in the target's stock; the Court held that the tippees owed no duty to the plaintiffs on an impersonal market).

(2) Plaintiffs have not had much greater success under § 20A, which was added by ITSFEA in 1988. Most (though not all) complaints have been dismissed or summary judgments for defendants have been entered before trial. Major issues have been how contemporaneous must "contemporaneous trading" be and how particularized allegations must be that the defendants in fact possessed material nonpublic information at the time of trading. Simon v. American Power Conversion Corp., 945 F.Supp. 416 (D.R.I.1996), held that trading that occurred during the same week was "contemporaneous" and refused to grant a motion to dismiss, while In re AST Research Securities Litigation, 887 F.Supp. 231 (C.D.Cal.1995), took the position that trading must occur on the same day if it is to meet the "contemporaneous trading" requirement. While some cases have suggested that a five- or six-day period is "contemporaneous," In re MicroStrategy, Inc. Securities Litigation, 115 F.Supp.2d 620 (E.D.Va.2000), holds that a purchase of stock three days after an officer's sale at a higher price was not "contemporaneous."

SECURITIES EXCHANGE ACT OF 1934 § 16

15 U.S.C. § 78p.

Section 16.   Directors, officers, and principal stockholders

(a) Disclosures required.—

(1) Directors, officers, and principal stockholders required to file.— Every person who is directly or indirectly the beneficial owner of more than 10 percent of any class of any equity security (other than an exempted security) which is registered pursuant to section 12, or who is a director or an officer of the issuer of such security, shall file the statements required by this subsection with the Commission.

(2) Time of filing.—The statements required by this subsection shall be filed—

(A) at the time of the registration of such security on a national securities exchange or by the effective date of a registration statement filed pursuant to section 12(g);

(B) within 10 days after he or she becomes such beneficial owner, director, or officer, or within such shorter time as the Commission may establish by rule;

(C) if there has been a change in such ownership, or if such person shall have purchased or sold a security-based swap agreement involving such equity security, before the end of the second business day following the day on which the subject transaction has been executed, or at such other time as the

Commission shall establish, by rule, in any case in which the Commission determines that such 2-day period is not feasible.

(3) Contents of statements.—A statement filed—

(A) under subparagraph (A) or (B) of paragraph (2) shall contain a statement of the amount of all equity securities of such issuer of which the filing person is the beneficial owner; and

(B) under subparagraph (C) of such paragraph shall indicate ownership by the filing person at the date of filing, any such changes in such ownership, and such purchases and sales of the security-based swap agreements or security-based swaps as have occurred since the most recent such filing under such subparagraph.

* * *

(b) For the purpose of preventing the unfair use of information which may have been obtained by such beneficial owner, director, or officer by reason of his relationship to the issuer, any profit realized by him from any purchase and sale, or any sale and purchase, of any equity security of such issuer (other than an exempted security) * * * within any period of less than six months, unless such security * * * was acquired in good faith in connection with a debt previously contracted, shall inure to and be recoverable by the issuer, irrespective of any intention on the part of such beneficial owner, director, or officer in entering into such transaction of holding the security * * * purchased or of not repurchasing the security * * * sold for a period exceeding six months. Suit to recover such profit may be instituted at law or in equity in any court of competent jurisdiction by the issuer, or by the owner of any security of the issuer in the name and in behalf of the issuer if the issuer shall fail or refuse to bring such suit within sixty days after request or shall fail diligently to prosecute the same thereafter; but no such suit shall be brought more than two years after the date such profit was realized. This subsection shall not be construed to cover any transaction where such beneficial owner was not such both at the time of the purchase and sale, or the sale and purchase, of the security * * * involved, or any transaction or transactions which the Commission by rules and regulations may exempt as not comprehended within the purpose of this subsection.

NOTES

(1) Section 16(b), enacted as part of the original 1934 Exchange Act, is probably the most quirky provision of federal securities law. Read § 16(b) again, carefully. From the first, the courts have held that this section establishes a "crude rule of thumb" and that it is no defense to argue that the offsetting transactions were entered into for innocent reasons unconnected with inside information about the corporation's affairs. If a purchase and sale

(or sale and purchase) by an officer, director, or 10% shareholder takes place within a six-month period, the "profit" is automatically recoverable by the corporation. Section 16(b) states that its purpose is to prevent "the unfair use of information which may have been obtained by [the] beneficial owner, director, or officer by reason of his relationship to the issuer." The conventional reading of this statement of purpose is rather literal— that it prevents an insider from trading on nonpublic information and then restoring his or her securities position after that information has become public. However, § 16(b) is almost completely ineffective to achieve this purpose since most persons trading on nonpublic information are willing to hold securities for more than six months in order to capitalize on that information. A more rational explanation of § 16(b) is that its true purpose is to prevent manipulation of market prices by insiders. Dennis W. Carlton & Daniel R. Fischel, The Regulation of Insider Trading, 35 Stan. L.Rev. 857, 892 (1983); Frank H. Easterbrook & Daniel R. Fischel, The Economic Structure of Corporate Law 273–74 (1991). Based on original research into the background and origins of § 16(b), other related explanations have been put forth. Steve Thel, The Genius of Section 16: Regulating the Management of Publicly Held Companies, 42 Hastings L.J. 391 (1991) (purpose was to discourage manipulation of corporate affairs to create opportunities to trade corporate stock profitably since insiders must invest for the long term); Karl Shumpei Okamoto, Rereading Section 16(b) of the Securities Exchange Act, 27 Ga. L.Rev. 183 (1992) (purpose was to deter insiders from sending false signals that artificially affect prices when in fact there was no inside information at all).

(2) How are violations discovered? Nothing could be easier, since the reports required by § 16(a) are promptly made publicly available by the SEC. It is simply a matter of comparing transactions.

(3) Is there any incentive to find violations given the fact that the recovery inures to the corporation? Again from the first, the courts recognized that attorneys for plaintiff shareholders who locate § 16(b) violations, bring them to the attention of the corporation, and if necessary, bring suit on them (as contemplated by § 16(b)) are entitled to attorneys' fees. Further, "[s]ince in many cases such as this the possibility of recovering attorney's fees will provide the sole stimulus for the enforcement of § 16(b), the allowance must not be too niggardly." Smolowe v. Delendo Corp., 136 F.2d 231, 241 (2d Cir.1943), cert. denied, 320 U.S. 751 (1943). Finally, it is not necessary to actually resort to litigation in order to earn the fee. Gilson v. Chock Full O'Nuts Corp., 326 F.2d 246 (2d Cir.1964). It is enough to find violations and report them to the corporation if they lead to payment to the corporation.

(4) How difficult is it to find a plaintiff in whose name a suit may be brought to recover for a § 16(b) violation? Not difficult at all, since there is no requirement that the plaintiff be a shareholder at the time of either the purchase or sale, and the ownership of a single share purchased specifically for bringing the suit is sufficient. See generally 9 Louis Loss & Joel Seligman,

Securities Regulation 4286–89 (3d ed. 1992). In a word, it is legalized champerty.

(5) How are profits computed if there is a series of transactions? In a word, punitively. "The only rule whereby all possible profits can surely be recovered is that of lowest price in, highest price out within six months." Smolowe v. Delendo Corp., 136 F.2d at 239; Gratz v. Claughton, 187 F.2d 46 (2d Cir.1951), cert. denied, 341 U.S. 920 (1951). To illustrate:

Assume that an insider enters into the following transactions, which are grouped together for simplicity of analysis:

(1)	7/1/75	Buys 100 shares	@	115
(2)	5/15/76	Sells 100 shares	@	93
(3)	5/18/76	Buys 100 shares	@	90
(4)	5/21/76	Buys 100 shares	@	95
(5)	5/23/76	Sells 100 shares	@	97
(6)	5/26/76	Buys 100 shares	@	105
(7)	5/29/76	Sells 100 shares	@	108
(8)	8/10/76	Sells 100 shares	@	115

A businessman examining this sequence of transactions would probably conclude that the insider made a profit of $300 on transactions (2) and (3), $200 on (4) and (5), $300 on (6) and (7), and $0 on (1) and (8), closing the account for a total trading profit of $800. However, by matching lowest price in with highest price out, the following tabulation is made:

Purchases	Sales	Profit
100 @ 90 (trans. (3))	100 @ 115 (trans. (8))	2500
100 @ 95 (trans. (4))	100 @ 108 (trans. (7))	1300
100 @ 105 (trans. (6))	100 @ 97 (trans. (5))	0

Thus, there is a total § 16(b) profit of $3,800. In this computation, all transactions which yield losses are to be ignored. The Supreme Court has not had occasion to consider specifically the propriety of this method of calculating "profits." See Andrew Chin, Accurate Calculation of Short Swing Profits Under Section 16(b) of the Securities Exchange Act of 1934, 22 Del.J.Corp.L. 587, 588 (1997) (The lowest-in, highest-out "algorithm * * * originated from an erroneous 1943 analysis that cannot be defended in today's complex, computerized environment.").

(6) An officer, director, or ten percent shareholder, subject to § 16(b), must accommodate his or her securities transactions to the requirements of that section, whether or not the transactions are motivated by nonpublic information. In order to avoid application of that section, a covered person who purchases or sells securities of the corporation must avoid entering into an offsetting transaction—a sale if the other transaction was a purchase, or a purchase if the other transaction was a sale—for a period that begins six

months before the transaction in question and ends six months after the transaction. In effect, in-and-out trading is proscribed for a one-year period surrounding every transaction. Of course, § 16(b) is not violated if there are either a succession of purchase transactions or a succession of sale transactions without any offsetting transactions, no matter how much nonpublic information is used. Further, there is no "profit" to return to the corporation if the highest sale price during every possible six-month period is below the lowest purchase price during every possible six-month period surrounding the transaction; however, as illustrated above, transactions are matched in such a way that a single purchase at a lower price than any sale price will always generate § 16(b) profits no matter what the net profit or loss in the account was over the same or a different period.

(7) Section 16(b), in short, is an *in terrorem* provision that appears to combine an effective enforcement system with virtually no loopholes for a violator. Since avoidance of the section is relatively easy—spacing offsetting transactions six months and one day apart provides complete protection—one might assume that violations are rather rare, the product of ignorance, carelessness or inattention. The history is far different. Before about 1980, the federal reports fairly bristle with cases in which § 16(b) was applied. In addition to reported cases, there were numerous instances in which officers and directors voluntarily repaid § 16(b) profits to the issuer because they had no plausible defense; certainly, in many of these transactions nonpublic information was not involved. Why were there so many inadvertent violations? In a few instances, persons clearly covered by § 16(b) violated the section because they were unaware of the section's existence, careless in calculating the six month period, or because they relied on uninformed or erroneous advice. However, many cases also arose because of uncertainty as to the applicability of § 16(b): Should a conversion of convertible preferred into common be viewed as a "sale" of the convertible or a "purchase" of the common, or both? Is a receipt of an option to purchase a "purchase"? Or does the "purchase" occur when the option is exercised? Is the writing of a call a "sale" or the writing of a put a "purchase"? Is a person who was not an officer or director at the time of the first transaction but was at the time of the second transaction covered by the section? What about a person who was an officer or director at the time of the first transaction but not at the time of the second? Is a "vice president" an "officer"? It is fair to say that in most of the reported cases during this era, the transactions did not in fact appear to involve the use of nonpublic information but liability was imposed because § 16(b) was an automatic liability section. Karl Shumpei Okamoto, Oversimplification and the SEC's Treatment of Derivative Securities Trading by Corporate Insiders, 1993 Wis.L.Rev. 1287, 1289–90 accurately summarized the law of § 16(b) when he wrote:

> It is difficult to accommodate the broad goal of deterring insider trading within this narrow prohibition of short-swing trading. There is no necessary correlation between the simple fact of a purchase and sale or a sale and purchase within six months and the abuse of inside information. Inside information can be abused with but one

trade, and matched trades are not ineluctably motivated by inside information. Therefore, courts have been forced to struggle with the innocent insider whose activity fits within the literal prohibition, as well as with the clearly culpable insider whose antics do not. Cohesive rules of application have evaded the courts as they seek to apply the basic statute to a purpose it was not well suited to achieve.

(8) The number of reported § 16(b) cases has declined significantly in the last two decades. One factor is improved distribution of information about the dangers of inadvertent violations. General counsel of issuers of registered securities regularly distribute cautionary memoranda to directors, officers, large shareholders, and employees who are subject to § 16(b). Since 1988, these memoranda have been virtually required by ITSFEA, but even before the enactment of that statute, they were widely used.

A second important factor are the exemptive regulations promulgated by the SEC in 1991 and 1996 that go a long way toward rationalizing the coverage of § 16(b). The last sentence of § 16(b) grants the SEC power to exempt transactions from that section if they are "not comprehended within the purpose of this subsection." Prior to 1991, the SEC had exercised this power of exemption sparingly and unsystematically. Perhaps the most important exemptions were § 240.16b–3 (relating to employee benefit plans and stock appreciation rights), and § 240.16b–6 (relating to the exercise of long-term options). In 1991, however, the SEC adopted new regulations that significantly reduce areas of uncertainty about the application of § 16(b) and modify to some extent policies previously adopted by the SEC. In 1996, the SEC returned to the task and smoothed out additional "rough edges," particularly in the director and officer compensation area. 17 C.F.R. § 240.16a–1 (1997), et seq.; Rel.No. 34–28869, 56 Fed. Reg. 7241 (Feb. 8, 1991), Rel.No. 34–37260 (June 14, 1996). These regulations constitute more than 15 densely packed pages of the Code of Federal Regulations and deal with a number of significant issues under § 16(b):

(a) The definition of "officers" is narrowed to include only the issuer's president, principal financial officer, principal accounting officer, any vice president in charge of a principal business unit, division, or function, and other persons performing policy-making functions for the issuer. Any executive officer identified as such in an issuer's 10–K Annual Report is presumed to be an "officer" for purposes of § 16.

(b) The definitions of "beneficial owner" and "equity security" are made more objective, defining direct and indirect pecuniary interests, but excluding ownership of derivatives such as options or warrants.

(c) The treatment of derivative securities—warrants, options, puts, and calls—are treated quite differently than before. Previously, acquiring an option or a call to purchase securities was not a § 16(b) purchase; the purchase occurred when the option or call was exercised. Under the regulations, the acquisition of an option is a § 16(b) purchase and its exercise is not. 16 C.F.R. §§ 240.16a–4, 240.16b–6 (1997). Previously, a covered person might speculate on inside information by matching the acquisition of a derivative with the purchase or sale of the underlying security without incurring § 16(b) liability. This is now prevented, but a covered person may now exercise a stock option and immediately sell the acquired shares without incurring § 16(b) liability. See Marc I. Steinberg & Daryl L. Landsdale, The Judicial and Regulatory Constriction of Section 16(b) of the Securities Exchange Act of 1934, 68 Notre Dame L. Rev. 33, 60–69 (1992); Karl Shumpei Okamoto, Oversimplification and the SEC's Treatment of Derivative Securities Trading by Corporate Insiders, 1993 Wisc.L.Rev. 1287.

(d) Purchases or sales made before a person becomes an officer or director need not be reported and therefore may not be matched with sales or purchases after the person becomes an officer or director. 17 C.F.R. § 240.16a–2(a) (1997). Steinberg & Landsdale criticize this change as giving away a "crown jewel" of the prohibitions against insider trading. Steinberg & Landsdale, supra at 69–78.

(e) The rules with respect to employee benefit plans were substantially reorganized and supplemented in 1991 and then completely revised in 1996 to meet criticisms and complaints about the complexity of the 1991 regulations. 17 C.F.R. § 240.16b–3 (1997). Basically, the 1996 regulations work from the premise that transactions between an issuer and its officers and directors who owe state law fiduciary duties to the issuer and its shareholders do not present the possibility of insider trading. The revised regulations completely exempt compensation and stock purchase plans that are qualified for favorable tax treatment. They also provide guidelines for the application of § 16(b) to "discretionary decisions" by participants in these plans. See Ronald O. Mueller, SEC Adopts Final, Section 16 Rule Revisions, Insights, Vol. 10, No. 8, at 2 (August 1996).

(f) The 1996 regulations also make numerous changes designed to simplify the reporting requirements for specific transactions under § 16(a).

(9) The 10 percent shareholder provision of § 16(b) makes the section potentially applicable in takeover situations wherever an aggressor acquires more than 10 percent of the target's shares but fails to acquire control of the target and thereafter disposes of the purchased shares within six months. That disposition may be to the target by private sale at a premium (greenmail), to a successful competitor for control, or on the open market by a series of sales, usually to risk arbitrageurs or conceivably to long-term investors who are not seeking control of the target. Since takeover disputes rarely extend for long periods, the probability is relatively high that offsetting transactions will occur within six months of the failed takeover bid. The United States Supreme Court addressed this issue in a series of opinions during the 1970s, and like the lower federal courts, became trapped by the irreconcilable tensions between § 16(b) as an objective crude rule of thumb on the one hand, and the unjust or irrational results often reached when that objective standard was literally applied on the other. The Court reached plausible results through a process of inconsistent interpretation:

(a) In Reliance Elect. Co. v. Emerson Elect. Co., 404 U.S. 418 (1972), an aggressor purchased 13.2 percent of the target's stock in an unsuccessful takeover attempt; when it was clear the battle was lost, the aggressor sold its shares to the successful purchaser in two sales, the first that reduced its holding to 9.6 percent, and the second the balance of its holding. In a 4–3 decision, the Supreme Court held that § 16(b) applied to the first sale but not to the second, since the seller was no longer a 10 percent shareholder.

(b) In Kern County Land Co. v. Occidental Petroleum Corp., 411 U.S. 582 (1973), Occidental purchased more than 10 percent of Kern County shares in a takeover attempt, but was blocked by a defensive merger between Kern County and Tenneco. As a result of the merger, Occidental received Tenneco preferred shares. Occidental requested the SEC to exempt the exchange, but the SEC refused. Occidental thereafter granted Tenneco the option to purchase its preference shares exercisable exactly six months and one-day after the Tenneco tender offer expired. In a 6–3 decision, the Supreme Court held that the exchange transaction and the grant of the option was not within § 16(b) because they did not lend themselves to the evil against which § 16(b) was directed—the utilization of confidential information.

(c) In Foremost-McKesson, Inc. v. Provident Sec. Co., 423 U.S. 232 (1976), the Court finally solved most § 16(b) problems in the takeover context by holding that the transaction by which a person becomes a 10 percent shareholder is not itself a purchase that may be matched with subsequent sales. On the perhaps debatable assumption that the aggressor who accepts cash tenders from tens or hundreds of thousands of shareholders does so in a single transaction, most of the problems of applying § 16(b) to takeover situations disappeared. Of course, all purchases after the one that increases the holding to above ten percent continue to be subject to § 16(b).

(10) Do you think that § 16(b) is now obsolete and should be repealed given the growth of Rule 10b–5, the enactment by Congress of ITSA and ITSFEA during the 1980s, and the development of the 1991 and 1996 regulations? For a strong argument supporting that suggestion, see Michael H. Dessent, Weapons to Fight Insider Trading in the 21st Century: A Call for the Repeal of Section 16(b), 33 Akron L.Rev. 481 (2000). Professor Dessent suggests Rule 10b–5, including the misappropriation doctrine approved in O'Hagan, provides more rational application of the prohibition against insider trading than § 16(b). Alternatively, Professor Dessent also suggests that it might be sensible to limit enforcement of § 16(b) actions to the SEC.

(11) Section 16(b) still prevents in-and-out trading by officers, directors, and large shareholders within a six month period. Is that a sufficient justification to retain this section, despite its quirky and erratic nature and the inequities and champertous litigation that it generates? The SEC has considered proposals to recommend the repeal of this section, but has never actually supported such a proposal.

C. JUDICIAL DEVELOPMENT OF LIABILITY FOR SECURITIES FRAUD

BASIC INC. V. LEVINSON
Supreme Court of the United States, 1988.
485 U.S. 224.

JUSTICE BLACKMUN delivered the opinion of the Court.

This case requires us to apply the materiality requirement of § 10(b) of the Securities Exchange Act of 1934, and the Securities and Exchange Commission's Rule 10b–5, in the context of preliminary corporate merger discussions. We must also determine whether a person who traded a corporation's shares on a securities exchange after the issuance of a materially misleading statement by the corporation may invoke a rebuttable presumption that, in trading, he relied on the integrity of the price set by the market.

I

Prior to December 20, 1978, Basic Incorporated was a publicly traded company primarily engaged in the business of manufacturing chemical refractories for the steel industry. As early as 1965 or 1966, Combustion Engineering, Inc., a company producing mostly alumina-based refractories, expressed some interest in acquiring Basic, but was deterred from pursuing this inclination seriously because of antitrust concerns it then entertained. In 1976, however, regulatory action opened the way to a renewal of Combustion's interest. The "Strategic Plan," dated October 25, 1976, for Combustion's Industrial Products Group included the objective: "Acquire Basic Inc. $30 million."

Beginning in September 1976, Combustion representatives had meetings and telephone conversations with Basic officers and directors,[2] * * * concerning the possibility of a merger.[3] During 1977 and 1978, Basic made three public statements denying that it was engaged in merger negotiations.[4] On December 18, 1978, Basic asked the New York Stock

---

[2] In addition to Basic itself, petitioners are individuals who had been members of its board of directors prior to 1979. * * *

[3] In light of our disposition of this case, any further characterization of these discussions must await application, on remand, of the materiality standard adopted today.

[4] On October 21, 1977, after heavy trading and a new high in Basic stock, the following news item appeared in the Cleveland Plain Dealer:

"[Basic] President Max Muller said the company knew no reason for the stock's activity and that no negotiations were under way with any company for a merger. He said Flintkote recently denied Wall Street rumors that it would make a tender offer of $25 a share for control of the Cleveland-based maker of refractories for the steel industry."

On September 25, 1978, in reply to an inquiry from the New York Stock Exchange, Basic issued a release concerning increased activity in its stock and stated that

"management is unaware of any present or pending company development that would result in the abnormally heavy trading activity and price fluctuation in company shares that have been experienced in the past few days."

Exchange to suspend trading in its shares and issued a release stating that it had been "approached" by another company concerning a merger. On December 19, Basic's board endorsed Combustion's offer of $46 per share for its common stock, and on the following day publicly announced its approval of Combustion's tender offer for all outstanding shares.

Respondents are former Basic shareholders who sold their stock after Basic's first public statement of October 21, 1977, and before the suspension of trading in December 1978. Respondents brought a class action against Basic and its directors, asserting that the defendants issued three false or misleading public statements and thereby were in violation of § 10(b) of the 1934 Act and of Rule 10b–5. Respondents alleged that they were injured by selling Basic shares at artificially depressed prices in a market affected by petitioners' misleading statements and in reliance thereon.

The District Court adopted a presumption of reliance by members of the plaintiff class upon petitioners' public statements that enabled the court to conclude that common questions of fact or law predominated over particular questions pertaining to individual plaintiffs. See Fed.Rule Civ.Proc. 23(b)(3). The District Court therefore certified respondents' class. On the merits, however, the District Court granted summary judgment for the defendants. It held that, as a matter of law, any misstatements were immaterial: there were no negotiations ongoing at the time of the first statement, and although negotiations were taking place when the second and third statements were issued, those negotiations were not "destined, with reasonable certainty, to become a merger agreement in principle."

The United States Court of Appeals for the Sixth Circuit affirmed the class certification, but reversed the District Court's summary judgment, and remanded the case. 786 F.2d 741 (1986). The court reasoned that while petitioners were under no general duty to disclose their discussions with Combustion, any statement the company voluntarily released could not be " 'so incomplete as to mislead.' " *Id.,* at 746, quoting *SEC v. Texas Gulf Sulphur Co.,* 401 F.2d 833, 862 (C.A.2 1968) (en banc), cert. denied *sub nom. Coates v. SEC,* 394 U.S. 976, 89 S.Ct. 1454, 22 L.Ed.2d 756 (1969). In the Court of Appeals' view, Basic's statements that no negotiations were taking place, and that it knew of no corporate developments to account for the heavy trading activity, were misleading. With respect to materiality, the court rejected the argument that preliminary merger discussions are immaterial as a matter of law, and held that "once a statement is made denying the existence of any

---

On November 6, 1978, Basic issued to its shareholders a "Nine Months Report 1978." This Report stated:

"With regard to the stock market activity in the Company's shares we remain unaware of any present or pending developments which would account for the high volume of trading and price fluctuations in recent months."

discussions, even discussions that might not have been material in absence of the denial are material because they make the statement made untrue." 786 F.2d, at 749.

The Court of Appeals joined a number of other circuits in accepting the "fraud-on-the-market theory" to create a rebuttable presumption that respondents relied on petitioners' material misrepresentations, noting that without the presumption it would be impractical to certify a class under Fed.Rule Civ.Proc. 23(b)(3).

We granted certiorari, 479 U.S. 1083, 107 S.Ct. 1284, 94 L.Ed.2d 142 (1987), to resolve the split among the Courts of Appeals as to the standard of materiality applicable to preliminary merger discussions, and to determine whether the courts below properly applied a presumption of reliance in certifying the class, rather than requiring each class member to show direct reliance on Basic's statements.

II

The 1934 Act was designed to protect investors against manipulation of stock prices. Underlying the adoption of extensive disclosure requirements was a legislative philosophy: "There cannot be honest markets without honest publicity. Manipulation and dishonest practices of the market place thrive upon mystery and secrecy." H.R.Rep. No. 1383, 73d Cong., 2d Sess., 11 (1934). This Court "repeatedly has described the 'fundamental purpose' of the Act as implementing a 'philosophy of full disclosure.'" *Santa Fe Industries, Inc. v. Green,* 430 U.S. 462, 477–478, 97 S.Ct. 1292, 1303, 51 L.Ed.2d 480 (1977), quoting *SEC v. Capital Gains Research Bureau, Inc.,* 375 U.S. 180, 186, 84 S.Ct. 275, 280, 11 L.Ed.2d 237 (1963).

* * *

The Court * * * explicitly has defined a standard of materiality under the securities law, see *TSC Industries, Inc. v. Northway, Inc.,* 426 U.S. 438, 96 S.Ct. 2126, 48 L.Ed.2d 757 (1976), concluding in the proxy-solicitation context that "[a]n omitted fact is material if there is a substantial likelihood that a reasonable shareholder would consider it important in deciding how to vote." *Id.,* at 449, 96 S.Ct., at 2132. Acknowledging that certain information concerning corporate developments could well be of "dubious significance," *Id.,* at 448, 96 S.Ct., at 2132, the Court was careful not to set too low a standard of materiality; it was concerned that a minimal standard might bring an overabundance of information within its reach, and lead management "simply to bury the shareholders in an avalanche of trivial information—a result that is hardly conducive to informed decisionmaking." *Id.,* at 448–449, 96 S.Ct., at 2132. It further explained that to fulfill the materiality requirement "there must be a substantial likelihood that the disclosure of the omitted fact would have been viewed by the reasonable investor as having significantly altered the 'total mix' of information made available." We now expressly adopt the *TSC Industries* standard of materiality for the § 10(b) and Rule 10b–5 context.

III

The application of this materiality standard to preliminary merger discussions is not self-evident. Where the impact of the corporate development on the target's fortune is certain and clear, the *TSC Industries* materiality definition admits straightforward application. Where, on the other hand, the event is contingent or speculative in nature, it is difficult to ascertain whether the "reasonable investor" would have considered the omitted information significant at the time. Merger negotiations, because of the ever-present possibility that the contemplated transaction will not be effectuated, fall into the latter category.

A

Petitioners urge upon us a Third Circuit test for resolving this difficulty. Under this approach, preliminary merger discussions do not become material until "agreement-in-principle" as to the price and structure of the transaction has been reached between the would-be merger partners. See *Greenfield v. Heublein, Inc.,* 742 F.2d 751, 757 (C.A.3 1984), cert. denied, 469 U.S. 1215 (1985). By definition, then, information concerning any negotiations not yet at the agreement-in-principle stage could be withheld or even misrepresented without a violation of Rule 10b–5.

Three rationales have been offered in support of the "agreement-in-principle" test. The first derives from the concern expressed in *TSC Industries* that an investor not be overwhelmed by excessively detailed and trivial information, and focuses on the substantial risk that preliminary merger discussions may collapse: because such discussions are inherently tentative, disclosure of their existence itself could mislead investors and foster false optimism. The other two justifications for the agreement-in-principle standard are based on management concerns: because the requirement of "agreement-in-principle" limits the scope of disclosure obligations, it helps preserve the confidentiality of merger discussions where earlier disclosure might prejudice the negotiations; and the test also provides a usable, brightline rule for determining when disclosure must be made.

None of these policy-based rationales, however, purports to explain why drawing the line at agreement-in-principle reflects the significance of the information upon the investor's decision. The first rationale, * * * "assumes that investors are nitwits, unable to appreciate—even when told—that mergers are risky propositions up until the closing." *Flamm v. Eberstadt,* 814 F.2d [1169], at 1175, [(7th Cir.) cert. denied 484 U.S. 853

(1987)]. Disclosure, and not paternalistic withholding of accurate information, is the policy chosen and expressed by Congress. * * *

The second rationale, the importance of secrecy during the early stages of merger discussions, also seems irrelevant to an assessment whether their existence is significant to the trading decision of a reasonable investor. To avoid a "bidding war" over its target, an acquiring firm often will insist that negotiations remain confidential, and at least one Court of Appeals has stated that "silence pending settlement of the price and structure of a deal is beneficial to most investors, most of the time." *Flamm v. Eberstadt,* 814 F.2d, at 1177.[11]

We need not ascertain, however, whether secrecy necessarily maximizes shareholder wealth * * * for this case does not concern the *timing* of a disclosure; it concerns only its accuracy and completeness. * * *

The final justification offered in support of the agreement-in-principle test seems to be directed solely at the comfort of corporate managers. A bright-line rule indeed is easier to follow than a standard that requires the exercise of judgment in the light of all the circumstances. But ease of application alone is not an excuse for ignoring the purposes of the securities acts * * *.

We therefore find no valid justification for artificially excluding from the definition of materiality information concerning merger discussions, which would otherwise be considered significant to the trading decision of a reasonable investor, merely because agreement-in-principle as to price and structure has not yet been reached by the parties or their representatives. * * *

C

Even before this Court's decision in *TSC Industries,* the Second Circuit had explained the role of the materiality requirement of Rule 10b–5, with respect to contingent or speculative information or events, in a manner that gave that term meaning that is independent of the other provisions of the Rule. Under such circumstances, materiality "will depend at any given time upon a balancing of both the indicated probability that the event will occur and the anticipated magnitude of the event in light of the totality of the company activity." *SEC v. Texas Gulf Sulphur Co.,* 401 F.2d [833, 849 (2d Cir.1968)]. * * *

In a subsequent decision, the late Judge Friendly, writing for a Second Circuit panel, applied the *Texas Gulf Sulphur* probability/magnitude approach in the specific context of preliminary merger negotiations. After acknowledging that materiality is something

---

[11] Reasoning backwards from a goal of economic efficiency, that Court of Appeals stated: "Rule 10b–5 is about *fraud,* after all, and it is not fraudulent to conduct business in a way that makes investors better off * * *." Flamm v. Eberstadt, 814 F.2d, at 1177.

to be determined on the basis of the particular facts of each case, he stated:

> Since a merger in which it is bought out is the most important event that can occur in a small corporation's life, to wit, its death, we think that inside information, as regards a merger of this sort, can become material at an earlier stage than would be the case as regards lesser transactions—and this even though the mortality rate of mergers in such formative stages is doubtless high. *SEC v. Geon Industries, Inc.,* 531 F.2d 39, 47–48 (1976).

We agree with that analysis.[16]

Whether merger discussions in any particular case are material therefore depends on the facts. Generally, in order to assess the probability that the event will occur, a factfinder will need to look to indicia of interest in the transaction at the highest corporate levels. Without attempting to catalog all such possible factors, we note by way of example that board resolutions, instructions to investment bankers, and actual negotiations between principals or their intermediaries may serve as indicia of interest. * * *

>   * * *

IV

A

We turn to the question of reliance and the fraud-on-the-market theory. Succinctly put:

> The fraud on the market theory is based on the hypothesis that, in an open and developed securities market, the price of a company's stock is determined by the available material information regarding the company and its business. * * * Misleading statements will therefore defraud purchasers of stock even if the purchasers do not directly rely on the misstatements. * * * The causal connection between the defendants' fraud and the plaintiffs' purchase of stock in such a case is no less significant than in a case of direct reliance on misrepresentations. *Peil v. Speiser,* 806 F.2d 1154, 1160–1161 (C.A.3 1986).

Our task, of course, is not to assess the general validity of the theory, but to consider whether it was proper for the courts below to apply a

---

[16] The SEC in the present case endorses the highly fact-dependent probability/magnitude balancing approach of *Texas Gulf Sulphur*. It explains: "The *possibility* of a merger may have an immediate importance to investors in the company's securities even if no merger ultimately takes place." The SEC's insights are helpful, and we accord them due deference.

rebuttable presumption of reliance, supported in part by the fraud-on-the-market theory.

* * * In their amended complaint, the named plaintiffs alleged that in reliance on Basic's statements they sold their shares of Basic stock in the depressed market created by petitioners. Requiring proof of individualized reliance from each member of the proposed plaintiff class effectively would have prevented respondents from proceeding with a class action, since individual issues then would have overwhelmed the common ones. The District Court found that the presumption of reliance created by the fraud-on-the-market theory provided "a practical resolution to the problem of balancing the substantive requirement of proof of reliance in securities cases against the procedural requisites of [Federal Rule of Civil Procedure] 23." The District Court thus concluded that with reference to each public statement and its impact upon the open market for Basic shares, common questions predominated over individual questions, as required by Federal Rule of Civil Procedure 23(a)(2) and (b)(3).

Petitioners and their *amici* complain that the fraud-on-the-market theory effectively eliminates the requirement that a plaintiff asserting a claim under Rule 10b–5 prove reliance. They note that reliance is and long has been an element of common-law fraud, see, e.g., Restatement (Second) of Torts § 525 (1977), and argue that because the analogous express right of action includes a reliance requirement, see, e.g., § 18(a) of the 1934 Act, as amended, so too must an action implied under § 10(b).

We agree that reliance is an element of a Rule 10b–5 cause of action. Reliance provides the requisite causal connection between a defendant's misrepresentation and a plaintiff's injury. There is, however, more than one way to demonstrate the causal connection. Indeed, we previously have dispensed with a requirement of positive proof of reliance, where a duty to disclose material information had been breached, concluding that the necessary nexus between the plaintiffs' injury and the defendant's wrongful conduct had been established. Similarly, we did not require proof that material omissions or misstatements in a proxy statement decisively affected voting, because the proxy solicitation itself, rather than the defect in the solicitation materials, served as an essential link in the transaction. See *Mills v. Electric Auto-Lite Co.,* 396 U.S. 375, 384–385 (1970).

The modern securities markets, literally involving millions of shares changing hands daily, differ from the face-to-face transactions contemplated by early fraud cases, and our understanding of Rule 10b–5's reliance requirement must encompass these differences.

In face-to-face transactions, the inquiry into an investor's reliance upon information is into the subjective pricing of that information by that investor. With the presence of a market, the market is interposed between seller and buyer and, ideally, transmits information to the investor in the processed form of a market price. Thus the market is performing a substantial part of the valuation process performed by the investor in a face-to-face transaction. The market is acting as the unpaid agent of the investor, informing him that given all the information available to it, the value of the stock is worth the market price. *In re LTV Securities Litigation,* 88 F.R.D. 134, 143 (N.D.Tex.1980).

Accord, *e.g., Peil v. Speiser,* 806 F.2d, at 1161 ("In an open and developed market, the dissemination of material misrepresentations or withholding of material information typically affects the price of the stock, and purchasers generally rely on the price of the stock as a reflection of its value"); *Blackie v. Barrack,* 524 F.2d 891, 908 (C.A.9 1975) ("[T]he same causal nexus can be adequately established indirectly, by proof of materiality coupled with the common sense that a stock purchaser does not ordinarily seek to purchase a loss in the form of artificially inflated stock"), cert. denied, 429 U.S. 816 (1976).

B

* * *

Arising out of considerations of fairness, public policy, and probability, as well as judicial economy, presumptions are * * * useful devices for allocating the burdens of proof between parties. The presumption of reliance employed in this case is consistent with, and, by facilitating Rule 10b–5 litigation, supports, the congressional policy embodied in the 1934 Act. In drafting that Act, Congress expressly relied on the premise that securities markets are affected by information, and enacted legislation to facilitate an investor's reliance on the integrity of those markets * * *.

The presumption is also supported by common sense and probability. Recent empirical studies have tended to confirm Congress' premise that the market price of shares traded on well-developed markets reflects all publicly available information, and, hence, any material misrepresentations.[24] It has been noted that "it is hard to imagine that there ever is a buyer or seller who does not rely on market integrity. Who would knowingly roll the dice in a crooked crap game?" *Schlanger v. Four-Phase Systems Inc.,* 555 F.Supp. 535, 538 (SDNY 1982). * * * Because most publicly available information is reflected in market price, an

---

[24] See *In re LTV Securities Litigation,* 88 F.R.D. 134, 144 (N.D.Tex.1980) (citing studies); Fischel, Use of Modern Finance Theory in Securities Fraud Cases Involving Actively Traded Securities, 38 Bus.Law. 1, 4, n. 9 (1982) (citing literature on efficient-capital-market theory). We need not determine by adjudication what economists and social scientists have debated through the use of sophisticated statistical analysis and the application of economic theory. For purposes of accepting the presumption of reliance in this case, we need only believe that market professionals generally consider most publicly announced material statements about companies, thereby affecting stock market prices.

investor's reliance on any public material misrepresentations, therefore, may be presumed for purposes of a Rule 10b–5 action.

C

The Court of Appeals found that petitioners "made public, material misrepresentations and [respondents] sold Basic stock in an impersonal, efficient market. Thus the class, as defined by the district court, has established the threshold facts for proving their loss." 786 F.2d, at 751. The court acknowledged that petitioners may rebut proof of the elements giving rise to the presumption, or show that the misrepresentation in fact did not lead to a distortion of price or that an individual plaintiff traded or would have traded despite his knowing the statement was false.

Any showing that severs the link between the alleged misrepresentation and either the price received (or paid) by the plaintiff, or his decision to trade at a fair market price, will be sufficient to rebut the presumption of reliance. For example, if petitioners could show that the "market makers" were privy to the truth about the merger discussions here with Combustion, and thus that the market price would not have been affected by their misrepresentations, the causal connection could be broken: the basis for finding that the fraud had been transmitted through market price would be gone.[28] Similarly, if, despite petitioners' allegedly fraudulent attempt to manipulate market price, news of the merger discussions credibly entered the market and dissipated the effects of the misstatements, those who traded Basic shares after the corrective statements would have no direct or indirect connection with the fraud.[29] Petitioners also could rebut the presumption of reliance as to plaintiffs who would have divested themselves of their Basic shares without relying on the integrity of the market. For example, a plaintiff who believed that Basic's statements were false and that Basic was indeed engaged in merger discussions, and who consequently believed that Basic stock was artificially underpriced, but sold his shares nevertheless because of other unrelated concerns, e.g., potential antitrust problems, or political pressures to divest from shares of certain businesses, could not be said to have relied on the integrity of a price he knew had been manipulated.
* * *

---

[28] By accepting this rebuttable presumption, we do not intend conclusively to adopt any particular theory of how quickly and completely publicly available information is reflected in market price. Furthermore, our decision today is not to be interpreted as addressing the proper measure of damages in litigation of this kind.

[29] We note there may be a certain incongruity between the assumption that Basic shares are traded on a well-developed, efficient, and information-hungry market, and the allegation that such a market could remain misinformed, and its valuation of Basic shares depressed, for 14 months, on the basis of the three public statements. Proof of that sort is a matter for trial, throughout which the District Court retains the authority to amend the certification order as may be appropriate. Thus, we see no need to engage in the kind of factual analysis the dissent suggests that manifests the "oddities" of applying a rebuttable presumption of reliance in this case.

The judgment of the Court of Appeals is vacated, and the case is remanded to that court for further proceedings consistent with this opinion.

It is so ordered.

THE CHIEF JUSTICE, JUSTICE SCALIA, and JUSTICE KENNEDY took no part in the consideration or decision of this case.

JUSTICE WHITE, with whom JUSTICE O'CONNOR joins, concurring in part and dissenting in part.

* * * I agree that the standard of materiality we set forth in *TSC Industries, Inc. v. Northway, Inc.,* 426 U.S. 438, 449 (1976), should be applied to actions under § 10(b) and Rule 10b–5. But I dissent from the remainder of the Court's holding because I do not agree that the "fraud-on-the-market" theory should be applied in this case.

I

Even when compared to the relatively youthful private cause-of-action under § 10(b), see *Kardon v. National Gypsum Co.,* 69 F.Supp. 512 (E.D.Pa.1946), the fraud-on-the-market theory is a mere babe.[1] Yet today, the Court embraces this theory with the sweeping confidence usually reserved for more mature legal doctrines. In so doing, I fear that the Court's decision may have many adverse, unintended effects as it is applied and interpreted in the years to come.

A

At the outset, I note that there are portions of the Court's fraud-on-the-market holding with which I am in agreement. Most importantly, the Court rejects the version of that theory, heretofore adopted by some courts, which equates "causation" with "reliance," and permits recovery by a plaintiff who claims merely to have been *harmed* by a material misrepresentation which altered a market price, notwithstanding proof that the plaintiff did not in any way *rely* on that price. I agree with the Court that if Rule 10b–5's reliance requirement is to be left with any content at all, the fraud-on-the-market presumption must be capable of being rebutted by a showing that a plaintiff did not "rely" on the market price. For example, a plaintiff who decides, months in advance of an alleged misrepresentation, to purchase a stock; one who buys or sells a stock for reasons unrelated to its price; one who actually sells a stock "short" days before the misrepresentation is made—surely none of these people can state a valid claim under Rule 10b–5. Yet, some federal courts

---

[1]   The earliest Court of Appeals case adopting this theory cited by the Court is *Blackie v. Barrack,* 524 F.2d 891 (C.A.9 1975), cert. denied, 429 U.S. 816 (1976). Moreover, widespread acceptance of the fraud-on-the-market theory in the Courts of Appeals cannot be placed any earlier than five or six years ago.

have allowed such claims to stand under one variety or another of the fraud-on-the-market theory.[3]

B

* * *

In general, the case law developed in this Court with respect to § 10(b) and Rule 10b–5 has been based on doctrines with which we, as judges, are familiar: common-law doctrines of fraud and deceit. * * * [W]ith no staff economists, no experts schooled in the "efficient-capital-market hypothesis," no ability to test the validity of empirical market studies, we are not well equipped to embrace novel constructions of a statute based on contemporary microeconomic theory.[4]

* * * [T]he Court today ventures into this area beyond its expertise, beyond—by its own admission—the confines of our previous fraud cases. Even if I agreed with the Court that "modern securities markets * * * involving millions of shares changing hands daily" require that the "understanding of Rule 10b–5's reliance requirement" be changed, I prefer that such changes come from Congress in amending § 10(b). * * *

For while the economists' theories which underpin the fraud-on-the-market presumption may have the appeal of mathematical exactitude and scientific certainty, they are—in the end—nothing more than theories which may or may not prove accurate upon further consideration. * * *

---

[3]   *Abrams v. Johns-Manville Corp.,* [1981–1982] CCH Fed.Sec.L.Rep. ¶ 98,348, p. 92,157 (SDNY 1981) * * *.

The *Abrams* decision illustrates the particular pliability of the fraud-on-the-market presumption. In *Abrams,* the plaintiff represented a class of purchasers of defendant's stock who were allegedly misled by defendant's misrepresentations in annual reports. But in a deposition taken shortly after the plaintiff filed suit, she testified that she had bought defendant's stock primarily because she thought that favorable changes in the federal tax code would boost sales of its product (insulation).

Two years later, after the defendant moved for summary judgment based on the plaintiff's failure to prove reliance on the alleged misrepresentations, the plaintiff resuscitated her case by executing an affidavit which stated that she "certainly [had] assumed that the market price of Johns-Manville stock was an accurate reflection of the worth of the company" and would not have paid the then-going price if she had known otherwise. Based on this affidavit, the District Court permitted the plaintiff to proceed on her fraud-on-the-market theory.

Thus, *Abrams* demonstrates how easily a *post hoc* statement will enable a plaintiff to bring a fraud-on-the-market action—even in the rare case where a plaintiff is frank or foolhardy enough to admit initially that a factor other than price led her to the decision to purchase a particular stock.

[4]   This view was put well by two commentators who wrote a few years ago:

Of all recent developments in financial economics, the efficient capital market hypothesis ('ECMH') has achieved the widest acceptance by the legal culture.* * * Yet the legal culture's remarkably rapid and broad acceptance of an economic concept that did not exist twenty years ago is not matched by an equivalent degree of understanding.

Gilson & Kraakman, The Mechanisms of Market Efficiency, 70 Va.L.Rev. 549, 549–550 (1984) (footnotes omitted; emphasis added).

While the fraud-on-the-market theory has gained even broader acceptance since 1984, I doubt that it has achieved any greater understanding.

Consequently, I cannot join the Court in its effort to reconfigure the securities laws, based on recent economic theories, to better fit what it perceives to be the new realities of financial markets. I would leave this task to others more equipped for the job than we.

C

At the bottom of the Court's conclusion that the fraud-on-the-market theory sustains a presumption of reliance is the assumption that individuals rely "on the integrity of the market price" when buying or selling stock in "impersonal, well-developed market[s] for securities." Even if I was prepared to accept (as a matter of common sense or general understanding) the assumption that most persons buying or selling stock do so in response to the market price, the fraud-on-the-market theory goes further. For in adopting a "presumption of reliance," the Court *also* assumes that buyers and sellers rely—not just on the market price—but on the "*integrity*" of that price. It is this aspect of the fraud-on-the-market hypothesis which most mystifies me.

To define the term "integrity of the market price," the majority quotes approvingly from cases which suggest that investors are entitled to " 'rely on the price of a stock as a reflection of its value' " (quoting *Peil v. Speiser,* 806 F.2d 1154, 1161 (C.A.3 1986)). But the meaning of this phrase eludes me, for it implicitly suggests that stocks have some "true value" that is measurable by a standard other than their market price. While the scholastics of medieval times professed a means to make such a valuation of a commodity's "worth," I doubt that the federal courts of our day are similarly equipped.

Even if securities had some "value"—knowable and distinct from the market price of a stock—investors do not always share the Court's presumption that a stock's price is a "reflection of [this] value." Indeed, "many investors purchase or sell stock because they believe the price *inaccurately* reflects the corporation's worth." See Black, Fraud on the Market: A Criticism of Dispensing with Reliance Requirements in Certain Open Market Transactions, 62 N.C.L.Rev. 435, 455 (1984) (emphasis added). If investors really believed that stock prices reflected a stock's "value," many sellers would never sell, and many buyers never buy (given the time and cost associated with executing a stock transaction). As we recognized just a few years ago: "[I]nvestors act on inevitably incomplete or inaccurate information, [consequently] there are always winners and losers; but those who have 'lost' have not necessarily been defrauded." *Dirks v. SEC,* 463 U.S. 646, 667, n. 27 (1983). Yet today, the Court allows investors to recover who can show little more than that they sold stock at a lower price than what might have been.[7]

---

[7]   This is what the Court's rule boils down to in practical terms. For while, in theory, the Court allows for rebuttal of its "presumption of reliance"—a proviso with which I agree—in

I do not propose that the law retreat from the many protections that § 10(b) and Rule 10b–5, as interpreted in our prior cases, provide to investors. But any extension of these laws, to approach something closer to an investor insurance scheme, should come from Congress, and not from the courts. * * *

III

Finally, the particular facts of this case make it an exceedingly poor candidate for the Court's fraud-on-the-market theory, and illustrate the illogic achieved by that theory's application in many cases.

Respondents here are a class of sellers who sold Basic stock between October 1977 and December 1978, a 14-month period. At the time the class period began, Basic's stock was trading at $20 a share (at the time, an all-time high); the last members of the class to sell their Basic stock got a price of just over $30 a share. It is indisputable that virtually every member of the class made money from his or her sale of Basic stock.

The oddities of applying the fraud-on-the-market theory in this case are manifest. First, there are the facts that the plaintiffs are sellers and the class period is so lengthy—both are virtually without precedent in prior fraud-on-the-market cases. * * * [T]hese two facts render this case less apt to application of the fraud-on-the-market hypothesis.

Second, there is the fact that in this case, there is no evidence that petitioner's officials made the troublesome misstatements for the purpose of manipulating stock prices, or with any intent to engage in underhanded trading of Basic stock. Indeed, during the class period, petitioners do not appear to have purchased or sold *any* Basic stock whatsoever. I agree with *amicus* who argues that "[i]mposition of damages liability under Rule 10b–5 makes little sense * * * where a defendant is neither a purchaser nor a seller of securities." In fact, in previous cases, we had recognized that Rule 10b–5 is concerned primarily with cases where the fraud is committed by one trading the security at issue. And it is difficult to square liability in this case with § 10(b)'s express provision that it prohibits fraud "*in connection with* the purchase or sale of any security."

Third, there are the peculiarities of what kinds of investors will be able to recover in this case. As I read the District Court's class certification order, there are potentially many persons who did not purchase Basic stock until *after* the first false statement (October 1977),

---

practice the Court must realize, as other courts applying the fraud-on-the-market theory have, that such rebuttal is virtually impossible in all but the most extraordinary case.

Consequently, while the Court considers it significant that the fraud-on-the-market presumption it endorses is a rebuttable one, the majority's implicit rejection of the "pure causation" fraud-on-the-market theory rings hollow. In most cases, the Court's theory will operate just as the causation theory would, creating a nonrebuttable presumption of "reliance" in future Rule 10b–5 actions.

but who nonetheless *will* be able to recover under the Court's fraud-on-the-market theory. Thus, it is possible that a person who heard the first corporate misstatement and *disbelieved* it—*i.e.,* someone who purchased Basic stock thinking that petitioners' statement was false—may still be included in the plaintiff-class on remand. How a person who undertook such a speculative stock-investing strategy—and made $10 a share doing so (if he bought on October 22, 1977, and sold on December 15, 1978)—can say that he was "defrauded" by virtue of his reliance on the "integrity" of the market price is beyond me.[10] And such speculators may not be uncommon, at least in this case.

Indeed, the facts of this case lead a casual observer to the almost inescapable conclusion that many of those who bought or sold Basic stock during the period in question flatly disbelieved the statements which are alleged to have been "materially misleading." Despite three statements denying that merger negotiations were underway, Basic stock hit record-high after record-high during the 14-month class period. It seems quite possible that, like Casca's knowing disbelief of Caesar's "thrice refusal" of the Crown,[11] clever investors were skeptical of petitioners' three denials that merger talks were going on. Yet such investors, the savviest of the savvy, will be able to recover under the Court's opinion, as long as they now claim that they believed in the "integrity of the market price" when they sold their stock (between September and December 1978). Thus, persons who bought after hearing and relying on the *falsity* of petitioners' statements may be able to prevail and recover money damages on remand.

And who will pay the judgments won in such actions? I suspect that all too often the majority's rule will "lead to large judgments, payable in the last analysis by innocent investors, for the benefit of speculators and their lawyers." Cf. *SEC v. Texas Gulf Sulphur Co.,* 401 F.2d 833, 867 (C.A.2 1968) (en banc) (Friendly, J., concurring), cert. denied, 394 U.S. 976 (1969). This Court and others have previously recognized that "inexorably broadening * * * the class of plaintiff[s] who may sue in this area of the law will ultimately result in more harm than good." *Blue Chip Stamps v. Manor Drug Stores, supra,* at 747–748. See also *Ultramares Corp. v. Touche,* 255 N.Y. 170, 179–180, 174 N.E. 441, 444–445 (1931) (Cardozo, C.J.). Yet such a bitter harvest is likely to be reaped from the seeds sewn by the Court's decision today. * * *

---

[10] The Court recognizes that a person who *sold* his Basic shares believing petitioners' statements to be false may not be entitled to recovery. Yet it seems just as clear to me that one who *bought* Basic stock under this same belief—hoping to profit from the uncertainty over Basic's merger plans—should not be permitted to recover either.

[11] See W. Shakespeare, Julius Caesar, Act I, Scene II.

NOTES

(1) Two preliminary aspects of this case should be noted. First, Justice Blackmun's opinion is a plurality opinion. Five of the nine sitting Justices did not sign this opinion, either by disqualification or dissent. Second, assuming that the various issues remanded by Justice Blackmun are resolved in favor of the plaintiffs, the defendants may be held liable for damages to all members of a class of plaintiffs who traded in Basic stock over a relatively long period. Depending on the number of members of the class and how damages are computed, the monetary liability of the defendants may be very substantial. May the defendants who are directors take advantage of Del.Gen.Corp.Law § 102(b)(7)? Two of the three false statements denying that merger negotiations were taking place were made by press releases. The third was made in a public statement by Max Muller, the President of Basic Incorporated, which appeared as a news item in the Cleveland Plain Dealer. No officer or director of Basic was accused of actually trading in Basic stock or otherwise personally benefiting from the violations. In both *Chiarella* and *Dirks*, discussed earlier in this Chapter, the Supreme Court went out of its way to emphasize that there must be a breach of a fiduciary duty in order for there to be a violation of Rule 10b–5. Where was the breach of fiduciary duty in *Basic*? For a discussion of this issue, see Jonathan Macey and Geoffrey Miller, Good Finance, Bad Economics: An Analysis of the Fraud on the Market Theory, 42 Stan. L. Rev. 1059 (1990).

(2) A controversial aspect of *Basic* is Justice White's stinging criticism of the "fraud on the market" thesis. For a strong defense of the "fraud on the market" thesis, see Daniel R. Fischel, Use of Modern Finance Theory in Securities Fraud Cases Involving Actively Traded Securities, 38 Bus.Law. 1 (1982). Professor Fischel is strongly identified with the "Chicago school" of law and economics. On the other hand, some post-*Basic* legal literature expresses serious reservations about the broad validity of the efficient capital market hypothesis and the desirability of the fraud on the market doctrine. See Donald C. Langevoort, Theories, Assumptions, and Securities Regulation: Market Efficiency Revisited, 140 U. Pa. L.Rev. 851, 853–54 (1992) ("In the 1980s, using more sophisticated data sets and computer technology, a number of economists began to question the accuracy of the tests that were thought to validate the efficiency model. * * * [T]he idea of strong capital market efficiency [is now] a legitimately debatable issue"); Carol Goforth, The Efficient Capital Market Hypothesis—An Inadequate Justification for the Fraud-on-the-Market Presumption, 27 Wake Forest L.Rev. 895, 897 (1992) ("While substantial empirical data supports certain aspects of the ECMH, much of the data is anomalous, and numerous aspects of the theory have not been researched adequately").

D. LIABILITY FOR SECURITIES FRAUD: STATUTORY REGULATION

As a result of the *Basic* decision, the number of class action lawsuits alleging securities fraud increased in the federal courts (though other factors, including the development of law firms specializing in plaintiff securities fraud litigation, undoubtedly also contributed to this increase). Much of this new-breed litigation was viewed as the product of entrepreneurial lawyers brought primarily for their own personal benefit. The result was the enactment of the Private Securities Litigation Reform Act of 1995, Pub.Law 104–67, 109 Stat. 737,[g] probably the most significant securities-related legislation since the original enactment of the classic statutes in the early 1930s. This Act is referred to as "PSLRA" or the "Reform Act" in the subsequent materials. Unanticipated consequences of PSLRA in turn led to enactment of the Securities Litigation Uniform Standards Act, Pub.L. 105–353, 112 Stat. 3227 (1998), referred to here as "SLUSA" or the "Standards Act."

RICHARD M. PHILLIPS AND GILBERT C. MILLER, THE PRIVATE SECURITIES LITIGATION REFORM ACT OF 1995: REBALANCING LITIGATION RISKS AND REWARDS FOR CLASS ACTION PLAINTIFFS, DEFENDANTS AND LAWYERS

51 Bus. Law. 1009, 1009–15 (1996).

The Reform Act came into being because sizeable bipartisan majorities of both houses of Congress became persuaded that the private securities litigation system was seriously out of balance. A properly balanced system would give appropriate weight to two competing interests: the interest in deterring securities fraud and remedying it when it occurs, and the interest in assuring that the litigation process is not used for abusive purposes and does not unfairly target defendants who are guilty of no wrongdoing.

The evidence presented in many months of congressional hearings strongly suggested that the second of these interests was not receiving adequate protection. The principal culprit was identified as the speculative securities class action lawsuit—a strike suit initiated not because plaintiffs or their class action lawyers had any persuasive evidence of fraudulent conduct on the part of the defendants but primarily as an *in terrorem* device for extracting settlements from the defendants irrespective of the merits of the underlying claims. * * * [U]nwarranted settlements could be extracted because plaintiffs and their counsel, at relatively little cost and risk to themselves, were able to

---

[g] Legislation dealing with securities fraud cases was part of the Republican "Contract with America." President Clinton vetoed this legislation but his veto was promptly overridden by Congress.

impose enormous discovery costs and the risks of astronomical damage awards on defendants.

* * *

Securities class action claims often are instituted after there has been a sudden, large decline in the price of a company's stock following a disappointing earnings announcement or other negative news about the company's operations. The typical fraud complaint alleges that the defendant company's public disclosures have been overly optimistic in light of negative information that management knew or was reckless in not knowing. Relying on the fraud-on-the-market theory that false or misleading public statements artificially inflate market prices, the suits allege that if the company had revealed the information sooner, the stock price would have been lower and all persons purchasing during the period that the negative news was not disclosed would have paid less. The claimed damages can be astronomical because millions of shares may have changed hands during the time the allegedly false information was influencing the price. Even if each share only loses a small amount of its value, the total loss for all affected shares can be immense.

* * * Because of the limited stakes that most investors have in * * * class action suits, however, they have tended to be sponsored and controlled not by aggrieved investors, but by a relatively small number of entrepreneurial law firms that specialize in this field. These firms typically do not have traditional client relationships with the named plaintiffs.[10] Prior to the Reform Act, these named plaintiffs often were called "professional plaintiffs," individuals who lent their names to the actions simply to accommodate plaintiffs' counsel and, in some cases, receive bonuses for their limited efforts. * * *

Because the lawyers who filed the first complaint often controlled the class litigation from the plaintiffs' side, there developed a "race to the courthouse" mentality that discouraged the plaintiffs' counsel from conducting reasonable factual investigations before initiating a class suit. Complaints frequently were filed within days or even hours of a stock price drop precipitated by an unexpected earnings decline or other negative news about the company's operations.[13] * * *

A high percentage of securities class action lawsuits have involved high-tech or other growth-oriented companies. * * * Such companies have

---

[10] One plaintiffs' class action lawyer rather famously observed: "I have the greatest practice * * * in the world. * * * I have no clients." William P. Barret, I have No Clients, Forbes, Oct. 11, 1993, at 32.

[13] Evidence adduced at the Senate hearings indicated that more than one in five actions was filed within 48 hours of negative news. * * * Melvyn Weiss, a noted securities litigator who frequently represents plaintiffs in securities class actions, provided information that, over a period three years, out of 229 Rule 10b–5 actions filed by his firm, 157 were filed within 10 days of a major adverse disclosure to the market by the defendant corporation.

been natural targets for class action securities suits because of the volatility of their stock prices. * * *

In the course of the Reform Act hearings, Congress became persuaded that speculative securities class action suits served to discredit the credibility of the private securities litigation system and operated to the general detriment of investors, corporations and the economy as a whole. * * *

Expert witnesses testified that the shareholders themselves, on whose behalves the suits ostensibly were instituted, were often indirect victims of class action litigation. Even if included within the class, shareholders generally recovered only a small fraction of their losses from the settlement process. Moreover, if they still held shares of the defendant companies, the value of their shares were diminished by the losses the companies suffered, directly and indirectly, as a consequence of the litigation. Congress came to understand that the only "winners" of these speculative lawsuits were the class action lawyers themselves whom Congress perceived to be richly rewarded, without commensurate risk, for their efforts at the expense of other participants in the system. * * *

Congress saw that speculative class action suits were able to thrive because talented and motivated class action lawyers were able to exploit the litigation system. Liberal notice pleading requirements under the Federal Rules made it relatively easy to frame fraud complaints with little if any supporting evidence. This was especially true in the case of forward-looking statements such as earnings projections that, by their very nature as prognostications, were prone to being erroneous. While Rule 9(b) of the Federal Rules requires fraud to be pled with particularity, it proved only partially successful in weeding out speculative class suits because many courts allowed the element of scienter to be pled generally, without any facts to support a charge that defendants knew or were reckless in not knowing that their statements were false or misleading. Moreover, many courts were generally reluctant to grant motions to dismiss unless complaints appeared frivolous on their face, in part, because Rule 12(b)(6) of the Federal Rules itself imposed rigorous standards for granting such motions and, in part, because the securities fraud allegations of the complaints normally turned on complex mixed issues of law and fact that were difficult to dispose of by pretrial motions.

Even before a court ruled on defendants' motions to dismiss, plaintiffs' counsel could begin blanketing defendants with discovery demands. Counsel knew, of course, that a major pressure point for defendants was the enormous costs and burdens that discovery entailed. Many courts, moreover, were unwilling to stay discovery even when a motion to dismiss was pending and the plaintiffs' case appeared weak. * * * Although courts had authority under Rule 11 of the Federal Rules [of Civil Procedure] to impose sanctions on counsel for instituting meritless class suits, they seldom did so, often to avoid creating additional contentious issues for resolution by an already overburdened federal judiciary.

From the perspective of plaintiffs' lawyers, there were no compelling reasons not to initiate speculative class action lawsuits. * * * The downside risks were small compared to the potential rewards because once the suits were filed, and motions to dismiss had been averted, settlements almost always could be achieved that compensated plaintiffs' lawyers handsomely quite irrespective of any lack of merit in the underlying claims.

By contrast, from the perspective of defendants, the legal terrain appeared much less hospitable. Defendant issuers realized that they could be exposed to huge damage claims regardless of the lack of evidence to support a complaint's allegations of fraud. * * *

Individual defendants in class action suits were particularly risk averse and prone to settle. For them, going to trial, even with a strong defense, ran the risk, however slight, of a personally ruinous damage award. This risk was greatly exacerbated by the rule of joint and several liability. * * * [A] defendant who had only peripheral responsibility for an allegedly fraudulent misstatement or omission, and who had no intent to commit a knowing fraud, could be forced to pay 100 percent of the class action damages. Insurance coverage available in settlements could be jeopardized if a defendant went to trial and lost on the merits. Moreover, the securities laws have been construed to prohibit defendants from enforcing indemnity contracts after an adjudication of fraud under Rule 10b–5. Thus, in order to preserve the ability to use insurance or indemnity agreements to defray all or part of their losses, individual defendants were strongly disposed to settle with no admission of liability rather than run any risk of losing at trial.

E. SALES OF CONTROL

DeBaun v. First Western Bank and Trust Co.

Court of Appeals of California, 1975.
120 Cal. Rptr. 354.

Thompson, Associate Justice.

This appeal primarily concerns the duty of a majority shareholder to the corporation whose shares he holds in selling the shares when possessed of facts establishing a reasonable likelihood that the purchaser intends to exercise the control to be acquired by him to loot the corporation of its assets. We conclude that in those circumstances the majority shareholder owes a duty of reasonable investigation and due care to the corporation.

Facts

Alfred S. Johnson Incorporated (Corporation) was incorporated by Alfred S. Johnson in 1955 to process color photographs to be reproduced in printed form. All of the 100 outstanding shares of Corporation were originally owned by Johnson. Subsequently, Johnson sold 20 of his shares to James DeBaun, Corporation's primary salesman, and 10 shares to Walter Stephens, its production manager. In November of 1964, Johnson was seriously ill so that managerial control of Corporation was assumed by DeBaun, Stephens, and Jack Hawkins, Corporation's estimator.

Johnson died testate on January 15, 1965. His will named appellant First Western Bank and Trust Company (Bank) as executor and trustee of a trust created by the will. The 70 shares of Corporation owned by Johnson at the time of his death passed to the testamentary trust. George Furman, an employee of Bank, was charged with the direct administration of the trust. While Bank took no hand in the management of Corporation leaving it to the existing management team, Furman attended virtually all directors' meetings. Bank, through its nominee, voted the 70 shares at stockholders' meetings.

Under the guidance of DeBaun and Stephens, the net after tax profit of Corporation increased dramatically as illustrated by the following table:

Fiscal year ending August 31	Net Profit
1964	$15,903
1965	$42,316
1966	$58,969
1967	$37,583
1968 (10 mos.)	$56,710

On October 27, 1966, Bank's trust department determined that the investment in Corporation was not appropriate for the trust and decided to sell the 70 shares. Bank also decided that no one connected with Corporation should be made aware of its decision to sell until a sale was firm. It caused an appraisal of Corporation to be made by General Appraisal Company which estimated the value of Corporation as a going concern at $326,000. Bank retained W.H. Daum Investment Company (Daum) to find a buyer and to assist it in the sale.

DeBaun and Stephens were not told of the Bank's plans. In March of 1968, a competitor of Corporation showed DeBaun a letter from Daum indicating that Corporation was for sale. Subsequently, both DeBaun and Stephens were contacted by two potential buyers who sought to purchase their shares. They refused to sell, agreeing to hold their shares because they had "* * * a good job * * * and percentage of the company * * *." At the request of Daum's representative, DeBaun submitted an offer for the 70 shares held by Bank. The offer was rejected as inadequate.

On May 15 and 20, 1968, Bank received successive offers for the 70 shares from Raymond J. Mattison, acting in the name of S.O.F. Fund, an inter vivos revocable trust of which he was both settlor and trustee. A sketchy balance sheet of S.O.F. Fund was submitted with the second offer. The offers were rejected. Anticipating a further offer from Mattison and his trust, Furman, acting for Bank, ordered a Dun & Bradstreet report on Mattison and the fund. The report was received on May 24, 1968. It noted pending litigation, bankruptcies, and tax liens against corporate entities in which Mattison had been a principal, and suggested that S.O.F. Fund no longer existed.

As of May 24, I. Earl Funk, a vice-president of Bank, had personal knowledge that: (1) on October 24, 1957, the Los Angeles Superior Court had entered a judgment against Mattison in favor of Bank's predecessor in interest for compensatory and punitive damages as the result of Mattison's fraudulent misrepresentations and a fraudulent financial statement to obtain a loan; and (2) the judgment remained unsatisfied in 1968 and was an asset of Bank acquired from its predecessor in an acquisition of 65 branch banks.

On May 27, 1968, Mattison submitted a third offer to purchase the 70 shares of Corporation held by Bank. The offer proposed that S.O.F. Fund would pay $250,000 for the shares, $50,000 in marketable securities as a down payment with the balance payable over a five-year period. Bank made a counter offer, generally accepting the terms of the Mattison proposal but providing that: (1) the $200,000 balance of the purchase price was to be secured by a pledge of marketable securities valued at a like amount; and (2) Corporation would pay no dividends out of "pre-sale" retained earnings. On June 4, 1968, representatives of Bank met with Oroville McCarrol, who had been a trust officer of Bank's predecessor in interest and was counsel for Mattison. McCarrol proposed that Corporation use its assets to secure the unpaid balance of the purchase price rather than Mattison supplying the security in the form of marketable securities. He proposed also the elimination of the restriction against dividends from pre-sale retained earnings. Despite reservations by Bank personnel on the legality of the use of corporate assets to secure an obligation of a major shareholder, Bank determined to pursue the McCarrol modification further. Troubled by the Dun & Bradstreet report, personnel of Bank met with Mattison and McCarrol on June 27. Mattison explained that it had been his practice to take over failing companies so that the existence of the litigation and tax liens noted in the Dun & Bradstreet report was not due to his fault. Not entirely satisfied, Furman wrote to McCarrol requesting a written report on the status of all pending litigation in which Mattison was involved. McCarrol telephoned his response, declining to represent the status of the litigation but noting that the information was publicly available. Partly because Ralph Whitsett, Furman's immediate superior at Bank, knew McCarrol as a former trust officer of Bank's predecessor in interest, and partly because during a luncheon with Mattison at the Jonathan Club Robert Q. Parsons, the officer at Daum in charge of the transaction, had noted that Mattison was warmly received by his fellow members and reported that fact to Furman, Bank did not pursue its investigation into the public records of Los Angeles County where a mass of derogatory information lay.

As of July 1, 1968, the public records of Los Angeles County revealed 38 unsatisfied judgments against Mattison or his entities totalling $330,886.27, and 54 pending actions claiming a total of $373,588.67 from them. The record also contained 22 recorded abstracts of judgments against Mattison or his entities totalling $285,704.11, and 18 tax liens aggregating $20,327.97. Bank did not investigate the public record and hence was unaware of Mattison's financial track record.

While failing to pursue the investigation of the known information adverse to Mattison, Bank's employees knew or should have known that if his proposal through McCarrol were accepted the payment of the $200,000 balance of the purchase price would necessarily come from Corporation. They assumed that the payments would be made by Mattison from distributions of the Corporation which he would cause it to make after assuming control. They were aware that Corporation would not generate a sufficient aftertax cash flow to pay dividends in a sufficient amount to permit the payments of interest and principal on the $200,000 balance as scheduled in the McCarrol proposal, and knew that Mattison could make those payments only by resorting to distribution of "pre-sale" retained earnings and assets of Corporation.

On July 11, 1968, Bank accepted the McCarrol modification by entering into an exchange agreement with S.O.F. Fund. The agreement obligated S.O.F. to retain a working capital of not less than $70,000, to refrain from intercompany transactions except in the ordinary course of business for adequate consideration, and to furnish monthly financial statements and a certified annual audit report to Bank. It provides that Bank is to transfer its 70 shares of Corporation to Mattison as trustee of S.O.F. Fund, and that the stock will be held by Bank in pledge to secure the fund's obligation. There is provision for acceleration of the unpaid balance of the purchase price if Mattison defaults in any provision of the agreement. The contract obligated Mattison to cause Corporation to execute a security agreement to secure Mattison's obligation to Bank covering all "furniture, fixtures and equipment of [Corporation]."

Mattison agreed also to cause Corporation's principal banking business to be maintained with Bank.

The exchange agreement having been executed, Bank gave Mattison a proxy to vote the 70 shares of Corporation at a special meeting of shareholders of Corporation to be held on July 11 at 3 p.m. Furman attended that meeting and an ensuing directors' meeting, as did Mattison. At the shareholders' meeting, DeBaun and Stephens were told that the shares of Corporation owned by Bank had been sold by it on an installment basis to Mattison and that Bank intended to take a pledge of those shares. A new board of directors was elected of which Mattison had control although DeBaun and Stephens remained as directors. DeBaun and Stephens were informed by Furman that a security agreement had been signed to protect Corporation in the event of death or default of Mattison and that in such an event Bank would "foreclose on the stock." Furman did not supply DeBaun or Stephens with a copy of the security agreement or inform them that in fact [it] hypothecated corporate assets as security for Mattison's debt to Bank. Relying upon Furman's statement of the effect of the agreement and misled by his failure to disclose its material terms, and by the further representation that the document was simply a formal requirement of Mattison's purchase of the majority shares, DeBaun and Stephens participated in a unanimous vote approving the execution by Corporation of the security agreement. A directors' meeting was then convened at which Mattison was elected president of Corporation.

At the moment of Bank's sale of the controlling shares to Mattison, Corporation was an eminently successful going business with a bright future. It had cash of $76,126.15 and other liquid assets of over $122,000. Its remaining assets were worth $60,000. Its excess of current assets over current liabilities and reserve for bad debts was $233,391.94, and its net worth about $220,000. Corporation's earnings indicated a pattern of growth. Mattison immediately proceeded to change that situation. Beginning with the date that he acquired control, Mattison implemented a systematic scheme to loot Corporation of its assets. His first step was to divert $73,144 in corporate cash to himself and to MICO, a shell company owned by Mattison. The transfer was made in exchange for unsecured noninterest bearing notes but for no other consideration. On August 2, 1968, Mattison caused Corporation to assign to MICO all of Corporation's assets, including its receivables in exchange for a fictitious agreement for management services. He diverted all corporate mail to a post office box from which he took the mail, opened it, and extracted all incoming checks to the corporation before forwarding the mail on. He ceased paying trade creditors promptly, as had been Corporation's practice, delaying payment of trade creditors to the last possible moment and, to the extent he could, not paying some at all. He delayed shipments on new orders. To cover his activities, Mattison removed the corporate books and records.

In September 1968, DeBaun left Corporation's employ as a salesman because of Mattison's policy of not filling orders and because Mattison had drastically reduced DeBaun's compensation. * * * Mattison continued to loot the corporation, although at a reduced pace by reason of its depleted assets. He collected payments from employees to pay premiums on a voluntary health insurance plan although the policy covering the plan was terminated in September for failure to pay premiums. He issued payroll checks without sufficient funds and continued not to pay trade creditors. Mattison did not supply Bank with the financial reports required by the exchange agreement.

While Bank was not aware of the initial transfer of cash to MICO, it did learn of the other misconduct of Mattison as it occurred. Although the conduct was a breach of the exchange agreement, Bank took no action beyond seeking an oral explanation from Mattison. In December 1968, Stephens also left Corporation's employ.

Bank took no action in the matter until April 25, 1969. On that date, it filed an action in the superior court seeking the appointment of a receiver. On April 30, Bank called a special shareholders' meeting of Corporation at which it voted its shares with those of DeBaun and Stephens to elect a new board of directors replacing the Mattison group. Faced with resistance from Mattison, Bank pursued neither its receivership nor its ouster of the board until June 20, 1969, when it shut down the operations of Corporation. By that time, Corporation was hopelessly insolvent. Its debts exceeded its assets by over $200,000, excluding its contingent liability to Bank, as a result of the fraudulently obtained hypothecation of corporate assets to secure Mattison's debt. Both the federal Internal Revenue Service and California State Board of Equalization had filed liens upon corporate assets and notices to withhold funds. A trade creditor had placed a keeper on the corporate premises.

On July 10, 1969, Bank, pursuant to the security agreement, sold all of Corporation's then remaining assets for $60,000. $25,000 of the proceeds of sale was paid to release the federal tax lien while the remaining $35,000 was retained by Bank. After the sale, Corporation had no assets and owed $218,426 to creditors.

Respondents filed two related actions against Bank. One asserted their right to recover, as shareholders, for damage caused by Bank. The other was a stockholders' [derivative] action brought on behalf of Corporation * * *. The two cases were consolidated. Bank demurred to both complaints. In the demurrer to the first action, it contended that respondents DeBaun and Stephens, as shareholders, lacked capacity to pursue their claim. In the demurrer to the second complaint, Bank took the opposite tack, contending that its liability did not run to Corporation. The demurrer to the first complaint was sustained without leave to amend, and the demurrer to the second complaint was overruled. The case at bench proceeded to trial before a judge as a [derivative] action. The trial court held for respondents, finding that Bank had breached duties it owed as a majority controlling shareholder to the corporation it controlled. It assessed monetary damages in the amount of $473,836, computed by adding to $220,000, the net asset value of the corporation at the date of transfer of the shares to Mattison, an amount equal to anticipated after-tax earnings of the corporation for the ensuing 10-year period, taking into account an 8 percent growth factor. The court additionally awarded Corporation an amount equal to the sum it would be required to pay and the cost of defending valid claims existing against it when it became defunct. Pursuant to Fletcher v. A.J. Industries, Inc., 266 Cal.App.2d 313, 320–321, the trial court awarded counsel for respondents attorneys' fees payable from the fund recovered for Corporation's benefit. It denied respondents' claim for punitive damages. This appeal from the resulting judgment followed. * * *

Breach of Duty

Early case law held that a controlling shareholder owed no duty to minority shareholders or to the controlled corporation in the sale of his stock. Decisional law, however, has since recognized the fact of financial life that corporate control by ownership of a majority of shares may be misused. Thus the applicable proposition now is that "[i]n any transaction where the control of the corporation is material," the controlling majority shareholder must exercise good faith and fairness "from the viewpoint of the corporation and those interested therein." (Remillard Brick Co. v. Remillard-Dandini, 241 P.2d 66, 75 quoted in Jones v. H.F. Ahmanson & Co., 460 P.2d 464, 472.) That duty of good faith and fairness encompasses an obligation of the controlling shareholder in possession of facts "[s]uch as to awaken suspicion and put a prudent man on his guard (that a potential buyer of his shares may loot the corporation of its assets to pay for the shares purchased) * * * to conduct a reasonable adequate investigation (of the buyer)." (Insuranshares Corporation v. Northern Fiscal Corp., 35 F.Supp. 22, 25 (E.D.Pa.1940)).

Here Bank was the controlling majority shareholder of Corporation. As it was negotiating with Mattison, it became directly aware of facts that would have alerted a prudent person that Mattison was likely to loot the corporation. Bank knew from the Dun & Bradstreet report that Mattison's financial record was notable by the failure of entities controlled by him. Bank knew that the only source of funds available to Mattison to pay it for the shares he was purchasing lay in the assets of the Corporation. The after-tax net income from the date of the sale would not be sufficient to permit the payment of dividends to him which would permit the making of payments. An officer of Bank possessed personal knowledge that Mattison, on at least one occasion, had been guilty of a fraud perpetrated on Bank's predecessor in interest and had not satisfied a judgment Bank held against him for damages flowing from that conduct.

Armed with knowledge of those facts, Bank owed a duty to Corporation and its minority shareholders to act reasonably with respect to its dealings in the controlling shares with Mattison. It breached that duty. Knowing of McCarrol's refusal to express an opinion on litigation against Mattison and his entities, and that the information could be obtained from the public records, Bank closed its eyes to that obvious source. Rather, it relied upon Mattison's friendly reception by fellow members of the Jonathan Club and the fact that he was represented by a lawyer who had been a trust officer of Bank's predecessor in interest to conclude that indicators that Mattison was a financial bandit should be ignored. Membership in a club, whether it be the Jonathan or the informal group of ex-trust officers of Bank, does not excuse investigation. Nor can Bank be justified in accepting Mattison's uncorroborated statement that the past financial disasters of his entities reported by Dun & Bradstreet were due to his practice of acquiring failing companies. Only one who loots a failed company at the expense of its creditors can profit from its acquisition. Mattison's constantly repeated entry into the transactions without ever pulling a company from the morass was a strong indication that he was milking the companies profitably. Had Bank investigated, as any prudent man would have done, it would have discovered from the public records the additional detail of Mattison's long, long trail of financial failure that would have precluded its dealings with him except under circumstances where his obligation was secured beyond question and his ability to loot Corporation precluded. * * *

Measure of Damages

Appellant contends finally that the trial court improperly multiplied the measure of damages by adding to net asset value on the date of Bank's tortious conduct an estimate for future net profit and an obligation that Bank discharge the valid existing obligations of Corporation. The record refutes the contention.

The trial judge arrived at a value of the corporation as a going concern at the time of appellant's breach by adding to the value of Corporation's tangible assets a goodwill factor computed on the basis of future net income reasonably to be anticipated from the Corporation's past record. This the trial court was authorized to do in determining "the amount which will compensate for all the detriment proximately caused * * *" by appellant's breach of duty. Appellant's breach damaged Corporation not only in the loss of its assets but also in the loss of its earning power. Since the trial court's determination of loss of earning power was based upon a past record of earnings and not speculation, it is supported by substantial evidence. The trial court's order requiring appellant to pay all valid claims of creditors against Corporation is also proper as necessary to restore Corporation to the condition in which it existed prior to the time that Bank contributed to its destruction. Prior to Bank's action, Corporation was a going concern with substantial net assets. As a proximate result of Bank's dereliction of duty, Corporation acquired a negative net worth of about $218,000. Total damage to Corporation is thus the sum necessary to restore the negative net worth, plus the value of its tangible assets, plus its going business value determined with reference to its future profits reasonably estimated. That is the measure which the trial court applied. Since the derivative action is equitable in nature, the court properly framed part of its judgment in terms of an obligation dependent upon future contingencies rather than at a fixed dollar amount.

Disposition

The judgment is affirmed. The matter is, however, remanded to the trial court with directions to hold a hearing to determine the additional amount payable to respondents from the fund recovered by them for benefit of Corporation for counsel fees due for services on this appeal.

NOTES

(1) The American Law Institute, Principles of Corporate Governance: Analysis and Recommendations § 5.16, provides:

> A controlling shareholder has the same right to dispose of voting equity securities as any other shareholder, including the right to dispose of those securities for a price that is not made proportionally available to other shareholders, but the controlling shareholder does not satisfy the duty of fair dealing to the other shareholders if:
>
> (a) The controlling shareholder does not make disclosure concerning the transaction to other shareholders with whom the controlling shareholder deals in connection with the transaction; or
>
> (b) It is apparent from the circumstances that the purchaser is likely to violate the duty of fair dealing * * * in such a way as to obtain a significant financial benefit for the purchaser or an associate.

Would "it [be] apparent" to First Western Bank that Mattison was likely to loot the corporation? Isn't the ALI test too lax? The comment discusses the language of § 5.16(b) further:

> * * * Affirmative investigation by the controlling shareholder is not required in the absence of facts that would alert a reasonable person to the need for further inquiry. What is necessary to trigger that inquiry, however, must be determined in the context of the transaction. The mere fact that the controlling shareholder receives a substantial premium for its shares, or that the purchaser has a general reputation for aggressive acquisitions, is not itself sufficient

to trigger such an inquiry. What is required are facts sufficient to put the controlling shareholder on notice that it would be imprudent to proceed with the transaction without making further inquiry as to the purchaser and its motives for acquiring control of the corporation.

Does the comment set forth a stricter test than § 5.16(b)?

(2) The leading decision in Delaware as to liability for sale to a looter is Harris v. Carter, 582 A.2d 222, 235 (Del.Ch.1990):

> Thus, I conclude that while a person who transfers corporate control to another is surely not a surety for his buyer, when the circumstances would alert a reasonably prudent person to a risk that his buyer is dishonest or in some material respect not truthful, a duty devolves upon the seller to make such inquiry as a reasonably prudent person would make, and generally to exercise care so that others who will be affected by his actions should not be injured by wrongful conduct.

(3) Many cases involve a purchase price that seems unreasonably high given the business being purchased. Should the manifest willingness of an unknown purchaser to pay an unreasonably high price be a suspicious circumstance? Some courts have refused to draw an adverse inference even though the premium seems extreme. In Clagett v. Hutchison, 583 F.2d 1259 (4th Cir.1978), for example, the majority shareholder was offered $43.75 per share at a time when the price in a "thinly traded * * * public market" varied between $7.50 and $10.00 per share; the Court held that this price "cannot be said to be so unreasonable as to place [the seller] on notice of the likelihood of fraud on the corporation or the remaining stockholders." 583 F.2d at 1262. One judge dissented.

(4) Frank H. Easterbrook & Daniel R. Fischel, The Economic Structure of Corporate Law 126, 129–31 (1991):

> Sales of controlling blocs of shares provide a good example of transactions in which the movement of control is beneficial. The sale of control may lead to new offers, new plans, and new working arrangements with other firms that reduce agency costs and create gains from new business relationships. The premium price received by the seller of the control bloc amounts to an unequal distribution of the gains. Sales at a premium are lawful, and the controlling shareholder generally has no duty to spread the bounty. * * *

> A specter of "looting" haunts opinions about corporate control transactions. * * * Certainly the sellers of control can detect knavery at a lower cost than the public shareholders who are not parties to the transaction. Yet it is difficult if not impossible to detect looters early on. Looting is by nature a one-time transaction. Once looters have plundered one firm, their reputation (or their residence in jail) prevents them from doing so again. But when they first obtain control, they may appear innocuous. Any rule that

blocks sales in advance is equivalent to a program of preventive detention for people who have never robbed banks but have acquisitive personalities.

Although sellers could spend substantial sums investigating buyers and investors and still more in litigating over the quality of investigation, almost all of these efforts would be wasted. If investigations blocked transfers, most of these refusals would be false positives. That is, they would be refusals that reduced the gains available from transferring control. * * *

We do not suggest that the legal system should disregard looting, but the best remedies are based on deterrence rather than prior scrutiny. Looters, when caught, may be fined or imprisoned. Penalties could be made high enough to be effective, making the transaction unprofitable *ex ante*. The costs of deterrence are less than the costs of dealing with looting through a system of prior scrutiny that would scotch many valuable control shifts as a by-product.

(5) Robert W. Hamilton, Private Sale of Control Transactions: Where We Stand Today, 36 Case W.Res.L.Rev. 248, 267–68 (1985):

It is possible that Easterbrook and Fischel are correct when they infer that the costs of an *ex ante* requirement exceed its benefits, but I doubt it. In the first place, in my personal experience, it is not true that looters abscond and only first-time looters ply their trade. Rather, persons on the fringe of the law often quietly merge into the general economy and surface from time to time, hoping that their background is not discovered, and if it is, quietly disappear again. As a result, routine and inexpensive credit checks on persons offering to buy asset-rich companies often turn up substantially negative factors. * * *

Second, while it is possible that the *ex ante* investigation would turn up some "false positives," I do not see why this should be so. What is supposed to be investigated is not whether the purchaser has dismantled companies in the past, but whether he has a reputation for honesty and the apparent wherewithal to finance a transaction of the magnitude under consideration without recourse to the corporation's assets in a way that defrauds creditors and minority shareholders. If a person does not meet this standard, one wonders whether he is really a "false positive."

Finally, the *ex post* deterrence proposed by Easterbrook and Fischel in the form of criminal sanctions is not very attractive. Even if it is assumed that punishment for this type of conduct will be quick and sure—hardly characteristics of current criminal sanctions against white-collar crime—the result is that the innocent shareholders and others "left behind" will usually suffer the entire economic loss, while the majority shareholders who sold to the thieves may keep the entire purchase price, premium and all. The thieves, of course, go to jail. This result seems so obviously unjust from the standpoint of the minority shareholders that it seems unreasonable to embrace it on the basis of entirely theoretical considerations of economic "efficiency."

PERLMAN V. FELDMANN

United States Court of Appeals, Second Circuit, 1955.
219 F.2d 173.

CLARK, CHIEF JUDGE.

This is a derivative action brought by minority stockholders of Newport Steel Corporation to compel accounting for, and restitution of, allegedly illegal gains which accrued to defendants as a result of the sale in August, 1950, of their controlling interest in the corporation. The principal defendant, C. Russell Feldmann, who represented and acted for the others, members of his family,[1] was at that time not only the dominant stockholder, but also the chairman of the board of directors and the president of the corporation. Newport, an Indiana corporation, operated mills for the production of steel sheets for sale to manufacturers of steel products, first at Newport, Kentucky, and later also at other places in Kentucky and Ohio. The buyers, a syndicate organized as Wilport Company, a Delaware corporation, consisted of end-users of steel who were interested in securing a source of supply in a market becoming ever tighter in the Korean War. Plaintiffs contend that the consideration paid for the stock included compensation for the sale of a corporate asset, a power held in trust for the corporation by Feldmann as its fiduciary. This power was the ability to control the allocation of the corporate product in a time of short supply, through control of the board of directors; and it was effectively transferred in this sale by having Feldmann procure the resignation of his own board and the election of Wilport's nominees immediately upon consummation of the sale.

The present action represents the consolidation of three pending stockholders' actions in which yet another stockholder has been permitted to intervene. Jurisdiction below was based upon the diverse citizenship of the parties. Plaintiffs argue here, as they did in the court below, that in the situation here disclosed the vendors must account to the nonparticipating minority stockholders for that share of their profit which is attributable to the sale of the corporate power. Judge Hincks denied the validity of the premise, holding that the rights involved in the sale were only those normally incident to the possession of a controlling block of

---

[1] The stock was not held personally by Feldmann in his own name, but was held by the members of his family and by personal corporations. The aggregate of stock thus held amounted to 33% of the outstanding Newport stock and gave working control to the holder. The actual sale included 55,552 additional shares held by friends and associates of Feldmann, so that a total of 37% of the Newport stock was transferred.

shares, with which a dominant stockholder, in the absence of fraud or foreseeable looting, was entitled to deal according to his own best interests. Furthermore, he held that plaintiffs had failed to satisfy their burden of proving that the sales price was not a fair price for the stock per se. Plaintiffs appeal from these rulings of law which resulted in the dismissal of their complaint.

The essential facts found by the trial judge are not in dispute. Newport was a relative newcomer in the steel industry with predominantly old installations which were in the process of being supplemented by more modern facilities. Except in times of extreme shortage Newport was not in a position to compete profitably with other steel mills for customers not in its immediate geographical area. Wilport, the purchasing syndicate, consisted of geographically remote end-users of steel who were interested in buying more steel from Newport than they had been able to obtain during recent periods of tight supply. The price of $20 per share was found by Judge Hincks to be a fair one for a control block of stock, although the over-the-counter market price had not exceeded $12 and the book value per share was $17.03. But this finding was limited by Judge Hincks' statement that "[w]hat value the block would have had if shorn of its appurtenant power to control distribution of the corporate product, the evidence does not show." It was also conditioned by his earlier ruling that the burden was on plaintiffs to prove a lesser value for the stock.

Both as director and as dominant stockholder, Feldmann stood in a fiduciary relationship to the corporation and to the minority stockholders as beneficiaries thereof. Pepper v. Litton, 308 U.S. 295. His fiduciary obligation must in the first instance be measured by the law of Indiana, the state of incorporation of Newport. Although there is no Indiana case directly in point, the most closely analogous one emphasizes the close scrutiny to which Indiana subjects the conduct of fiduciaries when personal benefit may stand in the way of fulfillment of trust obligations. In Schemmel v. Hill, 169 N.E. 678, 682, 683, McMahan, J., said: "Directors of a business corporation act in a strictly fiduciary capacity. Their office is a trust. When a director deals with his corporation, his acts will be closely scrutinized. Directors of a corporation are its agents, and they are governed by the rules of law applicable to other agents, and, as between themselves and their principal, the rules relating to honesty and fair dealing in the management of the affairs of their principal are applicable. They must not, in any degree, allow their official conduct to be swayed by their private interest, which must yield to official duty. In a transaction between a director and his corporation, where he acts for himself and his principal at the same time in a matter connected with the relation between them, it is presumed, where he is thus potential on both sides of the contract, that self-interest will overcome his fidelity to his principal, to his own benefit and to his principal's hurt." And the judge added: "Absolute and most scrupulous good faith is the very essence of a director's obligation to his corporation. The first principal duty arising from his official relation is to act in all things of trust wholly for the benefit of his corporation."

In Indiana, then, as elsewhere, the responsibility of the fiduciary is not limited to a proper regard for the tangible balance sheet assets of the corporation, but includes the dedication of his uncorrupted business judgment for the sole benefit of the corporation, in any dealings which may adversely affect it. Irving Trust Co. v. Deutsch, 2 Cir., 73 F.2d 121; Meinhard v. Salmon, 164 N.E. 545. Although the Indiana case is particularly relevant to Feldmann as a director, the same rule should apply to his fiduciary duties as majority stockholder, for in that capacity he chooses and controls the directors, and thus is held to have assumed their liability. Pepper v. Litton, supra, 308 U.S. 295. This, therefore, is the standard to which Feldmann was by law required to conform in his activities here under scrutiny.

It is true, as defendants have been at pains to point out, that this is not the ordinary case of breach of fiduciary duty. We have here no fraud, no misuse of confidential information, no outright looting of a helpless corporation. But on the other hand, we do not find compliance with that high standard which we have just stated and which we and other courts have come to expect and demand of corporate fiduciaries. In the often-quoted words of Judge Cardozo: [The Court quotes the classic language from Meinhard v. Salmon.][h] The actions of defendants in siphoning off for personal gain corporate advantages to be derived from a favorable market situation do not betoken the necessary undivided loyalty owed by the fiduciary to his principal.

The corporate opportunities of whose misappropriation the minority stockholders complain need not have been an absolute certainty in order to support this action against Feldmann. If there was possibility of corporate gain, they are entitled to recover. * * *

This rationale is equally appropriate to a consideration of the benefits which Newport might have derived from the steel shortage. In the past Newport had used and profited by its market leverage by operation of what the industry had come to call the "Feldmann Plan." This consisted of securing interest-free advances from prospective purchasers of steel in return for firm commitments to them from future production. The funds thus acquired were used to finance improvements in existing plants and to acquire new installations. In the summer of 1950 Newport had been negotiating for cold-rolling facilities which it needed for a more fully integrated operation and a more marketable product, and Feldmann plan funds might well have been used toward this end.

---

[h] See Chapter 3, Section E (discussing *Meinhard*).

Further, as plaintiffs alternatively suggest, Newport might have used the period of short supply to build up patronage in the geographical area in which it could compete profitably even when steel was more abundant. Either of these opportunities was Newport's, to be used to its advantage only. Only if defendants had been able to negate completely any possibility of gain by Newport could they have prevailed. It is true that a trial court finding states: "Whether or not, in August, 1950, Newport's position was such that it could have entered into 'Feldmann Plan' type transactions to procure funds and financing for the further expansion and integration of its steel facilities and whether such expansion would have been desirable for Newport, the evidence does not show." This, however, cannot avail the defendants, who—contrary to the ruling below—had the burden of proof on this issue, since fiduciaries always have the burden of proof in establishing the fairness of their dealings with trust property. Pepper v. Litton, supra.

Defendants seek to categorize the corporate opportunities which might have accrued to Newport as too unethical to warrant further consideration. It is true that reputable steel producers were not participating in the gray market brought about by the Korean War and were refraining from advancing their prices, although to do so would not have been illegal. But Feldmann plan transactions were not considered within this self-imposed interdiction; the trial court found that around the time of the Feldmann sale Jones & Laughlin Steel Corporation, Republic Steel Company, and Pittsburgh Steel Corporation were all participating in such arrangements. In any event, it ill becomes the defendants to disparage as unethical the market advantages from which they themselves reaped rich benefits.

We do not mean to suggest that a majority stockholder cannot dispose of his controlling block of stock to outsiders without having to account to his corporation for profits or even never do this with impunity when the buyer is an interested customer, actual or potential, for the corporation's product. But when the sale necessarily results in a sacrifice of this element of corporate good will and consequent unusual profit to the fiduciary who has caused the sacrifice, he should account for his gains. So in a time of market shortage, where a call on a corporation's product commands an unusually large premium, in one form or another, we think it sound law that a fiduciary may not appropriate to himself the value of this premium. Such personal gain at the expense of his coventurers seems particularly reprehensible when made by the trusted president and director of his company. In this case the violation of duty seems to be all the clearer because of this triple role in which Feldmann appears, though we are unwilling to say, and are not to be understood as saying, that we should accept a lesser obligation for any one of his roles alone.

Hence to the extent that the price received by Feldmann and his codefendants included such a bonus, he is accountable to the minority stockholders who sue here. And plaintiffs, as they contend, are entitled to a recovery in their own right, instead of in right of the corporation (as in the usual derivative actions), since neither Wilport nor their successors in interest should share in any judgment which may be rendered. See Southern Pacific Co. v. Bogert, 250 U.S. 483. Defendants cannot well object to this form of recovery, since the only alternative, recovery for the corporation as a whole, would subject them to a greater total liability.

The case will therefore be remanded to the district court for a determination of the question expressly left open below, namely, the value of defendants' stock without the appurtenant control over the corporation's output of steel. We reiterate that on this issue, as on all others relating to a breach of fiduciary duty, the burden of proof must rest on the defendants. Judgment should go to these plaintiffs and those whom they represent for any premium value so shown to the extent of their respective stock interests.

The judgment is therefore reversed and the action remanded for further proceedings pursuant to this opinion.

SWAN, CIRCUIT JUDGE (dissenting).

With the general principles enunciated in the majority opinion as to the duties of fiduciaries I am, of course, in thorough accord. But, as Mr. Justice Frankfurter stated in Securities and Exchange Comm. v. Chenery Corp., 318 U.S. 80, 85, "to say that a man is a fiduciary only begins analysis; it gives direction to further inquiry. To whom is he a fiduciary? What obligations does he owe as a fiduciary? In what respect has he failed to discharge these obligations?" My brothers' opinion does not specify precisely what fiduciary duty Feldmann is held to have violated or whether it was a duty imposed upon him as the dominant stockholder or as a director of Newport. Without such specification I think that both the legal profession and the business world will find the decision confusing and will be unable to foretell the extent of its impact upon customary practices in the sale of stock.

The power to control the management of a corporation, that is, to elect directors to manage its affairs, is an inseparable incident to the ownership of a majority of its stock, or sometimes, as in the present instance, to the ownership of enough shares, less than a majority, to control an election. Concededly a majority or dominant shareholder is ordinarily privileged to sell his stock at the best price obtainable from the purchaser. In so doing he acts on his own behalf, not as an agent of the corporation. If he knows or has reason to believe that the purchaser intends to exercise to the detriment of the corporation the power of management acquired by the purchase, such knowledge or reasonable suspicion will terminate the dominant shareholder's privilege to sell and will create a duty not to transfer the power of management to such purchaser. The duty seems to me to resemble the obligation which everyone is under not to assist another to commit a tort rather than the obligation of a fiduciary. But whatever the nature of the duty, a violation of it will subject the violator to liability for damages sustained by the corporation. Judge Hincks found that Feldmann had no reason to think that Wilport would use the power of management it would acquire by the purchase to injure Newport, and that there was no proof that it ever was so used. Feldmann did know, it is true, that the reason Wilport wanted the stock was to put in a board of directors who would be likely to permit Wilport's members to purchase more of Newport's steel than they might otherwise be able to get. But there is nothing illegal in a dominant shareholder purchasing from his own corporation at the same prices it offers to other customers. That is what the members of Wilport did, and there is no proof that Newport suffered any detriment therefrom.

My brothers say that "the consideration paid for the stock included compensation for the sale of a corporate asset," which they describe as "the ability to control the allocation of the corporate product in a time of short supply, through control of the board of directors; and it was effectively transferred in this sale by having Feldmann procure the resignation of his own board and the election of Wilport's nominees immediately upon consummation of the sale." The implications of this are not clear to me. If it means that when market conditions are such as to induce users of a corporation's product to wish to buy a controlling block of stock in order to be able to purchase part of the corporation's output at the same mill list prices as are offered to other customers, the dominant stockholder is under a fiduciary duty not to sell his stock, I cannot agree. For reasons already stated, in my opinion Feldmann was not proved to be under any fiduciary duty as a stockholder not to sell the stock he controlled.

Feldmann was also a director of Newport. Perhaps the quoted statement means that as a director he violated his fiduciary duty in voting to elect Wilport's nominees to fill the vacancies created by the resignations of the former directors of Newport. As a director Feldmann was under a fiduciary duty to use an honest judgment in acting on the corporation's behalf. A director is privileged to resign, but so long as he remains a director he must be faithful to his fiduciary duties and must not make a personal gain from performing them. Consequently, if the price paid for Feldmann's stock included a payment for voting to elect the new directors, he must account to the corporation for such payment, even though he honestly believed that the men he voted to elect were well qualified to serve as directors. He can not take pay for performing his fiduciary duty. There is no suggestion that he did do so, unless the price paid for his stock was more than its value. So it seems to me that decision must turn on whether finding 120 and conclusion 5 of the district judge are supportable on the evidence. They are set out in the margin.[1]

Judge Hincks went into the matter of valuation of the stock with his customary care and thoroughness. He made no error of law in applying the principles relating to valuation of stock. Concededly a controlling block of stock has greater sale value than a small lot. While the spread between $10 per share for small lots and $20 per share for the controlling block seems rather extraordinarily wide, the $20 valuation was supported by the expert testimony of Dr. Badger, whom the district judge said he could not find to be wrong. I see no justification for upsetting the valuation as clearly erroneous. Nor can I agree with my brothers that the $20 valuation "was limited" by the last sentence in finding 120. The controlling block could not by any possibility be shorn of its appurtenant power to elect directors and through them to control distribution of the corporate product. It is this "appurtenant power" which gives a controlling block its value as such block. What evidence could be adduced to show the value of the block "if shorn" of such appurtenant power, I cannot conceive, for it cannot be shorn of it. * * *

The final conclusion of my brothers is that the plaintiffs are entitled to recover in their own right instead of in the right of the corporation. This appears to be completely inconsistent with the theory advanced at the outset of the opinion, namely, that the price of the stock "included compensation for the sale of a corporate asset." If a corporate asset was sold, surely the corporation should recover the compensation received for it by the defendants. Moreover, if the plaintiffs were suing in their own right, Newport was not a proper party. The case of Southern Pacific Co. v. Bogert, 250 U.S. 483, relied upon as authority for the conclusion that the plaintiffs are entitled to recover in their own right, relates to a situation so different that the decision appears to me to be inapposite.

I would affirm the judgment on appeal.

NOTES

(1) On remand, Judge Hincks took a deep breath and concluded that the "enterprise value" of a share of Newport stock was $14.67, so that Feldmann had received a premium of $5.33 per share, or a total premium of $2,126,280. The plaintiffs, representing sixty-three percent of the stock, were therefore entitled to a judgment of $1,339,769, plus interest. Perlman v. Feldmann, 154 F.Supp. 436 (D.Conn.1957).

---

[1] "120. The 398,927 shares of Newport stock sold to Wilport as of August 31, 1950, had a fair value as a control block of $20 per share. What value the block would have had if shorn of its appurtenant power to control distribution of the corporate product, the evidence does not show."

"5. Even if Feldmann's conduct in cooperating to accomplish a transfer of control to Wilport immediately upon the sale constituted a breach of a fiduciary duty to Newport, no part of the moneys received by the defendants in connection with the sale constituted profits for which they were accountable to Newport."

(2) Accepting Judge Hincks' allocation, why should the recovery go to the plaintiffs personally rather than to the corporation, as would normally be the case with derivative suit recoveries? The ALI's Principles of Corporate Governance lists nine similar cases, and generalizes them in § 7.18(e) as follows:

(e) The court having jurisdiction over a derivative action may direct that all or a portion of the award be paid directly to individual shareholders, on a pro-rata basis, when such a payment is equitable in the circumstances and adequate provision has been made for the creditors of the corporation.

The comment states:

In general, when a substantial portion of the shares are held either by persons who had aided or abetted the defendants to commit the fiduciary breach or by non-contemporaneous holders who had suffered no injury because they had bought their shares at a price reflecting the injury done to the corporation, the case for a pro-rata recovery in favor of the other eligible shareholders will be strongest. However, it should not be assumed that pro-rata recovery should be granted merely because persons who committed or aided the breach remain as shareholders. A corporate recovery in such an instance does not mean that the defendants will receive unjust enrichment. To the contrary, proration of a partial recovery among other shareholders reduces the damages defendants must pay and thereby minimizes both the sanction against them and the amount of compensation that will benefit creditors and others affected by an injury to the corporation. That defendants continue as shareholders is, however, highly relevant if the court determines that there is a possibility that defendants will divert the recovery. This possibility will be greatest when the defendants remain in control of the corporation.

Another instance in which a pro-rata recovery is justified arises when shareholders who were earlier injured by a wrong for which they have not been adequately compensated have been eliminated as the result of a fundamental corporate change. In these circumstances, a derivative action is a more practical means by which to address such a wrong than is the appraisal remedy, because the appraisal remedy grants relief only against the corporation (and thus indirectly against its current shareholders) rather than against the alleged wrongdoer. * * *

(3) Is it desirable for courts to evolve a single, consistent position with respect to premiums paid for controlling shares? (To date they have not done so.) At least the following arguments seem defensible:

(a) In the absence of fraud or foreseeable looting, a person may sell his property for what he can get or refuse to sell it at all. That is what economic freedom is all about. (A number of cases have adopted this position which is the dominant position today.)

(b) A purchaser is really seeking control of the corporate assets when he buys the controlling shares. If he wants the assets, he should buy them from the corporation, in which case all the shareholders would receive the same amount per share. In effect, this translates all sale of control cases into corporate opportunity cases. (Some courts have adopted this position, particularly where the purchasers first approached the corporation seeking to buy its assets, and the controlling shareholder proposes a stock deal. See, e.g., Commonwealth Title Ins. & Trust Co. v. Seltzer, 76 A. 77 (Pa.1910)).

(c) If it is part of the deal for the selling shareholder to resign from his position with the corporation (as it almost always is), that is what the premium *really* is for. This approach in effect translates virtually all sale of control cases into sale of corporate office cases. (Some courts have tried this approach, particularly where the premium is set aside and its payment is made contingent on the resignations. E.g., Porter v. Healy, 91 A. 428 (Pa.1914)).

(d) It is simply immoral for a shareholder knowingly to take a greater price for his shares than other shareholders, since each share is actually identical with every other share. The additional amount must be for control, and that should belong to the corporation. See, e.g., David Cowan Bayne, The Noninvestment Value of Control Stock, 45 Ind.L.J. 317 (1970).

(4) William D. Andrews, The Stockholder's Right to Equal Opportunity in the Sale of Shares, 78 Harv.L.Rev. 505, 515–17 (1965), suggests the following rule:

> [W]henever a controlling stockholder sells his shares, every other holder of shares (of the same class) is entitled to have an equal opportunity to sell his shares, or a prorata part of them, on substantially the same terms. Or in terms of the correlative duty: before a controlling stockholder may sell his shares to an outsider he must assure his fellow stockholders an equal opportunity to sell their shares, or as high a proportion of theirs as he ultimately sells of his own. * * *

> Now let us look briefly at what the rule means. First, it neither compels nor prohibits a sale of stock at any particular price; it leaves a controlling stockholder wholly free to decide for himself the price above which he will sell and below which he will hold his shares. The rule only says that in executing his decision to sell, a controlling stockholder cannot sell pursuant to a purchase offer more favorable than any available to other stockholders. Second, the rule does not compel a prospective purchaser to make an open offer for all shares on the same terms. He can offer to purchase shares on the condition that he gets a certain proportion of the total. Or he can even make an offer to purchase 51 per cent of the shares, no more and no less. The only requirement is that his offer, whatever it

may be, be made equally or proportionately available to all stockholders.

(5) Frank H. Easterbrook & Daniel R. Fischel, The Economic Structure of Corporate Law 117–18 (1991):

> A sharing requirement also may make an otherwise profitable transaction unattractive to the prospective seller of control. Suppose the owner of a control bloc of shares finds that his perquisites or the other amenities of his position are worth $10. A prospective acquirer of control concludes that, by eliminating these perquisites and other amenities, it could produce a gain of $15. The shareholders in the company benefit if the acquirer pays a premium of $11 to the owner of the controlling bloc, ousts the current managers, and makes the improvements. The net gains of $4 inure to each investor according to his holdings, and although the acquirer obtains the largest portion because it holds the largest bloc, no one is left out. If the owner of the control bloc must share the $11 premium with all of the existing shareholders, however, the deal collapses. The owner will not part with his bloc for less than a $10 premium. A sharing requirement would make the deal unprofitable to him, and the other investors would lose the prospective gain from the installation of better managers.

Compare Robert W. Hamilton, Private Sale of Control Transactions: Where We Stand Today, 36 Case Western Res.L.Rev. 248, 256–57 (1985):

> There are several problems with this kind of analysis, however. The hypothetical the authors create assumes the correctness of their thesis. The assumption [is] that the purchasers of control will reduce the "perquisites or the other amenities" enjoyed as a result of the seller's position by $10, thereby producing a corporate gain of $15 * * *. One can equally plausibly assume that the buyer feels that he can enjoy the same "perquisites or the other amenities" as the seller enjoyed, and even increase them to, for instance, $14. On this assumption, the minority shareholders are clearly worse off as a result of the sale, and both the purchaser and seller of the control shares are benefiting at the minority shareholders' expense. * * *

> There is another problem with the Easterbrook-Fischel hypothetical. Assume that the control stock sold in the hypothetical consists of 55% of the outstanding shares; if the buyers are content to allow the $15 increase in value to remain in the corporation, they will obtain 55% of the $15 increase in value by reason of their 55% stock ownership, or $8.25. In other words, if they abandon the "perquisites and other amenities," they will pay $11 in order to obtain an increase in investment value of only $8.25. They would obviously be better off if they retain the sellers' "percs" worth $10 and seek to squeeze out another couple of dollars here and there from additional "percs," rather than eliminating the "percs." * * *

The basic question is: If the new purchasers are rational profit maximizers, why should they share the $15 increase in value with the minority? It is not true that minority shareholders always share ratably in all increases in value with the majority shareholders. It would appear to be rational (and certainly practical) to place the minority shareholders on "starvation returns" from the corporation while increasing salaries or other "percs" to the new controlling shareholders in order to obtain all the additional $15 in gains. Why should the minority be given any of it? Starvation returns may also persuade the minority to sell their shares at low prices to the majority so that at some time thereafter the purchasers may own all of the outstanding shares and obtain all of the benefits of their skills. In short, I do not view hypothetical examples, such as those put forth by Easterbrook and Fischel, to prove anything more than that there *may be* idealized situations where everyone is better off as a result of the transfer of control; they do not prove that there are such situations, or their frequency.

For an evaluation of all aspects of the sale of control issue, see Einer Elhauge, The Triggering Function of Sale of Control Doctrine, 59 U.Chi.L.Rev. 1465 (1992) (arguing the choice that courts must make when selecting between the two approaches (equal sharing versus the deregulatory school) is based on a classification of cases that effectively avoids underdeterring harmful transfers of control and overdeterring beneficial transfers of control).

(6) A purchaser of a controlling block of stock may specifically contract for immediate control of the corporation. This is usually accomplished by having the corporation's current directors resign one-by-one from the board, and by appointing the purchaser's nominees to fill the vacancies (the seller contractually promises that it will use its control over the existing board to effectuate this process). See, e.g., DGCL § 223(a) (allowing a majority of directors then in office to fill board vacancies). Is there anything wrong with allowing the purchaser to obtain control in this manner? Is it preferable to force the purchaser to call a formal shareholders' meeting to replace the directors?

(7) Courts typically allow a seriatim resignation and replacement of directors when a purchase of a controlling block has occurred, but only if the purchaser owns enough shares to constitute control. See, e.g., Essex Universal Corp. v. Yates, 305 F.2d 572, 575–76, 578–79 (2d Cir. 1962) (involving the purchase of a 28.3% block of voting stock in a public corporation and suggesting that seriatim resignation and replacement was likely proper because such a block "is usually tantamount to majority control" in a public corporation); Caplan v. Lionel Corp., 246 N.Y.S.2d 913, 915 (App. Div. 1964) (involving the purchase of a 3% block of stock in a public corporation and concluding that seriatim resignation and replacement was improper because such a block did not provide working control).

(8) Carter v. Muscat, 251 N.Y.S.2d 378 (App.Div.1964), involved seriatim resignations of directors in connection with transfer of 9.7 percent of the outstanding shares. Full disclosure of the change in control was made to the shareholders and some of the new directors were thereafter reelected at annual shareholders' meetings. After quoting from *Caplan,* the court said: "When a situation involving less than 50% of the ownership of stock exists, the question of what percentage of ownership of stock is sufficient to constitute working control is likely to be a matter of fact, at least in most circumstances." 251 N.Y.S.2d at 381. The change in control was upheld with the court relying on the disclosure, the absence of objection, and the subsequent election of directors as "endorsements" of the substituted directors.

(9) Section 14(f) of the Securities Exchange Act of 1934, added in 1970, provides that if there is an "arrangement or understanding" with persons acquiring more than five percent of the stock of a registered publicly traded corporation by tender offer or purchase, and "any persons are to be elected or designated as directors of the issuer, otherwise than at a meeting of security holders, and the persons so elected or designated will constitute a majority of the directors," the issuer must disseminate certain information to the SEC and to all holders of record entitled to vote at a meeting. The information must identify the persons to whom control was transferred, describe the transaction by which control was transferred, the source of any consideration paid, the identity of the new directors, transactions with the issuer, the remuneration to be paid to directors and management, and the amount of securities held by principal shareholders. See 17 C.F.R. § 240.14f–1.

CHAPTER 15

INDEMNIFICATION AND INSURANCE

■ ■ ■

A. A. Sommer, Jr., Review of Olson and Hatch, Director and Officer Liability: Indemnification and Insurance, 47 Bus. Law. 355, 355–56 (1991), captures the importance of the principles discussed in this Chapter:

> Before the onset of * * * litigation, directors are usually unconcerned with the mundane details of the corporation's indemnification provisions, the limitations upon indemnification permitted under state law or the terms of the corporation's directors' and officers' liability policy ("lawyer stuff!", they say). Let the complaint be filed naming him (or her), and here this reviewer speaks from personal experience as a director, and then those matters assume consuming importance, for on them may depend the prosperity of the director's future and the comfort of his or her retirement years. At that point limits on the ability of the corporation to indemnify, or even to advance expenses (most important given the costs of litigation and the increasing insistence by lawyers upon ongoing payments), and the exclusionary clauses of the D&O policy are examined with all the attention and devotion, and parsed as carefully for every nuance, as were once youthful love letters.

MERRITT-CHAPMAN & SCOTT CORP. v. WOLFSON
Superior Court of Delaware, 1974.
321 A.2d 138.

BALICK, JUDGE.

These actions arise over claims of Louis Wolfson, Elkin Gerbert, Joseph Kosow and Marshal Staub (claimants) for indemnification by Merritt-Chapman & Scott Corporation (MCS) against expenses incurred in a criminal action. All parties seek summary judgment.

Claimants were charged by indictment with participation in a plan to cause MCS to secretly purchase hundreds of thousands of shares of its own common stock. Count one charged all claimants with conspiracy to violate federal securities laws. Count two charged Wolfson and count three charged Gerbert with perjury before the * * * SEC. Counts four and five charged Wolfson, Gerbert, and Staub with filing false annual reports for 1962 and 1963 respectively with the SEC and New York Stock Exchange.

At the first trial the court dismissed part of the conspiracy count but the jury returned guilty verdicts on all charges against all claimants. At that stage this court held that Wolfson, Gerbert, and Kosow were not entitled to partial indemnification. Merritt-Chapman & Scott v. Wolfson, 264 A.2d 358 (Del.Super.1970). Thereafter the convictions were reversed. United States v. Wolfson, 437 F.2d 862 (2d Cir.1970).

There were two retrials of the perjury and filing false annual report charges against Wolfson and Gerbert. At the first retrial the court entered a judgment of acquittal on count four at the end of the State's case, and the jury could not agree on the other counts. At the second retrial the jury returned a guilty verdict on count three, but could not agree further.

The charges were then settled as follows: Wolfson entered a plea of *nolo contendere* to count five and the other charges against him were dropped. He was fined $10,000 and given a suspended sentence of eighteen months. Gerbert agreed not to appeal his conviction of count three, on which he was fined $2,000 and given a suspended sentence of eighteen months, and the other charges against him were dropped. The prosecution also dropped the charges against Kosow and Staub.

Indemnification of corporate agents involved in litigation is the subject of legislation in Delaware. Title 8 Delaware Code § 145. Subsection (a), which permits indemnification, and subsection (c), which requires indemnification, provide as follows:

(a) A corporation may indemnify any person who was or is a party or is threatened to be made a party to any threatened, pending or completed action, suit or proceeding, whether civil, criminal, administrative or investigative (other than an action by or in the right of the corporation) by reason of the fact that he is or was a director, officer, employee or agent of the corporation, or is or was serving at the request of the corporation as a director, officer, employee or agent of another corporation, partnership, joint venture, trust or other enterprise, against expenses (including attorneys' fees), judgments, fines and amounts paid in settlement actually and reasonably incurred by him in connection with such action, suit or proceeding if he acted in good faith and in a manner he reasonably believed to be in or not opposed to the best interests of the corporation, and, with respect to any criminal action or proceeding, had no reasonable cause to believe his conduct was unlawful. The termination of any action, suit or proceeding by judgment, order, settlement, conviction, or upon a plea of *nolo contendere* or its equivalent, shall not, of itself, create a presumption that the person did not act in good faith and in a manner which he reasonably believed to be in or not opposed to the best interests of the corporation, and, with respect to any criminal action or proceeding, had reasonable cause to believe that his conduct was unlawful. * * *

(c) To the extent that a director, officer, employee or agent of a corporation has been successful on the merits or otherwise in defense of any action, suit or proceeding referred to in [subsection (a)], or in defense of any claim, issue or matter therein, he shall be indemnified against expenses (including attorneys' fees) actually and reasonably incurred by him in connection therewith.

The policy of the statute and its predecessor has been described as follows, Folk, The Delaware General Corporation Law, 98 (1972):

The invariant policy of Delaware legislation on indemnification is to "promote the desirable end that corporate officials will resist what they consider" unjustified suits and claims, "secure in the knowledge that their reasonable expenses will be borne by the corporation they have served if they are vindicated." Beyond that, its larger purpose is "to encourage capable men to serve as corporate directors, secure in the knowledge that expenses incurred by them in upholding their honesty and integrity as directors will be borne by the corporation they serve."

MCS argues that the statute and sound public policy require indemnification only where there has been vindication by a finding or concession of innocence. It contends that the charges against claimants were dropped for practical reasons, not because of their innocence, and that in light of the conspiracy charged in the indictment, the judgment of acquittal on count four alone is not vindication.

The statute requires indemnification to the extent that the claimant "has been successful on the merits or otherwise." Success is vindication. In a criminal action, any result other than conviction must be considered success. Going behind the result, as MCS attempts, is neither authorized by subsection (c) nor consistent with the presumption of innocence.

The statute does not require complete success. It provides for indemnification to the extent of success "in defense of any claim, issue or matter" in an action. Claimants are therefore entitled to partial indemnification if successful on a count of an indictment, which is an independent criminal charge, even if unsuccessful on another, related count. * * *

Wolfson was sentenced upon a plea of *nolo contendere* to count five of the indictment * * * [while] Gerbert was sentenced upon a guilty verdict on count three * * *. Conviction of these offenses establishes that Wolfson and Gerbert were adjudged to have been derelict in the performance of their duty as director or officer, and they are therefore not entitled to indemnification against expenses incurred in connection with counts three and five. * * *

NOTES

(1) In its opinion in the earlier proceeding, 264 A.2d 358, 360 (Del.Super.1970), the court described the purpose of § 145 as follows:

> Indemnification statutes were enacted in Delaware, and elsewhere, to induce capable and responsible businessmen to accept positions in corporate management. [Section 145] is a new statute, enacted to clarify its predecessor, and to give vindicated directors and others involved in corporate affairs a judicially [enforceable] right to indemnification.

> It would be anomalous, indeed, and diametrically opposed to the spirit and purpose of the statute and sound public policy to extend the benefits of indemnification to these defendants under the circumstances of this case. * * *

If the corporation had wished to do so, could it have indemnified Wolfson and Gerbert for the expenses incurred in connection with claims three and five? See MBCA § 8.51.

(2) While fees paid to directors may seem relatively generous, they do not begin to cover the out-of-pocket costs incurred by a director who is named as a defendant in any major litigation. The decision of the Delaware Supreme Court in *Van Gorkom* (Chapter 10) doubtless contributed to the concern of directors about personal liability generally and the need for iron-clad indemnification rights against the corporation in particular.

(3) The need for indemnification to attract directors seems clearest in the case of litigation that ultimately vindicates the actions of the director on the merits. However, reflection should also indicate that a test requiring complete vindication on the merits is too narrow. For example, should directors be entitled to indemnification for costs if a settlement is available that involves a relatively nominal payment to the plaintiffs and their attorneys? Should not the corporation and the defendant directors be able to settle nuisance suits by nominal payments to or on behalf of the plaintiffs without shifting litigation costs from the corporation back to the defendant directors? Can one distinguish such settlements from situations where directors settle because the probability that they will lose is high? Should there be indemnification in such cases? Questions such as these raise the fundamental issue of what should be the outside limits of the power of indemnification.

(4) One court has held that a director who settles an administrative proceeding by voluntarily paying a fine has conclusively established that he lacked the requisite good faith necessary to be entitled to indemnification, even though indemnification was apparently authorized by a broadly phrased by-law provision. Waltuch v. Conticommodity Services, Inc., 88 F.3d 87 (2d Cir.1996). The *Waltuch* court also held that success "on the merits or otherwise" means not being required to pay anything; the fact that other similarly situated defendants did make payments in a settlement was not relevant.

(5) In VonFeldt v. Stifel Financial Corp., 714 A.2d 79 (Del.1998), the Delaware Supreme Court held that a person elected to be a director of a wholly owned subsidiary by the parent corporation was serving "at the request of" the parent corporation and was therefore entitled to indemnification from the parent corporation. The court went to some lengths to warn against "hyper-technical readings" of § 145. See Micah John Schreurs, VonFeldt v. Stifel Financial Corporation: Clarifying the Scope of Delaware Corporate Indemnification Law, 25 J.Corp.L. 161 (1999). In *Waltuch*, the Second Circuit had narrowly read the scope of indemnification permitted under § 145. See Kurt A. Mayr, II, Indemnification of Directors and Officers: The "Double Whammy" of Mandatory Indemnification under Delaware Law in Waltuch v. Conticommodity Services, Inc., 42 Vill.L.Rev. 223 (1997).

(6) When a corporation files for bankruptcy, the corporation's indemnification obligations become lumped in with the corporation's other obligations to creditors. Creditors frequently argue that payments to officers and directors should come after the corporation's obligations to third-party creditors are satisfied. The risk of bankruptcy provides yet another compelling reason why officers and directors should require corporations they serve to purchase directors' and officers' liability insurance.

(7) Subchapter E of Chapter 8 of the MBCA (§§ 8.50–8.59) defines the scope of permissible indemnification. Subchapter E was significantly amended in 1994 to integrate it with MBCA § 2.02(b)(4), which authorizes a corporation to limit the liability of directors by a provision in the articles of incorporation. Both liability limitations and indemnification effectively shift the economic cost for the director's acts or omissions from the director to the corporation. Both liability limitations and indemnification, therefore, raise the issue of whether it is appropriate to shift this cost to the corporation in the specific case.

(8) The policy considerations underlying the MBCA indemnification provisions are described in part as follows:

> * * * Today, * * * it would be difficult to persuade responsible persons to serve as directors if they were compelled to bear personally the cost of vindicating the propriety of their conduct in every instance in which it might be challenged. * * *

If permitted too broadly, however, indemnification may violate equally basic tenets of public policy. It is inappropriate to permit management to use corporate funds to avoid the consequences of certain conduct. For example, a director who intentionally inflicts harm on the corporation should not expect to receive assistance from the corporation for legal or other expenses and should be required to satisfy from his personal assets not only any adverse judgment but also expenses incurred in connection with the proceeding. * * *

A further policy issue is raised in connection with indemnification against liabilities or sanctions imposed under state or federal civil or criminal statutes. * * *

The fundamental issue that must be addressed by an indemnification statute is the establishment of policies consistent with these broad principles: to ensure that indemnification is permitted only where it will further sound corporate policies and to prohibit indemnification where it might protect or encourage wrongful or improper conduct. * * *

MBCA, Introductory Comment to Chapter 8, Subchapter E.

(9) What about indemnification of directors in derivative suits brought by shareholders in the name of the corporation? See MBCA § 8.51(d)(1), added in 1994. See also James J. Hanks, Jr., Evaluating Recent State Legislation on Director and Officer Liability Limitation and Indemnification, 43 Bus.Law. 1207, 1221, 1240 (1988):

At least ten states * * * have enacted statutes expanding the right of corporations to indemnify their directors for expenses, settlements, and adverse judgments in derivative suits. * * *

In the absence of any applicable liability limitation, the disadvantage of permitting indemnification against settlements and adverse judgments [in] derivative suits is its circularity. Any money recovered from the director or officer is paid, less the stockholders' attorneys' fees, by the individual to the corporation, which then returns the money, together with reimbursement for the individual's legal expenses, to the individual as indemnification. Although the individual is made whole, the corporation winds up paying not only the amount of the loss but also the stockholders' and individual's attorneys' fees and costs. * * * The real beneficiaries of circular indemnification are the stockholders' lawyers. * * *

Moreover, while statutes may permit a corporation to indemnify a director or officer held liable for negligence in a derivative suit, they do not * * * require indemnification. Thus, unless the charter or by-laws require indemnification in such circumstances, the individual is left in a state of uncertainty as to whether indemnification will actually be authorized in his particular case. This type of uncertainty has caused many directors to leave corporate boards. While expanded indemnifiability helps directors and officers by giving them at least one source of reimbursement (assuming the corporation can afford to pay at the time of the loss), it will not provide any relief for the insurance carriers. * * *

ALEYNIKOV V. GOLDMAN SACHS GROUP, INC.

United States District Court, District of New Jersey, 2013.
2013 WL 5739137.

KEVIN MCNULTY, U.S.D.J.:

[Sergey Aleynikov was employed by Goldman, Sachs & Co. ("GSCo") from May 7, 2007 through June 30, 2009. He worked as part of a team of computer programmers responsible for developing source code relating to GSCo's high frequency trading system. This proprietary code, alleged to be a trade secret, enhanced the quality of the firm's analysis and decisionmaking in the trading business.

GSCo is a "broker-dealer" limited liability partnership organized in New York. It is a subsidiary of GS Group, the Goldman Sachs parent company, which is incorporated in Delaware.

In April 2009, Aleynikov accepted an employment offer from Teza Technologies, a start-up company based in Chicago. Before leaving GSCo in June 2009, Aleynikov allegedly copied and transmitted to his home computer and other devices, via a server in Germany, hundreds of thousands of lines of confidential source code. About a month later, Aleynikov flew to Teza's offices carrying a laptop and flash drive that allegedly contained the stolen source code. Immediately upon his return, he was arrested by the FBI at Newark Liberty International Airport and charged federally in the Southern District of New York.

After an eight day jury trial, Mr. Aleynikov was convicted of (1) theft of trade secrets in violation of the Electronic Espionage Act, and (2) transportation of stolen property in interstate commerce in violation of the National Stolen Property Act. The federal court sentenced Aleynikov to 97 months of imprisonment. On direct appeal, the United States Court of Appeals for the Second Circuit reversed the district court's judgment, reasoning that, although Aleynikov had breached his confidentiality obligations to Goldman, his conduct did not fall within the scope of the charged federal offenses. On remand, a judgment of acquittal on both counts was entered.

On August 2, 2012, Aleynikov was rearrested in New Jersey. He was indicted by a Manhattan grand jury for two offenses under New York law based upon the same alleged theft of computer code that had been charged federally. The state case is currently pending.]

Aleynikov seeks indemnification for legal fees and expenses he has already incurred in [the] federal criminal case that concluded, after appeal, in dismissal of the charges (the "Federal Case"). He also seeks advancement of legal fees and expenses for his ongoing defense of [the] criminal case thereafter filed in New York state court based on the same facts (the "State Case"). There is a fundamental distinction between indemnification and advancement. Indemnification is a claim for fees incurred in a case that has already concluded in plaintiffs favor; it is a claim for damages based on events concluded in the past. Advancement of fees, on the other hand, is designed to fund an ongoing case, and the recipient of the funds is required to pay them back should he be unsuccessful in that case.

I will grant Aleynikov's motion for summary judgment with respect to his claim for advancement of fees only. Defendants shall pay to Aleynikov's counsel, Marino Tortorella & Boyle, P.C. ("MTB"), (1) reasonable fees and expenses incurred to date for Aleynikov's legal defense in the State Case; (2) reasonable fees and expenses that Aleynikov incurs for his ongoing defense in the State Case, on a rolling basis until a final judgment is reached; and (3) "fees on fees," *i.e.,* fees and expenses in this action that can reasonably be apportioned and attributed to the issue of advancement.

As to indemnification, summary judgment is denied * * * in part because any dollar amount due has not yet been proven; issues as to, for example, MTB's fee arrangements with Aleynikov in the federal criminal case may require exploration. But I am primarily motivated by concerns of procedural fairness. * * * Advancement is both time-sensitive (the funds are needed in pending legal proceedings now) and provisional (the funds must be paid back if plaintiff is not successful). As to indemnification, however, neither is true. * * * When both sides' remaining claims are ripe, I will entertain motions for summary judgment or try them, as appropriate.

* * *

The parties agree that the availability of advancement or indemnity depends heavily on one disputed issue: whether Aleynikov was an "officer" of GSCo within the meaning of Section 6.4 of the GS Group By-laws. * * *

* * * [T]he starting point is Section 145 of the Delaware General Corporation Law ("DGCL"). Delaware corporate law authorizes *indemnification* of legal expenses when the person has been successful in the underlying proceeding. "Section 145(a) and (b) of the Delaware General Corporation Law gives corporations the power to indemnify their

current and former corporate officials from expenses incurred in legal proceedings '*by reason of the fact* that the person is or was a director, officer, employee or agent of the corporation.'" Homestore, Inc. v. Tafeen, 888 A.2d 204, 211 (Del. 2005) (quoting Del. Code Ann. tit. 8, § 145(a) & (b)). Indemnification is not appropriate "until after the defense to legal proceedings has been successful on the merits or otherwise." Id.

In addition, DGCL Section 145(e) authorizes the *advancement* of expenses being incurred in pending proceedings. Its aim is to provide "immediate interim relief from the personal out-of-pocket financial burden of paying the significant on-going expenses inevitably involved with investigations and legal proceedings."

The right to indemnification and the right to advancement are "separate and distinct." Indemnification depends upon whether the officer's defense in underlying litigation has succeeded. Advancement, by contrast, depends on the pendency, not the merits, of the claims asserted against the corporate official. *See* Ridder v. CityFed Fin. Corp.*, 47 F.3d 85, 87 (3d Cir.1995) ("Under Delaware law, appellants' right to receive the costs of defense in advance does not depend upon the merits of the claims asserted against them, and is separate and distinct from any right of indemnification they may later be able to establish.").

* * * Section 6.4 of GS Group's By-laws provides for indemnity and advancement of legal fees as follows:

> The Corporation shall indemnify to the full extent permitted by law any person made or threatened to be made a party to any action, suit or proceeding, whether civil, criminal, administrative or investigative, by reason of the fact that such person or such person's testator or intestate is or was a director or officer of the Corporation, is or was a director, officer, trustee, member, stockholder, partner, incorporator or liquidator of a Subsidiary of the Corporation * * *. Expenses, including attorneys' fees, incurred by any such person in defending any such action, suit or proceeding shall be paid or reimbursed by the Corporation promptly upon demand by such person and, if any such demand is made in advance of the final disposition of any such action, suit or proceeding, promptly upon receipt by the Corporation of an undertaking of such person to repay such expenses if it shall ultimately be determined that such person is not entitled to be indemnified by the Corporation. The rights provided to any person by this by-law shall be enforceable against the Corporation by such person, who shall be presumed to have relied upon it in serving or continuing to serve as a director or officer or in such other capacity as provided above.

Thus, if certain conditions are met, indemnification and advancement are mandatory. By-laws § 6.4 *("shall* be paid or reimbursed by the Corporation"). The By-Laws do, however, restrict indemnification and advancement to particular persons, including "officers," a defined term:

> * * * the term "officer,"
>
> [1] when used with respect to the Corporation, shall refer to any officer elected by or appointed pursuant to authority granted by the Board of Directors of the Corporation pursuant to clauses (i), (ii), (iii) and (iv) of Section 4.1 of these by-laws,
>
> [2] when used with respect to a Subsidiary or other enterprise that is a corporation, shall refer to any person elected or appointed pursuant to the by-laws of such Subsidiary or other enterprise or chosen in such a manner as is prescribed by the by-laws of such subsidiary or other enterprise or determined by the board of directors of such Subsidiary or other enterprise, and
>
> [3] when used with respect to a Subsidiary or other enterprise that is not a corporation or is organized in a foreign jurisdiction, the term "officer" shall include in addition to any officer of such entity, any person serving in a similar capacity or as the manager of such entity. * * *

GSCo, a New York limited liability partnership, is "a Subsidiary or other enterprise that is not a corporation" and it therefore falls within By-laws Section 6.4 Category [3], quoted above. Under Section 6.4[3], an "officer" is defined as "any officer of such entity, [and] any person serving in a similar capacity or as the manager of such entity." Aleynikov does not claim that he served "in a similar capacity" to an officer or that he served as "manager" of GSCo. Rather, Aleynikov claims to be an "officer" of GSCo because he held the title of "vice president."

As I observed ten months ago, "the phrasing of Category [3] is less than clear. It begins by stating that 'the term 'officer' shall include in addition to any officer of such entity * * *.' Thus, for a non-corporate subsidiary, an 'officer' is defined as, *inter alia,* 'any officer.'"

* * * A "vice president"—Aleynikov indisputably held that title—would ordinarily be considered an "officer" in a corporate context. In a non-corporate partnership entity like GSCo, however, "officer" and "vice president" have no fixed definition. Moreover, it does not appear that Aleynikov, a computer programmer, performed functions normally associated with the status of officer or manager. The definition of a non-corporate "officer" in GS Group's By-laws is circular and unhelpful. Aleynikov argues that I should therefore let the burden of ambiguity fall on GS Group, take the title of "vice president" at face value, and declare

him eligible for advancement of fees. GS Group urges, however, that "vice president" can be something of a courtesy title in its industry. It further alleges that it has established a process of appointment that clearly distinguishes between officers and non-officers. If true, this would be highly relevant; an entity may decide whom to designate as an officer. But because GS Group points to no such written policy, because it is in possession of all the facts on this point, and because there has been no discovery, it would be unfair to conclude from a blanket statement in an affidavit that it is true. Aleynikov is entitled to probe these matters.

* * *

Despite a more developed factual record, a renewed round of briefing, and helpful oral advocacy from both sides, I still find this to be a close question. I do resolve the advancement issue in Aleynikov's favor. My decision * * * largely concerns the issue of whether Aleynikov, as a vice president of GSCo, is an "officer" for purposes of By-Laws § 6.4[3]. The following discussion has several interrelated components.

* * * I read the By-Laws in keeping with the Delaware state law policy favoring advancement of fees, a remedy that is intended to be emergent and provisional. Delaware case law confirms my conclusion that by-laws are to be read liberally to effectuate that policy.

* * *

* * * Delaware interprets potential ambiguities in by-laws under ordinary rules of construction of contracts. Plain language, supplemented by case law interpretations, suggests that a vice president be considered an officer. * * *

* * *

The public policy served by authorizing the advancement and indemnification of litigation expenses is well-settled. Without it, corporations would find it difficult to retain high-quality directors and officers, willing to make socially useful decisions that involve economic risk. By authorizing indemnity and advancement within certain guidelines, the General Assembly sought to encourage well-qualified persons to serve as directors and officers of Delaware corporations and, in that capacity, to be willing to commit their corporations, after the exercise of good faith and care, to risky transactions that promise a lucrative economic return.

That statutory policy, liberal enough as to indemnification, is particularly liberal as to advancement.

> [DGCL] Section 145(e), however, expressly contemplates that corporations may confer a right to advancement that is greater than the right to indemnification and recognizes that advances

must be repaid if it is ultimately determined that the corporate official is not entitled to be indemnified.

Homestore, 888 A.2d at 212–13.

* * * The By-Laws grant advancement "to the full extent permitted by law," and therefore must be read, at least in a general way, as implementing the policy of the Delaware statute.

* * *

It is not much of an exaggeration to say that the statue and By-Laws require immediate assistance, postponing the issue of whether such assistance is deserved. They do not distinguish between "worthy" and "unworthy" recipients. They do not distinguish between claims brought by Goldman and claims brought by outsiders. In contrast to indemnification, which is reserved for persons who prevail in the underlying case, advancement is indifferent as to the underlying merits. Thus the Court is not to predict, or base its decision on, the likelihood of Aleynikov's prevailing in the New York criminal case. In short, the advancement provision almost explicitly prioritizes speed over accuracy.

To put it another way, the statute and By-Laws contemplate that funds may be advanced to persons who in the end may not to be entitled to keep them—most commonly, perhaps, because such persons ultimately are convicted in the underlying criminal case or lose the underlying civil litigation. Of course, the advancement remedy has a backstop. It is provisional to the extent that a person who receives advancement of fees must furnish an "undertaking" to pay them back if he or she is unsuccessful in the underlying litigation. But an "undertaking," the parties agree, is nothing more than a promise; no further security is required.

The lesson to be drawn is that advancement is urgent; the applicant's defense is to be funded now, while the action is pending. * * *

* * *

Aleynikov argues that, as a "vice president," he is an officer under the "plain and commonly-understood meaning" of the term. Goldman replies that Aleynikov's job designation reflects title inflation in the financial services industry. "Vice president is merely a functional title, because it connotes a level of seniority between associate and managing director, and as distinguished from an officer title, which is somebody who has been appointed through the process." The title of vice president, says Goldman, is held by "thousands at the firm and across the financial services industry." According to Goldman, the indemnification provision of the By-laws could not have been intended to cover so many.

* * *

It may be the case that Goldman (or the industry of which it is a part) has been profligate in conferring the title of vice president. If so, Goldman must bear the consequences of that profligacy. Goldman might easily have chosen to be more sparing with job titles, or to confer them in some other way. It might easily have drafted its By-Laws to restrict indemnification to a well-defined class. It did not.

* * *

Pursuant to Section 6.4[3] of GS Group's By-Laws, Aleynikov is entitled to advancement of legal fees and expenses arising from his defense of the State Action, as well as duly apportioned "fees on fees" in this civil action [i.e., the fees incurred in this litigation to obtain advancement of Aleynikov's legal expenses].

* * *

As in any fee situation, bills will be scrutinized for reasonableness. The Court expects counsel to confer and reach reasonable accommodations, and it will not indiscriminately award "fees on fees" for the litigation of disputes it deems excessive or unreasonable.

* * *

NOTES

(1) This case illustrates that, as a practical matter, an optional provision authorizing advances is likely to provide no protection at all when it is needed the most. Recognizing this, sophisticated directors insist that advances should be mandatory to the maximum extent possible, and such provisions are very common in modern articles of incorporation and bylaws.

(2) As usual, outside of Delaware, the law is less clear. In Fidelity Fed. Sav. & Loan Ass'n v. Felicetti, 830 F.Supp. 262 (E.D.Pa.1993), the court found a conflict between the fiduciary obligation of directors to act only in the corporation's best interest and a bylaw provision that mandated advancement of expenses in all events. The court concluded that "the only reasonable interpretation requires that the directors abide by their fiduciary obligations to act only as they believe is in the best interest of the corporation. Accordingly, [the corporation] is not required to advance the funds necessary for Felicetti and Scarcia to defend themselves in this action." 830 F.Supp. at 269. Most courts, however, have rejected this approach in which preliminary judgments are made about the merits. See Ridder v. CityFed Financial Corp., 47 F.3d 85 (3d Cir.1995).

———

Directors' and Officers' (D&O) insurance pays the covered legal fees and liability awards for directors and officers of a company when they are sued in conjunction with the performance of their duties. Such policies usually provide protection for employment practices liability and sometimes provide limited protection from fiduciary liability.

D&O insurance is different from the Errors & Omissions insurance policies often carried by corporations. Errors & Omissions policies cover performance failures and negligence with respect to a company's products and services. D&O insurance covers liability resulting from the performance of directors and managers.

Sometimes both forms of insurance are needed for the same event. For example, in early 2014, Target Corporation, the third-largest retail store in the United States, experienced a massive data breach by sophisticated internet fraudsters that compromised the credit card and debit card information of some 70 million customers. "Well-placed sources who requested anonymity" told journalists covering the business insurance industry that Target had "at least $100 million of cyber insurance, including self-insured retentions, and $65 million of directors and officers liability coverage." Judy Greenwald, Target has $100M of Cyber Insurance, $65M of D&O Cover: Sources, Business Insurance, Jan. 14, 2014.

Candidates for board positions generally will not agree to serve on the board of a company unless the company has a D&O insurance policy that the candidate and her independent counsel consider adequate. Large investors such as venture capital funds also require companies to have D&O insurance as a pre-condition to investing.

Consider MBCA § 8.57. Even in states without express authorization, the purchase of D&O insurance may be implicit in other corporate powers relating to the compensation of officers and directors. Is such insurance erosive of the public policy underlying the securities acts and other rules providing for liability? Of course, § 8.57 is only enabling, and significant express exceptions and exclusions appear in all such policies.

MCCULLOUGH V. FIDELITY & DEPOSIT CO.

United States Court of Appeals, Fifth Circuit, 1993.
2 F.3d 110.

Before GOLDBERG, HIGGINBOTHAM, and DAVIS, CIRCUIT JUDGES.

W. EUGENE DAVIS, CIRCUIT JUDGE:

The Federal Deposit Insurance Corporation (FDIC) filed a declaratory judgment action against Fidelity and Deposit Company of Maryland (F & D) to determine whether F & D provided coverage under a directors' and officers' liability policy. The district court found no coverage under F & D's policy and granted summary judgment to F & D. Because the insured failed to give F & D adequate notice to trigger coverage under the "claims made" insurance policy, we affirm.

I.

F & D issued four directors' and officers' (D&O) liability policies to four affiliate banks, including Harris County Bankshares, Inc. and three of its subsidiaries (banks). The policy covers claims made against the insured officers and directors if the required notice is given to the insurer during the policy period. This coverage is expanded by Section 6(a) of the policy to cover claims made after expiration of the policy term if the insured gives F & D certain written notice during the policy period of potential claims. Section 6 of the policy provides, in pertinent part:

(a) If during the policy period, or during the extended discovery period * * * the Bank or the Directors and Officers shall:

(1) receive written or oral notice from any party that it is the intention of such party to hold the Directors and Officers, or any of them, responsible for a specified Wrongful Act; or

(2) become aware of any *act, error, or omission* which *may subsequently give rise to a claim* being made against the Directors and Officers, or any of them, for a *specified Wrongful Act*;

and shall during such period give written notice thereof to the Company as soon as practicable and prior to the date of termination of the policy, then any claim which may subsequently be made against the Directors and Officers arising out of such Wrongful Act shall, for the purpose of this policy, be treated as a claim made during the Policy Year or the extended discovery period in which such notice was first given. (emphasis added).

The summary judgment evidence focused on information the banks furnished F & D about their lending activities. The parties disagreed about whether that information was adequate to put F & D on notice of a potential claim under § 6 of the policy.

As requested by F & D, the banks provided F & D with June 1984–March 1985 Call Reports[1] that described increasing loan losses and delinquencies. In conjunction with the 1985 renewal of the policies, the banks provided F & D a 1984 annual report. Footnote M of that report referred to the issuance of a cease and desist order to one of the subsidiaries by its primary regulator, the Office of the Comptroller of the Currency (OCC). The bank did not send the order itself.

F & D continued to express concern about the banks' financial condition and continued to request Call Reports and other information. In one of F & D's letters, they expressed concern about the banks' "problem

---

[1]   A Call Report is a quarterly report of financial condition that each insured institution is required to furnish its primary regulator.

with the Feds." In September 1985, in response to the increasing loan losses, F & D informed the banks that it intended to cancel their policies mid-term, effective October 9.

* * * [T]he OCC declared the bank insolvent in February 1988 and declared the FDIC as Receiver. FDIC sued the banks' directors and officers for improperly or illegally making, administering, or collecting loans. F & D denied coverage to the officers and directors under the D&O policies. FDIC then filed its declaratory judgment action against F & D, seeking a determination that F & D provided coverage under the D&O liability policies.

In the declaratory judgment action, * * * [t]he court found that FDIC had failed to show that F & D received written notice of a potential claim under § 6(a)(2) of the policy, and on reconsideration it entered final judgment for F & D. FDIC timely appealed.

II.

FDIC * * * [argues] that a genuine issue of fact exists regarding whether, pursuant to § 6(a)(2) of the "claims made" policy, they provided F & D sufficient written notice of potential claims during the policy period. * * *

A.

The parties first contest the type of notice the policy requires the banks to give to F & D. F & D contends that the policy requires the bank to notify it of "specified Wrongful Acts" of directors and officers having claim potential. FDIC argues that the notice can be in the broader form of "any act, error or omission" which may give rise to a claim for specified wrongful acts.

We agree with F & D that the policy requires the insured to give notice of specified wrongful acts of officers and directors. First, the plain language supports F & D's argument. § 6 of the policy provides that coverage will be provided if the Bank notifies the insurer of:

> any act, error, or omission which may subsequently give rise to a claim being made against Directors and Officers, or any of them, for a specified Wrongful Act * * *

Notice, as provided in the policy, is required in a claims made policy to trigger coverage. Notice in a claims made policy therefore serves a very different function than prejudice-preventing notice required under an "occurrence" policy. If the policy requirement for notice of specified wrongful acts is relaxed, then policy coverage actually expands. For example, if notice that an insured attorney has a poor docket control system is accepted as coverage triggering notice of the attorney's wrongful act, the attorney's malpractice coverage would be triggered for any number of suits predicated on missed deadlines.[3] For all of the above reasons, we are persuaded that the policy requires the insured to give the insurer notice of specified wrongful acts to trigger coverage.

B.

* * * FDIC argues that even if notice of specified wrongful acts is required, a genuine issue of fact exists regarding whether it provided this notice. FDIC contends that reference to the cease and desist order and the reports of the banks' deteriorating financial condition put F & D on notice of acts or omissions of directors and officers which could later give rise to claims for specified wrongful acts. They argue that the policies define "wrongful act" to include a breach of duty, and the information they furnished F & D was adequate to inform F & D that the insureds breached their duty to properly supervise the banks' lending operations.

Critically, the banks did not furnish F & D with a copy of the cease and desist order. The banks' annual report simply referred to it. But even if we assume that notice of the issuance of a cease and desist order informs the insurer that the bank is having some difficulty, the issuance of such an order does not identify specified wrongful acts. The banks gave F & D no notice of the particular subsidiary involved, the particular agents, officers, or directors involved, the time period during which the events occurred, the identity of potential claimants, and the specific unsound practices made the basis of the order.

We agree with the district court that the insureds failed to give F & D adequate notice of specific wrongful acts to trigger coverage under § 6(a). Notice of an institution's worsening financial condition is not notice of an officer's or director's act, error, or omission. See *American Casualty Co. v. FDIC*, 944 F.2d 455, 460 (8th Cir.1991) and *California Union Ins. Co. v. American Diversified Savings Bank*, 914 F.2d 1271, 1277–78 (9th Cir.1990), cert. denied, 498 U.S. 1088, 111 S.Ct. 966, 112 L.Ed.2d 1052 (1991). Rising delinquencies and bad loan portfolios, especially in light of falling real estate prices, are insufficient to constitute such notice. The district court correctly granted summary judgment. * * *

AFFIRMED.

NOTES

(1) Do you understand the difference between a "claims made" policy and an "occurrence" policy? The former provides coverage for claims first made against an insured during the policy period, while the latter provides coverage for injuries that take place during the policy period regardless of when the claim is asserted. Originally, D&O policies were occurrence-based,

---

[3] See *Hirsch v. Texas Lawyers' Ins. Exchange*, 808 S.W.2d 561, 565 (Tex.Ct.App.1991) (court reluctant to permit expansion of "claims made" coverage through relaxation of coverage-triggering notice requirements).

but the practical difficulties created by the possibility that claims may be asserted many years later caused all companies to shift to claims made policies. For example, it is reported that many of the problems of Lloyds of London arose because of the issuance of occurrence policies covering asbestos liability and similar long-term events. Claims under these policies were asserted years after the close of the year for which the insurance was purchased.

(2) Claims made insurance policies open up the possibility that an insured who retires or leaves an employer may not have any insurance in force (or may be insured by an entirely different insurer) at the time a claim arising out of an earlier period is first asserted. For example, a claim that arose from conduct in 2012 may first be asserted in 2014; such a claim is covered only by the 2014 claims made policy. An employee who was covered in 2012 but has retired may not have any coverage in 2014.

(3) A major problem with D&O coverage is that defense counsel for litigation in corporate cases is very expensive. Some D&O policies have unrealistically low limits of coverage.

THOMAS D. LONG, HOW STRONG IS YOUR D&O SAFETY NET

Law 360 (Jan. 10, 2014).

[D&O insurance] is the most important insurance to protect directors and officers from personal liability. Corporations often broadly indemnify their directors and officers so gaps in D&O insurance will have no impact until the company fails. At that point, it is too late to repair deficiencies in the D&O insurance program. Directors and officers should evaluate D&O insurance the same way they evaluate their compensation packages.

Lawsuits arising out of hundreds of bank failures—as well as other corporate failures—across the country have highlighted strengths and weaknesses in existing D&O programs. Some of the lessons learned are the following:

Policy Limits are Often Not Adequate

The collapse of a corporation can spawn multiple lawsuits which can consume a large portion of the available limits even if few of the suits go to trial.

Carriers and brokers often suggest benchmarking a company's purchase of D&O insurance by comparing it to that of other companies. However, this approach may not take into account the real purpose of adequate policy limits. From the point of view of the director or officer, the D&O limits should be more attractive to a plaintiff than the director's or officer's own personal net worth even after a vigorous defense has exhausted a large portion of those limits.

The relatively low limits of D&O insurance programs are exacerbated by some of the features of how the program operates. The events which trigger coverage under the policy can be defined broadly and a defense can be available for investigations well before litigation begins. Insurers often market the broad scope of coverage provided by the D&O policies to demonstrate that the policies do a good job of providing a high-quality defense.

Perhaps for this reason, insurers for D&O policies accept very high rates—often as much as three to four times the rates that would be accepted under other corporate insurance programs—for defense counsel. The higher rates accepted for D&O defense and the possibility of multiple lawsuits arising out of the same "interrelated wrongful acts" being assigned to a single policy year create a significant risk that corporate problems will lead to rapid erosion of D&O policy limits.

A second problem with D&O policy limits is the sharing of limits among insureds who have conflicting interests. First, in the event of a corporate bankruptcy, the directors and officers may be in conflict with the corporation. The bankruptcy trustee will argue that the D&O policies are property of the bankruptcy estate and may seek to terminate coverage or sell back the policies to the insurers to augment the estate. D&O coverage is commonly divided into Side A, Side B and Side C coverage. Directors and officers obtain the best possible coverage from Side A which provides no protection to the company itself. Separate freestanding "Side A Only" policies are arguably not subject to the jurisdiction of the bankruptcy court at all since the company itself has no ownership interest in them. Directors and officers should insist on significant freestanding Side A Only coverage if available.

Directors and officers can also run into trouble when sharing limits with each other. If directors become enmeshed in litigation, it may be that inside directors are substantially more culpable than the outside directors and failed to properly inform the outside directors. If the directors and officers share limits they will often be pressured to share counsel as well. Such joint representation can present serious conflicts of interest. It is awkward for counsel representing both officers and outside directors to give full attention to all of the defenses that might otherwise be available to the outside directors.

Conflicts can emerge having insiders jointly represented as well. In cases involving bank failures, production officers charged with originating new business are sometimes represented by the same counsel who represent credit officers who are supposed to be guarding the bank's financial safety. Similarly, the chief executive officer and chief financial officer may be jointly represented even though the latter is supposed to honestly report financial performance of the company that in turn affects the compensation of the former. In each of these cases, joint representation may prevent the full development of one party's defense. At a minimum, conflict waivers are necessary. Waiving conflicts may be undesirable for the substantive defense but may be the only way to protect the D&O program against excessive defense costs.

For some D&O coverage plans, the problems with insufficient limits are exacerbated by other types of coverages being in the D&O policy. If it were possible to do so, a cautious outside director should demand his or her freestanding Side A Only D&O policy in limits sufficient to address his or her personal situation. If limits must be shared, they should be shared only with others who have a common interest—such as other outside directors. Even within the group of outside directors those on particular subcommittees (e.g. audit) may have greater exposure. In sum, the less a director or officer shares D&O policy limits with others, the better.

The Scope of Coverage Under the D&O Program May be Insufficient

D&O policies are structured in a fundamentally different way from commercial general liability policies. CGL policies are "occurrence based" and are triggered by damage that happens during the policy term regardless of when the claim was made and when a suit was filed. A significant weakness in all D&O insurance programs is that they are triggered only when there has been a "claim" during the policy period or in some cases a "circumstance."

The policy definitions of "claim" and "circumstance" and the timing requirements as to when they must be reported to trigger coverage under the D&O policy are extremely important. If the policy defines "claim" to include only written demands and does not allow the reporting of a "circumstance," both the insured and the insurer may learn of a situation which everyone knows ultimately will lead to a claim but which the insured cannot report so as to trigger coverage during the current policy term and which will be excluded during subsequent policy terms. This potential coverage gap can be minimized, but not entirely eliminated, by careful attention to the definition of "claim," "circumstance," and to the timing of the reporting obligations in the policy.

Once a D&O policy is triggered, the insured must demonstrate that the claim involves the types of exposures that fall within the basic coverage grant of the policy. Typically a "claim" for a "wrongful act" leading to "loss" or "claims expense" will trigger coverage. Some policies contain definitions of "claim" which include investigatory proceedings

[and] broaden the scope of coverage that would otherwise be provided and may provide a defense even where the indemnity obligation is limited.

Some D&O policies define "loss" to include "claims expenses." Arguably this means that "claims expenses" (defense costs) will be covered only if a covered loss is proven and only to the extent of the covered loss. As a result, some policies allow the insurer to allocate between covered and uncovered claims and to claw back defense payments that are advanced and that eventually prove to relate to claims that are later shown not to be covered. Such provisions can lead to conflicts not only between the insured and the insurance carrier but also among insureds competing for a limited amount of insurance.

Some D&O policy programs are structured to provide separate payments for "claims expenses" and "loss." Under such policies, once there is a "claim" arising out of a "wrongful act," the "claims expenses" of defending the claim are covered regardless of whether the claim itself leads to a covered "loss." These policies are more like CGL policies which provide that the insurance carriers have a duty to defend a claim even if there is only a potential for coverage and even if the claim ultimately ends up being not covered. Nonetheless, there may still be allocation of defense costs between covered and uncover[ed] claims.

The Ninth Circuit has held that D&O insurers have a duty to advance defense costs even though they may not have a duty to defend. If the insurers cannot demonstrate that all or a specifically identifiable portion of the loss is unquestionably uncovered at the time defense costs are incurred, they may incur those costs and have little practical ability to claw back the funds that have been spent. However, since only covered "loss" reduces the policy limits under many D&O programs, the advancement of defense costs for claims that prove not to be covered may not reduce the policy limits available for the resolution of other claims. No doubt D&O insurers will argue that once they have paid anything, those payments exhaust the remaining available limits. However, policyholders should not assume this is automatically the case.

A third area that affects the scope of coverage available under D&O insurance is exclusions. These exclusions can be couched as part of the coverage grant. For example, some banks were issued policies that defined "loss" to exclude losses on loans. Read literally, this language could be interpreted to make the D&O coverage sold to banks illusory since essentially all of the business of most banks arises out of loans. Insurers will put forth a panoply of exclusions designed on the one hand to try to narrow coverage as much as possible, but also to allow those marketing the policies to assert that the coverage remains broad. All of the insurer's policy exclusions should be reviewed carefully with a jaundiced eye for the impact they may have.

Another way in which the scope of coverage may be limited under D&O policies is through a "retroactive date" which limits or eliminates coverage for "prior acts." Even if a claim arises out of facts which occurred years prior to the policy, the claim still triggers the policy if it is made and timely reported during the policy term, unless there is a limitation on "prior acts" coverage. Such limitations are always a red flag particularly for a new or outside director who does not have knowledge of the company's history.

Protection Against Bad Actors May Not be Adequate

Misconduct by a director or officer or an inaccurate statement on an application—even an honest misstatement—may allow the insurer to rescind the policy. Insurers frequently use postclaim underwriting to aggressively pursue rescission in other lines of insurance and would do so with D&O insurance if the policies did not frequently contain provisions protecting against just such actions.

In D&O insurance, it is common to have severability provisions such that the misconduct and/or misstatements of individuals vitiate coverage only as to those particular individuals or perhaps as to those individuals and to the company but not as to others insured by the policy. Specifically, directors and officers insured under a freestanding Side A Only policy should justifiably expect that their coverage should be impacted only by their own particular misconduct.

Also, to the extent that insurance can be denied because of the fraudulent conduct of an insured, it is common for the policy to require that that fraud must be determined by a "final adjudication" of a court. To avoid the risk that the suit against the insured could be settled without such an adjudication, but that the insurer could seek a separate adjudication in a declaratory relief action, it is best to seek language that protects the insured unless fraud is established by a final adjudication against that particular insured in the precise case where the D&O coverage is being sought. Also, since many different claims against a director or officer will include accusations of misconduct for personal profit, any exclusions for misconduct based upon seeking personal profit should be as narrowly circumscribed as possible, and if possible, be triggered only by a final judgment to that effect.

Joseph P. Monteleone & John F. McCarrick, Directors' and Officers' Liability, A D & O Policy Road Map: The Coverage Exclusions

Insights, Vol. 7, No. 7, at 8 (July 1993).

* * *

Some of the more common exclusions found in the exclusions section of D&O policies include the following[:]

Personal profit or advantage exclusion. Most D&O policies exclude claims based upon or attributable to directors or officers gaining any personal profit or advantage to which they were not legally entitled. Some policy forms require that the personal profiting be established "in fact"[;] other policy forms require an adjudication of unentitled personal profit in the underlying litigation.

Dishonesty exclusion. Given the liberal pleading requirements in virtually every federal and state court, the dishonesty exclusion has potential applicability to virtually all D&O claims and, therefore, is frequently identified in insurers' reservation of rights letters as a potential coverage defense. First, the scope of the exclusion varies among different D&O policy forms in several respects. The conduct falling within the exclusion also may vary. Some policy forms exclude claims brought about or contributed to by the "dishonest" or the "fraudulent, dishonest or criminal" acts of the insureds. Other forms exclude "deliberately fraudulent" or "deliberately dishonest" conduct or a "willful violation of any statute, rule or regulation."

Second, the triggering conditions for the applicability of dishonesty exclusions vary. Some policy forms require a judgment or other final adjudication which establishes that "acts of active and deliberate dishonesty" were committed "with actual dishonest purpose and intent." Other forms simply require the requisite conduct to have occurred "in fact," while yet other forms have no expressed triggering condition. As to policy forms requiring a final adjudication, courts have consistently held that the adjudication must occur in the underlying D&O proceeding (and cannot be established in separate coverage litigation) and, therefore, the exclusion is inapplicable if the underlying D&O litigation is settled prior to a final adjudication. If the exclusion does not expressly require an adjudication, the exclusion has potential applicability even where the underlying lawsuit is settled.

Bodily injury/property damage exclusion. All D&O policies exclude coverage with respect to claims for bodily injury, sickness, disease or death, or property damage. More recent policy forms also may exclude emotional or mental distress, violation of a person's right of privacy, wrongful entry, eviction, false arrest and assault and battery, as well as libel, slander and defamation.

ERISA exclusion. Almost all D&O policy forms exclude claims arising under ERISA or a similar federal or state law. Given this wording, the D&O insurers' intent with respect to this exclusion appears to be to avoid providing overlapping coverage with that typically provided by fiduciary liability insurance. The exclusion may also be deemed sufficiently broad to apply to a claim for benefits in connection with a wrongful termination claim whether or not the claim for benefits is explicitly based on an alleged violation of ERISA.

Section 16(b) ("short-swing profit") exclusion. * * * Since the issue of intent or conduct is not relevant in determining whether liability should be imposed, D&O insurers typically separately exclude claims arising under Section 16(b) regardless of whether or not the trading constituted "personal profit" or "dishonesty."

Return of illegal remuneration exclusion. This exclusion was developed in response to D&O insurers' concerns that if a director or officer is forced to return to the corporation profits or excessive compensation, insureds might seek to obtain those funds under a D&O policy. Like the "short-swing profit" exclusion, it is not necessary that there be a factual finding or adjudication of "personal profit" or "dishonesty" in order for the D&O insurer to invoke this exclusion. Recent policies combine this exclusion with the "personal profit" exclusion.

Pollution exclusion. Virtually every D&O insurance policy contains a "broad form" pollution exclusion, although substantial variations in exclusionary wording exist among policy forms. The intent of most insurers is to exclude coverage for any type of direct or indirect pollution or environmental exposure. Some exclusions are drafted to be more comprehensive than others. Under the most commonly used "broad form" pollution exclusions, coverage is excluded not only for claims by parties seeking recovery for pollution damages, but also for secondary suits, such as shareholder derivative and nondisclosure suits against directors and officers arising out of environment-related losses incurred by the corporation.

In some instances, insureds may be able to obtain an exception to this exclusion through negotiation with D&O insurers and obtain coverage for non-indemnifiable secondary pollution suits.

Insured v. insured exclusion. Prior to the mid-1980s, most D&O policies did not exclude claims brought by the corporation or by some directors and officers against other directors and officers. However, in light of suits brought by corporations against their directors and officers under circumstances which created an appearance that the entities simply were converting their D&O policies to cash by suing their own directors and officers, virtually all D&O policy forms now exclude claims brought against directors and officers by other directors and officers or by the company. Most newer policy forms incorporate this exclusion into the Exclusions section of the policy. Older policy forms generally add this exclusion by endorsement.

The "insured v. insured" exclusion varies significantly from policy to policy, with the primary differences relating to which claims are excepted from the exclusion (and are therefore covered). Almost all policy forms contain an exception to the "insured v. insured" exclusion to provide coverage for derivative lawsuits brought without the solicitation, assistance or participation of an insured. Other exceptions to the "insured v. insured" exclusion may preserve coverage for claims for wrongful termination and claims for contribution or indemnity.

In recent years, the "insured v. insured" exclusion has been frequently litigated in the context of claims brought by the regulatory banking agencies against directors and officers of failed financial institutions. Courts have reached different results as to whether the "insured v. insured" exclusion applies to these claims. * * *

D&O policies typically exclude coverage for claims which may be covered under other insurance policies. This exclusion may be found in the exclusions section of the policy in some policy forms, or in separate provisions in other forms. Some policy forms apply this exclusion only to the extent of actual payments under other policies; others limit the exclusion to other "valid" or "valid and collectible" insurance. In virtually all policies, the exclusion applies only to the amount of such other insurance, with the D&O insurance policy affording coverage in excess of such other insurance.

ENDORSEMENTS

In addition to policy exclusions contained in standardized policy forms, D&O insurers may add further exclusions to the policy by endorsement and thus tailor the policy coverage to a specific risk or industry. The following are some commonly found endorsement exclusions[:]

Pending/prior litigation exclusion. When an insurer first issues a D&O policy to a corporation, an exclusion is frequently included which eliminates coverage for claims arising from pending or prior litigation or from any facts or circumstances involved in such litigation. In this way, the insurer's intent is to avoid exposure for a claim already in progress or which is likely to arise from existing litigation. The "pending/prior litigation" exclusion typically will reference a date—frequently the inception date of the policy—which is used to determine whether the litigation is "pending or prior." In evaluating different policy forms, one important inquiry should be which party is the subject of the pending or prior litigation. Some forms of this exclusion limit the scope of the exclusion to litigation, claims, demands, or proceedings *against* the insured directors and officers and, in some forms, the corporation. Other forms apply the exclusion to *any* pending or prior litigation, claims, demands or proceedings whether or not the corporation or any insured is a party or even knows of the existence of the matter.

Depending upon the specific wording, the "pending/prior litigation" exclusion may broadly apply and, therefore, may create inadvertent coverage gaps. For example, if the prior litigation asserts claims against only the corporation (or under the broader form of this exclusion, against only a third party), and insured directors and officers subsequently are named as defendants in the litigation or are subsequently subject to separate litigation based upon the same matters as alleged in the pending litigation, it is likely that no coverage will exist under the newly-issued policy. Thus, unless a notice of circumstances referencing the matters alleged in the prior litigation was submitted to the prior D&O insurer, if any, the defendant directors and officers may well be without any D&O coverage for such claims.

Regulatory exclusion. Although potentially applicable to any corporation subject to regulation by a governmental agency, this exclusion is most commonly endorsed onto D&O policies issued to financial institutions—and particularly where there are concerns that the institution may be taken over by regulators. Beginning in the late 1980s, some courts ruled that this exclusion was unenforceable as being ambiguous and against public policy because it frustrated the broad powers and duties bestowed upon financial institution regulators. During the past two years, however, courts have almost unanimously upheld the enforceability of this exclusion. * * *

NOTES

(1) The cost of D&O insurance has risen dramatically over the years. There are at least three explanations for this increase. First, the large number of high-profile corporate scandals since 2001 have increased the perceived liability risks of corporate directors and officers. Second, even before these scandals hit, there had been a steady increase in the average dollar amount of settlements in class action lawsuits against directors and officers. Third, the passage of Sarbanes-Oxley has significantly increased the duties and obligations of corporate officers and directors, thereby increasing potential liability. Some of the changes, such as the extension of the statutes of limitations in securities fraud actions and the creation of new securities fraud causes of action (such as having an "improper influence over a corporate audit") have obvious implications for insurers' potential liability.

(2) In a modern D&O policy, advancements of expenses to defend insureds usually reduce the available coverage by the amount of the payment. As a result, extended litigation may deplete the policy and limit the protection available to insureds. Not all policies are structured in this fashion.

(3) As the Long article makes clear, material misrepresentations made by an insured on a policy application give the insurance company the right to rescind insurance coverage. Of particular concern are questions on many insurance forms that ask companies to disclose "any facts and circumstances that might give rise to a claim in the future." When a lawsuit is filed, the insurance company can claim that it has the right to rescind on the grounds that the company failed to disclose the facts and circumstances that might have given rise to the claim being asserted. An issue that sometimes arises is whether a corporation's fraudulent failure to disclose material facts gives the insurance company the right to deny coverage to officers or directors who were unaware that a misrepresentation had been made. With this in mind, lawyers reviewing insurance policies for officers and directors often insist on "severability clauses." One such clause provides that a corporation's misrepresentations or failure to disclose facts or circumstances that might give rise to a claim "shall not be imputed, for the purpose of rescission of this Policy, to any other insured Persons who are not aware" of the fraud.

(4) Significant problems arise when litigation involves claims brought simultaneously against directors and officers who are insured and persons who are not insured: corporate agents and employees, directors of subsidiaries or affiliated corporations, and the corporation itself. (Traditional policies covered only the indemnification obligations of the corporation itself and not its direct liability; some policies now insure the corporation itself as well as directors and officers.) If a settlement is reached, the insurer must allocate the settlement payment among the insureds and the uninsureds based on relative fault or culpability. Not surprisingly, litigation has arisen over the propriety of specific allocations. See Caterpillar v. Great American Ins. Co., 62 F.3d 955 (7th Cir.1995); Safeway Stores v. National Union Fire Ins. Co., 64 F.3d 1282 (9th Cir.1995). Somewhat similar issues arise when the corporation is insolvent and settlement is proposed for some but not all of the defendants. See Joseph P. Monteleone and John F. McCarrick, Settlement Issues in Securities Litigation Involving Officers and Directors, Insights, Vol. 7, No. 9, Sept. 1996, at 7.

CHAPTER 16

TAKEOVERS

■ ■ ■

We live in an era in which publicly-held corporations are objects of commerce. Even the largest U.S. publicly-held corporation can become the target of a hostile acquisition attempt. Takeovers have become a major part of the U.S. economy, and thousands of lawyers across the country specialize in advising clients such as buyers, sellers, and financiers who are involved in takeovers. Takeovers appear to come in waves, the first of which occurred in the late 1960s. There was a strong wave in the 1980s, followed by a short pause in the early 1990s. A new wave began in the mid-1990s and continues into the twenty-first century.

In a takeover, corporations both large and small are routinely (1) bought and sold, (2) bought, recapitalized, and then reintroduced to the public markets as new and quite different publicly held corporations, (3) bought, broken up, and individual components sold, or (4) bought and retained by the purchaser as wholly-owned subsidiaries or divisions of the purchaser. The potential acquirer colloquially is known as the "bidder" and the sought-after corporation the "target." Sometimes two or more bidders compete against each other to acquire the target.

Investors love it when the companies in which they own shares become takeover targets because bidders offer target shareholders very substantial premiums over market prices. Premiums are approximately 35% on average, but sometimes much higher premiums are paid. For example, in 2012, the pharmaceutical company GlaxoSmithKline made an unsolicited $2.6 billion bid for Human Genome Sciences, which reflected an 81% premium over Human Genome Sciences' previous share price. Human Genome Sciences rejected the offer but, as targets often do in order to quell shareholder outrage at passing over such a rich premium, said that it was considering "strategic alternatives."

Top managers and boards of directors generally dislike being a takeover target. The announcement of a takeover sends a strong signal that the bidder thinks that the target is poorly managed, is not deploying its assets efficiently, or is not educating the investing public properly about the actual value of the company. In addition to hurt feelings, target management and boards are replaced by managers and directors selected by bidders who succeed in gaining control of the targets.

It is not surprising then that defensive strategies are an intense focus of the highly compensated group of lawyers that specialize in takeovers. Often, though by no means always, hostile takeover bids in the modern period end up either abandoned or negotiated directly with incumbent management. While from the outside these deals look like consensual transactions rather than the brutal, no-holds-barred battles that occurred during the earlier period, they are often highly competitive. While fending off other potential bidders, the aggressor seeks to acquire a target as well as a target management team that prefers either to remain independent or to negotiate with another, more congenial acquirer. Defensive strategies today usually permit incumbent management to defeat even attractive takeover bids if they are sufficiently motivated. Once a company becomes an acquisition target, however, it rarely remains independent because it usually is acquired by some outsider or another.

The power of management to defeat takeover bids raises serious policy questions about whether the interests of shareholders or the interests of management are paramount. It should be apparent that these two interests are usually in direct conflict: shareholders prefer to sell their shares to would-be acquirers at attractive prices considerably above the former market price, while management prefers to retain lucrative positions managing the enterprise. Similar questions about whether the interests of shareholders are being served by takeovers arise from the observation that, while shareholders of companies that are targets of hostile takeovers enjoy significant gains in the form of a high sales price, shareholders of the acquiring companies almost always fare less well. Indeed, the share prices of target firms usually increase dramatically when there is an outside bid, but the shares of the firms making the bids usually slightly decline in price.

A. THE BEGINNINGS OF THE TAKEOVER MOVEMENT

WILLIAM ALLEN, U.S. CORPORATE GOVERNANCE IN A POST-MANAGERIAL AGE

Text of speech given as the Fifth Distinguished Lecture in International Business and
Trade Law, University of Toronto Faculty of Laws.
Pages 6–12 (Oct. 20, 1993).

* * * [John Kenneth Galbraith, in his influential book, *The New Industrial State,* written in the 1960s,] saw the social landscape dominated by huge, virtually autonomous business institutions, under the control of an elite corps of professional managers. These corporations—or what, in this view, amounted to the same thing, these senior managers—had largely freed themselves from the constraints imposed by * * * capital markets by internally generating required funds. Berle and Means had long since shown that the modern U.S. corporation was managed free of

constraint from shareholders, who—widely dispersed and diversified—could be counted upon to affirm any proposal that management offered. The picture of autonomous management was completed by reference to long-term labor contracts in which management entered into peace treaties with labor and by the co-opting of the regulatory processes of government through revolving door employment practices. Atop these large and powerful institutions, of course, sat self-perpetuating hierarchies of senior management.

Galbraith saw these powerful corporations of * * * [this era]—General Motors, IBM, the Pennsylvania Railroad, U.S. Steel, etc.—as impervious, nearly governmental in nature and nearly permanent. We now know that this vision badly underestimated the power of markets, but at the time it reflected what I take to have been a widely held perception.

Businessmen * * *, I feel sure, never felt control over their environment to the degree that Mr. Galbraith posited. But the view of the corporation as a quasi-public institution was quite consistent with the dominant view among managers. If they did not view the public corporation as impervious to markets, business leaders did see the large-scale business enterprise as a quasi-public institution. This was the dogma of managerialism. It was one of managerial authority and managerial responsibility. It implied, of course, that corporations did not exist in a brutally competitive world. * * *

But changes began to undermine the secure suppositions of the managerialist ideology. Those changes included innovation and growth in credit markets and the evolution of takeover entrepreneurs; the explosive growth of pension funds and other institutional shareholders and the striking emergence of a global market place. These forces came together by the early 1980s to trigger a period of significant restructuring in the private sector of the U.S. economy. In that process the premises of the managerialist vision of the corporation were directly challenged by a device that might have come straight out of a neo-classical economics textbook: the hostile cash tender offer.

Historically, legal devices have long existed by which inefficient or dishonest corporate managers could be removed from office. In a few instances, individual shareholders or families owned sufficient shares to influence directly the decisions of boards of directors. Palace coups in which a majority of the directors determined secretly to oust incumbent management and replace them with more competent persons were also a possibility. In some instances, the management of publicly held corporations in dire financial straits voluntarily agreed to be taken over by more successful entities. An aggressor rebuffed by management of a target might obtain voting control over the target by going over the heads of incumbent management and the board of directors and approaching shareholders of the target with a proposal to exchange shares issued by the aggressor for the target's voting shares. Such an offer is a public offering of securities by the aggressor that requires registration under the Securities Act of 1933 and historically has been viewed as a high risk strategy that was unlikely to be successful.

1. PROXY FIGHTS

The most important traditional device used to oust incumbent managers who insisted on remaining independent—a device much more talked about than actually used—was the proxy fight. Since they are often used today, sometimes alone[a] but more often in connection with other takeover devices, a brief discussion of them is appropriate.

A traditional proxy fight was a struggle for control of a public corporation in which most of the high cards were held by management. The nonmanagement group owning a small minority of shares often recently acquired—the "insurgents"—competed with management in an effort to obtain sufficient proxy votes to elect a majority (or all) of the board of directors, and thereby take over control of the corporation. The insurgent group usually made some open market purchases of shares before publicly announcing its intentions, and in some instances assembled a substantial block of shares before management became aware that someone was accumulating shares. In order to solicit proxies successfully, the insurgents had to obtain a list of shareholders, which usually involved a trip to the courthouse and certainly warned incumbent management that an unfriendly proxy solicitation was being contemplated by someone.

After a proxy contest was announced by insurgents, proxies were actively solicited by both incumbent management and insurgents. Proxies were solicited by mailings, by personal contact, and by newspaper and radio commercials. Even though institutional investors did not have the holdings they do today, they were often individually courted. Specialized proxy solicitation firms assisted both the insurgents and management in what was essentially a political campaign for control of the corporation, somewhat similar to an election for public office.

Proxy fights obviously were expensive if the number of shareholders was large. The accepted view was that such fights were not feasible at all in very large corporations with hundreds of thousands of shareholders since the costs of solicitation were prohibitive. Furthermore, incumbent management could have the corporation assume most (or all) of its costs while the insurgents had to finance their campaign entirely out of their

---

[a]   In 1998, a pure proxy fight conducted by TIAA/CREF ousted the entire board of directors of Furr's/Bishop, Inc. a struggling publicly held restaurant chain. This apparently was the first modern instance of the use of a proxy fight by an institutional investor to effect a change in management of a substantial publicly held corporation.

own pockets. The expenses of an unsuccessful proxy fight by insurgents were likely to be sunk costs that were simply lost if the proxy fight failed, so that the insurgents had much more to lose than management. And, in addition, insurgents seeking proxy solicitations from numerous shareholders had the burden of persuading them that they would be better off if new (and often unknown) management were substituted for incumbent management. These burdens alone meant that proxy fights were likely to be successful only if the corporation's recent economic performance had been weak.

Is there any problem with management charging expenses of a proxy fight to the corporation even though the fight is basically designed to preserve their positions in the corporation? Is there any problem with insurgents, if successful, charging their expenses to the corporation after they take it over? Since the ousted management will have used corporate funds to finance their defense while they were in office, the usual result where the insurgents won was that the corporation paid the expenses of both sides. Is there anything wrong with that? There is a fair amount of law on the appropriateness of charging proxy contest expenses to the corporation. Delaware has adopted a "policy/personality" distinction that permits management to charge expenses relating to the development of policy issues but prohibits them from doing so when the issue is purely a personality contest. Palumbo v. Deposit Bank, 758 F.2d 113 (3d Cir.1985); Levin v. Metro-Goldwyn-Mayer, Inc., 264 F.Supp. 797 (S.D.N.Y.1967). Can one draw a meaningful distinction between "policy" and "personality"? Cannot all personality disputes be formulated in terms of a policy disagreement? New York narrowly avoided adopting an even more stringent test in Rosenfeld v. Fairchild Engine & Airplane Corp., 128 N.E.2d 291 (N.Y.1955). So far as the insurgents are concerned, the rule clearly is "no reimbursement" if the insurgents are unsuccessful (certainly it is highly unlikely that successful incumbent management will volunteer to pay the losing faction's expenses). If they are successful, insurgents may argue that they should be reimbursed by the corporation because of the benefit conferred by the change in management. Academic commentary suggested that the usual result where insurgents are successful (that the corporation in effect pays the expenses of both sides) was less than optimal, but there was little movement to try to change this result. Lucian Arye Bebchuk & Marcel Kahan, A Framework for Analyzing Legal Policy Towards Proxy Contests, 78 Cal. L.Rev. 1071 (1990); Franklin C. Latcham & Frank D. Emerson, Proxy Contest Expenses and Shareholder Democracy, 4 Western Res. L.Rev. 5 (1952). Should reimbursement of unsuccessful insurgents be required if their campaign leads to beneficial changes in policy? What kinds of restrictions or limitations might be built into such a plan to eliminate the risk that publicity seekers, cranks, and the like might institute hopeless proxy fights?

SEC proxy regulations contain detailed rules relating to disclosure requirements in connection with proxy solicitations. 17 C.F.R. §§ 240.14a–4 to 14a–6, 240.14a–12 to 14a–15, 240.14a–101. These regulations require "participants" other than management in a proxy contest to file specified information with the SEC and securities exchanges at least five days before a solicitation begins. "Participant" is defined so as to include anyone who contributes more than $500 for the purpose of financing the contest. The information that must be disclosed relates to the identity and background of the participants, their interests in securities of the corporation, when they were acquired, financing arrangements, participation in other proxy contests, and understandings with respect to future employment with the corporation. The solicitation of majority consents is also subject to these third-party proxy solicitation rules, as is a solicitation by an institutional investor to more than ten other institutional investors to act in concert on a matter relating to shareholder voting.

The general philosophy of these contested proxy regulations is described by Judge Clark as follows:

> Appellants' fundamental complaint appears to be that stockholder disputes should be viewed in the eyes of the law just as are political contests, with each side free to hurl charges with comparative unrestraint, the assumption being that the opposing side is then at liberty to refute and thus effectively deflate the "campaign oratory" of its adversary. Such, however, was not the policy of Congress as enacted in the Securities Exchange Act. There Congress has clearly entrusted to the Commission the duty of protecting the investing public against misleading statements made in the course of a struggle for corporate control.

Securities and Exch. Comm'n v. May, 229 F.2d 123, 124 (2d Cir.1956).

The number of proxy fights subject to SEC jurisdiction historically was rather small. For example, only thirty-seven companies were involved in proxy contests for the election of directors in fiscal 1977. Control was involved in twenty-six instances; in eight of these, management retained control, three were settled by negotiation, five were won by nonmanagement factions, and ten were pending at the end of the year. In eleven instances, representation, not control, was sought; management retained all places on the board in six contests and opposition candidates won places on the board in five cases. 1977 S.E.C. Annual Report, at 107. Similar SEC data are not available for more recent years.

The proxy fight was largely eclipsed as a takeover mechanism by the cash tender offer that evolved in the 1960s and is discussed in the following Section.[b] During the late 1980s, however, there was a brief resurgence of contested proxy campaigns in connection with purchase-type takeover attempts. During the period between October 1984 and September 1990, there were 165 proxy contests seeking full or partial control of the board of directors. Joseph A. Grundfest, Just Vote No: A Minimalist Strategy for Dealing with Barbarians Inside the Gates, 45 Stan. L. Rev. 857, 862 n. 17 (1993). In some instances, the target was simply too big for the aggressor to finance the purchase of a majority of the shares. If the aggressor had financial resources to acquire only fifteen or twenty percent of the outstanding shares, a proxy fight might be instituted in an effort to attract sufficient additional votes to oust incumbent management without purchasing an outright majority of the voting stock or, at least, mount a viable threat to encourage the target to negotiate. A well-known example of this strategy was Carl Icahn's proxy fight against the incumbent management of Texaco, Inc. in 1986. In other instances, takeover defenses proved to be impregnable against an outside cash tender offer, and the aggressor attempted an end run by launching a proxy fight in order to compel the removal of the defenses. See Christopher Power, Why the Proxy Fight is Back, Bus. Wk., Mar. 7, 1988, at 32; Judith Dobrzynski, et al., Whose Company Is It Anyway? Proxy Fights Are Spreading as Shareholders Seek More Power, Bus. Wk., Apr. 25, 1988, at 60. In yet another type of case, proxy fights were launched in an effort to persuade a target corporation to enter into a recapitalization or financial restructuring that involved an extraordinary distribution to shareholders. In about 50 percent of these situations, the insurgents were wholly or partially successful.[c] Grundfest, supra, at 863 n.17. In 1990, financing for all-cash takeovers began to dry up, and there was a spurt of more than a dozen proxy fights instituted against major corporations. This trend, however, did not last. The number of proxy fights again declined markedly by 1993.[d]

---

[b] Sophisticated defensive techniques developed against cash tender offers described in Sections B and C, *infra,* are routinely used to defeat outside proxy solicitations. See generally Randall Thomas, Judicial Review of Defensive Tactics in Proxy Contests: When Is Using a Rights Plan Right?, 46 Vand. L.Rev. 503 (1993); Irvin H. Warren & Kevin G. Abrams, Evolving Standards of Judicial Review of Procedural Defenses in Proxy Contests, 47 Bus. Law. 647 (1992); Mark A. Stach, An Overview of Legal and Tactical Considerations in Proxy Contests: The Primary Means of Effecting Fundamental Corporate Change in the 1990s, 13 George Mason U.L.Rev. 745 (1991).

[c] The major successful proxy fight during this period was won by a group headed by Robert Gintel, who began with a 21.6 percent voting interest in Xtra Corporation, and obtained sufficient proxy votes to oust the incumbent management. See Randall Smith, Storming the Barricades with a Proxy: Takeover Defenses Prove to be Flimsy, Wall St. J., May 10, 1990, at C1. In the situations where proxy fights were not directly successful, the target often felt the pressure of this tactic in its negotiations with the insurgents or with other possible aggressors.

[d] By 1992, the number of proxy fights had shrunk to less than half of the 1989 peak. See id.

2.   CASH TENDER OFFERS

ROBERT W. HAMILTON AND RICHARD BOOTH,
CORPORATION FINANCE: CASES AND MATERIALS
Pages 763–66 (3d ed. 2001).

Prior to the 1960s, most contests for corporate control took the form of a proxy fight. * * * There is, of course, a more direct way to gain the votes necessary to unseat the incumbent board. A bidder may simply buy up the shares of the target company either on the open market or [by] making an offer to the public shareholders (or both). Prior to the 1960s, most such offers took the form of exchange offers in which the bidder would offer its own stock or other securities to the stockholders of the target company. Such an offer is, of course, a public offering of securities and is therefore subject to registration under the 1933 Act. * * *

Cash is not a security, and there is no need to register an offer of cash in exchange for target company stock. Thus, cash tender offers were largely unregulated up to and through most of the 1960s. Essentially, a cash tender offer is a public invitation to the shareholders of the target corporation to *tender* their shares to the bidder for purchase for cash. As developed during the 1960s, the offering price was set usually 15 to 20 per cent in excess of the then current market price. The bidder sought enough shares to gain control of the target corporation, although sometimes the bidder sought a higher percentage or all of the outstanding shares. The bidder usually made a public offer or invitation for tenders of shares under which it was not obligated to purchase any shares unless the required amount was tendered. If an excess was tendered, the bidder could, at its option, purchase the excess shares or purchase the required amount only on a pro rata or first-come first-served basis. The tender offer was usually made by an advertisement in the financial press, and copies were often mailed to all shareholders as well. The offer usually provided for a generous commission to brokers who persuaded customers to tender shares.

* * * Initially, the probability of success of a tender offer appeared to be greater than a proxy fight in part because of the element of surprise. During this period it was not uncommon for management of target companies to learn of the offer only when the Wall Street Journal blossomed with a full page ad announcing the offer. Offers often remained open for a brief period so that little time was available to incumbent management to respond and shareholders were panicked into tendering quickly lest they lose out on the offer entirely. Indeed, the phrase *Saturday Night Special,* was coined to describe an offer after the close of the market on Friday and expiring at midnight on Sunday. Such an offer had the advantage (from the bidder's point of view) of denying target shareholders any information as to the reaction of the market. After all, if

the offer was a low ball, the market might actually react by bidding up the price of the shares over the offer price in anticipation of a higher offer to come, in which case the shareholders would have no reason to tender. They could sell in the market for more.

Another factor favoring the tender offer over the proxy fight is that in a cash tender offer, the individual shareholder's decision tends to be a simple investment decision rather than a choice between competing factions for control. In a proxy contest, the shareholder's choice is between competing factions for the right to run the corporation in which the shareholder will have a continuing interest.

When a cash tender offer was made, the open market price for the shares usually increased dramatically. (Whether it equaled or exceeded the tender offer price depended on a complex variety of factors, including the probability that a competing offer at a higher price might be made, whether the offer was likely to be over-subscribed, whether it was on a first-come first-served basis, and so forth.) Persons owning shares thus had the choice of selling their shares in the open market, retaining them, or tendering them. Most shares sold on the open market ultimately were tendered. A group of speculators, known as arbitrageurs, or simply arbs, purchased shares in the open market at prices below the tender offer price in order to tender them and profit by the difference between the two prices. In many tender offers, the arbs came to control enough shares to dictate the outcome of the offer.

This classic picture of the tender offer was significantly modified by the 1968 enactment of the Williams Act, which technically was an amendment to sections 13 and 14 of the Securities Exchange Act of 1934. The Williams Act does essentially two things. First, it provides for disclosures by the bidder. Unlike the 1933 Act or the proxy rules under the 1934 Act, however, these disclosures need not be made or filed in advance of the offer. In other words, the element of surprise is preserved under the Williams Act, although the act does require that anyone who acquires five percent or more of the stock of a registered company (or thereafter increases his or her holdings) must disclose the acquisition and notify the issuer within ten days. Second, the Williams Act provides a set of bidding rules to govern the conduct of tender offers. These rules have been modified somewhat over the years by the SEC, but in essence they provide (1) that there is a minimum period during which a tender offer must remain open (currently 20 business days), (2) that a tendering shareholder has the right during the offer to withdraw shares tendered, (3) that all tendering shareholders must receive the highest price paid in the offer, and (4) that if the offer is over-subscribed then all shareholders may have their shares purchased pro rata in proportion to the number of shares they tendered. In general, the Williams Act applies only to companies that are registered under the 1934 Act, although the catch-all anti-fraud rules adopted thereunder apply in connection with all tender offers in interstate commerce.

The central idea behind the Williams Act was not to stop tender offers altogether, but rather (1) to slow down the process, give shareholders information about the offer, and give target management a chance to respond, and (2) to assure that the shareholders would be treated equally and get the highest possible price, in part by increasing the chances for a competing bid to arise. Whether these goals are worthy and whether the Williams Act achieves them are separate questions.

Numerous devices were designed to avoid or minimize the impact of the Williams Act bidding rules. For example, a bidder might launch a front-end loaded two-tier tender offer, offering an attractive premium for 51 percent of the shares in the front-end tender offer and announcing that the remaining 49 percent of the shares will be cashed out in a later merger at the pre tender offer market price. The idea is to induce shareholders to tender their shares even if they might prefer to hold out for a higher price. Or a bidder might announce an offer for a bare controlling interest and say nothing about what might happen to the remaining minority interest if the bid were successful, raising the possibility that the bidder might loot the target after a successful bid and that the minority shares would end up worth even less than the pre-bid market price. Target management argued that such bids were coercive and that greater leeway should be allowed under principles of fiduciary duty in resisting such offers. Some also argued that such bids violated the spirit of the Williams Act and perhaps even its letter in that they were designed to manipulate the price at which the offer would succeed. Some even argued that the United States should adopt the United Kingdom rule that any offer for 30 percent or more of target shares must be an offer for all of the shares.

Although neither of these fixes came to pass, the courts did allow target management considerable flexibility in defending against coercive offers. Moreover, the SEC promulgated regulations designed to modify or eliminate some tactics, and the states enacted statutes designed to limit others. The overall result of these developments has been the creation of a regulatory scheme for tender offers of increasing, and sometimes bewildering, complexity. Ultimately, however, two tier and partial offers probably evolved away because of competitive forces. Given the choice, target shareholders would presumably favor an all-cash offer for any and all shares over any other sort of offer. Thus, anyone who made a two-tier or partial offer would likely find that another bidder would emerge offering the same price in cash for more of the shares, assuming, of course, that the cash was available.

During the late 1980s, both the size and number of transactions increased dramatically. The previously little known securities firms of

Drexel Burnham Lambert and Kohlberg Kravis Roberts & Co. became major players with access to billions of dollars for the purchase of large publicly owned corporations. Multi-billion dollar all-cash transactions became commonplace, culminating in the $24.8 billion leveraged buyout of RJR Nabisco, Inc. by KKR at the end of 1988, a year in which there were also about 85 hostile takeovers. According to Securities Data Company, there were 4239 priced deals valued at $5 million or more in 1990 of which 177 were leveraged buyouts. The peak year for leveraged buyouts was 1989 in which there were 293 such transactions valued at $75.5 billion or about 24 percent of the $317 billion in aggregate deal value that year. During the 1980s as a whole, 30 percent of the Fortune 500 companies were the target of a hostile offer. See John C. Coates IV, Measuring the Domain of Mediating Hierarchy: How Contestable Are U.S. Public Corporations?, 24 J. Corp. L. 837, 851 (1999).

NOTES

(1) The Williams Act also governs tender offers by an issuer for its own shares. The rules relating to such self-tender offers are roughly the same as those relating to third-party tender offers, although it is common for a self-tender offer to take the form of a Dutch auction[e] in which the shareholders specify the price within a range at which they are willing to sell. In this type of auction, bidding starts high and declines until a buyer claims the item. When multiple items are auctioned, more bidders claim the items as the price decreases; therefore, the first winner pays more than subsequent winners. However, if two buyers want the item at the initial suggested price, the buyers bid against each other until only one bidder is left to purchase at the final bid price.

(2) A variation of the cash tender offer is the "exchange offer," in which the aggressor offers to exchange a package of its own securities for the shares of the target. The package usually consists of both debt and equity interests, and might include highly-speculative warrants or options to acquire further equity interests in the aggressor. Such interests sometimes receive the derogatory label "funny money." In any event, cash tender offers and public exchange offers can be utilized by different bidders seeking control of a single target corporation. For example, in the fight for Armour & Co., a cash tender offer by Greyhound Lines, Inc. was met with a public exchange offer by rival bidder General Host Corporation.

In a broad sense, public exchange offers can be viewed as a type of financing device by aggressors. An aggressor might sell its own securities to create a pool of capital in order to make offers to shareholders of a target corporation to buy shares for cash. Alternatively, the aggressor might offer its own securities directly to the target shareholders in a public exchange offer,

---

[e]   The purchaser in a Dutch auction determines how many shares he wishes to buy and accepts all bids at (or below) the price that yields the desired quantity he wishes to buy.

eliminating the cash-raising step and making the target shareholders the source of capital for the takeover.

(3) Premiums in hostile deals tend to be somewhat higher than premiums in friendly deals. During the period from 1974–85, the average premium was around 75% over the pre-bid market price. See Nathan & O'Keefe, The Rise in Takeover Premiums: An Exploratory Study, 23 J. Fin. Econ. 101, 101 (1989). In 2012, the average premium for the year ended March 31, 1999 was approximately 35%, a level that has held more or less constant for the past 15 years.

3.   LEVERAGED BUYOUTS

The leveraged buyout (LBO) of the 1980s initially appeared to be a new and irresistible business form. An LBO involved an aggressor (an existing management, another corporation, or a corporate raider) who purchased all or most of the outstanding stock of the target for a substantial premium over market price. The acquisition was financed through loans that initially might involve short-term "mezzanine" or "bridge" loans (short-term financing with payment of only interest until the whole balance is due) plus low-grade high-interest debt instruments—noninvestment-grade junk bonds. The transaction was structured so that the repayment of this newly-created debt ultimately became the obligation of the target corporation. It was a classic bootstrap transaction: the proceeds of the debt assumed by the target were used to purchase the publicly-held shares of the target. Funds to pay the debt assumed by the target were to be obtained by the sale of components of the target's business or by use of the target's subsequent cash flow. This cash flow was increased by tax savings arising from the deductions for interest payments made on the new debt. In making the financial calculations to see how much debt a target can carry, the standard measure is "EBIT"— net "earnings before interest and taxes"—because the tax obligation is eliminated by the interest deductions for payments on the new debt. When the debt was paid down sufficiently, the target could again become a publicly-held corporation through the sale of shares to the general public. In the best of all worlds, everyone benefited. In the worst, the corporation was unable to carry the load of the new debt and went into bankruptcy; at that point, the issue became whether the LBO transaction itself could be attacked as a fraudulent conveyance.

ROBERT W. HAMILTON AND RICHARD A. BOOTH, BUSINESS BASICS FOR LAW STUDENTS: ESSENTIAL TERMS AND CONCEPTS
Pages 355, 360–61 (1997).

It is important to recognize that even if the bidder acquires over 50 percent of the outstanding shares and replaces the target's board of directors and management, it does not have a free hand with respect to the target's assets. The target is still a publicly owned company with the public owning 49.9 percent; the presence of this minority interest sharply circumscribes and limits what the bidder can do with the target's assets. For example, the bidder may not simply distribute to itself * * * $50,000,000 in excess cash or combine a manufacturing division owned by the target with a similar division owned by the bidder. Transactions of these types would almost certainly be viewed as in breach of the fiduciary duty new management has assumed to the former target company and would likely give rise to immediate shareholder derivative suits. Transactions between the bidder and its new partially owned subsidiary must be made at arms-length and, even then, there is a substantial opportunity for distracting litigation brought by minority shareholders of the target. * * *

* * * However, it is not possible, as a practical matter, to acquire 100 percent of the shares of a publicly held corporation by a tender offer. Even in an irresistibly attractive tender offer for all shares, a few shareholders always fail to tender by reason of inadvertence or inattention, and there always are a few small shareholders who hold out and refuse to accept an offer at any price. A follow-up transaction to eliminate the remaining shareholders is an essential step where 100 percent ownership is desired. These follow-up transactions, often called back-end or mop-up transactions, are statutory [cash-out] mergers [in which minority shares are converted into a specified amount of cash]. A back-end transaction is not necessary if the bidder is willing to accept the status of a majority shareholder in a publicly held corporation with minority shareholders.

In a public cash tender offer, the bidder may make the back-end transaction an affirmative weapon. The bidder may make a partial tender offer, seeking to acquire a controlling interest but less than all of the target's outstanding shares, and at the same time announce, as part of its takeover strategy, the terms of the back-end merger that will eliminate all of the remaining outstanding shares if the original partial offer is successful. Such an offer is known as a two-step offer or two-tier offer. The terms of the back-end part of the two-step offer, moreover, may be [considerably] less attractive than the terms of the original cash tender offer, thereby encouraging (or coercing) all shareholders to tender promptly to avoid the less attractive terms of the follow-up transaction. Such an offer is known as a front-end loaded offer and is sometimes referred to as a coercive offer (although coercion comes in many forms). Many states have enacted statutes restricting back-end transactions.

ROBERT W. HAMILTON, CORPORATE MERGERS AND ACQUISITIONS

The Guide to American Law Yearbook.
Pages 66, 72–75 (1990).

Most acquisition transactions since 1985 have involved all-cash purchases of the stock of the target corporation. * * * Even transactions involving little-known companies routinely involve all-cash transactions of hundreds of millions of dollars. The amounts involved in these transactions are so large as to have been almost unimaginable in a private transaction just two decades ago. An important question * * * [is] where [is] all the money * * * coming from[?]

In one sense, the answer is very simple: Most of the capital that goes into modern takeover attempts is borrowed. Borrowed money is what makes the modern takeover world go round; if that source of funding disappeared, the present takeover movement would stop instantly. It is true that aggressors such as Conoco and Texaco have immense operations of their own and can accumulate large amounts of cash, but even companies of that size cannot readily finance a multibillion dollar takeover entirely from internal sources. * * *

Loans from commercial banks are the source of most of the borrowed capital in large takeover bids, but other sources of high-risk financing also exist. During the 1980s, a market for high-risk, below-investment-grade debt instruments or "bonds," usually called "junk bonds," was largely created by Drexel Burnham Lambert, Inc. This market has grown to the point that it is able to absorb several billion dollars of high-risk debt to finance specific takeover bids. Many institutional investors are active in this market because junk bonds pay interest at rates considerably higher than can be obtained from the less risky "investment-grade" bonds.

In addition, a major source of equity capital has been created by takeover firms such as KKR, which has attracted takeover funds from sophisticated investors, including many institutional investors. The proposed financing by KKR of its purchase of RJR Nabisco illustrates the operation of these modern financing sources. KKR needed $20.1 billion in cash to purchase RJR. (The remaining $4.8 billion was represented by the debt securities being issued to tendering RJR shareholders.) KKR raised the $20.1 billion from the following sources:

1. Bank loans were obtained from a large consortium of domestic and foreign (largely Japanese) banks—$13.3 billion.

2. Five billion dollars in "bridge financing" was provided by the brokerage houses of Drexel Burnham Lambert, Inc. ($3.5 billion) and Merrill Lynch & Company ($1.5 billion). This bridge financing was to be refinanced within a year by the sale of junk bonds to investors.

3.   KKR limited partners put up $1.5 billion in equity capital. KKR itself put up only $15 million, or 1 percent of the entire risk capital and a tiny fraction of the total purchase price. Altogether, KKR raised $25.7 billion to cover the purchase price and expenses but invested only about $15 million of its own capital in order to acquire the nation's nineteenth largest commercial enterprise!

Why do banks and others agree to make such large loans to fund buyouts? For one thing, the return is good—interest rates on both takeover-directed bank loans and junk bonds are well above those available from other alternative investments. For another thing, fees for making loan commitments are earned whether or not the sale actually occurs. In the RJR Nabisco transaction, Merrill Lynch & Company and Drexel Burnham Lambert, Inc., received fees of about $200 million for their commitment to invest $5 billion, while the banks received a somewhat larger amount in commitment fees for making their much larger commitments. These fees are earned and paid when the commitment is made and are not dependent on the success of the bid.

Yet when all is said and done, commitment fees and high interest rates alone do not explain the attractiveness of these loans. One does not make money even from large loan commitment fees and high interest rates if the loans are so risky that they are unlikely to be repaid. These transactions are attractive because the risks are not as great as they first appear. An essential attribute of the ability of KKR and other takeover firms to raise immense amounts of capital is that these loans are in effect secured by the assets and cash flow of the target corporation itself. Such transactions are called "leveraged buyouts" or "bootstrap transactions." Approximately one-half of the recent takeover transactions were of this type. The banks were willing to lend more than $13 billion to KKR to purchase RJR Nabisco common stock because they were assured that, if the transaction succeeded, the assets and cash flow of RJR Nabisco would be used to pay the interest on and secure the repayment of the loans and junk bonds used to finance the purchase.

Of course, RJR Nabisco already had some indebtedness on its books. The new debt was simply added onto this existing debt and it is expected to repay the entire amount. Needless to say, Nabisco's existing creditors were not happy at these new obligations being assumed by RJR Nabisco. Since the proceeds of the new loans were used to pay shareholders, they did not benefit RJR Nabisco, and loans owed to existing creditors now were less secure and considerably more risky. But there was not very much they could do about the transaction.

After a leveraged buyout, the target may find that its total debt obligations greatly exceed its ability to repay them if business is continued as usual. Such a corporation may find it necessary to make Herculean efforts to reduce costs and increase cash flow. It may be compelled to sell portions of its business to third parties in order to liquidate at least a portion of the new indebtedness and permit the corporation to remain solvent. Transactions in which such later sales of components of the original business are contemplated at the time of the offer are called "bust-up transactions" or "bust-up acquisitions." Improvements in earnings and cash flow may also be achieved from the savings inherent in not being a reporting publicly-held corporation, from the immense tax deductions arising from the interest payments on its debt, from the elimination of dividends, and from economic improvements to the target's business. Indeed, the disciplinary effect of the increase in debt has been cited by some observers as a major benefit arising from leveraged transactions since it encourages increased efficiency and control of costs.

Many established businesses that have been acquired in leveraged buyouts have proven that they are able to carry large increases of indebtedness during periods of high economic activity. However, the recent spate of multibillion dollar leveraged buyouts, bust-up transactions, and junk bond financing because of the immense sums of money involved has caused concern among regulatory agencies, legislators, and the general public. The principal concern that has been expressed about the growth of such leveraged transactions generally is whether most of these debt-burdened businesses can survive when there is an economic downturn. Since there was no significant downturn during the 1980s, no one really knows the answer to this question. A secondary concern that has sometimes been expressed is whether the large investments by commercial banks and institutional investors in leveraged buyout loans and investments may harm the public's confidence in the nation's financial institutions during an economic downturn. If such a downturn occurs, the future of the spectacular mergers and acquisitions examined here will be in grave doubt. * * *

Corporate law firms thrived during the late 1980s as never before. Lawyers were close to the center of the takeover movement, charting strategy, devising defenses, and documenting and effectuating the transactions as they occurred. Immense acquisition transactions required structuring, the production of legal documents, of legal opinions, of tax analysis, and so forth. Securities and banking lawyers also played key roles in negotiating the financing of major transactions: the suppliers of huge amounts of capital required legal teams whose size rivaled those of the target and the aggressor. And finally there was the litigation that surrounded virtually every major takeover. Suits were often simultaneously pending in Delaware and six or seven other states as the target attempted to evade the grasp of the aggressor.

The largest takeover transaction ever attempted—the 1988 leveraged buyout of RJR-Nabisco, Inc. by the KKR firm * * * reflected both the high point and culmination of a movement that had shaken large American enterprise to its roots.

NOTES

(1) Is all this only of historical interest? Not entirely. In 2012, there were over a dozen leveraged buyout firms—each with assets in excess of three billion dollars. The largest LBO firm, KKR, has assets in excess of eight billion dollars. Leveraged buyouts were on the rise in 2011 and 2012, after a drop off attributable to the frozen credit markets in the financial crisis of 2007 and 2008. The recent boom is fueled in part by historically low borrowing costs. Total U.S. LBO volumes reached $28.87 billion in the third quarter of 2012, up 96 percent from the same period in 2011 and outperforming a 32 percent growth in global leveraged buyouts, according to data from Thomson Reuters. But the RJR Nabisco deal, which has an inflation-adjusted value of $55.38 billion, remains the biggest deal in history, in constant dollars. The 2007 LBO of Energy Future Holdings, with a deal value of $47.37 billion and an inflation-adjusted value of $47.23 billion, holds second place.

(2) Litigation over takeovers is a major industry in Delaware, New York, and other U.S. financial capitals. A study of litigation by Matthew Cain and Steven Davidoff found that fully 97.5 percent of takeovers in 2013 with a value over $100 million experienced a shareholder lawsuit. This was higher than the final figure in 2012 of 91.7 percent of transactions. In 2005, "only" 39.3 percent of transactions attracted a lawsuit. In 2013, the average takeover valued greater than $100 million had no less than seven lawsuits each brought by a different law firm. With regard to the settlements reached in these cases, the authors' findings are still preliminary because many of these cases are making their way through the courts, but more than 70 percent already have settled so far. Nearly 85 percent of the settlements required only additional disclosure, meaning that there must be an amendment to the company's proxy statement to provide additional disclosure to shareholders. Shareholders are not paid any amount in this settlement, but the plaintiffs' lawyers are paid fees awarded by the court, often generously. These disclosure-only settlements have been criticized for being "cheap" settlements that benefit only plaintiffs' lawyers and further encourage litigation without merit.

Professors Cain and Davidoff find that even though the courts in Delaware have been quick to award big fees where there is wrongdoing, the judges are "clearly tiring of disclosure-only settlements." The authors point to In re Paetec Holding Corp. S'holders Litig., C.A. No. 6761–VCG, 2013 WL 1110811 (Del. Ch. Mar. 19, 2013), in which Delaware Vice Chancellor Sam Glasscock III expressed concern that these settlements might be the subject of collusion between the defendants and the plaintiffs' lawyers, who agree to zero-dollar payouts to shareholders (good for the defendants) and big dollar payouts for the plaintiffs' lawyers (good for the plaintiffs' lawyers, not so much for the plaintiffs themselves) whose clients are unsophisticated small investors and not really in a position to monitor their self-appointed lawyers. As the court observed, the risk is that these parties have agreed to "trivial disclosures as the path of least resistance to a desired end." He recommended that the court scrutinize disclosure-only settlements. Even after the kvetching, however, Vice Chancellor Glasscock awarded a lawyers' fee of $500,000 for the disclosure-only settlement in the case. In another 2013 case, In re Gen-Probe, Vice Chancellor J. Travis Laster raised questions about the high lawyers' fees in disclosure-only settlements and awarded only $100,000. Expressing concern over the proliferation of takeover litigation, he admitted that there was a need for a "recalibrating" of the idea that the court was going to give out "left and right, 500 grand for" relatively meritless disclosure-only settlements. Michael C. Cain and Stephen Davidoff, Takeover Litigation in 2014, January 9, 2014 Working Paper, available at http://papers.ssrn.com/sol3/papers.cfm?abstract_id=2377001.

B. DEFENSES: STATE LEGISLATION

CTS CORP. v. DYNAMICS CORP. OF AMERICA

Supreme Court of the United States, 1987.
481 U.S. 69.

JUSTICE POWELL delivered the opinion of the Court.

This case presents the questions whether the Control Share Acquisitions Chapter of the Indiana Business Corporation Law, Ind.Code § 23–1–42–1 *et seq.* (Supp.1986), is preempted by the Williams Act or violates the Commerce Clause of the Federal Constitution, Art. I, § 8, cl. 3.

I

A

On March 4, 1986, the Governor of Indiana signed a revised Indiana Business Corporation Law, Ind.Code § 23–1–17–1 *et seq.* (Supp.1986). That law included the Control Share Acquisitions Chapter (Indiana Act or Act). Beginning on August 1, 1987, the Act will apply to any corporation incorporated in Indiana, § 23–1–17–3(a), unless the corporation amends its articles of incorporation or bylaws to opt out of the Act, § 23–1–42–5. Before that date, any Indiana corporation can opt into the Act by resolution of its board of directors. § 23–1–17–3(b). The Act applies only to "issuing public corporations." The term "corporation" includes only businesses incorporated in Indiana. See § 23–1–20–5. An "issuing public corporation" is defined as:

"a corporation that has:

"(1) one hundred (100) or more shareholders;

"(2) its principal place of business, its principal office, or substantial assets within Indiana; and

"(3) either:

"(A) more than ten percent (10%) of its shareholders resident in Indiana;

"(B) more than ten percent (10%) of its shares owned by Indiana residents; or

"(C) ten thousand (10,000) shareholders resident in Indiana." § 23–1–42–4(a).[1]

The Act focuses on the acquisition of "control shares" in an issuing public corporation. Under the Act, an entity acquires "control shares" whenever it acquires shares that, but for the operation of the Act, would bring its voting power in the corporation to or above any of three thresholds: 20%, 33 1/3%, or 50%. § 23–1–42–1. An entity that acquires control shares does not necessarily acquire voting rights. Rather, it gains those rights only "to the extent granted by resolution approved by the shareholders of the issuing public corporation." § 23–1–42–9(a). Section 23–1–42–9(b) requires a majority vote of all disinterested[2] shareholders holding each class of stock for passage of such a resolution. The practical effect of this requirement is to condition acquisition of control of a corporation on approval of a majority of the pre-existing disinterested shareholders.

The shareholders decide whether to confer rights on the control shares at the next regularly scheduled meeting of the shareholders, or at a specially scheduled meeting. The acquirer can require management of the corporation to hold such a special meeting within 50 days if it files an "acquiring person statement,"[4] requests the meeting, and agrees to pay the expenses of the meeting. See § 23–1–42–7. If the shareholders do not

---

[1]   These thresholds are much higher than the 5% threshold acquisition requirement that brings a tender offer under the coverage of the Williams Act.

[2]   "Interested shares" are shares with respect to which the acquirer, an officer, or an inside director of the corporation "may exercise or direct the exercise of the voting power of the corporation in the election of directors." § 23–1–42–3. If the record date passes before the acquirer purchases shares pursuant to the tender offer, the purchased shares will not be "interested shares" within the meaning of the Act; although the acquirer may own the shares on the date of the meeting, it will not "exercise * * * the voting power" of the shares.

As a practical matter, the record date usually will pass before shares change hands. Under Securities and Exchange Commission (SEC) regulations, the shares cannot be purchased until 20 business days after the offer commences. 17 CFR § 240.14e–1(a) (1986). If the acquirer seeks an early resolution of the issue—as most acquirers will—the meeting required by the Act must be held no more than 50 calendar days after the offer commences, about three weeks after the earliest date on which the shares could be purchased. See § 23–1–42–7. The Act requires management to give notice of the meeting "as promptly as reasonably practicable * * * to all shareholders of record as of the record date set for the meeting." § 23–1–42–8(a). It seems likely that management of the target corporation would violate this obligation if it delayed setting the record date and sending notice until after 20 business days had passed. Thus, we assume that the record date usually will be set before the date on which federal law first permits purchase of the shares.

[4]   An "acquiring person statement" is an information statement describing, *inter alia,* the identity of the acquiring person and the terms and extent of the proposed acquisition. See § 23–1–42–6.

vote to restore voting rights to the shares, the corporation may redeem the control shares from the acquirer at fair market value, but it is not required to do so. § 23–1–42–10(b). Similarly, if the acquirer does not file an acquiring person statement with the corporation, the corporation may, if its bylaws or articles of incorporation so provide, redeem the shares at any time after 60 days after the acquirer's last acquisition. § 23–1–42–10(a).

B

On March 10, 1986, appellee Dynamics Corporation of America (Dynamics) owned 9.6% of the common stock of appellant CTS Corporation, an Indiana corporation. On that day, six days after the Act went into effect, Dynamics announced a tender offer for another million shares in CTS; purchase of those shares would have brought Dynamics' ownership interest in CTS to 27.5%. Also on March 10, Dynamics filed suit in the United States District Court for the Northern District of Illinois, alleging that CTS had violated the federal securities laws in a number of respects no longer relevant to these proceedings. On March 27, the board of directors of CTS, an Indiana corporation, elected to be governed by the provisions of the Act, see § 23–1–17–3.

Four days later, on March 31, Dynamics moved for leave to amend its complaint to allege that the Act is preempted by the Williams Act, and violates the Commerce Clause, Art. I, § 8, cl. 3. Dynamics sought a temporary restraining order, a preliminary injunction, and declaratory relief against CTS' use of the Act. On April 9, the District Court ruled that the Williams Act preempts the Indiana Act and granted Dynamics' motion for declaratory relief. 637 F.Supp. 389 (N.D.Ill.1986). Relying on Justice White's plurality opinion in *Edgar v. MITE Corp.,* 457 U.S. 624 (1982), the court concluded that the Act "wholly frustrates the purpose and objective of Congress in striking a balance between the investor, management, and the takeover bidder in takeover contests." 637 F.Supp., at 399. A week later, on April 17, the District Court issued an opinion accepting Dynamics' claim that the Act violates the Commerce Clause. This holding rested on the court's conclusion that "the substantial interference with interstate commerce created by the [Act] outweighs the articulated local benefits so as to create an impermissible indirect burden on interstate commerce." *Id.,* at 406. The District Court certified its decisions on the Williams Act and Commerce Clause claims as final under Federal Rule of Civil Procedure 54(b). Ibid.

CTS appealed the District Court's holdings on these claims to the Court of Appeals for the Seventh Circuit. Because of the imminence of CTS' annual meeting, the Court of Appeals consolidated and expedited the two appeals. On April 23rd—23 days after Dynamics first contested application of the Act in the District Court—the Court of Appeals issued an order affirming the judgment of the District Court. The opinion followed on May 28. 794 F.2d 250 (C.A.7 1986).

After disposing of a variety of questions not relevant to this appeal, the Court of Appeals examined Dynamics' claim that the Williams Act preempts the Indiana Act. The court looked first to the plurality opinion in *Edgar v. MITE Corp., supra,* in which three Justices found that the Williams Act preempts state statutes that upset the balance between target management and a tender offeror. The court noted that some commentators had disputed this view of the Williams Act, concluding instead that the Williams Act was "an anti-takeover statute, expressing a view, however benighted, that hostile takeovers are bad." 794 F.2d, at 262. It also noted:

> [I]t is a big leap from saying that the Williams Act does not itself exhibit much hostility to tender offers to saying that it implicitly forbids states to adopt more hostile regulations * * *. But whatever doubts of the Williams' Act preemptive intent we might entertain as an original matter are stilled by the weight of precedent. *Ibid.*

Once the court had decided to apply the analysis of the *MITE* plurality, it found the case straightforward:

> Very few tender offers could run the gauntlet that Indiana has set up. In any event, if the Williams Act is to be taken as a congressional determination that a month (roughly) is enough time to force a tender offer to be kept open, 50 days is too much; and 50 days is the minimum under the Indiana act if the target corporation so chooses. *Id.,* at 263.

The court next addressed Dynamic's Commerce Clause challenge to the Act. Applying the balancing test articulated in *Pike v. Bruce Church, Inc.,* 397 U.S. 137 (1970), the court found the Act unconstitutional:

> Unlike a state's blue sky law the Indiana statute is calculated to impede transactions between residents of other states. For the sake of trivial or even negative benefits to its residents Indiana is depriving nonresidents of the valued opportunity to accept tender offers from other nonresidents.

> * * * Even if a corporation's tangible assets are immovable, the efficiency with which they are employed and the proportions in which the earnings they generate are divided between management and shareholders depends on the market for corporate control—an interstate, indeed international, market that the State of Indiana is not authorized to opt out of, as in effect it has done in this statute. 794 F.2d, at 264.

Finally, the court addressed the "internal affairs" doctrine, a "principle of conflict of laws * * * designed to make sure that the law of only one state shall govern the internal affairs of a corporation or other association." It stated:

> We may assume without having to decide that Indiana has a broad latitude in regulating those affairs, even when the consequence may be to make it harder to take over an Indiana corporation. * * * But in this case the effect on the interstate market in securities and corporate control is direct, intended, and substantial. * * * [T]hat the mode of regulation involves jiggering with voting rights cannot take it outside the scope of judicial review under the commerce clause. *Ibid.*

Accordingly, the court affirmed the judgment of the District Court.

Both Indiana and CTS filed jurisdictional statements. We noted probable jurisdiction and now reverse. * * *

II

The first question in these cases is whether the Williams Act preempts the Indiana Act. As we have stated frequently, absent an explicit indication by Congress of an intent to preempt state law, a state statute is preempted only

> 'where compliance with both federal and state regulations is a physical impossibility * * *,' *Florida Lime & Avocado Growers, Inc. v. Paul,* 373 U.S. 132, 142–143 (1963), or where the state 'law stands as an obstacle to the accomplishment and execution of the full purposes and objectives of Congress.' *Hines v. Davidowitz,* 312 U.S. 52, 67 (1941). * * * *Ray v. Atlantic Richfield Co.,* 435 U.S. 151, 158 (1978).

Because it is entirely possible for entities to comply with both the Williams Act and the Indiana Act, the state statute can be preempted only if it frustrates the purposes of the federal law.

A

Our discussion begins with a brief summary of the structure and purposes of the Williams Act. * * *

B

The Indiana Act differs in major respects from the Illinois statute that the Court considered in *Edgar v. MITE Corp.,* 457 U.S. 624 (1982). After reviewing the legislative history of the Williams Act, Justice White, joined by Chief Justice Burger and Justice Blackmun (the plurality), concluded that the Williams Act struck a careful balance between the interests of offerors and target companies, and that any state statute that "upset" this balance was preempted. *Id.,* at 632–634.

The plurality then identified three offending features of the Illinois statute. Justice White's opinion first noted that the Illinois statute provided for a 20-day precommencement period. During this time, management could disseminate its views on the upcoming offer to shareholders, but offerors could not publish their offers. The plurality found that this provision gave management "a powerful tool to combat tender offers." *Id.*, at 635. This contrasted dramatically with the Williams Act; Congress had deleted express precommencement notice provisions from the Williams Act. According to the plurality, Congress had determined that the potentially adverse consequences of such a provision on shareholders should be avoided. Thus, the plurality concluded that the Illinois provision "frustrate[d] the objectives of the Williams Act." *Ibid.* The second criticized feature of the Illinois statute was a provision for a hearing on a tender offer that, because it set no deadline, allowed management " 'to stymie indefinitely a takeover,' " *id.*, at 637. * * * The plurality noted that " 'delay can seriously impede a tender offer,' " 457 U.S., at 637 (quoting *Great Western United Corp. v. Kidwell*, 577 F.2d 1256, 1277 (C.A.5 1978) (Wisdom, J.)), and that "Congress anticipated that investors and the takeover offeror would be free to go forward without unreasonable delay," 457 U.S., at 639. Accordingly, the plurality concluded that this provision conflicted with the Williams Act. The third troublesome feature of the Illinois statute was its requirement that the fairness of tender offers would be reviewed by the Illinois Secretary of State. Noting that "Congress intended for investors to be free to make their own decisions," the plurality concluded that " '[t]he state thus offers investor protection at the expense of investor autonomy—an approach quite in conflict with that adopted by Congress.' " *Id.*, at 639–640 (quoting *MITE Corp. v. Dixon, supra,* at 494).

C

As the plurality opinion in *MITE* did not represent the views of a majority of the Court, we are not bound by its reasoning. We need not question that reasoning, however, because we believe the Indiana Act passes muster even under the broad interpretation of the Williams Act articulated by Justice White in *MITE*. As is apparent from our summary of its reasoning, the overriding concern of the *MITE* plurality was that the Illinois statute considered in that case operated to favor management against offerors, to the detriment of shareholders. By contrast, the statute now before the Court protects the independent shareholder against both of the contending parties. Thus, the Act furthers a basic purpose of the Williams Act, " 'plac[ing] investors on an equal footing with the takeover bidder,' " *Piper v. Chris-Craft Industries,* 430 U.S., at 30, (quoting the

Senate Report accompanying the Williams Act, S.Rep. No. 550, 90th Cong., 1st Sess., 4 (1967)).[7]

The Indiana Act operates on the assumption, implicit in the Williams Act, that independent shareholders faced with tender offers often are at a disadvantage. By allowing such shareholders to vote as a group, the Act protects them from the coercive aspects of some tender offers. If, for example, shareholders believe that a successful tender offer will be followed by a purchase of nontendering shares at a depressed price, individual shareholders may tender their shares—even if they doubt the tender offer is in the corporation's best interest—to protect themselves from being forced to sell their shares at a depressed price. As the SEC explains: "The alternative of not accepting the tender offer is virtual assurance that, if the offer is successful, the shares will have to be sold in the lower priced, second step." Two-Tier Tender Offer Pricing and Non-Tender Offer Purchase Programs, SEC Exchange Act Rel. No. 21079 (June 21, 1984) (hereinafter SEC Release No. 21079). See Lowenstein, Pruning Deadwood in Hostile Takeovers: A Proposal for Legislation, 83 Colum.L.Rev. 249, 307–309 (1983). In such a situation under the Indiana Act, the shareholders as a group, acting in the corporation's best interest, could reject the offer, although individual shareholders might be inclined to accept it. The desire of the Indiana Legislature to protect shareholders of Indiana corporations from this type of coercive offer does not conflict with the Williams Act. Rather, it furthers the federal policy of investor protection.

In implementing its goal, the Indiana Act avoids the problems the plurality discussed in *MITE*. Unlike the *MITE* statute, the Indiana Act does not give either management or the offeror an advantage in communicating with the shareholders about the impending offer. The Act also does not impose an indefinite delay on tender offers. Nothing in the Act prohibits an offeror from consummating an offer on the 20th business day, the earliest day permitted under applicable federal regulations. Nor does the Act allow the state government to interpose its views of fairness between willing buyers and sellers of shares of the target company.

---

[7] Dynamics finds evidence of an intent to favor management in several features of the Act. * * *

The Act * * * imposes some added expenses on the offeror, requiring it, *inter alia,* to pay the costs of special shareholder meetings to vote on the transfer of voting rights, see § 23–1–42–7(a). In our view, the expenses of such a meeting fairly are charged to the offeror. A corporation pays the costs of annual meetings that it holds to discuss its affairs. If an offeror—who has no official position with the corporation—desires a special meeting solely to discuss the voting rights of the offeror, it is not unreasonable to have the offeror pay for the meeting.

Of course, by regulating tender offers, the Act makes them more expensive and thus deters them somewhat, but this type of reasonable regulation does not alter the balance between management and offeror in any significant way. The principal result of the Act is to grant shareholders the power to deliberate collectively about the merits of tender offers. This result is fully in accord with the purposes of the Williams Act.

State laws also may provide for "dissenters' rights" under which minority shareholders who disagree with corporate decisions to take particular actions are entitled to sell their shares to the corporation at fair market value. See, e.g., MBCA § 13.02. By requiring the corporation to purchase the shares of dissenting shareholders, these laws may inhibit a corporation from engaging in the specified transactions.[12]

It thus is an accepted part of the business landscape in this country for States to create corporations, to prescribe their powers, and to define the rights that are acquired by purchasing their shares. A State has an interest in promoting stable relationships among parties involved in the corporations it charters, as well as in ensuring that investors in such corporations have an effective voice in corporate affairs.

There can be no doubt that the Act reflects these concerns. The primary purpose of the Act is to protect the shareholders of Indiana corporations. It does this by affording shareholders, when a takeover offer is made, an opportunity to decide collectively whether the resulting change in voting control of the corporation, as they perceive it, would be desirable. A change of management may have important effects on the shareholders' interests; it is well within the State's role as overseer of corporate governance to offer this opportunity. The autonomy provided by allowing shareholders collectively to determine whether the takeover is advantageous to their interests may be especially beneficial where a hostile tender offer may coerce shareholders into tendering their shares.

Appellee Dynamics responds to this concern by arguing that the prospect of coercive tender offers is illusory, and that tender offers generally should be favored because they reallocate corporate assets into the hands of management who can use them most effectively.[13] See

---

[12] Numerous other common regulations may affect both nonresident and resident shareholders of a corporation. Specified votes may be required for the sale of all of the corporation's assets. See MBCA § 12.02. The election of directors may be staggered over a period of years to prevent abrupt changes in management. See MBCA § 8.06. Various classes of stock may be created with differences in voting rights as to dividends and on liquidation. See MBCA § 6.01(c). Provisions may be made for cumulative voting. See MBCA § 7.28. Corporations may adopt restrictions on payment of dividends to ensure that specified ratios of assets to liabilities are maintained for the benefit of the holders of corporate bonds or notes. See MBCA * * * 6.40 (noting that a corporation's articles of incorporation can restrict payment of dividends) * * *. Where the shares of a corporation are held in States other than that of incorporation, actions taken pursuant to these and similar provisions of state law will affect all shareholders alike wherever they reside or are domiciled.

Nor is it unusual for partnership law to restrict certain transactions. For example, a purchaser of a partnership interest generally can gain a right to control the business only with the consent of other owners. See Uniform Partnership Act § 27, Revised Uniform Limited Partnership Act §§ 702, 704. These provisions—in force in the great majority of the States—bear a striking resemblance to the Act at issue in this case.

[13] It is appropriate to note when discussing the merits and demerits of tender offers that generalizations usually require qualification. No one doubts that some successful tender offers will provide more effective management or other benefits such as needed diversification. But there is no reason to assume that the type of conglomerate corporation that may result from repetitive takeovers necessarily will result in more effective management or otherwise be beneficial to shareholders. The divergent views in the literature—and even now being debated in

generally Easterbrook & Fischel, The Proper Role of a Target's Management in Responding to a Tender Offer, 94 Harv.L.Rev. 1161 (1981). * * * Indiana's concern with tender offers is not groundless. Indeed, the potentially coercive aspects of tender offers have been recognized by the SEC, see SEC Release No. 21079, and by a number of scholarly commentators, see, e.g., Bradley & Rosenzweig, Defensive Stock Repurchases, 99 Harv.L.Rev. 1377, 1412–1413 (1986). * * * The Constitution does not require the States to subscribe to any particular economic theory. We are not inclined "to second-guess the empirical judgments of lawmakers concerning the utility of legislation," *Kassel v. Consolidated Freightways Corp.,* 450 U.S., at 679, 101 S.Ct., at 1321 (Brennan, J., concurring in judgment). In our view, the possibility of coercion in some takeover bids offers additional justification for Indiana's decision to promote the autonomy of independent shareholders.

Dynamics argues in any event that the State has " 'no legitimate interest in protecting the nonresident shareholders.' " Dynamics relies heavily on the statement by the *MITE* Court that "[i]nsofar as the * * * law burdens out-of-state transactions, there is nothing to be weighed in the balance to sustain the law." 457 U.S., at 644, 102 S.Ct., at 2641. But that comment was made in reference to an Illinois law that applied as well to out-of-state corporations as to in-state corporations. We agree that Indiana has no interest in protecting nonresident shareholders *of nonresident corporations.* But this Act applies only to corporations incorporated in Indiana. We reject the contention that Indiana has no interest in providing for the shareholders of its corporations the voting autonomy granted by the Act. Indiana has a substantial interest in preventing the corporate form from becoming a shield for unfair business dealing. Moreover, unlike the Illinois statute invalidated in *MITE,* the Indiana Act applies only to corporations that have a substantial number of shareholders in Indiana. See Ind.Code § 23–1–42–4(a)(3) (Supp.1986). Thus, every application of the Indiana Act will affect a substantial number of Indiana residents, whom Indiana indisputably has an interest in protecting.

D

Dynamics' argument that the Act is unconstitutional ultimately rests on its contention that the Act will limit the number of successful tender offers. There is little evidence that this will occur. But even if true, this result would not substantially affect our Commerce Clause analysis. We reiterate that this Act does not prohibit any entity—resident or nonresident—from offering to purchase, or from purchasing, shares in Indiana corporations, or from attempting thereby to gain control. It only

---

the Congress—reflect the reality that the type and utility of tender offers vary widely. Of course, in many situations the offer to shareholders is simply a cash price substantially higher than the market price prior to the offer.

provides regulatory procedures designed for the better protection of the corporations' shareholders. We have rejected the "notion that the Commerce Clause protects the particular structure or methods of operation in a * * * market." *Exxon Corp. v. Governor of Maryland,* 437 U.S., at 127, 98 S.Ct., at 2215. The very commodity that is traded in the securities market is one whose characteristics are defined by state law. Similarly, the very commodity that is traded in the "market for corporate control"—the corporation—is one that owes its existence and attributes to state law. Indiana need not define these commodities as other States do; it need only provide that residents and nonresidents have equal access to them. This Indiana has done. Accordingly, even if the Act should decrease the number of successful tender offers for Indiana corporations, this would not offend the Commerce Clause.

IV

On its face, the Indiana Control Share Acquisitions Chapter evenhandedly determines the voting rights of shares of Indiana corporations. The Act does not conflict with the provisions or purposes of the Williams Act. To the limited extent that the Act affects interstate commerce, this is justified by the State's interests in defining the attributes of shares in its corporations and in protecting shareholders. Congress has never questioned the need for state regulation of these matters. Nor do we think such regulation offends the Constitution. Accordingly, we reverse the judgment of the Court of Appeals.

It is so ordered.

JUSTICE SCALIA, concurring in part and concurring in the judgment.

* * * [H]aving found * * * that the Indiana Control Share Acquisitions Chapter neither "discriminates against interstate commerce," nor "create[s] an impermissible risk of inconsistent regulation by different States," I would conclude without further analysis that it is not invalid under the dormant Commerce Clause. * * * Whether the control shares statute "protects shareholders of Indiana corporations," or protects incumbent management seems to me a highly debatable question, but it is extraordinary to think that the constitutionality of the Act should depend on the answer. Nothing in the Constitution says that the protection of entrenched management is any less important a "putative local benefit" than the protection of entrenched shareholders, and I do not know what qualifies us to make that judgment—or the related judgment as to how effective the present statute is in achieving one or the other objective—or the ultimate (and most ineffable) judgment as to whether, given importance-level x, and effectiveness-level y, the worth of the statute is "outweighed" by impact-on-commerce z. * * *

I also agree with the Court that the Indiana Control Shares Act is not preempted by the Williams Act, but I reach that conclusion without entering into the debate over the purposes of the two statutes. The Williams Act is governed by the antipreemption provision of the Securities Exchange Act of 1934, 15 U.S.C. § 78bb(a), which provides that nothing it contains "shall affect the jurisdiction of the securities commission (or any agency or officer performing like functions) of any State over any security or any person insofar as it does not conflict with the provisions of this chapter or the rules and regulations thereunder." Unless it serves no function, that language forecloses preemption on the basis of conflicting "purpose" as opposed to conflicting "provision." Even if it does not have literal application to the present case (because, perhaps, the Indiana agency responsible for securities matters has no enforcement responsibility with regard to this legislation), it nonetheless refutes the proposition that Congress meant the Williams Act to displace *all* state laws with conflicting purpose. And if any are to survive, surely the States' corporation codes are among them. It would be peculiar to hold that Indiana could have pursued the purpose at issue here through its blue-sky laws, but cannot pursue it through the State's even more sacrosanct authority over the structure of domestic corporations. Prescribing voting rights for the governance of state-chartered companies is a traditional state function with which the Federal Congress has never, to my knowledge, intentionally interfered. I would require far more evidence than is available here to find implicit preemption of that function by a federal statute whose provisions concededly do not conflict with the state law.

I do not share the Court's apparent high estimation of the beneficence of the state statute at issue here. But a law can be both economic folly and constitutional. The Indiana Control Share Acquisitions Chapter is at least the latter. I therefore concur in the judgment of the Court.

JUSTICE WHITE, with whom JUSTICE BLACKMUN and JUSTICE STEVENS join as to Part II, dissenting.

The majority today upholds Indiana's Control Share Acquisitions Chapter, a statute which will predictably foreclose completely some tender offers for stock in Indiana corporations. I disagree with the conclusion that the Chapter is neither preempted by the Williams Act nor in conflict with the Commerce Clause. The Chapter undermines the policy of the Williams Act by effectively preventing minority shareholders, in some circumstances, from acting in their own best interests by selling their stock. In addition, the Chapter will substantially burden the interstate market in corporate ownership, particularly if other States follow Indiana's lead as many already have done. The Chapter, therefore, directly inhibits interstate commerce, the very economic consequences the Commerce Clause was intended to prevent. The opinion of the Court of

Appeals is far more persuasive than that of the majority today, and the judgment of that court should be affirmed. * * *

Given the impact of the Control Share Acquisitions Chapter, it is clear that Indiana is directly regulating the purchase and sale of shares of stock in interstate commerce. Appellant CTS' stock is traded on the New York Stock Exchange, and people from all over the country buy and sell CTS' shares daily. Yet, under Indiana's scheme, any prospective purchaser will be effectively precluded from purchasing CTS' shares if the purchaser crosses one of the Chapter's threshold ownership levels and a majority of CTS' shareholders refuse to give the purchaser voting rights. This Court should not countenance such a restraint on interstate trade. * * *

NOTES

(1) Prior to the decision in the principal case, and based largely on language in the plurality opinion in *MITE,* a number of academic scholars of the Chicago "law and economics school" argued that an interstate market for corporate control existed and that states were powerless to regulate it. Under this approach, state statutes regulating tender offers seemed clearly unconstitutional, and perhaps even traditional state corporation law provisions could be invalidated if they unreasonably restricted or interfered with the market for corporate control. This type of argument was accepted by Judge Posner in the opinion reversed by the Supreme Court in the principal case. The "market for corporate control" idea appealed to economists but troubled many lawyers because, to the extent it applied to publicly held corporations, this "market" seemed to be a "slippery slope" that could federalize much of the state law of corporations. The CTS opinion is of major importance in the corporate area because of its dicta about the relative rules of federal and state law in this area.

(2) Pennsylvania's anti-takeover law is particularly restrictive. Section 25E of the statute requires a person who acquires 20 percent or more of the voting power of a target company to pay in cash the "fair value" for the shares of other shareholders who object to the transaction. This provision creates a form of dissenters' appraisal rights applicable to acquirers rather than to issuers. Corporations may opt-out of Section 25E but not the rest of the statute.

In addition, Pennsylvania has a strong "shareholder constituency" statute that expressly permits Pennsylvania companies that are the targets of hostile takeovers to take into consideration the interests of employees and communities affected by a takeover when deciding how to respond.

NORMAN VEASEY ET AL., THE DELAWARE TAKEOVER LAW: SOME ISSUES, STRATEGIES AND COMPARISONS

43 Bus.Law. 865, 866–69 (1988).

* * * New York in 1986 and New Jersey in 1987 adopted statutes prohibiting an acquirer from accomplishing a second-step "business combination"—such as a merger—with the target for a period of five years. Concern was raised that states were trying to outdo each other in their attempts to regulate tender offers of corporations domiciled in other states (notably Delaware), thus leading to a worrisome balkanization of state tender offer statutes. In *TLX Acquisition Corp. v. Telex Corp.,* the federal district court sitting in Oklahoma held that an Oklahoma statute that purported to regulate the tender offer process and thus the internal affairs of a Delaware corporation was unconstitutional even though there were substantial contacts with Oklahoma. * * *

The major question in that national puzzle was whether Delaware would adopt any legislation and, if so, how far it would go. Delaware, of course, is the principal architect and steward of a "national corporation law" since it is the domicile of over 180,000 corporations, many of which are major, national public corporations with no substantial operations in Delaware. Indeed, over half of the Fortune 500 companies are Delaware corporations. As at least one commentator has noted, Delaware has always been wary of antitakeover legislation for at least three reasons: doubts about constitutionality (at least pre-*CTS*); concerns over preemption; and the fact that such statutes simply don't fit comfortably into the mold of a state enabling statute governing internal corporate affairs.[15]

Nevertheless, there was an expectation following *CTS* that Delaware would do something, and it did. After a lengthy "on-again, off-again" process stretching from May 1987 through January 1988, the Delaware State Bar Association proposed a new takeover statute,[16] which was

---

[15] See Black, Why Delaware Is Wary of Anti-Takeover Law, Wall St.J., July 10, 1987, at 18, col. 3:

> Although Delaware prides itself on being a leader in corporation law, it has always been wary of laws regulating tender offers. For one thing, such laws have never fit well in corporation statutes. For another, they don't work. Efforts to regulate tender offers at the federal level under the Williams Act have distorted the process. Since the Williams Act was enacted in 1968, the Securities and Exchange Commission (and the states, through such acts as the now-validated Indiana law) has played an endless game of catch up, adopting rules that seem to fix one problem only to give rise to another.

[16] The Delaware statute is the product of a lengthy study by the Corporation Law Section of the Delaware State Bar Association. In June 1987, following the *CTS* decision, the Section studied and sought national comment on a draft control share acquisition statute of the type upheld by the Supreme Court in that case. CTS Corp. v. Dynamics Corp. of America, 107 S.Ct. 1637 (1987). There were many uncertainties regarding the operation and effect of such legislation, including concern that it may, ironically, help put "in play" corporations which might not otherwise become takeover targets. Accordingly, the Section determined that it would not be appropriate to propose such a statute for Delaware. Nevertheless, because of continued interest

adopted in late January substantially in *haec verba* by the Delaware General Assembly. It became effective with the signature of Governor Castle on February 2, 1988. The statute is codified as new section 203 of the Delaware General Corporation Law. Section 203 is a modified "business combination" statute based on the concept, adopted in New York and New Jersey, of regulating second-step transactions between acquirers and the corporation rather than regulating the initial acquisition of stock or voting rights.

With the enactment of section 203, Delaware became the twenty-eighth state to enact a post-*MITE* takeover statute. About half of these statutes were adopted in the wake of the Supreme Court opinion in *CTS*. California is the only major state (in terms of the number of incorporations) without a takeover law.

Operation of Section 203

Section 203 is not an enabling (or "opt-in") provision * * *. Rather, section 203 is an "opt-out" statute. It automatically applies (with certain exceptions) to every public corporation formed under the laws of Delaware unless (i) the corporation's original charter contains a provision opting out of the protection of the statute, or (ii) within ninety days of the effective date of the statute (February 2, 1988), the board of directors adopts a by-law opting out of the statute. In addition, the holders of a majority of shares entitled to vote can opt out by amending the certificate or the by-laws. Although such an amendment can be adopted at any time, it will not become effective for twelve months and will not apply to a business combination with a person who was an interested stockholder at or prior to the time of the amendment.

Assuming the statute is applicable and the corporation has not opted out, its operative effect can be briefly summarized as follows. If a person acquires fifteen percent or more of a corporation's voting stock (thereby becoming an "interested stockholder"), he may not engage in a wide range of transactions with the corporation [for three years], unless the board has approved the transaction or exempted the stockholder before he

---

in takeover legislation, the Council of the Section began a new study in the late summer of 1987. An exposure draft of a "business combination statute" was released for public comment in November. Over 150 comment letters were received from corporations, lawyers, Commissioners of the Securities and Exchange Commission and the Federal Trade Commission, executives, institutional investors, academics, and many others. Some comments were based on broad policy grounds, some made narrower policy suggestions, and still others recommended drafting changes. During the bar association debate and the legislative process, some law firms represented specific clients and took positions as a firm. Richards, Layton & Finger [the firm in which the authors are partners] did not take a position as a firm and would not accept representation by a client to lobby for or against the bill. Each lawyer in the firm had the freedom to express his or her own personal view since the clients of the firm had divergent views. Some members of the firm fully supported the statute; others supported it with a few specific reservations (for example whether 85% should be 80% and whether the grandfather date should be the effective date); others opposed it on broad policy grounds. Governor Castle strongly supported the legislation, but he said that the issue is "neither black nor white, but gray."

reaches the fifteen-percent threshold or unless one of two exceptions is satisfied: (i) Upon consummation of the transaction which resulted in such person becoming an interested stockholder, the interested stockholder owned at least eighty-five percent of the corporation's voting stock outstanding at the time the transaction commenced (excluding shares owned by officer-directors and shares owned by employee stock plans in which participants do not have the right to determine confidentially whether shares will be tendered in a tender or exchange offer); or (ii) after the acquirer becomes an interested stockholder, the business combination is approved by the board of directors and authorized by the affirmative vote (at an annual or special meeting, and not by written consent) of at least two-thirds of the outstanding voting stock excluding that owned by the interested stockholder.[f] * * *

C. DEFENSES: POISON PILLS

The "ultimate" in defensive tactics is the "shareholder rights plan," more commonly called a "poison pill." Here the preliminary question is not whether these potent anti-takeover devices are constitutional, but whether they are consistent with existing state corporate law for allocating rights and responsibilities within the corporation.

MORAN V. HOUSEHOLD INT'L, INC.
Supreme Court of Delaware, 1985.
500 A.2d 1346.

MCNEILLY, JUSTICE.

This case presents to this Court for review the most recent defensive mechanism in the arsenal of corporate takeover weaponry—the Preferred Share Purchase Rights Plan ("Rights Plan" or "Plan"). The validity of this mechanism has attracted national attention. *Amici curiae* briefs have been filed in support of appellants by the Securit[ies] and Exchange Commission ("SEC")[1] and the Investment Company Institute. An *amicus curiae* brief has been filed in support of appellees ("Household") by the United Food and Commercial Workers International Union.

In a detailed opinion, the Court of Chancery upheld the Rights Plan as a legitimate exercise of business judgment by Household. Moran v.

---

[f] A more candid statement of the intent and effect of this statute is that it makes a bidder either negotiate with management or make an offer so attractive that it garners virtually all of the target shares. Many (indeed probably most) legal scholars were critical of laws designed to protect target companies from takeover and were therefore critical of the Delaware statute. See, e.g., Easterbrook & Fischel, The Proper Role of a Target's Management in Responding to a Tender Offer, 94 Harv.L.Rev. 1161 (1981).

[1] The SEC split 3–2 on whether to intervene in this case. The two dissenting Commissioners have publicly disagreed with the other three as to the merits of the Rights Plan. 17 Securities Regulation & Law Report 400; The Wall Street Journal, March 20, 1985, at 6.

Household International, Inc., Del.Ch., 490 A.2d 1059 (1985). We agree, and therefore, affirm the judgment below.

I

*** A review of the basic facts is necessary for a complete understanding of the issues.

On August 14, 1984, the Board of Directors of Household International, Inc. adopted the Rights Plan by a fourteen to two vote.[2] The intricacies of the Rights Plan are contained in a 48-page document entitled "Rights Agreement." Basically, the Plan provides that Household common stockholders are entitled to the issuance of one Right per common share under certain triggering conditions. There are two triggering events that can activate the Rights. The first is the announcement of a tender offer for 30 percent of Household's shares ("30% trigger") and the second is the acquisition of 20 percent of Household's shares by any single entity or group ("20% trigger").

If an announcement of a tender offer for 30 percent of Household's shares is made, the Rights are issued and are immediately exercisable to purchase 1/100 share of new preferred stock for $100 and are redeemable by the Board for $0.50 per Right. If 20 percent of Household's shares are acquired by anyone, the Rights are issued and become non-redeemable and are exercisable to purchase 1/100 of a share of preferred. If a Right is not exercised for preferred, and thereafter, a merger or consolidation occurs, the Rights holder can exercise each Right to purchase $200 of the common stock of the tender offeror for $100.[g] This "flip-over" provision of the Rights Plan is at the heart of this controversy. ***

---

[2] Household's Board has ten outside directors and six who are members of management. Messrs. Moran (appellant) and Whitehead voted against the Plan. The record reflects that Whitehead voted against the Plan not on its substance but because he thought it was novel and would bring unwanted publicity to Household.

[g] In other words, each Household shareholder receives one "right" for each Household share of stock held. If a triggering event occurs, this right authorizes the holder to purchase $200 of the common stock of the offeror or purchaser for $100, thereby causing massive dilution of the value of the aggressor's shares. Prior to the triggering event, the right is automatically fixed (or, figuratively, "stapled") to the shares and cannot be traded separately from the shares. Hence the rights may remain in existence indefinitely without interfering with normal business transactions of Household. The option to purchase a fractional interest in a preferred share of Household was "window dressing" designed to assure that the "rights" would always be tied to Household shares; it was never intended that anyone would ever exercise that option, as indicated by the very high price for a very small fractional interest in a share of very limited value.

Before rights are triggered, Household may cancel them; if they have been triggered, Household may elect to redeem the rights at a nominal price. The power to cancel or redeem these rights at any time was thought to give Household flexibility to negotiate a voluntary merger or sale with the aggressor or some other corporation or entity.

In Leonard Loventhal Account v. Hilton Hotels Corp., 2000 WL 1528909 (Del.Ch. Oct. 10, 2000), the court held that poison pills attach automatically to all outstanding shares and cannot be rejected by a major shareholder.

Household did not adopt its Rights Plan during a battle with a corporate raider, but as a preventive mechanism to ward off future advances. The Vice-Chancellor found that as early as February 1984, Household's management became concerned about the company's vulnerability as a takeover target and began considering amending its charter to render a takeover more difficult. After considering the matter, Household decided not to pursue a fair price amendment.

In the meantime, appellant Moran, one of Household's own Directors and also Chairman of the Dyson-Kissner-Moran Corporation, ("D-K-M") which is the largest single stockholder of Household, began discussions concerning a possible leveraged buy-out of Household by D-K-M. D-K-M's financial studies showed that Household's stock was significantly undervalued in relation to the company's break-up value. It is uncontradicted that Moran's suggestion of a leveraged buy-out never progressed beyond the discussion stage.

Concerned about Household's vulnerability to a raider in light of the current takeover climate, Household secured the services of Wachtell, Lipton, Rosen and Katz ("Watchell, Lipton") and Goldman, Sachs & Co. ("Goldman, Sachs") to formulate a takeover policy for recommendation to the Household Board at its August 14 meeting. After a July 31 meeting with a Household Board member and a pre-meeting distribution of material on the potential takeover problem and the proposed Rights Plan, the Board met on August 14, 1984.

Representatives of Wachtell, Lipton and Goldman, Sachs attended the August 14 meeting. The minutes reflect that Mr. Lipton explained to the Board that his recommendation of the Plan was based on his understanding that the Board was concerned about the increasing frequency of "bust-up" takeovers, the increasing takeover activity in the financial service industry, such as Leucadia's attempt to take over Arco, and the possible adverse effect this type of activity could have on employees and others concerned with and vital to the continuing successful operation of Household even in the absence of any actual bust-up takeover attempt. Against this factual background, the Plan was approved.

Thereafter, Moran and the company of which he is Chairman, D-K-M, filed this suit. * * * The trial was held, and the Court of Chancery ruled in favor of Household. Appellants now appeal from that ruling to this Court.

II

The primary issue here is the applicability of the business judgment rule as the standard by which the adoption of the Rights Plan should be reviewed. Much of this issue has been decided by our recent decision in Unocal Corp. v. Mesa Petroleum Co., [493 A.2d 946 (Del.1985)]. In

Unocal, we applied the business judgment rule to analyze Unocal's discriminatory self-tender. We explained:

> When a board addresses a pending takeover bid it has an obligation to determine whether the offer is in the best interests of the corporation and its shareholders. In that respect a board's duty is no different from any other responsibility it shoulders, and its decisions should be no less entitled to the respect they otherwise would be accorded in the realm of business judgment.

* * * Other jurisdictions have also applied the business judgment rule to actions by which target companies have sought to forestall takeover activity they considered undesirable. * * * [The court cites ten cases, including Gearhart Industries, Inc. v. Smith International, 5th Cir., 741 F.2d 707 (1984) (sale of discounted subordinate debentures containing springing warrants); Treco, Inc. v. Land of Lincoln Savings and Loan, 7th Cir., 749 F.2d 374 (1984) (amendment to by-laws); Panter v. Marshall Field, 7th Cir., 646 F.2d 271 (1981) (acquisitions to create antitrust problems); Johnson v. Trueblood, 3d Cir., 629 F.2d 287 (1980), cert. denied, 450 U.S. 999, 101 S.Ct. 1704, 68 L.Ed.2d 200 (1981) (refusal to tender); and Crouse-Hinds Co. v. InterNorth, Inc., 2d Cir., 634 F.2d 690 (1980) (sale of stock to favored party).]

This case is distinguishable from the ones cited, since here we have a defensive mechanism adopted to ward off possible future advances and not a mechanism adopted in reaction to a specific threat. This distinguishing factor does not result in the Directors losing the protection of the business judgment rule. To the contrary, pre-planning for the contingency of a hostile takeover might reduce the risk that, under the pressure of a takeover bid, management will fail to exercise reasonable judgment. Therefore, in reviewing a pre-planned defensive mechanism it seems even more appropriate to apply the business judgment rule. * * *

Of course, the business judgment rule can only sustain corporate decision making or transactions that are within the power or authority of the Board. Therefore, before the business judgment rule can be applied it must be determined whether the Directors were authorized to adopt the Rights Plan.

III

Appellants vehemently contend that the Board of Directors was unauthorized to adopt the Rights Plan. First, appellants contend that no provision of the Delaware General Corporation Law authorizes the issuance of such Rights. Secondly, appellants, along with the SEC, contend that the Board is unauthorized to usurp stockholders' rights to receive hostile tender offers. Third, appellants and the SEC also contend that the Board is unauthorized to fundamentally restrict stockholders' rights to conduct a proxy contest. We address each of these contentions in turn.

A.

While appellants contend that no provision of the Delaware General Corporation Law authorizes the Rights Plan, Household contends that the Rights Plan was issued pursuant to 8 *Del.C.* §§ 151(g) and 157. It explains that the Rights are authorized by § 157[7] and the issue of preferred stock underlying the Rights is authorized by § 151.[8] Appellants respond by making several attacks upon the authority to issue the Rights pursuant to § 157.

Appellants begin by contending that § 157 cannot authorize the Rights Plan since § 157 has never served the purpose of authorizing a takeover defense. Appellants contend that § 157 is a corporate financing statute, and that nothing in its legislative history suggests a purpose that has anything to do with corporate control or a takeover defense. Appellants are unable to demonstrate that the legislature, in its adoption of § 157, meant to limit the applicability of § 157 to only the issuance of Rights for the purposes of corporate financing. Without such affirmative evidence, we decline to impose such a limitation upon the section that the legislature has not. Compare Providence & Worcester Co. v. Baker, Del.Supr., 378 A.2d 121, 124 (1977) (refusal to read a bar to protective voting provisions into 8 *Del.C.* § 212(a)).

As we noted in *Unocal:*

> [O]ur corporate law is not static. It must grow and develop in response to, indeed in anticipation of, evolving concepts and needs. Merely because the General Corporation Law is silent as to a specific matter does not mean that it is prohibited. * * * 493 A.2d at 957.

---

[7] The power to issue rights to purchase shares is conferred by 8 *Del.C.* § 157 which provides in relevant part:

> Subject to any provisions in the certificate of incorporation, every corporation may create and issue, whether or not in connection with the issue and sale of any shares of stock or other securities of the corporation, rights or options entitling the holders thereof to purchase from the corporation any shares of its capital stock of any class or classes, such rights or options to be evidenced by or in such instrument or instruments as shall be approved by the board of directors.

[8] 8 Del.C. § 151(g) provides in relevant part:

> When any corporation desires to issue any shares of stock of any class or of any series of any class of which the voting powers, designations, preferences and relative, participating, optional or other rights, if any, or the qualifications, limitations or restrictions thereof, if any, shall not have been set forth in the certificate of incorporation or in any amendment thereto but shall be provided for in a resolution or resolutions adopted by the board of directors pursuant to authority expressly vested in it by the provisions of the certificate of incorporation or any amendment thereto, a certificate setting forth a copy of such resolution or resolutions and the number of shares of stock of such class or series shall be executed, acknowledged, filed, recorded, and shall become effective, in accordance with § 103 of this title.

Secondly, appellants contend that § 157 does not authorize the issuance of sham rights such as the Rights Plan. They contend that the Rights were designed never to be exercised, and that the Plan has no economic value. In addition, they contend the preferred stock made subject to the Rights is also illusory, citing *Telvest, Inc. v. Olson,* Del.Ch., C.A. No. 5798, Brown, V.C. (March 8, 1979).

Appellants' sham contention fails in both regards. As to the Rights, they can and will be exercised upon the happening of a triggering mechanism, as we have observed during the current struggle of Sir James Goldsmith to take control of Crown Zellerbach. See Wall Street Journal, July 26, 1985, at 3, 12. As to the preferred shares, we agree with the Court of Chancery that they are distinguishable from sham securities invalidated in *Telvest,* supra. The Household preferred, issuable upon the happening of a triggering event, have superior dividend and liquidation rights. * * *

[Next], appellants contend that if § 157 authorizes the Rights Plan it would be unconstitutional pursuant to the Commerce Clause and Supremacy Clause of the United States Constitution * * * since it is an obstacle to the accomplishment of the policies underlying the Williams Act. Appellants put heavy emphasis upon the case of Edgar v. MITE Corp., 457 U.S. 624, 102 S.Ct. 2629, 73 L.Ed.2d 269 (1982), in which the United States Supreme Court held that the Illinois Business Takeover Act was unconstitutional, in that it unduly burdened interstate commerce in violation of the Commerce Clause. We do not read the analysis in *Edgar* as applicable to the actions of private parties. The fact that directors of a corporation act pursuant to a state statute provides an insufficient nexus to the state for there to be state action which may violate the Commerce Clause or Supremacy Clause. * * *

Having concluded that sufficient authority for the Rights Plan exists in 8 *Del.C.* § 157, we note [that] the inherent powers of the Board conferred by 8 *Del.C.* § 141(a), concerning the management of the corporation's "business and *affairs*" (emphasis added), also provides the Board additional authority upon which to enact the Rights Plan.

B.

Appellants contend that the Board is unauthorized to usurp stockholders' rights to receive tender offers by changing Household's fundamental structure. We conclude that the Rights Plan does not prevent stockholders from receiving tender offers, and that the change of Household's structure was less than that which results from the implementation of other defensive mechanisms upheld by various courts.

Appellants' contention that stockholders will lose their right to receive and accept tender offers seems to be premised upon an understanding of the Rights Plan which is illustrated by the SEC *amicus* brief which states: "The Chancery Court's decision seriously understates the impact of this plan. In fact, as we discuss below, the Rights Plan will deter not only two-tier offers, but virtually all hostile tender offers."

The fallacy of that contention is apparent when we look at the recent takeover of Crown Zellerbach, which has a similar Rights Plan, by Sir James Goldsmith. Wall Street Journal, July 26, 1985, at 3, 12. The evidence at trial also evidenced many methods around the Plan ranging from tendering with a condition that the Board redeem the Rights, tendering with a high minimum condition of shares and Rights, tendering and soliciting consents to remove the Board and redeem the Rights, to acquiring 50% of the shares and causing Household to self-tender for the Rights. One could also form a group of up to 19.9% and solicit proxies for consents to remove the Board and redeem the Rights. These are but a few of the methods by which Household can still be acquired by a hostile tender offer.

In addition, the Rights Plan is not absolute. When the Household Board of Directors is faced with a tender offer and a request to redeem the Rights, they will not be able to arbitrarily reject the offer. They will be held to the same fiduciary standards any other board of directors would be held to in deciding to adopt a defensive mechanism, the same standard as they were held to in originally approving the Rights Plan.

In addition, appellants contend that the deterrence of tender offers will be accomplished by what they label "a fundamental transfer of power from the stockholders to the directors." They contend that this transfer of power, in itself, is unauthorized.

The Rights Plan will result in no more of a structural change than any other defensive mechanism adopted by a board of directors. The Rights Plan does not destroy the assets of the corporation. The implementation of the Plan neither results in any outflow of money from the corporation nor impairs its financial flexibility. It does not dilute earnings per share and does not have any adverse tax consequences for the corporation or its stockholders. The Plan has not adversely affected the market price of Household's stock.

Comparing the Rights Plan with other defensive mechanisms, it does less harm to the value structure of the corporation than do the other mechanisms. Other mechanisms result in increased debt of the corporation. See Whittaker Corp. v. Edgar, supra (sale of "prize asset"), Cheff v. Mathes, supra, (paying greenmail to eliminate a threat), Unocal Corp. v. Mesa Petroleum Co., supra, (discriminatory self-tender).

There is little change in the governance structure as a result of the adoption of the Rights Plan. The Board does not now have unfettered discretion in refusing to redeem the Rights. The Board has no more discretion in refusing to redeem the Rights than it does in enacting any defensive mechanism.

The contention that the Rights Plan alters the structure more than do other defensive mechanisms because it is so effective as to make the corporation completely safe from hostile tender offers is likewise without merit. As explained above, there are numerous methods to successfully launch a hostile tender offer.

C.

Appellants' third contention is that the Board was unauthorized to fundamentally restrict stockholders' rights to conduct a proxy contest. Appellants contend that the "20% trigger" effectively prevents any stockholder from first acquiring 20% or more shares before conducting a proxy contest and further, it prevents stockholders from banding together into a group to solicit proxies if, collectively, they own 20% or more of the stock.[12] In addition, at trial, appellants contended that read literally, the Rights Agreement triggers the Rights upon the mere acquisition of the right to vote 20% or more of the shares through a proxy solicitation, and thereby precludes any proxy contest from being waged.[13]

Appellants seem to have conceded this last contention in light of Household's response that the receipt of a proxy does not make the recipient the "beneficial owner" of the shares involved which would trigger the Rights. In essence, the Rights Agreement provides that the Rights are triggered when someone becomes the "beneficial owner" of 20% or more of Household stock. Although a literal reading of the Rights Agreement definition of "beneficial owner" would seem to include those shares which one has the right to vote, it has long been recognized that the relationship between grantor and recipient of a proxy is one of agency, and the agency is revocable by the grantor at any time. Henn, *Corporations* § 196, at 518. Therefore, the holder of a proxy is not the "beneficial owner" of the stock. As a result, the mere acquisition of the right to vote 20% of the shares does not trigger the Rights.

The issue, then, is whether the restriction upon individuals or groups from first acquiring 20% of shares before waging a proxy contest fundamentally restricts stockholders' right to conduct a proxy contest. Regarding this issue the Court of Chancery found:

> Thus, while the Rights Plan does deter the formation of proxy efforts of a certain magnitude, it does not limit the voting power of individual shares. On the evidence presented it is highly

---

[12] Appellants explain that the acquisition of 20% of the shares trigger the Rights, making them non-redeemable, and thereby would prevent even a future friendly offer for the ten year life of the Rights.

[13] The SEC still contends that the mere acquisition of the right to vote 20% of the shares through a proxy solicitation triggers the rights. We do not interpret the Rights Agreement in that manner.

> conjectural to assume that a particular effort to assert shareholder views in the election of directors or revisions of corporate policy will be frustrated by the proxy feature of the Plan. Household's witnesses, Troubh and Higgins, described recent corporate takeover battles in which insurgents holding less than 10% stock ownership were able to secure corporate control through a proxy contest or the threat of one.

490 A.2d at 1080.

We conclude that there was sufficient evidence at trial to support the Vice-Chancellor's finding that the effect upon proxy contests will be minimal. Evidence at trial established that many proxy contests are won with an insurgent ownership of less than 20%, and that very large holdings are no guarantee of success. There was also testimony that the key variable in proxy contest success is the merit of an insurgent's issues, not the size of his holdings.

IV

Having concluded that the adoption of the Rights Plan was within the authority of the Directors, we now look to whether the Directors have met their burden under the business judgment rule.

The business judgment rule is a "presumption that in making a business decision the directors of a corporation acted on an informed basis, in good faith and in the honest belief that the action taken was in the best interests of the company." Aronson v. Lewis, Del.Supr., 473 A.2d 805, 812 (1984) (citations omitted). Notwithstanding, in *Unocal* we held that when the business judgment rule applies to adoption of a defensive mechanism, the initial burden will lie with the directors. The "directors must show that they had reasonable grounds for believing that a danger to corporate policy and effectiveness existed. * * * [T]hey satisfy that burden 'by showing good faith and reasonable investigation * * *'" *Unocal,* 493 A.2d at 955 (citing Cheff v. Mathes, 199 A.2d at 554–55). In addition, the directors must show that the defensive mechanism was "reasonable in relation to the threat posed." *Unocal,* 493 A.2d at 955. Moreover, that proof is materially enhanced, as we noted in *Unocal,* where, as here, a majority of the board favoring the proposal consisted of outside independent directors who have acted in accordance with the foregoing standards. *Unocal,* 493 A.2d at 955; *Aronson,* 473 A.2d at 815. Then, the burden shifts back to the plaintiffs who have the ultimate burden of persuasion to show a breach of the directors' fiduciary duties. *Unocal,* 493 A.2d at 958.

There are no allegations here of any bad faith on the part of the Directors' action in the adoption of the Rights Plan. There is no allegation that the Directors' action was taken for entrenchment purposes. Household has adequately demonstrated, as explained above, that the adoption of the Rights Plan was in reaction to what it perceived to be the threat in the market place of coercive two-tier tender offers. Appellants do contend, however, that the Board did not exercise informed business judgment in its adoption of the Plan. * * * Appellants contend the Delaware counsel did not express an opinion on the flip-over provision of the Rights, rather only that the Rights would constitute validly issued and outstanding rights to subscribe to the preferred stock of the company.

To determine whether a business judgment reached by a board of directors was an informed one, we determine whether the directors were grossly negligent. Smith v. Van Gorkom, Del.Supr., 488 A.2d 858, 873 (1985). Upon a review of this record, we conclude the Directors were not grossly negligent. The information supplied to the Board on August 14 provided the essentials of the Plan. The Directors were given beforehand a notebook which included a three-page summary of the Plan along with articles on the current takeover environment. The extended discussion between the Board and representatives of Wachtell, Lipton and Goldman, Sachs before approval of the Plan reflected a full and candid evaluation of the Plan. Moran's expression of his views at the meeting served to place before the Board a knowledgeable critique of the Plan. The factual happenings here are clearly distinguishable from the actions of the directors of Trans Union Corporation who displayed gross negligence in approving a cash-out merger.

In addition, to meet their burden, the Directors must show that the defensive mechanism was "reasonable in relation to the threat posed." The record reflects a concern on the part of the Directors over the increasing frequency in the financial services industry of "boot-strap" and "bust-up" takeovers. The Directors were also concerned that such takeovers may take the form of two-tier offers.[14] In addition, on August 14, the Household Board was aware of Moran's overture on behalf of D-K-M. In sum, the Directors reasonably believed Household was vulnerable to coercive acquisition techniques and adopted a reasonable defensive mechanism to protect itself.

V

* * * While we conclude for present purposes that the Household Directors are protected by the business judgment rule, that does not end the matter. The ultimate response to an actual takeover bid must be judged by the Directors' actions at that time, and nothing we say here relieves them of their basic fundamental duties to the corporation and its stockholders. Smith v. Van Gorkom, 488 A.2d at 872–73. Their use of the Plan will be evaluated when and if the issue arises.

Affirmed.

---

[14] We have discussed the coercive nature of two-tier tender offers in Unocal, 493 A.2d at 956, n. 12. We explained in *Unocal* that a discriminatory self-tender was reasonably related to the threat of two-tier tender offers and possible greenmail.

NOTES

(1) The "Rights Plan" approved in *Moran* was the first "poison pill." "Innovations" and "improvements" quickly followed. See Julian Velasco, The Enduring Illegitimacy of the Poison Pill, 27 J. Corp. L. 381 (2002).

(2) One federal district court case arising under Delaware law, Moore Corp., Ltd. v. Wallace Computer Services, Inc., 907 F.Supp. 1545 (D.Del. 1995), comes close to accepting the proposition that "management can do no wrong" and may "just say no" under Delaware law. The court refused to order a poison pill withdrawn even though 73 percent of Wallace's shareholders had accepted the aggressor's (Moore's) offer, and even though Wallace made no effort to find a more friendly bidder or make a share buyback offer. Furthermore, Wallace had a staggered board of directors, so that for Moore to have elected a majority of the directors of Wallace, proxy fights in two successive years would have been necessary. Following this decision, Moore withdrew its bid. See Andrew R. Brownstein, Face-off on Poison Pills, 11 Insights, No. 1, January 1997, 12, 15.

(3) Faced with an apparently unbreakable poison pill and an obdurate management, bidders began to seek a majority of the board of directors through a proxy fight. If successful, they could withdraw or redeem the poison pill, allowing the takeover to succeed. The response of incumbent management was immediate: poison pills were revised to provide that they could be withdrawn only by the vote of "continuing directors"—those who originally authorized the pill or persons nominated by those directors. Thus the "dead hand" pill was born. Bank of New York v. Irving Bank Corp., 528 N.Y.S.2d 482 (Sup.Ct.1988), invalidated such a poison pill on the grounds that it improperly intruded on the power of boards of directors to manage the company, and it was an attempt by one board of directors to limit improperly the powers of future boards. However, in Invacare Corp. v. Healthdyne Technologies, Inc., 968 F.Supp. 1578 (N.D.Ga.1997), a similar shareholder rights plan was upheld under Ga. Code Ann. § 14–2–624(c) that authorized terms of options and similar rights to be set in the "sole discretion" of the board of directors.

(4) Poison pills can be adopted to thwart activist hedge fund investors. For example, on December 30, 2013, the rent-a-car company Hertz adopted a poison pill. The Hertz shareholder rights plan will be triggered if an investor acquires a 10 percent stake or more of the company's shares. Hertz's shares, which had already gained 53 percent in 2013, climbed another 3.25 percent to $26.75 in after-hours trading after the pill was adopted. Hertz's largest listed shareholder is the hedge fund Wellington Management, which holds 9.15 percent of its shares. The hedge fund York Capital Management also has a 2.75 percent stake. Hertz said the plan would allow management to continue "strategic initiatives," including the integration of its recent $2.6 billion acquisition of Dollar Thrifty. Hertz acquired Dollar Thrifty last year after a protracted battle with its rival Avis. Alexandra Stephenson, Hertz Adopts "Poison Pill" to Thwart Activists, N.Y. Times, Dec. 30, 2013.

MENTOR GRAPHICS CORPORATION V. QUICKTURN DESIGN SYSTEMS, INC.

Court of Chancery of Delaware, 1998.
728 A.2d 25.

JACOBS, VICE CHANCELLOR.

In the ever-evolving field of corporate takeover jurisprudence, the defensive mechanism that has mutated more rapidly than others, and has prompted the most widespread debate, is the "poison pill" rights plan. Since making its legal debut in 1985, the story of the poison pill has been a work-in-progress, with each variation and innovation generating new litigation and occasions for judicial opinion writing. This case involves the pill's most recent incarnation—a "no hand" poison pill of limited duration and scope.[2] It marks the latest (but by no means the last) chapter of that work-in-progress.

To put this case into context, in Carmody v. Toll Brothers, Inc. ("Toll Brothers"), this Court, in denying a Rule 12(b)(6) motion to dismiss a complaint attacking a so-called "dead hand" poison pill,[4] ruled that that form of rights plan was subject to legal challenge under the Delaware General Corporation Law ("DGCL") and Delaware corporate fiduciary principles. The Toll Brothers dead hand poison pill plan provided that if there were a change of control of the board of directors, then for the entire lifetime of the pill only the "continuing directors" would be empowered to redeem the rights to facilitate an acquisition by a hostile bidder.

The "no hand" poison pill being challenged here is a variation of, and operates in a different manner from, the "dead hand" pill addressed in Toll Brothers. The pill in Toll Brothers created two classes of directors. One would have the power to redeem and the other would not. That limitation would last the entire lifetime of the pill. In contrast, the "no hand" pill in this case would create no classes. It would evenhandedly prevent all members of a newly elected target board, whose majority is nominated or supported by the hostile bidder, from redeeming the rights to facilitate an acquisition by the bidder. The duration of this "no hand" pill would be for six months after the new directors take office. Those nuanced distinctions and their legal effect, none of which were addressed in Toll Brothers, are what this lawsuit is about.

---

[2] Some practitioners of the art have described this iteration as a "slow hand" poison pill.

[4] A "dead hand" rights plan permits only the directors in office at the time the rights plan was adopted or their designated successors ("continuing directors") to redeem the rights. Thus, if the continuing directors are ousted from office in a proxy contest waged by a bidder making a hostile tender offer, the bidder's newly-elected board nominees could not redeem the rights to permit the bidder from acquiring the stock tendered to it. Only the previous incumbent directors (or their designated successors) could do so. See Jeffrey N. Gordon, "Just Say Never?" Poison Pills, Dead Hand Pills, and Shareholder Adopted Bylaws: An Essay for Warren Buffet, 19 Cardozo L. Rev. 511, 523, 531–32 (1997).

The dispute that underlies these actions for declarative and injunctive relief arises out of an ongoing effort by Mentor Graphics Corporation ("Mentor"), a hostile bidder, to acquire Quickturn Design Systems, Inc. ("Quickturn"), the target company. The plaintiffs are Mentor[6] and an unaffiliated stockholder of Quickturn; the named defendants are Quickturn and its directors. The plaintiffs challenge the validity, on Delaware fiduciary and statutory grounds, of a "no hand" rights plan of limited duration (the "Delayed Redemption Provision" or "DRP") that the target company board adopted in response to the hostile bidder's tender offer and proxy contest to replace that board as part of the bidder's larger effort to acquire the target company. In response to that hostile bid, the board also amended the company's by-laws to delay the holding of any special stockholders meeting requested by stockholders, for 90 to 100 days after the validity of the request is determined (the "Amendment" or "By-Law Amendment"). The plaintiffs also challenge the legality of that By-Law Amendment.

This is the Opinion of the Court, after trial on the merits. For the reasons discussed below, the Court determines that the DRP is invalid on fiduciary duty grounds, and that the By-Law Amendment is valid and will be upheld. * * *

I. Statement of Facts

* * * [Both Mentor (an Oregon corporation) and Quickturn (a Delaware corporation) are publicly held corporations engaged in the electronics business with securities traded on NASDAQ. Mentor sold a certain emulation product to Quickturn in 1992. Later, Mentor re-entered the emulation business when it acquired a French company called Meta Systems ("Meta"), and began to market Meta's products in the United States in December 1995. Quickturn reacted by commencing a proceeding before the International Trade Commission ("ITC") claiming that Meta and Mentor were infringing Quickturn's patents. Quickturn was ultimately successful in this litigation, and Mentor was barred from competing with Quickturn in the United States emulation market].

After it became clear that these legal barriers prevented Mentor from competing effectively against Quickturn, Mentor began exploring the possibility of acquiring Quickturn. If Mentor owned Quickturn, it would also own the patents, and be in a position to "unenforce" them by seeking to vacate Quickturn's injunctive orders against Mentor in the patent litigation.[19]

---

[6]   Mentor and MGZ Corp., a wholly owned Mentor subsidiary specially created as a vehicle to acquire Quickturn, are referred to collectively as "Mentor." Unless otherwise indicated, Mentor and Howard Shapiro, the shareholder plaintiffs * * * are referred to collectively as "plaintiffs."

[19]   Mentor assiduously denies that obtaining ownership of the patents, which effectively would enable Mentor to reenter the United States market, was a motivating factor for making its

The exploration process began when Mr. Bernd Braune, a Mentor senior executive, retained Arthur Andersen ("Andersen") to advise Mentor how it could successfully compete in the emulation market. The result was a report Andersen issued in October 1997, entitled "PROJECT VELOCITY" and "Strategic Alternatives Analysis." The Andersen report identified several advantages and benefits Mentor would enjoy if it acquired Quickturn.[21]

The Andersen report also analyzed whether Mentor would create more value by selling Meta or by purchasing Quickturn. Andersen concluded that selling Meta would eliminate (for Mentor) Meta's forecasted 1998 loss of $3.4 million and would possibly bring $50 million in a sale. Acquiring Quickturn, on the other hand, would enable Mentor to sell its Meta products worldwide; obtain Quickturn's product line, manufacturing facilities, and sales force; and ultimately provide Mentor $610–$640 million of value. Lastly, Andersen concluded that Mentor could pay $300 to $320 million—about $16.80 to $17.90 per share—to acquire Quickturn and still create an additional $290–$320 million in synergistic value for Mentor.

Six weeks later, in December 1997, Mentor retained Salomon Smith Barney ("Salomon") to act as its financial advisor in connection with a possible acquisition of Quickturn. [Salomon's study made in early 1998 concluded that the market price of Quickturn was so high that a takeover bid was not feasible. Later that year, however, Quickturn's stock price declined, and Mentor decided to make a public bid to purchase Quickturn.]

On August 11, 1998, the evening before Mentor launched its bid, Dr. Rhines [Chairman of Mentor's board of directors] scheduled a dinner with Glen Antle, Quickturn's board chairman. After dinner Dr. Rhines informed Mr. Antle that Mentor would be launching a hostile tender offer for the outstanding shares of Quickturn the next morning. Dr. Rhines then handed Mr. Antle a previously prepared letter to that effect. At no time during the three month planning period did Mentor ever attempt to contact Quickturn's management or its board to negotiate a consensual deal.[31]

---

hostile bid. I conclude, however, that was the primary, if not sole, motivation for Mentor's takeover bid, and reject * * * contrary testimony on this subject as lacking credibility.

[21] These included: (i) eliminating the time and expense associated with litigation; (ii) creating synergy from combining two companies with complementary core competencies; (iii) reducing customer confusion over product availability, which in turn would accelerate sales; and (iv) eliminating the threat of a large competitor moving into the emulation market. Mentor has utilized these reasons in public statements in which it attempted to explain why its bid made sense.

[31] What Dr. Rhines did not disclose to Mr. Antle at that dinner was that Mentor had already prepared two complaints, which Mentor planned to file the next day, naming Mr. Antle and the other Quickturn board members as defendants. Dr. Rhines claims that he did not disclose this because the subject "just didn't come up." Dr. Rhines also refused Mr. Antle's

The next morning, on August 12, 1998, Mentor announced an unsolicited cash tender offer for all outstanding common shares of Quickturn at $12.125 per share—a price representing an approximate 50% premium over Quickturn's immediate pre-offer price, and a 20% discount from Quickturn's February 1998 stock price levels. Mentor's tender offer, once consummated, would be followed by a second step merger in which Quickturn's nontendering stockholders would receive, in cash, the same $12.125 per share tender offer price. Mentor also announced its intent to solicit proxies to replace the board at a special meeting. Relying upon Quickturn's then-applicable by-law provision governing the call of special stockholders meetings, Mentor began soliciting agent designations from Quickturn stockholders to satisfy the by-law's stock ownership requirements to call such a meeting.[32] * * *

[After three board meetings to discuss Mentor's proposal,] the Quickturn board concluded that Mentor's offer was inadequate, and decided to recommend that Quickturn shareholders reject Mentor's offer. * * * At the August 21 board meeting, the Quickturn board adopted two defensive measures in response to Mentor's hostile takeover bid.

First, the board amended Article II, § 2.3 of Quickturn's by-laws, which permitted stockholders holding 10% or more of Quickturn's stock to call a special stockholders meeting. The By-Law Amendment provides that if any such special meeting is requested by shareholders, the corporation (Quickturn) would fix the record date for, and determine the time and place of, that special meeting, which must take place not less than 90 days nor more than 100 days after the receipt and determination of the validity of the shareholders' request.

Second, the board amended Quickturn's shareholder rights plan ("Rights Plan") by eliminating its "dead hand" feature and replacing it with the Deferred Redemption Plan ("DRP"), under which no newly elected board could redeem the Rights Plan for six months after taking office, if the purpose or effect of the redemption would be to facilitate a transaction with an "Interested Person" (one who proposed, nominated or financially supported the election of the new directors to the board).[40] Mentor would be an Interested Person.

---

requests that Quickturn be given time to consider Mentor's offer and perhaps proceed on a friendly basis, because it was "too late."

[32] The applicable by-law (Article II, § 2.3) authorized a call of a special stockholders meeting by shareholders holding at least 10% of Quickturn's shares. In their agent solicitation, Mentor informed Quickturn stockholders that Mentor intended to call a special meeting approximately 45 days after it received sufficient agent designations to satisfy the 10% requirement under the original by-law. The solicitation also disclosed Mentor's intent to set the date for the special meeting, and to set the record date and give formal notice of that meeting.

[40] The amended Rights Plan pertinently provides that: "[I]n the event that a majority of the Board of Directors of the Company is elected by stockholder action at an annual or special meeting of stockholders, then until the 180th day following the effectiveness of such election (including any postponement or adjournment thereof), the Rights shall not be redeemed if such

The effect of the By-Law Amendment would be to delay a shareholder-called special meeting for at least three months. The effect of the DRP would be to delay the ability of a newly-elected, Mentor-nominated board to redeem the poison pill for six months in any transaction with an Interested Person. Thus, the combined effect of the two defensive measures would be to delay any acquisition of Quickturn by Mentor for at least nine months. * * *

Mentor filed this action on August 12, 1998, seeking (i) a declaratory judgment that Quickturn's newly adopted takeover defenses are invalid, and (ii) an injunction requiring the Quickturn board to dismantle those defenses. After expedited discovery, the defendants moved for summary judgment. Following extensive briefing and oral argument, the Court denied defendants' motion * * * [and] a trial was held on October 19, 20, 23, 26, and 28, 1998, during which the parties amassed a voluminous record; thereafter, the parties submitted extensive post trial briefs on an expedited schedule.

During the course of the litigation, the Quickturn board, relying upon the By-Law Amendment, noticed the special meeting requested by Mentor from January 8, 1999—71 days after the October 1, 1998 meeting date originally noticed by Mentor. After the trial, Mentor announced in Amendments to its Schedule 14A–1 that were filed with the S.E.C., that it had received tenders of Quickturn shares which, together with the shares that Mentor already owned, represent over 51% of Quickturn's outstanding stock.

* * * [The court concluded that the bylaw amendment was valid, but it invalidated the DRP on the following analysis:]

At the time Mentor commenced its bid, Quickturn had in place a Rights Plan that contained a so-called "dead hand" provision. That provision had a limited "continuing director" feature that became operative only if an insurgent that owned more than 15% of Quickturn's common stock successfully waged a proxy contest to replace a majority of the board. In that event, only the "continuing directors" (those directors in office at the time the poison pill was adopted) could redeem the rights. During the same August 21, 1998 meeting at which it amended the special meeting by-law, the Quickturn board also amended the Rights Plan to eliminate its "continuing director" feature, and to substitute a "no hand" or "delayed redemption" rights plan.

---

redemption is reasonably likely to have the purpose or effect of facilitating a Transaction with an Interested Person."

An "Interested Person" is defined under the amended Rights Plan as "any Person who (i) is or will become an Acquiring Person if such Transaction were to be consummated or an Affiliate or Associate of such a Person, and (ii) is, or directly or indirectly proposed, nominated or financially supported, a director of [Quickturn] in office at the time of consideration of such Transaction who was elected at an annual or special meeting of stockholders."

The DRP provides that, if a majority of the directors are replaced by stockholder action, the newly elected board cannot redeem the rights for six months if the purpose or effect of the redemption would be to facilitate a transaction with an "Interested Person." * * * The plaintiffs attack the DRP on * * * [the ground that it] was a disproportionate response to any threat reasonably perceived by the Mentor bid and, therefore, violated the fiduciary principles articulated in Unocal and Unitrin. The plaintiffs contend, specifically, that the Quickturn board has failed to establish that (i) the Mentor offer and proxy contest constituted a legally cognizable threat, (ii) the DRP is not coercive or preclusive, and that (iii) the DRP falls within a range of reasonable potential responses to Mentor's hostile takeover efforts.[h] * * *

The Court concludes that, in adopting the DRP, the Quickturn board, even though motivated by a good faith belief that their actions were in the company's best interests, nonetheless transgressed their fiduciary duties under Unocal and Unitrin.[73] * * *

* * * Decisions made by a board of directors are normally subject to the business judgment form of review, which is a "presumption that in making a business decision, the directors of a corporation acted on an informed basis, in good faith and in the honest belief that the action was taken in the best interest of the Company."[74] Under that form of review, the burden to rebut that presumption rests on the party that challenges the board's decision, and a court will not substitute its judgment for that of the board if the decision is attributable to a "rational business purpose."[75] But where a board of a Delaware corporation takes action to resist or defend against a hostile bid for control, the review standard is quite different. In that case the target company board's defensive actions are subjected to "enhanced" judicial scrutiny, because of the "omnipresent specter" that the board may be acting in its own interests rather than the interests of the corporation or its unaffiliated stockholders.[76] For a target board's actions to be entitled to business judgment rule protection, the target board must first establish that (i) it had reasonable grounds to believe that the hostile bid constituted a threat to corporate policy and effectiveness, and (ii) that the defensive measures adopted were

---

[h] The plaintiff also alleged that the plan (1) violated the board's fiduciary duties to Quickturn and its shareholders, and (2) the plan was invalid because it impermissibly deprived a newly elected board of its core authority to manage the corporation. The court did not find it necessary to address either of these contentions.

[73] The Court acknowledges that a disposition of this issue on fiduciary, rather than upon statutory, grounds may appear counterintuitive. In this case, however, the statutory argument—which appears as the last in the sequence of arguments in Mentor's brief, and went virtually unanswered in the defendants' briefs—was not adequately developed by the parties. Because the briefing focused almost entirely upon the fiduciary claims, the Court rests its DRP ruling on those grounds as well.

[74] Unitrin, 651 A.2d at 1373 (quoting Aronson v. Lewis, 473 A.2d 805, 812 (1984)).

[75] Id. (citing Sinclair Oil Corp. v. Levien, Del.Supr., 280 A.2d 717, 720 (1971)).

[76] Id. (quoting Unocal, 493 A.2d at 954).

"proportionate," that is, reasonable in relation to the threat that the board reasonably perceived.[77] The DRP is reviewed under that standard.

The parties first dispute whether the Quickturn board has established the existence of a legally cognizable threat. On that issue, the board may satisfy its burden by showing that it conducted a reasonable investigation and took defensive action in good faith. That proof is enhanced if a majority of the board that approved the defensive measures were outside independent directors. Although Mentor contends that its offer did not pose a legally cognizable threat, I conclude otherwise * * *.

A major point of contention (and confusion) concerns what precisely the Quickturn board perceived to be the threat posed by Mentor's hostile bid. Our Supreme Court has recognized that three categories of threats normally arise in the corporate takeover context: (i) opportunity loss * * * [where] a hostile offer might deprive target shareholders of the opportunity to select a superior alternative offered by target management [or, we would add, offered by another bidder]; (ii) structural coercion, * * * the risk that disparate treatment of non-tendering shareholders might distort shareholders' tender decisions; and * * * (iii) substantive coercion, * * * the risk that shareholders will mistakenly accept an underpriced offer because they disbelieve management's representations of intrinsic value. * * *

Despite the defendants' diverse characterizations of the threat, the evidence, viewed as a whole, shows that the perceived threat that led the Quickturn board to adopt the DRP, was the concern that Quickturn shareholders might mistakenly, in ignorance of Quickturn's true value, accept Mentor's inadequate offer, and elect a new board that would prematurely sell the company before the new board could adequately inform itself of Quickturn's fair value and before the shareholders could consider other options. In so finding, I reject the effort by Quickturn's attorneys to characterize the threat differently in their briefs. * * *

Having concluded that the board reasonably perceived a cognizable threat, the issue then becomes whether the board's response—the DRP— was reasonable in relation to that threat. * * * A board " 'does not have unbridled discretion to defeat any perceived threat by any Draconian means available.' "[85] Accordingly, our law requires that Quickturn's board establish that the DRP was proportional to the threat posed by Mentor's offer.

For the reasons next discussed, the Court concludes that the DRP was disproportionate, because although the DRP is neither coercive nor

---

[77] Unocal, 493 A.2d at 955; see also Unitrin, 651 A.2d at 1372 (1995); Paramount Communications, Inc. v. Time Inc., Del.Supr., 571 A.2d 1140, 1152 (1989) ("Time").

[85] Unitrin, 651 A.2d at 1387 (quoting Unocal, 493 A.2d at 955).

preclusive in these particular circumstances, it does fall outside the range of reasonable responses to Mentor's hostile bid. * * *

The record establishes, and I therefore find, that the board's justification or rationale for adopting the DRP was to force any newly elected board (as distinguished from only a Mentor-nominated board) to take sufficient time to become familiar with Quickturn and its value, and to provide shareholders the opportunity to consider alternatives, before selling Quickturn to any acquirer.

Unfortunately, that justification renders the DRP a disproportionate response, because the justification is at war with how the DRP, as adopted by the board, would actually operate. The DRP does not create a six month pill redemption delay in all cases where a newly elected, Mentor-nominated board seeks to sell the company to any bidder. It creates such a delay only if a newly elected board seeks to sell Quickturn to an "Interested Person," which in this case is Mentor. It is undisputed that under the terms of the DRP, a new board could sell the company to anyone other than Mentor on its very first day in office, or at any time during the six month nonredemption period. An example of the inconsistency between the theory (the directors' justification for the DRP) and the reality (how the DRP would actually operate) makes the point. Suppose that the day after the new Mentor-nominated board takes office, a third party makes a $14 per share offer, which tops Mentor's $12.125 bid. An auction then ensues. Mentor decides to increase its offer to $15, and becomes the high bidder. Under the DRP, the new board could redeem the pill and accept the $14 bid immediately, but could not accept Mentor's $15 bid for six months. There is no evidence that when it decided to adopt that defensive measure the board considered that the DRP could operate in this way. Because the operative terms of the DRP cannot be reconciled with the directors' stated justification for adopting it, the board has not carried its burden of demonstrating that the DRP is reasonable in relation to the perceived threat.

The defendants have also failed to carry their burden because they are unable to articulate a cogent reason why a six month delay period is reasonable. The board did discuss alternate time periods, but it ultimately settled on six months because that period was "reasonable" and the "minimum" time a newly elected board would need to become sufficiently informed about Quickturn, based upon their own experience as to how long they, as directors, needed to learn about the company. * * * [However,] the board has offered no justification that is anchored to any objective fact or criterion for adopting the six month nonredemption period in the DRP.

Finally, the DRP cannot pass the proportionality test because its articulated purpose—to give a newly elected board time to inform itself of Quickturn's value—would already have been achieved by the conclusion of the three month delay period imposed by the By-Law Amendment. The purpose of the Amendment is to give shareholders 90 to 100 days' time to make an informed decision about which slate to vote for. The DRP would protract the delay by another six months, purportedly to enable the newly elected board to educate itself about Quickturn's value before committing to a sale of the company.

The problem with this rationale is that the subject matter about which the shareholders would be informing themselves during the By-Law Amendment 90 to 100 day delay period, and the subject about which a new board would be informing itself during the six month DRP nonredemption period, is the same: should the company be sold and, if so, when and at what price? If three months is an adequate time for shareholders to become informed, why should a new board require six months? More fundamentally, why would the Mentor director nominees be unable to inform themselves on that issue (as the Quickturn shareholders must) during the three month period imposed by the Amended By-Law? * * * The conclusion that must be drawn is that the board has failed to show why the additional six month delay imposed by the DRP is necessary to achieve the board's stated purpose for its adoption.

For these reasons the DRP cannot survive scrutiny under Unocal and must be declared invalid.[105]

NOTES

(1) On an expedited appeal, the Supreme Court of Delaware affirmed this decision, but on significantly broader grounds than that used by Chancellor Jacobs. See Quickturn Design Systems, Inc. v. Shapiro, 721 A.2d 1281, 1290–99 (Del.1998).

---

[105]   By way of postscript, this Court is mindful that higher level issues lurk behind the factual shadows of this dispute, issues that are not addressed in this Opinion. In this ever-changing area of the law where there is a potential (and, perhaps, also the need) to afford guidance to the corporate bar in the form of bright-line standards, for a Court to adjudicate the validity of an innovative takeover defense on the basis of equitable and fiduciary principles that by their nature are highly fact specific and particularized, is admittedly unsatisfying. That there are underlying policy issues is inevitable, given the tension between the directors' acknowledged authority to manage the affairs of the corporation, and the shareholders' independent right and authority to choose the corporation's ultimate destiny, whether by approving or disapproving a fundamental transaction or by electing a new board committed to a direction the shareholders think desirable. In a contest for corporate control where the incumbent board adopts a poison pill and an insurgent slate of board candidates vow to redeem it, should the target company shareholders have the final word on whether or not the pill should be redeemed? To express the question in fiduciary terms, should a proxy contest in this setting be viewed as a referendum on whether the company should be sold, and if so, should the board of directors be allowed to delay the effect of that referendum? To pose the issue in statutory terms, should a delayed redemption provision be found invalid under 8 Del. C. § 141(a) because it temporarily deprives a newly elected insurgent board of a portion of its core authority that the board arguably may need (or have a fiduciary duty) to exercise during the period of deprivation? * * * To craft a principle, or "bright line" test, that will readily enable a court to determine the validity of a limited duration "no hand" poison pill, would require a court to address issues of this kind. This Opinion does not meet that challenge * * *.

(2) A commentator made the cautious suggestion that "these decisions represent the first real shift in Delaware takeover law after more than a decade of decisions that all seemed to favor targets." Paul T. Schnell, From the Editor: A Good Year for Bidders in Delaware, 3 Glasser LegalWorks, No. 6, 2 (1999). This certainly does not intimate that a seismic change was underway in Delaware.

(3) If the principal case really does mean that current boards of directors cannot restrict the power of their successors (following a successful purchase offer), is there danger that publicly-held corporations might migrate to states more hospitable than their state of incorporation? Maryland was the first state specifically to validate a slow-hand provision in rights plans following the *Quickturn* decision. The Maryland statute, it may be noted, leaves open the measuring time for the beginning of the 180 day period. It also apparently gives the "stockholder rights plan" unlimited discretion to define "future director." Is there any room within these Maryland statutes for a judicial decision such as the Delaware Supreme Court's decision in Quickturn?

INTERNATIONAL BROTHERHOOD OF TEAMSTERS V. FLEMING COMPANIES

Supreme Court of Oklahoma, 1999.
975 P.2d 907.

SIMMS, J.

The United States Court of Appeals, Tenth Circuit, John C. Porfilio, Presiding Judge, * * * certified to the Oklahoma Supreme Court the following question of law:

> Does Oklahoma law [A] restrict the authority to create and implement shareholder rights plans exclusively to the board of directors, or [B] may shareholders propose resolutions requiring that shareholder rights plans be submitted to the shareholders for vote at the succeeding annual meeting?

We answer the first part of the question in the negative and the second part affirmatively. We hold under Oklahoma law there is no exclusive authority granted boards of directors to create and implement shareholder rights plans, where shareholder objection is brought and passed through official channels of corporate governance. We find no Oklahoma law which gives exclusive authority to a corporation's board of directors for the formulation of shareholder rights plans and no authority which precludes shareholders from proposing resolutions or bylaw amendments regarding shareholder rights plans. We hold shareholders may propose bylaws which restrict board implementation of shareholder rights plans, assuming the certificate of incorporation does not provide otherwise.

The International Brotherhood of the Teamsters General Fund [Teamsters] owns sixty-five shares of Fleming Companies, Inc. * * * In 1986, Fleming implemented a shareholder's rights plan with the term of the plan to expire in 1996. The rights plan implemented by Fleming is an anti-takeover mechanism. Such plans give boards of directors authority to adopt and execute discriminatory shareholder rights upon the occurrence of some triggering event, usually when a certain percentage of shares has been amassed by a single shareholder. A board can place "restrictions or conditions on the exercise, transfer or receipt of" shareholder rights which can severely dilute the shareholding power of one seeking control of a company.[1] The defensive plans usually result in entrenching existing management, making a takeover without the approval of incumbent management more difficult. These rights plans can make it far more expensive to effect a takeover. Because the rights plans make the merger of companies more painful for the suitor and assist incumbent management in maintaining control, the plans are often called "poison pill rights plans" or "poison pills."

From a target company's perspective, rights plans can often buy valuable time to implement merger strategy or even secure more lucrative offers from other suitors. In this context, a rights plan might serve not only the protectionist objectives of an existing management, but also the company's overall interests in the event of takeover, including the interests of shareholders.

However, rights plans can often stifle mergers, causing some shareholder groups to view them with increasing skepticism, because, company mergers can be financially lucrative for shareholders who own stock in a target company. A poison pill not only makes many mergers cost prohibitive and therefore might prevent a merger altogether, but it can decrease the profits in those mergers which do ultimately occur. As a result, poison pills have the ability to strip shareholders of financial benefit which might normally be associated with a takeover.

The stock market has had a long history of shareholder passivity, but this is likely a thing of the past. The rise of the institutional investor and the increased knowledge of stockholders as a whole is forcing an increased accountability to shareholders for many boards of directors. As a result, the demands of the Teamsters in its case against Fleming is something courts may encounter with increasing frequency in the years to come.

The trial court, which ruled in the Teamsters' (shareholders) favor, expressed concern with Fleming's position, stating that it effectively removed corporate authority regarding share marketability from the shareholders and vested it exclusively in a board of directors, which

---

[1]   John H. Matheson & Brent A. Olson, Shareholder Rights and Legislative Wrongs; Toward Balanced Takeover Legislation, 59 Geo.Wash.L.Rev. 1425, 1450 (1990).

might view the situation from the most self-interested point of view. Teamsters were critical of Fleming's rights plan, seeing it as a means of entrenching the current Fleming board of directors in the event Fleming became the target of a takeover. In 1996, the Teamsters organized and introduced a non-binding resolution for the annual shareholders meeting. The 1996 resolution called on the Fleming board to redeem the existing rights plan. The then current rights plan had been in effect since 1986 and was scheduled for renewal. The Teamsters proposal was met with apparent hostility from Fleming's board and the rights plan remained intact, despite a majority shareholder vote in agreement with the Teamsters' resolution to redeem it.

The following year, 1997, Teamsters mounted a more organized effort to change the continued implementation of the rights plan. Teamsters prepared a proxy statement for inclusion in the proxy materials for the 1997 annual shareholder's meeting. With the proxy effort, the Teamsters proposed an amendment to the company's bylaws which would require any rights plan implemented by the board of directors to be put to the shareholders for a majority vote.[3] The proposal was essentially a ratification procedure wherein the shareholders would force the board to formulate a rights plan both the board and shareholders could agree on or do away with such a plan altogether.

Fleming refused to include the resolution in its 1997 proxy statement, declaring the proposal was not a subject for shareholder action under Oklahoma law. Teamsters then brought an action in the Federal District Court for the Western District of Oklahoma. The district court ruled in favor of the Teamsters, the court finding that "shareholders, through the device of bylaws, have a right of review." Fleming appealed to the 10th Circuit Court of Appeals, which submitted the certified question to this Court.

---

[3]   The 1997 proxy proposal provided:

"Resolved, That shareholders hereby exercise their right under 18 O.S.A. Sec. 1013 to amend the bylaws of Fleming Companies, Inc. to add the following Article:

"Article X Poison Pills (Shareholder Rights Plans)

"A.   The Corporation shall not adopt or maintain a poison pill, shareholder rights plan, rights agreement or any other form of 'poison pill' which is designed to or has the effect of making acquisition of large holdings of the Corporation's shares of stock more difficult or expensive (such as the 1986 'Rights Agreement'), unless such plan is first approved by a majority shareholder vote. The Company shall redeem any such rights now in effect. The affirmative vote of a majority of shares voted shall suffice to approve such a plan.

"B.   This article shall be effective immediately and automatically as of the date it is approved by the affirmative vote of the holders of a majority of the shares, present, in person or by proxy at a regular or special meeting of shareholders.

"C.   Notwithstanding any other provision of these bylaws, this Article may not be amended, altered, deleted or modified in any way by the Board of Directors without prior shareholder approval."

Fleming sought to postpone any shareholder vote on the 1997 proxy issue until after the resolution of this case. But the U.S. District Court and later the 10th Circuit denied Fleming's motion to suspend the injunction. Fleming was then forced to allow its shareholders to vote on the Teamsters' proxy. The Teamsters' resolution passed with approximately 60% of the voted shares.

Fleming's position is that 18 O.S.1991 § 1038[5] gives the board of directors authority to create and issue shareholder rights plans, subject only to limits which might exist in the corporation's certificate of incorporation; and that shareholders cannot through bylaws restrict the board's powers to implement a rights plan. The Teamsters' position is that 18 O.S.1991 § 1013 gives shareholders of a publicly traded corporation, such as Fleming, the authority to adopt bylaws addressing a broad range of topics from a corporation's business, corporate affairs, and rights and powers of shareholders and directors.[6] It is this apparent conflict which brings this federal certified question to this Court.

This is a case of first impression in Oklahoma and there is little guidance from other states. Oklahoma and Delaware have substantially similar corporation acts, especially with regard to Title 18, §§ 1013 & 1038 which are of primary concern here. 8 Del.C. § 109(a) & (b); 8 Del.C. § 157. However, a review of Delaware decisions revealed no comparable case from that state. The 10th Circuit's question is ultimately one of corporate governance and what degree of control shareholders can exact upon the corporations in which they own stock.

In the scheme of corporate governance the role of shareholders has been purposefully indirect. Shareholders' direct authority is limited. * * * This is true for obvious reasons. Large corporations with perhaps thousands of stockholders could not function if the daily running of the corporation was subject to the approval of so many relatively attenuated people. However, the authority given a board of directors under the Oklahoma General Corporation Act, is not without shareholder oversight. * * *

Fleming's argument relies on this passage [from] 18 O.S.1991 § 1038: "Subject to any provisions in the certificate of incorporation, every

---

[5]   18 O.S.1991 § 1038, Rights and options respecting stock: "Subject to any provisions in the certificate of incorporation, every corporation may create and issue, whether or not in connection with the issue and sale of any shares of stock or other securities of the corporation, rights or options entitling the holders thereof to purchase from the corporation any shares of its capital stock of any instrument or instruments as shall be approved by the board of directors. * * *"

[6]   18 O.S.1991 § 1013(A) & (B), Bylaws: "* * * After a corporation has received any payment for any of its stock, the power to adopt, amend or repeal bylaws shall be in the shareholders entitled to vote * * *; provided, however, any corporation, in its certificate of incorporation, may confer the power to adopt, amend or repeal bylaws upon the directors * * *. The fact that such power has been so conferred upon the directors or governing body, as the case may be, shall not divest the shareholders or members of the power, nor limit their power to adopt, amend or repeal bylaws."

corporation may create and issue * * * rights or options entitling the holders thereof to purchase from the corporation any shares of its capital stock of any class or classes, such rights or options to be evidenced by or in such instrument or instruments as shall be approved by the *board of directors*. [Emphasis added] In making its argument, Fleming asserts that the word "corporation" is synonymous with "board of directors" as the term is used in 18 § 1038. Therefore, according to Fleming, "every corporation may create and issue * * * rights and options," can actually be read to say "[every corporation's board of directors] may create and issue * * * rights and options[.]" However, * * * this assertion is flawed. * * * [T]he former Business Corporation Act, 18 § 1.2(1) and (23), defines "corporation" and "director" differently. The statutes indicate our legislature has an understanding of the distinct definitions it assigns to these terms, and we find it unlikely the legislature would interchange them as Fleming contends. While this Court would agree with Fleming that a corporation may create and issue rights and options within the grant of authority given it in 18 § 1038, it does not automatically translate that the board of directors of that corporation has in itself the same breadth of authority.

A shareholder rights plan is essentially a variety of stock option plan. Its use as an anti-takeover mechanism does not change its essential character. While shareholder ratification of poison pills has not been tested in the courts, the same cannot be said for stock option plans as a whole. There is authority supporting shareholder ratification of stock option plans. * * * For example, in Michelson v. Duncan, 407 A.2d 211, 218–20 (Del.1979), shareholders ratified a stock option package, curing a voidable act of the corporation's board of directors. Unlike the instant case, Michelson does not focus on whether shareholders have the authority to ratify the stock option plan, but rather explains that shareholder approval can cure the invalidity of an otherwise voidable act of the company's board. Despite this distinction, however, the case does reveal that stock option plans themselves can be subject to shareholder approval. * * *

We find nothing in the Oklahoma General Corporation Act * * * or existing case law which indicates the shareholder rights plan is somehow exempt from shareholder adopted bylaws. Fleming argues that only the certificate of incorporation can limit the board's authority to implement such a plan * * *. While this Court might agree that a certificate of incorporation, which somehow precludes bylaw amendments directed at shareholder rights plans, could preclude the Teamsters from seeking the bylaw changes which are proposed in this case, neither party has indicated Fleming's certificate speaks in any way to the board's authority or shareholder constraints regarding shareholder rights plans. We find no authority to support the contention that a certificate of incorporation which is silent with regard to shareholder rights plans precludes shareholder enacted bylaws regarding the implementation of rights plans.

A number of states have taken affirmative steps to ensure their domestic corporations, and in many instances the board of directors itself, are able to implement shareholder rights plans to protect the company from takeover. The legislation is typically called a shareholders rights plan endorsement statute. However, the Oklahoma legislature has not passed such legislation. There are at least twenty-four states with these share rights plan endorsement statutes.[7]

[An example] of [a] shareholders rights plan endorsement statute[ ] which give[s] explicit authority to directors of the corporation read[s] as follows: Nothing contained in this chapter is intended or shall be construed in any way to limit, modify or restrict an issuing public corporation's authority to take any action *which the directors may appropriately determine* to be in furtherance of the protection of the interests of the corporation and its shareholders, *including without limitation* the authority to adopt or enter into plans, arrangements or instruments that deny rights, privileges, power or authority to the holder or holders of at least a specified number of shares or percentage of share ownership or voting power in certain circumstances. [Idaho] St. § 30–1706(1) (emphasis added). * * *

* * * [The Idaho statute illustrates] how a board of directors can operate with relative autonomy when a rights plan endorsement statute applies. This does not suggest the absence of a share rights plan endorsement statute in Oklahoma precludes the implementation of such a takeover defense. We merely find that without the authority granted in such an endorsement statute, the board may well be subject to the general procedures of corporate governance, including the enactment of bylaws which limit the board's authority to implement shareholder rights plans.

This Court understands much of the reasoning behind the enactment of rights plan endorsement statutes and why so many state legislatures are inclined to facilitate this takeover protection for their domestic corporations. In addition, we understand Fleming's desire to have a rights plan available for quick, and more effective, implementation. However, if, as in this case, the certificate of incorporation does not offer directors this broad authority to protect against mergers and takeover, corporations must look to Oklahoma's legislature, not this Court, which is more properly vested with the means to offer boards such authority.

---

[7] John H. Matheson & Brent A. Olson, Shareholder Rights and Legislative Wrongs: Toward Balanced Takeover Legislation, 59 Geo. Wash. L.Rev. 1425, 1554–58 (August 1991). * * * [S]tates with shareholder rights plan endorsement statutes are * * * Colorado, Georgia, Hawaii, Idaho, Illinois, Indiana, Iowa, Kentucky, Massachusetts, Michigan, Nevada, New Jersey, New York, North Carolina, Ohio, Oregon, Pennsylvania, Rhode Island, South Dakota, Tennessee, Utah, Virginia, Wyoming, [and] Wisconsin.

In answering this certified question, we do not suggest all shareholder rights plans are required to submit to shareholder approval, ratification or review; this is not the question presented to us. Instead, we find shareholders may, through the proper channels of corporate governance, restrict the board of directors authority to implement shareholder rights plans.

SUMMERS, C.J., HARGRAVE, V.C.J., LAVENDER, OPALA, WILSON, KAUGER, and WATT, JJ., concur. HODGES, J., no vote.

NOTES

(1) Some institutional investors that oppose poison pills have had success as proponents of nonbinding precatory shareholder proposals under Rule 14a–8 to redeem the poison pill. See also MBCA § 10.21, which provides explicitly for the primacy of shareholder-approved by-laws over directorial action.

(2) This issue has given rise to a substantial amount of law review commentary supporting the validity of shareholder rights bylaws. See e.g. Lawrence Hamermesh, Corporate Democracy and Stockholder Adopted Bylaws: Taking Back the Street?, 73 Tulane L.Rev. 409 (1998); Jonathan R. Macey, The Legality and Utility of the Shareholder Rights Bylaw, 26 Hofstra L.Rev. 835 (1998) ("concern about its legality is misplaced"); Robert Thompson, Preemption and Federalism in Corporate Governance: Protecting Shareholder Rights to Vote, Sell, and Sue, 62 Law & Contemp. Prob. 215 (1999); E. Norman Veasey, An Economic Rationale for Judicial Decisionmaking in Corporate Law, 53 Bus.Law. 681 (1998).

D. TAKEOVER DEFENSES AND JUDICIAL REVIEW

Assuming that a takeover offer—either all cash or cash and marketable securities—is made, does incumbent management have a duty to oppose it? To support it? To remain neutral and neither support nor oppose it? These questions raise fundamental issues about the roles of shareholders and management that are at the center of the modern debate over takeovers. If, as will normally be the case, the aggressor has the financial strength to carry out the contemplated offer, shareholders of the target corporation will almost certainly realize more for their shares if the offer succeeds than if it fails. If one accepts the basic proposition that the sole goal of management should be to maximize shareholder wealth, does it not follow that management certainly should not be permitted to actively oppose an offer, and that it should further have an affirmative obligation either to support the offer or seek even more favorable offers from other sources?

On the other hand, the underlying justification for the many state statutes that authorize consideration of non-shareholder constituencies (see Chapter 9, Section B) is to liberate management from the chains of this apparently-compelling theoretical argument that it has a duty always to maximize the financial interests of the shareholders. It is also clear that acceptance of a takeover bid is often not value-maximizing from the standpoint of incumbent management. These individuals face the loss of prestigious positions, six- or seven-figure salaries, desirable "perks," lucrative fringe benefits, and the loss of power to control a large enterprise. Thus, it is not surprising that management usually feels it is a matter of the highest urgency to defeat uninvited takeover bids at all costs.

The derogatory term "entrenchment" usually describes defensive tactics that are designed solely to defeat an offer in order to preserve management's position. Entrenchment is a breach of the fiduciary duty of loyalty (since the tactics are not for a corporate purpose but to preserve the position of the managers). Open descriptions of one's motive to entrench and preserve one's position are clear losers, therefore other justifications to defeat the offer must be developed. Examples include (1) the offered price is too low and does not reflect the "true" value of the corporation's business; (2) the aggressor's reputation for sound fiscal management is not good; (3) the aggressor is assuming debt obligations which it probably cannot meet without using the target's assets, thereby injuring remaining shareholders or senior security or debt holders; (4) it is simply in the best long-run interests of the shareholders for the corporation to remain independent (the "just say no" defense); (5) management has already embarked on long-range plans to improve the corporation's profits and stock price, and the decision to pursue those plans is protected by the business judgment rule; (6) the proposed transaction would result in a violation of the antitrust laws or some other federal or state statute; or (7) the offer is a partial one and is structured in a way that makes it unfair to shareholders by "coercing" them to tender. Whether or not such arguments are persuasive or even plausible obviously depends on the facts of the particular takeover. If one accepts the premise that takeovers occur primarily to weed out less efficient managers, the conclusions that management should be sharply restricted in the defensive tactics it may employ and that basic economic forces should decide the outcome are considerably strengthened.

The economic stakes in a takeover battle are so great that litigation to test the validity of any defenses employed by management—at least in the 1980s—was a virtual certainty. This litigation was traditionally in the form of suits for equitable relief based either on violations of the Williams Act or on breaches of the duty of care or loyalty by management, or both. However, where management effectively defeated a tender offer without providing an offsetting management buyout or leveraged recapitalization to replace some or all of the lost value to shareholders, there inevitably was a precipitous decline in the market price of the target stock, and litigation commenced on the theory that the directors should be held personally liable for the losses since they opposed the takeover in order to preserve their positions with the corporation.

Suits by shareholders against the directors and officers first foundered on the business judgment rule in its most permissive form. The leading case was Panter v. Marshall Field & Co., 646 F.2d 271 (7th Cir.1981), cert. denied, 454 U.S. 1092 (1981), where Marshall Field successfully fended off an unwanted takeover bid from Carter Hawley Hale (CHH), a national retail chain that operated Neiman-Marcus and other stores. Marshall Field adopted and vigorously pursued a policy to preserve its independence; among other things, it adopted an expansion program that led to Marshall Field stores coming into direct competition with Neiman-Marcus in several markets. When CHH withdrew its bid in part because of antitrust complications, the price of Marshall Field common stock precipitously declined from about $34 per share to $19 per share. The Court absolved the defendants of liability under the business judgment rule and the presumption of good faith that protects directors: "The plaintiffs also contend that the 'defensive acquisitions' of the five Liberty House stores and the Galleria were imprudent, and designed to make Field's less attractive as an acquisition, as well as to exacerbate any antitrust problems created by the CHH merger. It is precisely this sort of Monday-morning-quarterbacking that the business judgment rule was intended to prevent." 646 F.2d at 297.

This approach was too much for Judge Cudahy:

Unfortunately, the majority here has moved one giant step closer to shredding whatever constraints still remain upon the ability of corporate directors to place self-interest before shareholder interest in resisting a hostile tender offer for control of the corporation. There is abundant evidence in this case to go to the jury on the state claims for breach of fiduciary duty. I emphatically disagree that the business judgment rule should clothe directors, battling blindly to fend off a threat to their control, with an almost irrebuttable presumption of sound business judgment, prevailing over everything but the elusive hobgoblins of fraud, bad faith or abuse of discretion. * * *

Addressing first the state law claims of breach of fiduciary duty by the Board, the majority has adopted an approach which would virtually immunize a target company's board of directors against liability to shareholders, provided a sufficiently prestigious (and expensive) array of legal and financial talent were retained to furnish *post hoc* rationales for fixed and immutable policies of resistance to takeover. Relying on several recent decisions interpreting the Delaware business judgment rule, the majority fails to make the important distinction between the activity of a corporation in managing a business enterprise and its function as a vehicle for collecting and using capital and distributing profits and losses. The former involves corporate functioning in competitive business affairs in which judicial interference may be undesirable. *The latter involves only the corporation-shareholder relationship, in which the courts may more justifiably intervene to insist on equitable behavior. Note, Protection for Shareholder Interests in Recapitalizations of Publicly Held Companies,* 58 Colum.L.Rev. 1030, 1066 (1958) (emphasis supplied).

The theoretical justification for the "hands off" precept of the business judgment rule is that courts should be reluctant to review the acts of directors in situations where the expertise of the directors is likely to be greater than that of the courts. But, where the directors are afflicted with a conflict of interest, relative expertise is no longer crucial. Instead, the great danger becomes the channeling of the directors' expertise along the lines of their personal advantage—sometimes at the expense of the corporation and its stockholders. Here courts have no rational choice but to subject challenged conduct of directors and questioned corporate transactions to their own disinterested scrutiny. Of course, the self-protective bias of interested directors may be entirely devoid of corrupt motivation, but it may nonetheless constitute a serious threat to stockholder welfare. * * *

Directors of a New York Stock Exchange-listed company are, at the very least, "interested" in their own positions of power, prestige and prominence (and in their not inconsequential perquisites). They are "interested" in defending against outside attack the management which they have, in fact, installed or maintained in power—"their" management (to which, in many cases, they owe their directorships). And they are "interested" in maintaining the public reputation of their own leadership and stewardship against the claims of "raiders" who say that they can do better. Thus, regardless of their technical "independence," directors of a target corporation are in a very special position, where the slavish application of the majority's version of the good faith presumption is particularly disturbing.

646 F.2d, at 299–300.

It is debatable whether or not Panter v. Marshall Field involved a proper application of the business judgment rule. To some extent the decision may have been influenced by the threatened imposition of immense liabilities on outside directors who did not materially benefit from the transaction.[i] In any event, the development of numerous sophisticated and powerful defensive tactics caused the Delaware courts to reject the almost simplistic application of the business judgment rule of *Panter*, and to seek a "more balanced" analysis of the equities of the situation. These defenses often work in tandem with each other, while others are freestanding.

(1) Among the most common (and effective) are three-tier plans that include (a) a classification of the board of directors into three groups, with one group being elected each year, (b) a prohibition against removing directors except for cause, and (c) a provision that prohibited certain designated types of amendments to the articles of incorporation or bylaws (which could result in a change of control) unless approved by a supermajority (e.g., 80 percent) of the directors. The cumulative effect of these provisions is to prevent an aggressor that acquired even 100 percent of the shares from replacing a majority of the board of directors for two years. Compare MBCA §§ 7.27, 8.06, 8.24(a) and (c), 10.21. Delaware's statute is similar to these provisions. See Del. Gen. Corp. Law § 141(d). Do such provisions provide adequate protection to the shareholders or to the public against possible misuse of these entrenchment provisions?

(2) Poison pills and state takeover legislation discussed in the previous Sections.

(3) A requirement that 80 percent or more of the shareholders approve certain transactions (e.g., mergers) between the corporation and persons that own more than 10 percent of the corporate shares—adopted by Southwest Airlines and others.

(4) A requirement that a majority of the shares other than shares owned by a party to a proposed transaction approve the proposed transaction—adopted by Baldor Electric, Inc. and others.

(5) A requirement that 95 percent approval of certain transactions between the corporation and large shareholders be obtained unless the transaction meets certain precise price and other substantive terms set forth in the articles or bylaws—adopted by Anchor Hocking Corporation and others.

(6) A provision that allows minority shareholders to redeem their shares for cash from the corporation at a price set forth in the articles or bylaws for a limited period following any transaction in which a person acquires a majority of the outstanding shares or a majority shareholder increases his holdings—adopted by Rubbermaid Corporation and others.

---

[i] This type of litigation against directors for damages is probably not precluded by Del.Gen.Corp.L. § 102(b)(7) (see Chapter 10) because it involves an arguable breach of the duty of loyalty or the receipt of an improper, personal benefit. It may be barred by some statutes enacted after *Van Gorkom*. See Chapter 10.

(7) A provision creating special classes of preferred shares to be held by a limited number of holders and requiring approval of that class of shares for certain classes of transactions—e.g., Outdoor Sports Industries, Inc.

(8) Fair price amendments to articles of incorporation which mandate that shareholders receive equivalent consideration (both in terms of amount and form) on both ends of a two-tiered bid—adopted by numerous corporations.

(9) Anti-greenmail provisions: amendments to articles of incorporation prohibiting the repurchase by the company of stock at a premium from a three percent or greater holder unless the repurchase is approved by a majority vote of the shareholders—adopted by International Minerals & Chemical Corporation and others.

NOTES

(1) Staggered terms for corporate boards of directors are a popular defensive device available to management. A 'staggered board' is a board of directors that is usually divided into three groups with one group being elected each year. In a staggered board only a minority of directors are elected each year and directors stand for election only every third year. See Lucian Bebchuk, John Coates, and Guhan Subramanian, The Powerful Antitakeover Force of Staggered Boards: Theory, Evidence and Policy, 54 Stan. L. Rev. 887, 895 (2002). Staggered boards have defensive characteristics because they prevent a hostile acquirer from gaining control of the company in a single election.

(2) Other popular defensive devices include fair-price charter amendments that require (1) all shareholders be paid the same price, (2) a supermajority vote for proposed mergers, (3) dual class capitalization plans with different classes of voting shares, (4) cumulative voting, (5) provisions limiting the power of shareholders to act by written consent without a shareholders' meeting, (6) charter amendments limiting the power of shareholders to call special shareholders' meetings, (7) charter amendments discouraging greenmail, (8) provisions that acquire secret ballots, and (9) proposals specifically authorizing directors to consider the interests of other constituencies when evaluating outside acquisition attempts. Of course, many companies adopt several of these devices. In some states, these defensive devices are automatically in effect by reason of statute.

(3) Dual class capitalization plans led to major legal battles during the 1980s. A dual class capitalization plan builds on the basic notion that a corporation is totally takeover-proof if a majority of its voting shares are held by a single person, entity, or family group. During the 1980s, a number of publicly held corporations seriously considered the creation of "supervoting stock" as the ultimate antitakeover device. Supervoting stock gives holders of a class the right to cast multiple votes for each share owned. In other words,

Class A stock might have five votes per share while Class B stock had one vote per share.

(4) Supervoting shares ran afoul of a rule that existed on the New York Stock Exchange (but not on other exchanges or NASDAQ) that prohibited a registered corporation from having classes of shares with different voting rights. However, when General Motors proposed the creation of classes with different voting rights, the NYSE abandoned its one-share-one-vote rule in 1984 to assure that GM would remain listed on the NYSE.

In 1988, the SEC adopted Rule 19c–4, which not only replaced the NYSE's one-share-one-vote rule, but also expanded the rule to cover all publicly-traded securities. The rule prevented the NASD or the exchanges to bar the listing of a domestic corporation's securities if that company issued securities or took any other action that nullified, restricted or disparately reduced the per share voting rights of the common stockholders. However, the U.S. Court of Appeals for the D.C. Circuit, in Business Roundtable v. SEC, 905 F.2d 406 (D.C.Cir.1990), nullified Rule 19c–4 on the grounds that the SEC does not have the statutory authority to adopt rules of corporate governance. The adoption of corporate governance rules is the province of state law, unless there is a clear expression of intent by Congress to permit an administrative agency to enter this field. In the words of the court, giving the SEC the power to adopt rules concerning the internal corporate governance of firms would "overturn or at least impinge severely on the tradition of state regulation of corporate law." 905 F.2d 406, 411. This ruling, as Roberta Karmel pointed out in an excellent article on this subject, "did not put an end to the voting rights rule story." The exchanges and the NASD, knowing where their bread was buttered, "voluntarily" adopted rules that were "modified versions of former SEC Rule 19c–4." See Roberta Karmel, The Future of Corporate Governance Listing Requirements, 54 SMU L. Rev. 325 (2001).

There are three leading—but essentially inconsistent—cases involving takeover defenses in Delaware.

I.

Unocal Corporation v. Mesa Petroleum Co., 493 A.2d 946 (Del.1985). In this case, Mesa launched a takeover fight against Unocal, a major oil company. Mesa offered $54 per share for 64,000,000 shares, just enough to bring its ownership to 50 percent. The bulk of the $3.4 billion purchase price was to be borrowed in the form of junk bonds. At the same time, Mesa announced that if it were successful in the tender offer, it would thereafter purchase the balance of the Unocal stock it did not already own through a second-step merger in which the holders would receive "highly subordinated securities" (presumably subordinated to the borrowings needed to raise the initial $3.4 billion) with a value that the Delaware Supreme Court stated was "purportedly" also $54 per share. Unocal's ultimate defense was a flatly discriminatory proposal: an "exchange offer" that provided that if Mesa bought the 64,000,000 shares it sought, the remaining Unocal shareholders could exchange all of their remaining shares for debt securities worth $72 per share that would be senior to Mesa's junk bond financing. The exchange offer expressly provided that Mesa and persons affiliated with Mesa were not eligible to participate in the offer. The effect of the "Mesa exclusion"—the provision allowing Unocal to offer debt securities to all of its shareholders other than Mesa—devastated Mesa's financing. If it completed its tender offer and obtained control of Unocal, the remaining Unocal shareholders would swap their shares for senior Unocal debt, and Mesa would end up owning virtually 100 percent of a corporation that was awash in debt. Indeed, this defense involves such strong medicine and is so devastatingly effective that it seems ill-matched with the very permissive business judgment rule. The Delaware Supreme Court evolved a new standard for evaluating such proposals:

> In the board's exercise of corporate power to forestall a takeover bid our analysis begins with the basic principle that corporate directors have a fiduciary duty to act in the best interests of the corporation's stockholders. Guth v. Loft, Inc., Del.Supr., 5 A.2d 503, 510 (1939). As we have noted, their duty of care extends to protecting the corporation and its owners from perceived harm whether a threat originates from third parties or other shareholders.[10] But such powers are not absolute. A corporation does not have unbridled discretion to defeat any perceived threat by any Draconian means available.
>
> The restriction placed upon a selective stock repurchase is that the directors may not have acted solely or primarily out of a desire to perpetuate themselves in office. See Cheff v. Mathes, 199 A.2d 548, 556 (1964).
>
> Of course, to this is added the further caveat that inequitable action may not be taken under the guise of law. Schnell v. Chris-Craft Industries, Inc., Del.Supr., 285 A.2d 437, 439 (1971). The standard of proof established in Cheff v. Mathes * * * is designed to ensure that a defensive measure to thwart or impede a takeover is indeed motivated by a good faith concern for the welfare of the corporation and its stockholders, which in all circumstances must be free of any fraud or other misconduct. Cheff v. Mathes, 199 A.2d at 554–55. However, this does not end the inquiry.

---

[10] It has been suggested that a board's response to a takeover threat should be a passive one. Easterbrook & Fischel, 36 Bus.Law. at 1750. However, that clearly is not the law of Delaware, and as the proponents of this rule of passivity readily concede, it has not been adopted either by courts or state legislatures. Easterbrook & Fischel, supra, 94 Harv.L.Rev. at 1194.

A further aspect is the element of balance. If a defensive measure is to come within the ambit of the business judgment rule, it must be reasonable in relation to the threat posed. This entails an analysis by the directors of the nature of the takeover bid and its effect on the corporate enterprise. Examples of such concerns may include: inadequacy of the price offered, nature and timing of the offer, questions of illegality, the impact on "constituencies" other than shareholders (i.e., creditors, customers, employees, and perhaps even the community generally), the risk of nonconsummation, and the quality of securities being offered in the exchange. 40 Bus.Law. 1403 (1985). While not a controlling factor, it also seems to us that a board may reasonably consider the basic stockholder interests at stake, including those of short term speculators, whose actions may have fueled the coercive aspect of the offer at the expense of the long term investor.[11] Here, the threat posed was viewed by the Unocal board as a grossly inadequate two-tier coercive tender offer coupled with the threat of greenmail. * * *

In adopting the selective exchange offer, the board stated that its objective was either to defeat the inadequate Mesa offer or, should the offer still succeed, provide the 49% of its stockholders, who would otherwise be forced to accept "junk bonds," with $72 worth of senior debt. We find that both purposes are valid.

However, such efforts would have been thwarted by Mesa's participation in the exchange offer. First, if Mesa could tender its shares, Unocal would effectively be subsidizing the former's continuing effort to buy Unocal stock at $54 per share. Second, Mesa could not, by definition, fit within the class of shareholders being protected from its own coercive and inadequate tender offer.

Thus, we are satisfied that the selective exchange offer is reasonably related to the threats posed. It is consistent with the principle that "the minority stockholder shall receive the substantial equivalent in value of what he had before." Sterling v. Mayflower Hotel Corp., Del.Supr., 93 A.2d 107, 114 (1952).

---

[11] There has been much debate respecting such stockholder interests. One rather impressive study indicates that the stock of over 50 percent of target companies, who resisted hostile takeovers, later traded at higher market prices than the rejected offer price, or were acquired after the tender offer was defeated by another company at a price higher than the offer price. See Lipton, 35 Bus.Law. at 106–109, 132–133. Moreover, an update by Kidder Peabody & Company of this study, involving the stock prices of target companies that have defeated hostile tender offers during the period from 1973 to 1982 demonstrates that in a majority of cases the target's shareholders benefited from the defeat. The stock of 81% of the targets studied has, since the tender offer, sold at prices higher than the tender offer price. When adjusted for the time value of money, the figure is 64%. The thesis being that this strongly supports application of the business judgment rule in response to takeover threats. There is, however, a rather vehement contrary view. See Easterbrook & Fischel, supra 36 Bus.Law. at 1739–1745.

This concept of fairness, while stated in the merger context, is also relevant in the area of tender offer law. Thus, the board's decision to offer what it determined to be the fair value of the corporation to the 49% of its shareholders, who would otherwise be forced to accept highly subordinated "junk bonds," is reasonable and consistent with the directors' duty to ensure that the minority stockholders receive equal value for their shares.

NOTES

(1) Shortly after the Delaware Supreme Court's opinion in *Unocal,* the SEC adopted Rule 14d–10, 17 C.F.R. § 240.14d–10, 51 Fed.Reg. 25,882, popularly known as the "All Holders Rule," which required that an offer be open to all security holders of the same class of securities. It is clear that the purpose of this rule was to eliminate the *Unocal* strategy, though the SEC explained its purpose as follows:

> A major aspect of the legislative effort to protect investors was to avoid favoring either management or the takeover bidder. In implementing this policy of neutrality, the Commission has administered the Williams Act in an even-handed fashion favoring neither side in a contest. Also implicit in these provisions, and necessary for the functioning of the Williams Act are the requirements that a bidder make a tender offer to all security holders of the class of securities which is the subject of the offer and that the offer [be] made to all holders on the same terms.

> The investor protection purposes of the Exchange Act would not be achieved without these requirements because tender offers could be extended to some security holders but not to others or to all security holders but on different terms. * * *

SEC Rel. No. 34–22,198, 50 Fed.Reg. 27,976, 27,977. Is the all holders rule really neutral as between the aggressor and management?

(2) In Polaroid Corp. v. Disney, 862 F.2d 987 (3d Cir.1988), the Court upheld the all-holders rule on the theory that it broadly related to disclosure. The Court also held that disadvantaged shareholders had standing to enjoin violations of the all-holders rule by a third party, but that the issuer did not have standing to sue on its own behalf.

(3) From a relatively early time, courts have indicated that more or less brazen attempts to perpetuate incumbent management in office would be enjoined. The leading case is Schnell v. Chris-Craft Industries, Inc., 285 A.2d 430 (Del.Ch.1971), reversed, 285 A.2d 437 (Del.1971), discussed in *Unocal.* Later cases have struggled with the *Schnell* principle in the takeover context. Aprahamian v. HBO & Co., 531 A.2d 1204 (Del.Ch.1987), for example, enjoined a change of the date of the annual meeting after directors learned that a dissident shareholder had successfully obtained a large number of proxies. Blasius Indus., Inc. v. Atlas Corp., 564 A.2d 651 (Del.Ch.1988), enjoined the addition of two new persons to a staggered board that had the

effect of making impractical a transaction that was being proposed in a pending consent solicitation. In both of these cases, the enjoined actions would clearly have been protected by the business judgment rule in the absence of pending shareholder action on the same subject and an intention to defeat the shareholder-initiated action. On the other hand, Stroud v. Grace, 606 A.2d 75 (Del.1992), declined to apply the *Schnell* principle in a situation where the board of directors was not under a threat.

(4) *Stroud* and several other Delaware cases involve bylaw amendments that require names of potential board of director candidates to be submitted to management in advance of the meeting date. Nomad Acquisition Corp. v. Damon Corp., 1988 WL 383667, 14 Del.J.Corp.L. 814 (Del.Ch. Sept. 20, 1988), holds that such a provision is not invalid on its face, but it is clear from Lerman v. Diagnostic Data, 421 A.2d 906 (Del.Ch.1980), and Hubbard v. Hollywood Park Realty Enter., Inc., 1991 WL 3151, 17 Del. J. Corp. L. 238 (Del.Ch. Jan. 14, 1991), that such a provision cannot be applied inequitably in the heat of a takeover contest.

———

II.

Revlon, Inc. v. MacAndrews & Forbes Holdings, Inc., 506 A.2d 173 (Del.1986). This litigation arose after Pantry Pride, Inc. made a hostile tender offer for any and all shares of Revlon, Inc. for $47.50 per share. Viewing this price as inadequate, considering the value of Revlon's assets, and receiving information that Pantry Pride planned to break up and sell off Revlon's component businesses, Revlon management instituted a series of defensive tactics, particularly an offer to purchase 10,000,000 of its own shares in part for promissory notes that contained poison pill provisions.

Pantry Pride then increased its offer in a series of steps, first to $50 per share, then to $53, and then to $56.25, contingent in each case on Pantry Pride waiving the poison pill features of the notes. Faced with this steady pressure, Revlon decided to seek a more friendly purchaser, a "white knight." One potential white knight was Forstmann Little & Co. After some negotiations with Forstmann (during which Forstmann was given access to financial information about Revlon that had been denied to Pantry Pride), Forstmann and Revlon management agreed to a leveraged buyout transaction at a price of $57.25 per share. A critical aspect of the Forstmann agreement was that Forstmann received "a lock-up option[j] to purchase Revlon's Vision Care and National Health Laboratories divisions for $525 million, some $100–$175 million below the value ascribed to them by Lazard Freres, if another acquirer got 40% of Revlon's shares."

———

[j]   "Lock-ups" are discussed in Section E of this Chapter.

Pantry Pride then raised its price to $58 per share contingent upon removal not only of the poison pill provisions but also the Forstmann lock-up. When Revlon management decided to go through with the Forstmann sale (apparently in large part because Forstmann promised to support the price of the notes issued earlier by Revlon to create poison pill protection), the decision moved into the Delaware courts.

The Delaware Supreme Court upheld Revlon's actions to fight off Pantry Pride's initial "inadequate" offers but then enunciated a new legal principle:

> However, when Pantry Pride increased its offer to $50 per share, and then to $53, it became apparent to all that the break-up of the company was inevitable. The Revlon board's authorization permitting management to negotiate a merger or buyout with a third party was a recognition that the company was for sale. The duty of the board had thus changed from the preservation of Revlon as a corporate entity to the maximization of the company's value at a sale for the stockholders' benefit. This significantly altered the board's responsibilities under the *Unocal* standards. It no longer faced threats to corporate policy and effectiveness, or to the stockholders' interests, from a grossly inadequate bid. The whole question of defensive measures became moot. The directors' role changed from defenders of the corporate bastion to auctioneers charged with getting the best price for the stockholders at a sale of the company. * * *

> The original threat posed by Pantry Pride—the break-up of the company—had become a reality which even the directors embraced. Selective dealing to fend off a hostile but determined bidder was no longer a proper objective. Instead, obtaining the highest price for the benefit of the stockholders should have been the central theme guiding director action. Thus, the Revlon board could not make the requisite showing of good faith by preferring the noteholders and ignoring its duty of loyalty to the shareholders. * * *

> The Revlon board argued that it acted in good faith in protecting the noteholders because *Unocal* permits consideration of other corporate constituencies. Although such considerations may be permissible, there are fundamental limitations upon that prerogative. A board may have regard for various constituencies in discharging its responsibilities, provided there are rationally related benefits accruing to the stockholders. *Unocal,* 493 A.2d at 955. However, such concern for non-stockholder interests is inappropriate when an auction among active bidders is in progress, and the object no longer is to protect or maintain the corporate enterprise but to sell it to the highest bidder. * * *

While Forstmann's $57.25 offer was objectively higher than Pantry Pride's $56.25 bid, the margin of superiority is less when the Forstmann price is adjusted for the time value of money. In reality, the Revlon board ended the auction in return for very little actual improvement in the final bid. The principal benefit went to the directors, who avoided personal liability to a class of creditors to whom the board owed no further duty under the circumstances. Thus, when a board ends an intense bidding contest on an insubstantial basis, and where a significant by-product of that action is to protect the directors against a perceived threat of personal liability for consequences stemming from the adoption of previous defensive measures, the action cannot withstand the enhanced scrutiny which *Unocal* requires of director conduct. * * *

* * * [I]n granting an asset option lock-up to Forstmann, we must conclude that under all the circumstances the directors allowed considerations other than the maximization of shareholder profit to affect their judgment, and followed a course that ended the auction for Revlon, absent court intervention, to the ultimate detriment of its shareholders. No such defensive measure can be sustained when it represents a breach of the directors' fundamental duty of care. See Smith v. Van Gorkom, Del.Supr., 488 A.2d 858, 874 (1985). In that context the board's action is not entitled to the deference accorded it by the business judgment rule. * * *

NOTES

(1) The Revlon decision permits management to justify poison pills and other defensive tactics if they slow down an initial offeror and lead to an auction involving additional bidders. The theory is that an auction should produce a better price for shareholders than a sale to the first serious bidder. (For a case in which a poison pill in fact led to this result, see CRTF Corp. v. Federated Dep't Stores, Inc., 683 F.Supp. 422 (S.D.N.Y.1988).) Even though poison pills permit management to negotiate with potential aggressors, once the decision to sell the company has been made under the *Revlon* principle, the role of management shifts to obtaining the best price for shareholders.

(2) See John C. Coffee, Jr., Securities Law: Defining 'Sale' Is Paramount Concern, Nat'l L.J., Nov. 8, 1993, at 18, 20. As Professor Coffee indicates, the *Revlon* principle is easily stated, but its application in practice is difficult. For example, what is a "sale"? A management buyout? What about a merger between companies roughly equal in size? Further, how should an auction be conducted? When may the board of directors decide that it is concluded? What should the board of directors do if it receives "out of the blue" an unexpected offer at an attractive price? May it simply take that offer or should it publicly announce its intention, seek additional bids, and conduct

an auction? What if a board of directors enters into a contract to be acquired by an offeror, but then a second bidder unexpectedly arrives? Does not the board of directors commit a breach of contract if it then decides to conduct a *Revlon* auction? Should it therefore have included an "out" clause in the initial contract to guard against this possibility? What if it didn't?

(3) Subsequent Delaware Supreme Court cases nicely illustrate the difficulty of determining the relationship between the *Revlon* and *Unocal* principles. See, for example, Paramount Communications, Inc. v. Time Inc. 571 A.2d 1140 (Del.1989) (*Revlon* duty was not triggered when a cash tender offer was substituted for a merger transaction involving an exchange of shares in a strategic combination); and Paramount Communications v. QVC Network Inc., 637 A.2d 34 (Del.1994) (*Revlon* duty was triggered when a cash tender offer was substituted for a merger transaction involving an exchange of cash for shares).

However, the consistency of these two decisions (*Time* and *QVC*) is not intuitively obvious and the decisions have been criticized, both individually and collectively. See Alan E. Garfield, *Paramount*: The Mixed Merits of Mush, 17 Del. J. Corp. L. 33 (1992) (the Court in *Paramount* "took a decisive turn in takeover jurisprudence in favor of management" and "left no clear standards in its wake"); Marc I. Steinberg, Nightmare On Main Street: The *Paramount* Picture Horror Show, 16 Del. J. Corp. L. 1 (1991) (author was a "wishful thinker" when he earlier expressed the view that shareholders were protected in Delaware); John C. Coffee, Jr., The Battle to Control Paramount is Over, But the Legal and Strategic Questions Raised by This Epic Corporate Struggle May Have Just Begun, Nat'l L.J., Mar. 28, 1994, at B5. Professor Coffee suggests that "*Paramount* represents a half-step retreat from the Delaware Supreme Court's apparent position * * * that only a breakup or liquidation of the company triggers a duty to auction." The focus of when the *Revlon* duty is triggered, he states, appears to be whether the transaction involves the acquisition of control by a new controlling shareholder, but a number of questions remain unanswered.

———

III.

Unitrin, Inc. v. American General Corp., 651 A.2d 1361 (Del. 1995). The activism of the Delaware Supreme Court in reviewing defensive tactics was tempered by its decision in *Unitrin*. The target corporation, Unitrin, initiated a major share repurchase plan in the face of an unwanted all-cash tender offer and proxy contest. The Delaware Chancery Court enjoined this maneuver on the ground that it was a disproportionate response to the threat posed by American General's "inadequate" tender offer, but the Supreme Court reversed, applying the following analysis to a defensive tactic:

> This Court has recognized "the prerogative of a board of directors to resist a third party's unsolicited acquisition proposal or offer."

Paramount Communications, Inc. v. QVC Network Inc., Del.Supr., 637 A.2d 34, 43 n. 13 (1994). The Unitrin Board did not have unlimited discretion to defeat the threat it perceived from the American General Offer by any draconian[34] means available. Pursuant to the Unocal proportionality test, the nature of the threat associated with a particular hostile offer sets the parameters for the range of permissible defensive tactics. Accordingly, the purpose of enhanced judicial scrutiny is to determine whether the Board acted reasonably in "relation * * * to the threat which a particular bid allegedly poses to stockholder interests." Mills Acquisition Co. v. Macmillan, Inc., Del.Supr., 559 A.2d 1261, 1288 (1989).

* * * Courts, commentators and litigators have attempted to catalogue the threats posed by hostile tender offers. Commentators have categorized three types of threats: (i) opportunity loss * * * [where] a hostile offer might deprive target shareholders of the opportunity to select a superior alternative offered by target management [or, we would add, offered by another bidder]; (ii) structural coercion, * * * the risk that disparate treatment of non-tendering shareholders might distort shareholders' tender decisions; and (iii) substantive coercion, * * * the risk that shareholders will mistakenly accept an underpriced offer because they disbelieve management's representations of intrinsic value. * * *

* * * As common law applications of Unocal's proportionality standard have evolved, at least two characteristics of draconian defensive measures taken by a board of directors in responding to a threat have been brought into focus through enhanced judicial scrutiny. In the modern takeover lexicon, it is now clear that since Unocal, this Court has consistently recognized that defensive measures which are either preclusive or coercive are included within the common law definition of draconian.

If a defensive measure is not draconian, however, because it is not either coercive or preclusive, the Unocal proportionality test requires the focus of enhanced judicial scrutiny to shift to "the range of reasonableness." Paramount Communications, Inc. v. QVC Network Inc., Del.Supr., 637 A.2d 34, 45–46 (1994). Proper and proportionate defensive responses are intended and permitted to thwart perceived threats. When a corporation is not for sale, the board of directors is the defender of the

---

[34] Draconian, adj. of or pert. to Draco, an archon and member of the Athenian eupatridae, or the code of laws which is said to have been framed about 621 B.C. by him as thesmothete. In them the penalty for most offenses was death, and to a later age they seemed so severe that they were said to be written in blood. Hence, barbarously severe; harsh; cruel. Webster's New International Dictionary 780 (2d ed. 1951).

metaphorical medieval corporate bastion and the protector of the corporation's shareholders. The fact that a defensive action must not be coercive or preclusive does not prevent a board from responding defensively before a bidder is at the corporate bastion's gate.[38]

The ratio decidendi for the "range of reasonableness" standard is a need of the board of directors for latitude in discharging its fiduciary duties to the corporation and its shareholders when defending against perceived threats. The concomitant requirement is for judicial restraint. Consequently, if the board of directors' defensive response is not draconian (preclusive or coercive) and is within a "range of reasonableness," a court must not substitute its judgment for the board's. * * *

In this case, the Court of Chancery erred by substituting its judgment, that the Repurchase Program was unnecessary, for that of the Board. The Unitrin Board had the power and the duty, upon reasonable investigation, to protect Unitrin's shareholders from what it perceived to be the threat from American General's inadequate all-cash for all-shares Offer. The adoption of the poison pill and the limited Repurchase Program was not coercive and the Repurchase Program may not be preclusive. Although each made a takeover more difficult, individually and collectively, if they were not coercive or preclusive the Court of Chancery must determine whether they were within the range of reasonable defensive measures available to the Board.

If the Court of Chancery concludes that individually and collectively the poison pill and the Repurchase Program were proportionate to the threat the Board believed American General posed, the Unitrin Board's adoption of the Repurchase Program and the poison pill is entitled to review under the traditional business judgment rule. The burden will then shift "back to the plaintiffs who have the ultimate burden of persuasion [in a preliminary injunction proceeding] to show a breach of the directors' fiduciary duties." In order to rebut the protection of the business judgment rule, the burden on the plaintiffs will be to demonstrate, "by a preponderance of the evidence that the

---

[38] This Court's choice of the term draconian in Unocal was a recognition that the law affords boards of directors substantial latitude in defending the perimeter of the corporate bastion against perceived threats. Thus, continuing with the medieval metaphor, if a board reasonably perceives that a threat is on the horizon, it has broad authority to respond with a panoply of individual or combined defensive precautions, e.g., staffing the barbican, raising the drawbridge, and lowering the portcullis. Stated more directly, depending upon the circumstances, the board may respond to a reasonably perceived threat by adopting individually or sometimes in combination: advance notice by-laws, supermajority voting provisions, shareholder rights plans, repurchase programs, etc.

directors' decisions were primarily based on [(1)] perpetuating themselves in office or [(2)] some other breach of fiduciary duty such as fraud, overreaching, lack of good faith, or [(3)] being uninformed." Unocal, 493 A.2d at 958 (emphasis added).

E. LOCKUPS

MICHAEL G. HATCH, CLEARLY DEFINING PRECLUSIVE CORPORATE LOCK-UPS: A BRIGHT LINE TEST FOR LOCK-UP PROVISIONS IN DELAWARE
75 Wash.L.Rev. 1267–76 (2000).

Record-breaking merger and acquisition volume in each of the previous four years has placed the United States in the midst of an unprecedented merger phenomenon. Ten of the largest transactions in history were announced in 1998 and 1999. Fueling this merger boom is the fact that the merger, offering a quick solution for businesses seeking greater competitiveness, resources, market share, and new technology, has become the preferred tool for strategic and corporate development. This current wave of mega-mergers, coupled with the intense competition for merger partners, has resulted in merger battles with fiercely contested auctions[5] for control of corporations.

Merging corporations often seek to defend their deals from subsequent bidders with defensive measures known as lock-up provisions. Lock-ups are promises by a target company's board of directors to compensate the prospective acquirer if the target breaches or does not consummate the merger agreement. Lock-ups are designed to protect the negotiated deal by compensating the prospective acquirer and by imposing the threat of additional costs on other competitors who might decide to make offers. Under certain circumstances, courts must enjoin lock-ups that preclude shareholders the opportunity to receive other potentially higher offers in the merger transaction. However, courts are unable to make this determination accurately because it involves evaluating competing bids, an increasingly complex calculation in the current merger environment. As a result, the size and scope of defensive measures have skyrocketed as both courts and corporations have been unsure how to determine the validity of lock-ups.

In the 1990s, large corporations began to use mergers to gain advantage within their industries. This phenomenon, combined with rapidly increasing stock market values, has greatly increased the price paid in recent mergers. As a result, corporations seeking merger partners have faced increasing transaction costs. In addition, large corporations

---

[5]   An auction occurs when directors decide to sell the corporation to the highest bidder. In an auction, the target corporation will solicit bids and the highest bidder will obtain control of the corporation. * * *

are no longer content to sit by as competitors enter strategic mergers. Large corporations are willing to compete for targets[13] by making unsolicited bids after a competitor has announced a merger agreement. In partial response to these increased costs and competition, the size and scope of deal-protecting lock-up provisions have skyrocketed. * * *

A. The Strategic Merger

Corporations are increasingly using strategic mergers to gain advantages within their industries. Intense foreign competition has focused many corporations' strategic goals on increasing efficiency and dominating their markets. While efficiency increases shareholder value by reducing overhead, corporations appear to have concluded that a short-term increase in shareholder value may result from boosting market share either by eliminating competitors or acquiring an important supplier that competitors need. Typically, strategic mergers are negotiated deals focusing on long-term growth and increasing efficiency, either between former competitors or between a supplier and a producer. The merging corporations are often of similar size, and stockholders of the respective corporations own approximately an equal amount of the post-merger corporation.

A prospective acquirer must incur substantial costs in identifying and consummating a strategic merger. Initially, it may be expensive for the prospective acquirer to perform the research necessary to identify the target as a profitable opportunity. Once it identifies the target, the acquirer incurs additional costs negotiating the agreement and ensuring that the target is truthfully representing itself. These costly and time-consuming steps require expert analysis, due diligence reports[23] by lawyers, and fairness opinions[24] by investment bankers. All of these costs and efforts are expended to determine the core issue in the merger: that the price to be paid for the target is fair in the eyes of both parties.

Although the fair value of the target is the core issue in a merger, considerable uncertainty surrounds the determination of that value. Valuation begins with the determination of how much the target is worth as it stands alone, and then focuses on how much its value will increase when combined with the acquirer. To assist in the valuation, both sets of corporate directors will retain the services of investment bankers to determine a "fair" price for the target. However, valuation is a very

---

[13] The target is the corporation that is to be acquired in a merger or acquisition. * * *

[23] Due diligence refers to the legal audit performed on the target company. In a due diligence investigation, lawyers investigate the books and records of the target company, check the accuracy of factual representations, and look for potential problems. See Dale A. Oesterle, The Law of Mergers and Acquisitions 270 (1999). The due diligence investigation precedes the signing of the final acquisition agreement in order to give the acquirer a high level of confidence in the accuracy and completeness of the target's representations and warranties in the acquisition agreement.

[24] Fairness opinions are reports by investment bankers confirming that the acquisition price is within a range of fair prices that adequately compensates the target's shareholders.

inexact inquiry, and often involves a range of values rather than a specific price. Although valuation studies or fairness opinions may be important, a contested auction will often lead to prices that substantially exceed any fair price determination, a price that a board of directors cannot know without an auction. In addition, the current trend of "deal-jumping" followed by hotly contested bidding wars has further widened the disparity between a fair price determined by an investment banker and a price obtained through competitive bidding at an auction for a company.

B. The Threat of "Deal-Jumping"

Hostile takeovers, or "deal-jumping," by competitors represent the most serious threat to negotiated strategic mergers. According to one study, deal-jumpers or second bidders prevail in a "substantial majority" of contests. In a strategic merger, the acquirer and target will negotiate an initial offer; however, competitors within the industry may attempt to jump the deal by making unsolicited bids for the target corporation. In this situation, the initial prospective acquirer is at a disadvantage. Its initial bid may provide insights into the financial viability and long-term prospects of the target as well as a signal that existing management is amenable to a sale. This allows the deal-jumper to avoid incurring identification and research costs. The deal-jumper is then able to use the money saved on research costs in its attempt to top the initial bid. Absent a large lock-up, a bidding war may result where the original acquirer must compete with other bidders for control of the target corporation. Even if the initial bidder ultimately prevails, competition will likely force the final price much higher than the initial bid. For example, 1999 witnessed a number of high profile jumped deals: AT&T's successful $58 billion hostile takeover of MediaOne, which had previously agreed to a $53 billion merger with Comcast; Vodafone's successful $60 billion takeover of Airtouch, topping Bell Atlantic's original bid of $45 billion; and Pfizer's $90.27 billion hostile takeover of Warner-Lambert, dwarfing the original $72 billion bid by American Home Products. Given the deal-jumper's competitive advantage, acquiring corporations use a number of lock-up devices in an attempt to protect their negotiated deals.

C. Lock-Up Provisions in General

The current wave of mega-mergers, coupled with the growing threat of deal-jumping, has dramatically increased the size and scope of lock-up provisions as directors attempt to protect their merger costs and expected profits. An acquiring corporation will often demand some form of lock-up provision,[44] such as a stock option, termination fee or other device, in the

---

[44] Delaware courts have tended to define the term "lock-up" expansively. See Vincent F. Garrity, Jr. & Mark A. Morton, Would the CSX/Conrail Express Have Derailed in Delaware? A Comparative Analysis of Lock-Up Provisions Under Delaware and Pennsylvania Law, 51 U. Miami L.Rev. 677, 678 & n.4 (1997). Although the narrow interpretation of lock-ups only includes asset and stock options, for purpose of this Comment, such measures as termination fees and no shop provisions are also lock-up devices.

merger agreement to protect itself from deal-jumping as well as to guarantee some benefit in the event the merger is not consummated. The Supreme Court of Delaware, in its first evaluation of a lock-up, recognized that lock-ups may be necessary to facilitate mergers because they provide incentives to merging corporations to enter and complete the transaction.[46] However, lock-ups may also be excessive, deterring other, possibly better, offers.

D.   Types of Lock-Up Provisions

Lock-ups are promises by a target's board of directors to compensate the prospective acquirer in some fashion if the target breaches or does not consummate the merger agreement. Lock-ups are designed both to compensate the prospective acquirer in case of a breach and to protect the negotiated deal by imposing additional costs on other competitors who might decide to make offers. The acquirer may ask the target's board of directors to grant a number of lock-up provisions including: (1) an irrevocable stock option, (2) an asset option, (3) a "topping" fee, (4) an expense reimbursement provision, and (5) a termination or "break-up" fee.

The most common lock-up provision involves an irrevocable stock option by which the target corporation usually grants the acquirer the right to purchase ten to twenty percent of the target's stock at a favorable price. The right to exercise the option is usually conditioned upon the defeat of the favored bidder's attempt to acquire the target corporation. In addition, use of the stock option by the original bidder may preclude an intervening third party from using "pooling of interests" accounting,[54] a significant deterrent itself.

In an asset option or "crown jewel" defense, the target grants the acquirer the option to purchase a particularly desirable asset of the target at a negotiated price. If the deal is not consummated, this option compensates the prospective acquirer, because it will still acquire the desirable asset at a price below fair market value. In addition, an asset option may deter bidders as they may be unwilling to suffer the loss from a sale of the asset at below fair market value. Furthermore, regardless of

---

[46] See Revlon, Inc. v. MacAndrews & Forbes Holdings, Inc., 506 A.2d 173, 183 (Del.1985); see also Garrity & Morton, supra, at 69 (noting that Delaware courts recognize benefits of lock-ups to shareholders).

[54] See Linda Vincent, Equity Valuation Implications of Purchase Versus Pooling Accounting, J. Fin. Statement Analysis, Summer 1997, at 5. Pooling of interests accounting is a favorable accounting method under which the asset and liability accounts of the bidder and target are combined at book value as though the two firms had always been a single enterprise. See id. at 7. This method allows corporations to record their combined assets at historical values and the surviving entity to avoid recording goodwill. See id. Not recording goodwill results in greater annual earnings on paper and is the preferred method of accounting for business combinations. See Phillip J. Azzollini, Note, The Wake of Paramount v. QVC: Can a Majority Shareholder Avoid Triggering the Auction Duty During a Merger and Retain a Significant Equity Interest? Suggestion: A Pooling of Interests, 63 Fordham L. Rev. 573, 596 (1994).

the price, other bidders often lose interest once they cannot acquire the truly vital asset of the target.

Topping fees are a type of lock-up where the target must pay a fee to the initial bidder if the target accepts another bidder's offer. The fee is based on a percentage of the amount by which the accepted bid exceeds the initial bid. For example, in In re KDI Corp. Shareholders Litigation, the parties agreed to a topping fee or "override" equal to one-half of the difference between the stock price and any other future offer.

A fourth type of lock-up is an expense-reimbursement provision, which is similar to a liquidated-damages provision although not subject to the same analysis. In an expense-reimbursement provision, if the target accepts another bid, then the target reimburses the initial prospective acquirer for any costs incurred during the initial merger effort. The reimbursement covers any actual or estimated out-of-pocket expenses such as research or legal fees incurred by the prospective acquirer in its unsuccessful attempt to merge with the target. For example, in Kahn v. Dairy Mart Convenience Stores, Inc., Dairy Mart agreed to reimburse the acquirer for expenses up to $2.25 million if the merger failed for any reason other than a breach of warranty or representation by the acquirer.

Finally, an acquirer may negotiate for a termination or "break-up" fee. In the event the target terminates the merger, this provision requires the target to pay the acquirer often as much as three percent of the value of the transaction. For example, in 1995 the Supreme Court of Delaware approved a termination fee of $550 million designed to protect the $28 billion merger of Bell Atlantic and NYNEX. Recently, Warner-Lambert agreed to a record-breaking $1.8 billion termination fee to American Home Products as protection for their original merger agreement valued at $72 billion. * * *

E.   Lock-Ups Under the Business Judgment Rule

Depending on the form of the transaction, Delaware courts apply a doctrinal framework that contains three different standards used to determine the validity of a lock-up. The central inquiry in the doctrinal framework is whether the lock-up is preclusive. If the lock-up is not preclusive and if the transaction does not involve a change of control, the business judgment rule will protect the lock-up from court invalidation, provided the decision to grant the lock-up was reached in an informed manner. If the transaction involves a change of corporate control, under Revlon, Inc. v. MacAndrews & Forbes Holdings, Inc. the validity of a lock-up provision depends on whether it facilitates receipt by target-company shareholders of a maximum value for their shares. If the lock-up was intended solely as a defensive measure against a subsequent hostile threat and the merger involves no change of control, the lock-up's validity, under Unocal Corp. v. Mesa Petroleum Co., depends on whether the lock-up is a balanced response to the threat posed by the future bidder. * * *

A non-preclusive lock-up in a transaction that does not involve a change of control is protected by the business judgment rule and will not be disturbed provided it was reached in an informed manner. Following the business judgment rule, courts generally presume that "in making a business decision the directors of a corporation acted on an informed basis, in good faith and in an honest belief that the action was taken in the best interests of the company."[89] Any party challenging the applicability of the presumption has the burden of establishing facts rebutting the presumption. * * * A court's inquiry under the business judgment rule focuses on the process by which the board reached a decision, not the merits of the decision itself. Accordingly, a Delaware court will not interfere with the board's substantive decision to grant lock-up provisions provided there is any rational business purpose and the decision was reached in an informed manner.

F. The Limited Application of Revlon Duties to Lock-Ups in Transactions Involving a Change of Control or Break-Up of the Target

Under Revlon and its progeny, if a transaction involves a change of control the validity of the lock-up depends on whether it facilitates receipt by target-company shareholders of a maximum value for their shares. If it does not, then the lock-up is preclusive and should be enjoined. In *Revlon*, the Supreme Court of Delaware found that Revlon's directors effectively had put the company up for sale and granted lock-ups[98] that precluded further bids offering a higher value to Revlon's shareholders.[99] According to the *Revlon* court, the critical inquiry for lock-up provisions involves distinguishing "those lock-ups which draw bidders into the battle" from those that "end an active auction and foreclose further bidding."[100] Therefore, in a sale of a corporation implicating *Revlon* duties, courts must enjoin preclusive lock-ups that prevent the target corporation's shareholders from obtaining the maximum value for their shares. * * *

NOTES

(1) A theoretical debate has long continued over whether lock-ups should be permitted at all. Frank H. Easterbrook & Daniel R. Fischel, The Proper

---

[89] Aronson v. Lewis, 473 A.2d 805, 812 (Del.1984).

[98] Revlon's directors agreed to a $25 million termination fee and an asset lock-up option allowing Forstmann Little to acquire certain key Revlon divisions at $100–$175 million below market value. * * * Revlon, Inc. v. MacAndrews & Forbes Holdings, Inc., 506 A.2d 173, 183 (Del.1986).

[99] * * * According to the court, when the directors put the company up for sale, their "role changed from defenders of the corporate bastion to auctioneers charged with getting the best price for the stockholders at a sale of the company." *Id.* at 182.

[100] *Id.* at 183.

Role of a Target's Management in Responding to a Tender Offer, 94 Harv.L.Rev. 1161, 1164 (1981), believed that all lock-ups ultimately decreased shareholder wealth and therefore no defensive tactics should be permitted. Once it was realized that some lock-ups increased shareholder wealth, the issue became how desirable lock-ups should be distinguished from undesirable ones. Professor Bainbridge suggested a bright-line rule: invalidate all lock-ups equal to more than ten percent of the value of the favored bidder's proposal. Stephen Bainbridge, Exclusive Merger Agreements and Lock-Ups in Negotiated Corporate Acquisitions, 75 Minn.L.Rev. 239 (1990). The author of the above Comment suggested a bright line drawn at three percent of the bidder's proposal. 75 Wash. L. Rev., at 1292.

(2) The negotiation of a "deal" to acquire another business entity is costly. The potential purchaser naturally wishes to preserve its investment and will seek provisions designed to protect the deal from other suitors. The result is a variety of "no shop" clauses, lock-ups, termination fees, stock options, and the like. Is there anything wrong with that?

(3) Brazen v. Bell Atlantic Corp., 695 A.2d 43 (Del.1997), involved the merger between Bell Atlantic and NYNEX. The merger was viewed as a merger of equals. The parties negotiated an agreement under which Bell Atlantic agreed to pay NYNEX $200 million if Bell Atlantic withdrew. Furthermore, if Bell Atlantic was merged with another entity within 18 months, Bell Atlantic agreed to pay NYNEX an additional $350 million. The two payments together constituted approximately 2 percent of Bell Atlantic's net worth. The payments were defined in the Agreement to be liquidated damages for breach of contract and not a termination fee. The Delaware Supreme Court accepted this characterization of the payments and held that they were not a penalty and therefore enforceable.

F. FUNDAMENTAL TRANSACTIONS AND THE MBCA

The MBCA provisions relating to mergers, takeovers, and the appraisal remedy have been significantly revised over the years. These provisions diverge to some extent from the law of Delaware and other states. However, the net effect or spirit of these MBCA provisions is generally consistent with the way the law works in Delaware and elsewhere. Moreover, these provisions are much more detailed and precise and far better organized than the statutes of most states. However, potential problems with the revised MBCA are that new sections sometimes contain too much detail and are not phrased in traditional statutory language. In addition, the amendments deal primarily with publicly-traded corporations while most states that closely track the MBCA in their corporation statutes have relatively few publicly-traded corporations. Nevertheless, the current MBCA is definitely a logical construct, and its innovations should be seriously considered by important commercial states.

1. **Section 6.21(f).** Section 6.21(f) requires a shareholder vote on every transaction by a corporation that involves the issuance of shares (other than shares issued for cash) that carry more than 20 percent of the voting power in the corporation as measured before the issuance. Thus, shareholders of a surviving corporation must vote on significant share-for-share mergers whether or not they are structured as triangular mergers.

2. **Section 11.02(a).** The MBCA states that "[o]ne or more domestic business corporations may merge with one or more domestic or foreign business corporations or eligible entities pursuant to a plan of merger." Thus, a corporation may merge into a partnership, LLC, or other non-corporate entity (provided that the other entity is allowed under its governing statute to merge with a corporation). The surviving entity may be either the corporation or the non-corporate entity. This is an important option, particularly in light of the extraordinary growth of non-corporate entities in recent years. However, there are usually significant tax costs if a corporation is merged into a non-corporate entity since the IRS views such a transaction as a dissolution of the corporation and immediately taxes all unrealized appreciation in the value of the corporation's assets. This tax is avoided if the corporation is the surviving entity, but then the surviving entity is not eligible for Subchapter K taxation. Moreover, if any kind of entity has ownership interests that are publicly-traded, it is taxed as a C corporation no matter what its legal form is.

3. **Section 11.04(e).** The MBCA reduces the required vote to approve a merger or similar transaction from a majority of all shares eligible to vote to "approval of the shareholders at a meeting at which a quorum consisting of a majority of the votes entitled to be cast on the plan exists and, if any class or series of shares is entitled to vote as a separate group on the plan, the approval of each such separate group at a meeting at which a quorum consisting of at least a majority of the votes entitled to be cast on the plan by that class or series exists." MBCA § 11.04 cmt. 3. If a quorum is present, then under sections 7.25 and 7.26, "the plan will be approved if more votes are cast in favor of the plan than against it by the voting group or separate voting groups entitled to vote on the plan." Id.

4. **Section 11.04(h).** The shareholders of a corporation that is a party to a merger are not entitled to vote on the merger at all (i) if the corporation will be a surviving corporation or "is [an] acquiring corporation in a share exchange," (ii) its articles of incorporation will not be changed except for amendments permitted by section 10.05, (iii) its shareholders' rights and preferences will not be changed, and (iv) a vote is not required by section 6.21(f).

5. **Section 12.02.** The standards for determining what constitutes a sale of assets requiring a shareholder vote have been significantly revised. In earlier versions of the MBCA, only a disposition of "all or

substantially all" of the assets of a corporation triggered a mandatory shareholder vote. Section 12.02 now provides that a vote is required whenever the transaction would leave the corporation without a "significant continuing business activity," which in turn is defined as a situation where "a corporation retains a business activity that represented at least 25% of total assets at the end of the most recently completed fiscal year, and 25% of either income from continuing operations before taxes or revenues from continuing operations for that fiscal year, in each case of the corporation and its subsidiaries on a consolidated basis." The older "all or substantially all" test continues to appear in virtually all corporate statutes. In practice, however, courts applying this older test use language somewhat comparable to that embodied in section 12.02(a). For example, in *Gimbel v. Signal Cos.*, 316 A.2d 599 (Del.Ch.1974), aff'd, 316 A.2d 619 (Del.1974), the court stated, "While it is true that [the 'all or substantially all'] test does not lend itself to a strict mathematical standard to be applied in every case, the qualitative factor can be defined to some degree * * *. If the sale is of assets quantitatively vital to the operation of the corporation and is out of the ordinary [course] and substantially affects the existence and purpose of the corporation then it is beyond the power of the Board of Directors." The court added, "The need for shareholder * * * approval is to be measured not by the size of a sale alone, but also by its qualitative effect upon the corporation. Thus, it is relevant to ask whether a transaction 'is out of the ordinary' and substantially affects the existence and purpose of the corporation." 316 A.2d, at 606. The 25% safe harbor embodied in this section obviously represents a policy judgment that more certainty than is provided by interpretations of the current case law is desirable.

6. Chapter 13, Dissenters' Rights. This subchapter provides for a significant degree of private ordering (see section 13.02(a)(5)) and as a result, the scope of the statutory appraisal remedy in the revised Act is somewhat narrower than that provided in the 1984 Act. In general, the right of appraisal under the MBCA is available only for corporate actions that will result in a fundamental change in the shares to be affected by the action and then only when uncertainty concerning the fair value of the affected shares may cause reasonable differences about the fairness of the terms of the corporate action. There are several types of transactions that satisfy these criteria:

(1) *A merger pursuant to section 11.04 or a short-form merger pursuant to section 11.05.* Holders of any class or series that is to be exchanged or converted in connection with a merger under sections 11.04 or 11.05 are entitled to appraisal under section 13.02(a)(1). Although shareholders of a subsidiary that is a party to a merger under section 11.05 may not be entitled to vote on the merger, they are entitled to appraisal under 13.02(a)(1) because their interests will be extinguished by the merger. Section 13.02(a)(1)(i), however, denies appraisal rights to

any class or series of shares in the surviving corporation if such class or series remains outstanding after the transaction.

(2) *A share exchange under section 11.03 if the corporation is a party whose shares are being acquired in the exchange.* Consistent with the treatment in § 13.02(a)(1) of mergers requiring shareholder approval, an appraisal remedy is available only for holders of shares that will be exchanged.

(3) *A disposition of assets under section 12.02.* As a general rule, shareholders of all classes or series of the corporation, whether or not they are generally entitled to vote under section 12.02, will be entitled to assert appraisal rights. An exception from appraisal rights is also provided, however, in addition to the exception provided in section 13.02(b), if liquidation is required to take place within one year of the shareholder vote and shareholders are to receive cash in accordance with their respective interests, so long as the transaction is not an interested transaction. In these circumstances, where shareholders are being treated on a proportionate basis in accordance with the corporation's governing documents in an arm's-length transaction (akin to a distribution in dissolution), there is no need for the added protection of appraisal rights.

(4) *Reverse stock splits.* Appraisal rights are available in connection with amendments to the articles of incorporation that effectuate a reverse stock split that reduces the number of shares a shareholder owns to a fractional share if the corporation has the obligation or right to repurchase the fractional share so created. Section 13.02(a)(4). The reason for granting appraisal rights in this situation is similar to the reasons for granting such rights in all cases of cash-out mergers that compel affected shareholders to accept cash for their investment in an amount established by the corporation.

(5) *Voluntary appraisal rights.* Section 13.02(a)(5) provides that a corporation may voluntarily authorize appraisal rights with respect to a merger, share exchange, disposition of assets, or amendment to the articles of incorporation. Such an authorization may be by provision in the articles of incorporation, bylaws, or by a resolution of the board of directors. The theory is that a corporation may wish to grant appraisal rights in connection with important transactions even though the MBCA does not provide for them. A voluntary grant of appraisal rights may satisfy unhappy shareholders who otherwise might seek other remedies. Further, if the existence of the appraisal right is itself in dispute, a voluntary offer of an appraisal right may avoid litigation. An express grant of appraisal rights under section 13.02(a)(5) overrides the exceptions to the availability of appraisal rights in section 13.02(a) and automatically makes all provisions of chapter 13 applicable to the corporation and its holders.

7. Market exception to Appraisal Rights. Section 13.02(b) creates a market exception to appraisal rights. If a liquid and reliable market exists, shareholders do not have an appraisal right and they may either accept the consideration offered in the transaction or sell their shares at the market price. This provision assumes that an efficient market exists and the market price will therefore be an adequate proxy for the appraised value of the corporation's shares. This market exception reflects a judgment that the uncertainty, costs, and time commitment involved in appraisal proceedings are unwarranted where an efficient, fair, and liquid market exists.

Section 13.02(b)(1) is unusual in that it defines in great detail when a market is "liquid" and when the appraisal right is therefore unavailable. Liquidity is present if the class or series of stock is a covered security under section 18(b)(1)(A) or (B) of the Securities Act of 1933. This means that it must be listed on the New York Stock Exchange, the American Stock Exchange, the NASDAQ Global Select Market or the NASDAQ Global Market (successors to the NASDAQ National Market), or on certain other markets having comparable listing standards as determined by the Securities and Exchange Commission. If not in these categories, the class or series of stock must be traded in an organized market, must have at least 2,000 shareholders, and must have a market value of at least $20 million (excluding the value of shares held by the corporation's subsidiaries, senior executives, directors, and beneficial shareholders owning more than 10% of the class or series).

Section 13.02(b)(3) contains in even greater detail a series of exceptions to the exception: circumstances in which an appraisal right remains available even though a liquid market as defined in § 13.02(b)(1) exists. For example, the market exception is inapplicable if the transaction requires shareholders to accept anything other than cash or securities that meet the liquidity tests of section 13.02(b)(1). Thus, shareholders are assured of receiving either appraisal rights, cash from the transaction, liquid shares, or other proprietary interests in the survivor entity. Appraisal rights are also preserved in certain types of interested transactions where a corporation's management, controlling shareholders, or directors have conflicting interests that could, if not dealt with appropriately, adversely affect the consideration that otherwise could have been expected.

Section 13.02(c) permits the corporation to eliminate or limit appraisal rights for the holders of series or classes of preferred shares. Such a provision may initially appear in the corporation's articles of incorporation. If added thereafter by amendment, the provision does not become effective for one year with respect to outstanding shares or shares which the corporation is or may be required to issue or sell at some later date. Section 13.02 apparently does not permit the corporation to eliminate or limit appraisal rights with respect to common shares in similar situations.

NOTES

(1) As the Official Comment to § 13.01 notes, the 1999 revisions to the MBCA eliminated the right of shareholders to an appraisal in connection with amendments to the articles of incorporation in the absence of a merger, share exchange, or disposition of assets requiring a shareholder vote. Prior to the 1999 revisions, appraisal was available to a class of shares if an amendment *materially and adversely* affected the rights of that class of shares. (Under § 10.04, however, a class of shares is entitled to vote as a class on any amendment that changes the rights of that class in any way.) Appraisal remains available in connection with an amendment effecting a reverse stock split that has the effect of cashing out some of the shares of a class or series.

(2) As mentioned, the MBCA includes an exception to the stock market exception for interested transactions. This provision is described as applying to transactions in which there is a likelihood that the price being offered to the shareholders is on the low side. The provision is similar to many state anti-takeover statutes and may allow a target company in a hostile takeover to maintain an appraisal action in lieu of, or in addition to, litigation.

(3) Section 13.01(4) of the MBCA defines fair value for appraisal purposes to mean "the value of the corporation's shares determined: (i) immediately before the effectuation of the corporate action to which the shareholder objects; (ii) using customary and current valuation concepts and techniques generally employed for similar businesses in the context of the transaction requiring appraisal; and (iii) without discounting for lack of marketability or minority status except, if appropriate, for amendments to the articles pursuant to section 13.02(a)(5)."

CHAPTER 17

CORPORATE BOOKS AND RECORDS

■ ■ ■

Chapter 16 of the MBCA attempts to provide guidelines for certain issues relating to corporate books and records. Most older corporation statutes are silent on these issues, dealing only with the inspection rights of shareholders. In addition to the rules, lawyers advising corporations also need to be aware of regulatory guidelines concerning record-keeping promulgated by administrative agencies, such as the Securities and Exchange Commission, the Food and Drug Administration, and the Federal Trade Commission. For example, in December 2002, five prominent securities firms—Deutsche Bank Securities, Goldman Sachs, Morgan Stanley, Salomon Smith Barney, and U.S. Bancorp Piper Jaffray—each paid fines of $1.65 million to the SEC for failing to preserve internal e-mail communications as required by the securities laws.

MBCA Section 16.01(a) requires every corporation to "keep as permanent records" a minimum set of core documents that reflects decisions made by the directors and shareholders of the corporation. In addition, § 16.01(e) requires every corporation to "keep a copy" of specified basic corporate documents at the principal office of the corporation. These documents must be made available for routine inspection by any shareholder during regular business hours. MBCA § 16.02(a).

Section 16.01(b) requires every corporation to "maintain appropriate accounting records." The word "maintain" should be contrasted with the word "keep" in § 16.01(a) and (e); "keep" means permanent retention while "maintain" refers to current records only and does not address the question of how long financial and other records should be kept. Thus, the retention and destruction of all records, other than the limited records the corporation is directed to "keep" by the MBCA, is dictated by considerations or rules independent of the MBCA. In part, specific record retention rules may be established by state or federal tax or regulatory statutes, or perhaps by general state statutes. Many corporations have established internal policies that permit the destruction of records after some suitably long period of time, taking into account statutes of limitations and the possibility that products liability claims may arise long after the records relating to those products were generated.

The word "appropriate" with respect to accounting records in MBCA § 16.01(b) reflects a general recognition of the fact that the nature and size of the business largely determines its accounting system, which in turn largely determines its accounting records. The Official Comment suggests that "appropriate" records are "generally records that permit financial statements to be prepared which fairly present the financial position and transactions of the corporation. In some very small businesses operating on a cash basis, however, 'appropriate' accounting records may consist only of a check register, vouchers, and receipts." Today most accounting and financial records are maintained electronically, a development recognized in MBCA § 16.01(d).

MBCA § 16.01(c) requires every corporation to "maintain" a record of its shareholders. In larger corporations, records of shareholders are usually maintained electronically; this function is often delegated to transfer agents that have the responsibility of recording transfers of securities. In closely held corporations, the record may consist only of the filled-in stubs of stock certificates previously issued, if that.

Publicly held corporations registered under the Securities Exchange Act of 1934 are required to prepare detailed financial statements that are distributed to shareholders and to the public. See Chapter 9. Historically, state statutes did not contain an analogous requirement, so that shareholders of closely held or unregistered corporations did not have the right to receive routine financial statements from the corporation. However, this is gradually changing. The MBCA first introduced such a requirement in 1979. The current provision, MBCA § 16.20, is carefully constructed so as not to impose onerous requirements on very small corporations and yet to require larger corporations that have financial statements professionally prepared to distribute those statements to shareholders. Every corporation under this provision must furnish, at a minimum, a balance sheet, an income statement, and a statement of changes in shareholders' equity for the year. Financial statements require accounting principles to be established for their preparation; § 16.20 does not require the use of generally accepted accounting principles (GAAP) or any specific set of accounting principles, but if financial statements are prepared for the corporation on the basis of GAAP, the annual financial statements must likewise be prepared on a GAAP basis. Section 16.20(b) sets forth general principles for disclosing the "basis of preparation" of financial statements and whether the system used was consistent with that of the preceding year.

One issue that is more or less addressed in all state corporation statutes is the extent to which shareholders are entitled to inspect corporate books and records. Shareholders, as ultimate owners of the enterprise, enjoyed qualified rights at common law to inspect the corporate books and records, including shareholder lists, contracts, correspondence, tax returns, and other documents. Harry G. Henn & John R. Alexander, Laws of Corporations and Other Business Enterprises § 199 (3d ed. 1983).

This qualified common-law right continues to exist under the MBCA (see § 16.02(f)(2)) and in many states. In addition, many states supplement the common-law right with a statutory right. See, e.g., MBCA § 16.02.

At one time, most inspection cases revolved around the list of shareholders required to be maintained by the corporation. This list, of course, is a list of record shareholders only. Most statutes permit a virtually automatic right of inspection of the list of record shareholders entitled to vote at a scheduled shareholders' meeting shortly before and during the meeting itself. See MBCA § 7.20. At other times, a list of shareholders may be inspected only if the shareholder qualifies under the general shareholder inspection statutes. See MBCA § 16.02.

Shareholders continue to request shareholder lists in connection with proxy fights or takeover bids for publicly held corporations. However, access to this list by an insurgent or by outside bidders has become less important than it was twenty or thirty years ago. This shift is a result of the widespread use of nominees as record holders (thus limiting the usefulness of the list itself) and the growth of institutional investors, many of whom make information about their entire portfolios available as a matter of public record. Of course, access to a current shareholders' list may still be essential in situations involving closely held corporations or publicly held corporations with shares widely held of record by individuals rather than institutional investors.

THOMAS & BETTS CORPORATION V. LEVITON MANUFACTURING CO.

Supreme Court of Delaware, 1996.
681 A.2d 1026.

Before VEASEY, C.J., WALSH and BERGER, JJ.

VEASEY, CHIEF JUSTICE:

In this appeal we affirm the order of the Court of Chancery denying in part and limiting a stockholder's entitlement to inspection of books and records. In doing so, we rest our decision on the fact that the trial court's determination of the stockholder's failure to show a proper purpose turned on legal and credibility assessments well within the proper burden placed on a stockholder seeking an inspection. Such a stockholder has the burden of showing, by a preponderance of the evidence, a proper purpose entitling the stockholder to an inspection of every item sought. Here, the Court of Chancery overstated the burden on the stockholder as a "greater-than-normal evidentiary burden." The burden on the stockholder is a normal burden and this stockholder failed to adduce sufficient evidence to meet that burden.

I. Facts

Plaintiff below—appellant, Thomas & Betts Corporation ("Thomas & Betts" or "plaintiff"), appeals from a decision of the Court of Chancery granting in part and denying in part its request for inspection of certain books and records of defendant below—appellee, Leviton Manufacturing Co., Inc. ("Leviton" or "defendant").

Leviton is a closely held Delaware corporation engaged in the business of manufacturing electronic components and residential wiring devices. Thomas & Betts is a publicly traded New Jersey corporation engaged in the electronics business. Thomas & Betts and Leviton are not considered to be in competition with one another. This is due, in large part, to Leviton's focus on the residential market. For a number of years, Thomas & Betts has expressed an interest either in acquiring Leviton or engaging in some form of joint venture. During the summer of 1993, Thomas & Betts and Leviton engaged in preliminary negotiations concerning a possible union of the two companies, but no agreement was ever reached. To date, Leviton has not expressed any interest in participating in a change-of-control or joint venture transaction with Thomas & Betts.

Leviton's President and CEO, Harold Leviton, is also the company's majority stockholder. Harold Leviton and his wife control a voting trust which represents 76.45 percent of Leviton's Class A voting stock. He and the other Leviton insiders are members of the Leviton family and most bear some relationship to the company's founder. By all accounts, Harold Leviton is the dominant figure in the corporation, deciding the company's strategy, operations and future goals.

Thomas & Betts decided to seek a minority position in Leviton in order to force a sale of the company to Thomas & Betts. In April of 1994, without the knowledge of Harold Leviton, Thomas & Betts began negotiations with Leviton's former Group Vice President, Thomas Blumberg ("Blumberg"). Blumberg and his wife, who is Harold Leviton's niece, owned approximately 29.1 percent of Leviton's outstanding shares. Negotiations for the sale of the Blumberg stock to Thomas & Betts were clandestine. In furtherance of the transaction, Blumberg provided Thomas & Betts with confidential internal Leviton documents and disclosed various facets of Leviton's internal strategies and accounting figures. Ultimately, Thomas & Betts paid Blumberg $50 million for his Leviton stake, with a promise of up to an additional $20 million if Thomas & Betts were to accomplish its desired acquisition of Leviton. Thomas & Betts indemnified Blumberg against, inter alia, litigation by Leviton, and also agreed to pay up to $7.5 million to Blumberg, in equal quarterly installments, if the sale of his shares were enjoined. At the time of sale, Thomas & Betts was fully aware that Leviton did not pay dividends and that Leviton's accounting practices did not follow Generally Accepted Accounting Principles ("GAAP").

The sale of the Blumberg shares was consummated on July 12, 1994, and Harold Leviton was informed of the sale the following day. Harold Leviton immediately fired Blumberg, only to hire him back and fire him again days later, along with his children and their secretaries. Harold Leviton rebuffed overtures from Thomas & Betts to establish an amicable relationship. Instead, Harold Leviton sought to buy out the interest of Thomas & Betts. From July 1994 to February of 1995, various representatives of Thomas & Betts met with Leviton insiders in an attempt to cultivate a working relationship. On October 6, 1994, Kevin Dunnigan ("Dunnigan"), the CEO of Thomas & Betts, reported to the board of Thomas & Betts on his strategy:

> On the Leviton front, we are moving to the next phase. I will write to Harold Leviton next week to give him a rationale on why it is in everyone's best interests to start a dialogue. We will follow this up with a legal request to review all the books and records of Leviton which will start either a dialogue or a lawsuit.

Harold Leviton, however, remained obstinate in his opposition to Thomas & Betts' ownership position. Although some concessions were made and Thomas & Betts was allowed limited access to Leviton's books and records, by February 1995 it was abundantly clear that Harold Leviton intended to thwart any acquisition of Leviton by Thomas & Betts.

On February 8, 1995, Thomas & Betts served Leviton with a formal demand seeking inspection of the following documents:

1. Leviton's stockholder list,

2. Minutes of Leviton shareholder and directors meetings as well as written consents,

3. Audited financial statements for Leviton and its subsidiaries,

4. Internal financial statements for the current fiscal year provided on a monthly basis,

5. Tax returns filed for Leviton and its subsidiaries,

6. Organizational charts for Leviton and its subsidiaries,

7. Documents relating to interested party transactions between Leviton or its subsidiaries and its shareholders, directors or officers,

8. Documents relating to "key man" life insurance policies taken out by Leviton,

9. Material contracts between Leviton and its subsidiaries,

10. Documents relating to Leviton leases for real estate or equipment.

On February 16, 1995, Dunnigan wrote to Harold Leviton and offered to purchase the balance of Leviton's stock for $250 million, net of expenses. Dunnigan's letter threatened litigation if this final offer were rebuffed:

> You are forcing us down a road where given a choice, I am sure neither of us wants to go. Often, once this process gets started, it ends up with consequences that were never intended. Watch! It won't be long before the lawyers, the government and the courts are completely in charge, and in the end neither you nor I will have much say in the outcome. There will be only victims, but it won't be the lawyers.

On February 17, 1995, Leviton formally refused both Thomas & Betts' acquisition offer and its inspection demand.

On February 27, 1995, Thomas & Betts filed this action in the Court of Chancery seeking to compel inspection of Leviton's books and records pursuant to 8 Del.C. § 220. After a four-day trial, the Court of Chancery determined that: (1) plaintiff's demand was not motivated by its stated purposes of investigating waste and mismanagement * * * and [valuing its] shares; (2) plaintiff's actual motivation was to gain leverage in its efforts to acquire Leviton; (3) this motive was antithetical to the interests of Leviton; (4) despite the initially improper purpose of its demand, Thomas & Betts was entitled to limited inspection so it could value its Leviton shares since a fundamental change of circumstances had occurred; and (5) this inspection should be narrowly circumscribed. From this decision, Thomas & Betts appeals. Leviton has not cross-appealed.

II. Proper Purpose

Thomas & Betts' Demand Letter purported to state [two] separate purposes for its requested inspection of Leviton's books and records. Specifically, plaintiff asserted that the books and records were necessary: (1) to investigate possible waste and mismanagement; * * * and (2) to assist in the valuation of Thomas & Betts' Leviton shares. After trial, the Court of Chancery concluded that plaintiff's articulated purposes were not its actual purposes and that plaintiff's actual purpose was improper.[1] Specifically, the

---

[1]   See, e.g., BBC Acquisition Corp. v. Durr-Fillauer Medical, Inc., Del.Ch., 623 A.2d 85, 88 (1992):

> [W]hen seeking inspection of books and records other than the corporate stock ledger or stock list, a shareholder has the burden of proving that his purpose is proper. Since such a shareholder will often have more than one purpose, that requirement has been construed to mean that the shareholder's primary purpose must be proper; any secondary purpose, whether proper or not, is irrelevant. CM & M Group, Inc. v. Carroll, Del.Supr., 453 A.2d 788, 792 (1982); Helmsman Management Services, Inc. v. A & S Consultants, Inc., Del.Ch., 525 A.2d 160, 164 (1987).

See also Ostrow v. Bonney Forge Corp., Del.Ch., C.A. No. 13270, Allen, C., mem. op., 1994 WL 114807 (April 6, 1994) ("Once a shareholder has established a proper purpose for the demanded inspection, any secondary purpose he or she may have is generally considered to be irrelevant. * * * The primary purpose may not, however, be adverse to the corporation's best interests.") (citing CM

trial court held that Thomas & Betts was attempting to use the Section 220 proceeding as leverage in its efforts to acquire Leviton. The trial court concluded, however, that Thomas & Betts should be allowed to inspect those books and records necessary to value its investment in Leviton in view of the fact that there had been a change in circumstances.

Thomas & Betts now asserts that the * * * [purpose] for inspection not credited by the trial court—investigation of waste and mismanagement—constituted [a] proper purpose under Section 220 and that the trial court erred in refusing inspection of books and records relevant to [this purpose]. These contentions are addressed seriatim below.

"The question of a 'proper purpose' under Section 220(b) of our General Corporation Law is an issue of law and equity which this Court reviews de novo." Compaq Computer Corp. v. Horton, Del.Supr., 631 A.2d 1, 3 (1993) (citing Oberly v. Kirby, Del.Supr., 592 A.2d 445, 462 (1991)); Western Air Lines, Inc. v. Kerkorian, Del.Supr., 254 A.2d 240 (1969) (court reviewed proper purpose determination in stocklist case de novo). "The determination of whether [plaintiff's] * * * stated purpose for the inspection was its primary purpose, is a question of fact warranting deference to the trial court's credibility assessments." State ex rel. Scattered Corp., Del.Supr., No. 444, 1995, Veasey, C.J., 1996 WL 191023 (April 4, 1996) (ORDER); accord CM & M Group, Inc. v. Carroll, Del.Supr., 453 A.2d 788, 793 (1982).

III. Plaintiff's Claims of Waste and Mismanagement

As found by the Court of Chancery, plaintiff's claims of waste and mismanagement are grounded on Leviton's purportedly substandard financial performance, the company's failure to pay dividends, Leviton's poor cash flow and the company's higher than average expenses. As specific instances of misconduct, plaintiff asserted that: "(a) Leviton has paid for the Leviton family's personal expenses, including use of the company's accounting firm for tax and estate planning purposes; (b) Leviton has been overcompensating its officers and directors at the shareholders' expense; and (c) Leviton's lease agreements with members of the Leviton family are self-dealing transactions." The trial court found, however, that these claims "are so lacking in record support" that inspection could not be justified.

Plaintiff contends that the Court of Chancery applied an incorrect legal standard in determining that plaintiff's stated purpose lacked adequate record support. Specifically, Thomas & Betts points to portions of the trial court's holding which appear to impose on plaintiff "a greater-than-normal evidentiary burden," to "adduce evidence from which a credible possibility of mismanagement and waste may be inferred" and to "adduce specific evidence of waste and mismanagement."

& M Group, Inc. v. Carroll, Del.Supr., 453 A.2d 788, 792 (1982); Skoglund v. Ormand Indus., Inc., Del.Ch., 372 A.2d 204, 207 (1976)).

The Court of Chancery incorrectly articulated the governing legal standard. It is well established that investigation of waste and mismanagement is a proper purpose for a Section 220 books and records inspection. Nodana Petroleum Corp. v. State, Del.Supr., 123 A.2d 243, 246 (1956). When a stockholder seeks inspection of books and records, the burden of proof is on the stockholder to demonstrate that his purpose is proper. CM & M Group, 453 A.2d at 792.[2] In order to meet that burden of proof, a stockholder must present some credible basis from which the court can infer that waste or mismanagement may have occurred. Skouras v. Admiralty Enters., Inc., Del.Ch., 386 A.2d 674, 678 (1978) ("more than a general statement is required in order for the Court to determine the propriety of a demand"); Helmsman Management Servs., Inc. v. A & S Consultants, Inc., Del.Ch., 525 A.2d 160, 166 (1987) ("A mere statement of a purpose to investigate possible general mismanagement, without more, will not entitle a shareholder to broad '220 inspection relief'. There must be some evidence of possible mismanagement as would warrant further investigation of the matter."); Neely v. Oklahoma Publishing Co., Del.Ch., C.A. No. 5293, Brown, V.C. (Aug. 15, 1977); Everett v. Hollywood Park, Inc., Del.Ch., C.A. No. 14556, Jacobs, V.C., mem. op., 1996 WL 32171 (Jan. 19, 1996) ("Where, as here, the plaintiff's purpose is to investigate possible waste or mismanagement, she must also adduce evidence of potential mismanagement sufficient to support her suspicions and to warrant going forward."). While stockholders have the burden of coming forward with specific and credible allegations sufficient to warrant a suspicion of waste and mismanagement, they are not required to prove by a preponderance of the evidence that waste and [mis]management are actually occurring.[3]

A general standard that a stockholder seeking inspection of books and records bears "a greater-than-normal evidentiary burden" is unclear and could be interpreted as placing an unduly difficult obstacle in the path of stockholders seeking to investigate waste and mismanagement. Viewed in context, however, the articulation in dispute here accurately describes a stockholder's position in cases such as the one at bar, where substantial evidence supports a finding that plaintiff's primary motives for the inspection are improper.

---

[2]   While a stockholder has the burden to show a proper purpose for an inspection of books and records, the corporation has the burden of showing an improper purpose when a stockholder seeks only to inspect the stockholder list. 8 Del.C. § 220(c). The trial court held that plaintiff "has established a proper purpose for seeking inspection of Leviton's shareholder list," and the corporation failed to meet its burden that plaintiff's purpose was improper.

[3]   The Revised Model Business Corporation Act requires that a stockholder "describe with reasonable particularity his purpose and the records he desires to inspect." Revised Model Business Corp. Act § 16.02(c). See Grimes v. Donald, 673 A.2d 1207, 1217 (1996), for an analogous discussion of the reasonable doubt, or reason to believe, standard in the context of a derivative suit. * * * Contrary to plaintiff's assertion in the instant case, this Court in Grimes did not suggest that its reference to a Section 220 demand as one of the "tools at hand" was intended to eviscerate or modify the need for a stockholder to show a proper purpose under Section 220. Id. at 1216 n. 11 (noting that Section 220 can be used to secure information to support demand futility).

In the final analysis, the decision of the trial court did not turn solely on a legal conclusion that Thomas & Betts had failed to meet an elevated evidentiary burden. As discussed further, infra, the trial court's determination turned, in large part, on the Vice Chancellor's determination that plaintiff's witnesses were not credible. According appropriate deference to the factual findings of the Court of Chancery, we conclude that plaintiff failed to satisfy the appropriate standard for inspection of the books and records with regard to the claim of waste and mismanagement. Levitt v. Bouvier, Del.Supr., 287 A.2d 671, 673 (1972) ("When the determination of facts turns on a question of credibility and the acceptance or rejection of 'live' testimony by the trial judge, his findings will be approved upon review."); State ex rel. Scattered Corp., Del.Supr., No. 444, 1995, Veasey, C.J. (April 4, 1996) (ORDER) ("The determination of whether Scattered's stated purpose for the inspection was its primary purpose, is a question of fact warranting deference to the trial court's credibility assessments.") * * *

More significantly, the trial court did not exclude this testimony. Rather, the Vice Chancellor heard the testimony and found it unworthy of belief. In this posture, plaintiff's evidentiary objections carry little weight. Similarly, Thomas & Betts' citation to Skoglund v. Ormand Industries is unavailing. Skoglund, 372 A.2d at 208, 211–13. As in the case at bar, the Skoglund court allowed hearsay testimony regarding statements made by a corporate insider. Unlike the instant case, however, the trial court in Skoglund chose to credit that testimony as worthy of belief.

Finally, plaintiff's arguments ignore the underlying posture of this case. Unlike the cases relied on by plaintiff, this case does not involve a typical uninformed stockholder seeking to protect his or her investment. Thomas & Betts acquired its shares in Leviton with the acknowledged purpose of acquiring the company. Moreover, Thomas & Betts did so with full knowledge that Leviton's CEO would likely oppose any such transaction. Thomas & Betts first praised Harold Leviton for his expert management of the company, seeking an amicable union of the two corporations. When Thomas & Betts' friendly overtures proved unavailing, it filed an inspection demand to create leverage. Its self-avowed acquisition motives cast serious doubt on the genuineness of its claim that it seeks the books and records to investigate waste and mismanagement.

These facts were properly before the Court of Chancery. See, e.g., Helmsman Management Servs., 525 A.2d at 164 ("The propriety of a demanding shareholder's purpose must be determined from the facts in each case, and the burden of proving a proper purpose is upon the shareholder."). The Court of Chancery concluded that "Thomas & Betts' initial primary purpose in seeking a books and records inspection was * * * to exert pressure on Harold Leviton to negotiate a sale of his controlling interest or, alternatively, the entire company." Ultimately, the Court of

Chancery found Thomas & Betts' articulated purpose to be "highly opportunistic" and unworthy of belief. Thomas & Betts has provided no reason for this Court to revisit those factual determinations and credibility assessments. * * *

V. The Scope of the Inspection

After trial, the Court of Chancery found that Thomas & Betts had failed to meet its burden of establishing that it sought inspection in furtherance of its concerns regarding * * * mismanagement. The trial court found that Thomas & Betts' primary purpose for inspection was to further its plans for acquiring Leviton and that this interest was antithetical to the interests of the corporation. Despite Thomas & Betts' initially improper motives, the Court acknowledged that Thomas & Betts had experienced a fundamental change of circumstances. The court reasoned that, owing to Harold Leviton's unwillingness to negotiate a change-of-control transaction, Thomas & Betts was now in the unenviable position of a "locked-in" minority stockholder. Based on this fact, the trial court allowed inspection of certain Leviton books and records, but limited the scope of that inspection to those documents which are "essential and sufficient" to Thomas & Betts' valuation purpose. Thomas & Betts now contends that the Court of Chancery abused its discretion in limiting the scope of its inspection of Leviton's books and records.

Absent any apparent error of law, this Court reviews for abuse of discretion the decision of the trial court regarding the scope of a stockholder's inspection of books and records. 8 Del.C. § 220(c); CM & M Group, 453 A.2d at 794. The plaintiff bears the burden of proving that each category of books and records is essential to accomplishment of the stockholder's articulated purpose for the inspection. Helmsman Management Servs., 525 A.2d at 168.

The plain language of 8 Del.C. § 220(c) provides that "[t]he Court may, *in its discretion*, prescribe any limitations or conditions with reference to the inspection." (emphasis supplied). The responsibility of the trial court to narrowly tailor the inspection right to a stockholder's stated purpose is well established. See BBC Acquisition Corp., 623 A.2d at 88–89 (entitlement is restricted to those books and records needed to perform the task). In discharging this responsibility, the trial court has wide latitude in determining the proper scope of inspection. Undergirding this discretion is a recognition that the interests of the corporation must be harmonized with those of the inspecting stockholder.

Here, the trial court has found that Thomas & Betts' primary purpose for inspection is at odds with the interests of the corporation. In this posture, it was entirely appropriate for the Court of Chancery to limit plaintiff's inspection to those documents which are essential and sufficient to its valuation purpose.

Moreover, even in a case where no improper purpose has been attributed to the inspecting stockholder, the burden of proof is always on the party seeking inspection to establish that each category of the books and records requested is essential and sufficient to the stockholder's stated purpose. Helmsman Management Servs., 525 A.2d at 167. The trial court specifically found that Thomas & Betts had not met its burden of proof as to certain of the books and records of Leviton. This finding is supported by the record and is the product of an orderly and logical deductive process. Accordingly, the finding of the Court of Chancery and its concomitant decision to limit inspection will not be disturbed on appeal. * * *

We AFFIRM the order of the Court of Chancery.

NOTES

(1) Why should a shareholder's right of inspection be so limited? If a shareholder suspects that improper conduct may have occurred, should he not have the right to make a general search of corporate records and documents to see if his suspicions are justified? In a word, the answer is "no." The right of inspection reflects a balancing between the shareholder's right to have information about his investment and the fealty of "his" agents, and the competing interest of the corporation to be free from harassment by unhappy investors. See Randall S. Thomas, Improving Shareholder Monitoring and Corporate Management by Statutory Access to Information, 38 Ariz.L.Rev. 331, 334 (1996).

(2) All states adopt a "proper purpose" or similar test for shareholder inspection of records. Hundreds of cases have classified specific purposes (as set forth in trial testimony or deposition) as "proper" or "not proper." In resolving these disputes, courts tend to look beyond the formal statements of purpose put forth and inquire into the shareholder's motive and relationship with the corporation. For a good example in the publicly held corporation context, see State ex rel. Pillsbury v. Honeywell, Inc., 191 N.W.2d 406 (Minn.1971).

(3) Even if generalized purposes for an inspection are not acceptable, many cases state that a "proper purpose" is to examine financial records in order to determine the value of one's own shares. See, e.g., CM & M Group, Inc. v. Carroll, 453 A.2d 788 (Del.1982).

(4) The right of inspection is only one avenue to company information. See MBCA § 16.02(f). In modern litigation, broad discovery rights exist and these rights appear to be independent of the statutory or common law inspection rights of shareholders.

PAUL V. CHINA MEDIAEXPRESS HOLDINGS, INC.
Court of Chancery of Delaware, 2012.
2012 WL 28818.

PARSONS, VICE CHANCELLOR.

This is an action to inspect the books and records of a corporation under 8 Del. C. § 220. A shareholder brought this action after a series of reports and events, including the resignation of the company's independent auditor, raised suspicions that the company had engaged in fraud and falsified its financial statements. The company opposes the shareholder's demand on the ground that the shareholder has not established a proper purpose to inspect its books and records. Furthermore, the company argues that this action should be stayed pending resolution of a motion to stay these and other proceedings that is pending in a related federal court action.[a]

For the reasons stated in this Memorandum Opinion, I find that the shareholder has established proper purposes to inspect the books and records of the company. Those purposes are to investigate (1) fraud and mismanagement and (2) the ability of the board to act independently and in good faith. Therefore, I grant the shareholder's demand as to the documents discussed in this Memorandum Opinion, but only to the extent the documents are necessary for one of his proper purposes. I also deny the company's request to stay this action.

I. BACKGROUND

A. The Parties

Plaintiff, Marc Paul, is a resident of Tennessee and a shareholder of Defendant, China MediaExpress Holdings, Inc. ("CME" or the "Company"). Paul acquired stock in CME through personal online brokerage accounts he maintains for himself and his family.

Defendant, CME, is a Delaware corporation with its principal place of business in Hong Kong, China. CME is engaged in the business of television advertising on inter-city and airport express buses in China. Until recently, CME was publicly listed on the NASDAQ Stock Market. CME obtained its listing on NASDAQ through a merger with TM Entertainment and Media, Inc. * * * in 2009.

---

[a] The Private Securities Litigation Reform Act (PSLRA) was enacted in 1995 to stop nuisance suits for securities fraud that involved what the legislative history described as "manipulation by class action lawyers of the clients whom they purportedly represent." The PSLRA imposes heightened pleading standards, damage caps, and mandatory sanctions for frivolous litigation in securities class action lawsuits. As a result of the PSLRA, plaintiffs' class action attorneys began to file suits in state court rather than in federal court. Congress then enacted the Securities Litigation Uniform Standards Act of 1998 (SLUSA) to curb the practice of filing suits in state court to avoid the restrictions of the PSLRA.

B. Facts

This action arises from various allegations of fraud and mismanagement made against CME beginning in January 2011. Around that time, Citron Research, a financial analyst firm, released a report alleging that CME was engaging in fraudulent accounting practices and that most of CME's business could be a fraud. * * * Zheng Cheng, CME's Chairman, CEO, and President, responded to the allegations on February 7, 2011, denying any fraud * * *.

* * * On March 11, the Company's independent auditor, Deloitte Touche Tohmatsu ("DTT") formally resigned. In a press release following DTT's resignation, CME acknowledged that DTT had stated in its resignation letter that it was "no longer able to rely on the representations of management," that certain issues raised in the audit should be addressed through an independent investigation, and that the issues may have adverse implications for prior periods' financial reports. That same day, the Company requested that NASDAQ temporarily suspend trading in its stock.

Following the resignation of DTT, CME's situation quickly degenerated. Jacky Lam, a director and the Company's CFO, resigned on March 13, 2011, citing concerns over senior management's failure to respond properly to information which he had "learned in the past few days" following the resignation of DTT. Dorothy Dong, another CME director, resigned shortly after Lam, citing similar concerns over senior management's response to accounting irregularities related to DTT's resignation. * * * [In addition, several shortsellers began selling CME stock and issuing reports and press releases that were highly critical of the company and its management and financial reporting.]

As a result of the events unfolding at CME during the spring of 2011, Starr Investments Cayman II, Inc. ("Starr"), a CME investor, filed a complaint against CME, DTT, Cheng, and Lam in the United States District Court for the District of Delaware on March 18, 2011 (the "Federal Action"). In its complaint, Starr alleges various violations of state law and federal securities laws, including: (1) violation of § 10(b) of the Exchange Act and Rule 10b–5; (2) violation of § 20(a) of the Exchange Act against Cheng and Lam; (3) common law fraud; (4) breach of fiduciary duty against Cheng and Lam; (5) aiding and abetting a breach of fiduciary duty against DTT; and (6) negligent misrepresentation. * * *

C. Procedural History

* * * [W]hile the Federal Action was proceeding, Paul served CME with a written demand for inspection of the books and records of the Company pursuant to *8 Del. C. § 220*. CME did not respond to the demand. As a result, Paul filed the Complaint in this action on June 16.

CME answered the Complaint on July 6, and a trial date was set for October 11, 2011.

* * * At trial * * * both parties were given the opportunity to address CME's related request that this Court defer ruling on Paul's § 220 demand pending the district court's decision. * * *

D. Parties' Contentions

In this books and records action under 8 Del. C. § 220, Plaintiff asserts two purposes for his request to inspect the books and records of CME. They are: (1) to investigate "possible mismanagement and breaches of fiduciary duties by the directors and officers of the Company, including, but not limited to, mismanagement and breaches of fiduciary duties in connection with the Company's lack of oversight and possible participation in fraudulent conduct involving the Company's customer contracts, revenues and net income"; and (2) to "determin[e] whether the Company's directors are independent and have acted, and are capable of acting, in good faith with respect to the Company's potential misconduct."

CME opposes Paul's inspection demands on the basis that he has failed to state a proper purpose. CME also argues that, in any case, these proceedings should be stayed pending resolution of the motion in the Federal Action.

II. ANALYSIS

A. 8 Del. C. § 220

It is well-established that "[s]tockholders of Delaware corporations enjoy a qualified common law and statutory right to inspect the corporation's books and records." Under the common law, "[i]nspection rights were recognized * * * because, '[a]s a matter of self-protection, the stockholder was entitled to know how his agents were conducting the affairs of the corporation of which he or she was a part owner.'" This common law right was codified in Delaware under 8 Del. C. § 220, which provides in pertinent part that:

> Any stockholder, in person or by attorney or other agent, shall, upon written demand under oath stating the purpose thereof, have the right during the usual hours for business to inspect for any proper purpose, and to make copies and extracts from: (1) The corporation's stock ledger, a list of its stockholders, and its other books and records * * *.

Therefore, in asserting the right to inspect the books and records of a company, a shareholder must prove that he (1) is a stockholder of the company, (2) has made a written demand on the company, and (3) has a proper purpose for making the demand.

* * * The Company, however, resists Paul's demand on the ground that he does not have a proper purpose. * * *

1. Proper purpose

Where, as here, a shareholder seeks to inspect the books and records of a company other than the stock ledger or list of stockholders, the burden of proof is on the shareholder to demonstrate a proper purpose for inspection by a preponderance of the evidence. "Proper purpose," under Delaware law, means a purpose reasonably related to such person's interest as a stockholder. As this Court noted in *Melzer v. CNET Networks, Inc.*, "[t]here is no shortage of proper purposes under Delaware law." To plead a proper purpose successfully, however, the purpose asserted by the shareholder should be intended to "further[ ] the interest of all stockholders and should increase stockholder return."

2. Investigating waste and mismanagement

* * * [A] shareholder's investigation of wrongdoing or mismanagement at a company is a "proper purpose" for a § 220 action. To meet its burden of proving a proper purpose, however, a shareholder must make more than mere conclusory statements that waste and mismanagement have occurred or are occurring. Instead, the shareholder must present some credible basis "through documents, logic, testimony or otherwise" from which the Court can infer wrongdoing. Moreover, although shareholders have the burden of coming forward with specific and credible allegations sufficient to warrant a suspicion of waste and mismanagement, they are "not required to prove by a preponderance of the evidence that waste and [mis]management are actually occurring." Instead, shareholders only need to show a credible basis from which the Court can infer that there are reasonable grounds to suspect mismanagement that would warrant further investigation. This showing "may ultimately fall well short of demonstrating that anything wrong occurred."

Here, Plaintiff sufficiently has alleged a credible basis to warrant suspicion of waste and mismanagement at CME. In the Complaint, Paul alleges as proof of wrongdoing: (1) numerous third-party media reports alleging fraudulent conduct by CME's officers and directors; (2) the NASDAQ Stock Market's halting of trading in, and subsequent delisting of, CME shares; (3) the resignation of the Company's independent auditor; (4) the noisy resignations of three board members in the last year, including the Company's CFO, citing concerns about senior management and the Company's accounting practices; and (5) CME's initiation of its own internal investigation.

Each of these items arguably provides a credible basis from which the Court could infer that CME's officers and directors may have mismanaged the Company or engaged in wrongdoing in breach of their fiduciary duties. Collectively, these allegations and the evidence supporting them convince me that Paul has presented a credible basis for suspecting wrongdoing. The resignation of DTT, for example, implicates problems with CME's financial reporting and CME's ability or willingness to respond to those problems. The NASDAQ delisting similarly raises concerns about CME's financial reporting and corporate governance. Each of the resigning directors also expressed concerns about senior management, and the internal investigation by the Company itself tends to corroborate the existence of reasonable suspicion that raises concerns that wrongdoing or mismanagement may have occurred.

* * *

[With regard to the negative reports of the shortsellers of the company's stock, the defendants argued that such reports were hearsay and could not be used as evidence in support of the plaintiff's request to inspect books and records. The court responded as follows:]

Delaware law, * * * "d[oes] not endorse a categorical rule of law * * * that 'hearsay statements not offered for their truth fail as a matter of law to meet Section 220's evidentiary requirements.'" Instead, if the Court determines that such evidence is sufficiently reliable, "it may be considered in determining whether a credible basis exists to conclude that waste or mismanagement may have occurred * * *." Here, the events that occurred after the publication of the challenged reports, such as the resignation of the CME directors, reinforce the shortsellers' claims. Therefore, without addressing whether those reports ultimately may be used to prove the truth of the allegations of fraud that later may be brought against the Company, I find that, when considered in light of the other evidence upon which Paul relies, the reports do provide a credible basis upon which to infer that waste and mismanagement may have occurred at CME.

3. Determining whether the Company's directors are independent and capable of acting in good faith

As an alternative purpose, Paul demands inspection to determine whether CME's directors are independent and capable of acting in good faith with respect to the Company's potential misconduct. Paul acknowledged at trial that he seeks to investigate the independence of the directors in anticipation of alleging demand futility if he later decides to bring a derivative action on behalf of the Company. * * *

* * *

B. Scope of Demand

Inspection under § 220 is not discovery, but rather is a limited form of document production narrowly tailored to the express purposes of the shareholder requesting access to the company's books and records. Even where a shareholder has made a sufficient showing to satisfy the demand requirements of § 220, the right to inspection is not absolute; instead, "it is a qualified right depending on the facts presented." In ordering the production of documents under § 220, the Court "has wide discretion in determining the proper scope of inspection in relation to the stockholder's purpose." * * * "[T]he scope of inspection should be circumscribed with precision and limited to those documents that are necessary, essential and sufficient to the stockholder's purpose." Moreover, where the shareholder is seeking the more intrusive inspection of books and records, as opposed to shareholder lists or stock ledgers, "the level of judicial scrutiny is enhanced and the scope of relief more carefully tailored."

Here, because I find that Paul has stated proper purposes to investigate wrongdoing and mismanagement, as well as demand futility, he is entitled to inspect the books and records of CME that are necessary, essential, and sufficient to further those purposes. Paul's demand includes a detailed list of the documents he seeks to inspect. Therefore, I next examine that list in light of the proper purposes Paul has stated.

1. Requested documents

Paul seeks to inspect the following documents:

* * *

(2) Any documentation supporting the following contentions set forth in Chairman, CEO and President Zheng Cheng's letter to "Shareholders and Friends" dated February 7, 2011, including

    a. Any materials provided to the United States Patent Office or any patent office in any other country, including the People's Republic of China, relating to the Company's acquisition of a patent for the media player used by the Company;

    b. Any contracts entered into with Beijing A-er-sha Passenger Transaction Co. Ltd. and Beijing Xiang Long A-er-sha Passenger Transportation Co. Ltd.;

    c. The contract that was purportedly entered into by the Company with Apple Inc.'s alleged authorized distributor, the Eading Group, in December 2010;

(3) Copies of each version of the "media kit" used by Company employees;

(4) Books and records constituting any contracts or evidencing any business relationship between the Company and * * * [naming multiple entities];

(5) The resignation letter from Deloitte Touche Tohmatsu ("Deloitte"), or its affiliated subsidiary, in connection with Deloitte's resignation as the Company's independent auditor; and

(6) All memoranda, presentations, reports, correspondence, email, minutes, recordings, consents, agendas, resolutions, summaries, analyses, transcripts, notes, and board or committee packages created by, distributed to, or reviewed by or on behalf of CME's Board of Directors * * * or any committee thereof, concerning the subjects referenced in items 1–5 above.

In addition, Paul demands the right to inspect all books and records requested in his demand letter that are within the legal possession, custody, or control of the Company, including, but not limited to, such books and records that are within the possession, custody, or control of the Company's subsidiaries and outside legal counsel, special counsel, accountants, or consultants.

2. Permitted documents

* * *

Paul is entitled to production of all documents requested under Demands Two, Three, and Five (and their subparts) above. The documents requested under Demand Two directly relate to CME's claimed business relationships, intellectual property, and customer contracts. The existence, or nonexistence, of these contracts and documents would affect directly the Company's revenue and net income. Likewise, Demand Five, DTT's resignation letter, also directly relates to alleged wrongdoing and fraudulent accounting practices by CME. Finally, Demand Three, the media kits used by the Company, relate to representations made by the Company about its business relationships and profitability. All of these documents could impact the veracity of CME's financial reporting and would help confirm or repudiate Paul's suspicions of fraud and wrongdoing at the Company. Therefore, Paul is entitled to inspection of these documents.

Paul is also entitled to production of documents constituting any contracts between CME and the entities listed in Demand Four. Paul is not, however, entitled to production of documents "evidencing any business relationship between the Company" and the more than twenty entities listed in Demand Four. The latter clause is simply too broad for a § 220 demand, especially where there is reason for caution based on a co-pending motion for a stay under SLUSA. Paul made no showing that production of such an ill-defined group of documents is necessary to either of his proper purposes.

3. Denied documents

* * *

* * * Demand Six is objectionable in a couple of respects. First, Demand Six reads much more like a sweeping discovery request than a narrowly focused § 220 demand. This is apparent, for example, in its request for "all * * * emails [and] notes * * * created by, distributed to, or reviewed by or on behalf of CME's Board * * * or any committee thereof, concerning [well over two dozen subjects]." Second, the overbreadth and burdensomeness of Paul's request is exacerbated by his further request for all such books and records that are within the legal possession, custody, or control of the Company, its subsidiaries, or its agents, including outside legal counsel and accountants. Paul may be entitled to inspect certain documents that fall under the scope of Demand Six, but any such documents most likely would be among the documents the Court already has required CME to produce pursuant to Demands Two through Five. Accordingly, I deny Paul's request to inspect the documents called for in Demand Six in its entirety.

C. Confidentiality Agreement

Finally, when authorizing inspection under § 220, it is "entirely reasonable" to require the inspecting shareholder to enter into a confidentiality agreement as a prerequisite for inspection. Here, Paul has agreed to execute a confidentiality agreement to protect the information obtained through this § 220 action from being shared with the federal plaintiffs. Therefore, I condition Paul's right to receive documents pursuant to this Memorandum Opinion and any accompanying Order on his entering into such an agreement with CME and filing it for the Court's approval.

III. WHETHER THE § 220 ACTION SHOULD BE STAYED PENDING THE FEDERAL COURT'S RULING ON CME'S SLUSA MOTION

In granting in part Paul's § 220 demand, I recognize that the district court may have authority to stay this action if it determines that such inspection would interfere with the automatic stay in the Federal Action. At least one federal court has held that § 220 actions are "discovery proceedings" for the purposes of SLUSA, and that Act gives a federal court discretion to stay discovery proceedings in state courts if "necessary in aid of its jurisdiction, or to protect or effectuate its judgments." Federal courts generally rely on three factors in deciding whether to stay a state action: (1) whether there is a risk that the federal plaintiffs will obtain the state plaintiff's discovery, and to what extent a confidentiality agreement and/or protective order with defendants can minimize that risk; (2) whether the underlying facts and legal claims in the state and federal actions overlap; and (3) the burden that the state court discovery proceedings will impose on the federal defendants. In considering these factors, previous federal courts have invited "thoughtful and careful explanation[s]" from state courts regarding whether state actions should be stayed. Therefore, I briefly discuss my reasons for concluding this action should not be stayed.

A. Risk of the Federal Plaintiffs Obtaining State Discovery

The dispositive question with regard to this element is "whether some form of relevant discovery is likely to reach the federal plaintiffs during the pendency of a motion to dismiss in federal court." Relevant considerations include (1) the relationship between the plaintiffs in the state and federal cases and (2) the stage of the proceedings in the state action (*e.g.*, whether discovery hearings or even a public trial are likely to occur before the federal court has a chance to decide the motion).

Paul, the Plaintiff in this action, is not a party to the Federal Action. He is an individual investor and CME has not alleged that he has any relationship with Starr. Paul also has agreed to sign a confidentiality agreement that would restrict him from sharing information with the federal plaintiffs. * * *

B. Whether the State and Federal Actions have Overlapping Claims and Underlying Facts

The state and federal claims against CME relate to the same underlying facts, but they involve entirely different legal claims. A § 220 action is a proceeding by which a shareholder may inspect the books and records of a company in which he has an ownership interest. Although § 220 actions are often precursors to direct or derivative actions in state court for fraud or breaches of fiduciary duties, the actual judgments entered in § 220 cases are much more limited in scope. In this case, for example, a judgment in favor of Paul would mean that he has proven stock ownership, a formal written demand, and a proper purpose. Consequently, there is minimal risk of inconsistency between a judgment here and a ruling on the federal motion to dismiss. Moreover, to the extent this action could be deemed to constitute the "embryonic stages" of a state derivative action, it still is unlikely that any judgment will issue from such a future derivative action before the district court has an opportunity to decide the motion to dismiss.

C. The Burden of State Court Discovery on Defendants

Finally, when deciding whether to stay a related state action, a federal court will consider whether the state action would create an unreasonable discovery burden for the federal defendant. Relevant concerns include (1) whether discovery in the federal and state actions will be duplicative and (2) whether the defendant will be required to litigate and resolve the same discovery disputes in two different courts, wasting judicial resources and imposing substantial costs on the defendant.

Here, several of Paul's requests sought fairly limited production of targeted documents. To the extent certain other requests were not related to a proper purpose under § 220 or were overly broad, I denied the requests or limited their scope. Furthermore, in this action, CME will not be required to submit to any deposition discovery, will not have to answer interrogatories, and faces only a minimal risk of further disputes over the scope of production. Therefore, I do not expect complying with the production ordered in this action to be overly burdensome for CME.

IV. CONCLUSION

For the foregoing reasons, I grant Paul's § 220 demand to inspect the books and records of CME requested under Demands Two, Three, and Five of his demand letter, as listed *supra*, and under Demand Four, but only after the phrase "or evidencing any business relationship" is excised from that Demand. In all other respects, Paul's § 220 demand is denied. Furthermore, as a condition of his inspection, I direct Paul to enter into an appropriate confidentiality agreement with CME. Counsel for the parties promptly shall confer about a confidentiality agreement and submit a proposed form of such agreement to the Court within ten days of the date of this Memorandum Opinion.

It is so ordered.

NOTES

(1) In Cohen v. El Paso Corp., 2004 WL 2340046, at *1 (Del.Ch. Oct. 18, 2004), Cohen, a shareholder in the El Paso Corporation, proceeded in an action to inspect the company's books under Section 220 of the Delaware General Corporation Law. El Paso, also a defendant in a federal securities class action, argued that a stay of discovery in the federal case prevented Cohen from inspecting the corporate books and records. The Delaware court rejected El Paso's argument. The judge held that the Private Securities Litigation Reform Act and the Securities Litigation Uniform Standards Act, which allowed for the stay of discovery, only applied to federal class action cases. Because Cohen's demand had nothing to do with the federal class action, his action to inspect the company's books and records was allowed under Section 220.

(2) A demand for corporate books and records often is of critical importance to shareholders who want to commence a derivative suit. In order to get past an initial motion to dismiss the complaint, derivative plaintiffs must plead sufficient facts to excuse pre-suit demand on the corporation's board. The decision in *Paul* provides an example of a court allowing a plaintiff to use the inspection right to investigate the independence of the board members.

Similarly, in Beam v. Stewart, 845 A.2d 1040 (Del.2004), the court affirmed the dismissal of several claims in a derivative suit due to a lack of sufficient facts to excuse demand. The court was perplexed as to why the plaintiff did not first request to inspect the corporate books and records under Section 220: "[F]ailure to seek a books and records inspection that may have uncovered the facts necessary to support a reasonable doubt of independence has resulted in substantial cost to the parties and the judiciary." 845 A.2d at 1057.

(3) Over time, Section 220 of the Delaware General Corporation Law has become an increasingly powerful tool, allowing both record and beneficial owners of stock to inspect a company's books and records for "any proper purpose." DGCL § 220(b). The powers granted to shareholders under this section are sometimes referred to as the "tools at hand," and they represent a crucial element of many derivative and other shareholder-initiated suits. Indeed, it is precisely these tools at hand that allow shareholders in many cases to plead with the particularity necessary to reach a trial on the merits.

(4) In *Parsons v. Jefferson-Pilot Corp.*, 426 S.E.2d 685 (N.C.1993), the North Carolina Supreme Court upheld shareholders' common law and statutory rights of inspection. Less than a year later, the North Carolina legislature enacted the following provision:

> Notwithstanding the provisions of this section, or any other provisions of this Chapter or interpretations thereof to the contrary, a shareholder of a public corporation shall have no common law rights to inspect or copy any accounting records of the corporation or any other records of the corporation that may not be inspected or copied by a shareholder of a public corporation as provided in G.S. 55–16–02(b).

N.C. Gen. Stat. § 55–16–02(i).

(5) Enforcement of inspection rights has long been a problem. Prior to the enactment of statutes dealing specifically with shareholder inspection rights, the normal reaction of management to an inspection request was to refuse to provide anything, which required the shareholder to go to court. In an effort to make the inspection right more meaningful and less costly to shareholders, a variety of statutory inspection rights were created. Some placed the burden of showing an improper purpose on the corporation while others imposed penalties on corporate officers that failed to comply with inspection rights without reasonable cause. Some statutes required the corporation to pay a successful shareholder's expenses. The MBCA now addresses the enforcement problem in MBCA § 16.04.

(6) A related problem arises with respect to the scope of the inspection itself. An inspection is not very useful to a shareholder if, for example, the corporation produces a list of 26,000 shareholders of record at the corporation's principal office, but then refuses a request to provide a copy (or to let the shareholder make a copy) of the list. An inspection right is also of limited

usefulness if the corporation refuses to permit the shareholder to be accompanied by his attorney and accountant when inspecting the records. MBCA § 16.03 is intended to provide comprehensive answers to such problems.

(7) Many states adopting streamlined inspection rights limit them to "eligible" shareholders, usually defining eligible shareholders as those holding a specified number of shares or holding a number of shares for some period of time. The Model Act does not include these restrictions on the theory that they are ineffective.

CHAPTER 18

THE LIMITED PARTNERSHIP

■ ■ ■

A. INTRODUCTION

Like a corporation, a limited partnership is solely a creature of statute. Unlike a general partnership, which can be created simply by the owners behaving in a certain manner ("carrying on as co-owners a business for profit"), a limited partnership can only be created by complying with the formation requirements of the relevant statute.

A limited partnership is comprised of at least one general partner and at least one limited partner. While a general partner in a limited partnership has unlimited liability for the obligations of the firm, a limited partner has no liability for the debts of the venture beyond the loss of his investment. As you will learn, however, in certain circumstances that limited liability can be forfeited if a limited partner participates in the control of the business. Like a general partnership, a limited partnership provides its owners with pass-through tax treatment and structural flexibility (i.e., the parties can contractually arrange to run the business largely as they see fit).

The limited partnership has a long history in the United States. New York and Connecticut adopted the first limited partnership statutes in 1822, followed by Pennsylvania in 1836. The adoption of these statutes was motivated by a desire to avoid the liability implications of the general partnership form and by a related effort to facilitate investment and business development.

The first uniform act to focus on limited partnerships was the 1916 Uniform Limited Partnership Act ("ULPA"). ULPA was drafted by the National Conference of Commissioners on Uniform State Laws ("NCCUSL"), and the Act was widely adopted in this country. In 1976, NCCUSL promulgated the Revised Uniform Limited Partnership Act ("RULPA (1976)"). Modern limited partnerships had become much more sophisticated, and many of ULPA's provisions were outdated. As one authority explained:

> While the 1916 Act was motivated largely by the underutilization of its predecessors, the 1976 Act was motivated largely by the overutilization of its predecessor. Rising prosperity and high income-tax rates coupled with numerous special deductions and credits led to the creation and growth of a

1115

major tax shelter industry from the 1960s onward. The limited partnership was the favorite vehicle. * * * Into it, the syndicator or promoter (who often became or selected the general partner) put the oil and gas lease, apartment complex, or other asset. Shares were sold to investors in the form of interests (often called units) in the limited partnership. Investors thus could enjoy the tax benefits [such as interest expense, depletion, depreciation, and ultimate capital gain treatment] attached to ownership or development of the asset (until restricted by legislative changes) but with limited liability. The 1916 Act, which contemplated small numbers of limited partners, simple financial arrangements, and local operations, was not well suited to the hundreds or thousands of limited partners, intricate financial arrangements, and multistate operations in some of the modern firms.

III ALAN R. BROMBERG & LARRY E. RIBSTEIN, BROMBERG AND RIBSTEIN ON PARTNERSHIP § 11.02(c), at 11:26 to 11:27 (13th ed. 2005). RULPA (1976) made a number of important changes to limited partnership law, including, among others, increasing the relative importance of the limited partnership agreement over the certificate of formation, and reducing the circumstances under which a limited partner could be liable for participating in the control of the enterprise.

In 1985, NCCUSL significantly amended the 1976 act ("RULPA (1985)"). RULPA (1985) further established the limited partnership agreement as the more important organizational document, and it continued to reduce the circumstances under which a limited partner could be liable for the venture's obligations. The limited partnership statutes of most states are presently based upon RULPA (1985).

In 2001, NCCUSL approved a new Uniform Limited Partnership Act ("ULPA (2001)"). In contrast to its predecessors, ULPA (2001) is a stand-alone act. As a result, the Act is considered to be more than a mere revision, and the term "revised" was dropped from its title. Among other changes, ULPA (2001) completely eliminates a limited partner's liability for participating in the control of the business, and it removes buyout rights for dissociating general and limited partners. As of this writing, only eighteen states have adopted ULPA (2001). Limited partnerships in most of the country, therefore, are still governed by earlier versions of the Act. Consequently, the materials below focus on RULPA (1985), although the corresponding provisions of ULPA (2001) are noted as well.

For many years, the limited partnership stood alone as the only business form that provided the best of both worlds—the corporate trait of limited liability, and the partnership traits of pass-through taxation and structural flexibility. With the birth of the limited liability partnership ("LLP") and the limited liability company ("LLC"), however, the modern business owner now has multiple options that fuse limited liability, operational flexibility, and favorable tax treatment. As a result, a number of commentators have predicted that the usage of the limited partnership will dramatically wane. Nevertheless, keep the following in mind: (1) the relatively long history of use of limited partnerships in this country has produced a comfort level among many attorneys and business owners with that form; (2) that same history of use has generated a significant body of common-law precedent that makes the limited partnership's operation more "predictable" than newer business structures; (3) the legal framework of other business forms (particularly the LLC) derives, in large part, from limited partnership law; and (4) limited partnerships are still popular in certain specialized areas (e.g., estate planning, real estate, venture capital, oil and gas). Consequently, limited partnerships—and the law of limited partnerships—are likely to remain relevant for many years to come.

NOTE ON STATUTORY "LINKAGE" AND "DE-LINKAGE"

Limited partnership statutes have historically been "linked" to general partnership statutes. Because of this linkage, a jurisdiction's general partnership law would apply to a limited partnership issue when that issue was not covered by the limited partnership statute. For example, UPA § 6(2) states that "this act [UPA] shall apply to limited partnerships except in so far as the statutes relating to such partnerships are inconsistent herewith." Correspondingly, ULPA § 1 specifically defines a limited partnership as a "partnership," and § 9 states that a general partner, with some exceptions, "shall have all the rights and powers and be subject to all the restrictions and liabilities of a partner in a partnership without limited partners."

In contrast, RUPA § 202(b) indicates that "[a]n association formed under a statute other than this [Act], a predecessor statute, or a comparable statute of another jurisdiction is not a partnership under this [Act]," and the comment specifically states that "[a] limited partnership is not a partnership under this definition." The comment to RUPA § 101, however, states that the language of § 202(b) "was not intended to preclude the application of any RUPA general partnership rules to limited partnerships where limited partnership law otherwise adopts the RUPA rules." Further, the comment notes that "[t]he effect of these definitions leaves the scope and applicability of RUPA to limited partnerships to limited partnership law, not to sever [sic] the linkage between the two Acts in all cases." It is important to note, therefore, that § 101(7) of RULPA (1976) and RULPA (1985) defines a limited partnership as a "partnership," § 403 provides that a general partner in a limited partnership has the rights, powers, restrictions, and liabilities "of a partner in a partnership without limited partners," and § 1105 indicates that "[i]n any case not provided for in this [Act] the provisions of the Uniform Partnership Act govern."[a]

This linkage between limited partnership and general partnership statutes is useful to the extent that general partnership law can be used to answer questions when the limited partnership statute is silent. At times, however, general partnership law may be inappropriate for the limited partnership context. Statutory linkage, therefore, can be problematic.

Significantly, ULPA (2001) explicitly "de-links" itself from the general partnership statutes with the purpose of standing alone as a comprehensive limited partnership act. The "Prefatory Note" to ULPA (2001) sheds some light on this decision:

> The Committee saw several substantial advantages to de-linking. A stand alone statute would:
>
> - be more convenient, providing a single, self-contained source of statutory authority for issues pertaining to limited partnerships;
>
> - eliminate confusion as to which issues were solely subject to the limited partnership act and which required reference (i.e., linkage) to the general partnership act; and
>
> - rationalize future case law, by ending the automatic link between the cases concerning partners in a general partnership and issues pertaining to general partners in a limited partnership.

As stated above, ULPA (2001) has not yet been widely adopted. For most of the limited partnerships in this country, therefore, "linkage" is still an important concept—one that may determine the applicable law in a particular limited partnership dispute.

B. FORMATION

Unlike general partnerships, limited partnerships can only be formed by filing a certificate of limited partnership with the secretary of state (or equivalent official) of the appropriate jurisdiction. The certificate is a relatively skeletal document that includes basic information about the company, including, among other items, the name of the limited partnership and the identity of the general partners. *See, e.g.*, RULPA (1985) § 201. Of course, you should always check a state's limited partnership statute for precisely what is required in a particular jurisdiction.

---

[a] "States enacting R.U.P.A. have typically amended [RULPA (1985)] § 1105 to say that R.U.P.A. rather than U.P.A. governs, and courts are likely to construe it this way even if the state has not amended [RULPA (1985)] § 1105." IV ALAN R. BROMBERG & LARRY E. RIBSTEIN, BROMBERG AND RIBSTEIN ON PARTNERSHIP § 17.01(b)(2), at 17:11 (13th ed. 2005).

The real detail on the rights and duties of partners and on the overall operation of a limited partnership is contained in the partnership agreement—a separate, non-public document that the parties draft (or, more precisely, the parties' lawyers draft) to govern their particular firm. In general, a partnership agreement can be tailored to suit the specific needs of a limited partnership, and the agreement's terms will displace the default provisions of the statute.

NOTES

(1) When is a limited partnership formed? *See* RULPA (1985) § 201; ULPA (2001) § 201. Why do you think limited partnerships are required to make a public filing, but general partnerships are not? If a limited partnership plans to do business in a state other than its state of formation, appropriate filings should also be made in the non-formation state(s). *See* RULPA (1985) § 902; ULPA (2001) § 902.

(2) Under RULPA (1985) and ULPA (2001), a limited partnership is not required to have a partnership agreement. The default rules of the limited partnership statute (and, when RULPA (1985) is silent, the general partnership statute) would provide the operative terms. Nevertheless, most limited partnerships have a detailed partnership agreement, and you will likely need to draft one to meet your clients' needs.

(3) Does a limited partnership agreement have to be in writing? *See* RULPA (1985) § 101(9); ULPA (2001) § 102(13).

(4) In general, the function of a certificate of limited partnership is to provide notice to third parties. *See, e.g.*, Garrett v. Koepke, 569 S.W.2d 568, 570 (Tex. Civ. App. 1978) ("The purpose of the filing requirements under the [limited partnership] act is to provide notice to third persons dealing with the partnership of the essential features of the partnership arrangement * * *. [The legislature's] intent was to provide notice of limited liability of certain partners to third parties dealing with a partnership."). The partnership agreement, rather than the certificate, is intended to govern the partners' rights and duties to each other. Indeed, noncompliance with formation requirements is rarely important in suits between the partners themselves. *See, e.g.*, Fujimoto v. Au, 19 P.3d 699, 728 (Haw. 2001) ("[T]he purpose underlying the statutes requiring that a certificate of limited partnership be filed in order to form a limited partnership is to ensure notice to third persons, and failure to comply with the filing requirement does not affect the rights, among themselves, of the parties to the partnership agreement.").

(5) What happens when the relatively simple formation requirements of a limited partnership are not complied with? Section 201(b) of RULPA (1985) states that "[a] limited partnership is formed at the time of the filing of the certificate of limited partnership in the office of the Secretary of State * * * if * * * there has been substantial compliance with the requirements of this section." (Earlier limited partnership statutes had a similar provision, as does ULPA (2001) § 201(c)).

RULPA (1985) § 304 also mitigates the effect of defective formation. Section 304(a) provides protection to a person who makes a contribution to a business enterprise under the mistaken (but good faith) belief that he is a limited partner. According to the statute, such a person "is not a general partner in the enterprise and is not bound by its obligations" if, upon ascertaining the mistake, he either (1) "causes an appropriate certificate of limited partnership or a certificate of amendment to be executed and filed," or (2) "withdraws from future equity participation in the enterprise by executing and filing in the office of the Secretary of State a certificate declaring withdrawal under this section." If these requirements are met, § 304(b) indicates that the mistaken person is only liable as a general partner to any third party who transacts business with the enterprise before (1) or (2) above are accomplished. Even then, liability is only imposed "if the third party actually believed in good faith that the person was a general partner at the time of the transaction." Although § 304 is typically used to mitigate the effect of a limited partnership's defective formation, the statute has also been applied in the general partnership context. *See, e.g.*, Briargate Condo. Ass'n v. Carpenter, 976 F.2d 868, 870–71 & n.6 (4th Cir. 1992) (involving a partner who mistakenly believed that she was a limited partner in a limited partnership, even though she was actually a general partner in a business that was intentionally formed as a general partnership). ULPA (2001) § 306 is similar to RULPA (1985) § 304.

(6) Should a plaintiff's knowledge that a business is a limited partnership matter in defective formation disputes? *Compare* Garrett v. Koepke, 569 S.W.2d 568, 570–71 (Tex. Civ. App. 1978) ("Appellees [limited partners] admit that they had failed to file a certificate of limited partnership as required * * *. Since appellants [creditors of the limited partnership] knew that the entity with which they were dealing was a limited partnership, as well as the consequences of dealing with such an entity, they were in no way prejudiced by the failure to comply with the statute. * * * We hold, therefore, that where a party has knowledge that the entity with which he is dealing is a limited partnership, that status is not changed by failing to file * * *."), *with* Dwinell's Central Neon v. Cosmopolitan Chinook Hotel, 587 P.2d 191, 194 (Wash. Ct. App. 1978) ("[A] third party's knowledge regarding the status of a limited partnership is irrelevant when at the time of contracting, the partners have made no attempt to comply with the statutory information and filing requirements of the Limited Partnership Act * * *. A creditor has a right to rely upon there being substantial compliance * * * before the protection of [the limited partnership statute's] provisions are afforded to any member of a partnership. Here there was no compliance.").

(7) Partners in a limited partnership are usually required to make a contribution to the capital of the venture. The limited partnership statutes tend to define "contribution" broadly. *See, e.g.*, RULPA (1985) §§ 101(2), 501; ULPA (2001) §§ 102(2), 501.

(8) In response to the use of limited partnerships as vehicles for evading the double tax on corporations, § 7704 of the Internal Revenue Code now

mandates that, for federal income tax purposes, a "publicly traded partnership" shall be taxed as a corporation. *See* 26 U.S.C. § 7704. A "publicly traded partnership" is defined as "any partnership if (1) interests in such partnership are traded on an established securities market, or (2) interests in such partnership are readily tradable on a secondary market (or the substantial equivalent thereof)." *Id.* § 7704(b). An exception to the rule exists "if 90 percent or more of the gross income of such [publicly traded] partnership for such taxable year consists of qualifying [passive-type] income," such as interest, dividends, or rent. *Id.* § 7704(c)(2), (d)(1). Put differently, publicly traded partnerships meeting the exception will avoid corporation tax treatment.

(9) Can other business entities convert to limited partnerships, and can limited partnerships convert to other business entities? RULPA (1985) does not address conversion issues, but RUPA does. RUPA § 902 and § 903 state the requirements for converting a general partnership to a limited partnership (and vice-versa), and RUPA § 904 specifies the effects of conversion.

Unlike RULPA (1985), ULPA (2001) does address conversion issues. ULPA (2001) § 1102 allows "[a]n organization other than a limited partnership" to convert to a limited partnership. Conversely, the section also allows a limited partnership to convert "to another organization." *See also* ULPA (2001) § 1101(8) (defining "organization"). ULPA (2001) § 1105 prescribes the effects of conversion.

(10) Under most circumstances, limited partnership interests are treated as securities under federal and state securities laws. Ownership interests that are not specifically mentioned in the 1933 Securities Act, such as general and limited partnership interests, are usually analyzed under the "investment contract" term of the Act. The courts have interpreted "investment contract" to include situations where a person invests in a common enterprise expecting profits predominantly from the efforts of others. *See, e.g.*, SEC v. W.J. Howey Co., 328 U.S. 293 (1946). Courts typically conclude that limited partnership interests are investment contracts (and are therefore securities) because limited partners often lack the right to participate in management and usually depend on the efforts of the general partners for profit. In contrast, because general partners commonly have the right to participate in management, most courts hold that general partnership interests are not securities. *But see* Williamson v. Tucker, 645 F.2d 404, 424 (5th Cir. 1981) (suggesting that a general partnership interest can be a security if, as a practical matter, a general partner lacks meaningful partnership powers). When the securities laws apply, it generally means that, absent an exemption, a security (such as a limited partnership interest) cannot be sold to the public without going through a detailed registration and disclosure process—a process that is frequently time-consuming and expensive. Moreover, fraud in connection with the purchase or sale of a security can result in criminal, administrative, and civil liability under securities fraud statutes. *See* Chapter 14.

C. MANAGEMENT AND OPERATION

As RULPA (1985) § 403(a) indicates, a general partner in a limited partnership has the same rights and powers (and is subject to the same restrictions) as a general partner in a general partnership (except when RULPA (1985) otherwise provides). The statute explicitly links to general partnership law, in other words, on the subject of a general partner's management rights and powers. Those rights and powers would include, among others, the ability to participate in management (UPA § 18(e); RUPA § 401(f)), the ability to bind the partnership via apparent authority to transactions in the ordinary course of business (UPA § 9(1); RUPA § 301(1)), and the ability to vote (UPA § 18(h); RUPA § 401(j)). As § 403(a) makes clear, however, these linked rights and powers are only default rules—i.e., a partnership agreement can restrict or alter them.

RULPA (1985) does not explicitly grant or deny management rights to limited partners. Nevertheless, several cases have stated that limited partners cannot take part in the management of the business, *see, e.g.,* Goodman v. Epstein, 582 F.2d 388, 408 (7th Cir. 1978), and partnership agreements tend to explicitly deny management rights to limited partners. As discussed in Section F(1) of this Chapter, limited partners who participate in the control of the business risk liability for some or all of the obligations of the venture. *See, e.g.,* RULPA (1985) § 303. Indirectly, therefore, this control restriction helps to restrain limited partners from exercising substantial management rights.

RULPA (1985) does not speak to the issue of whether a limited partner is an agent of the limited partnership who can bind the venture, via apparent authority, to transactions in the ordinary course of business. There is some case law, however, stating that limited partners have no agency authority merely as a result of their limited partner status. *See, e.g.,* Berman v. Herrick, 231 F. Supp. 918, 921 (E.D. Pa. 1964) ("It should be observed at this point that although Kupin was a limited partner * * * that status alone did not vest Kupin with authority to act for or bind the partnership or the general partners.").

Absent provisions in a partnership agreement, a limited partner has no voting rights under RULPA (1985). *See* RULPA (1985) § 302. In practice, however, partnership agreements often provide voting rights, at least on some issues, to limited partners. For example, an Illinois formbook includes the following language as part of a sample partnership agreement:

5.1. Rights and Obligations of the Limited Partners.

(a) A Limited Partner is only liable to make the payment of its Capital Contribution. A Limited Partner will not be liable for any obligations of the Partnership * * *.

* * *

(c) No Limited Partner will participate in the management, nor have any control over the Partnership business, nor transact any business for the Partnership, nor have any power to sign for or bind the Partnership at any time.

12.1.　　Voting Rights.

(a) Unless otherwise specified in this Agreement, any matters which must be submitted to a vote of the Limited Partners will be deemed approved if at least 75 percent of the Interests vote in favor of any such matter. Each Limited Partner has the right to cast one vote for each Interest owned of record on the books of the Partnership by the Limited Partner, but no Limited Partner is entitled to cumulate votes. Any matters to be voted on may be presented for vote to the Limited Partners at a meeting called by the General Partner by notice given not less than 15 days and not more than 30 days or may be adopted without a meeting or vote by written consent of the holders of at least 75 percent of the Interests or such greater percentage as may be provided in this Agreement for the adoption of such matter.

(b) Unless otherwise specified in this Agreement, Limited Partners have the right to vote only upon the following matters affecting the basic structure of the Partnership:

> (i) Removal of the General Partner;

> (ii) Election of a successor General Partner;

> (iii) Amendment of this Agreement;

> (iv) Extension of the term of the Partnership;

> (v) A sale of substantially all of the assets of the Partnership; and

> (vi) Authorizing a competing business * * *.

9 ILL. FORMS LEGAL & BUS. § 30:58 (2005).

NOTES

(1) As mentioned, RULPA (1985) § 403(a) links to general partnership law on the rights, powers, and restrictions of a general partner. In *Connecticut National Bank v. Cooper*, 656 A.2d 215 (Conn. 1995), the court used this linkage provision (as well as others) to import the UPA rule that a third party is bound by its knowledge of a restriction on partner authority:

> General Statutes § 34–47(4) [based on UPA § 9(4)] provides: "No act of a partner in contravention of a restriction on authority shall bind the partnership to persons having knowledge of the

restriction." The partnership argues that because the bank's attorney acknowledged that he had received and had reviewed the limited partnership agreement prior to the stipulated judgment, the bank had knowledge of the restriction on Gordon's authority to agree to the stipulation. The partnership, therefore, argues pursuant to § 34–47(4) that it is not bound by the stipulation. * * *

Section 34–47, which is part of the Uniform Partnership Act (UPA), was codified in Connecticut in 1961. The UPA applies to limited partnerships except insofar as it is inconsistent with the Uniform Limited Partnership Act. [*See* UPA § 6(2)]. General Statutes § 34–17(a), which is part of the Uniform Limited Partnership Act, provides: "Except as provided in this chapter or in the partnership agreement, a general partner of a limited partnership shall have all the rights and powers and be subject to all the restrictions of a partner in a partnership without limited partners." Because § 34–47 is not inconsistent with § 34–17(a), the limitation provided in § 34–47(4) applies to the general partner of a limited partnership.

Id. at 219.

(2) Does RULPA (1985) provide a limited partner with a default right to vote for the removal of a general partner? A default right to vote against an amendment to the partnership agreement? *See* RULPA (1985) § 302. Do you think it is important for limited partners to have these rights? ULPA (2001) provides limited partners with default voting rights on a number of "extraordinary" matters, including the right to vote on the expulsion of a general partner (under certain circumstances), and the right to vote on amending the partnership agreement. *See, e.g.,* ULPA (2001) §§ 302 & cmt., 406(b)(1), 603(4).

(3) Limited partners who become dissatisfied with the performance of a general partner may want to remove that partner. RULPA (1985) § 402(3) states that a person ceases to be a general partner if the person "is removed * * * in accordance with the partnership agreement." The partnership agreement, therefore, controls whether limited partners have a removal right. *See also* RULPA (1985) § 302 ("[T]he partnership agreement may grant to all or a specified group of the limited partners the right to vote * * * upon any matter."). Nevertheless, keep in mind that other provisions of § 402 can result in a general partner's removal. For example, § 402(4) indicates that, subject to a contrary provision in a written partnership agreement, a general partner's bankruptcy (or comparable proceeding) causes the removal of that partner. The general partner can be retained, however, if all of the partners (including the limited partners) agree in writing (i.e., the preamble to § 402 states "[e]xcept as approved by the specific written consent of all partners at the time"). *See also* Curley v. Brignoli Curley & Roberts Assocs., 746 F. Supp. 1208, 1221 (S.D.N.Y. 1989) (involving a court that used its equitable powers to remove a general partner).

(4) RULPA (1985) § 305 provides limited partners with the right to inspect the limited partnership's records and the accompanying right to obtain information about the limited partnership. Why are these inspection and information rights particularly important for limited partners? RULPA (1985) does not specifically provide general partners with inspection and information rights, but general partnership law, via linkage, does provide them. *See* RULPA (1985) § 403(a); UPA §§ 19–20; RUPA § 403.

(5) Consistent with its effort to "delink" from general partnership law, ULPA (2001) addresses a general partner's rights and powers within the statute itself. *See, e.g.*, ULPA (2001) § 402 (addressing a general partner's agency authority); *id.* § 406 (addressing a general partner's right to participate in management and the accompanying right to vote); *id.* § 407 (addressing a general partner's inspection and information rights).

(6) With respect to a limited partner's rights and powers under ULPA (2001), § 302 indicates that a limited partner lacks management rights and agency authority. The section states that "[a] limited partner does not have the right or the power as a limited partner to act for or bind the limited partnership," and the comment clarifies that "[i]n this respect a limited partner is analogous to a shareholder in a corporation; status as owner provides neither the right to manage nor a reasonable appearance of that right." Similarly, § 406(a) conveys that a limited partner lacks voting rights for most limited partnership decisions: "Except as expressly provided in this [Act], any matter relating to the activities of the limited partnership may be exclusively decided by the general partner[s] * * *." (But see the note above regarding a limited partner's right to vote on extraordinary matters). Finally, § 304 provides a limited partner with inspection and information rights.

D. FINANCIAL RIGHTS AND OBLIGATIONS

RULPA (1985) § 503 and § 504 state that, unless otherwise agreed in a written partnership agreement, the profits, losses, and distributions of a limited partnership shall be allocated "on the basis of the value * * * of the contributions made by each partner to the extent they have been received by the partnership and have not been returned." *See also* RULPA (1985) §§ 101(2), 501 (defining "contribution" broadly). Notice that this default rule differs from the "equal sharing" default rule of general partnership law.

ULPA (2001) § 503 also allocates distributions on the basis of partner contributions, although it does so without regard to whether a limited partnership has returned any of those contributions. *See also* ULPA (2001) §§ 102(2), 501 (defining "contribution" broadly). ULPA (2001) is silent, however, on the allocation of profits and losses. The comment to § 503 suggests that the drafters of ULPA (2001) believed that a default rule for profit and loss allocation was inappropriate. *See* ULPA (2001) § 503 cmt. ("Nearly all limited partnerships will choose to allocate profits and losses in order to comply with applicable tax, accounting and other regulatory requirements. Those requirements, rather than this Act, are the proper source of guidance for that profit and loss allocation.").

RULPA (1985) contains several provisions that are designed to prevent partners from abusing their financial rights to the detriment of creditors. Section 502 gives a creditor the right, under certain circumstances, to enforce a limited partner's promise to contribute to the venture. Under § 607, a distribution to a partner is prohibited if it would leave the firm insolvent. Finally, § 608 makes partners liable to the limited partnership for wrongful distributions and, in some instances, for rightful distributions. These creditor protections can be viewed as a trade-off of sorts for the limited liability granted by the statute.

ULPA (2001) § 502 retains a creditor's right, under certain circumstances, to enforce a contribution obligation, and § 508 retains the prohibition on distributions that would render the firm insolvent. ULPA (2001) § 509 makes partners liable for wrongful distributions but, unlike RULPA (1985) § 608, § 509 does not impose liability for distributions that were rightfully made.

NOTES

(1) Does it make sense for limited partnership and general partnership statutes to have different default rules for the allocation of profits and losses?

(2) As a practical matter, the financial rights of general partners and limited partners are almost always specified in a partnership agreement. As a result, the above-mentioned default rules relating to the allocation of profits, losses, and distributions seldom apply.

(3) RULPA (1985) § 601 states that "[e]xcept as provided in this Article, a partner is entitled to receive distributions from a limited partnership before his [or her] withdrawal from the limited partnership and before the dissolution and winding up thereof to the extent and at the times or upon the happening of the events specified in the partnership agreement." Ordinarily, therefore, a partner (general or limited) has no default right to demand interim distributions, as the partnership agreement governs. Section 604, however, does provide general and limited partners with a default distribution right upon withdrawal (i.e., a default buyout right upon withdrawal).

(4) ULPA (2001) § 504 states that "[a] partner does not have a right to any distribution before the dissolution and winding up of the limited partnership unless the limited partnership decides to make an interim distribution." The comment to § 504 adds that "[u]nder Section 406(a), the general partner or partners make this decision for the limited partnership." In contrast to RULPA (1985), ULPA (2001) does not provide general or limited partners with a default distribution/buyout right upon withdrawal. *See* ULPA (2001) § 505; Chapter 18, Section I(1) (discussing dissociation).

E. ENTITY STATUS

Under RULPA (1985), is a limited partnership considered to be a separate legal entity? The statute does not directly speak to the question. Nevertheless, limited partnerships possess a number of characteristics that suggest a separateness between the partners and the business itself. As examples, limited partners possess limited liability for the obligations of the business (§ 303(a)), limited partners can bring derivative lawsuits on behalf of the limited partnership (§ 1001), and the dissociation of a partner (general or limited) does not necessarily result in the dissolution of the limited partnership (§ 801). Perhaps not surprisingly, therefore, courts have generally treated RULPA limited partnerships as legal entities distinct from their owners. *See also* ULPA (2001) § 104(a) ("A limited partnership is an entity distinct from its partners."). Even if a limited partnership is recognized as an entity under limited partnership law, however, a court may conclude that a limited partnership will not be treated as a distinct entity when policy considerations outside of limited partnership law are compelling. *See, e.g.,* Currier v. Amerigas Propane, L.P., 737 A.2d 1118, 1119–20 (N.H. 1999) (concluding that a general partner's immunity from suit under the workers' compensation laws extended to the limited partnership itself).

NOTE

In *Barr Lumber Co. v. Old Ivy Homebuilders, Inc.*, 40 Cal. Rptr. 2d 717 (Cal. App. Dep't Super. Ct. 1995), a creditor of a limited partnership filed a lawsuit to foreclose on the limited partnership's property. Unfortunately, the creditor only sued Old Ivy, the general partner of the limited partnership, Old Ivy/Lawndale II. The court refused to allow the foreclosure:

> In the present case, it is uncontradicted that the title to the subject real property is held by the limited partnership Old Ivy/Lawndale II, and not by its general partner Old Ivy, who is the only defendant in this case. * * *
>
>   * * *
>
> * * * As stated above, a judgment foreclosing a lien must name *all* parties having an interest in the subject property, and is not enforceable against any party who has an interest in the property who is not named as a defendant.
>
> * * * Here, despite defendant's interest in the property as a general partner of the titleholder, defendant does not, on its own, have any interest in the property that could properly be subject to foreclosure. Defendant, as general partner, has no individual interest in the subject property; the property is owned by the limited partnership. Defendant has only an intangible interest in the limited partnership, and there is no basis in this case for using the partnership property to satisfy a judgment against the general

partner. An individual partner is not, by operation of law, deemed the owner of specific partnership assets, simply by virtue of his status as a partner. In short, the property of the partnership belongs to the partnership, not to the general partner.

Simply put, plaintiff sued the wrong party, and failed to amend the complaint to name the proper party, in this case the limited partnership. Because plaintiff failed to name the proper party in the foreclosure action within 90 days of the filing of the mechanic's lien, the limited partner[ship] cannot be bound by the judgment and its property cannot be used to satisfy the claim in this case.

Id. at 719–21.

F. LIMITED LIABILITY

1. THE CONTROL RULE

A central feature of the limited partnership is the limited liability provided to limited partners. As mentioned, limited partners have no liability for the debts of the venture beyond the loss of their investments. A limited partner can lose her limited liability protection, however, if she participates in the control of the business—an inquiry that is the subject of much litigation.

Section 7 of the 1916 ULPA stated, in its entirety, that "[a] limited partner shall not become liable as a general partner unless, in addition to the exercise of his rights and powers as a limited partner, he takes part in the control of the business." There was considerable doubt under this sparse language as to how much activity by the limited partner would constitute "tak[ing] part in the control of the business" with the corresponding liability of a general partner. For example, may limited partners advise general partners and consult with them on business issues? May limited partners retain the power to remove a general partner and to elect another person for the position? May a limited partner also act as an employee, agent, or surety of the limited partnership? Finally, may a limited partner have the power to vote for or against amendments to the limited partnership agreement? Under ULPA, one could not be sure whether engaging in this type of conduct or providing these or similar rights would be viewed as "tak[ing] part in the control of the business." This uncertainty made the limited partnership form somewhat dangerous for investors relying on limited liability, and it played a substantial role in the decision to modernize the 1916 ULPA. The result was the development of RULPA (1976), RULPA (1985), and, ultimately, ULPA (2001). To get a sense of the changes brought about by the statutory developments, consider the following case:

GATEWAY POTATO SALES V. G.B. INVESTMENT CO.
Court of Appeals of Arizona, 1991.
822 P.2d 490.

TAYLOR, JUDGE.

Gateway Potato Sales (Gateway), a creditor of Sunworth Packing Limited Partnership (Sunworth Packing), brought suit to recover payment for goods it had supplied to the limited partnership. Gateway sought recovery from Sunworth Packing, from Sunworth Corporation as general partner, and from G.B. Investment Company (G.B. Investment) as a limited partner, pursuant to Arizona Revised Statutes Annotated (A.R.S.) § 29–319. Under § 29–319, a limited partner may become liable for the obligations of the limited partnership under certain circumstances in which the limited partner has taken part in the control of the business.

G.B. Investment moved for summary judgment, urging that there was no evidence that the circumstances described in A.R.S. § 29–319 had occurred in this case. It argued that, as a limited partner, it was not liable to the creditors of the limited partnership except to the extent of its investment. The trial court agreed, granting G.B. Investment's motion for summary judgment.

* * *

FACTS

* * * Sunworth Corporation and G.B. Investment formed Sunworth Packing in November 1985 for the purpose of engaging in potato farming in Arizona. The limited partnership certificate and agreement of Sunworth Packing, filed with the office of the Arizona Secretary of State, specified Sunworth Corporation as the general partner and G.B. Investment Company as the limited partner. The agreement recited that the limited partner would not participate in the control of the business. The agreement further stated that the limited partner would not become liable to the creditors of the partnership, except to the extent of its initial contribution and any liability it may incur with an Arizona bank as a signatory party or guarantor of a loan and/or line of credit.

In late 1985, Robert C. Ellsworth, the president of Sunworth Corporation, called Robert Pribula, the owner of Gateway, located in Minnesota, to see if Gateway would supply Sunworth Packing with seed potatoes. Pribula hesitated to supply the seed potatoes without receiving assurance of payment because Pribula was aware that Ellsworth had previously undergone bankruptcy. Pribula, however, decided to sell the seed potatoes to Sunworth Packing after being assured by Ellsworth that he was in partnership with a large financial institution, G.B. Investment Company, and that G.B. Investment was providing the financing, was actively involved in the operation of the business, and had approved the purchase of the seed potatoes. Thereafter, from February 1986 through April 1986, Gateway sold substantial quantities of seed potatoes to Sunworth Packing.

While supplying the seed potatoes, Pribula believed that he was doing business with a general partnership (i.e., Sunworth Packing Company, formed by Sunworth Corporation and G.B. Investment Company). The sales documents used by the parties specified "Sunworth Packing Company" as the name of the partnership. Pribula was neither aware of the true name of the partnership nor that it was a limited partnership.

All of Gateway's dealings were with Ellsworth. Pribula neither contacted G.B. Investment prior to selling the seed potatoes to the limited partnership nor did he otherwise attempt to verify any of the statements Ellsworth had made about G.B. Investment's involvement. The only direct contact between G.B. Investment and Gateway occurred some time after the sale of the seed potatoes. It is, however, disputed whether G.B. Investment ever provided any assurance of payment to Gateway.

G.B. Investment's vice-president, Darl Anderson, testified in his affidavit that G.B. Investment had exerted no control over the daily management and operation of the limited partnership, Sunworth Packing. This testimony was contradicted, however, by the affidavit testimony of Ellsworth which was presented by Gateway in opposing G.B. Investment's motion for summary judgment. According to Ellsworth, G.B. Investment's employees, Darl Anderson and Thomas McHolm, controlled the day-to-day affairs of the limited partnership and made Ellsworth account to them for nearly everything he did. This day-to-day contact included but was not limited to approval of most of the significant operational decisions and expenditures and the use and management of partnership funds without Ellsworth's involvement.[1]

---

[1]   Ellsworth described with some specificity the ways in which G.B. Investment's control was exerted:

a.   During the early months of the Partnership, Thomas McHolm and/or Darl Anderson were at the Partnership's offices on a daily basis directing the operation of the Partnership, and thereafter, they were at the Partnership's offices at least 2–3 times per week reviewing the operations of the business, directing changes in operations, and instructing me to make certain changes in operating the Partnership's affairs;

b.   G.B. Investment Company was solely responsible for obtaining a $150,000.00 line-of-credit loan for the Partnership with Valley National Bank of Arizona, and it also signed documents guaranteeing the repayment of the loan;

c.   As the President of the general partner, I was not permitted to make any significant independent business decisions concerning the operations of the Partnership, but was directed to have all business decisions approved with Darl Anderson and/or Thomas McHolm, or was directed to carry out decisions made by Darl Anderson and/or Thomas McHolm. For example, instead of using Partnership funds to pay certain creditors and suppliers, I was directed by Darl Anderson and/or Thomas McHolm to use the Partnership funds to purchase additional machinery and equipment;

Ellsworth testified further that he had described G.B. Investment's control of the business operation to Pribula. Pribula confirmed that Ellsworth had informed him that G.B. Investment's employees, McHolm and Anderson, were at the partnership's office on a frequent basis, that Ellsworth reported directly to them, that daily operations of the partnership were reviewed by representatives of G.B. Investment, and that Ellsworth had to get their approval before making certain business decisions.

DISCUSSION

* * *

Subsection (a) of A.R.S. § 29–319 [analogous to RULPA (1976) § 303] sets forth the general rule that a limited partner who is not also a general partner is not liable for the obligations of the limited partnership.

---

d.   Prior to constructing improvements to the packaging facilities of the Partnership, Thomas McHolm and/or Darl Anderson had to approve all construction bids, individually selected some of the suppliers and subcontractors, and individually selected the equipment to be installed;

e.   Thomas McHolm and/or Darl Anderson dictated the accounting procedures to be followed by the Partnership, reviewed the Partnership's books and accounts almost continually, dictated that the Partnership use the same accounting firm as that of G.B. Investment Company to do the Partnership accounting tasks, undertook the responsibility of having prepared all Partnership tax forms and returns, and I only signed tax returns after they had been prepared by G.B. Investment Company's accountants and reviewed by Darl Anderson or some other employee/agent of G.B. Investment Company;

f.   During a great portion of the duration of the Partnership, Thomas McHolm and/or Darl Anderson oversaw the daily operations of the Partnership because I had to have all expenditures approved by Thomas McHolm and/or Darl Anderson and Darl Anderson had to approve and sign checks issued by the Partnership, including without limitation payroll checks and invoices for telephone charges, utilities, publications, interest payments, bank card charges, supplies, etc. * * *;

g.   After it was decided to add a hydrocooler to the processing and packaging facilities of the Partnership, Thomas McHolm individually selected the refrigeration equipment and chose the contractor to install the refrigeration equipment on the hydrocooler, and even saw to it that G.B. Investment Company (not the Partnership) directly paid the contractor for all of his services;

h.   Thomas McHolm insisted that the Partnership use a particular supplier, to-wit: Allied Packaging, to supply packaging materials to the Partnership, he further took an active role in reviewing and modifying the art work for use on the packaging items, and personally approved the bid submitted for the art work;

i.   At least on two separate occasions, approximately in August, 1986 and again in November, 1986, Darl Anderson caused sums of monies (approximately $8,000 and $7,000 respectively) to be withdrawn from the Partnership account (No. 2270–8018) with Valley National Bank without the prior knowledge or consent of myself, as the President of the general partner of the Partnership. These monies were paid directly to G.B. Investment, and the withdrawals caused other checks of the Partnership to be dishonored due to insufficient funds and left the Partnership without sufficient funds to meet its payroll obligations;

j.   Darl Anderson and/or Thomas McHolm caused certain expenses of the Partnership to be paid directly by G.B. Investment Company, to-wit: refrigeration equipment; and

k.   After the Partnership defaulted on its loan payments to Valley National Bank, a loan which had been guaranteed by G.B. Investment Company, Darl Anderson, without my knowledge or consent, instructed the Valley National Bank to proceed with declaring the loan to be in default and to pursue its remedies under its Security Agreement with the Partnership, to-wit: to sell the equipment and machinery that it held as collateral at a foreclosure auction. At the foreclosure auction held on March 3, 1987, by Valley National Bank, Darl Anderson, on behalf of G.B. Investment Company, bought the equipment and machinery previously owned by Sunworth Corporation.

[A] limited partner is not liable for the obligations of a limited partnership unless he is also a general partner or, in addition to the exercise of his rights and powers as a limited partner, he takes part in the control of the business. However, if the limited partner's participation in the control of the business is not substantially the same as the exercise of the powers of a general partner, he is liable only to persons who transact business with the limited partnership with actual knowledge of his participation in control.

Subsection (a) does not discuss the types of activities that might be undertaken by a limited partner which would amount to "control of the business." Subsection (b), however, does contain a listing of activities that are permissible for a limited partner to undertake without being deemed to be taking part in "control of the business."

* * * In addition, subsection (c) of A.R.S. § 29–319 provides that "[t]he enumeration in subsection (b) does not mean that the possession or exercise of any other powers by a limited partner constitutes participation by him in the business of the limited partnership."

* * * Gateway argued that the statute imposes liability on a limited partner whose participation in the control of the business is substantially the same as the exercised power of a general partner. Gateway further argued that even if the person transacting business with the limited partnership did not know of the limited partner's participation in control, there is liability. Alternatively, Gateway argued that the statute imposes liability when the powers exercised in controlling the business might fall short of being "substantially the same as the exercise of powers of a general partner," but the person transacting business with the limited partnership had actual knowledge of the participation in control. Gateway asserted that the evidence it was presenting in response to the motion for summary judgment raised issues of material fact as to whether either of these situations had occurred. If either had occurred, Gateway argued, it would be entitled to recover from the limited partner, G.B. Investment.

In granting G.B. Investment's motion for summary judgment, the trial court gave two reasons for concluding that G.B. Investment could not be found liable under A.R.S. § 29–319(a) as a matter of law. First, as we interpret the trial court's comments, it read the statute as having a threshold requirement—that is, under all circumstances, a creditor of the limited partnership must have contact with the limited partner in order to impose liability on the limited partner. The evidence before the trial court showed that Gateway merely relied upon the statements made by Ellsworth, president of the general partner, and that Gateway did not contact G.B. Investment prior to transacting business with the limited partnership. Based upon these facts, the trial court concluded that liability could not be imposed upon G.B. Investment. * * *

To the extent that the trial court's ruling may have been based on a belief that a limited partner could never be liable under the statute unless the creditor had contact with the limited partner and learned directly from him of his participation and control of the business, we believe that ruling to be in error.

In A.R.S. § 29–319(a), the legislature stopped short of expressly stating that if the limited partner's participation in the control of the business is substantially the same as the exercise of the powers of a general partner, he is liable to persons who transact business with a limited partnership even though they have no knowledge of his participation and control. It has made this statement by implication, though, by stating to the opposite effect that "if the limited partner's participation in the control of the business is not substantially the same as the exercise of the powers of a general partner, he is liable only to persons who transact business with the limited partnership with actual knowledge of his participation in control." A.R.S. § 29–319(a).

We believe this interpretation is strengthened by an examination of the legislative history of Arizona's limited partnership statute. It is further strengthened by the legislature's refusal to modify this statute to correspond to the Revised Uniform Limited Partnership Act, as amended in 1985. Prior to 1982, Arizona's limited partnership statute was patterned after the Uniform Limited Partnership Act (ULPA), which was drafted in 1916. Section 7 of the ULPA provided that "[a] limited partner shall not become liable as a general partner unless, in addition to the exercise of his rights and powers as a limited partner, he takes part in the control of the business."

The Revised Uniform Limited Partnership Act (RULPA) was drafted in 1976. In 1982, the Arizona legislature adopted the RULPA after repealing its enactment of the ULPA. * * * The [RULPA (1976)] drafters' comment to section 303 explained that limited partners exercising all of the powers of a general partner would not escape liability by avoiding direct dealings with third parties. The comment stated:

> Section 303 makes several important changes in Section 7 of the prior uniform law. The first sentence of Section 303(a) carries over the basic test from former Section 7 whether the limited partner "takes part in the control of the business" in order to ensure that judicial decisions under the prior uniform law remain applicable to the extent not expressly changed. The second sentence of Section 303(a) reflects a wholly new concept. Because of the difficulty of determining when the "control" line has been overstepped, it was thought it unfair to impose general partner's liability on a limited partner except to the extent that a

third party had knowledge of his participation in control of the business. On the other hand, in order to avoid permitting a limited partner to exercise all of the powers of a general partner while avoiding any direct dealings with third parties, the "is not substantially the same as" test was introduced. * * *

Id. at 326 cmt.

In 1985, the drafters of the RULPA backtracked from the position taken in section 303(a) of the 1976 Act. The new amendments reflect a reluctance to hold a limited partner liable if the limited partner had no direct contact with the creditor. The 1985 revised RULPA section 303(a) was amended to provide as follows:

> Except as provided in Subsection (d), a limited partner is not liable for the obligations of a limited partnership unless he is also a general partner or, in addition to the exercise of his rights and powers as a limited partner, he participates in the control of the business. *However, if the limited partner participates in the control of the business, he is liable only to persons who transact business with the limited partnership reasonably believing, based upon the limited partner's conduct, that the limited partner is a general partner.*

Id. at 325 (emphasis added). The comment to section 303 was also revised to explain the reason for the amendment. The revised comment states:

> Section 303 makes several important changes in Section 7 of the 1916 Act. The first sentence of Section 303(a) differs from the text of Section 7 of the 1916 Act in that it speaks of participating (rather than taking part) in the control of the business; this was done for the sake of consistency with the second sentence of Section 303(a), not to change the meaning of the text. It is intended that judicial decisions interpreting the phrase "takes part in the control of the business" under the prior uniform law will remain applicable to the extent that a different result is not called for by other provisions of Section 303 and other provisions of the Act. The second sentence of Section 303(a) reflects a wholly new concept in the 1976 Act that has been further modified in the 1985 Act. It was adopted partly because of the difficulty of determining when the "control" line has been overstepped, but *also (and more importantly) because of a determination that it is not sound public policy to hold a limited partner who is not also a general partner liable for the obligations of the partnership except to persons who have done business with the limited partnership reasonably believing, based on the limited partner's conduct, that he is a general partner.* * * *

Id. at 326 cmt. (emphasis added).

The Arizona legislature, however, has not revised A.R.S. § 29–319(a) to correspond to the section 303 amendments. The Arizona statute continues to impose liability on a limited partner whenever the "substantially the same as" test is met, even though the creditor has no knowledge of the limited partner's control. It follows then that no contact between the creditor and the limited partner is required to impose liability.

Moreover, whereas section 303 of the RULPA states that the creditor's reasonable belief must be "based upon the limited partner's conduct," under A.R.S. § 29–319 the only requirement is that the creditor has had "actual knowledge of [the limited partner's] participation in control." The statute does not state that this knowledge must be based upon the limited partner's conduct. The comments to the original version of section 303 of the RULPA, from which Arizona's statute is taken, make it clear that only when the "substantially the same as" test is met is direct contact not a requirement. Conversely, if the "substantially the same as" test is not met, direct contact is required. Under the facts presented in this case, Gateway had no direct contact with G.B. Investment until after the sales were concluded. We conclude, therefore, that G.B. Investment would be liable only if the "substantially the same as" test was met.

Whether a limited partner has exercised the degree of control that will make him liable to a creditor has always been a factual question. This is so regardless of whether the particular statute involved is patterned after section 7 of the ULPA or after section 303 of the RULPA. Our current Arizona statute lists activities that a limited partner may undertake without participating in controlling the business. It also states that other activities may be excluded from the definition of such control. Where activities do not fall within the "safe harbor" of A.R.S. § 29–319(b), it is necessary for a trier-of-fact to determine whether such activities amount to "control." In the absence of actual knowledge of the limited partner's participation in the control of the partnership business, there must be evidence from which a trier-of-fact might find not only control, but control that is "substantially the same as the exercise of powers of a general partner."

We conclude that the evidence Gateway presented in this case should have allowed it to withstand summary judgment. The affidavit testimony of Ellsworth raises the issue whether he was merely a puppet for the limited partner, G.B. Investment. While a few of the activities Ellsworth listed may have fallen within the protected areas listed in A.R.S. § 29–319(b), others did not. Ellsworth's detailed statement raises substantial issues of material facts.

Viewing the facts in the light most favorable to Gateway, we cannot say as a matter of law that G.B. Investment was entitled to summary judgment. We conclude that Gateway is entitled to a determination by trial of the extent of control exercised by G.B. Investment over Sunworth Packing.

For the foregoing reasons, we reverse the judgment of the trial court and remand for further proceedings. * * *

NOTE ON THE STATUTORY EVOLUTION OF THE CONTROL RULE

With each subsequent version of NCCUSL's limited partnership statute, the control rule has become progressively more protective of limited partners. As mentioned, ULPA § 7 stated rather directly that "[a] limited partner shall not become liable as a general partner unless, in addition to the exercise of his rights and powers as a limited partner, he takes part in the control of the business." RULPA (1976) § 303(a) retained the control rule and added a new second sentence that narrowed the scope of a limited partner's liability: "However, if the limited partner's participation in the control of the business is not substantially the same as the exercise of the powers of a general partner, he [or she] is liable only to persons who transact business with the limited partnership with actual knowledge of his participation in control." RULPA (1976) § 303(b) also added a "safe harbor"—i.e., a list of protected limited partner activities that did not constitute "participat[ion] in the control of the business."

RULPA (1985) § 303(a) retained the control rule and altered the second sentence to further restrict a limited partner's liability: "However, if the limited partner participates in the control of the business, he [or she] is liable only to persons who transact business with the limited partnership reasonably believing, based upon the limited partner's conduct, that the limited partner is a general partner." RULPA (1985) § 303(b) also expanded the safe harbor list of protected limited partner activities.

ULPA (2001) § 303 completes the pro-limited partner evolution by wholly eliminating the control rule: "A limited partner is not personally liable, directly or indirectly, by way of contribution or otherwise, for an obligation of the limited partnership solely by reason of being a limited partner, even if the limited partner participates in the management and control of the limited partnership." As the comment to ULPA (2001) § 303 explains:

> In a world with [limited liability partnerships], [limited liability companies] and, most importantly, [limited liability limited partnerships], the control rule has become an anachronism. This Act therefore takes the next logical step in the evolution of the limited partner's liability shield and renders the control rule extinct.

NOTES

(1) Why have the control rule? What function(s) does it serve? What are its costs?

(2) Why is Ellsworth assisting Gateway in its efforts to hold G.B. Investment liable?

(3) In *Gateway*, how did the limited partner (G.B. Investment) participate in the control of the business (assuming that the allegations are proven at trial)? How would you define "control?"

(4) The *Gateway* court notes that there was no direct contact between G.B. Investment and Gateway until sometime after the sale of the potatoes. Gateway believed that G.B. Investment was a general partner based entirely on statements that Ellsworth made to Gateway about G.B. Investment's involvement. Under the language of RULPA (1976) § 303(a), are these facts enough to establish Gateway's "actual knowledge of [G.B. Investment's] participation in control?" Do you agree with the *Gateway* court that "direct contact" between Gateway and G.B. Investment is required to meet this "actual knowledge" standard?

(5) What result in *Gateway* under RULPA (1985) § 303(a)? Would Ellsworth's statements to Gateway about G.B. Investment's involvement suffice to establish a reasonable belief, "based upon [G.B. Investment's] conduct," that G.B. Investment was a general partner? What if Ellsworth's statements to Gateway about G.B. Investment's involvement closed with the following: "It's amazing that Anderson and McHolm call all the shots when their business is just a limited partner!"

(6) Reconsider footnote 1 of the *Gateway* opinion. Assuming that RULPA (1985) was applicable to the dispute, would some of G.B. Investment's activities have fallen within the safe harbor of § 303(b)?

(7) Under RULPA (1985) § 303(a), will limited partners who participate in the control of the business ever be liable for the limited partnership's tort obligations? Consider (1) a lawsuit by a pedestrian who is injured when the limited partnership's truck negligently runs a red light; and (2) a lawsuit by a supplier claiming that it was fraudulently induced to enter into a supply contract with the limited partnership.

(8) Even before ULPA (2001) was promulgated, a few states had eliminated the control rule in their limited partnership statutes. *See, e.g.*, GA. CODE § 14–9–303 ("A limited partner is not liable for the obligations of a limited partnership by reason of being a limited partner and does not become so by participating in the management or control of the business."); MO. REV. STAT. § 359.201 (same). The comment to the Georgia statute is particularly revealing:

> This Section eliminates the rule that a limited partner is liable as a general partner if he takes part in control of the partnership. The following is a summary of the reasons for eliminating the "control" rule:

(1) The control rule has, over the years, been greatly watered down, so that in its current version in RULPA there is no liability without creditor reliance and [there is] a broad safe harbor as to what constitutes control.

(2) Even in a watered down form, the control rule leaves some uncertainty as to liability of limited partners, and therefore operates as an important disincentive to limited partnership investments. In particular, many of the "safe harbor" categories of non-control acts are open to interpretation.

(3) Even without a control rule, third parties are protected if (despite their ability to check the certificate) they are misled by a limited partner's participation in control into believing that he is a general partner. Thus, a limited partner may be liable on estoppel (see Section 14–8–16 [partner by estoppel]) or fraud grounds, or on general equitable grounds under a "veil-piercing" theory. Fraud liability may be imposed, for example, if the limited partner's name is used in the name of the partnership in violation of Section 14–9–102 [analogous to RULPA (1985) § 303(d)]. This Section only eliminates liability imposed solely because a limited partner participates, as such, in control of the business.

(4) The control rule is not effective in fulfilling the objective of ensuring that only those with personal liability, and thus a strong incentive to be careful, will manage the business. General partners can always incorporate or delegate control to individuals other than limited partners. The control rule may actually serve to weaken the quality of management since the risk of liability for participation in control deters limited partners from monitoring the generals. If third party creditors want a limitation on partner participation in control, Section 14–9–303 does not prevent third parties from entering into agreements, similar to loan covenants, that provide for certain rights if the limited partners participate in control. * * *

(9) To avoid the effects of limited liability, can a third party assert a "piercing the veil" claim against a limited partner in a limited partnership? A Texas court gave a negative answer to this question:

> * * * The theory of alter ego, or piercing the corporate veil, is inapplicable to partnerships. * * * [I]n a limited partnership, the general partner is always liable for the debts and obligations of the partnership. * * *
>
> Under corporation law, officers and shareholders are not liable for the actions of the corporation absent an independent duty. Because officers and shareholders may not be held liable for the actions of the corporation, the theory of alter ego is used to pierce the corporate veil so the injured party might recover from an officer or shareholder who is otherwise protected by the corporate structure. Alter ego is inapplicable with regard to a partnership

because there is no veil that needs piercing, even when dealing with a limited partnership, because the general partner is always liable for the debts and obligations of the partnership to third parties.

Pinebrook Props., Ltd. v. Brookhaven Lake Prop. Owners Ass'n, 77 S.W.3d 487, 499–500 (Tex. App. 2002).

In the Virginia decision of *C.F. Trust, Inc. v. First Flight Limited Partnership*, 580 S.E.2d 806 (Va. 2003), the court, in the context of a reverse veil piercing claim, suggested that veil piercing principles were applicable to limited partnerships:

> Traditionally, a litigant who seeks to pierce a veil requests that a court disregard the existence of a corporate entity so that the litigant can reach the assets of a corporate insider, usually a majority shareholder. In a reverse piercing action, however, the claimant seeks to reach the assets of a corporation or some other business entity, as in this instance the assets of a limited partnership, to satisfy claims or a judgment obtained against a corporate insider. This proceeding, often referred to as "outsider reverse piercing," is designed to achieve goals similar to those served by traditional corporate piercing proceedings.

> We conclude that there is no logical basis upon which to distinguish between a traditional veil piercing action and an outsider reverse piercing action. In both instances, a claimant requests that a court disregard the normal protections accorded a corporate structure to prevent abuses of that structure. Therefore, we hold that Virginia does recognize the concept of outsider reverse piercing and that this concept can be applied to a Virginia limited partnership. Indeed, limited partnerships, like corporations, have a legal existence separate from the partners in the limited partnership, and the structure of the statutorily-created limited partnership limits the potential liability of each limited partner.

Id. at 810.

PROBLEM

Assume that a limited partnership agreement states the following:

§ 16.   Limitations on General Partners' Powers. No General Partner(s) shall, without the vote, written consent, or ratification of the specific act by all the other [Limited] Partners:

> (a) Assign, transfer, or pledge any of the claims of or debts due to the Partnership except upon payment in full, or arbitrate or consent to the arbitration of any disputes or controversies of the Partnership;

> (b) Sell, lease, or mortgage any part of Partnership real estate or any interest therein, or enter into any contract for any such purpose;

(c) Create an employment or independent contractor relationship with any person, or terminate the employment or independent contractor status of any person;

(d) Pledge or hypothecate or in any manner transfer his or her interest in the Partnership, except to the parties of this agreement; or

(e) Become a surety, guarantor, or accommodation party to any obligation except for Partnership business.

(Modified from 1B WEST LEGAL FORMS, BUSINESS ORGANIZATIONS § 10.32).

If limited partners vote on these issues, do they risk personal liability for at least some of the limited partnership's obligations? Consider § 303 of RULPA (1976) and RULPA (1985).

2. CONTROL OF THE ENTITY GENERAL PARTNER

ROBERT W. HAMILTON, CORPORATE GENERAL PARTNERS OF LIMITED PARTNERSHIPS

1 J. Small & Emerging Bus. L. 73, 78–87 (1997).

A limited partnership with a corporation as the sole general partner creates a totally different kind of entity than the traditional limited partnership. If the general partner is only marginally capitalized, the limited partnership becomes a limited liability entity not unlike a corporation. No individual is personally liable for the firm's debts. Most of the capital is provided by passive investors who, as limited partners, have no right to participate in management. Furthermore, control of the limited partnership is vested solely in the hands of the corporate general partner; in turn, control of that entity may be vested exclusively in the persons who organize the venture but provide only a small fraction of the capital needed by the enterprise. Since there is no legal prohibition against limited partners serving as shareholders, directors, or officers of the corporate general partner, organizers of the venture also may participate in the sharing of profits and losses as limited partners as well as through the corporate general partner.

What was the incentive that gave rise to the rather sudden development of corporate general partners beginning in about 1970? The answer, in a word, is taxes; federal income taxes, to be precise. The 1970s was the era of tax shelters. A business form was needed that assured that losses could be passed through to investors, that investors would have no personal responsibility for losses, and that the promoters of the tax shelter could run things without personal responsibility for debts and losses arising when the business ultimately collapsed. The limited partnership with a corporate general partner filled this need perfectly. During the 1970s, many thousands of real estate and oil and gas ventures were created in the limited partnership form primarily to provide tax deductions for affluent professionals and investors based on tax deductions for depreciation in real estate ventures, and for tangible and intangible drilling expenses and depletion in oil and gas ventures.

The era of tax shelters ended with the enactment of the Tax Reform Act of 1986. However, the changes in marginal tax rates for individuals and corporations made in that statute opened up entirely new tax saving devices that utilized limited partnerships with corporate general partners. * * * As a result, the creation of limited partnerships with corporate general partners continued at a faster rate after 1986 than before, despite the closing of tax shelters.

* * *

* * * [W]here limited partnerships are used today, it is the norm to use a corporation as the sole general partner. Probably the most common allocation of financial benefits is ninety-nine percent to the limited partners and one percent to the general partner. In these situations, the general partner is usually under the direct control of some but not all of the limited partners. This ninety-nine to one division minimizes the tax disadvantages * * *.

* * *

A corporate general partner differs from an individual general partner in several basic respects. * * * First, a corporate general partner is subject to the control of somebody else. With an individual as a general partner, there is no doubt as to whose decisions will be evaluated under applicable principles of fiduciary duty. Where a corporate general partner is involved, the decision maker may be a panel of individuals or a single person whose identity may or may not be known to the limited partners and whose financial interest in the limited partnership may be great or may be small.

Second, it is relatively easy to control transfers of managerial authority to third persons when individual general partners are involved. Restrictions on the transfer of general partnership interests without the consent of the limited partners appear both in statutes and in limited partnership agreements. While it may be possible to evade these limitations through a delegation of duties rather than an assignment of the interest itself, such a delegation does not eliminate the continuing responsibility of the general partner. In contrast, a corporate general partner is inherently an economic entity which itself may be purchased or sold. The individuals involved in the ownership and management of the business of the corporate general partner may change without a change in the identity of the general partner itself. The simplest example is the sale of shares by the shareholders of the general partner to an unrelated third person. The same result may be achieved through mergers or other transactions that arguably do not involve a sale or transfer at all. Thus, a corporate general partner is unlike an individual general partner in that control may be shifted from one group to another without apparently affecting the corporate general partner's continuous existence. From the standpoint of the inactive investors who are the limited partners, the identity of those in control of the general partner is usually more important than the formal identity of the general partner itself.

Third, a corporate general partner may be entirely acceptable and responsible as a general partner even though its assets are nominal or relatively insignificant in comparison to the size of the business it is managing. This is likely where the shareholders or managers of the corporate general partner also own substantial limited partnership interests. A claim of breach of fiduciary duty against a general partner is not worth very much if the general partner itself is a corporation with nominal assets. If there is to be recovery, it must be based on a theory that holds the parties that manage the general partner liable for the general partner's breach of duty.

Fourth, even if a corporate general partner is reasonably capitalized at the outset, subsequent transactions may bleed off these assets to the owners of the corporation without the consent of the limited partnership and without involving a fraudulent conveyance but greatly increasing the potential risks to the limited partners.

––––––––

By definition, a limited partnership has at least one general partner who is subject to unlimited personal liability for the debts of the venture. *See, e.g.*, RULPA (1985) §§ 101(7), 403(b). As the prior excerpt discusses, however, what if the general partner is an entity with limited liability of its own (e.g., a corporation)? Further, what if the managers of that entity general partner are also limited partners in the limited partnership? Can the control exercised by the managers over the entity general partner—in their positions as managers of the entity general partner—be "imputed" to them in their limited partner roles? If so, the control rule may be violated. Alternatively, perhaps liability for the limited partnership's obligations extends only to the entity general partner itself.

Some courts resisted the concept of entity general partners and the notion of limited liability for limited partners who participated in the control of such entities (usually as managers or controlling owners). The case of *Delaney v. Fidelity Lease Limited*, 526 S.W.2d 543 (Tex. 1975), is illustrative. In *Delaney*, a limited partnership was formed with a corporate general partner, Interlease Corporation. Interlease's sole officers, directors, and shareholders were W.S. Crombie, Jr., Alan Kahn, and William D. Sanders—individuals who were also limited partners in the limited partnership. *See id.* at 544. Creditors of the limited partnership sued for breach of a lease agreement, naming as defendants the limited partnership itself, Interlease, and all of the limited partners. The creditors alleged that Crombie, Kahn, and Sanders controlled the business of the limited partnership through their managerial roles in Interlease. *See id.* at 544–45. In response, Crombie, Kahn, and Sanders argued that they acted only as representatives of Interlease and that the corporation, Interlease, actually controlled the business of the limited partnership. *See id.* at 545. The court expressed concern that "the statutory requirement of at least one general partner with general liability in a limited partnership [could] be circumvented or vitiated by limited partners operating the partnership through a corporation with minimum capitalization and therefore minimum liability." *Id.* at 546. Moreover, the *Delaney* court held that "the personal liability, which attaches to a limited partner when 'he takes part in the control and management of the business,' cannot be evaded merely by acting through a corporation." *Id.* at 545.

These days, the use of entity general partners, and the provision of limited liability to limited partners who participate in the control of such entities, is far less controversial. Indeed, due in no small part to the evolution of limited partnership statutes, *Delaney*-like antagonism has largely disappeared.

PROBLEM

Assume that a dispute with facts identical to the *Delaney* facts described above arises in a jurisdiction that has adopted RULPA (1985).

(a) Under limited partnership law, what are the arguments for holding Crombie, Kahn, and Sanders individually liable for the limited partnership's breach of the lease agreement? What defenses can Crombie, Kahn, and Sanders raise? *See* RULPA (1985) §§ 101(5), (7), (11), 303(a), (b)(1), (c).

(b) Assume that the general partner was an LLC rather than a corporation. Assume further that Crombie, Kahn, and Sanders were acting as the sole managing members of that LLC. Does your analysis change? *See* RULPA (1985) §§ 101(5), (7), (11), 303(a), (b)(1), (c); *cf.* ULPA (2001) § 102(8), (11), (14).

(c) Putting aside limited partnership law, is there another legal theory that might reach Crombie, Kahn, and Sanders individually? What evidence would be needed to support such a theory?

NOTES

(1) Limited partners who participate in the control of an entity general partner should seek to ensure that third parties are aware of the capacity in which the limited partners are acting (e.g., the limited partners are acting solely as managers of the entity general partner). In *Gonzalez v. Chalpin*, 565 N.E.2d 1253 (N.Y. 1990)—a case decided before New York adopted a safe

harbor provision comparable to RULPA (1985) § 303(b)(1)—Excel was a New York limited partnership with one individual general partner (Lipkin), one corporate general partner (Tribute), and one limited partner (Chalpin). Chalpin was also the president, sole shareholder, and director of Tribute. Gonzalez was a creditor of the limited partnership who attempted to impose individual liability on Chalpin. Chalpin defended by arguing that his actions on Excel's behalf were performed only in his capacity as an officer of Tribute. *See id.* at 1253–54. The court rejected Chalpin's defense:

> Irrefutably, individual liability should not be imposed on a limited partner merely because that person happens also to be an officer, director and/or shareholder of a corporate general partner (*see, Frigidaire Sales Corp. v. Union Props.*, 88 Wash.2d 400, 562 P.2d 244). But that is not this case. Moreover and conversely, a limited partner who "takes part in the control of" the limited partnership's business should not automatically be insulated from individual liability merely by benefit of status as an officer and sole owner of the corporate general partner. That is this case.
>
> A limited partner who assumes such a dual capacity rightly bears a heavy burden when seeking to elude personal liability. For once a plaintiff meets the threshold burden of proving that a limited partner took an active individual part in effectuating the limited partnership's interests, the fulcrum shifts. The limited partner in such a dual capacity must then, at least, prove that any relevant actions taken were performed solely in the capacity as officer of the general partner.
>
> Defendant in this case failed to adjust to the shift and did not overcome the proof of involvement and responsibility for his actions undertaken in his individual capacity. * * * [T]here is no evidence that Chalpin ever asserted his identity and authority as a corporate officer of Tribute when conducting Excel's affairs with Gonzalez— except his own testimony, which was expressly discredited and characterized as unbelievable by the trial court. The clinching documentary evidence shows Chalpin signing Excel's checks in payment to Gonzalez in his own name and without naming Tribute or indicating that he was signing in any representative capacity.

Id. at 1254–55; *see also* Zeiger v. Wilf, 755 A.2d 608, 619 (N.J. Super. Ct. App. Div. 2000) (involving a manager of a corporate general partner who failed to consistently identify himself as a manager of the general partner when he acted on behalf of the limited partnership, but refusing to impose personal liability because "plaintiff was at all times fully aware of what [the manager] was doing and how [the manager] was doing it"); *id.* at 618–19 ("[T]here is no claim that plaintiff was misled, or that he relied on some impression that [the manager] was a general partner * * *. A failure to comply with some designated formality might have had some significance if, at any time or in any way, it misled plaintiff or prejudiced him. But, as we have noted several times, that is simply not the case.").

(2) For cases refusing to impose personal liability on limited partners who participated in the control of an entity general partner, see Western Camps, Inc. v. Riverway Ranch Enters., 138 Cal. Rptr. 918 (Ct. App. 1977); Zeiger v. Wilf, 755 A.2d 608 (N.J. Super. Ct. App. Div. 2000); Frigidaire Sales Corp. v. Union Props., Inc., 562 P.2d 244 (Wash. 1977).

G. FIDUCIARY DUTIES

1. GENERAL PARTNERS

RULPA (1985) does not explicitly address the topic of general partner fiduciary duties. Instead, as a result of the linkage created by RULPA (1985) § 403 (as well as § 1105), general partnership law is imported to deal with the topic. UPA § 21 and RUPA § 404, in other words, wind up governing fiduciary duty issues for general partners in limited partnerships. Thus, the fiduciary duty material that you studied in the general partnership area is important in the limited partnership area as well. Consistent with its "delinkage" theme, ULPA (2001) § 408 specifically addresses general partner fiduciary duties in a manner that is nearly identical to RUPA § 404.

Despite the linkage of RULPA (1985) to general partnership law, the topic of general partner duties in the limited partnership setting does present its own issues. First, although the subject of contractually modifying fiduciary duties arises in the general partnership and limited partnership contexts, most of the legal developments on this subject have occurred in the limited partnership area. Second, when a general partner of a limited partnership is a business entity, managers of the entity may personally owe fiduciary duties to the limited partners and the limited partnership.

As you learned in the general partnership materials, partners have broad latitude to modify traditional fiduciary duties by contract. That latitude clearly applies to the limited partnership context as well:

> Delaware's limited partnership jurisprudence begins with the basic premise that, *unless limited by the partnership agreement*, the general partner has the fiduciary duty to manage the partnership in its interest and in the interests of the limited partners. That qualified statement necessarily marries common law fiduciary duties to contract theory when it comes to considering actions undertaken in the limited partnership context. Thus, I think it a correct statement of law that principles of contract preempt fiduciary principles where the parties to a limited partnership have made their intentions to do so plain.

> * * *

In short, I think that under Delaware limited partnership law a claim of breach of fiduciary duty must first be analyzed in terms of the operative governing instrument—the partnership agreement—and only where that document is silent or ambiguous, or where principles of equity are implicated, will a Court begin to look for guidance from the statutory default rules, traditional notions of fiduciary duties, or other extrinsic evidence. * * *

Sonet v. Timber Co., 722 A.2d 319, 322, 324 (Del. Ch. 1998); *see also* Continental Ins. Co. v. Rutledge & Co., 750 A.2d 1219, 1236 n.37 (Del. Ch. 2000) ("Many opt for the limited partnership form in Delaware precisely in order to embrace this [contractual] flexibility. * * * [P]arties, otherwise unwilling to shoulder fiduciary burdens, maintain the opportunity to form limited partnerships precisely because the parties can contract around some or all of the fiduciary duties the general partner typically owes the limited partners.").

Until 2004, the Delaware Revised Uniform Limited Partnership Act ("DRULPA") stated that a "partner's or other person's duties and liabilities may be expanded or restricted by provisions in the partnership agreement." DRULPA § 17–1101(d)(2). In *Gotham Partners, L.P. v. Hallwood Realty Partners*, 817 A.2d 160 (Del. 2002), the Supreme Court of Delaware strongly suggested that this statutory language did not permit the *elimination* of fiduciary duties:

The Vice Chancellor's summary judgment opinion in this case, however, creates a separate problem. We refer to one aspect of the Vice Chancellor's discussion of the [DRULPA] in his summary judgment opinion in this case where he stated that section 17–1101(d)(2) "expressly authorizes the *elimination*, modification or enhancement of * * * fiduciary duties in the written agreement governing the limited partnership." It is at least the second time the Court of Chancery has stated in dicta that DRULPA at 6 *Del. C.* § 17–1101(d)(2) permits a limited partnership agreement to *eliminate* fiduciary duties.

Because the Vice Chancellor's summary judgment order in this matter has not been appealed, his opinion on this point is not before us for review on this appeal. In our view, however, this dictum should not be ignored because it could be misinterpreted in future cases as a correct rule of law. Accordingly, in the interest of avoiding the perpetuation of a questionable statutory interpretation that could be relied upon adversely by courts, commentators and practitioners in the future, we are constrained to draw attention to the statutory language and the underlying general principle in our jurisprudence that scrupulous adherence to fiduciary duties is normally expected.

Section 17–1101(d)(2) states: "the partner's or other person's duties and liabilities may be *expanded* or *restricted* by provisions in the partnership agreement." There is no mention in § 17–1101(d)(2), or elsewhere in DRULPA at 6 *Del. C.,* ch. 17, that a limited partnership agreement may *eliminate* the fiduciary duties or liabilities of a general partner.

Finally, we note the historic cautionary approach of the courts of Delaware that efforts by a fiduciary to escape a fiduciary duty, whether by a corporate director or officer or other type of trustee, should be scrutinized searchingly. Accordingly, although it is not appropriate for us to express an advisory opinion on a matter not before us, we simply raise a note of concern and caution relating to this dubious dictum in the Vice Chancellor's summary judgment opinion.

Id. at 167–68.

Two years after *Gotham Partners*, the Delaware legislature amended DRULPA § 17–1101 (effective August 1, 2004). The statute now provides that "[a] partner's or other person's duties may be expanded or restricted or eliminated by provisions in the partnership agreement; provided that the partnership agreement may not eliminate the implied contractual covenant of good faith and fair dealing." DRULPA § 17–1101(d); *see id.* § 17–1101(f). The statute also states that "[i]t is the policy of this chapter [on limited partnerships] to give maximum effect to the principle of freedom of contract and to the enforceability of partnership agreements." *Id.* § 17–1101(c).

NOTES

(1) With respect to freedom of contract in the limited partnership setting, other states may be unwilling to go as far as Delaware. *See, e.g.*, Labovitz v. Dolan, 545 N.E.2d 304, 313 (Ill. App. 1989) ("Defendants cite no authority, and we find none, for the proposition that there can be an *a priori* waiver of fiduciary duties in a partnership—be it general or limited."). Are there any limits on partners' contractual freedom under RULPA (1985)? Under ULPA (2001)? *See* RULPA (1985) §§ 101(7), 1105; RUPA § 103; ULPA (2001) § 110.

(2) The relationship between claims asserting a breach of fiduciary duty and claims asserting a breach of the implied covenant of good faith and fair dealing has become increasingly important in limited partnership and other business disputes. This is particularly true in jurisdictions, such as Delaware, that permit fiduciary duties, but not the implied covenant, to be eliminated by contract. *See, e.g.*, DRULPA § 17–1101(d). When fiduciary duties are eliminated, courts will need to decide the extent to which the implied covenant can be used to remedy allegations of unfair or abusive conduct. For

more on the implied covenant, see the "Note on Gerber and the Implied Covenant Under Delaware Law" in Chapter 20, Section G(2).

(3) Reconsider the general partnership materials on the topic of contractually modifying fiduciary duties. *See* Chapter 3, Section E(2)(c). Is the case for allowing contractual modification or elimination of fiduciary duties stronger or weaker in the limited partnership context?

(4) General partners may have an affirmative duty to disclose information to limited partners, even in the absence of a demand for information by the limited partners. The Minnesota decision of *Appletree Square I Limited Partnership v. Investmark, Inc.*, 494 N.W.2d 889 (Minn. App. 1993), is illustrative:

> This appeal [which apparently involved the sale of an office building by the general partners to the limited partners] turns on whether respondents [the sellers] had a fiduciary duty to disclose to appellants [the purchasers] the presence and danger of asbestos.
> * * *
>
> Absent a fiduciary relationship, one party to a transaction has "no duty to disclose material facts to the other." *Midland Nat'l Bank of Mpls. v. Perranoski*, 299 N.W.2d 404, 413 (Minn.1980). In this case, appellants and respondents were partners in a limited partnership. The relationship of partners is fiduciary and partners are held to high standards of integrity in their dealings with each other. Parties in a fiduciary relationship must disclose material facts to each other. Where a fiduciary relationship exists, silence may constitute fraud. Under the common law, respondents had a duty to disclose information regarding asbestos if they knew about it.
>
> The trial court held that the Uniform Limited Partnership Act changed the common law duties of disclosure. Minn.Stat. § 322A.28(2) [analogous to RULPA (1985) § 305] states that limited partners have the right, "upon reasonable demand," to obtain information from the general partners. This statute mirrors the disclosure requirement in the Uniform Partnership Act and should be interpreted similarly. The trial court held that because appellants did not demand information about asbestos, respondents had no obligation to disclose the information.
>
> The trial court's holding is contradicted by a proper interpretation of the disclosure statute. Minn.Stat. § 322A.28(2) addresses the narrow duty of partners to respond to requests for information. It does not negate a partner's broad common law duty to disclose all material facts. *See* H. Reuschlein and W. Gregory, *Handbook on the Law of Agency and Partnership*, 285 (1979) (the duty to render information is not the same as the duty to disclose). This view has been accepted by other jurisdictions that have adopted the uniform acts governing general and limited

partnerships. Minn.Stat. § 322A.28(2) did not eliminate respondents' common law duty to disclose material information to their partners.

Id. at 892–93.

(5) RULPA (1985) § 107 states that "[e]xcept as provided in the partnership agreement, a partner may lend money to and transact other business with the limited partnership and, subject to other applicable law, has the same rights and obligations with respect thereto as a person who is not a partner." *See also* ULPA (2001) § 112 (substantially the same); RUPA § 404(f) (substantially the same). In *BT-I v. Equitable Life Assurance Society*, 89 Cal. Rptr. 2d 811 (Ct. App. 1999), the court indicated that this section does not alter a general partner's fiduciary duties:

> We cannot discern anything in the purpose of Corporations Code section 15617 [analogous to RULPA (1985) § 107] that suggests an intent to affect a general partner's fiduciary duty to limited partners. Under the prior limited partnership rule, limited partners were prohibited from making secured loans to the partnership and any collateral received could be set aside as a fraud upon creditors. Corporations Code section 15617 is identical to Uniform Limited Partnership Act (1976) section 107, which was enacted to remove the fraudulent conveyances prohibition from the limited partnership law and leave the question to the general fraudulent conveyances statute. This change hardly sanctions Equitable's self-dealing.

Id. at 818; *see also* ULPA (2001) § 112 cmt. ("This section has no impact on a general partner's duty * * * [to] refrain[ ] from acting as or for an adverse party * * * and means rather that this Act does not discriminate against a creditor of a limited partnership that happens also to be a partner.").

IN RE USACAFES, L.P.

Court of Chancery of Delaware, 1991.
600 A.2d 43.

ALLEN, CHANCELLOR.

These consolidated actions arise out of the October 1989 purchase by Metsa Acquisition Corp. of substantially all of the assets of USACafes, L.P., a Delaware limited partnership (the "Partnership") at a cash price of $72.6 million or $10.25 per unit. Plaintiffs are holders of limited partnership units. They bring these cases as class actions on behalf of all limited partnership unitholders except defendants. The relief sought includes, *inter alia*, the imposition of constructive trusts on certain funds received by defendants in connection with the Metsa sale and an award of damages to the class resulting from the sale.

The Partnership was formed in the 1986 reorganization of the business of USACafes, Inc., a Nevada corporation. Also formed as part of that reorganization was USACafes General Partner, Inc. (the "General Partner"), a Delaware corporation that acts as the general partner of the Partnership. Both the Partnership and the General Partner are named as defendants in this action. A second category of defendants is composed of Sam and Charles Wyly, brothers who together own all of the stock of the General Partner, sit on its board, and who also personally, directly or indirectly, own 47% of the limited partnership units of the Partnership. Sam Wyly chairs the Board of the General Partner.

The third category of defendants are four other individuals who sit on the board of directors of the General Partner. All of these persons are alleged to have received substantial cash payments, loan forgiveness, or other substantial personal benefits in connection with the 1989 Metsa purchase.

The last of the defendants is Metsa, the buyer of the Partnership's assets. Metsa is not alleged to be related in any way to the Wylys or any other defendant except as a buyer in the transaction under review.

THE THEORIES OF THE AMENDED COMPLAINT

The amended complaint arrays four theories of liability against these defendants. The first and most central theory involves an alleged breach of the duty of loyalty. In essence, it claims that the sale of the Partnership's assets was at a low price, favorable to Metsa, because the directors of the General Partner all received substantial side payments that induced them to authorize the sale of the Partnership assets for less than the price that a fair process would have yielded. * * * In sum, it is alleged that between $15 and $17 million was or will be paid to the directors and officers of the General Partner by or with the approval of Metsa; those payments are alleged to constitute financial inducements to the directors of the General Partner to refrain from searching for a higher offer to the Partnerships. Plaintiffs add that, even assuming that Metsa was the buyer willing to pay the best price, some part at least of these "side payments" should have gone to the Partnership.

The second theory of liability reflected in the amended complaint asserts that the General Partner was (or the directors of the General Partner were) not sufficiently informed to make a valid business judgment on the sale. This theory focuses upon the absence of shopping of the Partnership's assets, or of any post-agreement market check procedure, and on the alleged weakness of the investment banker's opinion. Thus, this claim is that the defendants were uninformed when they authorized the sale to Metsa.

* * *

THE PENDING MOTIONS

* * * [T]he Wyly defendants and the other director defendants move under Rule 12(b)(6) to dismiss the breach of fiduciary duty claims in the amended complaint asserting that, while the General Partner admittedly did owe fiduciary duties to the limited partners, they as directors of the General Partner owe no such duties to those persons. The whole remedy of the limited partners for breach of the duties of loyalty and care, it is said, is against the General Partner only and not its directors.

* * *

I turn first to the director defendants' motion to dismiss for failure to state a claim with respect to the sale of the Partnership's assets. The gist of this motion is the assertion that the directors of the General Partner owed the limited partners no duty of loyalty or care. In their view their only duty of loyalty was to the General Partner itself and to *its* shareholders (*i.e.*, the Wyly brothers). Thus, in alleging that the director defendants breached duties of loyalty and care running to them, the directors say the limited partners have asserted a legal nullity.

In my opinion the assertion by the directors that the independent existence of the corporate General Partner is inconsistent with their owing fiduciary duties directly to limited partners is incorrect. Moreover, even were it correct, their position on this motion would have to be rejected in any event because the amended complaint expressly alleges that they personally participated in the alleged breach by the General Partner itself, which admittedly did owe loyalty to the limited partners.

The first basis of this holding is the more significant. While I find no corporation law precedents directly addressing the question whether directors of a corporate general partner owe fiduciary duties to the partnership and its limited partners, the answer to it seems to be clearly indicated by general principles and by analogy to trust law. I understand the principle of fiduciary duty, stated most generally, to be that one who controls property of another may not, without implied or express agreement, intentionally use that property in a way that benefits the holder of the control to the detriment of the property or its beneficial owner. There are, of course, other aspects—a fiduciary may not waste property even if no self interest is involved and must exercise care even when his heart is pure—but the central aspect of the relationship is, undoubtedly, fidelity in the control of property for the benefit of another.

The law of trusts represents the earliest and fullest expression of this principle in our law, but courts of equity have extended it appropriately to achieve substantial justice in a wide array of situations. Thus, corporate directors, even though not strictly trustees, were early on regarded as fiduciaries for corporate stockholders. When control over corporate property was recognized to be in the hands of shareholders who controlled the enterprise, the fiduciary obligation was found to extend to such persons as well.

While the parties cite no case treating the specific question whether directors of a corporate general partner are fiduciaries for the limited partnership, a large number of trust cases do stand for a principle that would extend a fiduciary duty to such persons in certain circumstances. The problem comes up in trust law because [modern] corporations may serve as trustees of express trusts. Thus, the question has arisen whether directors of a corporate trustee may personally owe duties of loyalty to *cestui que trusts* of the corporation. A leading authority states the accepted answer:

> The directors and officers of [a corporate trustee] are certainly under a duty to the beneficiaries not to convert to their own use property of the trust administered by the corporation. * * * Furthermore, the directors and officers are under a duty to the beneficiaries of trusts administered by the corporation not to cause the corporation to misappropriate the property. * * * The breach of trust need not, however, be a misappropriation * * *. Any officer [director cases are cited in support here] who knowingly causes the corporation to commit a breach of trust causing loss * * * is personally liable to the beneficiary of the trust. * * *

> Moreover, a director or officer of a trust institution who improperly acquires an interest in the property of a trust administered by the institution is subject to personal liability. He is accountable for any profit * * *. Even where the trustee [itself] is not liable, however, because it had no knowledge that the director was making the purchase * * *, the director * * * is liable to the beneficiaries. * * * The directors and officers are in a fiduciary relation not merely to the [corporation] * * * but to the beneficiaries of the trust administered by the [corporation].

4 A. Scott & W. Fratcher, *The Law of Trusts* § 326.3, at 304–306 (4th ed. 1989) (citing cases) ["Scott on Trusts"].

The theory underlying fiduciary duties is consistent with recognition that a director of a corporate general partner bears such a duty towards the limited partnership. That duty, of course, extends only to dealings with the partnership's property or affecting its business, but, so limited, its existence seems apparent in any number of circumstances. Consider, for example, a classic self-dealing transaction: assume that a majority of the board of the corporate general partner formed a new entity and then caused the general partner to sell partnership assets to the new entity at an unfairly small price, injuring the partnership and its limited partners. Can it be imagined that such persons have not breached a duty to the partnership itself? And does it not make perfect sense to say that the gist of the offense is a breach of the equitable duty of loyalty that is placed upon a fiduciary? It appears true that the same result might be rationalized as aider and abettor liability, but I am unsure what such indirection would add that is useful where a self-dealing transaction or other diversion of partnership property is alleged. Indeed in some instances, for example the use by a director of confidential information concerning the partnership's business not yet known by the board of the general partner, there may be no breach of loyalty or care by the general partner itself to abet, yet there may be director liability to the partnership by the director. *Cf.* cases cited at 4 *Scott on Trusts* § 326.3, at n. 7.

Two courts have, in fact, held a sole shareholder/director of a corporate general partner personally liable for breach of fiduciary duty to limited partners, although without much discussion of the issue here considered. *See Tobias v. First City National Bank and Trust Co.*, 709 F.Supp. 1266, 1277–78 (S.D.N.Y.1989); *Remenchik v. Whittington*, Tex.Ct.App., 757 S.W.2d 836 (1988); *see also In re Integrated Resources, Inc.*, Case No. 90–B–10411 (CB) (Bankr.S.D.N.Y. Oct. 22, 1990) (controlling shareholder held liable).

While these authorities extend the fiduciary duty of the general partner to a controlling shareholder, they support as well, the recognition of such duty in directors of the General Partner who, more directly than a controlling shareholder, are in control of the partnership's property. It is not necessary here to attempt to delineate the full scope of that duty. It may well not be so broad as the duty of the director of a corporate trustee.[3] But it surely entails the duty not to use control over the partnership's property to advantage the corporate director at the expense of the partnership. That is what is alleged here.

The amended complaint contains the following allegations:

16. The General Partner and its directors, the named individual defendants, are in a fiduciary relationship with the plaintiffs and the other Unitholders of USACafes * * *.

17. * * * Through their unit ownership and executive positions [the director defendants] have dominated and controlled the affairs of USACafes. Among other things, they have * * * failed to adequately solicit or consider alternative proposals for USACafes, have failed to negotiate in good faith to enhance Unitholders' values and, instead, have agreed to sell all of its assets to Metsa, which will result in the minority limited partners receiving the grossly inadequate price of $10.25 per

---

[3] For example, I imply nothing on such questions as whether a director of a corporate general partner might be held liable directly to the partnership on a "corporate" opportunity theory or for waste of partnership assets (two possible consequences of characterizing such persons as fiduciaries for the partnership).

Unit. As inducement to the individual defendants to agree to the Metsa proposal, Metsa offered to pay and the individual defendants agreed to accept, certain additional payments (approximately $17 million) that were not offered to the classes * * *.

19. The individual defendants and the General Partner participated in the wrongdoing complained of in order to divert the valuable assets of USACafes for their own benefit by entering into highly favorable compensation arrangements with Metsa as part of the liquidation of USACafes.

I therefore conclude that the amended complaint does allege facts which if true establish that the director defendants have breached fiduciary obligations imposed upon them as directors of a Delaware corporation or have participated in a breach of such duties by the General Partner. The amended complaint does, in my opinion, state a claim upon which relief can be granted.

* * *

The motions of the individual defendants, the General Partner, and the Partnership to dismiss the claims arising out of the sale of the Partnership's assets is denied. * * *

NOTES

(1) "Since the corporate general partner has complete control over the management of the limited partnership, and the managers of the corporation have complete power over the general partner, it seems plausible to impose the fiduciary duties owed by the general partner upon those managers. The justification for this conclusion is that the managers of the corporate general partner have complete control over the management of the limited partnership and therefore should have responsibility for abuse of that control to persons relying on them. Indeed, this is the classic situation in which courts imply the existence of fiduciary duty." Robert W. Hamilton, *Corporate General Partners of Limited Partnerships*, 1 J. OF SMALL & EMERGING BUS. L. 73, 87–88 (1997).

(2) With a corporate general partner, the following assertions seem clear: (1) the officers and directors of the corporation owe fiduciary duties to the corporation; and (2) the corporation itself, as the general partner, owes fiduciary duties to the limited partners and the limited partnership. When a court concludes that the individual officers and directors of the corporation also owe fiduciary duties to the limited partners and the limited partnership, doesn't that conclusion disregard the separate entity status of the corporation? Is that appropriate?

(3) Assume that a corporate general partner has breached its fiduciary duty to the limited partnership. Short of concluding directly that the

corporation's officers and directors owe fiduciary duties to the limited partnership, are there other theories for holding the corporation's officers and directors liable for the general partner's breach?

(4) Assume that a corporation serves as the general partner of a limited partnership. Assume further that an officer of the corporation discovers a business opportunity that would be of interest to the corporation and the limited partnership. To whom does the officer owe a fiduciary duty? Should the officer disclose the opportunity to the corporation? To the limited partnership? To both? Does *USACafes* help to answer these questions? Consider the observations of two commentators:

> *USACafes* was subject to criticism for relying on trust law principles while ignoring a fundamental distinction between the trustee's fiduciary duty of undivided loyalty and the contractual relationship between general and limited partners. A general partner and its affiliated limited partnership will have adverse or competing interests on many matters. When the two interests diverge, it is unclear under *USACafes* how the director is to balance his or her fiduciary duties to the corporate general partner and the partnership. If the higher duty is owed to the limited partners, by what standards is the "lesser" fiduciary duty to the corporation to be judged? * * * As a practical matter, *USACafes* left officers and directors in a position of substantial risk in any interested transaction, because of the likelihood that their duties to the limited partners of the partnership would always be given precedence over their duties to the corporate general partner.

Robert B. Robbins, *The Fiduciary Duties of Directors of Corporate General Partners: Ten Years After USACafes*, SH067 ALI-ABA 195, 205, 209 (2003).

> * * * The general partner obviously owes fiduciary duties to the limited partnership and to the limited partners. Corporate officers and directors also owe fiduciary duties to the shareholders of a corporate partner. These fiduciary duties may conflict. This conflict is likely to be particularly intense when there are shareholders of the corporate general partner who have no direct financial interest in the limited partnership. Indeed, one can argue that these duties have the same degree of intensity: If the shareholders of the corporate general partner gain more from a breach of fiduciary duty than the limited partners lose, it should be the duty of the managers of the corporate general partner to breach duties to the limited partners and maximize the gain to the corporate general partner. However, the rhetoric of fiduciary duties in this situation appears to indicate the contrary: The duties owed by the corporate general partner to the limited partners actually trump the duties owed by the officers and directors of the corporate general partner to the shareholders. Cases state that a corporation that is the sole general partner owes "the duty * * * to exercise the utmost good faith, fairness, and loyalty" for the benefit of the limited partnership. [*See*,

e.g., Boxer v. Husky Oil Co., 429 A.2d 995, 997 (Del. Ch. 1981).] This statement seems to require that officers and directors of the corporate general partner favor their duties to the limited partnership and to the limited partners above any duty to the shareholders.

* * *

* * * Any other rule leaves innocent parties without remedy, encourages directors to authorize breaches of fiduciary duty if they might profit personally from the breach, and almost certainly is inconsistent with the reasonable expectations of limited partners that invest capital in the venture.

Robert W. Hamilton, *Corporate General Partners of Limited Partnerships*, 1 J. OF SMALL & EMERGING BUS. L. 73, 87, 96 (1997).

(5) Does DRULPA § 17–1101(d) provide a way out of the *USACafes* thicket for managers of entity general partners? In *Brickell Partners v. Wise*, 794 A.2d 1 (Del. Ch. 2001), an affiliate of a corporate general partner sold assets to the limited partnership. Pursuant to the partnership agreement, a conflicts committee approved the transaction (the committee was comprised of directors of the corporate general partner). Limited partners sued the directors of the corporate general partner claiming that the directors could not fairly opine on the transaction because of their fiduciary duties to the corporation. *See id.* at 2–3. The *Brickell* court rejected the limited partners' claim:

* * * As this court has noted elsewhere, directors of corporate general partners occupy a strange and unsettling position. By definition, they find themselves in a position of on-going conflict because they owe fiduciary duties to the corporate general partner (on whose board they serve) and fiduciary duties to the limited partnership governed by the corporate general partner. Even when such directors have no material self-interest in the success of the corporate general partner as an entity or the partnership itself, they owe duties to two entities with potentially conflicting interests. * * *

* * *

Here, the plain and unambiguous language of * * * the Partnership Agreement displaces traditional fiduciary duty principles. In place of such principles, the Agreement provides limited partners solely with the protection of Conflicts and Audit Committee Review when [the corporate general partner] decides to seek "Special Approval" of a conflict transaction, as it did here. Such "Special Approval" is "conclusive[ ]" evidence of the "fair[ness] and reasonable[ness]" of a conflict transaction, and bars any challenge to the transaction based on the Agreement, other contracts, or default principles of law or equity. As a result, the plain language of the Agreement appears to compel a dismissal of the complaint * * *.

Id. at 4 (order of paragraphs reversed). Along these same lines, consider the following:

> * * * It is time to consider whether a partnership agreement should not contain a specific acknowledgement by the limited partners that the officers and directors of the corporate general partner owe duties both to the partnership and to the general partner, in connection with an agreement that those individuals will not be liable to the partnership for actions that they took in the good faith belief that the corporate general partner was acting in a manner consistent with its duties to the partnership. While provisions of this type are not yet customary, they fall squarely within the Delaware statute, and within the emerging line of Delaware cases that permit the partners of a limited partnership to define and to restrict the duties owed to the partnership by the partners and by persons associated with them.

Robert B. Robbins, *The Fiduciary Duties of Directors of Corporate General Partners: Ten Years After USACafes*, SH067 ALI-ABA 195, 210 (2003).

2. LIMITED PARTNERS

RULPA (1985) does not address the fiduciary duties of limited partners. In such circumstances, § 1105 indicates that general partnership law applies, but the general partnership statutes also fail to specifically address the duties of limited partners. Because RULPA (1985) § 101(8) defines "partner" to include a limited partner, one might argue (via linkage) that the general partnership law of "partner" fiduciary duties (e.g., UPA § 21; RUPA § 404) applies to limited partners as well. That results in a poor fit, however, as most limited partners do not exercise the degree of control over the business that typically calls for the imposition of fiduciary duties (due in large part, of course, to the control rule). These issues are discussed in the materials below.

KE PROPERTY MANAGEMENT INC. V. 275 MADISON MANAGEMENT CORP.

Court of Chancery of Delaware, 1993.
1993 WL 285900.

HARTNETT, VICE CHANCELLOR.

Although the procedural posture in this suit is complex, the gravamen of the suit is quite simple. The issue is the control of a limited partnership based in New York and whether, under the Partnership Agreement and New York law, the fraud by the agent of the managing general partner justified the general partner's removal by a limited partner.

There is no disputed fact that prevents summary judgment for the plaintiff, a general partner, on its claim that, as a matter of law, a limited partner affiliated with it was justified in removing the general managing partner because of the fraud committed by the agent of the partner that was removed.

* * *

The case is a procedural nightmare and is an example of the burden often placed on the Delaware courts by litigation arising from convoluted limited partnerships that have been formed in Delaware for a token fee.

THE PLEADINGS

I

The original plaintiff, KE Property Management Inc. ("KE Property"), one of the general partners of 275 Madison Associates L.P., a Delaware limited partnership ("the Partnership"), seeks a declaratory judgment that the purported removal of 275 Madison Management Corp. ("275 Madison Corp."), the managing general partner of the Partnership, by KJ Capital Management, Inc. ("KJ Capital"), an affiliate of plaintiff, was effective. It therefore seeks to enjoin 275 Madison Corp. from purporting to act as the managing general partner.

275 Madison Corp. has plead counterclaims against: (1) KE Property, the original plaintiff; (2) KJ Capital, one of the limited partners in the partnership; (3) Kawasaki Leasing International, Inc. ("Kawasaki Lender"), a lender to the partnership; and (4) seven other entities that purchased a portion of the loan to the partnership ("the Loan Participants"). KE Property, the original plaintiff, and KJ Capital, are affiliated and are collectively referred to as "The Kawasaki Partners."

* * *

THE FACTS

IV

The essential facts are undisputed. The Partnership was formed in October 1987 for the purpose of owning a building and a ground lease at 275 Madison Avenue in New York City. Originally, there were three general partners: Harry Skydell, Udi Toledano and Joseph Mizrachi. Skydell was the original managing general partner and he arranged for the Partnership to retain Hudson Park Management Co. ("Hudson Park"), an entity controlled by Skydell, to manage the building.

In 1988, KJ Capital invested $4 million in the Partnership and was admitted as a limited partner and its affiliate KE Property became a general partner. Two entities owned by the Nasser family, R.A.J.N. Corp. and Belmor Co., Inc. ("the Nasser Limited Partners"), invested $6 million in the Partnership and also became limited partners.

In February 1989, the Partnership borrowed $70 million from the Kawasaki Lender to refinance its existing obligations. This loan was secured by a mortgage on the building and ground lease. Portions of this loan were sold to the Loan Participants.

That same month, 275 Madison Corp. was formed to serve as managing general partner of the Partnership in lieu of Skydell. * * *

The original partnership agreement was revised in July 1989 to reflect the changes made among the partners. The Revised Partnership Agreement contemplated that Hudson Park, an entity controlled by Skydell, would continue to manage the building.

Between January and May 1990, Skydell misappropriated $2 million of Partnership funds by diverting money from the Partnership's accounts at Chase Manhattan Bank. 275 Madison Corp. claims that, although Skydell was its President at the time, he committed the fraud through Hudson Park, the manager of the building, rather than in his capacity as part-owner and officer of 275 Madison Corp. However, the signature cards for the Partnership's accounts from which the funds were siphoned showed, and a representative from Chase testified, that Skydell was authorized to sign in his capacity as a representative of the managing partner. On certain accounts, Skydell was the sole person with signatory authority while on others Toledano and Mizrachi—former general partners of the Partnership—also had signatory authority.

       * * *

In 1990 and 1991 the Partnership experienced financial difficulties and the Nassers negotiated with the Kawasaki Lender for a restructuring of the finances of the Partnership. On July 9, 1991, on behalf of itself and the Loan Participants, the Kawasaki Lender notified the Partnership that it was in default of the loan agreement and at risk of foreclosure. 275 Madison Corp. took the position that it would be in the best interests of the Partnership for the Partnership to seek protection from its creditors under the federal bankruptcy laws. However, KE Property refused to agree, allegedly because of improper loyalty to its affiliate the Kawasaki Lender in alleged violation of its fiduciary duty to the other partners.

On August 20, 1991, KJ Capital, an affiliate of KE Property, as one of the limited partners, sent 275 Madison Corp. a letter purportedly removing it as managing general partner. Paragraph 5.07(d) of the Partnership Agreement provides, in relevant part, that "the Limited Partners may * * * by a vote of not less than 25% of the Units then outstanding, expel any General Partner if he has * * * injured the Partnership as a result of his fraud or willful misconduct in the performance of his duties as a General Partner." KJ Capital claimed that Skydell's misappropriation of $2 million constituted fraud or willful misconduct on the part of 275 Madison Corp. in its capacity as the managing general partner of the Partnership. It is not disputed that 25% of the units outstanding favored the expulsion.

275 Madison Corp., however, claims that KJ Capital used Skydell's fraud as a pretext to remove it from its position as managing general partner to prevent 275 Madison Corp. from filing for bankruptcy on behalf of the Partnership. KJ Capital allegedly acted at the behest of the Kawasaki Lender in so doing.

On August 22, 1991, two days after its purported removal as managing general partner of the Partnership, 275 Madison Corp. filed a bankruptcy petition on behalf of the Partnership in the United States Bankruptcy Court for the Southern District of New York. * * * KE Property then brought this action seeking a declaratory judgment that the purported removal of 275 Madison Corp. as managing general partner by KJ Capital was effective and seeking an injunction prohibiting 275 Madison Corp. from acting on behalf of the Partnership.

* * *

In addition to its other defenses, 275 Madison Corp. argues that summary judgment should be denied because the Kawasaki entities acted in "bad faith" in that their real motivation in removing 275 Madison Corp. was to prevent it from taking the partnership into bankruptcy to block the foreclosure of the mortgage. Because * * * there is a presumption that the Kawasaki entities acted in good faith, defendant bears the burden of rebutting the presumption by showing the existence of bad faith.

275 Madison Corp.'s allegation of bad faith is predicated upon KJ Capital having owed a fiduciary duty to it. A general partner owes a fiduciary duty to its partners. It was, however, KJ Capital, a limited partner (rather than KE Property, a general partner) that acted to remove 275 Madison Corp. as managing general partner.

KJ Capital, a limited partner, is controlled by the same entity that controls KE Property, a general partner. This might be sufficient to impose on KJ Capital the same fiduciary duty that KE Property has as a general partner. It is not necessary to decide that issue, however, because although the Delaware Revised Uniform Limited Partnership Act does not specifically state that a limited partner owes a fiduciary duty to a general partner it, by reference to the Delaware Uniform Partnership Act, so provides.

6 *Del.C.* § 17–1105 states:

> In any case not provided for in [the Delaware Revised Uniform Limited Partnership Act] the Delaware Uniform Partnership Law and the rules of law and equity, including the Law Merchant, shall govern.

Under the Delaware Uniform Partnership Law all partners owe each other fiduciary obligations. Therefore, to the extent that a partnership agreement empowers a limited partner discretion to take actions affecting the governance of the limited partnership, the limited partner may be subject to the obligations of a fiduciary, including the obligation to act in good faith as to the other partners.

The Partnership Agreement does not leave the decision as to the removal of 275 Madison Corp. to the unlimited discretion of KJ Capital or any other partner, however. Instead, it provides that removal can only occur upon "fraud or willful conduct" injurious to the Partnership. As previously discussed, 275 Madison Corp. was legally guilty of "fraud or willful conduct" injurious to the Partnership because of the acts of its agent Skydell that are imputed to it.

An allegation of bad faith "raises essentially a question of fact," which means that such an allegation generally is sufficient to defeat a motion to dismiss or a motion for judgment on the pleadings. However, allegations unsupported by any competent evidence cannot defeat a motion for summary judgment. Where the non-moving party bears the burden of persuasion at trial, as 275 Madison Corp. does here as to overcoming the presumption of good faith, the non-moving party, after adequate opportunity for discovery, must introduce competent evidence which, if true, would rebut the presumption or summary judgment will be granted against it.

As noted above, the parties conducted extensive discovery on the issue of the propriety of 275 Madison Corp.'s removal in the bankruptcy proceedings. 275 Madison Corp. has not adduced any competent evidence to overcome the presumption of good faith of the Kawasaki Partners in removing 275 Madison Corp. All that 275 Madison Corp. has proffered is mere speculation as to what the Kawasaki Partners might do if they gain control of the enterprise. Such speculation cannot prevent the Kawasaki Partners from exerting their lawful right under the Partnership Agreement to remove 275 Madison Corp. for willful misconduct.

Summary judgment therefore must be granted to KE Property on its claim against 275 Madison Corp.

* * *

NOTES

(1) The analysis of the *KE Property* court was elaborated on in the later decision of *Bond Purchase, L.L.C. v. Patriot Tax Credit Properties, L.P.*, 746 A.2d 842 (Del. Ch. 1999). *Bond Purchase* involved a limited partnership that issued all of its limited partnership interests to an "Assignor Limited Partner." Third parties invested in the partnership by purchasing "BUC\$," which the partnership sold through its Assignor Limited Partner. A BUC was

a certificate that represented the assignment by the Assignor Limited Partner to the person or entity purchasing the BUC (a "BUC$holder") of all of the economic and substantially all of the ownership rights (except for record ownership and the right to vote directly on matters submitted to the limited partners for a vote) of one limited partnership interest. Bond was a BUC$holder who commenced a mini-tender offer for 4.9% of the outstanding BUC$. The partnership sued Bond, claiming that his mini-tender offer was coercive and deceptive. In reliance on *KE Property*, the partnership asserted that Bond's offer violated a fiduciary duty that he owed to the limited partners and BUC$holders. *See id.* at 847, 863. The court disagreed:

> In deciding whether a limited partner of a Delaware limited partnership owed a fiduciary duty to the general partner when removing the general partner pursuant to its contractual right under the partnership agreement, this Court in *K.E. Property Management* merely stated that "to the extent that a partnership agreement empowers a limited partner discretion to take actions affecting the governance of the limited partnership, the limited partner may be subject to the obligations of a fiduciary, including the obligation to act in good faith as to the other partners." In making this ruling, the Court relied on the proposition that under the Delaware Uniform Partnership Act ["DUPA"] all partners owe each other fiduciary obligations. The Court relied on this proposition because the Delaware Revised Uniform Limited Partnership Act does not specifically state whether a limited partner owes a fiduciary duty to a general partner and in such instances refers the Court to the DUPA. It is clear, however, through the Court's qualification of its ruling, that the *K.E. Property Management* Court was not adopting that proposition in its entirety but was limiting it to situations in which a "partnership agreement empowers a limited partner discretion to take actions affecting the governance of the limited partnership."

> Unlike the partnership agreement in *K.E. Property Management,* the Partnership Agreement does not grant BUC$holders any rights to take actions affecting the governance of the Partnership. Furthermore, Bond's mini-tender offer for 4.9% of the outstanding BUC$ will have no effect on the governance of the Partnership since, at this time, Bond only owns 5 of the 38,125 outstanding BUC$, and Bond's mini-tender offer is for only 4.9% of the Partnership's outstanding BUC$. In any event, Bond stipulated * * * that its proposed mini-tender offer would not affect the control of the Partnership. Finally, a fiduciary is typically one who is entrusted with the power to manage and control the property of another. As the holder of 5 BUC$ and in the absence of a provision in the Partnership Agreement granting BUC$holders the right to manage or control Partnership property, Bond stands in no such relationship to the other limited partners. Bond's mini-tender offer is akin to a minority shareholder making a mini-tender offer for a

corporation's stock—an action to which fiduciary duties would not normally apply. Therefore, in the absence of any provision in the Partnership Agreement engrafting fiduciary duties onto Bond, I conclude that Bond owes no fiduciary duties to the other limited partners or the other BUC\$holders.

Id. at 863–64; *cf.* Goldwasser v. Geller, 684 N.Y.S.2d 210, 210 (App. Div. 1999) ("Defendants-appellants, all limited partners in the partnership in which the nonappealing defendants were the general partners, assumed a fiduciary duty to plaintiff, also a limited partner aggrieved by the general partners' nonfeasance, when they took over managerial control of the partnership.").

(2) In *In re Villa West Associates*, 146 F.3d 798 (10th Cir. 1998), the court addressed the issue of limited partner fiduciary duties under Kansas law:

* * * Kansas courts have not directly addressed the issue of whether a limited partner owes fellow limited partners a fiduciary duty. However, the cases have clearly set forth what criteria must exist in order to establish a fiduciary relationship. *Gillespie v. Seymour*, 14 Kan.App.2d 563, 796 P.2d 1060 (1990), *rev'd in part on other grounds*, 250 Kan. 123, 823 P.2d 782 (1991), recites the necessary elements:

"It has been recognized that a fiduciary relationship between parties does not depend upon some technical relation created by, or defined in, law. It exists in cases where there has been a special confidence reposed in one who, in equity and good conscience, is bound to act in good faith and with due regard for the interests of the one reposing the confidence.

Fiduciary relationships recognized and enforceable in equity do not depend upon nomenclature; nor are they necessarily the product of any particular legal relationship. They may arise out of conduct of the parties evidencing an agreement to engage in a joint enterprise for the mutual benefit of the parties. But they necessarily spring from an attitude of trust and confidence and are based upon some form of agreement, either expressed or implied, from which it can be said the minds have met in a manner to create mutual obligations.

For the plainest of reasons, agreements establishing fiduciary relationships, if not in writing, must be clear and convincing. Because of the acuteness of the equitable remedies, courts will not reach out to establish legal relationships from which enforceable equitable rights may flow. A confidential relationship is never presumed, and the burden of proof is upon the party asserting it.

Mere concert of action, without more, does not establish a fiduciary relationship. Undoubtedly, parties may deal at arm's length for their mutual profit. It is only when, by their concerted action, they willingly and knowingly act for one another in a manner to impose mutual trust and confidence that a fiduciary relationship arises."

Id. at 1063 (quoting *Paul v. Smith*, 191 Kan. 163, 380 P.2d 421, 426 (1963)).

Summarizing the relevant considerations, the *Gillespie* court concluded that a "fiduciary relationship requires confidence of one in another and a certain inequity or dependence arising from weakness of age, mental strength, business intelligence, knowledge of facts involved, or other conditions which give one an advantage over the other." *Id.*

Villa West, 146 F.3d at 806–07.

(3) Can you articulate when a court is likely to hold that a limited partner owes a fiduciary duty? Is the analysis in *Villa West* consistent with *KE Properties*?

(4) Can a partnership agreement impose fiduciary duties on limited partners? In *Cantor Fitzgerald, L.P. v. Cantor*, No. 16297, 2000 WL 307370, at *19 (Del. Ch. Mar. 13, 2000), the court gave an affirmative answer to this question: "Nothing in DRULPA or our case law expressly prohibits a limited partnership agreement from providing that limited partners are subject to duties that the common law or equity does not independently impose upon them."

(5) ULPA (2001) § 305(a) states that "[a] limited partner does not have any fiduciary duty to the limited partnership or to any other partner solely by reason of being a limited partner." Under § 305(b), however, a limited partner "shall discharge the duties to the partnership and the other partners under this [Act] or under the partnership agreement and exercise any rights consistently with the obligation of good faith and fair dealing." The comment to § 305 states, in part, the following:

Fiduciary duty typically attaches to a person whose status or role creates significant power for that person over the interests of another person. Under this Act, limited partners have very limited power of any sort in the regular activities of the limited partnership and no power whatsoever justifying the imposition of fiduciary duties either to the limited partnership or fellow partners. It is possible for a partnership agreement to allocate significant managerial authority and power to a limited partner, but in that case the power exists not as a matter of status or role but rather as a matter of contract. The proper limit on such contract-based power is the obligation of good faith and fair dealing, not fiduciary duty, unless the partnership agreement itself expressly imposes a fiduciary duty or creates a role for a limited partner which, as a matter of other law, gives rise to a fiduciary duty. For example, if the partnership agreement makes a limited partner an agent for the limited partnership as to particular matters, the law of agency will impose fiduciary duties on the limited partner with respect to the limited partner's role as agent.

(6) RULPA (1985) and ULPA (2001) explicitly authorize derivative lawsuits. *See* RULPA (1985) §§ 1001–1004; ULPA (2001) §§ 1001–1005. As one leading treatise observed:

> Derivative suits in limited partnerships are generally easier to justify than in corporations (which have been the models for limited partnership derivative suits). Restraints on opportunistic behavior in many corporations are not present in many limited partnerships. General partners in most limited partnerships have permanent tenure; unlike corporate directors, they are not periodically elected. Most limited partnerships have no provision for removal of a general partner—except when state securities laws for public offerings have required a removal provision or when the limited partners have successfully negotiated for one. In contrast, corporate directors are usually removable by shareholders, at least for cause, and corporate officers are removable by directors. Often there is only one general partner in a limited partnership, with no collective decisionmaking to serve as a brake. Most corporations have several directors as well as several officers. There is no public market for the interests in most limited partnerships, so dissatisfied limited partners cannot follow "the Wall Street rule" and sell out. For the same reason, the market for entity control cannot operate for most limited partnerships. There is a public market for the shares of many corporations and therefore a market for control.

> With factors of this kind as background, most courts under [the 1916] U.L.P.A., and all legislatures under R.U.L.P.A., have authorized limited partner derivative suits * * *. At the same time they have imposed various requirements to reduce abuse and disruptive effects * * *. Corporate precedents are often used to interpret these requirements, as the derivative suit has been characterized as a "corporate action grafted onto the limited partnership form." [Gotham Partners, L.P. v. Hallwood Realty Partners, L.P., No. Civ. A. 15754–NC, 1998 WL 832631, at *5 n.14 (Del. Ch. Nov. 10, 1998).]

IV Alan R. Bromberg & Larry E. Ribstein, Bromberg and Ribstein on Partnership § 15.05(a), at 15:48.4 (13th ed. 2005).

H. OWNERSHIP INTERESTS AND TRANSFERABILITY

As you have learned, partners in limited partnerships may have management and financial rights (although limited partners are rarely given substantial management rights). Like general partnerships, the default rule in limited partnerships is that financial rights are transferable while management rights are not. *See, e.g.,* RULPA (1985)

§§ 101(10), 702; ULPA (2001) §§ 102(22), 701–702. Indeed, under RULPA (1985) § 704, an assignee of a partnership interest (including an assignee of a general partner interest) has the right to become a limited partner "if and to the extent that (i) the assignor gives the assignee that right in accordance with authority described in the partnership agreement, or (ii) all other partners consent." *See also* RULPA (1985) § 301 (addressing the admission of limited partners); ULPA (2001) § 301 (same); RULPA (1985) § 401 (addressing the admission of general partners); ULPA (2001) § 401 (same).

Entity general partners present interesting issues related to ownership and transferability. For example, the transfer of shares of a corporate general partner is technically distinct from the transfer of a general partner interest. That is, the corporation maintains its identity even if 100% of its shares are sold to a third party. One could argue, therefore, that limited partners have no basis for objecting when shareholders of a corporate general partner sell all or a controlling block of their shares in the corporation to a third party. Selling a controlling block of shares, however, shifts control of a corporate general partner to new owners, even if the identity of the corporate general partner remains the same. Such a result may adversely affect the interests of limited partners. The use of broad anti-transfer clauses may help to alleviate this problem. *See, e.g., In re* Asian Yard Partners, No. 95–333–PJW,1995 WL 1781675, at *7 (Bankr. D. Del. Sept. 18, 1995) (concluding that language in a limited partnership agreement that barred transfer of a partnership interest "directly or indirectly, or by operation of law or otherwise" prevented the transfer of a controlling stock interest in a corporate general partner: "By using the words 'directly or indirectly' the parties obviously meant that a partner could not do indirectly that which it was prohibited from doing directly. In my view, the plain meaning of the language encompasses a situation where there is a transfer of a controlling interest in a partner entity, because such a transaction effectively transfers a partner interest to the control of the party acquiring the controlling interest of the partner entity.").

A merger involving an entity general partner may also shift control of the general partner to new owners and possibly change the identity of the general partner itself. As a result, a merger might constitute a "transfer" or "assignment" in violation of prohibitions against transfers in limited partnership agreements or in breach of the general prohibition against assigning management powers by general partners. A leading case is *Star Cellular Telephone Co. v. Baton Rouge CGSA, Inc.*, Civ. A. No. 12507, 1993 WL 294847 (Del. Ch. Aug. 2, 1993). The agreement provided that:

> The General Partner may transfer or assign its General Partner's interest only after written notice to all the other Partners and the unanimous vote of all the other Partners to

permit such transfer and to continue the business of the Partnership with the assignee of the General Partner as General Partner. * * * Withdrawal of the General Partner (which will also be deemed its withdrawal as a Limited Partner) will cause the dissolution and termination of the Partnership * * * unless it is continued by the unanimous consent of the remaining Partners * * *.

The *Star Cellular* court concluded that the word "transfer" could not be read to encompass a merger, although it noted that the parties could have provided otherwise (e.g., by explicitly defining transfer to include transfers "by operation of law"). *See id.* at *5–7. Significantly, however, the court rested its decision on an analysis of the effect of the merger in the context of the relationships of the parties. It concluded that the merger created no material change in control or operations—i.e., the change was form and not substance:

> Antiassignment clauses are normally included in contracts to prevent the introduction of a stranger into the contracting parties' relationship and to assure performance by the original contracting parties.
>
> * * *
>
> * * * Here, in contrast, no "stranger" has been "forced" upon the plaintiffs in any meaningful sense. The defendants retained the same partner, but in a different corporate form.
>
> The record establishes that the Merger did not adversely impact the plaintiffs' position or rights. After the Merger, operational control of the Partnership remained in the hands of BellSouth, which made no material changes in the Partnership's management.
>
> * * *
>
> In short, the Merger created no material change in the control of the general partner or in the operations of the Partnership. The change was purely formal—the substitution of a new corporate entity for the entity that was the original general partner. That effected a change, to be sure, but one of legal form, not of substance. It altered none of the pre-Merger realities that were crucial to the limited partners' economic interests.

Id. at *8–11.

NOTES

(1) Do the default restrictions on transferability make sense for general partner interests? For limited partner interests?

(2) In *In re Asian Yard Partners*, No. 95–333–PJW, 1995 WL 1781675 (Bankr. D. Del. Sept. 18, 1995), the limited partnership agreement barred transfer of a partnership interest "directly or indirectly, or by operation of law or otherwise." *Id.* at *7. The court distinguished the *Star Partners* conclusion that the word "transfer" did not encompass a merger by noting that the parties clearly defined prohibited transfers as including transfers "by operation of law or otherwise." *See id.* at 8 ("I believe that if the *Star Cellular* court had before it the anti-transfer provision at issue here, it would have reached a different conclusion."). The court also suggested that any substantive inquiry into whether the merger caused a material change of control was unnecessary: "It may fairly be inferred from the broad scope of the description of a 'transfer' set forth in * * * the Partnership Agreement that the parties here intended to eliminate the need for a determination (including a litigated one) of whether a transfer by operation of law (such as by merger) would result in a material change in control of the general partner or in the operation of the partnership. They carried out that intent by providing a blanket prohibition to transfer * * *." *Id.*

(3) RULPA (1985) § 703 provides a charging order procedure whereby "the court may charge the partnership interest of the partner with payment of the unsatisfied amount of the judgment with interest," but "[t]o the extent so charged, the judgment creditor has only the rights of an assignee of the partnership interest." *See also* ULPA (2001) § 703 (providing for charging orders).

(4) In *Green v. Bellerive Condominiums Limited Partnership*, 763 A.2d 252 (Md. Ct. Spec. App. 2000), the court rejected a charging creditor's assertion that it had a right to be notified of a partnership opportunity— specifically, an opportunity to purchase the partnership's debt. The court observed:

> * * * [W]e hold that general partners of a limited partnership do not have a duty to notify a charging creditor about that partnership opportunity, and that the charging creditor does not have standing to assert the debtor partners' management rights to participate in or object to such a purchase.
>
> * * *
>
> As reflected in the unambiguous language of [RULPA (1985)] sections [702], [703], and [704], a charging order against a limited partnership interest does not operate as an unlimited assignment of all partnership rights, or as a judicial "swap" of the creditor for the debtor partner. When read *in pari materia,* these sections make it clear that a charging order against a limited partnership interest does not entitle the creditor *"to become a partner, or * * * exercise any rights of a partner."* § [702] (emphasis added). The "rights of a partner" include the right to information and the right to participate in partnership decisions that the receiver is demanding in this instance. These rights are not analogous to "distribution" or

"collection" rights, nor are they merely incidental or ancillary to the receiver's right to receive the debtor partner's distributions. Instead, we conclude that these rights are fundamental "management rights of a partner" that were not transferred to the receiver by the Charging Order.

Id. at 253, 260.

I.   DISSOCIATION AND DISSOLUTION

1.   DISSOCIATION

RULPA (1985) § 402 specifies the events of withdrawal for a general partner, including, among others, voluntary withdrawal, removal, and bankruptcy. Section 602 allows a general partner to withdraw at any time by giving written notice to the other partners, but if withdrawal violates the partnership agreement, the limited partnership may recover damages. Pursuant to § 604, a withdrawing partner (general or limited) is entitled to receive any distribution provided for in the partnership agreement. If the partnership agreement is silent, § 604 specifies that a partner shall receive, "within a reasonable time after withdrawal, the fair value of his [or her] interest in the limited partnership as of the date of withdrawal based upon his [or her] right to share in distributions from the limited partnership."

RULPA (1985) § 603 allows a limited partner to withdraw under circumstances specified in a written partnership agreement. If the agreement is silent, "a limited partner may withdraw upon not less than six months' prior written notice to each general partner." As noted above, when withdrawal occurs, § 604 provides for a "fair value" buyout.

The primary issue posed by the limited partnership dissociation provisions is their effect on the family limited partnership ("FLP"). An FLP is an estate planning device involving a business owner who creates a limited partnership with family members as the limited partners. The goal of the FLP, at least in part, is to ultimately transfer the business to the family members while minimizing estate and gift taxes. This "minimization" is accomplished by taking advantage of minority and marketability discounts—discounts that are commonly applied when valuing closely held business interests for tax purposes. Federal tax law, however, eliminates the ability to apply a marketability discount when limited partnership statutes provide default withdrawal and buyout rights. In the FLP context, in other words, the presence of exit rights under state law hinders the effort to minimize taxes.

LESLIE A. DROUBAY, THE CERTAINTY OF DEATH AND TAXES FOR FAMILY LIMITED PARTNERSHIPS

7 J. Small & Emerging Bus. L. 523, 524–25 (2003).

Traditionally, family limited partnerships have been created by wealthy parents with the intent of shifting family wealth to their children. Taxpayers use FLPs as receptacles into which they transfer assets such as corporate stock, securities, real property, bonds, and notes. Instead of making outright gifts of these assets to their children, the transferors use the FLP as a holding company. The parent, in his or her capacity as general partner, transfers interests in the partnership to the children, in their capacity as limited partners, instead of the underlying assets. This commonly used estate planning mechanism enables the transferor's estate to get valuation discounts on the interests in the partnership. It also allows the transferor to retain a sufficient amount of control over the assets transferred to the partnership. In short, FLPs reduce transfer taxes, and in certain cases, allow the parents, as general partners, to retain control.

* * *

In general, an FLP is a limited partnership that consists of family members. In a typical structure, the donors form a limited partnership, to which they contribute assets in exchange for general and limited partnership interests. The donors (commonly the parents or grandparents) will hold the general partnership interest, likely through a corporation, and over time, make gifts of limited partnership interests to the donees (commonly the children or grandchildren).

The most significant tax benefit of an FLP is the possible valuation discounts available for the gifts of limited partnership interests to the limited partners. When valuing FLP interests, courts consistently apply minority discounts for lack of control and lack of marketability. The availability of these discounts allows gifts of ownership interests to be made at values less than the proportionate share of the fair market value of the underlying assets. These discounts are also available for interests retained in the gross estate. A minority-interest discount recognizes the limited partner's lack of control within the partnership; a lack-of-marketability discount recognizes the inability of a limited partner to transfer his interest in the partnership * * *.

ROBERT T. DANFORTH, THE ROLE OF FEDERALISM IN ADMINISTERING A NATIONAL SYSTEM OF TAXATION

57 Tax Law. 625, 633–34 (2004).

Another recent development involves state legislative efforts designed to help taxpayers achieve substantial discounts when valuing family owned business interests for transfer tax purposes. * * * [S]ection

2704(b) of the [Internal Revenue] Code requires certain restrictions on liquidation rights in family-owned business entities to be disregarded for transfer tax purposes. "Applicable restrictions" on liquidation rights— generally speaking limitations on liquidation rights that are more restrictive than the default rules under state law—are disregarded under section 2704(b), producing an enhanced value of the business interest for transfer tax purposes. An example illustrates the point: Suppose a senior family member transfers to her child a limited partnership interest in a family-owned limited partnership established under the law of State X. Assume that the default rule under the State X limited partnership statute permits a limited partner to withdraw from the partnership and receive the liquidation value of her interest. If the partnership agreement were to restrict the withdrawal right of a limited partner, this restriction would be ignored for valuation purposes under section 2704(b). As a general proposition, the value of a limited partnership interest without a withdrawal right would be considerably lower than the value of a limited partnership [interest] with a withdrawal right.

Recall that section 2704(b) and its regulations make express reference to state law in determining what constitutes an applicable restriction. Not surprisingly, many state legislatures have read this as an invitation to enact limited partnership statutes designed to achieve favorable results under section 2704(b). For example, in 1997 the Virginia General Assembly modified its limited partnership statute to provide that "[a] limited partner may withdraw from a limited partnership only at the time or upon the happening of events specified in writing in the partnership agreement." Thus, in Virginia, there is no default rule granting a withdrawal right to a limited partner. Consequently, any restrictions on withdrawal rights in the limited partnership agreement would not constitute applicable restrictions for purposes of section 2704(b).

NOTES

(1) What are the advantages of eliminating the default withdrawal and buyout rights provided to limited partners under RULPA (1985) § 603 and § 604? Are there any disadvantages?

(2) A number of states have modified RULPA (1985) § 603 by eliminating a limited partner's default right of withdrawal. *See, e.g.*, TEX. BUS. ORGS. CODE § 153.110 ("A limited partner may withdraw from a limited partnership only at the time or on the occurrence of an event specified in a written partnership agreement."). Many states are eliminating default exit rights in the LLC setting as well. *See* Chapter 20, Section I. In both contexts, this elimination facilitates the business organization's use as an estate planning vehicle.

(3) Can you explain why general partners can withdraw at will from a limited partnership under RULPA (1985) § 602, but limited partners can withdraw only upon six months' notice under § 603?

(4) ULPA (2001) § 601(a) eliminates the *right* of a limited partner to dissociate before the firm's termination. Section 601(b)(1), however, recognizes a limited partner's *power* to dissociate by express will. Under § 602(a)(3), the effect of dissociation is that the former limited partner becomes a transferee of his own transferable interest. A right to payment upon dissociation is not provided. Under § 603 and § 604, a general partner has dissociation rights and powers similar to those in RUPA. Under § 605(a)(5), the effect of dissociation is that the former general partner becomes a transferee of his own transferable interest. Once again, a right to payment upon dissociation is not provided. *See also* ULPA (2001) § 505 ("A person does not have the right to receive a distribution on account of dissociation."). Sections 606 and 607 address, in a RUPA-like fashion (*see* Chapter 3, Section G), the effect of dissociation on a general partner's power to bind the limited partnership and a general partner's liability for the obligations of the limited partnership.

(5) NCCUSL's "Summary" of ULPA (2001) states the following:

> Another important change concerns a limited partner's right to disassociate from the partnership. Under RULPA a limited partner could theoretically withdraw from the partnership on six months notice unless the partnership agreement specified the withdrawal events for a limited partner. Due to estate planning concerns, the new ULPA default rule affords no right to disassociate as a limited partner before the termination of the limited partnership. The power to disassociate is expressly recognized, but may be exercised only through the partnership agreement or those events listed in section 601(b) of this Act.

The National Conference of Commissioners on Uniform State Laws, *Summary of the Uniform Limited Partnership Act (2001), at* http://uniform laws.org/ActSummary.aspx?title=Limited%20Partnership%20Act (last visited Jan. 18, 2014).

(6) ULPA (2001) § 601(b)(5) and § 603(5) allow for judicial expulsion of limited and general partners for misconduct. Such expulsion results in dissociation and could (at least in the case of general partner expulsion) lead to dissolution of the partnership under § 801(3).

2.   DISSOLUTION

Under RULPA (1985) § 801, a limited partnership is dissolved (1) at the time specified in the certificate of limited partnership; (2) upon the occurrence of events specified in a written partnership agreement; (3) upon the written consent of all partners; (4) upon an event of withdrawal of a general partner under § 402 (except when certain requirements are met); and (5) by the entry of a decree of judicial dissolution under § 802.

Section 802 provides that a court "may decree dissolution of a limited partnership whenever it is not reasonably practicable to carry on the business in conformity with the partnership agreement." Notice that dissolution is not caused by the dissociation of a limited partner. That comports with the typical structure of limited partnerships—i.e., limited partners are passive owners who mainly provide financing to the venture. Their departure does not normally cause a substantial change in the business.

NOTES

(1) ULPA (2001) § 801 states the grounds for non-judicial dissolution. The section provides that a limited partnership will not ordinarily dissolve upon the withdrawal of a general partner if another general partner remains (unless partners owning a majority of the distribution rights consent to dissolution). *See id.* § 801(3)(A). In addition, dissolution by partner consent does not require the consent of all of the limited partners. Instead, along with the consent of all of the general partners, only the consent of limited partners owning "a majority of the rights to receive distributions as limited partners" is required. *Id.* § 801(2).

(2) Like RULPA (1985) § 802, ULPA (2001) § 802 provides for judicial dissolution "if it is not reasonably practicable to carry on the activities of the limited partnership in conformity with the partnership agreement." Courts have applied this language to various forms of general partner misconduct, including the general partner's operation of the venture in a manner that violates the partnership agreement. Keep in mind that the standard is "not reasonably practicable," which presumably differs from "impossible."

(3) Linkage issues may exist between limited partnership and general partnership dissolution provisions. For example, RULPA (1985) § 802 covers the topic of judicial dissolution. By its terms, it applies to a dissolution application made "by or for a partner." What inference should a court draw from that language? Does it mean that the section has preemptive force—i.e., that only partners and partner representatives, and no one else, can seek judicial dissolution? If so, importing UPA § 32(2) or RUPA § 801(6) (which grant judicial dissolution rights to certain non-partners) would be improper. Alternatively, because § 802 does not address the rights of non-partners (e.g., assignees), perhaps it should be interpreted as silent on the issue. In that event, UPA § 32(2) or RUPA § 801(6) should be imported.

A similar issue arises with respect to RULPA (1985) § 801—i.e., are the grounds for nonjudicial dissolution under § 801 exclusive, or can they be supplemented by grounds under the general partnership statute? *Cf.* Active Asset Recovery, Inc. v. Real Estate Asset Recovery Servs., Inc., No. Civ. A. 15478, 1999 WL 743479, at *8–9 (Del. Ch. Sept. 10, 1999) (citing the equivalent of UPA § 31(2) (dissolution by express will) and finding that a limited partnership was dissolved when one of the partners expressed its will to dissolve).

The consequences of dissolution may also be affected by linkage issues. For example, while general partnership statutes include provisions on partners' post-dissolution agency authority (UPA §§ 33, 35; RUPA § 804), such provisions are absent in RULPA (1985) and its predecessors. As a stand-alone statute, of course, ULPA (2001) includes provisions on the consequences of dissolution. *See, e.g.*, ULPA (2001) §§ 804–808.

(4) In some limited partnerships, the partnership agreement specifies how distributions should be made in the event of the company's dissolution. When a partnership agreement is silent, however, the statute provides a distribution scheme. *See, e.g.*, RULPA (1985) § 804; ULPA (2001) § 812.

J. A FINAL LOOK

In a world of limited liability partnerships and limited liability companies, what role remains for the limited partnership? The Prefatory Note to ULPA (2001) provides some insight:

> The new Act has been drafted for a world in which limited liability partnerships and limited liability companies can meet many of the needs formerly met by limited partnerships. This Act therefore targets two types of enterprises that seem largely beyond the scope of LLPs and LLCs: (i) sophisticated, manager-entrenched commercial deals whose participants commit for the long term, and (ii) estate planning arrangements (family limited partnerships). This Act accordingly assumes that, more often than not, people utilizing it will want:
>
> • strong centralized management, strongly entrenched, and
>
> • passive investors with little control over or right to exit the entity
>
> The Act's rules, and particularly its default rules, have been designed to reflect these assumptions.

Family limited partnerships have previously been discussed in Section I(1) of this Chapter. Venture capital firms and leveraged buyout companies are two illustrations of modern limited partnerships that can be described as "sophisticated, manager-entrenched commercial deals whose participants commit for the long term." Both involve management and investment of huge amounts of capital—typically individual contributions in the millions of dollars—provided by wealthy individuals and institutional investors. The investors are limited partners who receive periodic distributions of income from the limited partnership. The venture capital or leveraged buyout managers typically form an entity to serve as the general partner in these limited partnerships. Withdrawals of capital by the limited partners are regulated by contract. The limited partnership structure assures continuous centralized management—i.e., investment decisions made by managers of the general partner free from involvement by the limited partners, who simply contribute capital and share in the economic returns.

Venture capital limited partnerships are professionally managed pools of capital that invest their money in equity securities of closely held companies at early and medium stages of their development. (The companies invested in are known as "portfolio companies.") Venture capitalists usually sit on the boards of the portfolio companies and take a very active role in the corporate governance of those firms.

Venture capital firms are often organized as limited partnerships run by a general partner with experience in all aspects of managing young companies. The limited partners provide virtually all of the capital that the firm uses to make investments. The general partner that manages the firm and that provides expertise to the portfolio companies contributes only a small portion of the capital. Venture capital general partners are able to help with brand development, financial controls, accounting, and marketing, as well as choosing lawyers, accountants, and investment bankers. Venture capitalists also assist portfolio companies in choosing managers. Simply put, venture capital general partners help with the development of their portfolio companies up to the point at which those companies sell shares to the public.

Usually, the partnership agreements between U.S. venture capital firms and their investors limit the term of the investment to a designated number of years, at which time the firm is liquidated and the money is returned to investors. Successful venture capital limited partnerships easily attract money from investors when they begin a new funding cycle.

Venture capital firms are often highly specialized. Some firms invest only in certain industry sectors such as biotechnology, computer peripherals, or fashion retailing. Other firms invest only in companies in certain geographic regions or only in companies that are in the very early stages of their development.

While venture capital investing is a modest fraction of overall capital investment in corporations, the U.S. venture capital industry is, by far, the largest in the world. Moreover, the venture capital industry is important in certain industry sectors, particularly biotechnology and high technology companies. A number of very successful companies including Apple Computer, Cisco Systems, Compaq, Lotus Development Corp., Seagate Technologies, and Sun Microsystems began life as portfolio companies of venture capital firms.

Although venture capitalists generally do not receive a majority of the equity in the companies in which they invest, they typically control a majority of the seats on the boards of portfolio companies. Venture capital firms receive preferred stock (or sometimes debt instruments) in portfolio companies, which has significant voting rights and which can be converted into common stock and liquidated if and when the portfolio company makes a public offering. These arrangements work well, as evidenced by the fact that, while there is a tremendous amount of litigation among investors in closely held corporations, there has been comparatively little litigation between venture capital firms and the portfolio companies they create, or between venture capital firms and their investors. This is particularly surprising in light of the high rate of failure of portfolio companies. A rough rule of thumb in the industry is that a failure rate of 80% is considered quite good for venture capitalists that specialize in investing in early stages of new ventures.

A leveraged buyout company collects money from investors and combines those funds with money borrowed from financial institutions to buy controlling interests in more established companies. The assets of the company being acquired (the "target company") are typically used as collateral to secure the repayment of the borrowed funds, and the earnings of the target company are typically used to service the debt. The ideal target, therefore, is a mature company with stable and predictable earnings.

Such an acquisition commonly involves the leveraged buyout company creating a holding company to effectuate the transaction. The holding company purchases all (or at least a majority of) the outstanding voting stock of the target company using cash obtained primarily from debt (indeed, the term "leverage" means debt) and secondarily from investors. The holding company then merges with the target to form a single firm with significant debt in relation to the amount of equity on its balance sheet. The hope is that the earnings of the new company will be sufficient to pay down the debt and to generate a significant return for the leveraged buyout company.

CHAPTER 19

THE LIMITED LIABILITY PARTNERSHIP

■ ■ ■

A. INTRODUCTION

The limited liability partnership ("LLP") is typically a general partnership that, depending on the relevant statute, provides the partners with limited liability for the firm's tort obligations or for both its tort and contract obligations. Because the LLP is ordinarily a general partnership rather than a limited partnership,[a] all of the partners have the right to participate in the management of the venture without risking a loss of their limited liability. More generally, because partnership statutes typically provide that an LLP is a "partnership," *see, e.g.*, RUPA § 101(5), general partnership law is applicable to LLPs when it is not explicitly altered by LLP-specific provisions.

ROBERT W. HAMILTON, REGISTERED LIMITED LIABILITY PARTNERSHIPS: PRESENT AT THE BIRTH (NEARLY)
66 U. Colo. L. Rev. 1065, 1065–67, 1069–71 (1995).

[The LLP's] birth date can be precisely identified as August 26, 1991, when Texas House Bill 278 became effective without Governor Ann Richards' signature. * * *

* * *

The original conception of an LLP—and the conception that has been accepted by the great bulk of the state LLP statutes—is that it provides what might be described as "peace of mind" insurance for innocent partners. The LLP is designed to avoid the fear by a partner that her personal assets may be at risk because of negligence or malpractice by a partner over whom she has no control and quite possibly whom she has never met.

A basic principle of general partnership law is that each individual partner is personally liable for all partnership obligations to the extent they exceed the assets of the partnership. This means not only that innocent partners may be required to discharge partnership obligations from their personal assets, but also they may be required to make contributions from their personal assets to the partnership to enable it to discharge all of its liabilities. In the original LLP concept, all partners

---

[a]   In some jurisdictions, limited partnerships can register as LLPs. *See* Section D.

have the benefits, responsibilities, and potential liability of general partners except that partners have no responsibility for malpractice claims or for liabilities arising from negligence or misconduct in which they were not personally involved. The protection provided innocent partners against personal liability is usually referred to as "the shield of limited liability" * * *.

* * *

The LLP is a direct outgrowth of the collapse of real estate and energy prices in the late 1980s, and the concomitant disaster that befell Texas's banks and savings and loan associations. Texas led the nation in bank and savings and loan failures during the 1980s. More than one-third of all the bank failures in the United States occurred in Texas.

Ever since the collapse of these financial institutions across the state, the Federal Deposit Insurance Corporation ("FDIC") and the Resolution Trust Corporation ("RTC") (and its predecessor, the Federal Savings and Loan Insurance Corporation ("FSLIC")) have devoted a significant part of their total resources to the recovery of funds lost in the collapse of Texas institutions. Suit was brought against hundreds of shareholders, directors and officers of failed financial institutions. However, the amounts recovered from the principal wrongdoers were only a tiny fraction of total losses and attention quickly turned to the roles of the lawyers and accountants who had represented the failed financial institutions before their collapse. "Where were the lawyers?" and "Where were the public accountants?" were cries figuratively heard across the state. Claims against lawyers and accountants for malpractice and breach of duty were attractive because the individual professionals sometimes had been deeply involved in the affairs of their clients. Also, these lawyers and accountants were usually associated with partnerships that had substantial malpractice insurance and numerous wealthy partners. As a result, several highly reputable law firms in Texas found themselves in deep trouble because of their bank and thrift work during the "salad days" of the 1980s.

The most vivid example is provided by a major Dallas law firm (hereafter referred to as the "Dallas Law Firm"). Long recognized as one of the leading corporate law firms in the state, the Dallas Law Firm in the early 1980s was a traditional general partnership. One Dallas Law Firm partner, Laurence Vineyard, along with four associates, did legal work for three savings and loan associations. Two of them, Brownfield Savings & Loan and State Savings & Loan were quite small; the third, Vernon Savings & Loan was somewhat larger and grew rapidly during this period. Vineyard severed his relationship with the Dallas Law Firm in 1983 and formed his own firm with his associates; this new firm continued to do work for the S & Ls. In addition to providing legal services, it turned out that Vineyard sat on the board of directors of at least one of the S & Ls and had profitable financial arrangements with the others. These three S & Ls were among the more flagrant "high fliers" which paid little attention to principles of sound financial management and provided lavish benefits and large unsecured loans for their owners. Losses from the collapse of these three S & Ls ran over one billion dollars. Vineyard was deeply involved. He was criminally prosecuted, convicted, sentenced to two five year prison terms, and disbarred. His personal assets were insubstantial in light of the losses incurred by the S & Ls, and the FSLIC and FDIC turned their attention to the malpractice insurer for the Dallas Law Firm and to all persons who were partners during the period the firm represented the S & Ls. Caught within the FSLIC/FDIC net were retired partners, partners who had since left the Dallas Law Firm to join other firms, partners who had been promoted from associate to partner, persons who had become "of counsel" to the Dallas Law Firm, and the forty-some partners who had nothing at all to do with representation of the various thrift institutions. The total claims asserted by the FSLIC greatly exceeded the liability insurance available to the firm and the assets of the firm itself. To emphasize this point, in one particularly chilling meeting, FSLIC personnel used an overhead projector to show a slide listing the names of each Dallas Law Firm defendant with estimates of total net worth and the amount likely to be available from each of them to satisfy the government's claims.

Needless to say, the Dallas Law Firm litigation caught the attention of the hundreds of law firms that had represented banks or thrifts during the 1980s. Thousands of lawyers in hundreds of Texas law firms watched this litigation closely as it unfolded in the late 1980s with a "there but for the grace of God go I" reaction. The lawsuit against the Dallas Law Firm was ultimately settled for approximately the amount of malpractice insurance carried by the firm.

B. FORMATION

As mentioned, partnership statutes typically provide that an LLP is a "partnership." *See, e.g.*, RUPA § 101(5). With respect to formation, therefore, an LLP must fall within the statutory definition of a partnership—i.e., an association of two or more persons to carry on as co-owners a business for profit. Beyond meeting the partnership definition, an LLP must satisfy certain statutory formalities. First, an LLP is required to file a document (generally called an application, registration, or certificate) with the secretary of state or other designated official. The document must provide prescribed information, which usually includes, among other items, the firm's name (which ordinarily must contain the "LLP" abbreviation or the "limited liability partnership" term), the firm's address, and a statement of its business or purpose. *See, e.g.*, RUPA § 1001 (prescribing the contents of the "statement of qualification"); *id.* § 1002 (addressing the LLP's name). Because of legislative variations, you should always check the relevant statute in your jurisdiction for the precise informational requirements.

Second, some jurisdictions require an LLP to provide a specified amount of liability insurance or, alternatively, a pool of funds designated and segregated for the satisfaction of judgments against the partnership. New Mexico, for example, requires a $1,000,000 liability insurance policy or a $1,000,000 pool of segregated funds. *See, e.g.*, N.M. STAT. § 54–1–47. An LLP that fails to comply with the insurance/segregated funds requirement presumably loses its limited liability protection, at least up to the amount that insurance or segregated funds should have provided. *See, e.g.*, OKLA. STAT. tit. 54, § 1–309(g) ("If a limited liability partnership * * * fails to comply with this [insurance/segregated funds] section, the partners thereof shall be liable jointly for the debts, obligations and liabilities of the partnership * * *; provided, however, that the aggregate amount for which the partners are jointly liable shall be limited to the difference between the amount of security required to be maintained * * * and the amount of security actually maintained by the partnership."). Even if there is no LLP-specific insurance/segregated funds provision, an LLP may still be subject to similar requirements under licensing or other statutes.

NOTES

(1) An LLP is simply a partnership that has availed itself of statutory procedures altering the traditional rule of partner liability. Thus, the registration filed with the state is not a document effectuating or evidencing formation of the entity in the same sense as articles of incorporation or a certificate of limited partnership. The partnership is formed with or without an effective LLP registration; it is the same entity as it was prior to registration. The filing merely changes the rule regarding the personal liability of the partners.

(2) In California and New York, the LLP is available only for partnerships that perform professional services. *See* CAL. CORP. CODE § 16101(8)(A); N.Y. P'SHIP LAW § 121–1500(a).

(3) What vote of the partners is needed to approve LLP registration? Depending on the statute, unanimous, "majority in interest," or majority approval may be required. Some statutes (such as RUPA § 1001(b)) provide that approval by the vote necessary to amend the partnership agreement is required, and some LLP statutes are silent on the issue. When silent, what vote should be required? Consider the following observations:

> Statutes that permit registration by majority or other subunanimous vote raise difficult policy and constitutional issues. LLP registration may, in effect, redistribute exposure to liability from the partners generally to those partners who are closely enough involved in the liability-generating aspects of the practice to

be exposed to direct liability for monitoring or supervision lapses. Directly affected partners arguably ought to be able to block the registration. On the other hand, a default unanimity rule might so greatly increase the bargaining costs associated with registration that some firms may be unable to become LLPs. The appropriate balance between these competing considerations may vary from firm to firm. * * *

* * * [P]ermitting LLP registration is a new development that partnerships in existence on adoption of the LLP statute did not anticipate in drafting their agreement. It is reasonable to suppose that many partnerships would have contracted for limited liability from the outset if they had been allowed to do so.

ALAN R. BROMBERG & LARRY E. RIBSTEIN, BROMBERG AND RIBSTEIN ON LIMITED LIABILITY PARTNERSHIPS, THE REVISED UNIFORM PARTNERSHIP ACT, AND THE UNIFORM LIMITED PARTNERSHIP ACT (2001) § 2.04(b), at 59 (2005).

(4) Most LLP statutes provide that limited liability begins as soon as the registration statement is filed. *See, e.g.*, RUPA § 1001(e). Nevertheless, the effect of LLP registration on existing contracts and relationships is not entirely clear:

> Since LLP registration continues the pre-existing partnership entity, it apparently does not affect the firm's contracts either among the partners or between the partnership and third parties. But there are many unanswered questions with respect to attributing liabilities to the pre-or post-registration period. Are post-registration loans pursuant to a pre-registration line of credit subject to the LLP liability limitation (under statutes that limit liability for contract debts)? Is a partner's malpractice covered by the registration if it was committed prior to registration but results in an injury afterward? Is a creditor who agreed to a lease or a line of credit prior to registration stuck with limited liability as to subsequent loans or rent?

> One possible place to look for answers to these questions is cases that have considered whether new partners are personally liable, or former partners not liable, for interest or other payments on preexisting partnership contracts or debts that accrue after dissociation or admission. The reasoning in these cases for and against liability, which is based on the creditors' expectations as to who would be liable on the loan, arguably also applies to the effect of the LLP liability limitation on post-registration charges or liabilities that accrue on pre-registration contracts or misconduct.

> Creditors can, of course, deal with these issues in their agreements with the partnership. The problem, of course, is that older agreements could not have anticipated the LLP.

LARRY E. RIBSTEIN, UNINCORPORATED BUSINESS ENTITIES 499–500 (3d ed. 2004).

(5) Most states require LLPs to pay registration fees. In Texas, for example, an LLP must pay $200 per partner every year. *See* TEX. BUS. ORGS. CODE §§ 4.158(1)–(2), 152.802(a), (e), (g) (noting that the fee for filing an initial LLP application is "$200 for each partner," and the fee for filing the required annual renewal of the application is "$200 for each partner on the date of renewal").

(6) In a state that requires an LLP to renew its registration, a failure to comply may jeopardize the partners' limited liability. In *Apcar Investment Partners VI, Ltd. v. Gaus*, 161 S.W.3d 137 (Tex. App. 2005), a partnership (Smith & West) registered as a Texas LLP on March 6, 1995. The LLP failed to subsequently renew its registration. On August 11, 1999, the LLP entered into a lease agreement. Apcar ultimately sued the LLP and its two individual partners (Gaus and West) for breach of the lease agreement. Gaus and West filed a summary judgment motion asserting that the Texas partnership statute shielded them from personal liability for LLP obligations. *See id.* at 138–39. The trial court granted the motion, *see id.* at 139, but the court of appeals reversed:

> * * * Apcar contends that the lease obligations were not incurred while Smith & West, L.L.P. was a registered limited liability partnership because Smith & West, L.L.P.'s status as a registered limited liability partnership expired in 1996—three years before the lease was executed. Therefore, Apcar asserts that Gaus and West are personally liable for the lease obligations. Gaus and West contend that Smith & West, L.L.P.'s initial registration as a registered limited liability partnership in 1995 protects them from individual liability in this case. To support their argument, Gaus and West rely on cases involving the statutory filing requirements for limited partnerships. They assert that, based on the reasoning of the limited partnership cases, Smith & West, L.L.P. did not need to comply with statutory renewal requirements for maintaining its status as a registered limited liability partnership in order to protect them from individual liability under the lease.

> * * *

> * * * In the context of limited partnerships, courts have held that it is not necessary for limited partnerships to strictly comply with statutory filing requirements for its limited partners to receive limited liability protection. [*See, e.g.*, Garrett v. Koepke, 569 S.W.2d 568 (Tex. App. 1978).] In each of these cases, the courts held that limited partners did not lose their limited liability status when the partnership failed to comply with filing requirements.

> * * *

> The limited partnership cases are distinguishable from registered limited liability partnership cases for two reasons. First, the clear language of Article 6132b–3.08(a)(1) [now TEX. BUS. ORGS. CODE § 152.801] provides that partners are protected from

individual liability only for debts and obligations that are incurred while the partnership is a registered limited liability partnership. Article 6132b–3.08(b)(5) and (b)(7) [now TEX. BUS. ORGS. CODE § 152.802] provides that registration expires in one year unless it is renewed prior to the expiration date. To apply the reasoning of the limited partnership cases would conflict with the clear language of Article 6132b–3.08. Second, the Texas Revised Limited Partnership Act * * * contains a ["substantial compliance" provision analogous to RULPA (1985) § 201(b)] that is not present in Article 6132b–3.08. * * *

Article 6132b–3.08 does not contain a "substantial compliance" section, nor does it contain a grace period for filing a renewal application. We hold that a partnership must be in compliance with the registration requirements in Article 6132b–3.08(b) for its partners to receive protection from individual liability under Article 6132b–3.08(a)(1). Smith & West, L.L.P. was not a registered limited liability partnership when it incurred the lease obligations; therefore, Gaus and West are not protected from individual liability for the lease obligations under Article 6132b–3.08(a)(1).

Id. at 140–42.

C. LIMITED LIABILITY

KUS V. IRVING

Superior Court of Connecticut, 1999.
736 A.2d 946.

HURLEY, JUDGE TRIAL REFEREE.

The two defendants, attorneys Narcy Z. Dubicki and Garon Camassar, claim in their motion for summary judgment that there is no genuine issue of material fact as to their liability and request, as a matter of law, that the motion be granted. The law firm is a limited liability partnership.

The plaintiff, Margaret Kus, claims that a third defendant, attorney Charles J. Irving, a partner in the firm of Irving, Dubicki and Camassar, induced her to sign a fee agreement to pay him a fee of 25 percent of what he collected on the life insurance policy of the husband of the plaintiff before suit was filed and 33 percent of any proceeds after suit was brought. The policy had a death benefit of $400,000. She claims that Irving had already received the $400,000, but nevertheless filed suit to collect the larger fee of 33 percent. Irving then paid the plaintiff $270,692.26 and took a fee of $135,365.63, which the plaintiff claims was $33,841.41 too high. The plaintiff sued all three partners in the firm.

Both Dubicki and Camassar have filed affidavits stating that they had no personal knowledge of the case or the dealings between Irving and the plaintiff until November 24, 1998, which was several days after the matter between the plaintiff and Irving was concluded. They claim that under General Statutes § 34–327, they are protected from liability for any actions by their partner, Irving.

Section 34–327 provides in pertinent part: ["(c) Subject to subsection (d) of this section, a partner in a registered limited liability partnership is not liable directly or indirectly, including by way of indemnification, contribution or otherwise, for any debts, obligations and liabilities of or chargeable to the partnership or another partner or partners, whether arising in contract, tort or otherwise, arising in the course of the partnership business while the partnership is a registered limited liability partnership."].

["(d) The provisions of subsection (c) of this section shall not affect the liability of a partner in a registered limited liability partnership for his own negligence, wrongful acts or misconduct, or that of any person under his direct supervision and control."].

In their affidavits, Dubicki and Camassar state that they had no personal knowledge of the dealings between the plaintiff and Irving, nor did they have any supervision or control of Irving. Furthermore, they state that under the partnership agreement, Irving retains all fees for his activities and does not share any of them with the other partners.

The plaintiff claims that the two defendants are guilty of negligence, wrongful acts and misconduct. She produced no affidavit or other documents, however, to support this claim. The court must, therefore, find that there is no genuine issue of material fact in this regard.

* * * [The plaintiff] claims [that the two defendants] admitted knowledge of what happened and did not attempt to rectify it. All they admitted was knowledge after the transaction was concluded. Again, the plaintiff's claims are made without supporting affidavits.

* * * Accordingly, since the two defendants shared no benefit, did not have direct supervision or control over Irving and did not know about the matter until nine days after the funds were distributed, the court finds that they are protected from liability by § 34–327(c).

The motion for summary judgment by defendants Dubicki and Camassar is granted.

NOTES

(1) Under the Connecticut statute involved in *Kus*, when is liability imposed on an LLP partner? What about under RUPA § 306? Are there any differences between these statutes?

(2) In *Kus*, the court concludes that "since the two defendants shared no benefit * * * and did not know about the matter until nine days after the

funds were distributed, the court finds that they are protected from liability by § 34–327(c)." What if the defendants did share fees from Irving's activities? Is that relevant to § 34–327(c) or (d)? What if the defendants knew about Irving's conduct before the funds were distributed, but they took no action in response? Is that relevant to § 34–327(c) or (d)?

(3) Some LLP provisions (such as § 34–327(d) of the Connecticut statute involved in *Kus*) specify that a partner is liable for the misconduct of others under the partner's supervision, direction, or control. *See also* WIS. STAT. § 178.12(3)(b) (imposing liability on a partner for the wrongful acts of a person acting under the partner's "actual supervision and control"). Is this "supervisory" liability sensible? If a partner makes reasonable attempts to supervise a subordinate, but the subordinate nevertheless commits an actionable wrong, will the supervising partner be liable? Should she be?

(4) The Utah statute states, in relevant part, the following:

(1) Except as provided in Subsection (2), all partners are liable [for partnership obligations] * * *.

(2)(a) A partner in a limited liability partnership is not liable, directly or indirectly, including by way of indemnification, contribution or otherwise, for a debt, obligation, or liability chargeable to the partnership arising from negligence, wrongful acts, or misconduct committed while the partnership is registered as a limited liability partnership and in the course of the partnership business by another partner, or an employee, agent, or representative of the limited liability partnership.

(2)(b) Notwithstanding Subsection (2)(a), a partner in a limited liability partnership is liable for his own negligence, wrongful acts, or misconduct.

UTAH CODE § 48–1–12.

Assume that an LLP obtains a bank loan to provide additional capital for its operations. After receiving the loan proceeds, the LLP experiences severe financial difficulties, and it ultimately defaults on the loan. The bank recovers a $600,000 judgment against the LLP for breach of contract, but it is unsuccessful in its efforts to collect from the LLP's assets. The bank seeks to recover the $600,000 from the personal assets of the partners. What result under § 306 of RUPA? Under § 48–1–12 of the Utah statute?

(5) Although many LLP provisions were originally like Utah's, most now limit a partner's liability for all types of claims. *See, e.g.,* RUPA § 306. Is it sensible for LLP provisions to furnish partners with limited liability for the firm's tort obligations, but not for the firm's contractual obligations?

(6) With respect to partner liability, how does the LLP compare to the limited partnership? To the corporation?

(7) When the assets of an LLP are insufficient to pay all of the firm's obligations, conflicts between the partners can arise:

Where different partners have different individual liability with respect to different partnership obligations, there will be a question of prioritizing the payment of these liabilities. These differences can arise in several ways. For example, all partners will be individually liable for obligations that arose before the registration, while only negligent or responsible partners will be liable for certain claims arising after registration. If there are insufficient assets within the partnership to pay all obligations, may the non-negligent partners determine to apply those assets to the payment of liabilities for which they are individually liable? If general firm debts, such as a lease or line of credit, are paid, the negligent partner will be required to use separate assets to pay any liability arising from such partner's negligence. Whether such a decision would constitute a breach of fiduciary duty to the negligent partner remains to be determined. If the liability for malpractice is paid with partnership assets, all the partners will be liable for the remaining firm obligations.

Robert R. Keatinge et al., *Limited Liability Partnerships: The Next Step in the Evolution of the Unincorporated Business Organization*, 51 BUS. LAW. 147, 184 (1995).

(8) The LLP is a popular business form for law firms. In 1996, the Ethics Committee of the American Bar Association concluded that the practice of law in the LLP form was consistent with the Model Rules of Professional Conduct. *See* Formal Opinion 96–401. The Committee disagreed, however, on the amount of disclosure that clients should receive about the LLP's limited liability:

Although the members of the ABA Ethics Committee agreed that the restriction on liability must be "made apparent to the client," they parted ways on the amount of disclosure necessary to inform clients as to the limitation on liability. A minority of the committee expressed concern "that the use of initials, without more, is not sufficient to make the limitation of liability apparent to the client." The majority believed that the use of abbreviations "places clients on notice that their lawyer is practicing in a particular business form, and encourages them to inquire if they are in doubt as to its implications for them." When clients do inquire about the form of entity, the ABA Ethics Opinion states that "a lawyer must clearly explain the limitation of liability features of his firm's business organization." Unless faced with such a client inquiry, the ABA opinion does not require that lawyers explain the restriction on liability.

Every statute creating limited liability entities specifies that the firm include in its name a notation or reference to its limited liability structure. Most statutes require the initials "LLP" (with or without periods), "Limited Liability Partnership," or "Registered Limited Liability Partnership" as the last letters or words in the partnership name. "The policy underlying the name requirement is to maximize notice to the world concerning the fact that a partnership has elected LLP status and is an LLP." [Martin I. Lubaroff, *Registered Limited Liability Partnerships—The Next Wave*, 8 No. 5 INSIGHTS 23, 27 (1994).] To give notice, a few states like New York require publication in a local newspaper for a certain number of days after the LLP registration date. Beyond the name change in all states and the publication [requirement] in a few states, LLP statutes do not require that the LLP notify its customers, creditors, clients, or patients.

Other than compliance with the minimum statutory requirement of using initials to designate the LLP, the ABA Ethics Opinion does not require notice to clients and others dealing with the LLP. Based upon "legislative approval of the use of initials and the relative unimportance, today, of the lawyer's business form for clients," most of the committee members opined "that the use of initials, without more, is adequate to meet ethical criteria."

Susan Saab Fortney, *Professional Responsibility and Liability Issues Related to Limited Liability Law Partnerships*, 39 S. TEX. L. REV. 399, 412–13 (1998).

(9) Do you think law firm clients know (or care) that partners in LLP law firms have no personal liability for the malpractice of their fellow partners? *Cf.* Jonathan D. Glater, *Fearing Liability, Law Firms Change Partnership Status*, N.Y. TIMES, Jan. 10, 2003, at C2 ("Despite the apparent advantages of L.L.P. status, the weight of tradition at law firms rests on the general partnership structure. There is a perception, several lawyers said, that firms' advice means more because all the partners ultimately put their own wealth behind it. But as more and more firms have converted to L.L.P.[s] and clients have not abandoned them, that concern has eased, lawyers said. 'Clients don't seem to care,' one senior partner said.").

PROBLEM

Arthur Andersen LLP is an Illinois LLP. Lawsuits have been filed against Arthur Andersen for the audit work that it performed for Enron Corporation. Assuming that the claims are successful and that the LLP will have insufficient assets to pay the claims, can the plaintiffs recover from the assets of Andersen's individual partners? At the time of the alleged misconduct, the Illinois statute stated, in relevant part, the following:

(b) Subject to subsection (c) of this Section, a partner in a registered limited liability partnership is not liable, directly or indirectly, including by way of indemnification, contribution, assessment or otherwise, for debts, obligations, and liabilities of or chargeable to the partnership, whether arising in tort, contract or otherwise, arising from negligence, wrongful acts, omissions, misconduct, or malpractice, committed while the partnership is a registered limited liability partnership and in the course of the partnership business by another partner or an employee, agent, or representative of the partnership. * * *

(c) Subsection (b) of this Section shall not affect (1) the liability of a partner in a registered limited liability partnership for his own negligence, wrongful acts, omissions, misconduct, or malpractice or that of any other person under his direct supervision and control, [or] (2) the joint liability of a partner for debts and obligations of the partnership arising from any cause other than those specified in subsection (b) of this Section, including the ordinary commercial debts of the registered limited liability partnership * * *.

805 ILL. COMP. STAT. 205/15.

EDERER V. GURSKY

Court of Appeals of New York, 2007.
881 N.E.2d 204.

READ, J.

[Ederer was a partner in Gursky & Ederer, LLP who withdrew from the firm before it ceased operations. Pursuant to a withdrawal agreement, the LLP was obligated to pay Ederer various sums of money. When those sums were not forthcoming, Ederer sued the LLP and its partners and alleged, among other claims, that the LLP had breached the withdrawal agreement. The individual partners moved to dismiss, asserting that New York's LLP liability provision (Partnership Law § 26(b)) shielded them from personal liability for the LLP's obligations. The lower courts denied the motion.]

This appeal calls upon us to explore the nature and scope of Partnership Law § 26(b). We hold that this provision does not shield a general partner in a registered limited liability partnership from personal liability for breaches of the partnership's or partners' obligations to each other.

* * *

This appeal comes down to a dispute over the effect of the Legislature's 1994 amendments to section 26 of the Partnership Law (L. 1994, ch. 576, § 8). As originally adopted by the Legislature in 1919 (L. 1919, ch. 408), section 26 was identical to section 15 of the Uniform Partnership Act (UPA), which was drafted by the National Conference of Commissioners on Uniform State Laws and approved by the Conference in 1914. Prior to its amendment in 1994, section 26 provided that

"[a]ll partners are liable

"1. Jointly and severally for everything chargeable to the partnership under sections twenty-four and twenty-five.

> "2. Jointly for all other debts and obligations of the partnership; but any partner may enter into a separate obligation to perform a partnership contract."

Section 24 specifies that

> "[w]here, by any wrongful act or omission of any partner acting in the ordinary course of the business of the partnership, or with the authority of his copartners, loss or injury is caused to any person, not being a partner in the partnership, or any penalty is incurred, the partnership is liable therefor to the same extent as the partner so acting or omitting to act."

Section 25 binds the partnership to "make good the loss"

> "1. Where one partner acting within the scope of his apparent authority receives money or property of a third person and misapplies it; and

> "2. Where the partnership in the course of its business receives money or property of a third person and the money or property so received is misapplied by any partner while it is in the custody of the partnership."

Partnership Law § 26, as originally enacted, and its prototype, section 15 of the UPA, have always been understood to mean what they plainly say: general partners are jointly and severally liable to nonpartner creditors for all wrongful acts and breaches of trust committed by their partners in carrying out the partnership's business, and jointly liable for all other debts to third parties. This proposition follows naturally from the very nature of a partnership, which is based on the law of principal and agent. Just as a principal is liable for the acts of its agents, each partner is personally responsible for the acts of other partners in the ordinary course of the partnership's business. In addition to this vicarious liability to nonpartner creditors, each partner concomitantly has an obligation to share or bear the losses of the partnership through contribution and indemnification in the context of an ongoing partnership (*see* Partnership Law § 40[1], [2] as originally enacted, which is identical to section 18[a] and [b] of the UPA); and contribution upon dissolution and winding up (*see* Partnership Law § 65 as originally enacted, which is identical to section 34 of the UPA; Partnership Law § 71[d] as originally enacted, which is identical to section 40[d] of the UPA).

The nationwide initiative to create a new business entity combining the flexibility of a partnership without the onus of this traditional vicarious liability originated with a law adopted

> "in Texas in 1991, following the savings and loan crisis. At that time, a number of legal and accounting firms faced potentially

ruinous judgments arising out of their professional services for banks and thrifts which thereafter failed. Because these professional firms were typically organized as general partnerships, this liability also threatened the personal assets of their constituent partners. The Texas LLP statute protected such partners (at least prospectively) from this unlimited personal exposure without requiring a reorganization of their business structure" (Walker, New York Limited Liability Companies and Partnerships: A Guide to Law and Practice § 14:3, at 344–345 [1 West's N.Y. Prac. Series 2002]).

In New York, the Legislature enacted limited liability partnership legislation as a rider to the New York Limited Liability Company Law. This legislation eliminated the vicarious liability of a general partner in a registered limited liability partnership by amending section 26 of the Partnership Law, and making conforming changes to sections 40(1), (2), 65 and 71(d). Specifically, new section 26(b) creates an exception to the vicarious liability otherwise applicable by virtue of section 26(a) (original section 26 [section 15 of the UPA]), by providing that

"[e]xcept as provided by subdivisions (c) and (d) of this section, no partner of a partnership which is a registered limited liability partnership is liable or accountable, directly or indirectly (including by way of indemnification, contribution or otherwise), for any debts, obligations or liabilities of, or chargeable to, the registered limited liability partnership or each other, whether arising in tort, contract or otherwise, which are incurred, created or assumed by such partnership while such partnership is a registered limited liability partnership, solely by reason of being such a partner."

Section 26(c) excludes from section 26(b)'s liability shield "any negligent or wrongful act or misconduct committed by [a partner] or by any person under his or her direct supervision and control while rendering professional services on behalf of [the] registered limited liability partnership." Section 26(d) allows partners to opt out from or reduce the reach of section 26(b)'s protection from vicarious liability.

As one commentator has noted, by "expressly provid[ing] that limited liability includes liability by way of indemnification or contribution," section 26(b) precludes the potential for a plaintiff to "attempt an end-run around the liability shield of [section 26(b)] by first asserting a claim against the [limited liability partnership] and then arguing that the general partnership statute requires the [limited liability partnership] partners to make contributions to the [limited liability partnership]" (Johnson, Limited Liability for Lawyers: General Partners Need Not Apply, 51 Bus. Law. 85, 110 [1995]). The Legislature further expressed its intention to negate a partner's indemnification or contribution obligations with respect to liabilities for which the partner was not vicariously liable by making sections 40(1), (2), 65 and 71(d) subject to section 26(b).

Defendants point out that section 26(b) eliminates the liability of a partner in a limited liability partnership for "any debts" without distinguishing between debts owed to a third party or to the partnership or each other. As a result, they contend, the Legislature did not "leave open to conjecture whether § 26(b) was intended to cover debts which may be owed by the [limited liability partnership] (or one partner) to other partners." This argument ignores, however, that the phrase "any debts" is part of a provision (section 26) that has always governed only a partner's liability to third parties, and, in fact, is part of article 3 of the Partnership Law ("Relations of Partners to Persons Dealing with the Partnership"), not article 4 ("Relations of Partners to One Another"). The logical inference, therefore, is that "any debts" refers to any debts owed a third party, absent very clear legislative direction to the contrary.

Defendants also note that chapter 576's legislative history illustrates the desire to enact liability protection for partners in limited liability partnerships that is "the same as that accorded to shareholders of a professional corporation organized under the [Business Corporation Law] [and] as that accorded to members of a professional LLC" (Senate Introducer Mem in Support, Bill Jacket, L. 1994, ch. 576). They point out that "the legislative history of the LLP Act plainly indicates that the Legislature intended to provide an *even greater shield* of individual liability to partners in LLPs than that enacted by other states as of the date of the legislation."

These observations are correct, but do not advance defendants' cause. Chapter 576 does, in fact, afford limited liability partners the same protection from third-party claims as New York law provides shareholders in professional corporations or professional limited liability companies. And unlike New York, most states "have adopted a partial liability shield protecting the partners only from vicarious personal liability for all partnership obligations arising from negligence, wrongful acts or misconduct, whether characterized as tort, contract or otherwise, committed while the partnership is an LLP" (*see* Prefatory Note Addendum to Uniform Partnership Act [1997] [explaining that RUPA, by contrast, "provid(es) for a corporate-styled liability shield which protects partners from vicarious personal liability for all partnership obligations incurred while a partnership is a limited liability partnership"]; *see also* Walker § 14:5, at 346 ["The type of LLP generally permitted by the states (other than Minnesota and New York) * * * offers less insulation against personal liability than many other types of organization"]). Nowhere in the voluminous commentary on limited liability partnerships has anyone suggested that New York (or any other state) has adopted a statute expanding the concept of limited liability in the way asserted by defendants.

* * *

In closing, we emphasize that the law of partnerships contemplates a written agreement among partners specifying the terms of their relationship. The Partnership Law's provisions are, for the most part, default requirements that come into play in the absence of an agreement. * * * Partners might agree, as among themselves, to limit the right to contribution or indemnification or to exclude it altogether. In this case, however, there was no written partnership agreement; therefore, the provisions of the Partnership Law govern.

Accordingly, the order of the Appellate Division, insofar as appealed from, should be affirmed, with costs * * *.

SMITH, J. (dissenting).

The text of Partnership Law § 26(b) seems clear to me: "no partner of a partnership which is a registered limited liability partnership is liable * * * for any debts, obligations or liabilities of * * * the registered limited liability partnership * * * whether arising in tort, contract or otherwise." The statute contains two specific exceptions, applicable when a partner acts wrongfully or when partners agree to vary the liability scheme (Partnership Law § 26[c], [d]), but there is no exception for liabilities to former partners claiming a share of the partnership's net assets. We should not create an exception that the Legislature did not. The majority draws a distinction between liability to "third parties" and liabilities to former partners—but a *former* partner is a third party where the partnership is concerned, and there is no good reason to treat him more favorably than any other third party.

No one suggests that section 26(b) exempts partners from any of their fiduciary duties; if a partner has diverted partnership funds to himself, or otherwise received more than his fair share, he will not escape liability and his former partners, as well as his existing partners, will be made whole. The issue is whether a former partner claiming his partnership share may reach the personal assets of partners who are no more blameworthy, and have no more been unjustly enriched, than he has.

I can think of two situations in which this issue may be important. First, without any fault by any partner, the business of the partnership may go badly after a partner withdraws from the firm but before he is paid his share, leaving the firm without enough assets to satisfy his claim. (This is apparently what happened here.) Secondly, the partnership's insolvency may result from the fault of a partner who is himself insolvent; in that case, the question is whether the former partner can proceed against the innocent remaining partners.

In the first case, there is no apparent reason why a former partner should be allowed to collect his debt when other third-party creditors may not; in fact, the Partnership Law provides in another context that debts to nonpartners have a preferred status (Partnership Law § 71[b] [equivalent to UPA § 40(b)]). In the second case, the rule adopted by the majority can produce even more clearly perverse results. Take an extreme example: Suppose there are three partners, two with a 49% interest each and one with a 2% interest. One of the 49% partners withdraws, and is entitled to 49% of the firm's assets. Before he can be paid, however, it is found that the other 49% partner has stolen all of those assets, lost them at a casino and gone bankrupt. Why should the innocent 2% partner have to make good the former partner's large loss?

If the Gursky & Ederer firm had remained a professional corporation, instead of turning itself into a limited liability partnership, the result in this case would not be in question: the individual shareholders of the corporation would not be liable for its obligation to Ederer. I do not see why the partners of an LLP should have an obligation that the shareholders of a PC do not, and I therefore dissent.

* * *

NOTES

(1) The *Ederer* court concludes that the LLP liability shield does not protect partners from claims by other partners. As a result, from a collection standpoint, partner creditors are better off than non-partner creditors. Moreover, partners in an LLP have less liability protection than shareholders in a corporation or members in an LLC, as shareholders and members are not vicariously liable for claims by their fellow owners. Do these results make sense?

(2) If RUPA 306(c) governed the dispute in *Ederer*, would the court have reached a different conclusion? What about under the Texas statute? *See* TEX. BUS. ORGS. CODE § 152.801(a) ("Except as provided by the partnership agreement, a partner is not personally liable to any person, including a partner, directly or indirectly, by contribution, indemnity, or otherwise, for any obligation of the partnership incurred while the partnership is a limited liability partnership.").

(3) In certain circumstances, courts could presumably impose personal liability on LLP partners under a "piercing the veil" theory. For example, in jurisdictions that provide for a full liability shield, partners may have an incentive to distribute partnership assets to themselves rather than to retain assets for the satisfaction of creditors. Because LLP statutes tend not to include restrictions on distributions that leave the firm undercapitalized, courts may turn to fraudulent transfer or veil-piercing doctrines. *See, e.g.*, COLO. REV. STAT. § 7–64–1009(1) ("In a case in which a party seeks to hold the general partners of a limited liability partnership or limited liability

limited partnership personally responsible for the alleged improper actions of the limited liability partnership or limited liability limited partnership, the court shall apply the case law that interprets the conditions and circumstances under which the corporate veil of a corporation may be pierced under Colorado law.").

(4) As mentioned, because partnership statutes typically provide that an LLP is a "partnership," *see, e.g.,* RUPA § 101(5), general partnership law is applicable to LLPs when it is not explicitly altered by LLP-specific provisions. Given that partners have limited liability in the LLP form, however, one can question whether general partnership law is suitable for the LLP setting. As a few specific examples, consider the following:

Management rights: Partnership law provides a default rule that each partner has a right to participate in the management of the business. *See* UPA § 18(e); RUPA § 401(f). When partners have personal liability for the obligations of the partnership, this rule can be justified on the ground that poor management decisions threaten a partner with substantial liability. As a consequence, each partner needs the ability to participate in (and hopefully influence) management decisions. When limited liability is present, however, the risk of personal liability from poor management decisions is lessened. Correspondingly, one can argue that the need to participate in management is lessened as well.

Profit sharing: Under partnership law, the default rule is that partners share profits equally. *See* UPA § 18(a); RUPA § 401(b). When partners have unlimited personal liability for partnership debts, this rule can be justified on the ground that each partner's "credit" contribution to the partnership (i.e., putting one's personal assets at risk) largely makes up for any inequality in financial contributions. When credit contributions are eliminated as a result of limited liability, however, this justification for equal sharing is weaker. Similarly, an LLP partner who practices in a high-risk area (e.g., a law firm partner who writes opinion letters and/or supervises a significant number of associates) may demand an increased share of the profits if, as a result of limited liability, her fellow partners no longer share in the risk.

Admitting new partners: Under partnership law, the default rule is that a unanimous vote of the partners is required to admit a new partner. *See* UPA § 18(g); RUPA § 401(i). At least part of the rationale for this rule is that the misconduct of a new partner can create partnership obligations and, therefore, personal liability for the partners. When limited liability is present, of course, this justification for unanimity is less compelling.

Even if these general partnership principles are applicable to the LLP setting, keep in mind that they are merely default rules. Thus, the partners in an LLP can contract around any unsuitable provisions.

D. THE LIMITED LIABILITY LIMITED PARTNERSHIP

Some states allow limited partnerships to register as LLPs. In effect, this creates a limited liability limited partnership ("LLLP")—a limited partnership where all of the partners have limited liability. (The alphabet soup seemingly never ends).

In contrast to a general partner in a traditional limited partnership, a general partner in an LLLP is liable for the obligations of the business only when a general partner in an LLP would be liable. *See, e.g.*, GA. CODE § 14–9–403(c) ("If a limited partnership is a limited liability partnership * * *, then * * * the liabilities of each general partner of such limited partnership shall be determined by reference to the provisions * * * regarding limited liability partnerships."). In some jurisdictions, a limited partner is granted the same protection. *See, e.g.*, ARIZ. REV. STAT. § 29–1026(D) ("If a limited partnership is a limited liability partnership, [the LLP liability protection] applies to its general partners and to any of its limited partners who * * * are liable for the debts or obligations of the partnership."). For limited partners, this protection presumably means that conduct that would result in control rule liability in a traditional limited partnership will not result in liability in an LLLP—unless a partner in an LLP would be liable for such conduct.

NOTES

(1) An LLLP is a limited partnership. As a consequence, a firm that is not a limited partnership (such as a firm that fails to comply with the filing requirements of the limited partnership statute) cannot be an LLLP.

(2) In general, if a limited partnership wishes to become an LLLP, it must comply with the registration and insurance/segregated funds requirements of the relevant LLP statute. Statutes typically specify the partner vote that is necessary to become an LLLP, and they usually provide for special name requirements as well. *See, e.g.*, TEX. BUS. ORGS. CODE § 153.351 (noting that a limited partnership can register as an LLP "as permitted by its partnership agreement" or, if the agreement is silent, "with the consent of partners required to amend its partnership agreement"); *id.* § 5.055 (requiring the name of an LLLP to include a designation of its limited partnership status and a designation of the limited liability of its partners, such as "Acme LP, LLP" or the more direct "Acme LLLP"); *see also* RUPA § 101 cmt. (suggesting an LLLP provision that specifies the necessary partner vote and that mandates compliance with the name requirements of the LLP statute).

(3) As noted, in some states the LLP liability protection is applied to all partners (general and limited) in an LLLP. In practical terms, this seems to reduce the importance of the control rule for limited partner liability in LLLPs. A limited partner who would be liable for violating the control rule in

a non-LLLP, in other words, has no liability in an LLLP unless the situation would result in liability for an LLP partner.

(4) Some LLLP provisions speak only of general partners receiving the LLP liability protection. In these jurisdictions, limited partner liability in an LLLP is presumably no different from limited partner liability in a traditional limited partnership. Notice, however, that this results in a peculiarity. In a RULPA (1985) limited partnership, a limited partner who participates in the control of the business can become personally liable for at least some of the venture's obligations. When a limited partnership has elected LLLP status, however, a general partner can participate in the control of the business without becoming personally liable for any of the venture's obligations. *See, e.g.,* RUPA § 306(c). LLLP status in a RULPA (1985) jurisdiction, therefore, may provide general partners with more liability protection than limited partners.

The drafters of RUPA clearly recognized this peculiarity. The Comment to RUPA § 101 states, in part, the following:

> * * * [According to RULPA (1985) § 303(a),] [u]nless also a general partner, a limited partner is not liable for the obligations of a limited partnership unless the partner participates in the control of the business and then only to persons reasonably believing the limited partner is a general partner. Therefore, arguably limited partners in a LLLP will have the specific RULPA Section 303 [(a)] liability shield while general partners will have a superior [RUPA] Section 306(c) liability shield [the LLP liability shield]. In order to clarify limited partner liability and other linkage issues, states that have adopted RUPA, these limited liability partnership rules, and RULPA may wish to consider an amendment to RULPA. A suggested form of such an amendment is:
>
> § 1107.   Limited Liability Limited Partnership.
>
> * * *
>
> (c) Sections 306(c) and 307(b) of the Uniform Partnership Act (1994) apply to both general and limited partners of a limited liability limited partnership.

(5) ULPA (2001) provides for LLLPs. If a limited partnership wishes to become an LLLP, it must state that it is an LLLP in its certificate of limited partnership. *See* ULPA (2001) §§ 102(9), 201(a)(4); *see also id.* § 108(c) (setting forth name requirements for LLLPs). If an LLLP is created, a full status-based liability shield is provided for the venture's general and limited partners. *See id.* §§ 303, 404(c). Under ULPA (2001), therefore, the peculiarity described in the prior note disappears.

PROBLEM

Acme is an LLLP in the state of Moll. Assume that an employee of Acme is working under the direct supervision of a limited partner. The employee engages in misconduct which gives rise to a partnership obligation. Does the limited partner face personal liability for this partnership obligation?

In working this problem, assume the following: (1) § 34–327 of the Moll general partnership statute is identical to § 34–327 in *Kus v. Irving*; (2) § 303 of the Moll limited partnership statute is identical to RULPA (1985) § 303; and (3) § 304 of the Moll limited partnership statute states that "[i]f a limited partnership is a limited liability partnership, § 34–327 of the general partnership statute applies to a general partner and to a limited partner who is liable under other provisions of this [limited partnership statute] for the debts or obligations of the limited partnership."

CHAPTER 20

THE LIMITED LIABILITY COMPANY

■ ■ ■

A. INTRODUCTION

The limited liability company ("LLC") is a noncorporate business structure that provides its owners, known as "members," with a number of benefits: (1) limited liability for the obligations of the venture, even if a member participates in the control of the business; (2) pass-through tax treatment; and (3) tremendous freedom to contractually arrange the internal operations of the venture. Because of this favorable combination of attributes, the LLC has emerged as the preferred business structure for many closely held businesses. Keep in mind, however, that the LLC is a relatively new form of business organization in this country. Although its "birth" dates back to 1977, its widespread use is more recent. Compared to other forms of business organization (such as the corporation or the partnership), therefore, the LLC is less established, and there are still a number of open questions for lawyers and courts to wrestle with. The materials in this Chapter focus on the operation of the LLC and on the advantages and disadvantages of conducting business in this form.

The LLC was the product of innovative professionals creating solutions when the current legal system failed to meet client needs. As described by one commentator: "Since the late 1960s, Hamilton Brothers Oil Company had been involved in international oil and gas exploration using foreign LLCs, primarily the Panamanian limitada. Unlike the U.S. entities available at that time, limitadas provided direct limited liability [for all owners] and the ability to secure partnership classification for * * * tax purposes." Susan Pace Hamill, *The Origins Behind the Limited Liability Company*, 59 OHIO ST. L.J. 1459, 1463 (1998).

Because no similar domestic entity existed in the United States, representatives of Hamilton Brothers Oil Company developed legislation that authorized an unincorporated domestic entity to be created that resembled the limitada. An initial effort to obtain enactment in Alaska failed, but the same legislation was introduced in Wyoming, where it was enacted on March 4, 1977, apparently without controversy. The critical question then became whether the Internal Revenue Service would issue a favorable ruling that an unincorporated entity that provided limited liability for all of its members would be eligible for partnership taxation. Such a favorable ruling was obtained in 1988. *See* Revenue Ruling 88–76,

1988–2 C.B. 360. Once the tax issue was resolved, states quickly adopted LLC statutes to take advantage of the flexibility of this new business form. By 1995, all 50 states had enacted statutes allowing for the creation of LLCs.

Because of concern that statutory diversity might create serious problems for interstate LLCs, attempts to develop prototype or uniform LLC statutes began almost immediately after the LLC's tax status was recognized. The rush by states to enact LLC statutes was underway, however, and most states enacted LLC statutes before efforts to develop standardized statutes came to fruition. The first standardized product was a "Prototype Limited Liability Company Act" that was proposed in 1992 by a committee of the American Bar Association.[a] Concepts developed in this prototype act were incorporated into many state statutes.

The Uniform Limited Liability Company Act ("ULLCA") was promulgated by the National Conference of Commissioners on Uniform State Laws ("NCCUSL") in 1996. As of this writing, only eight states and the U.S. Virgin Islands have adopted ULLCA. ULLCA's limited acceptance may be due in part to the fact that it embodies more partnership concepts than many existing state LLC statutes. For example, ULLCA retains the "at-will" versus "term" distinction for an LLC as well as the related dissociation and dissolution consequences that flow from that distinction. In 2006, ULLCA was substantially revised and updated. Only eight states and the District of Columbia, however, have presently adopted the revised Act ("RULLCA").[b] Nevertheless, ULLCA and RULLCA serve as useful templates for studying and debating LLC provisions, and the materials below will discuss both statutes. Many provisions of the Delaware LLC Act ("DLLCA") will also be referenced in the materials, as DLLCA and the Uniform Acts differ on a number of significant points and serve, to some extent, as competing statutory models.

Due to this developmental history of LLC legislation, there is less uniformity among LLC statutes than in the statutes governing other business forms. Indeed, even ULLCA's prefatory note points out that "state limited liability company acts display a dazzling array of diversity."

---

[a] The committee published a Revised Prototype Limited Liability Company Act in 2011.

[b] The prefatory note to RULLCA states the following:

Eighteen years have passed since the IRS issued its gate-opening Revenue Ruling 88–76, declaring that a Wyoming LLC would be taxed as a partnership despite the entity's corporate-like liability shield. More than eight years have passed since the IRS opened the gate still further with the "check the box" regulations. It is an opportune moment to identify the best elements of the myriad "first generation" LLC statutes and to infuse those elements into a new, "second generation" uniform act.

NOTES

(1) As noted above, a primary reason for forming an LLC is to create an entity that offers investors the protections of limited liability and the pass-through tax status of partnerships. *See* Chapter 1, Section D(4) (discussing pass-through taxation). The Treasury regulations in effect when the original LLC statutes were enacted provided that an unincorporated business organization such as an LLC would be taxed as a corporation (with the undesirable double taxation on distributions) if it possessed more "corporate" characteristics than "noncorporate" characteristics. More specifically, the so-called "Kintner regulations" provided that a firm would be taxed as a corporation rather than a partnership if it had three or more of the following "corporate" characteristics: (1) continuity of life; (2) free transferability of ownership interests; (3) centralized management; and (4) limited liability. Because LLC statutes provided limited liability and, typically, the possibility of centralized management, a state wanting to ensure partnership tax treatment for LLCs organized under its statute needed to deny both of the remaining corporate characteristics. As a result, early versions of LLC statutes tended to restrict the members' ability to transfer their ownership interests in order to deny the free transferability characteristic. Further, to deny the continuity of life characteristic, LLC statutes usually provided for dissolution of an LLC upon a member's withdrawal or other dissociation from the business. As critics of the Kintner regulations argued, these statutory provisions were driven largely by tax concerns rather than by broader business considerations.

In 1997, the IRS replaced the Kintner regulations with new "check the box" regulations. *See* Chapter 1, Section D(4). Under these new rules, an unincorporated business entity such as an LLC can simply elect whether to be taxed as a partnership (pass-through taxation) or a corporation (double taxation). (Technically, the unincorporated entity receives pass-through taxation by default and must only make an affirmative election if it wishes to be taxed as a corporation.) Certain entities, however, must be taxed as corporations. Such businesses include: (1) entities organized under a federal or state statute that refers to the entity as "incorporated" or a "corporation"; (2) certain foreign entities that are specifically listed in the regulations as per se corporations; and (3) business entities that are taxable as corporations under other provisions of the Internal Revenue Code, such as publicly traded firms and regulated investment companies. As a result of the check the box regulations, the federal income tax treatment of LLCs is now determined by a simple taxpayer choice rather than by the fact-specific "corporateness" inquiry called for by the Kintner regulations.

(2) "The check-the-box rule took the lid off of the growth of LLCs. Tax returns for the year 2000 report 718,704 domestic LLCs, up from 589,403 in 1999. The 2002 Annual Report of the Jurisdictions of the International Association of Corporation Administrators shows 521,953 domestic and foreign LLCs filing in 43 reporting states for 2001, compared to 474,791 for 2000. While LLC filings were rising by 47,000 from 2000 to 2001, domestic

for-profit business and professional corporation filings were dropping about 30,000 and limited partnership filings were dropping about 7,000. These figures indicate that LLCs are gradually replacing corporations and limited partnerships as the leading business entity." Larry E. Ribstein, *LLCs: Is the Future Here?*, 13 BUS. LAW TODAY 11, 13 (Nov./Dec. 2003).

(3) "The [LLC] is now undeniably the most popular form of new business entity in the United States. * * * Rising from near obscurity in the 1990s, the LLC has now taken its place as the new 'king-of-the-hill' among business entities, utterly dominating its closest rivals. As the research reported in this article indicates, the number of new LLCs formed in America in 2007 now outpaces the number of new corporations formed by a margin of nearly two to one. In several 'bellwether' states, the numbers are even more impressive. * * * Other business forms have fared no better against the LLC. While data for hybrid and newer business structures is more difficult to compile, the data in this Article relating to limited partnerships (LPs) demonstrate that the LLC's dominance of these entities is even more staggering. For example, the number of new LLCs formed in 2007 outpaced the number of new LPs formed in that same year by a margin of over 34 to 1." Rodney D. Chrisman, *LLCs are the New King of the Hill*, XV FORD. J. OF CORP. & FIN. L. 459, 459–62 (2010).

(4) As the above materials suggest, the combination of limited liability and pass-through taxation has contributed significantly to the LLC's popularity. Even without the LLC, however, limited liability and pass-through taxation can be obtained through the limited partnership, S-corporation, and LLP structures. What advantages does the LLC provide over these other business forms?

(5) Because LLC statutes often reflect a mishmash of corporation, partnership, and limited partnership principles, courts frequently analogize to existing doctrines from other business forms when confronting LLC issues—particularly when the LLC statute itself offers little guidance. One court explained its analytical approach as follows:

> It is important to keep the history of LLC development in perspective when working with LLCs and court interpretations of LLC acts. * * * The typical LLC act is usually a hybrid of provisions culled from the individual state's partnership statutes and business corporation law.
>
> * * *
>
> [W]hen a court is interpreting an LLC act or agreement, the court will focus on the particular aspect of the LLC that gives rise to the problem, with emphasis on the foundational business form from which that characteristic originated. Usually, the particular aspect can be traced to either the corporate components or the partnership components of the LLC act or agreement. In such cases where the characteristic originated from the partnership aspects of the LLC, the court will use the established [principles] and precedent of the

partnership law to resolve the issue * * *. In such cases where the characteristic originated from the corporate aspects of the LLC, the court will utilize the established [principles] and precedent of corporate law to resolve the issue.

Anderson v. Wilder, No. E2003–00460–COA–R3–CV, 2003 WL 22768666, at *4 (Tenn. Ct. App. Nov. 21, 2003) (quoting Annotation, *Construction and Application of Limited Liability Company Acts,* 79 A.L.R.5TH 689, 698). In all likelihood, many courts, either explicitly or implicitly, follow this analytical approach.

B. FORMATION

Like limited partnerships, corporations, and LLPs, LLCs are formed by filing a document, usually known as the "articles of organization" or "certificate of organization," with the secretary of state or equivalent official of the appropriate jurisdiction. The articles of organization are relatively skeletal and typically include only basic information about the company. (For the precise requirements of any given state, of course, check that state's LLC statute.) In Delaware, for example, the "certificate of formation" is required to include only the name of the LLC, the address of its registered office, and the name and address of its registered agent for service of process. *See* DLLCA § 18–201. ULLCA demands slightly more content in the "articles of organization" (e.g., the articles must specify whether the LLC is to be manager-managed), but the information required is still relatively basic. *See* ULLCA § 203; RULLCA § 201(b).

The real detail on the governance of an LLC is usually provided in a separate document known as an "operating agreement" or a "limited liability company agreement." The operating agreement is a nonpublic document (i.e., it is not filed with any state official) similar to a partnership agreement or a corporation's bylaws. It contains specifics on the rights, duties, and obligations of the LLC's members and managers and on the operation of the LLC as a whole. In general, the operating agreement can be tailored to suit the particular needs of an LLC's members, and the provisions of the operating agreement will displace most, if not all, of the statutory provisions. Freedom of contract, in other words, is central to the LLC's structure.

NOTES

(1) Under DLLCA and the Uniform Acts, is an LLC a separate legal entity? If so, when does its legal existence commence? *See* DLLCA § 18–201; ULLCA §§ 201–202; RULLCA §§ 104, 201.

Many practitioners and clients wish to have an LLC formed and on the public record before the precise identity and relationship of the members has been determined. When the prospective members complete the negotiation of their business deal, the LLC can be "waiting on the shelf" and business can commence without any filing delay. This concept of a "shelf LLC"—i.e., an LLC formed without having at least one member upon formation—poses difficulties under the statutes of some jurisdictions, as the statutes presuppose that an LLC has a member upon formation. *See, e.g.,* ULLCA § 202(a). RULLCA permits shelf LLCs, but two filings have to be made. First, the certificate of organization must be filed, and it must explicitly state that the LLC will have no members when the Secretary of State files the certificate. *See* RULLCA § 201(b)(3). Second, within 90 days from the filing of the certificate, an organizer of the LLC must file a notice stating that the LLC has at least one member and the date when the person or persons became the LLC's initial member or members. *See id.* § 201(e)(1). If this second filing is properly made, the LLC is deemed formed as of the date of initial membership stated in the notice. *See id.* § 201(e)(2). If the second filing is not properly made, the certificate lapses and is void. *See id.* § 201(e)(1).

(2) Under DLLCA and the Uniform Acts, must an LLC have an operating agreement? If so, does the operating agreement have to be in writing? *See* DLLCA §§ 18–101(7), 18–201; ULLCA §§ 101(13), 103; RULLCA §§ 102(13), 110; *cf. In re* Spires, 778 N.Y.S.2d 259, 262–63 (Sup. Ct. 2004) ("There is no provision in the [New York] Limited Liability Company Law imposing any type of penalty or punishment for failing to adopt a written operating agreement. The statute does not require an operating agreement prior to the formation of this type of entity. There is no statute or common law that leads to the conclusion that the failure to enter into an operating agreement transforms a limited liability company into a partnership. * * * Lighthouse Solutions LLC was formed at the time of the filing of the Articles of Organization * * * with the Department of State. According to the statute, the filing is conclusive evidence of the formation of the limited liability company * * *."). Even if an LLC statute permits oral operating agreements, they may still be problematic under the jurisdiction's statute of frauds. *See, e.g.,* RULLCA § 102(13) cmt. *But see* DLLCA § 18–101(7) (stating that "[a] limited liability company agreement is not subject to any statute of frauds").

(3) Contract principles have a vital role in the operation of the LLC. A number of LLC statutes explicitly promote freedom of contract and encourage the enforcement of the parties' private arrangements. *See, e.g.,* DLLCA § 18–1101(b). Moreover, LLC statutes usually contain far fewer governance rules than the statutory schemes of other business forms (e.g., LLC statutes typically contain few or no default rules on meetings, quorums, and notice). As a consequence, the operating agreement of the parties is often the only supplier of certain governance and operating terms.

(4) As between the articles of organization and the operating agreement, which one controls if there is a conflict? Only a few statutes speak to this issue. *Compare* N.Y. LTD. LIAB. CO. LAW § 417(a) ("Subject to the provisions of this chapter, the members of a limited liability company shall adopt a written operating agreement that contains any provisions not inconsistent with law or its articles of organization * * *."), *with* ULLCA § 203(c) ("[I]f any provision of an operating agreement is inconsistent with the articles of organization

* * * [then] (1) the operating agreement controls as to managers, members, and members' transferees; and (2) the articles of organization control as to persons, other than managers, members and their transferees, who reasonably rely on the articles to their detriment."), *and* RULLCA § 112(d) (substantially the same).

(5) As in the limited partnership context, some LLC statutes provide that an LLC is created so long as there has been "substantial compliance" with the formation requirements of the statute. *See, e.g.*, DLLCA § 18–201(b). Other statutes omit the substantial compliance language but provide that the filing of the articles is "conclusive proof" that formation requirements have been satisfied. *See, e.g.*, ULLCA § 202(c); RULLCA § 201(d)(3), (e)(3). The conclusive proof language should eliminate any uncertainty about whether an error in the articles prevents the formation of an LLC. Interestingly, unlike limited partnership statutes, LLC statutes do not typically provide any amendment/withdrawal protection for members who mistakenly (but in good faith) believe that an LLC has been formed. *Cf.* RULPA (1985) § 304 (providing amendment/withdrawal protection); ULPA (2001) § 306 (same).

(6) Some courts have concluded that the de facto corporation and estoppel doctrines apply to LLCs. *See, e.g.*, Duray Development, 792 N.W.2d 749, 759–60 (Mich. Ct. App 2010) (de facto corporation and estoppel doctrines); *In re* Hausman, 921 N.E.2d 191, 193 (N.Y. 2009) (de facto corporation doctrine); Simsbury-Avon Preservation Soc'y, LLC v. Metacon Gun Club, Inc., No. CV040834190S, 2004 WL 2094933, at *1–2 (Conn. Super. Ct. Aug. 20, 2004) (de facto corporation doctrine); *see also* Chapter 5, Section D(2) (discussing the doctrines in the corporate setting).

(7) Should an operating agreement be effective among the members if an LLC is improperly formed (e.g., the articles of organization are never filed)? Consider the following:

> * * * The underlying agreement is generally enforced in the analogous limited partnership situation. In most cases, the failure to comply with formalities such as central filing requirements affects only third parties whom the formalities were designed to protect.
>
> The only argument in favor of refusing to enforce the agreement among the parties is that this result would enhance the deterrent effect of the formal rules. Enforcing the operating agreement where formalities have not been complied with might encourage parties not to comply with the requirement. On the other hand, upsetting agreements through rigid enforcement of formal requirements might be more costly because it would discourage reliance on LLC agreements and encourage litigation over compliance issues. Moreover, nonenforcement is arguably an excessive penalty in light of the low probability of serious harm to third parties from failure to file.

1 LARRY E. RIBSTEIN & ROBERT R. KEATINGE, RIBSTEIN AND KEATINGE ON
LIMITED LIABILITY COMPANIES § 4:16, at 4–25 to 4–26 (2d ed. 2004).

(8) LLC members are usually required to make a contribution to the
capital of the company. Like limited partnership statutes, LLC statutes tend
to define "contribution" broadly. Cash, property, and services, for example,
typically count as contributions. *See, e.g.*, DLLCA § 18–101(3); ULLCA § 401;
RULLCA § 402.

(9) In *McConnell v. Hunt Sports Enterprises*, 725 N.E.2d 1193 (Ohio Ct.
App. 1999), the trial court ruled that the appellant was not a member of an
LLC prior to his execution of the operating agreement. The Ohio Court of
Appeals disagreed:

> As a preliminary matter, we note that the trial court erred in
> concluding appellant was not a member of [the LLC] prior to
> executing the operating agreement. R.C. [Revised Code] 1705.01(G)
> states that a member of a limited liability company is a person
> whose name appears on the records of the company as the owner of
> a membership interest in that company. Further, a person becomes
> a member of a limited liability company at the time the company is
> formed or at any later time that is specified in the records of the
> company for becoming a member. R.C. 1705.14(A).

> Section 1.2 of the [LLC] operating agreement states that the
> agreement becomes effective on the date that an executed copy of
> the articles of organization are filed with the Secretary of State.
> [The LLC]'s articles of organization were filed with the Secretary of
> State on October 31, 1996.

> Section 11.1*(l)*, article XI, of the operating agreement states
> that "Members" is defined in section 3.1. Section 3.1 states:

> *"Members. The members of the Company ('Members') shall be those
> persons or entities identified as such on Schedule A, as such
> Schedule shall be amended from time to time.* The names and
> addresses of the Members, the amount of their contribution to the
> capital of the Company, the number of Units credited to each
> Member and their Percentage Interests are set forth in Schedule A."
> (Emphasis added.)

> Appellant is identified on Schedule A and is credited with a
> capital contribution of $25,000 and as having twenty-five units.
> Appellant made such capital contribution on November 12, 1996.
> Therefore, pursuant to the Revised Code and the operating
> agreement, appellant was a member of [the LLC] from its inception
> even though appellant did not execute a copy of the operating
> agreement until June 6, 1997.

Id. at 1213; *see also* DLLCA §§ 18–101(11) (defining "member"), 18–301
(addressing the admission of members); RULLCA §§ 102(11) (defining
"member"), 401 (addressing the admission of members); *cf. id.* § 111(b)

(stating that "[a] person that becomes a member of a limited liability company is deemed to assent to the operating agreement").

(10) Most LLC statutes indicate that the law of the jurisdiction of an LLC's organization will govern a foreign LLC's internal affairs, organization, and the liability of its members and managers. *See, e.g.*, DLLCA § 18–901(a)(1); ULLCA § 1001(a); RULLCA § 801(a).

(11) Many LLC statutes formerly required LLCs to have at least two members, suggesting that LLCs were viewed more as partnerships than corporations. Modern-day statutes have largely eliminated this two-member requirement, however, and single-member LLCs are now permissible.

(12) In many jurisdictions, LLCs can be formed by converting existing non-LLC business structures into LLCs. Statutes typically specify the procedure for converting as well as the effects of conversion. *See, e.g.*, DLLCA § 18–214; ULLCA §§ 902–903; RULLCA §§ 1006–1009.

(13) Unlike a partnership, which by definition requires a profit motive, *see, e.g.*, RUPA §§ 101(6), 202(a), an LLC under many statutes need not be a profit-seeking enterprise. *See, e.g.*, DLLCA § 18–106(a); ULLCA §§ 101(3) & cmt., 112(a); RULLCA § 104(b) & cmt.

(14) Some state statutes authorize a so-called "low-profit LLC," or "L3C." As one commentator explained:

> The L3C is similar to a traditional LLC in that it is a for-profit entity that offers a flexible structure in which each member's management and financial interest may vary. The "structural flexibility" of LLCs permits individuals, foundations, non-governmental organizations, corporations, and government agencies to be part of the same entity. While both LLCs and L3Cs may generate profits, the major difference between the two is that L3C statutes require L3Cs to prioritize socially beneficial goals, with generating profit as a secondary priority. By contrast, a party can organize an LLC for any lawful purpose. Typically, L3C legislation amends a state's existing LLC statute to create a subcategory of LLCs that effectively retains the LLC's flexible nature but adds a requirement of meeting social goals.
>
>   * * *
>
>   * * * [The L3C's] major aim is to facilitate capital-raising for social causes in both the non-profit (e.g., foundations) and for-profit sectors (e.g., venture capital and other investors). Specifically, the L3C aims to attract program-related investments ("PRIs") from private foundations. * * * PRIs are investments that foundations make to further the foundation's social mission, and thus do not subject the foundation to a variety of penalty taxes. PRIs, by definition, cannot have a significant profit motive. As a result, social enterprises that can attract PRIs can make use of a tiered investment strategy, where foundations making PRIs take on the

most risk and accept the lowest return; this then facilitates investment by for-profit investors, who could receive a market rate of return, even though the social enterprise, as a whole, does not offer a market return.

Edward Xia, Note, *Can the L3C Spur Private Foundation Program-Related Investment?*, 2013 COLUM. BUS. L. REV. 242, 244, 248. The emergence of the L3C, however, has not escaped criticism, largely because there is no assurance that an investment in an L3C will qualify as a PRI. *See, e.g., id.* at 244 ("However, as L3C legislation has spread to nine different states, some critics have begun to question whether, given the case-by-case analysis required in a typical determination of whether a PRI meets IRS standards, the L3C facilitates the making of PRIs any more than a typical LLC does."); *see also* Daniel S. Kleinberger, *A Myth Deconstructed: The "Emperor's New Clothes" on the Low-Profit Limited Liability Company*, 35 DEL. J. CORP. L. 879, 881 (2010) (stating that the "glowing characterizations" of the L3C "are flatly wrong," and noting that the L3C "is an unnecessary and unwise contrivance" whose "very existence is inherently misleading").

C. MANAGEMENT AND OPERATION

1. GENERAL GOVERNANCE

Most LLC statutes assign, as a default rule, all management functions to members. *See, e.g.*, DLLCA § 18–402; ULLCA §§ 101(11), (12), 203(a)(6); RULLCA §§ 102(10), (12), 407. This member-managed structure resembles a general partnership, as each of the owners has management rights. In contrast, a few statutes default to management by a separate group of managers, who may or may not be members. This manager-managed structure resembles a corporation, as management is centralized in a smaller subset of actors. Because these are only default rules, member-managed jurisdictions allow the owners to elect manager-managed governance, and manager-managed jurisdictions allow the owners to elect member-managed governance.

The default rules for voting in an LLC differ among the statutes. About half of the LLC statutes default to members voting on a per capita basis (one vote per member), while the other half default to members voting on a pro rata basis (by financial or other contribution to the firm). For ordinary matters, majority rule (whether on a per capita or pro rata basis) typically carries the decision. For extraordinary matters, however, some statutes require a specified supermajority vote. In manager-managed LLCs, decisions are usually made by a majority vote of the managers (by number), although certain extraordinary decisions will often require a specified vote of the members as well. *See, e.g.*, ULLCA § 404(c); RULLCA § 407(c).

NOTES

(1) Why might LLC owners choose member-management or manager-management for their venture?

(2) As mentioned, LLC owners can choose to opt out of the default management structure in the statute. If such an opt out choice is made, most statutes require the deviation to be specified in the articles of organization, although some allow the specification to be made in the operating agreement. *See, e.g.,* ULLCA § 203(a)(6) (articles of organization); DLLCA § 18–402 (LLC agreement); RULLCA § 407(a) (operating agreement). From the standpoint of a third party transacting with an LLC, is this issue important? *See, e.g.,* ULLCA § 301(a)(1), (b)(1).

(3) An LLC may not have to be entirely member-managed or manager-managed. Some LLC statutes allow the management functions to be divided between members and managers. *See, e.g.,* VA. CODE § 13.1–1024(A) ("The articles of organization or an operating agreement of a limited liability company may delegate full or partial responsibility for managing a limited liability company to or among one or more managers."). Even without explicit statutory authorization, the members could presumably divide up management authority between members and managers in the operating agreement. For example, an LLC may choose manager-management for ordinary business decisions but member-management for some or all of the firm's extraordinary business decisions.

(4) As previously discussed, the default voting rule for members in LLC statutes splits between per capita voting and pro rata voting. The default rule for the allocation of financial rights among members (i.e., sharing profits and losses) follows a similar split. Why might LLC members prefer per capita voting and sharing? Pro rata voting and sharing?

(5) Some LLC statutes explicitly allow for the creation of multiple classes of LLC ownership interests with different rights and privileges (e.g., a class of ownership interests with superior or inferior voting rights). *See, e.g.,* DLLCA § 18–302(a). This is analogous to a corporation and the ability to have multiple classes of stock with varying rights and privileges.

(6) Corporation statutes usually include a number of provisions that address governance formalities (e.g., provisions on electing and removing directors, meetings, minutes, quorums, notice, proxies). By contrast, LLC statutes typically fail to include such provisions. Is this lack of detail beneficial or problematic?

PROBLEM

A, B, and C form a member-managed LLC. A contributes 60% of the start-up capital and B and C each contribute 20%. The operating agreement is silent as to voting rules, voting power, and profit and loss allocation.

(a) On a decision to hire a new employee, A votes one way while B and C vote the other. On a separate decision to amend the operating agreement, the same voting pattern occurs. Who prevails on these two decisions? *See* DLLCA §§ 18–101(3), 18–302, 18–402, 18–503; ULLCA § 404; RULLCA § 407.

(b) Assume that the LLC is manager-managed pursuant to the terms of its operating agreement. The operating agreement is silent, however, on the election and removal of managers. How are managers elected? How are they removed? *See* DLLCA §§ 18–101(10), 18–401 to 18–402; ULLCA § 404; RULLCA § 407.

(c) Assume again that the LLC is manager-managed. Assume further that the operating agreement specifies that a manager can be elected only by a unanimous vote of the members, but the agreement is silent on the vote needed to remove a manager. At the inception of the venture, C is unanimously elected as the sole manager. Personal animosity subsequently develops between A, B, and C. As a consequence, A and B seek to remove C as manager and to replace her with B. Under the Uniform Acts, will A and B be successful in their effort to remove C? To elect B? Is there a problem here? *See* ULLCA § 404; RULLCA § 407.

2. AUTHORITY

Under most statutes, members in member-managed LLCs possess partnership-like agency authority to bind the LLC, and managers in manager-managed LLCs have similar authority. Not surprisingly, members in manager-managed LLCs usually have no statutory authority to bind the venture. *See, e.g.*, ULLCA § 301(a), (b). *But see* DLLCA § 18–402 ("Unless otherwise provided in a limited liability company agreement, each member and manager has the authority to bind the limited liability company."). Efforts to restrict the authority of members or managers can sometimes be problematic, as the following case illustrates.

TAGHIPOUR V. JEREZ
Supreme Court of Utah, 2002.
52 P.3d 1252.

RUSSON, JUSTICE:

On a writ of certiorari, Namvar Taghipour, Danesh Rahemi, and Jerez, Taghipour and Associates, LLC, seek review of the decision of the court of appeals affirming the trial court's dismissal of their causes of action against Mount Olympus Financial, L.C. ("Mt. Olympus"). We affirm.

BACKGROUND

Namvar Taghipour, Danesh Rahemi, and Edgar Jerez ("Jerez") formed a limited liability company known as Jerez, Taghipour and Associates, LLC (the "LLC"), on August 30, 1994, to purchase and develop a particular parcel of real estate pursuant to a joint venture agreement. The LLC's articles of organization designated Jerez as the LLC's manager. In addition, the operating agreement between the members of the LLC provided: "No loans may be contracted on behalf of the [LLC] * * * unless authorized by a resolution of the [m]embers."

On August 31, 1994, the LLC acquired the intended real estate. Then, on January 10, 1997, Jerez, unbeknownst to the LLC's other members or managers, entered into a loan agreement on behalf of the LLC with Mt. Olympus. According to the agreement, Mt. Olympus lent the LLC $25,000 and, as security for the loan, Jerez executed and delivered a trust deed that conveyed the LLC's real estate property to a trustee with the power to sell the property in the event of default. Mt. Olympus then dispensed $20,000 to Jerez and retained the $5,000 balance to cover various fees. In making the loan, Mt. Olympus did not investigate Jerez's authority to effectuate the loan agreement beyond determining that Jerez was the manager of the LLC.

After Mt. Olympus dispersed the funds pursuant to the agreement, Jerez apparently misappropriated and absconded with the $20,000. Jerez never remitted a payment on the loan, and because the other members of the LLC were unaware of the loan, no loan payments were ever made by anyone, and consequently, the LLC defaulted. Therefore, Mt. Olympus foreclosed on the LLC's property. The members of the LLC, other than Jerez, were never notified of the default or pending foreclosure sale.

On June 18, 1999, Namvar Taghipour, Danesh Rahemi, and the LLC (collectively, "Taghipour") filed suit against Mt. Olympus and Jerez. Taghipour asserted three claims against Mt. Olympus: (1) declaratory judgment that the loan agreement and subsequent foreclosure on the LLC's property were invalid because Jerez lacked the authority to bind the LLC under the operating agreement, (2) negligence in failing to conduct proper due diligence in determining whether Jerez had the authority to enter into the loan agreement, and (3) partition of the various interests in the property at issue. In response, Mt. Olympus moved to dismiss all three claims, asserting that pursuant to Utah Code section 48–2b–127(2), the loan agreement documents are valid and binding on the LLC since they were signed by the LLC's manager. This section provides:

> Instruments and documents providing for the acquisition, mortgage, or disposition of property of the limited liability company shall be valid and binding upon the limited liability company if they are executed by one or more managers of a limited liability company having a manager or managers or if they are executed by one or more members of a limited liability company in which management has been retained by the members.

Utah Code Ann. § 48–2b–127(2) (1998). The trial court granted Mt. Olympus' motion and dismissed Taghipour's claims against Mt. Olympus, ruling that under the above section, "instruments and documents providing for the mortgage of property of a limited liability company are valid and binding on the limited liability company if they are executed by the manager," that the complaint alleges that Jerez is the manager of the LLC, and that therefore the loan documents Jerez executed are valid and binding on the LLC.

Taghipour appealed to the Utah Court of Appeals. Taghipour argued that the trial court's interpretation of section 48–2b–127(2) was in error, inasmuch as it failed to read it in conjunction with Utah Code section 48–2b–125(2)(b), which provides that a manager's authority to bind a limited liability company can be limited by the operating agreement. That section provides in relevant part:

> If the management of the limited liability company is vested in a manager or managers, any manager has authority to bind the limited liability company, unless otherwise provided in the articles of organization or operating agreement.

Id. § 48–2b–125(2)(b). The Utah Court of Appeals affirmed the trial court * * *.

* * *

ANALYSIS

The issue in this case is whether the loan agreement documents executed by Jerez, as manager of the LLC, are valid and binding on the LLC under section 48–2b–127(2) of the Utah Limited Liability Company Act (the "Act"), as the statute existed at the time Jerez executed the loan agreement, or whether the documents were not binding on the LLC because, consistent with section 48–2b–125(2)(b) of the Act, the operating agreement effectively denied Jerez the necessary authority to bind the LLC where the agreement provides: "No loans may be contracted on behalf of the [LLC] * * * unless authorized by a resolution of the [m]embers." Taghipour reasons that this operating agreement provision precludes Jerez from executing a loan without a resolution of the members since under section 48–2b–125(2)(b) of the Act a manager cannot bind a limited liability company if the articles of organization or operating agreement does not afford the manager the authority to do so.

I.   COMPETING STATUTORY PROVISIONS

To determine whether the loan agreement in this case is valid and binding on the LLC, it must first be determined whether this case is governed by section 48–2b–127(2), which makes certain kinds of documents binding on a limited liability company when executed by a manager, or section 48–2b–125(2)(b), which provides that a manager's authority to bind a limited liability company can be limited or eliminated by an operating agreement.

When two statutory provisions purport to cover the same subject, the legislature's intent must be considered in determining which provision applies. To determine that intent, our rules of statutory construction provide that "when two statutory provisions conflict in their operation, the provision more specific in application governs over the more general provision."

In this case, the Utah Court of Appeals, affirming the trial court, concluded that section 48–2b–127(2) was more specific than section 48–2b–125(2)(b), and therefore took precedence over it. However, Taghipour contends that in determining which of the two provisions is more specific, the more restrictive clause is more specific because it is more limiting and "would require authority in all situations." Accordingly, Taghipour contends that section 48–2b–125(2)(b) is the more restrictive, and consequently, the more specific, provision.

The question of which statute the legislature intended to apply in this case is determined by looking to the plain language of the statutes that purport to cover the same subject. * * *

Section 48–2b–127(2) is the more specific statute because it applies only to documents explicitly enumerated in the statute, i.e., the section expressly addresses "[i]nstruments and documents" that provide "for the acquisition, mortgage, or disposition of property of the limited liability company." Thus, this section is tailored precisely to address the documents and instruments Jerez executed, e.g., the trust deed and trust deed note. For example, a trust deed is similar to a mortgage in that it secures an obligation relating to real property, and a trust deed "is a conveyance" of title to real property, which is a disposition of property as contemplated by the statutory provision. Conversely, section 48–2b–125(2)(b) is more general because it addresses *every* situation in which a manager can bind a limited liability company.

Further, a statute is more specific according to the content of the statute, not according to how restrictive the statute is in application. Indeed, a specific statute may be either more or less restrictive than the statute more general in application, depending upon the intent of the legislature in enacting a more specific statute.

Moreover, if we were to hold that section 48–2b–125(2)(b) is the more specific provision, we would essentially render section 48–2b–127(2) "superfluous and inoperative," because section 48–2b–127(2) would simply restate section 48–2b–125(2)(b) and would therefore be subsumed by section 48–2b–125(2)(b). Accordingly, the court of appeals correctly concluded that section 48–2b–127(2) is more specific, and therefore, the applicable statute in this case.

II. VALID AND BINDING LOAN AGREEMENT DOCUMENTS

Section 48–2b–127(2) must be applied to the facts of this case to determine whether the documents are valid and bind the LLC. * * * According to this section, the documents are binding if they are covered by the statute and if executed by a manager. There are no other requirements for such documents to be binding on a limited liability company.

In this case, as Taghipour acknowledges in the complaint and Taghipour's brief on appeal, Jerez was designated as the LLC's manager in the articles of organization. Jerez, acting in his capacity as manager, executed loan agreement documents, e.g., the trust deed and trust deed note, on behalf of the LLC that are specifically covered by the above statute. As such, these documents are valid and binding on the LLC under section 48–2b–127(2). Therefore, the court of appeals correctly concluded that the LLC was bound by the loan agreement and, consequently, that Mt. Olympus was not liable to Taghipour for Jerez's actions.

CONCLUSION

The court of appeals correctly determined that section 48–2b–127(2) (1998) governs this case, that under this statutory section the loan agreement is valid and binding on the LLC, and that Mt. Olympus did all that was required by statute. Therefore, the court of appeals correctly affirmed the trial court's dismissal of Taghipour's claims against Mt. Olympus. Accordingly, we affirm.

NOTES

(1) In light of the *Taghipour* court's holding, how should the members of the LLC have protected themselves against Jerez's (the manager's) unauthorized disposition of the LLC's property?

(2) As part of its analysis, the *Taghipour* court states the following: "Moreover, if we were to hold that section 48–2b–125(2)(b) is the more specific provision, we would essentially render section 48–2b–127(2) 'superfluous and inoperative,' because section 48–2b–127(2) would simply restate section 48–2b–125(2)(b) and would therefore be subsumed by section 48–2b–125(2)(b)." Can you explain what the court means by this assertion?

(3) What is the purpose of a statutory provision like Utah Code § 48–2b–127(2)? Consider the following passage from a concurring opinion in the Court of Appeals decision in *Taghipour*:

> * * * I must note that I find the policy reflected in sections 48–2b–125(2)(b) and –127(2) to be quite curious. If, as in this case, there are restrictions in a limited liability company's organic documents on its managers' ability to unilaterally bind the

company, those restrictions will be effective across the range of mundane and comparatively insignificant contracts purportedly entered into by the company, but the restrictions will be ineffective in the case of the company's most important contracts. Thus, if the articles of organization or operating agreement provide that the managers will enter into no contract without the approval of the company's members, as memorialized in an appropriate resolution, the company can escape an unauthorized contract for janitorial services, coffee supplies, or photocopying, but is stuck with the sale of its property for less than fair value or a loan on unfavorable terms.

Surely this is at odds with the expectations of the business community. A manager or officer typically can bind the company to comparatively unimportant contracts, but, as is provided in the Operating Agreement in this case, needs member or board approval to borrow against company assets. Financial institutions know this and are able to protect themselves by insisting on seeing articles of incorporation, bylaws, and board resolutions—or the limited liability company equivalents—as part of the mortgage loan process. A cursory review of such documents in this case would have disclosed that Jerez lacked the authority to bind the company to the proposed loan agreement.

In short, I suspect that the strange result in this case is not so much the product of carefully weighed policy considerations as it is the product of a legislative oversight or lapse of some kind. That being said, I readily agree that the language of both statutory sections is clear and unambiguous and that it is not the prerogative of the courts to rewrite legislation. If the laws which dictate the result in this case need to be fixed, the repairs must come via legislative amendment rather than judicial pronouncement.

Taghipour v. Jerez, 26 P.3d 885, 889 (Utah Ct. App. 2001) (Orme, J., concurring).

(4) The concurrence in the Court of Appeals decision suspects that Utah Code § 48–2b–127(2) "is the product of a legislative oversight or lapse of some kind." One can find support for that suspicion in the fact that the section was repealed in Utah's revision to its LLC Act. Nevertheless, substantially similar provisions are found in other LLC statutes. *See, e.g.,* NEB. REV. STAT. § 21–2617 ("Instruments and documents providing for the acquisition, mortgage, or disposition of property of the limited liability company shall be valid and binding upon the limited liability company if executed by a manager of a limited liability company having a manager or, if management has been retained by one or more classes of members, by a member of any such class."); OHIO REV. CODE § 1705.35 (substantially the same); R.I. GEN. LAWS § 7–16–68 (substantially the same).

(5) If ULLCA § 301(c) had governed the dispute in *Taghipour*, what result? Consider RULLCA § 302(a), (g) as well.

(6) Under the default rules of DLLCA and ULLCA, can a member's unauthorized actions bind an LLC to a third-party transaction? Under what circumstances? *See* DLLCA § 18–402; ULLCA § 301.

(7) In a sharp break from prior Uniform Acts, RULLCA eliminates the concept of statutory agency authority. Section 301(a) states that "[a] member is not an agent of a limited liability company solely by reason of being a member," and there is no provision addressing the agency authority of managers. *See also id.* § 407 cmt. (stating that "[t]he actual authority of an LLC's manager or managers is a question of agency law," and further noting that "[t]he common law of agency will also determine the apparent authority of an LLC's manager or managers"). The comment to RULLCA § 301 provides the rationale for this elimination:

> Most LLC statutes, including the original ULLCA, provide for what might be termed "statutory apparent authority" for members in a member-managed limited liability company and managers in a manager-managed limited liability company. This approach codifies the common law notion of apparent authority by position and dates back at least to the original, 1914 Uniform Partnership Act. * * *

> This Act rejects the statutory apparent authority approach * * *:

> The concept [of statutory apparent authority] still makes sense both for general and limited partnerships. A third party dealing with either type of partnership can know by the formal name of the entity and by a person's status as general or limited partner whether the person has the power to bind the entity.

> Most LLC statutes have attempted to use the same approach but with a fundamentally important (and problematic) distinction. An LLC's status as member-managed or manager-managed determines whether members or managers have the statutory power to bind. But an LLC's status as member- or manager-managed is not apparent from the LLC's name. A third party must check the public record, which may reveal that the LLC is manager-managed, which in turn means a member as member has no power to bind the LLC. As a result, a provision that originated in 1914 as a protection for third parties can, in the LLC context, easily function as a trap for the unwary. The problem is exacerbated by the almost infinite variety of management structures permissible in and used by LLCs.

> The new Act cuts through this problem by simply eliminating statutory apparent authority.

Codifying power to bind according to position makes sense only for organizations that have well-defined, well-known, and almost paradigmatic management structures. Because:

- flexibility of management structure is a hallmark of the limited liability company; and

- an LLC's name gives no signal as to the organization's structure,

it makes no sense to:

- require each LLC to publicly select between two statutorily preordained structures (i.e., manager-managed/member-managed); and then

- link a "statutory power to bind" to each of those two structures.

Under this Act, other law—most especially the law of agency—will handle power-to-bind questions.

RULLCA § 301 cmt.

(8) RULLCA's elimination of statutory agency authority has not escaped criticism:

RULLCA essentially abandons the careful compromise and distinctive features embodied in the dominant state statutory approach, as well as seeking to halt its evolution, by imposing brand new agency rules on LLCs. While RULLCA preserves the distinction between member-managed and manager-managed LLCs, it undercuts the effect of the distinction. The firm need not disclose its status in the articles and, more importantly, members and managers have no statutory default agency power to bind the LLC. By eliminating positional agency power, RULLCA unmoors itself not only from every other LLC statute, but also from the LLC's partnership antecedents clarified in generations of partnership precedents. At the same time, RULLCA does not align the LLC with any other model. The RULLCA LLC becomes a sui generis business form regarding the important category of agency rules.

The reporters' main rationale for the change was that the standard LLC rule is a trap for the unwary because third parties may not be aware of whether an LLC is member-managed or manager-managed. * * *

The reporters exaggerated the third party's plight. The costs of checking the public record are low. A third party who checks and learns that the LLC is manager-managed is on notice that only a manager can bind the LLC. If a person represents herself to third parties as a manager, the third party usually can rely on this person having at least the power to bind as to ordinary business unless the third party is aware of limitations or circumstances limiting authority. * * *

Larry E. Ribstein, *An Analysis of the Revised Uniform Limited Liability Company Act*, 3 VA. L. & BUS. REV. 35, 59 (2008).

(9) As a general matter, should third parties be bound by limitations on a member's or manager's agency authority that are included in the articles of organization or the operating agreement? Why or why not? Some statutes address this issue, although most do not. *See, e.g.*, LA. REV. STAT. § 12:1317(B) ("Persons dealing with a member, if management is reserved to the members, or manager, if management is vested in one or more managers * * * of the limited liability company shall be deemed to have knowledge of restrictions on the authority of such a member or manager contained in a written operating agreement if the articles of organization of the limited liability company contain a statement that such restrictions exist.").

3. INSPECTION AND INFORMATION RIGHTS

Similar to partnership and corporation statutes, LLC statutes often provide members and managers with defined rights to inspect the records of the venture. *See, e.g.*, DLLCA § 18–305; ULLCA § 408; RULLCA § 410. The rights provided under LLC statutes, however, often differ in meaningful ways from the corresponding rights provided under other business organization statutes. The following case highlights the distinctions of the LLC setting and adds an "electronic age" twist to a classic books-and-records dispute.

KASTEN v. DORAL DENTAL USA, LLC

Supreme Court of Wisconsin, 2007.
733 N.W.2d 300.

LOUIS B. BUTLER, JR., J.

* * *

I

Doral Dental was organized on April 29, 1996, by, among others, Craig Kasten (Craig), who was then married to Marie Kasten (Marie). Doral Dental's primary business was creating and administering dental programs for health maintenance organizations (HMOs) and state governments. In the year 2000, Doral Dental reported revenues of $98.3 million. * * * In early 2001, Craig and Marie divorced, with each taking a 23.13% interest in Doral Dental. MOA Investments, a company managed and part-owned by Doral Dental Chief Executive Officer Greg Borca, held 51.4% of Doral Dental, the lion's share of the interest in the company not held by Craig or Marie.

In February 2003 Marie began asserting her rights under the operating agreement and Wis. Stat. § 183.0405(2) to inspect and copy company records and documents. Marie states that she made these requests because negotiations had begun with potential buyers for the sale of Doral Dental, and she was concerned that such a transaction would adversely impact her interest in the company. Marie asserts that after reviewing documents produced in response to her initial inspection request, she "began to suspect that Doral's management was engaging in various actions adverse to her interests, such as the transfer, without adequate consideration of Doral's assets, including the [software] at the heart of the Company's success, to entities which Craig Kasten/MOA [Investments] owned, but she did not."

* * *

From February to October 2003, Marie made numerous requests of Doral Dental managers and their attorneys to inspect company records. Doral Dental fulfilled to Marie's satisfaction some of these requests but not others. In November 2003 Marie filed an action in Ozaukee County Circuit Court seeking an order pursuant to the operating agreement and Wis. Stat. § 183.0405 requiring Doral Dental to provide Marie with copies of documents not yet produced and to respond to her requests for information about Doral Dental's attempts to sell the company. Doral Dental states that prior to and during the ensuing litigation, it provided for Marie's inspection over thirteen boxes containing 35,000 documents.

In April 2004 some of Doral Dental's assets * * * were sold to DentaQuest Ventures (DQV) for approximately $95 million. Marie received $17.9 million from the sale. In July 2004 Marie filed a motion to compel production of documents not yet provided for inspection by Doral Dental. The motion sought inspection of electronic files and document drafts first requested in two June 2004 letters to Doral Dental. Specifically, the motion requested the following: "For the years 2001 to the present, e-mails by/to/from Greg Borka, Craig Kasten or Lisa Sweeney"; "[a]ll internal communications between the officers or directors of Doral (e-mail, memo or correspondence) for the years 2001 to the present"; and "drafts of * * * sales documents and exhibits." * * *

Doral Dental opposed Marie's request to inspect e-mails and other electronically stored files, asserting that * * * the request was unreasonable under Wis. Stat. § 183.0405(2) and the operating agreement because it contained no limitation as to subject matter, and sought all e-mails over a three-year period. Doral Dental argued that the e-mails likely numbered in the hundreds of thousands and that it would have to review each e-mail to segregate those containing information to which Marie was not entitled, including attorney-client communications and personal communications not related to company business.

The circuit court held a hearing on July 30, 2004, on the motion to compel. In a bench decision, the circuit court concluded that * * * e-mails [and document drafts] were not subject to inspection under the WLLCL or the operating agreement * * *.

* * *

Marie appealed to the court of appeals, and the court of appeals certified this case to address the scope of an LLC member's right of inspection, and whether this right encompasses the right to inspect e-mails and document drafts.

II

This case requires us to examine the record inspection provisions of Wisconsin's Limited Liability Company Law (WLLCL) contained in Wis. Stat. § 183.0405, and the inspection provisions of the operating agreement of Doral Dental USA, LLC. Statutory interpretation and contract interpretation are matters of law subject to our independent review.

* * *

III

* * *

We first considered Wisconsin's limited liability company statute two years ago in *Gottsacker*. There, we noted that the LLC is a hybrid business form that combines structural elements of the corporation and the partnership forms:

> From the partnership form, the LLC borrows characteristics of informality of organization and operation, internal governance by contract, direct participation by members in the company, and no taxation at the entity level. From the corporate form, the LLC borrows the characteristic of protection of members from investor-level liability.

[*Gottsacker v. Monnier*, 281 Wis.2d 361, 697 N.W.2d 436.]

Wisconsin enacted its LLC statute, the Wisconsin Limited Liability Company Law (WLLCL), Chapter 183 of the state statutes, in 1993. The drafters of the WLLCL borrowed concepts from the state partnership and corporation statutes, Chapters 179 and 180 respectively, and the 1992 Prototype Limited Liability Company Act, a product of an ABA Business Law Section subcommittee.

The WLLCL contains an explicit statement of statutory purpose, which provides, in part, that "[i]t is the policy of this chapter to give maximum effect to the principle of freedom of contract and to the enforceability of operating agreements." Wis. Stat. § 183.1302(1). *LLCs and LLPs: A Wisconsin Handbook* § 1.11 (rev. ed. 1999), written by the members of the State Bar Business Law Committee who drafted the WLLCL, explains that the committee members sought to encourage LLCs to adopt their own rules by operating agreement, while establishing default statutory rules that were simple enough to be used by "mom and pop" operations * * *.

The default rules concerning the rights of LLC members to inspect company records, and the duties of LLC managers to disclose information to members, are provided in Wis. Stat. § 183.0405. Subsection (1) of § 183.0405 sets forth the records a limited liability company must keep at its principal place of business. These include a list of members, and, if applicable, manager(s); copies of the articles of organization and all amendments thereto; copies of tax returns and financial statements; copies of all operating agreements, all amendments thereto, and operating agreements no longer in effect; the value of each member's contribution to the LLC; information concerning additional contributions to be made by each member; events upon which the LLC is to be dissolved; and any other writings required under the operating agreement.

Wisconsin Stat. § 183.0405(2) addresses the right of a member to inspect company records. It provides as follows: "Upon reasonable request, a member may, at the member's own expense, inspect and copy during ordinary business hours any limited liability company record required to be kept under sub. (1) and, unless otherwise provided in an operating agreement, any other limited liability company record, wherever the record is located." Chapter 183 does not define what constitutes an LLC "record," or indicate what constitutes a "reasonable request" for inspection.

The WLLCL further addresses a member's right to company information by imposing a duty upon LLC managers to disclose "[to the extent that the circumstances render it just and reasonable,] true and full information of all things affecting the [LLC] members to any member * * * upon reasonable request of the member or [the member's] legal representative." Wisconsin Stat. § 183.0405(3) * * *.

Here, Doral Dental's operating agreement included two provisions regarding a member's right of inspection that were effective when Marie made the July 2004 inspection request that is the focus of this appeal. Section 6(k)(i) of Doral Dental's operating agreement provided as follows:

> *Books of Account.* The manager shall maintain full and accurate books of account for the Company at the principal Company office. Each Member shall have access and the right to inspect and copy such books and all other Company records at all reasonable times.

Section 8(e) of the operating agreement provides:

> *Company Books.* Upon reasonable request, each Member shall have the right, during ordinary business hours, to inspect and copy Company documents at the requesting Member's expense.

Doral Dental's operating agreement is silent on the company managers' duty to disclose information to Doral Dental members.

* * *

Doral Dental contends that Wis. Stat. § 183.0405 should not be read to authorize members to make unlimited record requests that amount to "corporate proctology exams." Doral Dental argues that a member's right to inspect company records hinges on the reasonableness of the request, citing language of § 183.0405(2) that authorizes inspections "upon reasonable request." It asserts that the operating agreement similarly provides that Doral Dental managers need comply only with "reasonable" member requests to access records. It further notes that the requirement of § 183.0405(3) that the * * * managers of an LLC provide "true and full information of all things affecting the members to any member" is only "to the extent that the circumstances render it just and reasonable."

Doral Dental asserts that the types of documents described in Wis. Stat. § 183.0405(1) (member lists, tax returns, copies of the operating agreement, values of member contributions, dissolution events and "other writings as required by an operating agreement") are illustrative of those that we should consider to be "records" under § 183.0405(2). It further notes that subsection (2) does not reference e-mails or drafts of documents.

* * *

We begin by examining the record inspection provisions of two closely-related statutes, the corporation and partnership statutes. As we noted above, the LLC is a hybrid of these two business forms, and the drafters of Wisconsin's LLC statute borrowed freely from these established forms in crafting the WLLCL.

Wisconsin Stat. § 179.05(1) of Wisconsin's Uniform Limited Partnership Act enumerates the records a limited partnership must keep. Section 179.05(2) then provides that records under that subsection "are subject to inspection and copying at the reasonable request, and at the expense, of any partner during ordinary business hours." Section 179.05 does not include explicit requirements concerning the form, timing and purpose of the request. Like the WLLCL, the limited partnership statute provides an interest holder with the right to inspect and copy records "at the reasonable request" of the interest holder. However, the limited partnership statute appears to restrict the right to inspect records to those enumerated by the statute, while the WLLCL contains no such limitation; LLC members may inspect and copy "any other LLC records" in addition to those enumerated in Wis. Stat. § 183.0405(1), "unless otherwise provided in an operating agreement." § 183.0405(2).

The corporation inspection statute, Wis. Stat. § 180.1602(2)(b), contains numerous limitations on shareholder access to corporate records, including requirements that the requests be made "in good faith and for a proper purpose," and that the request identify "with reasonable particularity" the records sought and the purpose of the request. Moreover, an inspection request must target only those records that "are directly connected with [the requester's] purpose." See § 180.1602(2)(b)3– 5.

Doral Dental urges us to look to the corporation inspection statute for guidance in interpreting Wis. Stat. § 183.0405. Doral Dental asserts that the explicit limitations on a shareholder's record inspection demand contained in the corporation statute strike a proper balance between the shareholder's legitimate need for information and the corporation's need to be protected from repeated, harassing record requests. It argues that language limiting a member's right to inspect records to requests that are "reasonable" establishes a similar balance in the LLC context between the inspection right of members and the need to protect companies from improper record requests.

However, consideration of the WLLCL's inspection provision in light of its corporate counterpart only serves to highlight the differences between the statutes. The corporation statute includes a host of explicit requirements not provided in the WLLCL's inspection statute, including that the requester either hold at least five percent of the company's shares or be a shareholder for at least six months prior to the request; that the request be made in writing, and at least five days prior to the desired inspection date; and that the records requested be directly connected to the purpose of the request. Wis. Stat. § 180.1602(2)(b).

Additionally, the corporation statute limits shareholder inspection rights to the types of records enumerated in Wis. Stat. § 180.1602(2)(a) [e.g., excerpts from minutes or records that the corporation is required to keep as permanent records, accounting records of the corporation, and the list of shareholders]. The WLLCL, by contrast, contains no explicit restrictions on the time and place of inspection, and allows access to "any * * * limited liability company record," unless otherwise provided by the operating agreement. Wis. Stat. § 183.0405(2). Indeed, the transparency of the business form established by the default rules of the WLLCL is further illustrated by its unique requirement that managers provide "true and full information of all things affecting the members to any member * * * upon reasonable request of the member." Wis. Stat. § 183.0405(3). There is no analogue to this provision in the corporation statute.

By the plain language of Wis. Stat. § 183.0405(2), an LLC member may inspect anything that is a "record," and access will be granted to the member "upon reasonable request." Thus, the scope of a member's right of inspection under the default inspection provisions of § 183.0405(2) is exceptionally broad, and hinges on what constitutes an LLC "record," and the degree and kind of restrictions on access that "upon reasonable request" may impose.

This interpretation is consistent with the purposes of simplicity and freedom of contract that are at the heart of the WLLCL. As we said in *Gottsacker,* the overriding goal of the WLLCL was "to create a business entity providing limited liability, flow-through taxation, and simplicity." *Gottsacker,* 281 Wis.2d 361, 697 N.W.2d 436 (citation omitted).

The default inspection rules provided in Wis. Stat. § 183.0405(2) were designed for less sophisticated companies that would be less likely to craft their own inspection rules in an operating agreement. Accordingly, the default provisions do not include cumbersome restrictions on records access that might burden such businesses. Conversely, the statutory scheme envisions that larger, more sophisticated companies with multiple members may [choose] to adopt inspection rules that may be more suited to their needs, and the statute permits them to do so by the operating agreement.[14]

In this case, we note that the inspection provisions of the operating agreement are not identical to those of Wis. Stat. § 183.0405(2). While the operating agreement, like the statute, provides for inspection "upon reasonable request," the agreement provides members a right to inspect "documents" as well as "records." We therefore examine first whether, under language of the operating agreement, informal stored information, document drafts and e-mails may be "records" and/or "documents."

* * *

The WLLCL does not define "record." Likewise, Doral Dental's operating agreement does not define "record" or "Company document."[15]

We therefore consult a dictionary to ascertain the common meaning of these words. *Merriam-Webster's Collegiate Dictionary* (11th ed. 2003) defines "record" as "an authentic official copy of a document deposited with a legally designated officer," *id.* at 1040, and "document" as "a writing conveying information" or "a computer file containing information input by a computer user and usually created with an application (as a word processor)." *Id.* at 368. *Merriam-Webster's* definition of "record"—"an authentic official copy of a document"—indicates that a "document" is a

---

[14] Under the WLLCL, larger, more sophisticated LLCs are free to adopt more restrictive inspection rules that may incorporate features of the corporation inspection statute. Of course, the statutory scheme also permits LLCs to adopt inspection rules that are less restrictive than the default statutory rules * * *.

[15] We note that items an LLC must keep "at its principal place of business" under § 183.0405(1) are referred to in subsection (2) as "records." As noted earlier, these items include a list of members, tax returns, and other items that record financial and organizational essentials of an LLC. However, while subsection (2) indicates recordings of these essentials are "records," it does not limit "records" to only these types of items. Likewise, the context in which the term "Company documents" appears in the operating agreement is of little assistance to us.

broader category of stored information than "record," capturing all "records" and many types of stored information that would not be "records." However, section 8(e) of the operating agreement does not permit inspection of "documents," but rather "Company documents." We conclude that Doral Dental's operating agreement, by permitting inspection of "Company documents" as well as the statutorily-provided "records," affords access to more forms of stored information than the default inspection provisions of the WLLCL. Thus, we do not address whether the right to access "any other records" under Wis. Stat. § 183.0405(2) embraces * * * e-mails and document drafts. We examine instead what constitutes a "Company document" subject to member inspection under Doral Dental's operating agreement, and, specifically, whether e-mails and document drafts may be "Company documents."

The circuit court concluded that e-mails and document drafts were categorically neither "records" nor "Company documents" and therefore were not subject to inspection. The circuit court reasoned that e-mail was a "communication," similar to a telephone call, and not a "record" or a "Company document."

We agree with the circuit court that some e-mails may properly be categorized as private communications between the sender and the receiver that are neither "Company documents" nor "records." Nevertheless, the circuit court's view fails to account for the ubiquity of e-mail in today's business world and the many purposes for which e-mail is now used. E-mail is a primary tool of modern business communication. One market research firm estimates that in 2006, there were 128.7 million business e-mail users, and that the typical business user sent and received 600 e-mails per week. David Ferris, *Industry Statistics* (2006), http://www.ferris.com/research-library/industry-statistics.

For most businesses, e-mail has all but replaced hardcopy correspondence and memoranda. A categorical holding that e-mail is never a "Company document" under Wis. Stat. § 183.0405(2) would be blind to the day-to-day volume of e-mail in the modern business setting and the business-related purposes for which e-mail is used. Moreover, such a holding would frustrate the purposes of the inspection statute by encouraging LLC managers to conduct business via e-mail to avoid the scrutiny of non-managing members.

However, without addressing the question of whether all e-mail created and stored on company equipment is necessarily a "document," we do not believe that all of the requested e-mails in this case are necessarily "*Company* documents" subject to Marie's inspection under the Doral Dental operating agreement. When construing the language of a contract, we give meaning to every word, avoiding constructions "which render[ ] portions of a contract meaningless, inexplicable or mere surplusage." *Goebel v. First Fed. Sav. and Loan Ass'n of Racine,* 83

Wis.2d 668, 680, 266 N.W.2d 352 (1978). We construe "Company" to limit "documents" available for inspection to those relating to the business. Stored information of a strictly personal or social nature, such as personal e-mails that do not touch upon business matters, are not "Company documents" subject to inspection under the operating agreement.[16] Subject to this limitation, we therefore conclude that information that is stored as e-mail may be a "Company document" subject to a member's reasonable inspection request under the operating agreement. Because the circuit court concluded information that is stored as e-mail was categorically not a "Company document," its decision was in error.

With regard to Marie's request to inspect company document drafts, we conclude that such drafts are clearly "a writing conveying information," [as per] *Merriam-Webster's* definition of "document." *Merriam-Webster's New Collegiate Dictionary* at 368. Accordingly, under the language of the operating agreement, document drafts are subject to inspection upon a member's reasonable request. We do not address here whether a document draft may be a "record" within the meaning of Wis. Stat. § 183.0405(2).

We have thus concluded that the operating agreement provides member access to business-related company e-mails and document drafts. This right is subject to "upon reasonable request" language contained in Wis. Stat. § 183.0405(2) and the operating agreement, which we consider in the next section. We pause first, however, to consider what impact, if any, the requirement of § 183.0405(3) that LLC managers provide "information" about "all things affecting the members" may have upon a request to inspect LLC records or documents.

Wisconsin Stat. § 183.0405(3) is not a "record" or "document" inspection statute per se. * * * It establishes a member right [upon reasonable request] to "true and full information," without regard to whether that information is recorded and stored as a "record" or "document." However, the requesting member is entitled under this section only to information "affecting the members." § 183.0405(3). Managers must provide such information to members "to the extent that the circumstances render [the provision of the information] just and reasonable." *Id.*

We construe the phrase "all things affecting the members" to mean all things affecting the requesting member's financial interest in the company. To the extent that records and documents requested by Marie

---

[16] Our determination that e-mails that are strictly personal or social in nature are not "Company documents" is based on a plain meaning interpretation of the operating agreement. We note that other factors not contained in the record before us may be relevant to a determination of what constitutes "Company documents," including whether Doral Dental had in effect a company policy regarding the use of e-mail, employment agreements addressing the ownership of e-mail with those employees whose e-mails were sought, and the terms of these policies and/or agreements.

under Wis. Stat. § 183.0405(2) contain information affecting her financial interest in the company, subsection (3) requires that the information contained in the records or documents be furnished to Marie.

Doral Dental contends that Wis. Stat. § 183.0405(3) limits the scope of records and documents subject to inspection under § 183.0405(2) and sections 6(k)(i) and 8(e) of the operating agreement to records and/or documents that "affect" the member's interest. However, nothing in the text of subsections (2) and (3) suggests that the two should be read to limit each other. Had the legislature intended to limit the scope of inspection provision to only those "records" that *affect* a member's membership interest, it would have done so in the text of the inspection provision.

* * *

Earlier, we rejected Doral Dental's argument that language in Wis. Stat. § 183.0405 and the operating agreement providing access to LLC records only "upon reasonable request" imposed on LLC members the specific limitations on inspection rights set forth in the corporation statute. We return now to this language to determine what constitutes a "reasonable request" with respect to LLC member inspection rights.

For her part, Marie argues that "upon reasonable request" does not relate to the scope of records subject to inspection, only to the timing of the inspection and the form of production requested. Marie asserts that where the legislature has provided access to records "upon reasonable request," it has not restricted the scope of the records requested, citing the inspection provisions of the limited partnership statute, Wis. Stat. § 179.05. Marie notes that § 179.05(2) already limits a partner's inspection right to records required to be kept under § 179.05(1), so the limited partnership statute's guarantee of access "upon reasonable request" in that statute applies only to time and manner of inspection. Marie reasons that because § 179.05(2) uses the phrase "upon reasonable request" in a very similar context, we should construe the phrase as having the same meaning in Wis. Stat. § 183.0405.

Doral Dental contends that "upon reasonable request" applies to more than just the timing and form of the inspection, but also to the breadth of the request, to whether the request is tied to the concerns of the requester and to the types of records or documents requested. Doral Dental argues that the reasonableness requirement attempts to strike a balance between member access to information and the LLC's ability to conduct its business. Doral Dental asserts that the "upon reasonable request" language prohibits requests that are not reasonably limited by the date the requested items were created, by the place the items may be stored, and/or by the reason for the request. Doral Dental also argues the reasonableness language should be read to limit the right of inspection to certain kinds of formal records, such as tax returns, financial records and sales tax documents.

We disagree with Doral Dental that "upon reasonable request" language limits the types of records that are subject to inspection. The statutory language unambiguously provides members with the right to inspect "any limited liability company record required to be kept under sub. (1) and, unless otherwise provided in an operating agreement, *any other* limited liability company record." Wis. Stat. § 183.0405(2) (emphasis added).

But we also disagree with Marie that the phrase "upon reasonable request" in Wis. Stat. § 183.0405(2) should be interpreted in the same manner in which it is used in the inspection provisions of the partnership statute, Wis. Stat. § 179.05(2). The partnership statute differs from the LLC statute in that it authorizes inspection of only certain specified records, *see* § 179.05(1), while § 183.0405(2) permits inspection of all records the LLC must keep under § 183.0405(1) and "any other limited liability company record." Because the right to inspect records under the partnership statute is already limited to only certain, specified records, the "reasonableness" of such a request would not encompass the types or scope of records sought by the request. By contrast, an inspection request under the LLC statute is not limited to specified records, as LLC members may inspect any records (or, as here, even more items under the terms of the operating agreement).

Chapter 183 does not explicitly address whether the reasonableness language encompasses the breadth of the request or whether it applies only to the timing and form of the request. Because neither the language of Wis. Stat. § 183.0405(2) nor the context in which it appears provides any guidance as to the factors that may be relevant to whether an inspection request is "reasonable," we conclude the provision is ambiguous. We therefore turn to extrinsic sources to ascertain the meaning of "upon reasonable request" within the context of Wis. Stat. § 183.0405(2).

The legislative history of the WLLCL contains no discussion of the LLC inspection statute in general terms, much less any specific consideration of "upon reasonable request." *The Wisconsin Handbook to LLCs*, authored by the drafters of the WLLCL, is similarly mute. Moreover, no Wisconsin cases have interpreted the inspection provision of the WLLCL, and no cases from other jurisdictions have interpreted similar "reasonable request" language contained in LLC inspection provisions of other states.

However, other state inspection statutes provide insight into the meaning of Wisconsin's inspection provisions and the phrase "upon reasonable request." As noted, the LLC is a new business form, and most state LLC statutes, including Wisconsin's, were adopted between 1990 and 1995. Because the drafters consulted other LLC statutes when drafting the WLLCL, *see Gottsacker*, 281 Wis.2d 361, 697 N.W.2d 436, differences between the WLLCL and other state LLC statutes suggest choices the drafters made that may be relevant to statutory meaning.

One leading treatise has surveyed the various state LLC record inspection statutes and has identified four general approaches to LLC record inspection. *Ribstein and Keatinge on LLCs,* App. 9–3. It notes that in approximately half of the states, LLC members are permitted to inspect records only "upon demand for a proper purpose," *id.*, a requirement familiar to corporation law and included in Wisconsin's corporation statute. *See* Wis. Stat. § 180.1602(2)(b)3.

Other states, including Wisconsin, do not include an explicit "proper purpose" requirement, but require, in some fashion, that the inspection request be "reasonable." *Ribstein and Keatinge on LLCs,* App. 9–3. Ribstein and Keatinge note that reasonableness limitations on LLC member inspection rights contained in many state LLC statutes are not as restrictive as limits on corporation shareholder inspection rights, and as a result, "courts may be more lenient in allowing inspection in LLCs than in publicly held corporations." *Ribstein and Keatinge on LLCs,* App. 9–3. The authors explain that corporation inspection and disclosure statutes are more restrictive and detailed than those of LLCs and partnerships "because of the need [for corporations] to spell out ground rules that both avoid unreasonable and costly requests by thousands of shareholders and ensure disclosure by managers who are remote from the owners." *Id.* at § 9:10.

* * *

Those states that have adopted "proper purpose" language permit LLC managers to deny an inspection request based on the member's intent, regardless of whether the records sought would otherwise be available for member inspection. Some commentators have argued that states that permit inspections without the showing of a "proper purpose" may be inviting record inspections that are contrary to the company's financial health. One state law treatise urges that the "reasonable request" requirement contained in the Louisiana statutes (and similar to the WLLCL) be read to prohibit such inspection abuses. It warns that

> without * * * [a] restrictive reading of the reasonable request requirement, even an LLC member who was starting up his own competing business would be entitled to copy his LLC's contracts, customer lists, and pricing calculations, as long as he was willing to do so with adequate notice and at a convenient time and place. Surely, this is not the result that the legislature would have expected had it considered the matter.

8 Glenn G. Morris and Wendell H. Holmes, *La. Civ. L. Treatise, Business Organizations* § 44.21 (1999).

We read the absence of "proper purpose" language in Wis. Stat. § 183.0405(2) to indicate the drafters of the WLLCL chose not to require LLC members to demonstrate, as a threshold matter, that their inspection request is not made for an improper motive. Moreover, this interpretation is in harmony with the intent of the WLLCL drafters to favor simple default rules suitable for "mom and pop" operations. However, this does not mean that the statute is blind to a member's motive for making an inspection request.

We conclude that a number of factors may be relevant to whether a request to inspect LLC records (or, here, "Company documents") was submitted "upon reasonable request." The scope of items subject to inspection under Wis. Stat. § 183.0405(2)—"any * * * record[s]," unless the operating agreement provides otherwise—is so broad that to permit any inspection request, no matter its breadth, could impose unreasonable burdens upon the operation of the company. Because we do not believe that the drafters intended the inspection statute to threaten the financial well being of the company, we read "upon reasonable request" to pertain to the breadth of an inspection request, as well as the timing and form of the inspection.

We therefore conclude that one purpose of the language "upon reasonable request" is to protect the company from member inspection requests that impose undue financial burdens on the company.[18] Whether an inspection request is so burdensome as to be unreasonable requires balancing the statute's bias in favor of member access to records against the costs of the inspection to the company. When applying this balancing test, a number of factors may be relevant, including, but not limited to: (1) whether the request is restricted by date or subject matter; (2) the reason given (if any) for the request, and whether the request is related to that reason;[19] (3) the importance of the information to the member's interest in the company; and (4) whether the information may be obtained from another source.

In the event that an LLC inspection request comes before a circuit court, the court within its discretion will take into account these purposes

---

[18] As noted, the statute requires that the member shoulder the costs of inspection. *See* Wis. Stat. § 183.0405(2) (providing a member may "inspect and copy" LLC records "at the member's own expense"). However, we observe that other costs, including labor and other indirect costs, may result from a member inspection request. Expenses incurred litigating an inspection request are not among those that may be factored into the reasonableness analysis.

[19] We note that while Wis. Stat. § 183.0405(2) does not require that a member's inspection request be made for a "proper purpose," the reason for the request may be a relevant factor in determining whether the request is reasonable under § 183.0405(2). Thus, a request that is made for an improper purpose may well be unreasonable. However, for a request to meet the reasonableness requirement, the requester need not always show that the request was submitted for a "proper purpose," or even give a reason for the request.

when determining whether an inspection request is reasonable under Wis. Stat. § 183.0405(2), provided the operating agreement does not require a different analysis. A circuit court's determination of the reasonableness of a member's request will depend on the circumstances of the case. Decisions of the circuit court regarding the reasonableness of an inspection request are addressed to its discretion.

* * *

Doral Dental contends that Marie's requests of July 2004 to inspect e-mails and draft documents were "unreasonably broad." * * * Doral Dental also argues that because Marie's actual requests were not limited to any stated concern, we should conclude that they were unreasonable under Wis. Stat. § 183.0405.

As noted, a member's inspection request need not necessarily be tied to a stated concern of the member to be reasonable. However, the question of whether a specific inspection request is reasonable under the WLLCL and the operating agreement is a question for the circuit court, applying the legal standards set forth above.

* * *

IV

In summary, we conclude that Doral Dental's operating agreement, which provides access to "Company documents" as well as "records," grants a right of inspection that embraces document drafts and some company e-mails. We therefore conclude that the circuit court's order denying inspection of company e-mails on grounds that they were, categorically, not "Company documents" was in error.

Additionally, we construe the language "upon reasonable request" included in Wis. Stat. § 183.0405(2) and the operating agreement to pertain to the financial burdens a request may place upon the company, as well as the timing and form of inspection. We conclude that the reasonableness inquiry seeks to weigh the statute's bias in favor of the member's right of inspection against the burden the specific request may place upon the company.

We therefore reverse the circuit court's orders denying Marie Kasten's request to inspect e-mail and document drafts * * *. We remand this matter to the circuit court to reconsider Marie's request of July 2004 to inspect e-mails and document drafts in a manner consistent with this opinion.

* * *

NOTES

(1) Because the *Kasten* court concluded that business-related e-mails and document drafts were "Company documents" under the operating agreement, it ducked the question of whether e-mails and drafts were "records" under the Wisconsin inspection statute. How would you answer that question?

(2) What differences exist between a member's inspection right under § 183.0405(2) of the Wisconsin LLC statute and a shareholder's inspection right under a typical corporation statute? Is a member's purpose for inspecting records relevant under § 183.0405(2)?

(3) The *Kasten* court remands to the circuit court to determine whether Marie Kasten's inspection requests were reasonable. Applying the legal standards set forth in the *Kasten* opinion, how should the circuit court rule?

(4) As the court discusses, § 183.0405(3) of the Wisconsin LLC statute provides:

> Members or, if the management of the limited liability company is vested in one or more managers, managers shall provide, to the extent that the circumstances render it just and reasonable, true and full information of all things affecting the members to any member or to the legal representative of any member upon reasonable request of the member or the legal representative.

Moreover, § 183.0405(2) states that "[u]pon reasonable request, a member may, at the member's own expense, inspect and copy during ordinary business hours any limited liability company record required to be kept under sub. (1) and, unless otherwise provided in an operating agreement, any other limited liability company record, wherever the record is located."

How do these two sections relate? Is the member's right to inspect records under § 183.0405(2) needed in light of management's obligation to provide information under § 183.0405(3)?

(5) The Uniform Acts also contain a statutory duty to disclose information. Similar to the RUPA § 403(c) provisions, ULLCA § 408(b)(1) requires an LLC to furnish to a member "without demand, information concerning the company's business or affairs reasonably required for the proper exercise of the member's rights and performance of the member's duties under the operating agreement or this [Act]." Moreover, § 408(b)(2) requires the LLC to furnish, "on demand, other information concerning the company's business or affairs, except to the extent the demand or the information demanded is unreasonable or otherwise improper under the circumstances." RULLCA follows a similar approach. *See* RULLCA § 410. Under the Delaware statute, however, there is no comparable provision.

(6) Can an operating agreement eliminate a member's rights to inspection and information? Consider DLLCA §§ 18–305, 18–1101; ULLCA §§ 103(b)(1), 408; RULLCA §§ 110(c)(6), 410.

D. FINANCIAL RIGHTS AND OBLIGATIONS

With respect to members' financial rights, LLC statutes tend to provide either a partnership-like equal allocation or a corporate/limited partnership-like pro rata allocation based upon contributions to the firm. Because these allocation schemes are merely default rules, the members can contract around them. Like partners in a general partnership, LLC members typically establish capital accounts and specify the allocation of financial rights in their operating agreement.

Although LLC statutes provide members with limited liability, the statutes often include provisions that protect creditors (to some extent) from member actions that can damage a creditor's position. For example, many statutes provide that a member may be liable to a creditor for an unpaid contribution to the firm, even if the other members have decided to waive that contribution obligation. *See, e.g.,* DLLCA § 18–502; ULLCA § 402(b); RULLCA § 403. Many statutes also indicate that members may have liability for receiving distributions that render the LLC insolvent. *See, e.g.,* DLLCA § 18–607; ULLCA §§ 406–407; RULLCA §§ 405–406. Fraudulent transfer law, however, offers similar protection.

NOTES

(1) Should an operating agreement allow members to make additional contributions to an LLC? What problems might additional contributions cause?

(2) Under DLLCA, how are profits and losses allocated among the members? *See* DLLCA § 18–503. Unlike the Delaware statute, the Uniform Acts do not contain a default rule for allocating profits and losses. *See* ULLCA § 405(a); RULLCA § 404(a); *see also* RULLCA § 404 cmt. ("This Act has no provision allocating profits and losses among the partners. Instead, the Act directly apportions the right to receive distributions. Nearly all [LLCs] will choose to allocate profits and losses in order to comply with applicable tax, accounting and other regulatory requirements. Those requirements, rather than this Act, are the proper source of guidance for that profit and loss allocation.").

(3) Does a member in a member-managed LLC have a right to compel the LLC to distribute some of its profits before dissolution? If so, how should the distribution be allocated among the members? *See* DLLCA §§ 18–504, 18–601; ULLCA §§ 404(c)(6), 405; RULLCA §§ 404, 407(b).

(4) As mentioned, LLC operating agreements often establish capital accounts for the members. A capital account gives a snapshot of a member's financial interest in the company at a particular point in time. In general, a capital account balance begins with the member's contribution, is increased by the member's share of the venture's profits, and is decreased by the member's share of the venture's losses and by any distributions made to the

member. Capital account provisions are often complicated and are significantly influenced by tax concerns. *See* Chapter 3, Section D(1).

(5) Many operating agreements provide that profits and losses (as well as voting rights) shall be allocated among the members according to an agreed "sharing ratio," which is usually based upon a member's financial contribution (but not always, particularly in firms with service-providing members).

E. ENTITY STATUS

Under most LLC statutes, an LLC is explicitly characterized as a separate legal entity whose identity is distinct from that of its owners. *See, e.g.*, DLLCA § 18–201(b); ULLCA § 201; RULLCA § 104(a). As a separate "legal person," an LLC can exercise rights and powers in its own name. For example, an LLC can bring a lawsuit (or be a defendant in one), and it can own property. *See, e.g.*, ULLCA § 112(b); RULLCA § 105. Nevertheless, judicial treatment of the LLC's entity status is not always predictable.

PREMIER VAN SCHAACK REALTY, INC. v. SIEG

Court of Appeals of Utah, 2002.
51 P.3d 24.

GREENWOOD, JUDGE:

Premier Van Schaack Realty, Inc. (Premier) seeks to enforce the brokerage fee payment provided in the listing agreement (the Agreement) it entered into with Thomas K. Sieg (Sieg) regarding the sale of real property located at 273 North East Capital, Salt Lake City, Utah (the Property). Premier appeals the trial court's grant of summary judgment to Sieg * * *. We affirm.

BACKGROUND

On February 7, 1997, Sieg entered into the Agreement with Coldwell Banker. Coldwell Banker subsequently assigned the Agreement to Premier. The Agreement provisions relevant to this appeal state:

> BROKERAGE FEE. If, during the Listing period, [12 months] [Premier], the Listing Agent, the Owner, another real estate agent, or anyone else locates a party who is ready, willing and able to buy, sell or exchange (collectively referred to as "acquire") the Property, or any part thereof, at the listing price and terms stated on the attached board/association property data information form, or any other price or terms to which the Owner may agree in writing, the Owner agrees to pay to [Premier] a brokerage fee in the amount of seven percent (7%) of such acquisition price * * *.

In March 1997, Premier's real estate agent introduced Sieg to Michael Davis, Marion Vaughn, and Jane Johnson (DVJ), who offered to purchase the Property for $1.3 million. Sieg made a counter-offer that DVJ accepted. However, the anticipated sale never closed, and Sieg returned DVJ's earnest money.

In June 1997, DVJ proposed that they form a limited liability company (LLC) with Sieg. On September 26, 1997, DVJ and Sieg signed an operating agreement (the Operating Agreement), forming the LLC, MJTM. The Operating Agreement provided that Sieg would convey the Property to MJTM and Sieg would receive a 40% interest in MJTM and a preferential return of 9% on future profits. The Operating Agreement also provided that Sieg had a beginning balance of $670,000 in his initial capital contribution account and that MJTM assumed $580,000 of Sieg's debt. The other members of MJTM agreed not to encumber the Property without Sieg's approval. The Operating Agreement stated that the agreed value of the Property was $1.3 million. * * * On January 21, 1998, Sieg transferred title to the Property to MJTM by warranty deed.

In January 1998, MJTM borrowed $1.413 million from Zions Bank secured by a lien on the Property. All of the members of MJTM personally guaranteed the loan. With the proceeds from this loan, MJTM paid off a $300,000 loan to Sieg secured by the Property.

When Premier discovered that Sieg had entered into this arrangement with MJTM, it demanded its commission of 7% of $1.3 million. Sieg refused to pay, claiming that his contribution of the Property was an investment and not a sale or exchange; thus Premier filed suit. On cross-motions for summary judgment the trial court ruled in favor of Sieg, holding that the transaction between Sieg and MJTM was not a sale or exchange pursuant to the Agreement because it lacked consideration. * * *

       * * *

ANALYSIS

I. Sale or Exchange

Premier argues that a sale or exchange occurred as defined in the Agreement; thus triggering the 7% commission provision. * * * Because this court interprets contracts according to their plain meaning, Premier must show the following to prevail: (1) that there was a party who was ready, willing, and able to buy or exchange the Property; (2) that Sieg agreed to a sale or exchange; and (3) that the sale or exchange occurred during the term of the Agreement. For purposes of this appeal, we assume that the alleged sale or exchange occurred during the term of the Agreement. Indeed, there is no dispute that the transfer to MJTM took place during the term of the Agreement.

Consequently, we are left to decide whether a sale or exchange occurred between Sieg and MJTM triggering the commission provisions of the Agreement. Under Utah law, "sale" has been defined as, "the conveyance of title to the purchaser for a valuable consideration consisting of the purchase price, or the execution and delivery of a valid and enforceable contract of sale whereby some estate in land, legal or equitable, passes to the purchaser." *Lewis v. Dahl,* 108 Utah 486, 161 P.2d 362, 365 (1945). While "exchange" has not been judicially defined in Utah, this court will apply its plain meaning when interpreting the Agreement. The plain meaning of "exchange" is, "the act of giving or taking one thing in return for another." Webster's Ninth New Collegiate Dictionary 432 (9th ed.1986); *see also* Black's Law Dictionary 585 (7th ed.1999). These definitions demonstrate that to have either a sale or an exchange, there must be consideration.

Premier argues that Sieg received consideration from MJTM in several different ways. First, Sieg received a 40% interest in MJTM in exchange for the Property. Second, Sieg was entitled to a 9% preferential return from MJTM on all future profits. Third, Sieg had a beginning balance of $670,000 in his initial capital contribution account. Finally, MJTM promised to assume $580,000 of Sieg's debt.[1]

Sieg contends that each of these alleged indicia of consideration fails for various reasons. Sieg argues that the interest in MJTM [that] Premier relies on cannot serve as consideration because Sieg maintained an ownership interest in the Property. Additionally, Sieg argues that the alleged debt relief fails as consideration because Sieg was personally liable for his personal debt plus the debt of MJTM to Zions Bank.

To support his argument, Sieg cites *Cooley Investment Co. v. Jones,* 780 P.2d 29 (Colo.Ct.App.1989), and *Dahdah v. Continent Realty, Inc.,* 434 So.2d 997 (Fla.Dist.Ct.App.1983) (per curiam), for the proposition that the 40% interest and 9% preferential return on future profits in exchange for the Property cannot be valuable consideration. In both *Cooley* and *Dahdah,* the property owner entered into a listing agreement with a realtor to sell his or her property. In both cases, the owner decided to convey the property to a partnership or joint venture in which the owner was a member in exchange for: (1) an interest in the joint venture; (2) a preferential interest in future profits; and (3) an initial capital contribution account balance that received no interest over time. In each case, the court held that no sale or exchange occurred. Each court reasoned:

---

[1]   Premier also argues that this court should find consideration because the other members of MJTM promised not to encumber the Property without Sieg's approval. However, "because [Premier] did not properly raise [this] issue[ ] in the trial court * * * and because [it] argued [this issue] for the first time in [its] reply brief, we decline to review [the issue]." Colemen v. Stevens, 2000 UT 98, ¶ 9, 17 P.3d 1122.

Thus, *because the defendant retained an ownership interest in the property,* there was only a change in the form of ownership, not a transfer of the property to another entity.

Further, the conveyance of the title to the property cannot be considered to be a "sale." Under the agreement between defendant and [the other partner], defendant received only a credit for a capital contribution of $500,000, which represented the market value of the property. She received no other compensation; there was no unconditional promise on the part of the partnership, or anyone else, to pay her anything; there was no security given to her; and she was not entitled to receive any interest payments on her capital account. Defendant's only right was to receive a share of future profits, if any.

Cooley, 780 P.2d at 31 (emphasis added) (internal citations omitted).

[A] sale did not occur because *the owner retained an ownership interest in the property.* Rather than assuming the risk of a seller, the owner assumed the risk of a participant in a joint venture with the potential for losses as well as profits. As such, the owner decided to develop the property herself.

The exclusive right of sale contract did not address the situation where the owner develops the property herself in the form of a joint venture. The exclusive right of sale contract should be construed against the broker as drafter of the document. Consequently, if the broker wanted a commission in the event the owner entered into a joint venture with other parties regarding the property, the broker should have spelled that out in the contract.

Dahdah, 434 So.2d at 998–99 (quoting *Miller, Cowherd & Kerver, Inc. v. De Montejo,* 406 So.2d 1196 (Fla.Dist.Ct.App.1981)) (emphasis added).

Like the property owners in *Cooley* and *Dahdah,* Sieg retained a substantial ownership interest in the Property that caused him to assume the risks of an investor instead of the risks of a seller. By illustration, when a person undertakes the risks of an investor, that person assumes the risk that the value of [the] investment will increase or decrease over time, or that the investment may be completely lost. However, as a general rule, once a person sells property, appreciation, depreciation, or total loss of the property is of no concern since the sale severs the seller from any interest in the property. Sieg still retained a significant ownership interest in the Property, including the potential value of its future sale and the present right to prevent MJTM from encumbering the Property without his permission. *See Pride Oil Co. v. Salt Lake County,* 13 Utah 2d 183, 370 P.2d 355, 356 (1962) (holding that "[the right to own property] includes the right to sell it"); *Ritholz v. City of Salt Lake,* 3 Utah

2d 385, 284 P.2d 702, 705 (1955) ("Clearly among the rights attendant upon ownership and enjoyment of property are the rights to exchange, pledge, sell or otherwise dispose of it * * *."). Moreover, the value of Sieg's interest in MJTM is directly tied to the value of the Property because the Property is the only asset MJTM owned. Therefore, because Sieg retained such a substantial ownership interest in the Property, the transaction between Sieg and MJTM does not constitute a sale or exchange as contemplated in the Agreement.

Additionally, Premier's argument that the debt relief is consideration fails because Sieg personally guaranteed the $1.413 million loan that MJTM used to pay $300,000 of Sieg's debt. Simply stated, MJTM did not actually relieve Sieg of debt, but rather caused him to personally incur nearly three times more debt than he owed on the Property prior to joining MJTM. MJTM had no ability to pay Sieg's debt itself, without securing a loan secured by the Property, MJTM's only asset. Therefore, under the facts of this case, the debt relief promised in the Agreement was illusory.[2]

Premier argues that, unlike the partnership and joint venture in *Cooley* and *Dahdah,* a limited liability company under Utah, Colorado, and Florida law is a separate legal entity that is able to buy property in its own name. *See* Utah Code Ann. § 48–2c–104 (Supp.2001); Colo.Rev.Stat. Ann. §§ 7–80–104; 7–80–107 (2001) (stating limited liability companies can own property separate from their owners); Fla. Stat. Ann. § 608.404 (2001) (same). Because a limited liability company is an entity distinct from its owners, Premier argues that if a seller of property transfers his property to a limited liability company or to a corporation of which he is the sole shareholder, such a transaction would constitute a sale or exchange. *See Hagan v. Adams Prop. Assocs., Inc.,* 253 Va. 217, 482 S.E.2d 805, 807 (1997) (holding that [a] limited liability company can exchange property for debt relief in its own name because it is an entity separate from its members). We believe, however, that focusing on the legal structure of the transferee averts attention from the critical question of whether there was valuable consideration.

Whether a sale or exchange for valuable consideration occurred is a fact-intensive inquiry that requires more than a mere showing that an owner transferred his property to a separate legal entity. In this case, Sieg's credit to his capital contribution account and debt assumption roughly approximate the $1.3 million value of the Property. The preferential interest in future profits and the Zions Bank loan reflect the

---

[2] Each of the cases in support of both Sieg's and Premier's argument do not consider the initial capital account balance as consideration unless it received interest payments. *See Cooley Inv. Co. v. Jones,* 780 P.2d 29, 31 (Colo.Ct.App.1989); *Dahdah v. Continent Realty, Inc.,* 434 So.2d 997, 998 (Fla.Dist.Ct.App.1983); *Hagan v. Adams Prop. Assocs., Inc.,* 253 Va. 217, 482 S.E.2d 805, 807 (1997). Since no interest was credited to Sieg's initial capital account, the account is not consideration.

investment nature of the transaction. Where the owner retains essentially the same ownership interest in the property as he had prior to the conveyance, with plans to develop the property by improving it with the possibility of future gains or losses, and can prevent the record owner from encumbering the property without his permission, such a transaction is not a sale or exchange. Therefore, because the facts in this case show Sieg continued to have substantially the same ownership interest in the Property after the deed to MJTM was executed, there was no consideration and a sale or exchange as contemplated in the Agreement did not occur.

* * *

CONCLUSION

In sum, the transfer of the Property from Sieg to MJTM was not supported by consideration so as to constitute a sale or exchange. Because no sale or exchange occurred, Sieg owes no commission under the Agreement. * * *

NOTES

(1) In *Sieg*, the court repeatedly states that Sieg, post-transfer, retained a significant ownership interest in the property. Is this assertion legally correct? More specifically, according to the court, the fact that the property cannot be encumbered without Sieg's permission indicates that Sieg still has an ownership interest in the property. Do you agree? *See* UTAH CODE § 48–2c–104 ("A company formed under this chapter is a legal entity distinct from its members."); *id.* § 48–2c–701(2) ("A member has no interest in specific property of a company."); *cf.* DLLCA § 18–701; ULLCA § 501(a); RULLCA § 501 cmt.

(2) Do you agree with the court's conclusion that Sieg did not receive consideration for the conveyance to the LLC?

(3) The *Cooley* and *Dahdah* cases cited by the court involved the conveyance of property to a UPA-governed partnership or joint venture. The dispute in *Sieg* involved the conveyance of property to an LLC. Is this distinction significant?

(4) In contrast to *Sieg*, consider the decision of *Hagan v. Adams Property Associates, Inc.*, 482 S.E.2d 805 (Va. 1997). In *Hagan*, Ralph and Maureen Hagan (collectively "Hagan") owned the Stuart Court Apartments. On April 30, 1994, Hagan executed an agreement with Adams Property Associates, Inc. ("Adams") giving Adams the exclusive right to sell the property for $1,600,000. The agreement provided that if the property was "sold or exchanged" within one year, with or without Adams' assistance, Hagan would pay Adams a fee of six percent of the "gross sales amount." Before the year expired, Hagan, Roy Tepper, and Lynn Parsons formed a limited liability company, Hagan, Parsons, & Tepper, LLC ("HPT"). By deed dated April 23,

1995, Hagan transferred the property to HPT. When Hagan refused to pay a commission to Adams, Adams sued. The Virginia Supreme Court held that a sale of the property had occurred and that a commission was required:

> When Hagan transferred the property to HPT, he received more than an interest in the new company. Under the terms of the operating agreement executed in conjunction with the formation of HPT, HPT agreed to assume all liabilities existing on the property, which included the $1,028,000 unpaid balance on a first deed of trust note on the property. The record does not indicate whether the holder of the first deed of trust note released Hagan and substituted HPT as the obligor on the note. Even assuming such substitution did not occur, Hagan nevertheless received substantial relief from his debt obligation because, upon assuming all liabilities on the property, HPT became liable to Hagan for any amount Hagan would have had to pay the holder of the first deed of trust note. Also as part of the property transfer transaction, HPT executed a second deed of trust on the property securing a note payable to Hagan for $323,000. This note was due and payable when the property was subsequently sold, and it had priority over payments to anyone other than the beneficiary of the first deed of trust. Thus, in exchange for transfer of title to the property, Hagan received relief from his debt on the first deed of trust note as well as the benefit of a second deed of trust note and an interest in HPT. These benefits received by Hagan constituted valid consideration.
>
>   * * *
>
> Under the Virginia Limited Liability Company Act, a limited liability company is an unincorporated association with a registered agent and office. It is an independent entity which can sue and be sued and its members are not personally liable for the debt or actions of the company. In contrast to a partnership, a limited liability company in Virginia is an entity separate from its members and, thus, the transfer of property from a member to the limited liability company is more than a change in the form of ownership; it is a transfer from one entity or person to another. Accordingly, we agree with the trial court's conclusion that Hagan transferred the title of the property in exchange for valuable consideration and that this transfer was a sale of the property.

Id. at 807.

(5) The entity-based analysis in *Hagan* is similar to the Ninth Circuit's rationale in *Abrahim & Sons Enterprises v. Equilon Enterprises, LLC*, 292 F.3d 958 (9th Cir. 2002). In *Abrahim*, Shell and Texaco formed an LLC called Equilon Enterprises. In exchange for 100% of the ownership interests in Equilon, Shell and Texaco contributed assets and assigned gas station leases and dealer agreements to Equilon. *See id.* at 960. A group of independent dealers operating gas stations leased from Shell or Texaco sued on the

grounds that Shell and Texaco violated California Business & Professions Code § 20999.25(a), which prohibits a franchisor from selling, transferring, or assigning an interest in a premises to another person unless he or she first makes a bona fide offer to sell that interest to the franchisee. *See id.* The court agreed that a violation of the Code had occurred, reasoning, in part, as follows:

> * * * Corporations and LLCs are distinct legal entities, separate from their stockholders or members. The acts of a corporation or LLC are deemed independent of the acts of its members. For this reason, both corporations and LLCs are included within the definition of "person" in the California Corporations Code. The purpose of forming these types of businesses is to limit the liability of their shareholders and members.

> * * * Because Equilon is an LLC, it is distinct from its members Shell and Texaco and is "another person" under Section 20999.25(a).

> Shell and Texaco argue that Equilon is not a distinct entity because they own and control Equilon. In essence, they ask us to disregard the corporate form they themselves created because the form does not benefit them here. We refuse to do so. Members own and control most LLCs, yet the LLCs remain separate and distinct from their members. Indeed, the separate and distinct nature of LLCs is their reason for existence. Just because it happens not to benefit Shell and Texaco here is no reason to disregard the formation of this entity. Based on the common understanding of how an LLC works, Equilon fits within the meaning of "another person."

> * * *

> Finally, under the California Corporations Code, Shell and Texaco have no interest in the property of Equilon. Once members contribute assets to an LLC, those assets become capital of the LLC and the members lose any interest they had in the assets. Thus, once Shell and Texaco contributed the gas stations to Equilon, they no longer had an interest in the stations and could not individually exert control over them. The oil companies no longer had title, possession, or control over the properties. Therefore, their contribution was a transfer to Equilon.

Id. at 962–63.

(6) In *Elf Atochem North America, Inc. v. Jaffari*, 727 A.2d 286 (Del. 1999), the operating agreement contained an arbitration clause covering all disputes. The agreement was signed by the two members of the LLC, Malek, Inc. and Elf, but not by the LLC itself. Elf attempted to avoid arbitration by bringing a derivative action on behalf of the LLC. *See id.* at 288–89. Despite the fact that the LLC was not a signatory to the operating agreement, the Supreme Court of Delaware concluded that the LLC was bound by the agreement, including the arbitration provision:

* * * Because Malek LLC never expressly assented to the arbitration and forum selection clauses within the Agreement, Elf argues it can sue derivatively on behalf of Malek LLC * * *.

We are not persuaded by this argument. Section 18–101(7) defines the limited liability company agreement as "any agreement, written or oral, *of the member or members* as to the affairs of a limited liability company and the conduct of its business." Here, Malek, Inc. and Elf, the members of Malek LLC, executed the Agreement to carry out the affairs and business of Malek LLC and to provide for arbitration and forum selection.

Notwithstanding Malek LLC's failure to sign the Agreement, Elf's claims are subject to the arbitration and forum selection clauses of the Agreement. The Act is a statute designed to permit members maximum flexibility in entering into an agreement to govern their relationship. It is the members who are the real parties in interest. The LLC is simply their joint business vehicle. This is the contemplation of the statute in prescribing the outlines of a limited liability company agreement.

Id. at 293; *see also id.* at 287 ("We hold that * * * the Agreement is binding on the LLC as well as the members * * *.").

Can the conclusion of the *Elf Atochem* court be reconciled with DLLCA § 18–201(b)? Notice that this issue is now addressed by statute. *See id.* § 18–101(7) ("A limited liability company is bound by its [LLC] agreement whether or not the [LLC] executes the [LLC] agreement."); *see also* RULLCA § 111(a) ("A limited liability company is bound by and may enforce the operating agreement, whether or not the company has itself manifested assent to the operating agreement.").

(7) The LLC's entity status is ignored for purposes of federal diversity jurisdiction. A number of courts have concluded that an LLC's citizenship is determined by looking at the citizenship of its individual members, regardless of whether state law views the LLC as a separate legal entity. *See, e.g.*, Cosgrove v. Bartolotta, 150 F.3d 729, 731 (7th Cir. 1998) ("Given the resemblance between an LLC and a limited partnership, and what seems to have crystallized as a principle that members of associations are citizens for diversity purposes unless Congress provides otherwise (as it has with respect to corporations, in 28 U.S.C. § 1332(c)(1) [deeming that a corporation is a citizen of the state where it incorporated and the state where it has its principal place of business]), we conclude that the citizenship of an LLC for purposes of the diversity jurisdiction is the citizenship of its members." (citations omitted)).

F. LIMITED LIABILITY

Like many of the other business entities that you have studied, the LLC provides its owners with limited liability for the venture's obligations. ULLCA § 303(a) indicates that "the debts, obligations, and liabilities of a limited liability company, whether arising in contract, tort, or otherwise, are solely the debts, obligations, and liabilities of the company," and it further states that "[a] member or manager is not personally liable for a debt, obligation, or liability of the company solely by reason of being or acting as a member or manager." *See also* DLLCA § 18–303(a) (substantially the same); RULLCA § 304(a) (substantially the same). Even limited liability, however, has its limits. The materials below will explore this point in greater detail.

1. THE SCOPE OF LIMITED LIABILITY

PEPSI-COLA BOTTLING CO. V. HANDY

Court of Chancery of Delaware, 2000.
2000 WL 364199.

JACOBS, VICE CHANCELLOR.

This case arises out of the purchase by the plaintiff, The Pepsi-Cola Bottling Company of Salisbury, Maryland ("Pepsi"), from the defendants, of a 66.19 acre parcel of undeveloped real property in Delmar, Delaware. Certain defendants (the "moving defendants") have moved to dismiss all five counts of the complaint under Rule 12(b)(6) * * *.

For the reasons stated below, [the] motion[ ] will be denied.

I.   BACKGROUND

The plaintiff, Pepsi, is a Maryland corporation that bottles soft-drink beverages. Pepsi's principal place of business is in Salisbury, Maryland.

The five named defendants are: (i) Handy Realty, Inc. ("Handy Realty"), which is a Delaware corporation engaged in the development, sale, and brokering of real property in Delaware; (ii) Willow Creek Estates, LLC ("Willow Creek"), which is a Delaware limited liability company created on August 18, 1997 to develop and sell real property in Delaware; (iii) Randall C. Handy, Jr. ("Handy"), who at all relevant times was an officer, director, and shareholder of Handy Realty and was also a member and the manager of Willow Creek; and (iv) Michael Ginsburg ("Ginsburg") and (v) C. Larry McKinley ("McKinley"), both of whom were members of Willow Creek.

On April 5, 1997, Handy, acting on his own behalf and the behalf of Ginsburg and McKinley, contracted to purchase a 66.13 acre parcel of undeveloped real property (the "Property") for development into a residential subdivision called "Willow Creek Estates." Before settling on the contract to purchase, Handy began taking steps to develop the Property into a residential subdivision. Shortly after he began development planning, Handy learned, from a study by Coastal & Estuarine Research, Inc. ("Coastal"), that the Property contained wetlands—a fact that adversely affected the Property's value and development potential.

* * *

After learning that the Property contained wetlands, the defendants abandoned their plans to develop the Property, and instead opted to sell it. To advertise and promote that sale, a Handy Realty sign was placed on the Property. The sign announced that the Property had "Excellent Development Potential," and remained on the Property at all relevant times.

In June, 1997, Pepsi became interested in the Property as a possible site to construct a new soft-drink bottling facility. Unaware of the existence of wetlands, Pepsi acquired an option to purchase the Property from Handy on August 5, 1997. At that time, Willow Creek had not yet been formed and Handy had not yet purchased the Property. Handy, Ginsburg, and McKinley formed the LLC, Willow Creek, on August 18, 1997.

During the option period, Pepsi hired soil engineering consultant John D. Hynes & Associates, Inc. to conduct a Phase I environmental investigation of the Property. As part of its investigation the Hynes firm interviewed Handy and sent him an "Owner/Operator Questionnaire." In his written answers to specific questions about the Property, Handy did not disclose on that questionnaire that the Property contained wetlands or that Coastal had already performed a written preliminary wetlands determination the month before. Moreover, in his response to the question whether any analytical tests or inspections had previously been performed on the Property, Handy falsely represented that no "analytical tests or inspections [had] been conducted on the groundwater, surface water, or soil of the Property." By that point Willow Creek had been formed, and Handy was acting as the agent on behalf of all defendants in their efforts to sell the Property.

On September 4, 1997, the defendants, through Willow Creek, settled on and took title to the Property for a purchase price of $174,000. Four months later, the Defendants, again through Willow Creek, sold the Property to Pepsi for $455,000. Willow Creek's members—Handy, Ginsberg, and McKinley—realized a profit of $281,000 on the sale.

After Pepsi learned that the Property contained wetlands, it brought this action for rescission and damages.

II. THE CONTENTIONS

Pepsi's complaint asserts five counts. Those counts allege: (1) violation of the Consumer Fraud Act, (2) common law fraud, (3) equitable fraud, (4) breach of express warranty, and (5) unjust enrichment. Although the counts plead different legal theories, all are grounded upon the same essential pleaded facts, namely that (i) neither Handy nor any other defendant told Pepsi that the Property contained wetlands, and (ii) the defendants knew that if Pepsi had been told about the wetlands, Pepsi would not have paid $455,000 for the Property. The prayer for relief, which also is common to all Counts, seeks either "resci[ssion of] Plaintiff's purchase of the Property and [an] order [for] the full return and refund of the purchase price, together with such other and further relief as required to reimburse Pepsi for all costs, damages and losses incurred as the result of its purchase of the Property," *or,* alternatively, "monetary damages suffered as a result of Defendants' actions."

The defendants have moved to dismiss all five counts under Court of Chancery Rule 12(b)(6) * * *. The motion to dismiss does not attack the sufficiency of the claims. Rather, it is grounded upon the argument that even if the claims are legally sufficient, no relief can be granted because there can be no recovery against individual members of the LLC in this particular case.

* * *

III. ANALYSIS

A.   The Motion to Dismiss

In considering a motion to dismiss under Court of Chancery Rule 12(b)(6), this Court will assume the truth of all well-pleaded allegations, giving the plaintiff the benefit of all reasonable inferences that can be drawn from the complaint. * * *

The essence of the moving defendants' argument is that the plaintiff cannot recover directly against the movants as LLC members, because none of the movants ever directly held legal or equitable title to the Property. The defendants argue that a plaintiff can recover distributions made to members of an LLC only if (i) the plaintiff pierces the LLC's corporate veil, or (ii) 6 *Del. C.* § 18–607 is applicable. Section 18–607(b) provides that if an LLC member receives a distribution that results in the LLC becoming insolvent, and knew at that time that the LLC would become insolvent as a result of the distribution, the LLC member is liable to the LLC for the amount of the distribution. The defendants argue that because neither of these two circumstances is alleged, the complaint must be dismissed as against Ginsburg, McKinley, and Handy, who are being sued in their capacity as members of Willow Creek.

Any analysis of the defendants' position begins with 6 *Del. C.* § 18–303(a), which codifies the liability of LLC members to third parties. [The court quotes DLLCA § 18–303(a).]

Section 18–303(a) protects members and managers of an LLC against liability for any obligations of the LLC solely by reason of being or acting as LLC members or managers. But, its phrase, "solely by reason of being a member * * *" does imply that there are situations where LLC members and managers would not be shielded by this provision. As two leading Delaware corporation law treatise commentators have observed:

> The word "solely," which is used in Section 18–303, indicates that a member or manager will not be liable for the debts, obligations, or liabilities of a Delaware LLC only by reason of being a member or manager; however, other acts or events could result in the imposition of liability upon or assumption of liability by a member or manager. [R. Franklin Balotti and Jesse A. Finkelstein, *The Delaware Law of Corporations & Business Organizations* 20–6 (3rd ed. 1998).]

The issue presented is whether the defendants here are being sued "solely by reason of being a member" of Willow Creek (the LLC) where the claim is based upon fraudulent acts committed by the LLC members before the LLC was formed and took title to the Property. To express it in terms of the facts at bar, if a person makes material misrepresentations to induce a purchaser to purchase a parcel of land at a price far above fair market value, and thereafter forms an LLC to purchase and hold the land, can that person later claim that his status as an LLC member protects him from liability to the purchaser under § 18–303? I think not.

In this case the complaint alleges that the sequence of relevant events is as follows:

> —*April 5, 1997*—Handy contracts to purchase the Property with intent of forming an LLC with Ginsburg and McKinley for the purpose of building a residential community on the Property.

> —*April 21, 1997*—Coastal provides conclusive evidence that the Property contains wetlands. Handy, Ginsburg, and McKinley abandon construction plans and instead decide to sell the Property.

> —*August 5, 1997*—Pepsi and Handy negotiate an option to purchase the Property. Pepsi discloses its intent to build a bottling facility on the Property and Handy has not disclosed the existence of wetlands.

> —*August 18, 1997*—Defendants Handy, Ginsburg, and McKinley form Willow Creek Estates, LLC.

> —*During option period*—Pepsi hires Hynes to do Phase I, during which time Hynes specifically asks Handy about the existence of wetlands, to which Handy responds in the negative.

> —*September 4, 1997*—The defendants, through Willow Creek, settle and take title to the Property.

> —*Four months later*—The defendants, through Willow Creek, sell the unimproved Property to Pepsi for over twice the amount

of their purchase price, and do not disclose the existence of wetlands.

Because the facts alleged in the complaint establish that the LLC was not formed (and the Property was not acquired by the LLC) until after the allegedly critical wrongful acts had been committed, it follows that the defendants could not have been acting "*solely* as members of the LLC when they committed those acts."[10] Therefore, the defendants are not protected by § 18–303.

The defendants[ ] next argue that they are protected by 6 *Del. C.* § 18–607(a) * * *. [The court quotes DLLCA § 18–607(a).]

The movants interpret this language as limiting the right of third parties to bring direct claims against LLC members to cases where the LLC makes a distribution to LLC members who know, at the time, that the distribution would leave the LLC insolvent. Section [18]–607(b) provides, in that circumstance, that an LLC member who knew of that fact at the time it received the distribution is liable to the LLC for the amount of the distribution. Here, the defendants contend that (i) § 18–607 is the only provision that allows a third party to recover from an LLC member without piercing the LLC's corporate veil, and (ii) because the complaint does not allege a claim under § 18–607, they cannot be held liable.

Section 18–607 prohibits the stripping of corporate assets so as to render an LLC insolvent, and creates a corporate cause of action against LLC members who improperly receive a distribution of those assets. The defendants, however, give a far more expansive reading to § 18–607 than its language warrants. They claim that the statute shields LLC members against *any* other claims against them, *i.e.,* against *all* claims except those that arise under § 18–607. Nothing in § 18–607 so provides. Moreover, and as previously discussed, under § 18–303, a third party may recover from an LLC member on claims that do not arise "*solely* by reason of being a member or acting as a manager of the limited liability company."

Because all five counts of the complaint are based on conduct that occurred before the LLC was formed, those claims are not barred by § 18–303. Under the Limited Liability Company Act, no protection against liability is afforded to LLC members who (as here) are sued in capacities other than as members of the LLC. Accordingly, there is no reason to address the alternative argument that the corporate veil of the LLC must be pierced in order to state a cognizable claim.

---

[10] The complaint alleges specifically that at least one of the members (Handy) had direct knowledge of the Coastal report, and made fraudulent [representations] to sell the Property, before the formation of Willow Creek. It is also inferable from the complaint that Ginsburg and McKinley had at least constructive knowledge that the Property contained wetlands and that the LLC would attempt to sell the Property without disclosing that fact.

For the above reasons, the motion to dismiss Pepsi's claims will be denied.

* * *

NOTES

(1) The *Handy* court rests its conclusion on the fact that "all five counts [were] based on conduct that occurred before the LLC was formed." Would the result change if the LLC had been formed (and if it had acquired the property) well before Pepsi-Cola became interested in purchasing the land? *Cf.* Allen v. Dackman, 991 A.2d 1216, 1229 (Md. 2010) ("An LLC member is liable for torts he or she personally commits, inspires, or participates in because he or she personally committed a wrong, not 'solely' because he or she is a member of the LLC.").

(2) Assume that Ginsburg and McKinley (the two other members of the LLC) had no actual or constructive knowledge of (1) the presence of wetlands on the property, and (2) the alleged misrepresentations made by Handy. (This is contrary, of course, to what was alleged in the complaint—see footnote 10 of the *Handy* opinion.) Under DLLCA § 18–303, could Ginsburg and McKinley be held personally liable in these circumstances for Handy's alleged misrepresentations?

(3) Based on your answers to the above questions, can you articulate what type of liability is "limited" by provisions such as DLLCA § 18–303, ULLCA § 303, and RULLCA § 304?

(4) DLLCA § 18–215 provides an additional form of limited liability protection. An operating agreement can designate a "series" or specified group of members, managers, LLC interests, or assets that have "separate rights, powers or duties with respect to specified property or obligations of the limited liability company or profits and losses associated with specified property or obligations." *Id.* § 18–215(a). If the operating agreement creates one or more of these series, and if certain requirements are met, then "the debts, liabilities, obligations and expenses incurred, contracted for or otherwise existing with respect to a particular series shall be enforceable against the assets of such series only, and not against the assets of the limited liability company generally or any other series thereof." *Id.* § 18–215(b). Similarly, "none of the debts, liabilities, obligations and expenses incurred, contracted for or otherwise existing with respect to the limited liability company generally or any other series thereof shall be enforceable against the assets of such series." *Id.*

Some other states have followed Delaware's lead in authorizing "series LLCs." RULLCA, however, does not permit them. As the Prefatory Note to RULLCA explains:

> The new Act also has a very noteworthy omission; it does not authorize "series LLCs." Under a series approach, a single limited liability company may establish and contain within itself separate series. Each series is treated as an enterprise separate from each

other and from the LLC itself. Each series has associated with it specified members, assets, and obligations, and—due to what have been called "internal shields"—the obligations of one series are not the obligation[s] of any other series or of the LLC.

Delaware pioneered the series concept, and the concept has apparently been quite useful in structuring certain types of investment funds and in arranging complex financing. Other states have followed Delaware's lead, but a number of difficult and substantial questions remain unanswered, including:

- *conceptual*—How can a series be—and expect to be treated as— a separate legal person for liability and other purposes if the series is defined as part of another legal person?

- *bankruptcy*—Bankruptcy law has not recognized the series as a separate legal person. If a series becomes insolvent, will the entire LLC and the other series become part of the bankruptcy proceedings? Will a bankruptcy court consolidate the assets and liabilities of the separate series?

- *efficacy of the internal shields in the courts of other states*—Will the internal shields be respected in the courts of states whose LLC statutes do not recognize series? Most LLC statutes provide that "foreign law governs" the liability of members of a foreign LLC. However, those provisions do not apply to the series question, because those provisions pertain to the liability of a member for the obligations of the LLC. For a series LLC, the pivotal question is entirely different—namely, whether some assets of an LLC should be immune from some of the creditors of the LLC.

- *tax treatment*—Will the IRS and the states treat each series separately? Will separate returns be filed? May one series "check the box" for corporate tax classification and the others not?

- *securities law*—Given the panoply of unanswered questions, what types of disclosures must be made when a membership interest is subject to securities law?

* * * Given the availability of well-established alternate structures (e.g., multiple single member LLCs, an LLC "holding company" with LLC subsidiaries), it made no sense for the Act to endorse the complexities and risks of a series approach.

2.   PIERCING THE VEIL

KAYCEE LAND & LIVESTOCK V. FLAHIVE

Supreme Court of Wyoming, 2002.
46 P.3d 323.

KITE, JUSTICE.

This matter comes before this court as a question certified to us by the district court for resolution * * *. The certified question seeks resolution of whether, in the absence of fraud, the entity veil of a limited liability company (LLC) can be pierced in the same manner as that of a corporation. We answer the certified question in the affirmative.

* * *

FACTS

* * * The district court submitted the following statement of facts in its order certifying the question of law:

1.   Flahive Oil & Gas is a Wyoming Limited Liability Company with no assets at this time.

2.   [Kaycee Land and Livestock] entered into a contract with Flahive Oil & Gas LLC allowing Flahive Oil & Gas to use the surface of its real property.

3.   Roger Flahive is and was the managing member of Flahive Oil & Gas at all relevant times.

4.   [Kaycee Land and Livestock] alleges that Flahive Oil & Gas caused environmental contamination to its real property located in Johnson County, Wyoming.

5.   [Kaycee Land and Livestock] seeks to pierce the LLC veil and disregard the [LLC] entity of Flahive Oil & Gas Limited Liability Company and hold Roger Flahive individually liable for the contamination.

6.   There is no allegation of fraud.

DISCUSSION

The question presented is limited to whether, in the absence of fraud, the remedy of piercing the veil is available against a company formed under the Wyoming Limited Liability Company Act (Wyo. Stat. Ann. §§ 17–15–101 to –144 (LexisNexis 2001)). To answer this question, we must first examine the development of the doctrine within Wyoming's corporate context. As a general rule, a corporation is a separate entity distinct from the individuals comprising it. Wyoming statutes governing corporations do not address the circumstances under which the veil can be pierced. However, since 1932, this court has espoused the concept that a corporation's legal entity will be disregarded whenever the recognition thereof in a particular case will lead to injustice. In *Miles v. CEC Homes, Inc.,* 753 P.2d 1021, 1023 (Wyo.1988), this court summarized the circumstances under which the corporate veil would be pierced pursuant to Wyoming law:

> " 'Before a corporation's acts and obligations can be legally recognized as those of a particular person, and vice versa, it must be made to appear that the corporation is not only influenced and governed by that person, but that there is such a unity of interest and ownership that the individuality, or separateness, of such person and corporation has ceased, and that the facts are such that an adherence to the fiction of the separate existence of the corporation would, under the particular circumstances, sanction a fraud or promote injustice.' Quoting *Arnold v. Browne,* 27 Cal.App.3d 386, 103 Cal.Rptr. 775 (1972) (overruled on other grounds)."

* * *

Wyoming courts, as well as courts across the country, have typically utilized a fact driven inquiry to determine whether circumstances justify a decision to pierce a corporate veil. This case comes to us as a certified question in the abstract with little factual context, and we are asked to broadly pronounce that there are no circumstances under which this court will look through a failed attempt to create a separate LLC entity and prevent injustice. We simply cannot reach that conclusion and believe it is improvident for this court to prohibit this remedy from applying to any unforeseen circumstance that may exist in the future.

We have long recognized that piercing the corporate veil is an equitable doctrine. The concept of piercing the corporate veil is a judicially created remedy for situations where corporations have not been operated as separate entities as contemplated by statute and, therefore, are not entitled to be treated as such. The determination of whether the doctrine applies centers on whether there is an element of injustice, fundamental unfairness, or inequity. The concept developed through common law and is absent from the statutes governing corporate organization. Appellee Roger Flahive suggests that, by the adoption of § 17–16–622(b)—a provision from the revised Model Business Corporation Act—the Wyoming legislature intended to explicitly authorize piercing in the corporate context and, by inference, prevent its application in the LLC context. A careful review of the statutory language and legislative history leads to a different conclusion. Section 17–16–622(b) reads: "Unless otherwise provided in the articles of incorporation, a shareholder of a corporation is not personally liable for the acts or debts of the corporation except that he may become personally liable by reason of his own acts or conduct." Mr. Flahive contrasts that language with the

LLC statute which simply states the underlying principle of limited liability for individual members and managers. Section 17–15–113 provides:

> Neither the members of a limited liability company nor the managers of a limited liability company managed by a manager or managers are liable under a judgment, decree or order of a court, or in any other manner, for a debt, obligation or liability of the limited liability company.

However, we agree with Commentator Gelb that: "It is difficult to read statutory § 17–15–113 as intended to preclude courts from deciding to disregard the veil of an improperly used LLC." Harvey Gelb, *Liabilities of Members and Managers of Wyoming Limited Liability Companies,* 31 Land & Water L.Rev. 133 at 142 (1996).

Section 17–16–622—the statute relied upon by Mr. Flahive as indicating legislative intent to allow piercing of the corporate veil—when considered in the context of its legislative history, provides no support for the conclusion that the legislature intended in any way to limit application of the common-law doctrine to LLCs. As previously explained, § 17–16–622 was adopted from the revised Model Business Corporation Act, and the comments therein clarify that subsection (b) "sets forth the basic rule of nonliability of shareholders for corporate acts or debts that underlies modern corporation law" and "recognizes that such liability may be assumed voluntarily or by other conduct." 1 Model Bus. Corp. Act Ann. § 6.22 at 6–94 to 6–95 (Supp.1997). This provision was added in 1984 and was not intended to "treat exhaustively the statutory bases for imposing liability on shareholders." *Id.* at 6–96. The official comments in the revised Model Business Corporation Act specifically recognize the separate existence of the common law by stating: "Shareholders may also become liable for corporate obligations by their voluntary actions or by other conduct under the common law doctrine of 'piercing the corporate veil.'" *Id.*

We note that Wyoming was the first state to enact LLC statutes. Many years passed before the Internal Revenue Service's approval of taxation of LLCs as partnerships led to other states adopting LLC legislation and the broad usage of this form for business organizations. Wyoming's statute is very short and establishes only minimal requirements for creating and operating LLCs. It seems highly unlikely that the Wyoming legislature gave any consideration to whether the common-law doctrine of piercing the veil should apply to the liability limitation granted by that fledgling statute. It is true that some other states have adopted specific legislation extending the doctrine to LLCs while Wyoming has not. However, that situation seems more attributable to the fact that Wyoming was a pioneer in the LLC arena and states which adopted LLC statutes much later had the benefit of years of practical experience during which this issue was likely raised.

Mr. Flahive insists that, if the legislature intended for liability to be asserted against the members of an LLC, it could have added similar language to the LLC chapter at the same time it adopted provisions of the revised Model Business Corporation Act. However, adoption of those amendments in 1989, twelve years after the enactment of the LLC statutes, while remaining silent on the issue of piercing the veil in the LLC statutes, is far too attenuated to indicate a clear legislative intent to restrict application of the common law to LLCs. It stands to reason that, because it is an equitable doctrine, "[t]he paucity of statutory authority for LLC piercing should not be considered a barrier to its application." [Karin Schwindt, *Limited Liability Companies: Issues in Member Liability,* 44 UCLA L. REV. 1541, 1552 (1997).] Lack of explicit statutory language should not be considered an indication of the legislature's desire to make LLC members impermeable. Moreover,

> " 'It is not to be presumed that the legislature intended to abrogate or modify a rule of the common law by the enactment of a statute upon the same subject; it is rather to be presumed that no change in the common law was intended unless the language employed clearly indicates such an intention * * *. The rules of common law are not to be changed by doubtful implication, nor overturned except by clear and unambiguous language.' " *McKinney v. McKinney,* [59 Wyo. 204,] 135 P.2d [940,] 942 [(1943)], quoting from 25 R.C.L. 1054, § 280.

Allstate Insurance Company v. Wyoming Insurance Department, 672 P.2d 810, 824 (Wyo.1983).

With the dearth of legislative consideration on this issue in Wyoming, we are left to determine whether applying the well established common law to LLCs somehow runs counter to what the legislature would have intended had it considered the issue. In that regard, it is instructive that: "Every state that has enacted LLC piercing legislation has chosen to follow corporate law standards and not develop a separate LLC standard." Philip P. Whynott, The Limited Liability Company § 11:140 at 11–5 (3d ed.1999). Statutes which create corporations and LLCs have the same basic purpose—to limit the liability of individual investors with a corresponding benefit to economic development. Statutes created the legal fiction of the corporation being a completely separate entity which could act independently from individual persons. If the corporation were created and operated in conformance with the statutory requirements, the law would treat it as a separate entity and shelter the individual shareholders from any liability caused by corporate action, thereby encouraging investment. However, courts throughout the country have consistently recognized [that] certain unjust circumstances can arise if immunity from liability shelters those who have failed to operate a corporation as a separate entity. Consequently, when corporations fail to follow the statutorily mandated formalities, co-mingle funds, or ignore the restrictions in their articles of incorporation regarding separate treatment of corporate property, the courts deem it appropriate to disregard the separate identity and do not permit shareholders to be sheltered from liability to third parties for damages caused by the corporations' acts.

We can discern no reason, in either law or policy, to treat LLCs differently than we treat corporations. If the members and officers of an LLC fail to treat it as a separate entity as contemplated by statute, they should not enjoy immunity from individual liability for the LLC's acts that cause damage to third parties. Most, if not all, of the expert LLC commentators have concluded the doctrine of piercing the veil should apply to LLCs. It also appears that most courts faced with a similar situation—LLC statutes which are silent and facts which suggest the LLC veil should be pierced—have had little trouble concluding the common law should be applied and the factors weighed accordingly. *See, e.g., Hollowell v. Orleans Regional Hospital,* No. Civ. A. 95–4029, 1998 WL 283298 (E.D.La. May 29, 1998); *Ditty v. CheckRite, Ltd., Inc.,* 973 F.Supp. 1320 (D.Utah 1997); *Tom Thumb Food Markets, Inc. v. TLH Properties, LLC,* No. C9–98–1277, 1999 WL 31168 (Minn.Ct.App. Jan. 26, 1999).

Certainly, the various factors which would justify piercing an LLC veil would not be identical to the corporate situation for the obvious reason that many of the organizational formalities applicable to corporations do not apply to LLCs. The LLC's operation is intended to be much more flexible than a corporation's. Factors relevant to determining when to pierce the corporate veil have developed over time in a multitude of cases. It would be inadvisable in this case, which lacks a complete factual context, to attempt to articulate all the possible factors to be applied to LLCs in Wyoming in the future. * * *

The certified question presents an interesting internal inconsistency. It begins, "In the absence of fraud," thereby presenting the assumption that a court may pierce an LLC's veil in a case of fraud. Thus, the certified question assumes that, when fraud is found, the courts are able to disregard the LLC entity despite the statutory framework which supposedly precludes such a result. Either the courts continue to possess the equitable power to take such action or they do not. Certainly, nothing in the statutes suggests the legislature gave such careful consideration and delineated the specific circumstances under which the courts can act in this arena. If the assumption is correct, individual LLC members can be held personally liable for damages to innocent third parties when the LLC has committed fraud. Yet, when the LLC has caused damage and has inadequate capitalization, co-mingled funds, diverted assets, or used the LLC as a mere shell, individual members are immune from liability. Legislative silence cannot be stretched to condone such an illogical result.

In *Amfac Mechanical Supply Co.* [*v. Federer*, 645 P.2d 73 (Wyo.1982)], this court clarified that a showing of fraud or an intent to defraud is not necessary to disregard a corporate entity. We clearly stated: "Fraud is, of course, a matter of concern in suits to disregard corporate fictions, but it is not a prerequisite to such a result." Other courts have echoed this view: "Liability on the basis of fraud, however, does not encompass the entire spectrum of cases in which the veil was pierced in the interest of equity." [Eric Fox, *Piercing the Veil of Limited Liability Companies*, 62 GEO. WASH. L. REV. 1143, 1169 (1994).] Thus, even absent fraud, courts have the power to impose liability on corporate shareholders. This same logic should naturally be extended to the LLC context. We have made clear that: "Each case involving the disregard of the separate entity doctrine must be governed by the special facts of that case." *Opal Mercantile* [*v. Tamblyn*, 616 P.2d 776, 778 (Wyo.1980)]. Determinations of fact are within the trier of fact's province. The district court must complete a fact intensive inquiry and exercise its equitable powers to determine whether piercing the veil is appropriate under the circumstances presented in this case.

CONCLUSION

No reason exists in law or equity for treating an LLC differently than a corporation is treated when considering whether to disregard the legal entity. We conclude the equitable remedy of piercing the veil is an available remedy under the Wyoming Limited Liability Company Act.

NOTES

(1) Should courts allow piercing in the LLC context? If so, should any differences exist between piercing in the LLC context and piercing in the corporation setting?

(2) Some LLC statutes explicitly state that corporate piercing the veil standards shall apply to LLCs. *See, e.g.*, MINN. STAT. § 322B.303(2) ("The case law that states the conditions and circumstances under which the corporate veil of a corporation may be pierced under Minnesota law also applies to [LLCs]."). Under some statutes, however, an LLC piercing analysis cannot consider a firm's failure to follow formalities. *See, e.g.*, WASH. REV. CODE § 25.15.060 ("[T]he failure to hold meetings of members or managers or the failure to observe formalities pertaining to the calling or conduct of meetings shall not be considered a factor tending to establish that the members have personal liability for any act, debt, obligation, or liability of the limited liability company if the certificate of formation and limited liability company agreement do not expressly require the holding of meetings of members or managers."); *see also* ULLCA § 303(b) ("The failure of [an LLC] to observe the

usual company formalities or requirements relating to the exercise of its company powers or management of its business is not a ground for imposing personal liability on the members or managers for liabilities of the company."); RULLCA § 304(b) (substantially the same); *id.* § 304 cmt. ("In the corporate realm, 'disregard of corporate formalities' is a key factor in the piercing analysis. In the realm of LLCs, that factor is inappropriate, because informality of organization and operation is both common and desired.").

(3) In *Martin v. Freeman*, 272 P.3d 1182, 1184–85 (Colo. App. 2012), the court affirmed a veil-piercing determination that Tradewinds Group, LLC was the alter ego of its sole member, Dean Freeman. The lower court had made the following findings: (1) Tradewinds' assets were commingled with Freeman's personal assets and the assets of one of his other entities; (2) Tradewinds maintained negligible corporate records; (3) the records concerning Tradewinds' substantive transactions were inadequate; (4) the fact that a single individual served as the entity's sole member and manager facilitated misuse; (5) the entity was thinly capitalized; (6) undocumented infusions of cash were required to pay all of Tradewinds' operating expenses, including its litigation expenses; (7) Tradewinds was never operated as an active business; (8) legal formalities were disregarded; (9) Freeman paid Tradewinds' debts without characterizing the transactions; (10) Tradewinds' assets were used for nonentity purposes without agreement or compensation; and (11) Tradewinds was operated as a mere assetless shell, and the proceeds of the sale of its only significant asset were diverted from the entity to Freeman's personal account.

On appeal, Freeman argued that "the court erred in not recognizing that * * * limited liability companies have fewer restrictions than corporations concerning maintaining formal corporate records." The *Martin* court cited a Colorado statute indicating that an LLC's failure "to observe the formalities or requirements relating to the management of its business and affairs is not in itself a ground for imposing personal liability on the members," but the court nevertheless stated that "factors in determining alter ego status" include whether "adequate corporate records are maintained" and whether "legal formalities are disregarded." The court observed that "the [lower] court considered the appropriate factors and its findings support a conclusion that Tradewinds was Freeman's alter ego."

(4) In *Litchfield Asset Management Corp. v. Howell*, 799 A.2d 298 (Conn. App. Ct. 2002), the plaintiff held a $657,207 judgment against Mary Ann Howell. Howell later formed two LLCs and contributed some of her personal assets to the companies. The court applied a "reverse piercing" analysis and allowed the plaintiff to reach the LLCs' assets in partial satisfaction of its judgment against Howell. As the court stated:

> * * * In the usual veil piercing case, a court is asked to disregard a corporate entity so as to make available the personal assets of its owners to satisfy a liability of the entity. In this case, an instance of what is known as "reverse piercing," the plaintiff

argues the opposite, that the assets of the corporate entities should be made available to pay the personal debts of an owner.

      * * *

We recognize that the separate existence of a corporate entity for liability purposes represents a public policy choice, as expressed in Connecticut's legislation governing the formulation and regulation of corporations and limited liability companies, and that the corporate or limited liability form should not be disregarded lightly. * * * However, "[w]hen the statutory privilege of doing business in the corporate [or limited liability company] form is employed as a cloak for the evasion of obligations, as a mask behind which to do injustice, or invoked to subvert equity, the separate personality of the corporation [or limited liability company] will be disregarded." (Internal quotation marks omitted.) [Toshiba Am. Med. Sys., Inc. v. Mobile Med. Sys., Inc., 730 A.2d 1219, 1224 (Conn. App. Ct. 1999).] We therefore conclude that the court properly disregarded Design's and Antiquities' structures as limited liability companies so as to hold them liable for the personal debt of Mary Ann Howell.

Id. at 311, 316.

G.   FIDUCIARY DUTIES

1.   THE BASIC DUTIES

In contrast to many corporation statutes, a number of LLC statutes address the concept of fiduciary duty. The statutes often state that members (in member-managed LLCs) and managers (in manager-managed LLCs) owe fiduciary duties of care and loyalty to the LLC, and at least some of the statutes indicate that those duties also run to the individual members. *See, e.g.*, FLA. STAT. § 605.04091(1) ("Each manager of a manager-managed limited liability company and member of a member-managed limited liability company owes fiduciary duties of loyalty and care to the limited liability company and members of the limited liability company."); *see also* ULLCA § 409 (setting forth duties and obligations of members and managers); RULLCA § 409 (same). Courts will be needed, of course, to resolve disputes over whether breaches of fiduciary duty have occurred. In jurisdictions where fiduciary duty is not addressed by statute, the courts will have an even greater role, as they must shape the contours of fiduciary duty doctrine without any legislative aid.

VGS, INC. V. CASTIEL

Court of Chancery of Delaware, 2000.
2000 WL 1277372.

STEELE, VICE CHANCELLOR.

* * *

I.   Facts

David Castiel formed Virtual Geosatellite LLC (the "LLC") on January 6, 1999 in order to pursue a Federal Communications Commission ("FCC") license to build and operate a satellite system which its proponents claim could dramatically increase the "real estate" in outer space capable of transmitting high speed internet traffic and other communications. When originally formed, it had only one Member—Virtual Geosatellite Holdings, Inc. ("Holdings"). On January 8, 1999, Ellipso, Inc. ("Ellipso") joined the LLC as its second Member. Several weeks later, on January 29, 1999, Sahagen Satellite Technology Group LLC ("Sahagen Satellite") became the third Member of the LLC.

David Castiel controls both Holdings and Ellipso. Peter Sahagen, an aggressive and apparently successful venture capitalist, controls Sahagen Satellite.

Pursuant to the LLC Agreement, Holdings received 660 units (representing 63.46% of the total equity in the LLC), Sahagen Satellite received 260 units (representing 25%), and Ellipso received 120 units (representing 11.54%). The founders vested management of the LLC in a Board of Managers. As the majority unitholder, Castiel had the power to appoint, remove, and replace two of the three members of the Board of Managers. Castiel, therefore, had the power to prevent any Board decision with which he disagreed. Castiel named himself and Tom Quinn to the Board of Managers. Sahagen named himself as the third member of the Board.

Not long after the formation of the LLC, Castiel and Sahagen were at odds. Castiel contends that Sahagen wanted to control the LLC ever since he became involved, and that Sahagen repeatedly offered, unsuccessfully, to buy control of the LLC. Sahagen maintains that Castiel ran the LLC so poorly that its mission had become untracked, additional necessary capital could not be raised, and competent managers could not be attracted to join the enterprise. Further, Sahagen claims that Castiel directed LLC assets to Ellipso in order to prop up a failing, cash-strapped Ellipso. At trial, these issues and other similar accusations from both sides were explored in great detail. For our purposes here, all that need be concluded is the unarguable fact that Castiel and Sahagen had very different ideas about how the LLC should be managed and operated.

Sahagen ultimately convinced Quinn that Castiel must be ousted from leadership in order for the LLC to prosper. As a result, Quinn (Castiel's nominee) covertly "defected" to Sahagen's camp, and he and Sahagen decided to wrest control of the LLC from Castiel. Many LLC employees and even some of Castiel's lieutenants testified that they believed it to be in the LLC's best interest to take control from Castiel.

On April 14, 2000, without notice to Castiel, Quinn and Sahagen acted by written consent to merge the LLC under Delaware law into VGS, Inc. ("VGS"), a Delaware corporation. Accordingly, the LLC ceased to exist, its assets and liabilities passed to VGS, and VGS became the LLC's legal successor-in-interest. VGS's Board of Directors is comprised of Sahagen, Quinn, and Neel Howard. Of course, the incorporators did not name Castiel to VGS's Board.

On the day of the merger, Sahagen executed a promissory note to VGS in the amount of $10 million plus interest. In return, he received two million shares of VGS Series A Preferred Stock. VGS also issued 1,269,200 shares of common stock to Holdings, 230,800 shares of common stock to Ellipso, and 500,000 shares of common stock to Sahagen Satellite. Once one does the math, it is apparent that Holdings and Ellipso went from having a 75% controlling combined ownership interest in the LLC to having only a 37.5% interest in VGS. On the other hand, Sahagen and Sahagen Satellite went from owning 25% of the LLC to owning 62.5% of VGS.

There can be no doubt why Sahagen and Quinn, acting as a majority of the LLC's board of managers did not notify Castiel of the merger plan. Notice to Castiel would have immediately resulted in Quinn's removal from the board and a newly constituted majority which would thwart the effort to strip Castiel of control. Had he known in advance, Castiel surely would have attempted to replace Quinn with someone loyal to Castiel who would agree with his views. Clandestine machinations were, therefore, essential to the success of Quinn and Sahagen's plan.

II.　Analysis

A.　The Board of Managers did have authority to act by majority vote.

The LLC Agreement does not expressly state whether the Board of Managers must act unanimously or by majority vote. Sahagen and Quinn contend that because a number of provisions would be rendered meaningless if a unanimous vote was required, a majority vote is implied. Castiel, however, maintains that a unanimous vote must be implied when the majority owner has blocking power.

Section 8.01(b)(i) of the LLC Agreement states that, "[t]he Board of Managers shall initially be composed of three (3) Managers." Sahagen Satellite has the right to designate one member of the initial board, and if the Board of Managers increased in number, Sahagen Satellite could "designate a number of representatives on the Board of Managers that is less than Sahagen's then current Percentage Interest." If unanimity were required, the number of managers would be irrelevant—Sahagen, and his minority interest, would have veto power in any event. The existence of language in the LLC Agreement discussing expansion of the Board is therefore quite telling.

Also persuasive is the fact that Section 8.01(c) of the LLC Agreement, entitled "Matters Requiring Consent of Sahagen," provides that Sahagen's approval is needed for a merger, consolidation, or reorganization of the LLC. If a unanimity requirement indeed existed, there would have been no need to expressly list matters on which Sahagen's minority interest had veto power.

Section 12.01(a)(i) of the LLC Agreement also supports Sahagen's argument. This section provides that the LLC may be dissolved by written consent by either the Board of Managers or by Members holding two-thirds of the Common Units. The effect of this Section is to allow any combination of Holdings and Sahagen Satellite, or Holdings and Ellipso, as Members, to dissolve the LLC. It seems unlikely that the Members designed the LLC Agreement to permit Members holding two-thirds of the Common Units to dissolve the LLC but denied their appointed Managers the power to reach the same result unless the minority manager agreed.

Castiel takes the position that while the Members can act by majority vote, the Board of Managers can act only by unanimous vote. He maintains that if the Board fails to agree unanimously on an issue, the issue should be put to an LLC Members' vote with the majority controlling. The practical effect of Castiel's interpretation would be that whenever Castiel and Sahagen disagreed, Castiel would prevail because the issue would be submitted to the Members where Castiel's controlling interest would carry the vote. If that were the case, both Sahagen's Board position and Quinn's Board position would be superfluous. I am confident that the parties never intended that result, or if they had so intended, that they would have included plain and simple language in the agreement spelling it out clearly.

B. By failing to give notice of their proposed action, Sahagen and Quinn failed to discharge their duty of loyalty to Castiel in good faith

Section 18–404(d) of the LLC Act states in pertinent part:

Unless otherwise provided in a limited liability company agreement, on any matter that is to be voted on by managers, the managers may take such action without a meeting, *without prior notice* and without a vote if a consent or consents in writing, setting forth the action so taken, shall be signed by the managers having not less than the minimum number of votes that would be necessary to authorize such action at a meeting (emphasis added).

Therefore, the LLC Act, read literally, does not require notice to Castiel before Sahagen and Quinn could act by written consent. The LLC Agreement does not purport to modify the statute in this regard.

Those observations cannot complete the analysis of Sahagen and Quinn's actions, however. Sahagen and Quinn knew what would happen if they notified Castiel of their intention to act by written consent to merge the LLC into VGS, Inc. Castiel would have attempted to remove Quinn, and block the planned action. Regardless of his motivation in doing so, removal of Quinn in that circumstance would have been within Castiel's rights as the LLC's controlling owner under the Agreement.

Section 18–404(d) has yet to be interpreted by this Court or the Supreme Court. Nonetheless, it seems clear that the purpose of permitting action by written consent without notice is to enable LLC managers to take quick, efficient action in situations where a minority of managers could not block or adversely affect the course set by the majority even if they were notified of the proposed action and objected to it. The General Assembly never intended, I am quite confident, to enable two managers to deprive, clandestinely and surreptitiously, a third manager representing the majority interest in the LLC of an opportunity to protect that interest by taking an action that the third manager's member would surely have opposed if he had knowledge of it. My reading of Section 18–404(d) is grounded in a classic maxim of equity—"Equity looks to the intent rather than to the form." In this hopefully unique situation, this application of the maxim requires construction of the statute to allow action without notice only by a *constant or fixed majority*. It cannot apply to an illusory, will-of-the wisp majority which would implode should notice be given. Nothing in the statute suggests that this court of equity should blind its eyes to a shallow, too clever by half, manipulative attempt to restructure an enterprise through an action taken by a "majority" that existed only so long as it could act in secrecy.

Sahagen and Quinn each owed a duty of loyalty to the LLC, its investors and Castiel, their fellow manager. Castiel or his entities owned a majority interest in the LLC and he sat as a member of the board representing entities and interests empowered by the Agreement to control the majority membership of the board. The majority investor protected his equity interest in the LLC through the mechanism of appointment to the board rather than by the statutorily sanctioned mechanism of approval by members owning a majority of the LLC's equity interests. It may seem somewhat incongruous, but this Agreement allows the action to merge, dissolve or change to corporate status to be taken by a simple majority vote of the board of managers rather than rely upon the default position of the statute which requires a majority vote of the equity interest. Instead the drafters made the critical assumption, known to all the players here, that the holder of the majority equity interest has the right to appoint and remove two managers, ostensibly guaranteeing control over a three member board. When Sahagen and Quinn, fully recognizing that this was Castiel's protection against actions adverse to his majority interest, acted in secret, without notice, they failed to discharge their duty of loyalty to him in good faith. They owed Castiel a duty to give him prior notice even if he would have interfered with a plan that they conscientiously believed to be in the best interest of the LLC.[4] Instead, they launched a preemptive strike that furtively converted Castiel's controlling interest in the LLC to a minority interest in VGS without affording Castiel a level playing field on which to defend his interest. "[Another] traditional maxim of equity holds that equity regards and treats that as done which in good conscience ought to be done." [DONALD J. WOLFE, JR. & MICHAEL A. PITTENGER, CORPORATE AND COMMERCIAL PRACTICE IN THE DELAWARE COURT OF CHANCERY § 2–3(b)(1)(i) (1998).] In good conscience, under these circumstances, Sahagen and Quinn should have given Castiel prior notice.

Many hours were spent at trial focusing on contentions that Castiel has proved to be an ineffective leader in whom employees and investors have lost confidence. I listened to testimony regarding delayed FCC licensing, a suggested new management team for the LLC, and the alleged unlocked value of the LLC. A substantial record exists fully flushing out the rancorous relationships of the members and their wildly disparate views on the existing state of affairs as well as the LLC's prospects for the future. But the issue of who is best suited to run the LLC should not be resolved here but in board meetings where all managers are present and all members appropriately represented, and/or in future litigation, if it unfortunately becomes necessary.

Likewise, the parties spent much time and effort arguing over the standard to be applied to the actions taken by Sahagen and Quinn. Specifically, the parties debated whether the standard should be entire fairness or the business judgment rule. It should be clear that the actions of Sahagen and Quinn, in their capacity as managers constituted a breach of their duty of loyalty and that those actions do not, therefore, entitle them to the benefit or protection of the business judgment rule. They intentionally used a flawed process to merge the LLC into VGS, Inc., in an attempt to prevent the member with majority equity interest in the LLC from protecting his interests in the manner contemplated by the very LLC Agreement under which they purported to act. Analysis beyond

---

[4] I make no ruling here as to whether I believe the merger and the resulting recapitalization of the LLC was in the LLC's best interests, nor do I rule here regarding the wisdom of Castiel's actions had he in fact been able to remove Quinn before the merger.

a look at the process is clearly unnecessary. Perhaps, had notice been given and an attempt then made to block Castiel's anticipated action to replace Quinn, the allegedly disinterested and independent member that Castiel himself had appointed, the analysis might be different. However, this, as all cases, must be reviewed as it is presented, not as it might have been.

III. Conclusion

For the reasons stated above, I find that a majority vote of the LLC's Board of Managers could properly effect a merger. But, I also find that Sahagen and Quinn failed to discharge their duty of loyalty to Castiel in good faith by failing to give him advance notice of their merger plans under the unique circumstances of this case and the structure of this LLC Agreement. Accordingly, I declare * * * the acts taken to merge the LLC into VGS, Inc. to be invalid and the merger is ordered rescinded. * * *

NOTES

(1) Why did Vice-Chancellor Steele have to parse the operating agreement to determine if the managers voted on a majority or unanimity basis? Because the operating agreement failed to cover the matter, shouldn't the default rule of DLLCA have applied? *See* DLLCA §§ 18–402, 18–404; *cf.* ULLCA § 404 (addressing the management of an LLC); RULLCA § 407 (same).

(2) Vice-Chancellor Steele finds that "the LLC Act, read literally, does not require notice to Castiel before Sahagen and Quinn could act by written consent," and he notes that "[t]he LLC Agreement does not purport to modify the statute in this regard." The actions of Sahagen and Quinn, therefore, did not violate any express provisions of the LLC Act or the LLC agreement. Why were their actions deemed unlawful?

(3) Vice-Chancellor Steele also finds that "Sahagen and Quinn each owed a duty of loyalty to the LLC, its investors and Castiel, their fellow manager." What is the Vice-Chancellor's authority for this finding?

(4) Should the business judgment rule apply to LLC disputes? Are the rationales supporting the business judgment rule in the corporation context also present in the LLC setting? In Oklahoma, the business judgment rule is explicitly applicable, by statute, to managerial decisions in an LLC. *See* OKLA. STAT. tit. 18, § 2016(4) ("A manager is not liable for any action taken as a manager, or any failure to take any action, if the manager performed the duties of the office in compliance with the business judgment rule as applied to directors and officers of a corporation * * *."). Similarly, RULLCA explicitly states that the fiduciary duty of care is "[s]ubject to the business judgment rule." RULLCA § 409(a), (c).

(5) Should the need for, and the content of, fiduciary duties be affected by (1) whether the owners have personal liability for the obligations of the

firm, and (2) whether the owners can easily liquidate their ownership interests?

(6) LLC statutes that explicitly define the duty of care provide either that a member or manager must act as a prudent person would act in similar circumstances, or that a member or manager must refrain from engaging in grossly negligent conduct. *See, e.g.*, N.Y. LTD. LIAB. CO. LAW § 409(a) ("A manager shall perform his or her duties as a manager, including his or her duties as a member of any class of managers, in good faith and with that degree of care that an ordinarily prudent person in a like position would use under similar circumstances."); ULLCA § 409(c) ("A member's duty of care to a member-managed company and its other members in the conduct of and winding up of the company's business is limited to refraining from engaging in grossly negligent or reckless conduct, intentional misconduct, or a knowing violation of law."). Is there a substantive difference between these articulations? *See also* RULLCA § 409(c) (stating that, "[s]ubject to the business judgment rule," the duty of care "is to act with the care that a person in a like position would reasonably exercise under similar circumstances and in a manner the member reasonably believes to be in the best interests of the company").

(7) With respect to the duty of loyalty, some LLC statutes state, in a partnership-like manner, that conflict of interest transactions require the consent of members or managers. Depending on the statute, either a disinterested majority or unanimous consent is required. *Cf.* ULLCA §§ 103(b)(2)(ii), 404(c)(2) (addressing conflict of interest transactions). Other statutes bear a closer resemblance to the corporate model, as a conflict of interest transaction can be validated through a disinterested member or manager vote, or upon a showing of fairness.

RULLCA seems to borrow from both the partnership and corporate models. Section 409(f) states that "[a]ll of the members of a member-managed limited liability company or a manager-managed limited liability company may authorize or ratify, after full disclosure of all material facts, a specific act or transaction that otherwise would violate the duty of loyalty." Moreover, with respect to claims under § 409(b)(2) (i.e., conflict of interest transactions), § 409(e) states that "[i]t is a defense to a claim under subsection (b)(2) and any comparable claim in equity or at common law that the transaction was fair to the limited liability company."

(8) The duty of loyalty in the LLC setting likely addresses the same issues that it covers in other business contexts—i.e., regulating conflict of interest transactions, preventing competition with the firm, restricting personal use of the firm's assets, and prohibiting the misappropriation of LLC business opportunities. *See, e.g.*, Anest v. Audino, 773 N.E.2d 202, 209–11 (Ill. App. Ct. 2002) (finding that a member of a member-managed LLC owed a fiduciary duty to another member, and remanding for a consideration of whether that duty had been breached by the usurpation of an alleged LLC opportunity); *see also* ULLCA § 409(b), (h) (addressing the duty of loyalty); RULLCA § 409(b), (g) (same).

(9) Following other Uniform Acts, ULLCA states that the "only" fiduciary duties owed by members and managers are the duties of loyalty and care set forth in the statute. ULLCA § 409(a). Moreover, the duty of loyalty is "limited to" the circumstances described in the statute. *Id.* § 409(b). In a sharp break from prior practice, RULLCA "uncabins" fiduciary duties by removing the "only" and "limited to" restrictions. *See* RULLCA § 409(a), (b). As the Comment to RULLCA § 409 explains:

> Until the promulgation of RUPA, it was almost axiomatic that: (i) fiduciary duties reflect judge-made law; and (ii) statutory formulations can express some of that law but do not exhaustively codify it. The original UPA was a prime example of this approach.

> In an effort to respect freedom of contract, bolster predictability, and protect partnership agreements from second-guessing, the Conference decided that RUPA should fence or "cabin in" all fiduciary duties within a statutory formulation. That decision was followed without re-consideration in ULLCA and ULPA (2001).

> This Act takes a different approach. After lengthy discussion in the drafting committee and on the floor of the 2006 Annual Meeting, the Conference decided that: (i) the "corral" created by RUPA does not fit in the very complex and variegated world of LLCs; and (ii) it is impracticable to cabin all LLC-related fiduciary duties within a statutory formulation.

> As a result, this Act: (i) eschews "only" and "limited to"—the words RUPA used in an effort to exhaustively codify fiduciary duty; (ii) codifies the core of the fiduciary duty of loyalty; but (iii) does not purport to discern every possible category of overreaching. One important consequence is to allow courts to continue to use fiduciary duty concepts to police disclosure obligations in member-to-member and member-LLC transactions.

(10) A number of LLC statutes include a corporate-like provision that protects members and managers from liability if they rely in good faith upon the information, opinions, reports, or statements of accountants, lawyers, or other experts. *See, e.g.,* DLLCA § 18–406; *see also* RULLCA § 409(c) (limiting the protection to alleged breaches of the duty of care). In *Flippo v. CSC Associates III, LLC,* 547 S.E.2d 216 (Va. 2001), the court interpreted a Virginia provision which stated, in relevant part, the following:

> Unless a manager has knowledge or information concerning the matter in question that makes reliance unwarranted, a manager is entitled to rely on information, opinions, reports or statements, including financial statements and other financial data, if prepared or presented by * * * [l]egal counsel, public accountants, or other persons as to matters the manager believes, in good faith, are within the person's professional or expert competence * * *.

VA. CODE § 13.1–1024.1(B). Flippo, the manager of an LLC, sought legal advice on how to accomplish some personal estate planning goals. *See Flippo,*

547 S.E.2d at 220. His lawyer advised him to transfer the LLC's assets to a joint venture (Flippo, as manager, had the power to do this), which would have the effect of causing the dissolution of the LLC. (For reasons that are not important to explain here, the LLC's dissolution would allow Flippo to achieve his estate planning goals.) *See id.* After following his lawyer's advice, Flippo was sued by a member of the LLC for breach of fiduciary duty. *See id.* The court rejected Flippo's claim that he was entitled to the protection of section 13.1–1024.1(B)—the good faith reliance on experts provision:

> * * * We have held that a corporate director is entitled to such protection from liability * * * only for acts related to the exercise of business judgment on behalf of the corporation of which he or she was the director. There is no basis to apply a different rule to managers seeking protection from liability under Code § 13.1–1024.1(B). In this case, therefore, to come within the protection of subsection (B) of Code § 13.1–1024.1, the legal advice which Carter Flippo received and acted upon must have been advice sought in good faith for the benefit of the company.
>
> The trial court found that the legal advice sought by Carter Flippo was not related to the business interests of [the LLC]. [The law firm] was not representing [the LLC] when it advised Carter Flippo to transfer the assets of [the LLC] to [the joint venture]. According to the trial court, [the law firm] was "representing their long-time client[ ], Carter Flippo * * *." Not only was the advice sought, delivered, and implemented for the personal benefit of the Flippos, Carter Flippo testified at trial that he thought the advice was not "very good" for [the LLC].
>
> The Flippos' argument that the advice upon which it acted involved acts which could "legally" be taken by a manager is irrelevant to the prerequisite for protection under Code § 13.1–[1024.1(B)]—whether an act was taken with the intent of benefiting the company. Furthermore, an act which is otherwise legal may, nevertheless, breach one's fiduciary duty. The advice relied and acted upon in this case was given solely for the purpose of implementing the Flippos' personal estate planning goals. Even if legal, the action was neither sought nor taken with the intent of benefiting [the LLC] and, in fact, had an adverse impact on the company. Following such advice cannot be the basis for a defense under subsection (B) of Code § 13.1–1024.1 * * *.

Id. at 221–22.

(11) Most LLC statutes explicitly authorize derivative lawsuits. *See, e.g.,* DLLCA §§ 18–1001 to 18–1004; ULLCA §§ 1101–1104; RULLCA §§ 902–906. The statutes (and the courts) typically prescribe rules that are similar to the rules applied to derivative lawsuits in the corporation setting. *See, e.g.,* Wood v. Baum, 953 A.2d 136, 138–41 (Del. 2008) (applying corporate law demand requirements and demand futility standards to a derivative lawsuit in the

LLC setting). Even when derivative lawsuits are not explicitly authorized by statute, courts have allowed them. *See, e.g.*, Weber v. King, 110 F. Supp. 2d 124, 131 (E.D.N.Y. 2000) ("[I]t seems peculiar that in drafting New York's Limited Liability Company Law, the New York State legislature chose not to include a provision expressly permitting derivative lawsuits by members of an LLC on behalf of the LLC. * * * We do not believe that the legislature's failure to include a derivative action provision in the [LLC statute] prevents us from recognizing such a right at common law."); *accord* Tzolis v. Wolff, 884 N.E.2d 1005, 1005 (N.Y. 2008). Rather than authorizing a single member to bring an action on behalf of an LLC, some LLC statutes require a vote of the disinterested members or managers to authorize a derivative lawsuit.

PROBLEM

A is a member of XYZ, LLC, a manager-managed LLC. (A is not a manager). Through conversations with other members in the company, A becomes aware that XYZ is negotiating with Seller for the purchase of a parcel of land. XYZ needs the land to expand its manufacturing facilities, and this particular parcel is ideal for XYZ's purposes. A decides to drive out to the parcel to look at it. When he sees it, he realizes that it would be perfect for a country home that he has always wanted to build. Without telling the XYZ managers, A calls Seller and purchases the parcel for himself.

Does XYZ have a cause of action against A for purchasing the parcel? Would it make a difference if A owned a controlling interest in the LLC? Consider ULLCA §§ 301, 409; RULLCA §§ 301, 409.

PROBLEM

A, B, and C form a manager-managed LLC with C as the sole manager. C procures loans for the business by fraudulently representing the financial position of the LLC to banks and other lenders. Ultimately, the LLC defaults on the loans.

(a) Assume that A and B have no knowledge of C's fraudulent activity. Are A and B personally liable to the banks and other lenders? *See* ULLCA § 303(a); RULLCA § 304(a).

(b) Assume that A and B have no knowledge of C's fraudulent activity, but if they had reviewed the company's books and records and paid more attention to the operation of the firm, they would have known about the wrongdoing. Are A and B personally liable to the banks and other lenders? *See* ULLCA §§ 303(a), 409; RULLCA §§ 304(a), 409.

(c) Assume that A and B have knowledge of C's fraudulent activity, but they do not object or attempt to stop C in any way. Are A and B personally liable to the banks and other lenders? *See* ULLCA §§ 303(a), 409; RULLCA §§ 304(a), 409.

2. THE ROLE OF CONTRACT

As mentioned, freedom of contract and the enforcement of the parties' private arrangements are central to the LLC. *See* Section B. In *Elf Atochem North America, Inc. v. Jaffari*, 727 A.2d 286 (Del. 1999), the Supreme Court of Delaware underscored this point:

> The basic approach of the Delaware Act is to provide members with broad discretion in drafting the Agreement and to furnish default provisions when the members' agreement is silent. The Act is replete with fundamental provisions made subject to modification in the Agreement (e.g. "unless otherwise provided in a limited liability company agreement * * *").

> * * *

> Section 18–1101(b) of the Act, like the essentially identical Section 17–1101(c) of the [limited partnership] Act, provides that "[i]t is the policy of [the Act] to give the maximum effect to the principle of freedom of contract and to the enforceability of limited liability company agreements." Accordingly, the following observation relating to limited partnerships applies as well to limited liability companies:

>> The Act's basic approach is to permit partners to have the broadest possible discretion in drafting their partnership agreements and to furnish answers only in situations where the partners have not expressly made provisions in their partnership agreement. Truly, the partnership agreement is the cornerstone of a Delaware limited partnership, and effectively constitutes the entire agreement among the partners with respect to the admission of partners to, and the creation, operation and termination of, the limited partnership. Once partners exercise their contractual freedom in their partnership agreement, the partners have a great deal of certainty that their partnership agreement will be enforced in accordance with its terms. [Martin I. Lubaroff & Paul Altman, *Delaware Limited Partnerships* § 1.2 (1999) (footnote omitted).]

> In general, the commentators observe that only where the agreement is inconsistent with mandatory statutory provisions will the members' agreement be invalidated. Such statutory provisions are likely to be those intended to protect third parties, not necessarily the contracting members.

Id. at 291–92.

Elf Atochem reflects the deference that many courts are willing to give to contractual arrangements between LLC owners. This deference, however, gives rise to the thorniest question in the legal development of the LLC—should freedom of contract have any limits? This question tends to arise in the context of fiduciary duties when the parties' operating agreement seeks to limit, or eliminate all together, the fiduciary duties otherwise owed.

FISK VENTURES, LLC V. SEGAL

Court of Chancery of Delaware, 2008.
2008 WL 1961156.

CHANDLER, CHANCELLOR.

* * *

I.　BACKGROUND

Petitioner Fisk Ventures, LLC ("Fisk") initiated this action to dissolve Genitrix, LLC ("Genitrix" or the "Company"), a limited liability company of which Fisk is a member, under 6 Del. C. §§ 18–801 and 18–802. Dr. Andrew Segal, the president and sole officer of Genitrix, answered the petition and filed counterclaims and third-party claims. Fisk and third-party respondents H. Fisk Johnson, Stephen Rose, and William Freund then moved to dismiss Segal's claims. * * *

The facts below are gleaned from the well-pleaded allegations of Segal's amended answer and counterclaims/third-party claims. On a motion to dismiss, the Court must assume such allegations are true and must make all reasonable inferences from such facts in favor of the non-movant. * * *

A.　The Company, its Structure, and the LLC Agreement

Genitrix, LLC, is a Delaware limited liability company formed to develop and market biomedical technology. Dr. Segal founded the Company in 1996 following his postdoctoral fellowship at the Whitehead Institute for Biomedical Research. Originally formed as a Maryland limited liability company, Genitrix was moved in 1997 to Delaware at the behest of Dr. H. Fisk Johnson, who invested heavily.

Equity in Genitrix is divided into three classes of membership. In exchange for the patent rights he obtained from the Whitehead Institute, Segal's capital account was credited with $500,000. This allowed him to retain approximately 55% of the Class A membership interest. The remainder of the Class A interest was apparently granted to other individuals not involved in this suit. In the initial round of investment, Johnson contributed $843,000 in return for a sizeable portion of the Class B membership interest. The remainder of the Class B interest is held by Fisk Ventures, LLC, and Stephen Rose. Finally, various other investors contributed over $1 million for membership interests in Class C. These Class C investors are apparently mostly passive; the power in the LLC is essentially divided by the LLC Agreement (the "Agreement") between the Class A and Class B members.

Under the Agreement, the Board of Member Representatives (the "Board") manages the business and affairs of the Company. As originally contemplated by the Agreement, the Board consisted of four members: two of whom were appointed by Johnson and two of whom were appointed by Segal. In early 2007, however, the balance of power seemingly shifted. Because the Company failed to meet certain benchmarks, the Board expanded to five seats and the Class B members were able to appoint a representative to the newly created seat. Nevertheless, because the Agreement requires the approval of 75% of the Board for most actions, the combined 60% stake of Fisk Ventures and Johnson is insufficient to control the Company. In other words, the LLC Agreement was drafted in such a way as to require the cooperation of the Class A and B members.

B.   The Parties

1.   Andrew Segal

Dr. Andrew Segal, fresh out of residency training, worked for the Whitehead Institute for Biomedical Research in Cambridge, Massachusetts from 1994 to early 1996. While there, Segal researched and worked on projects relating to how the human immune system could be manipulated effectively to attack cancer and infectious diseases. In early 1996, Dr. Segal left the Whitehead Institute and obtained a license to certain patent rights related to his research.

With these patent rights in hand, Dr. Segal formed Genitrix. Intellectual property rights alone, however, could not fund the research, testing, and trials necessary to bring Dr. Segal's ideas to some sort of profitable fruition. Consequently, Segal sought and obtained capital for the Company. Originally, Segal served as both President and Chief Executive Officer * * *.

As alluded to above and as discussed more fully later, much of that capital came from Johnson and Fisk, but, even with that capital, the Company has ultimately stalled. In his counterclaims and third-party claims, Dr. Segal contends that the Company's failings were caused by the counterclaim and third-party defendants' breaches of contractual and fiduciary obligations

2.   Fisk Ventures, LLC

Fisk Ventures is a Delaware limited liability company controlled by Dr. H. Fisk Johnson, who owns 99% of it. Fisk is a Class B member and is entitled to appoint one person to the Board. Fisk filed the initial petition in this action seeking dissolution of the Company.

3. H. Fisk Johnson

Dr. Johnson is the controlling member of Fisk and is himself a Class B shareholder in the Company who is personally now entitled to appoint two members to the Board. Johnson is also the chief executive officer and controlling shareholder of S.C. Johnson & Son, Inc. As discussed above, Dr. Johnson insisted that Genitrix be formed under Delaware law before he would invest in the Company. Although Johnson has previously served on the Board, he stepped down in 1998 and appointed others in his place, though he occasionally still attended board meetings.

* * *

4. Stephen Rose and William Freund

Stephen Rose and William Freund are Class B Members of the Company and are Class B Representatives on the Board who were appointed by Johnson. Johnson also employs both Rose and Freund in a number of capacities outside of Genitrix, and Segal alleges that they are therefore [dependent] on Johnson or his affiliates for their livelihood.

C. The Company's Woes

Over the course of its existence, the Company has encountered several periods of financial instability and hardship. The story of Genitrix—and of Dr. Segal's claims—is the story of many startup companies: difficulty raising money.

1. Early Difficulties, the Fisk Ventures Note, and the Class B Put Right

From its inception, Genitrix found itself strapped for cash. Segal's allegations contain numerous references to the tight budget and reminders that he worked for the Company for little or no pay in order to ease Genitrix's financial pain. In the earliest part of this decade, the Company hobbled along on grants from the National Institutes of Health and a series of relatively small financing transactions. Between November 2000 and August 2002, Johnson contributed another $550,000 in convertible debt, much of which was subsequently converted to Class B equity, and other investors provided $100,000 in convertible debt that was subsequently converted to Class C equity.

This influx of financing was insufficient, however. In the summer of 2003, Segal communicated to the Board that the Company would require $2.6 million to allow for human trials of the technology. Johnson, who by that point had contributed about $1.4 million, stated that he was unwilling to be the sole financier of the Company. Nevertheless, Johnson and Fisk Ventures agreed to contribute another $2 million in convertible debt if the Company agreed to try to raise an additional $5 million from other investors over the following two years.

Over the course of negotiating the terms of the Fisk Ventures note, Segal proposed that the "Put Right" of the Class B investors be suspended to allow him to more easily woo other investors. Pursuant to Section 11.5 of the LLC Agreement, the Class B Members may, at any time, force the Company to purchase any or all of their Class B membership interests at a price determined by an independent appraisal. If the purchase price exceeds 50% of the Company's tangible assets, the Members who exercised the Put Right would receive notes secured by all of the assets of the Company. In other words, the Put—if exercised—would subrogate what would otherwise be senior claims of new investors. Though Segal believed this right would scare off potential investors, the Class B Members refused to suspend or relinquish their contractual rights, though they did communicate that they had no immediate or foreseeable intention of exercising the right. Segal alleges that, based on his conversations with Rose, he believed the Class B Members would be "more flexible with respect to the Put" once there was a prospective investment "on the table."

2.   Failed Efforts to Raise Money from New Investors

To meet the $5 million challenge put forth in the Fisk Ventures Note, the Company retained an investment banking consultant to help it raise money from venture capital funds. This effort failed to generate any investment. By the summer of 2005—almost two years after the creation of the Fisk Ventures Note—the Company had failed to raise the needed $5 million, and the Fisk Ventures Note was scheduled to convert to Class B equity by the end of August. If the Company failed to meet the fundraising challenge by the conversion deadline, the Company's valuation would be adversely affected and, of course, the interests of the Class A and C members would be diluted. Segal threatened to resign if he could not raise the required funds by the conversion deadline, and Fisk Ventures agreed to postpone conversion.

While negotiating the terms of the postponement, Dr. Segal turned his attention to individual, high-net-worth investors. Early indications were positive, but, Segal alleges, several potential investors complained about the Class B Put Right, one of whom called it a "deal killer." Thus, Segal again asked the Class B members to relinquish or suspend the Put Right. The Class B members again refused. Segal alleges that an agent of the Class B Members orally represented to him that they were willing to suspend the Put Right and hold back on exercising the conversion for four months. However, Segal says, they changed their minds shortly thereafter and, in November 2005, the Class B Members exercised their conversion rights and maintained their Put Right. Despite his threats, Dr. Segal did not resign.

3. *The Private Placement Memorandum * * ***

Meanwhile, in August 2005, Segal took it upon himself to draft a proposed private placement memorandum ("PPM") for use in connection with any investment by the high-net-worth individuals.[13] Segal circulated a draft to the other Board members in August, but did not distribute it to potential investors until the Company nearly ran out of funds in December 2005. When he attempted to get the approval of the Board in December, the Class B representatives refused to consent, citing the haste with which Segal was then acting. Once again, moreover, Segal wanted the Class B members to suspend or relinquish their Put Right. The Class B members asked to discuss the PPM at a Board meeting, but no such meeting occurred.

Segal stressed the Company's need to quickly secure additional funding and encouraged the Class B members to authorize the use of his PPM, but the Class B Members instead offered a counterproposal of $500,000 in convertible debt from Fisk Ventures. The terms of that note would have required the Company to meet certain benchmarks. If the Company failed to meet them, the Class B members would obtain control of the Board. * * * [Segal rejected the counterproposal.]

* * *

5. *The Company's Current State*

In March 2006, the Company ran out of operating cash. Fisk Ventures provided another $125,000 capital contribution to pay the remaining employees and to cover some expenses, but larger problems loomed. The Board met in the third week of April to discuss its options.

Keeping with the common theme in this case, Dr. Segal and the Class B members had different ideas of what the Company should do. * * *

In August 2006 * * * the Company [was left] with just two employees (including Dr. Segal). That other employee left in May 2007. The Company has no office, no capital funds, no grant funds, and generates no revenue. The Board has not met since the fall of 2006 because the Class A representatives have refused to participate in any meetings. In May 2007 and at the invitation of the Class B members, Dr. Segal proposed terms under which the Class B members might purchase his interest in the Company. The Class B members rejected those terms in June 2007 and subsequently Fisk Ventures initiated this suit, seeking dissolution of Genitrix.

---

[13] Segal alleges that he was forced to draft the PPM because the Company's legal counsel, a partner with Ropes & Gray, "was busy."

D. The Counterclaims / Third-Party Claims and the Parties' Contentions

In answering the petition, Dr. Segal made counterclaims against Fisk Ventures and third-party claims against Johnson, Rose, and Freund. Specifically, Segal contends that the counterclaim/third-party defendants breached the LLC Agreement, breached the implied covenant of good faith and fair dealing implicit in the LLC Agreement, [and] breached their fiduciary duties to the Company * * *. Segal passionately contends that the Class B defendants failed to comply with their duties to Segal and to the Company by standing in the way of proposed financing.

The counterclaim/third-party defendants now seek to dismiss Segal's claims and reduce this suit to its original form as a petition for judicial dissolution. * * * All counterclaim/third-party defendants move under Rule 12(b)(6), claiming that Segal has failed to state a claim upon which relief can be granted because his allegations reflect little more than the exercise of their contractual rights.

* * *

III. FAILURE TO STATE A CLAIM

A. Breach of Contract

The *sine qua non* of pleading an actionable breach is demonstrating that there was something to be breached in the first place. In other words, before the Court can start worrying about whether or not there was a breach, the Court needs to determine that there was a *duty*. In the context of limited liability companies, which are creatures not of the state but of contract, those duties or obligations must be found in the LLC Agreement or some other contract. Because Segal's counterclaims and third-party claims fail to allege breaches of duties found in the Genitrix LLC agreement, the Court must dismiss Count I under Rule 12(b)(6).

Dr. Segal's counterclaims and third-party claims contend—perhaps reasonably—that Genitrix suffered because the Class B members refused to accede to Segal's proposals with respect to research, financing, and other matters. It may very well be that Genitrix would be a thriving company today if only the Class B members had seen things Segal's way. However, it may very well be that Genitrix would also be a thriving company today if only Dr. Segal had gone along with what the Class B members wanted. Indeed, the LLC Agreement endows both the Class A and Class B members with certain rights and protections. In no way does it obligate one class to acquiesce to the wishes of the other simply because the other believes its approach is superior or in the best interests of the Company. To find otherwise—that is, to find that the Court must decide whose business judgment was more in keeping with the LLC's best interests—would cripple the policy underlying the LLC Act promoting freedom of contract.

That, however, is precisely what Segal asks this Court to do. Specifically, Segal points to various sections of the LLC Agreement that he says establish a "standard of conduct" that binds members of Genitrix. First, he directs the Court to section 9.1, which reads:

> *Performance of Duties; no Liability of Officers.* No Member shall have any duty to any Member of the Company except as expressly set forth herein or in other written agreements. No Member, Representative, or Officer of the Company shall be liable to the Company or to any Member for any loss or damage sustained by the Company or to any Member, unless the loss or damage shall have been the result of gross negligence, fraud or intentional misconduct by the Member, Representative, or Officer in question * * *.

Segal contends that this section demonstrates that the Company *can* create duties for Members and *did* in fact create such a duty. Moreover, Segal argues that this section establishes a "duty to act without gross negligence, fraud or intentional misconduct." He subsequently points to sections 9.2, 9.5, 13.11, and 13.12 with a similarly tortured reading.

This Court adheres to an objective theory of contracts. As such, the Court must "interpret contracts to mean what they objectively say." *Seidensticker v. Gasparilla Inn, Inc.,* C.A. No. 2555–CC, [2007 WL 4054473, at *1 (Del. Ch. Nov. 8, 2007).] Nowhere in sections 9.1, 9.2, 9.5, 13.11, or 13.12 does the Genitrix LLC Agreement purport to create a code of conduct for all members; on the contrary, most of those sections expressly claim to limit or waive liability. Thus, Segal's interpretation rests all of its proverbial eggs in the single basket of the principle granting him, the nonmovant, all reasonable inferences. However, as the Supreme Court has noted in different circumstances, "[e]ven liberal construction has its limits." [*National Union Fire Ins. Co. of Pittsburgh v. Fisher,* 692 A.2d 892, 896 (Del. 1997).]

There is no basis in the language of the LLC Agreement for Segal's contention that all members were bound by a code of conduct, but, even if there were, this Court could not enforce such a code because there is no limit whatsoever to its applicability. Under Segal's reading, a Genitrix member would be liable to the Company or other members for *any* damage caused by gross negligence, willful misconduct, or a knowing violation of law. There is no guidance as to how or when this "code of conduct" applies, and this Court declines to follow Segal's invitation to turn an expressly exculpatory provision into an all encompassing and seemingly boundless standard of conduct.

Moreover, even if these provisions did somehow create a code of conduct for Genitrix members, Segal has not alleged facts sufficient to support a reasonable inference that Fisk, Rose, or Freund acted with gross negligence, willful misconduct, in bad faith, or by knowingly violating the law. At most, the facts in Segal's counterclaim/third-party claim demonstrate that the Class B members vigorously championed their own proposals and did not support Segal's plans. Perhaps Genitrix would have been more able to obtain financing if the Class B members had been willing to relinquish their Put Right, but their refusal to do so was not in bad faith,[41] Segal's conclusory assertions to the contrary notwithstanding.

* * *

B. Breach of the Implied Covenant of Good Faith and Fair Dealing

Every contract contains an implied covenant of good faith and fair dealing that "requires a 'party in a contractual relationship to refrain from arbitrary or unreasonable conduct which has the effect of preventing the other party to the contract from receiving the fruits' of the bargain." [Dunlap v. State Farm Fire & Cas. Co., 878 A.2d 434, 442 (Del. 2005) (quoting Wilgus v. Salt Pond Inv. Co., 498 A.2d 151, 159 (Del. Ch. 1985)).] Although occasionally described in broad terms, the implied covenant is not a panacea for the disgruntled litigant. In fact, it is clear that "a court cannot and should not use the implied covenant of good faith and fair dealing to fill a gap in a contract with an implied term unless it is clear from the contract that the parties would have agreed to that term had they thought to negotiate the matter."[47] Only rarely invoked successfully, the implied covenant of good faith and fair dealing protects the spirit of what was *actually bargained and negotiated for* in the contract. Moreover, because the implied covenant is, by definition, *implied,* and because it protects the *spirit* of the agreement rather than the form, it cannot be invoked where the contract itself expressly covers the subject at issue.[50]

Here, Segal argues that Fisk, Rose, and Freund breached the implied covenant of good faith and fair dealing by frustrating or blocking the financing opportunities proposed by Segal. However, neither the LLC Agreement nor any other contract endowed him with the right to unilaterally decide what fundraising or financing opportunities the

---

[41] *See In re Walt Disney Co. Derivative Litig.*, 907 A.2d 693, 755 (Del. Ch. 2005) (noting that "[d]eliberate indifference and inaction *in the face of a duty to act*" is bad faith conduct), aff'd, 906 A.2d 27 (Del. 2006). Here, there is no allegation that the Class B members had a *duty* to acquiesce to Segal's plans for Genitrix. On the contrary, the Class B members had a *right* to disagree and advocate their own position.

[47] *Corporate Prop. Assocs. 14 Inc. v. CHR Holding Corp.*, C.A. No. 3231–VCS, 2008 WL 963048, at *5 (Del. Ch. Apr. 10, 2008) (declining to use implied covenant to protect a party from dilution by cash dividends where parties failed to agree to such protection in the contractual language itself).

[50] *E.g., Allied Capital [Corp. v. GC-Sun Holdings, L.P.,* 910 A.2d 1020, 1032–33 (Del. Ch. 2006)] ("[I]mplied covenant analysis will only be applied when the contract is truly silent with respect to the matter at hand, and only when the court finds that the expectations of the parties were so fundamental that it is clear that they did not feel a need to negotiate about them."); *Dave Greytak Enters., Inc. v. Mazda Motors of Am., Inc.*, 622 A.2d 14, 23 (Del. Ch. 1992) ("[W]here the subject at issue is expressly covered by the contract * * * the implied duty to perform in good faith does not come into play."), *aff'd,* 609 A.2d 668 (Del. 1992).

Company should pursue, and his argument is "another in a long line of cases in which a plaintiff has tried, unsuccessfully, to argue that the implied covenant grants [him] a substantive right that [he] did not extract during negotiation." [*Allied Capital Corp. v. GC-Sun Holdings, L.P.*, 910 A.2d 1020, 1024 (Del. Ch. 2006).] Moreover, the LLC Agreement *does* address the subject of financing, and it specifically requires the approval of 75% of the Board. Implicit in such a requirement is the right of the Class B Board representatives to disapprove of and therefore block Segal's proposals. As this Court has previously noted, "[t]he mere exercise of one's contractual rights, without more, cannot constitute * * * a breach [of the implied covenant of good faith and fair dealing]." [*Shenandoah Life Ins. Co. v. Valero Energy Corp.*, C.A. No. 9032, 1988 WL 63491, at *8 (Del. Ch. June 21, 1988).] Negotiating forcefully and within the bounds of rights granted by the LLC agreement does not translate to a breach of the implied covenant on the part of the Class B members.

C. Breach of Fiduciary Duties

Count III of Segal's counterclaims/third-party claims merely dresses his breach of contract claim in fiduciary duties' clothing. In support of these supposed fiduciary duty claims, Segal cites the same provisions of the Genitrix LLC Agreement that he cited in support of his breach of contract claims. These makeweight fiduciary duty claims fail for at least two reasons.

First, the LLC Agreement, in accordance with Delaware law, greatly restricts or even eliminates fiduciary duties. Delaware's Limited Liability Act specifically provides:

> To the extent that * * * a member or manager or other person has duties (including fiduciary duties) to a limited liability company or to another member or manager or to another person that is a party to or is otherwise bound by a limited liability company agreement, the member's or manager's or other person's duties *may be expanded or restricted or eliminated* by provisions in the limited liability company agreement * * *.

Pursuant to this provision, the Genitrix LLC Agreement eliminates fiduciary duties to the maximum extent permitted by law by flatly stating that members have no duties other than those expressly articulated in the Agreement. Because the Agreement does not expressly articulate fiduciary obligations, they are eliminated.

Second, even if Segal were correct that in the LLC Agreement there remained a fiduciary duty to not act in bad faith or with gross negligence, Segal has manifestly failed to allege facts sufficient to support a claim that anyone has breached such a hypothetical duty. As discussed above, the hollow invocation of "bad faith" does not magically render a deficient complaint dismissal-proof; this Court will not blindly accept conclusory allegations.

* * *

IV. CONCLUSION

Anyone in Dr. Segal's position would be understandably frustrated by the demise of Genitrix, a company in which he has invested monetary, temporal, intellectual, and emotional resources. Nevertheless, such frustration cannot justify the *post hoc* refashioning of the bargain he struck with Johnson and the Class B investors in the LLC Agreement. For the reasons explained above * * * the allegations Segal makes in his amended response for breach of contract, breach of the implied covenant of good faith and fair dealing, [and] breach of fiduciary duty * * * fail to state a claim for which relief can be granted. Consequently, Segal's counterclaims/third-party claims are hereby dismissed * * *.

NOTE ON GERBER AND THE IMPLIED COVENANT UNDER DELAWARE LAW

In *Gerber v. Enterprise Products Holdings, LLC*, 67 A.3d 400 (Del. 2013), the Supreme Court of Delaware engaged in a lengthy discussion of the relationship between fiduciary duty and the implied covenant of good faith and fair dealing:

> The implied covenant seeks to enforce the parties' contractual bargain by implying only those terms that the parties would have agreed to during their original negotiations if they had thought to address them. Under Delaware law, a court confronting an implied covenant claim asks whether it is clear from what was expressly agreed upon that the parties who negotiated the express terms of the contract would have agreed to proscribe the act later complained of as a breach of the implied covenant of good faith—had they thought to negotiate with respect to that matter. While this test requires resort to a counterfactual world—what if—it is nevertheless appropriately restrictive and commonsensical.

> The temporal focus is critical. Under a fiduciary duty or tort analysis, a court examines the parties as situated at the time of the wrong. The court determines whether the defendant owed the plaintiff a duty, considers the defendant's obligations (if any) in light of that duty, and then evaluates whether the duty was breached. Temporally, each inquiry turns on the parties' relationship as it existed at the time of the wrong. The nature of the parties' relationship may turn on historical events, and past dealings necessarily will inform the court's analysis, but liability depends on the parties' relationship when the alleged breach occurred, not on the relationship as it existed in the past.

An implied covenant claim, by contrast, looks to the past. It is not a free-floating duty unattached to the underlying legal documents. It does not ask what duty the law should impose on the parties given their relationship at the time of the wrong, but rather what the parties would have agreed to themselves had they considered the issue in their original bargaining positions at the time of contracting. "Fair dealing" is not akin to the fair process component of entire fairness, *i.e.*, whether the fiduciary acted fairly when engaging in the challenged transaction as measured by duties of loyalty and care whose contours are mapped out by Delaware precedents. It is rather a commitment to deal "fairly" in the sense of consistently with the terms of the parties' agreement and its purpose. *Likewise "good faith" does not envision loyalty to the contractual counterparty, but rather faithfulness to the scope, purpose, and terms of the parties' contract. Both necessarily turn on the contract itself and what the parties would have agreed upon had the issue arisen when they were bargaining originally.*

The retrospective focus applies equally to a party's discretionary rights. The implied covenant requires that a party refrain from arbitrary or unreasonable conduct which has the effect of preventing the other party to the contract from receiving the fruits of its bargain. *When exercising a discretionary right, a party to the contract must exercise its discretion reasonably.* The contract may identify factors that the decision-maker can consider, and it may provide a contractual standard for evaluating the decision. Express contractual provisions always supersede the implied covenant, but even the most carefully drafted agreement will harbor residual nooks and crannies for the implied covenant to fill. In those situations, what is "arbitrary" or "unreasonable"—or conversely "reasonable"—depends on the parties' original contractual expectations, not a "free-floating" duty applied at the time of the wrong.

Id. at 418–19 (quoting ASB Allegiance Real Estate Fund v. Scion Breckenridge Managing Member, LLC, 50 A.3d 434, 440–42 (Del. Ch. 2012)).

In *Gerber*, § 7.9(b) of the limited partnership agreement eliminated the general partner's common-law fiduciary duties and replaced them with a contractual good faith standard, defined "for purposes of [the] [a]greement" as a "belie[f] that the determination or other action is in the best interests of the Partnership." Section 7.10(b) of the agreement then created a "conclusive presumption" that the general partner acted in good faith if the general partner relied upon the opinion of an expert believed to be competent. *See id.* at 409–11.

Gerber contended that the general partner breached his express contractual duties, as well as the implied covenant of good faith and fair dealing, under the partnership agreement. More specifically, Gerber contended that a 2009 sale transaction to a related party was not fair to the partnership and the limited partners because it did not provide adequate consideration. Moreover, the general partner relied upon a Morgan Stanley fairness opinion that did not opine on the specific consideration provided in the sale. Gerber also challenged a 2010 merger with a related party on similar grounds—i.e., the merger provided inadequate consideration and the general partner relied upon a Morgan Stanley fairness opinion that did not value two sets of legal claims that would be extinguished in the merger. *See id.* at 406–09.

The Court of Chancery dismissed Gerber's claims. With respect to claims for breach of the implied covenant, the court concluded that reliance upon the Morgan Stanley fairness opinions triggered the conclusive presumption of good faith in § 7.10(b), which precluded the implied covenant claims. The Supreme Court disagreed:

> The flaw in the court's reasoning stems from a decision by the LPA's [limited partnership agreement's] drafters to define a contractual fiduciary duty in terms of "good faith"—a term that is also and separately a component of the "implied covenant of *good faith* and fair dealing." Although that term is common, the LPA's contractual fiduciary duty describes a concept of "good faith" very different from the good faith concept addressed by the implied covenant.
>
> * * *
>
> * * * Under Section 7.9(b), [the general partner] must make all determinations and take or decline to take any action in "good faith." The LPA defines " 'good faith' for purposes of this Agreement" as a "belie[f] that the determination or other action is in the best interests of the Partnership." Like a common law fiduciary duty, Section 7.9(b)'s contractual fiduciary duty analysis looks to the parties as situated at the time of the wrong, and inquires whether [the general partner] "believe[d] that the determination or other action [was] in the best interests of the Partnership." That is different from the standard that is embedded in the implied covenant.
>
> LPA Section 7.10(b)'s conclusive presumption must be read together with Section 7.9(b). Section 7.9(b) imposes a contractual fiduciary duty to act in "good faith," and defines "good faith" for the "purposes of this [a]greement." Under Section 7.10(b), [the general partner] and its Affiliates are conclusively presumed to have met this standard if they rely upon the opinion of a qualified expert advisor. Nothing in Section 7.10(b) pertains to or addresses the implied covenant.
>
> The reasoning in the Vice Chancellor's opinion improperly conflates two distinct concepts—the implied covenant and the LPA's contractual fiduciary duty—and ignores the temporal distinction between them. Section 7.10(b) is a contractual provision that

establishes a procedure the general partner may use to conclusively establish that it met its contractual fiduciary duty. But, the implied covenant attaches to Section 7.10(b), as it attaches to the rest of the LPA. Therefore, [the general partner's] attempt to take advantage of Section 7.10(b) may itself be subject to a claim that it was arbitrary and unreasonable and in violation of the implied covenant. The conclusive presumption of "good faith" applies only to the contractual fiduciary duty. It cannot operate retroactively to alter the parties' reasonable expectations at the time of contracting, and it cannot be used to fill every gap in the LPA.

Were we to adopt the Vice Chancellor's construction of Section 7.10(b), that would lead to nonsensical results. Examples readily come to mind of cases where a general partner's actions in obtaining a fairness opinion from a qualified financial advisor themselves would be arbitrary or unreasonable, and "thereby frustrat[e] the fruits of the bargain that the asserting party reasonably expected." To suggest one hypothetical example, a qualified financial advisor may be willing to opine that a transaction is fair even though (unbeknownst to the advisor) the controller has intentionally concealed material information that, if disclosed, would require the advisor to opine that the transaction price is in fact not fair. More extreme would be a case where the controller outright bribes the financial advisor to opine (falsely) that the transaction is fair. In a third example, the financial advisor, eager for future business from the controller, compromises its professional valuation standards to achieve the controller's unfair objective. Although plaintiffs could properly challenge this conduct under the implied covenant, the court's reasoning, if upheld, would preclude those claims. We therefore conclude that the Court of Chancery erred in holding that Section 7.10(b) bars a claim under the implied covenant.

Having so determined, we next analyze whether Gerber has pled facts that, if true, would establish that [the general partner] breached the implied covenant. Applying the implied covenant is a "cautious enterprise" and we will only infer "contractual terms to handle developments or contractual gaps that the asserting party pleads neither party anticipated." Gerber must show that [the general partner] "acted arbitrarily or unreasonably, thereby frustrating the fruits of the bargain that [Gerber] reasonably expected." "When conducting this analysis, we must assess the parties' reasonable expectations at the time of contracting;" and will not imply terms to "rebalanc[e] economic interests after events that could have been anticipated, but were not, that later adversely affected one party to a contract."

* * * At the time of contracting, however, Gerber could hardly have anticipated that [the general partner] would rely upon a fairness opinion that did not fulfill its basic function—evaluating

the consideration the [limited partners] received for purposes of opining whether the transaction was financially fair. Although Section 7.10(b) does not prescribe specific standards for fairness opinions, we may confidently conclude that, had the parties addressed the issue at the time of contracting, they would have agreed that any fairness opinion must address whether the consideration received * * * in 2009 was fair, in order to satisfy Section 7.9(b)'s contractual fiduciary duty. Gerber has pled that [the general partner] engaged in a manifestly unfair transaction, and then relied on an unresponsive fairness opinion, to ensure that its contractual fiduciary duty would be conclusively presumed to have been discharged. That is the type of arbitrary, unreasonable conduct that the implied covenant prohibits.

A similar analysis applies equally to the 2010 Merger challenges. The Vice Chancellor held that the Complaint pled that a principal purpose of the 2010 Merger was to terminate the 2007 and 2009 Claims. Despite that purpose, Morgan Stanley did not independently value the 2007 and 2009 Claims in assessing the 2010 Merger's fairness in that firm's 2010 opinion, nor did [the general partner] obtain another valuation. * * * Although Section 7.10(b) does not explicitly so require, we conclude that the parties would certainly have agreed, at the time of contracting, that any fairness opinion contemplated by that provision would address the value of derivative claims where (as here) terminating those claims was a *principal purpose* of a merger. Therefore, Gerber has sufficiently pled that [the general partner] breached the implied covenant in the course of taking advantage of Section 7.10(b)'s conclusive presumption.

Id. at 418–23.

NOTES

(1) Why did the *Fisk Ventures* court dismiss Dr. Segal's claim for breach of fiduciary duty? Why did the court dismiss Dr. Segal's claim for breach of the implied covenant of good faith and fair dealing? Can you explain why the outcome in *Gerber* is different—i.e., why did Gerber's claims for breach of the implied covenant survive? *See* DLLCA § 18–1101.

(2) In *Fisk Ventures*, Chancellor Chandler states that LLCs "are creatures not of the state but of contract." Is this statement correct?

(3) Would Dr. Segal's claims have been dismissed under ULLCA? Under RULLCA? *See* ULLCA §§ 103, 409; RULLCA §§ 110, 409.

(4) Assume that the LLC agreement of a Delaware LLC states that LLC members shall have no duties or liability whatsoever—to each other or to the LLC—regardless of any claim of intentional or negligent action. *See* DLLCA § 18–1101(c), (e). Should a court enforce this provision? What if, for example, one of the members is stealing from the LLC? *Cf.* Abry Partners V, L.P. v. F

& W Acquisition LLC, 891 A.2d 1032, 1036 (Del. Ch. 2006) ("For these reasons, when a seller intentionally misrepresents a fact embodied in a contract—that is, when a seller lies—public policy will not permit a contractual provision to limit the remedy of the buyer to a capped damage claim. Rather, the buyer is free to press a claim for rescission or for full compensatory damages. By this balance, I attempt to give fair and efficient recognition to the competing public policies served by contractual freedom and by the law of fraud.").

(5) In *McConnell v. Hunt Sports Enterprises*, 725 N.E.2d 1193 (Ohio. Ct. App. 1999), Columbus Hockey Limited ("CHL") was an LLC formed to obtain and operate a National Hockey League franchise in Columbus, Ohio. The members of CHL included, among others, Hunt Sports Group and McConnell. CHL did not obtain the franchise; instead, the franchise was ultimately awarded to a separate ownership group headed by McConnell.

Section 3.3 of the CHL operating agreement stated that "Members shall not in any way be prohibited from or restricted in engaging or owning an interest in any other business venture of any nature, including any venture which might be competitive with the business of the Company." McConnell filed a complaint for declaratory judgment requesting a declaration that section 3.3 allowed CHL members to compete with CHL for the NHL franchise. Hunt Sports Group filed a counterclaim asserting that McConnell's competition had breached his fiduciary duty to CHL.

The trial court found that section 3.3 was clear and unambiguous and that McConnell's competition was permissible. The Court of Appeals agreed: "[The] evidence shows that appellees obtained the NHL franchise to the exclusion of CHL. This constituted direct competition with CHL. However, appellees were permitted under the operating agreement to compete with CHL and, as discussed above, this in and of itself cannot constitute a breach of fiduciary duty." *See id.* at 1200, 1202–03, 1206, 1216.

If the Uniform Acts had governed the dispute in *McConnell*, would the court have reached the same conclusion? *See* ULLCA §§ 103, 409; RULLCA §§ 110, 409.

(6) Can a member contractually waive his rights under a statutory provision if the provision does not contain language such as "unless otherwise provided in an operating agreement"? In Delaware, the absence of such language is not particularly significant:

> Petitioners proffer a far broader rule and argue that "[s]tatutory provisions that do not contain the qualification 'unless otherwise provided in a limited liability company agreement' (or a variation thereof) are mandatory and may not be waived." Petitioners, however, offer no authority for this assertion and, in fact, authorities they cite directly contradict it. In *Elf Atochem North America, Inc. v. Jaffari,* for example, a case on which petitioners heavily rely, the Supreme Court [of Delaware] held that a provision of the LLC Act *not* containing petitioners' magical

phrase was nonetheless permissive and subject to modification. Indeed, in *Elf,* the Supreme Court explicitly noted that the "unless otherwise provided" phrase was merely one example of the means by which a court could ascertain the intent of the General Assembly. Indeed, in other provisions, the General Assembly explicitly forbids waiver. For example, the Act overtly bars members from "eliminat[ing] the implied contractual covenant of good faith and fair dealing." [DLLCA § 18–1101(c).]

Sections 18–802, 18–803, and 18–805 are not mandatory provisions of the LLC Act that cannot be modified by contract. First, the Act does not expressly say that these provisions cannot be supplanted by agreement, and, in fact, section 18–803 does include the "unless otherwise provided" phrase. Second, the provisions employ permissive rather than mandatory language. Section 18–802 states that the "Court of Chancery *may* decree dissolution" and section 18–805 states that "the Court of Chancery * * * *may* either appoint" a trustee or receiver. Finally, and most importantly, none of the rights conferred by these provisions that are waived in the LLC Agreement is designed to protect third parties. * * * Because the waiver of a member's right to petition for dissolution or the appointment of a receiver does not violate the LLC Act and does not interfere with the rights of third parties, the waiver is valid and enforceable under the statute.

R & R Capital, LLC v. Buck & Doe Run Valley Farms, LLC, Civ. A. No. 3803–CC, 2008 WL 3846318, at *5–6 (Del. Ch. Aug. 19, 2008). In other jurisdictions, however, the absence of such language may be more relevant:

We have held, "It is elementary that no valid contract may be made contrary to statute, and that valid, applicable statutory provisions are parts of every contract." *Bell v. N. Ohio Tel. Co.* (1948), 149 Ohio St. 157, 158, 36 O.O. 501, 78 N.E.2d 42. * * * As a result, to the extent the operating agreement is in conflict with the statute, the statute takes precedence.

The statutory provisions that Epperson and the company rely upon, R.C. 1705.15, 1705.18, and 1705.20, contain the limiting words, "[u]nless," "if," or "except as otherwise provided in the operating agreement." They all discuss in general terms the rights of assignees of membership interests. These sections do not appear to be inconsistent with the operating agreement.

R.C. 1705.21(A), on the other hand, specifically sets forth the rights of legal representatives for a deceased member and grants the executor "all of [the deceased's] rights as a member for the purpose of settling his estate or administering his property." Because this section does not state "except as otherwise provided in the operating agreement," we can infer that the General Assembly did not intend R.C. 1705.21(A) to be restricted by contrary language within an operating agreement.

Holdeman v. Epperson, 857 N.E.2d 583, 587 (Ohio 2006).

PROBLEM

You are a Vice Chancellor on the Delaware Court of Chancery. In five different disputes pending before you, the plaintiff is a member of a Delaware manager-managed LLC who has brought a breach of fiduciary duty claim in a direct action seeking damages against a defendant manager. In each dispute, the defendant has moved to dismiss on the ground that the LLC agreement has either eliminated a manager's fiduciary duties to the members, or has eliminated monetary liability for breach of those duties. *See* DLLCA § 18–1101(c), (e).

The relevant provisions of the LLC agreements are set forth below. How would you rule on the motion to dismiss in each of the disputes? (Note: These provisions have all been taken from actual cases.)

Dispute #1:   *Section 6.1—Relationship of Managers.* Each Manager agrees that, to the fullest extent permitted by the Delaware Act and except as otherwise expressly provided in this Agreement, the Managers shall have the same duties and obligations that managers of a limited liability company formed under the Delaware Act have to the Company and the Members.

Section 6.2—Liability of Managers. Except for any duties imposed by this Agreement, each Manager shall owe no duty of any kind towards the Company or the other Members in performing its duties and exercising its rights hereunder or otherwise.

Dispute #2:   **Duties.** The Board of Managers shall manage the affairs of the Company in a prudent and businesslike manner and shall devote such time to the Company affairs as they shall, in their discretion exercised in good faith, determine is reasonably necessary for the conduct of such affairs. In carrying out their duties hereunder, the Managers shall not be liable for money damages for breach of fiduciary duty to the Company nor to any Member for their good faith actions or failure to act, but only for their own willful or fraudulent misconduct or willful breach of their contractual or fiduciary duties under this Agreement.

Dispute #3:   Whenever in this Agreement the Manager is permitted or required to make a decision (i) in its "sole discretion" or "discretion," with "absolute discretion" or under a grant of similar authority or latitude, the Manager shall be entitled to consider only such interests and factors as it desires and shall have no duty or obligation to give any consideration to any interest of or factors affecting the Company or the Members, or (ii) in its "good faith" or under another express standard, the Manager shall act under such express standard and shall not be subject to any other or different standards imposed by this Agreement or any other agreement contemplated herein.

(For dispute #3, assume that the plaintiff's breach of fiduciary duty claim challenges a decision made by the manager. The LLC agreement states that the manager is given the "sole and complete discretion" to make the decision.)

Dispute #4:   *Duties of Managers.* The Managers shall act in good faith and in the best interest of the Company and with such care as an ordinarily prudent person in a like position would use under similar circumstances.

Limitation of Liability. No Manager shall have any liability to the Company or any Member for any loss suffered by the Company or any Member that arises out of any act or omission by the Manager, if such Manager performs its duty in compliance with the standard set forth in the immediately preceding sentence, except loss or damage resulting from intentional misconduct, knowing violation of law, gross negligence or a transaction from which the Manager received a personal benefit in violation or breach of the provisions of this Agreement.

Dispute #5:   Whenever the Manager makes a determination or takes or declines to take any other action, then unless another express standard is provided for in this Agreement, the Manager shall make such determination or take or decline to take such other action in good faith, and shall not be subject to any other or different standards imposed by this Agreement, any other agreement contemplated hereby or under the Delaware Act or any other law, rule or regulation or at equity. In order for a determination or other action to be in "good faith" for purposes of this Agreement, the Manager making such determination or taking or declining to take such other action must believe that the determination or other action is in the best interests of the LLC.

PROBLEM

The sole manager of a Delaware LLC causes the LLC to enter into a transaction with another entity that the manager owns. The terms of the transaction are grossly unfair to the LLC. The LLC agreement includes the following provision:

> Whenever the Manager makes a determination or takes or declines to take any other action, the Manager is entitled to make such determination or take or decline to take such other action in its sole and absolute discretion, and shall not be subject to any other or different standards imposed: (i) by this Agreement; (ii) by any other agreement contemplated hereby; (iii) by the Delaware Act; or (iv) by any other law, rule, regulation, or common-law or equitable principle. For purposes of this Agreement, when the Manager exercises its sole and absolute discretion, the Manager shall be entitled to consider only such interests and factors as it desires and shall have no duty or obligation to give any consideration whatsoever to any interest of or factors affecting the Company or the Members.

A member of the LLC challenges the transaction by suing the manager for breach of fiduciary duty and for breach of the implied covenant of good faith and fair dealing. The manager moves to dismiss based on the above-stated provision of the LLC agreement. How would you rule on both claims? *See* DLLCA § 18–1101.

NOTE ON DEFAULT FIDUCIARY DUTIES UNDER DELAWARE LAW

Fiduciary duties in LLCs are typically viewed as default rules—i.e., they exist unless they are properly modified or eliminated by the parties' agreement. In a provocative 2009 article, former Chief Justice Myron Steele of the Supreme Court of Delaware advocated for a reversal of this default position in the LLC and limited partnership settings. Unless the parties contract *for* fiduciary duties, he argued, fiduciary standards should not be applied; instead, the parties' conduct should be evaluated under principles of contract. As Chief Justice Steele explained:

> First, I argue that default fiduciary duties violate the strong policy favoring freedom of contract enunciated by Delaware's legislature. Considering Delaware's strong policy favoring freedom of contract, Delaware courts should analyze mutually bargained-for LLC agreements that define the parties' conduct without any application of default fiduciary duties, even if the parties have not specifically provided for the elimination of fiduciary duties. Where an operating agreement provides for a specific set of conduct, the court should not read any default fiduciary duties into the agreement because the parties' prescribed and proscribed conduct contains the entire agreement that the parties intend and expect. Courts should favor the contracting parties' ex ante calculation of costs and benefits of fiduciary duties, and courts should not, on their own, endeavor to reassess that (albeit perhaps now imprudent) decision ex post.

> * * *

> Moreover, the wholly Byzantine approach, whereby parties must define the duties and rights they intend to keep while simultaneously disclaiming other duties that the parties wish to exclude, adds unnecessary chaos into the parties' contract negotiations, thereby increasing their contracting costs. Instead, assuming a clean slate where the organic agreement crafts the rights and duties owed among and between members and managers gives the parties clear expectations about which duties will apply and clear expectations about the other parties' conduct.

> Finally, from the prospect of potential litigation cost, without default duties, parties will focus their arguments specifically on the agreements they made, and not on default norms imposed on them by courts. To the extent that an answer to a party's contractual duty

is not clear, parties will focus their litigation on contract interpretation rather than fiduciary duties, which will eliminate litigation on claims that the parties never intended to include in their agreements.

Myron T. Steele, *Freedom of Contract and Default Contractual Duties in Delaware Limited Partnerships and Limited Liability Companies*, 46 AM. BUS. L.J. 221, 223–24 (2009).[c]

Despite Chief Justice Steele's argument, several Delaware LLC decisions indicate that fiduciary duties are default rules that apply in the absence of a contrary agreement. In *Auriga Capital Corp. v. Gatz Properties*, LLC, 40 A.3d 839 (Del. Ch. 2012), Chancellor Strine provided a lengthy justification for this position in a dispute involving a manager-managed LLC. He stated, in part, the following:

> The Delaware LLC Act does not plainly state that the traditional fiduciary duties of loyalty and care apply by default as to managers or members of a limited liability company. In that respect, of course, the LLC Act is not different than the DGCL, which does not do that either. In fact, the absence of explicitness in the DGCL inspired the case of *Schnell v. Chris-Craft* [285 A.2d 437 (Del. 1971)]. Arguing that the then newly-revised DGCL was a domain unto itself, and that compliance with its terms was sufficient to discharge any obligation owed by the directors to the stockholders, the defendant corporation in that case won on that theory at the Court of Chancery level. But our Supreme Court reversed and made emphatic that the new DGCL was to be read in concert with equitable fiduciary duties just as had always been the case, stating famously that "inequitable action does not become legally permissible simply because it is legally possible."

---

[c]   The Chief Justice noted, however, that his argument assumed active and sophisticated LLC participants:

> I assume that each partner, member, and manager had a bargained-for exchange when entering the relationship. By this I assume that the parties' organic agreement is not an agreement imposed on, for instance, a passive LLC member who simply purchased units in the LLC. Likewise, I assume that partners bargained for and received a benefit from the partnership agreement that they reached.
>
> * * *
>
> [I]t is important to note that sophisticated parties bargain for the obligations and duties provided in an LLC agreement. The choice of the LLC form was an intentional [one], chosen by sophisticated parties because that form provides the contracting parties with the maximum ability to customize their relationship. Understanding this key difference between LLCs and corporations points us away from adopting default corporate-like fiduciary duties and, instead, applying only Delaware's default contractual duties. To understand this point, in the context of LLC contracting by sophisticated parties, we can assume that the parties' choice to *not* provide fiduciary duties is a conscious and deliberate choice—rather than a "rational gap."

Id. at 225, 237; *see also id.* at 241 n.71 ("In this article, I focus only on sophisticated parties entering into a Delaware LLC. I do not imply that this analysis would apply to all members, specifically passive investors, who are not involved in the formation of the LLC * * *.").

The LLC Act is more explicit than the DGCL in making the equitable overlay mandatory. Specifically, § 18–1104 of the LLC Act provides that "[i]n any case not provided for in this chapter, *the rules of law and equity * * * shall govern.*" In this way, the LLC Act provides for a construct similar to that which is used in the corporate context. But unlike in the corporate context, the rules of equity apply in the LLC context *by statutory mandate,* creating an even stronger justification for application of fiduciary duties grounded in equity to managers of LLCs to the extent that such duties have not been altered or eliminated under the relevant LLC agreement.

> * * *

The manager of an LLC * * * easily fits the definition of a fiduciary. The manager of an LLC has more than an arms-length, contractual relationship with the members of the LLC. Rather, the manager is vested with discretionary power to manage the business of the LLC.

Thus, because the LLC Act provides for principles of equity to apply, because LLC managers are clearly fiduciaries, and because fiduciaries owe the fiduciary duties of loyalty and care, the LLC Act starts with the default that managers of LLCs owe enforceable fiduciary duties.

Id. at 849–51.

On appeal, the Supreme Court of Delaware affirmed *Auriga* on contractual grounds and explicitly noted that its ruling was not based on a determination that Delaware's LLC statute imposed default fiduciary duties. *See* Gatz Properties, LLC v. Auriga Capital Corp., 59 A.3d 1206, 1213–14 (Del. 2012). Further, the court criticized Chancellor Strine for addressing the default fiduciary duty issue:

> At this point, we pause to comment on one issue that the trial court should not have reached or decided. We refer to the court's pronouncement that the Delaware Limited Liability Company Act imposes "default" fiduciary duties upon LLC managers and controllers unless the parties to the LLC Agreement contract that such duties shall not apply. Where, as here, the dispute over whether fiduciary standards apply could be decided solely by reference to the LLC Agreement, it was improvident and unnecessary for the trial court to reach out and decide, *sua sponte,* the default fiduciary duty issue as a matter of statutory construction. The trial court did so despite expressly acknowledging that the existence of fiduciary duties under the LLC Agreement was "no longer contested by the parties." For the reasons next discussed, that court's statutory pronouncements must be regarded as dictum without any precedential value.

First, the * * * LLC Agreement explicitly and specifically addressed the "fiduciary duty issue" in Section 15, which controls this dispute. Second, no litigant asked the Court of Chancery or this Court to decide the default fiduciary duty issue as a matter of statutory law. In these circumstances we decline to express any view regarding whether default fiduciary duties apply as a matter of statutory construction. The Court of Chancery likewise should have so refrained.

Third, the trial court's stated reason for venturing into statutory territory creates additional cause for concern. The trial court opinion identifies "two issues that would arise if the equitable background explicitly contained in the statute were to be judicially excised now." The opinion suggests that "a judicial eradication of the explicit equity overlay in the LLC Act could tend to erode our state's credibility with investors in Delaware entities." Such statements might be interpreted to suggest (hubristically) that once the Court of Chancery has decided an issue, and because practitioners rely on that court's decisions, this Court should not judicially "excise" the Court of Chancery's statutory interpretation, even if incorrect. * * * It is axiomatic, and we recognize, that once a trial judge decides an issue, other trial judges on that court are entitled to rely on that decision as *stare decisis*. Needless to say, as an appellate tribunal and the court of last resort in this State, we are not so constrained.

Fourth, the merits of the issue whether the LLC statute does—or does not—impose default fiduciary duties is one about which reasonable minds could differ. Indeed, reasonable minds arguably could conclude that the statute—which begins with the phrase, "*[t]o the extent that,* at law or in equity, a member or manager or other person has duties (including fiduciary duties)"—is consciously ambiguous. That possibility suggests that the "organs of the Bar" (to use the trial court's phrase) may be well advised to consider urging the General Assembly to resolve any statutory ambiguity on this issue.

Fifth, and finally, the court's excursus on this issue strayed beyond the proper purview and function of a judicial opinion. "Delaware law requires that a justiciable controversy exist before a court can adjudicate properly a dispute brought before it." We remind Delaware judges that the obligation to write judicial opinions on the issues presented is not a license to use those opinions as a platform from which to propagate their individual world views on issues not presented. A judge's duty is to resolve the issues that the parties present in a clear and concise manner. To the extent Delaware judges wish to stray beyond those issues and, without making any definitive pronouncements, ruminate on what the proper direction of Delaware law should be, there are

appropriate platforms, such as law review articles, the classroom, continuing legal education presentations, and keynote speeches.
* * *

Id. at 1218–20.

Despite losing the battle, Chancellor Strine appears to have won the war. In 2013, the Delaware legislature amended DLLCA § 1104 to state the following (amended language in italics): "In any case not provided for in this chapter, the rules of law and equity, including *the rules of law and equity relating to fiduciary duties and* the law merchant, shall govern."[d]

ANDERSON V. WILDER

Court of Appeals of Tennessee, 2003.
2003 WL 22768666.

HOUSTON M. GODDARD, P.J.

This case involves a dispute between members of a limited liability company ("LLC") entitled FuturePoint Administrative Services, LLC. The Plaintiffs were expelled from the LLC by a vote of the Defendants, who together owned 53% of FuturePoint. The Plaintiffs received a buyout price of $150.00 per ownership unit in FuturePoint after they were expelled, pursuant to the operating agreement of the LLC. Shortly after the expulsion, the Defendants sold 499 ownership units, amounting to a 49.9% interest in the LLC, to a third party at a price of $250.00 per ownership unit. Plaintiffs filed this action, alleging, among other things, that the Defendants' actions violated their fiduciary duty and duty of good faith to Plaintiffs. Defendants moved for summary judgment, arguing that their actions were authorized by the operating agreement and that they acted in good faith in expelling the Plaintiffs. The Trial Court granted summary judgment in Defendants' favor. We vacate the order of summary judgment and remand.

FuturePoint Administrative Services, LLC, was created by the parties on or about January 1, 2000, at which time they executed the operating agreement for the company. * * *

The parties set up FuturePoint as a member-managed LLC. The operating agreement provides for a management committee "to oversee and manage the business operations of the Company." The operating agreement gives the management committee the power and authority to contract on behalf of the company by a majority vote. FuturePoint's management committee was comprised of Plaintiffs Michael Atkins, Charles Quade, and Bill Thompson, and Defendants Lamarr Stout and Brett Wilder.

---

[d] In January of 2014, Chancellor Strine became Chief Justice of the Supreme Court of Delaware. Strine replaced Myron Steele, who retired in November 2013.

On September 10, 2001, a members' meeting took place at the FuturePoint offices, at which two offers to purchase ownership units were discussed [one from Healthcare Economics Group, LLC, and one from Don Allen]. Each offer was at a price of $250.00 per ownership unit. At this time, FuturePoint had generated an amount of excess cash on hand in the amount of $63,000.00.

On September 14, 2001, [Plaintiffs were expelled from the LLC] by the Defendants * * *.

Pursuant to the terms of the operating agreement, the remaining members of the company bought the ownership interests of the expelled members at a price of $150.00 per membership unit. On October 11, 2001, the remaining members of FuturePoint sold a total of 499 membership units to a Don Allen at a price of $250.00 per unit.

The Plaintiffs brought this action on December 17, 2001, alleging breach of fiduciary duty and breach of the statutory and common law duty of good faith and fair dealing. Defendants moved for summary judgment, arguing that their actions were expressly permitted under the operating agreement, and that they acted in good faith in expelling the Plaintiffs. Specifically, Defendants relied upon the following provision of the operating agreement:

> 13.6 *Expulsion of a Member.* The Company may expel a Member, with or without cause, from the Company upon a vote or written consent of the Members who hold a majority of Units. In the event of a Member's expulsion, the remaining Members shall be obligated to purchase the expelled Member's Financial Rights at the Agreed Price and on the Agreed Terms within thirty (30) days of such expulsion. The remaining Members shall purchase the expelled Member's Financial Rights in proportion to their Financial Rights (excluding the Offered Financial Rights), or in such other proportion as they may agree.

The Trial Court granted the Defendants summary judgment, finding only that "no genuine issues of material fact exist for adjudication and the Defendants are entitled to summary judgment as a matter of law." Plaintiffs have appealed this ruling, raising the issue, which we restate, of whether the Trial Court erred in granting summary judgment.

* * *

We begin with the Plaintiffs' assertion that the majority shareholders in a member-managed, closely-held LLC stand in a fiduciary relationship to the minority shareholders, such as Plaintiffs in this case. * * *

* * *

It is well-recognized that a fiduciary relationship exists between members of either a partnership or a closely-held corporation under established principles of both partnership law and corporate law. In *Lightfoot v. Hardaway,* 751 S.W.2d 844 (Tenn.App.1988), the court stated as follows regarding business partnerships:

> The fundamental rule that the relationship of partners is fiduciary and imposes on them the obligation of the utmost good faith and integrity in their dealings with one another with respect to partnership affairs is universally recognized in the modern cases and is reinforced by the Uniform Partnership Act * * *. Also well established is the applicability of this fiduciary duty on the sale of one partner's interest to another partner, the courts often characterizing the duty as being "particularly" or "especially" applicable to this situation. Although it is no longer disputed, at least in theory, that such a sale will be sustained only when it is made in good faith, for a fair consideration, and on a full and complete disclosure of all important information as to value, the rule's application is by no means as clear and simple as its statement; and the specific content of such terms as "good," "fair," "full," and "important" can be known only by relating the particular conduct and circumstances of the parties to the results reached in the cases.

Lightfoot, 751 S.W.2d at 849 (quoting 4 A.L.R.4th at page 1128–29). * * *

The Supreme Court has provided the following guidance as regards members of corporate associations:

> This Court has stated that majority shareholders owe a fiduciary duty to minority shareholders. * * * The Court has not addressed specifically the issues presented in this case, the relationship between shareholders in a close corporation where there is no majority or dominant shareholder and the dispute relates to the shareholders' interests as shareholders. The Court of Appeals relied upon the decision in *Wilkes v. Springside Nursing Home, Inc.,* 370 Mass. 842, 353 N.E.2d 657 (1976), in which the Massachusetts court held there is a fiduciary relationship between shareholders of a close corporation. In *Wilkes,* the Court stated that "stockholders in the close corporation owe one another substantially the same fiduciary duty in the operation of the enterprise that partners owe to one another." *Id.* 353 N.E.2d at 661 (quoting *Donahue v. Rodd Electrotype Co.,* 367 Mass. 578, 328 N.E.2d 505, 515 (1975)). That standard of duty is one of "utmost good faith and loyalty." * * * Based on these principles, [defendants] * * *, together and separately, were obligated to deal fairly and honestly with [plaintiff] * * * and could not act

out of avarice, malice, or self-interest in violation of their fiduciary duty to him as a shareholder.

Nelson v. Martin, 958 S.W.2d 643, 647–49 (Tenn.1997), *overruled in part on other grounds* by *Trau-Med of America, Inc. v. Allstate Ins. Co.,* 71 S.W.3d 691 (Tenn.2002).

Defendants in the present case argue that an LLC is a "creature of statute" and because the LLC Act * * * does not specifically prescribe a fiduciary duty of majority shareholders to a minority, this Court should not recognize such a duty. Defendants cite the case of *McGee v. Best,* 106 S.W.3d 48 (Tenn.App.2002) in support of their argument. The *McGee* court stated as follows regarding the LLC Act:

> The statute in question defines the fiduciary duty of members of a member-managed LLC as one owing to the LLC, not to individual members. We cannot contravene the intent of the Legislature.

McGee, 106 S.W.3d at 64. The *McGee* case was in essence an employment dispute and did not involve an allegation of oppression by a majority shareholder group. The *McGee* Court noted that "this case boils down to a rather uncomplicated dispute controlled by the employment contract and the Operating Agreement. * * * The only issue involved is whether termination of the employment was for cause."

The statute at issue here is T.C.A. 48–240–102, and it provides in pertinent part as follows:

> (a) FIDUCIARY DUTY OF MEMBERS OF MEMBER-MANAGED LLC. Except as provided in the articles or operating agreement, every member of a member-managed LLC must account to the LLC for any benefit, and hold as trustee for it any profits derived by the member without the consent of the other members from any transaction connected with the formation, conduct, or liquidation of the LLC or from any use by the member of its property including, but not limited to, confidential or proprietary information of the LLC or other matters entrusted to the member as a result of such person's status as a member.

> (b) STANDARD OF CONDUCT. A member of a member-managed LLC shall discharge such member's duties as a member, including all duties as a member of a committee:

> (1) In good faith;

> (2) With the care an ordinarily prudent person in a like position would exercise under similar circumstances; and

> (3) In a manner the member reasonably believes to be in the best interest of the LLC.

Pursuant to the above analysis, we are of the opinion that finding a majority shareholder of an LLC stands in a fiduciary relationship to the minority, similar to the Supreme Court's teaching in *Nelson* regarding a corporation, is warranted in this case. Such a holding does not conflict with the statute, and is in keeping with the statutory requirement that each LLC member discharge all of his or her duties in good faith.

We now turn to the question of whether Defendants' actions, viewed in the light most favorable to Plaintiffs under our summary judgment standard, could reasonably be said to have violated their fiduciary duty of dealing fairly and honestly with the minority Plaintiffs, and acting in good faith toward them.

In support of their motion for summary judgment, Defendants Mr. Wilder, Mr. Cox, Mr. Stout, Mr. Freeman, Mr. Welles, and Ms. Shockley each filed an affidavit, identical in every aspect, which alleged as follows:

> Prior to the vote being taken to expel Plaintiff members, I was aware that the Plaintiff members of the management committee were planning to vote to distribute the remaining cash of the company, approximately $60,000, to the members, including themselves. I did not believe this would be beneficial to the company as it would not allow the company to meet payroll and other financial obligations, without most, if not all, of the members agreeing to loan that money back to the company.

As noted above, the members of FuturePoint met on September 10, 2001, to discuss two distinct offers to purchase ownership units in the company, one from Healthcare Economics Group, LLC, and one from Don Allen, who eventually purchased 499 ownership units. * * *

Plaintiff Mr. Quade testified by affidavit as follows:

> I have first hand knowledge of Brett Wilder's real reason for causing myself and the others to be expelled. In general, that reason was to expel us at a low price and sell the interests taken at a high price. As it specifically pertained to Bill Thompson and I, his reason no doubt included the fact that Bill and I would not go along with the plan he presented to us May 31, 2001, to expel certain members and take their interests and sell them at a higher price to one of the offerors at the time. Mr. Wilder even reduced his plan to a spreadsheet, a copy of which is attached as Exhibit A. He had it all figured out. That spreadsheet reflects how we would all gain by expelling 30% of the interests of the company. Those selected for the chopping block by Mr. Wilder were Mike Atkins, Pat Martin, Rhonda Shockley, Dennis Freeman, the Zimmermans, and Melinda Anderson. It was my view that these offers to purchase interests in the company were offers in general, and therefore to the members as a whole, and

not just for a few of us to usurp—simply because we knew about the offers and the other members at the time did not. Bill Thompson and I told Mr. Wilder that we would not go along with that scheme, it was not ethical, and that these offers needed to [be] presented to all members for discussion. It seems that my efforts to do right by my fellow partners in the company got me expelled and without a job at FuturePoint. This was most disappointing, especially to see that Rhonda [Shockley] and Dennis [Freeman] voted to expel me after I had stood up for not expelling them.

* * *

The basis for Defendants' argument that they expelled the Plaintiffs in good faith is their assertion that "the Plaintiff members of the management committee were planning to vote to distribute the remaining cash of the company, approximately $60,000, to the members, including themselves." FuturePoint's management committee had the authority and responsibility to distribute the net cash flow of the company to the members. Up until this point, it appears that no cash distributions had been made to any member of the company. The record reflects that after Plaintiffs were expelled, the company made cash distributions to the remaining members in amounts of $13,405.20 on March 27, 2002 and $40,000.00 on April 4, 2002. In their affidavits, Plaintiffs Mr. Quade and Mr. Atkins deny Defendants' allegation that they intended to distribute the remaining cash among the members.

Plaintiffs further argue that Defendants' assertion is false and pretextual for at least two reasons. First, several of the expelled members, Ms. Anderson, Mr. and Mrs. Zimmerman, and Mr. Martin, were not on the management committee and thus had no role in any alleged decision to make a cash distribution. Mr. Quade offered another reason in somewhat colorful fashion in his affidavit:

The Defendants claim in their affidavits that myself, Mike Atkins, and Bill Thompson, as members of the management committee, were planning to vote to distribute all the remaining cash of the company so as to cause the company to not meet its payroll and other financial obligations. This is just not true. For one thing, I WAS ONE SUCH PAYROLL OBLIGATION. That is, I worked at FuturePoint. The notion that *I* would vote to ruin my investment and put myself out of a job is nuts!

We find that there exists a genuine issue of material fact regarding whether the Defendants' actions in expelling the minority Plaintiffs were taken in good faith, as required by the LLC Act, or whether they expelled Plaintiffs solely in order to force the acquisition of their membership units at a price of $150.00 in order to sell them at $250.00 per unit, in violation of their fiduciary duty.

* * *

For the foregoing reasons, we find there are questions of material fact regarding whether the Defendant's actions in expelling the minority Plaintiffs were taken in good faith and in accordance with their fiduciary duty to them. The Trial Court's grant of summary judgment is vacated, and the cause remanded for proceedings consistent with this opinion.
* * *

NOTES

(1) Section 13.6 of the operating agreement in *Anderson* permitted expulsion of a member (with or without cause) upon a majority vote and required a buyout of the expelled member's interest. The facts indicate that a majority vote was obtained and that a buyout occurred according to the agreement's terms. Given this contractual compliance by the defendants, shouldn't the dispute be over?

(2) The *Anderson* court discusses the decision of *McGee v. Best*, 106 S.W.3d 48 (Tenn. Ct. App. 2002). In *McGee*, the plaintiff was a 33.3% owner, co-founder, and "Chief Manager" of an LLC who was responsible for the company's day-to-day operations. The operating agreement contemplated that the plaintiff would be an employee of the LLC. When the three other members voted to terminate the plaintiff's employment, he asserted that his termination breached the operating agreement because there was no "cause" for his firing. *See id.* at 59–60. The court rejected the claim on the grounds that the plaintiff was an employee at will—the operating agreement did not guarantee him "a specific term or duration of employment," nor did it indicate that he could only be terminated for cause. *Id.* at 60. (In addition, the plaintiff had signed an "Employment and Non Solicitation Agreement" that explicitly stated that his "indefinite term" employment could end, without good cause, upon fifteen days' notice. *Id.* at 55.)

The plaintiff further asserted that his termination breached the implied covenant of good faith and fair dealing. That claim was also rejected, as the court noted that "[t]here is no implied covenant of good faith and fair dealing in an employee-at-will contract." *Id.* at 67. (The trial court had additionally stated the following: "The performance of a contract according to its terms cannot be characterized as bad faith. Here, since the Operating Agreement allowed the very actions which Defendants took in terminating Plaintiff's employment, Plaintiff cannot state a claim for breach of the implied covenant of good faith and fair dealing." *Id.* at 61.)

The plaintiff also alleged that his termination constituted a breach of fiduciary duty that the other members owed to him. The court cited Tenn. Code § 48–240–102(a)—the statute referenced in *Anderson* that addresses the fiduciary duties of LLC members. After quoting the section, the court concluded that "[t]he statute in question defines the fiduciary duty of members of a member-managed LLC as one owing to the LLC, not to individual members." As a result, the breach of fiduciary duty claim was dismissed. *See id.* at 63–64. The operating agreement gave the company an option to purchase a terminated member's ownership interest at a prescribed "Formula Value." Because the company had exercised its option, the court remanded to the trial court to determine the proper amount owed to the plaintiff. *See id.* at 66–67.

Do you agree with the court's statement in *Anderson* that "[t]he *McGee* case was in essence an employment dispute and did not involve an allegation of oppression by a majority shareholder group?"

(3) After examining partnership and closely held corporation precedents, the *Anderson* court concludes that a "finding [that] a majority [member] of an LLC stands in a fiduciary relationship to the minority * * * is warranted in this case." Can that conclusion be squared with the court's statement in *McGee* that "[t]he statute in question defines the fiduciary duty of members of a member-managed LLC as one owing to the LLC, not to individual members?"

(4) The Uniform Acts state that managers of manager-managed LLCs, and members of member-managed LLCs, owe fiduciary duties to the LLC *and* its members. *See* ULLCA § 409; RULLCA § 409. As *Anderson* and *McGee* illustrate, however, when an LLC statute is less explicit, judicial conclusions may differ. As a further example, consider the decisions of *Remora Investments, L.L.C. v. Orr*, 673 S.E.2d 845 (Va. 2009), and *In re Allentown Ambassadors, Inc.*, 361 B.R. 422 (Bankr. E.D. Pa. 2007). In *Remora*, the Virginia LLC Act stated that "[a] manager shall discharge his or its duties as a manager in accordance with the manager's good faith business judgment of the best interests of the limited liability company." In rejecting the argument that a manager owed a fiduciary duty to an individual member, the court observed: "Nothing [in the LLC provision] imposes duties between * * * members and managers of an L.L.C. * * * By contrast, general partnership law in Virginia provides [by statute] that 'a partner owes to the partnership *and the other partners* * * * the duty of loyalty and the duty of care.'" *Id.* at 847; *see also id.* at 847–48 (discussing analogous corporate precedent holding that directors do not owe fiduciary duties to individual shareholders).

In *Allentown*, the North Carolina LLC Act similarly stated that "[a] manager shall discharge his duties as manager in good faith, with the care an ordinary prudent person in a like position would exercise under similar circumstances, and in the manner the manager reasonably believes to be in the best interests of the limited liability company." In contrast to *Remora*, however, the *Allentown* court concluded that a manager did owe a fiduciary duty to an individual member:

> * * * Defendant Wolff argues that in his actions as Manager of the NAB, LLC, his legal duty was to act in good faith and in the best

interests of the LLC and that he owed no fiduciary duty to the Debtor as an individual member of the LLC. * * *

Defendant Wolff's position is not unreasonable. Indeed, further support for the principle that a manager of a North Carolina LLC owes no fiduciary duty to an individual member can be derived by comparing the North Carolina statute to other state statutes governing LLC[s]. Some state statutes explicitly provide that the manager of an LLC owes a duty of loyalty or a fiduciary duty to both the entity and its individual members. The [North Carolina LLC Act] lacks such a provision.

Nevertheless, I conclude that the courts in North Carolina would hold that a manager of an LLC owes a duty to the individual members of the LLC that may be the subject of a claim for breach of fiduciary duty. I draw this conclusion from the well established principle under North Carolina law that majority shareholders owe a fiduciary duty to minority shareholders in a corporation. While my research has uncovered no controlling precedent, I predict that the North Carolina appellate courts would extend to LLC's the principles developed in the law of closely-held corporations that are designed to protect minority shareholders.

Since the majority members of an LLC have a duty to its minority members and Defendant Wolff's authority as manager of the NAB, LLC is derived entirely from the exercise of powers delegated by the "member-managers" of the LLC, it follows, and I find, that Defendant Wolff, too, owed a duty to the LLC's individual members, including the Debtor.

Id. at 461–62.

H. OWNERSHIP INTERESTS AND TRANSFERABILITY

An ownership interest in an LLC entitles a member to (1) the right to receive distributions and to share in the profits and losses of the venture (financial rights), and (2) the right to participate in the management and control of the business (management rights). Like partnerships, all LLC statutes provide that an assignment of an LLC ownership interest transfers a member's financial rights, but not his management rights. Indeed, the statutes usually specify that an assignee can acquire a member's management rights only with the consent of all of the nontransferring members. Unlike a shareholder but like a partner, therefore, an LLC member cannot freely transfer his full ownership interest (i.e., both his financial and management rights). Ordinarily, however, this limitation on transferability is simply a default rule that the parties can modify to permit (or further restrict) the free and full transferability of LLC ownership interests.

ACHAIAN, INC. v. LEEMON FAMILY LLC

Court of Chancery of Delaware, 2011.
25 A.3d 800.

STRINE, CHANCELLOR.

I. *Introduction*

Omniglow, LLC is a Delaware limited liability company engaged in the manufacture of chemiluminescent novelty items such as "glowsticks." When it was founded in 2005, Omniglow had a sole "Member," its "Parent" corporation. As part of a planned spin-off in 2006, Parent sold Omniglow to three business entities. That resulted in Omniglow having three Members, each owning the following Membership "Interests": (i) 50% were owned by the defendant Leemon Family LLC, a New York limited liability company controlled by its managing member, the individual defendant Ira Leemon (together, "Leemon"); (ii) 30% were owned by the non-party Randye M. Holland and Stanley M. Holland Trust, a revocable inter vivos trust controlled by non-parties Stanley and Randye Holland as trustees ("Holland"); and (iii) 20% were owned by the plaintiff Achaian, Inc., a Nevada corporation wholly owned by non-party William A. Heriot ("Achaian").

For two years, Holland and Leemon, together comprising 80% of the Interests, managed Omniglow's business with Achaian taking a passive role as an investor. In 2008, however, Leemon allegedly took sole control of Omniglow over the objection of both Achaian and Holland, and in contravention of Omniglow's "LLC Agreement" that vests managerial authority in the Members in proportion to their respective Interests. Holland, fed up with controversy, purported to transfer and assign its entire 30% Interest to Achaian in a January 25, 2010 "Purchase Agreement." Achaian then filed this suit on March 10, 2011, claiming that it and Leemon are now deadlocked, 50/50, as to the management of Omniglow and therefore an order of dissolution is warranted under 6 *Del. C.* § 18–802 because it is no longer "reasonably practicable to carry on [Omniglow's] business in conformity with [Omniglow's] [LLC] [A]greement." Leemon has moved to dismiss the complaint under Rule 12(b)(6), arguing that Holland's assignment was only effective to give Achaian an additional 30% economic interest in Omniglow. Specifically, Leemon says that in order for Achaian to have received a 30% *Membership* Interest in Omniglow, the LLC Agreement required Leemon's consent to the assignment because, in its view, Achaian was in effect being readmitted as a Member with respect to its newly acquired 30% Interest.

This case therefore presents a single question of law: may one member of a Delaware limited liability company assign its entire membership interest, including that interest's voting rights, to another existing member, notwithstanding the fact that the limited liability company agreement requires the affirmative consent of all of the members upon the admission of a new member, or, must the existing member assignee be readmitted with respect to each additional interest it acquires after its initial admission as a member? In this opinion, I find that, consistent with the Delaware Limited Liability Company Act, an enabling statute whose primary function is to fill gaps, if any, in a limited liability company agreement, the answer to that question depends in the first instance on the specific provisions governing the transferability of Interests in Omniglow's LLC Agreement. When Omniglow's LLC Agreement is read as a whole, as it must be, it allows an existing Member to transfer its entire Membership Interest, including voting rights, to another existing Member without obtaining the other Members' consent. Thus, Holland's assignment of its 30% Interest to an existing Member, Achaian, was effective to vest all of the rights associated with that Interest in Achaian, and Omniglow now has two coequal 50% Members.

II. *The Relevant Provisions Of The LLC Agreement And The Parties' Competing Interpretations*

This motion presents a discrete question of law. Both parties believe that their dispute must be determined by reference to the terms of the applicable statute, the Delaware Limited Liability Company Act, and Omniglow's LLC Agreement. Neither argues that there is any relevant parol evidence bearing on this dispute, especially because neither Achaian nor Leemon was involved in drafting the original LLC Agreement.

To resolve this dispute, it is useful to start with what is now a mundane notion, which is that under the Act, the parties to an LLC agreement have substantial authority to shape their own affairs and that in general, any conflict between the provisions of the Act and an LLC agreement will be resolved in favor of the LLC agreement.

That principle applies here. As Leemon stresses, the default provision of the Act dealing with the transfer of interests in an LLC states [in § 18–702(a), (b)(2)]:

> A limited liability company interest is assignable in whole or in part except as provided in a limited liability company agreement. The assignee of a member's limited liability company interest shall have no right to participate in the management of the business and affairs of a limited liability company *except as provided in a limited liability company agreement.* * * * *Unless otherwise provided in a limited liability company agreement,* [a]n assignment of a limited liability company interest does not entitle the assignee to become or to exercise any rights or powers of a member [and instead only] entitles the assignee to share in such profits and losses, to receive such distribution or distributions, and to receive such allocation of income, gain, loss,

deduction, or credit or similar item to which the assignor was entitled, to the extent assigned. * * *

Likewise, the Act provides that an assignee of a limited liability company interest "is admitted as a member of the limited liability company * * * as provided in § 18–704(a) of this title and at the time provided in and upon compliance with the limited liability company agreement. * * *"[14]

Thus, it is clear that the default rule under the Act is that an assignment of an LLC interest, by itself, does not entitle the assignee to become a member of the LLC; rather, an assignee only receives the assigning member's economic interest in the LLC to the extent assigned. It is equally clear, however, that the default rule may be displaced by the provisions of an LLC agreement itself and that in the event of a conflict, the LLC agreement prevails.

Here, Omniglow's LLC Agreement does contain specific provisions bearing on Interests in Omniglow and their transferability, namely §§ 7.1 and 7.2. In deciding the legal question surfaced by Leemon's motion to dismiss, therefore, I must first look to those provisions. If the LLC Agreement allowed Holland to transfer and assign the voting power associated with its Membership Interest to Achaian, that ends the matter notwithstanding that the default provisions in the Act, if applicable, might lead to a different result.

For starters, Omniglow's LLC Agreement defines a Member's Interest as meaning "the *entire ownership interest* of the Member in [Omniglow]." Two related sections of the LLC Agreement then deal specifically with the transfer of Interests. The first, § 7.1, allows a Member to transfer all or part of its Interest to any "Person," at any time:

> 7.1. *Transfer of Interest. [A] Member may transfer all or any portion of its Interest in [Omniglow] to any Person at any time.* If at any time such a transfer shall cause [Omniglow] to have more than one Member, then this [LLC] Agreement shall be appropriately amended to reflect the fact that [Omniglow] will

---

[14] 6 *Del. C.* § 18–301(b)(2). There are likely two motivations for the statutory default rules in §§ 18–702, 18–704(a), and 18–301 concerning the assignment of a limited liability company interest and the assignee's possible (and subsequent) admission as a member of the LLC. The first is tax-related. *See generally* Daniel S. Kleinberger, *Two Decades of "Alternative Entities": From Tax Rationalization Through Alphabet Soup To Contract As Deity,* 14 FORDHAM J. CORP. & FIN. L. 445, 447–54 (2009) (observing that the emergence of LLCs and statutory rules, sometimes mandatory, that prevented the free alienability of LLC interests was part of states' early attempts "to create an entity that, as a matter of tax law, is classified as a partnership with each owner treated as a partner, but whose owners are shielded by state law from automatic personal liability," and that such default statutory rules have now been rendered largely unnecessary after the United States Treasury Department adopted the "check-the-box" federal income tax classification regime in 1997 * * *"). Omniglow's LLC Agreement itself recognizes the desirability of partnership tax treatment. The second reason for the default rules in the Act regarding the transferability of interests may rest on the notion that one generally is entitled to select his own business associates in a closely held enterprise, like an LLC.

then be treated as a partnership for purposes of the [Internal Revenue] Code [of 1986].

Section 7.1's permissive grant of free transferability, however, is subject to the express restriction contained in § 7.2, which provides:

> 7.2. *Admission of New Members. No Person shall be admitted as a Member of [Omniglow]* after the date of this [LLC] Agreement without the written consent of the Member and delivery to [Omniglow] of a written acknowledgement (in form and substance satisfactory to the Member) of the rights and obligations of this [LLC] Agreement and [an] agreement [to] be bound hereunder.

Certain undisputed facts are also relevant to decide the current motion. The parties agree that each of Leemon, Achaian, and Holland were admitted as Members in 2006. The parties also agree that even though § 7.1 says that the LLC Agreement "shall be appropriately amended" in the event that Omniglow came to have more than one Member, there was never any such amendment. Notably, the parties also agree that despite the failure to amend the LLC Agreement, the reference in § 7.2 to the "written consent of the Member" must be read as now meaning "Members" affording any Member the right to object to the admission of a Person as a new Member.

From these undisputed facts, the key contractual provisions in the LLC Agreement, and the default provisions of the Act, the parties draw starkly different conclusions.

For its part, Leemon argues that none of the provisions in the LLC Agreement clearly reverse the default rule under the Act, which is that "[a]n assignment of a limited liability company interest does not entitle the assignee to become a member or to exercise any rights or powers of a member," and instead only entitles the assignee to the economic interest of the assigning member. Because, in Leemon's view, the LLC Agreement does not plainly provide that the assignee of an Interest will receive the voting rights along with the economic interest, Achaian only received the economic interest associated with Holland's 30% Interest and thus possesses only the original 20% voting power it received from Parent.

Alternatively, Leemon argues that the LLC Agreement itself unambiguously distinguishes between the transferability of a Member's economic interest (i.e., the right to share in Omniglow's profits, losses and other distributions) and that Member's voting rights (i.e., the right to manage). That is, Leemon says that although § 7.1 allows a Member to freely transfer its economic interest in Omniglow, § 7.2 makes plain that a Member's voting rights can only be transferred with the express written consent of the existing Members. Were it otherwise, argues Leemon, and a Member was allowed to transfer *both* his economic *and* voting interest under § 7.1 without first obtaining the consent of Omniglow's other Members, § 7.2's prohibition against the admission of a new Member without the written consent of existing Members would be "superfluous." To avoid that result, Leemon says that § 7.2 applies to transfers or assignments of an Interest to existing Members, like Achaian. That is, Leemon suggests that although Achaian was "admitted as a Member" with respect to its original 20% Interest, § 7.2 requires Leemon's written consent in order for Achaian to have been "admitted as a Member" with respect to the additional 30% Interest it acquired from Holland.

Achaian, for its part, admits that if Leemon is correct that the Act's default provisions it cites govern the transfer made by Holland to Achaian in the Purchase Agreement, "it is possible that the Court might find that Achaian did not acquire Holland's voting rights and does not hold a fifty percent full [I]nterest." But, says Achaian, the LLC Agreement's specific provisions bearing on transferability trump the Act's default rules and permitted Holland to assign its voting rights to another existing Member, like Achaian. To that end, Achaian first points to the LLC Agreement's broad definition of Interest, which means "the *entire ownership interest* of the Member in [Omniglow]." Achaian says that because § 7.1 allows a "Member [to] transfer all or any part of its Interest to any Person at any time," Holland was free to transfer its "entire ownership [I]nterest," including that Interest's voting rights, to Achaian in the Purchase Agreement. What's more, says Achaian, § 7.2 is far from superfluous, as Leemon contends. Instead, § 7.2 has an important role to play when a Member wishes to assign his Membership Interest to a "Person" who is not already "admitted as a Member." When a Person is already "admitted as a Member," Achaian says that § 7.2 has no relevance, and a Member need not be readmitted as to each subsequent Interest it acquires.

III. *Leemon's Motion To Dismiss Is Denied*

For the following reasons, I conclude that Achaian has the better of the argument. When read as a whole, as it must be, the LLC Agreement provides that all of the rights accompanying an Interest—including the voting rights—in Omniglow may be transferred to an already existing Member of Omniglow without the written consent of the other Members. Read in complete context, the LLC Agreement makes Interests in Omniglow freely transferable subject only to a limited proviso that requires the written consent of the existing Members in order for a transfer to confer the status of Member on a Person, who at the time of the transfer was not already a Member. Because Achaian was already a Member at the time of the Purchase Agreement and nothing in the LLC Agreement requires that it be readmitted as a Member with respect to each additional Interest it acquires in Omniglow, it was entitled to receive the "entire ownership interest" owned by Holland, including that Interest's corresponding voting rights.

I now explain that reasoning in more detail.

I start by noting that Achaian places substantial weight on the LLC Agreement's definition of Interest—"the entire ownership interest of the Member in [Omniglow]." Although it might be read as a way to ensure that partial positions can be transferred without saying anything about whether the Interest transferred included voting rights, the fact that § 7.1 already permits a Member to transfer "all or any portion of its Interest" casts doubt on that reading because that reading renders the LLC Agreement's specific definition of Interest unnecessary and superfluous. That is, if "entire," as used to describe the extent of a Member's "ownership interest" in Omniglow serves only to confirm that a Member can, under § 7.1, transfer "all or any portion of its Interest" in the sense that a 60% Member may transfer any percentage up to and including its full 60% Interest, but does not speak at all as to what rights are included in that 60% Interest, the two provisions of the LLC Agreement would in effect be saying the same thing. It is instead preferable to accord the specific definition of Interest in the LLC Agreement independent meaning and significance.

In that vein, given that the term "entire" is used only once in the LLC Act, in a vastly different context, and is not a statutorily defined term, it is also reasonably susceptible to a reading, as Achaian urges, that is consistent with its plain meaning. Under its plain meaning, entire would mean what it ordinarily does, as "[h]aving no part excluded or left out; [the] whole." It is in this sense that Achaian claims that "entire" must mean that a Member, like Holland, can transfer under § 7.1 "all or any portion of its Interest," i.e., all or any portion of its *entire ownership interest * * * in [Omniglow],"* including the Member's voting rights. That this is what entire is best read as meaning, however, need not be determined in isolation, and in candor only becomes clear and unambiguous when read in full contractual context.

To that point, it is only when the second sentence of § 7.1 and § 7.2 are considered that the LLC Agreement's broad definition of Interest emerges as unambiguously including all aspects of Membership in Omniglow, including managerial voting rights. The second sentence of § 7.1 provides that "[i]f at any time *such a transfer shall cause [Omniglow] to have more than one Member,* then this [LLC] Agreement shall be appropriately amended to reflect the fact that [Omniglow] will then be treated as a partnership for purposes of the [Internal Revenue] Code [of 1986]." The second sentence of § 7.1 makes clear that a Member's Interest—i.e., its "entire ownership interest * * * in [Omniglow]"— includes every aspect of a Member's Interest, including the portion that confers the status of Member, in whom, under § 4.1 of the LLC Agreement, managerial authority is vested. If it were otherwise, and an Interest in Omniglow represented *only* a Member's economic interest, as

Leemon argues, the second sentence of § 7.1 would seem to be unnecessary because in that case, an existing Member could not transfer or assign the voting rights included in its Interest to another Person such that as a result of such transfer or assignment, that Person could become a Member. In light of well settled principles of contract interpretation in Delaware, the reading proffered by Leemon would tend to render the second sentence of § 7.1, to phrase it in a word favored by Leemon, superfluous.

Of course, the fact that § 7.1 seems to permit the free transfer of the entire Interest, including that Interest's associated voting rights, does not end the inquiry. Instead, I must look at what effect the section of the LLC Agreement addressing the admission of Members has, keeping in mind that the Act affords maximum contractual flexibility to provide in an LLC agreement the precise mechanism by which an assignee of a limited liability company interest may become a member. As § 7.2 of the LLC Agreement provides in this case, *"[n]o Person shall be admitted as a Member* of [Omniglow] * * * without the written consent of the Member[s] * * *."* As noted, Leemon does not contest the fact that Achaian, like Leemon, was admitted as a Member of Omniglow when Parent assigned and sold all of Omniglow's Interests to Leemon, Holland, and Achaian in 2006. Instead, Leemon focuses on the specific 30% Interest that was transferred to Achaian under the Purchase Agreement and argues that "Achaian has not been admitted as a substituted [M]ember with respect to the 30% Interest, as provided by Section 7.2 of the LLC Agreement."

But nothing in the text of § 7.2 suggests that once a Person has been admitted as a Member, she must be admitted again in order to acquire additional voting rights when she acquires additional Interests in Omniglow. The reason for § 7.2's check on § 7.1's free grant of transferability is most naturally read as a manifestation of the unremarkable idea that one gets to choose one's own business partners (or in the case of an LLC, one's co-members). Leemon's argument relies on a very thinly sliced version of that, which is that once one chooses his initial co-members, one continues to hold a veto over how much additional voting power they may acquire. That is a strained extension of the traditional idea underlying partnerships and limited liability companies, and is not supported rationally by the LLC Agreement's text or by the context.

As it was, Leemon had already agreed in 2006 to become partners (or more properly, co-members) with Achaian and Holland in Omniglow's business. Thus, Leemon, as a 50% Interest holder, knew that Achaian and Holland could have voted together at any time to stymie Leemon from acting unilaterally. Leemon responds, however, that the LLC Agreement makes sure that if Holland and Achaian agreed to a transfer, in whatever direction, that vested all the voting power in one of them, the transferee had to be admitted as a Member for a second time—the first time being in 2006 when Parent sold its Interests to both Achaian, Holland and Leemon and approved their Membership.

The problem for Leemon is that nothing in the LLC Agreement supports Leemon's reading of it that would require an already admitted Member, like Achaian, to be become once, twice (or even three times) a Member each and every time that Member acquires an additional block of Interests.[54] By its plain terms, § 7.2 is directed at, and applies only to, a *"Person"* who is not yet "admitted as a Member." Because Achaian was already admitted as a Member at the time of Holland's 2010 transfer, § 7.2 has no application.[56] Nor has Leemon cited anything in the LLC Act, the Uniform LLC Act, or learned commentaries and treatises on alternative entities suggesting that such a serial admission scheme is standard practice. To the contrary, the Delaware LLC Act seems to contemplate a singular admission governed by the specific terms of the LLC agreement, providing that "[a]n assignee of a limited liability company interest *may become a member * * * as provided in the limited liability company agreement.*" To that point, Leemon's argument conflicts with the LLC Agreement's definition of a Member's Interest in Omniglow. That is, if § 7.2 requires, as Leemon argues, that Achaian be admitted as two Members, one with respect to each block of Interests it owns, the LLC Agreement's definition of Interest—"the *entire* ownership interest of *the Member* in [Omniglow]"—would make scant sense because in that case, a Member's Interest would not be its entire ownership interest in Omniglow, but, as in the case of Achaian, only a portion of it, the other portion also being owned by Achaian, albeit a "different" Achaian for purposes of Membership in Omniglow.

On the basis of the foregoing, I conclude that under the terms of the LLC Agreement, Holland was permitted, and did, transfer its entire 30% Interest to Achaian, including that Interest's voting rights. Thus, Achaian is entitled to the declaratory judgment it seeks, namely that Omniglow currently has two Members—Leemon and Achaian—each holding an identical 50% Membership Interest. * * *

NOTES

(1) Assume that the LLC Agreement in *Achaian* did not displace any of the provisions of DLLCA. What would have been the effect of Holland's transfer to a non-member? Would anything have changed if the transfer were

---

[54] *See* COMMODORES, *Three Times a Lady, on* NATURAL HIGH (Motown Records 1978) ("You're once, twice, three times a lady/And I love you. * * *").

[56] That § 7.2's restriction on transferability applies only to a Person who is not yet admitted as a Member does not, contrary to Leemon's argument, render § 7.2 superfluous. For instance, § 7.2's written consent requirement would clearly apply to the counterfactual situation in which Holland, instead of assigning its 30% Interest to Achaian (an existing Member), assigned that Interest to a non-Member. In the case where Holland assigned its Interest to the non-Member, § 7.2 would require both Leemon and Achaian's written consent as Members.

to a member (such as Achaian)? *See* DLLCA §§ 18–101(8), 18–301(b)(2), 18–402, 18–701, 18–702, 18–704, 18–801, 18–802.

(2) How did the provisions of the LLC Agreement in *Achaian* change what would have resulted under DLLCA?

(3) Assume that *Achaian* occurred in a Uniform Act jurisdiction, and that the LLC Agreement did not displace any of the provisions of the relevant Uniform Act. What would have been the effect of Holland's transfer to a non-member? Would anything have changed if the transfer were to a member (such as Achaian)? *See* ULLCA §§ 101(6), 404, 501–503, 601(3), 603(b)(1), 801(5); RULLCA §§ 102(21), 401(d), 407, 501–502, 602(4)(B), 701.

(4) Are restrictions on the transferability of ownership interests appropriate in the LLC setting? Why or why not?

(5) LLC statutes provide for the transfer of management rights only with the consent of the nontransferring members. As mentioned, that consent usually requires a unanimous vote, but some statutes provide that a majority vote or "majority in interest" vote will suffice. Under most statutes, the members can change these default provisions in the articles of organization or the operating agreement.

(6) Corporations reflect equity ownership through the issuance of stock that is typically represented by certificates. Section 3.201(e) of the Texas Business Organizations Code states that an LLC may "provide that an owner's ownership interest may be evidenced by a certificate of ownership interest issued by the entity," may "provide for the assignment or transfer of ownership interests represented by certificates," and may "make other provisions with respect to the certificate." Some other states have a similar statute, and even without such a statute, the use of certificates would presumably be permissible as a contractual matter.

Would you recommend that ownership certificates be used in an LLC? Assume that a member wishes to make a gift of a portion of his membership interest to a child. Would a statement in some obscure record that "Mr. X assigned a ten percent interest in his membership interest to his daughter" stand up at some later date? If certificates of membership are used in an LLC, is there a risk that they may be considered "securities" subject to registration, disclosure, and antifraud provisions? For more on whether LLC ownership interests should be characterized as securities, see the Notes in Section J.

NOTE ON CHARGING ORDERS

Most LLC statutes provide a charging order remedy that creditors can use against a member's interest. *See, e.g.*, DLLCA § 18–703; ULLCA § 504; RULLCA § 503. A charging order procedure is generally understood to trump the state's general execution statute. Indeed, despite the facts that (1) an LLC ownership interest is personal property, and (2) non-exempt personal property is typically subject to execution, allowing a judgment creditor to involuntarily seize and sell a debtor-member's ownership interest would be undesirable, as it would suggest that the buyer will become a full-fledged member with governance rights. Such a result would be contrary to the closely held nature of the LLC when the remaining members have not consented to the admission of a new owner.

The North Carolina decision of *Herring v. Keasler*, 563 S.E.2d 614 (N.C. Ct. App. 2002), exemplifies this general understanding. In *Herring*, the court prevented a judgment creditor plaintiff from seizing and selling defendant's 20% membership interests in several LLCs pursuant to a writ of execution. The trial court had denied defendant's request to seize and sell the LLC interests, and had instead granted a charging order:

> * * * With respect to the charging order, the trial court directed: Defendant's membership interests in the LLCs to be charged with payment of the judgment, plus interest; the LLCs to deliver to Plaintiff any distributions and allocations that Defendant would be entitled to receive on account of his membership interests in the LLCs; Defendant to deliver to Plaintiff any allocations and distributions he would receive; and Plaintiff to not obtain any rights in the LLCs, except as those of an assignee and under the respective operating agreement.

Id. at 615. The Court of Appeals affirmed:

> Generally, a trial court
>
> may order any property, whether subject or not to be sold under execution (except the homestead and personal property exemptions of the judgment debtor), in the hands of the judgment debtor or of any other person, or due to the judgment debtor, to be applied towards the satisfaction of [a] judgment.

N.C.G.S. § 1–362 (2001). North Carolina General Statutes § 57C–5–03, however, provides that with respect to a judgment debtor's membership interest in a limited liability company, a trial court "may charge the membership interest of the member with payment of the unsatisfied amount of the judgment with interest." This "charge" entitles the judgment creditor "to receive * * * the distributions and allocations to which the [judgment debtor] would be entitled." N.C.G.S. § 57C–5–02 (2001). The "charge" "does not dissolve the limited liability company or entitle the [judgment creditor] to become or exercise any rights of a member." *Id.* Furthermore, because the forced sale of a membership interest in a limited liability company to satisfy a debt would necessarily entail the transfer of a member's ownership interest to another, thus permitting the purchaser to become a member, forced sales of [this] type * * * are prohibited. *See* N.C.G.S. § 57C–3–03 (2001) (except as provided in the operating agreement or articles of organization, consent of all the members of a limited liability company required to "[a]dmit any person as a member").

In this case, despite Plaintiff's attempts to have Defendant's membership interests in the LLCs seized and sold, his only remedy is to have those interests charged with payment of the judgment under N.C.Gen.Stat. § 57C–5–03. Accordingly, the trial court did not err in ordering that the judgment be satisfied through the application of the distributions and allocations of Defendant's membership interests in the LLCs and in denying Plaintiff's motion to have Defendant's membership interests seized and sold.

Id. at 615–16.

In *Olmstead v. Federal Trade Commission*, 44 So. 3d 76 (Fla. 2010), the Supreme Court of Florida held that, in a single-member LLC, the statutory charging order procedure did not preclude a creditor from executing on an ownership interest. The court acknowledged that a charging order provision is generally designed to preserve a nondebtor member's right to block the admission of a new member (and the exercise of accompanying management rights), but it implied that this right was not implicated when the debtor was the sole member of the LLC. The court was particularly influenced by the fact that the Florida LLC statute did not indicate that a charging order was a creditor's exclusive remedy, while the Florida general partnership and limited partnership statutes did so provide. Although the court appeared to limit its holding to disputes involving a single-member LLC, the dissent noted that the court's emphasis on the lack of exclusivity language in the statute would seem to extend its holding to multi-member LLCs.

The Florida legislature reacted swiftly to the *Olmstead* decision. Acknowledging the "uncertainty of the breadth of the Court's holding in *Olmstead*," the legislature amended its LLC statute "to remediate the potential effect of the holding in *Olmstead* and to clarify that the current law does not extend to a member of a multimember LLC." In relevant part, the Florida statute now provides:

(5) Except as provided in subsections (6) and (7), a charging order is the sole and exclusive remedy by which a judgment creditor of a member or member's assignee may satisfy a judgment from the judgment debtor's interest in a limited liability company or rights to distributions from the limited liability company.

(6) In the case of a limited liability company having only one member, if a judgment creditor of a member or member's assignee establishes to the satisfaction of a court of competent jurisdiction that distributions under a charging order will not satisfy the judgment within a reasonable time, a charging order is not the sole and exclusive remedy by which the judgment creditor may satisfy the judgment against a judgment debtor who is the sole member of a limited liability company or the assignee of the sole member, and upon such showing, the court may order the sale of that interest in the limited liability company pursuant to a foreclosure sale. * * *

(7) In the case of a limited liability company having only one member, if the court orders [a] foreclosure sale of a judgment debtor's interest in the limited liability company or of a charging order lien against the sole member of the limited liability company pursuant to subsection (6):

(a) The purchaser at the court-ordered foreclosure sale obtains the member's entire limited liability company interest, not merely the rights of an assignee;

(b) The purchaser at the sale becomes the member of the limited liability company; and

(c) The person whose limited liability company interest is sold pursuant to the foreclosure sale or is the subject of the foreclosed charging order ceases to be a member of the limited liability company.

(8) In the case of a limited liability company having more than one member, the remedy of foreclosure on a judgment debtor's interest in such limited liability company or against rights to distribution from such limited liability company is not available to a judgment creditor attempting to satisfy the judgment and may not be ordered by a court.

FLA. STAT. § 608.433 & cmt. Other statutes explicitly provide that the charging order is the exclusive remedy for a judgment creditor of a member in single-member as well as multiple-member LLCs. *See, e.g.*, NEV. REV. STAT. § 86.401 ("This [charging order] section * * * [p]rovides the exclusive remedy by which a judgment creditor of a member or an assignee of a member may satisfy a judgment out of the member's interest * * *, whether the limited-liability company has one member or more than one member."); WYO. STAT. § 17–29–503(g) (substantially the same).

Does it make sense for a charging order to be a judgment creditor's sole remedy in a multiple-member LLC? In a single-member LLC? Could an *Olmstead*-like result be reached in Delaware or a Uniform Act jurisdiction? *See* DLLCA §§ 18–703(d), 18–1101(j); ULLCA § 504(e); RULLCA § 503(g).

I.   DISSOCIATION AND DISSOLUTION

LLC statutes typically state that a member dissociates from a venture upon the occurrence of certain specified acts—e.g., withdrawal, resignation, death, or bankruptcy. *See, e.g.*, ULLCA § 601; RULLCA § 602. Until relatively recently, member dissociation usually resulted in (1) a buyout of the dissociating member's ownership interest, or (2) dissolution of the LLC. If dissolution did not occur because the requisite percentage of the remaining members voted to continue the venture, then a buyout was required. If dissolution occurred, however, the dissociating member would receive her share of the company's dissolution value, and a buyout was no longer needed.

With the passage of the check-the-box regulations, there was no longer a tax-driven need for member dissociation to trigger a dissolution of the LLC. As a result, many states curtailed the buyout and dissolution rights that had previously arisen upon the dissociation of a member. Although statutes continue to provide other triggers of dissolution—e.g., expiration of the venture's term, consent of all or a specified percentage of the members, judicial decree based upon specified grounds—the easy liquidity provided by dissociation-triggered buyouts and dissolution has been eliminated in many jurisdictions. The materials that follow address these developments in greater detail.

DOUGLAS K. MOLL, MINORITY OPPRESSION & THE LIMITED LIABILITY COMPANY: LEARNING (OR NOT) FROM CLOSE CORPORATION HISTORY

40 Wake Forest L. Rev. 883, 925–40 (2005).

For tax purposes, a publicly-traded LLC is likely to be treated as a corporation. Because the desire to avoid the corporate "double tax" motivates, in large part, the founders' decision to choose an LLC structure, publicly-traded LLCs will be rare. Indeed, commentators have noted that the LLC is primarily used as a business structure for closely held ventures. As a result, a well-developed market for LLC ownership interests is typically nonexistent and, correspondingly, there is little possibility of sale. Moreover, even if a minority member could locate prospective outside purchasers, it would still be difficult to sell an LLC ownership position. Just as in the close corporation, the lack of control and lack of liquidity (at least compared to publicly-traded stock) associated with a minority LLC interest will severely reduce the likelihood of sale.

When the first LLC statutes were passed, most included provisions that provided liquidity to members if they chose to exit the business. These provisions took two forms. First, the majority of LLC statutes provided that members had the power to withdraw from the business in the absence of a contrary provision in the operating agreement. Upon withdrawal, the member was entitled to be paid the fair value of its ownership interest less any damages caused by a wrongful withdrawal. Second, most of the LLC statutes provided for dissolution of the LLC upon the member's withdrawal or other dissociation from the venture (e.g., dissociation due to a member's death, bankruptcy, or incompetency). An actual liquidation of the business could be avoided, however, if all (or a majority under some statutes) of the remaining members elected to continue the venture. Even if liquidation were averted, the withdrawing member was still entitled to a buyout of its ownership interest.

The inclusion of these provisions in the statutory scheme of the LLC was no accident. Before 1997, the IRS applied the "corporate resemblance" test to determine whether an LLC would be classified as a partnership or a corporation for tax purposes. * * *

* * * [T]he provisions calling for the LLC's dissolution upon the member's withdrawal or other dissociation from the business were designed to resist a continuity of life finding. Treasury Regulations at the time provided that "[i]f the death, insanity, bankruptcy, retirement, resignation, or expulsion of any member will cause a dissolution of the organization, continuity of life does not exist." As a result, most LLC statutory schemes included a dissolution provision with triggers that closely tracked the language of the Treasury Regulations.

In the first wave of LLC statutes, therefore, the inclusion of withdrawal and dissolution provisions provided exit rights and accompanying liquidity to LLC investors. The withdrawal provisions obviously provided liquidity by typically stating that a member would receive the fair value of its ownership interest upon withdrawal. The dissolution provisions provided liquidity by requiring the company to be sold (in the event of liquidation) and by allocating to each member its proportionate share of the company's sale value. If liquidation were avoided, the minority member was still entitled to its buyout upon withdrawal.

In late 1996, however, the IRS significantly altered the regulatory scheme that applied to LLCs. * * * Under the new "check-the-box" regulations, an unincorporated business entity, including an LLC, can simply choose whether it wants to be taxed as a corporation or a partnership. * * *

Following the passage of the "check-the-box" regulations, there was no longer a tax-driven need for state statutes to deny the LLC certain "corporate" characteristics. In response, many state legislatures eliminated or restricted the withdrawal and dissolution rights that had served to combat a continuity of life finding. With respect to withdrawal rights, for example, California's LLC statute previously provided the following:

> Upon a permitted withdrawal that does not cause dissolution of the limited liability company, any withdrawing member is entitled to receive any distribution to which that member is entitled under the operating agreement and, if not otherwise provided in the operating agreement, the member is entitled to receive, within a reasonable time after withdrawal, the fair market value of the member's interest in the limited liability company as of the date of withdrawal based upon the member's right to share in distributions from the limited liability company.

[CAL. CORP. CODE § 17252(c) (1996).] The 1997 version of the statute, however, eliminated this buyout right:

[U]nless the articles of organization or written operating agreement provide otherwise, the withdrawn member shall not be entitled to payment for the member's interest in the limited liability company, and, beginning on the date of the withdrawal, the withdrawn member shall have only the right of a holder of an economic interest with respect to that withdrawn member's interest in the limited liability company * * *.

[CAL. CORP. CODE § 17252(a) (1997).]

Similarly, California's LLC statute previously provided that dissolution of an LLC would occur "upon the death, withdrawal, resignation, expulsion, bankruptcy, or dissolution of a member, unless the business of the limited liability company is continued by a vote of all the remaining members within 90 days of the happening of that event." [CAL. CORP. CODE § 17350(d) (1996).] This language, however, was subsequently removed from the statute, and the grounds for dissolution were substantially narrowed. Since 1999, the statute has read as follows:

A limited liability company shall be dissolved and its affairs shall be wound up upon the happening of the first to occur of the following: (a) At the time specified in the articles of organization, if any, or upon the happening of the events, if any, specified in the articles of organization or a written operating agreement. (b) By the vote of a majority in interest of the members, or a greater percentage of the voting interests of members as may be specified in the articles of organization or a written operating agreement. (c) Entry of a decree of judicial dissolution pursuant to Section 17351 [an involuntary dissolution provision].

[CAL. CORP. CODE § 17350 (1999).]

Although one could attempt to justify the curbing of withdrawal and dissolution rights on the ground that "locking-in" capital helps to facilitate business development, the movement to restrict exit rights appears to be motivated primarily by a desire to make the family-owned LLC an attractive business structure for estate and gift tax purposes. To minimize the tax value of an ownership interest in a closely held business, an investor will frequently claim that the value of its ownership position should be reduced to reflect (1) that the interest is difficult to liquidate, and (2) that purchasers will generally pay less for illiquid positions. This well-accepted "marketability discount" is premised on empirical evidence indicating that investors will "extract a high discount relative to actively traded securities for stocks or other investment interests that lack [a] high degree of liquidity." [SHANNON P. PRATT, ROBERT F. REILLY, & ROBERT P. SCHWEIHS, VALUING A BUSINESS: THE ANALYSIS AND APPRAISAL OF CLOSELY HELD COMPANIES 333 (3d ed. 1996).] To qualify for a marketability discount in a family-owned LLC, however, state law must restrict an owner's ability to cash out of a business through withdrawal or dissolution. As a result, and with the blessing of estate tax planners, many jurisdictions amended their LLC statutes to restrict a member's ability to liquidate its ownership position. While perhaps accomplishing an estate tax goal, the elimination of default withdrawal and dissolution rights leaves minority members vulnerable to oppressive majority actions since the minority can no longer easily exit the venture with the value of its investment.

LIEBERMAN V. WYOMING.COM LLC

Supreme Court of Wyoming, 2004.
82 P.3d 274.

GOLDEN, JUSTICE.

Wyoming.com LLC (hereinafter "Wyoming.com") is a Wyoming limited liability company of which E. Michael Lieberman was a member. In 1998, Lieberman filed a notice of withdrawal of member with Wyoming.com, and the remaining members of Wyoming.com accepted Lieberman's withdrawal as tendered. The parties subsequently could not agree on the financial consequences of Lieberman's withdrawal and filed a petition for declaratory judgment on the issue. Ultimately, the district court, by way of summary judgment, ordered liquidation of Lieberman's equity interest at its capital account value as of the date of his withdrawal as a member. Lieberman appeals.

The Wyoming LLC Act contains no provision relating to the fate of a member's equity interest upon the member's dissociation. Thus, it was entirely up to the members of Wyoming.com to contractually provide for terms of dissociation. Upon careful review of all the agreements entered into by the parties regarding Wyoming.com, we determine that the agreements contain no provision regarding the equity interest of a dissociating member. Since we can find no provision mandating a different result, Lieberman retains his equity interest. Lieberman is under no obligation to sell his equity interest, and Wyoming.com is under no obligation to buy Lieberman's equity interest. The question of valuation is moot. The decision of the district court liquidating Lieberman's equity interest is reversed, and we remand to the district court for a declaration of the parties' rights consistent with this opinion.

* * *

FACTS

This is the second time this case has been before this Court on appeal. The facts as stated in *Lieberman v. Wyoming.com LLC*, 11 P.3d 353 (Wyo.2000) (*Lieberman I*), are as follows:

On September 30, 1994, Steven Mossbrook, Sandra Mossbrook, and Lieberman created Wyoming.com LLC by filing Articles of

Organization with the Wyoming Secretary of State. The initial capital contributions to Wyoming.com were valued at $50,000. Lieberman was vested with an initial capital contribution of $20,000, to consist of services rendered and to be rendered. According to the Articles of Organization, Lieberman's contribution represented a 40% ownership interest in the LLC. The Mossbrooks were vested with the remaining $30,000 capital contribution and 60% ownership interest. In August of 1995, the Articles of Organization of Wyoming.com were amended to reflect an increase in capitalization to $100,000. The increase in capitalization was the result of the addition of two members, each of whom was vested with a capital contribution of $25,000, representing a 2.5% ownership interest for each new member. Despite the increase in capitalization, Lieberman's ownership interest, as well as his stated capital contribution, remained the same.

On February 27, 1998, Lieberman was terminated as vice president of Wyoming.com and required to leave the business premises. The other members of Wyoming.com met the same day and approved and ratified the termination. On March 13, 1998, Lieberman served Wyoming.com and its members with a document titled "Notice of Withdrawal of Member Upon Expulsion: Demand for Return of Contributions to Capit[a]l." In addition to giving notice of his withdrawal from the company, Lieberman's notice demanded the immediate return of "his share of the current value of the company," estimating the value of his share at $400,000, "based on a recent offer from the Majority Shareholder."

In response to Lieberman's notice of withdrawal, the members of Wyoming.com held a special meeting on March 17, 1998, and accepted Lieberman's withdrawal. The members also elected to continue, rather than dissolve, Wyoming.com. Additionally, they approved the return of Lieberman's $20,000 capital contribution. However, Lieberman refused to accept the $20,000 when it was offered.

Wyoming.com filed suit in June of 1998 asking for a declaration of its rights against Lieberman. Lieberman filed suit the same month requesting dissolution of Wyoming.com, and the actions were consolidated. After a hearing on cross motions for summary judgment, the district court granted Wyoming.com's motion for summary judgment and denied Lieberman's motion for partial summary judgment. The district court ruled that, because the remaining members of Wyoming.com LLC agreed to continue the business under a right to do so in the Articles of Organization, the company was not in a state of dissolution. The district court further ruled that Lieberman had the right to demand return of only his stated capital contribution, $20,000, which the district court ordered to be paid in cash. Lieberman appealed.

[*Lieberman I*, 11 P.3d] at 355–56 (footnotes omitted).

In *Lieberman I,* this Court agreed that Wyoming.com was not in a state of dissolution. [The *Lieberman I* court, 11 P.3d at 357–58, stated the following:

> Turning to the issues presented, we first address whether Lieberman's withdrawal triggered dissolution of Wyoming.com. Wyo. Stat. Ann. § 17–15–123(a)(iii) requires that, upon [the death, retirement, resignation, expulsion, bankruptcy, dissolution, or occurrence of any other event which terminates the continued membership of a member], the LLC must dissolve unless all the remaining members of the company consent to continue under a right to do so stated in the articles of organization. Paragraph 9 of the Articles of Organization of Wyoming.com LLC permits continuation:

> **9.   Continuity.** The remaining members of the LLC, providing they are two or more in number, will have the right to continue the business on the death, retirement, resignation, expulsion, bankruptcy or dissolution of a member or occurrence of any other event which terminates the continued membership of a member in this LLC, in accordance with the voting provisions of the Operating Agreement of the Company.

> The minutes of a March 17, 1998, special meeting of Wyoming.com reflect that the remaining members of Wyoming.com elected to continue the LLC after Lieberman's departure.[e] This set of undisputed facts establishes there was no dissolution, and Lieberman is not entitled to distribution of assets * * * as he claimed.]

With regard to Lieberman's demand for the return of his capital contribution we stated:

> Lieberman claims the term "contribution to capital" found in Wyo. Stat. Ann. § 17–15–120[f] should be interpreted to

---

[e]   [This footnote is from *Lieberman I*, 11 P.3d at 357.] Although Lieberman argues he was expelled from the LLC, neither the Operating Agreement nor Wyo. Stat. Ann. § 17–15–123(a)(iii) draws a distinction between expulsion and withdrawal.

[f]   At the time of the dispute, Wyo. Stat. § 17–15–120, captioned "[w]ithdrawal or reduction of members' contributions to capital," stated:

(a) A member shall not receive out of limited liability company property any part of his or its contribution to capital until:

encompass the fair market value of his interest in the LLC and that his return should not be limited to the amount of his initial capital contribution. At this juncture, a distinction must be drawn between withdrawal of a member's capital contribution and the withdrawal from membership in an LLC, often termed dissociation. After a thorough review of § 17–15–120, we conclude nothing in that provision contemplates a member's rights upon dissociation. Besides the fact that § 17–15–120 speaks only to withdrawal of capital contributions, other provisions in the LLC act support our conclusion that § 17–15–120 does not govern dissociation. The following passage from § 17–15–119, which controls division of profits, envisions withdrawal of capital contribution without dissociation: "If the operating agreement does not so provide, distributions shall be made on the basis of the value of the contributions made by each member to the extent they have been received by the limited liability company and have not been returned." This quoted material clearly contemplates a situation where a member has withdrawn some (or even all) of his capital contribution but has not dissociated as a member. We conclude a withdrawal of capital contributions pursuant to § 17–15–120 does not also govern a member's rights upon dissociation.

(i) All liabilities of the limited liability company, except liabilities to members on account of their contributions to capital, have been paid or there remains property of the limited liability company sufficient to pay them;

(ii) The consent of all members is had, unless the return of the contribution to capital may be rightfully demanded as provided in this act;

(iii) The articles of organization are cancelled or so amended as to set out the withdrawal or reduction.

(b) Subject to the provisions of subsection (a) of this section, a member may rightfully demand the return of his or its contribution:

(i) On the dissolution of the limited liability company; or

(ii) Unless otherwise prohibited or restricted in the operating agreement, after the member has given all other members of the limited liability company prior notice in writing in conformity with the operating agreement. If the operating agreement does not prohibit or restrict the right to demand the return of capital and no notice period is specified, a member making the demand must give six (6) months prior notice in writing.

(c) In the absence of a statement in the articles of organization to the contrary or the consent of all members of the limited liability company, a member, irrespective of the nature of his or its contribution, has only the right to demand and receive cash in return for his or its contribution to capital.

(d) A member of a limited liability company may have the limited liability company dissolved and its affairs wound up when:

(i) The member rightfully but unsuccessfully has demanded the return of his or its contribution; or

(ii) The other liabilities of the limited liability company have not been paid, or the limited liability company property is insufficient for their payment and the member would otherwise be entitled to the return of his or its contribution.

[*Lieberman I*, 11 P.3d] at 359. This Court thus held that, pursuant to statute, Lieberman was entitled to the return of his capital contribution, regardless of his status as a member of Wyoming.com. Since Lieberman expected more, however, we remanded the case "because it is unclear what became of Lieberman's ownership or equity interest (as represented by a membership certificate)" requiring further proceedings "for a full declaration of the parties' rights."

Upon remand, no new evidence was introduced. Wyoming.com filed a motion for partial summary judgment requesting the district court to make two determinations: at what time should Lieberman's equity interest be valued and how should it be valued. Obviously, the parties proceeded under the assumptions that: Lieberman had withdrawn as a member and an equity owner; that he was entitled to his equity interest; and a valuation and buyout was necessary.

Wyoming.com relied upon language in the Operating Agreement to argue that Lieberman's equity interest should be limited to the value of his capital account. The district court agreed with Wyoming.com that the Operating Agreement provided the appropriate method to fully value Lieberman's equity interest. The district court also determined that Lieberman's equity interest should be valued as of the date of his withdrawal as a member. The district court therefore granted Wyoming.com's motion for partial summary judgment on these two issues, holding that "[t]he defendant is entitled to the balance of his capitol [sic] account as of the date of defendant's withdrawal from the LLC." Since it appears that the value of Lieberman's capital account at the date of his withdrawal was negative, Lieberman appeals.

* * *

DISCUSSION

* * *

In granting summary judgment, the district court relied upon paragraph 6.2 [of the Operating Agreement]. However, paragraph 6.2 contains no provision addressing the rights and obligations of the members with regard to a member who has withdrawn. Paragraph 6.2 provides a method for distributing capital upon liquidation. It contains no indication of when liquidation can or must occur. It does not mandate a buyout or a liquidation of a member's equity interest. As such, it has no application to the immediate issue and the district court's reliance upon it was misplaced.

Although we could end our discussion here, this appeal involves solely issues of law. In the interest of judicial economy, we deem it prudent to resolve the present issues. Returning then to our question upon remand, what has become of Lieberman's equity interest? This

Court began the process of attempting to determine the fate of Lieberman's equity interest in *Lieberman I*:

> Having determined that § 17–15–120 does not control a member's rights upon dissociation, we must determine what became of Lieberman's interest, other than his capital contribution, in Wyoming.com. Unfortunately, it is unclear from the district court's decision letter precisely what became of Lieberman's ownership interest. The Articles of Organization of Wyoming.com credited Lieberman with a 40% ownership interest in Wyoming.com, and he now argues he is entitled to payment for this interest at fair market value. In the alternative, he contends he retains that 40% interest because the district court has not resolved that portion of the parties' dispute. Wyoming.com disagrees.
>
> We begin by examining Lieberman's notice of withdrawal. Lieberman strongly disputes any contention that he has simply forfeited his interest, other than his capital contribution, in the LLC. After examining the notice of withdrawal, we cannot say, as a matter of law, that Lieberman forfeited his interest upon his withdrawal because nothing in his withdrawal indicates his intent to do so. Indeed, Lieberman's demand for "his share of the current value of the company," whose value he estimated at $400,000, "based on a recent offer from the Majority Shareholder," indicates he would not easily part with, much less forfeit, his interest. Because we cannot say that, as a matter of law, Lieberman's withdrawal amounted to forfeiture of his interest, and because there is no statutory provision governing dissociation, we look to Wyoming.com's Operating Agreement to determine Lieberman's remedy.
>
> Under * * * Wyoming.com's Operating Agreement, a member's equity interest was to be represented by a membership certificate. * * *
>
> * * * There is nothing in the record indicating what became of Lieberman's membership certificate; there is no indication it has been canceled or forfeited.
>
> * * *

Lieberman I, 11 P.3d at 360–61 (footnote omitted).

Essentially, in *Lieberman I* this Court determined that further information might be available to help identify the contractual rights and obligations of the members upon the withdrawal of a member. Despite this Court's suggestion that the membership certificates might contain applicable contractual language, upon remand, the parties elected to introduce no additional evidence. Thus, this case returns to us with the same record as was available in *Lieberman I.*

Since Lieberman has not voluntarily forfeited his equity interest, this Court must look to the agreements entered into by the members of Wyoming.com to determine the rights and obligations of the members with regards to a member who has dissociated.[2] The rights and obligations of the members of Wyoming.com are determined pursuant to the operating agreements of Wyoming.com. The record reveals that the parties entered into "Articles of Organization of Wyoming.com LLC" (the "Articles") and an "Operating Agreement of Wyoming.com LLC" (the "Operating Agreement"). These agreements establish Wyoming.com, provide for Wyoming.com's operation, and set forth the mutual obligations between each of Wyoming.com's members. At all times the members have been free to contract any provision they desired, so long as the provision did not conflict with the limited requirements of the Wyoming LLC Act. Determining the fate of Lieberman's equity interest requires this Court to construe these agreements.

A contract may consist of several documents, which this Court reviews as a whole with the goal of determining the intention of the contracting parties as expressed by their own words. * * *

The operating agreements of Wyoming.com vest Lieberman with an ownership interest. Lieberman can only be divested of this ownership interest if the members of Wyoming.com contracted for such divestment. Wyoming.com argues that Lieberman's withdrawal as a member mandates his withdrawal as an equity owner, thus triggering a liquidation of his equity interest. In *Lieberman I,* this Court clarified that "[u]nder the Wyoming LLC act, a member's interest in an LLC consists of economic and non-economic interests." [*Lieberman I*, 11 P.3d at 357.] These interests are distinct. It is clear from Lieberman's notice of withdrawal that he had no intention of forfeiting his economic, or equity, interest in the company. Lieberman's withdrawal regarded his non-economic membership interest only.

The operating agreements clearly anticipate a situation where a person could be an equity owner in Wyoming.com but not a member. Provision 4.3 of the Operating Agreement * * * provides that, if a transferee of an ownership interest is not unanimously approved by the remaining members, the transferee maintains the rights of equity ownership but will not be a member.[3] Logically, given the absence of any contractual provision to the contrary, there is no reason to treat a

---

[2] Our review is limited to the agreements between the parties because, as stated previously, there is no statutory provision regarding the rights and obligations of members upon the dissociation of a member.

[3] Wyo. Stat. Ann. § 17–15–122 contains a similar provision regarding the transferability of [an] interest. The transferee does not become a member without unanimous approval of all members.

withdrawing member any differently from someone who buys into Wyoming.com without becoming a member. Thus, Lieberman is not a member of Wyoming.com, but he maintains his equity interest and all rights and obligations attendant thereto.

The parties essentially admit this in their respective briefs. Lieberman argues that there is nothing in the agreements allowing Wyoming.com to acquire his ownership interest at less than fair market value, while Wyoming.com argues that there is nothing in the agreements requiring Wyoming.com to pay fair market value for Lieberman's ownership interest. Both arguments are correct. There simply is no contractual agreement that any party must buy or sell an ownership interest for any amount.

Having failed to contractually provide for mandatory liquidation or a buyout, the parties are left in status quo. We have long held that it is the duty of this Court to construe contracts made between parties, not to make a contract for them. We must abide by the terms of their contract. This is especially so since the parties are asking us to create terms and conditions which do not exist in their contract.[4] We decline to alter the contract as written and accepted by these parties in the name of contract interpretation. We will enforce the contract as written and accepted by the parties. Lieberman maintains his equity interest in Wyoming.com.

CONCLUSION

Lieberman has withdrawn as a member of Wyoming.com and all remaining members unanimously accepted his withdrawal as a member. Lieberman thus is no longer a member of Wyoming.com. Lieberman does, however, maintain his equity interest in Wyoming.com. There is no contractual provision for a buy-out of his equity interest. Therefore Lieberman cannot force Wyoming.com to buy his interest, and Wyoming.com cannot force Lieberman to sell his interest. Because the members of Wyoming.com failed to contractually provide for a buy-out, Lieberman remains an equity holder in Wyoming.com. There are no further rights or obligations of the parties for this court to construe with regards to this situation. The grant of summary judgment is reversed and the matter remanded to the district court for a declaration of the parties' rights consistent with this opinion.

LEHMAN, JUSTICE, dissenting, with whom KITE, JUSTICE, joins.

I respectfully dissent. I agree that paragraph 6.2 of the Operating Agreement only provides a method for distributing capital upon liquidation and that the district court erred in relying on that subsection to find that Lieberman was entitled to only his capital contribution upon

---

[4] This Court would be required to supply a liquidation or buy-out provision, including a valuation method, with no evidence as to what these parties intended when they formed Wyoming.com.

withdrawal. I also agree with the majority that a thorough review of the Operating Agreement discloses no express provision for dealing with a dissociated member's equity interest.

However, I must disagree with the majority's determination of the consequence for the failure to provide such a provision. As the majority noted * * * we must review the contract of the parties as a whole with the goal of determining the intent of the contracting parties. The right of a member to withdraw from membership in the LLC is evidenced in the provisions of the operating agreement. Also clearly expressed [in paragraph 9 of the Articles of Organization] is the right of the remaining members to continue the business after such a withdrawal. * * *

This provision allows any member to terminate his membership in Wyoming.com by taking any of the listed actions and provides the remaining members the right to continue the business. This provision evidences the parties' intent to allow a member to completely terminate his membership in the LLC without also terminating the LLC. Hand in hand with these rights is the implication that should the remaining members elect to continue, they will have to compensate the withdrawing member for his interest in some manner. It seems intuitive that if the parties allowed for withdrawal and continuation, they must have had some intent to deal with those events. Because the provision mentions nothing of forfeiting the interest or simply becoming a non-member equity owner, the agreement to continue thus implies that there must be some sort of buyout.

Furthermore, the LLC statutory scheme implies that, absent other agreement, a member has a right to terminate his continued membership in the LLC and be compensated for this interest. As we stated in *Lieberman I,* at 357, an LLC is a hybrid organization including characteristics of both a partnership and a corporation. At the time the legislature enacted the original LLC statutes, an important consideration was the tax ramifications of the newly created entity. At that time, in order to obtain taxation as a partnership, an LLC could have no more than two of four corporate characteristics: limited liability, central management, free transferability of interests, and continuity of life. The LLC entity provided for limited liability and central management. Therefore, to avoid corporate taxation, the typical LLC statutes choose to utilize partnership principles, rather than corporate principles, for exiting members in order to avoid the LLC having continuity of life.

Partnership exit rules ordinarily allow for any partner to dissolve the firm at any time and demand liquidation and accordingly be paid for his equity interest. The legislature clearly recognized this as the normal partnership rule and impliedly endorsed such a rule by providing for an exception to this rule if the members agreed otherwise in their operating agreement. In a sense, carrying on the business following a terminating event became the exception to the general rule that the business would cease when a member left for any reason. Thus, the resulting implication is a member may terminate his membership in an LLC and must be paid for this interest unless otherwise provided.

Therefore, I reach the conclusion that under the terms of the LLC as provided by the Articles of Organization and Operating Agreement, and under the statute, Lieberman could withdraw as a member of Wyoming.com resulting in a forced buyout of his entire interest. The majority concludes, "Lieberman's withdrawal regarded his non-economic membership interest only." I cannot agree with this conclusion. While a member's interest does in fact consist of an economic and non-economic interest, a withdrawing member does not envision that his withdrawal will result in this split in his interest. As we noted in *Lieberman I,* at 355–56, Lieberman demanded "his share of the current value of the company," which value he estimated at $400,000, "based on a recent offer from the Majority Shareholder." Clearly Lieberman intended to withdraw his entire interest from the LLC. As such, Lieberman essentially declared his intention to no longer be associated with the LLC. Having accepted this withdrawal, the remaining members were now required and expected to compensate Lieberman for his interest.

The majority has recognized this and stated, "the parties proceeded under the assumptions that: Lieberman had withdrawn as a member and an equity owner; that he was entitled to his equity interest; and a valuation and buyout was necessary." However, they now refuse to provide relief for this situation. In fact, the majority's resolution has created a situation where the remaining members are in a position of power to dictate the terms of any negotiations for a buyout. The remaining members are now conceivably in a position to retain earnings and avoid distributions, but as an equity owner Lieberman would still be required to pay taxes on those earnings. Additionally, Lieberman is no longer a member. He will not be drawing the salary of the member or controlling his equity interest in any manner. While it could be said that this situation arose because of Lieberman's withdrawal, it should be noted that under the majority's analysis the result would apply equally to an expelled member. In such an instance, some of the members could expel a member and then refuse to negotiate for a buyout. Such a result begs for the oppression of one party. While I agree with the majority that it is not our duty to write contract provisions for parties that have failed to do so, I believe it would be much worse to fail to provide a remedy.

Therefore, I would provide such a remedy. Because the Operating Agreement does not provide for a valuation method, I look to the statutes to see if the legislature provided a default valuation method. As we said in *Lieberman I,* express provisions for valuing a member's share when that member terminates his membership in the LLC do not exist.

However, I do not believe this requires us to unilaterally create a valuation method. The statute expressly provides for the distribution of assets on dissolution. Wyo. Stat. Ann. § 17–15–126.[g] Granted, as we stated in *Lieberman I,* Lieberman is not entitled to a distribution of assets upon dissolution under this section because there was no dissolution. *Lieberman I,* at 358. However, this statute would be a proper valuation tool. This conclusion logically flows from the fact that the general rule is that an LLC must be dissolved upon the termination of a member's membership in the LLC, and the exception to this rule is when the operating agreement contains a provision for carrying on the business. If such a carrying on provision is not placed in the operating agreement, the members receive a distribution in conformance with the provisions of Wyo. Stat. Ann § 17–15–126. The legislature has established this as the proper method of discharging members' equity interests. I see no reason to value the departing member's share differently when the business carries on and only one member departs.

Therefore, absent a provision in the operating agreement, a member's equity interest should be valued at what he would have received had the business been dissolved on the day he terminated his membership in the LLC. I recognize that, because the business is not actually dissolving, this valuation may be difficult and will have to be based to some extent on estimates and appraisals. However, a similar valuation method is used upon the dissociation of a partner from a partnership when the partnership agreement has failed to provide for a valuation method. Presumably, then, such estimates and appraisals are attainable.

Additionally, Wyo. Stat. Ann. § 17–15–126 provides that upon dissolution the proceeds are to be applied first to pay the creditors and then the remainder is to go to the members "in respect of their share of the profits and other compensation by way of income on their contributions" and then lastly to the members "in respect of their contributions to capital." As can be seen by that statute's wording, the proceeds upon dissolution are used to extinguish debt and then are used not only to return a member's capital contribution but also to provide for

---

[g]   At the time of the dispute, Wyo. Stat. 17–15–126, captioned "[d]istribution of assets upon dissolution," stated:

(a) In settling accounts after dissolution, the liabilities of the limited liability company shall be entitled to payment in the following order:

(i) Those to creditors, in the order of priority as provided by law, except those to members of the limited liability company on account of their contributions;

(ii) Those to members of the limited liability company in respect of their share of the profits and other compensation by way of income on their contributions; and

(iii) Those to members of the limited liability company in respect of their contributions to capital.

(b) Subject to any statement in the operating agreement, members share in the limited liability company assets in respect to their claims for capital and in respect to their claims for profits or for compensation by way of income on their contributions, respectively, in proportion to the respective amounts of the claims.

the member's share of profits and other compensation by way of income on that contribution. Such a provision can encompass many things including the increase in value of any assets, any retained profits, and the goodwill of the company. Therefore, fair market value, which generally accounts for these relevant factors, would be a reasonable alternative estimate of the departing member's share.

Lastly, in instances where a departing member's share is to be valued as detailed above, the remaining members have elected to continue the company. Therefore, some consideration must be given to the duties and hardship the company may encounter as a result of paying the departing member's equity interest. The whole of the LLC statutes evidences the legislature's overall concern for the protection of the LLC's creditors. It is evident that the legislature wanted to assure that the LLC's creditors were provided for before the LLC members. These observations lead me to conclude that the payment of the departing member's equity interest may take place over a reasonable period of time to avoid the liquidation of essential assets and the possible undercapitalization of the LLC. To be entitled to prolong the payment over a reasonable time, the LLC must show that immediate payment in full would jeopardize the company's ability to carry on its ordinary business and provide for its creditors. Should payment over time be required, such payment should be secured by a promissory note that provides for reasonable interest. Furthermore, until the member is paid in full, that member should still receive any distributions to which his interest is entitled much like a transferee without the right to participate in the management of the business * * *.

NOTES

(1) Under Wyoming law at the time of the dispute, did dissociation (through, for example, resignation or expulsion) trigger a buyout of the member's interest? Did dissociation trigger dissolution of the LLC? Why didn't Lieberman's expulsion, followed by withdrawal, force dissolution of the LLC? *See* WYO. STAT. §§ 17–15–120, 17–15–123 (quoted in the case).

(2) Do you think Lieberman was happy with the result of this decision? If the parties had explicitly considered this situation at the time they formed the venture, would they, in your opinion, have wanted this result?

(3) Should a state's LLC statute provide for buyout rights and/or dissolution of the venture upon a member's dissociation? What are the advantages and disadvantages of such "easy exit?"

(4) What result if *Lieberman* had taken place in Delaware? *See* DLLCA §§ 18–603, 18–604, 18–801. What result under the Uniform Acts? *See* ULLCA §§ 101(2), 101(19), 601–603, 701, 801; RULLCA §§ 404, 601–603, 701.

(5) In some LLCs, the operating agreement specifies how distributions are to be made in the event of the company's dissolution. In the absence of

such a provision, however, the applicable statute usually provides a distribution scheme. *See* DLLCA § 18–804; ULLCA § 806; RULLCA § 708.

(6) As mentioned, after the passage of the check-the-box regulations, many state legislatures eliminated or restricted the withdrawal and dissolution rights that had served to combat a continuity of life finding. Unless an operating agreement provides otherwise, a member who dissociates by withdrawal in these states has no ability to liquidate his investment. *See, e.g.,* R.I. GEN. LAWS § 7–16–29 (1996) (providing for a "fair value" buyout upon withdrawal); *id.* § 7–16–29 (1997) (eliminating the buyout right upon withdrawal); *id.* § 7–16–39 (1996) (providing for dissolution upon "the death, resignation, expulsion, bankruptcy, or dissolution of a member"); *id.* § 7–16–39 (1997) (retaining the dissolution triggers but adding that, even if a trigger occurs, dissolution is caused only "[u]pon the written consent of a majority of the capital values of the remaining members").

(7) Significantly, a number of other states do not expressly eliminate "buyout-upon-withdrawal" rights, but they do restrict a member's ability to withdraw before the dissolution of the LLC. These statutes, therefore, have the same effect of "locking-in" a minority member for the duration of the venture. *See, e.g.,* DLLCA §§ 18–603, 18–604 (providing that, "upon resignation any resigning member is entitled to receive * * * the fair value of such member's [LLC] interest," but also stating that "unless [an LLC] agreement provides otherwise, a member may not resign from [an LLC] prior to the dissolution and winding up of the [LLC]").

(8) Keep in mind that LLC statutes tend to be less uniform than statutes governing other business forms. Some states, for example, continue to provide buyout rights when a member withdraws or otherwise dissociates from an LLC. *See, e.g.,* 15 PA. CONS. STAT. § 8933 (granting a member a right to be bought out at "fair value" upon dissociation); ULLCA §§ 603, 701 (granting a member a right to be bought out at "fair value" upon dissociation, and indicating that the timing of the buyout will vary based upon the "at-will" or "term" status of the LLC at issue).

(9) When LLC statutes provide for a buyout of a member's ownership interest, the statutes may provide guidance on valuation issues, including whether discounts should be applied. *See, e.g.,* 15 PA. CONS. STAT. § 8933 cmt. (" '[F]air value' * * * is to be fixed generally with reference to the [member's] right * * * to share in distributions from the company. * * * [I]t should not include discounts for lack of marketability or minority interest and thus is different from 'fair market value,' which term has been specifically avoided.").

DUNBAR GROUP, LLC v. TIGNOR

Supreme Court of Virginia, 2004.

593 S.E.2d 216.

KEENAN, JUSTICE.

In this appeal from a judgment ordering the dissolution of a limited liability company, the dispositive issue is whether the evidence was sufficient to support the chancellor's judgment.

XpertCTI, LLC (Xpert), is a limited liability company that provides "computer telephony integration" (CTI) software to dealers and manufacturers for installation in certain telephone systems and equipment. CTI software enables the use of computers to "interface" with and control telephone systems.

Xpert was formed in March 2000, by The Dunbar Group, LLC (Dunbar), and Archie F. Tignor, who each owned a membership interest of 50 percent in Xpert. Edward D. Robertson, Jr., a computer software developer and consultant, was the sole member and manager of Dunbar.

Tignor, a commercial telephone and telecommunications equipment dealer and installer, owned 50 percent of the stock of X-tel, Inc. (X-tel), a telecommunications sales firm. Tignor served as the president of X-tel, which was a dealer in equipment for Samsung Telecommunications America, Inc. (Samsung), a manufacturer, distributor, and seller of telecommunications equipment.

Dunbar and Tignor executed an "Operating Agreement" for Xpert under which they were the sole managers of Xpert. Dunbar created Xpert's proprietary software, or "source code," and conducted the daily operations of the company. Tignor's main function was to provide Xpert with access to his business contacts in the telecommunications industry, including Samsung.

Xpert's operating agreement provided a procedure for a company member to assert a breach of the agreement by another company member. The agreement specified that if the breach was not timely cured by the defaulting member, the complaining member had the "right to petition a court of competent jurisdiction for dissolution of the Company." The agreement also stated that the "dissolution of a [m]ember or occurrence of any other event that terminates the continued membership of a [m]ember in the Company shall not cause the dissolution of the Company."

In December 2000, Xpert entered into a contract with Samsung to supply Samsung with software-driven security devices called "dongles," which were to be included in all telecommunications systems sold by Samsung. Xpert received about $20,000 per month from the Samsung contract. The Samsung contract contained a provision specifying the contract's duration:

> This Agreement shall come into force and effect on the date written above [December 5, 2000] and shall remain in full force and effect for consecutive periods of thirty-six (36) months thereafter * * *. After this time the contract will continue on an annual basis unless terminated by either party giving 90 days notice before the anniversary of the contract date.

Certain disputes arose between Robertson and Tignor over matters primarily related to the management and disbursement of Xpert's assets. In May 2002, Dunbar's counsel sent a letter to Tignor's counsel stating that it was apparent to Robertson that "his continued working relationship with Mr. Tignor [was] no longer possible." Dunbar's counsel further stated that "Mr. Robertson is of the opinion that it is in the parties' best interest to sever their ties as fully and quickly as possible."

In September 2002, Dunbar, Xpert, and Robertson, in his capacity as a manager of Xpert, (collectively, Dunbar) filed an amended bill of complaint against Tignor and X-tel requesting, among other things, entry of an order "expelling and dissociating Tignor as a member of Xpert pursuant to Virginia Code § 13.1–1040.1(5)." Dunbar alleged that Tignor engaged in "numerous acts of misconduct as a member and manager of Xpert," including the commingling of Xpert's funds with the funds of Tignor and "his corporate alter ego, X-tel."

Code § 13.1–1040.1, which provides for a court-ordered expulsion of a member of a limited liability company, states in relevant part:

> [A] member is dissociated from a limited liability company upon the occurrence of any of the following events:
>
> * * *
>
> 5.   On application by the limited liability company or another member, the member's expulsion by judicial determination because:
>
> a.   The member engaged in wrongful conduct that adversely and materially affected the business of the limited liability company;
>
> b.   The member willfully or persistently committed a material breach of the articles of organization or an operating agreement; or
>
> c.   The member engaged in conduct relating to the business of the limited liability company which makes it not reasonably practicable to carry on the business with the member.

Tignor filed a separate "Application for Judicial Dissolution" against Dunbar and Xpert. Tignor requested, among other things, the dissolution of Xpert under Code § 13.1–1047 on the ground that "it is not reasonably practicable to carry on the business of [Xpert] in conformity with the Articles of Organization and [the] Operating Agreement." Tignor alleged that "serious differences of opinion as to company management have arisen between the members and managers" of Xpert, and that the company was "deadlocked" in its ability to conduct its business affairs, including contracting with customers for goods and services and the "receipt and disbursement of [Xpert's] assets and company funds."

The chancellor consolidated for trial Dunbar's amended bill of complaint and Tignor's application for judicial dissolution. At a hearing, the chancellor received evidence relating to both pleadings.

The evidence showed that Tignor commingled Xpert's funds with X-tel's funds by placing several checks, which were made payable to Xpert, into X-tel's bank account. Tignor provided inaccurate information to Robertson concerning one of those checks, which was made payable to Xpert in the amount of about $47,000. Tignor used the proceeds from that check to pay some of X-tel's expenses and to meet X-tel's payroll, including the payment of Tignor's own salary.

Without informing Robertson, Tignor also authorized a change in the status of Xpert's checking account that prevented checks from being written on the account. When Robertson, who was unaware of the change, wrote a check payable to one of Xpert's vendors, the check "bounced."

Although Dunbar had been renting office space from X-tel, Tignor evicted Robertson from X-tel's premises. Tignor also restricted Robertson's access to various testing equipment located in X-tel's offices, reducing Robertson's ability to test Xpert's products. Robertson needed access to this equipment to ensure the quality of Xpert's products before they were delivered to Xpert's customers. Due to Robertson's restricted ability to test Xpert's products, Xpert's customers did not receive their orders in a timely manner and products were sent to customers "in less than quality condition."

Tignor also terminated Robertson's e-mail account with Xpert without giving him prior notice. This sudden termination of Robertson's e-mail account created "a lot of confusion" among Xpert's customers, giving the appearance that Xpert had "gone out of business."

In December 2002, the chancellor entered an order in which he found that Tignor commingled Xpert's funds with his own funds and the funds of X-tel. The chancellor also concluded that Tignor's actions had been contrary to Xpert's best interests and had "adversely affected Xpert's ability to carry on its business." The chancellor further determined that

Tignor had acted "in violation of" subparagraph five of Code § 13.1–1040.1.

The chancellor ordered that Tignor be "immediately expelled as an active member of Xpert" and that Robertson "shall continue to operate Xpert" and provide to Tignor a monthly accounting of Xpert's finances. The chancellor also ordered:

> Xpert * * * shall continue the arrangement pursuant to this order until its contract with [Samsung] expires or otherwise terminates, including any extensions. Following the fulfillment or non-renewal of the [Samsung] contract, the court orders that Xpert * * * be dissolved and its assets distributed pursuant to the Virginia Code and the operating agreement of Xpert.

Dunbar appeals.

Dunbar does not challenge that part of the chancellor's order expelling Tignor as a member of Xpert, but attacks only the portion of the order providing for the dissolution of Xpert. Dunbar argues that the evidence is insufficient to support the dissolution of Xpert because the evidence did not satisfy the standard required by Code § 13.1–1047 for the judicial dissolution of a limited liability company. In support of this argument, Dunbar primarily asserts that the record fails to show that after the expulsion of Tignor as a member of Xpert, it would not be reasonably practicable to carry on Xpert's business.

* * *

The chancellor resolved the dissolution issue in Tignor's favor. Thus, we consider the evidence relating to the dissolution determination in the light most favorable to Tignor.

This appeal presents our first opportunity to consider the statutory standard provided in Code § 13.1–1047 for the judicial dissolution of a limited liability company. The statute states that

> [o]n application by or for a member, the circuit court of the locality in which the registered office of the limited liability company is located may decree dissolution of a limited liability company if it is not reasonably practicable to carry on the business in conformity with the articles of organization and any operating agreement.

Id.

Because this statutory language is plain and unambiguous, we apply the plain meaning of that language. The statutory standard set by the General Assembly for dissolution of a limited liability company is a strict one, reflecting legislative deference to the parties' contractual agreement to form and operate a limited liability company. Only when a circuit court concludes that present circumstances show that it is not reasonably practicable to carry on the company's business in accord with its articles of organization and any operating agreement, may the court order a dissolution of the company.

The record here, however, does not show that the chancellor evaluated the evidence in light of the fact that Tignor was being expelled as a member and manager of Xpert. Although Tignor's actions in those capacities had created numerous problems in the operation of Xpert, his expulsion as a member changed his role from one of an active participant in the management of Xpert to the more passive role of an investor in the company. The record fails to show that after this change in the daily management of Xpert, it would not be reasonably practicable for Xpert to carry on its business pursuant to its operating authority.

Moreover, we observe that the terms of the chancellor's dissolution order refute a conclusion that dissolution was appropriate under the statutory standard of Code § 13.1–1047. While the chancellor concluded that judicial dissolution of Xpert was warranted, he nevertheless ordered that Xpert continue operating as a limited liability company for as long as the Samsung contract remained in effect. This provision in the chancellor's order indicates that he concluded that Tignor's expulsion from Xpert would make it reasonably practicable for Xpert to continue to operate for an extended period of time.

Accordingly, we hold that the evidence does not support that part of the chancellor's order providing for the dissolution of Xpert. Further, because the evidence is insufficient to support such a judicial dissolution, we do not reach Dunbar's additional argument that the chancellor erred under Code § 13.1–1047 in ordering that Xpert be dissolved at an uncertain, future date.

For these reasons, we will affirm that part of the chancellor's judgment expelling Tignor as a member of Xpert, reverse that part of the judgment ordering the dissolution of Xpert, and enter final judgment.
* * *

NOTES

(1) Why do you think Tignor was seeking dissolution of the LLC?

(2) Given that Robertson and Tignor clearly had serious problems with one another, why did the court decline to order dissolution? Can you think of circumstances when it is "not reasonably practicable to carry on the business in conformity with the articles of organization and any operating agreement?" *See, e.g.*, Fisk Ventures, LLC v. Segal, Civ. A. No. 3017–CC, 2009 WL 73957, at *1, 4 (Del. Ch. Jan. 13, 2009) ("This case presents the narrow question of whether it is 'reasonably practicable,' under 6 *Del. C.* § 18–802, for a Delaware limited liability company to continue to operate. When such a company has no office, no employees, no operating revenue, no prospects of

equity or debt infusion, and when the company's Board has a long history of deadlock as a result of its governance structure, more than ample reason and sufficient evidence exists to order dissolution. * * * If a board deadlock prevents the limited liability company from operating or from furthering its stated business purpose, it is not reasonably practicable for the company to carry on its business"); *In re* 1545 Ocean Ave., LLC, 893 N.Y.S.2d 590, 597–98 (App. Div. 2010) ("After careful examination of the various factors considered in applying the 'not reasonably practicable' standard, we hold that for dissolution of a limited liability company * * * the petitioning member must establish, in the context of the terms of the operating agreement or articles of incorporation, that (1) the management of the entity is unable or unwilling to reasonably permit or promote the stated purpose of the entity to be realized or achieved, or (2) continuing the entity is financially unfeasible."); McConnell v. Hunt Sports Enters., 725 N.E.2d 1193, 1220, 1222 (Ohio Ct. App. 1999) ("[T]he evidence does support the trial court's conclusion that it was no longer practicable to carry on the business of CHL [an LLC formed for the purpose of obtaining a National Hockey League franchise in Columbus, Ohio]. * * * The above evidence shows that the cause of it being no longer practicable to carry on the business of CHL was the fact that CHL was not the ownership group awarded the NHL franchise. * * * June 9, 1997 was the deadline for the ownership group to be identified. This ownership group was not CHL. Hence, as of June 9, 1997, the reason for CHL's existence was gone.").

(3) In a rather unusual application of the "not reasonably practicable" dissolution provision, a New York court ordered dissolution after determining that the LLC statute was the default "operating agreement" of the parties:

> When there is no written Operating Agreement, these statutory default provisions [of the New York LLC statute] become the terms, conditions, and requirements for the conduct of the members for the operation of the limited liability company. On an application for judicial dissolution, when there is no formal operating agreement of the entity, or any such agreement does not address specific issues, the Court must consider whether it is "not reasonably practicable" to carry on the business in conformity with the terms of a limited operating agreement or with the terms of the statutorily established operating agreement.
>
> * * *
>
> * * * [T]he issues raised in this dissolution application relating to the withdrawal or removal of one of the members [are] not addressed by this limited Operating Agreement. Thus, the only "Operating Agreement" that is applicable to this dissolution application is the Operating Agreement created by the default provisions contained in the [New York] Limited Liability Company Law.

The relevant issue in this application for dissolution is the withdrawal or removal of a member of Lighthouse [a three-member LLC]. The statutory default provision for withdrawal of a member of Lighthouse Solutions LLC states that "a member may not withdraw from a limited liability company prior to the dissolution and winding up of the limited liability company" (LLCL § 606[a]). This statute explicitly requires dissolution and winding up of the LLC prior to withdrawal of a member (*Id.*). Thus, under the applicable statutory Operating Agreement, Lighthouse must be dissolved and the business wound up prior to the withdrawal or removal of any of its members (*see* LLCL § 606[a]).

The evidence presented * * * demonstrates that Spires wanted to withdraw as a member of Lighthouse and/or that Casterline and Alamo wanted to remove Spires as a member of the LLC. The submitted information shows that all three wanted the business relationship to end, but they could not reach a consensus as to how to accomplish Spires leaving Lighthouse. * * *

This Court must now assess the ability to carry on the business of Lighthouse in conformity with the statutory Operating Agreement. Based on the terms of the default statutory Operating Agreement applicable to Lighthouse, it is "not reasonably practicable" for Lighthouse to carry on its business in conformity with the Operating Agreement. The terms of the Operating Agreement require the dissolution and winding up of Lighthouse prior to the withdrawal of its member, Timothy Spires (LLCL § 606[a]). * * * There is no other provision or mechanism in the statutory Operating Agreement for Timothy Spires, as a member of Lighthouse, to withdraw or be removed from the business.

Under the facts and circumstances presented, this Court exercises its discretion and decrees judicial dissolution of Lighthouse Solutions LLC as it is not reasonably practicable for Lighthouse to carry on its business in conformity with an Operating Agreement that explicitly requires the dissolution and winding up of Lighthouse prior to withdrawal of one of its members, Timothy Spires.

In re Spires, 778 N.Y.S.2d 259, 266–67 (Sup. Ct. 2004).

(4) In *In re Superior Vending*, 898 N.Y.S.2d 191, 192 (App. Div. 2010), the court affirmed a buyout award in lieu of dissolution on the grounds of reasonable impracticability. The court noted that "[a]lthough the Limited Liability Company Law does not expressly authorize a buyout in a dissolution proceeding, the Supreme Court properly determined that the most equitable method of liquidation in this case was to provide Plotkin a period of 45 days within which to purchase all of Tal's right, title, and interest in [the LLC]." *See also* Lyons v. Salamone, 821 N.Y.S.2d 188, 189 (App. Div. 2006) ("We reject plaintiff's argument that the absence of a provision in the Limited

Liability Company Law expressly authorizing a buyout in a dissolution proceeding rendered the * * * court without authority to grant the parties mutual buyout rights, and find that it is an equitable method of liquidation to allow either party to bid the fair market value of the other party's interest in the business, with the receiver directed to accept the highest legitimate bid.").

(5) Some LLC statutes include a corporate-like involuntary dissolution provision that allows a member to petition a court for dissolution on the grounds of deadlock, oppression, or other misconduct by those in control. *See, e.g.*, MINN. STAT. § 322B.833 (providing that a court may order dissolution of an LLC or other relief when a member establishes one of several grounds, including deadlock and "unfairly prejudicial" conduct); ULLCA § 801(4) (authorizing dissolution on the basis of "illegal, oppressive, fraudulent, or unfairly prejudicial" conduct by those in control); RULLCA § 701(a)(5) (substantially the same). Only a handful of states, however, include such provisions. *Cf.* Pointer v. Castellani, 918 N.E.2d 805, 808, 815–16 (Mass. 2009) (applying *Donahue* and *Wilkes* to an LLC dispute and upholding a finding that a minority member was frozen out of an LLC).

(6) Should members of an LLC be permitted to contractually waive their right to petition for judicial dissolution? In *R & R Capital, LLC v. Buck & Doe Run Valley Farms, LLC*, Civ. A. No. 3803–CC, 2008 WL 3846318 (Del. Ch. Aug. 19, 2008), the court upheld the following provision in an LLC agreement:

> *Waiver of Dissolution Rights.* The Members agree that irreparable damage would occur if any member should bring an action for judicial dissolution of the Company. Accordingly each member accepts the provisions under this Agreement as such Member's sole entitlement on Dissolution of the Company and waives and renounces such Member's right to seek a court decree of dissolution or to seek the appointment by a court of a liquidator for the Company.

Id. at *3, 6. As part of its rationale for enforcing the provision, the court stated the following:

> In addition to Delaware's general policy promoting the freedom of contract, there are legitimate business reasons why members of a limited liability company may wish to waive their right to seek dissolution or the appointment of a receiver. For example, it is common for lenders to deem in loan agreements with limited liability companies that the filing of a petition for judicial dissolution will constitute a noncurable event of default. In such instances, it is necessary for all members to prospectively agree to waive their rights to judicial dissolution to protect the limited liability company. Otherwise, a disgruntled member could push the limited liability company into default on all of its outstanding loans simply by filing a petition with this Court.

Id. at *7.

(7) In a member-managed firm, does a dissociated member retain the right to participate in management? What happens to the agency powers of a dissociated member? Many LLC statutes do not answer these questions. *See* ULLCA §§ 603, 703–704, 803–804; RULLCA §§ 603, 702.

(8) Can a member whose dissociation causes the dissolution of an LLC still participate in the winding up of the venture? In *Investcorp, L.P. v. Simpson Investment Co., L.C.*, 983 P.2d 265, 270–72 (Kan. 1999), the court, after examining the operating agreement and relevant statutory provisions, gave an affirmative answer to this question. In other jurisdictions, the statutory language may compel a different conclusion. *See, e.g.*, MD. CODE, CORPS. & ASS'NS § 4A–904(a) ("Unless otherwise agreed, the *remaining members* of a limited liability company may wind up the affairs of the limited liability company." (emphasis added)); ULLCA § 803(a) ("After dissolution, a member *who has not wrongfully dissociated* may participate in winding up a limited liability company's business * * *." (emphasis added)); RULLCA § 603(a)(1) (stating that "[w]hen a person is dissociated as a member" of an LLC, "the person's right to participate as a member in the management and conduct of the company's activities terminates").

PROBLEM

A, B, and C decide to form a Delaware manager-managed LLC to engage in the manufacture and distribution of T-shirts. They each invest $25,000 in the company in return for a 33.3% ownership stake. They quit their prior employment to work full-time at the company, and they all participate actively as managers of the venture. The LLC's operating agreement is skimpy, but it does specify manager-managed governance, it names A, B, and C as the initial managers, and it states that business decisions shall be made by the managers on a majority-rule basis.

After a few years of operation, personal animosity develops between the founders. A and B vote to terminate C's employment and to remove him as a manager of the venture. C's salary ceases, and the company continues its prior policy of reinvesting profits and avoiding distributions. C is upset by these decisions as he considers himself to be "frozen-out" of the business.

(a) Do you agree with C's assessment? Does C have any options in this situation? *See* DLLCA §§ 18–402, 18–601, 18–603, 18–604, 18–702, 18–801, 18–802.

(b) Would anything change if ULLCA governed (assume that the articles of organization make no mention of a term of existence for the LLC)? *See* ULLCA §§ 101(2), 101(19), 404, 409, 502–503, 601–603, 701, 801.

(c) Would anything change if RULLCA governed? *See* RULLCA §§ 404, 407, 409, 502, 601–603, 701.

J. THE NATURE OF THE LLC: REGULATORY ISSUES

Is an LLC more like a partnership or a corporation? The question is an important one, particularly because the applicability of various regulatory statutes may turn on the answer. Many of these statutes were enacted when partnerships and corporations were the only options for business organizations with more than one owner. As a result, the statutes tend to refer only to partnerships and corporations, leaving considerable uncertainty about whether new business forms, such as the LLC, fall within the statutory coverage.

POORE v. FOX HOLLOW ENTERPRISES

Superior Court of Delaware, 1994.
1994 WL 150872.

STEELE, JUDGE.

Pursuant to Superior Court Civil Rule 12(f), Tammy Poore filed a Motion to Strike Appellee's Answering Brief for failure to properly file an answer in Superior Court through Delaware counsel. * * * During the oral arguments concerning this Motion, Douglas E. Campbell admitted he drafted the answering brief himself. Although Mr. Campbell stated he did not have a license to practice law in Delaware, he believed because Fox Hollow Enterprises is a Limited Liability Company and not a corporation, he could represent this company in Superior Court without a Delaware licensed attorney. * * *

The Delaware Supreme Court has held a corporation cannot appear or conduct business in court without representation by Delaware counsel. Transpolymer Industries, Inc. v. Chapel Main Corp., Del.Supr., No. 284, 1990, Horsey, J. (Sept. 18, 1990) (ORDER). The Supreme Court reasoned "[a] corporation, though a legally recognized entity, is regarded as an artificial or fictional entity, and not a natural person. While a natural person may represent himself or herself in court even though he or she may not be an attorney licensed to practice, a corporation being an artificial entity, can only act through its agents and, before a court only through an agent duly licensed to practice law." Id. (citations omitted).

The threshold question presented to this Court concerns whether or not it should apply this theory of corporate representation to Delaware Limited Liability Companies. As an alternative business entity under Delaware law, the Court must decide if a Limited Liability Company more closely resembles a partnership, which may represent itself in Court, or a corporation, which requires representation by legal counsel. * * *

The Court recognizes the Delaware General Assembly enacted the DLLCA to serve as an alternative business entity which allows the combination of the best features of both partnerships and corporations. The Delaware statute treats a properly structured LLC as a partnership for federal income tax purposes while affording limited liability for members and managers, similar to the limited liability afforded to shareholders and directors of a Delaware corporation. 6 Del.C. § 18–303, 18–1106(a).

Although the statute treats an LLC as a partnership for federal income tax purposes, an LLC is largely a creature of contract—with management, economic, voting and other rights and obligations being primarily specified in the LLC agreement. Walter C. Tuthill & Denison H. Hatch, Jr., Delaware Limited Liability Companies, March 5, 1993, at 3. An LLC formed under the DLLCA constitutes a separate legal entity. 6 Del.C. § 18–201(b). Additionally, the interest of a member in the LLC is analogous to shareholders of a corporation. A member usually contributes personal property and has no interest in specific assets owned by the LLC. 6 Del.C. § 18–701. Moreover, a member or manager of an LLC cannot be held liable for the company's debts or obligations above his or her contribution to the company. 6 Del.C. § 18–303.

The Court finds these aspects of the LLC constitute a distinct, but artificial entity under Delaware law. Because of the limited liability inherent in the LLC and the contractual nature of this entity, the Court finds the Delaware Legislature did not intend [to say that] a member or manager of an LLC could appear in Court to represent the entity without representation by Delaware legal counsel. Ultimately, regulation of the practice of law rests in the Delaware Supreme Court, not the legislature. The underlying purpose of the rule prohibiting the appearance of a corporation by anyone other than a member of the Delaware Bar also applies to the representation of Limited Liability Companies.

Because Fox Hollow Enterprises did not obtain Delaware legal counsel to represent its interests in this appeal, the Court grants Appellant's Motion to Strike Appellee's Answering Brief pursuant to Superior Court Civil Rule 12(f).

NOTES

(1) Why did the *Poore* court conclude that Delaware legal counsel was needed to represent the LLC?

(2) *Poore* is one of several cases that address the applicability of regulatory statutes to LLCs. Another example is provided by *Meyer v. Oklahoma Alcoholic Beverage Laws Enforcement Commission*, 890 P.2d 1361 (Okla. Ct. App. 1995). At the time of the dispute in *Meyer*, the Oklahoma Constitution contained the following provisions with respect to the holders of liquor store licenses:

Not more than one retail package license shall be issued to any person or general or limited partnership.

OKLA. CONST., art. 28, § 4.

No retail package store or wholesale distributor's license shall be issued to:

(a) A corporation, business trust or secret partnership.

(b) A person or partnership unless such person or all of the copartners including limited partners shall have been residents of the State of Oklahoma for at least ten (10) years immediately preceding the date of application for such license.

(c) A person or a general or limited partnership containing a partner who has been convicted of a violation of a prohibitory law relating to the sale, manufacture, or the transportation of alcoholic beverages which constituted a felony or misdemeanor.

(d) A person or a general or limited partnership containing a partner who has been convicted of a felony.

OKLA. CONST., art. 28, § 10.

The *Meyer* court held that an LLC was not eligible to receive a liquor store license. The court reasoned as follows:

> Meyer argues that an LLC is essentially a partnership. However, the act creating the business form is in Title 18, which is entitled "Corporations." Furthermore, a provision in our Uniform Partnership Act states that "any association formed under any other statute of this state * * * is not a partnership under this act, unless such association would have been a partnership in this state prior to adoption of this act." 54 O.S.1991 § 206(2).

> Meyer claims that its expert witness, the only witness in all the proceedings, testified that an LLC was a partnership. However, contrary to Meyer's contention, the witness's testimony was not so unequivocal. The totality of the testimony was that an LLC is a hybrid that has attributes of both corporations and partnerships. The witness indicated an LLC is more like a partnership, but noted the primary difference is that all owners/members have limited liability in an LLC—something not found in partnerships. We conclude that the limitation of liability of all LLC members is a substantial difference especially relevant to the provisions of our liquor laws.

> Our examination of the pertinent constitutional provisions leads us to conclude that their evident purpose was the assignment of personal responsibility for compliance with the liquor laws. Thus, business forms that did not insure such personal responsibility were excluded from eligibility for licensing.

The [Oklahoma Limited Liability Company Act] does exactly what its name indicates. It creates a form of business that has as its most important feature the limitation of liability of its members. This liability limitation is also a shield from the very responsibility and accountability that the constitutional provisions regarding alcoholic beverage laws and enforcement sought to impose. * * *

Meyer, 890 P.2d at 1363–64.

(3) What result in *Meyer* if the business organization at issue was a limited partnership with an individual general partner? A limited partnership with a corporate general partner? An LLP? An LLLP?

(4) In *Exchange Point LLC v. United States Securities & Exchange Commission*, 100 F. Supp. 2d 172 (S.D.N.Y. 1999), the court concluded that an LLC did not meet the definition of a "person" under the Right to Financial Privacy Act of 1978 (the "RFPA"). Under the RFPA, a "person"—defined as "an individual or a partnership of five or fewer individuals"—has standing to object to a government subpoena of a financial institution's bank records so long as the person is a customer of the institution. *See id.* at 173–74. The court's conclusion was premised on two grounds. First, the court stated that an LLC is not covered by the plain meaning of the words "individual or a partnership of less than five individuals." Second, the court noted that the primary purpose of the RFPA is to protect the privacy rights of individuals and small partnerships. *See id.* at 175–76. Because LLCs resemble corporations to the extent that no one has personal liability for the debts of the company, the court suggested that privacy expectations for LLCs were weaker:

> * * * [T]he Court concludes that excluding LLC[s] from the protections of the RFPA will not thwart Congressional intent. Congress could have provided standing for LLC[s] of less than five members, or for ordinary corporations of five or fewer shareholders, but it chose not to by creating a very limited definition of "person" under the RFPA. The RFPA's protections are fully available to individuals and individuals who form small partnerships. If they so desire, individuals may choose instead to form an LLC with no member or manager fully liable for the company's debts. One price, however, of this greater separation between the business entity and its principals is that the entity will become less closely identified with the individuals who control it, and thus accorded a weaker privacy interest under the RFPA.

Id. at 176.

(5) There are likely numerous statutes, on both the state and federal levels, that were enacted when only partnerships and corporations existed. To the extent that these statutes are premised on the notion that all multiple-owner businesses are partnerships or corporations, how should they apply, if at all, to LLCs? Consider (1) having a legislature revise each statute to add "limited liability company" where appropriate; (2) providing a

legislative "quick fix" by including a statutory provision indicating that the word "corporation" and/or "partnership" shall always include an LLC; and (3) leaving courts to make these decisions on individual, statute-by-statute bases in litigated disputes.

(6) Should LLC ownership interests be characterized as "securities" that are subject to federal and state registration, disclosure, and anti-fraud provisions? As previously discussed in the limited partnership materials, *see* Chapter 18, Section B, ownership interests that are not specifically mentioned in the 1933 Securities Act, such as LLC interests, are usually analyzed under the "investment contract" term of the Act. The courts have interpreted "investment contract" to include situations where a person invests in a common enterprise expecting profits predominantly from the efforts of others. *See* SEC v. W.J. Howey Co., 328 U.S. 293 (1946). Should an LLC interest fall within the "investment contract" term and, consequently, be considered a security? Does the analysis depend on whether the LLC is member-managed or manager-managed? Consider the following:

> Precisely because LLCs lack standardized membership rights or organizational structures, they can assume an almost unlimited variety of forms. It becomes, then, exceedingly difficult to declare that LLCs, whatever their form, either possess or lack the economic characteristics associated with investment contracts. Even drawing firm lines between member-managed and manager-managed LLCs threatens impermissibly to elevate form over substance. Certainly the members in a member-managed LLC will often have powers too significant to be considered passive investors under the securities laws. And yet even members in a member-managed LLC may be unable as a practical matter to exercise any meaningful control, perhaps because they are too numerous, inexperienced, or geographically disparate. By the same token, while interests in manager-managed LLCs may often be securities, their members need not necessarily be reliant on the efforts [of] their managers.

Robinson v. Glynn, 349 F.3d 166, 174 (4th Cir. 2003).

A federal district court in Delaware expressed similar sentiments:

> The Delaware Limited Liability Company Act grants parties substantial flexibility in determining the character of an LLC. Accordingly, the terms of the operating agreement of each LLC will determine whether its membership interests constitute securities. The presumptions that courts have articulated with respect to general partnerships and limited partnerships do not apply to LLCs. Rather, to determine whether a member's profits are to come solely from the efforts of others, it is necessary to consider the structure of the particular LLC at issue, as provided in its operating agreement.
>
> In the present case, the Members of [the LLC] had no authority to directly manage [the LLC's] business and affairs. * * * The

Members, however, had the power to remove any Manager with or without cause, and to dissolve the company. * * * Because Great Lakes was the sole owner of [the LLC], its power to remove managers was not diluted by the presence of other ownership interests. *See* [Williamson v. Tucker, 645 F.2d 404, 423 (5th Cir. 1981)] (noting that a partner in a general partnership might be deemed to be a passive investor if there were a sufficient number of other partners to dilute the partner's voting rights). Great Lakes' authority to remove managers gave it the power to directly affect the profits it received from [the LLC]. Thus, the court finds that Great Lakes' profits from [the LLC] did not come solely from the efforts of others.

Great Lakes Chem. Corp. v. Monsanto Co., 96 F. Supp. 2d 376, 392 (D. Del. 2000).

(7) With respect to state law, some statutes explicitly characterize LLC interests as securities. *See, e.g.*, ALASKA STAT. § 45.55.990(32); N.M. STAT. § 58–13C–102(DD)(6); *see also* CAL. CORP. CODE § 25019 (characterizing an LLC interest as a security except when a person "can prove that all of the members are actively engaged in the management of the limited liability company"); *id.* (stating that "evidence that members vote or have the right to vote, or the right to information concerning the business and affairs of the limited liability company, or the right to participate in management, shall not establish, without more, that all members are actively engaged in the management of the limited liability company").

K. A FINAL LOOK

As you have learned, the LLC possesses many of the best features of other business organizations. It is worth asking, therefore, why anyone would choose to conduct a closely held business in a non-LLC form. Consider the following issues:

(1) *Differences in fees and franchise taxes.* In some states, filing and other statutory fees for LLCs are higher than for comparable business forms. In Illinois, for example, the filing fee for articles of incorporation is $150, while the filing fee for LLC articles of organization is $500. The fee for filing a corporation's annual report is $75, yet it is $250 for an LLC. *See, e.g.*, Howard M. Friedman, *The Silent LLC Revolution—The Social Cost of Academic Neglect*, 38 CREIGHTON L. REV. 35, 55–58 (2004) (discussing fee differentials in various states and observing that "[m]any LLCs are extremely small businesses with limited capital" such that "[a] few hundred dollars at the time of formation plus a few hundred dollars differential each year may be sufficient to affect the choice of entity"); *see also* Daniel M. Häusermann, *For a Few Dollars Less: Explaining State to State Variation in Limited Liability Company Popularity*, 20 U. MIAMI BUS. L. REV. 1, 8 (2011) (discussing the results of an empirical study on LLC formations: "I find that LLCs are * * * less popular in those states in

which the fees for organizing an LLC are higher than the fees for organizing a corporation. Formation fee differentials, which are highly visible at the moment the business entity is formed, account for 17% to 28% of the variation in LLC popularity. Their explanatory power is greater than the explanatory power of all other variables taken together."). Moreover, some states may impose income and franchise taxes on corporations and LLCs, but not on partnership structures.

(2) *Other taxes.* Federal social security and self-employment taxes, including Medicare taxes, may be higher in LLCs and partnerships than in corporations.

(3) *The relative complexity of the LLC.* A corporation is an established business form and corporate statutes provide numerous default governance rules that may very well be acceptable to the founders of a business. While the LLC has the advantage of flexibility, that flexibility also creates the need, in most instances, for a detailed operating agreement that is tailored to the wishes of the founders. This is particularly true given that most LLC statutes contain few or no default rules on basic governance procedures. This complexity may result in higher legal fees to form an LLC.

(4) *Attorney and business owner inertia.* Lawyers trained in the use of corporations and other closely held structures (and comfortable with existing shareholder and partnership agreements) may be reluctant to recommend a more unfamiliar business form and hesitant to tinker with "tried and true" operative documents. Similarly, business owners who have prior experience with corporations and other non-LLC ventures may prefer to avoid an unfamiliar business form.

(5) *Sparse case law.* Compared to the amount of judicial precedent on partnerships and corporations, there is less case law on LLC issues. Lawyers and business owners may feel less comfortable with LLCs because of this relative absence of judicial guidance. Given the number of LLC formations, however, this problem will lessen with the passage of time. Nevertheless, in light of the differences in LLC statutes, judicial opinions may have little precedential value in other jurisdictions.

(6) *Lack of exit rights.* LLC statutes often limit a member's ability to dissociate, dissolve the firm, or otherwise recover invested capital from the venture. Partnership default rules, however, provide broad dissociation and dissolution rights.

(7) *The desire to "go public."* Because the Internal Revenue Service taxes all publicly held business organizations as corporations (subject to a few narrow exceptions), a publicly traded LLC has no income-tax advantage over a corporation. In general, however, public investors are more familiar with the corporation than the LLC. Founders who desire to

sell all or part of a business to the public, therefore, may prefer the corporate form.

(8) *Ease of reorganization.* Some businesses may hope to be acquired in the future by a larger, publicly held corporation. The Internal Revenue Code allows a corporation to engage in a merger or other reorganization with another corporation on a tax-free basis. A merger or other reorganization between a corporation and an LLC, however, does not qualify for such tax-free treatment. Although an LLC could convert to a corporation at the time of the merger or other reorganization, it may be easier for a business to form as a corporation from inception to avoid the delay and expense of conversion (especially because pass-through tax treatment can be obtained in the S-corporation form).

INDEX

References are to Pages

DISCLOSURE DUTIES

3